D1201531

Short-Term Interest Rates, C
and the United States, 1979–

Canadian Inflation, 1966–1996

ECONOMICS

NINTH CANADIAN EDITION

Richard G. Lipsey
Simon Fraser University

Christopher T. S. Ragan
McGill University

Paul N. Courant
The University of Michigan

Addison-Wesley Publishers Limited

Don Mills, Ontario • Reading, Massachusetts
Menlo Park, California • New York • Wokingham, England
Amsterdam • Bonn • Sydney • Singapore • Tokyo • Madrid
San Juan • Paris • Seoul • Milan • Mexico City • Taipei

Senior Editor: Brian Henderson
Developmental Editor: Shirley Tessier
Project Coordination and Compositor: York Production Services
Text Designer: A Good Thing, Inc.
Cover Designer: Wycliff Smith Design
Cover Photo: © David Starrett
Art Studio: A Good Thing, Inc.
Senior Manufacturing Manager: Willie Lane
Printer and Binder: R. R. Donnelley & Sons Company
Cover Printer: The Lehigh Press, Inc.

ECONOMICS, Ninth Canadian Edition

Copyright © 1997 by Richard G. Lipsey, Christopher T. S. Ragan, and Paul N. Courant
Portions of this work were first published in the United Kingdom as
An Introduction to Positive Economics, © 1989 by Richard G. Lipsey.

All rights reserved. No part of this publication may be reproduced, stored in a retrieval
system, or transmitted, in any form or by any means, electronic, mechanical, photocopying, recording, or otherwise, without the prior written permission of the publisher.
Printed in the United States.

ISBN 0-673-98358-7

Canadian Cataloging-in-Publication Data

Lipsey, Richard G., 1928-
  Economics

9th Canadian ed.
Includes index.

ISBN 0-673-98358-7

1. Economics.   I. Ragan, Christopher.   II. Courant, Paul N.   III. Title.

HB171.5.L733   1997   330   C96-931260-1

12345678910—DOW—99989796

BRIEF CONTENTS

TO THE INSTRUCTOR

Economics is a living discipline, changing and evolving in response to developments in the world economy and in response to the research of many thousands of economists throughout the world. Through nine editions, *Economics* has evolved with the discipline. Our purpose in this edition, as in the previous eight, is to provide students with an introduction to the major issues facing the world's economies, to the methods that economists use to study those issues, and to the policy problems that those issues create. Our treatment is everywhere guided by three important principles:

1. Economics is *scientific,* in the sense that it progresses through the systematic confrontation of theory by evidence. Neither theory nor data alone can tell us much about the world, but combined they tell us a great deal.

2. Economics is *useful* and it should be seen by students to be so. An understanding of economic theory combined with knowledge about the economy produces many important insights about economic policy. Although we stress these insights, we are also careful to point out cases where too little is known to support strong statements about public policy. Appreciating what is not known is as important as learning what is known.

3. We strive always to be *honest* with our readers. Although we know that economics is not always easy, we do not approve of glossing over difficult bits of analysis without letting readers see what is happening and what has been assumed. We always take whatever space is needed to explain why economists draw their conclusions, rather than just asserting the conclusions. We also take pains to avoid simplifying matters so much that students would have to unlearn what they have been taught if they continue their study beyond the introductory course. In short, we have tried to follow Albert Einstein's advice:
Everything should be made as simple as possible, but not simpler.

THE ECONOMIC ISSUES OF THE 1990S

In writing the ninth edition, we have tried to reflect the major economic issues of the last decade of the twentieth century.

GLOBALIZATION AND GROWTH

Enormous changes have occurred throughout the world over the last few decades. Flows of trade and investment between countries have risen so dramatically that it is now common to speak of the "globalization" of the world economy. Today it is no longer possible to study any economy without taking into account developments in the rest of the world.

What is true for most countries is also true for Canada. Economic relations between Canada and the rest of the world have a significant impact on most of the major "domestic" issues in the news. Here are three examples that we discuss, along with many others, in the ninth edition of *Economics.*

1. Throughout most of this century, Canadians, Americans, and Europeans have each regarded the policies that they adopted to support their farmers as strictly their own concern. Now, with the globalization of agricultural markets, what one country does to support its own agricultural sector impacts greatly on farmers in other countries. No longer is any one nation an island unto itself. Each nation's agricultural policies affect agricultural producers throughout the world and therefore concern all countries.

2. Throughout most of the twentieth century, successive generations of Canadians have found themselves, on average, substantially better off than their parents as a result of the nation's economic growth. Over the last two decades, however, this generation-by-generation advance has applied to only the top income levels; for the rest, average incomes are little higher, and sometimes lower, compared with the previous generation. Although some of the causes may be peculiar to the Canadian economy, many have to do with worldwide changes in technology and in patterns of international trade.

3. Over the past fifteen years, Canadians have worried about large government budget deficits. They wonder if the failure to balance the budget will lead to higher taxes in the future. Canadian firms worry about how the budget deficits affect domestic interest rates and the external value of the Canadian dollar, and about how their competitive positions in world markets will be affected.

THE TRIUMPH OF MARKET CAPITALISM

Since the 1980s, the century-long ideological conflict between capitalism and communism has virtually ended. The most powerful communist economy in the world, the Soviet Union, has disappeared, both as a nation and as a planned economy. Mixed capitalism, the system of economic organization that has long prevailed in much of the industrialized world, now prevails in virtually all of it. Many of the less-developed economies are also moving in this direction. The reasons for the failure of the planned economies of Eastern Europe are discussed in Chapter 1 as a contrast to the reasons for the relative success of mixed capitalism. The difficulties of transition to mixed capitalism are also discussed in Chapter 3.

DECLINING GROWTH IN MARKET ECONOMIES

At the same time that the once communist world of Eastern Europe has begun to establish free markets, the economies of western Europe, the United States, Japan, and Canada have experienced a marked reduction in economic growth.

In Canada, average real wages, which rose steadily from 1900 to 1970, have remained nearly constant since the mid 1970s. Over the lifetimes of you who are now using this book, in contrast to readers of our first edition, steadily rising personal incomes have been the exception rather than the rule. Issues raised by the changing growth performance in most advanced industrial countries are discussed frequently in this book.

A GLOBALIZED ECONOMICS TEXTBOOK

Economic growth and the implications of globalization are pressing issues of the day. Much of our study of economic principles and the Canadian economy has been shaped by these issues.

In Chapter 6, foreign trade provides an example of demand and supply in action. Our discussion of agricultural policy in Chapter 6 also has an international dimension. Foreign direct investment and transnational corporations are introduced along with imperfect competition in Chapter 12, and they receive detailed attention in many subsequent chapters, including Chapter 14 on the organization of firms, Chapter 33 on economic growth, Chapter 34 on economic development, and Chapter 36 on trade policy. The newer method of "lean production" or "flexible manufacturing," first developed in Japan and now displacing the older mass-production techniques developed by Henry Ford, is discussed in connection with the firm (Chapters 8, 12, and 14), with economic growth (Chapter 33), and with economic development (Chapter 34).

Our basic framework for macroeconomic theory and policy is also organized around globalization and growth. In Chapters 23 through 26, we develop the theory of national income determination in an economy that is open to foreign trade and investment almost from the outset—rather than starting, as is so often done, with a closed economy and opening it to international trade and investment many chapters later. These chapters also discuss the long-run effects of national saving on economic growth.

Our analysis of the theory and practice of monetary policy in Chapters 27–29 highlights the role of exchange rates. Chapter 32, on government budget deficits, covers the effects of the budget deficit on the current account deficit (the "twin deficits"). In Chapter 33 we examine economic growth to an extent that is unusual in introductory texts. This treatment culminates in Chapter 34, which continues the growth theme with regard to less-developed economies with a major study of the newly emerging views concerning the effects of trade and foreign investment on growth of the poorer nations.

We treat international trade theory, trade policy and international finance in four chapters. Chapter 35 examines the basic theory of international trade. Chapter 36 provides a detailed discussion of policies that interfere with the free flow of international trade, and of trade-liberalizing arrangements such as the GATT and the North American Free Trade Agreement (NAFTA). Chapter 37 examines the balance of payments and the determination of exchange rates. Chapter 38 continues with a comprehensive treatment of macroeconomic policy in an open economy.

In addition to specific coverage of growth and internationally oriented topics, growth and globalization appear naturally throughout the book in the treatment of many topics once thought to be entirely "domestic."

MICROECONOMICS: STRUCTURE AND COVERAGE

Beginning Part 1, Chapter 1 introduces the issues of scarcity and choice and then briefly discusses alternative economic systems. The problems of converting command economies to market economies will be with us for some time, and comparisons with command economies help to establish what a market economy is *by showing what it is not*. We then survey a number of national and international trends to introduce students to many of the issues studied in detail later in the book. We end Chapter 1 with a discussion of the importance and role of economic policy. Chapter 2 makes the important distinction between positive and normative inquiries and goes on to an introductory discussion of the construction and testing of economic theories. Chapter 3 provides an overview of market economies, including a discussion of the important distinction between microeconomics and macroeconomics.

Part 2 deals with demand and supply. After introducing price determination and elasticity in Chapters 4 and 5, we apply these tools in Chapter 6. The case studies are designed to provide practice in applying the tools rather than a full coverage of each case.

Part 3 presents the foundations of demand and supply. The theory of consumer behaviour is developed via marginal utility theory in Chapter 7, which also provides an introduction to consumer surplus and an intuitive discussion of income and substitution effects. The Appendix to Chapter 7 covers indifference curves, budget lines, and the derivation of demand curves using indifference theory. Instructors' tastes differ greatly on how much demand theory is desirable in an introductory course, and the approach that we have taken in Chapter 7 allows the instructor to choose whether or not to use indifference curves without running into problems later in the book. (Further use of indifference curves is presented in appendices and optional boxes throughout the book.)

Chapter 8 introduces the firm as an institution and develops short-run costs. Chapter 9 covers long-run costs, the principle of substitution, and goes on to consider shifts in cost curves due to technological change. The latter topic is seldom if ever covered in the micro part of elementary textbooks, yet applied work on firms' responses to changing economic signals shows it to be extremely important. Although firms' short- and long-run responses matter, the response of their innovative activity is also highly significant. For example, a change in the wage rate, in capital costs, or in the exchange rate may cause firms to alter prices, outputs, and plans for capital expansion, but they will also cause firms to redirect their R&D expenditures. How firms choose to innovate their way out of unprofitable situations has come to be understood as a critical part of the microeconomic response to changes in market signals.

The first two chapters of Part 4, Chapters 10 and 11, present the standard theories of perfect competition and monopoly with some discussion of international cartels. Chapter 12 deals with monopolistic competition and oligopoly, which are the market structures most commonly found in Canadian industries. Strategic behaviour plays a central part in the analysis of this chapter. The first half of Chapter 13 deals with the efficiency of competition and the inefficiency of monopoly. The last half of the chapter is largely concerned with competition policy.

Part 5 begins in Chapter 15 by discussing the general principles of factor pricing and how factor prices are influenced by factor mobility. Chapter 16 then examines the operation of labour markets while Chapter 17 discusses capital and nonrenewable resources.

The first chapter of Part 6 (Chapter 18) provides a general discussion of market success and market failure, introduces social choice theory, and outlines the arguments for and against government intervention in a market economy. Chapter 19 deals with environmental and health and safety regulation. In addition to providing current applications of microeconomic theory to policymaking, it contains a boxed discussion of the U.S. experience with tradable emissions permits for sulphur dioxide. Chapter 20 analyzes taxes, public expenditure, and the main pillars of Canadian social policy.

These three chapters expand on the basics of microeconomic analysis by providing current illustrations of the relevance of economic theory to contemporary policy situations.

Strategic Behaviour

One of the most important advances in microeconomic analysis in recent years is the increased focus on strategic be-

haviour, including game theory and principal-agent analysis. In Chapter 12 we use elementary game theory in our discussion of competition among oligopolies. In Chapter 14 we introduce the principal-agent problem in the context of the market for corporate control. In Chapter 18 we discuss asymmetric information as a source of market failure.

Chapter 14 deals with the market for corporate control. A discussion of takeovers and mergers leads naturally to a brief consideration of why firms may and may not maximize their profits, since the possibility that existing management is not maximizing profits is widely viewed as an important motive for takeovers.

In all of these cases our approach is to introduce strategic behaviour when it is appropriate to the topic under discussion.

Economic Policy

Most chapters of the book contain some discussion of economic policy. We have two main goals in mind in these discussions:

1. We aim to give students practice in using economic theory, because applying theory is both a wonderfully effective teaching method and a reliable test of students' grasp of theory.

2. We want to introduce students to the major policy issues of the day.

Both goals reflect our view that students should see economics as useful in helping us to understand and deal with the world around us.

MACROECONOMICS: STRUCTURE AND COVERAGE

Our treatment of macroeconomics is divided into four parts following an introductory part: national income and fiscal policy; money, banking, and monetary policy; macroeconomic problems and policies; and international economics. The themes of internationalization and economic growth are interwoven throughout all four parts.

The first macro chapter, Chapter 21, identifies economic growth and the level of potential national income as the major determinants of a society's material standard of living. The discussion of national income accounting in Chapter 22 provides a thorough treatment of the distinction between real and nominal GDP, the distinction between GDP and GNP, and a discussion of what measures of national income *do not measure*.

In Part 8, the core macro chapters (23–26) develop what has become the standard aggregate-demand-aggregate-supply approach—an approach which this textbook was one of the first to pioneer. We start with a detailed exposition of the fixed-price (Keynesian cross) model of the determination of equilibrium income in Chapters 23 and 24. In Chapter 23 we consider a simplified economy, one with no international sector or government, in order to make the concepts of equilibrium income and the multiplier as teachable as possible. In Chapter 24 we add government and the international sector, thus opening our model economy to international trade at an early point.

In Chapters 23 and 24 we develop the saving-investment approach to equilibrium. This allows us to highlight the key temporal relationship between national savings and the accumulation of capital, both at home and abroad, that is a major source of economic growth. We also use the saving-investment approach to discuss the relationship between international trade and an economy's net accumulation of assets.

From the beginning of our treatment of macroeconomics, in contrast to many other introductory texts, we are careful to distinguish short-run fluctuations around potential national income from the long-term growth of potential national income. This reflects our desire to emphasize economic growth and to avoid trivializing it by confusing it with the rise in income caused by the removal of a recessionary gap.

In Chapter 25 we develop the aggregate demand (*AD*) curve and the short-run aggregate supply curve. Since we discuss the role of wealth in the consumption function in Chapter 23 and the international sector in Chapter 24, there is no mystery about why the *AD* curve slopes down—unlike other treatments where the *AD* curve is introduced prior to discussing these issues. Chapter 26 completes the core model by deriving the vertical long-run aggregate supply curve, which allows us to discuss the different effects of *AD* shifts in the short and long run. This leads directly to an introduction to fiscal policy and a discussion of business cycles in which both stabilization and growth are treated.

Part 9 focuses on the role of money and financial systems. Chapter 27 discusses the nature of money, including an overview of the evolution from metallic money to our modern system of fiat currency and deposit money. The chapter examines various components of the money supply, the commercial banking system and the Bank of Canada. In Chapter 28 we review the determinants of the demand for money. We then turn to a detailed discussion of the link between the money supply and other economic variables such as interest rates, the exchange rate, national income, and the price level. This chapter builds directly on the material in Chapters 25 and 26, with an emphasis on the distinction between short-run and long-run effects. In Chapter 29 we discuss monetary policy, covering the Bank of Canada's use of open-market operations and the switching of government deposits. The chapter ends with a review of Canadian monetary policy over the past 25 years. This provides some important historical context for policy discussions in later parts, as well as an opportunity to draw some general conclusions about the operation of monetary policy.

Part 10 deals with some of today's most pressing macroeconomic policy issues. It contains separate chapters on inflation, unemployment, budget deficits, economic growth, and growth in the developing countries, all of which are major concerns of the 1990s. Chapter 30 on inflation examines the central role of expectations in determining inflation, and the importance of credibility on the part of the central bank. Chapter 31 on unemployment examines the determinants of frictional and structural unemployment and discusses likely reasons for increases in the NAIRU over the past few decades. Chapter 32 on budget deficits stresses the effect of deficits on national saving and long-term economic growth.

Chapter 33 provides a comprehensive summary of what is and is not currently known about the causes of economic growth. Although some of the discussion ties directly into the emphasis of previous chapters on national saving, much of it examines current research on induced technological innovation and technological diffusion. The issue of globalization is revisited in a long section relating growth to international competitiveness. Our treatment of economic growth—which we regard as one of the most important macroeconomic issues facing Canada and the world today—goes well beyond the coverage in most other introductory texts. Chapter 34 continues the growth theme by providing a summary of current views about economic growth in the developing countries.

Virtually every macroeconomic chapter contains at least some discussion of international issues. However, the final part of *Economics* focuses primarily on international economics. Chapter 35 gives the basic treatment of international trade, developing both the traditional theory of static comparative advantage and newer theories based on imperfect competition and dynamic comparative advantage. Chapter 36 discusses both the positive and normative aspects of trade policy, as well as the GATT and prospects for regional free-trade areas. There is also a detailed discussion of NAFTA and a box on Canada-U.S. trade disputes.

Chapter 37 introduces the balance of payments and examines exchange-rate determination. Chapter 38 integrates the international material with the macroeconomic model developed earlier, thus providing an up-to-date discussion of monetary and fiscal policies in open economies. The discussion in Chapter 38 reemphasizes the distinction between the short run and the long run stressed in many earlier chapters. In addition to covering new open-economy issues, this chapter also reviews and integrates the macroeconomic theory and applications presented earlier.

We hope you find this menu both attractive and challenging; and we hope students find the material stimulating and enlightening. Many of the messages of economics are complex—if economic understanding were only a matter of common sense and simple observation, there would be no need for professional economists and no need for textbooks like this one. To understand economics, one must work hard. Working at this book should help readers gain a better understanding of the world around them and of the policy problems faced by all levels of government. Furthermore, in today's globalized world, the return to education is large. We like to think that we have contributed in some small part to the understanding that increased investment in human capital by the next generation is necessary to restore incomes to the rapid growth paths that so benefited our parents and our peers. Perhaps we may even contribute to some income-enhancing accumulation of human capital by some of our readers.

CHANGES TO THIS EDITION

We have done a major revision and update of the entire text with guidance from an extensive series of reviews and feedback from both users and nonusers of the previous editions of this book. As always, we have strived very hard to improve the teachability and readability of the book. Toward this goal, the revised text has been "test read" by a person *who is not an economics instructor* to locate difficult passages and confusing explanations and examples. This process led to the rewriting or considerable revision of many passages in the text; we are confident that students will have fewer difficulties with this edition.

OVERALL FORMAT

In addition to the usual tasks of rewriting and updating for the new edition, there are some changes to what might be called the "format" of the book. Here are some of the highlights.

Part Openers. Each part of the book (eleven in all) now begins with a brief description of what topics are covered in the part. There are a number of questions which we pose, not only to kindle the students' interest, but also to give them some indication of the type of questions they will be able to answer after successfully working through the material. In some cases, the questions are quite general; but in many cases the questions relate to specific examples that are covered within the following chapters.

Design. A completely new design for this edition helps to create a more open and logically accessible text.

Footnotes. Wherever possible, we have tried to shorten or eliminate footnotes, while at the same time making sure that we are not glossing over important details. We hope this makes the presentation of the central ideas less choppy.

Boxes. In this edition, we have added many new boxes and dropped many old ones (there are 24 new boxes). We have also differentiated the ways in which we use boxes in the text. All boxes are optional, and thus the student is able to skip all boxes without losing any *central economic principles*. The student's understanding of economics, however, will naturally be deeper if the material in the boxes is not skipped. In this edition, boxes are coded as one of two types.

1. *Applications* are meant to show economics in action, providing examples of how theoretical material relates to issues of current interest.

2. *Extensions* are designed to provide a deeper and more detailed treatment of a topic that is discussed in the text.

Chapter Summaries. In this edition, we have introduced a new format for our chapter summaries. The main section headings from the chapter now appear in the summaries, with the summary points organized appropriately. Making this change revealed to us that in previous editions we had not covered all parts of the chapter in the summary, and thus we have added many new summary points to fill these gaps. These revised and expanded summaries should be a more useful study tool for students.

End-of-Chapter Questions. We have updated and added to the list of questions at the end of each chapter. The answers to these questions are found in the Instructor's Manual (which is available for free to all adopters).

Mathematical Notes. Mathematical notes are collected in a separate section at the end of the book. Since mathematical notation and derivation is not necessary to understand the principles of economics but is helpful in more advanced work, this seems to be a sensible arrangement. Mathematical notes provide clues to the uses of mathematics for the increasing number of students who have some background in math, without loading the text with notes that are unnecessary and are a put-off to other readers.

Glossary. The glossary at the end of the book offers definitions of the terms that are used in boldface in the text. In addition, the glossary includes some commonly used terms that are not printed in boldface in the text because they are not, strictly speaking, technical terms.

Time Line of Great Economists. New to this edition, we have constructed a time line which runs from the mid 1700s to the middle of this century. Along this time line we have placed brief descriptions of the life and works of some great economists, most of whom the students encounter in the textbook. So that the students have a better appreciation of *when* these economists did their work, the time line also lists some major world events. We hope this will improve the students' sense of history and their sense of who these great economists are. The time line is located at the back of the book, immediately following the glossary.

CHANGES IN MICROECONOMICS

Here is a brief description of the major changes in the microeconomics half of the textbook.

Part 1 The Nature of Economics

- Chapter 1 has a new discussion of why opportunity cost changes along the production possibility boundary and there is a new box on the opportunity cost of a university education. There is a new final section in the chapter discussing the importance of economic policy.

- Chapter 2 has a new section on economic models, discussing the various ways in which economists use the term "model," and connecting model building to the process of developing and testing theories. In the appendix there is a clarified discussion of the difference between cross-sectional and time-series data.

- In Chapter 3, the box on comparative advantage has been completely rewritten. It now shows what happens when specialization occurs in the "wrong direction." There is also a new box on the difficulties involved in converting from command economies to market economies.

Part 2 An Introduction to Demand and Supply

- Chapter 4, which introduces the concepts of demand and supply, has a reworked discussion of what causes shifts in demand and supply curves. The existing box on "what really happens" has new examples of weather-generated demand and supply shocks. (The old appendix on foreign trade has been moved to Chapter 6.)

- In Chapter 5, the old box on the use of averages for computing elasticities has now been integrated into the text. In an effort to reduce the dryness of this chapter, we have added a new final section that presents "two examples where elasticity matters." This section examines the issue of tax incidence and the distinction between short-run and long-run elasticities.

- Chapter 6 has been substantially redesigned. It begins with a general discussion of government-controlled prices. It then goes on to examine the case of rent controls (this discussion has been extensively rewritten), agricultural policy, and foreign trade and tariffs. Each of these three applications can be covered independently. The chapter then ends with a section on "four lessons about resource allocation" which generalizes the specific lessons learned throughout the chapter.

Part 3 Consumption, Production, and Cost

- Chapter 7 has been completely rewritten. We now lay out the basic theory of consumer demand using marginal utility theory. This has proved to be the most accessible to students. Indifference curve analysis is now presented in the appendix. The more formal approach is thus still available to those instructors who prefer it. Consumer surplus, income and substitution effects, and the total-marginal distinction, all of which we view as key concepts, are developed in the text of Chapter 7.

- Chapter 8 is now the first chapter in the theory of the firm. It combines definitional material (economic profit, opportunity cost) with the analysis of cost and production in the short run. We have added a new box which presents a glossary of the different short-run cost concepts.

- Chapter 9 examines the firm in the long run and the very-long run. We have rewritten the discussion of the profit-maximizing factor mix. There is also a new box

on Jacob Viner's famous error. The appendix develops the long-run cost model via the use of isoquants and isocost curves.

Part 4 Pricing and Market Structure

- Chapter 10, which examines perfect competition, is unchanged in its basic structure. The box which contrasts the firm's and the industry's demand elasticity has been rewritten. We have also rewritten the discussion of entry and exit and the conditions required for long-run equilibrium.

- In the discussion of monopoly in Chapter 11, there is a new box on "fashion knockoffs" as an example of how technological change has lowered entry barriers.

- Chapter 12 has been retitled to reflect its added emphasis on strategic behaviour. The first section has been completely rewritten and now better motivates both the discussion of monopolistic competition and oligopoly. There is a new box on the prisoner's dilemma, and the discussion of strategic behaviour has been recast to emphasize game theory.

- In Chapter 13, we have tried to emphasize that allocative efficiency is a property of an *economy* rather than just a single industry. We have also made some clarifying changes in the discussion of marginal-cost and average-cost pricing. There is a new box on the pricing policies of the provincial hydro authorities.

- Chapter 14 combines institutional material from Chapter 9 of the previous edition with a streamlined discussion of the market for corporate control and the behaviour of foreign direct investment. We have added some data on the flows of inward- and outward-bound foreign investment since 1960.

Part 5 The Markets for Factors of Production

- In Chapter 15, the section on "the demand for factors" has been substantially reworked, emphasizing the distinction between the physical and revenue aspects of marginal revenue product. The section on "policy issues" now concludes with an examination of data on Canadian interprovincial labour mobility. This should emphasize the importance of the chapter's main theme of factor mobility.

- Chapter 16 now begins with a discussion of the conditions required to have a single wage in the labour market. The chapter then examines violations of these conditions. The discussion of wage differentials now leads to a new box on the puzzle of interindustry wage differentials in Canada. The section on labour unions has been substantially reworked, and a discussion of the union wage premium has been added. The final section presents the "good jobs—bad jobs" debate.

- Chapter 17 discusses the pricing of capital and nonrenewable resources. The discussion on present value has been clarified. A new box has been added on inflation and the distinction between nominal and real interest rates. The section of the equilibrium interest rate has been substantially reworked.

Part 6 Government Policy in the Market Economy

- In Chapter 18 we now make a very clear distinction between what we call the "formal" and the "informal" defences of free markets. The section on externalities has been completely rewritten and now ends with a new example of the Coase theorem. There is a new box on the Atlantic fishery illustrating the Tragedy of the Commons. The existing box on the "lemons problem" has been moved to this chapter to complement the discussion on information asymmetries.

- Chapter 19 examines environmental and safety regulation. The discussion on pollution regulation is now complemented with a new box on the U.S. experience with tradable emissions permits for sulphur dioxide.

- Chapter 20 examines government taxation and expenditure, and is the merger of Chapters 22 and 23 from the previous edition. It has also been extensively rewritten. The discussion on equity and efficiency of the tax system now leads to a new box on the negative income tax. There are considerable changes in the discussion of fiscal federalism. The final section of the chapter examines what we call the five pillars of Canadian social policy—education, health care, income support, unemployment insurance, and retirement support.

CHANGES IN MACROECONOMICS

Here is a brief description of the major changes in the macroeconomics half of the textbook.

Part 7 An Introduction to Macroeconomics

- The first two chapters have now been put into their own section, which is an introduction to macroeconomics. Chapter 21 has a substantially rewritten section of the major macroeconomic issues. The chapter brings the calculation of the CPI forward into a simple discussion box (rather than in an appendix).

- Chapter 22 has a new box on the arbitrary decisions involved in national income accounting. There is an expanded discussion of the distinction between GDP and GNP.

Part 8 National Income and Fiscal Policy

- Chapter 23 now uses two approaches for examining equilibrium national income: (1) desired aggregate expenditure equals actual national income and (2) desired saving equals desired investment. Some Canadian data have

been added so that students can see the empirical relevance of the consumption function.

- As in the previous chapter, the discussion of equilibrium in Chapter 24 now uses both approaches. This includes a discussion of private versus national saving and then introduces the concept of "national asset formation." The discussion of fiscal policy in Chapter 24 has been streamlined. The final section of the chapter, "lessons and limitations of the income-expenditure approach," has been considerably expanded and we have tried to emphasize the assumptions underlying the demand-determined nature of the model. This then motivates the discussion of aggregate supply in the next chapter.

- We have tried in Chapter 25 to clarify the distinction between the demand side and the supply side of the economy. The old box on why the *AD* curve slopes down has been integrated into the text. A new section has been added which reconciles the central results in this chapter with the results from the two previous chapters.

- In Chapter 26, the old box on *AD* shocks and business cycles has been integrated into the text. We have reworked the discussion of the paradox of thrift.

Part 9 Money, Banking, and Monetary Policy

- In Chapter 27, there is a new discussion of "joint responsibility" in the operation of the Bank of Canada, and how this dates from the Coyne Affair. We have tried to clarify the discussion of deposit creation, partly by being very clear about what is meant by a "new deposit." M2+ now appears in the discussion of the money supply.

- Chapter 28 has a new introduction, and there are new introductory paragraphs in several sections. The box on the open-economy transmission mechanism has been entirely rewritten (and is clearly indicated as being optional material).

- In Chapter 29, we now make it clear that open-market operations and the switching of government deposits are similar in their effect on the reserves of the banking system. Emphasis is then placed on the central bank's effect on reserves, rather than on a specific action. There is a new box on the bank rate and how this is now connected to the overnight interest rate. In the discussion of intermediate targets, there is a new discussion of the open-economy transmission mechanism and this leads to a new box on the *Monetary Conditions Index* and how the Bank uses this in its conduct of monetary policy. There is also a new box on "two views of the role of money in the Great Depression."

Part 10 Macroeconomic Problems and Policies

- Chapter 30 includes an updated discussion of the Bank of Canada's inflation policy. The Crow-to-Thiessen transition is discussed, and the policy change toward "price stability" is emphasized.

- In Chapter 31, there is a new section which discusses gross flows in the labour market. This leads to a new box which shows how flows data can be used to think about the expected duration of unemployment spells. The discussion of frictional unemployment has been modified, and this leads to a new box on search unemployment. We have also added a section on "policy and labour market flexibility" which argues that policies reducing flexibility are likely to raise the NAIRU.

- Chapter 32, which examines government debt and deficits, has been completely rewritten. The opening section on facts and definitions highlights the distinction between overall deficits and primary deficits, a distinction which returns later in the chapter. The second section examines the Ricardian Equivalence proposition, which is then revisited when the effects of deficits are examined in the third section. There are two boxes: (1) computing changes in the debt-to-GDP ratio and (2) two myths about government debt.

- Chapter 33 examines economic growth. We have changed the ordering of topics in this chapter to improve the flow of ideas. In the section on saving and investment, there is some data which shows the correlation between saving and investment in G7 countries since the 1960s.

- Chapter 34 is a new chapter on growth in the developing economies. This chapter examines traditional views about development and contrasts them with newer views, many of which relate to the discussion in the previous chapter. The chapter ends with a box presenting a case study of the South Korean experience.

Part 11 International Economics

- Chapter 35 examines the theory of international trade. The section on the sources of comparative advantage now contains a discussion of acquired comparative advantage. The box on the gains from trade has been changed to apply to an economy with a concave production possibilities boundary. In the final section, we have added data on Canada's terms of trade.

- Chapter 36, which discusses trade policy, has been substantially rewritten. In addition to thorough discussions of the theoretical arguments for and against free trade, there is an extensive discussion of the GATT, the formation of the WTO and the creation of NAFTA. There is a new discussion of trade creation and trade diversion. There is also a new box on Canada-U.S. trade disputes which discusses the cases of softwood lumber, supply-managed agricultural products, and cultural industries.

- Chapter 37, which examines exchange rates and the balance of payments, has been completely rewritten.

We have clarified the meaning of payments and receipts, especially as these terms apply to the central bank's actions. In the section on purchasing power parity, there is a new discussion which warns against applying PPP to broad price indices. There is also a new box on beggar-my-neighbour policies

- Chapter 38 discusses open-economy macroeconomic policy. We have made some substantial changes to the section on international capital mobility. There is a new section on the relationship between the government's budget deficit and the current account deficit—the twin deficits.

SUPPLEMENTS TO THE TEXTBOOK

There are several products to accompany *Economics,* either for the student or for the instructor.

Study Guide.   Our book is accompanied by a Study Guide, written by Kenneth Grant and William Furlong. The Study Guide can be used either in the classroom or by the students on their own. It offers additional study support and essential reinforcement for each text chapter, including chapter overviews, objectives, multiple-choice questions, exercises, short problems, and answers. It is available in one- or two-volume editions.

Instructor's Manual.   Prepared by us, the Instructor's Manual includes an explanation of the approach used in each text chapter, along with a chapter overview, answers to all end-of-chapter questions, and additional teaching suggestions.

Test Bank.   The Test Bank to accompany *Economics* has been completely overhauled by Ingrid Kristjanson-Ragan and Christopher Ragan. Approximately one-third of the questions in each chapter have been replaced by new questions. Many others have been revised or corrected. The questions are now organized within each chapter according to topic, which should make it easier for the instructor to select questions. We have also added two new levels of difficulty for questions. Each question was previously coded as either Difficulty 1, 2, or 3. These categories still exist (though we have in many cases reclassified the difficulty of the question). Difficulty 4 now pertains *only* to questions that are based on material found in the appendices. Difficulty 5 now pertains *only* to material found in the boxes. This is in keeping with our general approach that boxes and appendices are optional.

The Test Bank is free to adopters; it is also available in a microcomputerized version for IBM PCs or Macintosh computers called *Test Master,* which provides customized testing capabilities.

Transparencies.   For this edition, over 100 illustrations from 18 key theory chapters are reproduced as four-color transparency acetates. In addition, the remaining figures in the text are reproduced in the form of transparency masters. All of these are available free to adopters.

Software.   Also available with this text is a student software package. It contains an interactive tutorial with multicoloured graphs and exercises to help students learn key material from fifteen chapters. Interactive learning can make it much easier to absorb graphically presented concepts. The student software also offers a self-test program which asks questions about any text chapter and scores the results.

Using the book

Needs of students differ: Some want material that goes beyond the average class level, but others have gaps in their backgrounds. To accommodate the former we have included more material than we would assign to every student. Also, because there are many different kinds of first-year economics courses in colleges and universities, we have included more material than normally would be included in any single course.

Although instructors can best design their own courses, it may help if we indicate certain views of our own as to how this book might be adapted to different courses.

SEQUENCE

The choice of whether to study macro first or micro first is partly a personal one that cannot be decided solely by objective criteria. We believe that in the 1990s there are good reasons for preferring the micro-macro order. The thrust over the last 25 years has been to examine the micro underpinnings of macro functions and to erect macroeconomics on a firmer base of micro behavioural relations. Virtually every current macro controversy turns on some micro underpinning. For "micro-firsters" this poses no problem. For "macro-firsters" it is often hard to explain what is at issue.

Changes occur not only in economic theory but also in the problems that excite students. Many of today's problems that students find most challenging—mergers and takeovers, foreign direct investment, poverty, pollution—are microeconomic in character. The micro-macro order, moreover, reflects the historical evolution of the subject. A century of Classical and Neoclassical development of microeconomics preceded the Keynesian development of macroeconomics.

For those who prefer the macro-micro order, we have attempted to make reversibility easy. The overview in Chapter 3 (in Part 1) provides a base on which to build either the microeconomics beginning in Part 2 or the macroeconomics beginning in Part 7. Chapters 4 and 5 should be assigned after Chapter 3, even in macro-first courses. Where further microeconomic concepts are required—as in the discussion of investment in the core macro model—we have added brief sections to make the treatment self-contained, while providing review material for those who have covered the microeconomic section.

POSSIBLE OUTLINE FOR A ONE-SEMESTER COURSE IN ECONOMICS

Many first courses in economics are only one semester (or equivalent) in length, but cover both microeconomics and macroeconomics. Our book can be easily adapted to such courses. Here is our proposed outline for a one-semester course in economics principles. Core chapters for such a course are shown with an *. Chapters shown with a † are particularly appropriate for courses with a heavy policy orientation.

Note: A one-semester course can cover no more than 24 full chapters (and even that is a very full course!). The core consists of about 13 chapters. Selections from other chapters can produce courses with various emphases.

ACKNOWLEDGMENTS

The starting point for this book was *Economics*, Eleventh Edition, by Richard G. Lipsey and Paul N. Courant. It would be impossible to acknowledge here all the teachers, colleagues, and students who contributed to that book. Hundreds of users have written to us with specific suggested improvements, and much of the credit for the fact that the book does become more and more teachable belongs to them. We can no longer list them individually but we thank them all most sincerely.

Ian Christensen provided research assistance for which we are thankful. A number of individuals provided reviews of the eighth Canadian edition that were most helpful in preparing the present edition. At a later stage, we were also aided by the comments from several reviewers of the revised manuscript. These people are:

Steve Ambler
  (*Université du Québec à Montréal*)

David Andolfatto
  (*University of Waterloo*)

Robert Cherneff
  (*University of Victoria*)

David Cox
  (*University of Waterloo*)

Kieran Furlong
  (*University of Toronto*)

Irwin Gillespie
  (*Carleton University*)

David Gray
  (*University of Ottawa*)

Michael Hare
  (*University of Toronto*)

Ibrahim Hayani
  (*Seneca College*)

Cheryl Jenkins
  (*John Abbott College*)

David Johnson
  (*Wilfred Laurier University*)

Colin Jones
  (*University of Victoria*)

Marion Jones
  (*University of Regina*)

Ian King
  (*University of Victoria*)

George Kondor
  (*Lakehead University*)

Irwin Lipnowski
  (*University of Manitoba*)

Bill Morrison
  (*Wilfred Laurier University*)

A. Gyasi Nimarko
  (*Vanier College*)

Sonja Novkovic
  (*Saint Mary's University*)

Arnold Paus-Jenssen
  (*University of Saskatchewan*)

Balbir S. Sahni
  (*Concordia University*)

Brian Scarfe
  (*University of Regina*)

George Slasor
  (*University of Toronto*)

Brenda Spotton
  (*York University*)

Weiqiu Yu
  (*University of New Brunswick*).

We thank them all for their contribution to improving this textbook.

In addition, the following people reviewed the supplements that accompany this book: Study Guide—Peter Tsigaris (University College of the Cariboo), David Gray (University of Ottawa), Keith MacKinnon (York University), Eva Lau (University of Waterloo), Suki Badh (Doublas University College); Test Bank—Peter Kantrowitz (Douglas University College).

Our special thanks goes to Ingrid Kristjanson-Ragan, who closely read the entire manuscript and provided excellent comments and suggestions for improving some of the most difficult passages. She also helped tremendously with the biographical sketches of the economists for the timeline at the back of the book. For her diligence and hard work we are especially grateful.

Richard G. Lipsey
Christopher T. S. Ragan
Paul N. Courant

TO THE STUDENT

A good course in economics will give you insight into how an economy functions and into some currently debated policy issues. Like all rewarding subjects, economics will not be mastered without effort. A book on economics must be worked at. It cannot be read like a novel.

Each of you must develop an individual technique for studying, but the following suggestions may prove helpful. It is usually a good idea to read a chapter quickly in order to get the general run of the argument. At this first reading, you may want to skip the boxes and any footnotes. Then, after reading the Chapter Summary and the Key Concepts (both at the end of each chapter), reread the chapter more slowly, making sure that you understand each step of the argument.

With respect to the figures and tables, be sure you understand how the conclusions that are stated in the brief tag lines with each table or figure have been reached. You must not skip the captions. They provide the core of economic reasoning. You should be prepared to spend time on difficult sections; occasionally, you may spend an hour on only a few pages. Paper and pencil are indispensable equipment in your reading. It is best to follow a difficult argument by building your own diagram while the argument unfolds rather than by relying on the finished diagram as it appears in the book. It is often helpful to invent numerical examples to illustrate general propositions.

The end-of-chapter questions require you to apply what you have studied. We advise you to outline answers to some of the questions. In short, you should seek to understand economics, not to memorize it.

We call your attention to the glossary at the end of the book, beginning on page G-1. Any time that you encounter a concept that seems vaguely familiar but is not clear to you, check the glossary. Chances are that it will be there and that its definition will remind you of what you once understood. If you are still in doubt, check the index entry to find where the concept is discussed more fully. Incidentally, the glossary, along with the captions that accompany figures and tables and the end-of-chapter summaries, may prove to be very helpful when you are reviewing for examinations.

The bracketed boldface numbers in the text itself refer to a series of mathematical notes that are found starting on page M-1 at the end of the book. For those of you who like mathematics or prefer mathematical argument to verbal or geometric exposition, these may prove useful. Others may ignore them.

There is also a time line of great economists, immediately following the Glossary located at the back of the book. While reading the textbook, you will encounter the names of many great economists that have shaped the way modern-day economists think. But in the text we usually do not have the space to say more than a few words about these economists. The time line at the back of the book offers a more complete (but still brief) description of the life and works of many of these great economists. They are placed on a time line that begins in the mid 1700s and continues through the middle of this century. On this time line are also placed major world events, so that you will be better able to appreciate the world in which these economists lived when they were developing their thoughts. Our hope is that your sense of history and your sense of the origins of economics will be enhanced by glancing through this time line. Do so at your leisure!

We strongly suggest you make use of the excellent Study Guide written expressly for this text It will test and reinforce your understanding of the concepts and analytical techniques stressed in each chapter of the text and will help prepare you for your examinations. The ability to solve problems and to communicate and interpret your results are important goals in an introductory course in economics. The Study Guide can play an important role in your acquisition of these skills.

We hope you will find the book rewarding and stimulating. Students who used earlier editions made some of the most helpful suggestions for revision, and we hope that you will carry on the tradition. If you are moved to write to us (and we hope that you will be!), please do. You can send any comments or questions regarding the text (or any of the supplementary material, such as the Study Guide) to:

Christopher Ragan
Department of Economics
McGill University
855 Sherbrooke St. West
Montreal, Quebec
H3A 2T7

Or, if you prefer to communicate through E-mail,
send your comments to:

ragan@leacock.lan.mcgill.ca

PART ONE

THE NATURE OF ECONOMICS

What is economics all about? How will the study of economics help you to understand how modern economies function, and how modern economies differ from the economies of the past? Why does it appear that economists seldom agree on anything among themselves, or is this only an illusion? What makes some economic theories more sensible than others? What is the difference between microeconomics and macroeconomics, and is one more important than the other? These are questions that you will be able to answer after reading the following three chapters.

Chapter 1 introduces you to the concepts of *scarcity, choice, and opportunity cost*; each is central to understanding any economic system. You will then learn about various types of economic systems, ranging from the primarily *command economies* of the former Soviet Union to the primarily *market economies* of Canada, the United States, or Japan. This chapter also discusses the importance of *economic policy,* and emphasizes that *trade offs* between various policy goals are inevitable, and are often the source of disagreements about what constitutes the "best" policy.

Chapter 2 discusses the study of economics itself. You are introduced to the distinction between *positive statements* and *normative statements,* a distinction upon which the progress of economics as a social science is based. We then examine the role of *theory* in economics, and we explain why economists—like physicists or chemists—build *models* to help them think about the complex world they are trying to understand. Finally, you will learn about the way economists *test* their theories by confronting the *predictions* of their theories with the *evidence* drawn from the real world.

Chapter 3 presents a broad outline of the way market economies function. You are first shown how economies developed from ones in which all individuals were largely self sufficient to modern economies in which *specialization* and *trade* play a crucial role. You then meet the economy's main cast of characters—*households, firms, and governments*. Like characters in a play need the props and the lighting, you will see that a modern economy needs *markets* and *institutions* in order to operate smoothly. Finally, we examine the two separate but complementary ways of viewing the economy—*microeconomics* and *macroeconomics*. The questions and the emphasis differ markedly between the two, but we need both to understand the whole economy.

CHAPTER 1

THE ECONOMIC PROBLEM

Turn on the TV news, read your local newspaper or *The Globe and Mail,* glance at *Maclean's* or *The Economist* magazines and you will see for yourself that many of the world's most pressing problems are economic.

Why did communism fail to deliver acceptable living standards to the citizens of the countries of Eastern Europe and the republics of the former USSR? Why is the transition from communism to markets proving so difficult for many of these countries? Are the developed nations right in making the adoption of more market-oriented economic policies a precondition of increased foreign aid to the less-developed countries of the world? What is the impact of the growth of vast transnational corporations that conduct business over much of the world? Will the growth of mouths to feed outrun the growth of food to feed those mouths? Are economists right in arguing that environmental protection is often best accomplished using market incentives rather than direct government intervention?

Your media survey of press, radio, and TV will also show the importance of economic issues in the problems facing Canada today.

How is it that when the average Canadian citizen enjoys one of the highest living standards the world has ever seen, a standard vastly higher than has been achieved by most of the people who have ever lived on the earth, many Canadians are living below the so-called "poverty line" and worrying about how to feed their children? Should Canada feel threatened by Japanese economic power, or by the emerging economic power of the countries known as the "Asian Tigers"? Has the North American Free Trade Agreement (NAFTA) been a good or bad thing for the average Canadian? Why are so many large and established companies engaged in re-engineering (often a euphemism for downsizing, which in turn is a euphemism for laying workers off), and what does this imply for people's job prospects?

Does the size of the Federal government's budget deficit affect the average Canadian's living standards? Is the Bank of Canada right in believing that a low inflation rate is good for the country? Why has labour productivity in Canada and most other developed countries grown more slowly in the past two decades than through most of this century? Does it pay you to go on to higher education? Does it pay the nation to subsidize you to do so?

Of course, not all the world's problems are primarily economic. Political, biological, social, cultural, and philosophical issues often predominate. However, as the following examples suggest, no matter how noneconomic a particular problem may seem, it will almost always have a significant economic dimension.

1. The crises that lead to wars often have economic roots. Nations often fight for oil and rice and land to live on, even when the rhetoric of their leaders evokes God, glory, and nation.

2. It took 100,000 years, from the time *Homo sapiens* first appeared on earth until the year 1800, for the human population to reach 1 billion. In the next 100 years, a second billion was added. Three billion more came in the next 80 years. The world's population is predicted to reach 10 billion by the middle of the twenty-first century. The economic consequences are steady pressures on the environment and the food supply. Unless the human race can find ways to deal with these pressures, increasing millions of people face starvation, and increasing billions face rising levels of environmental degradation.

3. *Global warming* describes the possibility of a gradual warming of the earth's climate due to a cumulative buildup of carbon dioxide (CO_2) in the atmosphere. If the possibility proves a reality, the warming will have significant economic consequences, changing both production possibilities and consumption patterns.

WHAT IS ECONOMICS?

We have mentioned a handful of important current issues on which economics can shed some light. One way to define *economics* is to say that it is the social science that deals with such problems. A better known definition comes from the great economist Alfred Marshall (1842–1924), whom we will encounter at several points in this book: "Economics is a study of mankind in the ordinary business of life." A more penetrating definition is the following:

Economics is the study of the use of scarce resources to satisfy unlimited human wants.

Scarcity is inevitable and is central to economic problems. What are society's resources? Why is scarcity inevitable? What are the consequences of scarcity?

RESOURCES AND PRODUCTS

A society's resources consist of natural endowments such as land, forests, and minerals; human resources, both mental and physical; and manufactured aids to production such as tools, machinery, and buildings. Economists call such resources **factors of production**[1] because they are used to produce the outputs that people desire. We divide these outputs into goods and services. **Goods** are tangible (e.g., cars and shoes), and **services** are intangible (e.g., haircuts and education). Notice the implication of positive value contained in the terms *goods* and *services*. (Compare the terms *bads* and *disservices*.)

People use goods and services to satisfy many of their wants. The act of making them is called **production,** and the act of using them to satisfy wants is called **consumption.** Goods are valued for the services they provide. An automobile, for example, helps to satisfy its owner's desires for transportation, mobility, and possibly status.

SCARCITY

For most of the world's 6 billion people, scarcity is real and ever present. In relation to desires (for more and better food, clothing, housing, schooling, entertainment, and so forth), existing resources are woefully inadequate; there are enough to produce only a small fraction of the goods and services that are wanted.

But are not the advanced industrialized nations rich enough that scarcity is nearly banished? After all, they have been characterized as affluent societies. Whatever affluence may mean, it does not mean the end of the problem of scarcity. Most households that earn $80,000 per year (a princely amount by world standards) have no trouble spending it on things that seem useful to them. Yet it would take nearly twice the present output of the Canadian economy to produce enough to allow all Canadian households to earn that amount.

CHOICE

Because resources are scarce, all societies face the problem of deciding what to produce and how much each person will consume. Societies differ in who makes the choices and how they are made, but the need to choose is common to all. Just as scarcity implies the need for choice, so choice implies the existence of cost. A decision to have more of something requires a decision to have less of something

else. The less of "something else" can be thought of as the cost of having the more of "something."

Scarcity implies that choices must be made, and making choices implies the existence of costs.

Opportunity Cost

To see how choice implies cost, we look first at a trivial example and then at one that vitally affects all of us; both examples involve precisely the same fundamental principles.

Consider the choice that must be made by a young girl who has 50 cents to spend and who is determined to spend it all on candy. For the child, there are only two kinds of candy in the world: gumdrops, which sell for 5 cents each, and chocolates, which sell for 10 cents each. The child would like to buy 10 gumdrops and 10 chocolates but soon discovers that this is not possible: It is not an *attainable combination* given the scarce resources available. However, several combinations are attainable: 8 gumdrops and 1 chocolate, 4 gumdrops and 3 chocolates, 2 gumdrops and 4 chocolates, and so on. Some of these combinations leave money unspent, and the child is not interested in them. Only six combinations, as shown in Figure 1-1, are both attainable and use the entire 50 cents.

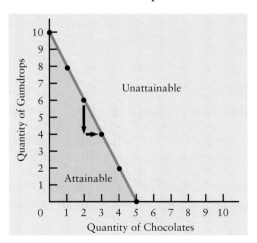

FIGURE 1-1
A Choice Between Gumdrops and Chocolates

A limited amount of money forces a choice among alternatives. Six combinations of gumdrops and chocolates are attainable and use all of the child's money. The negatively sloped line provides a boundary between attainable and unattainable combinations. The arrows show that the opportunity cost of 1 more chocolate is 2 gumdrops.

---

[1]Definitions of the terms in boldface can be found in the glossary at the back of the book.

APPLICATION 1-1

THE OPPORTUNITY COST OF YOUR UNIVERSITY DEGREE

As discussed in the text, the opportunity cost of choosing one thing is what must be given up as *the best alternative.* Computing the opportunity cost of a college or university education is a good example to illustrate which factors are included (and which are excluded) from the computation of opportunity cost. You may also be surprised to learn how expensive your university degree really is!*

Suppose that a Bachelor's degree requires four years of study and that each year you spend $2,500 for tuition fees—approximately the average at Canadian universities in 1996—and a further $1,000 per year for books and materials. Does this mean that the cost of a university education is only $14,000? Unfortunately not; the true cost of a university degree is much higher.

The key point is that the opportunity cost of a university education does not just include the out-of-

---

* This box considers only the cost *to the student* of a university degree. For reasons that will be discussed in detail in Part 6 of this book, the government heavily subsidizes post-secondary education in Canada. Because of this subsidy, the cost *to society* of a university degree may be quite different from the cost to an individual student.

pocket expenses on tuition and books. You must also take into consideration *what you are forced to give up* by choosing to attend university. Of course, if you were not studying you could have been doing any one of a number of things, but the relevant one is *the one you would have chosen instead*—your best alternative to attending university.

Suppose that your best alternative to attending university was to get a job. In this case, the opportunity cost of your university degree must include the earnings that you would have received had you taken that job. Suppose that your (after-tax) annual earnings would have been $18,000 per year, for a total of $72,000 if you stayed at that job for four years. To the direct expenses of $14,000, we must therefore add $72,000 for the earnings that you gave up by not taking a job. This brings the true cost of your university degree—the opportunity cost—up to $86,000!

Notice that the cost of food, lodging, clothing, and other living expenses did not enter the calculation of the opportunity cost in this example. This is because living expenses must be incurred in either case—whether you attend university or get a job. Of course, it is possible that your total living ex-

---

After careful thought, the child has almost decided to buy 6 gumdrops and 2 chocolates, but at the last moment she decides that she simply must have 3 chocolates. What will it cost to get this extra chocolate? One answer is 2 gumdrops. As seen in the figure, this is the number of gumdrops the child must forgo to get the extra chocolate. Economists describe the 2 gumdrops as the *opportunity cost* of the third chocolate.

Another answer is that the cost of the third chocolate is 10 cents. However, given the child's budget and her intentions, this answer is less revealing than the first one. Though the real choice is between more of this and more of that, the cost of "this" is usefully viewed in terms of what one cannot have of "that."

The idea of opportunity cost is one of the central insights of economics. Here is a precise definition. The **opportunity cost** of using resources for a certain purpose is defined to be *the benefit given up by not using them in the best alternative way.* That is, it is the cost measured in terms of other goods and services that could have been obtained instead. If, for example, resources that could have produced 20 miles of road are used instead to produce two small hospitals, the opportunity cost of a hospital is 10 miles of road; looked at the other way round, the opportunity cost of 1 mile of road is one-tenth of a hospital.

Every time a choice is made, opportunity costs are incurred.

penses as a student are different from what they would have been had you taken the job. In this case, the calculation of opportunity cost would need to be adjusted. For example, perhaps the job you would have taken *required* you to spend $3,000 for clothes so that you could look presentable to customers. In contrast, you find that your university classmates and professors are pretty relaxed about fashion and that your old jeans are perfectly adequate. In this case, the opportunity cost of your university degree would be only $83,000 because by attending university you "saved" $3,000 that you otherwise would have had to spend on clothes.

Notice also that the higher is your earning potential in a job, the higher is the opportunity cost of attending university. For example, if your best alternative to attending university was to get a job that paid $25,000 per year (instead of $18,000), the opportunity cost of your degree rises from $86,000 to $114,000. When your earning potential is high, the opportunity cost of getting a degree is high because you are giving up a lot to go to university. The reverse is also true; when high school graduates can only expect low-paying jobs, or when the prospects of getting any job is poor (when the unemployment rate is high), the opportunity cost of attending university is lower. This suggests that university enrollments should be higher during periods of high unemployment, and this is indeed the case in Canada.

If the opportunity cost of a university degree is so high, why do students choose to go to university? The simple answer is that they believe that they are better off by going to university than by not going (otherwise they would not go!). Maybe the students simply enjoy learning, and thus are prepared to incur the high cost to be in the university environment. Or maybe they believe that a university degree will significantly increase their future earning potential. In this case, they are giving up four years of earnings at one salary so that they can invest in their own skills in the hopes of enjoying many more years in the future at a considerably higher salary.

Whatever the case, the recognition that a university degree is very expensive should convince students to make the best use of their time while they are there. Read on!

See Application 1-1 for an example of opportunity cost which should seem quite familiar to you—the opportunity cost of getting a university degree.

Production Possibilities

Although the choice between gumdrops and chocolates is a minor consumption decision, the essential nature of the decision is the same whatever the choice being made. Consider, for example, the important choice between producing military and civilian goods.

If resources are fully employed, it is not possible to have more of both. However, as the government cuts defence production, resources needed to produce civilian goods will be freed up. The opportunity cost of increased civilian goods is therefore the forgone military output. (Or, if we were considering an increase in military output, the opportunity cost of military output would be the foregone civilian goods.)

The choice is illustrated in Figure 1-2. Because resources are limited, some combinations—those that would require more than the total available supply of resources for their production—cannot be attained. The negatively sloped curve on the graph divides the combinations that can be attained from those that cannot. Points above and to the right of this curve cannot be attained because there are not enough resources; points below and to the left of the curve can be attained without using all of the available resources; and points on the curve can just be attained if all the available resources are used. The curve is called the **production possibility boundary** or **production possibility curve.** It has a negative slope because when all resources are being used, producing more of one kind of good requires producing less of the other kind.

A production possibility boundary illustrates three concepts: scarcity, choice, and opportunity cost. Scarcity is indicated by the unattainable combinations above the boundary; choice, by the need to choose among the alternative attainable points along the boundary; and opportunity cost, by the negative slope of the boundary.

The shape of the production possibility boundary in Figure 1-2 implies that an increasing amount of civilian production must be given up to achieve equal successive increases in military production. This shape, referred to as *concave* to the origin, indicates that the opportunity cost of either good grows larger and larger

as we increase the amount of it that is produced. A straight-line boundary, as in Figure 1-1, indicates that the opportunity cost of one good in terms of the other stays constant, no matter how much of it is produced.

The concave shape in Figure 1-2 occurs because each factor of production is not equally useful in producing all goods. To see why differences among factors of production are so important, consider beginning at a point where all resources are devoted to the production of military goods, and then consider gradually shifting more and more resources toward the production of civilian goods. The first resources you shift might be, just to take an example, nutrient-rich land that is particularly well-suited to growing wheat. This land may not be very useful for making military equipment, but it is very useful for making certain civilian goods (like bread). This shift of resources will therefore lead to a very small reduction in military ouptut, but a substantial increase in civilian output. Thus the opportunity cost of producing the first unit of civilian goods, which is equal to the foregone military output, is very small. But as we shift more and more resources toward the production of civilian goods, we must shift more and more resources that are actually quite well suited to the production of military output, like airplane mechanics or the minerals needed to make gunpowder. This implies that as we produce more and more civilian goods (by having more and more resources devoted to producing them), the amount of military output that must be foregone to produce one *extra* unit of civilian goods rises. That is, the opportunity cost of producing one good rises as more of that good is produced.

FOUR KEY ECONOMIC PROBLEMS

Modern economies involve thousands of complex production and consumption activities. While this complexity is important, many of the basic kinds of decisions that must be made are not very different from those made in primative economies in which people work with few tools and barter with their neighbours. Whatever the economic system, most problems studied by economists can be grouped under four main headings.

What Is Produced and How?

The allocation of scarce resources among alternative uses, called **resource allocation,** determines the quan-

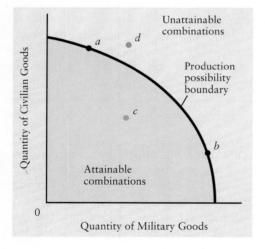

FIGURE 1-2
A Production Possibility Boundary

Unattainable combinations

Production possibility boundary

Attainable combinations

Quantity of Civilian Goods

Quantity of Military Goods

The negatively sloped boundary shows the combinations that are just attainable when all of the society's resources are efficiently employed. The production possibility boundary separates the attainable combinations of goods, such as *a, b,* and *c,* from unattainable combinations, such as *d.* Points *a* and *b* represent full and efficient use of society's resources. Point *c* represents either inefficient use of resources or failure to use all the available resources.

tities of various goods that are produced. What determines which goods get produced? Choosing to produce a particular combination of goods means choosing a particular allocation of resources among the industries or regions producing the goods.

Further, because resources are scarce, it is desirable that they be used efficiently. Hence it matters which of the available methods of production is used to produce each of the goods. What determines which methods of production get used and which ones do not?

In terms of Figure 1-2, these questions relate to where the economy will produce. Will the economy be inside the production possibility boundary because resources are used inefficiently? If resources are used efficiently, then at which point on the boundary will production take place?

What Is Consumed and by Whom?

What is the relationship between an economy's production of goods and the consumption enjoyed by its citizens? Economists seek to understand what determines the distribution of a nation's total output among its people. Who gets a lot, who gets a little, and why?

If production takes place on the production possibility boundary, then how about consumption? Will the economy consume exactly the same goods as it produces? Or will the country's ability to trade with other countries permit the economy to consume a different combination of goods?

Questions relating to what is produced and how, and what is consumed and by whom, fall within the realm of microeconomics. Microeconomics is the study of the allocation of resources as it is affected by the workings of the price system and government policies that seek to influence it.

Why are Resources Sometimes Idle?

When an economy is in a recession, many workers who would like to have jobs are unable to find employers to hire them. At the same time, the managers and owners of offices and factories would like to operate at a higher level of activity—that is, they would like to produce more goods and services. Similarly, during recessions raw materials are typically available in abundance. For some reason, however, these resources—labour, factories and equipment, and raw materials—are idle. In terms of Figure 1-2, this means that the economy is operating within its production possibility boundary.

Why are resources sometimes idle? Should governments worry about such idle resources, or is there some reason to believe that such occasional idleness is appropriate in a well-functioning economy? Is there anything that the government could do to reduce such idleness?

Is Productive Capacity Growing?

The capacity to produce goods and services grows rapidly in some countries, expands slowly in others, and actually declines in others. Growth in productive capacity can be represented by an outward shift of the production possibility boundary, as shown in Figure 1-3. If an economy's capacity to produce goods and services is growing, combinations that are unattainable today will become attainable tomorrow. Growth makes it possible to have more of all goods. What are the determinants of growth? Can governments do anything to increase economic growth?

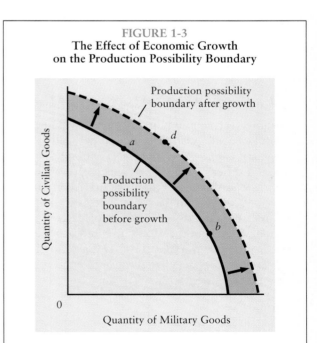

FIGURE 1-3
The Effect of Economic Growth on the Production Possibility Boundary

Economic growth shifts the boundary outward and makes it possible to produce more of all products. Before growth in productive capacity, points *a* and *b* were on the production possibility boundary and point *d* was an unattainable combination. After growth, as shown by the dark shaded band, point *d* and many other previously unattainable combinations are attainable.

Questions relating to the idleness of resources during recessions, and the growth of productive capacity, fall within the realm of macroeconomics. Macroeconomics is the study of the determination of economic aggregates such as total output, total employment, the price level, and the rate of economic growth.

ALTERNATIVE ECONOMIC SYSTEMS

An economic system is a distinctive method of providing answers to the basic economic questions just discussed. All such systems are complex. They include producers of every sort—public and private, domestic and foreign. They include consumers of every sort—young and old, rich and poor, working and nonworking. They include laws—such as those relating to property rights—rules, regulations, taxes, subsidies, and everything else that governments use to influence what is produced, how it is produced, and who gets it. They also include customs of every conceivable kind and the entire range of contemporary mores and values.

TYPES OF ECONOMIC SYSTEMS

Although every economy is in some ways unique, it is helpful to distinguish three pure types, called *traditional, command,* and *market* economies. These economies differ in the way in which economic decisions are coordinated. But no actual economy fits neatly into one of these three categories—all real economies contain some elements of each type. Of particular interest in the 1990s are the so-called *transition economies,* notably those of Eastern Europe, which are moving away from the command form toward a market orientation.

Traditional Systems

A traditional economic system is one in which behaviour is based primarily on tradition, custom, and habit. Young men follow their fathers' occupations. Women do what their mothers did. There is little change in the pattern of goods produced from year to year, other than those imposed by the vagaries of nature. The techniques of production also follow traditional patterns, except when the effects of an occasional new invention are felt. Finally, production is allocated among the members according to long-

established traditions. In short, the answers to the economic questions of what to produce, how to produce, and how to distribute are determined by traditions.

Such a system works best in an unchanging environment. Under static conditions, a system that does not continually require people to make choices can prove effective in meeting economic and social needs.

Traditional systems were common in earlier times. The feudal system, under which most people in medieval Europe lived, was a largely traditional society. Peasants, artisans, and most others living in villages inherited their positions in that society. They also usually inherited their specific jobs, which they handled in traditional ways. For example, the blacksmith made customary charges for dealing with horses brought to him, and it would have been unthinkable for him to decline his services to any villager who requested them.

Today, only a few small, isolated, self-sufficient communities still retain mainly traditional systems. Examples can be found in the Canadian Arctic and in Patagonia. Also, in many less-developed countries, significant aspects of economic behaviour are still governed by traditional patterns.

Command Systems

In command systems, economic behaviour is determined by some central authority, usually the government, which makes most of the necessary decisions on what to produce, how to produce it, and who gets it. Such economies are characterized by the *centralization* of decision making. Because centralized decision makers usually lay down elaborate and complex plans for the behaviour that they wish to impose, the terms **command economy** and **centrally planned economy** are usually used synonymously.

The sheer quantity of data required for central planning of an entire economy is enormous, and the task of analyzing it to produce a fully integrated plan can hardly be exaggerated. Moreover, the plan must be continually changing to take account not only of current data but also of future trends in labour supplies, technological developments, and people's tastes for various goods and services. Doing so involves the planners in *forecasting.* This is a notoriously difficult exercise, not least because of the unavailability of all essential, accurate, and up-to-date information.

A decade ago, more than one third of the world's population lived in countries that relied heavily on central planning to deal with the basic economic questions. Today, the number of such countries is small. Even in countries where planning is the proclaimed system, as in China or Cuba, increasing amounts of market determination are being quietly permitted.

Market Systems

In the third type of economic system, the decisions about resource allocation are made without any central direction. Instead, they result from innumerable independent decisions made by individual producers and consumers. Such a system is known as a **free-market economy** or, more simply, a **market economy**. In such an economy, decisions relating to the basic economic issues are *decentralized*. Despite the absence of a central plan, these many decentralized decisions are nonetheless coordinated. The main coordinating device is the set of market-determined prices—which is why free-market systems are often called *price systems*. Because much of this book is devoted to studying how market systems work, little more needs to be said about them at this point.

Mixed Systems

Economies that are fully traditional or fully centrally controlled or wholly free-market are pure types that are useful for studying basic principles. When we look in detail at any real economy, however, we discover that its economic behaviour is the result of some mixture of central control and market determination, with a certain amount of traditional behaviour as well. In practice, every economy is a **mixed economy** in the sense that it combines significant elements of all three systems in determining economic behaviour.[2] Furthermore, within any economy, the degree of the mix will vary from sector to sector. For example, in some planned economies, the command principle was used more often to determine behaviour in heavy-goods industries, such as steel, than in agriculture. Farmers were often given substantial freedom to produce and sell what they wished in response to varying market prices.

When we speak of a particular economy as being centrally planned, we mean only that the degree of the mix is weighted heavily toward the command principle. When we speak of one as being a market economy, we mean only that the degree of the mix is weighted heavily toward decentralized decision making in response to market signals. It is important to

realize that such distinctions are always matters of degree and that almost every conceivable mix can be found across the spectrum of the world's economies.

Although no country offers an example of either system working alone, some economies, such as those of Canada, the United States, France, and Singapore, rely much more heavily on market decisions than others, such as the economies of China, North Korea, and Cuba. Yet even in Canada, the command principle has some sway. Crown corporations, legislated minimum wages, rules and regulations for environmental protection, quotas on some agricultural outputs, and restrictions on the import of items such as textiles and shoes are the obvious examples.

OWNERSHIP OF RESOURCES

We have seen that economies differ as to the principle used for coordinating their economic decisions. They also differ as to *who owns* their productive resources. Who owns a nation's farms and factories, its coal mines and forests? Who owns its railways, streams, and golf courses? Who owns its houses and hotels?

In a private-ownership economy, the basic raw materials, the productive assets of the society, and the goods produced in the economy are predominantly privately owned. By this standard, Canada has primarily a private-ownership economy. However, even in Canada, public ownership extends beyond the usual basic services such as schools and local transportation systems to include such other activities as housing projects, forest and range land, and electric power utilities.

In contrast, a public-ownership economy is one in which the productive assets are predominantly publicly owned. This was true of the former USSR, and it is true to a significant extent in present-day China. In China, however, private ownership exists in many sectors, including the rapidly-growing part of the manufacturing sector that is foreign owned, mainly by Japanese and by Chinese from Taiwan, Hong Kong, and Singapore.

The Coordination-Ownership Mix

Leaving aside tradition because it is not the predominant coordinating method in any modern market economy, there are four possible combinations of coordination and ownership principles. Of the two most common combinations, the first is the private-ownership market economy, in which the market principle is the main coordinating mechanism and most productive assets are privately owned. The second most common combination during the twen-

---

[2]Although tradition influences behaviour in all societies, we shall have little to say about it in the rest of this chapter because we are primarily interested in the consequences of making economic decisions through the market and command principles.

APPLICATION 1-2

THE FAILURE OF CENTRAL PLANNING

In 1989, communism collapsed throughout Central and Eastern Europe, and the economic systems of formerly communist countries began the transition from centrally planned to market economies. (See Application 3-3 in Chapter 3 for further discussion of these transitions.) Although political issues surely played a role in these events, the economic changes generally confirmed the superiority of a market-oriented price system over central planning as a method of organizing economic activity. The failure of central planning had many causes, but four were particularly significant.

THE FAILURE OF COORDINATION

In centrally planned economies, a body of planners tries to coordinate all the economic decisions about production, investment, trade, and consumption that are likely to be made by producers and consumers throughout the country. Without the use of prices to signal relative scarcity and abundance, central planning generally proved impossible to do with any reasonable degree of success. Bottlenecks in production, shortages of some goods, and gluts of others plagued the Soviet economy for decades. For example, for years there was an ample supply of black-and-white television sets but severe shortages of toilet paper and soap. In 1989, much of a bumper harvest rotted due to shortages of storage and transportation facilities.

FAILURE OF QUALITY CONTROL

Central planners can monitor the number of units produced by any factory and reward plants that exceed their production targets and punish ones that fall short. Factory managers operating under these conditions will meet their quotas by whatever means are available, and once the goods pass out of their factory, what happens to them is someone else's headache.

In market economies, poor quality is punished by low sales, and retailers soon give a signal to factory managers by shifting their purchases to other suppliers. The incentives that obviously flow from such private-sector purchasing discretion are generally absent from command economies, where purchases and sales are planned centrally and prices and profits are not used to signal customer satisfaction or dissatisfaction.

Not surprisingly, very few Eastern European manufactured products were able to stand up to the newly permitted competition from superior goods produced in the advanced market societies.

MISPLACED INCENTIVES

In market economies, relative wages and salaries provide incentives for labour to move from place to place, and the possibility of losing one's job provides an incentive to work diligently. This is a harsh mechanism that punishes losers with loss of income (although social programs provide floors to the amount of economic punishment that can be suffered). In planned economies, workers usually have complete job secu-

tieth century has been the public-ownership planned economy, in which central planning is the primary means of coordinating economic decisions and property is primarily publicly owned.

The two other possible combinations are a market economy in which the resources are publicly owned, and a command economy in which the resources are privately owned. No modern economy has operated under either hybrid type. Nazi Germany from 1932 to 1945 went some way toward combining private own-

ership with the command principle. The United Kingdom from 1945 to 1980 went quite a way toward a public-ownership market economy in that many industries and much housing were publicly owned. On balance, however, Germany and the United Kingdom were still best described as private-ownership market economies. (The United Kingdom's privatization program in the 1980s returned most publicly-owned assets to private ownership, firmly placing that country back in the ranks of private-ownership market economies.)

rity. Industrial unemployment is rare, and even when it does occur, new jobs are usually found for all who lose theirs. Although the high level of security is attractive to many people, it proved impossible to provide sufficient incentives for reasonably hard and efficient work under such conditions. In the words of Oxford historian Timothy Garton Ash, who wrote eyewitness chronicles of the developments in Eastern Europe from 1980 to 1990, the social contract between the workers and the government in the Eastern countries was "We pretend to work, and you pretend to pay us."

Because of the absence of a work-oriented incentive system, income inequalities do not provide the normal free-market incentives. Income inequalities were used instead to provide incentives for party members to toe the line. The major gap in income standards was between party members (in positions of power) on the one hand and non-members on the other. The former had access to such privileges as special stores where imported goods were available, special hospitals providing sanitary and efficient medical care, and special resorts where good vacations could be enjoyed. Non-members had none of these things.

ENVIRONMENTAL DEGRADATION

Fulfilling production plans became the all-embracing goal in planned economies, to the exclusion of most other considerations, including the environment. As a result, environmental degradation occurred in all the countries of Eastern Europe on a scale unknown in advanced Western nations. A particularly disturbing example occurred in central Asia where high quotas for cotton output led to indiscriminate use of pesticides and irrigation. Birth defects are now found in nearly one child in three, and the vast Aral Sea has been half drained, causing major environmental effects.

This failure to protect the environment stemmed from the pressure to fulfill production plans and the absence of a "political marketplace" where citizens could express their preferences for the environment versus economic gain. Imperfect though the system may be in democratic market economies—and in some particular cases it has been quite poor—their record of environmental protection has been vastly better than that of the command economies.

THE PRICE SYSTEM

In contrast to the failures of command economies, the performance of the free-market price system is impressive. One theme of this book is *market success:* how the price system works to coordinate with relative efficiency the decentralized decisions made by private consumers and producers, providing the right quantities of relatively high-quality outputs and incentives for efficient work. It is important, however, not to conclude that doing things better means doing things perfectly. Another theme of this book is *market failure:* how and why the unaided price system sometimes fails to produce efficient results and fails to take account of social values that cannot be expressed through the marketplace.

COMMAND VERSUS MARKET DETERMINATION

For over a century, a great debate raged on the relative merits of the command principle versus the market principle for coordinating economic decisions in practice. The former Soviet Union, the countries of Eastern Europe, and China were command economies for much of this century. Canada, the United States, and most of the countries of Western Europe were, and still are, primarily market economies. The successes of the Soviet Union and China in the early stages of industrialization suggested to many observers that the command principle was at least as good for organizing economic behaviour as the market principle, if not better. Over the long run, however, planned economies proved a failure of such disastrous proportions that they seriously depressed the living standards of their citizens.

Rarely in human history has such a decisive verdict been delivered on two competing systems. Application 1-2 gives some of the reasons why central planning was a failure in Eastern Europe and the former Soviet Union. The discussion is of more than purely historical interest because the reasons for the failure of central planning give insight into the reasons for the relative success of market economies. The current and recent problems of the Eastern European economies also show that markets do not simply happen—rather, they need to be supported by a complex set of institutions, customs, and rules, all of which are currently being developed in Eastern Europe. We discuss the progress of these Eastern European *transition economies* in some detail in Chapter 3.

Still Room for Disagreement

The failure of centrally planned economies suggests the superiority of decentralized markets over centrally planned ones as mechanisms for allocating an economy's scarce resources. Put another way, it demonstrates the superiority of mixed economies with substantial elements of market determination over fully planned command economies. However, it does *not* demonstrate, as some observers have asserted, the superiority of completely free-market economies over mixed economies.

There is no guarantee that completely free markets will, on their own, handle such urgent matters as controlling pollution or providing public goods (like national defence). Indeed, as we shall see in later chapters, much economic theory is devoted to explaining why free markets often fail to do these things. Mixed economies, with significant elements of government intervention, are needed to do these jobs.

Furthermore, acceptance of the free market over central planning does not provide an excuse to ignore a country's pressing social issues. Acceptance of the benefits of the free market still leaves plenty of scope to debate the kinds, amounts, and directions of government interventions into the workings of our market-based economy that will help to achieve social goals.

It follows that there is still considerable room for disagreement about the degree of the mix of market and government determination in any modern mixed economy—room enough to accommodate such divergent views as could be expressed by conservative, liberal, and modern social democratic parties. People can accept the free market as an efficient way of organizing economic affairs and still disagree about many things. A partial list includes the optimal amount and types of government regulation of various parts of the economy; the types of measures needed to protect the environment; whether health care should be provided by the public or the private sector; and the optimal amount and design of social services and other policies intended to redistribute income from more to less fortunate citizens.

Aspects of a Modern Economy

Throughout this book, we study the functioning of a modern, market-based, mixed economy such as is found in Canada today. By way of introduction, this section introduces a few salient aspects that should be kept in mind from the outset.

ORIGINS

The modern market economies that we know today first arose in Europe out of the ashes of the feudal system. As we have already mentioned, the feudal system was a traditional one in which people did jobs based on heredity (the miller's son became the next generation's miller) and received shares of their village's total output based on custom. Peasants were tied to the land. Much land was owned by the crown and granted to the lord of the manor in return for military services. Some of it was made available for the common use of all villagers. Property such as the village mill and blacksmith's shop never belonged to the people who worked there and therefore could never be bought and sold by them.

In contrast, modern economies are based on market transactions between people who voluntarily decide whether or not to engage in them. They have the right to buy and sell what they wish, to accept or refuse offered work, and to move where they want when they want. Key institutions are *private property* and *freedom of contract,* both of which must be maintained by active government policies. The government creates laws of ownership and contract and then provides courts to enforce these laws. It is precisely these sorts of institutions that the transition economies of Eastern Europe did not have when their command systems broke down in the late

1980s. Successful transition to fully developed market economies depends on the development of such institutions, which has so far proved more difficult than many economists had anticipated.

LIVING STANDARDS

The material living standards of any society depend on how much it can consume of various goods and services. What is available to consume, however, depends on what is produced. If the productive capacity of a society is small, the living standards of its typical citizen will be low. Only by raising that productive capacity can average living standards be raised. No society can generate increased real consumption merely by voting its citizens higher money incomes.

How much a society can produce depends on how many of that society's factors of production are employed to produce things and on the productivity of those factors. Labour is perhaps the single most important factor of production. How well has the Canadian economy performed with respect to the employment and the productivity of its labour?

Employment

In spite of some short-term ups and downs, the trend of total employment has been upward over most of modern Canadian history. For example, in 1975 there were just over 9.5 million Canadians employed, whereas in 1995 the figure was almost 13.5 million. This is a net creation of almost 4 million new jobs, a 42 percent increase over that 20-year period.

These new jobs provided employment for a rising labour force. The number of people over the age of 15 who were in the labour force (either working or looking for work) increased from about 10.2 million in 1975 to just over 15 million in 1995. This 47 percent increase in the labour force reflects not only an increase in the population, but also a five percentage point increase in the labour-force participation rate (the fraction of the population in the labour force).

This overall increase in both the level of employment and the size of the labour force, however, does not reveal some important changes in the *composition* of the labour force. In particular, the share of women in the labour force (and in total employment) has increased markedly over the past 20 years. Women accounted for 37 percent of the labour force in 1975; by 1995, women made up 45 percent of the Canadian labour force.

Labour Productivity

Labour productivity refers to the amount produced per hour of work. Rising living standards are closely linked to the rising productivity of the typical worker. If each worker produces more, then (other things being equal) there will be more production in total and hence more for each person to consume on average.

From 1750 to 1900, the market economies in Europe and North America became industrial economies. With industrialization, modern market economies have raised ordinary people out of poverty by raising productivity at rates that appear slow from year to year but have dramatic effects on living standards when sustained over long periods of time.

> Over a year, or even over a decade, the economic gains [of the late eighteenth and the nineteenth centuries], after allowing for the growth of population, were so little noticeable that it was widely believed that the gains were experienced only by the rich, and not by the poor. Only as the West's compounded growth continued through the twentieth century did its breadth become clear. It became obvious that Western working classes were increasingly well off and that the Western middle classes were prospering and growing as a proportion of the whole population. Not that poverty disappeared. The West's achievement was not the abolition of poverty but the reduction of its incidence from 90 percent of the population to 30 percent, 20 percent, or less, depending on the country and one's definition of poverty.[3]

Figure 1-4 shows the rise in the productivity of Canadian labour from 1946 to 1995. In spite of many short-term variations, the general trend is unmistakably upward. Every hour worked has produced more and more total output during the entire course of this half century. Over the period shown in the figure, labour productivity doubled and then doubled again. As a result, each person produces four times as much now as he or she did in 1946. The basis of our rising living standards is our ability to produce more and more as time passes. This comes not only from technological im-

---

[3]N. Rosenberg and L. E. Birdzell Jr., *How the West Grew Rich* (New York: Basic Books, 1986).

FIGURE 1-4
Output per Hour Worked in Canada

Output per hour worked in Canada has increased four-fold since 1946. The graph is based on a measure of total output in Canada (the GDP) divided by the total number of hours worked by the Canadian labour force. The data are expressed as a percentage of the value of the output per hour worked in 1986 (1986 is therefore shown as 100). The steady rise in outout per hour, which is the basis for rising living standards, is quite apparent. So also is the slowdown in the growth rate of output per hour that began in the mid 1970s.

Source: Statistics Canada, 15-204.

provements, but also from increases in the average skill of the labour force.

These are potent sources of increases in living standards. Over the long period of rising productivity, Canadian citizens (as well as the citizens of most industrial countries) got used to each generation being substantially better off than each preceding generation. In the period from 1938 to 1974, individuals whose income relative to their contemporaries was the same as their parents' could expect to earn about *twice the real income* their parents had enjoyed.

In the mid 1970s, this productivity growth slowed substantially. By the mid 1990s, the typical individual 25 years younger than his or her parents could expect to be *no more than 30 percent better off* than his or her parents were at the same age. This is a remarkable reduction in the rate that each gener-

ation is becoming wealthier. Over long periods of time, however, even 1 percent productivity growth is still a potent force for change, because it doubles real output per worker about every 72 years, or about one human lifetime. (A helpful device is the *rule of 72:* Divide 72 by the annual growth rate, and the result is approximately the number of years required for income to double.) [1][4]

Distribution of Income

Not only has the rate of increase in aggregate income slowed dramatically in recent years, but the way in

---

[4]Notes giving mathematical demonstrations of the concepts presented in the text are designated by reference numbers. These notes can be found at the back of the book, beginning on page M-1.

which that income is distributed among the various income groups has also altered.

Some of the most dramatic shifts have occurred in the United States. Incomes became progressively more equally distributed up through the 1960s. In the 1970s, the trend reversed, and ever since the distribution of income has slowly become more unequal. For example, the share of income received by the lowest 20 percent in the U.S. income distribution rose from 5.0 percent in 1947 to 5.7 percent in 1968, then fell to 4.4 percent in 1992. That is a 20 percent decrease in the share of total income going to the poorest group over a 25-year period. At the other end of the U.S. income distribution, the share of income going to the richest 20 percent fell from 43.0 percent in 1947 to 40.5 percent in 1968, then rose to 44.6 percent by 1992. That is close to a 10 percent increase in the share of total income going to the richest group in the society.

Though similar changes have been observed in several advanced industrial economies, it is interesting that Canadian data do not show this turnaround. Instead, inequalities in income have continued to narrow right up to the middle of the 1990s. For example, the poorest 20 percent of families received only 2.8 percent of total income in 1967; by 1993 the same group earned 6.7 percent of total income. While they are still poor by our standards, they did more than double their share of an increasing total of the nation's income. In contrast, the richest 20 percent of families received 46.3 percent of the nation's total income in 1967; by 1993, their share had fallen to 39.9 percent.

The difference between Canada and the United States appears to be largely due to the different effectiveness of the tax-and-transfer systems in the two countries—that is, the systems whereby resources are transfered from high-income to low-income families. The *pre-tax* distribution of income over the past several years has been very similar in the two countries, but the stronger presence of taxes and transfers in Canada has resulted in reduced *after-tax* income inequality over the same period in which (after-tax) income inequality has been increasing in the United States.

ONGOING CHANGE

The growth in incomes over the centuries since market economies first arose has been accompanied by continual technological change. Our technologies are our ways of doing things. New ways of making old things, and new things to make, are continually being invented and brought into use. These technological changes make labour more productive, and they are constantly changing the nature of our economy. Old jobs are destroyed and new jobs are created as the technological structure slowly evolves.

Job Structure

Figure 1-5 shows the change in industrial structure of Canadian employment since the end of the last century. The most dramatic changes are associated with the decline of jobs in agriculture and the rise of jobs in the service sector (including government). The share of total employment in the manufacturing sector rises for the early part of the century, peaks during the Second World War, and then declines continually to the current day. This decline in the relative importance of manufacturing has been the focus of much attention; indeed, many observers lament the "deindustrialization" of the Canadian economy. If that term applies to the Canadian economy, it also applies to the economies of the United States and most Western European countries, where similar changes have been observed.

Services in Manufacturing. The enormous growth in what are recorded as service jobs overstates the decline in the importance of the manufacturing of goods in our economy. This is because many of the jobs recorded as service jobs in fact are an integral part of the production of manufactured goods.

First, some of the growth has occurred because many services that used to be produced within manufacturing firms have now been "out-sourced" to specialist firms. These often include design, quality control, accounting, legal services, and marketing. Indeed, one of the most significant of the new developments in production is the breakdown of the old hierarchical organization of firms and the development of the production unit as a loosely knit grouping of organizations, each responsible for part of the total activities; some units are owned by the firms, but many are under contract to it.

Second, as a result of the rapid growth of international trade, production and sales have required growing quantities of service inputs for such things as transportation, insurance, banking, and marketing.

Third, as more and more products become high-tech, increasing amounts are spent on product design

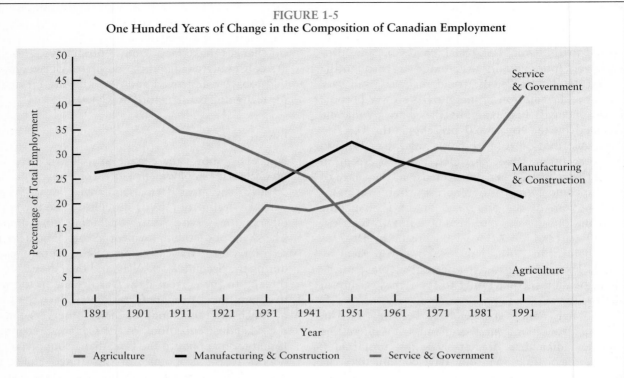

FIGURE 1-5
One Hundred Years of Change in the Composition of Canadian Employment

Over the past century, major shifts in employment have taken place between sectors of the economy. In 1891, over 45 percent of Canadian employment was in agriculture, and only 9 percent in services (including government). One hundred years later, agriculture accounted for only 3 percent of employment, while services had increased to 41 percent. The share of employment in manufacturing and construction increased from 26 percent in 1891 to 32 percent just after the Second World War, and then declined back to 20 percent by 1991.

Source: Canadian Census, various years, authors' calculations.

at one end and customer liaison at the other end. These activities, which are all related to the production and sale of goods, are often recorded as service activities.

Services for Final Consumption. As households' incomes have risen over the decades, households have spent a rising proportion of their incomes on services rather than goods. Today, for example, eating out is common; for our grandparents, it was a luxury. This does not mean, however, that we spend more on food. The extra expenditure goes to pay for the services of the people who prepare and serve in restaurants the same ingredients that our grandparents prepared for themselves at home. Young people spend far more on attending live concerts than they used to, and all of us spend vastly more on travel. In 1890, the salesman in a small town was likely to be

the best-traveled citizen because he had gone 600 kilometres by train to the provincial capital. Today, such a person would be regarded by many as an unworldly stay-at-home.

New Products

When we talk of each generation having more real income than previous generations, we must not think of just having more and more money to spend on the same set of products that our parents or grandparents consumed. In fact, we consume very few of the products that were the mainstays of expenditure for our great-grandparents.

One of the most important aspects of the change that permeates market economies is the continual introduction of new products. It was not until well into this century that electricity was brought to rural areas. Most of the myriad instruments and tools in a modern dentist's office, doctor's office, and hospital did not exist 50 years ago. Penicillin, painkillers, bypass operations, movies, stereos, videocassettes and recorders, pocket calculators, computers, ballpoint pens, compact discs, and everyday travel on aircraft have all been introduced within living memory. So also have the products that have eliminated much of the drudgery formerly associated with housework. Dishwashers, detergents, disposable diapers, washing machines, vacuum cleaners, refrigerators, frozen foods, and their complement, the supermarket, were not there to help your great-grandparents when they first set up house.

Globalization

A relatively new aspect of the constant change that occurs in evolving market economies is the *globalization* that has been occurring at an accelerating rate over the past two decades. At the heart of globalization lies the rapid reduction in transportation costs and the revolution in information technology. The cost of moving products around the world has fallen greatly in recent decades. More dramatically, our ability to transmit and to analyze data has been increasing dramatically, while the cost of doing so has been decreasing equally dramatically.

Many *markets* are globalizing; for example, as some tastes become universal to young people, we can see the same designer jeans and leather jackets in virtually all big cities. Many *corporations* are globalizing, as they increasingly become what are called *transnationals*. These are massive firms with a physical presence in many countries and an increasingly decentralized management structure. Many *product markets* are globalizing, as the revolutions in communications and transportation allow the various components of any one product to be produced all over the world. A typical compact-disc player or automobile contains components made in literally dozens of different countries. We still know where a product is assembled, but it is becoming increasingly difficult to say where it is *made*.

One result of this globalization of production is that components that can be produced by unskilled labour can now be produced in any low-wage country around the world, where previously they were usually produced in the country that did the assembly. This has proved valuable for developing countries. They have a better chance of becoming competitive in a small range of components than in the integrated production of whole products. However, unskilled labour in developed countries is losing (relatively, and possibly absolutely for a while), as their labour becomes less scarce relative to the need for it. In short, the market for unskilled labour is globalizing, throwing unskilled labour in advanced countries into direct competition with unskilled labour in poorer countries.

Globalization has greatly increased the amount of international trade. This has risen roughly twice as fast as total production over the decades since the end of the Second World War in 1945. Canada has always depended greatly on foreign trade. Most of its exports went to the United Kingdom up until 1945. Today, however, the United States is Canada's most important market, in most years taking over 70 percent of all Canadian exports.

Globalization has also increased U.S. dependence on foreign markets. In 1959, exports amounted to only 4.1 percent of total U.S. production (as measured by its gross domestic product, or GDP). The rest was used domestically. In 1994, the figure was 10.6 percent. The proportion of total U.S. production of *goods* that is exported is much larger than 10 percent. Without the export market, many of the existing sources of U.S. employment and income would not exist.

On the investment side, the most important result of globalization is that large firms are seeking a physical presence in many major countries. In the 1950s and 1960s, most foreign investment was made by U.S. firms investing abroad to establish a presence in foreign markets. Today, most developed countries see major flows of investment in both directions, inward as foreign firms invest in their markets and outward as their own firms invest abroad.

In 1967, fully 50 percent of all outward-bound foreign investment came from the United States and went to many foreign countries. In 1989, according to United Nations figures, the United States accounted for less than 30 percent of all outward-bound foreign investment. At the same time, the United Kingdom accounted for 16 percent, Japan and Germany accounted for just under 10 percent each, and Canada for 2.1 percent.

On the inward-bound side, the change is more dramatic. In 1967, the United States attracted only 9 percent of all foreign investment made in that year. In 1989, however, it attracted 27 percent. Not only do U.S. firms hold massive foreign investments in foreign countries, but foreign firms now hold massive investments in the United States. In 1990, Canada, a much smaller country, received 3.2 percent of all inward-bound foreign investment.

Being a small country with enormous resources beyond the power of domestic capital to develop fully, Canada has always relied heavily on foreign investment for much of its growth. As the Canadian economy matured and Canadian firms grew in size, however, Canadian firms began to finance their own investment and also began to look outward, making Canada a growing source of outward-bound investment. Foreign ownership of Canadian industry peaked in the early 1970s and has been declining ever since—with a small upsurge around 1990 when Canada's Free Trade Agreement with the United States increased Canada's attractiveness to foreign firms seeking to locate in the North American market.

The world is truly globalizing in both its trade and investment flows. Today, no country can take an isolationist economic stance and hope to take part in the global economy, where an increasing share of jobs and incomes are created. Not only do a large number of Canadians work for foreign-owned companies operating in Canada, but a growing number of foreigners work for Canadian-owned companies operating abroad.

CONCLUSION

In this section, we have briefly discussed how people's living standards are affected by the availability of jobs, the productivity of labour in those jobs, and the distribution of the income produced by those jobs. We have seen how the economy is characterized by ongoing change in the structure of jobs, in the production techniques used by the workers, and in the kinds of goods and services produced. We have also seen that these changes exist in the context of a rapidly globalizing economy, one in which events occuring in any one country have major consequences in many other countries.

These issues will arise at many places throughout this book. We will study what is happening in more detail and will use economic theory to explain why it is happening. Because most of the issues are interrelated, it helps to know the basic outlines of all of them before studying any one in more depth.

ECONOMIC ANALYSIS AND ECONOMIC POLICY

So far in this chapter, very little has been said about economic policy, but the analysis of economic policy plays a large role in many parts of this book. This chapter concludes by making some general points about some issues related to the analysis and evaluation of economic policies.

THE PERVASIVENESS OF POLICY DECISIONS

Governments derive their authority to form and carry out policy from their police power—indeed, the words "policy" and "police" come from the Greek word for state, *politeia.*

Some governments lean toward a policy of not intervening with the workings of the free market. Such a policy is often referred to as a *laissez-faire* policy. Other governments lean toward a policy of attempting strict control over every facet of the economy. Note that both of these extreme cases involve a choice of particular economic policies.

All governments have economic policies. Even the decision not to act but to let nature take its course is a policy decision.

Every year thousands of economic policy decisions are made by municipal, provincial, and federal governments. Most of them are never seriously debated. Nor is every facet of existing policy debated anew each year; indeed, many policy decisions now in force (such as giving unions the right to organize) were made decades ago. Only a few policy issues attract attention and become the subject of earnest and heated argument in any particular year.

Debates Over Means and Ends

To understand the debate associated with any given issue of economic policy, it is important to distinguish between the goals of our actions and the methods that we use to achieve those goals. Our goals are called **ends;** they are the things that we strive for. The things that we use to achieve our ends are our **means;** they are the methods of achieving our goals.

The debate over the "right" degree of government involvement in the economy is often really a debate about the alleged potency of *alternative means to achieve agreed ends*. For example, command and free-market economies were both seen (by different people) as means to higher living standards and better control over the environment. Starting in 1989, the countries of Eastern Europe made the choice to move toward a free-market system, in part because their citizens came to believe that it was a superior means to the end of higher living standards.

Other examples are the debates over government intervention in the markets for rental housing and farm production. Supporters of such intervention do not value intervention for its own sake. Rather, they hope that such intervention will be a means toward higher incomes for producers or lower prices to consumers, which in turn means a rise in the living standards of the people concerned. Opponents agree that a rise in living standards is desirable but argue that these means are an inappropriate way of achieving this end.

Economic debates also arise when various groups who are *pursuing different ends* come into conflict. For example, everyone may agree that a particular agricultural policy makes farmers better off, but only at the expense of consumers who must pay higher prices for their products. In this case, there is a real conflict between groups. The issue then becomes deciding between competing ends— improving the lot of farmers or of consumers— rather than judging between alternative means to agreed ends.

Conflicts can also emerge over ends because different groups put *different values on alternative ends*. When environmental groups oppose the establishment of a local pulp mill while potential employees support it, the two groups are applying different values to two competing ends: more local job creation and more environmental protection.

FOUR COMMON QUESTIONS ABOUT ECONOMIC POLICIES

Though each issue typically has its own special characteristics, most issues of economic policy share some common elements. Here are four main questions which can be asked about every proposed economic policy.

1. What are the policy goals?

2. Does the proposed policy achieve those goals?

3. Does the proposed policy have adverse side effects?

4. Are there alternative means of achieving the goals?

As an illustration of how these four questions may be applied in practice, consider the position of a team of economists asked to examine the case for and against the government enacting a policy to control the rents of apartments and houses. How should the economists go about evaluating this policy proposal?

First, the economists would ask what goals such "rent control" is meant to achieve. They might find that it is primarily intended to redistribute income from rich to poor.

Second, the economists would ask if rent control does in fact help to realize this policy goal. Rent control means that tenants pay less rent than they otherwise would and landlords receive less income than they otherwise would; thus rent control redistributes income from landlords to tenants. But do landlords tend to be richer than their tenants? If a survey shows that most tenants are, in fact, richer than their landlords, the economists can conclude that rent control does not achieve the redistributive goal for which it was being used. Then the case against rent control is clear, and that is the end of the story. If, however, the survey indicates that most tenants have lower incomes than their landlords, the economists will conclude that rent control is a means of obtaining the desired goal of income redistribution. Further study is then needed.

Third, the economists would ask if rent control has effects that conflict with other policy objectives. Rent controls may, for example, lead to the deterioration into slums of some areas where landlords do not find it economically worthwhile to maintain their property. It may also lead to a decrease in the total amount of rental housing as some owners shift their property out of rental uses and potential new investors do not find it worthwhile to construct apartment buildings and other rental units. When a policy action helps to achieve one goal but hinders the attainment of another, it is necessary to establish a trade off between goals. Usually there will be some rate at which people will trade a loss in one direction for a gain in another.

Fourth, the economists need to consider alternatives to see if there are other measures that will achieve the goals at a lower sacrifice in terms of setbacks to other policy objectives. It is probable, for example, that the progressive income tax redistributes income from rich to poor with more certainty and precision and with fewer undesired side effects than does rent control.

At any one of the four stages of their investigation, the economists may conclude that rent control is not a very effective means of achieving the policymakers' objectives. (In fact many economists *have* reached that conclusion about rent controls. We discuss rent controls in detail in Chapter 6.) But suppose that the team of economists concludes that rent control *does* achieve the desired goals, that the undesirable effects in other directions are judged (by the policymakers) to be less important than the desirable effects in achieving the stated policy goals, and that there are no other practicable measures that would better achieve the goals? The team will then conclude that there is a strong case in favour of rent controls.

Do not the views—and prejudices—of the investigators have a great deal to do with the outcome of their investigation? A particular group of economists may have strong views on the particular measure it is attempting to assess. If the economists do not like the measure, they are likely to be relentless in searching out possible unwanted effects and somewhat less than thorough in discovering effects that help to achieve the desired goals. It is therefore important (though often difficult) to guard against an unconscious bias of this sort. Fortunately there are likely to be others with different biases. One advantage of publishing evaluations and submitting them to review and discussion is that it provides opportunities for those with different biases to discover arguments and evidence originally overlooked.

CONFLICTS OF POLICY

Governments have many policy goals. A particular policy that serves one goal may hinder another and have no effect on yet a third. Unemployment insurance, for example, may protect unemployed families from debilitating hardship; at the same time it may hinder the quickness with which labour moves from labour-surplus to labour-scarce occupations, thereby increasing total unemployment in the country. Moreover, it will almost certainly have no effect one way or the other on the levels of air pollution.

The significance of this point is too frequently overlooked. It is never enough to show that a proposed policy advances one of society's objectives. What must be shown about the policy is that it advances certain objectives sufficiently to overcome the cost in terms of the amount that it retards other objectives. In order to do this, it is necessary to determine how much of one must be given up to get how much more of the others. This involves the question of opportunity cost, on which the studies of economists can shed light. It is also necessary to decide whether the opportunity cost is worth incurring, and this is a matter of social valuation.

Economic and Political Objectives

Actual policymaking is more complicated than the previous discussion suggests, and a few of the many reasons policy issues get settled in a less systematic fashion deserve mention.

Decisions on interrelated issues of policy are made by many different bodies. Federal and provincial parliaments pass laws, the courts interpret laws, and the governments decide which laws to enforce with vigor and which to soft-pedal. The Department of Finance and the Bank of Canada, both agents of the federal government, influence financial markets through their actions. And a host of other agencies and semi-independent bodies determine actions in respect to different aspects of policy goals. Because of the multiplicity of decision makers it would be truly amazing if fully consistent behaviour resulted.

Furthermore, in a system such as ours, inconsistent decisions may result from political compromises between two or more interested groups, factions, or agencies. Compromises are frequently necessary to reconcile conflicting interests among the provinces or between the federal government and the provinces.

Another problem arises because legislators in a democracy have their own and their party's reelection as one of their important goals. This means, for example, that any measure that imposes large costs and few benefits obvious to the electorate over the next few years is unlikely to find favour, no matter how large the long-term benefits are. There is a strong bias toward myopia in an elective system.

Although much of this bias stems from shortsightedness and selfishness, another part reflects genuine uncertainty about the future. The further into the future the economist is calculating, the wider is the margin of possible error in his or her statements. Thus it is not surprising that politicians who must worry about the next election often tend to worry less about the long-term effects of their actions.

SUMMARY

A. WHAT IS ECONOMICS?

- Most of the world's pressing problems have an economic aspect, and many are primarily economic. A common feature of such problems is that they concern the use of limited resources to satisfy virtually unlimited human wants.
- Scarcity is a fundamental problem faced by all economies. Not enough resources are available to produce all the goods and services that people would like to consume. Scarcity makes it necessary to choose. All societies must have a mechanism for choosing what goods and services will be produced and in what quantities.
- The concept of opportunity cost emphasizes the problem of scarcity and choice by measuring the cost of obtaining a unit of one product in terms of the number of units of other products that could have been obtained instead.
- Four basic questions must be answered in all economies: What is produced and how? What is consumed and by whom? Why are resources sometimes idle? Is productive capacity growing?

B. ALTERNATIVE ECONOMIC SYSTEMS

- Different economies resolve these four basic questions in different ways and with varying degrees of efficacy. Economists study how these problems are addressed in various societies and the consequences of using one method rather than another to provide solutions.
- We can distinguish three pure types of economies: traditional, command, and free-market. In practice, all economies are mixed economies in that their economic behaviour responds to mixes of tradition, government command, and price incentives.
- In the late 1980s, events in Eastern Europe and the USSR led to the general acceptance that the system of fully centrally planned economies had failed to produce minimally acceptable living standards for its citizens. All of these countries are now moving toward greater market determination and less state command in their economies.

C. ASPECTS OF A MODERN ECONOMY

- Market economies are based on private property and freedom of contract. They have generated sustained growth, which, over long periods, has raised material living standards greatly.
- Market economies are characterized by constant change in such things as the structure of jobs, the structure of production, the technologies in use, and the types of products produced.
- Driven by the revolution in transportation and communications, the world economy is rapidly globalizing. National and regional boundaries are becoming less important as transnational corporations locate the production of each component part of a product in the country that can produce it at the best quality and the least cost.
- As part of this globalization, most countries are much more heavily involved in foreign trade than in the past. Most advanced countries have become both host countries for investment by foreign firms and source countries for investment located in foreign countries.

D. ECONOMIC ANALYSIS AND ECONOMIC POLICY

- All governments have economic policies. Even the decision not to interfere with the workings of the free market is a policy decision. Understanding debates about economic policy requires that a distinction be made between the ends and means of policy actions.
- There are four basic questions which should be asked about any proposed policy. What are the policy goals? Does the proposed policy achieve those goals? Does the proposed policy have adverse side effects? Are there alternative means of achieving the goals?
- It is not sufficient to show that a proposed policy advances one of society's objectives. What must be shown is that the policy advances certain objectives enough to offset the amount that it retards others. Policy trade offs are therefore pervasive.

KEY CONCEPTS

Scarcity and the need for choice
Choice and opportunity cost
Production possibility boundary
Resource allocation

Growth in productive capacity
Traditional economies
Command economies

Market economies
Globalization
Policy means and ends

DISCUSSION QUESTIONS

1. What does each of the following questions tell you about the policy conflicts perceived by the person making the statement and about how that person has resolved them?

   a. "It is an industry worth several hundred jobs to our province; we cannot afford to forgo it." A provincial premier explaining the decision to organize a killing of wolves in his province so that more game animals could grow up to be shot by hunters.

   b. "The annual seal hunt must be stopped, even if it destroys the livelihood of the seal hunters." An animal-rights advocate opposing the seal hunt in Canada.

   c. "Considering our limited energy resources and the growing demand for electricity, Canada really has no choice but to use all of its possible domestic energy sources, including nuclear energy. Despite possible environmental and safety hazards, nuclear power is a necessity." A provincial hydro authority replying to critics.

   d. "The proposed pulp mills must be opposed because of the pollution they cause, even though they bring new and diversified jobs and even though they are based on the most advanced, pollution-minimizing technologies." An opponent of the proposal to construct new pulp and paper mills in the Peace River District of northern Canada during the 1990s.

   e. "Damn the pollution—we want the jobs!" A labour leader in Brazil advocating permission to build new pulp mills in his area.

2. What is the difference between scarcity and poverty? If everyone in the world had enough to eat, could we say that food was no longer scarce?

3. Consider the right to free speech in political campaigns. Suppose that the Flat Earth Society, the Communists, the Reform Party, the Conservatives, the Liberals, the Bloc Quebecois, and the NDP all demand equal time on network television in an election campaign. What economic questions are involved? Can there be freedom of speech without free access to the scarce resources needed to make one's speech heard?

4. Evidence accumulates that the use of chemical fertilizers, which increases agricultural production greatly, damages water quality. Analyze the choice between more food and cleaner water involved in using such fertilizers. Use a production possibility curve with agricultural output on the vertical axis and water quality on the horizontal axis. In what ways does this production possibility curve reflect scarcity, choice, and opportunity cost? How would an improved fertilizer that increased agricultural output without further worsening water quality affect the curve? Suppose that a pollution-free fertilizer were developed; would this mean that there would no longer be any opportunity cost in using it?

5. Pick one of the major socialist countries that have recently introduced market-oriented reforms and discuss the start-up problems that the reforms encounter. Explain why you think these problems will or will not persist over the next few years.

6. Many opponents of Canada's participation in the North American Free Trade Agreement (NAFTA) predicted that many Canadian jobs would flow south to Mexico. Proponents of this view based their arguments on the substantially lower wages of Mexican workers compared to Canadian workers and on the perception that Mexican workers are somehow willing to accept lower standards of living, *ceteris paribus*. Evaluate the strength of these arguments. What is one factor that might account for the differences in real wages between the two countries? How might this affect the conclusion that Canadian jobs must necessarily flow to lower-priced labour?

7. Discuss the following statement by a leading U.S. economist: "One of the mysteries of semantics is

why the government-managed economies ever came to be called planned and the market economies unplanned. It is the former that are in chronic chaos, in which buyers stand in line hoping to buy some toilet paper or soap. It is the latter that are in reasonable equilibrium—where if you want a cake of soap or a steak or a shirt or a car, you can go to the store and find that the item is magically there for you to buy. It is the liberal economies that reflect a highly sophisticated planning system, and the government-managed economies that are primitive and unplanned."

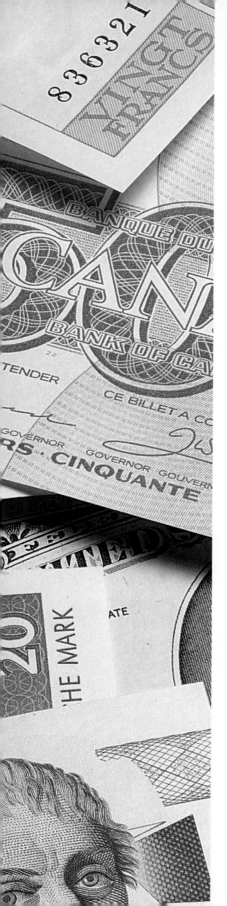

CHAPTER 2

ECONOMICS AS
A SOCIAL SCIENCE

Economics is regarded as a social science. But unlike many sciences such as chemistry or physics, many economists would say that a training in economics provides the student more with a "way of thinking" than with a collection of facts. This does not mean that facts are unimportant to the economist—quite the contrary. It means only that facts are typically harder to establish in economics than in the "hard" sciences and often economists do not know which facts are important without first having a way to organize their thinking.

Central to the economist's way of thinking is the distinction between *positive statements* and *normative statements*. Also of crucial importance to the economist is the role of *theory* and, in particular, the use of economic *models* to provide a framework for thinking about complex issues. Such models can be used to generate *testable hypotheses*.

In this chapter, we explore what it means to be "scientific" in the study of human behaviour and to establish criteria for evaluating how well economics succeeds in meeting that goal.

26

THE DISTINCTION BETWEEN POSITIVE AND NORMATIVE

The success of modern science rests partly on the ability of scientists to separate their views on what *does* happen from their views on what *they would like* to happen.

Positive statements concern what is, was, or will be. Positive statements, assertions, or theories may be simple or complex, but they are basically about matters of fact. Positive statements assert things about the world. If it is possible for a positive statement to be proved wrong by empirical evidence, we call it a *testable statement*.

Normative statements concern what one believes ought to be. They state, or are based on, judgments about what is good and what is bad. They are thus bound up with philosophical, cultural, and religious systems. Normative statements are not testable. Disagreements over such normative statements as "It is wrong to steal" or "It is immoral to have sexual relations out of wedlock" cannot be settled by an appeal to empirical observations.

Many positive statements are testable, and disagreements over such statements are appropriately handled by an appeal to the facts. Different techniques are needed for studying normative and positive questions.

It is therefore useful to separate normative and positive inquiries. We do this not because we think one is less important than the other but merely because they must be handled in different ways.

Here is a simple example. The statement "It is impossible to break up atoms" is a positive statement that can be (and of course has been) refuted by empirical observations. In contrast, the statement "Scientists ought not to break up atoms" is a normative statement that involves ethical judgments. The questions "What government policies will reduce unemployment?" and "What policies will prevent inflation?" are positive ones, whereas the question "Should we be more concerned about unemployment than about inflation?" is a normative one.

As we said above, disagreements over positive statements are appropriately handled by an appeal to the facts, whereas disagreements over normative statements involve competing value judgments.

Economists are often maligned for their apparent inability to agree on anything, including the facts. Extension 2-1 examines why this may be so.

THE IMPORTANCE OF THE DISTINCTION

As an example of the importance of this distinction, consider the question "Has the payment of unemployment benefits increased the amount of unemployment?" This positive question can be turned into a testable hypothesis such as "The higher the benefits paid to the unemployed, the higher will be the total amount of unemployment." If we are not careful, however, attitudes and value judgments may get in the way of the study of this hypothesis. Some people are opposed to all welfare measures and believe in an individualistic self-help ethic. They may hope that the hypothesis is correct because its truth could then be used as an argument against welfare measures in general. Others feel that welfare measures are desirable, reducing misery and contributing to human dignity. They may hope that the hypothesis is wrong because they do not want any welfare measures to come under attack. In spite of different value judgments and social attitudes, however, evidence is accumulating on this particular hypothesis. As a result, we have more knowledge than we had 20 years ago of why and to what extent unemployment benefits increase unemployment. This evidence could never have been accumulated or accepted if investigators had not been able to differentiate their feelings about how they wanted the answer to turn out from their assessment of evidence on how people actually behaved.[1]

The distinction between positive and normative statements allows us to keep our views on how we would like the world to work separate from our views on how the world actually does work. We may

---

[1] Of course, economists, like all scientists, are not immune from the possibility that what they find will be influenced by what they want to find. For a study of this problem in a different context, see Stephen Jay Gould, *The Mismeasure of Man* (New York: Norton, 1981). The more likely it is that value judgments will affect our judgments of positive issues, the more important it is that the test of consistency with facts be accepted as an important criterion for the acceptance of theories.

WHY ECONOMISTS DISAGREE

If you listen to a discussion among economists on *The National* or *Morningside* or read about their debates in the daily press or weekly magazines, you will find that economists frequently disagree among themselves. Why do economists disagree, and what should we make of this fact?

In a *Newsweek* column, Charles Wolf Jr. suggested four reasons:

1. Different economists use different benchmarks (e.g., inflation is down compared with last year but up compared with the 1950s).

2. Economists fail to make it clear to their listeners whether they are talking about short-term or long-term consequences (e.g., tax cuts will stimulate consumption in the short run and investment in the long run).

3. Economists often fail to acknowledge the full extent of their ignorance.

4. Different economists have different values, and these normative views play a large part in most public discussions of policy.

There is surely some truth in each of these assessments, but there is also a fifth reason: the public's *demand for disagreement*. For example, suppose that most economists were in fact agreed on some proposition, such as "Unions are not a major cause of inflation." This view would be unpalatable to some individuals. Those who are hostile to unions, for instance, would like to blame inflation on them and would be looking for an intellectual champion. Fame and fortune would await the economist who espoused their cause, and a champion would soon be found.

Notice also that any disagreement that does exist will be exaggerated, possibly unintentionally, by the media. When the media cover an issue, they naturally wish to give both sides of it. Normally, the public will hear one or two economists on each side of a debate, regardless of whether the profession is divided right down the middle or is nearly unanimous in its support of one side. Thus the public will not know that in one case a reporter could have chosen from dozens of economists to present each side, whereas in another case the reporter had to spend three days finding someone willing to take a particular side because nearly all the economists contacted thought it was wrong. In their desire to show both sides of all cases, however, the media present the public with the appearance of a profession equally split over all matters.

Thus anyone seeking to discredit some particular economist's advice by showing that there is disagreement among economists will have no trouble finding evidence of some disagreement. But those who wish to know if there is a majority view or even a strong consensus will find one on a surprisingly large number of issues. For example, a survey published in the *American Economic Review* showed strong agreement among economists on many propositions such as "Rent control leads to a housing shortage" (85 percent yes).

These results illustrate that economists do agree on many issues—where the balance of evidence seems strongly to support certain predictions that follow from economic theories.

---

be interested in both. It can only obscure the truth, however, if we let our views on what we would like bias our investigations of what actually is. For this reason, the separation of positive from normative statements is one of the foundations of science. It is also for this reason that scientific inquiry, as it is normally understood, is usually confined to positive questions. Some important limitations on the distinc-

tion between positive and normative are discussed in Extension 2-2.

POSITIVE AND NORMATIVE STATEMENTS IN ECONOMICS

We have seen that normative questions cannot be settled by a mere appeal to facts. In democracies,

LIMITS ON THE POSITIVE-NORMATIVE DISTINCTION

Although the distinction between positive and normative statements is useful, it has a number of limitations.

The Classification Is Not Exhaustive. The positive and normative classifications do not cover all statements that can be made. For example, there is an important class, called *analytic statements,* whose validity depends only on the rules of logic. Thus the sentence "If all humans are immortal and if you are a human, then you are immortal" is a valid analytic statement. It tells us that if two things are true, then a third thing must also be true. The validity of this statement is not dependent on whether or not its individual parts are in fact true. Indeed, the sentence "All humans are immortal" is a positive statement that has been decisively refuted. Yet no amount of empirical evidence on the mortality of humans can upset the truth of the if-then sentence quoted. Analytic statements—which proceed by logical analysis—play an important role in scientific work and form the basis of much of our ability to theorize.

Not All Positive Statements Are Testable. A positive statement asserts something about some aspect of the universe in which we live. It may be empirically true or false in the sense that what it asserts may or may not be true of the world. If it is true, it adds to our knowledge of what can and cannot happen. Many positive statements are refutable: If they are wrong, this can be ascertained (within a margin for error of observation) by checking them against data. For example, the positive statement that the earth is less than 5,000 years old was tested and refuted by a mass of evidence accumulated in the eighteenth and nineteenth centuries.

The statement "Extraterrestrials exist and frequently visit the earth in visible form" is also a positive statement. It asserts something about the universe, but we could never refute this statement with evidence because no matter how hard we searched, believers could argue that we did not look in the right places or in the right way, that extraterrestrials do not reveal themselves to nonbelievers, or a host of other reasons. Thus some positive statements are irrefutable.

The Distinction Is Not Unerringly Applied. The fact that the positive-normative distinction aids the advancement of knowledge does not necessarily mean that all scientists automatically and unerringly apply it. Scientists are human beings. Many have strongly-held values, and they may let their value judgments get in the way of their assessment of evidence. Nonetheless, the desire to separate what is from what we would like to be is a guiding light, an ideal of all science. The ability to do so, albeit imperfectly, is attested to by the acceptance, first by scientists and then by the general public, of many ideas that were initially extremely unpalatable—ideas such as the close relationship between humans and other primates.

normative questions relating to government policies are often settled by voting. So on the one hand, we look to observations to shed light on the issue of the extent to which unemployment insurance deters people from working. On the other hand, we use the political process to decide whether or not, when all the pros and cons are considered, we should have such insurance.

Economists need not confine their discussions to positive, testable statements. Economists can usefully hold and discuss value judgments. Indeed, the pursuit of what appears to be a normative statement, such as "Unemployment insurance ought to be abol-ished," will often lead to positive hypotheses that underlie the normative judgment. In this case, there are probably relatively few people who believe that government provision of unemployment insurance is in itself good or bad. Their advocacy or opposition will be based on beliefs that can be stated as positive rather than normative hypotheses—for example, "Unemployment insurance causes people to remain unemployed when they would otherwise take a job" or "Unemployment insurance increases the chance that workers will locate the jobs for which they are best suited by supporting them while they search for the right job."

THE SCIENTIFIC APPROACH IN ECONOMICS

An important aspect of the scientific approach consists of relating questions to evidence. When presented with a controversial issue, investigators, whether in the natural or the social sciences, will look for relevant evidence.

In some fields, scientists are able to generate observations that provide evidence for use in testing their hypotheses. Experimental sciences such as chemistry and some branches of psychology have an advantage because it is possible for them to produce relevant evidence through controlled laboratory experiments.

Other sciences, such as astronomy, cannot do this. They must wait for natural events to produce observations that can be used as evidence in testing their theories. The evidence that then arises does not come from controlled laboratory conditions. Instead, it arises from situations in which many things are changing at the same time, and great care is therefore needed in drawing conclusions from what is observed.

Not long ago, economics would have been put wholly in the group of nonexperimental sciences. It is still true that the majority of evidence that economists use is generated by observing what happens in the economy from day to day. However, a significant and growing amount of evidence is now being generated under controlled laboratory conditions. In this book, we concentrate on the nonlaboratory aspect of economic evidence both because it is still the predominant aspect and because the significance of laboratory-generated evidence in economics remains controversial.

Later in this chapter, we will consider some of the problems that arise when analyzing evidence generated by observing day-to-day behaviour that does not take place under controlled laboratory conditions. For the moment, however, we shall consider some general problems that are common to most sciences and are particularly important in the social sciences.

IS HUMAN BEHAVIOUR PREDICTABLE?

Social scientists seek to understand and to predict human behaviour. A scientific prediction is based on discovering stable response patterns, but are such patterns possible with anything so complex as human beings?

Does human behaviour show sufficiently stable responses to factors influencing it to be predictable within some stated margin of error? This positive question can be settled only by an appeal to evidence and not by armchair speculation. The question itself might concern either the behaviour of groups or that of isolated individuals.

Group Behaviour Versus Individual Behaviour

There are many situations in which group behaviour can be predicted accurately without certain knowledge of individual behaviour. The warmer the weather, for example, the more people visit the beach and the higher the sales of ice cream. It may be hard to say if or when one individual will buy an ice cream cone, but a stable response pattern can be seen among a large group of individuals. Although social scientists cannot predict which particular individuals will be involved in auto accidents during the next holiday weekend, they can come very close to knowing the total number who will. The more objectively measurable data they have (e.g., the state of the weather on the days in question and the trend in gasoline prices), the more closely they will be able to predict total accidents.

Economists can also predict with considerable accuracy what employees as a group will do when their take-home pay rises. Although some individuals may do surprising and unpredictable things, the overall response of workers in spending more when their take-home pay rises is predictable within a quite narrow margin of error. This relatively stable response is the basis of economists' ability to predict successfully the outcome of major changes in income-tax rates that permanently alter people's take-home pay.

Nothing we have said implies that people never change their minds or that future events can be foretold simply by projecting past trends. For example, we cannot safely predict that people will increase their spending next year just because they increased their spending this year. The stability we are discussing relates to a cause-effect response. For example, the next time take-home pay rises significantly (cause), spending by employees will rise (effect).

The Law of Large Numbers

Successfully predicting the behaviour of large groups of people is made possible by the statistical "law" of large numbers. Broadly speaking, this law asserts that random movements of many individual items tend to offset one another.

What is implied by this law? Ask any one person to measure the length of a room, and it will be almost impossible to predict in advance what sort of error of measurement will be made. Dozens of things will affect the accuracy of the measurement; furthermore, the person may make one error today and a quite different one tomorrow. But ask 1,000 people to measure the length of the same room, and we can predict within a small margin just how this *group* will make its errors. We can assert with confidence that more people will make small errors than will make large errors; that the larger the error, the fewer will be the number making it; that roughly the same number of people will overstate as will understate the distance; and that the larger the number of people making the measurement, the smaller the average of their errors will tend to be.

If a common cause acts on each member of the group, the average behaviour of the group can be predicted even though any one member may act in a surprising fashion. For example, let each of the 1,000 individuals be given a tape measure that understates actual distances. On average, the group will now understate the length of the room. It is, of course, quite possible that one member who had in the past been reading her tape measure correctly will now read more than it measures as a result of developing an eye defect. However, something else may have happened to another individual that causes him to underread his tape measure where before he was reading it correctly. Individuals may alter their behaviour for many different reasons, but the group's behaviour, when the inaccurate tape is substituted for the accurate one, is predictable precisely because the odd things that one individual does tend to cancel out the odd things that some other individual does.

Irregularities in individual behaviour tend to cancel each other out, and the regularities tend to show up in repeated observations.

THE IMPORTANCE OF THEORIES

When some regularity between two or more things is observed, curious people ask why. A *theory* provides an explanation, and by doing so, it enables us to predict as yet unobserved events.

For example, the simple theory of market behaviour that we will study in Part 2 shows how the output of a product affects the price at which it sells and hence affects the incomes of the people who produce it. As we will see in Chapter 6, this theory allows us to predict that a partial failure of the potato crop will *increase* the income of the average potato farmer.

Theories are used in explaining existing observations. A successful theory enables us to predict things that we have not yet seen.

Any explanation whatsoever of how given observations are linked together is a theoretical construction. Theories are used to impose order on our observations, to explain how what we see is linked together. Without theories, there would be only a shapeless mass of observations.

To illustrate this point, think about the common observation that something is "true in theory but not in practice." The next time you hear someone say this, you might reply, "All right, then, tell me what does happen in practice." Usually you will not be told mere facts, but you will be given an alternative theory—a different explanation of the facts. The speaker should have said, "The theory in question provides a poor explanation of the facts in question or is contradicted by some other facts. I have a different theory that does a much better job."

The choice is not between theory and observation but between better or worse theories to explain observations.

THE STRUCTURE OF THEORIES

A theory consists of:

1. a set of definitions that clearly define the variables to be used,

2. a set of assumptions about the behaviour of the variables, and

3. predictions (often called hypotheses) that are deduced from the assumptions of the theory and can be tested against actual empirical observations.

We shall consider these constituents one by one.

Variables

A **variable** is a magnitude that can take on different possible values. Variables are the basic elements of theories, and each one needs to be carefully defined.

Price is an example of an important economic variable. The price of a product is the amount of money that must be given up to purchase one unit of that product. To define a price, we must first define the product to which it is attached. Such a product might be one dozen Grade A large eggs. The price of such eggs sold in, say, supermarkets in Gimli, Manitoba, defines a variable. The particular values taken on by that variable might be $1.79 on July 1, 1997; $1.84 on July 8, 1998; and $1.95 on July 15, 1999.

In understanding any theory, it is crucial to distinguish between endogenous variables and exogenous variables. An **endogenous variable** is a variable that is explained within a theory. An **exogenous variable** influences endogenous variables but is itself determined by factors outside the theory.

Consider the theory that the price of apples in Calgary on a particular day depends on several things, one of which is the weather in the Okanagan Valley during the previous apple-growing season. We can safely assume that the state of the weather is not determined by economic conditions. The price of apples in this case is an endogenous variable—something determined within the framework of the theory. The state of the weather in the Okanagan Valley is an exogenous variable; changes in it influence prices because the changes affect the output of apples, but the state of the weather is not influenced by apple prices.

Other words are sometimes used for the same distinction. One frequently used pair is *induced* for endogenous and *autonomous* for exogenous; another is *dependent* for endogenous and *independent* for exogenous. Thus, economists use the words "exogenous," "independent," and "autonomous" interchangably; they also use the words "endogenous," "dependent," and "induced" interchangably.

Assumptions

A key element of any theory is a set of assumptions about the behaviour of the variables in which we are interested. Usually these state how the behaviour of two or more variables relate to each other.

In some cases, these linkages are provided by physical or biological laws. One example is the relation between the resources each firm uses, which economists call *inputs,* and that firm's *output.* In the case of the egg farmer, the output of eggs is related to inputs of chicken feed, farm labour, and all the other things the farmer uses.

In other cases, these linkages are provided by human behaviour. For example, economists make two basic assumptions about consumers. The first concerns how each consumer's satisfaction, or *utility,* is related to the quantities of all the goods and services consumed by that person. The second is that in making their choices on how much to consume, people seek to maximize the satisfaction they gain from that consumption.

Although assumptions are an essential part of all theories, students are often concerned about those that seem unrealistic. An example will illustrate some of the issues involved. Much of the theory that we are going to study in this book uses the assumption that the sole motive of the owners of firms is to maximize their profits. The assumption of profit maximization allows economists to make predictions about the behaviour of firms. They study how firms' profits are affected by the choices firms make. They then predict that the alternative that produces the most profits will be the one selected.

Profit maximization may seem like a rather crude assumption. Surely, for example, the managers of firms sometimes choose to protect the environment rather than pursue certain highly polluting but profitable opportunities. Does this not discredit the assumption of profit maximization by showing it to be unrealistic?

The answer is no; to make successful predictions, the theory does not require that managers be solely and unwaveringly motivated by the desire to maximize profits. All that is required is that profits be a sufficiently important consideration that a theory based on the assumption of profit maximization will lead to explanations and predictions that are substantially correct.

This illustration shows that it is not always appropriate to criticize a theory because its assumptions seem unrealistic. All theory is an abstraction from reality. If it were not, it would merely duplicate the world in all its complexity and would add nothing to our understanding of it. A good theory abstracts in a useful way; a poor theory does not. If a theory has ignored some genuinely important factors, its predictions will be contradicted by the evidence—at least where an ignored factor exerts an important influence on the outcome.

Predictions

A theory's predictions are the propositions that can be deduced from that theory; they are often called *hypotheses*. An example of a prediction concerning profit maximizing firms is: *if* the going wage for labour increases, *then* the amount of labour employed will fall.

A scientific prediction is a conditional statement that takes the following form: *If* this occurs, *then* such and such will follow.

For example, if a city government forces down the rents on residential accommodation (through a policy of *rent controls*), then a housing shortage will develop.

It is important to realize that this prediction is different from the statement "I predict that in two years' time, there will be a housing shortage in my city because I believe its municipal government will decide to impose rent controls." The government's decision to introduce rent controls in two years' time will be the outcome of many influences, both economic and political. If the economist's prophecy about a housing shortage turns out to be wrong because in two years' time the government does not impose rent controls, then all that has been learned is that the economist is not a good guesser about the behaviour of the government. However, if the government does impose rent controls and a housing shortage does not then develop, a conditional (if-then) prediction based on economic theory will have been contradicted.

Expressing Relations Among Variables

Economists deal with many relations among variables. A **function**, also known as a *functional relation*, is a formal expression of a relationship between two or more variables. When two variables are related in such a way that an increase in one is associated with an increase in the other, they are said to be positively related. When two variables are related in such a way that an increase in one is associated with a decrease in the other, they are said to be negatively related.

The prediction that the quantity of eggs people want to buy is negatively related to the price of eggs is an example of a functional relation in economics. In its most general form, it merely says that quantity demanded is related to price. The more specific hypothesis is that as the price of eggs rises, the quantity of desired purchases falls.

In many relations of this kind, economists can be even more specific about the nature of the functional relation. On the basis of detailed studies, economists often have a pretty good idea of by how much the quantity demanded will change as a result of specified changes in price; that is, they can predict magnitude as well as direction.

ECONOMIC MODELS

Economists often proceed by way of constructing what are referred to as *economic models*. Because the term *model* is used in several contexts, it is important to understand the range of meanings.

First, model is sometimes used merely as a synonym for a theory or a particular subset of theories, such as the Keynesian model of national income determination or the Neoclassical model of price determination in competitive markets.

Second, model is sometimes applied to a specific quantitative formulation of a theory. In this case, specific numbers are attached to the mathematical relationships implied by the theory, the numbers often being based on empirical evidence. The theory in its specific form can then be used to make precise predictions about, say, the behaviour of prices in the potato market or the course of national income and total employment. Forecasting models used by the Bank of Canada and the federal Department of Finance are of this type.

Third, a model is often an application of a general theory in a specific context. The successful model may then explain behaviour that previously seemed inexplicable or even perverse. An example is provided by a branch of economics known as *principal-agent theory*. The principal is the person who wants something done, and the agent is the person hired by the principal to do it. For example, managers of firms may be thought of as agents, while the owners are principals. Both principal and agent are assumed to wish to maximize their own well-being, and the principal's problem is to design a set of incentives that give the agent a self-interest in doing what the principal requires.

Specific principal-agent models have been applied successfully to many problems and have provided a rational explanation of what at first sight seemed to be perverse behaviour. For example, people put in positions of trust are often paid much more than is needed to induce people to take these jobs. Why should principals pay their agents more than they need to pay to fill the jobs? The explanation is that if the agent is paid more than she could earn in another job, she has an incentive not to violate the trust placed in her. If she does violate the trust and is caught, she loses the extra pay attached to the job.

Finally, a model may be just an illustrative abstraction which helps to organize our thoughts about a particular issue. For example, we may wish to gain insight into the consequences of the observation that the amount of research that goes into developing a new product often depends on the product's current sales (because profits to finance research and development are generated by sales). To do this, we may build a very simple model in which the amount of current research is positively related to the amount of current sales. This creates what is called *positive feedback:* The higher current sales are, the more research is done; the more research is done, the more rapidly the product improves; the more rapidly the product improves, the more current sales rise. If extended to allow several competing products, this model will reveal one key tendency of positive-feedback systems: Initial advantages tend to be reinforced, making it more and more difficult for competitors to keep up. No one believes that this simple model catches everything about the complex interactions when various new products compete in the early stages of their development. But it does alert us to certain forces to watch for when we build more complex models or create more general theories of the competition among new products and new technologies. Interestingly, these self-reenforcing characteristics have been observed in many circumstances such as the competition to be the power source of the first automobiles early in the twentieth century, the competition among alternative technologies to produce nuclear power after the Second World War, and the recent competition to produce the operating system of personal computers.

Testing theories

A theory is tested by confronting its predictions with evidence. It is necessary to discover if certain events are followed by the outcomes predicted by the theory. For example, is an increase in the wage rate followed by a decline in the amount of labour employed? Theories are sometimes tested in conscious attempts to do just that. They are also tested every time an economist uses one to predict the outcome of

some specific event. If economists continued to be mistaken every time they used some theory to make predictions, the theory would eventually be called into question.

Theories tend to be abandoned when they are no longer useful, and theories cease to be useful when they cannot predict the outcomes of actions better than the next best alternative. When a theory consistently fails to predict better than the available alternatives, it is either modified or replaced. Figure 2-1 summarizes the discussion of theories and their testing.

REFUTATION VERSUS CONFIRMATION

An important part of a scientific approach to any issue consists of setting up a theory that will explain it and then seeing if that theory can be refuted by evidence.

The alternative to this approach is to set up a theory and then look for confirming evidence. Such an approach is hazardous because the world is sufficiently complex that some confirming evidence can be found for any theory, no matter how unlikely the theory may be. For example, flying saucers, the Loch Ness monster, fortune-telling, and astrology all have their devotees who can quote confirming evidence in spite of the failure of attempts to discover systematic, objective evidence for these things.

An example of the unfruitful approach of seeking confirmation is frequently seen when a national leader is surrounded by followers who provide only evidence that confirms the leader's existing views. This approach is usually a road to disaster because the leader becomes more and more out of touch with reality.

A wise leader adopts a scientific approach instinctively, constantly checking the accuracy of accepted views by encouraging criticism from subordinates. This tests how far the leader's existing views correspond to all available evidence and encourages adjustments in the light of conflicting evidence.

STATISTICAL ANALYSIS

Statistical analysis is used to test the hypothesis that two or more things are related and to estimate the numerical values of the function that describes the relationship. In practice, the same data can be used simultaneously to test whether a relationship exists and, if it does exist, to provide a measure of it.

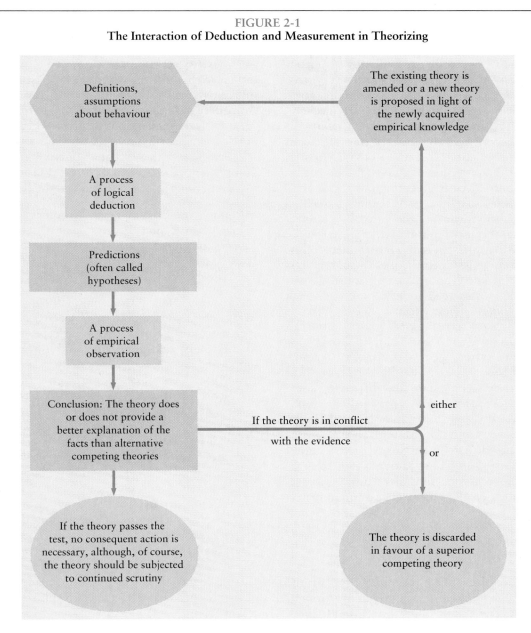

FIGURE 2-1
The Interaction of Deduction and Measurement in Theorizing

Definitions, assumptions about behaviour

A process of logical deduction

Predictions (often called hypotheses)

A process of empirical observation

Conclusion: The theory does or does not provide a better explanation of the facts than alternative competing theories

If the theory passes the test, no consequent action is necessary, although, of course, the theory should be subjected to continued scrutiny

The existing theory is amended or a new theory is proposed in light of the newly acquired empirical knowledge

If the theory is in conflict with the evidence

either

or

The theory is discarded in favour of a superior competing theory

Theory and observation are in continuous interaction. Starting (at the top left) with the assumptions of a theory and the definitions of relevant terms, the theorist deduces by logical analysis everything that is implied by the assumptions. These implications are the predictions or the hypotheses of the theory. The theory is then tested by confronting its predictions with evidence. If the theory is in conflict with facts, it will usually be amended to make it consistent with those facts (thereby making it a better theory); in extreme cases, it will be discarded, to be replaced by a superior alternative. The process then begins again: The new or amended theory is subjected first to logical analysis and then to empirical testing.

Because economics is primarily a nonlaboratory science, it lacks the controlled experiments that are central to sciences like physics and chemistry. Economics must therefore use millions of uncontrolled experiments that are going on every day. Households are deciding what to purchase given changing prices and incomes, firms are deciding what to produce and how, and governments are involved in the economy through their various taxes, subsidies, and regulations. Because all these activities can be observed and recorded, a mass of data is continually being produced by the economy.

The variables that interest economists, such as the level of unemployment, the price of compact discs, and the output of automobiles, are generally influenced by many forces that vary simultaneously. If economists are to test their theories about relations among variables in the economy, they must use statistical techniques designed for situations in which other things *cannot* be held constant.

Fortunately, such techniques exist, although their application is usually neither simple nor straightforward. The appendix to this chapter provides a discussion of some tabular and graphical techniques for describing data and displaying some of the more obvious relationships. Further examination of data involves techniques studied in elementary statistics courses. More advanced courses in econometrics deal with the array of techniques designed to test economic hypotheses and to measure economic relations in the complex circumstances in which economic evidence is often generated.

THE DECISION
TO ACCEPT OR REJECT

Nothing is ever absolutely certain. Some of the things we now think are true will eventually turn out to be false, and some of the things we currently think are false will eventually turn out to be true. Yet even though we can never be certain, we can assess the balance of available evidence. Some hypotheses are so unlikely to be true in the light of current evidence that for all practical purposes we may regard them as false. Other hypotheses are so unlikely to be false, given current evidence, that for all practical purposes we may regard them as true. This kind of practical decision must always be regarded as tentative. Every once in a while, we will find that we have to change our mind. Something that looked right will begin to look doubtful, or something that looked wrong will begin to look possible.

Making such decisions requires accepting some theories (to act as if they were true) and rejecting others (to act as if they were false). Just as a jury can make two kinds of errors (finding an innocent person guilty or letting a guilty person go free), so statistical decision makers can make two kinds of errors. They can reject hypotheses that are true, and they can accept hypotheses that are false. Fortunately, like a jury, they can also make correct decisions—and indeed, they expect to do so most of the time.

Although the possibility of error cannot be eliminated when testing theories against observations, it can be controlled.

The method of control is to decide in advance how large a risk to take in accepting a hypothesis that is in fact false.[2] Conventionally in statistics, this risk is often set at 5 percent or 1 percent. When the 5 percent cutoff point is used, we accept the hypothesis if the results that appear to establish it could have happened by chance no more than 1 time in 20. Using the 1 percent decision rule gives the hypothesis a more difficult test. A hypothesis is accepted only if the results that appear to establish it could have happened by chance no more than 1 time in 100.

Consider the hypothesis that a certain coin is "loaded," favouring heads over tails. The test consists of flipping the coin 100 times. Suppose that on a single test, the coin comes up heads 53 times. This result is not strong evidence in favour of the hypothesis because such an unbalanced result could happen by chance in more than 22 percent of such tests. Thus the hypothesis of a head-biased coin would not be accepted on the basis of this evidence using either a 1 percent or a 5 percent cutoff. Had the test produced 65 heads and 35 tails, a result that would occur by chance in less than 1 percent of such tests, we would (given either a 1 percent or a 5 percent cutoff) accept the hypothesis of the coin being loaded.[3]

---

[2]Return to the jury analogy: Our notion of a person's being innocent unless the jury is persuaded of guilt "beyond a reasonable doubt" rests on our wish to take only a small risk of accepting the hypothesis of guilt if the person tried is in fact innocent.

[3]The actual statistical testing process is more complex than this example suggests but must be left to a course in statistics.

When action must be taken, some rule of thumb is necessary, but it is important to understand, first, that no one can ever be certain about being right in rejecting any hypothesis and, second, that there is nothing magical about arbitrary cutoff points. Some cutoff point must be used whenever decisions have to be made.

Finally, recall that the rejection of a hypothesis is seldom the end of inquiry. Decisions can be reversed if new evidence comes to light. Often the result of a statistical test of a theory suggests a new hypothesis that "fits the facts" better than the old one.

CAN ECONOMICS BE MADE VALUE-FREE?

We have made two key statements about the positive-normative distinction. First, the ability to distinguish positive from normative questions is a key part of the foundation of science. Second, economists, in common with all scientists, seek to answer positive questions.

Some people who have accepted these points have gone on to argue that there can be a completely value-free inquiry into any branch of science, including economics. After long debate over this issue, the conclusion that most people seem to accept is that a *completely* value-free inquiry is impossible.

Our values become involved at all stages of any inquiry. For example, we must allocate our scarce time. This means that we choose to study some problems rather than other problems. This choice is often influenced by our value judgments about the relative importance of various problems. Also evidence is never conclusive and so is always open to more than one interpretation. It is difficult to assess such imperfect evidence without giving some play to our values. Further, when reporting the results of our studies, we must use words that we know will arouse various emotions in the people who read them. So the words we choose and the emphasis we give to the available evidence (and to the uncertainties surrounding it) will influence the impact that the study has.

For these and many other reasons, most people who have discussed this issue believe that there can be no totally value-free study of economics.

This does not mean that economists and other scientists should conclude that *everything* is a matter of subjective value judgments. The very real advancements of knowledge in all sciences, natural and social, show that science is not just a matter of opinion or of debating competing value judgments.

Science has been successful in spite of the fact that individual scientists have not always been totally objective. Individual scientists have sometimes passionately resisted the apparent implications of evidence. The rules of the scientific game—that facts cannot be ignored and must somehow be fitted into the accepted theoretical structure—tend to produce scientific advance in spite of what might be thought of as unscientific, emotional attitudes on the part of some scientists.

But if people engaged in scientific debate, in economics or any other science, ever succeed in changing the rules of the game to allow inconvenient facts to be ignored or defined out of existence, a major blow would be dealt to the power of scientific inquiry.

SUMMARY

A. THE DISTINCTION BETWEEN POSITIVE AND NORMATIVE

- It is useful to distinguish between positive and normative statements. Positive statements concern what is, was, or will be, whereas normative statements concern what ought to be. Disagreements over positive, testable statements are appropriately settled by an appeal to the facts. Disagreements over normative statements cannot be settled in this way.

B. THE SCIENTIFIC APPROACH IN ECONOMICS

- Successful scientific inquiry requires separating positive questions about the way the world works from normative questions about how one would like the world to work, formulating positive questions precisely enough so that they can be settled by an appeal to evidence, and then finding means of gathering the necessary evidence.

- Social scientists have observed many stable human behaviour patterns. These form the basis for successful predictions of how people will behave under certain conditions.
- The fact that people sometimes act strangely, even capriciously, does not destroy the possibility of scientific study of group behaviour. The odd and inexplicable things that one person does will tend to cancel out the odd and inexplicable things that another person does. The law of large numbers thus means that group behaviour is often easier to predict than individual behaviour.
- Theories are designed to give meaning and coherence to observed sequences of events. A theory consists of a set of definitions of the variables to be employed and a set of assumptions about how things behave. Any theory has certain logical implications that must be true if the theory is true. These are the theory's predictions or hypotheses.
- Economists use models to help them think about the complex interactions of different economic phenomena. Such models often generate testable predictions.

C. TESTING THEORIES

- A theory is conditional in the sense that it provides predictions of the type "if one event occurs, then another event will also occur." An important method of testing theories is to confront their predictions with evidence.

- The progress of any science lies in finding better explanations of events than are now available. Thus in any developing science, one must expect to discard some existing theories and replace them with demonstrably superior alternatives.
- Theories are tested by checking their predictions against evidence. In some sciences, these tests can be conducted under laboratory conditions in which only one thing changes at a time. In other sciences, testing must be done using the data produced by the world of ordinary events. (The appendix to this chapter provides a brief discussion of some of the elementary statistical techniques used to test hypotheses when many variables are changing at once.)

D. CAN ECONOMICS BE MADE VALUE-FREE?

- Although distinguishing positive from normative questions and seeking to answer positive questions are important aspects of science, it does not follow that economic inquiry can be totally value-free. Although values intrude at almost all stages of scientific inquiry, the rule that theories should be judged against evidence wherever possible tends to produce advances of positive knowledge over time.

KEY CONCEPTS

Positive and normative statements
Testable statements
The law of large numbers and the predictability of human behaviour

Variables, assumptions, and predictions in theorizing
Uses of models
Functional relations

Conditional prediction versus prophecy

DISCUSSION QUESTIONS

1. What are some of the positive and normative issues that lie behind the disagreements in the following cases?

   a. Economists disagree on whether the Government of Canada should try to stimulate the economy in the next six months.

   b. European and North American negotiators disagree over the desirability of reducing European farm subsidies.

   c. Economists argue about the merits of a voucher system that allows parents to choose the schools their children will attend.

   d. Economists debate the use of a two-tier medical system in Canada (whereby health care continues to be publicly provided, but individuals are permitted to be treated by doctors who bill the patient directly—"extra billing").

2. Much recent public debate has centred on the pros and cons of permitting continued unrestricted sale of cigarettes. Proposals for the control of cigarettes range from increasing excise taxes to the mandatory use of plain packaging to an outright ban on their sale. Identify the positive and normative assumptions that underlie the national mood to reduce the consumption of tobacco products.

3. A baby doesn't know about the theory of gravity, yet in learning to walk and eat, the child makes use of the principles of gravity. Distinguish between behaviour and the explanation of behaviour. Does a business executive or a farmer have to understand economic theory to behave in a pattern consistent with it?

4. "If human behaviour were completely capricious and unpredictable, life insurance could not be a profitable business." Explain. Can you think of any businesses that do not depend on predictable human behaviour?

5. Write five statements about unemployment. Classify each statement as positive or normative. If your list contains only one type of statement, try to add a sixth statement of the other type.

6. Each of the following unrealistic assumptions is sometimes made when economists construct models. See if you can imagine some situations in which each of these assumptions might be a useful simplification in order to think about some aspect of the real world.

   a. The earth is flat.
   b. There are no differences between men and women.
   c. There is no tomorrow.
   d. There are only two periods—this year and next year.
   e. A country produces only two types of goods.
   f. People are wholly selfish.

7. What may at first appear to be untestable statements can often be reworded so that they can be tested by an appeal to evidence. How might you do that with respect to each of the following assertions?

   a. Free-market economic systems are the best in the world.
   b. Unemployment insurance is eroding the work ethic and encouraging people to become wards of the state rather than productive workers.
   c. Robotics ought to be outlawed because it will destroy the future of working people.
   d. Laws requiring equal pay for work of equal value will make women better off.
   e. Free trade improves the welfare of a country's citizens.

8. "The simplest way to see that capital punishment is a strong deterrent to murder is to ask yourself whether you might be more inclined to commit murder if you knew in advance that you ran no risk of ending up in the electric chair, in the gas chamber, or on the gallows." Comment on the methodology of social investigation implied by this statement. What alternative approach would you suggest?

9. There are hundreds of eyewitnesses to the existence of flying saucers and other UFOs. There are films and eyewitness accounts of Nessie, the Loch Ness monster. Are you convinced of their existence? If not, what would it take to persuade you? If so, what would it take to make you change your mind?

APPENDIX TO CHAPTER 2

Graphing Relations Among Variables

The popular saying "The facts speak for themselves" is almost always wrong when there are many facts. Theories are needed to explain how facts are linked together, and summary measures are needed to assist in sorting out what facts show in relation to theories. The simplest means of providing compact summaries of a large number of observations is the use of tables and graphs. Graphs play an important role in economics by representing geometrically both observed data and the relations among variables that are the subject of economic theory.

Because the surface of a piece of paper is two-dimensional, a graph may readily be used to represent pictorially any relation between two variables. Flip through this book and you will see dozens of examples. Figure 2A-1 shows generally how a coordinate graph can be used to represent any two variables.[1]

UNDERSTANDING GRAPHS

Figure 2A-2 shows a simple two-variable graph, which will be analyzed in detail in Chapter 4. For now it is sufficient to notice that the graph permits us to show the relationship between two variables, the price of carrots on the vertical axis and the quantity of carrots (per month) on the horizontal axis.[2] The downward-sloping curve, labeled D for a *demand curve,* shows the relationship between the price of carrots and the quantity of carrots that buyers wish to purchase.

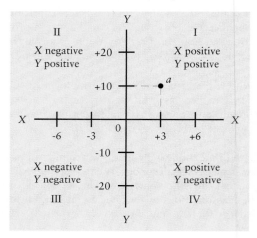

FIGURE 2A-1
A Coordinate Graph

The axes divide the total space into four quadrants according to the signs of the variables. In the upper right-hand quadrant, both X and Y are greater than zero; this is usually called the *positive quadrant.* Point a has *coordinates* $X = 3$ and $Y = 10$ in the coordinate graph. These coordinates define point a.

Figure 2A-3 is very much like Figure 2A-2, with one difference. It generalizes from the specific example of carrots to an unspecified product and focuses on the slope of the demand curve rather than on specific numerical values. Note that the quantity labeled q_0 is associated with the price p_0, and the quantity q_1 is associated with the price p_1.

STRAIGHT LINES AND THEIR SLOPES

Figure 2A-4 illustrates a variety of straight lines. They differ according to their slopes. **Slope** is defined as the

---

[1]Economics is often concerned only with the positive values of variables, and the graph is then confined to the upper right-hand (or "positive") quadrant. Whenever a variable has a negative value, one or more of the other quadrants must be included.
[2]The choice of which variable to put on which axis is discussed in math note 9 at the back of the book.

FIGURE 2A-2
The Relationship Between the Price of Carrots and the Quantity of Carrots That Purchasers Wish to Buy: A Numerical Example

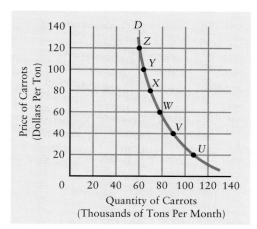

A two-dimensional graph can show how two variables are related. The two variables, the price of carrots and the quantity that people wish to purchase, are shown by the downward-sloping curve labeled D. Particular points on the curve are labeled U through Z. For example, point Z shows that at a price of $120 per ton, the demand to purchase carrots is 60,000 tons per month.

FIGURE 2A-3
The Relationship Between the Price of a Product and the Quantity of the Product That Purchasers Wish to Buy

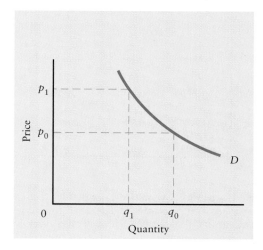

Graphs can illustrate general or specific relationships between variables. Here, in contrast to Figure 2A-2, price and quantity are shown as general variables. The demand curve illustrates a quantitatively unspecified negative relationship between price and quantity. For example, at the price p_0, the quantity that purchasers demand is q_0, whereas at the higher price of p_1, purchasers demand the lower quantity q_1.

FIGURE 2A-4
Four Straight Lines with Different Slopes

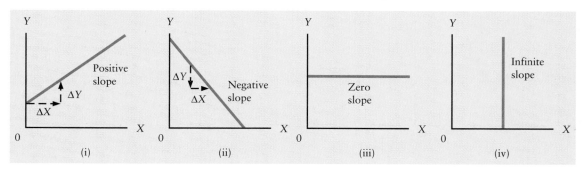

The slope of a straight line is constant but can vary from one line to another. The direction of slope of a straight line is characterized by the signs of the ratio $\Delta Y/\Delta X$. In part (i), that ratio is positive because X and Y vary in the same direction; in part (ii), the ratio is negative because X and Y vary in opposite directions; in part (iii), it is zero because Y does not change as X changes; in part (iv), it is infinite.

FIGURE 2A-5
Two Straight Lines with Different Slopes

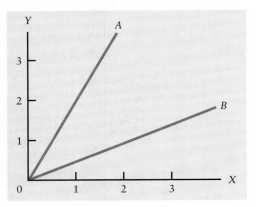

Slope is a quantitative measure. Both lines have positive slopes and thus are similar to Figure 2A-4(i). However, line A is steeper (has a greater slope) than line B. For each 1-unit increase in X, the value of Y increases by 2 units along line A but only one-half unit along line B. The ratio $\Delta Y/\Delta X$ is 2 for line A and one-half for B.

ratio of the vertical change to the corresponding horizontal change as one moves along a straight line.

The symbol Δ (which is the Greek upper-case delta) is used to indicate a change in any variable. Thus ΔX means "the change in X," and ΔY means "the change in Y." The ratio $\Delta Y/\Delta X$ is the slope of a straight line. When ΔX and ΔY have the same signs, the ratio is positive and the line is positively sloped, as in part (i) of Figure 2A-4. When ΔY and ΔX have opposite signs, that is, when one increases while the other decreases, the ratio is negative and the line is negatively sloped, as in part (ii). When ΔY is zero (as X changes), the line is horizontal, as in part (iii), and the slope is zero. When ΔX is zero (as Y changes), the line is vertical, as in part (iv), and the slope is often said to be infinite, although the ratio $\Delta Y/\Delta X$ is undefined. [2]

Slope is a quantitative measure, not merely a qualitative one. For example, in Figure 2A-5, two upward-sloping straight lines have different slopes. Line A has a slope of 2 ($\Delta Y/\Delta X = 2$); line B has a slope of ½ ($\Delta Y/\Delta X = 0.5$).

CURVED LINES AND THEIR SLOPES

Figure 2A-6 shows four curved lines. The line in part (i) is plainly upward sloping; the line in part (ii) is downward sloping. The other two change from one to the other, as the labels indicate. Unlike a straight line, which has the same slope at every point on the line, the slope of a curve changes. The slope of a curve must be measured at a particular point and is defined as *the slope of a straight line that just touches (is tangent to) the curve at that point.* This is illustrated in Figure 2A-7. The slope at point A is

FIGURE 2A-6
Four Curved Lines

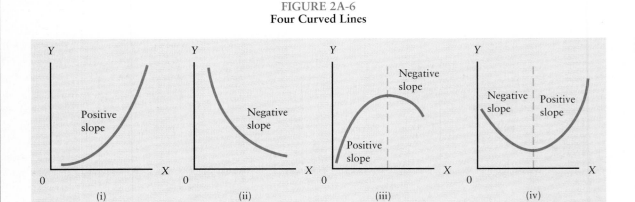

The slope of a curved line is not constant and may change direction. The slopes of the curves in parts (i) and (ii) change in size but not in direction, whereas those in parts (iii) and (iv) change in both size and direction. Unlike that of a straight line, the slope of a curved line cannot be represented by a single number because it changes as the value of X changes.

FIGURE 2A-7
Defining the Slope of a Curved Line

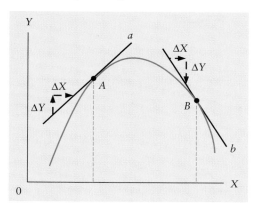

The slope of a curve at any point on the curve is defined by the slope of the straight line that is tangent to the curve at that point. The slope of the curve at point *A* is defined by the slope of the line *a*, which is tangent to the curve at point *A*. The slope of the curve at point *B* is defined by the slope of the tangent line *b*.

FIGURE 2A-8
A Scatter Diagram Relating Taxes Paid to Family Income

The scatter pattern shows a clear tendency for taxes paid to rise with family income. Family income is measured along the horizontal axis, and federal income taxes paid are measured along the vertical axis. Each dot represents a single family in the sample and is located on the graph according to the family's income and taxes paid. The dots fall mainly within a narrow rising band, suggesting the existence of a systematic relationship between income and taxes paid, but they do not fall along a single line, which suggests that things other than family income affect taxes paid.

measured by the slope of the tangent line *a*. The slope at point *B* is measured by the slope of the tangent line *b*.

GRAPHING DATA

A coordinate graph such as that shown in Figure 2A-1 can be used to show the observed values of two variables as well as the theoretical relationships between them. For example, curve *D* in Figure 2A-2 might have arisen as a freehand line drawn to generalize actual observations of the points labeled *U, V, W, X, Y,* and *Z*.

CROSS-SECTIONAL DATA

Although Figure 2A-2 was not constructed from actual observations, many graphs are. To illustrate, we examine the very simple hypothesis that the income taxes paid by families increase as their incomes increase.

To test this hypothesis about the relationship between incomes and income taxes, we have chosen a random sample of 212 families from data collected by the Survey Research Center of the University of Michigan. We have recorded each family's income and the federal income tax it paid in 1979. (1979 was a long time ago, but the principles illustrated in this discussion apply equally to any year.) This data is called **cross-sectional data** because data is collected *across space for the same time period*; the incomes and taxes paid by different households are compared for a single year.

One way in which the data may be used to evaluate the hypothesis is to draw what is called a **scatter diagram,** which plots paired values of two variables. Figure 2A-8 is a scatter diagram that relates family income to federal income tax payments. Income is measured on the horizontal axis and taxes paid on the vertical axis. Any point in the diagram represents a particular family's income combined with the tax payment of that family. Thus each family for which there is an observation is represented on the diagram by a dot, the coordinates of which indicate the family's income and the amount of taxes paid.

The scatter diagram is useful because if there is a simple relationship between the two variables, it will be apparent to the eye once the data are plotted. For example, Figure 2A-8 makes it apparent that more taxes tend to be paid as income rises. It also makes it apparent that the relationship between taxes and income is approximately linear. An upward sloping straight line fits the data reasonably well between about $10,000 and $40,000 of income. Above $40,000 and below $10,000 the line does not fit the data as well, but because more than two-thirds of the families sampled had incomes in the $10,000-to-$40,000 range, we may conclude that the straight line provides a fairly good description of the basic relationship for middle-income families in 1979.

The graph also gives some idea of the strength of the relationship. If income were the only determinant of taxes paid, all the dots would cluster closely around a line or a smooth curve. As it is, the points are somewhat scattered, and several households with the same income show different amounts of taxes paid.

There is some scattering of the dots because the relationship is not perfect; in other words, there is some variation in tax payments that cannot be associated with variations in family income. These variations in tax payments occur mainly for two reasons. First, factors other than income influence tax payments, and some of these other factors will undoubtedly have varied among the families in the sample. Second, there will inevitably be some errors in measurement. For example, a family might have incorrectly reported its tax payments to the person who collected the data.

TIME-SERIES DATA

The data used in the example of Figure 2A-8 are cross-sectional data because several observations are available (one for each family) at the same point in time. Scatter diagrams may also be drawn for a number of observations taken on two variables at successive periods of time.

For example, if we wanted to know whether there was any simple relationship between personal

| | TABLE 2A-1 | |
| | **Personal Income and Consumption in Canada, 1970–1994 (1986 dollars)** | |
Year	Disposable Personal Income Per Capita	Personal Consumption Expenditures Per Capita
1970	$ 8424	$ 7854
1971	8703	8009
1972	9385	8467
1973	10065	8874
1974	10562	9229
1975	11047	9511
1976	11480	9981
1977	11581	10121
1978	11868	10228
1979	12145	10358
1980	12323	10433
1981	12643	10436
1982	12461	9980
1983	12252	10274
1984	12647	10596
1985	12903	11022
1986	12902	11352
1987	13040	11645
1988	13498	11981
1989	13845	12141
1990	13610	12024
1991	13130	11609
1992	13078	11556
1993	12943	11567
1994	13011	11847

Real disposable income per capita and real personal consumption expenditures have both grown since 1970. The former has increased from $8,424 to just over $13,000 over the period, while the latter grew from $7,854 to just under $12,000.

Source: Statistics Canada, 11-210.

income and personal consumption in Canada between 1970 and 1994, data would be collected for the levels of personal income and expenditure per capita in each year from 1970 to 1994, as is done in Table 2A-1. This information could be plotted on a scatter diagram, with consumption on the X axis and income on the Y axis. The data are plotted in Figure 2A-9, and they do indeed suggest a systematic, almost linear relationship.

Figure 2A-9 is a scatter diagram of observations taken repeatedly over successive periods of time.

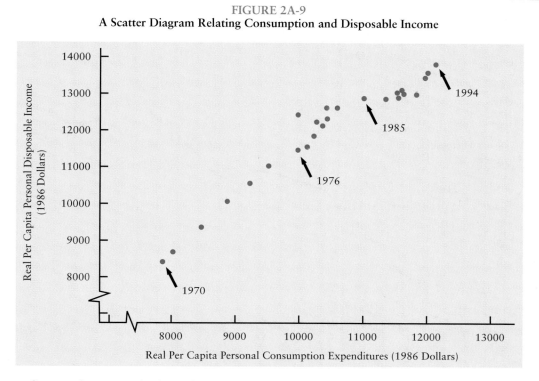

FIGURE 2A-9
A Scatter Diagram Relating Consumption and Disposable Income

This scatter diagram shows paired values of two variables. The data of Table 2A-1 are plotted here. Each dot shows the values of per capita personal consumption expenditures and per capita disposable income for a given year. A close positive linear relationship between the two variables is obvious. Note that in this diagram, the axes are shown with a break in them to indicate that not all the values of the variables between $8,000 and zero are given. Because no observations occurred in those ranges, it is unnecessary to provide space for them.

Such data are called **time-series data,** and plotting them on a scatter diagram involves no new techniques. When cross-sectional data are plotted, each point gives the values of two variables for a particular unit (say, a family); when time-series data are plotted, each point tells the values of two variables for a particular period (say, a year).

Rather than studying the relationship between income and consumption, we might instead be interested in the pattern taken in either *one* of these variables over time. Figure 2A-10 shows this information for personal consumption expenditures per capita. Time is one variable, and consumption expenditure is the other. However, time is a special variable; the order in which successive events happen is important. The year 1994 followed 1993; they were not two independent and unrelated years.

In contrast, two randomly selected households are independent and unrelated. For this reason, it is customary to draw in the line segments connecting the successive points, as has been done in Figure 2A-10.

Such a figure is called a *time-series graph,* or simply a time series. This kind of graph makes it easy to see if the variable being considered has changed in a systematic way over the years or if its behaviour has been more or less erratic.

RATIO (LOGARITHMIC) SCALES

All the foregoing graphs use axes that plot numbers on a natural arithmetic scale, with distances between two values shown by the size of the nu-

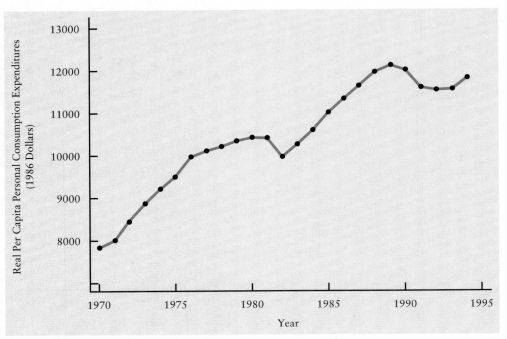

FIGURE 2A-10
A Time Series of Consumption Expenditures, 1970–1994

A time series plots values of a single variable in chronological order. This graph shows that with only minor interruptions, consumption measured in 1986 dollars rose from 1970 to 1994. The data are given in Table 2A-1.

merical difference. If *proportionate* rather than *absolute* changes in variables are important, it is more revealing to use a ratio scale than a natural scale. On a **natural scale,** the distance between numbers is proportionate to the absolute difference between those numbers. Thus 200 is placed halfway between 100 and 300. On a **ratio or logarithmic scale,** the distance between numbers is proportionate to the percentage difference between the two numbers (which can also be measured as the absolute difference between their logarithms). Equal distances anywhere on a ratio scale represent equal percentage changes rather than equal absolute changes. On a ratio scale, the distance between 100 and 200 is the same as the distance between 200 and 400, between 1,000 and 2,000, and between any two numbers that stand in the ratio 1:2.

| | TABLE 2A-2 | |
| | **Two Series** | |
Time Period	Series A	Series B
0	$10	$10
1	18	20
2	26	40
3	34	80
4	42	160

Series A shows constant absolute growth ($8 per period) but declining percentage growth. Series B shows constant percentage growth (100 percent per period) but rising absolute growth.

Table 2A-2 shows two series, one growing at a constant absolute amount of 8 units (dollars) per period and the other growing at a constant rate of 100 percent per period. In Figure 2A-11, the series

FIGURE 2A-11
The Difference Between Natural and Ratio Scales

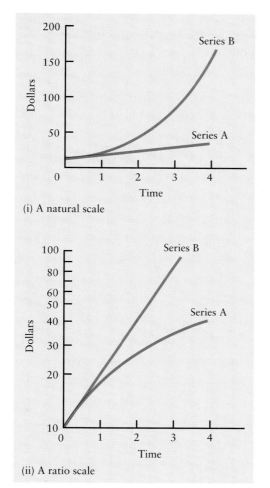

(i) A natural scale

(ii) A ratio scale

On a natural scale, equal distances represent equal amounts; on a ratio scale, equal distances represent equal percentage changes. The two series in Table 2A-2 are plotted in each chart. Series A, which grows at a constant absolute amount, is shown by a straight line on a natural scale but by a curve of diminishing slope on a ratio scale because the same absolute growth represents a decreasing percentage growth. Series B, which grows at a rising absolute rate but a constant percentage rate, is shown by a curve of increasing slope on a natural scale but by a straight line on a ratio scale.

are plotted first on a natural scale and then on a ratio scale. The natural scale makes it easy for the eye to judge absolute variations, and the ratio scale makes it easy for the eye to judge proportionate variations.[3]

GRAPHING THREE VARIABLES IN TWO DIMENSIONS

Often we want to show graphically more than two dimensions. For example, a topographic map shows latitude, longitude, and altitude on a two-dimensional page. This is done by using contour lines, as in Figure 2A-12.

FIGURE 2A-12
A Contour Map of a Small Mountain

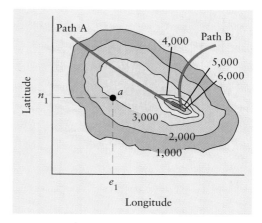

A contour map shows three variables in two-dimensional space. This familiar kind of three-variable graph shows latitude and longitude on the axes and altitude on the contour lines. The contour line labeled 1,000 connects all locations with an altitude of 1,000 metres, the contour line labeled 2,000 connects those with an altitude of 2,000 metres, and so forth. Point a, for example, has latitude n_1, longitude e_1, and an altitude of 3,000 metres. Where the lines are closely bunched, they represent a steep ascent; where they are far apart, a gradual one. Clearly, path A is a gentler climb from 3,000 to 4,000 metres on this mountain than path B.

---

[3] Graphs with a ratio scale on one axis and a natural scale on the other are frequently encountered in economics. In the case just illustrated, there is a ratio scale on the vertical axis and a natural scale on the horizontal (or time) axis. Such graphs are often called semilog graphs. In scientific work, graphs with ratio scales on both axes are frequently encountered. Such graphs are often referred to as double-log graphs.

Though topographic maps are rarely used in economics, there are many cases where economists wish to show three variables in two dimensions. The information usually takes the following general form. Consider the function $XY = a$, where X, Y, and a are variables. Figure 2A-13 plots this function for three different values of a. The variables X and Y are represented on the two axes. The variable a is represented by the labels on the curves. Several examples of this procedure occur throughout this book (for example, in the Appendix to Chapter 7 and the Appendix to Chapter 9).

FIGURE 2A-13
Three Variables Shown in Two Dimensions

This graph illustrates examples of the three-variable function $XY = a$. The function $XY = a$ is called a *rectangular hyperbola*. The figure shows three members of the family. For example, point A represents $Y = 2.0$, $X = 2.5$, and $a = 5.0$.

CHAPTER 3

AN OVERVIEW OF THE MARKET ECONOMY

All market economies have certain elements in common, although no two are exactly alike. In this chapter, we explore the main features of market economies, the details of which will occupy us for the rest of the book.

THE DEVELOPMENT OF MARKET ECONOMIES

Until about 10,000 years ago, all human beings were hunter-gatherers, providing for their wants and needs with foods that were freely provided in nature. The Neolithic agricultural revolution changed all that. People gradually abandoned their nomadic life of hunting and food gathering and settled down to tend crops and domesticated animals.

49

EXTENSION 3-1

THE GAINS FROM SPECIALIZATION

A simple case will illustrate the principles involved in the gains from specialization. A crucial point—and a major source of confusion in the popular press and elsewhere—is that the gains from specialization depend on *comparative advantage* but *not* on *absolute advantage*.

ABSOLUTE AND COMPARATIVE ADVANTAGE

Suppose that we consider two individuals, Jacob and Maria, and two products, sweaters and potatoes. Working full time on his own, Jacob can produce *either* 100 kilograms of potatoes *or* 50 sweaters per year. Maria can produce *either* 400 kilograms of potatoes *or* 100 sweaters per year. In this example, Maria is said to have an **absolute advantage** in the production of both goods because she can make more of each good than Jacob (for equal amount of work effort). It is immaterial *why* Maria has the absolute advantage; the key point is simply that she is better at producing both goods than Jacob.

Note that the pattern of absolute advantage is determined simply by how much of a certain product each individual can make with given inputs (in this case, one year's work). In contrast, the pattern of *comparative advantage* is determined by how much of one product must be given up in order to produce one unit of the other product. Thus *the pattern of comparative advantage depends crucially on opportunity costs*.

To see Jacob's opportunity costs in this example, suppose that he is initially devoting all of his time to producing potatoes with an output of 100 kg. He now considers switching to producing only sweaters. The opportunity cost of the 50 sweaters that he can produce is the 100 kg of potatoes that he no longer produces. It therefore *costs* him 2 kg of potatoes for every sweater he produces; or, expressing it the other way around, Jacob's cost of producing 1 kilogram of potatoes is one-half of a sweater. Using a similar argument for Maria, we see that Maria's opportunity cost of producing 100 sweaters is the 400 kilograms of potatoes that she must forego. Thus, Maria's cost per sweater is 4 kilograms of potatoes; her cost per kilogram of potatoes is one-quarter of a sweater.

Maria is said to have a **comparative advantage** in the production of potatoes because she produces them at a lower opportunity cost than Jacob. Similarly, Jacob has a comparative advantage in sweaters because his opportunity cost for producing sweaters is lower than Maria's.

Note that although Maria is better at producing both goods than Jacob—and thus has an absolute advantage in both goods—she is relatively better *only* in the production of potatoes—and thus Maria has a comparative advantage only in potato production. In this example and more generally, the pattern of absolute advantage tells us very little about the pattern of comparative advantage.

THE GAINS FROM SPECIALIZATION

Table 1 shows the output of each good per person, and the total output, in the situation where both Maria and Jacob divide their time equally between the production of the two goods.

To see the connection between comparative advantage and the gains from specialization, consider what happens when Jacob and Maria specialize

---

SPECIALIZATION, SURPLUS, AND TRADE

Along with permanent settlement, the agricultural revolution brought surplus production. Farmers could produce substantially more than they needed for survival. The agricultural surplus allowed the creation of new occupations. Freed from having to grow their own food, people formed new classes—artisans, soldiers, priests, government officials—as they turned their talents to performing specialized services and producing goods other than food. They also produced more than they themselves needed and traded the excess to obtain other goods.

TABLE 1
Production of Potatoes and Sweaters with Each Person's Time Divided Equally Between the Two Commodities

	Potatoes (kg)	Sweaters
Jacob	50	25
Maria	200	50
Total	250	75

along the lines suggested by the pattern of comparative advantage. Specifically, suppose that Jacob decides to specialize in the production of sweaters (he therefore produces no potatoes) and that Maria decides to spend 70 percent of her time producing potatoes (and 30 percent of her time producing sweaters). Table 2 shows the results in this case. The reason why production of both goods is higher in Table 2 than in Table 1 is that Jacob and Maria have each specialized toward the production of the good for which they have the lowest opportunity cost—that is, toward the good in which they have the comparative advantage.

Now consider what happens if Jacob and Maria specialize in the "wrong" direction. The numbers in parentheses in Table 2 show what happens if Jacob produces only potatoes and Maria spends 70 percent

TABLE 2
Production of Potatoes and Sweaters with Partial Specialization

	Potatoes (kg)		Sweaters	
Jacob	0	(100)	50	(0)
Maria	280	(120)	30	(70)
Total	280	(220)	80	(70)
Change from Table 1	+30	(−30)	+5	(−5)

of her time making sweaters and 30 percent making potatoes.

By specializing along the lines of comparative advantage, Jacob gives up only 2 kg of potatoes for each new sweater produced; Maria gives up only one-quarter of a sweater for each new kg of potatoes produced. By specializing in the opposite direction—against the pattern of comparative advantage—the cost of each new sweater is 4 kg of potatoes and the cost of each new kg of potatoes is one-half of a sweater. Comparing these opportunity costs, it is no wonder that total output is increased *only when specialization takes place along the pattern of comparative advantage!*

This example is obviously quite special, but the principles involved are very general. These principles can be generalized as follows:

- The pattern of absolute advantage is often very different from the pattern of comparative advantage.

- Total production can be increased when each person specializes in the production of the product in which he or she has a comparative advantage.

A more detailed study of the important concept of comparative advantage and its many applications to international trade and specialization must await the chapter on international trade (which is sometimes studied in courses on microeconomics and sometimes in courses on macroeconomics). In the meantime, it is worth noting that the comparative advantage of individuals and of whole nations may change. Maria may learn new skills and develop a comparative advantage in sweaters that she does not currently have. Similarly, whole nations may develop new abilities and know-how that will change their pattern of comparative advantage.

The allocation of different jobs to different people is called **specialization of labour.** Specialization has proved extraordinarily efficient compared with self-sufficiency, for two important reasons.

First, individual talents and abilities differ, and specialization allows each person to do the job he or she can do best while leaving everything else to be done by others. That production is greater with specialization than with self-sufficiency is one of the most fundamental principles in economics, known as the principle of *comparative advantage.* An example is given in Extension 3-1, and a much fuller discussion is found in Chapter 35.

Second, a person who concentrates on one activity becomes better at it than a jack-of-all-trades could. This is called "learning by doing," and was a factor much stressed by early economists. Modern research into what are called learning curves shows that learning by doing is important in many industries.

The exchange of goods and services in early societies commonly took place by simple mutual agreement among neighbours. In the course of time, however, trading became centred in particular gathering places called markets. Today we use the term *market economy* to refer to a society in which people specialize in productive activities and satisfy most of their material wants through exchanges.

Specialization must be accompanied by trade. People who produce only one thing must trade much of their production to obtain all the other things they require.

The earliest market economies depended to some considerable extent on **barter,** the trading of goods directly for other goods.[1] But barter can be a costly process in terms of the time spent searching out satisfactory exchanges. The evolution of money has made trading easier. Money eliminates the inconvenience of barter by allowing the two sides of the barter transaction to be separated. Farmers who have wheat and want hammers do not have to search for individuals who have hammers and want wheat. They take money in exchange, then find people who wish to trade hammers, and offer money for the hammers.

By eliminating the need for barter, money greatly facilitates trade and specialization.

THE DIVISION OF LABOUR

Market transactions in early economies involved mainly consumption goods. Producers specialized in making a product and then traded it for the other products they needed. Over the past several hundred years, many technical advances in methods of production have made it efficient to organize agriculture and industry on a large scale. These technical developments have made use of what is called the **division**

---

[1]Barter was common in the earliest societies that flourished before the invention of money and in medieval villages and it survived in isolated cases into more recent times. For example, much of the early North American fur trade was barter, with trinkets, gems, cloths, and firearms being traded directly for furs.

of labour, a further step in the specialization of labour involving specialization within the production process of a particular good or service. The labour involved is divided into a series of repetitive tasks, and each individual performs a single task that may be just one of hundreds of tasks necessary to produce the product.

To gain the advantages of the division of labour, it became necessary to organize production in large factories. Typical workers no longer earned their incomes by selling goods and services they had personally produced; rather, they sold their labour services to firms and received money wages in return. With this development, most urban workers lost their status as artisans and became dependent on their ability to sell their labour. Adam Smith (1723–1790), the great eighteenth-century Scottish political economist, was the first to study the division of labour in detail, as discussed in Extension 3-2.

Interestingly, recent changes have led to an increasing number of self-employed workers who are more like the artisans of old than like factory workers. Even within the factory, a new organizational principle called *lean production* or *flexible manufacturing*, pioneered by Japanese automobile manufacturers, has led to a more craft-based form of organization within the factory. In this technique, employees work as a team; each employee is able to do every team member's job rather than one very specialized task at one point on the assembly line. These important developments are discussed further in Chapter 9.

MARKETS AND RESOURCE ALLOCATION

As explained in Chapter 1, *resource allocation* refers to the distribution of the available factors of production among their various uses. There are not enough resources to produce all the goods and services that could be consumed. It is therefore necessary to allocate the available resources among their various possible uses and in so doing to choose what to produce and what not to produce. In a market economy, millions of consumers decide what goods and services to buy and in what quantities; a vast number of firms produce these goods and services and buy the factor services (labour and capital) that are needed to produce them; and millions of factor owners decide to whom they will

EXTENSION 3-2

THE DIVISION OF LABOUR

Adam Smith begins his classic *The Wealth of Nations* (1776) with a long study on the division of labour.

> The greatest improvements in the productive powers of labour . . . have been the effects of the division of labour.
>
> To take an example . . . the trade of the pin-maker, a workman not educated to this business (which the division of labour has rendered a distinct trade), nor acquainted with the use of the machinery employed in it could scarce, perhaps, with his utmost industry, make one pin in a day, and certainly could not make twenty. But in the way in which this business is now carried on . . . it is divided into a number of branches . . . One man draws out the wire, another straightens it, a third cuts it, a fourth points it, a fifth grinds it at the top for receiving the head; to make the head requires two or three distinct operations; to put it on is a peculiar business, to whiten the pins is another; it is even a trade by itself to put them into the paper; and the important business of making a pin is, in this manner, divided into about eighteen distinct operations, which, in some manufactories, are all performed by distinct hands, though in others the same man will sometimes perform two or three of them.

Smith observes that even in smallish factories, where the division of labour is exploited only in part, output is as high as 4,800 pins per person per day!

Later, Smith discusses the general importance of the division of labour and the forces that limit its application:

> Each animal is still obliged to support and defend itself, separately and independently, and derives no sort of advantage from that variety of talents with which nature has distinguished its fellows. Among men, on the contrary, the most dissimilar geniuses are of use to one another; the different produces of their respective talents, by the general disposition of truck, barter, and exchange, being brought, as it were, into a common stock, where every man may purchase whatever part of the produce of other men's talents he has occasion for.
>
> As it is the power of exchanging that gives occasion to the division of labour, so the extent of this division must always be limited by the extent of that power, or, in other words, by the extent of the market. When the market is very small, no person can have any encouragement to dedicate himself entirely to one employment for want [i.e., lack] of the power to exchange all that surplus part of the produce of his own labour, which is over and above his own consumption, for such parts of the produce of other men's labour as he has occasion for.

Smith notes that there is no point in specializing to produce a large quantity of pins, or anything else, unless there are enough persons making other goods and services to provide a market for all the pins that are produced. Thus the larger the market, the greater is the scope for the division of labour and the higher are the resulting opportunities for efficient production.

sell these services. These individual decisions collectively determine the economy's allocation of resources.

In a market economy, the allocation of resources is the outcome of countless independent decisions made by consumers and producers, all acting through the medium of markets.

This chapter provides an overview of the market mechanism.

THE DECISION MAKERS

Economics is about the behaviour of people. Much that we observe in the world and that economists assume in their theories can be traced back to decisions made by individuals. There are millions of individuals in most economies. To make a systematic study of their behaviour more manageable, economists categorize them into three important groups: households, firms, and government, collectively known as **agents.**[2] Members of these groups are economic theory's cast of characters.

HOUSEHOLDS

A **household** is defined as all the people who live under one roof and who make joint financial decisions or are subject to others who make such decisions for them. The members of households are often referred to as *consumers* because they buy and consume most of the consumption goods and services. Economic theory gives households a number of attributes.

First, economists assume that each household makes consistent decisions, as though it were composed of a single individual. Thus economists typically ignore many interesting problems of how each household reaches its decisions, including family conflicts and the moral and legal problems concerning parental control over minors.[3]

Second, economists assume that when buying goods and services and selling factor services, households are the principal owners of factors of production. They sell the services of these factors to firms and receive their incomes in return.

Finally, economists assume that each household seeks maximum *satisfaction* or what economists call *utility*. The household tries to do this within the limits set by its available resources.

FIRMS

A **firm** is defined as the unit that employs factors of production to produce goods and services that it sells to other firms, to households, or to government. For obvious reasons, a firm is often called a *producer*. Economic theory gives firms several attributes.

First, each firm is assumed to make consistent decisions, as though it were composed of a single individual. This strand of theory ignores the internal problems of how particular decisions are reached by assuming that the firm's internal organization is irrelevant to its decisions. This allows the firm to be treated, at least in elementary theory, as the unit of behaviour on the production or supply side of product markets, just as the household is treated as the unit of behaviour on the consumption or demand side.[4]

Second, economists assume that in their role as producers, firms are the principal users of the services of factors of production. In *factor markets*, where factor services are bought and sold, the roles of firms and households are thus reversed from what they are in product markets: In factor markets, firms do the buying and households do the selling.

Finally, economists assume that most firms make their decisions with a single goal in mind: to make as much profit as possible. This goal of *profit maximization* is analogous to the household's goal of utility maximization.

GOVERNMENT

The term **government** is used in economics in a broad sense to include all public officials, agencies, government bodies, and other organizations belonging to or under the direct control of federal, provincial, and local governments. For example, in Canada, the term government includes, among others, the prime minister, the Bank of Canada, city councils, commissions and regulatory bodies, legislative bodies, and police forces. It is not important to draw up a comprehensive list, but one should have in mind a general idea of the organizations that have legal and political power to exert control over individual decision makers and over markets.

It is *not* a basic assumption of economics that government always acts in a consistent fashion. Two important reasons for this may be mentioned here.

First, what we call "government" has many levels and many branches. For example, the mayor of Toronto, an MLA from Alberta, and a senator from Nova Scotia represent different constituencies.

---

[2]Although we can get away with just three sets of decision makers, it is worth noting that there are others. Probably the most important of those omitted are nonprofit organizations such as private universities and hospitals, charities, and research organizations such as the C. D. Howe Institute and the Institute for Research on Public Policy. These bodies have a significant influence on the allocation of the economy's resources.

[3]Some economists have studied resource allocation within households. This field of study, pioneered by University of Chicago economist and Nobel laureate Gary Becker, is often treated in advanced courses in labour economics.

---

[4]At the more advanced level, many studies look within the firm to ask questions such as "Does the firm's internal organization affect its behaviour?" We briefly consider such questions in Chapter 14.

Similarly, the federal departments of Finance, Human Resources, and International Trade represent different interests, each with its own goals. Therefore, different and conflicting views and objectives are typically found within "government."

Second, decisions on interrelated issues of policy are made by many different bodies. Federal and provincial legislatures pass laws, the courts interpret laws, governments decide which laws to enforce with vigour and which not to enforce, the Department of Finance and the Bank of Canada influence monetary conditions, and a host of other agencies and semiautonomous bodies determine actions in respect to different aspects of policy goals. Because of the multiplicity of decision makers, it would be amazing if fully consistent behaviour resulted.

Individual public servants, whether elected or appointed, have personal objectives (such as staying in office, promotion, power, and prestige) as well as public service objectives. Although the balance of importance given to the two kinds of objectives will vary among persons and among types of office, both will almost always have some influence. For example, in a free vote in Parliament, most MPs would vote in favour of a popular measure—even if they believed it was detrimental to the public good—if voting against it meant likely defeat in the next election.

As this discussion reveals, an important goal of legislators and political officials is electoral success—their own and that of their political party. As a result, governments often fail to adopt measures that impose large costs and yield few obvious benefits over the short run, even if the long-term benefits may be large. In other words, there tends to be a bias toward shortsightedness in an elective system. At the same time, in a democratic system, government actions cannot get too far away from what a majority of the electorate will approve. These and other issues of government motivation are discussed further in Chapter 18.

Markets and economies

If households, firms, and government are the main actors in the economy, markets are the stage on which their drama takes place.

MARKETS

Originally, *markets* were places where goods were bought and sold. The Granville Island Market in Vancouver is a modern example of a market in the everyday sense, and many cities and towns have their own "farmers' markets." Much early economic theory explained price behaviour in just such markets. Why, for example, can you get great bargains at the end of some days, but at the end of other days you buy at prices that appear exorbitant compared to the prices quoted only a few hours earlier?

As theories of market behaviour were developed, they were extended to cover commodities such as wheat. Wheat produced anywhere in the world can be purchased almost anywhere else in the world, and the price of a given grade of wheat tends to be nearly uniform. When we talk about the wheat market, the concept of a market has been extended well beyond the idea of a single place where the producer and consumer meet to sell and buy.

Similarly, the foreign exchange market has no specific location. Instead, it operates through international telephone and computer networks whereby dealers buy and sell dollars, sterling, francs, yen, and other national currencies. Markets may indeed use all conceivable means of communication, including the press, as in the case of the markets for many second-hand goods such as automobiles. If you have a car to sell or want to buy one, you will discover that "the market" comprises the local newspapers and bulletin boards, specialized magazines, and used-car dealers.

In the modern sense, a **market** refers to any situation in which buyers and sellers can negotiate the exchange of some product. In the past, high transportation costs and perishability made many markets quite local. Fresh fruits and vegetables, for example, would only be sold close to their points of production. Today, advances in preservation, the falling cost of transportation, and the development of worldwide communications networks have led to the globalization of many markets. A visit to the supermarket will confirm that food products such as Bulgarian jam, Chilean apples, and Indian rice are no longer confined to markets within their country of origin.

ECONOMIES

An **economy** is rather loosely defined as a set of interrelated production and consumption activities. It may refer to this activity in a region of one country (e.g., the economy of the Maritimes), in a country (the Canadian economy), or in a group of countries (the North American economy). In any economy, the allocation of resources is determined by the production, sales, and purchase decisions made by firms, households, and governments.

In Chapter 1, we learned three important things about economies. First, a *free-market economy* is one in which the decisions of individual households and firms (as distinct from the government) exert the major influence over the allocation of resources. Second, the opposite of a free-market economy is a *command economy,* in which the major decisions about the allocation of resources are made by the government and in which firms produce and households consume only as directed. Third, in practice, all economies are *mixed economies* in that some decisions are made by firms, households, and the government acting through markets while other decisions are made by the government using the command principle.

The past decade has brought a fourth type of economy into prominence—the *transition economy.* The countries of Eastern and Central Europe, along with the countries of the former Soviet Union, began the difficult transition from centrally planned economies toward free-market economies in the early 1990s. These economies displayed many unique characteristics, many of which related to the absence of certain *institutions.* This is discussed in Application 3-1.

THE SECTORS OF AN ECONOMY

Parts of an economy are usually referred to as **sectors** of that economy. For example, the agricultural sector is the part of the economy that produces agricultural commodities, and the manufacturing sector produces finished goods, such as automobiles and electric shavers.

The Market and Nonmarket Sectors

Producers make goods and provide services. Consumers use them. Goods and services may pass from one group to the other in two ways. They may be sold by producers and bought by consumers through markets, or they may be given away.

When goods and services are bought and sold, producers expect to cover their costs with the revenue they obtain from selling the product. We call

this *marketed production,* and we refer to this part of the economy's activity as belonging to the **market sector.** When the product is given away, the costs of production must be covered from some source other than sales revenue. We call this *nonmarketed production,* and we refer to this part of the economy's activity as belonging to the **nonmarket sector.**

In the case of private charities, the money required to pay for factor services may be raised from the public by voluntary contributions. In the case of production by government—which accounts for the bulk of nonmarketed production—the money is provided from government revenue, which in turn comes mainly from taxes.

Whenever a government enterprise *sells* its output, its production is in the market sector. Most of government's output, however, is in the nonmarket sector, often by the very nature of the product provided. For example, one could hardly expect the criminal to pay the judge for providing the service of criminal justice. Other products are in the nonmarket sector because governments have decided that there are advantages to removing them from the market sector. This is the case, for example, with public school education and medical and hospital services in Canada. Public policy places it in the nonmarket sector even though much of it could be provided by the market sector.

The economic significance of this distinction lies in the "bottom line." (In accounting, the bottom line refers to profits.) In the market sector, firms face the bottom-line test of profitability. If a product cannot be sold for a price that will cover its costs and provide sufficient profit for its makers, the product will not be made. Production in the nonmarket sector faces no such profitability test. Because the product is provided free and its costs are met by contributions, the decision to produce it depends on the willingness of government and private bodies to pay its costs and not on its ability to be sold at a cost-covering price.

The Private and Public Sectors

An alternative division of an economy's productive activity is between the private and public sectors. The private sector refers to all production that is in private hands, and the public sector refers to all production that is in public hands—that is, owned by government. The distinction between the two sectors depends on the legal distinction of ownership. In the **private sector,** the organization that does the producing is owned by households or other firms; in the **public sector,** it is owned and controlled by government. The public sector includes all production of goods and services by government plus all production of all publicly owned companies and other government-operated industries that is sold to consumers through markets.

The distinction between the market and nonmarket sectors is economic; it depends on whether or not producers cover their costs from revenue earned by selling output to users. The distinction between the private and public sectors is legal; it depends on whether the producing organizations are privately or publicly owned.

Some examples will illustrate these important distinctions. The Aluminum Company of Canada (ALCAN) is in the private and market sectors; a Salvation Army soup kitchen is in the private and nonmarket sectors. The provincial hydro authorities are in the public and market sectors. The Canadian Coast Guard is in the public and nonmarket sectors.

INSTITUTIONS

In discussions about markets, economies, and sectors, it is easy to forget about the importance of *institutions* in the operation of a market economy. In developed countries like Canada, these institutions have been operating for so many years that they are now taken for granted.

The most important example is the legal system. The existence of laws to facilitate the writing and enforcement of contracts between buyers and sellers clearly aids in the operation of a market economy. Imagine your reluctance to purchase a new car if there did not exist a civil court system which would enforce your claim to ownership, or the difficulty of operating a restaurant if your food suppliers did not honour their contractual obligations to supply your meat or fresh produce.

Laws which define and protect *property rights* and the *enforcement of contracts* are crucial to the smooth operation of market economies. In the absence of private property rights, there would be little incentive to improve land or to build plant and equipment (which could be arbitrarily confiscated at some later date). Without enforceable contracts, there would be no incentive to train workers who could not be tied by a contractual agreement to a specific period of work. Nor would there be anything like insurance or *forward markets*—there would be no

payment in advance for goods and services to be delivered at some point in the future.

The experiences of Eastern and Central Europe in recent years have brought to our attention the fact that for mixed economies to function effectively, their markets must be supported by a complicated set of governmental and private institutions. The special problems and lessons of these transition economies are discussed in Application 3-1.

MICROECONOMICS AND MACROECONOMICS

As we saw in Chapter 1, there are two different but complementary ways of viewing the economy. The first, **microeconomics,** studies the detailed workings of individual markets and interrelationships among markets. The second, **macroeconomics,** suppresses much of the detail and concentrates on the behaviour of broad aggregates.[5]

Microeconomics and macroeconomics differ in the questions each asks and in the level of aggregation each uses. Microeconomics deals with the determination of prices and quantities in individual markets and with the relationships among these markets. Thus it looks at the details of the market economy. It asks, for example, how much labour is employed in the fast-food industry and why the amount is increasing. It asks about the determinants of the output of broccoli, pocket calculators, automobiles, and hamburgers. It asks, too, about the prices of these goods—why some prices go up and others down. For example, economists interested in microeconomics analyze how a new invention, a government subsidy, or a drought will affect the price and output of wheat and the employment of farmworkers.

In contrast, macroeconomics focuses on much broader aggregates. It looks at such things as the total number of people employed and unemployed, the average level of all prices, national output, and aggregate consumption. Macroeconomics asks what determines these aggregates and how they respond to changing conditions. Whereas microeconomics looks at demand and supply with regard to particular goods and services, macroeconomics looks at aggregate demand and aggregate supply.

---

[5]The prefixes "micro" and "macro" derive from the Greek words *mikros,* for small and *makros,* for large.

| APPLICATION 3-1 |

THE TRANSITION ECONOMIES OF CENTRAL AND EASTERN EUROPE AND THE FORMER SOVIET UNION*

The countries of the former Soviet Union became a command economy after the Russian Revolution of 1917. The other countries of Eastern Europe became command economies when they fell under Soviet domination after the end of the Second World War in 1945. After the fall of the Berlin Wall in 1989, the Central and Eastern European countries then began the long process of transition from command economy to market economy. The republics of the former Soviet Union began this process in earnest in 1991. Because command economies and market economies are fundamentally different in both their essentials and their details, the transition process is proving to be lengthy and difficult. As of 1996, none of the affected economies can be considered fully command economies, but many are still far from functioning well as market economies.

The period of transition between command and market economy is generally characterized by the enactment of various economic reforms. As the transition began, most of the transition economies saw sharp drops in output followed by large decreases in employment. Many citizens experienced a fall in their living standards, and inflation greatly eroded the incomes of pensioners and others with fixed incomes. Although the difficulties of transition have been taken by some observers to signal the failure of the market system, economists generally see these hardships as a reflection of the extreme difficulty of transition from one system to the other.

Transition requires changes in institutions, custom, and the relationships between economy and government. These changes simply cannot be accomplished overnight. Several issues highlight the complexity of reform and help explain why transition takes a long time and is so painful.

THE CREDIBILITY OF REFORMS

The motivations of agents in a command economy are very different from those that operate in a market economy. To transform an economic system, agents in the economy must change their economic behaviour and learn to respond to prices, taking seriously the relationship between profit-seeking behaviour and their own economic well-being. Many people are reluctant to change their behaviour until they are certain that the reforms will indeed carry through. That is why, for transition to proceed, it is crucial that the reforms be credible—that the agents believe that the government will not reverse them.

The most obvious credibility problem in the formerly communist countries of Central and Eastern Europe and the former Soviet Union is the general disbelief that the government will allow bankrupt firms to shut down. In the days of central planning and command, the government bailed out firms that experienced financial losses. Now governments have announced that bankruptcy is possible and therefore firms need to earn profits if they want to remain in business. However, during the transition, especially in the early period of high inflation and unemployment, many firms were losing money. Governments were unwilling to allow a large proportion of productive capacity to shut down but could not easily determine which firms had the potential to become profitable in the long run. Where governments refrained from closing down firms, they made the bankruptcy reforms incredible. Firms came to believe that they would be bailed out in spite of the announced reforms, and therefore the incentive to minimize costs and maximize profits was weakened.

---

*For a very interesting discussion of the early progress made in the Eastern European transition economies, see O. J. Blanchard et al., *Reform in Eastern Europe* (MIT Press 1991); see also the subsequent progress report, O. J. Blanchard et al., *Post-Communist Reform* (MIT Press 1993).

THE RULE OF LAW

Although we often think of market economies as being governed only by the forces of demand and supply, they have a myriad of laws that help to govern economic behaviour and allow markets to run smoothly. For example, there are laws that facilitate the writing and enforcement of contracts between buyers and suppliers and between firms and workers, laws that dictate bankruptcy conditions and procedures, and laws that control the operation of stock markets and guarantee stockholders' rights as owners. Generally, these laws define and protect *property rights* in economic enterprises.

The command economies did not have such laws or the legal apparatus to support them, such as an extensive civil court system. To function effectively as market economies, each of these countries must enact laws that fit its desired political and economic structure and that establish property rights in economic activities. Often the procedure of passing the new legislation is even more time-consuming than the initial process of devising the policies and writing the legislation. Establishing institutions for enforcement takes longer still. Until the laws and institutions are in place, legal uncertainty hinders exchanges between economic agents.

One example of a crucial commercial law that is missing or nascent in transition economies is company law. Company law regulates the governance of firms; it stipulates what rights certain agents, such as stockholders and investors, have in firms' decision making. Without company law to protect these rights, agents are reluctant to invest in firms. Consequently, many firms in transition economies have been unable to attract desperately needed investment from either foreign or domestic investors.

SECTORAL ADJUSTMENT

Transition in the formerly communist countries entails two major sectoral adjustments. The first is the transfer of production from the public sector to the private sector. Such *privatization* of the economy involves both the transfer of existing physical assets from state ownership to private ownership and the entry of new private firms into the economy. Whereas facilitating new entry is relatively easy, the privatization of existing assets is very complicated, and there are many political and economic debates about how it should be done. The success of privatization to date has varied widely from one country to another.

The second necessary sectoral adjustment is a change in the proportions of economic activity accounted for by the military sector and the consumer goods sector. Central planning allowed the countries of the Soviet bloc to invest heavily in the production of military and industrial goods like weapons and machinery while skimping on the production of consumer goods like televisions and clothing. Under the market system, although the government will still be one of the economy's consumers, households will account for the majority of the demand for goods. Households want firms to produce far more consumer goods and fewer military goods. Unfortunately, it is not easy for a firm to change its production. The machines used to make missiles cannot be used to sew clothing. Thus the sectoral shift requires large-scale retooling and in many cases the rebuilding of factories. It also requires the retraining of many employees.

THE GOOD NEWS

Most of the economies in transition are making good progress. Different countries have succeeded in different areas so far, but most have passed the point of no return. In many Central and Eastern European countries, output has begun to increase and inflation has stabilized.

AN OVERVIEW OF MICROECONOMICS

Early economists observed the market economy with wonder. They saw that even though goods and services were made by many independent producers, the amounts of goods and services produced approximately equaled the amounts that people wanted to purchase. Natural disasters aside, there were neither vast surpluses nor severe shortages of products. They also saw that in spite of the ever-changing geographical, industrial, and occupational patterns of demand for labour services, most workers were able to sell their services to employers most of the time. Visitors from highly regulated economies often have a similar reaction. How, they ask, can there be such an abundance of the right things, produced at the right time, and delivered to the right place—something that planned economies have conspicuously failed to do?

The Price System as a Coordination Mechanism

How does the market produce this order in the absence of conscious coordination? It is one thing to have the same good produced year in and year out when people's wants and incomes do not change; it is quite another thing to have production adjusting continually to changing wants, incomes, and techniques of production. Yet this adjustment is accomplished relatively smoothly by markets—albeit with occasional, and sometimes serious, interruptions.

Markets work without conscious central control because individual agents make their private decisions in response to publicly known signals such as prices, wages, and profits, and these signals, in turn, respond to the collective actions entailed by the sum of all individual decisions. In short:

The great discovery of eighteenth-century economists was that the price system is a mechanism that coordinates decentralized decision making.

In *The Wealth of Nations,* Adam Smith (1723–1790) spoke of the price system as "the invisible hand." The system allows decision making to be decentralized to millions of individual producers and consumers but nonetheless to be coordinated. A simple example may help to illustrate how this coordination occurs; Part 2 of this book develops these ideas more formally.

An Example

Suppose that under prevailing conditions, farmers find it equally profitable to produce either of two crops, carrots or broccoli. As a result, they are willing to produce some of both commodities, thereby satisfying the demands of households to consume both. Now suppose that consumers develop a greatly increased desire for broccoli and a diminished desire for carrots. This change might have occurred because of the discovery of hitherto unsuspected nutritive or curative powers of broccoli.

When consumers buy more broccoli and fewer carrots, a shortage of broccoli and a surplus of carrots develop. To unload their surplus stocks of carrots, merchants reduce the price of carrots because it is better to sell them at a reduced price than not to sell them at all. Merchants find, however, that they are unable to satisfy all their customers' demands for broccoli. Broccoli has become more scarce, so merchants charge more for it. As the price rises, fewer people are willing and able to purchase broccoli. Thus the rise in its price limits the quantity demanded to the available supply.

Farmers see that broccoli production has become more profitable than in the past because the costs of producing broccoli remain unchanged while its market price has risen. Similarly, they see that carrot production has become less profitable than in the past because costs are unchanged while the price has fallen. Attracted by high profits in broccoli and deterred by low profits or potential losses in carrots, farmers expand the production of broccoli and reduce the production of carrots. Thus the change in consumers' tastes, working through the price system, causes a reallocation of resources—land and labour—out of carrot production and into broccoli production.

The reaction of the market to a change in demand leads to a reallocation of resources. Carrot producers reduce their production; they will therefore be laying off workers and generally demanding fewer factors of production. Broccoli producers expand production; they will therefore be hiring workers and generally increasing their demand for factors of production.

Labour can probably switch from carrot to broccoli production without much difficulty. Certain types of land, however, may be better suited for growing one crop than the other. When farmers increase their broccoli production, their demands for the factors especially suited to growing broccoli also increase—and this creates a shortage of these resources and a consequent rise in their prices. Meanwhile, with carrot production falling, the demand for land and other factors of production especially suited to growing carrots is reduced. A surplus results, and the prices of these factors decline.

Thus factors particularly suited to broccoli production will earn more and will obtain a higher share of total national income than before. Factors particularly suited to carrot production, however, will earn less and will obtain a smaller share of total national income than before.

All of the changes illustrated in this example will be studied more fully in subsequent parts of this book; the important thing to notice now is how changes in demand cause reallocations of resources in the directions required to cater to the new pattern of demand.

This example illustrates the point made earlier: *The price system is a mechanism that coordinates individual, decentralized decisions.*

AN OVERVIEW OF MACROECONOMICS

We can group together all the buyers of the nation's output and call their total desired purchases *aggregate demand.* We can also group together all the producers of the nation's output and call their total desired sales *aggregate supply.*

Sudden changes in aggregate demand are called *demand shocks,* and sudden changes in aggregate supply are called *supply shocks.* Shocks cause important changes in the broad averages and aggregates that are the concern of macroeconomics, including total output, total employment, and average levels of prices and wages. Government actions sometimes cause demand or supply shocks; at other times, governments are reacting to the shocks. In the latter case, the government may attempt to cushion or change the effects of a particular shock.

The Circular Flow of Income

One way to gain insight into aggregate demand and aggregate supply is to view the economy as a giant set of flows. We build up a picture of such flows in stages.

In Figure 3-1, all producers of goods and services are grouped together in the lower coloured

area. All consumers of goods and services are grouped together in the upper coloured area.[6]

The interactions between producers and consumers take place through two kinds of markets. Goods and services that are produced by firms are sold in markets that are usually referred to as *goods markets.* The services of factors of production (land, labour, and capital) are sold in markets called *factor markets.* The interactions involve flows going in two directions. Flows of goods and services, called *real flows,* are shown flowing counterclockwise in part (i) of the figure. Flows of payments for these goods and services, called *money flows,* are shown flowing clockwise in part (ii) of the figure.

We may now look in a little more detail at the relations just outlined.

Goods Markets.   The outputs of goods and services flow from producers to consumers through what are usually known as **goods markets** (or product markets), which includes both goods and services. Note the use of the plural *markets:* Just as firms produce many products, so there are many markets in which products are sold. Households constitute one major group of consumers—indeed, the largest, by amount consumed. They buy, for their own use, goods and services such as food, clothing, train journeys, legal services, and cars. Other consumers include firms that purchase capital goods produced by yet other firms, and foreigners who purchase exports.

Factor Markets.   Most people earn their incomes by selling factor services to producers. (Exceptions are people receiving payments from such schemes as pension plans and unemployment insurance; they receive an income, but not in return for providing their factor services to help in current production.) Most of those who do sell factor services are employees. They sell their labour services to firms in return for wages. Some others own capital and receive interest or profits for providing it. Others own land and derive rents from it. The buying and selling of these factor services takes place in **factor**

---

[6]Most individuals and firms have a double role. As buyers of goods and services, they play a part in consuming that output; as sellers of factor services and other inputs, they play a part in producing that output.

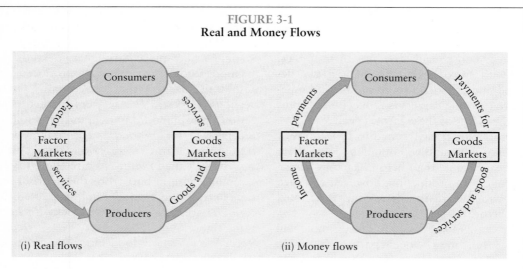

FIGURE 3-1
Real and Money Flows

Real flows of goods and services go in one direction between producers and consumers, whereas money flows of payments go in the opposite direction. The blue arrows in part (i) show real flows. Goods and services made by producers are sold to the people who consume them, and factor services owned by consumers are sold to producers. The red arrows in part (ii) show money flows. Income payments go to consumers in return for the factor services they sell. Expenditures flow from consumers to producers in return for the goods and services they buy.

markets. The buyers are producers. They use the services that they purchase as inputs for the production of goods and services that are sold to consumers.

The Circular Flow of Income.   What we have just described involves two circular *flows*. This concept of circularity in economic relations is a crucial one. It helps us to understand how the separate parts of the economy are related in a system of mutual interaction. For example, the activities of producers directly affect household incomes because the wages that producers pay make up the largest part of people's incomes. The activities of households directly affect firms because the goods and services that households buy account for the largest part of the sales revenues of firms.

The two parts of Figure 3-1 provide alternative ways of looking at the same transactions. Every market transaction is a two-sided exchange in the sense that for every sale there is a purchase and for every seller there is a buyer. The buyer receives goods or services and parts with money; the seller receives money and parts with goods or services.

The blue arrows in part (i) of the figure show the flows of goods and services through markets. They are shown flowing counterclockwise, from consumers to producers and from producers to consumers. The red

arrows in part (ii) of the figure show the corresponding flows of money payments. Flows of payments are going in the opposite direction—clockwise. Payments flow from producers to consumers to pay for factor services, and they flow from consumers to producers to pay for goods and services.[7]

To distinguish these two sets of flows, each of which is the counterpart of the other, the blue flows in part (i) are called real flows, and the red flows in part (ii) are called money flows.

Both of these ways of looking at the flows of economic transactions carry an important message. When firms produce goods and services, they create through factor payments the incomes needed to purchase their outputs; when users buy the outputs of firms, their payments create the revenues that firms need to pay for the factors of production that they employ. The main circular flow is shown passing from domestic producers to domestic households

---

[7]The direction (clockwise or counterclockwise) is of no significance. What is significant is that the real and the money flows are in opposite directions. Any real flow is matched by a corresponding money flow going in the other direction.

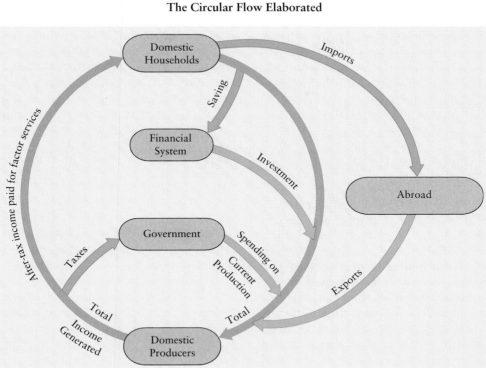

FIGURE 3-2
The Circular Flow Elaborated

Taxes, savings, and imports withdraw expenditures from the circular flow; government purchases, investment, and exports inject expenditures into the circular flow. Some of the total income created by domestic producers leaks out of the circular flow because of government taxes on incomes. Some household income leaks out of the circular flow because of saving and imports; the rest is spent on purchasing the output of domestic firms. The injections of investment, government expenditure, and exports plus household expenditure on domestic output account for the total purchases of domestic output.

and back again. On the way, however, there are several leakages from and injections into this flow around the main circuit.

Other Flows

Figure 3-2 elaborates on the money flows shown in part (ii) of Figure 3-1. It does so by allowing for private-sector saving and investment, government taxing and spending, and foreign trade. Because we are going to allow for foreign trade, the bottom box is labeled "Domestic Producers" to distinguish them from foreign producers. In addition, because we are going to allow for several classes of consumers of output, the top box is now labeled "Domestic Households" to distinguish that group from the

other purchasers of domestic output: foreigners, government, and firms that purchase capital goods.

Leakages.   As shown in Figure 3-2, payments flow from domestic producers to domestic households by way of payments for factor services. On the way, however, there is a **leakage** of some payments out of the circular flow because of government taxes, which reduce the flow of income payments that would otherwise go to households.[8]

---

[8]Government transfers to households, such as unemployment insurance and Social Security pensions, act as injections into the flow. The taxes shown in Figure 3-2 are the net leakage—total taxes minus total government transfers to households.

Payments pass from domestic households to domestic producers when households spend their incomes to buy goods and services made by producers. Some household income leaks out of the circular flow when households save part of their incomes. The part that is saved is not spent on goods and services. Instead it is shown flowing into the financial system, which happens, for example, when households deposit their savings in banks, credit unions, or with investment trust companies. Money payments also leak out of the flow because of imports, which are purchases by domestic consumers that create incomes for *foreign* producers.

Injections. The spending of domestic households on domestically produced output creates income for domestic producers. Income is also created by three additional expenditures, often called **injections,** that cause additions to the circular flow. The first is investment expenditure, which goes to purchase the output of other firms. It is expenditure that firms make on capital goods such as machinery or factories that are produced by other firms. This expenditure is shown as a flow coming from the financial system. Such investment expenditures include a firm financing its own investment with funds raised by selling stocks or bonds to households, which is done through intermediary agents, or directly borrowing money from a bank or other financial institu-

tion. The second injection is the funds that the government spends on a whole range of goods and services, from national defense through the provision of justice to the building of schools and roads. The third injection comes from the selling of exports in response to the demand from foreign consumers for the output of domestic producers.

Together, the expenditure of domestic households, the investment expenditure of domestic firms, government purchases of goods and services, and exports constitute the aggregate demand for domestic output. When any one of these elements of aggregate demand changes, aggregate output and total income earned by households are likely to change as a result. Hence studying the determinants of total consumption, investment, government spending, and imports and exports is crucial to understanding the causes of changes in the nation's total output.

The Next Step

Soon you will be going on to study microeconomics or macroeconomics. Whichever branch of the subject you study next, it is important to remember that microeconomics and macroeconomics are complementary, not competing, views of the economy. Both are needed for a full understanding of the functioning of a modern economy.

SUMMARY

A. THE DEVELOPMENT OF MARKET ECONOMIES

- Modern market economies are based on the specialization and division of labour, which necessitate the exchange of goods and services. Exchange takes place in markets and is facilitated by the use of money. Much of economics is devoted to the study of how markets work to coordinate millions of individual, decentralized decisions.

B. THE DECISION MAKERS

- Three groups of agents make the relevant decisions. Households, firms, and government all interact in markets. Households are assumed to maximize their satis-

faction and firms to maximize their profits. Government may have multiple objectives.

C. MARKETS AND ECONOMIES

- A free-market economy is one in which the allocation of resources is determined by production, sales, and purchase decisions made by firms and households acting in response to such market signals as prices and profits.
- Economies are commonly divided into the market and nonmarket sectors and into the public and private sectors. These divisions cut across each other; the former is based on the economic distinction of how costs are covered, and the latter is based on a legal distinction of ownership.

- Many institutions are crucial for the operation of a market economy. Most important among these is probably the legal system which is necessary for the enforcement of private contracts and for the establishment of private property rights.

D. MICROECONOMICS AND MACROECONOMICS

- The key difference between microeconomics and macroeconomics is in the level of aggregation. Microeconomics looks at prices and quantities in individual markets and how they respond to various shocks that impinge on those markets. Macroeconomics looks at broader aggregates such as aggregate production, employment, and the price level.

- The questions asked in microeconomics and macroeconomics differ, but they are complementary parts of economic analysis. They study different aspects of a single economic system, and both are needed for a complete understanding of the whole.

- Microeconomics deals with the determination of prices and quantities in individual markets and the relationships among those markets. It shows how the price system provides signals that reflect changes in demand and supply and to which producers and consumers react in a decentralized but nonetheless coordinated manner.

- The macroeconomic interactions between households and firms through markets may be illustrated in a circular flow diagram that traces real and money flows between producers and consumers. These flows are the starting point for studying the circular flow of aggregate income that is the key element of macroeconomics.

KEY CONCEPTS

Specialization and division of labour
Economic decision makers
Markets and market economies
Transition economies

Market and nonmarket sectors
Private and public sectors
The importance of institutions

Microeconomics and macroeconomics
The price system as a coordination mechanism
Circular flow of income

DISCUSSION QUESTIONS

1. In recent years, many productive activities in Canada have been moved out of the public and nonmarket sector. Can you give examples of some that have gone to the public and market sector and others that have gone to the private and market sector? What activities currently in the public and nonmarket sector could be moved into the private and market sector? Do you think such a move would be desirable?

2. Describe the tasks you performed in a job you held over the summer and discuss your duties, and those of your co-workers, in relation to the principle of the division of labour. If you were in charge, would you have divided up tasks and responsibilities differently? Why?

3. Consider the market for physicians' services. In what way has this market taken advantage of the specialization of labour?

4. Define the household of which you are a member. Consider your household's income last year. What proportion of it came from the sale of factor services? Identify other sources of income. Approximately what proportion of the expenditures by your household became income for firms?

5. "It is not from the benevolence of the butcher, the brewer, or the baker that we expect our dinner, but from their regard to their self-interest. We address ourselves, not to their humanity, but to their self-love, and never talk to them of our necessities, but of their advantages." Do you agree with this quotation from *The Wealth of Nations?* How are "our dinner" and "their self-interest" related to the price system? What are assumed to be the motives of firms and of households?

6. Discuss the effect of a sharp change in consumer demand away from fatty red meat and toward skinless

poultry as a result of continuing reports that too much fat in the diet is unhealthy.

7. Discuss some significant microeconomic and macroeconomic effects of an aging population, such as is predicted for many industrialized countries in the twenty-first century.

8. Which, if any, of the arrows in Figure 3-2 does each of the following affect initially?

a. Households increase their consumption expenditures by reducing saving.
b. The government lowers income tax rates.
c. Because of a recession, firms decide to postpone production of some new products.
d. Consumers like the new-model cars and borrow money from the banking system to buy them in record numbers. (Hint: Borrowing may be thought of as negative saving.)

PART TWO

AN INTRODUCTION TO DEMAND AND SUPPLY

In August of 1992, Hurricane Andrew struck the Florida coast, causing considerable damage to businesses and homes. Did this event cause the dramatic increase in the price of plywood that occurred in subsequent weeks, or was this just a coincidence? In the summer of 1994, Brazil experienced two frosts which severely damaged that country's coffee crop. Did this cause the large increase in the price of coffee that occurred almost immediately, or was that also a coincidence? Was Toronto's housing shortage in the 1980s related to the Ontario government's policy of *rent controls,* and if so, what is the connection? What determines the prices of specific products? What determines whether there will be a lot produced or only a little? What are the effects of government policies that seek to "administer" prices? These are the types of questions that you will be able to answer after reading the next three chapters.*

Chapter 4 introduces you to the basic concepts of *demand* and *supply.* You will see that the prices of goods in *free markets* are determined by the interaction of demand and supply. You will learn the meaning of *equilibrium,* and how equilibrium changes in response to changes to either demand or supply. With this apparatus in place, you will be returned briefly to Hurricane Andrew and to Brazil's damaged coffee crop (the price increases were *not* coincidences!).

Chapter 5 then introduces the important idea of *elasticity*—the sensitivity of one variable to a change in some other variable. This concept is central to our understanding of whether a change in the demand or supply of some commodity primarily affects *quantity* or *price.* As an application of the concept of elasticity, you will then examine the important policy issue of who bears the *burden* of commodity taxes. Do firms pay such taxes, or do consumers, or do both? How does elasticity affect the answer?

In Chapter 6 you get some practice in using what you learned in Chapters 4 and 5. We start with a general discussion of *government-controlled prices,* and then consider two examples. The first is *rent controls*—you will see that the government policy probably contributed to Toronto's housing shortage in the 1980s. The second is *agricultural price-support policies*—you will see what effects such policies have, both on farmers' incomes and on the allocation of resources. Finally, the chapter discusses the markets for internationally traded goods. You will see why Canada exports some goods and imports others, and how this pattern of trade depends on the *world prices* of the various products.

---

*Chapter 6 does not appear in *Macroeconomics.*

CHAPTER 4

DEMAND, SUPPLY, AND PRICE

Some people believe that economics begins and ends with the "laws" of supply and demand. "Economics in one lesson", however, is too much to hope for. (An unkind critic of a book with that title remarked that the author needed a second lesson.) Still, the so-called laws of supply and demand are an important part of our understanding of the market system.

As a first step, we need to understand what determines the demand for and the supply of particular products. Then we can see how demand and supply together determine the prices of products and the quantities that are bought and sold. Finally, we examine how the price system allows the economy to respond to the many changes that impinge on it. Demand and supply help us to understand the price system's successes and failures. They also help us to understand the consequences of such government policies as price controls, minimum-wage laws, and sales taxes.

DEMAND

What determines the demand for any given product? Why did the fraction of total consumer expenditure on food in Canada decline from more than 33 percent in 1910 to less than 13 percent in 1996? Why has the proportion of income spent on services increased significantly over the same period? How did Canadian consumers react to the large increases in fuel prices in the 1970s, followed by the large decreases in the 1980s? We seek to understand how much of each product consumers will buy. We start by developing a theory that is designed to explain consumption of some typical product.

WHAT IS "QUANTITY DEMANDED"?

The total amount of any particular good or service that an economy's consumers wish to purchase in some time period is called the **quantity demanded** of that product.[1] It is important to notice three things about this concept.

First, quantity demanded is a *desired* quantity. It is the amount that consumers wish to purchase, given the price of the product, other prices, their incomes, their tastes, and everything else that might matter.[2] It may be different from the amount that consumers actually succeed in purchasing. If sufficient quantities are not available, the amount that consumers wish to purchase may exceed the amount that they actually purchase. To distinguish these two concepts, the term *quantity demanded* is used to refer to desired purchases, and a phrase such as *quantity actually bought* or *quantity exchanged* is used to refer to actual purchases.

Second, *desired* does not refer to idle dreams but to *effective* demands, the amounts that people are actually willing to buy, given the price they must pay for the product.

Third, quantity demanded refers to a continuous *flow* of purchases. It must therefore be expressed as so much per period of time: 1 million units per day, 7 million per week, or 365 million per year. For example, being told that the quantity of new television sets demanded (at current prices) in Canada is 50,000 means nothing unless you are also told the period of time involved. Fifty thousand TVs de-

manded per day would be an enormous rate of demand; 50,000 per year would be a very small rate. The important distinction between stocks and flows is discussed in Extension 4-1.

The amount of some product that consumers wish to buy in a given time period is influenced by the following important variables: [3]

- Product's own price
- Average household income
- Prices of related products
- Tastes
- Distribution of income
- Population

It is difficult to determine the separate influence of each of these variables if we consider what happens when everything changes at once. Instead, we consider the influence of the variables one at a time. To do this, we hold all but one of them constant. Then we let the selected variable vary and study how it affects quantity demanded. We can do the same for each of the other variables in turn, and in this way we can come to understand the importance of each.[3] Once this is done, we can combine the separate influences of the variables to discover what happens when several things change at the same time—as they often do.

Holding all other influencing variables constant is often described by the expressions "other things being equal," "other things given," or the equivalent Latin phrase, *ceteris paribus.* When economists speak of the influence of the price of wheat on the quantity of wheat demanded, *ceteris paribus,* they refer to what a change in the price of wheat would do to the quantity of wheat demanded *if all other forces that influence the demand for wheat did not change.*

---

[1]In this chapter, we concentrate on the demand of all consumers, added together, for products. Of course, what all households do is only the sum of what each individual household does. In Chapter 7, we study the behaviour of individual consumers in more detail.
[2]When economists say that something is "given," they mean that it is held constant. The expression "given the price of the product" therefore means that the price of the product is assumed not to change during the period under discussion.

---

[3]A relationship in which many variables (in this case, average income, population, tastes, and many prices) influence a single variable (in this case, quantity demanded) is called a *multivariate* relationship. The technique of studying the effect of each of the influencing variables one at a time, while holding the others constant, is common in mathematics, and there is a specific concept, the *partial derivative,* designed to measure such effects.

THE DISTINCTION BETWEEN STOCKS AND FLOWS

One important conceptual issue that arises frequently in economics is the distinction between stock and flow variables. Economic theories use both, and it takes a little practice to keep them straight.

As noted in the text, a flow variable has a time dimension—it is so much *per unit of time.* For example, the quantity of Grade A large eggs purchased in Edmonton is a flow variable. No useful information is conveyed if we are told that the number purchased was 2,000 dozen eggs unless we are also told the period of time over which these purchases occurred. Two thousand dozen eggs per hour would indicate a much more active market in eggs than would 2,000 dozen eggs per month.

In contrast, a stock variable is a variable whose value has meaning *at a point in time.* Thus the number of eggs in the egg producer's warehouse on a particular day—for example, 20,000 dozen eggs on September 3, 1997—is a stock variable. All those eggs are there at one time, and they remain there until something happens to change the stock held in the warehouse. The stock variable is just a number at a point in time, not a rate of flow of so much per unit of time.

The terminology of stocks and flows can be understood in terms of an analogy to a bathtub. At any moment, the tub holds so much water. This is the stock, and it can be measured in terms of the volume of water, say, 100 litres. There might also be water flowing into the tub from the tap; this *flow* is measured as so much water per unit time, say, 500 litres per hour.

The distinction between stocks and flows is important. Failure to keep them straight is a common source of confusion and even error. Note, for example, that because they have different dimensions, a stock variable and a flow variable cannot be added together without specifying some time period for which the flow persists. One cannot add the stock of 100 litres of water in the tub to the flow of 500 litres per hour to get 600 litres. The new stock of water will depend on how long the flow persists; if it lasts for half an hour, the new stock will be 350 litres; if the flow persists for two hours, the new stock will be 2,100 litres (or the tub will overflow!).

In economics, the amount of income earned is a flow; there is so much per year or per month or per hour. The amount of a consumer's expenditure is also a flow—so much spent per week or per month or per year. The amount of money in a bank account or a miser's hoard (earned, perhaps, in the past but unspent) is a stock—just so many thousands of dollars. The key test is always whether a time dimension is required to give the variable meaning.

QUANTITY DEMANDED AND PRICE

We are interested in developing a theory of how prices are determined. To do this, we need to study the relationship between the quantity demanded of each product and that product's price. This requires that we hold all other influences constant and ask, "How will the quantity of a product demanded change as its price changes?"

A basic economic hypothesis is that the price of a product and the quantity demanded are related negatively, other things being equal. That is, the lower the price, the higher the quantity demanded; and the higher the price, the lower the quantity demanded.[4]

Why might this be so? Products are used to satisfy desires and needs, and there is almost always more than one product that will satisfy any desire or need. Hunger may be alleviated by meat or vegetables; a desire for green vegetables can be satisfied by

---

[4]The British economist Alfred Marshall (1842–1924) called this fundamental relation the "law of demand." In Chapter 7, we derive the law of demand as a prediction that follows from more basic assumptions about consumer behaviour.

broccoli or spinach. The desire for a vacation may be satisfied by a trip to the seashore or to the mountains; the need to get there may be satisfied by different airlines, a bus, a car, or a train. For any general desire or need, there are many different products that will satisfy it.

Now consider what happens if income, tastes, population, and the prices of all other products remain constant and the price of only one product changes. As the price goes up, that product becomes an increasingly expensive way to satisfy a desire. Some consumers will stop buying it altogether; others will buy smaller amounts; still others may continue to buy the same quantity. Because many consumers will switch wholly or partly to other products to satisfy the same desire, less will be bought of the product whose price has risen. As meat becomes more expensive, for example, consumers may to some extent switch to meat substitutes; they may also forgo meat at some meals and eat less meat at others.

Conversely, as the price goes down, the product becomes a cheaper method of satisfying a desire. Households will buy more of it. Consequently, they will buy less of similar products whose prices have not fallen and as a result have become expensive *relative* to the product in question. When a bumper tomato harvest drives prices down, shoppers switch to tomatoes and cut their purchases of many other vegetables that now look relatively more expensive.

THE DEMAND SCHEDULE AND THE DEMAND CURVE

A **demand schedule** is one way of showing the relationship between quantity demanded and the price of a product, other things being equal. It is a numerical tabulation showing the quantity that is demanded at certain prices.

Table 4-1 is a hypothetical demand schedule for carrots. It lists the quantity of carrots that would be demanded at various prices on the assumption that all other influences on quantity demanded are held constant. We note in particular that average household income is fixed at $30,000 because later we will want to see what happens when income changes. The table gives the quantities demanded for six selected prices, but in fact a separate quantity would be demanded at each possible price from 1 cent to several hundreds of dollars.

	Price Per Ton ($)	Quantity Demanded When Average Household Income Is $30,000 Per Year (thousands of tons per month)
U	20	110.0
V	40	90.0
W	60	77.5
X	80	67.5
Y	100	62.5
Z	120	60.0

TABLE 4-1
A Demand Schedule for Carrots

The table shows the quantity of carrots that would be demanded at various prices, *ceteris paribus*. For example, row W indicates that if the price of carrots were $60 per ton, consumers would desire to purchase 77,500 tons of carrots per month, given the values of the other variables that affect quantity demanded.

A second method of showing the relationship between quantity demanded and price is to draw a graph. The six price-quantity combinations shown in Table 4-1 are plotted on the graph shown in Figure 4-1. Price is plotted on the vertical axis, and quantity is plotted on the horizontal axis.

The smooth curve drawn through these points is called a **demand curve**. It shows the quantity that purchasers would like to buy at each price. The negative slope of the curve indicates that the quantity demanded increases as the price falls. Each point on the demand curve indicates a single price-quantity combination. The demand curve as a whole shows something more.

The demand curve represents the relationship between quantity demanded and price, other things being equal.

When economists speak of the demand in a particular market as being given or known, they are referring not just to the particular quantity being demanded at the moment (i.e., not just to one point on the demand curve) but to the entire demand curve— to the relationship between desired purchases and all the possible prices of the product.

Thus the term **demand** refers to the entire relationship between the quantity demanded of a product and the price of that product (as shown, for example, by the demand schedule in Table 4-1 or the

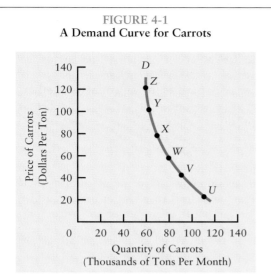

FIGURE 4-1
A Demand Curve for Carrots

This demand curve, labeled *D*, relates quantity of carrots demanded to the price of carrots; its downward slope indicates that quantity demanded increases as price falls. The six points correspond to the price-quantity combinations shown in Table 4-1. The smooth curve drawn through all of the points and labeled *D* is the demand curve.

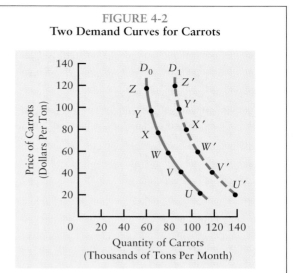

FIGURE 4-2
Two Demand Curves for Carrots

The rightward shift in the demand curve from D_0 to D_1 indicates an increase in the quantity demanded at each price. The lettered points correspond to those in Table 4-2.

demand curve in Figure 4-1). In contrast, a single point on a demand schedule or curve is the *quantity demanded* at that point. This distinction between "demand" and "quantity demanded" is an extremely important one and will be examined more closely later in this chapter.

Shifts in the Demand Curve

The demand schedule is drawn under the assumption that everything except the product's own price is being held constant. But what if other things change, as surely they do? For example, consider an increase in household income while price remains constant. If households increase their purchases of the product, the new quantity demanded cannot be represented by a point on the original demand curve. It must be represented on a new demand curve which is to the right of the old curve. Thus the rise in consumer income shifts the demand curve to the right, as shown in Figure 4-2. This illustrates the operation of an important general rule.

A demand curve is drawn under the assumption that everything except the product's own price is held

constant. A change in any of the variables previously held constant will shift the demand curve to a new position.

A demand curve can shift in many ways; two of them are particularly important. In the first case, more is bought at each price—the demand curve shifts rightward so that each price corresponds to a higher quantity than it did before. In the second case, less is bought at each price—the demand curve shifts leftward so that each price corresponds to a lower quantity than it did before.

The influence of changes in variables other than price may be studied by determining how changes in each variable shift the demand curve. Any change will shift the demand curve to the right if it increases the amount that households wish to buy, other things remaining equal. It will shift the demand curve to the left if it decreases the amount that households wish to buy, other things remaining equal. Note that changes in people's *expectations about future values* of variables such as income and prices can also influence current demand; however, for simplicity, we consider only the influence of changes in the current values of these variables.

Average Household Income. If consumers receive more income on average, they can be expected

TABLE 4-2
Two Alternative Demand Schedules for Carrots

Price Per Ton ($) P	Quantity Demanded When Average Consumer Income Is $30,000 Per Year (thousands of tons per month) D_0		Quantity Demanded When Average Consumer Income Is $36,000 Per Year (thousands of tons per month) D_1	
20	110.0	U	140.0	U'
40	90.0	V	116.0	V'
60	77.5	W	100.8	W'
80	67.5	X	87.5	X'
100	62.5	Y	81.3	Y'
120	60.0	Z	78.0	Z'

An increase in average consumer income increases the quantity demanded at each price. When average income rises from $30,000 to $36,000 per year, quantity demanded at a price of $60 per ton rises from 77,500 tons per month to 100,800 tons per month. A similar rise occurs at every other price. Thus the demand schedule relating columns P and D_0 is replaced by one relating columns P and D_1. The graphical representations of these two functions are labeled D_0 and D_1 in Figure 4-2.

to purchase more of most products even though product prices remain the same.[5] We therefore expect that a rise in average consumer income shifts the demand curve for most products to the right, indicating that more will be demanded at any given price. This is illustrated in Table 4-2 and Figure 4-2.

Prices of Related Goods.   We saw that the negative slope of a product's demand curve occurs because the lower its price, the cheaper the product becomes relative to other products that can satisfy the same needs or desires. These other products are called **substitutes.** Another way for the same change to come about is for the price of the substitute product to rise. For example, carrots can become cheap relative to cabbage either because the price of carrots falls or because the price of cabbage rises. Either change will increase the amount of carrots that consumers wish to buy as consumers substitute away from cabbage and toward carrots. Thus a rise in the price of a substitute for a product shifts the demand curve for the product to the right. More will be demanded at each price.

Complements are products that tend to be used jointly. Cars and gasoline are complements; so are CD players and speakers, golf clubs and golf balls, electric stoves and electricity, and airplane flights to Calgary and ski-lift tickets in Banff. Because complements tend to be consumed together, a fall in the price of one will increase the demand for *both* products. Thus a fall in the price of a complement for a product will shift that product's demand curve to the right. More will be demanded at each price.

For example, a fall in the price of airplane trips to Calgary will lead to a rise in the demand for ski-lift tickets in Banff, even though the price of those lift tickets is unchanged.

Tastes.   Tastes have an effect on people's desired purchases. A change in tastes may be long-lasting, such as the shift from fountain pens to ballpoint pens or from typewriters to computers; or it may be a short-lived fad such as hula hoops, CB radios, or Pogs. In either case, a change in tastes in favour of a product shifts the demand curve to the right. More will be demanded at each price.

Distribution of Income.   If a constant total of income is redistributed among the population, demands may change. If, for example, the government increases the deductions that may be taken for children on income-tax returns and compensates by raising basic tax rates, income will be transferred from childless persons to households with large families. Demands for products more heavily bought by childless persons will decline, while demands for products more heavily bought by households with large families will increase. A change in the distribution of income will therefore cause an increase in the demand for products bought most by households whose incomes increase and a decrease in the demand for products bought most by households whose incomes decrease.

Population.   Population growth does not create new demand unless the additional people have the means to purchase goods—that is, unless they have purchasing power. If there is an increase in population with purchasing power—for example, the immigration of wealthy foreigners—the demands for all the products purchased by the new people will rise. Thus we expect that an increase in population will shift the demand curves for most products to the right, indicating that more will be demanded at each price.

The reasons that demand curves shift are summarized in Figure 4-3.

---

[5]Such products are called *normal goods.* Products for which the quantity demanded falls as income rises are called *inferior goods.* These concepts are defined and discussed in Chapter 5.

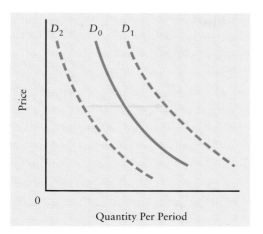

FIGURE 4-3
Shifts in the Demand Curve

A rightward shift in the demand curve from D_0 to D_1 indicates an increase in demand; a leftward shift from D_0 to D_2 indicates a decrease in demand. An increase in demand means that more is demanded at each price. Such a rightward shift can be caused by a rise in income, a rise in the price of a substitute, a fall in the price of a complement, a change in tastes that favours that product, an increase in population, or a redistribution of income toward groups that favour the product.

A decrease in demand means that less is demanded at each price. Such a leftward shift can be caused by a fall in income, a fall in the price of a substitute, a rise in the price of a complement, a change in tastes that disfavours the product, a decrease in population, or a redistribution of income away from groups that favour the product.

Movements Along the Curve Versus Shifts of the Whole Curve

Suppose that you read in today's newspaper that the soaring price of carrots has been caused by a greatly increased demand for carrots. Then tomorrow you read that the rising price of carrots is greatly reducing the typical consumer's purchases of carrots, as shoppers switch to potatoes, yams, and peas. The two stories appear to contradict each other. The first associates a rising price with a rising demand; the second associates a rising price with a declining demand. Can both statements be true? The answer is yes—because they refer to different things. The first describes a shift in the demand curve; the second describes a movement along a demand curve in response to a change in price.

Consider first the statement that the increase in the price of carrots has been caused by an increased demand for carrots. This statement refers to a shift in the demand curve for carrots. In this case, the demand curve must have shifted to the right, indicating more carrots demanded at each price. This shift, as we will see later in this chapter, will increase the price of carrots.

Now consider the statement that fewer carrots are being bought because carrots have become more expensive. This refers to a movement along a given demand curve and reflects a change between two specific quantities being bought, one before the price rose and one afterward.

Possible explanations for the two stories are given in the following:

1. A rise in the population is shifting the demand curve for carrots to the right as more carrots are demanded at each price. This in turn raises the price of carrots (for reasons we will soon study in detail). This was the first newspaper story.

2. The rising price of carrots is causing each individual household to cut back on its purchase of carrots. This causes an upward movement to the left along any particular demand curve for carrots. This was the second newspaper story.

To prevent the type of confusion caused by our two newspaper stories, economists use a specialized vocabulary to distinguish between shifts of curves and movements along curves.

We have seen that demand refers to the *whole* demand curve, whereas quantity demanded refers to a specific quantity that is demanded at a specified price, as indicated by a particular *point* on the demand curve. In Figure 4-1, for example, demand is given by the curve D; at a price of $40, the quantity demanded is 90 tons, as indicated by the point V.

Economists reserve the term **change in demand** to describe a change in the quantity demanded at *every* price. That is, a change in demand refers to a shift of the entire demand curve. The term **change in quantity demanded** refers to a movement from one point on a demand curve to another point on the same demand curve.

A change in quantity demanded can result from a shift in the demand curve, with the price constant; from a movement along a given demand curve due to a change in the price; or from a combination of the two. [4]

We consider each of these possibilities in turn.

An increase in demand means that the whole demand curve shifts to the right; a decrease in demand means that the whole demand curve shifts to the left. At a given price, an increase in demand causes an increase in quantity demanded, whereas a decrease in demand causes a decrease in quantity demanded. For example, in Figure 4-2, the shift in the demand curve from D_0 to D_1 represents an increase in demand, and at a price of $40, quantity demanded increases from 90,000 tons to 116,000 tons, as indicated by the move from V to V'.

A movement down and to the right along a demand curve causes an increase in quantity demanded; a movement up and to the left along a demand curve causes a decrease in quantity demanded. For example, in Figure 4-2, with demand given by the curve D_1, an increase in price from $40 to $60 causes a movement along D_1 from V' to W', and quantity demanded decreases from 116,000 tons to 100,800 tons.

When there is a change in demand *and* a change in the price, the overall change in quantity demanded is the net effect of the shift in the demand curve and the movement along the new demand curve. Figure 4-4 shows the combined effect of an increase in demand, shown by a rightward shift in the whole demand curve, and an upward movement to the left along the new demand curve due to an increase in price. The rise in demand causes an increase in quantity demanded at the initial price, whereas the movement along the demand curve causes a decrease in the quantity demanded. Whether quantity demanded rises or falls overall depends on the relative magnitudes of these two changes.

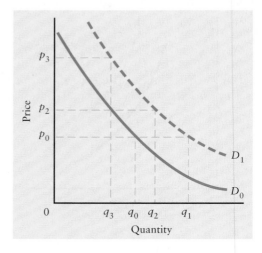

FIGURE 4-4
Shifts of and Movements Along the Demand Curve

An increase in demand means that the demand curve shifts to the right, and hence quantity demanded will be higher at each price. A rise in price causes an upward movement to the left along the demand curve, and hence quantity demanded will fall. The demand curve is originally D_0 and price is p_0, which means that quantity demanded is q_0. Suppose that demand increases to D_1, which means that at any particular price, there is a larger quantity demanded; for example, at p_0, quantity demanded is now q_1. Now suppose that the price rises above p_0. This causes a movement up and to the left along D_1, and quantity demanded falls below q_1.

The net effect of these two changes can be either an increase or a decrease in the quantity demanded. In this figure, a rise in price to p_2 means that the quantity demanded q_2 is still in excess of the original quantity demanded q_{01}; a rise in price to p_3 means that the final quantity demanded q_3 is below the original quantity demanded q_0.

SUPPLY

The Canadian economy produced goods and services worth about $800 billion in 1996. Economists have as many questions to ask about production and its changing composition as they do about consumption. What determines the amount produced? What determines its composition? Why does the quantity of goods and services produced change? Why has manufacturing output fallen from almost 30 percent of total private-sector production in the early 1950s to about 20 percent in 1996? Why have agriculture, forestry, and fisheries, as a group, fallen from almost 7 percent in the 1950s to approximately 3 percent in 1996?

Dramatic changes have occurred within each of these market categories. Why, for example, did the aluminum industry grow much faster than the steel industry? Even within any single industry, some firms prosper and grow while others decline. A large fraction of the firms in a typical industry at the beginning of any decade are no longer present at the end of that decade. Why and how do new jobs, new firms, and new industries come into being while other jobs, firms, and industries shrink or disappear altogether?

All of these questions and many others are aspects of a single question: *What determines the quantities of products that will be produced and offered for sale?*

A full discussion of these questions of supply will come later (in Part 4). For now, it suffices to examine the basic relationship between the price of a product and the quantity produced and offered for sale and to understand what forces lead to shifts in this relationship.

WHAT IS "QUANTITY SUPPLIED"?

The amount of a product that firms wish to sell in some time period is called the **quantity supplied** of that product. Quantity supplied is a flow; it is so much per unit of time. Note also that quantity supplied is the amount that firms are willing to offer for sale; it is not necessarily the amount that they succeed in selling, which is expressed by *quantity actually sold* or *quantity exchanged*. Although households may desire to purchase an amount that differs from what firms desire to sell, they obviously cannot succeed in buying what someone else does not sell. A purchase and a sale are merely two sides of the same transaction. Viewed from the buyer's side, there is a purchase; viewed from the seller's side, there is a sale.

Because desired purchases do not have to equal desired sales, quantity demanded does not have to equal quantity supplied. However, the quantity actually purchased must equal the quantity actually sold because whatever someone buys, someone else must sell.

The amount of a product that firms are willing to produce and offer for sale is influenced by the following important variables: [5]

- Product's own price
- Prices of inputs
- Technology
- Number of suppliers

The situation with supply is the same as with demand: There are several influencing variables, and we will not get far if we try to discover what happens when they all change at the same time. So, again, we use the convenient *ceteris paribus* assumption to study the influence of the variables one at a time.

QUANTITY SUPPLIED AND PRICE

We begin by holding all other influences constant and ask, "How do we expect the quantity of a product supplied to vary with its own price?"

A basic hypothesis of economics is that for many products, the price of the product and the quantity supplied are related *positively,* other things being equal. That is to say, the higher the product's own price, the more its producers will supply; and the lower the price, the less its producers will supply.[6]

Why might this be so? It is true because the profits that can be earned from producing a product will increase if the price of that product rises while the costs of inputs used to produce it remain unchanged. This will make firms, which are in business to earn profits, wish to produce more of the product whose price has risen.

THE SUPPLY SCHEDULE AND THE SUPPLY CURVE

The general relationship just discussed can be illustrated by a **supply schedule,** which shows the relationship between quantity supplied of a product and the price of the product, other things being equal. A supply schedule is analogous to a demand schedule; the former shows what producers would be willing to sell, whereas the latter shows what households would be willing to buy, at alternative prices of the product. Table 4-3 presents a hypothetical supply schedule for carrots.

A **supply curve,** the graphical representation of the supply schedule, is illustrated in Figure 4-5. Each point on the supply curve represents a specific price-quantity combination; however, the whole curve shows something more.

The supply curve represents the relationship between quantity supplied and price, other things being equal; its positive slope indicates that quantity supplied varies in the same direction as does price.

When economists make statements about the conditions of supply, they are not referring just to the particular quantity being supplied at the moment—

---

[6]In this chapter, we introduce this key relation as a hypothesis. In later chapters, we will derive it as a prediction from more basic assumptions about the behaviour of firms.

TABLE 4-3
A Supply Schedule for Carrots

	Price Per Ton ($)	Quantity Supplied (thousands of tons per month)
u	20	5.0
v	40	46.0
w	60	77.5
x	80	100.0
y	100	115.0
z	120	122.5

The table shows the quantities that producers wish to sell at various prices, *ceteris paribus*.

that is, not to just one point on the supply curve. Instead, they are referring to the entire supply curve, to the complete relationship between desired sales and all possible prices of the product.

Supply refers to the entire relationship between the quantity supplied of a product and the price of that product, other things being equal. A single point on the supply curve refers to the *quantity supplied* at that price.

FIGURE 4-5
A Supply Curve for Carrots

This supply curve, labeled S, relates quantity of carrots supplied to the price of carrots; its upward slope indicates that quantity supplied increases as price increases. The six points correspond to the price-quantity combinations shown in Table 4-3.

Shifts in the Supply Curve

A shift in the supply curve means that at each price, a different quantity will be supplied than previously. An increase in the quantity supplied at each price is shown in Table 4-4 and is graphed in Figure 4-6. This change appears as a rightward shift in the supply curve. In contrast, a decrease in the quantity supplied at each price appears as a leftward shift. A shift in the supply curve must be the result of a change in one of the factors that influence the quantity supplied other than the product's own price. We now briefly consider the major possible causes of such shifts.

For supply, as for demand, there is an important general rule:

A change in any of the variables (other than the product's own price) that affects the amount of a product that firms are willing to produce and sell will shift the supply curve to a new position.

Consider the effect of changes in the following variables:

Price of Inputs. All things that a firm uses to produce its outputs, such as materials, labour, and machines, are called the firm's *inputs*. Other things being equal, the higher the price of any input used to make a product, the less will be the profit from making that product. We expect, therefore, that the higher the price of any input used by a firm, the lower will be the amount that the firm will produce and offer for sale at any given price of the product. A rise in the price of inputs therefore shifts the supply curve to the left, indicating that less will be supplied at any given price; a fall in the cost of inputs shifts the supply curve to the right.

Technology. At any time, what is produced and how it is produced depends on what is known. Over time, knowledge changes; so do the quantities of individual products supplied. The enormous increase in production per worker that has been going on in industrial societies for about 200 years is due largely to improved methods of production. The Industrial Revolution is more than a historical event; it is a present reality. Discoveries in chemistry have led to lower costs of production for well-established products, such as paints, and to a large variety of new products made of plastics and synthetic fibers. Such inventions as silicon chips have radically changed products such as computers, televisions, and tele-

TABLE 4-4
Two Alternative Supply Schedules for Carrots

Price Per Ton ($) P	Quantity Supplied Before Cost-Saving Innovation (thousands of tons per month) S_0		Quantity Supplied After Innovation (thousands of tons per month) S_1	
20	5.0	u	28.0	u'
40	46.0	v	76.0	v'
60	77.5	w	102.0	w'
80	100.0	x	120.0	x'
100	115.0	y	132.0	y'
120	122.5	z	140.0	z'

A cost-saving innovation increases the quantity supplied at each price. As a result of a cost-saving innovation, the quantity that is supplied at $100 per ton rises from 115,000 to 132,000 tons per month. A similar rise occurs at every price.

phones, and the consequent development of smaller computers has revolutionized the production of countless other nonelectronic products.

Any technological innovation that decreases production costs will increase the profits that can be earned at any given price of the product. Because in-creased profitability leads to increased production, this change shifts the supply curve to the right, indicating an increased willingness to produce the product and offer it for sale at each possible price.

Number of Suppliers. For given prices and technology, the total amount of any product supplied depends on the number of firms producing that product and offering it for sale. For example, in Chapter 10 we will examine the situation where profits made by existing firms producing a particular good attract other firms to enter the industry in pursuit of those profits. The effect of this increase in the number of suppliers is to shift the supply curve to the right. Similarly, if the existing firms are losing money, then they will eventually leave the industry; this reduction in the number of suppliers shifts the supply curve to the left.

Movements Along the Curve Versus Shifts of the Whole Curve

As with demand, it is important to distinguish movements along supply curves from shifts of the whole curve. Economists reserve the term **change in supply** to describe a shift of the whole supply curve—that is, a change in the quantity that will be supplied at every price. The term **change in quantity supplied** refers to a movement from one point on a supply curve to another point on the same supply curve. In other words, an increase in supply means that the whole supply curve has shifted to the right, so that the quantity supplied at any given price has increased; a movement up and to the right along a supply curve indicates an *increase in the quantity supplied* in response to an increase in the price of the product.

A change in quantity supplied can result from a change in supply, with the price constant; from a movement along a given supply curve due to a change in the price; or from a combination of the two.

FIGURE 4-6
Two Supply Curves for Carrots

The rightward shift in the supply curve from S_0 to S_1 indicates an increase in the quantity supplied at each price. The lettered points correspond to those in Table 4-4. A rightward shift in the supply curve indicates an increase in supply such that more carrots are supplied at each price.

THE DETERMINATION OF PRICE BY DEMAND AND SUPPLY

So far, demand and supply have been considered separately. What we really want to know, however, is how these two forces *interact* to determine price in a

TABLE 4-5
Demand and Supply Schedules for Carrots and Equilibrium Price

(1) Price Per Ton ($) p	(2) Quantity Demanded (thousands of tons per month) D	(3) Quantity Supplied (thousands of tons per month) S	(4) Excess Demand (+) or Excess Supply (−) (thousands of tons per month) D − S
20	110.0	5.0	+105.0
40	90.0	46.0	+44.0
60	77.5	77.5	0.0
80	67.5	100.0	−32.5
100	62.5	115.0	−52.5
120	60.0	122.5	−62.5

Equilibrium occurs where quantity demanded equals quantity supplied—when there is neither excess demand nor excess supply. These schedules are those from Tables 4-1 and 4-3. The equilibrium price is $60.

competitive market.[7] Table 4-5 brings together the demand and supply schedules from Tables 4-1 and 4-3. The quantities of carrots demanded and supplied at each price may now be compared.

There is only one price, $60 per ton, at which the quantity of carrots demanded equals the quantity supplied. At prices less than $60 per ton, there is a shortage of carrots because the quantity demanded exceeds the quantity supplied. This is a situation of **excess demand.** At prices greater than $60 per ton, there is a surplus of carrots because the quantity supplied exceeds the quantity demanded. This is a situation of **excess supply.**

To examine the determination of market price, suppose first that the price is $100 per ton. At this price, 115,000 tons are offered for sale, but only 62,500 tons are demanded. There is an excess supply of 52,500 tons per month. We assume that sellers will then cut their prices to get rid of this surplus and that purchasers, observing the stock of unsold carrots, will pay less for what they are prepared to buy. Thus *excess supply causes downward pressure on price.*

Next consider the price of $20 per ton. At this price, there is excess demand. The 5,000 tons produced each month are snapped up quickly, and

105,000 tons of desired purchases cannot be made. Rivalry between would-be purchasers may lead them to offer more than the prevailing price to outbid other purchasers. Also, perceiving that they could sell their available supplies many times over, sellers may begin to ask a higher price for the quantities that they do have to sell. Thus *excess demand causes upward pressure on price.*

Finally, consider the price of $60. At this price, producers wish to sell 77,500 tons per month, and purchasers wish to buy that same quantity. There is neither a shortage nor a surplus of carrots. There are no unsatisfied buyers to bid the price up, nor are there unsatisfied sellers to force the price down. Once the price of $60 has been reached, therefore, there will be no tendency for it to change.

Equilibrium implies a state of rest, or balance, between opposing forces. The **equilibrium price** is the one toward which the actual market price will tend. It will persist, once established, unless it is disturbed by some change in market conditions which shifts the demand curve, the supply curve, or both. A condition that must be fulfilled if equilibrium is to be obtained in some market is called an **equilibrium condition.** The equality of quantity demanded and quantity supplied is an equilibrium condition. [6]

The price at which the quantity demanded equals the quantity supplied is called the equilibrium price, or the market-clearing price.

---

[7]Roughly speaking, a competitive market is one that has a large number of firms and a large number of consumers, each small relative to the size of the market. The concept of a competitive market is defined more precisely in Chapter 10.

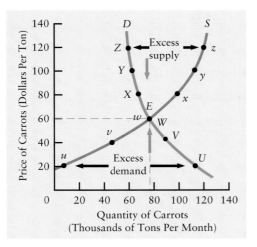

FIGURE 4-7
Determination of the Equilibrium Price

The equilibrium price corresponds to the intersection of the demand and supply curves. Equilibrium is indicated by E, which is point W on the demand curve and point w on the supply curve. At a price of $60, quantity demanded equals quantity supplied. At prices above equilibrium, there is excess supply and downward pressure on price. At prices below equilibrium, there is excess demand and upward pressure on price. The pressures on price are represented by the vertical arrows.

Any price at which the market does not clear—that is, quantity demanded does not equal quantity supplied—is called a **disequilibrium price.** Whenever there is either excess demand or excess supply in a market, that market is said to be in a state of **disequilibrium,** and the market price will be changing.

This same story is told in graphical terms in Figure 4-7. The quantities demanded and supplied at any price can be read off the two curves; the excess supply or excess demand is shown by the horizontal distance between the curves at each price. The figure makes it clear that the equilibrium price occurs where the demand and supply curves intersect. Below that price, there is excess demand and hence upward pressure on the existing price. Above that price, there is excess supply and hence downward pressure on the existing price. These pressures are represented by the vertical arrows in the figure.

THE LAWS OF DEMAND AND SUPPLY

Changes in any of the variables, other than price, that influence quantity demanded or supplied will cause a shift in the supply curve, the demand curve, or both. There are four possible shifts: a rise in demand (a rightward shift in the demand curve), a fall in demand (a leftward shift in the demand curve), a rise in supply (a rightward shift in the supply curve), and a fall in supply (a leftward shift in the supply curve).

To discover the effects of each of the possible curve shifts, we use the method known as **comparative statics,** short for *comparative static equilibrium analysis.*[8] Using this method, we derive predictions by analyzing the effect on the equilibrium position of some change in which we are interested. We start from a position of equilibrium and then introduce the change to be studied. The new equilibrium position is determined and compared with the original one. The difference between the two positions of equilibrium must result from the change that was introduced because everything else has been held constant.

Each of the four possible curve shifts causes changes that are described by one of the four so-called "laws" of demand and supply. Each of the laws summarizes what happens when an initial position of equilibrium is disturbed by a shift in either the demand curve or the supply curve. By using the term "law" to describe what happens, economists do not mean that they are absolutely certain of the outcome. The term "law" in science is used to describe a theory that has stood up to substantial testing. The laws of demand and supply are thus hypotheses that predict certain kinds of behaviour in certain situations, and the predicted behaviour occurs sufficiently often that economists continue to have confidence in the underlying theory.

The four laws of demand and supply are derived in Figure 4-8, which generalizes our specific discussion about carrots. Study the figure carefully. Previously, we had given the axes specific la-

---

[8]The term *static* is used because we are not concerned with the actual path by which the market goes from the first equilibrium position to the second or with the time taken to reach the second equilibrium. Analysis of these movements would be described as *dynamic analysis.*

FIGURE 4-8
The Four "Laws" of Demand and Supply

(i) The effect of shifts in the demand curve

(ii) The effect of shifts in the supply curve

The effects on equilibrium price and quantity of shifts in either demand or supply are known as the laws of demand and supply.

A rise in demand. In part (i), assume that the original demand and supply curves are D_0 and S, which intersect to produce equilibrium at E_0, with a price of p_0 and a quantity of q_0. An increase in demand shifts the demand curve to D_1, taking the new equilibrium to E_1. Price rises to p_1 and quantity to q_1.

A fall in demand. In part (i), the original demand and supply curves are D_1 and S, which intersect to produce equilibrium at E_1, with a price of p_1 and a quantity of q_1. A decrease in demand shifts the demand curve to D_0, taking the new equilibrium to E_0. Price falls to p_0, and quantity falls to q_0.

A rise in supply. In part (ii), the original demand and supply curves are D and S_0, which intersect to produce equilibrium at E_0, with a price of p_0 and a quantity of q_0. An increase in supply shifts the supply curve to S_1, taking the new equilibrium to E_1. Price falls to p_1, and quantity rises to q_1.

A fall in supply. In part (ii), the original demand and supply curves are D and S_1, which intersect to produce equilibrium at E_1, with a price of p_1 and a quantity of q_1. A decrease in supply shifts the supply curve to S_0, taking the new equilibrium to E_0. Price rises to p_0, and quantity falls to q_0.

bels, but from here on we will simplify. Because it is intended to apply to any product, the horizontal axis is simply labeled "Quantity." This should be understood to mean quantity per period in whatever units output is measured. "Price," the vertical axis, should be understood to mean the price measured as dollars per unit of quantity for the same product.

The four laws of demand and supply are as follows:

1. A rise in demand causes an increase in both the equilibrium price and the equilibrium quantity exchanged.

2. A fall in demand causes a decrease in both the equilibrium price and the equilibrium quantity exchanged.

3. A rise in supply causes a decrease in the equilibrium price and an increase in the equilibrium quantity exchanged.

4. A fall in supply causes an increase in the equilibrium price and a decrease in the equilibrium quantity exchanged.

Demonstrations of these laws are given in the caption to Figure 4-8. The intuitive reasoning behind each is as follows:

1. A rise in demand creates a shortage at the initial equilibrium price, and the unsatisfied buyers bid up the price. This causes a larger quantity to be produced, with the result that at the new equilibrium, more is bought and sold at a higher price.

2. A fall in demand creates a glut at the initial equilibrium price, and the unsuccessful sellers bid the price down. As a result, less of the product is produced and offered for sale. At the new equilibrium, both price and quantity bought and sold are lower than they were originally.

3. An increase in supply creates a glut at the initial equilibrium price, and the unsuccessful suppliers force the price down. This increases the quantity demanded, and the new equilibrium is at a lower price and a higher quantity bought and sold.

4. A reduction in supply creates a shortage at the initial equilibrium price that causes the price to be bid up. This reduces the quantity demanded, and the new equilibrium is at a higher price and a lower quantity bought and sold.

In this chapter, we have studied many forces that can cause demand or supply curves to shift. By combining this analysis with the four laws of demand and supply, we can link many real-world events that cause demand or supply curves to shift with changes in market prices and quantities. Application 4-1 shows how demand-and-supply analysis can be used to examine two real-world shocks; the effects of Florida's 1992 Hurricane Andrew, and Brazil's 1994 coffee-crop failure.

The theory of the determination of price by demand and supply is beautiful in its simplicity. Yet as we shall see throughout this book, it is powerful in its wide range of applications.

PRICES AND INFLATION

The theory we have developed explains how individual prices are determined by the forces of demand and supply. To facilitate matters, we have made *ceteris paribus* assumptions. Specifically, we have assumed the constancy of all prices except the one we are studying (and occasionally one other price, when we wish to see how a change in that price affects the market being studied). Does this mean that our theory is inapplicable to an inflationary world in which all prices are rising at the same time? Fortunately, the answer is no.

The price of a product is the amount of money that must be spent to acquire one unit of that product. This is called the **absolute price** or **money price**. A **relative price** is the ratio of two absolute prices; it expresses the price of one good in terms of (relative to) another.

We have mentioned several times that what matters for demand and supply is the price of the product in question relative to the prices of other products; that is, what matters is the *relative price*.

In an inflationary world, we are often interested in the price of a given product as it relates to the average price of all other products. If, during a period when all prices are increasing by an average of 40 percent, the price of oranges rose by 60 percent, then the price of oranges rose relative to the prices of other goods as a whole. Oranges became *relatively* expensive. However, if oranges had risen in price by only 30 percent when other prices increased by 40 percent, then the relative price of oranges would have fallen. Although the money price of oranges rose substantially, oranges became *relatively* cheap.

In Lewis Carroll's famous story, *Through the Looking Glass*, Alice finds a country where one has to run in order to stay still. So it is with inflation. A product's price must rise as fast as the general level of prices just to keep its relative price constant.

It has been convenient in this chapter to analyze changes in particular prices in the context of a constant price level. The analysis is easily extended to an inflationary period by remembering that any force that raises the price of one product when other prices remain constant will, given general inflation, raise the price of that product faster than the price level is rising. For example, a change in tastes in favour of carrots that would raise their price by 20 percent when other prices were constant would raise their price by 32 percent if, at the same time, the general price level rises by 10 percent.[9] In each case, the price of carrots rises 20 percent *relative to the average of all prices*.

In price theory, whenever we refer to a change in the price of one product, we mean a change in that product's relative price. That is, a change in the price of that product relative to the prices of all other goods.

If the price level is constant, this change requires only a rise in the money price of the product in question. If the price level is itself rising, this change requires that the money price of the product in question rise faster than the price level.

---

[9]Let the price level be 100 in the first case and 110 in the second. Let the price of carrots be 120 in the first case and x in the second. To preserve the same relative price, we need x such that $120/100 = x/110$, which makes $x = 132$.

APPLICATION 4-1

DEMAND AND SUPPLY: WHAT REALLY HAPPENS

"The theory of supply and demand is neat enough," said the sceptic, "but tell me what really happens."

"What really happens," said the economist, "is that demand curves have a negative slope; supply curves have a positive slope. Prices rise in response to excess demand; prices fall in response to excess supply."

"But that's theory," insisted the sceptic. "What about reality?"

"That is reality as well," said the economist. "Changes in the prices you pay when you go to the grocery story, the hardware store, or the mall are all responses to excess supply or excess demand."

"Explaining why prices change is a pretty impressive claim," replied the sceptic. "For this to make sense, you have to convince me that these situations of excess supply and excess demand ever occur. Prices change every time I go to the grocery store, but the only time I can remember seeing excess demand was when I tried to get tickets to see the Rolling Stones."

"Shifts in the demand curve or the supply curve for some product cause excess supply and excess demand to occur. These shifts may be caused by a whole range of factors, but the key is that they reflect information and events that have not already been incorporated in the model. The reason why you rarely observe excess demand or excess supply is that prices usually change rapidly to eliminate these gaps," lectured the economist.

"Still too abstract," replied the sceptic.

"Let me show you a couple of examples of how the weather—something that varies in unpredictable ways—helps to illustrate this whole theoretical apparatus."

THE WEATHER AND A DEMAND SHOCK

On August 24, 1992, Hurricane Andrew struck the Florida coast, causing considerable damage to homes and business. Immediately after the storm, people needed plywood to patch roofs and cover windows.

This immediate need for plywood meant that the demand curve for plywood shifted out—upward and

SUMMARY

A. DEMAND

- The amount of a product that consumers wish to purchase is called the *quantity demanded*. It is a flow expressed as so much per period of time. It is determined by tastes, average household income, the product's own price, the prices of related products, the size of the population, and the distribution of income among consumers.
- The relationship between quantity demanded and price is represented graphically by a demand curve that shows how much will be demanded at each market price. Quantity demanded is assumed to increase as the price of the product falls, other things held constant. Thus demand curves are downward sloping.
- It is important to make the distinction between a movement along a demand curve and a shift of a demand curve. A change in the product's price will cause a movement along the demand curve. This is called a *change in quantity demanded*.
- A shift in a demand curve represents a change in the quantity demanded at each price and is referred to as a *change in demand*. The demand curve shifts to the right (an increase in demand) if average income rises, if population rises, if the price of a substitute rises, if the price of a complement falls, or if there is a change in tastes in favour of the product. The opposite changes shift the demand curve to the left (a decrease in demand).

B. SUPPLY

- The amount of a product that firms wish to sell is called the *quantity supplied*. It is a flow expressed as so much to the right. At the prehurricane price, there would have been excess demand. As expected, the price of plywood rose to remove the excess demand. In Florida, there were reports that the price of plywood had doubled. The events in Florida affected the price of plywood nationwide, with prices jumping 18 percent in the two weeks after the storm.

THE WEATHER AND A SUPPLY SHOCK

In 1994, Brazil, which produces one-third of the world's coffee, experienced unusually severe weather. Two killing frosts in June and July and a period of drought thereafter severely damaged the next year's crop. Some experts estimated that the frosts had destroyed as much as 45 percent of Brazil's 1995 harvest.

This crop damage meant that the supply curve of coffee shifted in—upward and to the left. Without a change in price, there would have been excess demand for coffee, with more people wanting to buy than wanting to sell. Predictably, the market forces reacted swiftly, and coffee prices soared by nearly 100 percent on the wholesale commodity market on July 14. Consumers also felt the impact of the supply shock, with retail prices climbing by about $5 per kilogram.

BACK TO THE SCEPTIC

"Hey, that's kind of neat," said the sceptic, "I think I'm starting to get the hang of this. But I have just one problem. You said that prices usually change to eliminate the excess demands or supplies, but that doesn't explain the huge lineups I saw when I was trying to buy the Rolling Stones tickets."

"You're right," replied the economist, "but that situation can also be explained with the demand-and-supply apparatus. The situation with the Rolling Stones concert was that there was a fixed supply of tickets and a large demand for them, suggesting a high equilibrium price. But for various reasons, the concert promoters set the ticket prices below the market-clearing price and the result was exactly as predicted—excess demand leading to large lineups and ticket resales ("scalping") well above the official price."

per period of time. It depends on the product's own price, the costs of inputs, the number of suppliers, and the state of technology.

- The relationship between quantity supplied and price is represented graphically by a supply curve that shows how much will be supplied at each market price. Quantity supplied is assumed to increase as the price of the product increases, other things held constant. Thus, supply curves are upward sloping.

- It is important to make the distinction between a movement along a supply curve and a shift of a supply curve. A change in the product's price will cause a movement along the supply curve. This is called a *change in quantity supplied*.

- A shift in the supply curve indicates a change in the quantity supplied at each price and is referred to as a *change in supply*. The supply curve shifts to the right (an increase in supply) if the costs of producing the product fall or if, for any reason, producers become more willing to produce the product. The opposite changes shift the supply curve to the left (a decrease in supply).

C. THE DETERMINATION OF PRICE BY DEMAND AND SUPPLY

- The *equilibrium price* is the price at which the quantity demanded equals the quantity supplied. At any price below equilibrium, there will be excess demand; at any price above equilibrium, there will be excess supply. Graphically, equilibrium occurs where the demand and supply curves intersect.

- Price rises when there is excess demand and falls when there is excess supply. Thus the actual market price will be pushed toward the equilibrium price. When it is reached, there will be neither excess demand nor excess supply, and the price will not change until either the supply curve or the demand curve shifts.

- Using the method of *comparative statics,* the effects of a shift in either demand or supply can be determined. A rise in demand raises both equilibrium price and equilibrium quantity; a fall in demand lowers both. A rise in supply raises equilibrium quantity but lowers equilibrium price; a fall in supply lowers equilibrium quantity but raises equilibrium price. These are called the laws of demand and supply.

- Price theory is most simply developed in the context of a constant price level. Price changes discussed in the theory are changes relative to the average level of all prices. The absolute price of a product is its price in terms of money; its relative price is its price in relation to other products. In an inflationary period, a rise in the *relative price* of one product means that its absolute price rises by more than the price level; a fall in its relative price means that its absolute price rises by less than the price level.

KEY CONCEPTS

"Ceteris paribus" or "other things being equal"
Quantity demanded and quantity actually bought
Demand schedule and demand curve
Change in quantity demanded versus change in demand

Quantity supplied and quantity actually sold
Supply schedule and supply curve
Change in quantity supplied versus change in supply

Equilibrium, equilibrium price, and disequilibrium
Comparative statics
Laws of supply and demand
Relative price

DISCUSSION QUESTIONS

1. What shifts in demand or supply curves would produce the following results? (Assume in each case that only one of the two curves has shifted.)

   a. The price of pocket calculators has fallen over the past few years, and the quantity exchanged has risen greatly.
   b. Summer sublets in Kingston, Ontario, are at rents well below the regular rentals.
   c. Sales of designer jeans first rose, then declined.
   d. "Gourmet coffee market grows as affluent shoppers indulge."
   e. Du Pont increased the price of synthetic fibers, although it acknowledged that demand was weak.
   f. The Edsel was a lemon when it was produced in 1958–1960 but is now a best-seller among cars of its vintage.

2. Recently, a government economist predicted that this spring's excellent weather would result in larger crops of wheat and canola than farmers had expected. But the economist warned consumers not to expect prices to decrease because the cost of production was rising and foreign demand for Canadian crops was increasing. "The classic pattern of supply and demand won't work this time," the economist said. Discuss his observation.

3. What would be the effect on the equilibrium price and quantity of marijuana if its sale and consumption were legalized?

4. The relative price of personal computers has dropped drastically over the past 15 years. Would you explain this falling price in terms of demand or supply changes? What factors are likely to have caused the demand or supply shifts that did occur?

5. Classify the effect of each of the following as (i) a decrease in the demand for fish, (ii) a decrease in the quantity of fish demanded, or (iii) other. Illustrate each diagrammatically.

   a. The government of Canada closes the Atlantic Cod fishery.
   b. People buy less fish because of a rise in fish prices.
   c. The Catholic Church relaxed its ban on eating meat on Fridays.
   d. The price of beef falls, and as a result, consumers buy more beef and less fish.
   e. Fears of mercury pollution lead locals to shun fish caught in nearby lakes.
   f. It is generally alleged that eating fish is better for one's health than eating meat.

6. Predict the effect on the price of at least one product of each of the following:

   a. Winter snowfall is at a record high in the interior of British Columbia, but drought continues in Quebec ski areas.
   b. A recession decreases employment in Oshawa automobile factories.
   c. The French grape harvest is the smallest in 20 years.
   d. The province of Ontario cancels permission for citizens to cut firewood in provincial camp grounds.

7. Are the following two observations inconsistent? (a) Rising demand for housing causes prices of new homes to soar. (b) Many families refuse to buy homes as prices become prohibitive for them.

ELASTICITY

The laws of demand and supply predict the *direction* of changes in price and quantity in response to various shifts in demand and supply. However, it usually is not enough to know merely whether price and quantity each rise or fall; it is also important to know by *how much* each changes.

When flood damage led to major destruction of the U.S. onion crop in the 1990s, onion prices rose sharply. Not surprisingly, overall consumption of onions fell. The press reported that many consumers stopped using onions altogether and substituted onion salt, sauerkraut, cabbage, and other products. Other consumers still bought onions but in reduced quantities. Was the dollar value (price times quantity) higher or lower? The answer is important. A government concerned with the effect of a bad crop on farm income (because it has policies aimed at stabilizing farm income) will not be satisfied with being told that food prices will rise and quantities consumed will fall; it will need to know by approximately how much each will change if it is to assess the effects on farmers.

Measuring and describing the extent of the responsiveness of quantities to changes in prices and other variables is often essential if we are to understand the significance of these changes. This is what the concept of *elasticity* does.

PRICE ELASTICITY OF DEMAND

Suppose that there is an increase in the supply of some farm crop, that is, a rightward shift in the supply curve. We saw in Figure 4-8 when we examined the laws of supply and demand that such an increase in supply will cause the equilibrium price to fall and the equilibrium quantity to rise. By how much will each change? The answer depends on what is called the *elasticity of demand*.

This is illustrated in the two parts of Figure 5-1, each of which reproduces the analysis of Figure 4-8 but using two different demand curves. The two parts of Figure 5-1 have the same initial equilibrium, and

that equilibrium is disturbed by the same rightward shift in the supply curve. But because the demand curves are different in the two parts of the figure, the new equilibrium position is different, and hence the magnitude of the effects of the increase in supply on equilibrium price and quantity are different.

A shift in supply will have different quantitative effects, depending on the shape of the demand curve. The difference may be significant for government policy. Consider what would happen if the rightward shift of the supply curve shown in Figure 5-1 occurs because the government has persuaded farmers to produce more of a certain crop. (For example, it might have paid a subsidy to farmers for producing that crop.)

Part (i) of Figure 5-1 illustrates a case in which the quantity that consumers demand is relatively responsive to price changes. The rise in production brings down the price, but because the quantity demanded is quite responsive, only a small change in price is necessary to restore equilibrium. The effect of the government's policy, therefore, is to achieve a large increase in the production and sales of this product and only a small decrease in price.

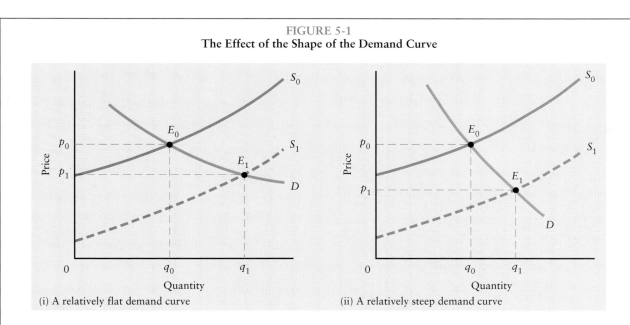

FIGURE 5-1
The Effect of the Shape of the Demand Curve

(i) A relatively flat demand curve

(ii) A relatively steep demand curve

The more responsive the quantity demanded is to changes in price, the less the change in price and the greater the change in quantity resulting from any given shift in the supply curve. Both parts of the figure are drawn to the same scale. They show the same initial equilibrium and the same shift in the supply curve. In each part, initial equilibrium is at price p_0 and output q_0 and the new equilibrium is at p_1 and q_1. In part (i), the effect of the shift in supply from S_0 to S_1 is a slight fall in the price and a large increase in quantity. In part (ii), the effect of the identical shift in the supply curve from S_0 to S_1 is a large fall in the price and a relatively small increase in quantity.

Part (ii) of Figure 5-1 shows a case in which the quantity demanded is relatively unresponsive to price changes. As before, the increase in supply at the original price causes a surplus that brings the price down. However, this time the quantity demanded by consumers does not increase much in response to the fall in price. The result is that equilibrium price falls more, and equilibrium quantity rises less, than in the first case. The effect of the government's policy is to achieve a large decrease in the price of this product and only a small increase in the quantity produced and sold.

In both of the cases shown in Figure 5-1, the government's policy has exactly the same effectiveness as far as the farmers' willingness to supply the commodity is concerned—the shifts of the supply curve are identical. The magnitude of the effects on the *equilibrium* price and quantity, however, are different because of the different degrees to which the quantity demanded by consumers responds to price changes.

If the purpose of the government's policy is to increase the quantity of this commodity produced and consumed, the policy will be more successful if the demand curve is similar to the one shown in part (i) of Figure 5-1 than if it is similar to the one shown in part (ii). If, however, the goal of the policy is to achieve a large reduction in the price of the commodity, the policy will be less successful if demand is as shown in part (i) than if it is as shown in part (ii).

THE MEASUREMENT OF PRICE ELASTICITY

In Figure 5-1, we were able to say that the curve in part (i) showed a demand that was more responsive to price changes than the curve in part (ii) because two conditions were fulfilled. First, both curves were drawn on the same scale. Second, the initial equilibrium prices and quantities were the same in both parts of the figure. Let us see why these conditions matter.

First, by drawing both figures on the same scale, the curve that looked steeper actually did have the larger absolute slope. (The slope of a demand curve tells us the number of dollars by which price must change to cause a unit change in quantity demanded.) If we had drawn the two curves on different scales, we could have concluded nothing about the relative price changes needed to get a unit change

TABLE 5-1
Price Reductions and Corresponding Increases in Quantity Demanded

Commodity	Reduction in Price (cents)	Increase in Quantity Demanded (per month)
Cheese	40 per kilogram	7,500 kilograms
T-shirts	40 per shirt	5,000 shirts
CD players	40 per CD player	100 CD players

The data show, for each of the three products, the change in quantity demanded in response to the same absolute fall in price. The data are fairly uninformative about the responsiveness of demand to price because they do not tell us either the original price or the original quantity demanded.

in quantity demanded by comparing their appearances on the graph.[1]

Second, because we started from the same price-quantity equilibrium in both parts of the figure, we did not need to distinguish between percentage changes and absolute changes. If the initial prices and quantities are the same in both cases, the larger absolute change is also the larger percentage change. However, when we wish to deal with different initial price-quantity equilibria, we need to decide whether we are interested in absolute or percentage changes. To see which is relevant, assume that we have the information shown in Table 5-1. Should we conclude that the demand for compact-disc players is not as responsive to price changes as the demand for cheese? After all, price cuts of 40 cents cause quite a large increase in the quantity of cheese demanded but only a small increase in the quantity demanded of compact-disc players.

This discussion raises the issue of absolute versus percentage changes. First, a reduction in the price of 40 cents will be a large price cut for a low-priced product and an insignificant price cut for a high-

---

[1]It is misleading to infer anything about the responsiveness of quantity to a price change by inspecting the apparent steepness of a graph of a demand curve. By the same token, it can be misleading to infer anything about the relative responsiveness of two different demands by comparing the appearance of their two curves. The reason is that you can make any curve appear as steep or as flat as you wish by changing the scales on the graph. For example, a curve that looks steep when the horizontal scale is 1 cm = 100 units will look much flatter when it is drawn on a graph with the same vertical scale but a horizontal scale of 1 cm = 1 unit.

TABLE 5-2
Price and Quantity Information Underlying Data of Table 5-1

Product	Unit	Original Price ($)	New Price ($)	Average Price ($)	Original Quantity	New Quantity	Average Quantity
Cheese	kg	3.40	3.00	3.20	116,250	123,750	120,000
T-shirts	shirt	16.20	15.80	16.00	197,500	202,500	200,000
CD players	player	80.20	79.80	80.00	9,950	10,050	10,000

These data provide the appropriate context for the data given in Table 5-1. The table relates the 40-cent-per-unit price reduction of each product to the actual prices and quantities demanded.

priced product. The price reductions listed in Table 5-1 represent different proportions of the total prices. It is usually more revealing to know the percentage change in the prices of the various products. Second, by an analogous argument, knowing the quantity by which demand changes is not very revealing unless the initial level of demand is also known. An increase of 7,500 kilograms is quite a significant reaction to demand if the quantity formerly bought was 15,000 kg, but it is insignificant if the quantity formerly bought was 10 million kg.

Table 5-2 shows the original and new levels of price and quantity. Changes in price and quantity expressed as percentages of the *average* prices and quantities are shown in the first two columns of Table 5-3. The **price elasticity of demand,** the measure of responsiveness of quantity of a product demanded to a change in that product's price, is symbolized by the Greek letter eta, η. It is defined as follows:

$$\eta = \frac{\text{percentage change in quantity demanded}}{\text{percentage change in price}}$$

TABLE 5-3
Calculation of Demand Elasticities

Product	(1) Percentage Decrease in Price	(2) Percentage Increase in Quantity	(3) Elasticity of Demand (2) ÷ (1)
Cheese	12.5	6.25	0.5
T-shirts	2.5	2.50	1.0
CD players	0.5	1.00	2.0

Elasticity of demand is the percentage change in quantity demanded divided by the percentage change in price. The percentage changes are based on average prices and quantities shown in Table 5-2. For example, the 40-cent-per-kilogram decrease in the price of cheese is 12.5 percent of $3.20. A 40-cent change in the price of CD players is only 0.5 percent of the average price per CD player of $80.00.

This measure is called the **elasticity of demand,** or simply *demand elasticity.* Because the variable causing the change in quantity demanded is the product's own price, the term *own-price elasticity of demand* is also used.

The Use of Average Price
and Quantity in Computing Elasticity

The caption in Table 5-3 stresses that the demand elasticities are computed using changes in price and quantity measured in terms of the *average* values of each. Averages are used to avoid the ambiguity caused by the fact that when a price or quantity changes, the change is a different percentage of the original value than it is of the new value. For example, the 40-cent change in the price of cheese shown in Table 5-2 is a different percentage of the original price, $3.40, than it is of the new price, $3.00 (11.8 percent versus 13.3 percent).

Using average values for price and quantity also means that the measured elasticity of demand between any two points on the demand curve, call them A and B, is independent of whether the movement is from *A* to *B* or from *B* to *A*. In the example of cheese in Tables 5-2 and 5-3, the 40-cent change in the price of cheese is unambiguously 12.5 percent of the average price of $3.20, and that percentage applies to a price increase from $3.00 to $3.40 as well as to the decrease discussed in the text.

The implications of using average values for price and quantity for calculating elasticity can be seen as follows. Consider a change from an initial price of p_0 and quantity of q_0 to a new price of p_1 and quantity of q_1. The formula for elasticity is then

$$\eta = \frac{(q_1 - q_0)/q}{(p_1 - p_0)/p} \qquad [1]$$

where p and q are the average price and average quantity, respectively. (Thus $p = (p_1 + p_0)/2$ and $q = (q_1 + q_0)/2$.) These expressions can be substituted for p and q in Equation 1 and, after canceling the 2s, we get

$$\eta = \frac{(q_1 - q_0)/(q_1 + q_0)}{(p_1 - p_0)/(p_1 + p_0)} \quad [2]$$

which provides a very convenient formula for calculating demand elasticity. For example, for the case of cheese in Tables 5-2 and 5-3, we have

$$\eta = \frac{7,500/240,000}{.40/6.40} = \frac{0.03125}{0.0625} = 0.5$$

which is as in Table 5-3. Further discussion of the use of averages to calculate elasticity and of alternative methods is found in the appendix to this chapter. [7]

Interpreting Numerical Elasticities

Because demand curves have negative slopes, an increase in price is associated with a decrease in quantity demanded, and vice versa. Because the percentage changes in price and quantity have opposite signs, demand elasticity is a negative number. However, we will follow the usual practice of ignoring the negative sign and speak of the measure as a positive number, as we have done in the illustrative calculations in Table 5-3. Thus the more responsive the quantity demanded (for example, CD players relative to cheese), the greater the elasticity of demand and the higher the measure (e.g., 2.0 compared with 0.5).

The numerical value of demand elasticity can vary from zero to infinity. Elasticity is zero when quantity demanded does not respond at all to a price change. As long as the percentage change in quantity is less than the percentage change in price, the elasticity of demand has a value of less than one (economists sometimes say less than *unity*). When the two percentage changes are equal, elasticity is equal to one. When the percentage change in quantity exceeds the percentage change in price, the elasticity of demand is greater than one (greater than unity).

When the percentage change in quantity is less than the percentage change in price (elasticity less than 1), there is said to be **inelastic demand.** When the percentage change in quantity is greater than the percentage change in price (elasticity greater than 1), there is said to be **elastic demand.** This terminology is important, and you should become familiar with it. It is summarized in part A of Extension 5-1.

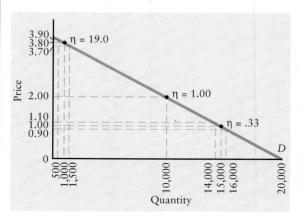

FIGURE 5-2
Elasticity Along a Straight-Line Demand Curve

Moving down a straight-line demand curve, elasticity falls continuously. On this straight-line demand curve, a reduction in price of $0.20 always leads to the same increase (1,000 units) in quantity demanded.

Near the upper end of the curve, where price is $3.80 and quantity demanded is 1,000 units, a reduction in price of $0.20 (from $3.90 to $3.70) is just slightly more than a 5 percent reduction, but the 1,000-unit increase in quantity demanded is a 100 percent increase. Here, elasticity (η) is 19.

Near the lower end, at a price of $1.00 and a quantity of 15,000 units, a price reduction of $0.20 (from $1.10 to $0.90) leads to the same 1,000-unit increase in quantity demanded. However, the $0.20 price reduction represents a 20 percent fall, whereas the 1,000-unit increase in quantity demanded represents only a 6.67 percent increase. Here, elasticity is 0.33.

A demand curve need not, and usually does not, have the same elasticity over every part of the curve. Figure 5-2 shows that a negatively sloped straight-line demand curve does not have a constant elasticity. A straight line has constant elasticity only when it is vertical or horizontal. Figure 5-3 illustrates these two cases, plus a third case of a particular *nonlinear* demand curve that also has a constant elasticity.

WHAT DETERMINES ELASTICITY OF DEMAND?

Table 5-4 shows some estimated price elasticities of demand. Evidently, elasticity varies considerably across different goods. The main determinant of demand elasticity is the availability of substitutes.

EXTENSION 5-1

THE TERMINOLOGY OF ELASTICITY

Term	Symbol	Numerical Measure of Elasticity	Verbal Description
A. Price elasticity of demand (supply)	η (η_S)		
Perfectly or completely inelastic		Zero	Quantity demanded (supplied) does not change as price changes.
Inelastic		Between zero and one	Quantity demanded (supplied) changes by a smaller percentage than does price.
Unit elastic		One	Quantity demanded (supplied) changes by exactly the same percentage as does price.
Elastic		Greater than one but less than infinity	Quantity demanded (supplied) changes by a larger percentage than does price
Perfectly, completely, or infinitely elastic		Infinity	Purchasers (sellers) are prepared to buy (sell) all they can at some price and none at all at an even higher (lower) price.
B. Income elasticity of demand	η_Y		
Inferior good		Negative	Quantity demanded decreases as income increases.
Normal good		Positive	Quantity demanded increases as income increases:
Income-inelastic		Less than one	Less than in proportion to income increase
Income-elastic		Greater than one	More than in proportion to income increase
C. Cross elasticity of demand	η_{XY}		
Substitute		Positive	Price increase of a substitute leads to an increase in quantity demanded of this good.
Complement		Negative	Price increase of a complement leads to a decrease in quantity demanded of this good.

Some products, such as margarine, cabbage, lamb, and Fords, have quite close substitutes—butter, other green vegetables, beef, and Chevrolets. A change in the prices of these products, *with the prices of the substitutes remaining constant,* can be expected to cause much substitution. A fall in price leads consumers to buy more of the product and less of the substitutes, and a rise in price leads consumers to buy less of the product and more of the substitutes. Products defined more broadly, such as *all* foods and *all* clothing, have few, if any, satisfactory substitutes. A rise in their prices can be ex-

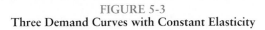

FIGURE 5-3
Three Demand Curves with Constant Elasticity

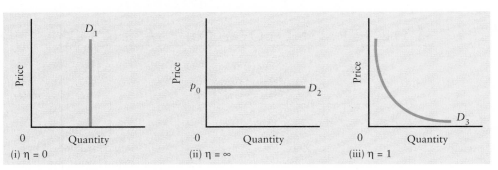

(i) $\eta = 0$ (ii) $\eta = \infty$ (iii) $\eta = 1$

Each of these demand curves has a constant elasticity. D_1 has zero elasticity: The quantity demanded does not change at all when price changes. D_2 has infinite elasticity at the price p_0: A small price increase from p_0 decreases quantity demanded from an indefinitely large amount to zero. D_3 has unit elasticity: A given percentage increase in price brings an equal percentage decrease in quantity demanded at all points on the curve; it is a rectangular hyperbola for which price times quantity is a constant.

TABLE 5-4
Estimated Price Elasticities of Demand[a]

(*selected products*)

Demand significantly inelastic (η less than 0.9)	
Potatoes	0.3
Sugar	0.3
Public transportation	0.4
All foods	0.4
Cigarettes	0.5
Gasoline	0.6
All clothing	0.6
Consumer durables	0.8
Demand approximately unit elastic (η between 0.9 and 1.1)	
Beef	
Beer	
Marijuana	
Demand significantly elastic (η more than 1.1)	
Furniture	1.2
Electricity	1.3
Lamb and mutton (U.K.)	1.5
Automobiles	2.1

[a]For the United States except where noted.

The wide range of price elasticities is illustrated by these selected measures. These elasticities, from various studies, are representative of literally hundreds of existing estimates. Some of the differences are discussed in the text.

pected to cause a smaller fall in quantities demanded than would be the case if close substitutes were available.

A product with close substitutes tends to have an elastic demand; a product with no close substitutes tends to have an inelastic demand.

Availability of substitutes—and hence measured demand elasticity—depends on both how the product is defined and the time period being considered. This is explored next.

Definition of the Product

For food taken as a whole, demand is inelastic over a large price range. It does not follow, however, that any one food, such as white bread or corned beef, is a necessity in the same sense. Individual foods can have quite elastic demands, and they frequently do.

Clothing provides a similar example. Clothing as a whole is less elastic than individual kinds of clothes. For example, when the price of wool sweaters rises, many households may buy cotton sweaters or down vests instead of buying an additional wool sweater. Thus, although purchases of wool sweaters fall, total purchases of clothing do not.

Any one of a group of related products will have a more elastic demand than the group taken as a whole.

Long-Run and Short-Run Elasticity of Demand

Because it takes time to develop satisfactory substitutes, a demand that is inelastic in the short run may prove to be elastic when enough time has passed. For example, at the time when cheap electric power was first brought to rural areas (long after it had come to cities), few farm households were wired for electricity. The initial measurements showed rural demand for electricity to be very inelastic; this is because many farmers did not rush to get hooked up to the electricity distribution system. Some commentators even argued that it was foolish to invest so much money in bringing cheap electricity to farmers because they would not buy it, even at low prices. Gradually, though, farm households became electrified, and as they purchased more and more electric appliances, measured elasticity increased considerably.

Petroleum provides a more recent example. In the early 1970s, the Organization of Petroleum Exporting Countries (OPEC) cartel shocked the world with its first sudden and large increase in the price of oil. At that time, the short-run demand for oil proved to be highly inelastic. Large price increases were met in the short run by very small reductions in quantity demanded. In this case, the short run lasted for several years. Gradually, however, the high price of petroleum products led to such adjustments as the development of smaller, more fuel-efficient cars, economizing on heating oil by installing more efficient insulation, and replacement of fuel oil in many industrial processes with such other power sources as coal and hydroelectricity. The long-run elasticity of demand, relating the change in price to the change in quantity demanded after all adjustments were made, turned out to have an elasticity of well over 1, although the long-run adjustments took as much as a decade to work out.

The degree of response to a price change, and thus the measured price elasticity of demand, will tend to be greater the longer the time span considered.

Because the elasticity of demand for a product changes over time as consumers adjust their habits and substitutes are developed, the demand curve also changes; hence a distinction can be made between short-run and long-run demand curves. Every demand curve shows the response of consumer demand to a change in price. For such products as cornflakes and pillowcases, the full response occurs quickly, and there is little reason to worry about longer-term effects. But other products are typically used in connection with highly durable appliances or machines. A change in the price of, say, electricity and gasoline may not have its major effect until the stock of appliances and machines using these products has been adjusted. This adjustment may take a long time to occur.

For products for which substitutes are developed over a period of time, it is helpful to identify two kinds of demand curves. A *short-run demand curve* shows the response of quantity demanded to a change in price for a given structure of the durable goods that use the product and for the existing sets of substitute products. A different short-run demand curve will exist for each such structure.

The *long-run demand curve* shows the response of quantity demanded to a change in price after enough time has passed to ensure that all adjustments to the changed price have occurred. The relationship between long-run and short-run demand curves is shown in Figure 5-4. The principal conclusion, already suggested in our discussion of elasticity, is this:

The long-run demand curve for a product will tend to have a substantially higher elasticity than the short-run demand curve for that product.

PRICE ELASTICITY AND CHANGES IN TOTAL EXPENDITURE

In the absence of sales taxes, the total amount spent by purchasers is also the total revenue received by the sellers, so we can use the terms *total expenditure* and *total revenue* interchangeably.[2] How does total expenditure react when the price of a product is changed? It turns out that the response of total expenditure depends on the price elasticity of demand.

To see the relationship between the price elasticity of demand and changes in total expenditure, we begin by noting that total expenditure is equal to price times quantity:

$$\text{Total Expenditure} = \text{price} \times \text{quantity}$$

Because price and quantity move in opposite directions along a demand curve, one falling when the other rises, the change in total expenditure appears

---

[2]Allowing for sales taxes complicates the analysis substantially but does not change the central results regarding the relationship between price, elasticity, and total expenditure. We examine sales taxes in detail in the final section of this chapter.

to be ambiguous. It is easily shown, however, that the direction of change in total expenditure depends on the percentage change in the two variables, price and quantity. If the percentage change in price exceeds the percentage change in quantity, the price change will dominate, and total expenditure will change in the same direction as the price changes; this is, of course, the case of elasticity less than unity. If the percentage change in the price is less than the percentage change in the quantity demanded (elasticity exceeds unity), the quantity change will dominate, and total expenditure will change in the same direction as quantity changes (that is, in the opposite direction to the change in price). If the two percentage changes are equal, total expenditure is unchanged—this is the case of unit elasticity.

The general relationship between demand elasticity, changes in price, and changes in total expenditure can be summarized as follows:

1. If demand is elastic, price and total expenditure are negatively related. A fall in price increases total expenditure, and a rise in price reduces it.

2. If demand is inelastic, price and total expenditure are positively related. A fall in price reduces total expenditure, and a rise in price increases it.

3. If elasticity of demand is unity, total expenditure is constant and therefore unrelated to price. A rise or a fall in price leaves total expenditure unaffected.

Table 5-5 and Figure 5-5 illustrate the relationship between elasticity of demand and total expenditure; both are based on the straight-line demand curve in Figure 5-2. Total expenditure at each of a number of points on the demand curve is calculated in Table 5-5, and the general relationship between total expenditure and quantity demanded is shown in Figure 5-5; there we see that expenditure reaches its maximum when elasticity is equal to 1. [8]

For example, when a bumper potato crop recently sent prices down 50 percent (a rightward shift in the supply curve), quantity sold increased by only 15 percent. Demand was clearly inelastic, and the result of the bumper crop was that potato farmers experienced a sharp *fall* in revenues.

Other examples are easily constructed from the information in Table 5-2. The reader can compute

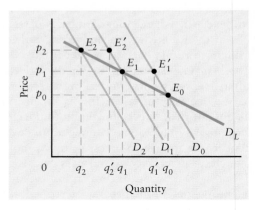

FIGURE 5-4
Short-Run and Long-Run Demand Curves

The long-run demand curve is more elastic than the short-run demand curve. D_L is a long-run demand curve. Suppose that consumers are fully adjusted to price p_0. Equilibrium is then at E_0, with quantity demanded q_0. Now suppose that price rises to p_1. In the short run, consumers will react along the short-run demand curve D_0 and adjust consumption to q_1'. Once time has permitted the full range of adjustments to price p_1, however, a new equilibrium E_1 will be reached with quantity q_1. At E_1 there is a new short-run demand curve D_1. A further rise to price p_2 would lead first to a short-run equilibrium at E_2' but eventually to a new long-run equilibrium at E_2. The long-run demand curve D_L is more elastic than any of the short-run curves.

TABLE 5-5
Changes in Total Expenditure for the Demand Curve of Figure 5-2

Price	Quantity	Expenditure
3.80	1,000	3,800
3.00	5,000	15,000
2.50	7,500	18,750
2.00	10,000	20,000
1.50	12,500	18,750
1.00	15,000	15,000

As price falls along a linear demand curve, total expenditure first rises and then falls. Along the range where price is greater than 2.00, elasticity is greater than one. As a result, the percentage fall in price is smaller than the resulting percentage increase in quantity, and total expenditure rises.

Along the range where price is less than 2.00, elasticity is less than one. As a result, the percentage fall in price is greater than the resulting percentage increase in quantity, and total expenditure falls.

FIGURE 5-5
Elasticity of Demand and Total Expenditure

The change in total expenditure on a product in response to a change in price depends on the elasticity of demand. The total expenditure for each possible quantity demanded is plotted for the demand curve in Figure 5-2. For quantities demanded that are less than 10,000, elasticity of demand is greater than one, and hence any increase in quantity demanded will be proportionately larger than the fall in price that caused it. In that range, total expenditure is increasing. For quantities greater than 10,000, elasticity of demand is less than one, and hence any increase in quantity demanded will be proportionately smaller than the fall in price that caused it. In that range, total expenditure is decreasing. The maximum of total expenditure occurs where the elasticity of demand equals one.

total expenditure for cheese, T-shirts, and CD players both before and after the 40-cent price reduction to confirm the relationship between price, elasticity, and total expenditure.

Other Demand Elasticities

The price of the product is not the only important variable determining demand for that product. Income and other prices also matter, and elasticity is a useful concept in measuring their effects.

INCOME ELASTICITY OF DEMAND

One of the most important determinants of demand is the income of the potential customers. When the Food and Agriculture Organization (FAO) of the United Nations wants to estimate the future demand for some crop, it needs to know by how much world income will grow and how much of that additional income will be spent on that particular foodstuff. As nations get richer, their consumption patterns typically change, with relatively more spent, for example, on meat and relatively less spent on staples such as rice and potatoes.

The responsiveness of demand to changes in income is termed the **income elasticity of demand** and is symbolized η_Y.

$$\eta_Y = \frac{\text{percentage change in quantity demanded}}{\text{percentage change in income}}$$

For most goods, increases in income lead to increases in demand—their income elasticity is positive. These are called **normal goods.** Goods for which demand decreases in response to a rise in income have negative income elasticities and are called **inferior goods.**

The income elasticity of normal goods may be greater than unity (elastic) or less than unity (inelastic), depending on whether the percentage change in the quantity demanded is greater or less than the percentage change in income that brought it about. It is also common to use the terms *income-elastic* and *income-inelastic* to refer to income elasticities of greater or less than unity. (See Extension 5-1 for a summary of the different elasticity concepts.)

The reaction of demand to changes in income is extremely important. We know that in most Western countries, economic growth caused the level of income to double every 20 to 30 years over a sustained period of at least a century. This rise in income has been shared to some extent by most citizens. As they found their incomes increasing, they increased their demands for most products, but the demands for some products, such as food and basic clothing, did not increase as much as the demands for other products. In developing countries, such as Ireland and Mexico, the demand for durable goods is increasing most rapidly as household incomes rise, while in North America and Western Europe, the demand for services has risen most rapidly. The uneven impact of the growth of income on the demands for different products has important economic effects, which are studied at several points in this book.

TABLE 5-6
Estimated Income Elasticities of Demand[a]

(selected products)

Inferior goods (η_Y less than zero)	
Whole milk	−0.5
Pig products	−0.2
Starchy roots	−0.2
Inelastic normal goods (η_Y between zero and one)	
Wine (France)	0.1
All food	0.2
Poultry	0.3
Cheese	0.4
Elastic normal goods (η_Y greater than one)	
Gasoline	1.1
Wine	1.4
Cream (U.K.)	1.7
Consumer durables	1.8
Poultry (Sri Lanka)	2.0
Restaurant meals (U.K.)	2.4

[a]For the United States except where noted.

Income elasticities vary widely across commodities and sometimes across countries. The basic source of food estimates by country is the Food and Agriculture Organization of the United Nations, but many individual studies have been made. Some of the differences are discussed in the text.

What Determines Income Elasticity of Demand?

The variations in income elasticities shown in Table 5-6 suggest that the more basic or staple a product, the lower its income elasticity. Food as a whole has an income elasticity of 0.2, consumer durables of 1.8. In Canada, starchy roots such as potatoes are inferior goods; their quantity demanded falls as income rises.

Does the distinction between luxuries and necessities help to explain differences in income elasticities? The table suggests that it does. The case of meals eaten away from home is one example. Such meals are almost always more expensive, calorie for calorie, than meals prepared at home. It would thus be expected that at lower ranges of income, restaurant meals would be regarded as an expensive luxury but that the demand for them would expand substantially as consumers became richer. This is in fact what happens.

Does this mean that the market demand for the foodstuffs that appear on restaurant menus will also have high income elasticities? Generally, the answer is no. When a household eats out rather than preparing meals at home, the main change is not in what is eaten but in who prepares it. The additional expenditure on "food" goes mainly to pay cooks and waiters and to yield a return on the restaurateur's capital. Thus, when a household increases its expenditure on restaurant food by 2.4 percent in response to a 1 percent rise in its income, most of the extra expenditure on "food" goes to workers in service industries; little, if any, finds its way into the pockets of farmers. This is a striking example of the general tendency for consumers to spend a rising proportion of their incomes on services and a lower proportion on foodstuffs as their incomes rise.

The more basic an item is in the consumption pattern of consumers, the lower is its income elasticity.

So far we have focused on differences in income elasticities among products. However, income elasticities for any one product also vary with the level of a consumer's income. When incomes are low, consumers may eat almost no green vegetables and consume lots of starchy foods such as bread and potatoes; when incomes are higher, they may eat cheap cuts of meat and more green vegetables along with their bread and potatoes; when incomes are higher still, they are likely to substitute frozen vegetables for canned and to eat a greater variety of foods.

What is true of individual consumers is also true of countries. Empirical studies show that for different countries at comparable stages of economic development, income elasticities are similar. However, the countries of the world are at various stages of economic development and so have widely different income elasticities for the same products. Notice in Table 5-6 the different income elasticity of poultry in the United States, where it is a standard item of consumption, and in Sri Lanka, where it is a luxury good.

Graphical Representation of Income Elasticity

Increases in income shift the demand curve to the right for a normal good and to the left for an inferior good. Figure 5-6 shows a different kind of graph, an *income-consumption curve*. The curve resembles an ordinary demand curve in one respect: It shows the relationship of quantity demanded to one other variable, *ceteris paribus*. The other variable is not price, however, but consumer income. (An in-

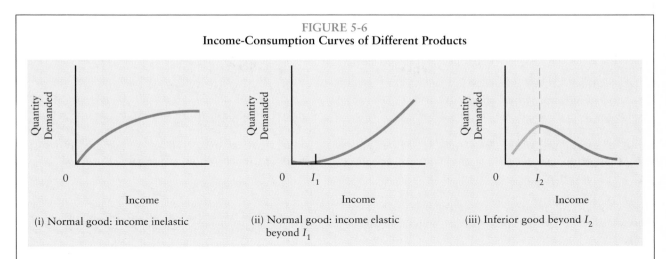

FIGURE 5-6
Income-Consumption Curves of Different Products

(i) Normal good: income inelastic

(ii) Normal good: income elastic beyond I_1

(iii) Inferior good beyond I_2

Different shapes of the curve relating quantity demanded to income correspond to different ranges of income elasticity. Normal goods have upward-sloping curves; inferior goods have downward-sloping curves. The good in part (i) is a typical normal good that is a necessity. The good in part (ii) is a luxury good that is income elastic beyond income I_1. The good in part (iii) is a necessity (normal) at low incomes but becomes an inferior good at incomes beyond I_2.

crease in the price of the product, holding income constant, would shift the curves shown in Figure 5-6 downward.)[3]

The figure shows three different patterns of income elasticity. Goods that consumers regard as necessities will generally have low income elasticities beyond some level of income. The obvious reason is that as incomes rise, it becomes possible for consumers to devote a smaller proportion of their incomes to meeting basic needs and a larger proportion to buying things that they have always wanted but could not afford. Some of the necessities may even become inferior goods. So-called luxury goods will not tend to be purchased at low levels of income but will have high income elasticities once incomes

rise enough to permit consumers to sample the better things of life available to them.

CROSS ELASTICITY OF DEMAND

The responsiveness of demand to changes in the price of another product is called the **cross elasticity of demand.** It is often denoted η_{XY} and defined as follows:[4]

$$\eta_{XY} = \frac{\text{percentage change in quantity demanded of good X}}{\text{percentage change in price of good Y}}$$

Cross elasticity can vary from minus infinity to plus infinity. Complementary products, such as cars and gasoline, have negative cross elasticities. A large rise in the price of gasoline will lead (as it did in Canada in the 1970s) to a decline in the demand for cars, as some people decide to do without a car and others decide not to buy an additional car. Substitute products, such as cars and public transport, have positive cross elasticities. A large rise in the price of cars (relative to public transport)

---

[3]In Figure 5-6, in contrast to the ordinary demand curve, quantity demanded is on the vertical axis. This follows the usual practice of putting the variable to be explained (called the dependent variable) on the vertical axis and the explanatory variable (called the independent variable) on the horizontal axis. It is the ordinary demand curve that has the axes "backward". The explanation is buried in the history of economics and dates to Alfred Marshall's *Principles of Economics* (1890), the classic that is one of the foundations of modern price theory. [9] For better or worse, Marshall's scheme is now used by everybody, although mathematicians never fail to wonder at this example of the odd ways of economists.

[4]The change in the price of good Y causes the *demand curve* for good X to shift. Holding the price of good X constant allows us to measure the shift in the demand curve in terms of the change in quantity demanded of good X at the given price of good X.

would lead to a rise in the demand for public transport as some people shift from cars to public transport. (See Extension 5-1 for a summary of elasticity terminology.)

Measures of cross elasticity sometimes prove helpful in defining whether producers of similar products are in competition. For example, glass bottles and tin cans have a high cross elasticity of demand. The producer of bottles is thus in competition with the producer of cans. If the bottle company raises its price, it will lose substantial sales to the can producer. Men's shoes and women's shoes have a low cross elasticity. A producer of men's shoes is not in close competition with a producer of women's shoes. If the former raises its price, it will not lose many sales to the latter. Knowledge of cross elasticities can be important in anticombines investigations in which the issue is whether a firm in one industry is or is not competing with firms in another industry. Whether waxed paper and plastic wrap or aluminum cable and copper cable are or are not substitutes may determine questions of monopoly under the law.

The positive or negative sign of cross elasticities tell us whether or not goods are substitutes.

ELASTICITY OF SUPPLY

The concept of elasticity can be applied to supply as well as to demand. **Elasticity of supply** measures the responsiveness of the quantity supplied to a change in the product's price. It is denoted η_S and defined as follows:

$$\eta_S = \frac{\text{percentage change in quantity supplied}}{\text{percentage change in price}}$$

This is often called *supply elasticity*. The supply curves considered in this chapter all have positive slopes: An increase in price causes an increase in quantity supplied. Such supply curves all have positive elasticities because price and quantity change in the same direction.

There are important special cases. If the supply curve is vertical—the quantity supplied does not change as price changes—then elasticity of supply is zero. A horizontal supply curve has an infinite elasticity of supply: A small drop in price would reduce the quantity that producers are willing to supply from an indefinitely large amount to zero. Between these two extremes, elasticity of supply varies with the shape of the supply curve.[5]

DETERMINANTS OF SUPPLY ELASTICITY

Supply elasticities are important for many problems in economics. Much of the treatment of demand elasticity carries over to supply elasticity and so we can cover the main points quickly.

Substitution and Production Costs

The ease of substitution can vary in production as well as in consumption. If the price of a product rises, how much more can be produced profitably? This depends in part on how easy it is for producers to shift from the production of other products to the one whose price has risen. If agricultural land and labour can be readily shifted from one crop to another, the supply of any one crop will be more elastic than if they cannot.

Supply elasticity depends to a great extent on how costs behave as output is varied, an issue that will be treated at length in Part 3 of this book. If the costs of producing a unit of output rise rapidly as output rises, then the stimulus to expand production in response to a rise in price will quickly be choked off by increases in costs. In this case, supply will tend to be rather inelastic. If, however, the costs of producing a unit of output rise only slowly as production increases, a rise in price that raises profits will elicit a large increase in quantity supplied before the rise in costs puts a halt to the expansion in output. In this case, supply will tend to be rather elastic.

Long-Run and Short-Run Elasticity of Supply

As with demand, length of time for response is important. It may be difficult to change quantities supplied in response to a price increase in a matter of weeks or months but easy to do so over a period of years. An obvious example is the planting cycle of crops. Also, new oil fields can be discovered, wells drilled, and pipelines built over a period of years but

---

[5]Steepness, which is related to absolute rather than percentage changes, is not always a reliable guide. For example, as is shown in the appendix to this chapter, *any* upward-sloping straight line passing through the origin has an elasticity equal to 1 over its entire range.

not in a few months. Thus the elasticity of oil supply is much greater over five years than over one year. We explore some of the implications of the distinction between short-run and long-run elasticity in the next section.

TWO EXAMPLES WHERE PRICE ELASTICITY MATTERS

We have examined the meaning of price elasticity and the determinants of it, and we have shown how shifts in demand or supply have different effects on equilibrium price and quantity depending on the degree of price elasticity. In this chapter's final section, we examine two important situations where the elasticity of demand and supply take the centre stage.

SHORT-RUN AND LONG-RUN MARKET ADJUSTMENT

We have discussed the distinction between short-run and long-run demand curves and hence between short-run and long-run demand elasticity. Similarly, we noted the distinction between short-run and long-run supply curves and hence between short-run and long-run supply elasticity. These distinctions have important implications for the market response to shifts in either demand or supply.

Shifts in Supply

In the short run, when demand is relatively inelastic, a shift in supply leads to a sharp change in the equilibrium price but only a small change in the equilibrium quantity. However, as we saw earlier in this chapter, demand will be more elastic in the long run than in the short run. This responsiveness of demand means that in the long run, the shift in supply results in a smaller change in the equilibrium price and a larger change in quantity.

Figure 5-7 shows the effects of an increase in supply. In the short run, the supply increase leads to a movement down the relatively inelastic short-run demand curve; it thus causes a large fall in price but only a small increase in quantity. In the long run, demand is more elastic, so long-run equilibrium has

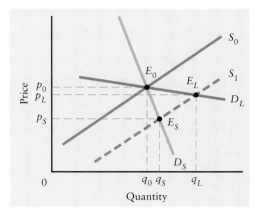

FIGURE 5-7
Short-Run and Long-Run Equilibrium Following an Increase in Supply

The magnitude of the changes in the equilibrium price and quantity following a shift in supply depends on the time allowed for demand to adjust. The change in the price is greater and the change in quantity is less in the short run than in the long run. The initial equilibrium is at E_0, with price p_0 and quantity q_0. Supply then increases such that the supply curve shifts from S_0 to S_1.

On impact, the relevant demand curve is the short-run curve D_S, and the new equilibrium immediately following the supply shock is E_S. Price falls sharply to p_S, and quantity rises only to q_S. In the long run, the demand curve is the more elastic one given by D_L, and equilibrium is at E_L. The long-run equilibrium price is p_L (greater than p_S), and quantity is q_L (greater than q_S).

price and quantity above those that prevailed in short-run equilibrium.

This pattern is often referred to as *overshooting* of the price. The overshooting of price that is evident in the figure is the way in which markets clear when demand is less elastic in the short run than in the long run. Note also that there is *undershooting* of quantity—that is, the equilibrium quantity rises by less in the short run than in the long run.

Shifts in Demand

In the short run, when supply is relatively inelastic, a shift in demand leads to a sharp change in the equilibrium price but only a small change in the equilibrium quantity exchanged. However, in the

FIGURE 5-8
Short-Run and Long-Run Equilibrium
Following an Increase in Demand

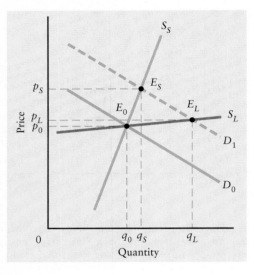

The magnitude of the changes in the equilibrium price and quantity following a shift in demand depends on the time frame of the analysis. In the short run, the change in the price is greater and the change in quantity is less than in the long run. The initial equilibrium is at E_0, with price p_0 and quantity q_0. Demand then increases such that the demand curve shifts from D_0 to D_1.

On impact, the relevant supply curve is the short-run curve S_S, so that the new equilibrium immediately following the demand shock is at E_S. Price rises sharply to p_S, and quantity rises only to q_S. In the long run, the supply curve is the more elastic one given by S_L. The long-run equilibrium is at E_L; price is p_L (less than p_S), and quantity is q_L (greater than q_S).

long run, when supply is more elastic than in the short run, the shift in demand leads to a smaller change in the equilibrium price and a larger change in quantity.

Figure 5-8 illustrates the effects of an increase in demand. The short-run overshooting of price, and the undershooting of quantity, that is evident in the figure is analogous to that shown in Figure 5-7 in response to a shift in supply. Here it arises following a shift in demand and is the market-clearing response when supply is less elastic in the short run than in the long run.

THE INCIDENCE OF SALES TAXES

The federal and provincial governments levy sales taxes on many goods. The Goods and Services Tax (GST) introduced in 1991 is a tax that applies to most goods and services at a uniform rate across the country. Special taxes (called **excise taxes**) also apply to goods such as cigarettes, alcohol, and gasoline. All such *commodity taxes* work in the following way. At the point of sale of the product, the sellers collect the tax on behalf of the government and then periodically remit the tax collections.

When the sellers write their cheques to the government, these firms feel—with some justification—that they are the ones paying the tax. Consumers, however, argue—again, with some justification—that *they* are the ones who are shouldering the burden of the tax because the tax causes the price of the product to rise.

The question of who *bears the burden* of a tax is called the question of **tax incidence**. A straightforward application of demand-and-supply analysis will show that tax incidence has nothing to do with whether the government collects the tax directly from consumers or from firms.

The burden of a sales tax is distributed between consumers and sellers in a manner that depends on the relative elasticities of supply and demand.

Consider the market for gasoline, as illustrated in Figure 5-9. To simplify the problem, we analyze the case where there is initially no sales tax. The equilibrium without taxes is illustrated by the solid supply and demand curves. What happens when a sales tax of t per litre of gasoline is introduced? A sales tax means that the price paid by the consumer, called the *consumer price,* and the price received by the seller, called the *seller price,* must now differ by the amount of the tax, t.

In terms of the figure, the effect of the sales tax can be analyzed by considering a new supply curve S' that is above the original supply curve S by the amount of the tax per litre of gasoline, t. To understand this new curve, consider the firm's situation at the original equilibrium quantity q_0. To supply that quantity, producers must receive p_0 per litre of gas sold. However, for producers to receive p_0 when there is a sales tax on gasoline, the consumer must

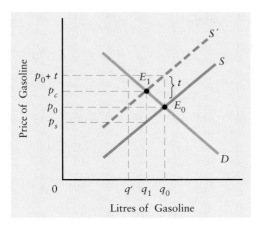

FIGURE 5-9
The Incidence of a Sales Tax

The burden of a sales tax is shared by consumers and producers. The original supply and demand curves for gasoline are given by the solid lines S and D; equilibrium is at E_0 with price p_0 and quantity q_0. When a sales tax of t per litre is imposed, the supply curve shifts up to the dashed line S', which lies above the original supply curve by the amount of the tax t.

nal demand curve D with the tax-shifted supply curve S'. At this new equilibrium, E_1, the consumer price rises to p_c (greater than p_0), the seller price falls to p_s (less than p_0), and the equilibrium quantity falls to q_1.

Note that the quantity demanded *at the consumer price* is equal to the quantity supplied *at the seller price*, which is required for equilibrium. As shown in the figure, compared to the original equilibrium, the consumer price is higher and the seller price is lower, although in each case the change in price is less than the full extent of the sales tax.

After the imposition of a sales tax, the difference between the consumer and seller prices is equal to the tax, and hence the sum of the increase in the consumer price and the decrease in the seller price is equal to the tax. In the new equilibrium, the quantity exchanged is less than that exchanged prior to the imposition of the tax.

The role of the relative elasticities of supply and demand in determining the incidence of the sales tax is illustrated in Figure 5-10. In part (i), demand is inelastic relative to supply; as a result, the fall in quantity is quite small, whereas the price paid by consumers rises by almost the full extent of the tax. Because neither the price received by sellers nor the quantity sold changes very much, sellers bear little of the burden of the tax. In part (ii), supply is inelastic relative to demand; in this case, consumers continue to purchase almost the same quantity with little change in the price, and hence they bear little of the burden of the tax, which falls mostly on suppliers. Notice in Figure 5-10 that the size of the upward shift in supply is the same in the two cases, indicating the same tax increase in both cases.

Now we can examine who really pays for cigarette and gasoline tax increases. The demand for cigarettes is inelastic both overall and relative to supply, suggesting that a cigarette-tax increase would be borne more by consumers than by producers. Thus, the large *reductions* in cigarette taxes which took place in the summer of 1994 in Ontario and Quebec benefited consumers more than producers. The demand for gasoline is also inelastic, but much more so in the short run than in the long run. In the long run, drivers can change

pay a total price of $p_0 + t$. This is true whether the consumer "pays the tax directly" by giving p_0 to the firm and t to the government or whether the consumer pays the total $p_0 + t$ to the firm and the firm then remits the tax t to the government. Either way, the total amount that consumers must pay to obtain a given quantity from firms has increased by the amount of the tax t.

This upward shift in the supply curve for gasoline is depicted in Figure 5-9 as the dashed curve, S'. This shift in the supply curve, caused by the tax, will generally also cause a movement *along* the demand curve, reducing the equilibrium quantity exchanged.

Consider the situation at the consumer price of $p_0 + t$. Firms will still be willing to sell the original quantity, but households will demand less because the price has risen; there is excess supply and hence pressure for the consumer price to fall.

The new equilibrium after the imposition of the sales tax occurs at the intersection of the origi-

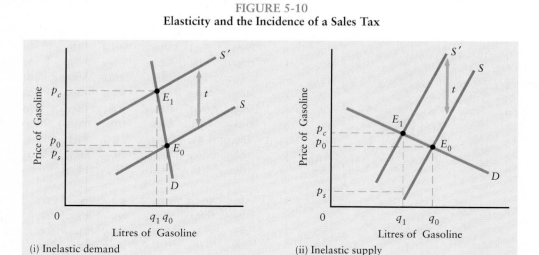

FIGURE 5-10
Elasticity and the Incidence of a Sales Tax

(i) Inelastic demand

(ii) Inelastic supply

The distribution of the burden of a sales tax between consumers and producers depends on the relative elasticities of supply and demand. In both parts of the figure, the initial supply and demand curves are given by S and D; the initial equilibrium is at E_0 with equilibrium price p_0 and quantity q_0. A sales tax of t per litre is imposed, causing the supply curve to shift up by the amount of the tax to S'. The new equilibrium is at E_1. The consumer price rises to p_c, the seller price falls to p_s, and the quantity falls to q_1. Sellers bear little of the burden of the tax in the first case (and consumers bear a lot), whereas consumers bear little of the burden in the second case (and sellers bear a lot).

their driving routines and improve the efficiency of their vehicles. In the short run, changes of both types are more costly. The supply of gasoline, given world trade in petroleum and petroleum products, is elastic relative to demand, implying that most of the tax falls on consumers.

SUMMARY

A. PRICE ELASTICITY OF DEMAND

- *Price elasticity of demand,* also called *elasticity of demand,* is a measure of the extent to which the quantity demanded of a product responds to a change in its price. Represented by the symbol η, it is defined as

$$\eta = \frac{\text{percentage change in quantity demanded}}{\text{percentage change in price}}$$

The percentage changes are usually calculated as the change divided by the *average* value. Elasticity is defined to be a positive number, and it can vary from zero to infinity.

- When the numerical measure of elasticity is less than unity, demand is *inelastic.* This means that the percentage change in quantity demanded is less than the percentage change in price that brought it about. When the numerical measure exceeds unity, demand is *elastic.* This means that the percentage change in quantity demanded is greater than the percentage change in price that brought it about.

- The main determinant of the price elasticity of demand is the availability of substitutes for the product. Any one of a group of close substitutes will have a more elastic demand than the group as a whole. Elasticity of demand tends to be greater the longer the time over which adjustment occurs. Items that have few substitutes in the short run may develop many substitutes when consumers and producers have time to adapt.

- Elasticity and total expenditure (or revenue) are related in the following way: If elasticity is less than unity, total expenditure is positively related with price; if elasticity is greater than unity, total expenditure is negatively related with price; and if elasticity is unity, total revenue does not change as price changes.

B. OTHER DEMAND ELASTICITIES

- *Income elasticity of demand* is a measure of the extent to which the quantity demanded of some product changes as income changes. Represented by the symbol η_Y, it is defined as

$$\eta_Y = \frac{\text{percentage change in quantity demanded}}{\text{percentage change in income}}$$

The income elasticity of demand for a product will usually change as income varies. For example, a product that has a high income elasticity at a low income (because increases in income bring it within reach of the typical household) may have a low or negative income elasticity at higher incomes (because with further rises in incomes, it is gradually replaced by a superior substitute).

- *Cross elasticity of demand* is a measure of the extent to which the quantity demanded of one product changes when the price of a different product changes. Represented by the symbol η_{XY}, it is defined as

$$\eta_{XY} = \frac{\text{percentage change in quantity demanded of good X}}{\text{percentage change in price of good Y}}$$

It is used to define products that are substitutes for one another (positive cross elasticity) and products that complement one another (negative cross elasticity).

C. ELASTICITY OF SUPPLY

- *Elasticity of supply* is an important concept in economics. It measures the extent to which the quantity supplied of some product changes when the price of that product changes. Represented by the symbol η_S, it is defined as

$$\eta_S = \frac{\text{percentage change in quantity supplied}}{\text{percentage change in price}}$$

It is the analogue on the supply side to the elasticity of demand. Supply tends to be more elastic in the long run than in the short run.

D. TWO EXAMPLES WHERE PRICE ELASTICITY MATTERS

- Since price elasticities are larger in the long run than in the short run, a shift in supply (or demand) will lead to a larger change in price and a smaller change in quantity in the short run than in the long run.
- The distribution of the burden of a sales tax between consumers and producers is independent of who actually remits the tax to the government. Rather, it depends on the relative elasticities of the supply and the demand for the product.

KEY CONCEPTS

Price elasticity of demand
Inelastic and perfectly inelastic demand
Elastic and infinitely elastic demand
Relationship between demand elasticity and total expenditure
Income elasticity of demand

Income-elastic and income-inelastic demands
Normal goods and inferior goods
Cross elasticity of demand
Substitutes and complements
Elasticity of supply

Short-run and long-run responses to shifts in demand and supply
Consumer price and seller price
Tax incidence

DISCUSSION QUESTIONS

1. From the following quotations, what, if anything, can you conclude about elasticity of demand?

   a. "Good weather resulted in record wheat harvests and sent wheat prices tumbling. The result has been disastrous for many wheat farmers."
   b. "Ridership always went up when bus fares came down, but the increased patronage never was enough to prevent a decrease in overall revenue."
   c. "As the price of compact-disc players fell, producers found their revenues soaring."
   d. "Coffee to me is an essential good—I've just gotta have it no matter what the price."
   e. "The soaring price of condominiums does little to curb the strong demand in Vancouver."

2. A provincial MLA proposes legislation that would privatize all primary and secondary education. The MLA argues that the province should, in return, provide each family a subsidy of $4,000 per child—the current per student expenditure. As a result, he argues, families will actually consume more education. Is this possible? What would be required for this argument to be correct?

3. What would you predict about the relative price elasticity of demand of (a) food, (b) vegetables, (c) artichokes, and (d) artichokes sold at the local supermarket? What would you predict about their relative income elasticities?

4. "Avocados have a limited market not greatly affected by price until the price falls to less than 80 cents per kilogram wholesale. Then they are much demanded by manufacturers of dog food." Interpret this statement in terms of price elasticity.

5. Home computers were a leader in sales appeal through much of the 1980s. But per capita sales are much lower in Mexico than in Canada, and lower in Newfoundland than in Alberta. Manufacturers are puzzled by the big differences. Can you offer an explanation in terms of elasticity?

6. What elasticity measure or measures would be useful in answering the following questions?

   a. Will cheaper transport into the central city help to keep downtown shopping centres profitable?
   b. Will raising the bulk postage rate increase or decrease the revenues for Canada Post?
   c. Are producers of toothpaste and mouthwash in competition with each other?
   d. What effect will rising gasoline prices have on the sale of cars that use propane gas?

7. Interpret the following statements in terms of the relevant elasticity concept.

   a. "As fuel for tractors has become more expensive, many farmers have shifted from plowing their fields to no-till farming. No-till acreage increased dramatically in the past 20 years."
   b. "Fertilizer makers brace for dismal year as fertilizer prices soar."
   c. "When farmers are hurting, small towns feel the pain."
   d. "The development of the Hibernia oil field may bring temporary prosperity to Newfoundland merchants."

8. Suggest products that you think might have the following patterns of elasticity of demand.

   a. High income elasticity, high price elasticity
   b. High income elasticity, low price elasticity
   c. Low income elasticity, low price elasticity
   d. Low income elasticity, high price elasticity

9. Assume a stamp collector buys the only two copies of a stamp at an auction. After the purchase, the collector goes to the front of the room and burns one of the stamps in front of the shocked audience. What must the collector believe for this to be a rational, wealth-maximizing action?

10. When the New York City Opera faced a growing deficit, it cut its ticket prices by 20 percent, hoping to attract more customers. At the same time, the New York Transit Authority raised subway fares to reduce its growing deficit. Was one of these two opposite approaches to reducing a deficit necessarily wrong?

11. When an MLA proposed an increase in the provincial sales-tax rate, one critic responded that this

would hurt both producers and consumers. Discuss the sense in which this is true. From the data in Table 5-4, how would you expect the distribution of the costs between the two groups to vary between, say, the market for automobiles and the market for clothing? Would you expect the distribution in each market to be different in the short run than in the long run?

APPENDIX TO CHAPTER 5

A Formal Analysis of Elasticity

The definition of elasticity used in the text may be written symbolically in the following form:[1]

$$\eta = \frac{\Delta q}{\text{average } q} \div \frac{\Delta p}{\text{average } p}$$

where the averages are over the range, or arc, of the demand curve being considered. Rearranging terms, we can write

$$\eta = \frac{\Delta q}{\Delta p} \times \frac{\text{average } p}{\text{average } q}.$$

This is called **arc elasticity,** and it measures the average responsiveness of quantity to price over an interval of the demand curve.

Most theoretical treatments use a different but related concept called **point elasticity.** This is the measure of responsiveness of quantity to price *at a particular point* on the demand curve. The precise definition of point elasticity uses the concept of a derivative, which is drawn from differential calculus.

In this appendix, we first study arc elasticity, which may be regarded as an approximation of point elasticity. Then we study point elasticity.

Before proceeding, we should note one further change. In the text of Chapter 5, we reported our price elasticities as positive values and thus implicitly multiplied all our calculations by −1. In theoretical work, it is more convenient to retain the concept's

---
[1]The following notation is used throughout this appendix.
$\eta \equiv$ elasticity of demand
$\eta_S \equiv$ elasticity of supply
$q \equiv$ initial quantity
$\Delta q \equiv$ change in quantity
$p \equiv$ initial price
$\Delta p \equiv$ change in price

natural sign. Hence normal demand elasticities will have negative signs, and statements about "more" or "less" elasticity must be understood to refer to the absolute, not the algebraic, value of demand elasticity.

ARC ELASTICITY AS AN APPROXIMATION OF POINT ELASTICITY

Point elasticity measures elasticity at some price-quantity point. In the approximate definition, however, the responsiveness is measured over a small range starting from that point. For example, in Figure 5A-1, the elasticity at point 1 can be measured by the responsiveness of quantity demanded to a change in price that

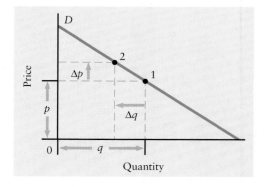

FIGURE 5A-1
A Straight-Line Demand Curve

Because p/q varies with $\Delta q/\Delta p$ constant, the elasticity varies along this demand curve; it is high at the left and low at the right.

takes price and quantity from point 1 to point 2. The algebraic formula for this elasticity concept is

$$\eta = \frac{\Delta q}{\Delta p} \times \frac{p}{q} \qquad [A1]$$

This is similar to the definition of arc elasticity above except that because elasticity is being measured at a point, p and q corresponding to that point are used (rather than the average p and q over an arc of the curve).

Equation A1 splits elasticity into two parts: $\Delta q/\Delta p$ (the ratio of the change in quantity to the change in price), which is related to the *slope* of the demand curve, and p/q, which is related to the *point* on the curve at which the measurement is made.

Figure 5A-1 shows a straight-line demand curve. To measure the elasticity at point 1, take p and q at that point and then consider a price change, say, to point 2, and measure Δp and Δq as indicated. The slope of the straight line joining points 1 and 2 is $\Delta p/\Delta q$. Therefore, the first term in the elasticity formula is the *reciprocal* of the slope of the straight line joining the two price-quantity positions under consideration.

Although point elasticity of demand refers to a price-quantity point on the demand curve, the first term in Equation A1 still refers to changes over an arc of the curve. This is the part of the formula that involves approximation, and, as we shall see, it has some unsatisfactory results. Nonetheless, some interesting theorems can be derived by using this formula as long as we confine ourselves to straight-line demand and supply curves.

1. *The elasticity of a downward-sloping straight-line demand curve varies from zero at the quantity axis to infinity at the price axis.* First notice that a straight line has a constant slope, so the ratio $\Delta p/\Delta q$ is the same everywhere on the line. Therefore, its reciprocal, $\Delta q/\Delta p$, must also be constant. The changes in η can now be inferred by inspecting the ratio p/q. Where the line cuts the quantity axis, price is zero, so the ratio p/q is zero; thus $\eta = 0$. Moving up the line, p rises and q falls, so the ratio p/q rises; thus elasticity rises. Approaching the top of the line, q approaches zero, so the ratio becomes very large. Thus elasticity increases without limit as the price axis is approached.

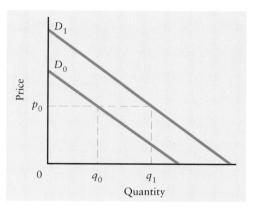

FIGURE 5A-2
Two Parallel Straight-Line Demand Curves

For any given price, the quantities are different on these two parallel curves; thus the elasticities are different, being higher on D_0 than on D_1.

2. *Where there are two straight-line demand curves of the same slope, the one farther from the origin is less elastic at each price than the one closer to the origin.* Figure 5A-2 shows two parallel straight-line demand curves. Compare the elasticities of the two curves at any price, say, p_0. Because the curves are parallel, the ratio $\Delta q/\Delta p$ is the same on both curves. Because elasticities at the same price are being compared on both curves, p is the same, and the only factor left to vary is q. On the curve farther from the origin, quantity is larger (i.e., $q_1 > q_0$) and hence p_0/q_1 is smaller than p_0/q_0; thus η is smaller. It follows that parallel shifts of a straight-line demand curve lower elasticity (at each price) when the line shifts outward and raise elasticity when the line shifts inward.

3. *The elasticities of two intersecting straight-line demand curves can be compared at the point of intersection merely by comparing slopes, the steeper curve being the less elastic.* In Figure 5A-3, there are two intersecting curves. At the point of intersection, p and q are common to both curves, and hence the ratio p/q is the same. Therefore, η varies only with $\Delta q/\Delta p$. On the steeper curve, $\Delta q/\Delta p$ is smaller than on the flatter curve, so elasticity is lower.

4. *If the slope of a straight-line demand curve changes while the price intercept remains con-*

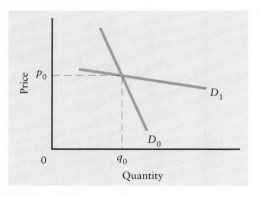

FIGURE 5A-3
Two Intersecting Straight-Line Demand Curves

Elasticities are different at the point of intersection of these demand curves because the slopes are different, being higher on D_0 than on D_1. Therefore, D_1 is more elastic than D_0 at p_0.

stant, elasticity at any given price is unchanged. This is an interesting case for at least two reasons. First, when more customers having similar tastes to those already in the market enter the market, the demand curve pivots outward in this way. Second, when more firms enter a market that is

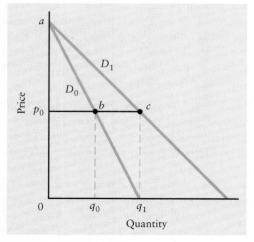

FIGURE 5A-4
Two Straight-Line Demand Curves
from the Same Price Intercept

The elasticity is the same on D_0 and D_1 at any given price. This situation occurs because the steeper slope of D_0 is exactly offset by the smaller quantity demanded at any price.

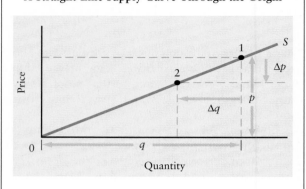

FIGURE 5A-5
A Straight-Line Supply Curve Through the Origin

At every point on the curve, p/q equals $\Delta p/\Delta q$; hence elasticity equals unity at every point.

shared proportionally among all firms, each firm's demand curve shifts inward in this way.

Consider in Figure 5A-4 the elasticities at point b on demand curve D_0 and at point c on demand curve D_1. We shall focus on the two triangles abp_0 on D_0 and acp_0 on D_1 formed by the two straight-line demand curves emanating from point a and by the price p_0. The price p_0 is the line segment $0p_0$. The quantities q_0 and q_1 are the line segments p_0b and p_0c, respectively. The slope of D_0 is $\Delta p/\Delta q = ap_0/p_0b$, and the slope of D_1 is $\Delta p/\Delta q = ap_0/p_0c$. From Equation A1 we can represent the elasticities of D_0 and D_1 at the points b and c, respectively, as

η at point $b = (p_0b/ap_0) \times (0p_0/p_0b) = (0p_0/ap_0)$

η at point $c = (p_0c/ap_0) \times (0p_0/p_0c) = (0p_0/ap_0)$

The two values of the elasticity are the same. The reason is that the distance corresponding to the quantity demanded at p_0 appears in both the numerator and the denominator and thus cancels out. Put differently, if the straight-line demand curve D_0 is twice as steep as D_1, it has half the quantity demanded at p_0. Therefore, in Equation A1 the steeper slope (a smaller Δq for the same Δp) is exactly offset by the smaller quantity demanded (a smaller q for the same p).

5. *Any straight-line supply curve through the origin has an elasticity of one.* Such a supply curve is shown in Figure 5A-5. Consider the two triangles with the sides p, q, and the S curve and

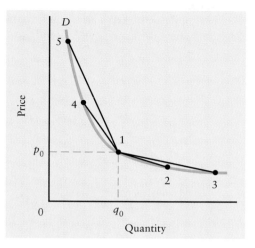

FIGURE 5A-6
**Point Elasticity of Demand Measured
by the Approximate Formula**

When the approximation of $\eta = (\Delta q / \Delta p) \times (p/q)$ is used, many elasticities are measured from point 1 because the slope of the chord between point 1 and every other point on the curve varies.

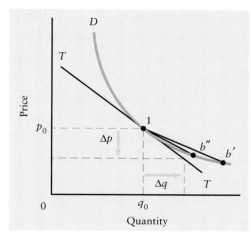

FIGURE 5A-7
**Point Elasticity of Demand Measured
by the Exact Formula**

When the exact definition $\eta = (dq/dp) \times (p/q)$ is used, only one elasticity is measured from point 1 because there is only one tangent to the demand curve at that point.

Δp, Δq, and the S curve. Clearly, these are similar triangles. Therefore, the ratios of their sides are equal; that is,

$$\frac{p}{q} = \frac{\Delta p}{\Delta q} \qquad [A2]$$

Elasticity of supply is defined as

$$\eta_S = \frac{\Delta q}{\Delta p} \times \frac{p}{q}$$

which, by substitution from Equation A2, gives

$$\eta_S = \frac{q}{p} \times \frac{p}{q} = 1$$

6. *The demand elasticity measured from any point (p,q), according to Equation A1, depends on the direction and magnitude of the change in price and quantity.* Except for a straight line (for which the slope does not change), the ratio $\Delta q/\Delta p$ will not be the same over different ranges of a curve. Figure 5A-6 shows a demand curve that is not a straight line. To measure the elasticity from point 1, the ratio $\Delta q/\Delta p$—and thus η—will vary according to the size and the direction of the price change. This result is very inconvenient

and is avoided by using the concept of point elasticity in its exact form.

THE PRECISE DEFINITION OF POINT ELASTICITY

To measure the point elasticity *exactly*, it is necessary to know the reaction of quantity to a change in price *at that point*, not over a range of the curve.

The reaction of quantity to price change at a point is called dq/dp, and this is defined as the reciprocal of the slope of the straight line tangent to the demand curve at the point in question. In Figure 5A-7, the elasticity of demand at point 1 is the ratio p/q (as it has been in all previous measures), now multiplied by the ratio of $\Delta q/\Delta p$ measured along the straight line T, tangent to the curve at point 1, that is, by dq/dp. Thus the exact definition of point elasticity is

$$\eta = \frac{dq}{dp} \times \frac{p}{q} \qquad [A3]$$

The ratio dq/dp, as defined, is in fact the differential calculus concept of the *derivative* of quantity with respect to price.

This definition of point elasticity is the one normally used in economic theory. Equation A1 is mathematically only an approximation of this expression. In Figure 5A-7, the measure of arc elasticity will come closer to the measure of point elasticity as a smaller price change is used to calculate the arc elasticity. The $\Delta q/\Delta p$ in Equation A1 is the reciprocal of the slope of the chord connecting the two points being compared. As the chord becomes shorter, its slope gets closer to that of the tangent T. (Compare the chords connecting point 1 to b' and b'' in Figure 5A-7.) Thus the error in using Equation A1 as an approximation of Equation A3 tends to diminish as the size of Δp diminishes.

DEMAND AND SUPPLY IN ACTION

Now that you have mastered the theory of how prices are determined by demand and supply, you have a very powerful tool at your command. However, a full understanding of any theory comes only with practice. This chapter is designed to give you that practice by examining some cases drawn from real-world experience. These include the effects of government-administered prices (a special case of which is rent controls), the pattern of a country's imports and exports, an examination of who actually "pays" for tariffs, and the effectiveness of agricultural income-support policies. Although we hope that these illustrations are interesting in themselves, the most important reason for studying them is to practice using the theory so that you can use it to understand the many other cases where the theory applies.

GOVERNMENT-CONTROLLED PRICES

In a number of important cases, governments fix the price at which a product must be bought and sold in the domestic market. Here we examine the consequences of such policies. Later, we look at rent controls and agricultural price supports, which are examples of government-controlled prices.

The equilibrium price in a free market occurs at the price at which quantity demanded equals quantity supplied. Government *price controls* are policies that attempt to hold the price at some disequilibrium value that could not be maintained in the absence of the government's intervention. Some controls hold the market price below its equilibrium value; this creates a shortage, with quantity demanded exceeding quantity supplied at the controlled price. Other controls hold price above the equilibrium price; this creates a surplus, with quantity supplied exceeding quantity demanded at the controlled price.

DISEQUILIBRIUM PRICES

As we discussed in Chapter 4, market price generally changes whenever quantity supplied does not equal quantity demanded. Price then moves toward its equilibrium value, at which point there are neither unsatisfied suppliers nor unsatisfied demanders.

When controls hold price at some disequilibrium value, what determines the quantity *actually traded*

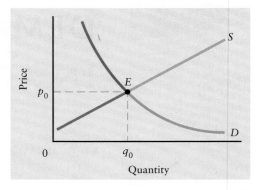

FIGURE 6-1
The Determination of Quantity Exchanged in Disequilibrium

In disequilibrium, quantity exchanged is determined by the lesser of quantity demanded and quantity supplied. At p_0, the market is in equilibrium, with quantity demanded equal to quantity supplied. For prices below p_0, the quantity exchanged will be determined by the supply curve. For prices above p_0, the quantity exchanged will be determined by the demand curve. Thus the darker portions of the S and D curves show the actual quantities exchanged at different prices.

on the market? The key to the answer is the fact that any voluntary market transaction requires both a willing buyer and a willing seller. This implies that if quantity demanded is less than quantity supplied, demand will determine the amount actually exchanged, while the rest of the quantity supplied will remain in the hands of the unsuccessful sellers. Conversely, if quantity demanded exceeds quantity supplied, supply will determine the amount actually exchanged, while the rest of the quantity demanded will represent desired purchases of unsuccessful buyers. This argument is spelled out in more detail in Figure 6-1, which establishes the following general conclusion:

At any disequilibrium price, quantity exchanged is determined by the *lesser* of quantity demanded or quantity supplied.

PRICE FLOORS

Governments sometimes establish a *price floor*, which is the minimum permissible price that can be charged for a particular good or service. A price floor that is set at or below the equilibrium price has no effect because equilibrium remains attainable. If,

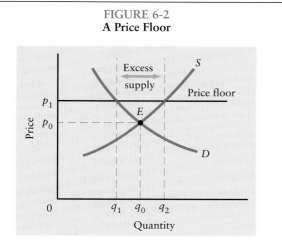

FIGURE 6-2
A Price Floor

If a price floor is above the equilibrium price, quantity supplied will exceed quantity demanded. The free-market equilibrium is at E, with price p_0 and quantity q_0. The government now establishes an effective price floor at p_1. Quantity supplied exceeds quantity demanded by $q_1 q_2$.

however, the price floor is set above the equilibrium, it will raise the price, in which case it is said to be *binding* or *effective*.

Price floors may be established by rules that make it illegal to sell the product below the prescribed price, as in the case of the minimum wage (examined in Chapter 16). Further, the government may establish a price floor by announcing that it will guarantee a certain price by buying any excess supply of the product that emerges at that price. Such guarantees are a feature of many agricultural support policies (examined later in this chapter).

The effects of binding price floors are illustrated in Figure 6-2, which establishes the following key result:

Effective price floors lead to excess supply. Either an unsold surplus will exist, or someone must enter the market and buy the excess supply.

The consequences of excess supply will, of course, differ from product to product. If the product is labour, subject to a minimum wage, excess supply translates into people without jobs. If the product is wheat, and more is produced than can be sold to consumers, the surplus wheat will accumulate in grain elevators or government warehouses. These consequences may or may not be worthwhile in

terms of the other goals achieved. Whether they are worthwhile or not, these consequences are inevitable whenever a price floor is set above the market-clearing equilibrium price.

Why might the government wish to incur these consequences? One reason is that the people who succeed in selling their products at the price floor are better off than if they had to accept the lower equilibrium price. Workers and farmers are among the politically active, organized groups who have gained much by persuading the government to establish price floors that enable them to sell their goods or services at prices above free-market levels. The losses are spread across the large and diverse set of purchasers, each of whom suffers only a small loss (although the *total* loss may be considerable).

PRICE CEILINGS

Governments sometimes establish a *price ceiling*, which is the maximum price at which certain goods and services may be exchanged. Price controls on oil, natural gas, and rental housing have been frequently imposed by federal and provincial governments.

Although sometimes referred to as *fixed* or *frozen* prices, these price controls actually specify a maximum price that producers may legally charge, and are thus price ceilings. If the price ceiling is set above the equilibrium price, it has no effect because the equilibrium remains attainable. If, however, the price ceiling is set below the equilibrium price, the price ceiling lowers the price and is said to be *binding* or *effective*. The effects of price ceilings are shown in Figure 6-3, which establishes the following conclusion:

Effective price ceilings lead to excess demand, with the quantity exchanged being less than its equilibrium amount.

Allocating a Product in Excess Demand

The free market eliminates excess demand by allowing prices to rise, thereby allocating the available supply among would-be purchasers. Because this cannot happen with price ceilings, some other method of allocation must be adopted. Experience suggests what we can expect.

If stores sell their available supplies on a *first-come, first-served* basis, then people will rush to

FIGURE 6-3
A Price Ceiling and Black-Market Pricing

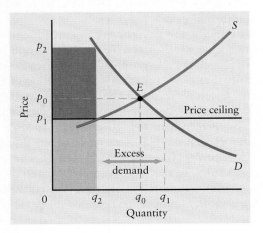

An effective price ceiling causes excess demand and invites a black market. Equilibrium price is at p_0. If a price ceiling is set at p_1, the quantity demanded will rise to q_1 and the quantity supplied will fall to q_2. Quantity actually exchanged will be q_2. Price is not legally permitted to restore equilibrium. If all the available supply of q_2 were sold on a black market, the price to consumers would rise to p_2, with black marketeers earning receipts shown by the two shaded areas. Because they buy at the ceiling price of p_1 and sell at the black-market price of p_2, their profits are represented by the dark shaded area.

government imposed price controls and rationing of gasoline, many gas station operators sold only to regular customers. When sellers decide to whom they will and will not sell their scarce supplies, allocation is said to be by **sellers' preferences.**

If the government dislikes these allocation systems, it can choose to ration the product. To do so, it prints only enough ration coupons to match the available supply and then distributes the coupons to would-be purchasers, who then need both money and coupons to buy the product. The coupons may be distributed equally among the population or on the basis of some criterion such as age, family status, or occupation. Rationing of this sort was used by Canada and many other countries during both the First and Second World Wars.

Black Markets

Price ceilings usually give rise to black markets. A *black market* is any market in which goods are sold illegally at prices that violate a legal price control.

Many manufactured products are produced by only a few firms but are sold by many retailers. Thus although it may be easy to police the few producers, it is often impossible to enforce the price at which the many retailers sell to the general public. If the government is able to control the price received by producers but not by retailers, production remains at a level consistent with the price ceiling because the producers receive only the controlled price. At the retail level, however, the opportunity for a black market arises because consumers are willing to pay more than the price ceiling for the limited amounts of the product that are available.

Effective price ceilings create the potential for a black market because a profit can be made by buying at the controlled price and selling at the black-market price.

Figure 6-3 illustrates the extreme case in which all the available supply is sold on a black market.[1]

Does the existence of a black market mean that the goals sought by imposing price ceilings have been

stores that are said to have stocks of the product. In some developing countries (and until recently, under communist regimes in many Eastern European countries), prices of essentials are subject to effective price ceilings, and even the rumour that a shop is selling supplies of a scarce product can cause a local stampede. Buyers may wait hours to get into the store, only to find that supplies are exhausted before they can be served. This is why standing in lines has been a way of life in command economies.

In market economies, "first-come, first-served" is often the basis for allocating tickets to concerts and sporting events when promoters set a price at which demand exceeds the supply of available seats. In these cases, a secondary market often develops, in which ticket scalpers resell tickets at market-clearing prices. Storekeepers (and some ticket sellers) often respond to excess demand by keeping goods "under the counter" and selling only to customers of their own choosing. For example, in 1979, when the U.S.

---

[1]This case is extreme because there are law-abiding people in every society and because governments ordinarily have considerable power to enforce their price ceilings. Although some of a product subject to an effective price ceiling will be sold on the black market, it is unlikely that all of that product will be.

thwarted? The answer depends on what the goals are. A government might have three main goals.

1. To restrict production (perhaps to release resources for war production)

2. To keep prices down

3. To satisfy notions of equity in the consumption of a product that is temporarily in short supply

When price ceilings are accompanied by a black market, only the first objective is achieved. Black markets frustrate the second objective. Effective price ceilings on manufacturers plus an extensive black market at the retail level may produce the opposite of the third goal. There will be less to go around than if there were no controls, and the available quantities will tend to go to the people with the most money or the least social conscience.

Rent controls: a case study of price ceilings

For long periods over this century, rent controls have existed in London, Paris, New York, and many other large cities. In Sweden and Britain, where rent controls on unfurnished apartments existed for decades, shortages of rental accommodations were chronic. When British controls were extended to furnished apartments in 1973, the supply of such accommodations dried up, at least until loopholes were found in the law. When rent controls were initiated in Ontario in 1975 and Rome in 1978, severe housing shortages developed, especially in those areas where demand was rising.

Rent controls are perhaps the most extensively studied form of price ceilings and provide a vivid illustration of the short- and long-term effects of this type of market intervention. Note, however, that the specifics of rent-control laws vary greatly and have changed significantly since they were first imposed many decades ago. In particular, current laws often permit exemptions for new buildings and allowances for maintenance costs and inflation. Moreover, in many countries rent controls have evolved into a "second generation" where they focus more on *regulating* the rental housing market rather than simply *controlling the price* of rental accomodation.

In this section, we confine ourselves to an analysis of rent controls which are aimed primarily at holding the price of rental housing below the free-market equilibrium value. It is this "first generation" of rent controls which produced serious results in cities like London, Paris, New York and, at times, Toronto.

THE PREDICTED EFFECTS OF RENT CONTROLS

Binding rent controls are a specific case of price ceilings and therefore Figure 6-3 can be used to predict some of their effects:

1. There will be a housing shortage in the sense that quantity demanded will exceed quantity supplied. Since rents are held below their free-market levels, the available quantity of rental housing will be less than if free-market rents had been charged.

2. The shortage will lead to alternative allocation schemes. Landlords may allocate by sellers' preferences, or the government may intervene, often through security-of-tenure laws, which protect tenants from eviction and thereby give them priority over prospective new tenants.

3. Black markets will appear. For example, landlords may require large "entrance fees" from new tenants, which reflect the difference in value between the free-market and the controlled rents. In the absence of security-of-tenure laws, landlords may force tenants out when their leases expire in order to extract a large entrance fee from new tenants.

The unique feature of rent control, however, as compared to price controls in general, is that they are applied to a highly *durable good* that provides services to consumers for a long period of time. Once built, an apartment can be used for decades. As a result, the immediate effects of rent control are typically quite different from the long-term effects.

The short-run supply response to the imposition of rent controls is quite limited. Some conversions of apartment units to condominiums and cooperatives may occur but the quantity of apartments does not change much. This implies that the short-run supply curve is quite *inelastic*.

In the long run, however, the supply response to rent controls can be quite dramatic. If the expected

FIGURE 6-4
The Effects of Rent Control in the Short Run and the Long Run

Rent control causes housing shortages that worsen as time passes. The controlled rent of r_c forces rents below their free-market equilibrium value of r_1. The short-run supply of housing is shown by the perfectly inelastic curve S_S. Thus quantity supplied remains at q_1 in the short run, and the housing shortage is q_1q_2. Over time, the quantity supplied shrinks, as shown by the long-run supply curve S_L. In the long run, there are only q_3 units of rental accommodations, fewer than when controls were instituted. The housing shortage of q_3q_2, which occurs after supply has fully adjusted, is larger than the initial shortage of q_1q_2.

return from investing in new rental housing falls significantly below what can be earned on comparable investments, funds will go elsewhere. New construction will be halted, and old buildings will be converted to other uses, or will simply be left to deteriorate. This implies that the long-run supply curve of rental accommodations (which refers to the quantity supplied after all adjustments have been made) is highly *elastic*.

Figure 6-4 illustrates the housing shortage that worsens as time passes under rent control. Because the short-run supply of housing is inelastic, the controlled rent causes only a moderate housing shortage in the short run. Indeed, most of the shortage comes from an increase in the quantity demanded rather than from a reduction in quantity supplied. As time passes, however, fewer new apartments are built, more conversions take place, and older buildings are not replaced as they wear out. As a result, the quantity supplied shrinks steadily. At the same time there

will be an incentive for landlords to allow the existing stock of rental housing to deteriorate. Since investment in maintenance may not be profitable, general maintenance and repair are no longer worthwhile.

Along with the growing housing shortage comes an increasingly inefficient use of rental accommodation space. Existing tenants will have an incentive to stay where they are even though their family size, location of employment, or economic circumstances may change. Since they cannot move without giving up their low-rent accommodation, some may take lower-paying jobs or even become unemployed to avoid the necessity for moving. Thus a situation will arise in which existing tenants will hang on to accommodation even if it is poorly suited to their needs while new individuals and families will be unable to find any rental accommodation except at black-market prices.

The province of Ontario instituted rent controls in 1975 and tightened them on at least two subsequent occasions. The controls permitted significant increases in rents only where these were needed to pass on cost increases. As a result, the restrictive effects of rent controls were felt mainly in areas where demand was increasing rapidly (as opposed to areas where only costs were increasing rapidly). In areas that were not growing, however, and in most areas during the severe recession of the early 1990s including Toronto, the demand for housing was not rising. As a result, many of the controls did not bind because the free-market rents were at or below the controlled ceilings on rents. Application 6-1 discusses the experience with rent controls in Toronto in the 1980s.

TEMPORARY VERSUS PERMANENT INCREASES IN DEMAND

We have seen that the effects of binding rent controls are more serious in the long run than in the short run. This suggests that a policy of rent controls *imposed only for a short time* may have few costs (and may actually be beneficial). Here we consider the distinction between temporary and permanent increases in housing demand, and the effects of rent controls in each case.

When Rent Controls May Work: Short-Term Shortages

Pressure for rent controls is strongest when prices are rising most rapidly. The case for stemming the rapid

APPLICATION 6-1

Rent controls in Toronto in the 1980s

Throughout the 1980s, Toronto was expanding rapidly. As a result, the demand for rental accommodations grew while the Ontario government's rent controls held rents down. The housing shortage at the controlled rents grew, as did the difference between the controlled rents and the rents that would have existed on the free market. This difference created a valuable asset to those tenants lucky enough to live in a rent-controlled apartment. For example, if you only have to pay $400 per month for an apartment that would rent on the free market for $700 per month, you have $300 of value per month that you do not pay for.

Naturally, people scrambled to appropriate such values. *Key money*—the price charged by landlords to gain access to a rent-controlled flat—became prevalent, and the press reported payments running into many thousands of dollars. (Such lump-sum payments are most burdensome on the low-income people that the rent-control policy is supposed to be aiding.) Subletting became common: A tenant pays the landlord the controlled rent and then sublets to someone else at the free-market rent. This is the worst of both worlds: The supplier gets the controlled price and hence supplies only a small quantity, while the occupier pays the market price, which, because of the control-induced shortage, is higher than the uncontrolled free-market price would have been. The gain goes to the tenant who is subletting. It serves no allocative purpose since that person is responsible neither

for maintaining the existing building nor for erecting new ones.

Another way of side-stepping the controlled rents—and to take advantage of the excess demand for housing—was for landlords to convert their rental apartments into condominiums which they then sold. Because the condominiums were put up for *sale*, rather than for *rent*, they were not subject to rent controls. This occurred on a significant scale until the provincial government passed legislation which effectively removed the owners' right to use their own property as they saw fit.

The Toronto housing shortage led to frantic searches for available space. A feature article in the *Toronto Star* told of searches involving bribing caretakers, hunting through obituary columns, and finding elderly tenants in the hope of being first on the scene when death made a flat available. Younger people, particularly those in less skilled jobs, told of landlord preferences for middle-aged, middle-class tenants holding white-collar jobs and earning higher incomes—a predictable allocation by sellers' preferences that tended to discriminate against some of the very groups the policy was supposed to help.

The experience of Toronto in the 1980s is no surprise to anyone who has studied the effects of rent controls elsewhere in the world. They are the all-too-predictable consequences of the system. City and provincial politicians and many other rent control advocates, however, expressed surprise at these events—being understandably unwilling to accept the responsibility for the situation.

rise of rents is strongest when the shortages causing the increasing rents are temporary. For example, construction of a pipeline gave rise to an enormous increase in demand for rental accommodations in Anchorage, Alaska, but it was anticipated that few of the influx of workers would remain behind once the job was done. When a temporary population floods in, market rents will rise. New construction of

apartments will not occur, however, because investors recognize that the rise in demand for rental accommodation is only temporary. In such a situation, rent controls may stop existing owners from making large profits and may result in few harmful supply effects because a long-run supply response is not expected in any case. After the boom is over, demand will fall, and free-market equilibrium rents will fall.

FIGURE 6-5
Rent Controls in Response to Increasing Demand

Quantity of Rental Accommodations

Rent controls prevent a temporary skyrocketing of rents when demand rises but also prevent the long-term supply adjustment where it is required.

Temporary demand fluctuations. The short-run supply curve S_S applies. In the free market, a temporary shift in demand from D_0 to D_1 and then back to D_0 will change rents from r_0 to r_1 and back to r_0. Rent control would hold rents at r_0 throughout. There would be a housing shortage of q_0q_1 because of excess demand, as long as demand was D_1, but rent control would not affect the quantity of housing supplied.

Permanent changes in demand. The long-run supply curve S_L applies. A permanent rise in demand from D_0 to D_1 will cause free-market rents to rise temporarily from r_0 to r_1 and then to fall to r_2 as the quantity of accommodations supplied grows from q_0 to q_2. Controlling the rent at r_0 then produces a *permanent* housing shortage of q_0q_1.

Rent controls may then be removed with little further effect. This is illustrated in Figure 6-5.

Although the rent controls have no long-run adverse effect under these circumstances, they will still have some disadvantages. At controlled rents, there will be a severe housing shortage but no *price incentive* for existing tenants to economize on housing or for potential suppliers to find ways to convert existing space into short-run accommodations, as would occur if rents were allowed to rise. Even though the supply of permanent apartments does not change, the supply of temporary accommodations can increase (mobile homes, and the subletting of bedrooms, for example). Such reactions are encouraged by the signal of rising rents but are inhibited by rent controls.

When Rent Controls Fail: Long-Term Shortages

Consider what happens when there is a long-term increase in the demand for rental accommodations. This has occurred most recently in Vancouver, and other cities of the lower mainland of British Columbia, where a rapidly increasing population has created local housing shortages and has forced rents to increase. Such increases in rents give the signal that apartments are highly profitable investments. A consequent building boom will lead to increases in the quantity supplied, and it will continue as long as high profits can be earned on rental housing.

If rent controls are imposed in the face of such long-term increases in demand, they will prevent landlords from earning high profits, but they will also prevent the needed long-run construction boom from occurring. Thus binding controls will convert a temporary shortage into a permanent one. This is also shown in Figure 6-5.

WHO GAINS AND WHO LOSES?

Existing tenants in rent-controlled accommodations are the principal gainers from a policy of rent control. As the gap between the controlled and the equilibrium rents grows, those who are lucky enough to be tenants gain more and more.

Landlords suffer because they do not get the return that they had expected on their investments. Some landlords are large companies, and others are wealthy individuals. Neither one of these groups attracts great public sympathy, even though the rental companies' stockholders are not all rich. Some landlords are people of modest means who have put their retirement savings into a small apartment or a house or two. They find that the value of their savings is diminished, and sometimes they find themselves in the ironic position of subsidizing tenants who are far better off than they are.

The other important group of people who suffer from rent controls are *potential future* tenants. The housing shortage hurts them because the rental housing they will require will not be there in the future. These people, who wind up living elsewhere, farther from their places of employment and study, are invisible in debates over rent control because they cannot obtain housing in the rent-controlled jurisdiction. Because of this, rent control is often stable politically even when it causes a long-run housing shortage. The current tenants benefit, and the potential tenants, who are harmed, are nowhere to be seen or heard.

POLICY ALTERNATIVES

Most rent controls today are meant to protect lower-income tenants, not only against "profiteering" by landlords in the face of severe local shortages but also against the steadily rising cost of housing. The market solution is to let rents rise sufficiently to cover the rising costs. If people decide that they cannot afford the market price of apartments and will not rent them, construction will cease. Given what we know about consumer behaviour, however, it is more likely that people will make agonizing choices, both to economize on housing and to spend a higher proportion of total income on it, which means consuming less housing and less of other things as well.

If governments do not wish to accept this market solution, there are many things they can do, but they cannot avoid the fundamental fact that the opportunity cost of good housing is high. Rent controls, as we have seen, create housing shortages. The shortages can be removed only if the government, at taxpayer expense, either subsidizes housing production or produces public housing directly.

Alternatively, the government can make housing more affordable to lower-income households by providing income-assistance to these households, allowing them access to higher-quality housing than they could otherwise afford. Whatever policy is adopted, it is important to recognize that providing rental accommodations has a resource cost. The costs of providing additional housing cannot be voted out of existence; all that can be done is to transfer the costs from one set of persons to another.

The final section of this chapter provides four general lessons concerning resource allocation and government attempts to control prices—lessons that apply to all parts of the economy, including the housing market, which we have just studied, and the agricultural sector, which we discuss next.

AGRICULTURE AND THE FARM PROBLEM

For over 80 years, policymakers in many western countries, including Canada, have been challenged and frustrated by what is often called the "farm problem." There are actually two separate farm problems, and supply-and-demand analysis can help to make it clear why they are so difficult to deal with.

LONG-TERM AND SHORT-TERM PROBLEMS

The first problem is that there is a long-run tendency for farm incomes to fall below urban incomes. The second problem is that agricultural prices fluctuate substantially from year to year, causing a great deal of variability in farm incomes. The farm policies implemented by most western countries are nominally directed at *stabilizing* farm incomes. However, the underlying trend of declining farm incomes also puts pressure on governments to implement polices which *raise* farm incomes.

Long-Term Trends

Agriculture's long-term problems arise from both the demand and the supply sides of agricultural markets.

Increasing Domestic Supply. Since 1900, the output per worker in Canadian agriculture has increased tenfold, roughly twice as fast as manufacturing productivity has increased. In 1900, one farm worker could produce enough food to feed about $2^1/_2$ people. By the year 2000, the figure will be approximately 65 people! Such growth of farm productivity means that the supply curves of farm products have been shifting rapidly to the right in Canada and most of the rest of the world.

Lagging Domestic Demand. The overall growth of output throughout the entire Canadian economy has resulted in a rising trend for the real income of the average Canadian family during the last 150 years. However, at the levels of income existing in Canada and in other advanced industrial nations, most foodstuffs have low income elasticities of demand because most people are already well fed. Thus increases in incomes are often spent mostly on consumer durables, entertainment, and travel. Thus as Canadian incomes grow, the Canadian demand for agricultural goods also grows, but less rapidly.

Export Demand. The contribution of export markets to demand for domestic production has been variable over recent decades. Explosive growth of world population in the past half century has provided an expanding demand for foodstuffs, which, over much of the period, translated into a growing export market for North American produce. This tended to alleviate somewhat the domestic pressures just discussed. Throughout the 1970s, however, many less developed countries succeeded in dramatically increasing their own food production.

Furthermore, large European agricultural subsidies turned the countries of western Europe into exporters of agricultural products rather than importers. By the beginning of the 1980s, therefore, international developments tended to exacerbate the domestic problem of agricultural surpluses instead of alleviating it.

For example, the world price of wheat fell from its peak of $6 per bushel in 1981 to about $2 in 1993. In real terms, this is the lowest price of wheat in Canadian history, including the prices at the depth of the Great Depression of the 1930s.

Excess Supply.   Both the demand and the supply curves in typical agricultural markets have been shifting to the right over the whole of this century, with the demand curve shifting more slowly than the supply curve. As a result, there is a continuing tendency for an excess supply of agricultural produce to develop at existing market prices. This naturally tends to depress world prices

for agricultural products. And since most agricultural products tend to have price elasticities of demand that are significantly less than one, it follows that the fall in the price tends to depress agricultural incomes.

Resource   Reallocation.   Depressed   prices, wages, and farm incomes signal the need for resources to move out of agriculture and into other sectors. However necessary they may be, adjustments of this kind prove to be painful to those who live and work on farms, especially when resources move slowly in response to depressed incomes. It is one thing for farmers' sons and daughters to move to the city; it is quite another for existing farmers and their parents to be displaced.

The magnitude of the required supply response has been enormous. In 1900, over 45 percent of the Canadian labour force worked in agriculture; by 1930 it was down to 29 percent, and by 1995 it had fallen to approximately 3 percent.

FIGURE 6-6
The Effect on Price of Unplanned Variations in Output

An unplanned fluctuation in output of a given size leads to a much sharper fluctuation in price when demand is inelastic than when it is elastic. Suppose that the expected price is p_0 and the planned output is q_0. The two curves D_i and D_e are *alternative* demand curves. If actual production always equaled planned production, the equilibrium price and quantity would be p_0 and q_0 with either demand curve. Unplanned variation in output, however, causes quantity to fluctuate year by year between q_1 (a bad harvest) and q_2 (a good harvest). When demand is inelastic (shown by the green curve), prices will show large fluctuations. When demand is elastic (shown by the light blue curve), price fluctuations will be much smaller.

Short-Term Fluctuations

The second part of the farm problem is the short-term price volatility which is typical of many agricultural markets. It occurs mainly because of factors beyond farmers' control. For example, pests, floods, and drought can reduce farm output drastically, whereas exceptionally favourable weather can cause production to exceed expectations. By now you should not be surprised to hear that such unplanned fluctuations in supply cause fluctuations in farm prices and in farm incomes.

Fluctuating Supply with Inelastic Demand. The basic situation is shown in Figure 6-6. Variations in farm output cause price fluctuations in the direction opposite to crop size. A bumper crop sends prices down; a small crop sends them up. The less elastic the demand curve, the bigger the fluctuations in price arising from given variations in output.

What are the effects on farmers' revenues? In typical cases where demand is inelastic, increases in supply cause *decreases* in farmers' revenues.

Because demands for farm products are typically inelastic, unplanned fluctuations in production tend to cause relatively large fluctuations in price. Therefore, good harvests bring reductions in total farm receipts, and bad harvests bring increases in total farm receipts.

Thus the inelasticity of demand for most farm products explains the apparently paradoxical experience that when nature is bountiful and produces a bumper crop, farmers' receipts dwindle, whereas when nature is moderately unkind and output falls unexpectedly, farmers' receipts rise. The interests of the farmer and the consumer are exactly opposed in such cases.

Fluctuating Demand with Inelastic Supply. As the tide of business activity ebbs and flows, demand curves for all products fluctuate. The magnitude of the effects on prices and outputs depends on the elasticity of *supply*.

Agricultural products typically have rather inelastic supply curves because land, labour, and machinery devoted to agricultural uses are neither quickly transferred to nonagricultural uses when demand falls nor quickly returned to agriculture when demand rises.

Given an inelastic supply curve for most agricultural products, farm prices and farm income will be sensitive to demand shifts.

This is illustrated in Figure 6-7. As shown, a reduction in demand will cause hardship among people whose incomes depend on farm crops.

THE THEORY OF AGRICULTURAL POLICY

Governments throughout the world intervene in agricultural markets in attempts both to *stabilize* agricultural incomes and to *raise* average farm incomes. We deal with three cases that are relevant to much of Canadian agriculture. The first two cases deal purely with the stabilization of farm income—first, the production of commodities mainly for export and, second, the production of commodities mainly for domestic consumption. The third case deals with price supports above the free-market equilibrium price. In what follows, we assume that all supply curves refer to planned production per year but that actual production fluctuates around that level for reasons beyond the control of farmers.

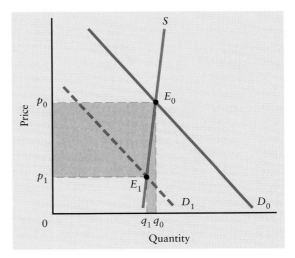

FIGURE 6-7
The Effect on Receipts of a Decrease in Demand

Inelastic supply can lead to sharp decreases in prices in response to decreases in demand. When demand decreases from D_0 to D_1, price and quantity decrease to p_1 and q_1, and total receipts decline by the shaded area. The fall in total receipts is mainly due to the sharp decrease in price. Output and employment remain high, but the drastic fall in price will reduce profits. This is typical in the agricultural sector.

Exports at World Market Prices

When Canadian production is sold on world markets, the prices are largely independent of the amount sold by Canadian producers because they contribute only a small proportion of total world supply. Thus domestic producers face a perfectly elastic demand curve, indicating that they can sell all that they wish at the given world price. A government stabilization policy then faces two key problems: first, how to cope with short-term supply fluctuations at home and second, how to react to fluctuations in world prices.

Output Fluctuations at Given World Prices. Figure 6-8 illustrates sales at a given world price when domestic output fluctuates. In years of bumper crops, sales will rise and so incomes will rise. In years of poor crops, sales will fall and so incomes will fall. In neither case do the fluctuations in domestic output affect the world price.

When domestic farmers sell at a given world price that is unaffected by their own volume of sales, their incomes fluctuate in the same direction as their short-term fluctuations in output.

The incomes of farmers who produce nonperishable crops could be stabilized if the government developed a scheme allowing farmers to store their outputs in years of bumper crops and to sell from their accumulated stocks in years of poor crops. Effectively, sales would always be equal to planned output. Any unplanned excess of production would be stored, and any shortfall would be made up out of sales from stocks. But storage costs money and postpones the receipt of revenue until the sales occur. An alternative would be to sell all the crop each year and then save the extra money received in good years to spend in bad years. This is something that farmers can do on their own without assistance from the government.

Fluctuations in World Prices. When world prices fluctuate, it may pay to hold stocks. When the government judges that this year's price is unusually low, it can store some of the output in the hope of selling it later at a better price. When the government judges that this year's price is unusually high, it can sell some of the stocks that it put aside in years when the price was low.

In a world in which future prices were known with certainty, the government would merely calculate the extra revenue that could be obtained by selling at some future price higher than the present one and subtract the costs of storage to see if the crop should be sold now or held. In practice, the future is not known, and the government must use its knowledge of market conditions to guess its best policy. The government will be inclined to store a larger amount this year the more it expects prices to rise in future years and to sell more from stocks if it expects prices to fall in future years. If the government is good at predicting the future state of the market, it will increase farmers' revenues by selling less when prices are low and more when prices are high, as compared with a policy of selling the whole crop each year. If the government's market predictions are wrong, however, the scheme can bring losses.

Sales on the Domestic Market Only

Quite a few Canadian agricultural goods are sold mainly on the domestic market. The difference between this case and the one just considered is that the demand curve facing domestic producers is now negatively sloped and typically inelastic. The analysis of Figure 6-6 now applies, so farm income will fluctuate in the direction opposite to output. Can farm income be stabilized in this case?

Price Stabilization. Suppose that the government enters the market, buying and thereby adding to its own stocks when there is a surplus, and selling and thereby reducing its stocks when there is a shortage. If it had enough grain elevators and warehouses, and if its support price were set at a realistic level, the government could stabilize *prices* indefinitely. But this would not stabilize farmers' revenues, which would be high with bumper crops and low with poor crops.

In effect, the government policy imposes a demand curve that is perfectly elastic at the support price. The situation is then analogous to the one analysed in Figure 6-8: The product can be sold at a given price, and income fluctuates in the same direction as output.

A policy which stabilizes prices received by farmers will not stabilize farm revenues. Such a policy would, however, reverse the pattern of revenue fluctuation.

Revenue Stabilization. When the government does not intervene at all in domestic agricultural markets, farm income fluctuates in the *opposite* direction as farm output. If the government intervenes to stabilize price, then farm income fluctuates in the *same* direction as farm output. This suggests that there must exist *some* government buying-and-selling policy that is able to stabilize farmers' incomes. What are the characteristics of such a policy? As has

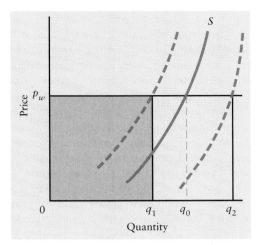

FIGURE 6-8
Exports at a Given World Price

A country that exports only a small portion of the world's supply of some product faces a perfectly elastic demand because the world price is not affected by its own sales. The given world price is p_w. The domestic supply curve shows that intended output is q_0 at that price. Unintended fluctuations cause output between q_1 and q_2. When output is q_1 (a partial crop failure), farm income is given by the dark shaded area. When output is q_2 (a bumper crop), farm income is given by the total of the bordered areas.

FIGURE 6-9
Price Supports Above the Equilibrium Price

The price support becomes a price floor, and the government must purchase the excess supply at that price. Average annual demand and supply are D and S, respectively. The free-market equilibrium is at E_0. If the government will buy any quantity at p_s, the demand curve becomes the light blue curve D_1 and equilibrium changes to E_1. The *average* addition to storage is the quantity q_1q_2. The government's purchases, financed by the taxpayer, add to farmers' incomes.

been seen, too much price stability causes receipts to vary directly with production, and too little price stability causes receipts to vary inversely with production. Thus it appears that the government should aim at some intermediate degree of price stability. If the government allows prices to vary in inverse proportion to variations in production, receipts will be stabilized. A 10 percent rise in production should be met by a 10 percent fall in price, and a 10 percent fall in production by a 10 percent rise in price.

To stabilize farmers' receipts, the government must make the effective demand curve unit elastic. It must buy in periods of high output and sell in periods of low output, but only enough to let prices change in inverse proportion to farmers' output.

Prices Above Equilibrium

Actual stabilization plans, whether they seek to fix prices completely or merely to dampen free-market fluctuations, often seek to maintain an average price above the average free-market equilibrium level. This is

because stabilization is not the only goal; governments aim to *raise* farm incomes as well as stabilize them.

The government buys in periods of high output and sells in periods of low output, but as shown in Figure 6-9, it buys much more on average than it sells, with the result that unsold surpluses accumulate. Taxpayers will generally be paying farmers for producing goods that no one is willing to purchase, at least at prices that come near to covering costs.

Subsidies.   This is the route taken by the countries in the European Union (EU) with its Common Agricultural Policy (CAP). This policy has supported the existing farm population of Europe by guaranteeing both stable and high prices. It has also meant that Western Europe has changed from being a net importer of agricultural products—which it had been for over a century and would still be under free markets—into a net exporter. As a result of the CAP, the EU is now faced with mounting stockpiles of many agricultural products.[2] Periodically, it seeks to sell

---

[2]Some attempts are made to restrict supply, but these are insufficient to prevent an excess of quantity supplied over quantity demanded at the support price.

some of the surpluses to outside countries, charging prices well below the costs of production. The net result is that taxpayers in the EU are subsidizing consumers in foreign countries by allowing them to buy goods at prices much below their cost of production. Payments under the CAP now account for well over half of the EU's entire budget, and concern is mounting that the ever-growing payments to farmers may soon outrun the EU's ability to pay.

Quotas.   Another way of holding the price above its free-market equilibrium level is to reduce the supply through quotas. Under this system, no one can produce the product without having a government-issued quota. Sufficient quotas are issued to hold production at any desired level below the free-market output. This drives prices above their free-market level. This quota system, which is analysed in Figure 6-10, has the advantage of not causing the accumulation of massive unsold surpluses. It is widely used in Canada.

The quota system, which is called *supply management* in Canada, affects both the short-term and the long-term behaviour of agricultural markets. Consider short-term fluctuations first. There will still be good crops and poor crops and other natural dis-

turbances, such as outbreaks of crop disease, that will cause short-term fluctuations in output. A shortfall of output below the quota will drive price upward. Farmers with no crop to sell will lose, but farmers whose outputs fall proportionally less than the price rise will gain. Since most agricultural products have inelastic demands, the typical farmer must gain—the percentage increase in market price will exceed the percentage fall in the aggregate crop.

What about unplanned extra output due to favourable conditions? The farmer is allowed to sell only the amount covered by the quota. The rest must be either destroyed or sold on some secondary market not covered by the quota system. Farm income is stabilized. The quota output is sold at the market price for that output even when there is surplus output (and the rest goes for what it can get). Given that demand is typically inelastic, without quotas the free-market price would fall by a larger percentage than output would rise, and producers' incomes would shrink drastically.

A quota system guarantees that farmers will get the free-market price of the total quota output when output equals or exceeds the quota and more when output falls short of the quota and demand is inelastic.

Thus, the quota system is superior to the subsidy system in that it really does remove the down-side risks caused by unexpected increases in output, and unlike the CAP, it does not lead to accumulating stockpiles of unsold output. The main cost is met by consumers, who on average pay a price that is higher, and consume an output that is lower, than would occur under free-market conditions.

Now consider the long term. We have seen that the quota drives price above its free-market level by restricting output. For purposes of illustration, let us suppose that the quota is for eggs. Those who are producing eggs when the quota system is first instituted must gain. Since production falls, total costs must fall; since demand is inelastic, total revenue must rise. Therefore, egg producers find their profits rising, since they spend less to earn more revenue. No wonder quotas are popular among the original producers!

But do quotas really increase farm income in the long run? Because people leave the industry for such reasons as death and retirement and new people must enter to replace them, existing holders are allowed to transfer their quotas to new would-be egg producers. But the quota is valuable, since it confers the right to produce eggs that earn a large profit as a

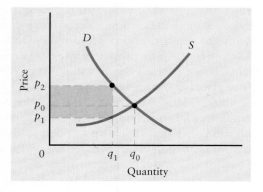

FIGURE 6-10
Price Support Through the Use of Quotas

The quota below the free-market equilibrium quantity maintains the price above the free-market equilibrium level without generating surpluses. If the total quota of q_1 is enforced, the price will rise to p_2. Since the supply curve indicates that in a free market producers would be willing to sell the quantity q_1 at the price p_1, the effect of the quota is to increase the revenues (by the shaded area) to those producers who hold quota.

result of the supply restriction. Therefore, the quota commands a price which naturally reflects the current value of the extra future profits that ownership of the quota allows.

The free-market price of a quota to produce any good will be such that the profitability of that good's production will, after deducting the cost of the quota, be no more than the profitability of other lines of activity carrying similar risks.

In other words, the whole extra profitability created by the quota system becomes embodied in the price of the quota. The extra profits created by the quota will just provide an acceptable return on the money invested in buying the quota—if it provided more, the price of the quota would be bid up; if it provided less, the price of the quota would fall.

For this reason, *new entrants* to the industry will earn no more than the return available in other lines of production. Since that would also be the case under market-determined prices and outputs, the quota does not raise the profitability of producing eggs. What it does do is reduce some of the uncertainty due to unexpected short-term fluctuations of output. Farming becomes a somewhat less risky operation than before.

AGRICULTURAL POLICY IN CANADA

The main tools of agricultural stabilization in Canada are marketing boards and income supplement programs. Sales through marketing boards account for about half of all farm cash receipts.

Marketing Boards

There are essentially two types of government marketing boards. The first seeks to influence prices by controlling supply. The second takes prices as given and acts as a selling agency for producers.

Supply Management. The supply-management schemes typically are provincially administered systems that restrict output of commodities sold in the Canadian market through quotas issued by provincial marketing boards. They vary from province to province but often cover milk, eggs, cheese, butter, and poultry. The farm profits created by these schemes are enormous and are reflected by the high prices farmers must pay to purchase quotas.

Schemes of this type, analyzed in Figure 6-10, are successful in reducing short-term fluctuations.

However, they also greatly increase the cost of becoming a producer, because a quota must be purchased in addition to the physical capital needed for production. The schemes are popular among farmers because they reduce risk in the short term and because the value of the quotas often rises over the long term. The gains to farmers and food importers are paid for by consumers in the form of higher prices.

Recently, two other important effects of supply management systems have become apparent. First, they harm Canadian manufacturers of food products. Canadian firms producing frozen and canned foods must pay high prices for Canadian produce, whereas their foreign competitors can buy their raw foodstuffs at the lower world prices. Second, they reduce competition among users of agricultural products. For example, to allocate scarce supplies of milk, the Fraser Valley Milk Marketing Board channels supplies to selected users of raw milk. These milk processors have no incentive to compete for market share or to introduce new products, because a successful competitor could not get the larger supplies of raw milk needed to increase sales.

The high domestic prices caused by supply management would normally lead to a flood of imports. To prevent this, the federal government used to impose fixed and small quotas on imports of goods subject to supply management. Under the Uruguay Round of the General Agreement on Tariffs and Trade (the GATT), Canada agreed to replace these quotas in 1994–1995 with tariffs which had an equivalent effect. In some cases the tariff rates exceeded 300 percent! The slow speed at which these tariff rates are to be reduced under the GATT will allow supply management to persist for many years. Consumers will have to wait for future tariff reductions before they get real relief from the high-price effects of Canadian marketing boards.

Orderly Marketing Schemes. The prime example of an orderly marketing scheme is the Canadian Wheat Board, which markets Canadian wheat at prices set on the world wheat market. Each year, the Wheat Board estimates the average price at which it expects the wheat crop to be sold. Seventy-five percent of that price is then paid to each farmer on delivery of the wheat. After the board sells the wheat, any proceeds in excess of the initial payments are distributed to the producers in proportion to the amount of wheat supplied by each.

The goal of the Wheat Board is not to influence world prices. Instead, by paying farmers 75 percent of the estimated average selling price over the year, the Board provides farmers with a secure cash flow early in the selling period. The Board also serves to secure farmers' incomes against intrayear fluctuations in wheat prices. It does this by pooling all of its receipts and paying them out to farmers according to the amount of wheat delivered by each farmer but irrespective of the date within the year of that delivery. So the farmer is relieved of worry about what the spot price of wheat may be on the day of delivery.

Income Supplements

The system of providing financial assistance to farmers was reorganized with the passage in 1991 of the Farm Income Protection Act (FIPA). The first programs to be established under this new legislation were the Net Income Stabilization Account (NISA) and the Gross Revenue Insurance Plan (GRIP). These two programs, combined with a system of crop insurance (and other companion programs) make up what might be called the "safety net programs" for Canadian farmers.

NISA is a voluntary program designed to help producers set aside money in good years to be used in bad years; producers' contributions of up to 2 percent of their net sales are matched by contributions from the federal and relevant provincial governments. Thus, although part of this program involves the individual producers saving their own financial resources, there is also a considerable portion of government money being used to supplement farmers' incomes.

GRIP offers producers protection from revenue loss due to output or price changes beyond their control. It provides producers with a guaranteed target revenue. Though GRIP is essentially just an insurance program, it also has an income support component. This comes from the fact that two-thirds of the insurance premiums are paid by the federal and relevant provincial governments.

All in all, the level of direct financial assistance to farmers is quite considerable, especially when seen relative to total farm income. In 1994 (an apporoximately typical year in the 1990s for Canadian farming), net cash income to Canadia farmers totalled $5.9 billion. In that same yeat, direct cash payments to farmers equalled $1.7 billion; thus direct financial assistance to farmers represented roughly 30 percent of their net cash income.

The Future of Agricultural Policy

Is there a better way to make farming an occupation in which people can invest and work without being disadvantaged relative to other citizens and without needing large payments of funds raised from the nation's taxpayers? Most economists believe that a more efficient system would assist farm workers to change occupations and farm producers to change products rather than subsidize them to stay where they are not needed and to produce products that cannot be marketed profitably. Such assistance would require significant outlays—as do the present schemes—but would allow the market to do the job of allocating resources to agriculture.

There is no doubt that a policy of allowing agricultural prices and outputs to be determined on free markets would avoid surplus production, but the human and political costs of this policy have been judged to be unacceptable. The challenge has been to respond to the real hardships of the farm population without intensifying the long-term problems. Canadian farm policy has not always succeeded in doing so; the economic analysis in the previous sections helps us to understand why.

THE DETERMINATION OF IMPORTS AND EXPORTS

In the previous chapter we examined the determination of price by demand and supply. So far in this chapter, however, we have examined situations in which the price of some commodity is determined by forces *other than* demand and supply—in particular, prices set by government as either a price floor or a price ceiling. We discovered that in such situations some mechanism other than price must be used to allocate scarce resources for the simple reason that prices are not permitted to adjust to excess demands or excess supplies. In the case of government-administered rent controls, which is a case of a price ceiling, we examined the problems associated with having the price held below the equilibrium price. In the case of agricultural subsidies or quotas, we examined the problems associated with having the price held above the equilibrium price.

We now examine a situation in which price *appears* to be determined by forces other than demand and supply. But a more accurate description of what follows is a situation where price is determined by forces other than *domestic* demand and supply. This is the situation where Canada produces some commodity where the price is determined by demand and supply *for the world as a whole* rather than by demand and supply *just in Canada*. We will see that the world price will play a key role in determining whether

Canada is an exporter or an importer of any particular product. Though international trade and trade policy are studied in detail in Chapters 35 and 36, we can use the basic tools of demand-and-supply analysis to provide some insights into a country's pattern of trade.

There are some products, such as coffee and bananas, that Canada does not produce (and will probably never produce). Any domestic consumption of these products must therefore be satisfied by imports from other countries. At the other extreme, there are some products, such as nickel or potash, where Canada is one of the world's major suppliers, and thus demand in the rest of the world must be satisfied partly by exports from Canada. There are also some products, such as housing, that are so expensive to transport that every country produces approximately what it consumes.

Our interest here is in the many intermediate cases in which Canada is only one of many producers of an internationally traded product, as with beef, oil, automobiles, wheat, and lumber. Will Canada be an exporter or an importer of such products, or will it just produce exactly enough to satisfy its domestic demand?

THE LAW OF ONE PRICE

Whether Canada imports or exports a product for which it is only one of many producers depends to a great extent on the product's price. This brings us to the so-called *law of one price*.

The law of one price states that when a product which can be cheaply transported is traded throughout the entire world, it will tend to have a single worldwide price—the world price.

Many basic products, such as copper wire, steel pipe, iron ore, and computer RAM chips, fall within this category. The world price for each good is the price that equates the quantity demanded worldwide with the quantity supplied worldwide.

The world price of an internationally traded product may be influenced greatly, or only slightly, by the demand and supply coming from any one country. The extent of one country's influence will depend on how important its demands and supplies are in relation to the worldwide totals.

The simplest case for us to study arises when the country, which we will take to be Canada, accounts for only a small part of the total worldwide demand and supply. In this case, Canada does not itself produce enough to influence the world price significantly. Similarly, Canadian purchases are too small a proportion of worldwide demand to affect the world price in any significant way. Producers and consumers in Canada thus face a world price that they cannot influence by their own actions.

Notice that in this case, the price that rules in the Canadian market must be the world price (adjusted for the exchange rate between the Canadian dollar and the foreign currency). The law of one price says that this must be so. What would happen if the Canadian domestic price diverged from the world price? If the Canadian price were below the world price, no supplier would sell in the Canadian market because more money could be made by selling abroad. Thus from the perspective of Canadian consumers, this world price is a supply curve—consumers can buy whatever amount of the product they choose at that price, but they cannot buy anything at a lower price.

Conversely, if the Canadian domestic price were above the worldwide price, no buyers would buy from a Canadian seller because money could be saved by buying abroad. Thus from the perspective of Canadian producers, the world price is a demand curve—producers can sell all of their output on the world market at the world price, but they cannot sell at a higher price.

THE PATTERN OF FOREIGN TRADE

Now let us see what determines the pattern of Canadian-foreign trade in such circumstances.

An Exported Product

To determine the pattern of Canadian trade, we first show the Canadian domestic demand and supply curves for some product, say, lumber. The intersection of these two curves tells us what the price and quantity would be *if there were no foreign trade.* Now compare this no-trade price with the world price of that product.[3] If the world price is higher, the actual price in Canada will exceed the no-trade price, there will be an excess of Canadian supply over Canadian demand, and the surplus production will be exported for sale abroad.

Countries export products whose world price exceeds the price that would rule domestically if there were no foreign trade.

---

[3]If the world price is stated in terms of some foreign currency (as it often is), then the price must be converted into Canadian dollars using the current exchange rate between the foreign currency and Canadian dollars.

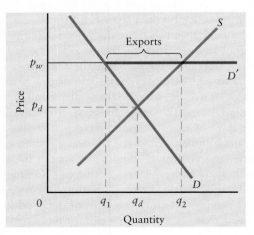

FIGURE 6-11
The Determination of Exports

Exports occur whenever there is excess supply domestically at the world price. The domestic demand and supply curves are D and S, respectively. The domestic price in the absence of foreign trade is p_d, with q_d produced and consumed domestically. The world price of p_w is higher than p_d. At p_w, q_1 is demanded while q_2 is supplied domestically. The excess of the domestic supply over the domestic demand is exported.

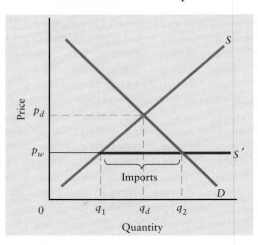

FIGURE 6-12
The Determination of Imports

Imports occur whenever there is excess demand domestically at the world price. The domestic demand and supply curves are D and S, respectively. The domestic price in the absence of foreign trade is p_d, with q_d produced and consumed domestically. The world price of p_w is less than p_d. At p_w, q_2 is demanded, whereas q_1 is supplied domestically. The excess of domestic demand over domestic supply is satisfied through imports.

This result is demonstrated in Figure 6-11.

An Imported Product

Now consider some other product—for example, oil. Once again, look first at the domestic demand and supply curves, shown this time in Figure 6-12. The intersection of these curves determines the no-trade price that would rule *if there were no foreign trade.* The world price of oil is below the Canadian no-trade price so that at the price ruling in Canada, domestic demand is larger and domestic supply is smaller than if the no-trade price had ruled. The excess of domestic demand over domestic supply is met by imports.

Countries import products whose world price is less than the price that would rule domestically if there were no foreign trade.

WHO PAYS FOR TARIFFS?

We have now developed the basic theory of how imports and exports are determined in competitive markets. In Chapters 35 and 36, this theory will be used

to study a number of issues relating to Canadian trade and trade policy. Here we briefly examine an issue of recurrent interest in Canada, the use of tariffs to protect domestic industries from foreign competition.

An import tariff is simply a tax on imports, imposed at the border, when the product is imported. A tariff at rate t would raise the price of an imported product by the amount of the tariff, as shown in Figure 6-13, which is based on the analysis in Figure 6-12. Note that the tariff acts exactly like a sales tax of the same amount. It shifts the supply curve, in this case the world price, upward by the amount of the tariff. As shown in Figure 6-13, domestic consumers, facing a tariff of t, will pay $p_w + t$. Tariffs clearly make domestic consumers worse off.

Figure 6-13 also shows that the tariff has beneficial effects for domestic producers of that good. The price that they receive rises to $p_w + t$, and the quantity that they produce also rises. With the tariff in place, domestic output rises to the point where the domestic supply curve reaches the price $p_w + t$. This explains why producers of imported products often

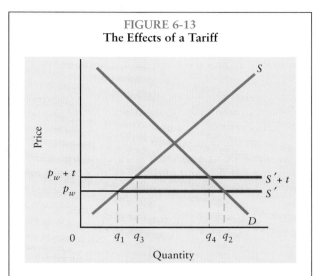

FIGURE 6-13
The Effects of a Tariff

A tariff increases the price faced by domestic consumers above the world price. Before the tariff, things are exactly as in Figure 6-12, with domestic production of q_1 and imports of $q_2 - q_1$. A tariff of t raises the domestic price to $p_w + t$, increasing domestic production to q_3 and reducing domestic consumption to q_4.

favour the imposition of tariffs. The tariffs are effective protection, increasing the portion of the domestic supply curve on which it is profitable for the domestic producers to operate.

A tariff causes conflict between domestic producers, who are benefited by it, and domestic consumers, who are made worse off due to the higher prices they pay.

In Chapter 36, we will show that the producers' well-being generally improves by less than the amount that consumers are hurt, so that the tariff makes the country as a whole worse off. But that analysis is considerably more complicated and will need more than simple demand and supply curves.

FOUR GENERAL LESSONS ABOUT RESOURCE ALLOCATION

In this chapter, we have examined several examples of government intervention in markets that might have been left unregulated. In all cases that we have examined, the government interventions generated

some problems (though they may also have helped achieve certain goals). Our discussion suggests four general lessons about resource allocation.

COSTS CAN BE SHIFTED, BUT NOT AVOIDED

Production, whether in response to free-market signals or to government controls, uses resources; thus it involves costs to members of society. If it takes 5 percent of the nation's resources to provide housing at some stated average standard, those resources will not be available to produce other products. If resources are used to produce unwanted wheat, those resources will not be available to produce other products. For society as a whole, there is no such thing as free housing or free wheat.

The average standard of living depends on the amount of resources available to the economy and the efficiency with which these resources are used. It follows that *costs are real* and are incurred no matter who provides the goods. Rent controls or subsidies to agriculture can change the share of the costs paid by particular individuals or groups, lowering the share for some and raising the share for others, but they cannot make the costs go away.

Different ways of allocating the costs may also affect the total amount of resources used and thus the amount of costs incurred. For example, controls that keep prices and profits of some product below free-market levels will lead to increased quantities demanded and decreased quantities supplied. Unless government steps in to provide additional supplies, fewer resources will be allocated to producing the product. If government chooses to supply all the demand at the controlled prices, more resources will be allocated to it, which means that fewer resources will be devoted to other kinds of goods and services.

MARKET PRICES ENCOURAGE ECONOMICAL USE OF RESOURCES

Prices and profits in a market economy provide signals to both demanders and suppliers. Prices that are high (relative to other prices) provide an incentive to purchasers to economize on the product. They may choose to satisfy the want in question with substitutes whose prices have not risen so much (because they are less costly to provide) or to satisfy less of that want by shifting expenditure to the satisfaction of other wants.

On the supply side, rising prices tend to produce rising profits. High profits attract further resources into production. Short-term profits that bear no relation to current costs repeatedly occur in market economies. They cause resources to move into industries with profits until profits fall to levels that can be earned elsewhere in the economy.

Falling prices and falling profits provide the opposite motivations. Purchasers are inclined to buy more; sellers are inclined to produce less and to move resources out of the industry and into more profitable undertakings.

The price system responds to the need for a change in the allocation of resources—say, in response to an external event such as the loss of a source of a raw material or the outbreak of a war. Changing relative prices and profits signal the need for change to which consumers and producers respond.

GOVERNMENT INTERVENTION AFFECTS RESOURCE ALLOCATION

Governments intervene in the price system sometimes to satisfy generally agreed social goals and sometimes to help politically influential interest groups. Government intervention changes the allocation of resources that the price system would achieve.

Interventions have allocative consequences because they inhibit the free-market allocative mechanism. Some controls, such as rent controls, prevent prices from rising (in response, say, to an increase in demand with no change in supply). If the price is held down, the signal is not given to consumers to economize on a product that is in short supply. On the supply side, when prices and profits are prevented from rising, the profit signals that would attract new resources into the industry are never given. The shortage continues, and the movements of demand and supply that would resolve it are not set in motion.

Other controls, such as agricultural price supports, prevent prices from falling (in response, say, to an increase in supply with no increase in demand). This leads to excess supply, and the signal is not given to producers to produce less or to buyers to increase their purchases. Surpluses continue, and the movements of demand and supply that would eliminate them are not set in motion.

INTERVENTION REQUIRES ALTERNATIVE MECHANISMS

During times of shortages, allocation will be by sellers' preferences, on a first-come, first-served basis, or by some system of government rationing. During periods of surplus, there will be unsold supplies unless the government buys and stores the surpluses. Because long-run changes in demand and costs do not induce resource reallocations through private decisions, the government will have to step in. It will have to force resources out of industries in which prices are held too high, as it has tried to do in agriculture, and into industries in which prices are held too low, as it can do, for example, by providing public housing.

Intervention almost always has both benefits and costs. Economics cannot answer the question of whether a particular intervention with free markets is desirable, but it can clarify the issues by identifying benefits and costs and who will enjoy or bear them. In doing so, it can identify the competing values involved. This matter will be discussed in detail in Part 6 of this book.

SUMMARY

A. GOVERNMENT-CONTROLLED PRICES

- Government price controls are policies that attempt to hold the price of some good or service at some disequilibrium value—a value that could not be maintained in the absence of the government's intervention. A binding price floor is set above the equilibrium price; a binding price ceiling is set below the equilibrium price.
- Effective price floors lead to excess supply. Either the potential seller is left with quantities that cannot be sold, or the government must step in and buy the surplus. Effective price ceilings lead to excess demand and provide a strong incentive for black marketeers to buy at the controlled price and sell at the higher free-market price.

B. RENT CONTROLS: A CASE STUDY OF PRICE CEILINGS

- Rent controls are a persistent and widespread form of price ceiling. The major consequence of effective rent controls is a shortage of rental accommodations that gets worse because of a decline in the quantity of rental housing.
- Rent controls can be an effective response to temporary situations in which there is a ban on building or a tran-

sitory increase in demand. They usually fail when they are introduced as a response to a long-run increase in demand.

C. AGRICULTURE AND THE FARM PROBLEM

- Agricultural products are subject to wide fluctuations in market prices, which cause fluctuations in farmers' incomes. This is because of year-to-year unplanned fluctuations in supplies combined with inelastic demands, and because of cyclical fluctuations in demands combined with inelastic supplies. Where demand is inelastic, large crops tend to be associated with low total receipts for farmers, and small crops tend to be associated with high total receipts.
- To stabilize farm incomes, the government should not stabilize prices. Instead, it should buy and sell just. enough to allow prices to vary in proportion to changes in quantity, thus causing the elasticity of demand for the product to be unity.
- Agricultural prices and incomes are depressed by chronic surpluses in agricultural markets. Government policies to protect farm incomes have included buying farmers' output at above free-market prices, limiting production and acreage through quotas, and paying farmers to leave crops unproduced. Such policies tend to inhibit the reallocation mechanism and thus to increase farm surpluses above what they would otherwise be and to lead to accumulating stocks.
- Canadian farm policy illustrates that government intervention to prevent the working of the market mechanisms affects resource allocation and requires alternative allocative mechanisms. While farm policy has protected farmers from certain hardships, it has slowed

the required outflow of resources that alone would solve the problem of chronic excess supply.

D. THE DETERMINATION OF IMPORTS AND EXPORTS

- For goods that are internationally traded, the equilibrium price of the good is determined by supply and demand *for the world as a whole* rather than for each country individually. This means that the world price of the good may be above or below the domestic equilibrium price *that would exist if there were no international trade.*
- A country will export goods when the domestic-market price is below the world price; a country will import goods for which the domestic-market price is above the world price.
- A tariff on some product causes conflict between domestic producers of that product, who are benefited by it, and domestic consumers, who are made worse off due to the higher prices they are forced to pay.

E. FOUR GENERAL LESSONS ABOUT RESOURCE ALLOCATION

- The examples of rent controls, farm policy, and tariffs seen in this chapter illustrate four important lessons about resource allocation.
  1. Costs can be shifted, but they cannot be avoided.
  2. Market-determined prices encourage the economical use of resources.
  3. Government intervention affects the allocation of resources.
  4. Intervention with the price mechanism means that other allocative mechanisms (often arbitrary) must be used.

KEY CONCEPTS

Price controls: floors and ceilings
Allocation by sellers' preferences and by black markets
Rent controls
Short-run and long-run supply curves of rental accommodations

The farm problem: short-run fluctuations and long-run trends
Price stabilization versus income stabilization
Quotas and supply management
Law of one price

Supply and demand curves at the world price
Imported and exported products
The effects of tariffs

DISCUSSION QUESTIONS

1. Discuss the following statements about the housing problem in Vancouver.
   a. "Zoning laws requiring that most of Vancouver be single-family dwellings reflect the exploitation of the poor by the middle class."

   b. "The world is awash with agricultural surpluses while land-starved Vancouver is prevented from spreading into much of the adjacent Fraser Valley by government 'land banks' designed to preserve agricultural land from urbanization."

c. "More than 40 percent of all rented apartments in Vancouver are illegal and would not be permitted if their owners applied for permission to rent their space legally."

2. "When an item is vital to everyone, it is easier to start controlling the price than to stop controlling it. Such controls are popular with consumers, regardless of their harmful consequences." Explain why it may be inefficient to have such controls, why they may be popular, and why, if they are popular, the government might nevertheless choose to decontrol these prices.

3. Commenting on a shortage of natural gas in the United States, the columnist William Safire called it "the unnatural shortage of natural gas." He wrote: "Be angry at the real villains: the Washington-knows-best Congressmen, the self-anointed consumer 'protectors' and the regulatory bureaucracy. They thought they could protect the consumer by breaking the laws of supply and demand, and as a result have made a classic case against government intervention." From these remarks, what do you judge the policy to have been? How would you define a "shortage?" Is there a useful distinction between a "natural shortage" and an "unnatural shortage?"

4. A top-ranked Canadian law school has 1,000 qualified applicants for 200 places in the first-year class. It is debating whether or not to institute a number of alternative admission criteria: (a) a lottery, (b) LSAT score, (c) recommendations from alumnae and alumni, (d) place of residence of applicant. An economist on the faculty determined that if the tuition level is doubled, the excess demand will disappear. Argue for (or against) using tuition fees to replace each of the other suggested criteria.

5. It is sometimes asserted that the rising costs of construction are putting housing out of the reach of ordinary citizens. Who bears the heaviest cost when rentals are kept down by (a) rent controls, (b) a subsidy to tenants equal to some fraction of their rent payments, and (c) low-cost public housing?

6. "This year the weather smiled on us, and we made a crop," says a wheat farmer near Minedosa in Manitoba. "But just as we made a crop, the economic situation changed." This quotation brings to mind the old saying, "If you are a farmer, the weather is always bad." Discuss the sense in which this saying might be true.

7. The Kenya Meat Commission (KMC) decided that it was undemocratic to allow meat prices to be out of reach of the ordinary citizen. It decided to freeze meat prices. Six months later, in a press interview, the managing commissioner of the KMC made the following statements.

a. "Cattle are scarce in the country, but I do not know why."
b. "People are eating too much beef, and unless they diversify their eating habits and eat other foodstuffs, the shortage of beef will continue."

Can you explain to the commissioner why these things have happened?

8. Consider a proposal to change trucking regulations such that trucks pulling smaller rigs (and so fewer tons) are permitted to use radar detectors while trucks pulling larger rigs (and more cargo) are prohibited from doing so. How can you interpret this as an income-support policy for the small-rig segment of the trucking industry? What are the income redistribution effects of this policy change? What is likely to be the effect on the supply curves of industries that rely on trucking to deliver raw materials or finished products?

9. During the summer of 1993, severe floods swept through the American Midwest. Although many homes that flooded that year do not typically flood, for many people this was only one in a long string of floods. However, after the waters receded, most people rebuilt their homes, despite the long history of destruction, generally with low-interest loans and disaster relief grants from the federal government. Discuss how the policy of subsidizing the reconstruction of property following floods affects the market for real estate in flood-prone areas. Is the outcome more or less efficient in the long run with such government intervention?

10. Gary Storey, a professor of agricultural economics at the University of Saskatchewan, made the following statement: "One of the sad truths of the agricultural policies in Europe and the United States is that they do very little for the future generations of farmers. Most of the subsidies get capitalized into higher land prices, creating windfall gains for current landowners (i.e., gains that they did not expect). It creates a situation where the next generation of farmers require, and ask for, increased government support."

a. Explain why subsidies to farmers would increase land values and generate windfall gains to current landowners.
b. As we have seen in this chapter, many Canadian agricultural policies are based on supply management, which involves the use of production quotas. Does such a system avoid the problem described by Professor Storey?

PART THREE

CONSUMPTION, PRODUCTION, AND COST

Why does water, which is essential to life and which we all value dearly, have such a low price? Why do diamonds, a more-or-less unnecessary part of life, have such a high price? Does this mean that the demand-and-supply apparatus that you just learned is all wrong? How many times have you heard the suggestion that a product, such as a new line of cosmetics, will sell more easily at a higher price than at a lower one? Does this mean that demand curves can have a positive slope? What determines the cost of specific products, and why does the cost sometimes depend on how many units are produced? For example, why is the production cost of a widely-used textbook significantly less than a similar textbook used only by a few universities? Why has the declining cost of computer-related equipment led some firms to reduce their number of employees? These are the sort of questions you will be able to answer after reading the next three chapters.

In Part 2, we saw that demand and supply are important for determining market prices and quantities. You also saw that the *shapes* of demand and supply curves influence the way prices and quantities respond to changes in income, technology, or commodity taxes. In the next three chapters, we go "behind the scenes" of demand and supply to examine in more detail the behaviour of consumers and the behaviour of firms. This will give you a deeper understanding of what demand and supply are all about.

In Chapter 7, you will explore the *theory of consumer behaviour*. There you will see how economists think about the way consumers make decisions. You will be introduced to the important concept of *utility*, and to the distinction between *marginal* and *total* utility. It is this distinction that explains why water has a low price and diamonds have a high price. You will also see how demand curves are derived from the underlying consumer behaviour, and you will see that (except in some very unusual cases) demand curves are indeed negatively sloped.

Chapters 8 and 9 explore the *theory of the firm*. You will learn about *profits* and *costs*, and how these terms are used differently in economics than in everyday life. The important concepts of *average cost* and *marginal cost* will be developed, at which point you will know why 50,000 textbooks can be produced at a lower cost per book than can 10,000 textbooks. You will be introduced to the *principle of substitution*, which explains why the falling cost of computers has led some firms to reduce their workforces (and increase their use of computers). Finally, you will see how changes in technology lead to changes in firms' behaviour.

CHAPTER 7

THE THEORY OF CONSUMER BEHAVIOUR

Imagine that you are walking down the aisle of a supermarket looking for something for your late-night snack (to have while you are studying!). With only a $5 bill in your pocket, you must choose how to divide this $5 between frozen burritos and cans of coke. How do you make this decision? In this chapter, we introduce you to the way economists think about such problems—the theory of consumer behaviour. Not surprisingly, economists (being consumers themselves) think about consumers as caring both about the prices of the goods and the amount of satisfaction that they get from the goods.

MARGINAL UTILITY AND CONSUMER CHOICE

Consumer *choice* is fundamental to market economies, and consumers make all kinds of decisions—they choose to drink coffee or tea (or neither), to go to the movies, to dine out, to buy excellent (or not so good) stereo equipment. As we discussed in Chapter 1, economists assume that in making their choices, consumers are motivated to maximize their **utility,** the total satisfaction that they derive from the goods and services that they consume.[1]

Neither economists nor psychologists can measure utility directly. However, it turns out that we can construct a useful theory of consumer behaviour based on utility maximization without directly measuring utility. In Chapter 1, we defined the *opportunity cost* of a given action as the benefit given up by choosing that action rather than the next best alternative. This chapter's theory of consumer behaviour is based on the idea that we can use the opportunity cost of making choices to measure the utility that consumers derive from the products they consume.

In developing our theory of consumer behaviour in general, we begin by considering the consumption of a single product. It will be useful to distinguish between the consumer's **total utility,** which is the full satisfaction resulting from the consumption of that product by a consumer, and the consumer's **marginal utility,** which is the *change* in satisfaction resulting from consuming a little more of that product. For example, the total utility of consuming seven eggs per week is the total satisfaction that those seven eggs provide. The marginal utility of the seventh egg consumed is the additional satisfaction provided by the consumption of that egg. Hence marginal utility is the difference in total utility gained by consuming six eggs per week and by consuming seven eggs per week.[2]

DIMINISHING MARGINAL UTILITY

The basic hypothesis of utility theory, often called the *law of diminishing marginal utility,* is as follows:

The utility that any consumer derives from *successive* units of a particular product diminishes as total consumption of the product increases, holding the consumption of all other products constant.

---

[1]We discuss two theories of consumer choice. In the chapter, we present the marginal utility theory of demand. In the appendix to this chapter, we present a more formal version of essentially the same theory using indifference curves.

[2]Technically, *incremental* utility is measured over a discrete interval, such as from 6 to 7, whereas *marginal* utility is a rate of change measured over an infinitesimal interval. However, common usage applies the word marginal when the last unit is involved, even if a one-unit change is not infinitesimal. [10]

Consider water. Some minimum quantity is essential to sustain life, and a person would, if necessary, give up his or her entire income to obtain that quantity of water. Thus the marginal utility of that basic quantity of water is extremely high. More than this bare minimum will be consumed, but the marginal utility of successive glasses of water drunk over a period of time will decline steadily.

Evidence for this hypothesis will be considered later, but you can convince yourself that it is at least reasonable by asking a few questions. How much money would induce you to reduce your consumption of water by one glass per week? The answer is very little. How much would induce you to reduce it by a second glass? By a third glass? To only one glass consumed per week? The answer to the last question is quite a bit. The fewer glasses you are consuming already, the higher the marginal utility of one more glass of water.

Water has many uses other than for drinking. A fairly high marginal utility will be attached to some minimum quantity for bathing, but much more than this minimum will be used for more frequent baths or longer showers than are absolutely necessary. The last weekly litre used for bathing is likely to have a low marginal utility. Again, some small quantity of water is necessary for brushing teeth, but many people leave the water running while they brush. The water going down the drain between wetting and rinsing the brush surely has a low utility. When all the extravagant uses of water by the modern consumer are considered, the marginal utility of the last, say, 30 percent of all units consumed is probably very low, even though the total utility of all the units consumed is extremely high.

UTILITY SCHEDULES AND GRAPHS

The hypothetical schedule in Table 7-1 is constructed to illustrate the assumptions that have been made about utility, using movie attendance as an example. The table shows that total utility rises as the number of movies attended (per month) rises. Everything else being equal, the more movies the consumer attends each month, the more satisfaction is obtained—at least over the range shown in the table. However, the marginal utility of each additional movie per month is less than that of the previous one, even though each movie adds something to the consumer's satisfaction. The schedule in Table 7-1 shows that mar-

TABLE 7-1
Total and Marginal Utility Schedules

Number of Movies Attended Per Month	Total Utility	Marginal Utility
0	0	
1	30	30
2	50	20
3	65	15
4	75	10
5	83	8
6	89	6
7	93	4
8	96	3
9	98	2
10	99	1

Total utility rises, but marginal utility declines as consumption increases. The marginal utility of 20, shown as the second entry in the third column, arises because total utility increases from 30 to 50—a difference of 20—with attendance at the second movie. To indicate that the marginal utility is associated with the change from one rate of movie attendance to another, the figures in the third column are recorded between the rows of the figures in the second column. When plotting marginal utility on a graph, it is plotted at the midpoint of the interval over which it is computed.

ginal utility declines as quantity consumed rises. [11] The data are graphed in the two parts of Figure 7-1.

MAXIMIZING UTILITY

A basic assumption of the theory of consumer behaviour is that consumers try to make themselves as well off as they possibly can in the circumstances in which they find themselves. In other words, the members of a household seek to maximize their total utility.

The Consumer's Decision

How can a consumer adjust expenditure so as to maximize total utility? A simple answer would be that the consumer should consume such that the marginal utility of each product is the same—that is, such that the last unit of each product consumed is valued equally. But this would make sense only if each product had the same price per unit. Consider a consumer buying two goods who must spend $3 to obtain an additional unit of one product and only $1 to obtain one unit of another. The first product would repre-

sent a poor use of money if the marginal utility of each were equal. The consumer would be spending $3 to get satisfaction equal to what could have been acquired for only $1 by buying the other good.

A consumer who is maximizing utility will allocate expenditures so that the utility obtained from the last dollar spent on each product is equal.

Imagine that the consumer is in a position in which the utility of the last dollar spent on cashews yields three times the utility of the last dollar spent on toffee. In this case, total utility can be increased by switching a dollar of expenditure from toffee to cashews and by gaining the difference between the utilities of a dollar spent on each.

The utility-maximizing consumer will continue to switch expenditure from toffee to cashews as long as a dollar spent on cashews yields more utility than a dollar spent on toffee. This switching, however, reduces the quantity of toffee consumed and, given the law of diminishing marginal utility, raises the marginal utility of toffee. At the same time, switching increases the quantity of cashews consumed and thereby lowers the marginal utility of cashews.

Eventually, the marginal utilities will have changed enough so that the utility of a dollar spent on cashews is just equal to the utility of a dollar spent on toffee. At this point, there is nothing to be gained by a further switch of expenditure from toffee to cashews. If the consumer persists in reallocating expenditure, she will further reduce the marginal utility of cashews (by consuming more of them) and raise the marginal utility of toffee (by consuming less of them). Total utility will no longer be at its maximum because the utility of a dollar spent on toffee will now exceed the utility of a dollar spent on cashews.

So much for the simple example. Now, what can we say more generally about utility maximization? Suppose we denote the marginal utility of the last unit of product X by MU_X and its price by p_X. Let MU_Y and p_Y refer, respectively, to the marginal utility of a second product Y and its price. The marginal utility per dollar of X will be MU_X/p_X. For example, if the last unit adds 30 units to utility and costs $2, its marginal utility per dollar is 30/2 = 15.

The condition required for a consumer to be maximizing utility, for any pair of products (X and Y), is

$$\frac{MU_X}{p_X} = \frac{MU_Y}{p_Y} \qquad [1]$$

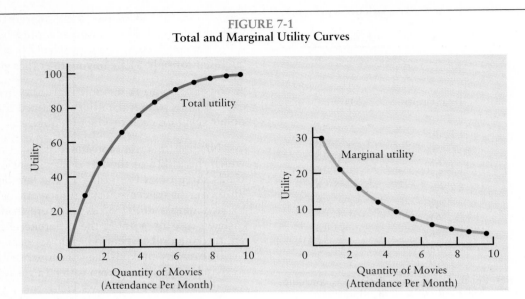

FIGURE 7-1
Total and Marginal Utility Curves

The total utility curve rises, but the marginal utility curve falls as the quantity consumed rises. The dots correspond to the values listed in Table 7-1; smooth curves have been drawn through them.

This says that the consumer will allocate expenditure so that the utility gained from the last dollar spent on each product is equal.

This is the fundamental equation of marginal utility theory. A consumer demands each good up to the point at which the marginal utility per dollar spent on it is the same as the marginal utility of a dollar spent on every other good. When this condition is met for all goods, the consumer cannot increase utility by shifting a dollar of expenditure from one product to another.

Utility and Opportunity Cost Revisited

When a consumer is deciding how much of a given product to purchase, the consumer compares the utility from that product to the utility that could be derived from spending the same money on other things. Thus for some good X, the consumer consumes to the point where the marginal utility obtained per dollar's worth of X is just equal to the marginal utility obtained per dollar of money.

The value to the consumer of consuming the last unit of some good (the marginal unit) is just equal to the opportunity cost—the value to the consumer of the money used to make the purchase.

This conclusion depends only on the assumption that the consumer maximizes utility and has preferences that exhibit diminishing marginal utility.

An Alternative Interpretation

If we rearrange the terms in Equation 1, we can gain additional insight into consumer behaviour.

$$\frac{MU_X}{MU_Y} = \frac{p_X}{p_Y} \qquad [2]$$

The right side of this equation states the *relative* price of the two goods. It is determined by the market and is outside the control of the individual consumer; the consumer reacts to these market prices but is powerless to change them. The left side states the relative ability of an additional unit of each good to add to the consumer's satisfaction. This is within the control of the consumer because in determining the quantities of different goods to buy, the consumer also determines their marginal utilities. (If you have difficulty seeing why, look again at the right side of Figure 7-1.)

If the two sides of Equation 2 are not equal, the consumer can increase total utility by rearranging purchases. To see this, suppose that the price of a unit of X is twice the price of a unit of Y ($p_X/p_Y =$ 2) and that the marginal utility of a unit of X is three times that of a unit of Y ($MU_X/MU_Y = 3$). Under these conditions, it is worthwhile for the consumer to buy more of X and less of Y. For example, if the consumer reduces purchases of Y by two units, enough purchasing power is freed to buy a unit of X. Because one extra unit of X bought yields 1½ times the satisfaction of two units of Y forgone, the switch is worth making. What about a further switch of X for Y? As the consumer buys more of X and less of Y, the marginal utility of X falls and the marginal utility of Y rises. The consumer will go on rearranging purchases, reducing Y consumption and increasing X consumption, until, in this example, the marginal utility of X is only twice that of Y. At this point, total satisfaction cannot be increased further by rearranging purchases between the two products.

The example in the previous paragraph illustrates a simple general point: Consumers face a set of prices that they cannot change and maximize their utility by adjusting the things that they can change—the quantities of the various goods they purchase—until Equation 2 is satisfied for all pairs of products.

This sort of equation—one side representing the choices made available to the individual by the outside world and the other side representing the effect of those choices on the individual's welfare—recurs often in economics. It reflects the position reached when decision makers have made the best adjustment possible to the external forces that limit their choices.

All consumers face the same set of market prices when they enter the market. When all consumers are fully adjusted to these prices, each will have identical ratios of marginal utilities for each pair of goods. Of course, a rich consumer may consume more of each product than a poor consumer. However, the rich and the poor consumers (and every other consumer) will adjust their *relative* purchases of each product so that the *relative* marginal utilities are the same for all. Thus if the price of X is twice the price of Y, each consumer will purchase X and Y to the point at which, for that consumer, the marginal utility of X is twice the marginal utility of Y. Consumers with different tastes will have different marginal utility schedules and so may consume differing relative quantities of products, even though the ratios of these marginal utilities are the same for all consumers.

DERIVATION OF THE CONSUMER'S DEMAND CURVE

To derive the consumer's demand curve for a product, it is only necessary to ask what happens when there is a change in the price of that product. As an example, let us do this for cashews. Consider Equation 2 and let X represent cashews and Y represent *all other products taken together*. In this case, the price of Y is interpreted as the average price of all other products. What will happen if, with all other prices remaining constant, there is an increase in the price of cashews? When the price of cashews rises, the right side of Equation 2 increases but until the consumer adjusts consumption, the left side is unchanged. Thus, after the price changes but before the consumer reacts, the consumer will be in a position in which the following circumstance prevails:

$$\frac{MU \text{ of cashews}}{MU \text{ of } Y} < \frac{\text{price of cashews}}{\text{price of } Y} \qquad [3]$$

What does the consumer do to restore the equality? The hypothesis of diminishing marginal utility tells us that as the consumer buys fewer cashews, the *marginal* utility of cashews will rise, thereby increasing the ratio on the left side. Thus in response to an increase in the price of cashews, with all other prices constant, the consumer will reduce his consumption of cashews (and increase his consumption of other goods) until the marginal utility of cashews rises sufficiently that Equation 2 is restored.[3]

The consumer began with the utility of the last dollar spent on cashews equal to the utility of the last dollar spent on all other goods, but the rise in cashew prices changes this. The consumer buys fewer cashews (and more of other goods) until the marginal utility of cashews rises enough to make the utility of the last dollar spent on cashews the same as

---

[3]For most consumers, cashews absorb only a small proportion of their total expenditures. If, in response to a change in its price, expenditure on cashews changes by $5 per month, this represents a large change in cashew consumption but only a negligible change in the consumption of other products. Hence in the text we proceed by assuming that the marginal utilities of other products do not change when the price and the consumption of cashews change.

MARKET AND INDIVIDUAL DEMAND CURVES

Market demand curves show how much is demanded by all purchasers. For example, in Figure 4-1, the market demand for carrots is 90,000 tons when the price is $40 per ton. This 90,000 tons is the sum of the quantities demanded by millions of different consumers. The demand curve in Figure 4-1 also tells us that when the price rises to $60, the total quantity demanded falls to 77,500 tons per month. This quantity, too, can be traced back to individual consumers. Notice that we have now described two points not only on the market demand curve but also on the demand curves of each of the millions of individual consumers.

The market demand curve is the horizontal sum of the demand curves of individual consumers. It is the horizontal sum because we wish to add quantities demanded at a given price, and quantities are measured in the horizontal direction on a conventional demand curve.

The figure illustrates aggregation over two consumers. At a price of $3, Consumer A purchases 2 units and Consumer B purchases 4 units; thus together they purchase 6 units, yielding one point on the market demand curve. No matter how many consumers are involved, the process is the same: Add the quantities demanded by all consumers at each price, and the result is the market demand curve.

(i) Consumer A   (ii) Consumer B   (iii) Consumers A and B

---

it was originally. This analysis leads to the basic prediction of demand theory:

A rise in the price of a product (holding all other things constant) will lead to a decrease in the quantity of the product demanded by each consumer.

If this is what each household does, it is also what all households taken together do. Thus the theory of consumer behaviour that we have presented here predicts a negatively sloped market demand curve in addition to a negatively sloped demand curve for each individual consumer. Extension 7-1 shows how a market demand curve can be obtained by adding up the demand curves of individual consumers.

THE DISTINCTION BETWEEN TOTAL AND MARGINAL UTILITY

An instinctive appreciation for the difference between *total* utility and *marginal* utility is important for understanding demand theory. Here are three important applications which will help to illustrate this difference.

CONSUMER SURPLUS

Imagine yourself facing an either-or choice concerning some particular product, say, ice cream: You can have the amount you are now consuming, or you can have none of it. Suppose that you would be willing to pay as much as $100 per month for the 8 litres of gourmet ice cream that you now consume, rather than do without it. Further suppose that you actually buy those 8 litres for only $50 instead of $100. What a bargain! You have paid $50 less than the most you were willing to pay. Strikingly, this sort of bargain occurs every day in any economy in which prices do the rationing. Indeed, it is so common that the $50 "saved" in this example has been given a name: *consumer surplus*. In general, **consumer surplus** is the difference between the total value that consumers place on all the units consumed of some product and the payment they must make to purchase that amount of the product.

Consumer surplus is a direct consequence of negatively sloped demand curves. To illustrate this connection, suppose that we have collected the information in Table 7-2 on the basis of an interview with Mr. Wally Ranney. Our first question to Mr. Ranney is, "If you were getting no milk at all, how much would you be willing to pay for one glass per week?" With no hesitation he replies $3.00. We then ask, "If you had already consumed that one glass, how much would you pay for a second glass per week?" After a bit of thought, he answers $1.50. Adding one glass per week with each question, we discover that he would be willing to pay $1.00 to get a third glass per week and 80, 60, 50, 40, 30, 25, and 20 cents for successive glasses from the fourth to the tenth glass per week.

The sum of the values that he places on each glass of milk gives us the *total value* that he places on all 10 glasses. In this case, Mr. Ranney values 10 glasses of milk per week at $8.55. This is the amount he would be willing to pay if he faced the either-or choice of 10 glasses or none. This is also the amount he would be willing to pay if he were offered the milk one glass at a time and charged the maximum he was willing to pay for each.

However, Mr. Ranney does not have to pay a different price for each glass of milk he consumes

TABLE 7-2
Consumer Surplus on Milk Consumption by One Consumer

(1) Glasses of Milk Consumed Per Week	(2) Amount the Consumer Would Pay to Obtain This Glass	(3) Consumer Surplus on Each Glass if Milk Costs 30 Cents Per Glass
First	$3.00	$2.70
Second	1.50	1.20
Third	1.00	0.70
Fourth	0.80	0.50
Fifth	0.60	0.30
Sixth	0.50	0.20
Seventh	0.40	0.10
Eighth	0.30	0.00
Ninth	0.25	—
Tenth	0.20	—

Consumer surplus on each unit consumed is the difference between the market price and the maximum price that the consumer is willing to pay to obtain that unit. The table shows the value that one consumer puts on successive glasses of milk consumed each week. His negatively sloped demand curve shows that he would be willing to pay progressively smaller amounts for each additional unit consumed. As long as he would be willing to pay more than the market price for any unit, he obtains consumer surplus on it when he buys it. The marginal unit is the one valued just at the market price and on which no consumer surplus is earned.

each week; he can buy all he wants at the prevailing market price. Suppose that the price is 30 cents per glass. He will buy eight glasses per week because he values the eighth glass just at the market price but all earlier glasses at higher amounts. He does not buy a ninth glass because he values it at less than the market price.

Because he values the first glass at $3.00 but gets it for 30 cents, he makes a "profit" of $2.70 on that glass. Between his $1.50 valuation of the second glass and what he has to pay for it, he clears a "profit" of $1.20. He clears a "profit" of 70 cents on the third glass, and so on. This "profit", which is shown in column 3 of Table 7-2, is his consumer surplus on each glass.

His total consumer surplus of $5.70 per week can be calculated by summing his surplus on each glass; the same total can be calculated by first summing what he would pay for all eight glasses, which is $8.10, and then subtracting the $2.40 that he does pay.

The value placed by each consumer on the total consumption of some product can be estimated in at least two ways: The valuation that the consumer places on each successive unit may be summed, or the consumer may be asked how much he or she would be willing to pay to consume the amount in question if the alternative were to have none of that product.[4]

Although other consumers would put different numerical values into Table 7-2, the negative slope of the demand curve implies that the values in column 2 would be declining for each consumer. Because a consumer will go on buying additional units until the value placed on the last unit equals the market price, it follows that there will be consumer surplus on every unit consumed except the last one.

The data in columns 1 and 2 of Table 7-2 give Mr. Ranney's demand curve for milk. It is his demand curve because he will go on buying glasses of milk as long as he values each glass at least as much as the market price he must pay for it. When the market price is $3.00 per glass, he will buy only one glass; when it is $1.50, he will buy two glasses; and so on. The total valuation is the area below his demand curve, and consumer surplus is the part of the area that lies above the price line. This is shown in Figure 7-2.

Figure 7-3 shows that the same relationship holds for the smooth market demand curve that indicates the total amount that all consumers would buy at each price.[5]

Consumer surplus is an important and useful concept. Understanding it is the key to understanding the theory of demand. In other parts of this chap-

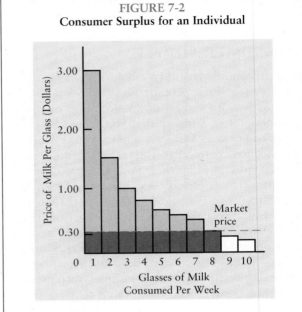

FIGURE 7-2
Consumer Surplus for an Individual

Consumer surplus is the sum of the extra valuations placed on each unit above the market price paid for each. This figure is based on the data in Table 7-2. The consumer pays the amounts shown in the dark shaded area for the eight glasses of milk he will consume per week when the market price is 30 cents per glass. The total value he places on these eight glasses is the entire shaded area. Hence his consumer surplus is the light shaded area.

ter, we will see how it helps us to explain some real-world events that on the surface seem paradoxical. Consumer surplus will also prove useful in later chapters when we evaluate aspects of the performance of the market system.

THE PARADOX OF VALUE

Early economists, struggling with the problem of what determines the relative prices of products, encountered what they called the *paradox of value*: Many necessary products, such as water, have prices that are low compared to the prices of luxury products, such as diamonds. Water is necessary to our existence, whereas diamonds are used mostly for frivolous purposes and could disappear from the face of the earth tomorrow without causing any real hardship. Does it not seem odd, then, these economists

---

[4]This is only an approximation, but it is good enough for our purposes. Although more advanced analysis indicates that it is sometimes necessary to account for the income effect discussed later in this chapter, no amount of refinement upsets the general result that we establish here: When consumers can buy all the units they require at a single market price, they pay less than they would be willing to pay if facing a choice between having the quantity they consume and having none.

[5]Figure 7-2 is a bar chart because we only allowed the consumer to vary his consumption in discrete units of one glass at a time. Had we allowed him to vary his consumption of milk one drop at a time, we could have traced out a continuous curve similar to the one shown in Figure 7-3.

FIGURE 7-3
Consumer Surplus for the Market

Quantity Consumed Per Period

Total consumer surplus is the area under the demand curve and above the price line. The demand curve shows the amount consumers would pay for each unit of the product if they had to buy their units one at a time. The area under the demand curve shows the total valuation that consumers place on all units consumed. For example, the total value that consumers place on q_0 units is the entire shaded area under the demand curve up to q_0. At a market price of p_0, the amount paid for q_0 units is the dark shaded area. Hence consumer surplus is the light shaded area.

asked, that water is so cheap and diamonds are so expensive? It took a long time to resolve this apparent paradox, so it is not surprising that even today, analogous confusions cloud many policy discussions.

The key to resolving this apparent paradox lies in the important distinction between what one would pay to avoid having one's consumption of a product *reduced to zero* and what one would pay to avoid losing the consumption of the product by *one unit*. This point involves a distinction between total and marginal values that is frequently encountered in many branches of economics.

We have seen already that the area under the demand curve shows what a consumer would pay for the product if required to purchase it unit by unit. It is thus a measure of the total value placed on all of the units that the consumer consumes. For all consumers together, the total value of q_0 units is the entire shaded area (light and dark) under the demand curve in Figure 7-3.

What about the *marginal value* that each consumer places on one more unit than is currently being consumed? This is given by the product's market

price, which is p_0 in this case. Facing a market price of p_0, each consumer buys all the units that he or she values at p_0 or greater but does not purchase any units valued at less than p_0. It follows that each consumer places on the last unit consumed of any product a value that is measured by the product's price. (Look back at Figure 7-2.)

Now look at the total *market* value of the product. This is the amount that everyone spends to purchase it. It is price multiplied by quantity. In Figure 7-3, this is the dark shaded rectangle defined by the vertical distance to p_0 and the horizontal distance to q_0.

We have seen that the total value that consumers place on a given amount of a product, as measured by the relevant area under the demand curve, is different from the total market value of a product, as given by the product's price multiplied by the quantity consumed. Not only are the two values different, but they are generally unrelated, except that the total area under the demand curve is always greater than the total market value. Figure 7-4 illustrates a case in which a good with a high total value has a low market value and vice versa.

FIGURE 7-4
Total Value Versus Market Value

The market value of the amount of some product bears no necessary relationship to the total value that consumers place on that amount. The graph presents hypothetical demand curves for water and diamonds that are meant to be stylized versions of the real curves. The total value that consumers place on water, as shown by the area under the demand curve, is great—indeed, we do not even show the curve for very small quantities because people would pay all they had rather than be completely deprived of water. The total valuation that consumers place on diamonds is shown by the area under the demand curve for diamonds. This is clearly less than the total value placed on water.

The large supply of water makes water plentiful and makes water low in price, as shown by p_w in part (i) of the figure. Thus the total *market* value of water consumed, indicated by the dark shaded area, is low. The low supply of diamonds makes diamonds scarce and keeps diamonds high in price, as shown by p_d in part (ii) of the figure. Thus the total *market* value of diamonds sold, indicated by the light shaded area, is high.

The resolution of the paradox of value is that a good that is very plentiful, such as water, will have a low price and will thus be consumed to the point where all consumers place a low value on the last unit consumed, whether or not they place a high value on their total consumption of the product. By contrast, a product that is relatively scarce will have a high market price, and consumption will therefore stop at a point where consumers place a high value on the last unit consumed, regardless of the value that they place on their total consumption of the good.

We have now reached an important conclusion:

Because the market price of a product depends not only on demand but also on supply, there is nothing paradoxical in there being a product on which con-sumers place a high total value (such as water) selling for a low price and hence having only a small amount spent on it.

FREE AND SCARCE GOODS

Consider a product for which the quantity supplied exceeds the quantity demanded at a price of zero. Such goods will not command positive prices in a market economy and hence are called **free goods.** A consumer can become better off by increasing consumption of free goods as long as the extra units consumed have positive value. It follows that free goods will be consumed up to the point at which the value that consumers place on another unit consumed is zero. At some times in some places, air, water, salt, sand, and wild fruit have been free goods.

Note that a good may be free at one time or place but not at another.

A **scarce good** is one for which the quantity demanded exceeds the quantity supplied at a price of zero. If all such goods had zero prices, the total amount that people would want to consume would greatly exceed the amount that could be produced. Such goods will therefore command positive prices in a market economy. Most goods are scarce goods.

Many people have strong views about the prices that are charged for certain products. These views are often an emotional reaction to the total values of the goods rather than to their marginal values. Here is an example: "Because water is such a complete necessity of life, both to the rich and the poor, it is wrong to make people pay for water. Instead, the government should provide free water for everyone."

When deciding between a zero price and a modest price for water, the relevant question for the consumer is not "Is water so necessary that we want everyone to be provided with some of it?" but rather "Are the marginal uses of water so important that we are willing to use scarce resources to provide the necessary quantities?" The distinction is important because the two questions have different answers.

The evidence that we have about the consumption of water at various prices suggests that the demand curve for water has a shape similar to the curve shown in part (i) of Figure 7-4. If so, the difference in consumption that results from providing water free or charging a modest price for it will be large. The additional water consumed, however, is costly to provide, and its provision requires scarce resources that could have been used to produce other goods. If the value that consumers place on the products forgone is higher than the value that they place on the extra water consumed, consumers are worse off as a result of receiving water for free. A charge for water would release resources from water production to produce goods that consumers value more highly at the margin. Of course, some minimum quantity of water could be provided free to every consumer, but the effects of this would be quite different from the effects of making *all* water free.

It follows that if we want to know the gain to consumers from consuming a little more of some product (or the loss from consuming a little less), then we need to know the *marginal value* to them of consuming the product. It is not enough simply to know the *total value* they place on consuming all units of the product.

Similar considerations apply to food, medical services, and a host of other products that are necessities of life but that also have numerous low-value uses that will be encouraged if a scarce product is provided at a zero price.

INCOME AND SUBSTITUTION EFFECTS OF PRICE CHANGES

In the first section of this chapter, we examined the relationship between the *law of diminishing marginal utility* and the slope of the consumer's demand curve for some product. In this section, we introduce an alternative method for thinking about the slope of an individual's demand curve. From the discussion in Extension 7-1, this alternative method can also be used to think about the slope of a market demand curve.

A fall in the price of one good (let's go back to our example of ice cream) affects the consumer in two ways. First, as we have emphasized throughout this chapter, relative prices change, providing an incentive to buy *more* ice cream because it is cheaper. Second, because the price of ice cream has fallen, the consumer has more *purchasing power* available to spend on all products. Suppose that the price of premium ice cream fell from $5.00 to $4.00 per litre and your friend Emil was in the habit of eating half a litre of ice cream a day. In the course of a 30-day month, Emil could keep his ice cream habit unchanged but save $15.00, money that would be available for any purpose—more ice cream, a trip to the movies, or photocopies of your economics notes.

The price fall induces an increase in Emil's **real income,** which we define as the quantity of goods and services that can be purchased with a given amount of money income. This rise in real income in turn provides an incentive to buy more of all normal goods. (Recall from Chapter 5 that when real income rises, the consumer buys more of all normal goods and less of all inferior goods.)

In general, the *extent* of the rise in real income depends on the share of total expenditures that the

CAN DEMAND CURVES HAVE A POSITIVE SLOPE?

What the great English economist Alfred Marshall (1842–1924) called the law of demand asserts that, other things being constant, the market price of a product and the quantity demanded in the market are negatively associated; that is, demand curves have a negative slope. Challenges to the law have taken various forms, focusing on Giffen goods, "conspicuous consumption" goods, and goods whose demands are perfectly inelastic. Let us consider each of these in turn.

GIFFEN GOODS

Great interest was attached to the apparent refutation of the law of demand by the English economist Sir Robert Giffen (1837–1910). He is alleged to have observed that when a rise in the price of imported wheat led to an increase in the price of bread, members of the British working class *increased* their consumption of bread. This meant that their demand curve for bread was positively sloped.

Two things must be true in order for a good to be a so-called **Giffen good**: The good must be an inferior good, and the good must take a large proportion of total household expenditure; that is, its in-

come effect must be both negative and large. Bread was indeed a dietary staple of the British working classes during the nineteenth century. A rise in the price of bread would cause a large reduction in their real income. This could lead to increased consumption of bread as households cut out their few luxuries in order to be able to consume enough bread to keep alive. Though possible, such cases are all but unknown in the modern world. The reason is that in all but the poorest societies, typical households do not spend large proportions of their incomes on a single inferior good.

CONSPICUOUS CONSUMPTION GOODS

Thorstein Veblen (1857–1929), in *The Theory of the Leisure Class,* noted that some products were consumed not for their intrinsic qualities but because they had "snob appeal." He suggested that the more expensive such a commodity became, the greater might be its ability to confer status on its purchaser.

Consumers might value diamonds, for example, precisely because diamonds are expensive. Thus a fall in price might lead them to stop buying dia-

consumer spends on each good. For example, consider the extreme case of a consumer who spends all of her income on ice cream. If the price of ice cream falls by half, she will find that her real income has doubled because she can buy twice as much as before. At the other extreme, a consumer who spends none of his income on ice cream and all of it on other things finds that his consumption opportunities are unchanged—he can still buy exactly what he bought before the price of ice cream fell. For intermediate cases where both ice cream and other goods are purchased, there will be some positive effect on real income when the price of ice cream

falls, the strength of which depends on the share of food expenditures in the consumer's budget.

THE SUBSTITUTION EFFECT

To isolate the effect of the change in relative price when the price of food falls, we can consider what would happen if we also reduce the consumer's money income to restore the original purchasing power. Suppose, in our example, that Emil's uncle sends him a monthly allowance for ice cream, and that when the price of ice cream falls, the allowance is reduced so that Emil can buy just as much ice monds and to switch to a more satisfactory object of conspicuous consumption. They may behave in the same way with respect to luxury cars, buying them *because* they are expensive.

Consumers that behave in this way will have positively-sloped *individual* demand curves for diamonds and cars. However, no one has ever observed a positively-sloped *market* demand curve for such commodities. The reason is easy to discover. The fact that countless lower-income consumers would be glad to buy diamonds or Cadillacs only if these commodities were sufficiently inexpensive suggests that positively-sloped demand curves for a few individual wealthy households are much more likely than a positively-sloped *market* demand curve for the same commodity.*

PERFECTLY INELASTIC DEMAND CURVES

Quite often, people implicitly assume that demand curves are vertical. It was once widely argued that the market demand for gasoline was almost perfectly inelastic on the grounds that people who had paid thousands of dollars for cars would not balk at pay-

ing a few cents extra for gasoline. Events have proved how wrong this argument is: Higher gasoline prices in the early 1980s led to production of smaller cars, to more car pools, to more economical driving speeds and habits, and to less pleasure driving. Falling gasoline prices in the mid-1980s led to a reversal of these trends.

MARKET DEMAND CURVES

Even if some individual consumers exhibited one or more of the "exceptions" to the law of demand discussed here, in most cases their actions would be swamped by those of consumers whose behaviour conformed to the law of demand. Thus the *market* demand curve would still be negatively sloped.

All in all, the mass of accumulated evidence confirms that demand curves generally have a negative slope. Exceptions are extremely rare.

*Of course, even with conspicuous consumption goods, the quantity demanded may rise when the price of the good goes down as long as its *perceived* price remains high. As one advertising slogan for a discount department store puts it: "Only you know how little you paid."

cream—and everything else—as he could before. Emil's purchasing power will be unchanged. If his behaviour remains unchanged, however, he will not be maximizing his utility. Recall that utility maximization requires that the ratio of marginal utility to price be the same for all goods. In our hypothetical example, with no change in behaviour, the quantities (and hence marginal utilities) and the prices of all goods other than ice cream are unchanged. The quantity of ice cream is also unchanged, but the price has fallen. To maximize his utility, Emil must therefore increase his consumption (reduce his marginal utility) of ice cream and reduce his consumption of all other goods.

In general, *holding purchasing power constant*, the change in the quantity demanded of a good whose relative price has changed is called the **substitution effect** of the price change.[6] With real income unchanged, consumers will always substitute toward goods whose relative prices have fallen and away from goods whose relative prices have increased.

[6]This measure, which isolates the substitution effect by holding the consumer's *purchasing power* constant, is known as the *Slutsky Effect*. A related but slightly different measure that holds the consumer's level of utility constant is discussed in the appendix to this chapter.

The substitution effect always increases the quantity demanded of a good whose price has fallen and always reduces the quantity demanded of a good whose price has risen.

THE INCOME EFFECT

To examine the substitution effect, we reduced Emil's *money* income following the price reduction so we could see the effect of the relative price change, holding purchasing power constant. Now we want to see the effect of the change in purchasing power, *holding relative prices constant at their new value*. To do this, suppose that after Emil has adjusted his purchases to the new price and his reduced income, he then calls his uncle and pleads to have his allowance restored to its original (higher) amount. Emil's uncle agrees, and so Emil's money income is returned to its original level. Assuming that we are dealing with normal goods, Emil will increase consumption of both ice cream and other goods. The change in the quantity of ice cream demanded as a result of the consumer's reaction to increased real income is called the **income effect**. Of course, if ice cream were an inferior good, the income effect of a price fall would lead Emil and other consumers to purchase less ice cream. This raises the possibility that demand curves could have positive slopes, which we considered in Extension 7-2.

The income effect leads consumers to buy more of a product whose price has fallen, provided that the product is a normal good.

We have now broken down the reaction to a change in the price of a product into a substitution effect and an income effect. Of course, when the price of a good falls, the consumer moves directly from the initial consumption pattern to the final one; we do not observe any "halfway" consumption pattern. By breaking this movement into two parts for analytical purposes, however, we are able to study the consumer's total change in quantity demanded as a response to a change in relative prices and a response to a change in real income.

Notice that the size of the income effect depends on the amount of income spent on the good whose price changes and on the amount by which the price changes. In our example, if Emil were initially spending one-half of his income on ice cream, a $1 fall in the price of ice cream would be equivalent to a 10 percent increase in income (20 percent of 50 percent). Now consider a different case: The price of petroleum falls by 20 percent. For a consumer who was spending only 5 percent of income on gas and oil, this is equivalent to only a 1 percent increase in purchasing power (20 percent of 5 percent).

THE SLOPE OF THE DEMAND CURVE

We have seen that the substitution effect always leads consumers to increase their demand for goods whose prices fall and to reduce their demand for goods whose prices rise. The income effect leads consumers to buy more of all normal goods whose prices fall.

Putting the income and substitution effects together gives the following support for the law of demand:

Because of the combined operation of the income and substitution effects, the demand curve for any normal commodity will be negatively sloped, indicating that a fall in price will increase the quantity demanded.

For most inferior goods, the demand curve also has a negative slope. The theoretical possibility that demand curves might not have a negative slope is considered in Extension 7-2.

SUMMARY

A. MARGINAL UTILITY AND CONSUMER CHOICE

- Marginal utility theory distinguishes between the total utility from the consumption of *all units* of some product and the incremental (or marginal) utility derived from consuming *one more unit* of the product.
- The basic assumption in marginal utility theory is that the utility that consumers derive from the consumption of successive units of a product diminishes as the number of units consumed increases.
- Consumers are assumed to make their decisions in a way which maximizes their utility. They thus make their choices such that the utility derived from the last dollar spent on each product is equal. Another way of putting this is that the marginal utilities derived from the last unit of each product consumed will be proportional to their prices.

- Demand curves have negative slopes because when the price of one product, X, falls, each consumer responds by increasing purchases of X sufficiently to restore the ratio of that product's marginal utility to its now lower price (MU_X/p_X) to the same level achieved for all other products.

B. THE DISTINCTION BETWEEN TOTAL AND MARGINAL UTILITY

- The total value that consumers place on some quantity of a product consumed is given by the area under the demand curve up to that quantity. The market value is given by an area below the market price up to that quantity. Consumer surplus is the difference between the two. In other words, consumer surplus is the difference between what the consumers would be *prepared to pay* for some quantity of the good and what the consumers *actually pay* for that quantity of the good.
- Consumer surplus arises because a consumer can purchase every unit of a product at a price equal to the value placed on the last unit purchased. The negative slope of demand curves implies that the value that consumers place on all other units purchased exceeds the value of the last unit purchased and hence that all but the last unit purchased yields consumer surplus.
- It is important to distinguish between total and marginal values because choices concerning a bit more and a bit less cannot be predicted from a knowledge of total

values. The paradox of value involves a confusion between total value and marginal value.
- Price is related to the *marginal* value that consumers place on having a bit more or a bit less of some product; it bears no necessary relationship to the *total* value that consumers place on all of the units consumed of that product.
- Consumers will consume any good that has a zero price up to the point where the marginal value that they place on further consumption is zero.

C. INCOME AND SUBSTITUTION EFFECTS OF PRICE CHANGES

- A change in the price of a product generates both an income effect and a substitution effect. The substitution effect is the reaction of the consumer to the change in relative prices, with purchasing power held constant. The substitution effect leads the consumer to increase purchases of the product whose relative price has fallen.
- The income effect is the reaction of the consumer to the change in purchasing power that is caused by the price change, holding relative prices constant. A fall in one price will lead to an increase in the consumer's purchasing power and thus to an increase in purchases of all normal goods.
- The combined income and substitution effects ensure that the quantity demanded of any normal good will increase when its money price falls, other things being equal. This means that normal goods have negatively sloped demand curves.

KEY CONCEPTS

Total utility and marginal utility	Slope of the demand curve	Income effect and substitution effect
Utility maximization	Consumer surplus	The law of demand and its possible
Equality of MU/p across different goods	The paradox of value	exceptions
	Free goods and scarce goods	

DISCUSSION QUESTIONS

1. In an effort to promote responsible drinking and to encourage the use of designated drivers, many campus bars in the country have started offering soft drinks at very low prices, sometimes even free. Describe the results you would expect in terms of the income and substitution effects.

2. Describe the difference in behaviour at a campus party at which drinks are free between someone who im-

bibes up to the point where the *marginal* value of more alcohol consumed is zero and someone who imbibes up to the point where the *average* value of alcohol consumed is zero.

3. Between 1980 and 1994, the cost of purchasing a representative bundle of consumer goods rose by almost 100 percent, as measured by the Consumer Price Index. What else would you need to know to

find out what had happened to the average Canadian's real income?

4. Compare and contrast the consequences of the income effect of a drastic fall in food prices with the consequences of a rise in incomes when prices are constant.

5. Mary is willing to pay $10 for the first widget that she purchases each year, $9 for the second, $8 for the third, and so on down to $1 for the tenth and nothing for the eleventh. How many widgets will she buy, and what will be her consumer surplus, if widgets cost $3 each? What will happen if the price of widgets rises to $5? Can you state a generalization about the relationship between consumer surplus obtained and the price of a product?

6. Two economics professors in the United States recently estimated that a 25 percent increase in wages will cause the average individual to reduce the time that he or she spends sleeping by about 1 percent. Interpret this in terms of the substitution effect. Would you expect to find an income effect on the amount of time that a person spends sleeping?

7. Consider the following common scenario. An economist is attending a conference in an unfamiliar city. She is in the mood for a high-quality dinner and wanders through the centre of the city looking for a restaurant. After narrowing her search to two establishments, she ultimately selects the restaurant with the higher prices. Because she is an economist, we know that she is rational. What might account for this behaviour?

8. Predict the relative magnitudes of changes in consumption due to a 10 percent rise in the prices of the following commodities. Pay particular attention to the expected size of the income effects.

a. Salt
b. Blue jeans
c. Gasoline
d. Automobiles
e. Aspirin

9. One often-touted characteristic of the "information superhighway" is the ability of consumers to have access to 500-channel cable systems. However, recent experiments by selected telecommunication companies with such super cable systems met with only lukewarm consumer response. Why might consumers not respond positively to a 200 to 500 percent increase in viewing options?

10. Medical and hospital services in Canada are provided at zero cost to all Canadians and are paid for out of general government revenues. What will be the *marginal value* of such services consumed by each Canadian if the government provides funds to meet all demand? What will differ when the government reduces the supply of these services (in order to save money to reduce their budget deficits)?

APPENDIX TO CHAPTER 7

Indifference Curve Analysis

In Chapter 7, we covered some basic material concerning the theory of demand; here we extend the treatment of demand theory by considering in more detail the assumptions about consumer behaviour that underlie the theory of demand.

The history of demand theory has seen two major breakthroughs. The first was *marginal utility theory*, which we used in Chapter 7. By distinguishing total and marginal values, this theory helped to explain the so-called paradox of value. The second breakthrough came with *indifference theory*, which showed that all that is required to develop demand theory is to assume that consumers can always say which of two consumption bundles they prefer without having to say *by how much* they prefer it.

Indifference theory, which is sometimes called the modern theory of demand, is based on *indifference curves*.

INDIFFERENCE CURVES

Start with an imaginary consumer who currently has available some specific bundle of goods, say, 18 units of clothing and 10 units of food. Now offer the consumer an alternative bundle of, say, 13 units of clothing and 15 units of food. This alternative combination of goods has 5 fewer units of clothing and 5 more units of food than the first one. Whether the consumer prefers this new bundle depends on the relative valuation that he places on 5 more units of food and 5 fewer units of clothing. If he values the extra food more than the forgone clothing, he will prefer the new bundle to the original one. If he values the extra food less than the foregone clothing, he will prefer the original bundle. If the consumer values the extra food the same as the forgone clothing, he is said to be *indifferent* between the two bundles.

Suppose that after much trial and error, we have identified several bundles between which the consumer is indifferent. In other words, each bundle gives the consumer equal satisfaction or utility. They are shown in Table 7A-1.

There will, of course, be combinations of the two products other than those enumerated in Table 7A-1 that will give the same level of satisfaction to the consumer. All of these combinations are shown in Figure 7A-1 by the smooth curve that passes through the points plotted from the table. This curve, called an **indifference curve**, shows all combinations of products that yield the same satisfaction to the consumer; the consumer is indifferent between the combinations indicated by any two points on one indifference curve.

Any points above the curve show combinations of food and clothing that the consumer would prefer to points on the curve. Consider, for example, the combination of 20 units of food and

---

TABLE 7A-1
Alternative Bundles Giving a Consumer Equal Utility

Bundle	Clothing	Food
a	30	5
b	18	10
c	13	15
d	10	20
e	8	25
f	7	30

These bundles all lie on a single indifference curve. Because all of these bundles of food and clothing give the consumer equal utility, the consumer is indifferent between them.

FIGURE 7A-1
An Indifference Curve

This indifference curve shows combinations of food and clothing that yield equal utility and between which the consumer is indifferent. Points *a* through *f* are plotted from Table 7A-1. The smooth curve through them is an indifference curve; each combination on it gives equal satisfaction to the consumer. Point *g* above the line is a preferred combination to any point on the line; point h below the line is an inferior combination to any point on the line. The slope of the line *T* gives the marginal rate of substitution at point *b*. Moving down the curve from *b* to *f*, the slope flattens, showing that the more food and the less clothing the consumer has, the less willing the consumer will be to sacrifice further clothing to get more food.

and to the left of the curve represent bundles that are inferior to bundles represented by points on the curve.

DIMINISHING MARGINAL RATE OF SUBSTITUTION

How much clothing would the consumer be prepared to give up to get one more unit of food? The answer to this question measures what is called the marginal rate of substitution of clothing for food. The **marginal rate of substitution (MRS)** is the amount of one product that a consumer is prepared to give up to get one more unit of another product.

The first basic assumption of indifference theory is that the algebraic value of the *MRS* is always negative.

A negative *MRS* means that to increase consumption of one product, the consumer is prepared to decrease consumption of a second product. The negative value of the marginal rate of substitution is indicated graphically by the negative slope of all indifference curves. (See, for example, the curve in Figure 7A-1.)

The second basic assumption of indifference theory is that the marginal rate of substitution between any two products depends on the amounts of the products currently being consumed.

Consider a case in which the consumer has a lot of clothing and only a little food. Common sense suggests that the consumer might be willing to give up quite a bit of plentiful clothing to get one unit more of scarce food. It suggests as well that a consumer with a little clothing and a lot of food would be willing to give up only a little scarce clothing to get one more unit of already plentiful food.

This example illustrates the hypothesis of **diminishing marginal rate of substitution.** The less of one product, *A*, and the more of a second product, *B*, that the consumer has already, the smaller the amount of *A* that the consumer will be willing to give up to get one additional unit of *B*. The hypothesis says that the marginal rate of substitution changes when the amounts of two products consumed change. The graphical expression of this is that any indifference curve becomes flatter as the consumer moves downward and to the right along the curve. In Figure 7A-1, a movement downward and to the right means that less clothing and more

18 units of clothing, represented by point *g* in Figure 7A-1. Although it may not be obvious that this bundle must be preferred to bundle *a* (which has more clothing but less food), it is obvious that it will be preferred to bundle *c* because both less clothing and less food are represented at *c* than at *g*. Inspection of the graph shows that any point above the curve will be superior to some points on the curve in the sense that it will contain both more food and more clothing than those points on the curve. However, because all points on the curve are equal in the consumer's eyes, any point above the curve must be superior to all points on the curve. By a similar argument, all points below

TABLE 7A-2
The Marginal Rate of Substitution Between Clothing and Food

Movement	(1) Change in Clothing	(2) Change in Food	(3) Marginal Rate of Substitution (1) ÷ (2)
From *a* to *b*	−12	5	−2.4
From *b* to *c*	−5	5	−1.0
From *c* to *d*	−3	5	−0.6
From *d* to *e*	−2	5	−0.4
From *e* to *f*	−1	5	−0.2

The marginal rate of substitution of clothing for food declines (in absolute value) as the quantity of food increases. This table is based on Table 7A-1. When the consumer moves from *a* to *b*, he gives up 12 units of clothing and gains 5 units of food; he remains at the same level of overall satisfaction. The consumer at point *a* is prepared to sacrifice 12 units of clothing for 5 units of food (i.e., 12/5 = 2.4 units of clothing per unit of food obtained). When the consumer moves from *b* to *c*, he sacrifices 5 units of clothing for 5 units of food (a rate of substitution of 1 unit of clothing for each unit of food).

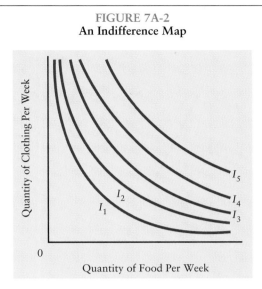

FIGURE 7A-2
An Indifference Map

Quantity of Clothing Per Week

I_1 I_2 I_3 I_4 I_5

0

Quantity of Food Per Week

An indifference map consists of a set of indifference curves. All points on a particular curve indicate alternative combinations of food and clothing that give the consumer equal satisfaction. The farther the curve is from the orgin, the higher is the level of satisfaction it represents. For example, I_5 is a higher indifference curve than I_4, which means that all the points on I_5 yield a higher level of satisfaction than do the points on I_4.

food is being consumed. The decreasing steepness of the curve means that the consumer is willing to sacrifice less and less clothing to get each additional unit of food. [12]

The hypothesis is illustrated in Table 7A-2, which is based on the example of food and clothing in Table 7A-1. The last column of the table shows the rate at which the consumer is prepared to sacrifice units of clothing per unit of food obtained. At first, the consumer will sacrifice 2.4 units of clothing to get 1 unit more of food, but as his consumption of clothing diminishes and his consumption of food increases, the consumer becomes less and less willing to sacrifice further clothing for more food.

THE INDIFFERENCE MAP

So far, we have constructed only a single indifference curve. However, starting at any other point of Figure 7A-1, such as *g*, there will be other combinations that will yield equal satisfaction to the consumer. If the points indicating all of these combina-

tions are connected, they will form another indifference curve. This exercise can be repeated as many times as we wish, and we can generate as many indifference curves as we wish. The farther any indifference curve is from the origin, the higher will be the level of satisfaction given by any of the points on the curve.

A set of indifference curves is called an **indifference map,** an example of which is shown in Figure 7A-2. It specifies the consumer's tastes by showing his rate of substitution between the two products for every possible level of current consumption of these products.

When economists say that a consumer's tastes are *given,* they do not mean that the consumer's current consumption pattern is given; rather, they mean that the consumer's entire indifference map is given.

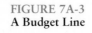

FIGURE 7A-3
A Budget Line

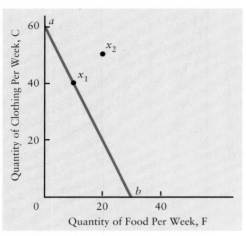

The budget line shows the quantities of goods available to a consumer given money income and the prices of goods. Any point in this diagram indicates a combination (or bundle) of so much food and so much clothing. Point x_1, for example, indicates 40 units of clothing and 10 units of food per week.

With an income of $720 a week and prices of $24 per unit for food and $12 per unit for clothing, the consumer's budget line is ab. This line shows all the combinations of F and C available to a consumer spending this income at these prices. The consumer could spend all of this money income on clothing and obtain 60 units of clothing and zero food each week. The consumer could likewise go to the other extreme and purchase only food, buying 30 units of F and zero units of C. The consumer could also choose an intermediate position and consume some of both goods—for example, spending $240 to buy 10 units of F and $480 to buy 40 units of C (point x_1). Points above the budget line, such as x_2, are not attainable.

THE BUDGET LINE

Indifference curves illustrate consumers' tastes. To develop a complete theory of their choices, we must also illustrate the alternatives available to them. These we show as the solid line ab in Figure 7A-3. That line, called a **budget line,** shows all the combinations of food and clothing that the consumer can buy if he spends a fixed amount of money, in this case his entire money income of $720 per week, at

fixed prices of the products. (It is also sometimes called an *isocost line* because all points on it represent bundles of goods with the same total cost.)

PROPERTIES OF THE BUDGET LINE

The budget line has several important properties:

1. Points on the budget line indicate bundles of products that use up the consumer's entire income. (Try, for example, the point 20C, 20F.)

2. Points between the budget line and the origin indicate bundles of products that cost less than the consumer's income. (Try, for example, the point 20C, 10F.)

3. Points above the budget line indicate combinations of products that cost more than the consumer's income. (Try, for example, the point 30C, 40F.)

The budget line shows all combinations of products that are available to the consumer given his money income and the prices of the goods that he purchases.

We can also show the consumer's alternatives with an equation that uses symbols to express the information contained in the budget line. Let E stand for the consumer's money income, which must be equal to the consumer's total expenditure on food and clothing. If P_F and P_C represent the money prices of food and clothing, respectively, and F and C represent the quantities of food and clothing chosen, then spending on clothing is equal to P_F times F, and spending on clothing is P_C times C. Thus the equation for the budget line is

$$E = P_F \times F + P_C \times C$$

THE SLOPE OF THE BUDGET LINE

Look again at the budget line shown in Figure 7A-3. The vertical intercept is 60 units of clothing, and the horizontal intercept is 30 units of food. Thus the slope is equal to −2. The minus sign means that increases in purchases of one of the goods must be accompanied by decreases in purchases of the other. The numerical value of the slope indicates how much of one good must be given up to obtain an additional unit of the other; in our example, the slope of −2 means that it is necessary to forgo the purchase of 2 units of clothing to acquire 1 extra unit of food.

Recall that in Chapter 4, we contrasted the *absolute,* or *money,* price of a product with its *relative* price, which is the ratio of its absolute price to that of some other product or group of products. One important point is that the relative price determines the slope of the budget line. In terms of our example of food and clothing, the slope of the budget line is determined by the relative price of food in terms of clothing, P_F/P_C; with the price of food (P_F) at $12 per unit and the price of clothing (P_C) at $6 per unit, the slope of the budget line (in absolute value) is -2. [13]

The significance of the slope of the budget line for food and clothing is that it reflects the *opportunity cost* of food in terms of clothing. To increase food consumption while maintaining expenditure constant, one must move along the budget line and therefore consume less clothing; the slope of the budget line determines how much clothing must be given up to obtain an additional unit of food.

The opportunity cost of food in terms of clothing is measured by the slope of the budget line, which is equal to the relative price ratio, P_F/P_C.

In the example, with fixed income and with the relative price of food in terms of clothing (P_F/P_C) equal to 2, it is necessary to forgo the purchase of 2 units of clothing to acquire 1 extra unit of food. The opportunity cost of a unit of food is thus 2 units of clothing. Notice that the relative price (in our example, $P_F/P_C = 2$) is consistent with an infinite number of absolute prices. If $P_F = 40 and $P_C = 20, it is still necessary to sacrifice 2 units of clothing to acquire 1 unit of food.[1] This shows that relative, not absolute, prices determine opportunity cost.

THE CONSUMER'S UTILITY-MAXIMIZING CHOICE

An indifference map describes the preferences of a consumer, and a budget line describes the possibili-

ties available to a consumer. To predict what a consumer will actually do, both sets of information must be combined. This is done in Figure 7A-4. The consumer's budget line is shown by the straight line, and the curves from the indifference map are also shown. Any point on the budget line is attainable, but which point will actually be chosen by the consumer?

Because the consumer wishes to maximize utility, he wishes to reach the highest attainable indifference curve. Inspection of Figure 7A-4 shows that if the consumer purchases any bundle on the budget line at a point cut by an indifference curve, a higher indifference curve can be reached. Only when the bundle purchased is such that the indifference curve is tangent to the budget line is it impossible for the consumer to reach a higher curve by altering his purchases.

The consumer's utility is maximized at the point where an indifference curve is tangent to the budget line. At that point, the consumer's marginal rate of substitution for the two goods is equal to the relative prices of the two goods.

The intuitive explanation for this result is that if the consumer values goods differently than the market does, there is room for profitable exchange. The consumer can give up some of the good that he values relatively less than the market does and take in return some of the good that he values relatively more than the market does. When the consumer is prepared to exchange goods at the same rate as they can be traded on the market, there is no further opportunity for the consumer to raise utility by substituting one product for the other.

The theory thus proceeds by supposing that the consumer is presented with market prices that he cannot change and then analyzing how the consumer adjusts to these prices by choosing a bundle of goods such that, at the margin, his own subjective evaluation of the goods coincides with the valuations given by market prices.

We now use this theory to predict the typical consumer's response to a change in income and in prices.

THE CONSUMER'S REACTION TO A CHANGE IN INCOME

A change in the consumer's money income will, *ceteris paribus*, shift the budget line. For example, if the

---

[1]Of course, with a given income, the consumer can afford much less of each at these higher money prices, but the opportunity cost of food in terms of clothing remains unchanged.

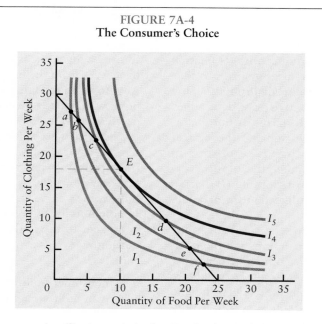

FIGURE 7A-4
The Consumer's Choice

The consumer's utility is maximized at *E*, where an indifference curve is tangent to the budget line. The consumer has a money income of $750 per week and faces money prices of $25 per unit for clothing and $30 per unit for food. A combination of units of clothing and food indicated by point *a* on I_1 is attainable, but by moving along the budget line, higher indifference curves can be reached. The same is true at *b* on I_2 and at *c* on I_3. At *E*, however, where an indifference curve (I_4) is tangent to the budget line, it is impossible to reach a higher curve by moving along the budget line. A consumer who altered the consumption bundle by moving from *E* to *d*, for example, would move to the lower indifference curve I_3 and hence to a lower level of utility.

consumer's income doubles, he will be able to buy twice as much of both goods compared with any combination on his previous budget line. The budget line will therefore shift out parallel to itself to indicate this expansion in the consumer's consumption possibilities. (The fact that it will be a parallel shift is established by our previous demonstration that the slope of the budget line depends only on the relative price of the two products.)

For each level of income, there will be a utility-maximizing point at which an indifference curve is tangent to the relevant budget line. Each such utility-maximizing position means that the consumer is doing as well as possible at that level of income. If we move the budget line through all possible levels of income and if we join up all the utility-maximizing points, we will trace out what is called an **income-consumption line,** an example of which is shown in Figure 7A-5. This line shows how the consumption bundle changes as income changes, with relative prices being held constant.

THE CONSUMER'S REACTION TO A CHANGE IN PRICE

We already know that a change in the relative price of the two goods changes the slope of the budget line. Given the price of clothing, for each possible price of food there is a utility-maximizing consumption bundle for the consumer. If we connect these bundles, at a given money income, we will trace out a **price-consumption line,** as shown in Figure 7A-6. Notice that in this example, as the relative prices of food and clothing change, the relative quantities of

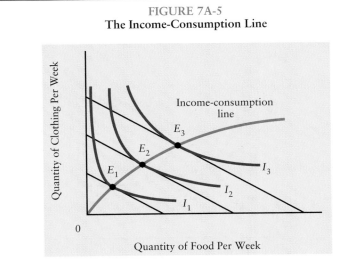

FIGURE 7A-5
The Income-Consumption Line

Quantity of Clothing Per Week

Income-consumption
line

E_3

E_2

I_3

E_1

I_2

I_1

0

Quantity of Food Per Week

**The income-consumption line shows how the consumer's purchases re-
act to a change in money income with relative prices being held constant.** Increases in money income cause a parallel outward shift of the
budget line, moving the utility-maximizing point from E_1 to E_2 to E_3.
By joining all the utility-maximizing points, an income-consumption
line is traced out.

food and clothing purchased also change. In particular, as the price of food falls, the consumer buys
more food and less clothing.

DERIVATION OF
THE DEMAND CURVE

What happens to the consumer's demand for some
product, say, gasoline, as the price of that product
changes, *holding constant the prices of all other goods?*

If there were only two products purchased by
consumers, we could derive a demand curve for one
of the products from the price-consumption line like
the one shown in Figure 7A-6. When there are many
products, however, a change in the price of one product generally causes substitution toward (or away
from) *all other goods.* Thus we would like to have a
simple way of representing the individual's tastes in a
world of many products.

In part (i) of Figure 7A-7, a new type of indifference map is plotted in which litres of gasoline per

month are measured on the horizontal axis and the
value of all other goods consumed per month is plotted
on the vertical axis. We have in effect used "everything
but gasoline" as the second product. The indifference
curves in this figure then show the rate at which the
consumer is prepared to substitute gasoline for money
(which allows him to buy all other goods) at each level
of consumption of gasoline and of all other goods.

To illustrate the derivation of demand curves, we
use the numerical example shown in Figure 7A-7.
The consumer is assumed to have an after-tax money
income of $4,000 per month. This level of money in-
come is plotted on the vertical axis, showing that if
the consumer consumes no gasoline, he can consume
$4,000 worth of other goods each month. When
gasoline costs $1.50 per litre, the consumer could
buy a maximum of 2,667 litres per month. This gives
rise to the innermost budget line. Given the consumer's tastes, utility is maximized at point E_0, consuming 600 litres of gasoline and $3,100 worth of
other products.

Next let the price of gasoline fall to $1.00 per
litre. Now the maximum possible consumption of

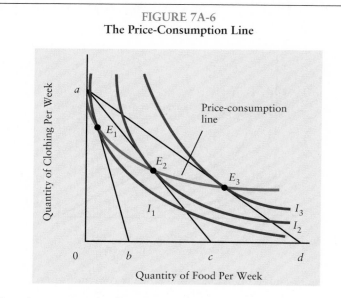

FIGURE 7A-6
The Price-Consumption Line

The price-consumption line shows how the consumer's purchases react to a change in one price with money income and other prices being held constant. Decreases in the price of food (with money income and the price of clothing being held constant) pivot the budget line from *ab* to *ac* to *ad*. The utility-maximizing bundle moves from E_1 to E_2 to E_3. By joining all the utility-maximizing points, a price-consumption line is traced out, showing more food and less clothing bought as the price of food falls.

gasoline is 4,000 litres per month, giving rise to the middle budget line in the figure. The consumer's utility is maximized, as always, at the point where the new budget line is tangent to an indifference curve. At this point, E_1, the consumer is consuming 1,200 litres of gasoline per month and spending $2,800 on all other goods. Finally, let the price fall to 50 cents per litre. The consumer can now buy a maximum of 8,000 litres per month, giving rise to the outermost of the three budget lines. The consumer maximizes utility by consuming 2,200 litres of gasoline per month and spending $2,900 on other products.

If we let the price vary over all possible amounts, we will trace out a complete price-consumption line, as shown in the figure. The points derived in the preceding paragraph are merely three points on this line.

We have now derived all that we need to plot the consumer's demand curve for gasoline, now that we

know how much the consumer will purchase at each price. To draw the curve, we merely replot the data from part (i) of Figure 7A-7 onto a demand graph, as shown in part (ii) of Figure 7A-7.

Like part (i), part (ii) has quantity of gasoline on the horizontal axis. By placing one graph under the other, we can directly transcribe the quantity determined on the upper graph to the lower one. We first do this for the 600 litres consumed on the innermost budget line. We now note that the price of gasoline that gives rise to that budget line is $1.50 per litre. Plotting 600 litres against $1.50 in part (ii) produces the point x, derived from point E_0 in part (i). This is one point on the consumer's demand curve. Next we consider the middle budget line, which occurs when the price of gasoline is $1.00 per litre. We take the figure of 1,200 litres from point E_1 in part (i) and transfer it to part (ii). We then plot this quantity against the price of $1.00 to get the point y on the demand curve. Doing the same thing for point E_2

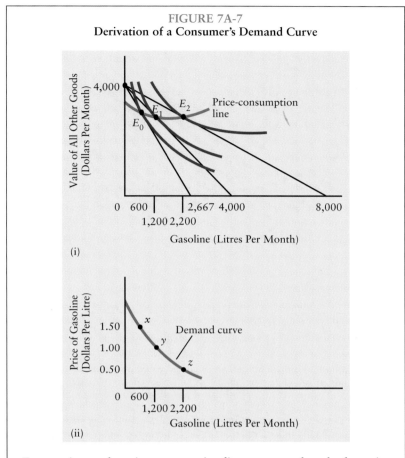

FIGURE 7A-7
Derivation of a Consumer's Demand Curve

Every point on the price-consumption line corresponds to both a price of the product and a quantity demanded; this is the information required for a demand curve. In part (i), the consumer has a money income of $4,000 and alternatively faces prices of $1.50, $1.00, and $0.50 per litre of gasoline, choosing positions E_0, E_1, and E_2 at each price. The information for litres demanded at each price is then plotted in part (ii) to yield the consumer's demand curve. The three points x, y, and z in part (ii) correspond to the points E_0, E_1, and E_2 in part (i).

yields the point z in part (ii): price 50 cents, quantity 2,200 litres.

Repeating the operation for all prices yields the demand curve in part (ii). Note that the two parts of Figure 7A-7 describe the same behaviour. Both parts measure the quantity of gasoline on the horizontal axes; the only difference is that in part (i) the price of gasoline determines the slope of the budget line, whereas in part (ii) the price of gasoline is plotted explicitly on the vertical axis.

THE SLOPE OF THE DEMAND CURVE

The price-consumption line in part (i) of Figure 7A-7 indicates that as price decreases, the quantity of gasoline demanded increases, thus giving rise to the negatively sloped demand curve in part (ii). As we saw in Chapter 7, the key to understanding the negative slope of the demand curve is to distinguish between the income effect and the substitution effect of a change in

FIGURE 7A-8
The Income Effect and the Substitution Effect of a Price Change

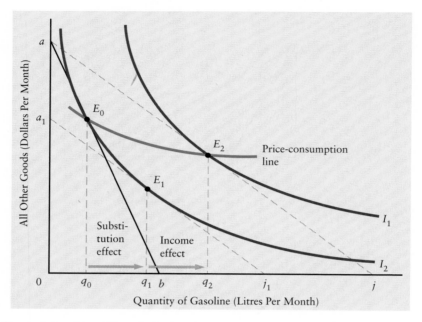

The substitution effect is defined by sliding the budget line around a fixed indifference curve; the income effect is defined by a parallel shift of the budget line. The original budget line is at ab, and a fall in the price of gasoline takes it to aj. The original utility-maximizing point is at E_0 with q_0 of gasoline being consumed, and the new utility-maximizing point is at E_2 with q_2 of gasoline being consumed. To remove the income effect, imagine reducing the consumer's money income until the original indifference curve is just attainable. We do this by shifting the line aj to a parallel line nearer the origin a_1j_1 that just touches the indifference curve that passes through E_0. The intermediate point E_1 divides the quantity change into a substitution effect q_0q_1 and an income effect q_1q_2.

price. This distinction can be made more precisely, and somewhat differently, using indifference curves.

Income and Substitution Effects

In Chapter 7, we examined the substitution effect of a reduction in price by eliminating the income effect. We did this by reducing money income until the consumer could just purchase the original bundle of goods. We then examined how the change in relative prices affected the consumer's choices. In indifference theory, however, the income effect is removed by changing money income until the *original level of utility*—the original indifference curve—can just be achieved. This results in a slightly different measure of the income effect, but the principle involved in separating the total change into an income effect and a substitution effect is exactly the same as in Chapter 7.[2]

The separation of the two effects according to indifference theory is shown in Figure 7A-8. The figure

shows in greater detail part of the price-consumption line first drawn in Figure 7A-7. Points E_0 and E_2 are on the price-consumption line for gasoline. We can think of the separation occurring in the following way. After the price of the good has fallen, we reduce money income *until the original indifference curve can just be obtained*. This leads the consumer to move from point E_0 to an intermediate point E_1, and this response is defined as the substitution effect. Then, to measure the income effect, we restore money income. The consumer moves from the point E_1 to the final point E_2, and this response is defined as the income effect.

[2]The approach used in Chapter 7 defines constant real income as constant purchasing power. The introduction of indifference curves allows a slightly more sophisticated concept of constant real income: constant utility as captured by the original indifference curve. However, the two are very similar in practice, and indeed, in most empirical applications, the approach taken in Chapter 7 is used.

SUMMARY

A. INDIFFERENCE CURVES

- Indifference curves describe consumers' tastes or preferences. A single indifference curve joins combinations of products that give consumers equal satisfaction and among which they are therefore indifferent. An indifference map is a set of indifference curves.
- The basic hypothesis about tastes is that of *diminishing marginal rate of substitution*. This hypothesis states that the less of one good and the more of another the consumer has, the less willing she will be to give up some of the first good to get an additional unit of the second. This means that indifference curves are downward sloping and convex to the origin.

B. BUDGET LINES

- The budget line shows all combinations of products that are available to a consumer with a given amount of money income who faces given prices of the products. The slope of the budget line is determined by the relative prices of the products; the position of the budget line is determined by both prices and income.

C. UTILITY MAXIMIZATION

- Given the constraint of the budget line, the consumer's utility is maximized by consuming a bundle of goods such that the indifference curve through that bundle is tangent to the budget line.
- The income-consumption line shows how quantity consumed changes as income changes with relative prices being held constant.
- The price-consumption line shows how quantity consumed changes when the price of one product changes. When prices change, the consumer will consume more of the product whose relative price falls.
- The price-consumption line relating the purchases of one particular product to all other products contains the same information as a conventional demand curve. The horizontal axis measures quantity, and the slope of the budget line measures price. Transferring this price-quantity information to a diagram whose axes represent price and quantity yields a demand curve.
- The effect of a change in price of one product, all other prices and money income being held constant, changes not only relative prices but also real incomes. A change in price affects consumption through both the substitution effect and the income effect.

DISCUSSION QUESTIONS

1. We have all seen people who consume too much alcohol at parties. Often, even though these individuals are quite sick, they continue to drink. Draw an indifference curve for alcohol for a person who has begun to get ill but still continues to drink. Explain your representation.

2. Figure 7A-5 shows the behaviour of a hypothetical consumer as income increases. Do you think that such responses would hold globally? How might the response differ if the individual has $10,000 in income versus $1 million in income? Would there ever be a time when a person might exhibit no response to an increase in income? If so, what would the indifference map look like in that case?

CHAPTER **8**

PRODUCTION AND COST IN THE SHORT RUN

To find out how market prices and quantities are determined, we know that we must consider the interaction of demand *and* supply. In Chapter 7, we examined the theory of demand. In this chapter and the next, we build a theory of how firms behave. To understand supply, we must find out, among other things, what determines the cost of various goods and services. It turns out that for most products, cost and output are closely related. This implies that a convincing theory of cost is inextricably intertwined with a theory of the level of production. Chapters 8 and 9 develop just such a theory. Extension 8-1 considers the question of why firms even exist in the first place.

EXTENSION 8-1

WHY ARE THERE FIRMS?

Throughout this book, we study the role of markets in allocating resources. Markets work through the forces of supply and demand: People with a particular good or service to sell and people who wish to purchase that good or service satisfy their mutual desires by exchanging with each other.

However, not all mutually advantageous trade occurs through markets; often it occurs within institutions and, in particular, within firms. Most economists, like most other people, are inclined simply to take the existence of firms for granted. But in a famous article published in 1937, Professor Ronald Coase of the University of Chicago, the recipient of the 1991 Nobel Prize in economics, took up the question posed in the title of this box.*

The key to understanding Coase's argument is to recognize that there are costs associated with transactions, known, appropriately enough, as **transactions costs.** When a firm purchases something, it must identify the market and then find what different quantities and qualities are available at what prices. This takes time and money; it usually involves some uncertainty. When the firm decides instead to produce the thing itself, it uses the command principle and orders the commmodity to be made to its desired specifications. The transactions costs may be lower, but the advantages of buying in a competitive market are lost. Furthermore, as the firm gets larger, the inefficiencies of the command system tend to become large compared with the efficiencies involved in decentralizing through the market system.

The firm must choose when to transact internally and when to transact through the market. For example, a car manufacturer must decide whether to purchase a certain component by contracting with a parts manufacturer to supply it or to "supply the component to itself" by producing it. Coase viewed the firm as an institution that economizes on transactions costs, and thus he argued that the market works best when transactions costs are low, but when transactions costs are high, the firm has an incentive to use internal mechanisms in place of market transactions.

Coase's insights have stimulated a great deal of further research by economists such as Professor Oliver Williamson of the University of California at Berkeley. This research has contributed to the understanding of the interaction of institutions and markets. Organization theorists have stressed that firms sometimes require less information than do markets for certain types of transactions; for example, transactions within firms do not require that the decision makers know market prices. Some research even shows that transactions within firms sometimes generate information that is useful to the firm; for example, a close relationship between the producer of a particular component and the user might lead to improvements in its design. Another aspect is that when firms internalize a production process, they use one type of contract (say, with employees) to replace a set of often more complicated contracts with external suppliers.

Coase's analysis has proved remarkably robust over the years, and its influence has spread throughout economics. As economic historian and 1993 Nobel laureate Douglass North recently put it, "Whenever transactions costs are high, institutions become important."

---

* "The Nature of the Firm," *Economica* (1937).

PROFITS AND COSTS

The theory of the firm is based on the assumption that firms maximize profits, an assumption that we will examine and criticize in Chapter 14. An immediate corollary of the assumption that firms maximize profits is that, given any particular level of output, they minimize costs.[1]

Before we begin our analysis of how profit-maximizing (and cost-minimizing) firms behave, it is worth taking a little time to be precise about exactly what economists mean when they use the words *profit* and *cost* and to examine some general consequences of profit maximization and cost minimization.

MOTIVATION: PROFIT MAXIMIZATION

Economists predict the behaviour of firms by studying the effect that making each choice available to the firm would have on profits. They then predict that firms will select the alternative that yields the largest profits. This theory does not say that profit is the *only* factor that influences the firm's behaviour; rather, it says that profits are important enough that assuming profits to be the firm's sole objective will produce predictions that are substantially correct.

FACTORS OF PRODUCTION

Firms seek profits by producing and selling products. In order to make their products, firms purchase materials such as metal, wood, electricity, and paint. They also purchase the services of factors of production—they hire workers, purchase or rent land, and purchase or rent machines. Economists use the word **inputs** to refer to all such purchases. They refer to the goods and services that result from the production process as **outputs.** One way of looking at the production process is to regard the inputs as being combined to produce the outputs. Another equally useful way is to regard the inputs as being used up, or sacrificed, to gain the outputs.

It is important to make the distinction among the different types of inputs. For example, among the inputs used to produce automobiles are steel, rubber, spark plugs, electricity, land, machinists, cost accountants, forklift operators, managers, designers, robots, drill presses, and painters. These inputs can be grouped into four broad classes: (1) those that are inputs for the automobile manufacturer but outputs for some other manufacturer, such as spark plugs, electricity, and steel; (2) those that are provided directly by nature, such as the land used by the automobile plant; (3) those that are provided directly by households, such as the services of workers; and (4) those that are provided by machines, such as drill presses and robots.

Inputs in the first group just mentioned are called **intermediate products.** They are goods that are produced by other firms, and they appear as inputs only because the stages of production are divided among different firms so that at any one stage, some firms are using as inputs goods produced by other firms. If these products are traced back to their sources, all production can be accounted for by the services of only three kinds of inputs, which we call **factors of production.** The three fundamental factors of production are:

- **Land.** Includes all gifts of nature, such as land and raw materials.[2]

- **Labour.** All physical and mental contributions that are provided by people are called labour.

- **Capital.** All manufactured aids to further production, such as machines, are referred to as capital.

Extensive use of capital is one distinguishing feature of modern production. Instead of making consumer goods with only the aid of simple natural tools, productive effort goes into the manufacture of tools, machines, and other goods that are desired not in themselves but as aids to making other goods.

---

[1]A firm's plant and equipment can be useful in its strategic behaviour against other firms. For example, a firm may sensibly invest in *unused* capacity as a means of detering entry into the industry by other firms. In this case, the firm would not be minimizing its costs for a given level of output, though such a strategy may be a profit-maximizing one. In our basic theory we ignore such strategic behaviour by firms and assume that the only purpose of plant and equipment is to produce current output. In this case, the assumption of profit maximization implies cost minimization. We examine strategic behaviour by firms in Chapter 12.

[2]Economists have begun to distinguish between land and the natural resources found on or below the land, such as oil, natural gas, or minerals. In Chapter 17, we discuss the pricing and use of nonrenewable natural resources.

The Short Run

The **short run** is a time period in which the quantity of some inputs, called **fixed factors,** cannot be increased.[3] A fixed factor is usually an element of capital (such as plant and equipment), but it might be land, the services of management, or even the supply of skilled labour. Inputs that can be varied in the short run are called **variable factors.**

The short run does not correspond to a specific number of months or years. In some industries, it may extend over many years; in others, it may be a matter of months or even weeks. In the electric power industry, for example, it takes three or more years to acquire and install a steam turbine generator. An unforeseen increase in demand will involve a long period during which the extra demand must be met with the existing capital equipment. In contrast, a machine shop can acquire new equipment or sell existing equipment in a few weeks. An increase in demand will have to be met with the existing stock of capital for only a brief time, after which it can be adjusted to the level made desirable by the higher demand.

The Long Run

The **long run** is a time period in which all inputs may be varied but in which the basic technology of production cannot be changed. Like the short run, the long run does not correspond to a specific length of time.

The long run corresponds to the situation the firm faces when it is planning to go into business, to expand the scale of its operations, to branch out into new products or new areas, or to change its method of production. The firm's *planning decisions* are long-run decisions because they are made from given technological possibilities but with freedom to choose from a variety of production processes that will use factor inputs in different proportions.

The Very-Long Run

Unlike the short run and the long run, the **very-long run** is a period of time in which the technological possibilities available to a firm will change. Modern industrial societies are characterized by continuously changing technologies that lead to new and improved products and production methods.

Some of these technological advances are made by the firm's own research and development efforts. For example, much of the innovation in computer hardware and software has been made by IBM, Apple, and Microsoft. Some firms adopt technological changes developed by others. For example, liquid crystal displays and microprocessor chips have revolutionized dozens of industries that had nothing to do with developing them. Firms must regularly decide how much to spend in efforts to change technology either by developing new techniques or by adapting techniques that have been developed by others.

CONNECTING THE RUNS: THE PRODUCTION FUNCTION

The **production function** describes the precise physical relationship between factor inputs and output.

The various runs are simply different aspects of the same basic problem: getting output from inputs efficiently. They differ in terms of what the firm is able to change.

A simplified production function in which there are only two factors of production, labour and capital, will be considered here, but the conclusions apply equally when there are many factors. In the short run, which is the focus of the remainder of this chapter, capital is taken to be the fixed factor and labour the variable one. This chapter deals with the short-run situations in which output and cost change as different amounts of the variable input, labour, are used. Long-run situations in which both factors can be varied and very-long-run situations in which the production function changes are both covered in Chapter 9.

---

[3]Sometimes it is physically impossible to increase the quantity of a fixed factor in a short time. For instance, there is no way to build a hydroelectric dam or a power plant in a few months. In other cases, it might be physically possible but prohibitively expensive to increase the quantity of a fixed factor in a short time. For example, a suit-manufacturing firm could conceivably rent a building, buy and install new sewing machines, and hire a trained labour force in a few days if money were no consideration. Prohibitive costs and physical impossibility are both determinants of fixed factors.

Short-run choices for the firm

Suppose that a firm starts with a fixed amount of capital (say, 4 units) and contemplates applying various amounts of labour to it. Table 8-2 shows three different ways of looking at how output varies with the quantity of the variable factor.

Total, Average, and Marginal Products

Total product *(TP)* is the total amount that is produced during a given period of time. If the inputs of all but one factor are held constant, total product will change as more or less of the variable factor is used. This variation is shown in columns 1 and 2 of Table 8-2, which gives a total product schedule. Part (i) of Figure 8-1 shows such a schedule graphically. (The shape of the curve will be discussed shortly.)

Average product *(AP)* is the total product divided by the number of units of the variable factor used to

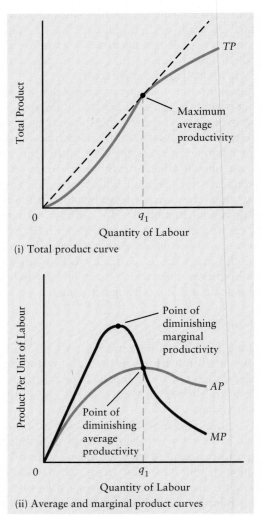

FIGURE 8-1
Total Product, Average Product, and Marginal Product Curves

(i) Total product curve

(ii) Average and marginal product curves

Total product *(TP)*, **average product** *(AP)*, **and marginal product** *(MP)* **curves often have the shapes shown here.** The total product curve in part (i) shows the total product steadily rising, first at an increasing rate and then at a decreasing rate. This causes both the average and the marginal product curves in part (ii) to rise at first and then to decline. The point of diminishing average productivity is q_1. At this point, $MP = AP$.

TABLE 8-2
Variation of Output with Fixed Capital and Variable Labour

(1) Quantity of Labour (L)	(2) Total Product (TP)	(3) Average Product (AP)	(4) Marginal Product (MP)
0	0	–	
			15
1	15	15.0	
			19
2	34	17.0	
			14
3	48	16.0	
			12
4	60	15.0	
			2
5	62	12.4	

The relationship between changes in output and changes in the quantity of labour can be looked at in three ways. Capital is assumed to be fixed at 4 units. As the quantity of labour increases, the level of output (the total product) increases. Average product increases at first and then declines. The same is true of marginal product. Marginal product is shown between the lines because it refers to the *change* in output from one level of labour input to another. When the schedule is graphed, marginal products are plotted at the midpoint of the interval. For example, the marginal product of 12 would be plotted to correspond to a quantity of labour of 3.5.

produce it. If we let the number of units of labour be denoted by L, the average product is given by

$$AP = \frac{TP}{L}$$

Notice in column 3 of Table 8-2 that as more of the variable factor is used, average product first rises and then falls. The level of output at which average product reaches a maximum (34 units of output in the example) is called the **point of diminishing average productivity.** Up to that point, average productivity is increasing; beyond that point, average productivity is decreasing.

Marginal product (MP), sometimes called *incremental product* or **marginal physical product (MPP),** is the change in total product resulting from the use of *one additional unit* of the variable factor:[4] **[14]**

$$MP = \frac{\Delta TP}{\Delta L}$$

Computed values of marginal product are shown in column 4 of Table 8-2. The figures in this column are placed between the other lines of the table to stress that the concept refers to the *change* in output caused by the *change* in quantity of the variable factor. For example, the increase in labour from 3 to 4 units ($\Delta L = 1$) raises output by 12 from 48 to 60 ($\Delta TP = 12$). Thus the *MP* equals 12, and it is recorded between 3 and 4 units of labour. Note that the *MP* in the example first rises and then falls as output increases. The level of output at which marginal product reaches a maximum is called the **point of diminishing marginal productivity.**

Part (ii) of Figure 8-1 plots average product and marginal product curves. Although three different schedules are shown in Table 8-2 and three different curves are shown in Figure 8-1, they are all aspects of the same single relationship described by the production function. As we vary the quantity of labour, with capital being fixed, output changes. Sometimes it is interesting to look at total product, sometimes at average product, and sometimes at the marginal product.

Finally, bear in mind that the schedules in Table 8-2 and the curves in Figure 8-1 all assume a specified quantity of the fixed factor. If the quantity of capital were, say, 10 units instead of the 4 that we assumed, there would be a different set of total product, average product, and marginal product curves. The reason is that if for any specified amount of labour there is more capital to work with, labour can then produce more output; that is, the total product will be greater.

AVERAGE AND MARGINAL PRODUCT CURVES

A great deal of important economic information is given by the shapes of the average and marginal product curves.

The Law of Diminishing Returns

The variations in output that result from applying more or less of a variable factor to a given quantity of a fixed factor are the subject of a famous economic hypothesis, referred to as the **law of diminishing returns.**

The law of diminishing returns states that if increasing amounts of a variable factor are applied to a given quantity of a fixed factor, eventually a situation will be reached in which each additional unit of the variable factor adds less to total product than the previous unit did; that is, the marginal product of the variable factor will decline.

The commonsense explanation of the law of diminishing returns is that as output is increased in the short run, more and more of the variable factor is combined with a given amount of the fixed factor. As a result, each unit of the variable factor has less and less of the fixed factor to work with. When the fixed factor is capital and the variable factor is labour, each unit of labour gets a declining amount of capital to assist it as the total output grows. It is not surprising, therefore, that sooner or later, equal increases in labour eventually begin to add less and less to total output.

It is possible that marginal product might diminish from the outset, so that the first unit of labour contributes most to total production and each successive unit contributes less than the previous unit. It is also possible for the marginal product to rise at first and to decline only at some higher level of output. In this case, the law might more accurately be described as the law of *eventually diminishing marginal returns.*

To illustrate this second case, let us consider the use of workers in a manufacturing operation. If there is only one worker, that worker must do all the tasks, shifting from one to another and becoming competent at each. As a second, third, and subsequent workers are added, each can specialize in one task, becoming expert at it. This process, as we noted in Chapter 3, is called the *division of labour.* If additional workers allow more efficient divisions of

---

[4]Δ is read "the change in." For example, ΔL is read "the change in quantity of labour."

labour, marginal product will rise: Each newly hired worker will add more to total output than each previous worker did. However, according to the law of diminishing returns, the scope for such increases must eventually disappear, and sooner or later, the marginal products of additional workers must decline. When this happens, each additional worker that is hired will increase total output by less than the previous worker did. This case, in which marginal product rises at first and then declines, is illustrated in part (ii) of Figure 8-1.

Eventually, as more and more of the variable factor is employed, marginal product may reach zero and even become negative. It is not hard to see why if you consider the extreme case, in which there would be so many workers in a limited space that additional workers would simply get in the way, thus reducing the total output.

We have so far examined the concept of diminishing *marginal* returns; but *average* returns are also expected to diminish. The *law of diminishing average returns* states that if increasing quantities of a variable factor are applied to a given quantity of fixed factors, the average product of the variable factor will eventually decrease. Diminishing marginal and average products are both illustrated in Table 8-2 and Figure 8-1. [15]

The Significance of Diminishing Returns

Empirical confirmation of both diminishing marginal and diminishing average returns occurs frequently. Some examples are illustrated in Application 8-1. But one might wish that it were not so. There would then be no reason to fear a food crisis caused by the population explosion in less-developed countries. If the marginal product of additional workers applied to a fixed quantity of land were constant, food production could be expanded in proportion to population growth merely by keeping a constant fraction of the population on farms. With fixed techniques, however, diminishing returns dictate an inexorable decline in the marginal product of each additional labourer because an expanding population must work with a fixed supply of agricultural land.

Thus, were it not for the steady improvement in the techniques of production, continuous population growth would bring with it, according to the law of diminishing returns, declining average living standards and eventually widespread famine. This gloomy prediction of the English economist Thomas Malthus (1766–1834) is discussed further in Application 9-2 in Chapter 9.

THE AVERAGE-MARGINAL RELATIONSHIP

Notice that in part (ii) of Figure 8-1, the *MP* curve cuts the *AP* curve at the *AP*'s maximum point. This is not a matter of luck or the way the artist just happened to draw the figure. Rather, it illustrates a fundamental property of the relationship between average and marginal product curves, one that is very important to understand. [16]

The average product curve slopes upward as long as the marginal product curve is *above* it; whether the marginal product curve is itself sloping upward or downward is irrelevant. If an additional worker is to raise the average product of all workers, that additional worker's output must be greater than the average output of the other workers. It is immaterial whether the new worker's contribution to output is greater or less than the contribution of the worker hired immediately before; all that matters is that the new worker's contribution to output exceeds the *average* output of all workers hired previously.

The relationship between marginal and average measures is very general. If the marginal is greater than the average, the average must be rising; if the marginal is less than the average, the average must be falling. For example, if you have a 3.6 cumulative grade point average (GPA) through last semester and in this (marginal) semester you have a 3.4, your cumulative GPA will fall. To increase your cumulative GPA, you must score better in this (marginal) semester than you have on average in the past—that is, to increase the average, the marginal must be greater than the average.

SHORT-RUN VARIATIONS IN COST

We now shift our attention from the firm's production function to its costs. The majority of firms cannot influence the prices of the inputs that they employ; instead they must pay the going market price for their inputs. For example, a shoe factory in

---

| APPLICATION 8-1 |

DIMINISHING RETURNS

The law of diminishing returns operates in a wide range of circumstances. Here are four examples.

British Columbia's Campbell River, a noted sport-fishing area, has long been the centre of a thriving, well-promoted tourist trade. As sport-fishing has increased over the years, the total number of fish caught has steadily increased, but the number of fish *per person fishing* has decreased and the average hours fished for each fish caught has increased.*

When Southern California Edison was required to modify its Mojave power plant to reduce the amount of pollutants emitted into the atmosphere, it discovered that a series of filters applied to the smokestacks could do the job. A single filter eliminated one-half of the discharge. Five filters in series reduced the discharge to the 3 percent allowed by law. When a state senator proposed a new standard that would permit no more than 1 percent of the pollutant to be emitted, the company brought in experts who testified that this would require at least 15 filters per stack and would triple the cost.

Public opinion pollsters, as well as all students of statistics, know that you can use a sample to estimate characteristics of a large population. Even a relatively small sample can provide a useful estimate—at a tiny fraction of the cost of a complete enumeration of the population. However, sample estimates are subject to sampling error. If, for example, 38 percent of a sample approves of a certain policy, the percentage of the population that approves of it is likely to be close to 38 percent, but it might well be anywhere from 36 to 40 percent. The theory of statistics shows that the size of the expected sampling error can be reduced by increasing the sample size. However, the theory also shows that successive reductions in the sampling error require larger and larger increases in the sample size. Suppose that the original sample was 400; if quadrupling the sample to 1,600 would halve the chance of an error of any given size from occurring, then to halve it again, the new sample would have to be quadrupled again—to 6,400. In other words, increasing the sample size leads to diminishing marginal returns in terms of accuracy.

During the early days of World War II, so few naval ships were available that each North Atlantic convoy had only a few escort vessels to protect it from German submarines. The escorts dashed about from one side of the convoy to the other and ended up sinking very few submarines. As the construction program made more ships available, the escorts could stay in one position in the convoy: Some could close in on the various flanks; others could hunt farther afield. Not only did the total number of submarines sunk per convoy crossing rise, but also the number of submarines sunk per escort vessel rose. Still later in the war, as each successive convoy was provided with more and more escort vessels, the number of submarines sunk per convoy crossing continued to rise, but the number of submarines sunk per escort vessel began to fall sharply.

---

*For a *given stock of fish* and increasing numbers of boats, this example is a good illustration of the law of diminishing returns. But in recent years the story has become more complicated as overfishing has depleted the stock of fish. We examine the reasons for overfishing in Chapter 18.

Montreal, a metals manufacturer in Sarnia, a rancher in Red Deer, and a boat builder in Prince Rupert are each too small a part of the total demand for the factors that they use to be able to influence their prices significantly. The firms must pay the going rent for the land that they need, the going wage rate for the labour that they employ, and the going interest rate that banks charge for loans; so it is with

---

EXTENSION 8-2

A SUMMARY OF SHORT-RUN COST CONCEPTS

TOTAL COSTS:

Total Cost *(TC)* = Total Fixed Cost *(TFC)* + Total Variable Cost *(TVC)*

> **Total Cost** is the total cost to the firm of producing a given level of output.
>
> **Total Fixed Cost** is the sum of all costs of production that do not vary with the level of output. Also called overhead costs.
>
> **Total Variable Cost** varies directly with the level of output; it rises as more ouptut is produced and falls as less output is produced.

AVERAGE COSTS:

Average Total Cost *(ATC)* = Average Fixed Cost *(AFC)* + Average Variable Cost *(AVC)*

> **Average Total Cost** is the total cost *per unit*

of output: $ATC = \dfrac{TC}{\text{Units of Output}}$.

Average Fixed Cost is the fixed cost *per unit* of output: $AFC = \dfrac{TFC}{\text{Units of Output}}$.

Average Variable Cost is the variable cost *per unit* of output: $AVC = \dfrac{TVC}{\text{Units of Output}}$.

MARGINAL COSTS:

> Marginal Cost is the increase in total cost resulting from increasing the level of output by one unit. Also called incremental cost.

$$MC = \frac{\text{Change in Total Cost}}{\text{Change in Output}} = \frac{\Delta TC}{\Delta Q}$$

Note: Since some of total costs are fixed costs, which do not change as the level of output changes, marginal cost is also equal to the increase in variable cost that results when output is increased by one unit.

---

most other firms.[5] Given these prices and the physical returns summarized by the product curves, the costs of different levels of output can be calculated.

COST CONCEPTS DEFINED

The following definitions of several cost concepts are closely related to the product concepts just introduced.

Total cost *(TC)* is the full cost of producing any given level of output. Total cost is divided into two parts, *total fixed cost* and *total variable cost*. **Total fixed cost** *(TFC)* does not vary with the level of output; it is the same whether output is 1 unit or 1 million units. Such a cost is also referred to as an *over-*

head cost. A cost that varies directly with output, rising as more output is produced and falling as less output is produced, is called a **total variable cost** *(TVC)*. In the example in Table 8-2, labour is the variable factor of production, and wages are therefore a variable cost.

Average total cost *(ATC)*, also called **average cost** *(AC)*, is the total cost of producing any given number of units of output divided by that number. Average total cost is therefore the (average) cost *per unit of output*. ATC can be separated into **average fixed costs** *(AFC)*, fixed cost divided by quantity of output, and **average variable costs** *(AVC)*, variable cost divided by quantity of output.

Although average *variable* costs may rise or fall as production is increased, it is clear that average *fixed* costs decline continuously as output increases. A doubling of output always leads to a halving of fixed costs per unit of output. This is a process popularly known as *spreading one's overhead*.

Marginal cost *(MC)*, sometimes called *incremental cost*, is the increase in total cost resulting

---

[5]The firm that is a large enough employer of labour or user of land or capital to affect the prices of its factor services is the exception rather than the rule. The exceptions are very large firms who employ much of the world's total of a given factor and firms in isolated towns that have only one large employer. Even in these cases, the firm does not have complete control over the wages it pays, as we shall see in Chapters 15 and 16.

FIGURE 8-2
Total Cost, Average Cost, and Marginal Cost Curves

Total cost (TC), average cost (AC), and marginal cost (MC) curves often have the shapes shown here. Total fixed cost does not vary with output. Total variable cost and the total of all costs (*TC = TVC + TFC*) rise with output, first at a decreasing rate and then at an increasing rate. The total cost curves in part (i) give rise to the average and marginal cost curves in part (ii). Average fixed cost *(AFC)* declines as output increases. Average variable cost *(AVC)* and average total cost *(ATC)* fall and then rise as output increases. Marginal cost *(MC)* does the same, intersecting *ATC* and *AVC* at their minimum points. Capacity output is q_c, the minimum point on the *ATC* curve.

from raising the rate of production by one unit. Because fixed costs do not vary with output, marginal fixed costs are always zero. Therefore, marginal costs are necessarily marginal variable costs, and a change in fixed costs will leave marginal costs unaffected. For example, the marginal cost of producing a few more potatoes by farming a given amount of land more intensively is not affected by the rent paid for the land. [17]

See Extension 8-2 for a summary of the firm's short-run cost concepts.

SHORT-RUN COST CURVES

Using the production relationships found in Table 8-2, suppose that the price of labour is $10 per unit and that the price of capital is $25 per unit. The cost schedules that result from these values are shown in Table 8-3.

Figure 8-2 shows some hypothetical cost curves. The shape of these curves are similar to the ones that would result from plotting the data in Table 8-3. Notice that the marginal cost curve cuts the average

total cost curve and the average variable cost curve at their lowest points. This is another example of the relationship between a marginal and an average curve. The *ATC* curve, for example, slopes downward as long as the *MC* curve is below it; it makes no difference whether the *MC* curve is itself sloping upward or downward.

To see this, consider an example in which 10 units are produced each week at an average cost of $5 per unit (total cost equals $50). The average cost of producing 11 units will exceed $5 if the eleventh unit adds more than $5 to total cost (*MC* exceeds *AC*) and will be less than $5 if the eleventh unit adds less than $5 to total cost (*MC* is less than *AC*). (The marginal cost of the tenth unit does not matter for this calculation. It could be above, below, or equal to the eleventh unit's marginal cost.)

Short-Run Average Variable Cost

In Figure 8-2, the average variable cost curve reaches a minimum and then rises. For given factor prices, when average product per worker is at a

TABLE 8-3
Variation of Costs with Capital Fixed and Labour Variable

(1) Labour (L)	(2) Output (q)	Total Cost ($)			Marginal Cost ($ per unit)	Average Costs ($ per unit)		
		(3) Fixed (TFC)	(4) Variable (TVC)	(5) Total (TC)	(6) (MC)	(7) Fixed (AFC)	(8) Variable (AVC)	(9) Total (ATC)
0	0	100	0	100		—	—	—
1	15	100	10	110	0.67	6.67	0.67	7.33
2	34	100	20	120	0.53	2.94	0.59	3.53
3	48	100	30	130	0.71	2.08	0.62	2.71
4	60	100	40	140	0.83	1.67	0.67	2.33
5	62	100	50	150	5.00	1.61	0.81	2.42

The relationship of cost to level of output can be looked at in several ways. These cost schedules are computed from the product schedule of Table 8-2, given the price of capital of $25 per unit and the price of labour of $10 per unit. Marginal cost (in column 6) is shown between the lines of total cost because it refers to the change in cost divided by the change in output that brought it about. For example, the MC of $0.71 is the $10 increase in total cost (from $120 to $130) divided by the 14-unit increase in output (from 34 to 48). In constructing a graph, marginal costs should be plotted midway in the interval over which they are computed. For example, the MC of $0.71 would be plotted at an output of 41.

maximum, average variable cost is at a minimum. [18] Common sense tells us that each additional worker adds the same amount to cost but a different amount to output, so when output per worker rises, the cost per unit of output must fall, and vice versa.

Eventually diminishing average productivity implies eventually increasing average variable costs.

Short-Run Average Total Cost

Short-run ATC curves are often U-shaped. This reflects the assumption that average productivity increases when output is low but that at some level of output, average productivity begins to fall fast enough so that average variable costs increase faster than average fixed costs are falling. When this happens, ATC increases.

Marginal Cost

In part (ii) of Figure 8-2, the marginal cost curve is shown as a declining curve that reaches a minimum and then rises. This is the reverse of the shape of the marginal product curve in part (ii) of Figure 8-1. The reason for the reversal is as follows: If extra units of a variable factor that is bought at a fixed price per unit result in increasing quantities of out-

put (marginal *product rising*), the cost per unit of extra output must be falling (marginal *cost falling*). However, if marginal product is falling, marginal cost will be rising.

The law of eventually diminishing marginal product implies eventually increasing marginal cost. [19]

Total Variable Cost

In part (i) of Figure 8-2, total variable cost is shown as an upward-sloping curve, indicating that total variable cost rises with the level of output. This is true as long as marginal cost is positive because the total variable cost of producing any given level of output is just the sum of the marginal costs of producing each unit of output up to the given level of output. [20]

CAPACITY

The level of output that corresponds to the minimum short-run average total cost is often called the *capacity* of the firm. In this sense, capacity is the largest output that can be produced without encountering rising average costs per unit. In part (ii) of Figure 8-2, capacity output is q_c units, but higher outputs can be achieved, provided that the firm is willing to accept the higher per-unit costs that accompany any level of output that is "above capacity." A firm that is producing at an output less than the point of minimum average total cost is said to have **excess capacity**.

The technical definition gives the word *capacity* a meaning that is different from the one used in everyday speech, in which it often means an upper limit that cannot be exceeded. The technical definition is, however, a useful concept in economic and business discussions.

SHIFTS IN SHORT-RUN COST CURVES

So far, we have seen how costs vary as output varies, with input prices being held constant. Figure 8-3 shows the effect on a firm's cost curves of a change in the price of any variable input. A rise in the price of any input used by the firm must raise the price of producing any given quantity of output. A fall in the price of any input has the opposite effect. This is a very simple relationship, but it is important nonetheless.

A change in the price of any variable input used by the firm will shift its marginal and average cost curves—upward for a price increase and downward for a price decrease.

There is thus a set of average and marginal cost curves that correspond to each price of the variable factor.

A FAMILY OF SHORT-RUN COST CURVES

A short-run cost curve shows how costs vary with output for a given quantity of the fixed factor, say, a given size of plant.

There is a different short-run cost curve for each given quantity of the fixed factor.

A small plant that manufactures nuts and bolts will have its own short-run cost curve. A medium-size plant and a large plant will each have its own short-run cost curve. If a firm expands and replaces its small plant with a medium-size plant, it will move from one short-run cost curve to another. This change from one plant size to another is a long-run change, which brings us to the next chapter, in which we discuss how short-run cost curves for plants of different sizes are related to each other.

FIGURE 8-3
The Effect of a Change in Input Prices

A change in any input price shifts the average total cost curve and the marginal cost curve. The original average total cost and marginal cost curves are shown by ATC_0 and MC_0. A rise in the price of a variable input—for example, the wage rate—raises the cost of producing each level of output. As a result, the average total cost curve and the marginal cost curve shift upward to ATC_1 and MC_1.

SUMMARY

A. PROFITS AND COSTS

- The key behavioural assumption in the theory of the firm is that the firm seeks to maximize its profit.
- Production consists of transforming inputs into outputs. It is often convenient to divide factors of production into categories. One common classification is land, labour, and capital. Land includes land and natural resources, labour refers to all human services, and capital denotes all manufactured aids to further production. An outstanding feature of modern production is the use of capital goods.
- The opportunity cost of using a resource is the value of that resource in its best alternative use. Measuring opportunity cost to the firm requires *imputing* the cost of resources not purchased or hired for current use. Among these imputed costs are those for the use of the owners' money, depreciation, risk taking, and any special advantages, such as trademarks, that the firm possesses.
- A firm that is maximizing profits (the difference between revenue and the opportunity cost of all the resources that it uses) is making the best allocation of the resources under its control, according to the firm's evaluation of its alternatives. When a firm is earning zero *economic profits,* its revenue is covering all of its opportunity costs. This means that it could do just as well (but not better) by using its resources in other ways.
- Economic profits and losses provide important signals concerning the allocation of resources. Profits earned in an industry provide a signal that more resources can profitably move into the industry. Losses show that resources have more profitable uses elsewhere and serve as a signal that some of these resources should be transferred out of that industry.

B. CHOICES OPEN TO THE FIRM

- A firm's production decisions can be classified into three groups:
  - The Short Run: How best to employ existing plant and equipment
  - The Long Run: What new plant and equipment and production processes to select, given known technical possibilities
  - The Very-Long Run: How to encourage or to adapt to technological changes
- The short run involves decisions in which one or more factors of production are fixed. The long run involves decisions in which all factors are variable but technology is given. The very long run involves decisions in which technology can change.
- The production function shows the output that results from each possible combination of inputs. Short-run and long-run situations can be interpreted as implying different kinds of constraints on the production function. In the short run, the firm is constrained to use no more than a given quantity of some fixed factor; in the long run, it is constrained only by the available techniques of production.

C. SHORT-RUN CHOICES FOR THE FIRM

- The theory of short-run costs is concerned with how output varies as different amounts of the variable factors are combined with given amounts of the fixed factors. The concepts of total, average, and marginal product represent alternative relationships between output and the quantity of the variable factors of production.
- The law of diminishing returns asserts that if increasing quantities of a variable factor are combined with given quantities of fixed factors, the marginal and the average products of the variable factor will eventually decrease. For given factor prices, this hypothesis implies that marginal and average costs will eventually rise.

D. SHORT-RUN VARIATIONS IN COST

- Given physical productivity schedules and the prices of inputs, it is a matter of simple arithmetic to develop the whole family of short-run cost curves, one for each quantity of the fixed factor.
- Short-run average total cost curves are often U-shaped. Average productivity increases at low levels of outputs but eventually declines sufficiently and rapidly to offset advantages of spreading overheads. The output corresponding to the minimum point of a short-run average total cost curve is called the plant's capacity.
- Changes in factor prices shift the short-run cost curves—upward when prices rise and downward when prices fall. Thus there is a whole family of short-run cost curves, one for each set of factor prices.

KEY CONCEPTS

The role of profit maximization
Inputs and factors of production
Opportunity costs
Imputed costs
The economics of durable capital: de-
preciation and sunk costs
Alternative definitions of profits

Profits and resource allocation
Short run, long run, and very-long run
Total product, average product, and
marginal product
The law of diminishing returns
Marginal product curves and average
product curves

The relationship between productivity
and cost
Total cost, marginal cost, and average
cost
Short-run cost curves
Capacity and excess capacity

DISCUSSION QUESTIONS

---

1. Can the economic theory of the firm be of any help in analyzing the decisions of such nonprofit organizations as governments, churches, and universities? What role, if any, does the notion of opportunity cost play for them?

2. "There is no such thing as a free lunch." Can anything be free? In earlier decades, gasoline stations routinely provided many free services, including windshield cleaning, tire inflation, and road maps. Now many sell road maps and have discontinued free services. Indeed, self-service stations have become increasingly popular with motorists, who like the lower gasoline prices at these stations. Under what conditions will profit-maximizing behaviour lead to the coexistence of full-service and self-service gasoline stations? What would determine the proportions in which each occurs?

3. Having bought a used car from Smiling Sam for $2,000, you drive it for two days, and it breaks down. You now find that it requires an extra $1,500 before it will run. Assuming that the car is worth less than $3,500 repaired, should you make the repairs? How does the concept of sunk cost enter your analysis?

4. Which concept of profits is implied in the following quotations?

   a. "Profits are necessary if firms are to stay in business."
   b. "Profits are signals for firms to expand production and investment."
   c. "Accelerated depreciation allowances lower profits and thus benefit the company's owners."

5. Does the short run consist of the same number of months for increasing output as for decreasing it? Must the short run in an industry be the same length for all firms in the industry? Under what circumstances

might the short run actually involve a longer time span than the very-long run for one particular firm?

6. In 1921, a classic set of experiments with chemical fertilizers was performed at the Rothampsted Experimental Station, an agricultural research institute in Hertfordshire, England. Researchers applied different amounts of a particular fertilizer to 10 apparently identical quarter-acre plots of land. The results for one test, using identical seed grain, are listed in the following table. Compute the average and marginal product of fertilizer, and identify the (approximate) points of diminishing average and marginal productivity.

Plot	Fertilizer Dose	Yield Index*
1	15	104.2
2	30	110.4
3	45	118.0
4	60	125.3
5	75	130.2
6	90	131.4
7	105	131.9
8	120	132.3
9	135	132.5
10	150	132.8

* Yield without fertilizer = 100.

7. Indicate whether each of the following conforms to the hypothesis of diminishing returns and, if so, whether it refers to marginal returns, average returns, or both.

   a. "The bigger they are, the harder they fall."
   b. "As more and more of the population receives chicken pox vaccinations, the reduction in the

chicken pox disease rate for each additional 100,000 vaccinations becomes smaller."

c. "Five workers produce twice as much today as 10 workers did 40 years ago."

d. "Diminishing returns set in last year when the rising rural population actually caused agricultural output to fall."

8. Consider the education of a person as a process of production. Regard years of schooling as one variable factor of production. What are the other factors? What factors are fixed? At what point would you expect diminishing returns to set in? For an Einstein, would diminishing returns set in during his lifetime?

9. Suppose that you are hungry and between classes. You go to a vending machine for a candy bar, deposit the required money, and press the button for your selection. Unfortunately, you do not pay enough attention and inadvertently press a button for an empty bay. Based on the discussion in the chapter, and assuming that you have more money, what should you do next? Why?

10. A carpenter quits his job at a furniture factory to open his own cabinetmaking business. In his first two years of operation, his sales average $100,000 and his operating costs for wood, workshop and tool rental, utilities, and miscellaneous expenses average $70,000. Now his old job at the furniture factory is again available. Should he take it or remain in business for himself? How would you make this decision?

11. Suppose that a large telecommunications firm launches a set of new communications satellites that carry twice the traffic of their previous satellites. Further assume that the only costs of this decision are the initial satellite construction and launch. Discuss how the cost curves for this firm may be affected.

12. The point of minimum average cost is referred to as the capacity of the firm. Yet we draw the average cost curve extending both to the left and to the right of this point. Obviously, a firm can operate below capacity, but how can a firm operate above capacity? Are there any types of firms for which it may be desirable to have a capacity below the level at which the firm may have to produce occasionally or even relatively frequently? Explain.

CHAPTER

9

PRODUCTION AND COST IN THE LONG RUN AND THE VERY-LONG RUN

In the first part of this chapter, we look at the *long run*, in which firms are free to vary all factors of production. Picking up from the end of Chapter 8, the choice that a firm faces in the long run is *which* of the family of short-run cost curves it should be on. Some firms use a great deal of capital and only a small amount of labour. Others use less capital and more labour. Here we examine the effects that these choices have on firms' costs, and we look at the conditions that determine these choices.

In the second part of the chapter, we examine the *very-long run*, in which the technology itself (the whole family of short-run cost curves) changes. The discussion concerns the improvements in technology and productivity that have dramatically increased output and incomes in all industrial countries over centuries. Firms are among the most important economic actors that cause technological advances to take place. Evidence shows that the hypotheses of profit maximization and cost minimization can help us to understand technological changes. Here, as in the short and long run, firms respond to such signals as changes in factor prices.

Throughout this chapter, we should remember that the lengths of the various runs under consideration are defined by the kinds of changes that can take place, not by calendar time. Thus we would expect actual firms in any given time period to minimize costs in the short run, as described in Chapter 8; to choose among short-run cost curves in the long run, as described in the first part of this chapter; and to change technologies as described in the latter part of this chapter.

THE LONG RUN: NO FIXED FACTORS

In the short run, in which only one factor can be varied, the only way to produce a given output is to adjust the input of the variable factor. Thus once the firm has decided on a rate of output, there is only one possible way of achieving it. In the long run, all factors can be varied, so there are numerous technically possible ways to produce any given output. The firm must decide on both a level of output *and* how to produce that output. Specifically, this means that firms in the long run must choose the type and amount of plant and equipment and the size of their labour force.

In making these choices, the firm will wish to be *technically efficient* by using no more of all inputs than necessary—that is, the firm does not want to waste any of its valuable inputs. Technical efficiency is not enough, however. To be *economically efficient,* the firm must choose from among the many technically efficient options the one that produces a given level of output at the lowest possible cost. (The distinction between various types of efficiency sometimes causes confusion, particularly when engineers and economists are involved in the same decision-making process. Extension 9-1 elaborates on this important distinction.)

Long-run planning decisions are important. A firm that decides to build a new steel mill and invest in the required machinery will choose among many alternatives. Once installed, that equipment is fixed for a long time. If the firm makes a wrong choice, its survival may be threatened; if it estimates correctly, it may be rewarded with large profits.

Long-run decisions are risky because the firm must anticipate what methods of production will be efficient not only today but also for many years in the future, when the costs of labour and raw materials will no doubt have changed. The decisions are also risky because the firm must estimate how much output it will want to produce. Is the industry to which it belongs growing or declining? Will new products emerge to render its existing products less useful than an extrapolation of past sales suggests?

PROFIT MAXIMIZATION AND COST MINIMIZATION

Any firm that is trying to maximize its profits in the long run should select the economically efficient method, which is the method that produces its output at the lowest possible cost. As we noted in the previous chapter, this implication of the hypothesis of profit maximization is called **cost minimization:** From the alternatives open to it, the profit-maximizing firm will choose the least costly way of producing whatever specific output it chooses.

Choice of Factor Mix

If it is possible to substitute one factor for another to keep output constant while reducing total cost, the firm is not using the least costly combination of factors. In such a situation, the firm should substitute one factor for another factor as long as the marginal product of the one factor *per dollar spent on it* is greater than the marginal product of the other factor *per dollar spent on it*. The firm is not minimizing its costs whenever these two magnitudes are unequal. For example, if an extra dollar spent on labour produces more output than an extra dollar spent on capital, the firm can reduce costs by spending less on capital and more on labour.

If we use K to represent capital, L to represent labour, and P_L and P_K to represent the prices per unit of the two factors, the necessary condition for cost minimization is as follows:

$$\frac{MP_K}{P_K} = \frac{MP_L}{P_L} \qquad [1]$$

Whenever the ratio of the marginal product of some factor to its price is not equal for all factors, there are possibilities for factor substitutions that will reduce costs.

EXTENSION 9-1

CONCEPTS OF EFFICIENCY

In popular discussion, business decision making, and government policies, three different types of efficiency concepts are encountered. These are engineering, technical, and economic efficiency. Each is a valid concept, and each conveys useful information. However, the use of one concept in a situation in which another is appropriate is a frequent source of error and confusion.

Engineering efficiency refers to the physical amount of some *single key input* that is used in production. It is measured by the ratio of that input to output. For example, the engineering efficiency of an engine refers to the ratio of the amount of energy in the fuel burned by the engine to the amount of usable energy produced by the engine. The difference goes in friction, heat loss, and other unavoidable sources of waste. Saying that a steam engine is 40 percent efficient means that 40 percent of the energy in the fuel that is burned in the boiler is converted into work that is done by the engine, while the other 60 percent is lost.

Technical efficiency is related to the physical amount of *all factors* used in the process of producing some product. A particular method of producing a given output is technically *inefficient* if there are other ways of producing the output that will use less of at least one input while not using more of any others.

Economic efficiency is related to the *value* (rather than the physical amounts) of all inputs used in producing a given output. The production of a given output is economically efficient if there is no other way of producing the output that will use a smaller total value of inputs.

What is the relationship between economic efficiency and these other two concepts? We have seen that engineering efficiency measures the efficiency with which a single input is used. Although knowing the efficiency of any given gasoline, electric, or diesel engine is interesting, increasing this efficiency is not necessarily economically efficient because doing so usually requires the use of other valuable resources. For example, the engineering efficiency of a gas turbine engine can be increased by using more and stronger steel in its construction. Raising the engineering efficiency of an engine saves on fuel, but at the cost of using more of other inputs. To know whether this is worth doing, the firm must compare the value of the fuel saved with the value of the other inputs used.

Technical efficiency is desirable as long as inputs are costly to the firm in any way. If a technically inefficient process is replaced by a technically efficient process, there is a saving. We do not need to put a precise value on the cost of inputs to make this judgment. All we need to know is that inputs have a positive cost to the firm, so that saving on these costs is desirable.

Usually, however, any given output may be produced in any one of many alternative technically efficient ways. Achieving technical efficiency is clearly a *necessary* condition for producing any output at the least cost. The existence of technical inefficiency means that costs can be reduced by reducing some inputs and not increasing any others. Achieving technical efficiency, however, is not a *sufficient* condition for producing at the lowest possible cost. The firm must still ask which of the many technically efficient methods it should use. This is where the concept of economic efficiency comes in. The appropriate method is the one that uses the smallest *value* of inputs. This ensures that the firm spends as little as possible producing its given output; in terms of opportunity cost, the firm sacrifices the least possible value with respect to other things that it might do with those inputs.

To see why Equation 1 must be satisfied when costs are being minimized, consider an example where the equation is *not* satisfied. Suppose that the marginal product of capital is 40 and the price of a unit of capital is $10, making the left side of Equation 1 equal to 4. Suppose also that the marginal product of labour is 20 and the price of a unit of labour is $2, making the right side equal to 10.

Thus the last dollar spent on capital adds only 4 units to output, whereas the last dollar spent on labour adds 10 units to output. In this case, it is possible for the firm to keep its output constant but reduce its costs by using more labour and less capital. Specifically, if the firm spent an additional $4 on labour, output would rise by 40 units; but then it could spend exactly $10 less on capital and output would fall back by 40 units. Making such a substitution of labour for capital would leave output unchanged but it would reduce costs by $6. Thus the original combination of factors was not a cost-minimizing one.[1]

By rearranging the terms in Equation 1, we can look at the cost-minimizing condition a bit differently.[2]

$$\frac{MP_K}{MP_L} = \frac{P_K}{P_L} \qquad [2]$$

The ratio of the marginal products on the left side compares the contribution to output of the last unit of capital and the last unit of labour. The right side shows how the cost of an additional unit of capital compares to the cost of an additional unit of labour. If the two sides of Equation 2 are the same, then the firm cannot make any substitutions between labour and capital to reduce costs (holding output constant). However, with the marginal products and factor prices used in the example above, the left side of the equation equals 2 but the right side equals 5; the last unit of capital is twice as productive as the last unit of labour but it is five times as expensive. It will thus pay the firm to switch to a method of production that uses less capital and more labour. If, however, the ratio on the right side were less than the ratio on the left, then it would pay the firm to switch to a method of production that used less labour and more capital.

We have seen that when the ratio MP_K/MP_L is greater than the ratio P_K/P_L, the firm will substitute capital for labour. This substitution is measured by changes in the **capital-labour ratio**—the amount of capital per worker used by the firm.

How far does the firm go in making this substitution? There is a limit because as the firm uses more

capital, the marginal product of capital falls, and as it uses less labour, the marginal product of labour rises. Thus the ratio MP_K/MP_L falls. When the ratio of marginal products reaches the ratio of factor prices, the firm need substitute no further.

Firms adjust the elements over which they have control (the quantities of factors used and thus the marginal products of the factors) to the prices of the factors given by the market.

Long-Run Cost Minimization

The firm will have achieved its cost-minimizing capital-labour ratio when there is no opportunity for cost-reducing substitutions. This occurs when the marginal product per dollar spent on each factor is the same (Equation 1) or, equivalently, when the ratio of the marginal products of factors is equal to the ratio of their prices (Equation 2). The preceding discussion suggests that cost-minimizing firms will react to changes in factor prices by changing their methods of production. We refer to this as the **principle of substitution**.

THE PRINCIPLE OF SUBSTITUTION

Suppose that a firm is currently meeting the cost-minimizing conditions and that the cost of labour increases while the cost of capital remains unchanged. The least-cost method of producing any output will now use less labour and more capital than was required to produce the same output before the factor prices changed.

Methods of production will change if the relative prices of factors change. Relatively more of the cheaper factor and relatively less of the more expensive factor will be used.

This is called the principle of substitution, and it follows from the assumption that firms minimize their costs.

The principle of substitution plays a central role in resource allocation because it relates to the way in which individual firms respond to changes in relative factor prices that are caused by the changing relative scarcities of factors in the economy as a whole. Individual firms are motivated to use less of factors that become scarcer to the economy and more of factors that become more plentiful. Here are two examples of the principle of substitution in action.

In recent decades, the price of "smart" word processors has fallen sharply relative to the wages of clerical workers. One result of this change has

---

[1] The argument in this paragraph assumes that the marginal products do not change when expenditure changes by a small amount.
[2] The appendix to this chapter provides a graphical analysis of this condition, which is similar to the analysis of consumer behaviour in the appendix to Chapter 7.

been the near demise of the form letter, beginning "Dear Sir or Madam." Nowadays, even total strangers send you letters that are customized by name and sometimes more. Twenty years ago, such customized attention would have required that a secretary look up the information in a file and type it into a letter. Now a well-designed mail-merge program can do the job at much lower cost, and we see the result every day. Here we see the substitution toward capital and away from labour as their relative prices change.

Some countries have plentiful land and relatively small populations. Their land prices are low, and because their labour is in short supply, their wage rates are high. In response, their farmers make lavish use of the cheap land while economizing on expensive labour; thus their production processes use low ratios of labour to land. Other countries are small in area but have large populations. The demand for land is high relative to its supply, and land is relatively expensive whereas labour is relatively cheap. In response, farmers economize on land by using much labour per unit of land; thus their production processes use high ratios of labour to land.

Once again, we see the price system functioning as an automatic control system. No single firm needs to be aware of national factor surpluses and scarcities. These are reflected by market prices, so individual firms that never look beyond their own profits are led to economize on factors that are scarce to the nation as a whole and to use factors that are abundant.

This discussion suggests why methods of producing the same product differ across countries. In Canada, where labour is generally highly skilled and expensive, a farmer with a large farm may use elaborate machinery to economize on labour. In China, where labour is abundant and capital is scarce, a much less mechanized method of production is appropriate. The Western engineer who believes that the Chinese are inefficient because they are using methods long ago discarded in the West is missing the truth about efficiency in the use of resources: Where factor scarcities differ across nations, so will the most efficient methods of production.

COST CURVES IN THE LONG RUN

When all factors can be varied, there exists a least-cost method of producing each possible level of output. Thus with given factor prices, there is a mini-

mum achievable cost for each level of output; if this cost is expressed in terms of dollars per unit of output, we obtain the long-run average cost of producing each level of output. When this cost of producing each level of output is plotted on a graph, the result is called a **long-run average cost (*LRAC*) curve.** Figure 9-1 shows one such curve.

This cost curve is determined by the technology of the industry (which is assumed to be fixed in the long run) and by the prices of the factors of production. It is a "boundary" in the sense that points below it are unattainable; points on the curve, however, are attainable if sufficient time elapses for all inputs to be adjusted. To move from one point on the *LRAC* curve to another requires an adjustment in *all* factor inputs, which may, for example, require building a larger, more elaborate factory.

The *LRAC* curve is the boundary between cost levels that are attainable, with known technology and given factor prices, and those that are unattainable.

Just as the short-run cost curves discussed in Chapter 8 relate to the *production function* describing the physical relationship between factor inputs and output, so does the *LRAC* curve. The difference is that in deriving the *LRAC* curve, there are no fixed factors of production. Thus, since all costs are variable in the long run, we do not need to distinguish between *AVC*, *AFC*, and *ATC*, as we did in the short run; in the long run, there is only one *LRAC* for any given set of input prices.

The Shape of the Long-Run Average Cost Curve

The *LRAC* curve shown in Figure 9-1 first falls and then rises. This curve is often described as U-shaped, although "saucer-shaped" might be a more accurate description of the evidence from many empirical studies. Consider the three portions of any such saucer-shaped *LRAC* curve.

Decreasing Costs. Over the range of output from zero to q_m, the firm has falling long-run average costs: An expansion of output permits a reduction of costs per unit of output. Technologies with this property are referred to as exhibiting **economies of scale.** Because the *LRAC* curve is drawn under the assumption of constant factor prices, the decline in long-run average cost occurs because output is increasing *more than* in proportion to inputs as the scale of the firm's production expands. Over this

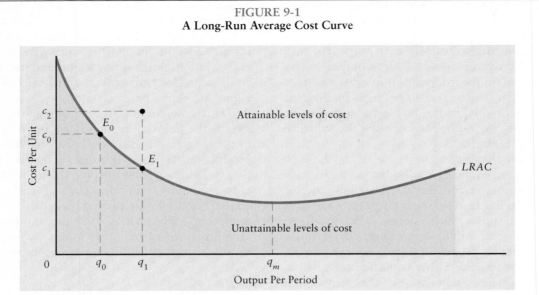

FIGURE 9-1
A Long-Run Average Cost Curve

The long-run average cost *(LRAC)* curve provides a boundary between attainable and unattainable levels of costs. If the firm wishes to produce output q_0, the lowest attainable cost level is c_0 per unit. Thus point E_0 is on the *LRAC* curve. E_1 represents the lowest possible average cost of producing q_1. Suppose that a firm is producing at q_0 and desires to increase output to q_1. In the long run, a plant optimal for output q_1 can be built, and the cost of c_1 per unit can be attained. However, in the short run, it will not be able to vary all factors, and thus costs per unit will be above c_1, say, c_2. At output q_m, the firm attains its lowest possible per unit cost of production for the given technology and factor prices.

range of output, the decreasing-cost firm is often said to enjoy long-run **increasing returns.**[3]

Increasing returns may occur as a result of increased opportunities for specialization of tasks made possible by the division of labour. Adam Smith's classic discussion of this important point is given in Extension 3-2 in Chapter 3. Even the most casual observation of the differences in production techniques used in large and small plants will show that larger plants use greater specialization.

These differences arise because large, specialized equipment is useful only when the volume of output that the firm can sell justifies employment of that equipment. For example, assembly-line techniques and body-stamping machinery in automobile production are economically efficient only when individual operations are repeated thousands of times. Use of elaborate harvesting equipment (which combines many individual tasks that would otherwise be done by hand and by tractor) provides the least-cost method of production on a big farm but not on a few acres.

Typically, as the level of planned output increases, capital is substituted for labour and complex machines are substituted for simpler machines. Robotics is a contemporary example. Electronic devices can handle huge numbers of operations quickly, but unless the level of production requires such a large volume of operations, robotics or other forms of automation will not provide the least-cost method of production.

The foregoing discussion refers to the technology of production, which is one major source of increasing returns to scale. A second source lies in the geometry that is intrinsic to the three-dimensional world in which we live. To illustrate how geometry matters, consider a firm that wishes to store a gas or a liquid. The firm is interested in the *volume* of storage space. However, the materials cost of a storage container is related to the *area* of its surface. When the size of a container is increased, the storage capacity (volume) increases faster than its surface area. This is a genuine case of increasing returns—the output, in terms

---

[3]Economists shift back and forth between speaking in physical terms ("increasing returns") and cost terms ("decreasing costs"). As the text explains, the same relationship can be expressed in either terms.

of storage capacity, increases more proportionately than the increase in the costs of the required construction materials.

A third source of increasing returns consists of inputs that do not have to be increased as the output of a product is increased, even in the long run. For example, there are often large fixed costs in developing new products, such as a new generation of airplanes or a more powerful computer. These R&D costs have to be incurred only once for each product and hence are independent of the scale at which the product is subsequently produced. Even if the product's *production costs* increase in proportion to output in the long run, average total costs, including *product development costs,* will fall as the scale of output rises. The influence of such once-and-for-all costs is that, other things being equal, they cause average total costs to be falling over the entire range of output. (The significance of such once-and-for-all costs is discussed further in Chapter 12.)

Constant Costs. In Figure 9-1, the firm's long-run average costs fall until output reaches q_m and rise thereafter. Another possibility should be noted. The firm's *LRAC* curve might have a flat portion over a range of output around q_m. With such a flat portion, the firm would be encountering constant costs over the relevant range of output. This means that the firm's long-run average costs per unit of output do not change as its output changes. Because factor prices are assumed to be fixed, the firm's output must be increasing *exactly in proportion to* the increase in inputs. When this happens, the constant-cost firm is said to be exhibiting **constant returns.**

Increasing Costs. Over the range of outputs greater than q_m, the firm encounters rising long-run average costs. An expansion in production, even after sufficient time has elapsed for all adjustments to be made, is accompanied by a rise in average costs per unit of output. If factor prices are constant, the firm's output must be increasing *less than* in proportion to the increase in inputs. When this happens, the increasing-cost firm is said to encounter long-run **decreasing returns.**[4] Decreasing returns imply that the

firm suffers some *diseconomy of scale.* As its scale of operations increases, diseconomies are encountered that increase its per-unit cost of production.

Such diseconomies may be associated with the difficulties of managing and controlling an enterprise as its size increases. For example, planning problems do not necessarily vary in direct proportion to size. At first there may be scale economies as the firm grows, but sooner or later, planning and coordination problems may multiply more than in proportion to the growth in size. If so, management costs per unit of output will rise. Other sources of scale diseconomies are the possible alienation of the labour force as size increases; it becomes more difficult to provide appropriate supervision as more and more tiers of supervisors and middle managers come between the person at the top and the workers on the shop floor. Control of middle-range managers may also become more difficult. As the firm becomes larger, managers may begin to pursue their own goals rather than devote all of their efforts to making profits for the firm. Much of the "reengineering" of large firms in the 1990s has been aimed at reducing the extent to which management difficulties increase with firm size, but the problem has not been, and probably cannot be, eliminated entirely.

The Relationship Between Long-Run and Short-Run Costs

The short-run cost curves mentioned at the conclusion of Chapter 8 and the long-run curve studied in this chapter are all derived from the same production function. Each curve assumes given prices for all factor inputs. In the long run, all factors can be varied; in the short run, some must remain fixed. The long-run average cost *(LRAC)* curve shows the lowest cost of producing any output when all factors are variable. Each short-run average total cost *(SRATC)* curve shows the lowest cost of producing any output when one or more factors are held constant at some specific level.

No short-run cost curve can fall below the long-run curve because the *LRAC* curve represents the lowest attainable cost for each possible output. As the level of output is changed, a different-size plant is normally required to achieve the lowest attainable cost. This is shown in Figure 9-2, where the *SRATC* curve lies above the *LRAC* curve *at all levels of output except q_0.*

---

[4]Long-run decreasing returns differ from short-run diminishing returns. In the short run, at least one factor is fixed, and the law of diminishing returns ensures that returns to the variable factor will eventually diminish. In the long run, all factors are variable, and it is possible that physically diminishing returns would never be encountered—at least as long as it was genuinely possible to increase inputs of all factors.

FIGURE 9-2
Long-Run Average Cost and Short-Run Average Cost Curves

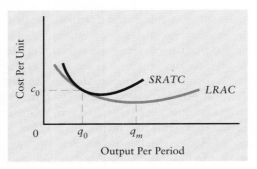

The short-run average total cost *(SRATC)* curve is tangent to the long-run average cost *(LRAC)* curve at the output for which the quantity of the fixed factors is optimal. For all other levels of output, there is either too little or too much of the fixed factors, and *SRATC* lies above *LRAC*. If output exceeds q_0, there is too little of the fixed factors; if output is less than q_0, there is too much of the fixed factor. If some level of output other than q_0 is to be sustained, costs can be reduced to the level of the long-run average cost curve when sufficient time has elapsed to adjust the plant and equipment.

As we observed at the end of Chapter 8, an *SRATC* curve is one of many such curves. The *SRATC* curve in Figure 9-2 shows how costs vary as output is varied from a base output, holding the fixed factor at the quantity most appropriate to that output. Figure 9-3 shows a family of short-run average total cost curves, along with a single long-run average cost curve. The long-run average cost curve is sometimes called an **envelope** because it encloses a series of short-run average total cost curves by being tangent to them. Each *SRATC* curve is tangent to the long-run average cost curve at the level of output for which the quantity of the fixed factor is optimal and lies above it for all other levels of output.

The relationship between the *LRAC* curve and the many different *SRATC* curves has a famous history in economics. The economist who is credited with first working out this relationship, Jacob Viner, initially made a serious mistake which ended up being published; Extension 9-2 explains his mistake and shows how it illustrates an important difference between short-run and long-run costs.

SHIFTS IN COST CURVES

The cost curves derived so far show how cost varies with output, given constant factor prices and fixed

FIGURE 9-3
The Envelope Relationship Between the Long-Run Average Cost Curve and All of the Short-Run Average Total Cost Curves

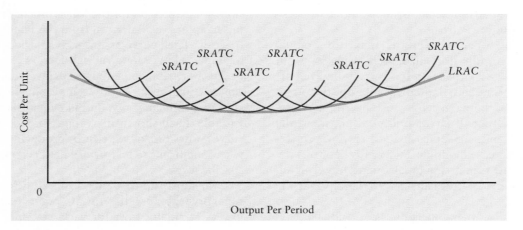

To every point on the long-run average cost (LRAC) curve, there is an associated short-run average total cost (SRATC) curve tangent at that point. Each short-run curve shows how costs vary if output varies, with the fixed factor being held constant at the level that is optimal for the output at the point of tangency.

EXTENSION 9-2

JACOB VINER AND THE CLEVER DRAFTSMAN

Jacob Viner (1892–1970) was born in Montreal and studied economics at McGill University under Stephen Leacock (1869–1944). Viner was clearly an outstanding student and, according to some of his McGill classmates, knew much more about economics than did Leacock, who was actually better known as a humourist than an economist. Viner was such a good economist that he was the first person to work out the relationship between a firm's long-run average costs and its short-run average costs. He went on to teach economics at the University of Chicago and at Princeton University and became one of the world's leading economic theorists.

The student who finds the relationship between *SRATC* and *LRAC* hard to understand may take some comfort from the fact that when Jacob Viner first worked out this relationship, and published it in 1931, he made a crucial mistake. In preparing a diagram like Figure 9-3, he instructed his draftsman to draw the *LRAC* curve through the *minimum points* of all the *SRATC* curves, "but so as to never lie above" the *SRATC* curves. Viner later said of the draftsman: "He is a mathematician, however, not an economist, and he saw some mathematical objection to this procedure which I could not succeed in understanding. I could not persuade him to disregard his scruples as a craftsman and to follow my instructions, absurd though they might be."

Viner's mistake was to require that the draftsman connect all of the *minimum* points of the *SRATC* curves rather than to construct the curve which would be the *lower envelope* of all the *SRATC* curves. The former curve can of course be drawn, but it *is not* the *LRAC* curve. The latter curve *is* the *LRAC* curve, and is tangent to each *SRATC* curve.

Since Viner's article was published in 1931, generations of economics students have experienced great satisfaction when they finally figured out his crucial mistake. Viner's famous article was often reprinted, for its fame was justly deserved, despite the importance of the mistake. But Viner always rejected suggestions that he correct the error because he did not wish to deprive other students of the pleasure of feeling one up on him.

The economic sense of the fact that tangency is *not* at the minimum points of *SRATC* rests on the subtle distinction between the *most efficient way to utilize a given plant* and the *most efficient way to produce a given level of output*. The first concept defines the minimum of any given *SRATC* curve, while the second defines a point on the *LRAC* curve for any given level of output. It is the second concept that interests us in the long run. If bigger plants can achieve lower costs per unit, there will be a gain in building a bigger plant *and underutilizing it* whenever the gains from using the bigger plant are enough to offset the costs of being inefficient in the use of the plant. If there are gains from building bigger plants (i.e., if *LRAC* is declining), there is always some underutilization that is justified.

---

technology. Changes in either technological knowledge or factor prices will cause the entire family of short-run and long-run average cost curves to shift. Loss of existing technological knowledge is rare, so technological change normally causes change in only one direction, shifting cost curves downward. Improved ways of producing existing products make lower-cost methods of production available.

Changes in factor prices can exert an influence in either direction. If a firm has to pay more for any factor that it uses, the cost of producing each level of output will rise; if the firm has to pay less for any factor that it uses, the cost of producing each level of output will fall.

A rise in factor prices shifts the family of short-run and long-run average cost curves upward. A fall in factor prices or a technological advance shifts the entire family of average cost curves downward.

Although factor prices usually change gradually, sometimes they change suddenly and drastically. For example, in the mid 1980s, oil prices fell dramatically; the effect was to shift downward the cost curves of all users of oil and oil-related products.

Technological change is constantly occurring and is typically more gradual. To this issue we now turn.

THE VERY-LONG RUN: CHANGES IN TECHNOLOGY

In the long run, profit-maximizing firms do the best they can to produce known products with the techniques and the resources currently available. This means being *on*, rather than above, their long-run cost curves. In the very-long run, the techniques and resources that are available change. Such changes cause *shifts* in long-run cost curves.

The decrease in costs that can be achieved by choosing from among available factors of production, known techniques, and alternative levels of output is necessarily limited. Improvements by invention and innovation are potentially limitless, however, and hence sustained growth in living standards is critically linked to technological change.

Technological change refers to all changes in the available techniques of production. To measure its extent, economists use the notion of **productivity**, defined as a measure of output produced per unit of resource input. The rate of increase in productivity provides a measure of the progress caused by technological change. The significance of such growth is explored further in Application 9-1.[5]

INNOVATION, INVENTION, AND TECHNOLOGICAL CHANGE

Technological change was once thought to be mainly a random process, brought about by inventions made by crackpots and eccentric scientists working in garages and scientific laboratories. As a result of recent research by economists, we now know better.

Changes in technology are often *endogenous responses* to changing economic signals; that is, they result from responses by firms to the same things that induce the substitution of one factor for another within the confines of a given technology.

_____
[5]One widely used measure of productivity is output per hour of labour. Other possible measures include output per worker, output per person, and output per unit of inputs, measured by an index number.

In our discussion of long-run demand curves in Chapter 5, we looked at just such technological changes in response to rising relative prices when we spoke of the development, in the 1970s, of smaller, more fuel-efficient cars in the wake of rising gasoline prices. Similarly, much of the move to substitute capital for labour in manufacturing, transportation, communications, mining, and agriculture in response to rising wage rates has taken the form of inventing new labour-saving methods of production.

Invention and Innovation

Invention is the creation of something new, such as a production technique or a product. **Innovation** is the introduction of an invention into methods of production. Invention is thus a precondition to innovation.

Innovation is a costly and very risky activity engaged in by firms in the hope of gaining profits; it results from responses to signals of current and expected prices and costs—that is, responses to profit incentives. Profit incentives are in turn affected by many aspects of the economic climate, among them the rate of growth of the economy, the cost and availability of money for investment, and all sorts of government policies, from taxes to regulations.

Invention is cumulative in effect. A useful invention is adopted; a useless one is discarded. The cumulative impact of many small, useful devices and techniques may be as great as the impact of one occasional dramatic mechanism such as the steam engine, the sewing machine, or the computer chip. Indeed, few famous inventions have sprung from a single act of creative genius; usually, each builds on the contributions of prior inventors. The backlog of past inventions constitutes society's technical knowledge, and that backlog in turn feeds innovation.

Kinds of Technological Change

Consider three kinds of change that influence production and cost in the very-long run.

New Techniques. Throughout the nineteenth and twentieth centuries, changes in the techniques available for producing existing products have been dramatic; this is called *process innovation*. About the same amount of coal is produced in North America today as was produced 50 years ago, but the number of coal miners is less than one-tenth what it was then. Eighty years ago, roads and railways were built by gangs of workers who used buckets, spades, and draft horses. Today, bulldozers, giant trucks, and other spe-

APPLICATION 9-1

THE SIGNIFICANCE OF PRODUCTIVITY GROWTH

Economics used to be known as the "dismal science" because some of its predictions were grim. Thomas Malthus (1766–1834) and other Classical economists predicted that the pressure of more and more people on the world's limited resources would cause a decline in output per person due to the law of diminishing returns. Human history would see more and more people living less and less well and the surplus population, which could not be supported, dying off from hunger and disease.

This prediction has proved wrong for the developed countries, for two main reasons. First, their populations have not expanded as rapidly as predicted by early economists, who were writing before birth-control techniques were widely used. Second, pure knowledge and its applied techniques have expanded so rapidly during the past 150 years that the ability to squeeze more out of limited resources has expanded faster than the population. We have experienced sustained growth in productivity that has permitted increases in output per person.

Growth in productivity permits increases in output per person and thus contributes to rising living standards.

Productivity increases are a powerful force for increasing living standards. Our great-grandparents would have regarded today's standard of living in most industrialized countries as unattainable. An apparently modest rate of increase in productivity of 2 percent per year leads to a doubling of output per hour of labour every 35 years. Productivity in Canada has increased at a rate somewhat greater than this throughout most of the twentieth century.

The growth rates of other countries have been even higher. Between 1945 and 1980, German productivity increased at 5 percent per year, doubling its output every 14 years. In Japan, it increased at more than 9 percent per year, a rate that doubles output per hour of labour approximately every 8 years! In many countries, a stable rate of productivity growth came to be taken for granted as an automatic source of ever-increasing living standards.

During the 1970s, the rate of productivity growth in most industrialized countries dropped sharply below its historical trend, and the slowdown was particularly acute in Canada and the United States. Although productivity growth has increased somewhat in the first part of the 1990s, almost no one expects the doubling of productivity in every generation to return anytime soon.

A permanent slowdown in productivity growth means that living standards rise more slowly than before.

cialized equipment have banished the workhorse completely from construction sites and to a great extent have displaced the pick-and-shovel worker.

An important new production technique called *lean production* (also often called *flexible manufacturing*) is rapidly replacing long-established *mass production, assembly line* techniques in many industries. Lean production, which was pioneered by the Japanese automobile industry and is spreading throughout the Western industrialized countries, is a more flexible, lower-cost method of production that produces higher-quality products and reduces the cost of developing new products. Lean production typically has a lower long-run cost curve than conventional mass production and a more rapidly downward-shifting cost curve in the very-long run. Lean production is discussed further in Application 9-2.

New Products.   New goods and services are constantly being invented and marketed; this is called *product innovation*. Videocassette players, personal computers, compact discs, and many other current consumer products did not exist a mere generation ago. Other products have changed so dra-

---

THE LEAN PRODUCTION REVOLUTION*

In many industries and in many countries, production techniques are currently being revolutionized by the introduction of so-called *lean production techniques* or *flexible manufacturing*. This is the most fundamental change to occur since the introduction of mass production—a technique brought to full development by Henry Ford early in the twentieth century. To understand the lean production revolution, pioneered by the Japanese, we must distinguish the three types of production methods used today.

Craft methods employ highly-skilled workers to make nonstandardized products that are often tailor-made for individual purchasers. The result is usually an expensive product of high quality, made by artisans who get considerable job satisfaction.

Mass-production methods are based on specialization and division of labour (see Extension 3-2 in Chapter 3). They use skilled personnel to design products and production methods. They then employ relatively unskilled labour to produce standardized parts and to assemble them using highly specialized, single-purpose machines. The parts are usually manufactured in separate locations, often by distinct companies, and then assembled at a central production facility, often called an *assembly line*. The design of the product is centralized, and manufacturers bid competitively to produce parts to the stated specifications. The cost of changing the specialized equipment from the production of one product variant to another is high, and hence specific product types are

produced for as long as possible. The result is a standardized product, made in a fairly small number of variants and produced at low cost with moderate quality. The work is repetitive, and workers are regarded as variable costs to be laid off or taken on as the desired rate of production varies.

Lean production methods combine the flexibility and high-quality standards of craft production with the low cost of mass production techniques. They are lean because they use less of all inputs, including time, labour, capital, and inventories, compared with either of the other techniques. They are flexible because the costs of switching from one product line to another are minimized.

In lean production, workers are organized as teams; each worker is encouraged to do all of the tasks assigned to the team, using equipment that is less highly specialized than is used in mass production techniques. This emphasizes individuality and initiative rather than a mind-numbing repetition of one unskilled operation. It also helps workers to identify places where improvements can be made and encourages them to follow up on these.

In mass-production plants, stopping an assembly line to correct a problem at one point stops work at all points. Stopping the line is therefore regarded as a serious matter, and keeping the assembly line running is the sole responsibility of a senior line manager. To reduce stoppages, large stocks of each part are held, and defective parts are discarded. Faults in assembly, which are treated as random events, are left to be corrected after the product has been assembled—often an expensive procedure. In lean production, by contrast, every worker has the ability to stop production whenever

*This material is adapted from J. P. Womack, D. T. Jones, and D. Ross, *The Machine That Changed the World* (New York: Macmillan, 1990).

---

matically that the only connection they have with the "same" product that was produced in the past is the name. A 1997 Ford is very different from a 1920 Ford, and it is even different from a 1970 Ford in size, safety, and gasoline consumption. Modern jets are revolutionary compared with the first jet aircraft, which were in turn many times larger and faster than

the DC–3, the workhorse of the airlines during the 1930s and 1940s. Beyond having wings and engines, the DC–3 itself bore little resemblance to the Wright brothers' original flying machine.

Improved Inputs. Improvements in such intangibles as health and education raise the quality of labour services. Today's workers and managers are a fault is discovered. Parts are delivered by the suppliers to the work stations "just in time." Defective parts are put aside for their source to be identified, and any defects are treated as events with patterns of causes that need to be understood. When lean methods are first introduced, stoppages are frequent as problems are identified and investigated. As the sources are found and removed, work stoppages diminish, and the typical mature lean production line, in which any worker can stop the line, stops much less frequently than the typical mass production assembly line, where only the line foreman can press the stop button.

The result for labour is much more worker identification with the job and much more worker satisfaction than under mass production techniques. Employers find that their labour force develops substantial skills, and they try to hold on to workers rather than treating them as strictly variable factors. (This can often result in some transitional difficulties as both unions and management adjust to new ways of dealing with each other.)

Product design is expensive. Mass-production firms try to reduce costs by using specialist designers. For example, one person may spend a lifetime trying to improve window-opening mechanisms. Specialization creates problems both in coordinating the work of various designers and in getting good feedback from parts producers and assembly line workers to designers. Lean producers use design teams that are nonspecialized and work closely with production engineers and parts producers. This creates more flexibility and better feedback, from the practical problems that arise in production to the basic design of products.

Although lean production methods generally still have scale economies—unit costs fall as the volume of output increases—their main effect is to shift the whole long-run cost curve downward. Lean methods are also effective in the very-long run, especially in developing successful new products that can be produced efficiently and cheaply.

Japanese automobile firms using these methods have been able to achieve unit costs of production below those of mass-production-based North American car factories that have twice their volume of output. They have also been able to lead in international competition to design new products efficiently and rapidly. Lean production methods are a major source of the Japanese competitive advantage, in automobiles and in a range of other manufactured goods. The ability of firms in other countries to compete successfully with these Japanese firms may depend on the speed with which they can institute lean methods in their own production processes.

Many Canadian and U.S. firms have redesigned their systems of operation to implement lean production methods in a process referred to as "reengineering." This has often involved a reduction in middle management, whose output is of little value in a lean system, with reduced heirarchy and more participation on the part of workers. In some cases, however, reengineering has become a euphemism for widespread layoffs. "Downsizing" of a firm may or may not be associated with moving toward lean production, and it is important to look at each case to see if the changes being made are simply efforts to cut costs by increasing the load on remaining employees or if they truly change the way that the firm is organized to produce its output.

healthier and better educated than their grandparents. Many of today's unskilled workers are literate and competent in arithmetic, and their managers are apt to be trained in methods of business management and computer science.

Similarly, improvements in material inputs occur. For example, the type and quality of metals have changed. Steel has replaced iron, and aluminum substitutes for steel in a process of change that makes a statistical category such as "primary metals" seem unsatisfactory. Even for a given category, say, steel, today's product is lighter, stronger, and more flexible than the "same" product manufactured only 20 years ago.

THE CHOICES THAT FIRMS FACE IN THE VERY-LONG RUN

When firms receive signals that the economic environment they currently face and can expect to face in the future is changing, they can respond in a number of ways.

Suppose that the price of an important input rises and that this increase is expected to persist into the future. One option for the firm is to make what we have called a long-run response by substituting away from the use of the input by changing its production techniques within the confines of existing technology. Another option is to invest in research in order to develop new production techniques that innovate away from the input. Often, both responses are adopted, but because both involve the use of costly resources, the responses are often substitutes in the sense that a particular firm may have to choose one or the other.

It is important to recognize that the two options can involve quite different actions and can ultimately have quite different implications for productivity. For example, consider three possible responses to an apparently permanent increase in labour costs.

One firm might reallocate its production activities to Mexico or Southeast Asia, where labour costs are relatively low and hence labour-intensive production techniques remain quite profitable. A second firm might elect to replace existing equipment with alternative machines that are more expensive but use less labour and hence become more attractive in the face of increased labour costs. A third firm might elect to devote resources to developing new production techniques—perhaps using robotics or other new equipment—that innovate the increased labour costs away.

All three are possible reactions to the changed circumstances. The first two are largely well understood in advance and will lead to improved efficiency relative to continued reliance on the original production methods. The third response, depending on the often unpredictable results of the innovation, may reduce costs sufficiently to warrant the investment in research and development and may even lead to substantially more effective production techniques that allow the firm to maintain an advantage over its competitors for a number of years.

In trying to understand any industry's response to changes in its operating environment, it is important to consider the effects of endogenous innovations in technology as well as substitution based on changes in the use of existing technologies.

SUMMARY

A. THE LONG RUN: NO FIXED FACTORS

- There are no fixed factors in the long run. Profit-maximizing firms choose from the alternatives open to them the least-cost method of achieving any specific output. A long-run cost curve represents the boundary between attainable and unattainable levels of cost for the given technology.
- The principle of substitution says that efficient production will use cheaper factors lavishly and more expensive ones more prudently. If the relative prices of factors change, relatively more of cheaper factors and relatively less of more expensive ones will be used.
- The shape of the long-run cost curve depends on the relationship of inputs to outputs as the whole scale of a firm's operations changes. Increasing, constant, and decreasing returns lead, respectively, to decreasing, constant, and increasing long-run average costs.

- The long-run and short-run cost curves are related. Every long-run cost corresponds to some quantity of each factor and is thus on some short-run cost curve. The short-run cost curve shows how costs vary when that particular quantity of a fixed factor is used to produce outputs greater than or less than the output for which it is optimal.
- Cost curves shift upward or downward in response to changes in the prices of factors or changes in technology. Increases in factor prices shift cost curves upward. Decreases in factor prices and technological advances shift cost curves downward.

B. THE VERY-LONG RUN: CHANGES IN TECHNOLOGY

- Over the very-long run, the most important influence on costs of production and on standards of living has been increases in output made possible by technological change—all the various changes in available techniques of production that lead to an increase in measured productivity.

- Changes in technology are often *endogenous responses* to changing economic signals; that is, they result from responses by firms to the same things that induce the substitution of one factor for another in a given technology.
- Innovation is the key to productivity growth. It requires invention but also profitable opportunities for the introduction of available knowledge. The state

of the economy, the institutional climate, and differences in technological possibilities in sectors where demand is growing and declining all affect the opportunities for innovation. Innovation can lead to technological change due to the introduction of new techniques, new products, and improved inputs.

- In trying to understand any industry's response to changes in its operating environment, it is important to consider the effects of endogenous innovations in technology as well as substitution based on changes in the use of existing technologies.

KEY CONCEPTS

The implication of cost minimization
The interpretation of $MP_K/MP_L = P_K/P_L$
The principle of substitution
Increasing, decreasing, and constant returns

Economies of scale
Envelope
Technological change and productivity growth
Changes in technology as endogenous responses

Determinants of innovation
Invention and innovation

DISCUSSION QUESTIONS

1. In *The Competitive Advantage of Nations,* Professor Michael Porter of Harvard University claimed: "Faced with high relative labor cost, . . . American consumer electronics firms moved to locate labor-intensive activities in . . . Asian countries, leaving the product and production process essentially the same. . . . Japanese rivals . . . set out instead to eliminate labor through automation. Doing so involved reducing the number of components which further lowered cost and improved quality. Japanese firms were soon building assembly plants in the United States, the place American firms had sought to avoid." Discuss these reactions in terms of changes over the long run and the very-long run.

2. Why does the profit-maximizing firm choose the least-cost method of producing any given output? Might a non-profit-maximizing organization such as a university, church, or government intentionally choose a method of production other than the least-cost one?

3. The chairman of a multinational oil company recently said, "Our government has adopted a gratuitously hostile attitude. Industry has been compelled to spend more and more of its research dollars to comply with

environmental, health, and safety regulations—and to move away from longer-term efforts aimed at major scientific advance." If this is true, is it necessarily a sign that government policies are misguided?

4. Use the principle of substitution to predict the effect of each of the following.

   a. During the 1960s, salaries of professors rose much more rapidly than those of teaching assistants. During the 1970s, salaries of teaching assistants rose more than those of professors. During the 1980s, the relative salaries of these two groups did not change greatly.

   b. The ratio of land costs to building costs is much higher in big cities than in smaller cities.

   c. Gold leaf is produced by pounding gold with a hammer. The thinner it is, the more valuable it is. The price of gold is set on the world market, but the price of labour varies among countries.

   d. Wages of textile workers and shoe machinery operators are higher in Canada than in the southern United States.

5. The long-run average cost curve can be thought of as consisting of a series of points, one taken from each

of a number of short-run average total cost curves. Explain in what sense any point on the long-run average cost curve is also on some short-run average total cost curve. What is the interpretation of a move from one point on a long-run average cost curve to another point on the same curve? Contrast this with a movement along a short-run average total cost curve.

6. Israel, a very small country, imports the "insides" of its automobiles, but it manufactures the bodies. If this makes economic sense, what does it tell us about cost conditions of automobile manufacturers?

7. Name five important modern products that were not available at the time you were born. Consider to what extent the items on your list may reflect product or process innovation.

8. Each of the following is a means of increasing productivity. Discuss which groups in a society might oppose each one.

   a. A labour-saving invention that permits all goods to be manufactured with less labour than before

   b. Rapidly increasing population growth in the economy
   c. The removal of all government production safety rules
   d. A reduction in corporate income taxes
   e. A reduction in production of services and an increase in agricultural production

9. Think of an industry with which you are familiar. Discuss the characteristics that may lead to economies of scale. Discuss the characteristics that would cause diseconomies of scale as production is continually increased.

10. Many people have called the transistor and the integrated circuit, which are the heart of the modern computer, the most important inventions of this century. Discuss the process of innovation with respect to computers. How many applications has this device found? Has the application of computers to a device or a task always resulted in a downward shift in the average cost curve?

APPENDIX TO CHAPTER 9

Isoquant Analysis

The production function gives the relationship between the factor inputs that the firm uses and the output that it obtains. In the long run, the firm can choose among many different combinations of inputs that yield the same output. The production function and the long-run choices open to the firm can be represented graphically using *isoquants*.

ISOQUANTS

Table 9A-1 illustrates a hypothetical example in which several combinations of two inputs, labour and capital, can produce a given quantity of output. The data from Table 9A-1 are plotted graphically in Figure 9A-1. A smooth curve is drawn through the points to indicate that there are additional ways, which are not listed in the table, of producing the same output.

This curve is called an **isoquant.** It shows the whole set of technologically efficient factor combinations for producing a given level of output—6 units, in this case. This is an example of graphing a relationship between three variables in two dimensions. It is analogous to the contour line on a map, which shows all points of equal altitude, and to an indifference curve (discussed in the Appendix to Chapter 7), which shows all combinations of products that yield the consumer equal utility.

As we move from one point on an isoquant to another, we are *substituting one factor for another* while holding output constant. If we move from point *b* to point *c,* we are substituting 1 unit of labour for 3 units of capital. *The marginal rate of substitution measures the rate at which one factor is substituted for another with output being held con-*

TABLE 9A-1
Alternative Methods of Producing 6 Units of Output:
Points on an Isoquant

Method	K	L	ΔK	ΔL	Rate of Substitution $\Delta K/\Delta L$
a	18	2			
b	12	3	−6	1	−6.00
c	9	4	−3	1	−3.00
d	6	6	−3	2	−1.50
e	4	9	−2	3	−0.67
f	3	12	−1	3	−0.33
g	2	18	−1	6	−0.17

An isoquant describes the firm's alternative methods for producing a given output. The table lists some of the methods available to produce 6 units of output. The first combination uses a great deal of capital *(K)* and very little labour *(L)*. As we move down the table, labour is substituted for capital in such a way as to keep output constant. Finally, at the bottom, most of the capital has been replaced by labour. The rate of substitution between the two factors is calculated in the last three columns of the table. Note that as we move down the table, the absolute value of the rate of substitution declines.

stant. Graphically, the marginal rate of substitution is measured by the slope of the isoquant at a particular point.[1] Table 9A-1 shows the calculation of some rates of substitution between various points on the isoquant. **[21]**

---

[1]Sometimes the term *marginal rate of technical substitution* is used to distinguish this concept from the analogous one for consumer theory (marginal rate of substitution) that we examined in Chapter 7. From here on, we adopt the standard convention of defining the marginal rate of substitution as the negative of the slope of the isoquant so that it is a positive number.

FIGURE 9A-1
An Isoquant for Output Equal to 6 Units

Isoquants are downward sloping and convex. The downward slope reflects the requirement of technical efficiency: Keeping the level of output constant, a reduction in the use of one factor requires an increase in the use of the other factor. The convex shape of the isoquant reflects a diminishing marginal rate of (technical) substitution. The lettered points on the graph are plotted from the data in Table 9A-1. Starting from point *a*, which uses relatively little labour and much capital, and moving to point *b*, 1 additional unit of labour can substitute for 6 units of capital (while holding production constant). However, from *b* to *c*, 1 unit of labour substitutes for only 3 units of capital. This diminishing rate is expressed geometrically by the flattening of the slope of the isoquant.

The marginal rate of substitution is related to the marginal products of the factors of production. To see how, consider an example. Suppose that at the present level of inputs of labour and capital, the marginal product of labour is 2 units of output and the marginal product of capital is 1 unit of output. If the firm reduces its use of capital and increases its use of labour to keep output constant, it needs to add only one-half unit of labour for 1 unit of capital given up. If, at another point on the isoquant with more labour and less capital, the marginal products are 2 for capital and 1 for labour, the firm will have to add 2 units of labour for every

unit of capital it gives up. The general proposition is this:

The marginal rate of (technical) substitution between two factors of production is equal to the ratio of their marginal products.

Isoquants satisfy two important conditions: They are downward sloping, and they are convex when viewed from the origin. What is the economic meaning of these conditions?

The downward slope indicates that each factor input has a positive marginal product. If the input of one factor is reduced and that of the other is held constant, output will be reduced. Thus if one input is decreased, production can be held constant only if the other factor input is increased. The marginal rate of substitution has a negative value. Decreases in one factor must be balanced by increases in the other factor if output is to be held constant.

To understand the convexity of the isoquant, consider what happens as the firm moves along the isoquant of Figure 9A-1 downward and to the right. Labour is being added and capital reduced to keep output constant. If labour is added in increments of exactly 1 unit, how much capital may be dispensed with each time? The key to the answer is that both factors are assumed to be subject to the law of diminishing returns. Thus the gain in output associated with each additional unit of labour added is *diminishing*, whereas the loss of output associated with each additional unit of capital forgone is *increasing*. It therefore takes ever-smaller reductions in capital to compensate for equal increases in labour. This implies that the isoquant is convex viewed from the origin.

AN ISOQUANT MAP

The isoquant of Figure 9A-1 is for 6 units of output. There is another isoquant for 7 units, another for 7,000 units, and a different one for every other rate of output. Each isoquant refers to a specific level of output and connects combinations of factors that are technologically efficient methods of achieving that output. If we plot a representative set of these isoquants from the same production function on a single graph, we get an *isoquant map* like that in

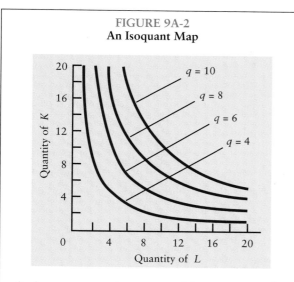

FIGURE 9A-2
An Isoquant Map

An isoquant map shows a set of isoquants, one for each level of output. Each isoquant corresponds to a specific level of output and shows factor combinations that are technologically efficient methods of producing that output.

Figure 9A-2. The higher the level of output along a particular isoquant, the farther the isoquant is from the origin.

Conditions for cost minimization

Finding the *economically efficient* way of producing any output requires finding the least-cost factor combination. To do this requires that when both factors are variable, factor prices be known. Suppose, to continue the example, that capital is priced at $4 per unit and labour at $1 per unit. In the Appendix to Chapter 7, a budget line was used to show the alternative combinations of goods that a household could buy; here an *isocost line* is used to show alternative combinations of factors that a firm could buy for a given total cost. Four different isocost lines appear in Figure 9A-3. The slope of each reflects *relative* factor prices, just as the slope of the budget line in Chapter 7 represented relative product prices. For

given factor prices, a series of parallel isocost lines will reflect the alternative levels of expenditure on factor purchases that are open to the firm. The higher the level of expenditure, the farther the isocost line is from the origin.

In Figure 9A-4, the isoquant and isocost maps are brought together. Recall that economic efficiency requires any given level of output to be produced at minimum possible cost. Thus, the economically efficient method of production must be a point on an isoquant that just touches (is tangent to) an isocost line. If the isoquant cuts the isocost line, it is possible to move along the isoquant and reach a lower level of cost. Only at a point of tangency is a movement in either direction along the isoquant a movement to a higher cost level. The lowest attainable cost of producing 6 units is $24. This cost level can be achieved only by operating at A, the point where the $24 isocost line is tangent to the 6-unit isoquant. The lowest average cost of producing 6 units is thus $24/6 = $4 per unit of output.

The least-cost position is given graphically by the tangency point between the isoquant and the isocost lines.

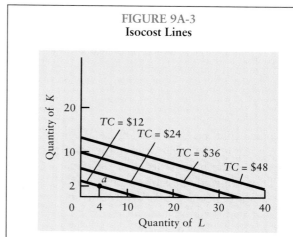

FIGURE 9A-3
Isocost Lines

Each isocost line shows alternative factor combinations that can be purchased for a given outlay. The graph shows the four isocost lines that result when labour costs $1 per unit and capital $4 per unit and when expenditure is held constant at $12, $24, $36, and $48, respectively. The line labeled *TC* = $12 represents all combinations of the two factors that the firm could buy for $12. Point *a* represents 2 units of *K* and 4 units of *L*.

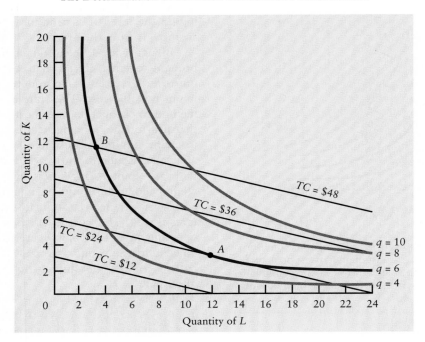

FIGURE 9A-4
The Determination of the Least-Cost Method of Production

Least-cost methods of production are represented by points of tangency between isoquant and isocost lines. The isoquant map of Figure 9A-2 and the isocost lines of Figure 9A-3 are brought together. Consider point A. It is on the 6-unit isoquant and the $24 isocost line. Thus it is possible to achieve the output q = 6 for a total cost of $24. There are other ways to achieve this output, for example, at point B, where TC = $48. Moving along the isoquant from point A in either direction increases cost. Similarly, moving along the isocost line from point A in either direction lowers output. Thus either move would raise cost per unit.

Notice that point A in Figure 9A-4 indicates not only the lowest level of cost for 6 units of output but also the highest level of output for $24 of cost. Thus we find the same solution if we set out *either* to minimize the cost of producing 6 units of output *or* to maximize the output that can be produced for $24. One problem is said to be the *dual* of the other.

The slope of the isocost line is given by the ratio of the prices of the two factors of production. The slope of the isoquant is given by the ratio of their marginal products. When the firm reaches its least-cost position, it has equated the price ratio (which is given to it by the market) with the ratio of the marginal products (which it can adjust by varying the proportions in which it hires the factors). In symbols,

$$\frac{MP_K}{MP_L} = \frac{P_K}{P_L}$$

We have now derived this result by use of the isoquant analysis of the firm's decisions. [22] Note the similarity of this condition for a cost-minimizing firm to Equation 2 in Chapter 7 where we showed how utility maximization for a consumer requires that the ratio of marginal utilities of consuming two products must equal the ratio of the two product prices.

FIGURE 9A-5
The Effects of a Change in Factor Prices on Costs and Factor Proportions

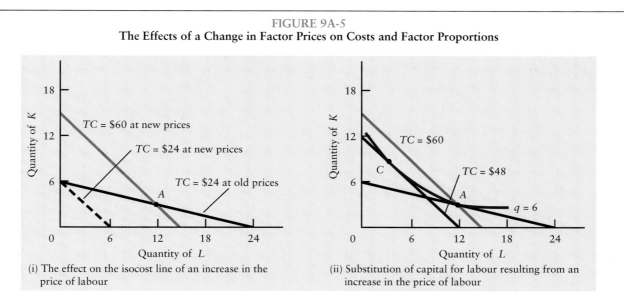

(i) The effect on the isocost line of an increase in the price of labour

(ii) Substitution of capital for labour resulting from an increase in the price of labour

An increase in the price of labour pivots the isocost line inward, increasing its slope. This changes the least-cost method of producing any output. In part (i), the rise in the price of L from $1 to $4 per unit (with the price of K being held constant at $4) pivots the $24 isocost line inward to the dashed line. Any output previously produced for $24 will cost more at the new prices if it uses any labour. The new cost of using the factor combination at A rises from $24 to $60. In part (ii), the steeper isocost line is tangent to the isoquant at C, not A, so that more capital and less labour is used. Costs at C are $48, higher than they were before the price increase but not as high as they would be if the factor substitution had not occurred.

THE PRINCIPLE OF SUBSTITUTION

Suppose that with technology unchanged (that is, for a given isoquant map), the price of one factor changes. Let us say that with the price of capital unchanged at $4 per unit, the price of labour rises from $1 to $4 per unit. Originally, the efficient factor combination for producing 6 units of output was 12 units of labour and 3 units of capital. Total cost was $24. To produce that same output in the same way would now cost $60 at the new factor prices. Figure 9A-5 shows why this is not efficient. The slope of the isocost line has changed, which makes it efficient to substitute the now relatively cheaper capital for the relatively more expensive labour. This illustrates the principle of substitution.

Changes in relative factor prices will cause a partial replacement of factors that have become relatively more expensive by factors that have become relatively cheaper.

Of course, substitution of capital for labour cannot fully offset the effects of a rise in cost of labour, as Figure 9A-5(i) shows. Consider the output attainable for $24. In the figure, there are two isocost lines representing $24 of outlay—at the old and new prices of labour. The new isocost line for $24 lies inside the old one (except where no labour is used). The $24 isocost line must therefore be tangent to a lower isoquant. This means that if production is to be held constant, higher costs must be accepted. However, because of substitution, it is not necessary to accept costs as high as those that would accompany an unchanged factor proportion. In the example, 6 units can be produced for $48 rather than the $60 that would be required if no change in factor proportions were made.

This leads to the following predictions:

A rise in the price of one factor with all other factor prices being held constant will (1) shift the cost curves of products that use that factor upward and (2) lead to a substitution of factors that are now relatively cheaper for the factor whose price has risen.

Both of these predictions were stated in Chapter 9; now they have been derived formally using isoquants.

PART FOUR

PRICING AND MARKET STRUCTURE

Do wheat farmers in Saskatchewan and Manitoba compete with each other in the same way that Nike competes with Reebok? How would the Saskatchewan farmer respond to an improvement in techniques used by the Manitoba farmer? How would Nike respond to a price reduction by Reebok? Are markets with many firms different in important ways from markets with only a few firms? Why does the government sometimes worry about (and prevent) two firms from merging to form one larger firm? Are there special considerations when one of the merging firms is a foreign firm? These are the types of questions you will be able to answer after reading the next five chapters.

Chapter 10 discusses the *theory of perfect competition*. This is the theory that describes markets in which there are a very large number of firms producing very similar products, like the wheat farmers in Saskatchewan and Manitoba. You will be introduced to the important concept of *price taking*. You will see how the existence of profits in such an industry leads to the *entry* of new firms, and why such entry leads to the dissipation of those profits. Similarly, you will see why losses lead existing firms to *exit*, and why this increases the profits of the remaining firms.

Chapter 11 introduces you to *monopoly*—a situation in which there is only a single seller of a product. You will see that monopolies typically produce less ouput and have higher prices than do firms under perfect competition. You will understand why several firms often try to join together to form a *cartel*—like the OPEC oil cartel—in which case they act as if they were a monopoly seller. You will also see why such cartels often break down.

Chapter 12 discusses the idea of *imperfect competition*, which describes markets that are in between the polar cases of perfect competition and monopoly. You will learn about industries with many firms but *differentiated products*, and you will also learn about industries with very few firms, in which *strategic behaviour* between the firms is important. It is here that you will see how economists—using simple *game theory*—think about Nike's likely response to Reebok's price reduction.

The concept of *economic efficiency* is examined in Chapter 13. You will see why perfectly competitive markets are more efficient than monopolized markets, and you will then understand why Canadian *competition policy* is designed to prevent the occurrence of some monopolies. In Chapter 14, we examine several issues related to what goes on inside firms. You will see why the *owners* of firms sometimes have different interests than the *managers* of firms, and how the *market for corporate control* enters the picture. We explore the hypothesis of *profit maximization* and examine what might happen if firms did not act to maximize profits. Finally, we look at some issues concerning the costs and benefits of *foreign investment*.

COMPETITIVE MARKETS

Does PetroCanada compete with Esso in the sale of gasoline? Does American Express compete with Visa? Does a wheat farmer from Biggar, Saskatchewan compete with a wheat farmer from Brandon, Manitoba? If we use the ordinary meaning of the word *compete*, the answer to the first two questions is plainly yes, and the answer to the third is no.

PetroCanada and Esso both advertise extensively to persuade car drivers to buy their products. All sorts of things, from free dishes to performance-enhancing gasoline additives, are used to tempt drivers to buy one brand of gasoline rather than another. A host of world travelers in various tight spots attest on television or in magazines to the virtues of American Express, while other happy faces advise us that only with a Visa card can their pleasures be ours.

When we shift our attention to wheat farmers, however, we see that there is nothing that the Saskatchewan farmer can do to affect either the sales or the profits of the Manitoba farmer. There would be no point in doing so even if they could, since the sales and profits of the Manitoba farm have no effect on those of the Saskatchewan farm.

To sort out the questions of who is competing with whom and in what sense, it is useful to distinguish between the behaviour of individual firms and the type of market in which they operate. In everyday use, the word *competition* usually refers to competitive behaviour. Economists, however, are interested both in the competitive behaviour of individual firms and in a quite distinct concept—competitive market structure.

MARKET STRUCTURE AND FIRM BEHAVIOUR

The term **market structure** refers to all the features that may affect the behaviour and performance of the firms in a market (for example, the number of firms in the market or the type of product that they sell).

COMPETITIVE MARKET STRUCTURE

The competitiveness of the market is the extent to which individual firms have power to influence market prices or the terms on which their product is sold. *The less power an individual firm has to influence the market in which it sells its product, the more competitive that market is.*

The extreme form of competitiveness occurs when each firm has zero market power. In such a case, there are so many firms in the market that each must accept the price set by the forces of market demand and market supply. The firms perceive themselves as being able to sell as much as they choose at the prevailing market price and as having no power to influence that price. If the firm charged a higher price, it would make no sales; so many other firms

would be selling at the market price that buyers would take their business elsewhere.

This extreme is called a *perfectly competitive market structure* or, more simply, a *perfectly competitive market*. In such a market there is no need for individual firms to compete actively with one another because none has any power over the market. One firm's ability to sell its product does not depend on the behaviour of any other firm. For example, the Saskatchewan and Manitoba wheat farms operate in a perfectly competitive market over which they have no power. Neither can change the market price for its wheat by altering its own behaviour.

COMPETITIVE BEHAVIOUR

In everyday language, the term *competitive behaviour* refers to the degree to which individual firms actively vie with one another for business. For example, PetroCanada and Esso clearly engage in competitive behaviour. It is also true, however, that both companies have some real power over their market. Each has the power to decide the price that people will pay for their gasoline and oil, within limits set by buyers' tastes and the prices of competing products. Either firm could raise its prices and still continue to attract some customers. So even though they actively compete with each other, they do so in a market that does not have a perfectly competitive structure.

In contrast, the Saskatchewan and Manitoba wheat farmers do not engage in competitive behaviour because the only way they can affect their profits is by changing their own outputs of wheat or their own production costs.

The distinction that we have just made between behaviour and structure explains why firms in perfectly competitive markets (e.g., the Saskatchewan and Manitoba wheat producers) do not compete actively with each other, whereas firms that do compete actively with each other (e.g., PetroCanada and Esso) do not operate in perfectly competitive markets.

THE SIGNIFICANCE OF MARKET STRUCTURE

PetroCanada and Esso are two of several large firms in the oil *industry*. They produce petroleum products and sell them in various *markets*. The terms *industry* and *market* are familiar from everyday use.

However, economists give them precise definitions that we need to understand.

We noted in Chapter 3 that a market consists of an area over which buyers and sellers can negotiate the exchange of some product. The firms that produce a well-defined product or a closely related set of products constitute an **industry**. In earlier chapters, we developed and used market demand curves; here we note that the market demand curve for any particular product is the demand curve facing the industry that produces the product.

When the managers of a firm make their production and sales decisions, they need to know what quantity of a product their firm can sell at various prices. Their concern is therefore not with the *market* demand curve for their industry's product but rather with the demand curve for their own firm's output of that product. If they know the demand curve that their own firm faces, they know the sales that their firm can make at each price it might charge, and thus they know its potential revenues. If they also know their firm's costs for producing the product, they can calculate the profits that would be associated with each rate of output. With this information, they can choose the output that maximizes profits.

Recall that economists define market structure as the characteristics that affect the behaviour and performance of firms that sell in that market. These characteristics determine, among other things, the relationship between the market demand curve for the industry's product and the demand curve that each firm in that industry faces.

To reduce the analysis of market structure to manageable proportions, economists focus on four theoretical market structures that cover most actual cases: *perfect competition, monopoly, monopolistic competition,* and *oligopoly.* Perfect competition will be dealt with in the rest of this chapter, the others in the chapters that follow.

THE THEORY OF PERFECT COMPETITION

The perfectly competitive market structure—usually referred to simply as **perfect competition**—applies directly to a number of markets. It also provides an important benchmark for comparison with other market structures.

THE ASSUMPTIONS OF PERFECT COMPETITION

The theory of perfect competition is built on a number of key assumptions relating to each firm and to the industry as a whole.

1. All the firms in the industry sell an identical product. Economists say that the firms sell a **homogeneous product.**

2. Customers know the nature of the product being sold and the prices charged by each firm.

3. The level of a firm's output at which its long-run average cost reaches a minimum is small relative to the *industry's* total output. (This is the precise way of saying that the firm is small relative to the size of the industry.)

4. Each firm in the industry is a **price taker.** This means that the firm can alter its rate of production and sales without affecting the market price of its product. This is why a firm operating in a perfectly competitive market has no power to influence that market through its own individual actions. It must passively accept whatever happens to be the ruling price, but it can sell as much as it wants at that price.[1]

5. The industry is assumed to be characterized by *freedom of entry and exit;* that is, any new firm is free to enter the industry and start producing if it so wishes, and any existing firm is free to cease production and leave the industry. Existing firms cannot bar the entry of new firms, and there are no legal prohibitions or other artificial barriers to entering or exiting the industry.

The Saskatchewan and Manitoba wheat farmers we considered earlier provide us with good illustrations of firms that are operating in a perfectly competitive market. Because each individual wheat farmer is just one of a very large number of producers who are all growing the same product, one firm's contribution to the industry's total production is a tiny drop in an extremely large bucket. Each firm will correctly assume that variations in its output

---

[1]To emphasize its importance, we identify price taking as a separate assumption, although, strictly speaking, it is implied by the first three assumptions.

have no significant effect on the world price of wheat. Thus each firm, knowing that it can sell as much or as little as it chooses at that price, adapts its behaviour to a given market price of wheat. Furthermore, there is nothing that existing farmers can do to stop another farmer from growing wheat, and there are no legal deterrents to becoming a wheat farmer. Anyone who has enough money to buy or rent the necessary land, labour, and equipment can become a wheat farmer.

The difference between the wheat farmers and PetroCanada is in the *degree of market power.* Each firm that is producing wheat is an insignificant part of the whole market and thus has no power to influence the price of wheat. The oil company does have power to influence the price of gasoline because its own sales represent a significant part of the total sales of gasoline.

THE DEMAND CURVE FOR A PERFECTLY COMPETITIVE FIRM

A major distinction between firms operating in perfectly competitive markets and firms operating in any other type of market is in the shape of the firm's own demand curve.

The demand curve that each firm in perfect competition faces is horizontal because variations in the firm's output have no noticeable effect on price.

The horizontal (perfectly elastic) demand curve does not mean that the firm could actually sell an infinite amount at the going price. It means, rather, that the variations in production *that it will normally be possible for the firm to make* will leave price unchanged because their effect on total industry output will be negligible.

Figure 10-1 contrasts the market demand curve for the product of a competitive industry with the demand curve that a single firm in that industry faces. Application 10-1 provides an example of the important difference between the firm's demand curve and the market demand curve. It shows a detailed calculation of why the demand curve facing any individual wheat farmer is very nearly perfectly elastic, even though the *market* demand for wheat is quite inelastic.

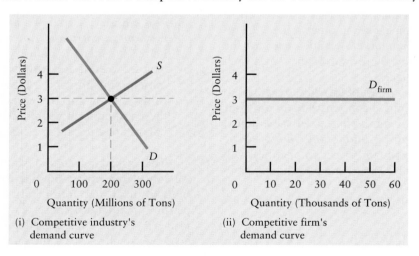

FIGURE 10-1
The Demand Curve for a Competitive Industry and for One Firm in the Industry

(i) Competitive industry's demand curve

(ii) Competitive firm's demand curve

The industry's demand curve is negatively sloped; the firm's demand curve is virtually horizontal. Notice the difference in the quantities shown on the horizontal scale in each part of the figure. The competitive industry has an output of 200 million tons when the price is $3. The individual firm takes that market price as given and considers producing up to, say, 60,000 tons. The firm's demand curve in part (ii) appears horizontal because the quantity scale represents a very small part of the industry's demand curve in part (i). The firm's output variation has only a tiny percentage effect on industry output. If we plotted the industry demand curve from 199,970,000 tons to 200,030,000 tons on the scale used in part (ii), the D curve would also appear virtually horizontal.

APPLICATION 10-1

DEMAND UNDER PERFECT COMPETITION: FIRM AND INDUSTRY

Consider an individual wheat farmer and the market for wheat. Since products have negatively sloped market demand curves, *any* increase in the industry's output (caused by a shift in supply) will cause *some* fall in the market price. However, as the calculations made below show, any conceivable increase that one wheat farm could make in its output has such a negligible effect on the industry's price that the farmer correctly ignores it—the individual wheat farmer is thus a price taker. Although the arithmetic used in reaching this conclusion is unimportant, it is crucial to understand why an individual wheat farmer is a price taker.

Here is the argument that the calculations summarize. The *market* elasticity of demand for wheat is approximately 0.25. Thus, if the quantity of wheat supplied in the world increased by 1 percent, the price of wheat would have to fall by roughly 4 percent to induce the world's wheat buyers to purchase the extra wheat.

Even huge farms produce a very small fraction of the total world crop. In a recent year, one large farm produced 1,750 metric tons of wheat. This was only 0.0035 percent of that year's world production of 500 million metric tons. Suppose that the farmer decided in one year to produce nothing and in another year managed to produce twice the normal output of 1,750 metric tons. This is an extremely large variation in one farm's output.

The increase in output from zero to 3,500 metric tons represents a 200 percent variation measured around the farm's average output of 1,750 metric tons. Yet the percentage increase in world output is only (3,500 / 500 million) × 100 = 0.0007 percent. This increase would lead to a decrease in the world price of 0.0028 percent. This price change, together with the 200 percent change in the farm's *own* output, implies that the farm's own demand curve has

an elasticity of over 71,000! This is an enormous elasticity of demand. The farm would have to increase its output by over 71,000 percent to bring about a 1 percent decrease in the price of wheat! Because the farm's output cannot be varied this much, it is not surprising that the farmer regards the price of wheat as unaffected by any change in output that he could conceivably make. For all intents and purposes, the individual farmer faces a perfectly elastic demand curve for its product and is thus a *price taker*.

CALCULATION OF THE FIRM'S DEMAND ELASTICITY FROM THE MARKET'S DEMAND ELASTICITY

We begin by taking as given the world elasticity of demand ($\eta = 0.25$) and world output (500 million metric tons). A large farm with an average output of 1,750 metric tons varies its output between 0 and 3,500 tons. The variation of 3,500 tons represents 200 percent of the farm's average output of 1,750 metric tons. This causes world output to vary by only 0.0007 percent.

Step 1: Find the percentage change in world price. We know that the market elasticity is 0.25. This means that the percentage change in price must be *four* times as big as the percentage change in quantity. Since world quantity changes by 0.0007 percent, world price must change by 0.0028 percent.

Step 2: Find the firm's elasticity of demand. This is the percentage change in its *own output* divided by the resulting percentage change in the world price: 200 percent divided by 0.0028 percent. Clearly, the percentage change in quantity vastly exceeds the percentage change in price, making elasticity very high. Its precise value is 200 / 0.0028 = 71,429.

TOTAL, AVERAGE, AND MARGINAL REVENUE

To study the revenues that firms receive from the sales of their products, economists define three concepts called *total*, *average*, and *marginal revenue*. These are the revenue counterparts of the concepts of total, average, and marginal cost that we considered in Chapter 8.

   Total revenue *(TR)* is the total amount received by the seller from the sale of a product. If q units are sold at p dollars each, $TR = p \times q$.

   Average revenue *(AR)* is the amount of revenue per unit sold. It is equal to total revenue divided by the number of units sold, and is thus equal to the price at which the product is sold: $AR = (p \times q)/q = p$.

   Marginal revenue *(MR)*, sometimes called *incremental revenue*, is the change in a firm's total revenue resulting from a change in its sales by 1 unit. Whenever output changes by more than 1 unit, the change in revenue must be divided by the change in output to calculate marginal revenue. For example, if an increase in output of 3 units per month is accompanied by an increase in revenue of $1,500, the marginal revenue resulting from the sale of 1 extra unit per month is $1,500/3, or $500. At any existing level of sales, marginal revenue shows what revenue the firm would gain by selling 1 unit more (or what revenue it would lose by selling 1 unit less). **[23]**

   To illustrate each of these revenue concepts, consider a firm that is selling an agricultural product in a perfectly competitive market at a price of $3 per bushel. Total revenue rises by $3 for every bushel sold. Because every bushel brings in $3, the average revenue per bushel sold is clearly $3. Furthermore, because each *additional* bushel sold brings in $3, the marginal revenue of an extra bushel sold is also $3. Table 10-1 shows calculations of these revenue concepts for a range of outputs between 10 and 13 bushels.

   The important point illustrated in Table 10-1 is that as long as the firm's own level of output cannot affect the price of the product it sells, then the firm's marginal revenue is equal to its average revenue (which is *always* equal to price). Thus, for a price-taking firm, $AR = MR$ = price. Graphically, as shown in part (i) of Figure 10-2, average revenue and marginal revenue are the same horizontal line drawn at the level of market price. Because the firm can sell any quantity it chooses at this price, the horizontal line is also the *firm's demand curve;* it shows that

---

TABLE 10-1
Revenue Concepts for a Price-Taking Firm

Price p	Quantity q	$TR = p \times q$	$AR = TR/q$	$MR = \Delta TR/\Delta q$
$3	10	$30	$3	
3	11	33	3	$3
3	12	36	3	3
3	13	39	3	3

When the firm is a price taker, $AR = MR = p$. Marginal revenue is shown between the lines because it represents the change in total revenue (e.g., from $33 to $36) in response to a change in quantity (from 11 to 12 units): $MR = (36 - 33)/(12 - 11) = \$3$ per unit.

---

any quantity the firm chooses to sell will be associated with this same market price.

If the market price is unaffected by variations in the firm's output, then the firm's demand curve, its average revenue curve, and its marginal revenue curve all coincide in the same horizontal line.

   This result can be stated in a slightly different way that turns out to be important for our later study:

For a firm in perfect competition, price equals marginal revenue.

This means, of course, that total revenue rises in direct proportion to output, as shown in part (ii) of Figure 10-2.

SHORT-RUN DECISIONS

We learned in Chapters 8 and 9 how each firm's costs vary with its output. In the short run, the firm has one or more fixed factors, and the only way in which it can change its output is by using more or less of its variable factor inputs. Thus the firm's short-run cost curves are relevant to its decision regarding output.

RULES FOR ALL PROFIT-MAXIMIZING FIRMS

We have just learned how the revenues of each price-taking firm vary with its output. The next step is to combine information about the firm's costs and revenues to determine the level of output that will

FIGURE 10-2
Revenue Curves for a Price-Taking Firm

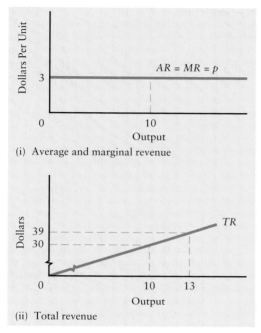

(i) Average and marginal revenue

(ii) Total revenue

This is a graphical representation of the revenue concepts in Table 10-1. Because price does not change as a result of the *firm* changing its output, neither marginal revenue nor average revenue varies with output. When price is constant, total revenue (which is price times quantity) is an upward-sloping straight line starting from the origin.

FIGURE 10-3
The Short-Run Profit-Maximizing Output Choice of a Competitive Firm

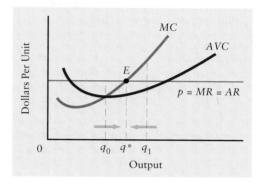

The firm chooses the output for which $p = MC$ above the level of AVC. When $p = MC$, as at q^*, the firm would decrease its profits if it changed its output. At any point to the left of q^*, say, q_0, price is greater than the marginal cost, and it is worthwhile for the firm to increase output (as indicated by the arrow on the left). At any point to the right of q^*, say, q_1, price is less than the marginal cost, and it is worthwhile for the firm to reduce output (as indicated by the arrow on the right).

maximize its profits. We start by stating two rules that apply to *all* profit-maximizing firms, whether or not they operate in perfectly competitive markets. The first determines whether the firm should produce at all, and the second determines how much it should produce.

Should the Firm Produce at All?

The firm always has the option of producing nothing. If it exercises this option, it will have an operating loss that is equal to its fixed costs. If it decides to produce, it will add the variable cost of production to its costs and the receipts from the sale of its product to its revenue. Therefore, since it must pay its fixed costs in any event, it will be worthwhile for the firm to produce as long as it can find some level of

output for which revenue exceeds *variable* cost. However, if its revenue is less than its variable cost at every level of output, the firm will actually lose more by producing any level of output than by not producing at all.

Rule 1: A firm should not produce at all if for *all* levels of output, the total variable cost of producing that output exceeds the total revenue derived from selling it or, equivalently, if the average variable cost of producing the output exceeds the price at which it can be sold. [24]

The price at which the firm can just cover its average variable cost, and so is indifferent between producing and not producing, is often called the **shut-down price.** At any price below this price, the firm will shut down. Such a price is shown in part (i) of Figure 10-5. (We will return in a moment to Figures 10-3 and 10-4.) At the price of $2, the firm can just cover its average variable cost by producing q_0 units. At this price, any other output would not produce enough revenue to cover variable costs. For any price below $2, there is no output at which variable costs can be covered. The price of $2 in part (i) is therefore the shut-down price.

How Much Should the Firm Produce?

If a firm decides that, according to Rule 1, production is worth undertaking, it must decide *how much* to produce. The key to understanding how much the firm should produce is to think about it on a unit-by-unit basis. If any unit of production adds more to revenue than it does to cost, producing and selling that unit will increase profits. However, if any unit adds more to cost than it does to revenue, producing and selling that unit will decrease profits. Using the terminology introduced earlier, a unit of production raises profits if the *marginal* revenue obtained from selling it exceeds the *marginal* cost of producing it; it lowers profits if the marginal revenue obtained from selling it is less than the marginal cost of producing it.

Now let a firm with some existing rate of output consider increasing or decreasing that output. If a further unit of production will increase the firm's profits, the firm should expand its output. However, if the last unit produced reduced profits, the firm should contract its output. From this it follows that the only time the firm should leave its output unaltered is when the last unit produced adds the same amount to revenues as it does to costs (i.e., $MR = MC$).

The results in these two paragraphs can be combined in the following rule:

Rule 2: Assuming that it is worthwhile for the firm to produce at all, the firm should produce the output at which marginal revenue equals marginal cost. [25]

The two rules that we have stated refer to each firm's own costs and revenues, and they apply to all profit-maximizing firms, whatever the market structure in which they operate.[2]

Rule 2 Applied to Price-Taking Firms

Rule 2 tells us that any profit-maximizing firm that produces at all will produce at the point where marginal cost equals marginal revenue. However, we

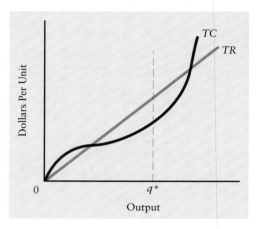

FIGURE 10-4
The Short-Run Profit-Maximizing Output Choice of a Firm Using Total Cost and Revenue Curves

The firm chooses the output for which the gap between the total revenue and the total cost curves is the largest. At each output, the vertical distance between the *TR* and the *TC* curves shows by how much total revenue exceeds total cost. In the figure, the gap is largest at output q^*, which is thus the profit-maximizing output.

have already seen that for price-taking firms, marginal revenue is the market price. Combining these two results gives us an important conclusion:

A firm that is operating in a perfectly competitive market will produce the output that equates its marginal cost of production with the market price of its product (as long as price exceeds average variable cost).

In a perfectly competitive industry, the market determines the price at which the firm sells its product. The firm then picks the quantity of output that maximizes its profits. We have seen that this is the output for which price equals marginal cost. When the firm has reached a position where its profits are maximized, it has no incentive to change its output. Therefore, unless prices or costs change, the firm will continue to produce this output because it is doing as well as it can do, given the market situation. This is illustrated in Figures 10-3 and 10-4.

The perfectly competitive firm is a quantity-adjuster, adjusting its level of output in response to changes in the price which are determined in the market.

Figure 10-3 shows the profit-maximizing choice of the firm using average cost and revenue curves. We

---

[2]A third rule is needed to distinguish between profit-maximizing and profit-*minimizing* positions: The marginal cost curve must cut the marginal revenue curve from below. This rule is not, however, needed for the discussion that follows, so we say nothing further about it. We consider only situations in which it is met.

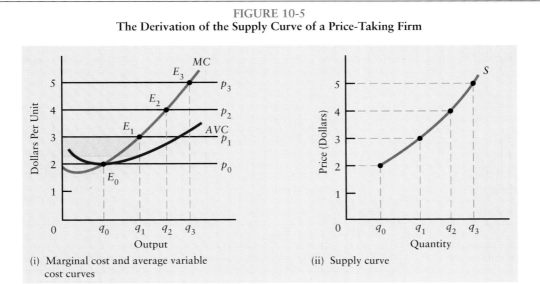

FIGURE 10-5
The Derivation of the Supply Curve of a Price-Taking Firm

(i) Marginal cost and average variable
     cost curves

(ii) Supply curve

The supply curve of the price-taking firm, shown in part (ii), is the same as its MC curve, shown in part (i). For prices below $2, output is zero because there is no output at which AVC can be covered. Thus the point E_0, where the price of $2 is just equal to AVC, is the point at which the firm will shut down. As price rises to $3, $4, and $5, the profit-maximizing point changes to E_1, E_2, and E_3, taking output to q_1, q_2, and q_3. At any of these prices, the firm's revenue exceeds its variable costs of production. An example of the excess is shown in part (i) of the figure by the shaded area associated with price p_1 and output q_1. This amount is available to help cover fixed costs and, once these are covered, to provide a profit.

can, if we wish, show the same result using total cost and revenue curves as done in Figure 10-4. Figure 10-4 combines the total cost curve first drawn in Figure 8-2 with the total revenue curve first shown in Figure 10-2. It shows the profit-maximizing output as the output with the largest positive difference between total revenue and total cost. This must of course be the same output as we located in Figure 10-3 by equating marginal cost and marginal revenue.

SHORT-RUN SUPPLY CURVES

We have seen that in a perfectly competitive market, the firm responds to a price that is set by the forces of demand and supply. By adjusting the quantity it produces in response to the current market price, the firm helps to determine the market supply. The link between the behaviour of the firm and the behaviour of the competitive market is provided by the *market supply curve.*

The Supply Curve for One Firm

The firm's supply curve is derived in part (i) of Figure 10-5, which shows a firm's marginal cost curve and

four alternative prices. The horizontal line at each price is the firm's demand curve when the market price is at that level. The firm's marginal cost curve gives the marginal cost corresponding to each level of output. We require a supply curve that shows the quantity that the firm will supply at each price. For prices below average variable cost, the firm will supply zero units (Rule 1). For prices above average variable cost, the firm will equate price and marginal cost (Rule 2, modified by the proposition that $MR = p$ in perfect competition). This leads to the following conclusion:

In perfect competition, the firm's supply curve is given by its marginal cost curve for those levels of output for which marginal cost exceeds average variable cost.

The Supply Curve for an Industry

To illustrate what is involved, Figure 10-6 shows the derivation of an industry supply curve for an industry containing only two firms. The general result is as follows:

In perfect competition, the industry supply curve is the horizontal sum of the marginal cost curves

(i) Firm A   (ii) Firm B   (iii) Firms A and B

The industry's supply curve is the horizontal sum of the supply curves of each of the firms in the industry. At a price of $3, Firm A would supply 4 units and Firm B would supply 3 units. Together, as shown in part (iii), they would supply 7 units. If there are hundreds of firms, the process is the same. Each firm's supply curve (derived as in Figure 10-5) shows what the firm will produce at any given price p. The industry supply curve relates the price to the sum of the quantities produced by each firm. In this example, because Firm B does not enter the market at prices below $2, the supply curve S_{A+B} is identical to S_A up to price $2 and is the sum of S_A and S_B above $2.

(above the level of average variable cost) of all firms in the industry.

The reason for this is that each firm's marginal cost curve shows how much that firm will supply at each given market price, and the industry supply curve is the sum of what each firm will supply.

This supply curve, based on the short-run marginal cost curves of all the firms in the industry, is the industry's supply curve that was first encountered in Chapter 4. We have now established the profit-maximizing behaviour of individual firms that lies behind that curve. It is sometimes called a **short-run supply curve** because it is based on the short-run, profit-maximizing behaviour of all the firms in the industry. It should not be confused with the long-run industry supply curve, which relates quantity supplied to the price that exists *when the industry is in long-run equilibrium* (which we will study later in this chapter).

SHORT-RUN EQUILIBRIUM IN A COMPETITIVE MARKET

The price of a product sold in a perfectly competitive market is determined by the interaction of the industry's short-run supply curve and the market demand curve. Although no single firm can influence the market price significantly, the collective actions of all

firms in the industry (as shown by the industry supply curve) and the collective actions of households (as shown by the market demand curve) together determine the equilibrium price. This occurs at the point where the market demand curve and the industry supply curve intersect.

When a perfectly competitive industry is in **short-run equilibrium,** each firm is producing and selling a quantity for which its marginal cost equals price. No firm is motivated to change its output in the short run. Because total quantity demanded equals total quantity supplied, there is no reason for market price to change in the short run.

Short-Run Profitability of the Firm

We know that when an industry is in short-run equilibrium, each firm is maximizing its profits. However, we do not know *how large* these profits are. It is one thing to know that a firm is doing as well as it can, given its particular circumstances; it is another thing to know how well it is doing.

Figure 10-7 shows three possible positions for a firm when the industry is in short-run equilibrium. In all cases, the firm is maximizing its profits by producing where price equals marginal cost, but in part (i) the firm is suffering losses, in part (ii) it is just

FIGURE 10-7
Alternative Short-Run Profits of a Competitive Firm

When the industry is in short-run equilibrium, a competitive firm may be suffering losses, breaking even, or making profits. The diagrams show a firm with given costs that faces three alternative prices p_1, p_2, and p_3. In each part of the figure, $MC = MR$ = price. Because in all three cases price exceeds AVC, the firm produces positive output in each case.

In part (i), price is p_1 and the firm is suffering losses, shown by the shaded area, because price is below average total cost. Because price exceeds average variable cost, it is worthwhile for the firm to keep producing, but it is not worthwhile for it to replace its capital equipment as it wears out.

In part (ii), price is p_2 and the firm is just covering its total costs. It is worthwhile for the firm to replace its capital as it wears out, since it is covering the full opportunity cost of its capital.

In part (iii), price is p_3 and the firm is earning profits, shown by the shaded area.

covering all of its costs (breaking even), and in part (iii) it is making profits because average revenue exceeds average total cost. In part (i), we could say that the firm is minimizing its losses rather than maximizing its profits, but both statements mean the same thing. In all three cases, the firm is doing as well as it can, given its costs and the market price.

LONG-RUN DECISIONS

Although Figure 10-7 shows three possible positions for a typical firm when the industry is in short-run equilibrium, not all of them are possible outcomes in the long run.

THE EFFECT OF ENTRY AND EXIT

The key difference between a perfectly competitive industry in the short run and in the long run is the entry or exit of firms. We have seen that firms may be making profits, suffering losses, or just breaking

even when the industry is in short-run equilibrium. Because costs include the opportunity cost of capital, firms that are just breaking even are doing as well as they could do by investing their capital elsewhere. Hence there will be no incentive for such firms to leave the industry. Similarly, if new entrants expect just to break even, there will be no incentive for firms to enter the industry, because capital can earn the same return elsewhere in the economy. If, however, existing firms are earning revenues in excess of all costs, including the opportunity cost of capital, new capital will enter the industry to share in these profits. Conversely, if existing firms are suffering losses, capital will leave the industry because a better return can be obtained elsewhere in the economy. Let us now consider this process in a little more detail.

An Entry-Attracting Price

First, suppose that there are 100 firms in a competitive industry, all in the position of the firm shown in part (iii) of Figure 10-7. New firms, attracted by the profitability of existing firms, will enter the industry.

FIGURE 10-8
The Effect of New Entrants

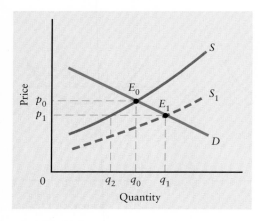

New entrants shift the supply curve to the right and lower the equilibrium price. Initial equilibrium is at E_0. The entry of new firms shifts the supply curve to S_1. Equilibrium price falls to p_1, while output rises to q_1. Before the entry of new firms, only q_2 would have been produced had the price been p_1. The extra output is supplied by the new productive capacity.

Suppose that in response to the high profits that the 100 existing firms are making, 20 new firms enter. The market supply curve that formerly added up the outputs of 100 firms must now add up the outputs of 120 firms. At any price, more will be supplied because there are more producers. This is a rightward shift in the industry supply curve.

With an unchanged market demand curve, this shift in the short-run industry supply curve means that the previous equilibrium price will no longer prevail. The shift in supply will lower the equilibrium price, and both new and old firms will have to adjust their output to this new price. This is illustrated in Figure 10-8. New firms will continue to enter, and the equilibrium price will continue to fall, until all firms in the industry are just covering their total costs. All firms will then be in the position of the firm shown in part (ii) of Figure 10-7, which is called a *zero-profit equilibrium*.

Profits in a competitive industry are a signal for the entry of new firms; the industry will expand, pushing price down until profits fall to zero.

An Exit-Inducing Price

Now suppose that all of the firms in the industry are in the position of the firm shown in part (i) of Figure 10-7. Although the firms are covering their variable costs, the return on their capital is less than the opportunity cost of capital. They are not covering their total costs. This is a signal for the exit of firms. Old plants and equipment will not be replaced as they wear out. As a result, the industry's short-run supply curve shifts leftward, and the market price rises. Firms will continue to exit, and the market price will continue to rise, until the remaining firms can cover their total costs—that is, until they are all in the zero-profit equilibrium illustrated in part (ii) of Figure 10-7. The exit of firms then ceases.

Losses in a competitive industry are a signal for the exit of firms; the industry will contract, driving the market price up until the remaining firms are just covering their total costs.

LONG-RUN EQUILIBRIUM IN A COMPETITIVE MARKET

Because firms exit when they are motivated by their losses and enter in pursuit of profits, we get the following conclusion:

The long-run equilibrium of a competitive industry occurs when firms are earning zero profits.

When a perfectly competitive industry is in long-run equilibrium, each firm will be like the firm in part (ii) of Figure 10-7. For such firms, the price P_z is sometimes called the **break-even price**. It is the price at which all costs, including the opportunity cost of capital, are being covered. The firm is just willing to stay in the industry. It has no incentive to leave, nor do other firms have an incentive to enter.

In the preceding analysis, we see profits serving the function of providing signals that guide the allocation of scarce resources among the economy's industries. It is also worth noting that freedom of entry will tend to push profits toward zero in any industry, whether it is perfectly competitive or not.

Conditions for Long-Run Equilibrium

The previous discussion suggests four conditions for a competitive industry to be in long-run equilibrium.

1. Existing firms must be maximizing their profits, given their existing capital. This means that short-run marginal costs of production must be equal to market price.

2. Existing firms must not be suffering losses. If they are suffering losses, they will not replace their capital and the size of the industry will decline over time.

3. Existing firms must not be earning profits. If they are earning profits, then new firms will enter the industry and the size of the industry will increase over time.

4. Existing firms must not be able to increase their profits by changing the size of their production facilities. This implies that each existing firm must be at the minimum point of its long-run average cost curve.

This last condition is new to our discussion. Figure 10-9 shows that if the condition does not hold, a firm can increase its profits. Although the firm is maximizing its profits with its existing production facilities, there are unexploited economies of scale. By building a new plant with a larger capacity than its existing plant, the firm can reduce its average cost. Because in its present position, average cost is just equal to price, any reduction in average cost must yield profits.

For a price-taking firm to be maximizing its long-run profits, it must be producing at the minimum point on its *LRAC* curve.

The level of output at which *LRAC* reaches a minimum is known as the firm's **minimum efficient scale (MES)**.[3]

When each firm in the industry is producing at the minimum point of its long-run average cost curve and just covering its costs (i.e., each is in the position shown in Figure 10-10), the industry is in long-run equilibrium. Because marginal cost equals price, no firm can improve its profits by varying its output in the short run. Because *LRAC* is above price at all possible outputs except the current one, where it is equal to the price, there is no incentive for any existing firm to move along its long-run cost curve by al-

FIGURE 10-9
Short-Run Versus Long-Run Profit Maximization for a Competitive Firm

A competitive firm that is not at the minimum point on its *LRAC* curve is not maximizing its long-run profits. A competitive firm with short-run cost curves *SRATC* and *MC* faces a market price of p_0. The firm produces q_0, where *MC* equals price and total costs are just being covered. However, the firm's long-run average cost curve lies below its short-run curve at output q_0. The firm could produce output q_0 at cost c_0 by building a larger plant so as to take advantage of economies of scale. Profits would rise, because average total costs of c_0 would then be less than price p_0. The firm cannot be maximizing its long-run profits at any output below q_m because with any such output, average total costs can be reduced by building a larger plant. The output q_m is the *minimum efficient scale* of the firm.

tering the scale of its operations. Because there are neither profits nor losses, there is no incentive for entry into or exit from the industry.

In long-run competitive equilibrium, each firm's average cost of production is the lowest attainable, given the limits of known technology and factor prices.

To summarize, the conditions for long-run equilibrium for a competitive industry are as follows: (1) Existing firms produce at the point where marginal cost equals price, (2) existing firms are not making losses and thus have no incentive to exit, (3) existing firms are not making positive profits, and thus potential new firms have no incentive to enter, and (4)

---

[3]With a U-shaped cost curve, as in Figure 10-10, there is only one point of efficient scale, so the qualification "minimum" is redundant. In Chapter 12, however, we will encounter cost curves that are flat over a range of minimum average cost. The qualification "minimum" is then needed to indicate the *smallest* output at which average costs are minimized.

FIGURE 10-10
A Typical Firm When the Industry is in Long-Run Equilibrium

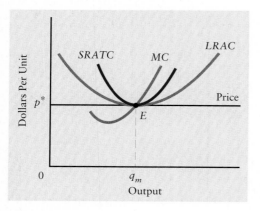

In long-run competitive equilibrium, each firm is operating at the minimum point on its *LRAC* curve. In long-run equilibrium, each firm must be (1) maximizing short-run profits, $MC = p$; (2) earning profits of zero on its existing plant, $SRATC = p$; and (3) unable to increase its profits by altering the scale of its operations. These three conditions can be met only when the firm is at E, the minimum point on its *LRAC* curve, with price p^* and output q_m.

existing firms produce at the minimum point on their long-run average cost curve. This is the position shown in Figure 10-10.

THE LONG-RUN INDUSTRY SUPPLY CURVE

Consider a competitive industry that is in long-run equilibrium. Suppose now that the market demand for the industry's product increases. The reactions to this demand shift should by now be a familiar story. First, price will rise, and in response, existing firms will increase their outputs and earn profits. New firms then enter the industry, attracted by the profits. As the industry's output expands, price will fall, and this process continues until profits have been eliminated. At that time, existing firms will once again be just covering their full costs. Note that in *both* of the long-run equilibrium positions just discussed—the one before and the one after the change in demand—all firms in the industry are producing at the lowest point on their *LRAC* curves.

This is now familiar ground, but there is one further question that we could ask. When all the dust has settled, will the new long-run equilibrium price be higher than, lower than, or the same as the price at the initial long-run equilibrium? A similar analysis could be made for a fall in demand, and the same question could be asked.

The adjustment of a competitive industry to the types of changes that we have just discussed is shown by what is sometimes called the **long-run industry supply (*LRS*) curve.** This curve shows the relationship between the market price and the quantity produced in a competitive industry *when it is in long-run equilibrium*. Note, however, that the curve does not take *very* long-run reactions into account and so is drawn on the assumption that technological knowledge is constant. (Changes in technology will *shift* the *LRS* curve.) Figure 10-11 shows the derivation of this curve and its various possible shapes.

Horizontal Long-Run Supply Curve.   In part (i) of the figure, the *LRS* curve is horizontal. This indicates that the industry will adjust its size to provide whatever quantity is demanded at a constant price. An industry with a horizontal *LRS* curve is said to be a **constant-cost industry.** This situation occurs when the long-run expansion of the industry, due to the entry of new firms, leaves the long-run cost curves of existing firms unchanged. Because new firms have access to the same technology and face the same factor prices as existing firms, their cost curves will be the same as those of existing firms. It follows that the cost curves of all firms, new or old, will be unaffected by expansion or contraction of the industry. Thus long-run equilibrium can be reestablished only when price returns to its original level. In other words, because cost curves are unaffected by the expansion or contraction of the industry, each firm must start from, and return to, the long-run equilibrium position shown in Figure 10-10—*which means that market price must also do the same.*

Upward-Sloping Long-Run Supply Curve. When an increase in demand for an industry's product leads that industry to expand, more of its inputs will be needed. The increase in demand for these inputs tends to bid up their prices.

If costs rise with increasing levels of industry output, so too must the price at which the producers are able to cover their costs. As the industry ex-

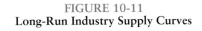

FIGURE 10-11
Long-Run Industry Supply Curves

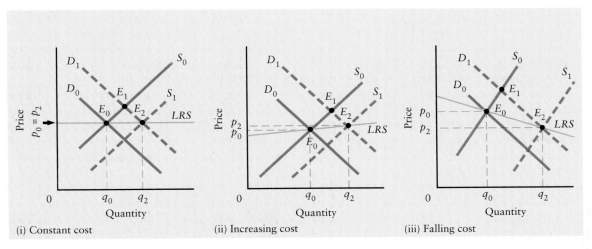

(i) Constant cost   (ii) Increasing cost   (iii) Falling cost

The long-run industry supply curve may be horizontal, positively sloped, or negatively sloped. In all three parts, the initial curves are at D_0 and S_0, yielding equilibrium at E_0, with price p_0 and output q_0. A rise in demand shifts the demand curve to D_1, taking the short-run equilibrium to E_1. New firms now enter the industry, shifting the supply curve outward, pushing down price until pure profits are no longer being earned. At this point, the supply curve is S_1 and the new equilibrium is E_2, with price at p_2 and output q_2.

In part (i), price returns to its original level, making the long-run industry supply curve horizontal. In part (ii), profits are eliminated, and a new long-run equilibrium acheived, at a price higher than p_0. This gives the *LRS* curve a positive slope. In part (iii), the price falls below its original level before profits are eliminated, giving the *LRS* curve a negative slope.

pands, the short-run supply curve shifts outward, but the firms' *SRATC* curves shift upward because of rising factor prices. The expansion of the industry comes to a halt when price is equal to minimum *LRAC* for existing firms. Because costs have risen, this must occur at a higher price than prevailed before the expansion began, as illustrated in part (ii) of Figure 10-11. A competitive industry with rising long-run supply prices is often called an **increasing-cost industry**.

Downward-Sloping Long-Run Supply Curve. So far we have suggested that the long-run supply curve may be flat or upward sloping. Could it ever be downward sloping, thereby indicating that higher outputs were associated with lower prices in long-run equilibrium?[4]

It is tempting to answer yes because of the opportunities of more efficient scales of operation using greater mechanization and more effective specilization of labour. However, this answer would not be correct for perfectly competitive industries because in long-run equilibrium each firm must already be at the lowest point on its *LRAC* curve. If a firm could lower its costs by building a larger, more mechanized plant, it would be profitable to do so without waiting for an increase in demand. Because any single firm perceives that it can sell all it wishes at the going market price, it will be profitable for the firm to expand the scale of its operations as long as it is on the downward-sloping portion of its *LRAC*.

The scale economies that we have just considered are within the control of the firm; they are said to be **internal economies of scale**. A perfectly competitive industry might, however, have falling long-run costs if industries that supply its inputs have increasing returns to scale. Such effects are outside the control of the perfectly competitive firm and are called **external economies of scale**. Whenever expansion of an industry leads to a fall in the prices of some of its

---

[4]The discussion of economies of scale in Chapter 9 is relevant here.

inputs, the firms will find their cost curves shifting downward as they expand their outputs.

As an illustration of how the expansion of one industry could cause the prices of some of its inputs to fall, consider the early stages of the growth of the automobile industry. As the output of automobiles increased, the industry's demand for tires grew greatly. This increased the demand for rubber and tended to raise its price, but it also provided the opportunity for tire manufacturers to build larger plants that exploited the scale economies available in tire production. These economies were large enough to offset any factor price increases, and tire prices charged to automobile manufacturers fell. Thus automobile costs fell because of lower prices of an important input. This case is illustrated in part (iii) of Figure 10-11. An industry that has a declining long-run supply curve is often called a **declining-cost industry.**

Notice in this example that although the economies of scale were *external* to the automobile industry, they were *internal* to the tire industry. This in turn requires that the tire industry *not* be perfectly competitive; if it were, all of its scale economies would already have been exploited as firms locate at the minimum of their *LRAC* curves in the long run. So this case refers to a perfectly competitive industry that uses an input produced by a non-perfectly-competitive industry whose own scale economies have not yet been fully exploited because demand is insufficient.

We can now use our long-run theory to understand the behaviour of firms in two commonly encountered but often misunderstood situations—changes in technology and declining industries.

CHANGES IN TECHNOLOGY

Consider a competitive industry in long-run equilibrium. Because the industry is in long-run equilibrium, each firm must be earning zero profits. Now suppose that some technological development lowers the cost curves of newly built plants. Because price is just equal to the average total cost *for the existing plants,* new plants will be able to earn profits, and some of them will now be built. The resulting expansion in capacity shifts the short-run supply curve to the right and drives price down.

The expansion in industry output and the fall in price will continue until price is equal to the short-run average total cost of the *new* plants. At this price, old plants will not be covering their long-run costs. As long as price exceeds their average variable cost, however, such plants will continue in production. As the outmoded plants wear out, they will gradually be closed. Eventually, a new long-run equilibrium will be established in which all plants will use the new technology.

What happens in a competitive industry in which technological change does not occur as a single isolated event but instead happens more or less continuously? Plants built in any one year will tend to have lower costs than plants built in any previous year. This common occurrence is illustrated in Figure 10-12.

Industries that are subject to continuous technological change have three common characteristics. The first is that plants of different ages and at different levels of efficiency exist side by side. This characteristic is dramatically illustrated by the many different vintages of farm equipment found in the agricultural sector; some farms have much newer and better equipment than others. Indeed, even any individual farm that has been established for a long time will have various vintages of equipment, all of which are in use. In this case, and in many others that you can think of, different vintages of plant and equipment, each with different efficiencies, exist side by side; older models are not discarded as soon as a better model comes on the market.

Critics who observe the continued use of older, less efficient plants and equipment often urge that something be done to "eliminate these wasteful practices." These critics miss the point of economic efficiency. If the plant or piece of equipment is already there, it can be profitably operated as long as its revenues more than cover its *variable* costs. As long as a plant or equipment can produce goods that are valued by consumers at an amount above the value of the resources currently used up for their production (variable costs), the value of society's total output is increased by using it.

A second characteristic of a competitive industry that is subject to continuous technological change is that price is governed by the minimum *ATC* of the *most efficient* plants. Firms will enter the industry until plants of the latest vintage are just expected to earn normal profits over their lifetimes. The benefits of the new technology are passed on to consumers because all of the units of the product, whether pro-

FIGURE 10-12
Plants of Different Vintages in an Industry with Continuous Technological Progress

Entry of progressively lower-cost firms forces price down, but older plants with higher costs remain in the industry as long as price covers average variable cost. Plant 3 is the newest plant with the lowest costs. Long-run equilibrium price will be determined by the average total costs of plants of this type because entry will continue as long as the owners of the newest plants expect to earn profits from them. Plant 1 is the oldest plant in operation. It is just covering its AVC, and if the price falls any further, it will be closed down. Plant 2 is a plant of intermediate age. It is covering its variable costs and earning some contribution toward its fixed costs. In parts (ii) and (iii), the excess of revenues over variable costs is indicated by the shaded area.

duced by new or old plants, are sold at a price that is related solely to the $ATCs$ of the new plants. Owners of older plants find that their returns over variable costs fall steadily as more and more efficient plants drive the price of the product down.

A third characteristic is that old plants are discarded (or "mothballed") when the price falls below their $AVCs$. This may occur well before the plants are physically worn out. In industries with continuous technological progress, capital is usually discarded because it is *economically obsolete,* not because it is physically worn out. Old capital is obsolete when the market price of output does not even cover its average variable cost of production. Thus a steel mill that is still fully capable of producing top-quality steel may be shut down for perfectly sensible reasons; if the price of steel cannot cover the average variable cost of the steel produced, then profit-maximizing firms will shut down the plant.

DECLINING INDUSTRIES

What happens when a competitive industry in long-run equilibrium begins to suffer losses due to a con-

tinual decrease in the demand for its products? One example of this might be a long-term change in tastes that leads households to substitute away from red meat and toward fish and poultry. As market demand for red meat declines, market price falls, and firms that were previously covering average total costs are no longer able to do so. They find themselves in the position shown in part (i) of Figure 10-7. Firms suffer losses instead of breaking even; the signal for the exit of capital is given, but exit takes time.

The Response of Firms

The economically efficient response to a steadily declining demand is to continue to operate with existing equipment as long as its variable costs of production can be covered. As equipment becomes obsolete because it cannot cover even its variable cost, it will not be replaced unless the new equipment can cover its total cost. As a result, the capacity of the industry will shrink. If demand keeps declining, capacity must keep shrinking.

Declining industries typically present a sorry sight to the observer. Revenues are below long-run total costs, and as a result, new equipment is not brought in to replace old equipment as it wears out. The average age of equipment in use thus rises steadily. The untrained observer, seeing the industry's plight, is likely to blame it on the old equipment.

The antiquated equipment in a declining industry is often the effect rather than the cause of the industry's decline.

An interesting illustration of the importance of the distinction between fixed and variable costs—one that is familiar to many hotel users—is given in Application 10-2.

The Response of Governments

Governments are often tempted to support declining industries because they are worried about the resulting job losses. Experience suggests, however, that propping up genuinely declining industries only delays their demise—at significant national cost. When the government finally withdraws its support, the decline is usually more abrupt and hence more difficult to adjust to than it would have been had the industry been allowed to decline gradually under the market force of steadily declining demand.

Once governments recognize the decay of certain industries and the collapse of certain firms as an inevitable aspect of economic growth, a more effective response is to provide retraining and income-support schemes that cushion the impacts of change. These can moderate the effects on the incomes of workers who lose their jobs and make it easier for them to transfer to expanding industries. Intervention that is intended to increase mobility while reducing the social and personal costs of mobility is a viable long-run policy; trying to freeze the existing industrial structure by shoring up an inevitably declining industry is not.

THE APPEAL OF PERFECT COMPETITION

Consider an economy in which all markets are perfectly competitive. In this economy, there are many firms and many households. Each is a price taker, responding as it sees fit to signals that are sent to it by the market. No single firm or consumer has any power over the market; instead, each is a passive quantity adjuster that merely responds to market signals. Yet the impersonal force of the market produces an appropriate response to all changes. If tastes change, for example, prices will change, and the allocation of resources will change in the appropriate direction. Throughout the entire process, no one firm has any power over any other firm. Dozens of firms react to the same price changes, and if one firm refuses to react, countless other profit-maximizing firms will be eager to make the appropriate changes.

Market reactions, not public policies, eliminate shortages or surpluses. There is need neither for regulatory agencies nor for bureaucrats to make arbitrary decisions about who may produce what, how to produce it, or how much it is permissible to charge for the product. If there are no government officials to make such decisions, no bribes will be necessary to influence their decisions.

In the impersonal decision-making world of perfect competition, neither private firms nor public officials wield economic power. The market mechanism, like an invisible hand, determines the allocation of resources among competing uses.

The theory of perfect competition is an intellectual triumph in showing how a price system can work to coordinate the decisions of millions of decentralized households and firms. The price system allows all necessary adjustments to occur, despite the fact that no single individual foresees them or provides any overall plan for them. Moreover, as we shall see in Chapter 13, a perfectly competitive economy will generally be economically efficient.

The British historian Lord Acton once observed, "Power tends to corrupt; absolute power corrupts absolutely." To someone who fears power, either in the hands of the state or in such private organizations as large firms, the perfectly competitive model has a strong appeal. It describes an economy that functions effectively without any private or public group exercising any significant market power.

Economic and social policy would be much simpler if the entire economy were perfectly competitive. Although the price system often allocates resources in ways that are quite similar to the perfectly competitive economy, and although some markets are indeed perfectly competitive, in our world many groups have power over many markets. Large firms often set

---

APPLICATION 10-2

THE PARABLE OF THE SEASIDE INN

Why do some resort hotels stay open during the off-season, even though to do so they must offer bargain rates that do not even cover their "full costs?" Why do the managers of other hotels allow them to fall into disrepair even though they are able to attract enough customers to stay in business? Are the former being overly generous, and are the latter being irrational penny-pinchers?

To illustrate what is involved, consider an imaginary resort hotel called the Seaside Inn. Its revenues and costs of operating during the four months of the high-season and during the eight months of the off-season are shown in the accompanying table. When the profit-maximizing price for its rooms is charged in the high-season, the hotel earns revenues of $58,000 and incurs variable costs equal to $36,000. Thus there is an "operating profit" of $22,000 during the high-season. This surplus goes toward meeting the hotel's fixed costs of $24,000. There is then $2,000 of the fixed costs which need yet to be paid.

If the Seaside Inn were to charge the same rates during the off-season, it could not attract enough customers even to cover its costs of maids, bellhops, and managers. However, the hotel discovers that by charging lower rates during the off-season, it can rent some of its rooms and earn revenues of $20,000. Its costs of operating (variable costs) during the off-season are $18,000. So, by operating at reduced rates in the off-season, the hotel is able to contribute another $2,000 toward its annual fixed costs, thereby eliminating the shortfall. Therefore, the hotel stays open during the whole year by offering off-season bargain rates to grateful guests.

(Indeed, if it were to close during the off-season, it would not be able to cover its total fixed and variable costs solely through its high-season operations.)

Now assume that the off-season revenues fall to $19,000 (everything else remaining the same). The short-run condition for staying open, that total revenue (TR) must exceed total variable cost (TVC), is met both for the high-season and for the off-season. However, the long-run condition is not met, since the TR over the whole year of $77,000 is less than the total costs of $78,000, all of which are variable in the long run. The hotel will remain open as long as it can do so with its present capital—it will produce in the short run. However, it will not be worthwhile for the owners to replace the capital as it wears out.

It will become one of those run-down hotels about which guests ask, "Why don't they do something about this place?"—but the owners are behaving quite sensibly. They are operating the hotel as long as it covers its variable costs, but they are not putting any more investment into it because it cannot cover its fixed costs. Sooner or later, the fixed capital will become too old to be run, or at least to attract customers, and the hotel will be closed.

The Seaside Inn: Total Costs and Revenues ($)

Season	Total Revenue *(TR)*	Total Variable Cost *(TVC)*	Contribution to Fixed Costs *(TR-TVC)*	Total Fixed Costs
High-Season	58,000	36,000	22,000	
Off-Season	20,000	18,000	2,000	
Total	78,000	54,000	24,000	24,000

---

prices, determine what will be produced, and decide what research will take place. Labour unions often influence wages by offering or withdrawing their labour services. Governments influence many markets by being the dominant purchaser, as well as by regulating

many others. As it is, observers who fear the concentration of market power can only regret that the perfectly competitive model does not describe the world in which we live; so many problems would disappear if only it did.

SUMMARY

A. MARKET STRUCTURE AND FIRM BEHAVIOUR

- Market behaviour is concerned with the degree to which individual firms compete against one another; market structure is concerned with the type of market in which firms operate. Market structure affects the degree of power that individual firms have to influence the price of the product.

B. THE THEORY OF PERFECT COMPETITION

- Five key assumptions of the theory of perfect competition are as follows:

  1. All firms produce a homogeneous product.
  2. Purchasers know the nature of the product and the price charged for it.
  3. Each firm's minimum efficient scale occurs at a level of output that is small relative to the industry's total output.
  4. Firms are price takers.
  5. The industry displays freedom of entry and exit.

- Any profit-maximizing firm will produce at a level of output at which (a) price is at least as great as average variable cost and (b) marginal cost equals marginal revenue. In perfect competition, firms are price takers, so marginal revenue is equal to price. Thus a profit-maximizing firm operating in a perfectly competitive market equates marginal cost to price.

C. SHORT-RUN DECISIONS

- If a profit-maximizing firm is to produce at all, it must be able to cover its variable costs. However, such a firm may be suffering losses (price is less than average total cost), making profits (price is greater than average total cost), or just breaking even (price is equal to average total cost).
- Under perfect competition, each firm's short-run supply curve is identical to its marginal cost curve above average variable cost. The perfectly competitive industry's short-run supply curve is the horizontal sum of the supply curves of the individual firms (the horizontal sum of the firms' marginal cost curves).

D. LONG-RUN DECISIONS

- In the long run, profits or losses will lead to the entry or the exit of capital into or out of the industry. This pushes any competitive industry to a long-run, zero-profit equilibrium and moves production to the level that minimizes average cost.
- The long-run response of an industry to steadily changing technology is the gradual replacement of less efficient plants by more efficient ones. Older plants will be discarded and replaced by more modern ones only when price falls below average variable cost.
- The long-run response of a declining industry will be to continue to satisfy demand by employing its existing plants as long as price exceeds short-run average variable cost. Despite the antiquated appearance that results, this response is the correct one.

E. THE APPEAL OF PERFECT COMPETITION

- The great appeal of perfect competition as a means of organizing production lies in the decentralized decision making of myriad firms and households. No individual firm or household exercises power over the market. At the same time, it is not necessary for the government to intervene to determine resource allocation and prices.

KEY CONCEPTS

Competitive behaviour and competitive market structure
Rules for maximizing profits
Perfect competition
Price taking and a horizontal demand curve

Average revenue, marginal revenue, and price under perfect competition
The relationship of supply curves to marginal cost curves
Short-run and long-run equilibrium of competitive industries

Entry and exit in achieving long-run equilibrium
Long-run industry supply curves
Constant, increasing, and decreasing cost industries

DISCUSSION QUESTIONS

1. A number of agricultural products, such as milk, eggs, and chickens, are produced under conditions that come close to perfect competition whenever governments do not regulate these markets. What are the main features of these industries that make them perfectly competitive? Use the theory you have learned in this chapter to predict the consequences of the introduction of government supply-management schemes that attempt to raise farmers' incomes by restricting total output through a system of quotas.

2. Discuss the common allegation that when all firms in an industry are charging the same price, this indicates the absence of competition and the presence of some form of price-setting agreement.

3. Which of the five assumptions of the theory of perfect competition does the following newspaper story relate to?

   > Recently, Ken Chapman booked a $932 round-trip ticket at noon. While he slept that night, a new computer program searched for a better deal. Sixteen hours later, a new fare became available, and Chapman is now ticketed to travel for $578.

   Will this new procedure make the airline industry more or less competitive? Will it make it perfectly competitive? Why or why not?

4. Which of the following observed facts about an industry are inconsistent with its being a perfectly competitive industry?

   a. Different firms use different methods of production.
   b. The industry's product is extensively advertised by a trade association.
   c. Individual firms devote a large fraction of their sales receipts to advertising their own product brands.
   d. There are 24 firms in the industry.
   e. The largest firm in the industry makes 40 percent of the sales, and the next largest firm makes 20 percent of the sales, but the products are identical, and there are 61 other firms.
   f. All firms made large profits in 1995.

5. In which of the following sectors of the Canadian economy might you expect to find competitive behaviour? In which might you expect to find industries that are classified as operating under perfectly competitive market structures?

   a. Manufacturing
   b. Agriculture
   c. Transportation and public utilities
   d. Wholesale and retail trade
   e. Illegal drugs

6. The typical office in 1997 contains personal computers of various vintages, with the newest machines having the largest output per unit of cost. There are also old machines that, though still able to function, are not in use at all. What determines the secondhand price of the older machines? What is the economic value of the machines that are no longer used?

7. Suppose that entry into an industry is not artificially restricted but takes time because of the need to build plants, acquire technical know-how, and establish a marketing organization. Can such an industry be characterized as perfectly competitive? Does ease of entry imply ease of exit, and vice versa?

8. What, if anything, does each one of the following tell you about ease of entry into or exit from an industry?

   a. Profits have been very high for two decades.
   b. No new firms have entered the industry for 20 years.
   c. The average age of the firms in the 40-year-old industry is less than 7 years.
   d. Most existing firms are using obsolete equipment alongside newer, more modern equipment.
   e. Profits are low or negative; many firms are still producing, but from steadily aging equipment.

9. Suppose all of the potentially arable land in Canada was currently being used for growing either wheat or barley. Both crop markets are in equilibrium. Discuss exactly how decentralized competitive markets would respond to shift resources from wheat to barley production following a report that barley helps to reduce cancer risk.

10. Discuss the entry and exit histories of the following industries. What are the implications of this with respect to these markets' competitive behaviour?

    a. Canadian automobile manufacturing
    b. Canadian passenger air travel
    c. Mail and small package delivery
    d. Breakfast cereal
    e. Local telephone service

11. Explain why perfectly competitive agricultural industries may have external economies of scale—and thus
may be declining-cost industries—arising from the behaviour of the farm machinery industry. Is it relevant
that the farm machinery industry is dominated by a
small number of very large firms?

CHAPTER 11

MONOPOLY

Perfect competition is at one end of the spectrum of market structures. At the other end is monopoly. The word **monopoly** comes from the Greek words *monos polein,* which mean "alone to sell". Economists say that a monopoly occurs when the output of an entire industry is produced and sold by a single firm, called a **monopolist** or a *monopoly firm.* Examples of monopoly are rare at the national level but are much more common for smaller geographical areas. The company that supplies electric power to your home is almost certainly a monopoly, as is the firm that provides local (but not long-distance) telephone service. Because monopoly is the market structure that allows for the maximum possible exercise of market power on the part of the firm, monopoly markets and perfectly competitive markets provide two extremes of behaviour that are useful to economists as they study market structure.

A SINGLE-PRICE MONOPOLIST

The first part of this chapter deals with a monopoly firm that charges a single price for its product. The firm's profits, like those of all firms, will depend on the relationship between its production costs and its sales revenues.

COST AND REVENUE IN THE SHORT RUN

We saw in Chapter 8 that U-shaped short-run cost curves are a consequence of the law of diminishing returns. Because this law applies to the conditions under which goods are produced rather than to the market structure in which they are sold, monopolists have U-shaped short-run cost curves for the same reasons as do perfectly competitive firms.

Because a monopolist is the sole producer of the product that it sells, its demand curve is simply the market demand curve for that product. The market demand curve, which shows the total quantity that buyers will purchase at each price, also shows the quantity that the monopolist will be able to sell at each price. Thus the monopolist, unlike the perfectly competitive firm, faces a negatively sloped demand curve. This means that it faces a trade off between the price it charges and the quantity it sells. Sales can be increased only if price is reduced, and price can be increased only if sales are reduced.

Average Revenue and Marginal Revenue

Starting with the market demand curve, the monopolist's average and marginal revenue curves can be readily derived. When the monopolist charges the same price for all units sold, average revenue per unit is equal to price. Thus the market demand curve is also the firm's *average revenue* curve.

Now consider the monopolist's *marginal revenue*—the revenue resulting from the sale of an additional (or marginal) unit of production. Because its demand curve is negatively sloped, the monopolist

TABLE 11-1
A Numerical Example of a Monopolist's Average, Marginal, and Total Revenues

(1) Price (Average Revenue)	(2) Quantity Sold	(3) Total Revenue ($p \times q$)	(4) Change in Total Revenue ΔTR	(5) Marginal Revenue $\Delta TR/\Delta q$
10	0	0		
9	10	90	90	9
8	20	160	70	7
7	30	210	50	5
6	40	240	30	3
5	50	250	10	1
4	60	240	−10	−1
3	70	210	−30	−3
2	80	160	−50	−5
1	90	90	−70	−7
0	100	0	−90	−9

Marginal revenue is less than price because price must be lowered to sell an extra unit. Columns 1 and 2 of the table give specific points on the demand curve shown in Figure 11-1. The data show that every time the firm lowers its price by $1, its sales increase by 10 units. Column 3 gives the total revenue associated with each price, which is that price multiplied by the quantity sold. Column 4 gives the change in total revenue as the price is altered by $1. To calculate the change in revenue associated with a unit change in quantity, the change in column 4 must be divided by 10 to get the change in revenue *per unit change in quantity*. The result is recorded in column 5, which is the marginal revenue.

must lower the price that it charges on *all* units in order to sell an extra unit.

It follows that the addition to its revenue resulting from the sale of an extra unit is less than the price that it receives for that unit (less by the amount that it loses as a result of cutting the price on all the units that it was selling already).

The monopolist's marginal revenue is less than the price at which it sells its output. [26]

The relationship between marginal revenue and price is shown in detail in Table 11-1 and Figure 11-1. Consider Table 11-1 first. Notice that the numbers in columns (4) and (5) are both plotted between the rows that refer to specific prices. This is done because the figures refer to what happens when the price is changed between the amounts shown in two adjacent rows.

Notice also that when price is reduced starting from $10, total revenue rises at first and then falls. The maximum total revenue is reached in this exam-

FIGURE 11-1
A Monopolist's Average and Marginal Revenue Curves

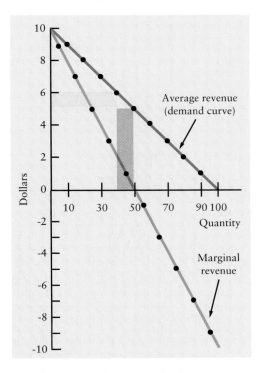

Marginal revenue is less than price because the price at which existing units are sold must be reduced in order to sell more units. The figure shows an example of a demand curve that a monopolist faces and the associated marginal revenue curve. The specific points shown by the black dots on the *AR* curve and the *MR* curve are recorded in Table 11-1.

the specific points on it that were calculated in the table. For purposes of illustration, a straight-line demand curve has been chosen.[1]

Notice that marginal revenue is positive up to 50 units of sales, indicating that reductions in price between $10 and $5 increase total revenue. Notice also that marginal revenue is negative for sales greater than 50 units, indicating that reductions in price below $5 cause total revenue to fall.

The figure also illustrates the two opposing forces that are present whenever the price is changed. As an example, consider the reduction in price from $6 to $5. First, the units already sold bring in less money at the new lower price than at the original higher price. This loss in revenue is the amount of the price reduction multiplied by the number of units already being sold (40 units × $1 per unit = $40). This is shown in the blue shaded area in the figure. The second force, operating in the opposite direction, is that new units are sold, which brings in more revenue. This gain in revenue is given by the number of new units sold multiplied by the price at which they are sold (10 units × $5 = $50). This is shown in the purple shaded area. The *net change* in total revenue is the *difference* between these two amounts ($10). In the example shown in the figure, the increase resulting from the sale of new units exceeds the decrease resulting from existing sales now being made at a lower price. Marginal revenue is thus positive. Furthermore, the change in total revenue is $10 whereas the change in the number of units sold is 10 units. Thus marginal revenue, given by $\Delta TR / \Delta q$, is equal to $10/10 = $1.

The proposition that marginal revenue is always less than average revenue, which has been illustrated numerically in Table 11-1 and graphically in Figure 11-1, provides an important contrast with perfect competition. Recall that in perfect competition, the firm's marginal revenue from selling an extra unit of output is *equal to* the price at which that unit is sold. The reason for the difference is not difficult to understand. The perfectly competitive firm is a price taker; it can sell all it wants at the given market price. In contrast, the monopolist faces a negatively sloped

ple at a price of $5. Because marginal revenue gives the change in total revenue resulting from the sale of one more unit of output, marginal revenue is positive whenever total revenue is increased by selling more, but it is negative when total revenue is reduced by selling more.

The method of calculating marginal revenue shown in the table involves subtracting the total revenue associated with one price from the total revenue associated with another price and then dividing this change by the change in the number of units sold.

Now look at Figure 11-1. It plots the entire demand curve that gave rise to the individual figures for price and quantity shown in Table 11-1. It also plots the entire marginal revenue curve and locates

---

[1]When drawing these curves, note that if the demand curve is a negatively sloped straight line, the *MR* curve also has a negative slope but is twice as steep. Its price intercept (where $q = 0$) is the same as that of the demand curve, and its quantity intercept (where $p = 0$) is one-half that of the demand curve. **[27]**

FIGURE 11-2
The Relationship Between Total, Average, and Marginal Revenue and Elasticity of Demand

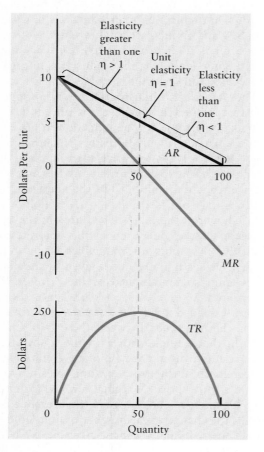

For a monopolist, *MR* is always less than price. When *TR* is rising, *MR* is greater than zero and elasticity is greater than one. When *TR* is falling, *MR* is less than zero and elasticity is less than one. The monopolist's demand curve is its *AR* curve; the *MR* curve is below the *AR* curve because the demand curve has a negative slope.

demand curve; it must reduce the market price to increase its sales.

Marginal Revenue and Elasticity

Now look at Figure 11-2. This duplicates the demand and marginal revenue curves shown in Figure

11-1.[2] In Chapter 5, we discussed the relationship between the elasticity of the market demand curve and the total revenue derived from selling the product. Figure 11-2 summarizes this earlier discussion and extends it to cover marginal revenue.

Over the range in which the demand curve is elastic, total revenue rises as more units are sold; marginal revenue must therefore be positive. Over the range in which the demand curve is inelastic, total revenue falls as more units are sold; marginal revenue must therefore be negative.

SHORT-RUN PROFIT MAXIMIZATION FOR A MONOPOLIST

To show the profit-maximizing position of a monopolist, we bring together information about its revenues and its costs and then apply the two rules developed in Chapter 10: (1) The firm should not produce at all unless there is some level of output for which price is at least equal to total variable cost, and (2) if the firm does produce, its output should be set at the point where marginal cost equals marginal revenue.

When the monopolist equates marginal cost with marginal revenue, its situation is as shown in Figure 11-3. The output is found as the quantity for which marginal cost equals marginal revenue. The price is read off the demand curve, which shows the price corresponding to that output.

Notice that because marginal revenue is always less than price for the monopolist, when marginal revenue is equated with marginal cost, both are less than price.

When a monopolist is maximizing its profit, its marginal cost is always less than the price it charges for its output.

Monopoly Profits

The fact that a monopolist produces the output that *maximizes* its profits tells us nothing about *how*

---

[2]To fit the figure onto the page, the scale on the vertical price axis has been shrunk somewhat. This makes the curve look flatter than the curve in Figure 11-1, even though they each show *exactly* the same data. This illustrates the point made in Chapter 5 that the apparent steepness of one curve is not a good guide to its elasticity because that steepness can be altered merely by changing the scale on the axes.

FIGURE 11-3
Short-Run Profit Maximization for a Monopolist

(i) Positive profits

(ii) Zero profits

The profit-maximizing output is q_0, where $MR = MC$; price is p_0, which is above MC at that output. The rules for profit maximization require $MR = MC$ and $p > AVC$. (*AVC* is not shown in the graph, but it must be below *ATC*.) Whether profits at q_0 are positive or negative (or zero) depends on the position of the *ATC* curve. In part (i), where average total cost is ATC_1, there are positive profits, as shown by the shaded area. In part (ii), where average total cost is ATC_2, profits are zero. If average total costs were ATC_3, the monopolist would suffer the losses shown by the purple shaded area.

large these profits will be or even whether there will be any profits at all. Profits may be positive, as shown in part (i) of Figure 11-3. As part (ii) of Figure 11-3 shows, however, the profit-maximizing monopolist may break even or suffer losses. Nothing guarantees that a monopolist will make profits in the short run, but if it suffers persistent losses, it will eventually go out of business.

No Supply Curve for a Monopolist

In describing the monopolist's profit-maximizing behaviour, we did not introduce the concept of a supply curve, as we did in the discussion of perfect competition. In perfect competition, the industry short-run supply curve depends only on the marginal cost curves of the individual firms. This is true because under perfect competition, profit-maximizing firms equate marginal cost with price. Given marginal costs, it is possible to know how much will be produced at each price. This is not the case, however, with a monopoly firm.

For a monopolist, there is no unique relationship between market price and quantity supplied.[3]

Firm and Industry

Because the monopolist is the only producer in an industry, there is no need for separate theories about the firm and the industry, as is necessary with perfect competition. The monopolist *is* the industry. Thus the short-run, profit-maximizing position of the firm, as shown in Figure 11-3, is also the short-run equilibrium of the industry.

---

[3]This can be proved by drawing a monopolist's marginal cost curve and any marginal revenue curve to intersect the *MC* curve at some output that we call q^*. Now draw as many other different *MR* curves as you like, all of which intersect *MC* at q^*. All of these curves give rise to profit-maximizing output of q^*, but because each *MR* curve is different, each must be associated with a different demand curve and hence a different price at which q^* is sold. This shows that a given quantity may be associated with many different prices, depending on the slope of the demand curve that the monopolist faces.

Competition and Monopoly Compared

The comparison of a monopoly firm with firms in perfect competition is important. In perfect competition, firms face perfectly elastic demand curves, so price and marginal revenue are the same. Thus when they equate marginal cost and marginal revenue, they ensure that marginal cost also equals price. In contrast, a monopolist faces a negatively sloped demand curve for which marginal revenue is less than price. Thus when it equates marginal cost and marginal revenue, it ensures that marginal cost will be less than price.

The relationship between elasticity and revenue just discussed has an interesting implication for the monopolist's profit-maximizing level of output. Because marginal cost is always greater than zero, a profit-maximizing monopolist (which produces where $MR = MC$) will always produce where marginal revenue is also greater than zero—that is, where demand is elastic. If the firm were producing where demand was inelastic, it could reduce its output, thereby increasing its total revenue and reducing its total costs.

A profit-maximizing monopolist will never produce a level of output where the demand curve is inelastic.

Note that no such restriction applies to firms in perfect competition. Each adjusts to its own perfectly elastic demand curve, not to the market demand curve. Thus equilibrium in a perfectly competitive industry can occur where the market demand curve is either elastic or inelastic.

LONG-RUN EQUILIBRIUM IN A MONOPOLIZED INDUSTRY

In a monopolized industry, as in a perfectly competitive one, losses and profits provide incentives for exit and entry.

If the monopoly is suffering losses in the short run, it will continue to operate as long as it can cover its variable costs. In the long run, however, it will leave the industry unless it can find a scale of operations at which its full opportunity costs can be covered.

If the monopoly is making profits, other firms will wish to enter the industry in order to earn more than the opportunity cost of their capital. If such entry occurs, the monopoly's position shown in part (i) of Figure 11-3 will change, and the firm will cease to be a monopoly.

In order for positive monopoly profits to lead to the entry of new firms into the industry, these new firms must *be able* to enter the industry. This leads us to a discussion of *entry barriers*.

Entry Barriers

Impediments that prevent entry are called **entry barriers**; they may be either natural or created.

If monopoly profits are to persist in the long run, the entry of new firms into the industry must be prevented by effective entry barriers.

Natural Entry Barriers. Natural barriers most commonly arise as a result of economies of scale. When the long-run average cost curve is negatively sloped over a large range of output, big firms have significantly lower average total costs than small firms.

Recall from Chapter 10 that the *minimum efficient scale (MES)* is the smallest-size firm that can reap all of the economies of large-scale production. It occurs at the level of output where the firm's long-run average total cost curve reaches a minimum.

Now suppose that the technology of an industry is such that one firm's *MES* would be 10,000 units per week at an average total cost of $10 per unit. Further assume that at a price of $10, the quantity demanded in the entire market is 11,000 units per week. Under these circumstances, only one firm can operate at or near its *MES*.

A **natural monopoly** occurs when the industry's demand conditions allow only one firm, at most, to cover its costs while producing at its *MES*. In a natural monopoly, there is no price at which two firms can both sell enough to cover their total costs at *MES*. Electrical power transmission is a natural monopoly—it will always be cheaper to have only one set of power lines (rather than two or more) serving a given region.

Another type of natural barrier is *setup cost*. If a firm could be catapulted fully grown into the market, it might be able to compete effectively with the existing monopolist. However, the cost to the new firm of entering the market, developing its products, and establishing such things as its brand image and its dealer network may be so large that entry would be unprofitable.

Created Entry Barriers. Many entry barriers are created by conscious government action and are therefore condoned by it. Patent laws, for instance, may prevent entry by conferring on the patent holder the sole legal right to produce a particular product for a specific period of time.

Patent protection has led to a major and prolonged battle among nations fought out in international organizations that seek to enforce conditions for fair trade and investment. The major developed countries, where much of the research and development is done, have sought to extend patent rights to other countries. They argue that without the temporary monopoly profits that a patent creates, the incentive to develop new products will be weakened. The less-developed countries have sought to maintain weak or nonexistent patent laws. This allows them to produce new products under more competitive conditions and so avoid paying monopoly profits to the original patent holders in developed countries.

A firm may also be granted a charter or a franchise that prohibits competition by law. Canada Post, for example, has a government-sanctioned monopoly on the delivery of mail. In other cases the regulation and/or licensing of firms severely restricts entry. Professional organizations for dentists or engineers, for example, might restrict the number of places in acredited dental or engineering schools, and thus restrict entry into those industries.

Other barriers can be created by the firm or firms already in the market. In extreme cases, the threat of force or sabotage can deter entry. The most obvious entry barriers of this type are encountered in organized crime, where operation outside of the law makes available an array of illegal but potent barriers to new entrants. Law-abiding firms must use legal tactics in an attempt to increase a new entrant's setup costs. Such tactics range from the threat of price cutting—designed to impose unsustainable losses on a new entrant—to heavy brand-name advertising. (These and other created entry barriers will be discussed in more detail in Chapter 12.)

The Significance of Entry Barriers

Because there are no entry barriers in perfect competition, profits cannot persist in the long run. In monopolized industries, however, profits can persist in the long run whenever there are effective barriers to entry.

In competitive industries, profits attract entry, and entry erodes profits. In monopolized industries, entry barriers frustrate the adjustment mechanism that would otherwise push profits to zero in the long run.

THE VERY-LONG RUN AND CREATIVE DESTRUCTION

In the very-long run, technology changes. New ways of producing old products are invented, and new products are created to satisfy both familiar and new wants. This is related to the concept of entry barriers; a monopoly that succeeds in preventing the entry of new firms capable of producing its product will sooner or later find its barriers circumvented by innovations. One firm may be able to use new processes that avoid some patent or other barrier that the monopolist relies on to bar entry of competing firms. Another firm may compete by producing a somewhat different product that satisfies the same need as the monopolist's product. Yet another firm might get around a natural monopoly by inventing a technology that produces at a low *MES* and ultimately allows several firms to enter the market and still cover costs.

One distinguished economist, Joseph Schumpeter (1883–1950), took the view that entry barriers were not a serious problem in the very-long run. He argued that monopoly profits provide one of the major incentives for people who risk their money by financing inventions and innovations. In his view, the large short-run profits of a monopoly provide a strong incentive for others to try to usurp some of these profits for themselves. If a frontal attack on the monopolist's entry barriers is not possible, the barriers will be circumvented by such means as the development of similar products against which the monopolist will not have entry protection.

Schumpeter called the replacement of one monopolist by another through the invention of new products or new production techniques the *process of creative destruction*. "Creative" referred to the rise of new products; "destruction" referred to the demise of the existing monopoly. Schumpeter argued that this process prevents the very-long run persistence of barriers to entry into industries that earn large profits.

He pushed this argument further and argued that because creative destruction thrives on innovation, the existence of monopoly profits is a major incentive to economic growth. A key part of his argument can be found in the following words:

> What we have got to accept is that it [monopoly] has come to be the most powerful engine of progress and in particular of the long-run expansion of total output not only in spite of, but to a

considerable extent through, this strategy [of creating monopolies], which looks so restrictive when viewed in the individual case and from the individual point of time.

In this respect, perfect competition is not only impossible but inferior, and has no title to being set up as a model. It is hence a mistake to base the theory of government regulation of industry on the principle that big business should be made to work as the respective industry would work in perfect competition.[4]

Schumpeter was writing at a time when the two dominant market structures studied by economists were perfect competition and monopoly. His argument easily extends, however, to any market structure that allows profits to exist in the long run. Today, pure monopolies are few, but there are many industries in which profits can be earned for long periods of time. Such industries, which are called *oligopolies,* are candidates for the operation of the process of creative destruction. We study these industries in detail in Chapter 12. In the mean time, see Application 11-1 for some everyday examples of the process of creative destruction.

CARTELS AS MONOPOLIES

So far in our discussion, a monopoly has meant that there is only one firm in an industry. A second way a monopoly can arise is for many firms in an industry to agree to cooperate with one another, to behave as if they were a single seller, in order to maximize joint profits, eliminating competition among themselves. Such a group of firms is called a **cartel.** A cartel that includes *all* the firms in the industry can behave in the same way as a single-firm monopoly. The firms can agree among themselves to restrict their total output to the level that maximizes their joint profits.[5]

---

[4]Joseph Schumpeter, *Capitalism, Socialism, and Democracy,* 3rd ed. (New York: Harper & Row, 1950), p. 106.
[5]In this chapter, we deal with the simple case in which *all* of the firms in a perfectly competitive industry form a cartel in order to act as if they were a monopoly. Cartels are sometimes formed by a group of firms that account for a significant part, but not all, of the total supply of some product. The effect is to create what is called an *oligopoly.* The most famous example of this type is the Organization of Petroleum Exporting Countries (OPEC). We examine this type of cartel in Chapter 12.

THE EFFECTS OF CARTELIZATION

Because perfectly competitive firms are price takers, they accept the market price as given and increase their output until their marginal cost equals price. In contrast, a monopolist knows that increasing its output will depress the market price. Taking account of this, the monopolist increases its output only until marginal revenue is equal to marginal cost. If all the firms in a perfectly competitive industry form a cartel, they too will be able to take account of the effect of their *joint output* on price. They can agree to restrict industry output to the level that maximizes their joint profits (where the industry's marginal cost is equal to the industry's marginal revenue). The incentive for firms to form a cartel lies in the cartel's ability to restrict output, thereby raising price and increasing profits.

When a perfectly competitive industry is cartelized, the firms can agree to restrict their joint output to the profit-maximizing level. One way to do this is to establish a quota for each firm's output. Say that the joint-profit-maximizing output is two-thirds of the perfectly competitive output. When the cartel is formed, each firm could be given a quota equal to two-thirds of its competitive output.

The effect of cartelizing a perfectly competitive industry and of reducing its output through production quotas is shown in more detail in Figure 11-4.

PROBLEMS THAT CARTELS FACE

Cartels encounter two characteristic problems. The first is ensuring that members follow the behaviour that will maximize the industry's *joint* profits. The second is preventing these profits from being eroded by the entry of new firms.

Enforcement of Output Restrictions

The managers of any cartel want the industry to produce its profit-maximizing output. Their job is made more difficult if individual firms either stay out of the cartel or enter and then cheat on their output quotas. Any one firm, however, has an incentive to do just this—to be either the one that stays out of the organization or the one that enters and then cheats on its output quota. For the sake of simplicity, assume that all firms enter the cartel, so enforcement problems are concerned strictly with cheating by its members.

If Firm X is the only firm to cheat, it is in the best of all possible situations. All other firms restrict

SOME EVERYDAY EXAMPLES OF THE PROCESS OF CREATIVE DESTRUCTION

Creative destruction, the elimination of one product by a superior product and one production process by a superior process, is a major characteristic of all advanced countries. It eliminates the strong market position of the firms and workers who make the threatened product or operate the threatened process.

The steel-nibbed pen eliminated the quill pen with its sharpened bird's feather nib. The fountain pen eliminated the steel pen and its accompanying ink well. The ball-point pen virtually eliminated the fountain pen. Who knows what will come next in writing implements?

The silent films eliminated vaudeville. The talkies eliminated the silent film and colour films have all but eliminated black and white. The TV seriously reduced the demand for films (and radio) while not eliminating either of them. Cable greatly reduced the demand for direct TV reception by offering better pictures and a more varied selection. The satellite is threatening to eliminate cable by offering much more selection. Predictably, the cable operators appealed to the Canadian regulators to protect their market by disallowing satellite TV.

For long-distance passenger travel by sea, the steamship eliminated the sailing vessel around the turn of the twentieth century. The airplane eliminated the ocean liner in the 1950s and 1960s. For passenger travel on land, the train eliminated the stage coach while the bus competed with the train without eliminating it. The airplane wiped out the passenger train in most of North America while leav-ing the bus still in a low-cost niche used mainly for short and medium distances.

The above are all product innovation. Production process also undergoes the same type of creative destruction. The laborious hand-setting of metal type for printing was replaced by the linotype that allowed the type to be set by a keyboard operator but which still involved a costly procedure for making corrections. The linotype was swept away by computer typesetting and much of the established printing shop operations have recently been replaced by desktop publishing.

Masses of assembly-line workers, operating highly specialized and inflexible machines replaced the craftsman when Henry Ford perfected the techniques of mass production. A smaller number of less specialized flexible manufacturing workers, operating sophisticated and less specialized machinery, have replaced the assembly line workers who operated the traditional factory.

The cases can be extended almost indefinitely and they all illustrate the same general message. Technological change transforms the products we consume, how we make those products, and how we work. It continually sweeps away positions of high income and economic power established by firms that were in the previous wave of technological change and by those who work for them. It is an agent of dynamism in our economy, an agent of change and economic growth, but it is not without its dark side in terms of the periodic loss of privileged positions on the part of the replaced firms and their workers.

---

output and hold the industry price up near its monopoly level. They earn profits but only by restricting output. Firm X can then reap the full benefit of the other firms' output restraint and sell some additional output at the high price that has been set by the cartel's actions. However, if all of the firms cheat, the price will be pushed back to the competitive level, and all of the firms will return to their competitive position.

This conflict between the interests of the group and the interests of the individual firm is the cartel's main dilemma. Provided that enough firms cooperate in restricting output, all firms are better off than they would be if the industry remained perfectly

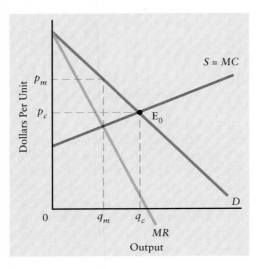

FIGURE 11-4
The Effect of Cartelizing a Perfectly Competitive Industry

Cartelization of a perfectly competitive industry can always increase that industry's profits. Equilibrium for a perfectly competitive industry occurs at E_0, where the supply and the demand curves intersect. Equilibrium price and output are p_c and q_c. Because the industry demand curve is negatively sloped, marginal revenue is less than price.

If the industry is cartelized, profits can be increased by reducing output. All units between q_m and q_c add less to revenue than to cost—the marginal revenue curve lies below the marginal cost curve. (Recall from Figure 10-6 that the industry's supply curve is the sum of the supply curves, and hence of the marginal cost curves, of each of the firms in the industry.) If the units between q_m and q_c are not produced, output is reduced to q_m and price rises to p_m. This price-output combination maximizes the industry's profits because it is where industry marginal revenue equals industry marginal cost.

competitive. Any one firm, however, is even better off if it remains outside or if it enters and cheats. However, if all firms act on this incentive, all will be worse off than if they had joined the cartel and restricted output.

Cartels tend to be unstable because of the incentives for individual firms to violate the output quotas needed to enforce the monopoly price.

The conflict between the motives for cooperation and for independent action is analyzed in more detail in Figure 11-5. In Chapter 12, we present an

explicit theory, called *game theory,* that economists use to analyze conflicts of this kind.

Cartels and similar output-restricting arrangements have a long history. For example, schemes to raise farm incomes by limiting crops bear ample testimony to the accuracy of the predicted instability of cartels. Industry agreements concerning crop restriction often break down, and prices fall as individual farmers exceed their quotas. This is why most crop restriction plans are now operated by governments rather than by private cartels. Government marketing boards of the type discussed in Chapter 6, backed by the full coercive power of the state, can force monopoly behaviour on existing producers and can effectively bar the entry of new ones.

Restricting Entry

A cartel must not only police the behaviour of its members but must also be able to prevent the entry of new producers. An industry that can support a number of individual firms must have no overriding natural entry barriers. Thus if it is to maintain its profits in the long run, a cartel of many separate firms must create barriers that prevent the entry of new firms that are attracted by the cartel's profits. Successful cartels are often able to license the firms in the industry and to control entry by restricting the number of licenses. This practice is often used by professionals, from physicians to beauticians. At other times, the government has operated a quota system and has given it the force of law. If no one can produce without a quota and the quotas are allocated among existing producers, entry is successfully prevented.

Application 11-2 discusses how technical change has severely lowered the entry barriers into the high-fashion industry. Though the industry was never fully monopolized, the lowering of entry barriers has naturally led to the quick erosion of profits as new firms enter the industry.

A MULTIPRICE MONOPOLIST: PRICE DISCRIMINATION

So far in this chapter, we have assumed that the monopolist charges the same price for every unit of its product, no matter where or to whom it sells that

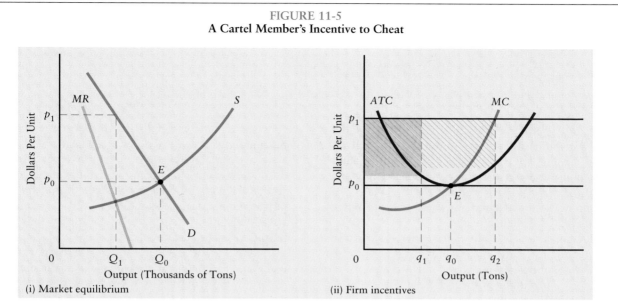

FIGURE 11-5
A Cartel Member's Incentive to Cheat

(i) Market equilibrium

(ii) Firm incentives

Cooperation leads to the monopoly price, but individual self-interest leads to production in excess of the monopoly output. Market conditions are shown in part (i), and the situation of a typical firm is shown in part (ii). (Note the change of scale between the two graphs.) Initially, the market is in competitive equilibrium with price p_0 and quantity Q_0. The individual firm is producing output q_0 and is just covering its total costs.

The cartel is formed and then enforces quotas on individual firms that are sufficient to reduce the industry's output to Q_1, the output where the supply curve cuts the marginal revenue curve. Q_1 is thus the output that maximizes the joint profits of the cartel members. Price rises to p_1 as a result. The typical firm's quota is q_1. The firm's profits rise from zero to the amount shown by the gray shaded area in part (ii). Once price is raised to p_1, however, the individual firm would like to increase output to q_2, where marginal cost is equal to the price set by the cartel. This would allow the firm to earn profits, shown by the diagonally striped area. However, if all firms increase their outputs above their quotas, industry output will increase beyond Q_1, and the profits earned by all firms will fall.

product. But as we shall soon see, a monopolist will find it profitable to sell different units of the same product at different prices whenever it gets the opportunity. This practice is prevalent in oligopolistic markets as well as monopoly, and so the range of examples we will discuss cover both types of market structure.

Airlines often charge less to people who stay over a Saturday night than to those who come and go within the week. Raw milk is often sold at one price when it is to be used as fluid milk but at a lower price when it is to be used to make ice cream or cheese. In countries where medical services are provided by the market, physicians in private practice often charge for their services according to the incomes of their patients. Movie theaters often have lower admission prices for children than for adults, and typically also have lower prices for seniors.

Railroads charge different rates for different products. Electric companies sell electricity at one rate to homes and at a different rate to firms.

Price discrimination occurs when a producer charges different prices for different units of the same product for reasons not associated with differences in cost. Not all price differences represent price discrimination. Quantity discounts, differences between wholesale and retail prices, and prices that vary with the time of day or the season of the year may not represent price discrimination because the same product sold at a different time, in a different place, or in different quantities may have different costs. If an electric power company has unused capacity at certain times of the day, it may be cheaper for the company to provide service at those hours than at peak demand hours. If price differences reflect cost differences, they are not discriminatory.

APPLICATION 11-2

EASE OF ENTRY AND TECHNICAL CHANGE: THE CASE OF FASHION KNOCKOFFS

Once upon a time, the *haute couture* (high fashion) industry maintained a franchise of exclusivity and profits by its lead in the introduction of new fashions. For women who wanted to be in step with the trends set on the fashion runways of Paris and Milan, it was necessary to pay the high prices of designer originals, often in excess of $10,000 for a dress. A substantial time lag separated the introduction of the "designer original" and the arrival of the *knockoff*—a more affordable copy of the designer original—at local department stores.

The entry of high technology and global communications into the fashion industry has eroded the ability of designers to extract these high prices for their new collections. As the *Wall Street Journal* noted, "A photograph snapped at a fashion show in Milan can be faxed overnight to a Hong Kong factory, which can turn out a sample in a matter of hours. That sample can be FedExed back to a New York showroom the next day, ready for retail buyers to preview." In economic terms, the increased ease of replicating haute couture designs has meant that the costs of entry have been dramatically reduced.

Designers such as Donna Karan and Yves Saint-Laurent worry that the disappearance of the lag between the presentation of the designer originals and the arrival of the knockoffs will make it more difficult to recoup the cost of investment and development of the new designs.

Forgery of designer products (claiming that a knockoff is in fact the real thing), such as the imitation Gucci scarves and handbags that are often sold on the streets in major metropolitan areas, is illegal under Canadian and U.S. trademark law. However, substantiating in court that a dress or suit has been plagiarized is very difficult because fashion is a derivative art that often revives motifs from earlier periods. Moreover, knockoffs may duplicate a general style, such as bell bottoms or a latex miniskirt, without copying a designer's work exactly—for example, by adding or subtracting a button or by slightly altering the color scheme.

While some sceptics in the fashion industry fear that the current increase in knockoffs may lead to the demise of the long tradition of haute couture, others believe that the industry will adapt. For example, the designer Bill Blass has addressed the challenge by issuing ready-to-wear knockoffs of his own couture stock. Realizing that a pearl-strapped black cocktail dress priced at nearly $2,000 could be easily replicated, he countered by releasing a $150 copy of this dress in his lower-priced collection. For designers, such two-tier pricing may constitute a viable response to the growth of knockoffs so long as designers are able to maintain some differentiation between the copy and the original.

The phenomenon of knockoffs is by no means unique to women's fashion, though the very short time lag between the arrival of the original and the entry of the copy is somewhat anomalous. Product imitation occurs in all sorts of industries. In the computer industry, a wave of "clones" followed IBM's introduction of the PC in 1984. Similarly, generic drugs are knockoffs in the pharmaceutical industry, though the mechanisms of patent protection and regulation explicitly define the time lag between the launch of the original and the entry of the copy.

When a price difference is based on different buyers' valuations of the same product, it is discriminatory. It does not cost a movie theater operator less to fill seats with children than with adults, but it may be worthwhile for the movie theater to let the children in at a discriminatory low price if few of them would attend at the full adult fare and if they take up seats that would otherwise be empty.

DIFFERENT FORMS OF PRICE DISCRIMINATION

Why should a firm want to sell some units of its output at a price that is well below the price that it receives for other units of its output? The simple answer is because it is profitable to do so. Why should it be profitable?

Persistent price discrimination is profitable either because different buyers are willing to pay different amounts for the same product or because one buyer is willing to pay different amounts for different units of the same product. The basic point about price discrimination is that in either of these circumstances, sellers may be able to capture some of the consumer surplus that would otherwise go to buyers. (Review the discussion of consumer surplus in Chapter 7.) We first discuss the ideas behind each type of price discrimination; we then examine its implications.

Discrimination Among Units of Output

Look back to Table 7-2 in Chapter 7, which shows the consumer surplus received by one consumer when buying eight glasses of milk at a single price. If the firm could sell the consumer each glass separately, it could capture this consumer surplus. It would sell the first unit for $3.00, the second unit for $1.50, the third unit for $1.00, and so on until the eighth unit was sold for 30 cents. The firm would get total revenues of $8.10 rather than the $2.40 obtained from selling eight units at the single price of 30 cents each. In this example, the firm is able to discriminate perfectly and to extract all of the consumer surplus.

Perfect price discrimination occurs when the entire consumer surplus is obtained by the firm. This usually requires that each unit be sold at a separate price. In practice, perfect discrimination is seldom possible. Suppose, however, that the firm could charge two different prices, one for the first 4 units sold and one for the next 4 units sold. If it sold the first 4 units for 80 cents and the next 4 units for 30 cents, it would receive $4.40—less than it would receive if it could discriminate perfectly but more than it would receive if it sold all units at 30 cents.

Discrimination Among Buyers

Think of the demand curve in a market that is made up of individual buyers, each of whom has indicated the maximum price that he or she is prepared to pay

for a single unit. Suppose, for the sake of simplicity, that there are only four buyers for the product; the first is prepared to pay any price up to $4 for one unit of the good, the second is prepared to pay up to $3, the third up to $2, and the fourth up to $1. Suppose that the product has a marginal cost of production of $1 per unit for all units. If the selling firm is limited to a single price, we know it will maximize its profits by setting marginal revenue equal to marginal cost. It will thus charge $3, sell 2 units, and earn profits of $4. (You can compute for yourself the firm's marginal revenue schedule.)

However, if the seller is able to discriminate among the buyers, it could charge the first buyer $4 and the second $3, thus increasing its profits from the first 2 units to $5. Moreover, it could also sell the third unit for $2, thus increasing its profits to $6. It would be indifferent about selling a fourth unit because the price would just cover marginal cost.

Discrimination Among Markets

Suppose now that the monopolist sells its product in two different markets. For example, it might be the only seller in a tariff-protected home market while in foreign markets it sells in competition with so many other firms that it is a price taker. In this case, the firm would equate its marginal cost to the price in the foreign market but to marginal revenue in the domestic market. As a result, it would charge a higher price on sales in the home market than on sales abroad.

Price Discrimination More Generally

Demand curves have a negative slope because different units are valued differently, either by one individual or by different individuals. This fact, combined with a single price for a product, gives rise to consumer surplus.

The ability to charge multiple prices gives a seller the opportunity to capture some (or, in the extreme case, all) of the consumer surplus.

In general, the larger the number of different prices that can be charged, the greater the firm's ability to increase its revenue at the expense of consumers. This is illustrated in Figure 11-6.

It follows that if a selling firm is able to discriminate through price, it can increase revenues received (and thus also profits) from the sale of any

FIGURE 11-6
Price Discrimination

Multiple prices permit a seller to capture consumer surplus. Suppose in either graph that if a single price were charged, it would be the price p_0. Quantity q_0 would be sold, and consumer surplus would be the entire area above p_0 and below the demand curve.

Part (i) assumes that the market can be segregated in such a way that two prices are charged: p_1 for the first q_1 units and p_0 for the remaining q_1q_0 units. Consumer surplus is reduced to the two light blue triangles, and the seller's revenue is increased by the dark blue square.

Part (ii) assumes that the market can be segregated in such a way that four prices are charged: p_2 for the first q_2 units, p_1 for the units between q_2 and q_1, and so on. Consumer surplus is reduced to the light blue triangles, and the seller's revenue is further increased by the two dark blue squares. At the extreme, if a different price could be charged for each unit, producers could extract every bit of the consumer surplus, and the price discrimination would be perfect.

given quantity. [28] However, price discrimination is not always possible, even if there are no legal barriers to its use.

WHEN IS PRICE DISCRIMINATION POSSIBLE?

Discrimination *among units of output* sold to the same buyer requires that the seller be able to keep track of the units that a buyer consumes in each period. Thus the tenth unit purchased by a given buyer in a given month can be sold at a price that is different from the fifth unit *only* if the seller can keep track of who buys what. This can be done by an electric company through its meter readings or by a magazine publisher by distinguishing between renewals and new subscriptions. It can also be done by distributing certificates or coupons that allow, for example, a car wash at a reduced price on a return visit.

Discrimination *among buyers* is possible only if the buyers who face the low price cannot resell the goods to the buyers who face the high price. However, even though the local butcher might like to charge the banker twice as much for steak as he charges the taxi driver, he cannot succeed in doing so. The banker can always shop for meat in the supermarket, where her occupation is not known. Even if the butcher and the supermarket agreed to charge her twice as much, she could hire the taxi driver to shop for her. The surgeon, however, may succeed in discriminating (especially if other reputable surgeons do the same) because it will not do the banker much good to hire the taxi driver to have her operation for her.

Price discrimination is possible if the seller can either distinguish individual units bought by a single buyer or separate buyers into groups such that resale between groups is impossible.

The ability to prevent resale tends to be associated with the nature of the product or the ability to classify buyers into readily identifiable groups. Services are less easily resold than goods; goods that require installation by the firm (e.g., heavy equipment or cable TV service) are less easily resold than movable goods such as household appliances. One simple example of nonresalability occurs in the case of plate glass. Small pieces of plate glass are much cheaper to buy per square metre than bigger pieces, but the person who needs glass for a picture window that is 2 metres by 4 metres obviously cannot use four pieces of glass that are each 1 by 2 metres. Thus the seller can succesfully price discriminate by charging more *per square metre* for large plate glass than for small plate glass.

In general, transportation costs, tariff barriers, and import quotas are among the factors that separate groups of buyers geographically and may make discrimination possible.

Of course, it is not enough to be able to separate different buyers or different units into separate groups. The seller must also be able to control the supply going to each group. For example, there is no point in asking more than the competitive price from some buyers if they can simply go to other firms who sell the good at the competitive price.

THE CONSEQUENCES OF PRICE DISCRIMINATION

The consequences of price discrimination are summarized in the following two propositions.

For any given level of output, the most profitable system of discriminatory prices will provide higher total revenue (and higher profits) to the firm than the profit-maximizing single price.

This first proposition, which was illustrated in Figure 11-6, requires only that the demand curve have a negative slope. To see that the proposition is correct, remember that a monopolist with the power to discriminate could produce exactly the same quantity as a single-price monopolist and charge everyone the same price. Therefore, it need never receive less revenue, and it can do better if it can raise the price on even one unit sold, as long as the price need not be lowered on any other.

Output under price discrimination will be larger than under a single-price monopolist.

To understand this second proposition, remember that a monopolist that must charge a single price for a product will produce less than would all the firms in a perfectly competitive industry. It does this because it knows that selling more depresses the price. Price discrimination allows it to avoid this disincentive. To the extent that the firm can sell its output in separate blocks, it can sell another block without spoiling the market for blocks that are already sold. In the case of perfect price discrimination, in which every unit of output is sold at a different price, the profit-maximizing monopolist will produce every unit for which the price charged is greater than or equal to its marginal cost. *A perfect-price-discriminating monopolist will therefore produce the same quantity of output as would all firms combined in a perfectly competitive industry.*

NORMATIVE ASPECTS OF PRICE DISCRIMINATION

The predicted combination of higher average revenue and higher output does not in itself have any *normative* significance. It will typically lead to a different distribution of income and a different level of output than when the seller is limited to a single price. The ability of the discriminating monopolist to capture some of the consumer surplus will seem undesirable to consumers but obviously not to the monopolist. How outsiders view the transfer may depend on who gains and who loses.

For instance, when railroads discriminate against small farmers, the results arouse public anger. It seems acceptable to many people, however, that doctors practice price discrimination in countries where medical services are provided by the market, charging lower prices to poor patients than to wealthy ones. Not everyone disapproves when airlines discriminate by giving senior citizens and vacationers lower fares than business travelers.

An interesting further example comes from abroad. For many years, government policy prevented British railways from discriminating among passengers in different regions. To prevent discrimination, a fixed fare per passenger-kilometre was specified and charged on all lines, regardless of passenger traffic or elasticity of demand for the services of the particular line. In the interests of economy, branch lines that could not cover costs were closed. Some lines stopped operating, even though their users preferred rail transport to any alternatives and the strength of their preference was such that they would have willingly paid a price that would have allowed the line to operate profitably. However, the lines were closed because it was thought to be inequitable to "discriminate against" the passengers on these lines.

Two quite separate issues are involved in evaluating any particular example of price discrimination. One is the effect of discrimination on the level of output, and the other is the effect of discrimination on the distribution of income. Price discrimination results in a higher output than would occur if a single price were charged. Often, however, it is the effect of discrimination on income distribution that accounts for people's strong emotional reactions to it. By increasing the seller's profits, price discrimination transfers income from buyers to sellers. When buyers are poor and sellers are rich, this may seem undesirable. However, as we saw in the case of doctors' fees and senior citizens' discounts, discrimination sometimes allows lower-income people to buy a product that they would be unable to afford if it were sold at the single price that maximized the producers' profits.

SUMMARY

A. A SINGLE-PRICE MONOPOLIST

- Monopoly is a market structure in which an entire industry is supplied by a single firm. The monopolist's own demand curve is identical to the market demand curve for the product. The market demand curve is the monopolist's average revenue curve, and its marginal revenue curve always lies below its demand curve.
- A single-price monopolist is maximizing its profits when its marginal revenue is equal to marginal costs. Since marginal costs are positive, profit maximization means that marginal revenue is positive. This in turn means that elasticity of demand is greater than unity at the monopolist's profit-maximizing level of output.
- The amount of profits that a monopoly earns may be large, small, zero, or negative in the short run, depending on the relationship between demand and cost.
- For monopoly profits to persist in the long run, there must be effective barriers to the entry of other firms. Entry barriers can be natural or created.
- Monopoly power is limited by the presence of substitute products, the development of new products, and the entry of new firms. In the very-long run, it is difficult to maintain entry barriers in the face of the process

of creative destruction—the invention of new processes and new products to attack the entrenched position of existing monopolies.

B. CARTELS AS MONOPOLIES

- A group of firms may form a cartel by agreeing to restrict their joint output to the monopoly level. Cartels tend to be unstable because of the strong incentives for each individual firm to cheat by producing more than its quota allows.

C. A MULTIPRICE MONOPOLIST: PRICE DISCRIMINATION

- A price-discriminating monopolist can capture some of the consumer surplus that exists when all of the units of a product are sold at a single price. Successful price discrimination requires that the firm be able to control the supply of the product offered to particular buyers and to prevent the resale of the product.
- A profit-maximizing monopolist that can enforce discriminatory prices will produce higher output and earn larger profits than will a single-price monopolist.

KEY CONCEPTS

The relationship between price and marginal revenue for a monopolist

The relationships among marginal revenue, total revenue, and elasticity for a monopolist

Short-run monopoly profits

Natural and created entry barriers

Cartels as monopolies

The instability of cartels

The causes and consequences of price discrimination

Perfect price discrimination

DISCUSSION QUESTIONS

1. Suppose that only one professor teaches economics at your university. Would you say that this professor is a monopolist who can exact any "price" from students in the form of readings assigned, tests given, and material covered? Suppose now that two additional professors have been hired. Has the original professor's monopoly power been decreased? What if the three professors form a cartel agreeing on common reading lists, workloads, and the like?

2. Three of the four companies that manufacture matzos—the unleavened bread eaten during the Jewish Passover celebration—recently combined to control 90 percent of the total market. When the owner of the new firm was approached by a marketing specialist about doing special promotions, he replied, "Why? We already own the market." What does this tell you about the new firm's attitude with respect to competitive behaviour? In analyzing the firm's price and output decisions, would it be reasonable to use monopoly theory? What does the quotation tell you about the firm's belief about the sensitivity of market demand to promotion schemes?

3. Imagine a monopolist that has fixed costs but no variable or marginal costs. For example, consider a firm that owns a spring of water that can produce indefinitely once certain pipes are installed in an area where no other source of water is available. What would be the firm's profit-maximizing price? What elasticity of demand would you expect at that price? Would this seem to be an appropriate pricing policy if the water monopoly were instead owned by the municipal government, and operated in the interests of the residents of the municipality?

4. Which of these industries—licorice candy, copper wire, outboard motors, coal, or the local newspaper—would it be most profitable to monopolize? Why? Does your answer depend on several factors or

on just one or two? Which would you as a consumer least like to have monopolized by someone else? If your answers to the two questions are different, explain why.

5. Aristotle Murphy owns movie theatres in two towns of roughly the same size, 100 kilometres apart. In Monopolia, he owns the only chain of theatres; in Competitia, there is no theatre chain, and he is only one of a number of independent theatre operators. Would you expect movie prices to be higher in Monopolia or in Competitia in the short run? In the long run? If differences occur in his prices, would Murphy be discriminating in price?

6. Liquor retailing is a competitive industry in most U.S. states but a government-owned monopoly in most Canadian provinces. In what ways would you expect the industry in the two countries to be different? In Alberta, the previously government-owned retail liquor stores were privatized. What would you expect to happen to the price and quantity of retail liquor in Alberta after the privatization?

7. Airline fares to Europe are higher in summer than in winter. Some railroads charge lower fares during the week than on weekends. Electric companies charge consumers lower rates the more electricity they use. Are these all examples of price discrimination? What additional information would you like to have before answering this question?

8. Discuss whether each of the following represents price discrimination. In your view, which are the most socially harmful?

   a. Weekend airline fares that are less than full fare
   b. First-class fares that are 50 percent higher than tourist fares, recognizing that two first-class seats use the space of three tourist seats

c. Discounts negotiated from list price, for which sales personnel are authorized to bargain and to get as much in each transaction as the traffic will bear

d. Higher tuition for out-of-state students at state-supported colleges and universities in the United States.

e. Higher tuition for law students than for graduate students in economics.

9. Acme Department Store has a sale on luggage. It is offering $30 off any new set of luggage to customers who trade in an old suitcase. Acme has no use for the old luggage and throws it away at the end of each day. Is this price discrimination? Why or why not? Which of the conditions necessary for price discrimination are or are not met?

10. The world price of coffee has declined in real terms over the past 40 years. In 1950, coffee was priced at just under $3 per pound (in 1994 U.S. dollars), whereas by 1995 the world price had fallen to just over $1 per pound. On July 29, 1995, *The Economist* magazine reported that,

> On July 26 the Association of Coffee Producing Countries agreed in New York to limit exports to 60m bags for 12 months. The current level is 70m bags. . . . Coffee prices rallied a bit on the news, but few expect the pact to last: some big coffee producers such as Mexico have not signed up, and even those who have will probably cheat.

Explain why "few expect the pact to last", keeping in mind the two characteristic problems for cartels that were discussed in this chapter.

CHAPTER 12

IMPERFECT COMPETITION AND STRATEGIC BEHAVIOUR

The two market structures that we have studied so far—perfect competition and monopoly—are polar cases; they define the two extremes of a firm's market power over an industry. Under perfect competition, firms are price takers, price is driven to the level of marginal cost, and economic profits in the long run are zero, which means that firms are just covering the opportunity cost of their capital. Under monopoly, the firm is a price setter, it sets price above marginal cost, and it may earn more than the opportunity cost of its capital.

Although they provide important insights, these two polar cases are insufficient for understanding the behaviour of all firms. Indeed, most of the products that we easily recognize—computers, breakfast cereals, automobiles, photographic equipment, and fast food, to name a few—are produced by firms that have *some* market power but are neither perfect competitors or monopolists.

This chapter is devoted to the discussion of the theory of industries that are neither perfectly competitive nor monopolistic. Before discussing the theory, however, we turn to a brief discussion of some characteristics of the Canadian economy.

THE STRUCTURE OF THE CANADIAN ECONOMY

Most industries in the Canadian economy lie between the two extremes of monopoly and perfect competition. Within this spectrum of market structure we can divide Canadian industries into two broad groups—those with a large number of relatively small firms and those with a small number of relatively large firms.

INDUSTRIES WITH MANY SMALL FIRMS

About two-thirds of Canada's gross domestic product is produced by industries made up of firms that are either small in absolute size, as most independent retailers are, or small relative to the size of the market in which they sell, like even the largest of Canadian farms.

The perfectly competitive model, extended to allow for the impact of government intervention where necessary, does quite well in explaining the behaviour of some of these industries. These are the ones in which individual firms produce more-or-less identical products and so are price takers. Forest and fish products provide many examples. Agriculture also fits fairly well in most ways since individual farmers are clearly price takers. Entry into farming is easy, and exit does occur, often making news when it happens on a large scale. Many basic raw materials, such as iron ore, tin, and copper, are sold on world markets where most individual firms lack significant market power and prices fluctuate continually in response to changing market conditions.

Other industries, however, do not exhibit the behaviour that is predicted by the perfectly competitive model, even though they contain many firms. In retail trade and in services, for example, most firms have some influence over prices. The local grocery, supermarket, discount house, and department store not only consider weekend specials and periodic sales to be important to their success, but also spend a good deal of money advertising—something that they would not have to do if they faced perfectly-elastic demand curves. Moreover, each store in these industries has a unique location that may give it some local monopoly power over nearby customers. In wholesaling, the sales representative is regarded as a key figure who must compete with other representatives to sell to reluctant purchasers.

As a result, industries with many relatively small firms can be divided into two categories. In one category, the firms' behaviour can be explained by the perfectly competitive model; in the other category, the perfectly competitive model does not apply because the firms, though small, are not price takers. It is this second group of industries that we examine in this chapter.

INDUSTRIES WITH A FEW LARGE FIRMS

About one third of Canada's gross domestic product is produced by industries that are dominated by either a single firm or a few large ones.

The most striking cases of single-firm monopolies in today's economy are the electric utilities and the firms which provide local telephone service. In the first case they are typcially owned by provincial governments; in the second they are subject to government regulation (which we examine in Chapter 13). Other than these and similar cases in which government ownership or regulation plays an important role, cases of single-firm monopoly are very rare in Canada today. However, there are some notable examples of monopoly (or near monopoly) from many years ago. For example, the Eddy Match Company was virtually the sole producer of wooden matches in Canada between 1927 and 1940, and Canada Cement Limited produced nearly all of the output of cement until the 1950s.

This type of market dominance by a single large firm is now largely a thing of the past. Most modern industries which are dominated by large firms contain several. Their names are part of the average Canadian's vocabulary: Canadian National and Canadian Pacific; Canadian Airlines and Air Canada; Banque National, Toronto Dominion, and Scotia Bank; Imperial Oil, Petro Canada, and Irving; Stelco, Dofasco, and Alcan; Falconbridge and INCO; Abitibi Price and MacMillan Bloedel; and Ford, Chrysler, and GM. Many service industries that used to be dominated by small independent producers have in recent decades seen the development of large firms operating on a world-wide basis. In accounting, firms such as Price-Waterhouse and Deloitte-Touche are enormous and clearly have some market power. SNC-Lavalin and Acres are two examples of very large engineering firms that have business contracts all over the world.

INDUSTRIAL CONCENTRATION

An industry that is highly concentrated contains few firms, whereas an industry that has a low degree of concentration contains many firms. Recall that monopoly and perfect competition lie at the two extremes of concentration; a monopoly is an industry with only one firm, and perfect competition is an industry with so many firms that no one of them has any influence on market price. As we have just seen, most industries lie between these two extremes of concentration.

Concentration Ratios

When measuring whether an industry has power concentrated in the hands of only a few firms or dispersed over many, it is not sufficient to count the number of firms. For example, an industry with one enormous firm and 29 small ones is more concentrated in any meaningful sense than an industry with only five equally-sized firms. One approach to this problem is to calculate what is called a **concentration ratio,** which shows the fraction of total market sales controlled by the largest sellers. Common types of concentration ratios cite the share of total market sales made by the largest four or eight firms.

One important problem associated with using concentration ratios is to *define the market* with reasonable accuracy. On the one hand, the market may be much smaller than the whole country. For example, concentration ratios in national cement sales are low, but they understate the market power of cement companies because high transportation costs divide the cement *industry* into a series of regional *markets,* with each having relatively few firms. On the other hand, the market may be larger than one country. This is a particularly important consideration in a small trading country such as Canada.

Indeed, the globalization of competition brought about by the falling costs of transportation and communication has been one of the most significant developments in the world economy in recent decades. As the world has "become smaller" through the advances in communication technologies, the nature of domestic markets has changed dramatically. The presence of only a single firm in one industry in Canada in no way implies monopoly power when it is in competition with five foreign firms that can easily sell in the Canadian market. Application 12-1 discusses how the communication revolution which has taken place in the past two decades has altered the nature of production and competition in Canada and around the world.

However, the use of concentration ratios, adjusted appropriately to correctly define the relevant

APPLICATION 12-1

GLOBALIZATION AND THE COMMUNICATION REVOLUTION

A mere 150 years ago, people and news traveled by sailing ship, and it took months to communicate across various parts of the world. Advances in the first 60 years of the twentieth century sped up both communications and travel. In the past three decades, the pace of change in communication technology has accelerated. The world has witnessed a communication revolution that has dramatically changed the way business decisions are made and implemented.

Four decades ago, telephone links were labouriously and unreliably connected by operators, satellites were newfangled and not especially useful toys for rocket scientists, photocopying and telecopying were completely unknown, mail was the only way to send hard copy and getting it to overseas destinations often took weeks, computers were in their infancy, and jets were just beginning to replace the much slower and less reliable propeller aircraft. Today, direct dialing is available to most parts of the world, at a fraction of what long-distance calls cost 40 years ago, and faxes, satellite links, jet travel, computer networks, cheap courier services, and a host of other developments have made communication that is reliable and often instantaneous available throughout the world.

The communication revolution has been a major contributor to the development of what has become known as the "global village," a term first used by Canadian author Marshall McLuhan in his writing about the social implications of changes in communication technology. Three important characteristics of the global village are a *globalization* of production, an increase in competition, and a decline in the power of the nation-state.

PRODUCTION

The communication revolution has allowed many large international companies, known as *transnational corporations (TNCs)*, to decentralize their production process. They are now able to locate their research and development (R&D) where the best scientists are available. They can produce various components in dozens of places, locating each activity in a country where costs are cheapest for that type of production. They can then ship all the parts, as they are needed, to an assembly factory where the product is "made."

The globalization of production has brought employment, and rising real wages, to people in many less-developed countries. At the same time, it has put

---

market, can give us useful information about the degree to which production in a given market is concentrated in the hands of a few firms.

Industrial Concentration in Canada

The concentration ratios that are typical of various sectors of the Canadian economy differ greatly from one sector to another. In agriculture, concentration ratios are very low. The market structure is close to perfectly competitive, except where government supply-management schemes have created cartels. In forestry, four firms account for approximately 20 percent of the total sales, but the remainder is accounted for by numerous small firms. Most of these firms, large and small, sell in highly competitive international markets. In transportation, communication, and energy utilities, the degree of concentration is higher. There are two firms in rail transportation and two main firms (with some fringe competitors) in air transport and in television networks. There is either monopoly or publicly owned firms in telecommunication, electric energy, and water and natural gas pipelines. Various parts of the wholesale trade have relatively low degrees of concentration, while in the retail trades, the ratios range from low to high. In community, business, and personal services, concentration tends to be quite low (except perhaps in small less-skilled labour in the developed countries under strong competitive pressures.

COMPETITION

The communication revolution has also caused a globalization of competition in almost all industries. National markets are no longer protected for local producers by high costs of transportation and communication or by the ignorance of foreign firms. Walk into a local supermarket or department store today, and you will have no trouble finding products representing most nations of the world.

Consumers gain by being able to choose from an enormous range of well-made, low-priced goods and services. Firms that are successful gain worldwide sales. Firms that fall behind even momentarily may, however, be wiped out by competition coming from many quarters. Global competition is fierce, and firms need to be fast on the uptake—of other people's new ideas or their own—if they are to survive.

ECONOMIC POLICY

The international character of TNCs means that national economic policies have been seriously constrained. Much international trade takes place between segments of single TNCs. This gives them the opportunity, through their accounting practices, to localize their profits in countries where corporate taxes are lowest and to localize their costs in countries where cost write-offs are highest.

The globalization of production also allows TNCs to shift production around the world. Tough national policies that reduce profitability in one country may be self-defeating as firms move production elsewhere. Generous policies that seek to attract production may succeed in attracting only small and specialized parts of it. For example, Sweden has given generous tax treatment to R&D expenditures, seeking to attract firms to do their high-tech, high-wage production in that country. Instead, however, many firms have come to Sweden to do their R&D and then have transferred the knowledge to countries where production costs are lower. The net result is that Swedish taxpayers are subsidizing world consumers by paying for R&D that is generating production in other countries.

The examples given here illustrate an important development: Globalization of production, and consequently of competition, means a great reduction in the scope for individual countries, especially small countries like Canada, to implement distinctive economic policies.

---

towns). In insurance and real estate, concentration is quite low, while in the financial industries concentration is typically quite high.

This is quite a varied story, and we can gain further insight into this experience of concentration by examining the Canadian manufacturing sector in detail.

Even in the Canadian manufacturing sector, the degree of concentration ranges from very high to very low. Table 12-1 shows the four-firm concentration ratios in selected Canadian manufacturing industries. Few, if any, of the industries shown in the table come close to monopoly. None of the industries in the table have a concentration ratio of 100 percent for four firms, let alone for one firm.

At the other extreme, there are many industries with low concentration ratios. The perfectly competitive model could conceivably fit these industries. But even here there are doubts. Manufacturers of clothing, for example, have some control over price because of style and fashion. This is also true for furniture manufacturers. Yet in both cases the four-firm concentration ratios are less than 10 percent.

Although similarities in standards of living, consumption patterns, and education in Canada and the United States have led to many similarities in industrial structure, the Canadian manufacturing sector is substantially *more concentrated* than the American.

TABLE 12-1
Four-Firm Concentration Ratios for Selected Canadian Manufacturing Industries, 1988

Industry	Percent of Revenue Controlled by Leading Four Firms
Tobacco Products	98.9
Petroleum and Coal Products	74.5
Transportation Equipment	68.4
Primary Metals	63.3
Beverages	59.2
Metal Mining	58.9
Paper and Allied Industries	38.9
Textile Mills	32.5
Electrical Products	32.1
Chemical Products	25.5
Food	19.6
Wood Industries	17.8
Knitting Mills	11.4
Machinery	11.3
Furniture Industries	7.6
Clothing Industries	6.6

Source: Douglas West, *Modern Canadian Industrial Organization* (HarperCollins, 1994), p. 37.

TABLE 12-2
Distribution of Concentration Ratios for 140 Canadian Manufacturing Industries

Concentration ratio categories (%)	Number of Industries in Each Group	
	Official data	Adjusted data
0–24.9	17	41
25–49.9	50	58
50–74.9	45	34
75–100	28	7
All industries	140	140

The standard concentration ratios overstate the degree of concentration in Canadian industries due to the openness of the Canadian economy. The first column shows the range for the four-firm concentration ratio. For example, the first row indicates a low degree of concentration, since the four largest firms account for less than 25 percent of the sales, whereas the last row indicates a high level of concentration, with the four largest firms accounting for more than 75 percent of all sales. The second column gives the number of industries in each concentration ratio class according to the official figures. The last column gives the distribution of the same industries when corrections are made for plants with multi-industry outputs and for the importance of imports in the Canadian market. When the corrected figures are substituted for the official ones, the fall in measured concentration of the typical Canadian industry is striking.

(Source: John Baldwin, Paul Gorecki, and John McVey, *Economic Council of Canada, Discussion Paper #263,* 1984.)

This is partly because the small size of the Canadian economy leaves room for fewer firms operating at minimum efficient scale than does the larger American economy. (Recall from Chapter 10 that minimum efficient scale is the level of output where *LRAC* is minimized.) Working in the other direction, however, is the fact that the Canadian economy is a very *open economy,* and for many industries the relevant market includes foreign countries, especially the United States.

Some economists have corrected the "official" concentration ratios (i.e., those published by Statistics Canada) to allow for foreign as well as domestic competition. They estimate market size on the basis of what is sold, whether or not it is produced in Canada. The importance of one firm in that market is estimated on the basis of what it sells in that market no matter where these goods were produced.

Table 12-2 gives the results based on the official four-firm concentration ratios for Canada as well as the corrected figures. It shows that when the corrections are made, there is significantly *less concentration* in Canadian manufacturing than one would infer by inspecting the published data alone. In

particular, they find that correcting for the openness of the Canadian economy results in more industries having low concentration ratios and fewer industries having high concentration ratios.

The data used in Table 12-2 is from 1979, and thus the study is considerably dated. Unfortunately, the data required to carry out such a correction are not easily available, and are not available on an on-going basis. But the changes in the structure of the Canadian economy over the past twenty years actually serve to reinforce the central point. The trend toward more international trade, partially driven by the FTA and NAFTA, have made Canada a more open economy today than it was in 1979. Thus a similar study today would likely find that there is *even less* industrial concentration than suggested in Table 12-2.

The table shows that even with the corrected data, in about 70 percent of Canadian manufacturing industries, the four largest firms control over 25 percent of the value of sales. Such industries are not monopolies, because there are several firms in the industry, and these firms engage in rivalrous behaviour. But neither do these firms operate in perfectly competitive markets. Often there are only a few major rival firms in an industry, but even when there are many, they are not price takers. Virtually all consumer goods are differentiated products, and any one firm will typically have several lines of a product that differ more or less from one another and from competing lines produced by other firms. To explain and predict behaviour in these markets, we must go beyond simple concentration ratios; we need to develop theories of the behaviour of firms in market structures other than monopoly and perfect competition.

IMPERFECTLY COMPETITIVE MARKET STRUCTURES

The market structures that we are now going to study are called *imperfectly competitive*. The word *competitive* emphasizes that we are not dealing with monopoly, and the word *imperfect* emphasizes that we are not dealing with perfect competition (in which firms are price takers). What is referred to, then, is rivalrous competitive behaviour among firms that have some amount of market power.

We begin by noting a number of important characteristics of behaviour that are typical of imperfectly competitive firms. To help organize our thoughts, we classify these under two main headings. First, firms choose the *variety* of the product that they produce and sell. Second, firms choose the *price* at which they will sell that product.

FIRMS SELECT THEIR PRODUCTS

If a new farmer enters the wheat industry, the full range of products that can be produced is already in existence. In contrast, if a new firm enters the snack food industry, that firm must decide on the characteristics of the new snacks that it is to produce. It will not produce snacks that are identical to those already in production. Rather, it will develop variations on existing snack foods or even a totally new food. Each of these will have its own distinctive characteristics. As a result, firms in the snack food industry sell an array of differentiated products, no two of which are identical.

The term **differentiated product** refers to a group of commodities that are similar enough to be called the same product but dissimilar enough that they can be sold at different prices. For example, although one brand of face soap is similar to most others, soaps differ from each other in chemical composition, colour, smell, softness, brand name, packaging, reputation, and a host of other characteristics that matter to customers. So all face soaps taken together can be regarded as one differentiated product.

Most (but not all) firms in imperfectly competitive markets sell differentiated products. In such industries, the firm itself must decide on what characteristics to give the products that it will sell.

FIRMS CHOOSE THEIR PRICES

Because firms in perfect competition sell a homogeneous product, they face a market price that they are unable to influence. In all other market structures, firms have negatively sloped demand curves and thus face a trade off between the price that they charge and the quantity that they sell.

Whenever different firms' products are not perfect substitutes, each firm must decide on a price to quote. For example, no market sets a single price for razor blades or television sets by equating overall demand with overall supply. What is true for razor blades and for television sets is true for virtually all consumer goods and many capital goods. Any one manufacturer will typically have several product lines that differ from each other and from the competing product lines of other firms. Each product has a price that must be set by its producer. Of course, a certain amount of haggling is possible, particularly at the retail level, but this is usually within well-defined limits set by the price charged by the manufacturer.

In such circumstances, economists say that firms *administer* their price. An **administered price** is a price set by the conscious decision of an individual firm rather than by impersonal market forces. Firms that administer their prices are said to be **price makers.**

Each firm has expectations about the quantity it can sell at each price that it might set. *Unexpected* market fluctuations then cause unexpected variations in the quantities that are sold at the administered prices.

In market structures other than perfect competition, firms set their prices and then let demand determine sales. Changes in market conditions are signaled to the firm by changes in the quantity that the firm sells at its current administered price.

The changed conditions may or may not then lead firms to change their prices.

One striking contrast between perfectly competitive markets, on the one hand, and markets for differentiated products, on the other, concerns the behaviour of prices. In perfect competition, prices change continually in response to changes in demand and supply. In markets where differentiated products are sold, prices often change less frequently. Manufacturers' prices for automobiles, radios, television sets, and men's suits do not change with anything like the frequency that prices change in markets for basic materials or stocks and bonds.

Modern firms that sell differentiated products typically have hundreds, and sometimes even thousands, of distinct products on their price lists. Changing such a long list of administered prices at the same frequency that competitive market prices change would be extremely costly if not impossible. Even changing them only occasionally involves costs. These include the costs of printing new list prices and notifying all customers, the difficulty of keeping track of frequently changing prices for purposes of accounting and billing, and the loss of customer and retailer goodwill due to the uncertainty caused by frequent changes in prices. These costs are often a significant consideration to multiproduct manufacturing firms.

Because producers of differentiated products must administer their own prices, firms must decide on the *frequency* with which they change these prices. In making this decision, the firm will balance the cost of making price changes against the revenue lost by not making price changes. Clearly, the likelihood that the firm will make costly price changes rises with the size of the disturbance to which it is adjusting and the probability that the disturbance will not be reversed.

Thus transitory fluctuations in demand may be met by changing output with prices constant, while changes in costs that accompany inflation are typically passed on through price increases. Because few firms expect inflationary price increases to be reversed, they know that they must raise their prices to cover them. Even in these cases, however, they do so periodically, rather than continuously, because of the costs incurred in making such changes.

OTHER ASPECTS OF FIRM BEHAVIOUR

Several other important aspects of the observed behaviour of firms in imperfect competition could not occur under either perfect competition or monopoly.

Nonprice Competition

Many firms spend large sums of money on advertising. They do so in an attempt both to shift the demand curves for the industry's products and to attract customers from competing firms. Many firms engage in a variety of other forms of non-price competition, such as offering competing standards of quality and product guarantees. Any kind of sales-promotion activity undertaken by a single firm would not happen under perfect competition; any such scheme directed at competing firms in the same industry is, by definition, inconsistent with monopoly.

Unexploited Scale Economies

Many firms in industries that contain more than one firm appear to be operating on the downward-sloping portions of the long-run average cost curves for many of the individual product lines that they produce. Although this is possible under monopoly, firms in perfect competition must, in the long run, be at the minimum point of their long-run average cost curves. (See Figure 10-10 in Chapter 10.)

One set of reasons is found in high development costs and short product lives. Many modern products involve large development costs and are sold for only a few years before they are replaced by new, superior products. For example, for Ford, Toyota or any of the other car manufacturers it takes many millions of dollars (and several years) to develop each new model-year, and many of the changes that are introduced into a new model-year are eliminated the very next year. In such cases, firms face steeply falling long-run average cost curves. The more units that are sold, the less the fixed development costs per unit. Given perfect competition, these firms would go on increasing outputs and sales until rising marginal costs of production balanced the falling fixed unit costs. As it is, they often face falling average cost curves all through the product's life cycle.

Entry Prevention

Firms in many industries engage in activities that appear to be designed to hinder the entry of new firms, thereby preventing existing pure profits from being eroded by entry. We will consider these activities in much more detail later in the chapter.

MONOPOLISTIC COMPETITION

The theory of **monopolistic competition** was originally developed to deal with the phenomenon of product differentiation.[1] This market structure is similar to perfect competition in that the industry contains many firms and exhibits freedom of entry and exit. It differs, however, in one important respect: Whereas firms in perfect competition sell a *homogeneous product* and are price takers, firms in monopolistic competition sell a *differentiated product* and have some power over setting price.

Product differentiation leads to, and is enhanced by, the establishment of brand names and advertising, and it gives each firm a degree of monopoly power over its own product. Each firm can raise its price, even if its competitors do not, without losing all its sales. This is the *monopolistic* part of the theory. However, each firm's monopoly power is severely restricted in both the short run and the long run. The short-run restriction comes from the presence of similar products sold by many competing firms; this causes each firm's demand curve to be very elastic. The long-run restriction comes from free entry into the industry. These restrictions comprise the *competition* part of the theory.

THE ASSUMPTIONS OF MONOPOLISTIC COMPETITION

The theory of monopolistic competition is based on three key assumptions.

1. *Each firm produces one specific variety, or brand, of the industry's differentiated product.*

---

[1]This theory was first developed by the U.S. economist Edward Chamberlin in his pioneering book, *The Theory of Monopolistic Competition* (Cambridge, Mass.: Harvard University Press, 1933).

Each firm thus faces a demand curve that, although it is negatively sloped, is highly elastic because competing firms produce many close substitutes.

2. *The industry contains so many firms that each one ignores the possible reactions of its many competitors when it makes its own price and output decisions.* There are so many firms in the industry that each is negligibly affected by the actions of any other one firm, and thus each firm ignores the actions of the others. In this way, firms in monopolistic competition are similar to firms in perfect competition. They make decisions based on their own demand and cost conditions and do not consider interdependence between their own decisions and those of the other firms in the industry. This is the key aspect that distinguishes the market structure of monopolistic competition from the market structure of oligopoly, which we discuss later in the chapter.

3. *There is freedom of entry and exit in the industry.* If profits are being earned by existing firms, new firms have an incentive to enter. When they do, the demand for the industry's product must be shared among more brands, and this is assumed to take demand equally from all existing firms.

PREDICTIONS OF THE THEORY

Product differentiation, which is the *only* thing that makes monopolistic competition different from perfect competition, has important consequences for behaviour in both the short and the long run.

The Short-Run Decision of the Firm

In the short run, a firm that is operating in a monopolistically competitive market structure is similar to a monopoly. It faces a negatively sloped demand curve and maximizes its profits by equating marginal cost with marginal revenue. If the demand curve cuts the average total cost curve, as is shown in part (i) of Figure 12-1, the firm can make pure profits over and above the opportunity cost of its capital.

The Long-Run Equilibrium of the Industry

Profits, as shown in part (i) of Figure 12-1, provide an incentive for new firms to enter the industry. As

FIGURE 12-1
Profit-Maximization for a Firm in Monopolistic Competition

(i) A typical firm in the short run

(ii) A typical firm when the industry is in long-run equilibrium

The short-run position for a monopolistically competitive firm is similar to that of a monopolist. In the long run, firms in a monopolistically competitive industry have zero profits and excess capacity. Short-run profit-maximization occurs in part (i) at E_S, the output for which $MR = MC$. Price is p_S and quantity is q_S. Profits may exist; in this example they are shown by the shaded area. Starting from the short-run position shown in part (i), entry of new firms shifts the firm's demand curve to the left and eliminates profits. In part (ii), point E_L, where demand is tangent to ATC, is the position of each firm when the industry is in long-run equilibrium. Price is p_L and quantity is q_L. Price is greater and quantity is less than the perfectly competitive equilibrium price and quantity (p_C and q_C). When the industry is in long-run equilibrium, each monopolistically competitive firm has excess capacity of $q_L q_C$.

they do so, the total demand for the industry's product must be shared among this larger number of firms, so each gets a smaller share of the total market. This shifts the demand curve for each existing firm's product to the left. Entry, and the consequent leftward shifting of the existing firms' demand curves, continues until profits are eliminated. When this has occurred, each firm is in the position shown in part (ii) of Figure 12-1. Its demand curve has shifted to the left until the curve is *tangent* to the average total cost curve. At this output, the firm is just covering all of its costs. At any other output, it would be suffering losses because average total costs would exceed average revenue.

To see why this "tangency solution" provides the only possible equilibrium for the industry, consider the two possible alternatives. First, suppose that the firm's demand curve *nowhere touched* the average total cost curve. There would then be no output at which costs could be covered, and exit would occur. The exit of firms from the industry would then lead each *remaining* firm's demand curve to shift to the right, until it eventually touched the average total cost curve. Second, suppose that the demand curve

cut the average total cost curve. There would then be a range of output over which profits could be earned. These profits would lead firms to enter the industry, and this would shift each *remaining* firm's demand curve to the left until it was just tangent to the average total cost curve.

The Excess-Capacity Theorem

Part (ii) of Figure 12-1 makes it clear that monopolistic competition results in a long-run equilibrium of zero profits, even though each individual firm faces a negatively sloped demand curve. It does this by forcing each firm into a position in which it has *excess capacity*; that is, each firm is producing an output less than that corresponding to the lowest point on its long-run average cost ($LRAC$) curve. If the firm were to increase its output, it would reduce its cost per unit, but it does not do so because selling more would reduce revenue by more than it would reduce cost. This result is often called the **excess-capacity theorem.**

In monopolistic competition, commodities are produced at a point where average total costs are falling, in contrast to perfect competition, where they are produced at their lowest possible cost.

EVALUATION OF THE THEORY

Alleged Inefficiency

The excess-capacity theorem once aroused passionate debate among economists because it seemed to show that all industries that sell differentiated products would produce them at a higher cost than was necessary. Because product differentiation is a characteristic of virtually all modern consumer goods industries, this suggested that modern market economies were systematically inefficient. A few decades ago, many critics of market economies called for government intervention to eliminate unnecessary product differentiation, thereby ensuring cost-minimizing levels of production in consumer goods industries.

Subsequent analysis by economists has shown that the charge of inefficiency has not been proved. The excess capacity of monopolistic competition does not necessarily indicate a waste of resources because when firms can choose the characteristics of their own products, minimizing the costs of producing a *given set of products* is not necessarily the best thing to do. Differentiated products provide consumers with a choice among a variety of products, and it is clear that consumers have different tastes and needs with respect to differentiated products.[2]

From society's point of view, there is a trade off between producing more brands to satisfy diverse tastes and producing fewer brands at a lower cost per unit.

Monopolistic competition produces a wider range of products but at a somewhat higher cost per unit than perfect competition. Consumers clearly value variety, so the benefits of variety must be matched against the extra cost that variety imposes in order to find the *socially optimal* amount of product differentiation. Product differentiation is wasteful only if the costs of providing variety exceed the benefits conferred by providing that variety.

The socially optimal number of varieties of a differentiated product is attained when the gain to consumers from adding one more variety equals the loss from having to produce each existing variety at a higher cost because less of each is produced.

Depending on consumers' tastes and firms' costs, monopolistic competition may result in too much, too little, or the optimal amount of product variety.

Empirical Relevance

A long controversy raged over several decades as to the empirical relevance of monopolistic competition. Of course, product differentiation is an almost universal phenomenon in industries producing consumer goods and capital goods. Nonetheless, many economists maintained that the monopolistically competitive market structure was almost never found in practice.

To see why, we need to distinguish between products and firms. Single-product firms are extremely rare in manufacturing industries. Typically, a vast array of differentiated products is produced by each of the few firms in the industry. Most of the vast variety of breakfast cereals, for example, is produced by only three firms (Kellogg's, Nabisco, and General Foods). Similar circumstances exist in soap, chemicals, cigarettes, and numerous other industries where many competing products are produced by a few very large firms. These industries are clearly not perfectly competitive and neither are they monopolies. Are they monopolistically competitive? The answer is no because they contain few enough firms for each to take account of the others' reactions when determining its own behaviour. Furthermore, these firms often earn large profits without attracting new entry (thereby violating the third assumption of monopolistic competition). In fact, they operate under the market structure called *oligopoly*, which we consider in the next section.

Although monopolostic competition is not applicable to differentiated products produced in industries with high concentration, the theory remains useful for analyzing industries where concentration

---

[2]By saying that consumers clearly value variety we are not saying that *each* consumer necessarily values variety. You might like only one of the many brands of dish soap, for example, and thus you might be better off if only that one brand were produced and the price were lower. But other consumers would prefer one of the other brands. Thus it is the differences in tastes *across many consumers* that gives rise to the social value of variety, and the price of that greater variety is the higher price per unit.

ratios are low and products are differentiated, as in the cases of restaurants and gas stations.

The 1980s witnessed a great outburst of theorizing concerning all aspects of product differentiation. The newer theories are consistent with Edward Chamberlin's (1899–1967) famous propositions that it pays firms to differentiate their products, to advertise heavily, and to engage in many other forms of competitive behaviour. These are characteristics to be found in the world, but not in perfect competition. Most modern industries that sell differentiated products, however, contain only a few firms. This is the market structure of oligopoly, to which we turn now.

OLIGOPOLY

Table 12-2 indicates that 41 Canadian manufacturing industries have four-firm concentration ratios that exceed 50 percent—that is, in these industries the largest four firms account for over 50 percent of the industry's total output.

The market structure that embraces such industries is called *oligopoly,* from the Greek words *oligos polein,* meaning "few to sell." An **oligopoly** is an industry that contains two or more firms, at least one of which produces a significant portion of the industry's total output. Whenever there is a high concentration ratio for the firms that are serving one particular market, that market is oligopolistic.

CHARACTERISTICS OF OLIGOPOLY

The market structures of oligopoly, monopoly, and monopolistic competition are similar in that firms in all of these markets face negatively sloped demand curves.

In contrast to a monopoly (which has no competitors) and to a monopolistically competitive firm (which has many competitors), an oligopolistic firm faces only a few competitors. The number of competitors is small enough for each firm to realize that its competitors may respond to anything that it does and that it should take such possible responses into account. In other words, *oligopolists are aware of the interdependence among the decisions made by the various firms in the industry.*

This is the key difference between oligopolists on the one hand and perfect or monopolistic competitors and monopolies, on the other. Oligopolists are aware of their impact on competing firms, and they may take their competitors' expected reactions into account when deciding on any course of action. We say that they exhibit **strategic behaviour,** which means that they take explicit account of the impact of their decisions on competing firms and of the reactions they expect competing firms to make. In contrast, firms in perfect competition or monopolistic competition engage in **nonstrategic behaviour,** which means they make decisions based on their own costs and their own demand curves without considering any possible reactions from their large number of competitors. Monopolists also do not engage in strategic behaviour—simply because they have no competitors to worry about.

Oligopolistic industries are of many types. In some industries, there are only a few firms. In others, there are many firms, but only a few dominate the market. For example, there are 38 manufacturers of mixed fertilizers, of which the largest 4 account for 70 percent of total sales. Oligopoly is consistent with a large number of small sellers, called a "competitive fringe," as long as a "big few" dominate the industry's production.

In oligopolistic industries, prices are typically administered. Products are usually differentiated. The intensity and the nature of rivalrous behaviour vary greatly from industry to industry and from one period of time to another. This variety has invited extensive theorizing and empirical study.

WHY BIGNESS?

Several factors contribute to explaining why so many industries are dominated by a few large firms. Some are "natural," and some are created by the firms themselves.

Natural Causes of Bigness

Economies of Scale. Much factory production uses the principle of the division of labour that we first studied in Chapter 3. The production of a commodity is broken up into hundreds of simple, repetitive tasks. This type of division of labour is the basis of the assembly line, which revolutionized the production of many goods in the early twentieth century, and it still underlies economies of large-scale production in many industries. Such division of labour is, as Adam Smith observed long ago, dependent on the size of the market (see Extension 3-2 in

Chapter 3). If only a few units of a product can be sold each day, there is no point in dividing its production into a number of tasks, each of which can be done in a few minutes. So big firms with large sales have an advantage over small firms with small sales whenever there are opportunities for economies based on an extensive division of labour.

Economies of Scope.   Modern industries produce many differentiated products that give rise to a different type of large-scale advantage. It is costly to develop a new product, and it may be only a matter of a few years before it is replaced by some superior version of the same basic product. These *fixed costs* of product development must be recovered in the revenues from sales of the product. The larger the firm's sales, the less the fixed cost that has to be recovered from each unit sold. Consider a product that costs $1 million to develop and to market. If 1 million units are to be sold, $1 of the selling price of each unit must go toward recovering the development costs. If, however, the firm expects to sell 10 million units, each unit need contribute only 10 cents to these costs, and the market price can be lowered accordingly. With the enormous development costs of some of today's high-tech products, firms that can sell a large volume have a distinct pricing advantage over firms that sell a smaller volume.

Other economies of scope are related to financing and to marketing. It is costly to enter a market, to establish a sales force, and to make consumers aware of a product. These costs are often nearly as high when a small volume is being marketed as when a large volume is being marketed. Thus the smaller the volume of the firm's sales, the higher the price must be if the firm is to cover all of these costs. Notice that these economies, which are related to the size of the firm, are related neither to the amount the firm produces of any one of its differentiated products nor to the size of any one of its plants. Economies that depend on the overall size of the *firm* rather than on the size of its *plants* or the volume of production of any one commodity are called **economies of scope.**

Where size confers a cost advantage through economies of either scale or scope, there may be room for only a few firms, even when the total market is quite large. This cost advantage of size will dictate that the industry be an oligopoly unless government regulation prevents the firms from growing to their efficient size.

Firm-Created Causes of Bigness

The number of firms in an industry may be decreased while the average size of the survivors rises due to strategic behaviour of the firms themselves. Firms may grow by buying out rivals (acquisitions) or merging with them (mergers) or by driving rivals into bankruptcy through predatory practices. This process increases the size and market shares of the survivors and may, by reducing competitive behaviour, allow them to achieve larger profit margins.

The surviving firms must then be able to create and sustain barriers to entry where natural ones do not exist. The industry will then be dominated by a few large firms only because they are successful in preventing the entry of new firms that would lower the industry's concentration ratio.

Is Bigness Natural or Firm-Created?

Most observers would agree that bigness results from a mix of both natural and firm-created causes. Some industries have high concentration ratios because the efficient size of the firm is large relative to the overall size of the industry's market. Other industries may have higher concentration ratios than efficiency considerations would dictate because the firms are seeking enhanced market power through entry restriction. The issue that is debated is the relative importance of these two forces, the one coming from efficiencies of scale and scope and the other coming from the desire of firms to create market power by growing large.

Harvard economist Alfred D. Chandler Jr. is a champion of the view that the major reason for the persistence of oligopolies in the manufacturing sector is the efficiency of large-scale production. His monumental work, *Scale and Scope: The Dynamics of Industrial Capitalism,* argues this case in great detail for the United States, the United Kingdom, and Germany.[3]

The set of laws in the United States designed to promote competition among firms—known as antitrust laws—is based on the presumption that large firms are undesirable and are not justified by the benefits of scale and scope economies. If Chandler is right, however, size efficiency is the most important reason for high concentration ratios, and although strategic reasons are probably important in some cases, they are of secondary importance as an overall explanation. Canadian competition policy is more in

---

[3]A. D. Chandler Jr., *Scale and Scope: The Dynamics of Industrial Capitalism* (Cambridge, Mass.: Harvard University Press, 1990).

line with Chandler's views, since the policy condemns neither size nor high market shares per se. We examine Canadian competition policy in the next chapter.

STRATEGIC BEHAVIOUR AND THE BASIC DILEMMA OF OLIGOPOLY

Oligopoly behaviour is necessarily strategic behaviour. Oligopolists must take into account the ways in which their rivals will react to what they do. In deciding on strategies, oligopolists face a basic dilemma between *competing* and *cooperating*.

The firms in an oligopolistic industry will make more profits as a group if they cooperate; any one firm, however, may make more profits for itself if it defects while the others cooperate.

This result is similar to the one established in Chapter 11 for the cartelization of a perfectly competitive industry.[4] In a perfectly competitive industry, however, there are so many firms that they cannot reach a cooperative outcome unless some central governing body is formed, by either themselves or the government, to force the necessary behaviour on all firms. In contrast, the few firms in an oligopolistic industry will themselves recognize the possibility of cooperating to avoid the loss of profits that will result from competitive behaviour.

Cooperative and Noncooperative Outcomes

If the firms in an oligopolistic industry cooperate, either overtly or tacitly, to produce among themselves the monopoly output, they can maximize their joint profits. If they do this, they will reach what is called a **cooperative outcome**, which is the position that a single monopoly firm would reach if it owned all the firms in the industry.

We have seen that if all the firms in an oligopolistic industry are at the cooperative outcome, it will usually be worthwhile for any one of them to cut its price or to raise its output, as long as the others do not do so. However, if everyone does the same thing, they will be worse off as a group and may all be worse off individually. An industry outcome that is reached when firms proceed by calculating only their own gains, without considering the reactions of others, is called a **noncooperative outcome**.

An Example from Game Theory

Game theory is used to study decision making in situations in which a number of players compete, each knowing that others will react to their moves and each taking account of others' expected reactions when making moves. For example, suppose that a firm is deciding whether to raise, lower, or maintain its price. Before arriving at an answer, it asks: "What will the other firms do in each of these cases, and how will their actions affect the profitability of whatever decision I make?" Game theory has become increasingly important in economics and is a very active area of economic research. The 1994 Nobel Prize in Economics went to three important contributors to game theory: John Harsanyi, John Nash, and Reinhard Selten.

When game theory is applied to oligopoly, the players are firms, their game is played in the market, their strategies are their price or output decisions, and the payoffs are their profits.

An illustration of the basic dilemma of oligopolists, to cooperate or to compete, is shown in Figure 12-2 for the case of a two-firm oligopoly, called a **duopoly**. In this simplified game there are only two strategies for each firm: to produce an output equal to either one-half of the monopoly output or two-thirds of the monopoly output. Even this simple game, however, is sufficient to illustrate several key ideas in the modern theory of oligopoly.

Figure 12-2 presents what is called a *payoff matrix*. The data in the matrix show that if both firms cooperate, *each* producing one-half of the monopoly output, they achieve the cooperative outcome and jointly earn the monopoly profits by *jointly* producing the output that a monopolist would produce. As a group, they can do no better.

Once the cooperative outcome is attained, the data in the figure show that if A cheats and produces more, its profits will increase. However, B's profits will be reduced: A's behaviour drives the industry's price down, so B earns less from its unchanged output. Because A's cheating takes the firms away from the joint-profit-maximizing monopoly output, their joint profits must fall. This means that B's profits fall by more than A's rise.

Figure 12-2 shows that similar considerations also apply to B. It is worthwhile for B to depart from the joint-profit-maximizing output, as long as A does

---

[4]The basic reason is that when only one firm increases its output by 1 percent, the price falls by less than when all firms do the same. Thus when the point is reached at which profits will be reduced if all firms expand output together, it will still pay one firm to expand output if the others do not do the same.

FIGURE 12-2
The Oligopolist's Dilemma: To Cooperate or to Compete?

		A's output		
		One-half monopoly output		Two-thirds monopoly output
B's output	One-half monopoly output	20 20		15 22
	Two-thirds monopoly output	22 15		17 17

Cooperation to determine the overall level of output can maximize joint profits, but it leaves each firm with an incentive to alter its production. The figure gives what is called a payoff matrix for a two-firm duopoly game. Only two levels of production are considered in order to illustrate the basic problem. A's production is indicated across the top, and its payoffs (profits in millions of dollars) are shown in the blue circles within each square. B's production is indicated down the left side, and its payoffs are shown in the red circles within each square. For example, the top right square tells us that if B produces one-half while A produces two-thirds of the output that a monopolist would produce, A's profits will be 22, while B's will be 15.

If A and B cooperate, each produces one-half the monopoly output and receives a payoff of 20, as shown in the upper left box. However, at that position, known as the cooperative outcome, each firm can raise its profits by producing two-thirds of the monopoly output, provided that the other firm does not do the same.

Now assume that A and B make their decisions noncooperatively. A reasons that whether B produces either one-half or two-thirds of the monopoly output, A's best output is two-thirds. B reasons similarly. In this case, they reach the noncooperative outcome, where each produces two-thirds of the monopoly output, and each makes less than it would if the two firms cooperated. In this example, the noncooperative outcome is a Nash equilibrium.

has an incentive to do so as well. When each follows this "selfish" strategy, both reach the noncooperative outcome at which they jointly produce 1 ⅓ times as much as the monopolist would. Each then has profits that are lower than at the cooperative outcome.

Nash Equilibrium. The noncooperative outcome shown in Figure 12-2 is called a **Nash equilibrium,** after the U.S. mathematician John Nash, who developed the concept in the 1950s and received the Nobel Prize in Economics in 1994 for this work. In a Nash equilibrium, each firm's best strategy is to maintain its present behaviour *given the present behaviour of the other firms.*

It is easy to see that there is only one Nash equilibrium in Figure 12-2. In the bottom-right cell, the best decision for each firm, given that the other firm is producing two-thirds of the monopoly output, is to produce two-thirds of the monopoly output itself. Between them, they produce a joint output of 1 ⅓ times the monopoly output. Neither firm has an incentive to depart from this position except through cooperation with the other. In any other cell, each firm has an incentive to alter its output *given the output of the other firm.*

The basis of a Nash equilibrium is rational decision-making in the absence of cooperation. Its particular importance in oligopoly theory is that it is the only type of self-policing equilibrium. It is self-policing in the sense that there is no need for group behaviour to enforce it. Each firm has a self-interest to maintain it because no move will improve its profits, given what other firms are currently doing.

If a Nash equilibrium is established by any means whatsoever, no firm has an incentive to depart from it by altering its own behaviour.

Strategic Behaviour. We have seen how the Nash equilibrium in Figure 12-2 can be arrived at when both firms cheat on an agreement to reach the cooperative outcome. The same equilibrium will be attained if each firm behaves strategically by choosing its optimal strategy taking into account what the other firm may do. Let us see how this works.

Suppose that Firm A reasons as follows: "B can do one of two things; what is the best thing for me to do in each case? First, what if B produces one-half of the monopoly output? If I do the same, I receive a profit of 20, but if I produce two-thirds of the monopoly output, I receive 22. Second, what if B produces two-thirds of the monopoly output? If I produce one-half of the monopoly output, I receive a

not do so. So both A and B have an incentive to depart from the joint-profit-maximizing level of output.

Finally, Figure 12-2 shows that when either firm does depart from the cooperative outcome, the other profit of 15, whereas if I produce two-thirds, I receive 17. Clearly, my best strategy is to produce two-thirds of the monopoly output in either case."

B will reason in the same way. As a result, they end up producing 1 ⅓ times the monopoly output between themselves, and each earns a profit of 17. This type of game, in which the noncooperative equilibrium makes *both players worse off* than if they were able to cooperate, is called a *prisoner's dilemma*. The reason for this curious name, and some further applications, are discussed in Extension 12-1.

COOPERATION OR COMPETITION?

We have seen that although oligopolists have an incentive to cooperate, they may be driven, through their own individual decisions, to produce more and earn less than they would if they cooperated. Our next step is to look in more detail at the types of cooperative and competitive behaviour that oligopolists may adopt. We can then go on to study the forces that influence the balance between cooperation and competition in actual situations.

Types of Cooperative Behaviour

When firms agree to cooperate in order to restrict output and raise prices, their behaviour is called **collusion.** Collusive behaviour may occur with or without an explicit agreement to collude. Where explicit agreement occurs, economists speak of *overt or covert collusion,* depending on whether the agreement is open or secret. Where no explicit agreement actually occurs, economists speak of *tacit collusion.* In this case, all firms behave cooperatively without an explicit agreement to do so. They merely understand that it is in their mutual interest to restrict output and to raise prices.

In terms of Figure 12-2, Firm A decides to produce one-half of the monopoly output, hoping that Firm B will do the same. Firm B does what A expects, and they achieve the cooperative outcome without ever explicitly cooperating.

Explicit Collusion.   The easiest way for firms to ensure that they will all maintain their joint-profit-maximizing output is to make an explicit agreement to do so. Such collusive agreements have occurred in the past, although they have been illegal among privately owned firms in Canada for a long time. When they are discovered today, they are rigorously prose-

cuted. We shall see, however, that such agreements are not illegal everywhere in the world, particularly when they are supported by national governments.

We saw in Chapter 11 that when a group of firms get together to act in this way, it is called a *cartel.* Cartels show in stark form the basic conflict between cooperation and competition that we just discussed. Full cooperation always allows the industry to achieve the result of monopoly. It also always presents individual firms with the incentive to cheat. The larger the number of firms, the greater the temptation for any one of them to cheat. After all, cheating by one small firm may not be noticed because it will have a negligible effect on price. The problems all cartels face are seen most vividly, therefore, in the case that we studied in Chapter 11, in which the number of firms is so large that most of them are price takers. This is why cartels that involve firms in industries that would otherwise be perfectly competitive tend to be unstable.

Cartels may also be formed by a group of firms that would otherwise be in an oligopolistic market. The smaller the group of firms that forms a cartel, the more likely that the firms will let their joint interest in cooperating guide their behaviour. Although cheating may still occur, the few firms in the industry can easily foresee the outcome of an outbreak of rivalrous behaviour among themselves.

The most famous modern example of a cartel that encourages explicit cooperative behaviour among oligopolists is the Organization of Petroleum Exporting Countries (OPEC). This cartel is discussed in more detail in Application 12-2.

Tacit Collusion.   Although collusive behaviour that affects prices is illegal, a small group of firms that recognize the influence that each has on the others may act without any explicit agreement to achieve the cooperative outcome. In such tacit agreements, the two forces that push toward cooperation and competition are still evident.

First, firms have a common interest in cooperating to maximize their joint profits at the cooperative solution. Second, each firm is interested in its own profits, and any one of them can usually increase its profits by behaving competitively.

Types of Competitive Behaviour

Although the most obvious way for a firm to violate the cooperative solution is to produce more than its share of the joint-profit-maximizing output, there are other ways in which rivalrous behaviour can occur.

THE PRISONER'S DILEMMA

The game shown in Figure 12-2 is often known as a prisoner's dilemma game. This is the story that lies behind the name:

Two men, John and William, are arrested for jointly committing a crime and are interrogated separately. They know that if they both plead innocence, they will get only a light sentence, and if they both admit guilt they will both receive a medium sentence. Each is told, however, that if *either* protests innocence while the *other* admits guilt, the one who claims innocence will get a severe sentence while the other will be released with no sentence at all.

Here is the payoff matrix for that game:

John reasons as follows: William will plead either guilty or innocent. First assume that he pleads innocent. I get a light sentence if I also plead innocent but no sentence at all if I plead guilty, so guilty is my better plea. Now assume that he pleads guilty. I get a severe sentence if I plead innocent and a medium sentence if I plead guilty. So once again guilty is my preferred plea. William reasons in the same way and, as a result, they both plead guilty and

get a medium sentence, whereas if they had been able to communicate and coordinate their pleas, they could both have agreed to plead innocent and get off with a light sentence.

Another example of a prisoner's dilemma can arise when two firms are making sealed bids on a contract. For simplicity, suppose that only two bids are permitted, either a high or a low price. The high price yields a profit of $10 million, whereas the low price yields a profit of $7 million. If they put in the same price, they share the job, and each earns half the profits. If they give different bids, the firm submitting the lower bid gets the job and all the profits. You should have no trouble in drawing up the payoff matrix and determining the outcomes under noncooperative and cooperative behaviour.

The prisoner's dilemma has been used to consider aspects of social behaviour that seem far removed from economics. For example, Professor Robert Axelrod of the University of Michigan has used the model to study the *evolution of cooperation*. In particular, he showed that in a *repeated* prisoner's dilemma, where the same players played the game many times, the best strategy was one that would support both players' cooperating rather than defecting. It turns out that the very simple rule of "tit for tat" works well: Cooperate if the other player cooperated on the most recent move, and defect (don't cooperate) if the player defected on the most recent move. In an environment with many players, those who use the tit-for-tat strategy will generally reap benefits of cooperation, while still effectively preventing themselves from being exploited by players who routinely do not. Thus players of the tit-for-tat strategy can come to dominate a population. This idea has been extended to a wide variety of human behaviours and of the behaviour of other organisms.*

*See Robert Axelrod, *The Evolution of Cooperation* (New York: Basic Books, 1984), and Robert Axelrod and Douglas Dion, "The Further Evolution of Cooperation", *Science* 9 (1988): p.1385–1389.

EXPLICIT COOPERATION IN OPEC

The experience of the Organization of Petroleum Exporting Countries (OPEC) in the 1970s and 1980s illustrates the power of cooperative behaviour to create short-run profits, as well as the problems of trying to exercise long-run market power in an industry without substantial entry barriers.

OPEC did not attract worldwide attention until 1973, when its members voluntarily restricted their output by negotiating quotas among themselves. In that year, OPEC countries accounted for about 70 percent of the world's supply of crude oil and 87 percent of the world's oil exports. So although it was not a complete monopoly, the cartel came close to being one. By reducing output, the OPEC countries were able to drive up the world price of oil and to earn massive profits both for themselves and for non-OPEC producers, who obtained the high prices without having to limit their output. After several years of success, however, OPEC began to experience the typical problems of cartels.

ENTRY

Entry became a problem for the OPEC countries. The high price of oil encouraged the development of new supplies, and within a few years, new productive capacity was coming into use at a rapid rate in non-OPEC countries.

LONG-RUN ADJUSTMENT OF DEMAND

The short-run demand for oil proved to be highly inelastic. Over time, however, adaptations to reduce the demand for oil were made within the confines of existing technology. Homes and offices were insulated more efficiently, and smaller, more fuel-efficient cars became popular. This is an example of the distinction between the short-run and long-run demand for a commodity first introduced in Chapter 5.

INNOVATION IN THE VERY-LONG RUN

Innovation further reduced the demand for oil in the very-long run. Over time, technologies that were more efficient in their use of oil, as well as alternative energy sources, were developed. Had the oil prices stayed up longer than they did, major breakthroughs in solar and geothermal energy would surely have occurred.

This experience in both the long run and the very-long run shows the price system at work, signal-

---

Competition for Market Shares.   Even if *joint* profits are maximized, there is the problem of market shares. How is the profit-maximizing level of sales to be divided among the colluding firms? Competition for market shares may upset the tacit agreement to hold to joint-profit-maximizing behaviour. Firms often compete for market shares through various forms of non-price competition, such as advertising and variations in the quality of their product. Such costly competition may reduce industry profits.

Covert Cheating.   In an industry that has many differentiated products and in which sales are often by contract between buyers and sellers, covert rather than overt cheating may seem attractive. Secret discounts and rebates can allow a firm to increase its sales at the expense of its competitors while appearing to hold to the tacitly agreed monopoly price.

Very-Long-Run Competition.   As we first discussed in Chapter 11, very-long-run considerations may also be important. When technology and product characteristics change constantly, there may be advantages to behaving competitively. A firm that behaves competitively may be able to maintain a larger market share and earn larger profits than it would if it cooperated with the other firms in the industry, even though all the firms' joint profits are lower. In our world of constant change, a firm that thinks it can *keep* ahead of its rivals through innovation has an incentive to compete even if that competition lowers the joint profing the need for adaptation and providing the incentives for that adaptation. It also provides an illustration of Schumpeter's concept of creative destruction, which we first discussed in Chapter 11. To share in the profits generated by high energy prices, new technologies and new substitute products were developed, and these destroyed much of the market power of the original cartel.

CHEATING

At first, there was little incentive for OPEC countries to violate quotas. Members found themselves with such undreamed-of increases in their incomes that they found it difficult to use all of their money productively. As the output of non-OPEC oil grew, however, OPEC's output had to be reduced to hold prices high. Incomes in OPEC countries declined sharply as a result.

Many OPEC countries had become used to their enormous incomes, and their attempts to maintain them in the face of falling output quotas brought to the surface the instabilities inherent in all cartels. In 1981, the cartel price reached its peak of U.S. $35 per barrel. In real terms, this was about five times as high as the 1972 price, but production quotas were less than one-half of OPEC's capacity. Eager to increase their oil revenues, many individual OPEC members gave in to the pressure to cheat and produced in excess of their production quotas. In 1984, Saudi Arabia indicated that it would not tolerate further cheating by its partners and demanded that others share equally in reducing their quotas yet further. However, agreement proved impossible. In December 1985, OPEC decided to eliminate production quotas and let each member make its own decisions about output.

AFTER THE COLLAPSE

OPEC's collapse as an output-restricting cartel led to a major reduction in world oil prices. Early in 1986, the downward slide took the price to $20 per barrel, and it fell to $11 per barrel later in the year. Allowing for inflation, this was around the price that had prevailed just before OPEC introduced its output restrictions in 1973. Prices have been volatile since then, oscillating between about $12 per barrel, which is close to the perfectly competitive price, and $20 per barrel, which seems to be all that can be sustained under the modest output restrictions that can currently be obtained.

its of the whole industry. Such competitive behaviour contributes to the long-run growth of living standards and may provide social benefits over time that outweigh any losses due to the restriction of output at any point in time.

For these and other reasons, there are often strong incentives for oligopolistic firms to compete rather than to maintain the cooperative outcome, even when they understand the inherent risks to their joint profits.

Cooperative or Noncooperative Outcomes?

Empirical research by economists suggests that the relative strengths of the incentives to cooperate and to compete vary from industry to industry in a systematic way, depending on observable characteristics of firms, markets, and products. What are some of the characteristics that will affect the strength of the two incentives?

The tendency toward joint maximization of profits is greater for smaller numbers of sellers than for larger numbers of sellers. This involves both motivation and ability. When there are few firms, they will know that one of them cannot gain sales without inducing retaliation by its rivals. Also, a few firms can tacitly coordinate their policies with less difficulty than a large number of firms.

The tendency toward joint maximization of profits is greater for producers of similar products than for producers of sharply differentiated products. The more nearly identical the products of sellers, the closer the direct rivalry for customers and the less able one firm is to gain a lasting advantage over its rivals. Such sellers will tend to prefer joint efforts to achieve a larger pie over individual attempts to increase their own shares.

The tendency toward joint maximization of profits is greater in a growing market than in a contracting market. When demand is growing, firms can produce at full capacity without any need to "steal" customers from their rivals. When firms have excess capacity, they are tempted to give price concessions to attract customers. When their rivals retaliate, price cuts become general.

The tendency toward joint maximization of profits is greater when the industry contains a dominant firm rather than a group of more-or-less equal competitors. A dominant firm may become a **price leader**, setting the industry's price while all other firms fall into line. Even if a dominant firm is not automatically a price leader, other firms may look to it for judgment about market conditions, and its decisions may become a tentative focus for tacit agreement.

The tendency toward joint maximization of profits is greater when non-price rivalry is absent or limited. When firms are not competing with each other through price, rivalry will tend to break out in other forms. Firms may seek to increase their market shares through extra advertising, changes in the quality of the product, the establishment of new products, giveaways, and a host of similar schemes that leave their prices unchanged but increase their costs and so reduce their joint profits.

The tendency toward joint maximization of profits is greater when the barriers to entry of new firms are greater. The high profits of existing firms attract new entrants, who will drive down price and reduce profits. The greater the barriers to entry, the less this will occur. Thus the greater the entry barriers, the closer the profits of existing firms can be to their joint maximizing level without being reduced by new entrants.

THE IMPORTANCE OF ENTRY BARRIERS

Suppose that firms in an oligopolistic industry succeed in raising prices above long-run average costs and earn substantial profits that are not completely eliminated by nonprice competition. In the absence of significant entry barriers, new firms will enter the industry and erode the profits of existing firms, as they do in monopolistic competition. Natural barriers to entry were discussed in Chapter 11. They are an important part of the explanation of the persistence of profits in many oligopolistic industries.

Where such natural entry barriers do not exist, however, oligopolistic firms can earn profits in the long run only if they can *create* entry barriers. To the extent this is done, existing firms can move toward joint profit maximization without fear that new firms, attracted by the high profits, will enter the industry. We discuss next some types of created entry barriers.

Brand Proliferation

By altering the characteristics of a differentiated product, it is possible to produce a vast array of variations on the general theme of that product. Think, for example, of automobiles with a little more or a little less acceleration, braking power, top speed, cornering ability, fuel efficiency, and so on, compared with existing models.

Although the multiplicity of existing brands is no doubt partly a response to consumers' tastes, it can have the effect of discouraging the entry of new firms. To see why, suppose that the product is the type for which there is a substantial amount of brand switching by consumers. In this case, the larger the number of brands sold by existing firms, the smaller the expected sales of a new entrant.

Suppose, for example, that an industry contains three large firms, each selling one brand of cigarettes, and say that 30 percent of all smokers change brands in a random fashion each year. If a new firm enters the industry, it can expect to pick up one-third of the smokers who change brands (a smoker who switches brands now has three *other* brands to choose between). This would give the new firm 10 percent (one-third of 30 percent) of the total market the first year merely as a result of picking up its share of the random switchers, and it would keep increasing its share for some time thereafter. If, however, the existing three firms have five brands each, there would be 15 brands already available, and a new firm selling one new brand could expect to pick up only one-fifteenth of the brand switchers, giving it only 2 percent of the total market the first year, with smaller gains also in subsequent years. This is an extreme case, but it illustrates a general result.

The larger the number of differentiated products that are sold by existing oligopolists, the smaller the market share available to a new firm that is entering with a single new product. Brand proliferation can therefore be an effective entry barrier.

Setup Costs

Existing firms can create entry barriers by imposing significant fixed costs on new firms that enter their market. This is particularly important if the industry has only weak natural barriers to entry because the minimum efficient scale occurs at an output that is low relative to the total output of the industry.

Advertising is one means by which existing firms can impose heavy setup costs on new entrants. Advertising, of course, serves purposes other than that of creating barriers to entry. Among them, it performs the useful function of informing buyers about their alternatives, thereby making markets work more smoothly. Indeed, a new firm may find that advertising is essential, even when existing firms do not advertise at all, simply to call attention to its entry into an industry in which it is currently unknown.

Nonetheless, advertising can also operate as a potent entry barrier by increasing the setup costs of new entrants. Where heavy advertising has established strong brand images for existing products, a new firm may have to spend heavily on advertising to create its own brand images in consumers' minds. If the firm's sales are small, advertising costs *per unit sold* will be large, and price will have to be correspondingly high to cover those costs. Consider Nike, Reebok, and their competitors. They advertise not so much the quality of their athletic shoes as images that they wish consumers to associate with the shoes. The ads are lavishly produced and photographed. They constitute a formidable entry barrier for a new producer.

Figure 12-3 illustrates how heavy advertising can shift the cost curves of a firm with a low minimum efficient scale *(MES)* to make it one with a high *MES*. In essence, what happens is that a high *MES* of advertising is added to a low *MES* of production, with the result that the overall *MES* is raised.

A new entrant with small sales but large setup costs finds itself at a substantial cost disadvantage relative to its established rivals.

Any one-time cost of entering a market has the same effect as a large initial advertising expenditure.

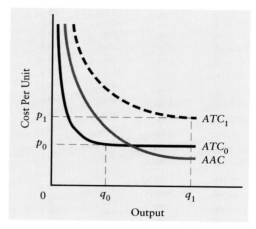

FIGURE 12-3
Advertising Cost as a Barrier to Entry

Large advertising costs can increase the minimum efficient scale *(MES)* of production and thereby increase entry barriers. The ATC_0 curve shows that the *MES* without advertising is at q_0. The curve AAC (for average advertising cost) shows that advertising cost per unit falls as output rises. Advertising increases average total cost to ATC_1, which is downward sloping over its entire range. The new *MES* is given by q_1. Advertising has given a scale advantage to large sellers and has thus created a barrier to entry.

For example, with many consumer goods, the cost of developing a new product that is similar but not identical to existing products may be quite substantial. Even if there are few economies of scale in the production of the product, its large fixed *development* cost can lead to a falling long-run average cost curve over a wide range of output.

An Example

The combined use of brand proliferation and advertising as an entry barrier helps to explain one apparent paradox of everyday life—that one firm often sells multiple brands of the same product, which compete actively against one another as well as against the products of other firms.

The soap and beer industries provide classic examples of this behaviour. Because all available scale economies can be realized by quite small plants, both industries have few natural barriers to entry. Both contain a few large firms, each of which produces an array of heavily advertised products. The numerous existing products make it harder for a new entrant to obtain a large market niche with a single new product. The heavy advertising, although directed against existing products, creates an entry barrier by increasing the setup costs of a new product that seeks to gain the attention of consumers and to establish its own brand image.

Predatory Pricing

A firm will not enter a market if it expects continued losses after entry. One way in which an existing firm can create such an expectation is to cut prices below costs whenever entry occurs and to keep them there until the entrant goes bankrupt. The existing firm sacrifices profits while doing this, but it sends a discouraging message to potential future rivals, as well as to present ones. Even if this strategy is costly in terms of lost profits in the short run, it may pay for itself in the long run by creating *reputation effects* that deter the entry of new firms at other times or in other markets that the firm controls.

Predatory pricing is controversial. Some economists argue that pricing policies that appear to be predatory can be explained by other motives and that existing firms only hurt themselves when they engage in such practices instead of accommodating new entrants. Others argue that predatory pricing has been observed and that it is in the long-run interests of existing firms to punish the occasional new entrant even when it is costly to do so in the short run.

The courts have taken the position that predatory pricing does indeed occur and a number of firms have been convicted of using it as a method of restricting entry. Canadian competition policy is discussed in Chapter 13.

CONTESTABLE MARKETS

We have been discussing the role played by entry barriers in determining the long-run characteristics of an oligopolistic industry. In general, we expect profits made by existing firms to lead new firms to enter the industry. Such entry will, in turn, reduce profits toward their competitive level. We now turn to a theory which emphasizes not the role of *actual entry*, but rather the role of *potential entry* in keeping industry profits near their competitive level.

The theory of *contestable markets* holds that markets do not have to contain many firms or expe-

rience *actual* entry for profits to be held near the competitive level. *Potential* entry can do the job just as well as actual entry, as long as (1) entry can be easily accomplished and (2) existing firms take potential entry into account when making price and output decisions.

The Theory of Contestable Markets

Entry is usually costly to the entering firm. It may have to build a plant, develop new versions of the industry's differentiated product, or advertise heavily to call attention to its product. These and many other initial expenses are often called *sunk costs of entry*. A sunk cost of entry is a cost that a firm must incur to enter the market and that *cannot be recovered if the firm subsequently exits*. For example, if an entering firm builds a product-specific factory that has no resale value, this is a sunk cost of entry. However, the cost of a factory that is not product-specific and can be resold for an amount that is close to its original cost is not a sunk cost of entry.

A market in which new firms can enter and leave without incurring any sunk costs of entry is called a perfectly **contestable market.** A market can be perfectly contestable even if the firm must pay some costs of entry, as long as these can be recovered when the firm exits. Because all markets require at least some sunk costs of entry, contestability must be viewed as a variable. The lower the sunk costs of entry, the more contestable the market.

In a contestable market, the existence of profits, even if they are due to transitory causes, will attract entry. Firms will enter to gain a share of these profits and will exit when the transitory situation has changed.

As an example, consider the market for air travel in the lucrative Toronto-Ottawa-Montreal triangle. This market would be quite contestable *if* counter and loading space were available to new entrants at the three cities' airline terminals. An airline that was not currently serving the cities in question could shift some of its existing planes to the market with small sunk costs of entry. Some training of personnel would be needed for them to become familiar with the route and the airport. This is a sunk cost of entry that could not be recovered if the cities in question were no longer to be served. However, most of the airline's costs are not sunk costs of entry. If it were to subsequently decide to leave a city, the rental of terminal space would stop and the airplanes and the ground equipment could be shifted to another location.

Sunk costs of entry constitute a barrier to entry, and the larger these are, the larger the profits of existing firms can be without attracting new entrants. The flip side of this coin is that firms operating in markets without large sunk costs of entry will not earn large profits. Strategic considerations will lead them to keep prices near the level that would just cover their total costs. They know that if they charge higher prices, firms will enter to capture the profits while they last and then exit.

Contestability, where it is possible, is a force that can limit the profits of existing oligopolists. Even if entry does not occur, the ease with which it can be accomplished may keep existing oligopolists from charging prices that would maximize their joint profits.

Contestability is just another example, in somewhat more refined form, of the key point that the possibility of entry is the major force preventing the exploitation of market power to restrict output and to raise prices.

Empirical Relevance

Most economists take the view that although the theory of contestable markets is an elegant extension of the theory of competitive markets, there are at least *some* barriers to entry in almost all real markets and very large barriers in many markets. Setting up an effective organization to produce or sell almost anything incurs sunk costs. In the case of airlines, for instance, the new company at a given airport must hire and train staff, advertise extensively to let customers know that it is in the market, set up baggage-handling facilities, and overcome whatever loyalties customers have to the preexisting firms. New firms in almost all industries face entry costs that are analogous to these. Entering a manufacturing industry usually requires a large investment in industry-specific (and sometimes product-specific) plants and equipment, in addition to considerable expenditures in product-development and marketing.

These considerations suggest that contestability, in practice, is something to be measured rather than simply asserted. The higher the sunk costs of entry, the less contestable the market, and the higher the profits that existing firms can earn without inducing

entry. Current evidence suggests that a high degree of contestability is in practice quite rare.

OLIGOPOLY: AN OVERVIEW

Oligopoly is found in many industries and in all advanced economies. It typically occurs in industries where both perfect and monopolistic competition are made impossible by the existence of major economies of scale or scope (or both). In such industries, there is simply not enough room for a large number of firms all operating at or near their minimum efficient scales.

Three questions are important for the evaluation of the performance of the oligopolistic market structure. First, do oligopolistic markets allocate resources very differently than perfectly competitive markets? Second, in their short-run and long-run price-output behaviour, where do oligopolistic firms typically settle between the extreme outcomes of earning zero profits and earning the profits that would be available to a monopolist? Third, how much do oligopolists contribute to economic growth by encouraging innovative activity in the very-long run? We consider each of these questions in turn.

The Market Mechanism Under Oligopoly

We have seen that under perfect competition, prices are set by the impersonal forces of demand and supply, whereas firms in oligopolistic markets administer their prices. The market signaling system works slightly differently when prices are administered rather than being determined by the market. Changes in the market conditions for both inputs and outputs are signaled to the perfectly competitive firm by changes in the prices of its inputs and its outputs. Changes in the market conditions for inputs are signaled to oligopolistic firms by changes in the prices of their inputs. Changes in the market conditions for the oligopolist's output, however, are typically signaled by changes in the volume of sales at administered prices.

Increases in costs of inputs will shift cost curves upward, and oligopolistic firms will be led to raise prices and lower outputs. Increases in demand will cause the sales of oligopolistic firms to rise. Firms will then respond by increasing output, thereby increasing the quantities of society's resources that are allocated to producing that output. They will then decide whether or not to alter their administered prices.

The market system reallocates resources in response to changes in demands and costs in roughly the same way under oligopoly as it does under perfect competition.

Profits Under Oligopoly

Some firms in some oligopolistic industries succeed in coming close to joint profit maximization in the short run. In other oligopolistic industries, firms compete so intensely among themselves that they come close to achieving competitive prices and outputs.

In the long run, those profits that do survive competitive behaviour among existing firms will tend to attract entry. These profits will persist only insofar as entry is restricted either by natural barriers, such as large minimum efficient scales for potential entrants, or by barriers created, and successfully defended, by the existing firms.

Very-Long-Run Competition

Once we allow for the effects of technological change, we need to ask which market structure is most conducive to the sorts of very-long-run changes that we discussed in Chapter 9. These are the driving force of the economic growth that has so greatly raised living standards over the past two centuries. They are intimately related to Schumpeter's concept of creative destruction, which we first encountered in our discussion of entry barriers in Chapter 11.

As we saw in Application 11-1, examples of creative destruction abound. In the nineteenth century, railways began to compete with wagons and barges for the carriage of freight. In the twentieth century, trucks operating on newly-constructed highways began competing with trains. During the 1950s and 1960s, airplanes began to compete seriously with trucks and trains.

The slide rule is an example of a product that had its market destroyed by a new one, which resulted in the elimination of a firm's monopoly power. Keuffel & Esser had achieved a dominant position in the manufacture and sale of slide rules, which were essential tools for engineers and applied scientists. Its dominant position and highly-profitable operations were wiped out, not by a better slide rule, but by the pocket calculator. When they were first introduced in

the early 1970s, pocket calculators were relatively expensive, often costing over $100. They were also relatively crude in their capabilities. Nonetheless, they proved to be popular; sales and profits rose, and firms rushed to enter the lucrative new field. Competition led simultaneously to product improvements and price reductions. Today, calculators that perform basic calculations can be bought for a few dollars, and sophisticated scientific and programmable pocket calculators can be bought for under $20. Few of today's university students have heard of Keuffel & Esser, but most of them know about Texas Instruments and Hewlett-Packard.

In recent years, the development of facsimile transmission and electronic mail eliminated the monopoly of the postal service in delivering hard-copy (printed) communications. In their myriad uses, microcomputers for the home and the office swept away the markets of many once-thriving products and services. For instance, in-store computers answer customer questions, decreasing the need for salespeople. Aided by computers, "just in time" inventory systems greatly reduce the investment in inventories required of existing firms and new entrants alike. Computer-based flexible manufacturing systems allow firms to switch production easily and inexpensively from one product line to another, thereby reducing the minimum scale at which each can be produced profitably. One day soon, your textbooks may be replaced by computers.

An important defense of oligopoly relates to this process of creative destruction. Some economists have adopted Joseph Schumpeter's concept of creative destruction to develop theories that intermediate market structures, such as oligopoly, lead to more innovation than would occur in either perfect competition or monopoly. They argue that the oligopolist faces strong competition from existing rivals and cannot afford the more relaxed life of the monopolist. At the same time, however, oligopolistic firms expect to keep a good share of the profits that they earn from their innovative activity.

The empirical evidence is broadly consistent with this view. Professor Jesse Markham of Harvard University concluded a survey of empirical findings with the following:

> If technological change and innovational activity are, as we generally assume, in some important way a product of organized R&D activities financed and executed by business companies, it is

clear that the ... payoffs that flow from them can to some measurable extent be traced to the doorsteps of large firms operating in oligopolistic markets.

Everyday observation provides some confirmation of this finding. Leading North American firms that operate in highly concentrated industries, such as Alcan, Bombardier, Du Pont, Kodak, General Electric, Northern Telecom, and Xerox, have been highly innovative over many years.

This is not meant to suggest that *only* oligopolistic industries are innovative. Much innovation is also done by very small new firms; and if today's new firms are successful in their innovation, they may become tomorrow's corporate giants. For example,

Hewlett-Packard, Microsoft, and Apple, which are enormous firms today, barely existed two decades ago; their rise from new start-up firms to corporate giants reflects their powers of innovation.

A Final Word

Oligopoly is an important market structure in modern economies because there are many industries in which the minimum efficient scale is simply too large to support many competing firms. The challenge to public policy is to keep oligopolists competing, rather than colluding, and using their competitive energies to improve products and to lower costs, rather than merely to erect entry barriers.

SUMMARY

A. THE STRUCTURE OF THE CANADIAN ECONOMY

- Most industries in the Canadian economy lie between the two extremes of monopoly and perfect competition. Within this spectrum of market structure we can divide Canadian industries into two broad groups—those with a large number of relatively small firms and those with a small number of relatively large firms. Such intermediate market structures are called imperfectly competitive.
- When measuring whether an industry has power concentrated in the hands of only a few firms or dispersed over many, it is not sufficient to count the number of firms. Instead, economists consider the concentration ratio, which shows the fraction of total market sales controlled by the largest group of sellers.
- One important problem associated with using concentration ratios is to define the market with reasonable accuracy. Since many goods produced in Canada compete with foreign-produced goods, the concentration ratios of Canadian industries should be adjusted to include foreign production. Such an adjustment significantly reduces the estimated concentration ratios in many Canadian industries.

B. IMPERFECTLY COMPETITIVE MARKET STRUCTURES

- Most firms operating in imperfectly competitive market structures sell differentiated products whose characteristics they choose themselves. They also administer their

prices, do not change their prices as often as prices change in perfectly competitive markets, engage in nonprice competition, sometimes have unexploited economies of scale, and sometimes take actions designed to prevent the entry of new firms.

C. MONOPOLISTIC COMPETITION

- Monopolistic competition is a market structure that has the same characteristics as perfect competition except that the many firms each sell one variety of a differentiated product rather than all selling a single homogeneous product. Firms face negatively sloped demand curves and may earn monopoly profits in the short run.
- As in a perfectly competitive industry, the long run in monopolistic competition sees new firms enter the industry whenever profits can be made. Long-run equilibrium in the industry requires that each firm earns zero profits. But unlike perfect competition, the long-run equilibrium in monopolistic competition has each firm producing less than its minimum-cost level of output. This is because firms with differentiated products face downward-sloping demand curves. Zero profits then requires that the demand curve is tangent to the average total cost curve, which in turn means that the firm will be on the downward-sloping part of its average total cost curve. This is the excess-capacity theorem associated with monopolistic competition.
- Such excess capacity in the long-run equilibrium of monopolistic competition does not necessarily result in inefficiency. Even though each firm produces at a cost

that is higher than the minimum attainable cost, the resulting product choice is valued by consumers and so may be worth the extra cost.

D. OLIGOPOLY

- Oligopolies are dominated by a few large firms that usually sell differentiated products and have significant market power. They can maximize their joint profits if they cooperate to produce the monopoly output. By acting individually, each firm has an incentive to depart from this cooperative outcome, but rivalrous behaviour reduces profits and may lead to a noncooperative Nash equilibrium from which no one firm has an incentive to depart.
- Strategic behaviour, in which each firm chooses its best strategy in light of other firms' possible decisions, may also lead to a Nash equilibrium. Economists use game theory to study strategic behaviour.
- Tacit cooperation is possible but often breaks down as firms struggle for market share, indulge in non-price competition, and seek advantages through the introduction of new technology. Oligopolistic industries are likely to come closer to the joint-profit-maximizing cooperative outcome (a) the smaller the number of firms in the industry, (b) the less differentiated their products, (c) when the industry's demand is growing rather than shrinking, (d) when the industry contains a dominant firm, (e) the less the opportunity for non-price competition, and (f) the smaller the barriers to entry.
- Oligopolistic industries will exhibit profits in the long run only if there are significant barriers to entry. Natural barriers relate to the economies of scale and scope in production, finance and marketing, and also to large entry costs. Firm-created barriers can be created by proliferation of competing brands, heavy brand-image advertising, and the threat of predatory pricing when new entry occurs.
- The theory of contestable markets holds that *potential* entry may be sufficient to hold profits down and emphasizes the importance of sunk costs as an entry barrier.
- In the presence of major scale economies, oligopoly may be the best of the feasible alternative market structures. Evaluation of oligopoly depends on how much interfirm competition (a) drives the firms away from the cooperative, profit-maximizing solution and (b) leads to innovations in the very-long run.

KEY CONCEPTS

Concentration ratios
Reasons for the persistence of large firms
Administered prices
Product differentiation
Monopolistic competition
The excess-capacity theorem

The alleged inefficiency of monopolistic competition
Strategic behaviour
Cooperative and noncooperative outcomes
Game theory
Nash equilibrium

Explicit and tacit collusion
OPEC as a cartel
Natural and firm-created entry barriers
Contestable markets
The social benefits of oligopoly in the very-long run.

DISCUSSION QUESTIONS

1. It is sometimes said that there are more drugstores and gasoline stations than are needed. In what sense might this be correct? Does the consumer gain anything from this plethora of retail outlets?

2. Do you think any of the following industries might be monopolistically competitive? Why or why not?

   a. Textbook publishing (more than 50 elementary economics textbooks are in use on campuses in North America this year)
   b. Postsecondary education
   c. Cigarette manufacturing
   d. Restaurant operation
   e. Automobile retailing

3. What bearing did each of the following have on the eventual inability of OPEC to maintain a monopoly price for oil?

   a. Between 1979 and 1985, OPEC's share of the world oil supply decreased by half.
   b. "Saudi Arabia's interest lies in extending the life span of oil to the longest possible period," said Sheik Yamani.
   c. During the 1970s, government policies in many oil-importing countries protected consumers from oil price shocks by holding domestic prices well below OPEC levels.
   d. To earn Western currency to pay for grain, the Soviet Union increased its oil exports to the West during the 1980s, becoming the world's second largest oil exporter.
   e. In the late 1980s, Iran became increasingly concerned with maximizing its oil revenues in order to pay for its war with Iraq.
   f. Iraq in 1990 occupied Kuwait, and many wells there were set on fire before Iraq was driven out in 1991 by Operation Desert Storm.
   g. Other OPEC countries are able to make up for the lost Kuwait production by raising their outputs at a marginal cost far below the current world price.

4. "The periods following each of the major OPEC price shocks proved to the world that there were many available substitutes for gasoline, among them bicycles, car pools, moving closer to work, cable TV, and Japanese cars." Discuss how each of these may be a substitute for gasoline.

5. Can you think of other examples of competition among a few firms that might be of the prisoner's dilemma type?

6. The Canadian airline industry is essentially a duopoly (an oligopoly with two firms). Do the firms price-discriminate? Why or why not? Which features of the market facilitate price discrimination, and which make it difficult or impossible? Does the behaviour of the firms seem likely to get them close to or far away from the cooperative outcome? Until recently, European airlines operated under a price-setting arrangement. How would you expect prices to differ between Canada and Europe?

7. Compare the effects on the automobile and the wheat industries of each of the following. In light of your answers, discuss general ways in which oligopolistic industries fulfill the same general functions as perfectly competitive industries.

   a. A large rise in demand
   b. A large rise in the costs of production
   c. A temporary cut in supplies coming to market due to a three-month rail strike
   d. A rush of cheap foreign imports

8. Evidence suggests that the profits earned by all the firms in many oligopolistic industries are less than the profits that would be earned if the industry were monopolized. What are some reasons why this might be so?

9. Assume that you operate one of two self-service photocopying firms in your market. Due to space constraints, the businesses must be set up right next to each other, and each has room for only five identical machines. The only dimension on which you can compete is price. In fact, your services are so similar that if your competitor charges 1 cent less than you per copy, all customers will go to your competition. If the marginal cost per copy is 5 cents for each of you, what price do you think will dominate in the market?

10. What is the key difference between monopolistic competition and oligopoly? Assume that you are in an industry that is monopolistically competitive. What actual steps might you take to transform your industry into a more oligopolistic form?

ECONOMIC EFFICIENCY AND PUBLIC POLICY

Monopoly has long been regarded with suspicion. In *The Wealth of Nations*, Adam Smith (1723–1790) developed a stinging attack on monopolists. Since then, most economists have criticized monopoly and advocated competition.

In this chapter, we first consider what economic theory has to say about the relevant advantages of the two polar market structures of monopoly and perfect competition. Next we examine intermediate market forms and then go on to study public policies that are directed at encouraging competition and discouraging monopoly.

Part of the appeal of competition and the distrust of monopoly is noneconomic, being based on a fear of concentration of power. This was discussed in Chapter 11. Much of the attraction of competition and the dislike of monopoly, however, has to do with the understanding that competition is efficient in ways that monopoly is not. To understand the issue, we must first define *efficiency*.

Economic efficiency

Economic *efficiency* requires that resources not be wasted. In this context, when economists speak of avoiding the waste of resources, they are *not* referring to those situations where labour is unemployed or factories are idle (as occurs in recessions). Though situations of such idleness might be viewed as wasteful in the sense that valuable resources are not being used, when defining economic efficiency economists usually consider situations where factors are *fully employed*. However, full employment of resources by itself is not enough to prevent the waste of resources. Even when resources are fully employed, they may be used inefficiently. Let us look at three examples of inefficiency in the use of fully employed resources.

1. If firms do not use the least-cost method of producing their chosen outputs, they waste resources. For example, a firm that produces 30,000 pairs of shoes at a resource cost of $400,000 when it could have been done at a cost of only $350,000 is using resources inefficiently. The lower-cost method would allow $50,000 worth of resources to be transferred to other productive uses.

2. If within an industry, the cost of producing its last unit of output is higher for some firms than for others, the industry's overall cost of producing its output is higher than necessary.

3. If too much of one product and too little of another product are produced, resources are being used inefficiently. To take an extreme example, suppose that so many shoes are produced that every consumer has all the shoes he or she could possibly want and so places a zero value on obtaining an additional pair of shoes. Further suppose that fewer coats are produced relative to demand, so that each consumer places a positive value on obtaining an additional coat. In these circumstances, each consumer can be made better off if resources are reallocated from shoe production, where the last shoe produced has a low value in the eyes of each consumer, to coat production, where one more coat produced would have a higher value to each consumer.

PRODUCTIVE AND ALLOCATIVE EFFICIENCY

These examples suggest that we must refine our ideas of the waste of resources beyond the simple notion of ensuring that all resources are employed. The sources of inefficiency just outlined suggest important conditions that must be fulfilled if economic efficiency is to be attained. These conditions are conveniently collected into two categories, called *productive efficiency* and *allocative efficiency*, which were studied in the nineteenth century by the Italian economist Vilfredo Pareto (1848–1923). Indeed, efficiency in the use of resources is often called Pareto-optimality or Pareto-efficiency in his honour.

Productive Efficiency

Productive efficiency has two aspects, one concerning production within each firm and one concerning the allocation of production among the firms in an industry.

The first condition for productive efficiency is that each firm should produce *any given level of output* at the lowest possible cost. In the short run, with only one variable factor, the choice of technique is not a problem for the firm. It merely uses enough of the variable factor to produce the desired level of output. In the long run, however, more than one method of production is available. Productive efficiency requires that the firm use the least costly of the available methods of producing any given output. This means that firms will be located on, rather than above, their long-run average cost curves.

In Chapter 9, we studied the condition for productive efficiency within the firm:

Productive efficiency requires that each firm produce its given output by combining factors of production so that the ratios of the marginal products of each pair of factors equals the ratio of their prices.

This is the same thing as saying that $1 spent on every factor should yield the same output. If this were not so, the firm could reduce the resource costs of producing its given output by altering the inputs it uses. It could substitute the input for which $1 of expenditure yields the higher output for the input for which $1 of expenditure yields the lower output.[1]

Any firm that is not being productively efficient is producing at a higher cost than is necessary. This must reduce its profits. It follows that any profit-maximizing firm will seek to be productively efficient no matter which market structure it operates within—perfect competition, monopoly, oligopoly, or monopolistic competition.

There is a second condition for productive efficiency. It ensures that the total output of each industry is allocated among its individual firms in such a way that the total cost of producing the industry's output is minimized.

Productive efficiency at the level of the industry requires that the marginal cost of production must be the same for each firm.

If an industry is productively *inefficient,* it is possible to reduce the industry's total cost of producing any given output by reallocating production among the industry's firms. To illustrate, suppose that the Jones Brothers shoe manufacturing firm has a marginal cost of $70 for the last shoe of some standard type that it produces, while Gonzales, Inc., has a marginal cost of only $65 for the same type of shoe. If the Jones plant were to produce one less pair of shoes and the Gonzales plant were to produce one more, total shoe output is unchanged, but total industry costs are reduced by $5. Thus $5 worth of resources would be released to increase the production of other goods.

Clearly, this cost saving can go on as long as the two firms have different marginal costs. However, as the Gonzales firm produces more shoes, its marginal cost rises, and as the Jones firm produces fewer shoes, its marginal cost falls. (By producing more,

the Gonzales firm is moving upward along its given *MC* curve, whereas by producing less, the Jones firm is moving downward along its given *MC* curve.) Say, for example, that after the Gonzales firm increases its production by 1,000 shoes per month, its marginal cost rises to $67, whereas when Jones Brothers reduces its output by the same amount, its marginal cost falls to $67. Now there are no further cost savings to be obtained by reallocating production between the two firms.

Figure 13-1 shows a production possibility curve of the sort that was first introduced in Chapter 1. Productive *inefficiency* implies that the economy is at some point *inside* the production possibility curve. In such a situation, it is possible to produce more of some goods without producing less of others. *Thus productive efficiency implies being on, rather than inside, the economy's production possibility curve.*

Allocative Efficiency

Allocative efficiency concerns the relative quantities of the products to be produced. It concerns the choice between alternative points on the curve such as points *b, c,* and *d* in Figure 13-1.

Allocative efficiency is defined as a situation in which it is impossible to change the allocation of resources in such a way as to make someone better off without making someone else worse off. Changing the allocation of resources implies producing more of some goods and less of others, which in turn means moving from one point on the production possibility curve to another. This is called changing the *mix* of production.

From an allocative point of view, resources are said to be used *inefficiently* when using them to produce a different bundle of goods makes it *possible* for at least one person to be better off while making no other person worse off. Conversely, resources are said to be used *efficiently* when it is *impossible,* by using them to produce a different bundle of goods, to make any one person better off without making at least one other person worse off.

This tells us what is meant by allocative efficiency, but how do we find the efficient point on the production possibility curve? For example, how many shoes, dresses, and hats should be produced to achieve allocative efficiency? The answer is as follows:

The economy is allocatively efficient when, for each good produced, its marginal cost of production is equal to its price.

---

[1]As we saw in Extension 9-1, producing at least cost within the firm also involves a more obvious type of efficiency, called *technical efficiency.* Technical efficiency requires that the firm not adopt a method of production if there exists another method that uses *less of all inputs.* Productive efficiency then ensures that the firm chooses the method that uses the lowest *value* of resources from among the technically efficient methods.

FIGURE 13-1
Productive and Allocative Efficiency

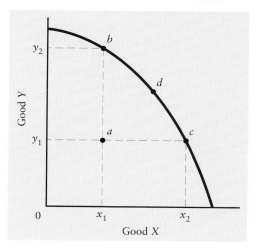

Any point on the production possibility curve is productively efficient; not all points on this curve are allocatively efficient. The curve shows all combinations of two goods X and Y that can be produced when the economy's resources are fully employed and being used with productive efficiency.

Any point inside the curve, such as *a*, is productively inefficient. If the inefficiency exists in industry X, production could be reallocated among firms in that industry in such a way as to raise production of X from x_1 to x_2. This would take the economy from point *a* to point *c*, raising production of X without any reduction in production of Y. Similarly, if the inefficiency exists in industry Y, production of Y could be increased from y_1 to y_2, which would take the economy from point *a* to point *b*. If both industries are productively inefficient, production can be increased to take the economy to some point on the curve between *b* and *c*, thereby increasing the production of both products.

Allocative efficiency concerns being at the most efficient point on the production possibility curve. Assessing allocative efficiency requires comparing various points on the curve, such as *b*, *c*, and *d*. Usually only one such point will be allocatively efficient (though all of them are productively efficient).

To understand the reasoning behind this answer, we need to recall a point that was established in our discussion of consumer surplus in Chapter 7. The price of any product indicates the value that each consumer places on the last unit consumed of that product. Faced with the market price of some product, the consumer goes on buying units until the last one is valued exactly at its price. Consumer surplus arises because the consumer would be willing to pay more than the market price for all but the last unit that is bought. On the last unit bought (the marginal unit), however, the consumer only "breaks even" because the valuation placed on it is just equal to its price.

Now let us return to our shoe example. Suppose that shoes sell for $60 per pair but the marginal cost is $70. If one less pair of shoes were produced, the value that all households would place on the pair of shoes not produced would be $60. Using the concept of opportunity cost, however, we see that the resources that would have been used to produce that last pair of shoes could instead produce another good (say, a coat) valued at $70. If society can give up something that its members value at $60 and get in return something that its members value at $70, the original allocation of resources is inefficient. Someone can be made better off, and no one need be worse off.

This is easy to see when the same consumer gives up the shoes and gets the coat, but it follows even when different consumers are involved. In this case, the market value of the gains to the household that gets the coat exceeds the market value of the loss to the household that gives up the shoes. The gaining household *could afford* to compensate the losing household and still come out ahead.

Suppose next that shoe production is cut back until the price of a pair of shoes rises from $60 to $65, while its marginal cost falls from $70 to $65. Efficiency is achieved in shoe production because $p = MC = \$65$. Now if one less pair of shoes were produced, $65 worth of shoes would be sacrificed, while at most, $65 worth of other products could be produced with the freed resources.

In this situation, it is not possible to change the allocation of resources to shoe production to make someone better off without making someone else worse off. If one household were to sacrifice one pair of shoes, it would give up goods worth $65 and would then have to obtain for itself all of the new production of the alternative commodity produced just to break even. It cannot gain without making another household worse off. The same argument can be repeated for every product, and it leads to the conclusion that we have stated already: The allocation of resources is efficient when each product's price equals its marginal cost of production.

One final comment about allocative efficiency. Whereas an individual firm or an individual industry may be *productively efficient*, it does not make sense to say that a given firm or industry is *allocatively efficient*. Allocative efficiency is a property of the overall economy, concerning the relative outputs of its various industries, and it is achieved when price equals marginal cost in *all* industries. Thus if we were to observe price greater than marginal cost in some individual industry, we would know that the economy is not allocatively efficient. But if we were to see price equal to marginal cost in that one industry, we must still check *all* other industries before we know whether the economy is allocatively efficient.

EFFICIENCY IN PERFECT COMPETITION AND MONOPOLY

We now know that for productive efficiency, marginal cost should be the same for all firms in any one industry and that for allocative efficiency, marginal cost should be equal to price in each industry. Do the market structures of perfect competition and monopoly lead to productive and allocative efficiency?

Perfect Competition

Productive Efficiency.   We saw in Figure 10-9 that in the long run under perfect competition, each firm produces at the lowest point on its long-run average cost curve. Therefore, no one firm could lower its costs by altering its own production.

We also know that in perfect competition, all firms in an industry face the same price of their product and that they equate marginal cost to that price. It follows immediately that marginal cost will be the same for all firms. Because all firms in the industry have the same cost of producing their last unit of production, no reallocation of production among the firms could reduce the total industry cost of producing a given output. Thus productive efficiency is achieved under perfect competition because all firms in an industry have identical marginal costs and identical minimum costs in long-run equilibrium.

Allocative Efficiency.   We have already seen that perfectly competitive firms maximize their profits by equating marginal cost to price. Thus when perfect competition is the market structure for the whole economy, price is equal to marginal cost in each line of production, resulting in allocative efficiency.

Monopoly

Productive Efficiency.   Monopolists have an incentive to be productively efficient because their profits will be maximized when they adopt the lowest-cost method that can be used to produce whatever level of output they choose. Hence profit-maximizing monopolists will operate on their *LRAC* curves. Furthermore, when they have more than one plant producing the same product, they will allocate production among those plants so that the cost of producing the last unit of output is the same in all plants.

Allocative Efficiency.   Although a monopoly firm will be productively efficient, it will choose a level of output that is too low to achieve allocative efficiency. This follows from what we saw in Chapter 11—that the monopolist chooses an output at which the price charged is *greater than* marginal cost. This violates the conditions for allocative efficiency because the amount that consumers pay for the last unit of output exceeds the opportunity cost of producing it.

Consumers would be prepared to buy additional units for an amount that is greater than the cost of producing these units. Some consumers could be made better off, and none need be made worse off, by shifting extra resources into production of the monopolized product, thus increasing the output of the product. From this follows the classic efficiency-based preference for competition over monopoly:

Monopoly creates allocative inefficiency because the monopolist's price always exceeds its marginal cost.

This result has important policy implications for economists and for policymakers, as we shall see later in this chapter.

Efficiency in Other Market Structures

Note that the result just stated extends beyond the case of a simple monopoly. Whenever a firm has any power over the market, in the sense that it faces a negatively sloped demand curve rather than one that is horizontal, its marginal revenue will be less than its price. Thus when it equates marginal cost to marginal revenue, as all profit-maximizing firms do, marginal cost will also be less than price. This implies allocative inefficiency. Thus oligopoly and monopolistic competition are also allocatively inefficient.

Oligopoly is an important market structure in today's economy because in many industries the minimum efficient scale is simply too high to support a large number of competing firms. Although oligopoly does not achieve the conditions for allocative efficiency, it may nevertheless produce more satisfactory results than monopoly. We observed one reason why this might be so in Chapter 12: Competition among oligopolists may encourage very-long-run adaptations that result in both new products and cost-reducing methods of producing old ones.

An important defense of oligopoly as an acceptable market structure is that it may be the best of the available alternatives when minimum efficient scale is large. As we observed at the end of Chapter 12, the challenge to public policy is to keep oligopolists competing and using their competitive energies to improve products and to lower costs rather than to restrict interfirm competition and to erect entry barriers. As we shall see later in this chapter, much public policy has just this purpose. What economic policymakers call *monopolistic practices* include not only output restrictions operated by firms with complete monopoly power but also anticompetitive behaviour among firms that are operating in oligopolistic industries.

ALLOCATIVE EFFICIENCY AND TOTAL SURPLUS

By using the concepts of price and marginal cost, we have established the basic points of productive and allocative efficiency. A different way of thinking about allocative efficiency—though completely consistent with the first approach—is to use the concepts of consumer and producer surplus.

Consumer and Producer Surplus

Recall from Chapter 7 that consumer surplus is the difference between the total value that consumers place on all the units consumed of some product and the payment that they actually make for the purchase of that product. Consumer surplus is shown once again in Figure 13-2.

Producer surplus is analogous to consumer surplus. It occurs because all units of each firm's output are sold at the same market price, while, given an upward-sloping supply curve, each unit except the last is produced at a marginal cost that is less than the market price.

Producer surplus is defined as the amount that producers are paid for a product minus the total

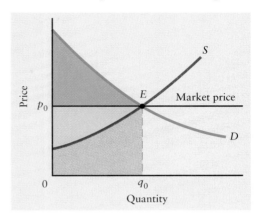

FIGURE 13-2
Consumer Surplus and Producer Surplus

Consumer surplus is the area under the demand curve and above the market price line. Producer surplus is the area above the supply curve and below the market price line. The total value that consumers place on q_0 of the commodity is given by the sum of the three shaded areas. The amount they pay is the rectangle p_0q_0. The difference, shown as the dark blue shaded area is consumer surplus.

The receipts to producers from the sale of q_0 units are also p_0q_0. The area under the supply curve, the red shaded area, is the minimum amount producers require to supply the output. The difference, shown as the light blue shaded area, is producer surplus.

variable cost of producing the product. The total variable cost of producing any output is shown by the area under the supply curve up to that output.[2] Thus producer surplus is the area above the supply curve and below the market price line. Producer surplus is also shown in Figure 13-2.

The Allocative Efficiency of Perfect Competition Revisited

If the total of consumer and producer surplus is not maximized, the industry's output could be altered to

---

[2]Marginal cost is the change in total cost caused by producing one more unit of output. Summing these additions over each unit of output, starting with the first, yields the total variable cost of output. Graphically, this process of summation is shown by the whole area under the marginal cost curve. Because, as we have already seen, the industry supply curve under perfect competition is merely the sum of the marginal cost curves of all the firms in the industry, the area under that supply curve up to some given output is the total of all the firms' variable costs of producing that output.

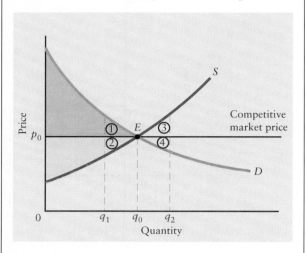

FIGURE 13-3
The Allocative Efficiency of Perfect Competition

Competitive equilibrium is allocatively efficient because it maximizes the sum of consumer and producer surplus. The competitive equilibrium occurs at the price-output combination $p_0 q_0$. At this equilibrium, consumer surplus is the dark shaded area above the price line, while producer surplus is the light shaded area below the price line.

For any output that is less than q_0, the sum of the two surpluses is less than at q_0. For example, reducing the output to q_1 but keeping price at p_0 lowers consumer surplus by area 1 and lowers producer surplus by area 2.

For any output that is greater than q_0, the sum of the surpluses is also less than at q_0. For example, if producers are forced to produce output q_2 and to sell it to consumers, who are in turn forced to buy it at price p_0, producer surplus is reduced by area 3 (the amount by which variable costs exceed revenue on those units), while the amount of consumer surplus is reduced by area 4 (the amount by which expenditure exceeds consumers' satisfactions on those units).

Only at competitive output q_0 is the sum of the two surpluses maximized.

increase that total. The additional surplus could then be used to make some consumers better off without making any others worse off.

Allocative efficiency occurs where the sum of consumer and producer surplus is maximized.

The allocatively efficient output occurs under perfect competition where the demand curve intersects the supply curve—that is, the point of equilibrium in a competitive market. This is shown in Figure 13-3. For any output that is less than the com-

petitive output, the demand curve lies above the supply curve, which means that the value that consumers put on the last unit of production exceeds its marginal cost of production. Suppose that the current output of shoes is such that consumers value at $70 an additional pair of shoes that adds $60 to costs. If it is sold at any price between $60 and $70, both producers and consumers gain; there is $10 of potential surplus to be divided between the two groups. In contrast, the last unit produced and sold in a competitive equilibrium adds nothing to either consumer or producer surplus because consumers value it at exactly its market price, and it adds the full amount of the market price to producers' costs.

If production were pushed beyond the competitive equilibrium, the sum of the two surpluses would fall. Suppose, for example, that firms were forced to produce and sell further units of output at the competitive market price and that consumers were forced to buy these extra units at that price. (Note that neither group would do so voluntarily.) Firms would lose producer surplus on those extra units because their marginal costs of producing the extra output would be above the price that they received for it. Purchasers would lose consumer surplus because the valuation that they placed on these extra units, as shown by the height of the demand curve, would be less than the price that they would have to pay.

The sum of producer and consumer surplus is maximized only at the perfectly competitive level of output. This is the only level of output that is allocatively efficient.

The Allocative Inefficiency of Monopoly Revisited

We have just seen in Figure 13-3 that the output in perfectly competitive equilibrium maximizes the sum of consumer and producer surplus. It follows that the lower monopoly output must result in a smaller total of consumer and producer surplus.

The monopoly equilibrium is not the outcome of a voluntary agreement between the one producer and the many consumers. Instead, it is imposed by the monopolist by virtue of the power it has over the market. When the monopolist chooses an output below the competitive level, market price is higher than it would be under perfect competition. As a result, consumer surplus is diminished, and producer surplus is increased. In this way, the monopolist gains at the expense of consumers. This is not the whole story, however.

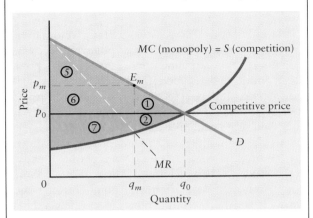

FIGURE 13-4
The Allocative Inefficiency of Monopoly

Monopoly is allocatively inefficient because it produces less than the competitive output and thus does not maximize the sum of consumer and producer surplus. If this market were perfectly competitive, price would be p_0, output would be q_0, and consumer surplus would be the sum of areas 1, 5, and 6 (the blue shaded areas). When the industry is monopolized, price rises to p_m and consumer surplus falls to area 5. Consumers lose area 1 because that output is not produced; they lose area 6 because the price rise has transferred it to the monopolist.

Producer surplus in a competitive equilibrium would be the sum of areas 7 and 2 (the gray shaded areas). When the market is monopolized and price rises to q_m, the surplus area 2 is lost because the output is not produced. However, the monopolist gains area 6 from consumers (6 is known to be greater than 2 because p_m maximizes profits).

Whereas area 6 is surplus that is transferred from consumers to producers by the price rise, areas 1 and 2 are lost altogether. They represent the deadweight loss resulting from monopoly and account for its allocative inefficiency.

When output is below the competitive level, there is always a *net loss* of surplus: More surplus is lost by consumers than is gained by the monopolist. Some surplus is lost because output between the monopolistic and the competitive levels is not produced. This loss of surplus is called the *deadweight loss of monopoly*. It is illustrated in Figure 13-4.

It follows that there is a conflict between the private interest of the monopoly producer and the public interest of all the nation's consumers. This creates grounds for government intervention to prevent the formation of monopolies or at least to control their behaviour.

ALLOCATIVE EFFICIENCY AND MARKET FAILURE

We have seen that perfect competition is allocatively efficient and that monopoly, in general, is not. Most of the remainder of the chapter discusses ways in which public policy has attempted to deal with problems raised by monopoly. Before we go on, however, it is important to reemphasize that perfect competition is a theoretical ideal that is at best only approximated in actual market economies and that the markets for many products do not even closely resemble this ideal. Hence to say that perfect competition is allocatively efficient is not to say that real-world market economies are ever allocatively efficient.

In Chapter 18, we provide a detailed analysis of the most important ways (other than monopoly) that market economies may fail to produce efficient outcomes. In Chapters 19 and 20, we discuss and evaluate the most important public policies that have been used to try to correct for these *market failures*. The most important problems arise when market transactions—production and consumption—impose costs or confer benefits on economic agents who are not parties to the transaction. Cases like these, which are called *externalities* because they involve economic effects that are external to the transaction, generally raise the possibility that market outcomes will be allocatively inefficient.

A simple example can illustrate the problem. We have argued that markets for agricultural commodities are highly competitive, with many relatively small producers who are unable to affect the price of the goods that they are producing. At the same time, it turns out that the technology of agricultural production involves the extensive use of fertilizers that pollute nearby streams and rivers. This pollution in turn imposes costs on downstream fisheries and on households downstream who use the water for drinking and cleaning. Because these costs are not taken into account in the market for the agricultural products, they will be external to transactions in those markets. Generally, when production of a good or service causes pollution, the quantity produced in a perfectly competitive industry will exceed the efficient amount.

One of the most important issues in public policy is whether, and under what circumstances, government action can increase the allocative efficiency of market outcomes.

As we will see later in this book, there are many circumstances in which there is room to increase the efficiency of market outcomes, but there are also many cases in which the cure is worse than the disease. In the remainder of this chapter, we consider an important set of examples of both of these phenomena—those arising from public policy toward monopoly and competition.

ECONOMIC REGULATION TO PROMOTE EFFICIENCY

Monopolies, cartels, and price-fixing agreements among oligopolists, whether explicit or tacit, have met with public suspicion and official hostility for over a century. These and other noncompetitive practices are collectively referred to as *monopoly practices*. Such practices go far beyond what actual monopolists do and include noncompetitive behaviour of firms that are operating in other market structures. The laws and other instruments that are used to encourage competition and discourage monopoly practices make up **competition policy** and are used to influence both the market structure and the behaviour of individual firms. By and large, Canadian competition policy has sought to create more competitive market structures where possible, to discourage monopolistic practices, and to encourage competitive behaviour where competitive market structures cannot be established. In addition, federal, provincial, and local governments all employ *economic regulations,* which prescribe the rules under which firms can do business and in some cases determine the prices that businesses can charge for their output. Railway freight rates, passenger airline fares, cable television, and local telephone service are examples of services that are subject to this kind of regulation.

The quest for allocative efficiency provides rationales both for competition policy and for economic regulation. Competition policy is used to promote allocative efficiency by increasing competition in the marketplace. Where effective competition is not possible (as in the case of a natural monopoly, such as an electric power company), economic regulation of privately owned firms or public ownership can be used as a substitute for competition. Consumers can

then be protected from the high prices and reduced output that result from the use of monopoly power.[3]

Public policies are indeed used in these ways, but they are also often used in ways that reduce economic efficiency. One reason is that economic efficiency is not the only concern of policymakers when designing and implementing competition policy. Most public policies have the potential to redistribute income, and people often use them for private gain, regardless of their original public purpose. This is studied more generally in Chapter 18.

In the remainder of this chapter, we look at a variety of ways in which policymakers have chosen to intervene in the workings of the market economy using economic regulation and competition policy. We will study three important aspects of Canadian policy: the control of natural monopolies, the control of oligopolies, and the creation of competitive conditions.

DIRECT CONTROL OF NATURAL MONOPOLIES

The clearest case for public intervention arises with what is called a **natural monopoly**—an industry in which scale effects are so dominant that there is room for *at most* one firm to operate at the minimum efficient scale. (Indeed, scale effects could be so important that even a single firm could satisfy the entire market demand before reaching its minimum efficient scale.) In the past, there have been many natural monopolies. Today, they are found mainly in public utilities, such as electricity generation and cable television.

One response to natural monopoly is for government to assume *ownership* of the single firm. In Canada, such government-owned firms are called **crown corporations.** In these cases, the government appoints managers and directors who are supposed to set prices guided by their understanding of the national interest. Another response to the problem of natural monopoly is to allow private ownership but to regulate the monopolist's behaviour. In Canada, both government ownership (e.g., Canada Post and the provincial hydro authorities) and regulation (e.g.,

---

[3]A second kind of regulation, *social regulation,* involves the legislated rules that require firms to consider the health, safety, environmental, and other social consequences of their behaviour. Social regulation is discussed in Chapter 19.

cable television and local telephone) are used actively. In the United States, with a few notable exceptions, regulation has been the preferred alternative.

Whether the government owns or merely regulates natural monopolies, the industry's pricing policy is determined by the government. The industry is typically asked to follow some pricing policy that conflicts with the goal of profit maximization. We will see that such government intervention must deal with problems that arise in the short run, the long run, and the very-long run.

Short-Run Price and Output

In the short run, there are three general types of pricing policies that the natural monopoly—either state owned or privately owned but regulated—might be required to follow. These are *marginal-cost pricing*, *two-part tariffs*, and *average-cost pricing*. We discuss them in turn.

Marginal-Cost Pricing.   Sometimes the government dictates that the natural monopoly should try to set price equal to short-run marginal cost in an effort to maximize the sum of consumer and producer surplus in that industry. In principle, this policy, called **marginal-cost pricing,** induces the allocatively efficient level of output (i.e., where price equals marginal cost). This is not, however, the profit-maximizing output (which is where marginal cost equals marginal revenue). Thus marginal-cost pricing sets up a tension between the regulators' desire to achieve the allocatively efficient level of output and the monopolist's desire to maximize profits.

Marginal-cost pricing creates different problems in each of two important cases. In the first case, the natural monopoly has unexploited economies of scale when producing the allocatively efficient output because it is still operating on the downward-sloping portion of its average total cost curve. In this case, marginal cost will be less than average total cost. It follows that when price is set equal to marginal cost, price will therefore be less than average cost, and so marginal-cost pricing will lead to losses. This is shown in part (i) of Figure 13-5.

In the second case, demand is sufficient to allow the firm to produce a level of output beyond its minimum efficient scale and thus on the upward-sloping portion of its average total cost curve. At any such level of output, marginal cost exceeds average total cost. Thus if the firm is directed to equate price with

marginal cost, it is clear that price will be above average total cost. Marginal-cost pricing will therefore lead the firm to earn positive profits. This is shown in part (ii) of the figure.[4]

When a natural monopoly with falling average costs sets price equal to marginal cost, it will suffer losses. When a natural monopoly with rising average costs sets price equal to marginal cost, it will earn positive profits.

Two-Part Tariff.   Though marginal-cost pricing achieves allocative efficiency, a natural monopoly with declining average costs cannot be expected to incur losses indefinitely. One way of trying to cover total costs in this case is to allow the firm to charge a **two-part tariff** in which customers pay one price to gain access to the product and a second price for each unit consumed. Consider the case of a regulated electric utility. In principle, the "hookup fee" covers fixed costs, and then each unit of output can be priced at marginal cost. In practice, some electric utilities use a modified form of the two-part tariff. Each customer pays a high price for the first block of kilowatts of electricity consumed each month and then pays a price that is closer to marginal cost for the remaining consumption. This is referred to as *block pricing.*

Average-Cost Pricing.   Another method of regulating a natural monopoly is to set prices just high enough to cover total costs, thus earning neither profits nor losses. This means that the firm produces to the point where average revenue equals average total cost, which is where the demand curve cuts the average total cost curve. Part (i) of Figure 13-5 shows that for a firm with declining costs, this pricing policy requires producing at less than the optimal output. The firm's financial losses that would occur under marginal-cost pricing are avoided by producing less than

---

[4]Sometimes a natural monopoly is defined as one where long-run costs are falling when price equals marginal cost. This, however, is only *sufficient* for a natural monopoly; it is not *necessary*. Demand may be such that one firm is producing, when price equals marginal cost, on the rising portion of its long-run cost curve, while there is no price at which two firms could both cover their total costs. For example, if a firm's minimum efficient scale is 1 million units of output and demand is sufficient to allow the firm to cover costs at 1.2 million units, there may be no price at which two firms, with their combined *MES* of 2 million units, can cover their full costs.

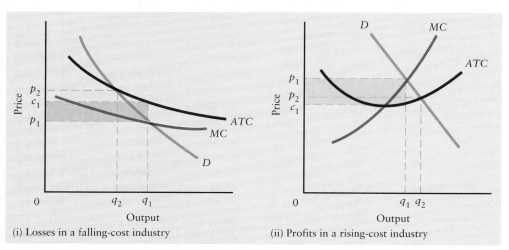

FIGURE 13-5
Pricing Policies for Natural Monopolies

(i) Losses in a falling-cost industry

(ii) Profits in a rising-cost industry

Marginal-cost pricing leads to profit or losses, whereas average-cost pricing violates the efficiency condition. In each part, the output at which marginal cost equals price is q_1 and price is p_1.

In part (i), average costs are falling at output q_1, so marginal costs are less than the average cost c_1. There is an average loss of $c_1 - p_1$ on each unit, making a total loss equal to the shaded area.

In part (ii), average cost c_1 is less than price at output q_1. There is an average profit of $p_1 - c_1$ on each unit sold, making a total profit equal to the shaded area.

In each part of the diagram, the output at which average cost equals price is q_2 and the associated price is p_2. In part (i), marginal cost is less than price at q_2, so output is below its optimal level. In part (ii), marginal cost exceeds price at q_2, so output is greater than its optimal level.

the efficient output.[5] Part (ii) shows that for a firm with rising costs, the policy requires producing at more than the optimal output. The profits that would occur under marginal-cost pricing are dissipated by producing more than the efficient output.

Generally, average-cost pricing will not result in allocative efficiency because price will not equal marginal cost.

On what basis do we choose between marginal-cost pricing and average-cost pricing? One the one hand, marginal-cost pricing generates allocative efficiency, but the firm may incur losses. In this case, the firm will eventually go out of business unless someone is prepared to cover the firm's costs. If the government is unwilling to do so, seeing no reason why

taxpayers should subsidize the users of the product in question, then average-cost pricing is preferable to monopoly pricing. It provides the lowest price that can be charged and the largest output that can be produced, given the requirement that sales revenue must cover the total cost of producing the product.

Long-Run Investment

So far, we have examined the implications for different pricing policies in the short run. Recall that in the short run the level of the firm's capital is fixed. The allocatively efficient pricing policy sets price equal to short-run marginal cost. The position of the short-run marginal cost curve depends, however, on the amount of fixed capital that is currently available to be combined with the variable factors. What should determine the long-run investment decision to accumulate capital?

The efficient answer follows from comparing the current market price with the *long-run* marginal cost of producing the product. The current market price

[5]Note that the losses are financial losses, not social welfare losses. Every unit produced between the points where AC equals price and MC equals price brings private financial losses to the producer even though total (consumer plus producer) surplus increases.

reflects the value consumers place on one additional unit of output. The long-run marginal cost reflects the full resource cost (including capital costs) of providing an extra unit of output. Thus if the current price exceeds long-run marginal cost, then the natural monopoly should increase its capacity; if current price is less than long-run marginal cost, the natural monopoly should allow its capacity to decline as its capital wears out.

For given capacity in the short run, the allocatively efficient pricing system determines output by setting price equal to the short-run marginal cost of production. It also adjusts capacity in the long run until the long-run marginal cost of production is equal to the price.

Application 13-1 discusses the example of provincial hydro authorities and the long-run investment problems associated with average-cost pricing.

Very-Long-Run Innovation

Natural monopoly is a long-run concept, meaning that given *existing technology*, there is room for only one firm to operate profitably. In the very-long run, however, technology changes. Not only does today's competitive industry sometimes become tomorrow's natural monopoly, but today's natural monopoly often becomes tomorrow's competitive industry.

A striking example is found in the telecommunications industry. Thirty years ago, hard-copy message transmission was close to a natural monopoly belonging to the post office. Today, technological developments such as satellite transmission, electronic mail, and fax machines have made this activity highly competitive. In many countries, an odd circumstance has now arisen: Publicly owned, or privately owned but regulated, post offices seek to maintain their profitability by prohibiting entry into what would otherwise become a highly competitive industry. Because it has the full force of the legal system behind it, the government-sanctioned monopolist may be more successful than the unregulated privately owned firm would have been in preserving its monopoly long after technological changes have destroyed its "naturalness." What started out as policies to facilitate efficiency of a natural monopoly ends up being a protection of an artificial monopoly against would-be competitors.

Not only is this true of many publicly owned or regulated post offices around the world, but it is also true of a number of other industries that once were natural monopolies but that could now be highly competitive. For example, many countries continue to operate such artificial monopolies in railways, airlines, telephones, and the generation of electricity (the *distribution* of electricity continues to be a natural monopoly). The basic lesson is this: Market economies change continually under the impacts of innovation and growth; to be successful, government policy must also adapt continually to keep it relevant to the ever-changing environment.

DIRECT CONTROL OF OLIGOPOLIES

Governments have from time to time intervened in industries that were oligopolies (rather than natural monopolies), seeking to enforce the type of price and entry behaviour that was thought to be in the public interest. Such intervention has typically taken two distinct forms. In the United Kingdom, it was primarily nationalization of whole oligopolistic industries such as railways, steel, and coal mining, which were then to be run by government-appointed boards. In the United States, firms such as airlines, railways, and electric power companies were left in private hands, but their decisions were regulated by government-appointed bodies that set prices and regulated entry. As so often happens, Canada followed a mixture of British and American practices. Many Canadian crown corporations were set up, and many firms that remained in private hands were regulated. For example, in the regulated railway industry, Canadian Pacific was privately owned while Canadian National, until very recently, was a crown corporation.

Scepticism About Direct Control

Policymakers have become increasingly sceptical of their ability to improve the behaviour of oligopolistic industries by having governments control the details of their behaviour either through ownership or regulation. Three main experiences have been important in developing this scepticism.

Oligopolies and Economic Growth. First, oligopolistic market structures have provided much of the economic growth in the twentieth century. New products and new ways of producing old products have followed each other in rapid succession, all lead-

APPLICATION 13-1

PRICING IN THE PROVINCIAL POWER AUTHORITIES

The use of average-cost pricing in natural monopolies tends to distort investment decisions. One example which illustrates this idea is the case of the provincially-owned power authorities, such as Manitoba Hydro, Ontario Hydro, or New Brunswick Power. There are essentially three different methods of generating electricity used by the power authorities: hydroelectric, fuel burning (coal, oil, and other fuels), and nuclear power. Across the various provincial hydro authorities, there is considerable variation in the methods used. For example, in British Columbia and Manitoba almost all power is hydroelectric; Ontario makes considerable use of nuclear power; and almost all electricity in Alberta is generated in fuel-burning plants. New Brunswick is the most diversified of the power authorities, having large amounts of its electricity being produced by each of the three methods.

COSTS OF PRODUCTION

The three methods of generating electricity differ markedly in their costs. Producing hydroelectricity involves high fixed costs but extremely low marginal costs—this reflects the high cost of building a dam but the very low costs of having an extra unit of water flow through a turbine. Fuel-burning plants have smaller fixed costs, but higher marginal costs—a fuel-burning plant can be easily built, but expensive fuel must be used for every unit of power produced. Nuclear plants have extremely high fixed costs, but do not have the advantage of the very low marginal costs typical of hydro plants—uranium and heavy water are important and expensive *variable* factors of production.

The combination of these very different cost structures is that hydro plants tend to produce electricity at the lowest average total cost, with power from fuel-burning plants being slightly more expensive. The extreme fixed costs of building nuclear plants (and storage facilities for the spent fuel bundles) tend to give nuclear power the highest average total costs.

AVERAGE-COST PRICING

Now consider a typical problem faced by the hydro authorities—especially Ontario Hydro—until the early 1990s. Suppose that there are no sites in Ontario where new hydroelectric plants can be built, and that new fuel-burning plants are considered undesirable on environmental grounds. This means that any new capacity which is to be built must come from new high-cost nuclear plants.

If Ontario Hydro uses a policy of average-cost pricing, then the price of each unit of electricity sold (a kilowatt hour) is set equal to the average total cost of *all* units produced. With all three methods of electricity generation being used, the policy of average-cost pricing implies that the price of electricity is greater than the average cost from the hydro and fuel-burning plants but less than the average cost from the nuclear plants.

Now suppose that when Ontario Hydro follows this policy of average-cost pricing, it finds that there is excess demand for electricity. That is, when price is set equal to overall average cost, the quantity of electricity demanded exceeds what Ontario Hydro can currently provide. In this situation, should Ontario Hydro build new capacity?

ing to higher living standards and higher productivity. Many of these innovations have been provided by firms in oligopolistic industries such as automobiles, agricultural implements, steel, petroleum refining, chemicals, and telecommunications. As long as oli-

gopolists continue to compete with each other, rather than cooperating to produce monopoly profits, most economists see no need to regulate such things as the prices at which oligopolists sell their products and the conditions of entry into oligopolistic industries.

The relevant test is not the existence of excess demand at the current price (which equals average cost), because the long-run cost of providing more electricity exceeds the current price. The relevant cost is the long-run *marginal* cost of providing electricity *from nuclear plants* (which includes the high fixed costs of nuclear plants). On efficiency grounds, another plant should be built only if there is excess demand at a price that equals that long-run marginal cost.

This case illustrates the inefficient policies often adopted by nationalized and regulated industries that face rising long-run costs. If they priced at marginal cost, they would make profits on all units of output except the marginal one. Instead, they price at average cost. As a result, market price does not then provide the correct signal about the social value of further investment. If a regulated or nationalized firm installs capacity to satisfy all of the demand when price is set equal to average cost, then there will be more capacity than what is socially optimal. Such socially wasteful policies were adopted by several of the provincial power authorities, including Ontario Hydro.

NEW PROBLEMS

Technological improvements and deregulation have introduced new problems for the provincial power authorities in the past few years. First, technological improvements in the generation of electricity have removed many of the economies of scale that for many years were typical of this industry. In particular, the development of small-scale gas-combustion turbines has permitted the inexpensive construction of small generating stations that can produce electricity at a lower average cost than the much larger existing stations owned by the power authorities. This improvement in technology has led regulators to the view that the provincial power authorities should be deregulated and forced to face competition from private power generators.

Such competition introduces serious problems for the power authorities. Faced with low-price competition from the private power producers, the provincial power authorities have been forced to reduce their prices. But such price reductions imply that price is no longer high enough to cover their high fixed costs, especially those associated with nuclear plants. The result is that competition has driven prices down—which is clearly good for consumers—but has left the provincial power authorities unable to cover their average costs.

This situation is now occurring in some of the provincial power authorities in Canada, especially those like Ontario Hydro that use so much nuclear power. How the provincial authorities will respond is not yet known, but there are two broad possibilities, neither of which are promising. The first is that the power authorities will continue to produce power with their large facilities and sell it at a price below their average cost. The losses incurred will be absorbed by the shareholders of the companies—which in these cases are the provincial taxpayers. The second possibility is that the power authorities will moth-ball their high-fixed-cost production facilities. This is the so-called *stranded investment* problem—the ownership of capacity that is unable to compete with the new small-scale private power generators and is therefore economically obsolete.

Over the next few years we will see how the provincial power authorities deal with this difficult situation.

Cross Subsidization. Second, many regulatory bodies have imposed policies that were not related to the cost of each of the services being priced. These prices involved what is called *cross subsidization*, whereby profits that are earned in the provision of one service are used to subsidize the provision of another at a price below cost. When they were in control, regulators typically required that long-distance telephone calls subsidize local calls, first-class mail subsidize third-class mail, and long-haul airline rates subsidize short-haul rates. These pricing policies forced users of the profitable service to subsidize users of the unprofitable service. When these users are firms that compete with firms in other countries where regulators do not require cross subsidization, international competitiveness can be reduced. Furthermore, cross subsidizing is never welfare maximizing. Instead, it reduces the sum of producer and consumer surplus because price exceeds marginal cost in some lines of output but is less than marginal cost in others.

Protection from Competition. Third, the record of postwar government intervention into regulated industries seemed poorer in practice than its supporters had predicted. Research by the University of Chicago Nobel Laureate George Stigler (1911–1991) and others established that in many industries, regulatory bodies were "captured" by the very firms that they were supposed to be regulating. As a result, the regulatory bodies that were meant to ensure competition often acted to enforce monopoly practices that would have been illegal if instituted by the firms themselves.

For example, Canadian and U.S. railroad rates were originally regulated in order to keep profits down by establishing schedules of *maximum* rates. By the 1930s, however, concern had grown over the depressed economic condition of the railroads and the emerging vigorous competition from trucks and barges. The regulators then became the protectors of the railroads, permitting them to establish *minimum* rates for freight of different classes, allowing price discrimination, and encouraging other restrictive practices.

The regulators also advocated including trucking under the regulatory umbrella. Restricting entry into trucking and setting minimum rates for trucks was unmistakably designed to protect the producers, not the consumers. The only reason for regulating the large carriers was to control their competition with the railroads. Regulation limited the big road carriers' routes and set *floors* to the prices they could charge. As a result, they became targets for small, unregulated truckers, who could cut rates and thus draw away customers without fear of retaliation. To eliminate the rate competition, regulation was extended to small truckers.

Airline regulation in Canada and the United States provides another example. When airline routes and fares were first regulated, it was possible to argue that demand was too low to permit effective competition among many firms. Whatever the validity of that argument in earlier times, by the mid 1960s the regulation was plainly protecting the industry, allowing it to charge higher fares, earn higher profits, and pay higher wages than it would under more competitive conditions. For decades, Canadian and U.S. regulation of airline prices consistently prevented price competition. For example, until recently airlines other than Air Canada and Canadian Airlines were prevented from introducing cheap fares between Canada and Europe. This regulation could not be explained as protecting the interests of passengers against the predatory behaviour of the carriers.

Why did regulatory bodies shift from protecting consumers to protecting firms? One reason is that the regulatory commissions were gradually captured by the firms they were supposed to regulate. In part, this capture was natural enough. When regulatory bodies were hiring staff, they needed people who were knowledgeable in the industries they were regulating. Where better to go than to people who had worked in these industries? Naturally, these people tended to be sympathetic to firms in their own industries. Also, because many of them aspired to go back to those industries once they had gained experience within the regulatory bodies, they were not inclined to arouse the wrath of industry officials by imposing policies that were against the firms' interests.

Deregulation and Privatization

The 1980s witnessed a movement in many advanced industrial nations to reduce the level of government control over industry. Various experiences in these countries have been pushing in this direction:

- The realization that regulatory bodies often sought to reduce, rather than increase, competition

- The dashing of the hopes that publicly owned industries would work better than privately owned firms in the areas of efficiency, productivity growth, and industrial relations

- The realization that replacing a private monopoly with a publicly owned one would not greatly change the industry's performance and that replacing privately owned oligopolists by a publicly owned monopoly might actually worsen the industry's performance

- The awareness that falling transportation costs and revolutions in data processing and communications exposed local industries to much more widespread international competition than they had previously experienced domestically

The natural outcomes of these revised views were deregulation, intended, among other things, to leave prices and entry free to be determined by private decisions, and the privatization of publicly operated activities such as municipal garbage collection and the operation of local transit services.

Privatization went a long way in the United Kingdom. In the United States, where regulation rather than government ownership had been the adopted policy, many industries were deregulated. In Canada, hundreds of crown corporations that the government had acquired for a variety of reasons, but were neither natural monopolies nor operating in highly concentrated industries, were sold off. Also, many large crown corporations operating in oligopolistic industries, such as Air Canada, Petro Canada, and Canadian National, were privatized. (In 1995, the federal government began exploring the privatization of the air traffic control network and the various ports.) Also, many industries, such as airlines and gas and oil, were deregulated. Prices were freed, to be set by the firms in the industries, and entry was no longer restricted by government policy.

The effects (and thus the wisdom) of these changes are the subject of both economic analysis and political debate. A considerable lapse of time is needed, however, before any industry settles into a stable post-regulation pattern, at which point a more informed debate about the effects of deregulation can take place.

INTERVENTION TO KEEP FIRMS COMPETING

The least stringent form of government intervention is designed neither to force firms to sell at particular prices nor to regulate the conditions of entry and exit; it is designed, instead, to create conditions of competition by preventing firms from merging unnecessarily or from engaging in anticompetitive practices such as colluding to set monopoly prices. This is referred to as **competition policy**. Here the policy seeks both to create the most competitive market structure possible and to prevent firms from reducing competition by engaging in certain forms of cooperative behaviour. We discuss the details of Canadian competition policy in the next section.

CANADIAN COMPETITION POLICY

Laws designed for the purposes of preventing anticompetitive behaviour are called **combine laws** in Canada. They have provided the main thrust of Canadian competition policy since its inception in the nineteenth century. They prohibit monopolies, attempts to monopolize, and conspiracies in restraint of trade. Throughout the history of Canadian competition policy, legislation has been directed chiefly at the misuse of market power by single firms or groups of firms and only rarely at mergers per se.

This acceptance of the need for relatively large firms in the business sector was partly a function of the small size of the Canadian economy in the days when most production was solely for the domestic market. Firms that were large enough to exploit the available economies of scale were likely to be large in relation to the total market. This meant that there would be fewer firms in Canadian industries dominated by scale effects than would be found in similar industries in such relatively large economies as the United States.

THE EVOLUTION OF CANADIAN POLICY

The first Canadian combine laws were adopted in 1889 and 1890, when legislation made it an offense to combine, to agree to lessen competition unduly, or to restrain trade. Because the proscribed behaviour was illegal, an offense was a criminal act to be handled by the criminal justice system. The laws have been changed frequently since that time, but their basic procompetition stance still prevails in current legislation.

By the 1950s, Canadian anticombine laws had evolved to make illegal three broad classes of activity:

- combinations, such as price-fixing agreements that unduly lessen competition

- mergers or monopolies that may operate to the detriment of the public interest

- unfair trade practices

Many cases of unfair trade practices were successfully pursued under these laws, but compared to the United States, few cases were brought against mergers, and none of those that were brought were successful. The reason most often cited for this lack of success was the inability of criminal legislation to cope with complex economic issues. Under criminal law, the government must prove *beyond a reasonable doubt* that the accused party has committed the offense. As an added complication, Canadian courts have been much less willing than American courts to assess economic evidence.

A major review of Canadian legislation was undertaken in the late 1960s by the now-disbanded Economic Council of Canada. Its recommendations, published in a report in 1969, together with those of a committee of experts appointed by the then-named Department of Consumer and Corporate Affairs, formed the basis of the amendments to the Combines Investigation Act that are still in force. Of the recommendations that were accepted, some were put into effect in 1976 and the remainder in 1986.

The 1976 amendments included several provisions:

- extending the Combines Investigation Act to service industries

- allowing *civil* (rather than criminal) actions to be brought for damages resulting from contravention of the act

- strengthening legislation against misleading advertising

Claims about product quality must now be based on adequate tests. Advertising a product at a bargain price when the supplier does not supply the product in reasonable quantities is prohibited. Also prohibited is the supplying of a product at a price higher than the advertised price. In 1992, the court levied a record fine against one individual of $500,000 for seriously misleading advertising. Also, the Restrictive Trade Practices Commission was given the power to protect customers by prohibiting suppliers from (1) refusing to supply without good

reason, (2) requiring exclusive dealerships, (3) restricting the way a good is sold, or (4) requiring tied sales. As a result, retailing practices for many goods have changed considerably.

In 1986, after four previous attempts had failed, the final set of amendments to the Combines Investigation Act were passed. The resulting Act—now called the Competition Act—has three central themes: economic efficiency, adaptability, and international trade. The new Act creates a specialized Competition Tribunal to deal with civil matters now that competition policy has been taken out of the sphere of the criminal law. This tribunal is empowered to hear applications and issue orders in respect of reviewable practices contained in the Act.

The Competition Tribunal can also accept consent orders from the director of investigations on terms agreed on by the parties involved without hearing further evidence. When this happens, Canadian procedures, which used to be very public ones (what economists call *transparent*), now go on very much behind closed doors in private negotiations between the firms involved and the Director of Investigations. Furthermore, in the important case of the takeover of Texaco Oil Company by Imperial Oil, a carefully worked out agreement among the parties and the director of investigations was seriously amended by the tribunal. This showed that the tribunal was unwilling merely to rubber-stamp agreements worked out behind the scenes under the auspices of the director.

Perhaps the most important of the 1986 amendments was the one which placed mergers under civil (rather than criminal) law—the statutory test being whether or not the merger "substantially lessens competition." For the first time in Canada, economic considerations are stated to be directly relevant in judging the acceptability of a merger. When reviewing a merger, the Director of Investigations is obliged to consider such things as effective competition after the merger, the degree of foreign competition, barriers to entry, the availability of substitutes, and the financial state of the merging firms. Furthermore, an allowable defense of a merger is that the gains in efficiency more than offset any reductions in competition.

This new merger legislation has had some substantial effects on business mergers for the first time in the history of Canadian competition policy. Many firms have consulted with the Director of

Investigations before concluding a merger. As a result, some proposed mergers have been amended, and a few have been abandoned. Many mergers that have gone forward have been investigated, and the terms of some have been substantially modified.

Several provisions of the Act have been challenged in the courts, and many times these cases reached the Supreme Court of Canada. In summarizing the effects of the Supreme Court's rulings, the Director of Investigation and Research of the Bureau of Competition Policy had this to say:[6]

> The recent case law, together with the release of enforcement guidelines concerning mergers (April 1991), price discrimination (September 1992), predatory pricing (May 1992) and misleading advertising (September 1991), have considerably advanced the important objectives of providing guidance to the business and legal communities with respect to the enforcement of Canada's competition law. Enforcement guidelines, in particular, have become an important

tool in the Bureau of Competition Policy's efforts towards articulating and clarifying enforcement policies and practices.

Looking Forward

The 1986 Competition Act will not be the end of the evolution of Canadian competition policy, but it appears to have marked the end of a major chapter. Canadian legislation has for a long time provided substantial protection to consumers against the misuse of market power by large firms. For the first time, it now also seems to provide some substantial protection against the creation, through mergers, of market power that is not justified by gains to efficiency or international competitiveness. Many observers are optimistic that these laws, no doubt to be further refined in the future, will provide more protection to consumers than direct government intervention did—either through government ownership of particular firms or through government control of prices and conditions of entry.

SUMMARY

A. ECONOMIC EFFICIENCY

- Economists distinguish two main kinds of efficiency: productive and allocative.
- Productive efficiency exists for given technology when whatever output is being produced is being produced at the lowest attainable cost. This requires, first, that firms be on, rather than above, their relevant cost curves and, second, that all firms in an industry have the same marginal cost.
- Allocative efficiency is achieved when it is impossible to change the mix of production in such a way as to make someone better off without making someone else worse off. The allocation of resources will be efficient when each product's price equals its marginal cost.
- Perfect competition achieves both productive and allocative efficiency. Productive efficiency is achieved because the same forces that lead to long-run equilibrium lead to production at the lowest attainable cost. Allocative effi-

ciency is achieved because in competitive equilibrium, price equals marginal cost for every product.

- The economic case against monopoly rests on its allocative inefficiency, which arises because profit maximization for a monopolist implies that price exceeds marginal cost. Some economists (notably Joseph Schumpeter) have argued that the incentive to innovate is so much greater under monopoly that monopoly is to be preferred to perfect competition, despite its allocative inefficiency. Though few modern economists go that far, the empirical evidence suggests that technological change and innovation can to a measurable extent be traced to the efforts of large firms operating in oligopolistic industries.

B. ECONOMIC REGULATION TO PROMOTE EFFICIENCY

- There are two broad types of policies designed to promote allocative efficiency in imperfectly competitive markets. These can be divided into *economic regulations* and *competition policy*. Economic regulation is used both in the case of a natural monopoly and in the case of an oligopolistic industry. Competition policy applies more to the latter.

---

[6]Public Lecture, Fordham Corporate Law Institute, New York, October 22, 1992.

- Efficient operation of natural monopolies requires that price be set equal to short-run marginal cost (marginal-cost pricing) and that investment be undertaken whenever that price exceeds the full long-run marginal cost of production. Average-cost pricing results in too little output in the short run and too little investment in the long run in falling-cost industries and too much output and too much investment in rising-cost industries.
- Direct control of pricing and entry conditions of some key oligopolistic industries has been common in the past, but deregulation is reducing such control. The move to deregulation is largely the result of the experiences that oligopolistic industries are a major engine of growth, as long as their firms are kept competing; that direct control of such industries has produced disap-

pointing results in the past; and that forced cross subsidization can have serious consequences for some users.

C. CANADIAN COMPETITION POLICY

- Canadian combine laws have always recognized the need for firms that are large in relation to the domestic market if economies of scale and scope are to be exploited. Such laws seek to restrict growth in size through mergers where the size is not justified by efficiencies and seek to prevent the unwarranted exploitation of market power.
- In 1976, such laws were removed from the criminal code, where enforcement proved difficult, and placed in the civil code, where enforcement appears to be easier.

KEY CONCEPTS

Productive and allocative efficiency
Consumer and producer surplus
The efficiency of competition

The inefficiency of monopoly
Regulation of natural monopolies
Marginal- and average-cost pricing

Regulation and effects on innovation
Deregulation
Canadian competition policy

DISCUSSION QUESTIONS

1. Suppose that allocative inefficiency of some economy amounts to 5 percent of the value of production. What does this statement mean? If it is true, would consumers *as a whole* be better off if policy measures were successful in moving the economy to an allocatively efficient outcome? Would *every* consumer be better off if the economy moved to an allocatively efficient outcome?

2. If the many plants producing a product were built at different times, with different levels of capacity and different cost curves, is it possible that the industry can ever be productively efficient? Use a diagram of the various firms' marginal cost curves to show why or why not.

3. When theme parks charge a price of admission and then a price for each ride, what type of pricing policy are they following? What alternative pricing policies

might be available? What are the advantages or disadvantages of each policy to the operators?

4. Would combine laws be necessary in an economy of perfect competition? Would they be beneficial in an economy of natural monopoly?

5. Evaluate the wisdom of having the Bureau of Competition Policy use profits as a measure of monopoly power in deciding whether to prosecute a case. Would such a rule be expected to affect the behaviour of firms with high profits? In what ways might any changes induced by such a rule be socially beneficial, and in what ways might they be socially harmful?

6. It is often asserted that whenever a regulatory agency is established, ultimately it will become controlled by the people whom it was intended to regu-

late. (This argument raises the question of who regulates the regulators.) Can you identify why this might happen? How might the integrity of regulatory boards be protected?

7. The chapter identifies several strategies for dealing with natural monopolies and their associated inefficiencies. Alternatively, assume that you are a regulator and that the monopoly you face is able to price discriminate—perhaps perfectly. Does this change the options you have for encouraging the efficient level of production? Would you choose to use this additional option? Why or why not?

8. Until 1983, AT&T was the sole provider of long-distance telephone service in the United States—a position enforced by U.S. federal law. What are some arguments that might have been in favour of supporting such a monopoly with government action early in this century? Which of these arguments do you think are

no longer valid? What has been the consequence of such structural changes?

9. "Canadian air travellers opting for U.S. carriers were [partly] responsible for Canadian airlines deregulation."—C. D. Howe Institute.

   "Canadian consumers crossing the border to buy cheap U.S. agricultural products may be responsible for the end of supply management in Canada."—Canadian economist

   What market forces lie behind each of these quotations? What difficulties do they reveal for the regulation of particular industries?

10. "Allocative efficiency is really about whether the economy 'has the quantities right'—it is not really about prices at all. Prices are only important in a discussion about allocative efficiency because *in a free market* changes in prices bring about the efficient allocation of resources." Comment.

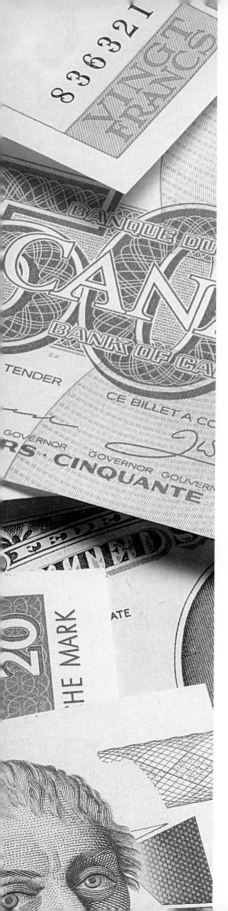

CHAPTER 14

INSIDE THE FIRM

Up to now, we have abstracted from much of the rich detail that distinguishes one firm from another, treating all firms merely as entities that assemble resources to produce goods and services with the ultimate objective of maximizing profits. But other than profit maximization, we have said nothing about what goes on inside firms, about how firms raise the necessary financial capital to conduct their business, or about the potentially different roles of managers versus owners.

In this chapter, we look at some of the details that are important in specific situations. We look in particular at how firms are organized and financed. We also see how the markets of many firms have expanded from just the country in which they are located to include international sales which, in many cases, now cover the entire world. We also consider why the management of firms may not succeed in maximizing profits and what may happen if they do not.

THE ORGANIZATION OF FIRMS

FORMS OF BUSINESS ORGANIZATION

There are three major forms of business organization in the private sector: the single proprietorship, the partnership, and the corporation. In the **single proprietorship,** one owner makes all the decisions and is personally responsible for all of the firm's actions and debts. In the **partnership,** there are two or more joint owners, each of whom may make binding decisions and may be personally responsible for all of the firm's actions and debts. In the **corporation,** the firm has a legal existence separate from that of the owners. The owners are the firm's shareholders, and they risk only the amount of money that they put up to purchase their shares. The owners elect a board of directors, which hires managers to run the firm under the board's supervision.

In manufacturing, transportation, public utilities, and finance, corporations do almost all of the nation's business. In trade and construction, they do about one-half of the total business. Only in agriculture and in services is the corporation relatively unimportant, and its importance has been increasing in these sectors as well.

The Single Proprietorship and the Partnership

The major advantage of the single proprietorship is that the owner is the boss who maintains full control over the firm. The disadvantages are, first, that the size of the firm is limited by the amount of capital that the owner can personally raise and, second, that the owner is personally responsible by law for all debts of the firm; this is called *unlimited liability.*

The partnership overcomes to some extent the first disadvantage of the single proprietorship but not the second. Ten partners may be able to finance a much bigger enterprise than one owner could, but

they are still subject to unlimited liability. Each partner is fully liable for all of the debts of the firm. Partnerships are traditional in many professions, including law, dentistry, engineering, and (until recently) brokerage. Partnerships survive in these professions partly because they depend heavily on a relationship of trust between owners and clients, and the partners' unlimited liability for one another's actions is thought to enhance public confidence in the firm.

The **limited partnership,** which has two classes of partners, general and limited, provides protection against some of the risks of the general partnership. The firm's *general partners,* who are responsible for the operation of the firm, have unlimited liability; the firm's *limited partners* are liable only for the amount that they have invested; this is called **limited liability.** Limited partners can neither participate in the running of the firm nor make agreements on its behalf.

The Corporation

The corporation is regarded by law as an entity separate from the individuals who own it. It can enter into contracts, sue and be sued, own property, contract debts, and generally incur obligations that are the legal obligations of the corporation but *not* of its owners. The corporation's right to be sued may not seem to be an advantage; but it is, because it allows others to enter into enforceable contracts with the corporation that otherwise would not take place.

Although some corporations are owned by just a few persons, who also manage the business, the most important type of corporation is one that sells shares to the general public. The people who invest their money by buying its stock, called its **stockholders** or **shareholders,** are the corporation's owners. All profits belong to the stockholders. Profits that are paid out to them are called **dividends;** profits that are retained to be reinvested in the firm's operations are called **undistributed profits** or **retained earnings.**

Stockholders, who are entitled to one vote for each share that they own, elect a board of directors. This board of directors defines general policy and hires senior managers whose job it is to translate this general policy into detailed decisions. This chain of command, from owner to director to manager, gives rise to what is called a *principal-agent problem*— wherein managers do not always have the incentive to act in the best interests of the shareholders. The principal-agent problem is discussed later in this chapter.

Should the corporation go bankrupt, the personal liability of any one stockholder is limited to whatever money that stockholder has actually invested in the firm. Thus from a stockholder's viewpoint, one of the most important aspects of the corporation is its limited liability.

The limited liability corporation was one of the great institutional inventions of early capitalism. Its advantage over the proprietorship or partnership is that it can raise capital from a large number of individuals. Each of the individuals who invest money in the firm shares in the firm's profits but has no personal liability beyond risking the loss of the amount invested. Thus investors know how much they have at risk. Because shares are easily transferred from one person to another, a corporation has a continuity of life that is unaffected by changes in investors. Without limited liability, the large amounts of capital needed for many trading and manufacturing enterprises would have been difficult if not impossible to amass.

Fifty years ago, most corporations had a physical presence in only one country. Of course, many corporations exported some or even all of their production, and some corporations imported some of their inputs, but they did not produce outside of the country in which they were incorporated. Today, a great deal of production takes place in **transnational corporations (TNCs),** which have a physical presence in more than one country. This development has many important implications for the functioning of the economy. TNCs are discussed later in this chapter.

THE RISE OF THE MODERN CORPORATION

The direct predecessors of the modern corporation were the English chartered companies of the sixteenth century. The Muscovy Company, chartered in 1555; the East India Company, chartered in 1600; and the Hudson's Bay Company, chartered in 1609 and still operating in Canada nearly 400 years later, are famous examples of early joint-stock ventures with limited liability. Their need for many investors to finance a ship that would not return with its cargo for years—if it returned at all—made this form of organization desirable.

In the next three centuries, the need to commit large amounts of capital for long periods of time and to diversify risks was felt in other fields, and charters were granted for insurance, turnpikes and canals, and banks, as well as for foreign trade. Exploiting the new techniques of the Industrial Revolution required the growth of large firms in many branches of manufacturing. The increasing need for large firms led to the passage of laws permitting incorporation with limited liability *as a matter of right rather than as a special grant of privilege.* Such laws became common in England and in North America during the late nineteenth century.

In their widely-read book, *How the West Grew Rich,* economic historians Nathan Rosenberg and L. E. Birdzell argue the importance of these institutional innovations in response to changing circumstances. Countries that develop new institutions that are better suited to the circumstances of the changing world environment, and in particular to the rapid developments in information and communication technology, may gain a large competitive advantage; some commentators argue that new management techniques and industrial structure explain much of Japan's rapid growth in the past quarter century.

THE FINANCING OF FIRMS

The money that a firm raises for carrying on its business is sometimes called its **financial capital** (or *money capital*). This is distinct from its **real capital** (or *physical capital*), the physical assets of the firm that constitute plant, equipment, and inventories. Financial capital may be broken down into **equity capital,** which refers to funds provided by the owners of the firm, and **debt,** which refers to the funds that have been borrowed from persons or institutions who are not owners of the firm.

Use of the term *capital* is sometimes confusing—economists use *capital* to refer to an amount of money, but they also use it to refer to a physical input to the production process (like plant and equipment). Fortunately, it is usually clear from the context which concept is being referred to. Notice also that the two uses are not entirely independent, for much of the financial capital raised by a firm will be used to purchase the physical capital that the firm requires for production.

Equity Financing

The firm can raise equity capital in two ways. One is to sell newly issued shares. The other is to reinvest, or plow back, some of its own profits. Although shareholders do not receive reinvested profits directly as their dividend income, they benefit from the rise in value of their shares (called *capital gains*) that occurs if the funds are reinvested profitably. Reinvestment has become an important source of funds in modern times.

Debt Financing

Firms can also raise money by issuing debt, either by selling bonds or by borrowing from financial institutions. A **bond** is a promise to pay interest each year and to repay the principal at a stated time in the future (say, 20 years hence). Bank loans are often short-term; sometimes the firm even commits to repaying the principal on demand. Debtholders are *creditors,* not owners, of the firm: They have loaned money to the firm in return for the firm's promise to pay interest on the loan and, of course, to repay the principal. The commitment to make interest payments is a legal obligation that must be met independently of whether profits are made. Many firms that would have survived a temporary crisis had all their capital been equity-financed have been forced into bankruptcy because they could not meet their contractual obligations to pay interest to their creditors. Creditors have the first claim on the firm's funds. Only when they have been repaid in full can the stockholders attempt to recover anything for themselves.

THE GOALS OF MODERN FIRMS

One hundred years ago, the single-proprietor firm, whose manager was its owner, was common in many branches of industry. In such firms, the single-minded pursuit of profits would be expected. Today, however, ownership is commonly diversified among thousands of stockholders, and the firm's managers are rarely its owners. Arranging matters so that managers always act in the best interests of stockholders is, as we shall see, anything but straightforward.

Thus there is potential for managers to maximize something other than profits.

THE SEPARATION OF OWNERSHIP FROM CONTROL

In corporations, the stockholders elect directors, and those directors then appoint managers. Directors are supposed to represent stockholders' interests and to determine broad policies that the managers will carry out. To conduct the complicated business of running a large firm, a full-time professional management group must be given broad powers of decision making. Although managerial decisions can be reviewed from time to time, they cannot be closely monitored on a day-to-day basis. The links between the directors and the managers are typically weak enough so that top management often truly controls the corporation over long periods of time.

As long as directors have confidence in the managerial group, they accept and ratify their proposals. Stockholders in turn elect and reelect directors who are proposed to them. If the managerial group does not satisfy the directors' expectations, it may be replaced. Until recently, boards of directors replaced managers only very rarely. In the past few years, boards have become somewhat more active, and in a number of cases, the top management of major firms has been removed by directors. Examples of leadership changes initiated by board action include the replacement of CEOs at GM, Eastman Kodak, IBM, and American Express. Still, such action remains unusual.

Within fairly broad limits, then, effective control of the corporation's activities generally resides with the managers. Although the managers are legally employed by the stockholders, they remain largely independent of them. Indeed, the management group typically asks for, and gets, the *proxies* of enough stockholders to elect directors who will reappoint it, and thus it perpetuates itself in office. (A proxy authorizes a person who is attending a stockholders' meeting to cast a stockholder's vote.) In the vast majority of cases, nearly all votes cast are in the form of proxies.

None of this matters unless the managers pursue different interests from those of the stockholders. Do the interests of the two groups diverge? To study this question, we need to look at what is called principal-agent theory.

PRINCIPAL-AGENT THEORY

If you (the *principal*) hire a girl down the block (your *agent*) to mow your lawn while you are away, all you can observe is how the lawn looks when you come back. She could have mowed it every 10 days, as you agreed, or she could have waited until two days before you were due home and mowed it only once. By prevailing on a friend or a neighbor to *monitor* your agent's behaviour, you could find out what she actually did, but only at some cost.

When you visit a doctor for a diagnosis and for treatment of your lower back pain, it is almost impossible for you to monitor the physician's effort and diligence on your behalf. You have not been to medical school, and much of what the physician does will be a mystery to you.

This latter situation is close to the relationship that exists between stockholders and managers. The managers have information and expertise that the stockholders do not have—indeed, that is why they are the managers. The stockholders can observe profits, but they cannot directly observe the managers' efforts. To complicate matters further, even when the managers' behaviour can be observed, the stockholders do not generally have the expertise to evaluate whether that behaviour was the best available. Everyone can see how well the firm performs, but it takes very detailed knowledge of the firm and the industry to know how well it *could have performed*. Boards of directors, who represent the firm's stockholders, can acquire some of the relevant expertise and monitor managerial behaviour, but, again, this is costly.

These examples illustrate the **principal-agent problem**—the problem of designing mechanisms that will induce agents to act in their principals' interests. In general, unless there is close monitoring of the agent's behaviour, the problem cannot be completely solved. Hired managers (like hired gardeners) will generally wish to pursue their own goals. They cannot ignore profits because if they perform badly enough, they will lose their jobs. Just how much latitude they have to pursue their own goals at the expense of profits will depend on many things, including the degree of competition in the industry and the possibility of takeover by more profit-oriented management.

Principal-agent analysis shows that when a firm's ownership and control are separated, the self-interest of agents will tend to make profits lower than in a "perfect" world in which principals act as their own agents.

We know that in the case of firms, the principals (the stockholders) are interested in maximizing profits. What different motives might their agents (the managers) have, and what market forces might limit their ability to act on these motives?

Sales Maximization

If agents do not maximize profits on behalf of the principals, what do they do? One alternative is that they seek to maximize *sales*. Suppose that the managers need to make some minimum level of profits to keep the stockholders satisfied. Beyond this, they are free to maximize their firm's sales revenue. This might be a sensible policy on the part of management because salary, power, and prestige all rise with the size of a firm as well as with its profits. Generally, the manager of a large, normally profitable corporation will earn a salary that is considerably higher than the salary earned by the manager of a small but highly profitable corporation.

The sales-maximization hypothesis says that managers of firms seek to maximize their sales revenue, subject to a profit constraint.

Sales maximization subject to a profit constraint leads to the prediction that a firm's managers will sacrifice some profits by setting price below and output above their profit-maximizing levels. See Figure 14-1 for a demonstration of this point.

Failure to Minimize Costs

The sales-maximization hypothesis implies that the firm's managers will choose to produce more than the profit-maximizing level of output. It is also possible that firms will produce their chosen output at greater than minimum cost. Why would a firm's managers fail to minimize costs?

There are many possible answers, but the most straightforward one is that minimizing costs can demand a great deal of detailed managerial attention, and if management can avoid doing so, it would prefer not to make the necessary effort. Moreover, it is usually costly for a firm to change its routine behaviour. If this is so, one firm may operate at a higher cost than another, but it will still not be worthwhile for the first firm to copy the behaviour of the second firm. The *transactions costs* of making the change

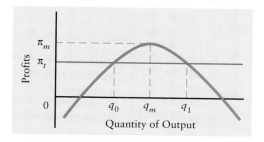

FIGURE 14-1
Output of the Firm Under Profit Maximizing, Sales Maximizing, and Satisficing Behaviour

The "best" level of output depends on the motivation of the firm. The curve shows the level of profits associated with each level of output. A profit-maximizing firm produces output q_m and earns profit π_m. A sales-maximizing firm, with a minimum profit constraint of π_t, produces the output q_1.

A satisficing firm with a target level of profits of π_t is willing to produce any output between q_0 and q_1. Thus satisficing allows a range of outputs on either side of the profit-maximizing level, whereas sales maximization results in a higher output than profit maximization.

could outweigh the benefits. As with sales maximization, pressure from stockholders, competition from other firms, and threat of takeover will limit the extent to which economic or technological inefficiency can survive, but they may not eliminate inefficiency.

THE MARKET FOR CORPORATE CONTROL

Managers who stray too far from profit maximization face the risk that their firms will be taken over by more profit-oriented ownership. **Mergers** and **takeovers** can be interpreted as transactions in a **market for corporate control.** This market, like any other, has both buyers (people who would acquire the rights to control a firm) and sellers (the current stockholders of the firm). As in other markets, the expected outcome is that the assets being bought and sold will wind up in the hands of the parties who value them most. These will tend to be those who can come closest to maximizing the firm's profits.

A takeover begins when the management of the acquiring firm makes a **tender offer** to the stockholders of the target firm. Tender offers are promises to purchase stock at a specified price for a limited pe-

riod of time, during which the acquiring firm hopes to gain control of the target company. Typically, the prices offered are considerably higher than the prevailing stock market price. This action is called a *hostile takeover* when the current management of the target firm opposes it.

Do takeovers improve economic efficiency? The main argument in their favour is that after a takeover, the new management can make more efficient use of the target firm's assets. The acquiring firm should be able to exploit profit opportunities that the target management is not exploiting. This can be done by such means as operating the target firm more efficiently, providing funds that the target firm could not obtain, or providing access to markets that would be too expensive for the target firm to open up on its own. If this is true, the value of the target firm will rise in response to a takeover, reflecting the expectation of increased future profits.[1] Further, if the *acquiring* firm's managers are acting in the best interest of *their* stockholders, the value of the acquiring firm should also rise when it is successful in a takeover bid.

Although stock values of acquiring and acquired firms show considerable variability following takeovers, most economists believe that takeovers provide a useful discipline that helps to restrain managers from acting in non-profit-maximizing ways. Such discipline helps to improve the allocation of resources as managers are under pressure to use the assets under their management in the most efficient way. In the absence of evidence to show that takeovers reduce economic efficiency (either productive or allocative), most economists would probably favour leaving the market for corporate control free from major government intervention.

NONMAXIMIZING THEORIES

Many students of corporate behaviour, particularly economists based in business schools, criticize the profit-maximization assumption from a perspective different from that given by principal-agent theory. They argue that there are other reasons for doubting that modern corporations are "simple profit-maximizing computers." They believe that corporations

---

[1]Any takeover bid is likely to raise the value of a firm on the stock market. A profitable takeover raises these values permanently; a misjudged takeover does so only temporarily.

are *profit-oriented* in the sense that, other things being equal, more profits are preferred to less profits. They do not believe, however, that corporations are profit *maximizers*.

A major group of critics of profit maximization develop their argument as follows: Firms operate in highly uncertain environments. Their long-term success or failure is determined largely by their ability to administer innovation and change. But the risks of innovation are large, and the outcomes are highly uncertain. Rational firms therefore tend to be quite risk-averse. They develop routines of behaviour that they follow as long as they are successful. Only when profits fall low enough to threaten their survival do they significantly change their course of action.

Supporters of this view argue on the basis of considerable evidence that firms react to the "stick" of threatened losses of existing profit more than to the "carrot" of possible increases in profit. Others argue that firms simply cannot handle the task of scrutinizing all possibilities, calculating the probable outcomes, and then choosing among these so as to maximize their expected profits. Instead, in their view, firms carry on with existing routines as long as these produce satisfactory profits, and only when profits fall to unacceptably low levels do the firms search for new ways of doing old things or new lines of activity.

One way of formalizing these views is the *theory of satisficing*. It was first put forward by Professor Herbert Simon of Carnegie-Mellon University, who in 1978 was awarded the Nobel Prize in Economics for his work on the behaviour of firms. He wrote, "We must expect the firm's goals to be not maximizing profits but attaining a certain level or rate of profit, holding a certain share of the market or a certain level of sales." In general, a firm is said to be **satisficing** if it does not change its behaviour, provided that a *satisfactory* (rather than optimal) level of performance is achieved.

According to the satisficing hypothesis, firms could produce any one of a range of outputs that produce profits at least equal to the target level. This contrasts with the unique output that is predicted by profit-maximizing theory. Figure 14-1 compares satisficing behaviour with sales- and profit-maximizing behaviour.

The theory of satisficing predicts not a unique level of output but a range of possible outputs that includes the profit-maximizing output.

THE IMPORTANCE OF NONMAXIMIZING BEHAVIOUR

An impressive array of empirical and theoretical evidence can be gathered in support of nonmaximizing theories. What would be the implications if they were accepted as being better theories of the behaviour of the economy than the "standard model," which is based on the assumption of profit maximization?

The Implications of Nonmaximizing Behaviour

To the extent that existing non-profit-maximizing theories are accurate, the economic system does not perform with the delicate precision that follows from profit maximization. Firms will not always respond quickly and precisely to small changes in market signals from either the private sector or government policy. Nor are they certain to make radical changes in their behaviour even when the profit incentives to do so are large.

The nonmaximizing theories imply that in many cases, firms' responses to small changes in market signals will be of uncertain speed and direction.

According to all existing theories, maximizing and nonmaximizing, firms will tend to sell more when demand increases and less when it decreases. They will also tend to alter their prices and their input mixes when they face sufficiently large changes in input prices. Moreover, there are limits to the extent to which the nonmaximizing behaviour can survive in the marketplace. Failure to respond to profit opportunities can lead to takeover by a more profit-oriented management. Although this does not mean that profits are being precisely maximized at all times, it does put real limits on the extent to which firms can ignore profits.

Profits are a potent force in the life and death of firms. The resilience of profit-maximizing theory and its ability to predict the economy's reactions to many major changes (such as the dramatic variations in energy prices that have occurred over the past two decades) suggest that firms are at least strongly motivated by the pursuit of profits.

Three key points are at issue here.

1. The extent to which firms respond predictably to changes in such economic signals as output and input prices, taxes, and subsidies

2. The extent to which nonmaximizing behaviour provides the opportunity for profit-oriented takeovers, mergers, and buyouts

3. The way in which firms manage very-long-run change

Regarding the third point, one of the most important lessons learned by economists in the past decade is that much oligopolistic competition takes place over the very-long run. How the firm performs relative to its domestic or foreign competitors with respect to product and process innovation will be the major determinant of its competitive performance over a decade or so. These matters require making decisions on highly uncertain issues. Many investigators believe that the performance of firms in these matters is best understood by theories that take account of the firm's organizational structure and the routines that it uses to guide its decision making.

Over the past decade or so, the question of how firms behave in detail has received renewed attention from both economists and organization theorists. Almost everyone in the field agrees that firms do not *exactly* maximize profits at all times and in all places. At the same time, almost everyone agrees that firms cannot stray too far from the goal of profit maximization. Just how far is too far depends on the circumstances in which firms operate and the mechanisms that firms' owners can use to influence managers. Just how much firms' nonmaximizing behaviour influences how they manage change is another important unsettled issue. These areas are at the frontier of current economic research.

Profit Maximization as an Evolutionary Equilibrium

U.S. economist Armen Alchian has suggested that in long-run equilibrium, firms will evolve to become profit maximizers. The basic argument is based on the principle of *survival of the fittest*. In a competitive environment, firms that pursue goals or adopt rules that are inconsistent with profit maximization will be unable to stay in business; firms that either choose or happen upon rules that are closer to profit maximization will displace those that do not. Eventually, only the profit-maximizing firms will survive in the marketplace.

A similar kind of argument can be applied to firms that operate in oligopolistic or monopolistic markets. Here it is not competition that forces the firm toward profit maximization in the long run but the possibility of a takeover. A firm that does not maximize profits will be less valuable than one that does maximize profits. Thus the non-profit-maximizing firm can be bought by profit-maximizing managers, who will increase its value as they increase its profits, as described earlier in this chapter.

Alchian's argument suggests the following conclusion:

Even if no firm starts out with the intention of maximizing profits, in the long run the firms that survive in the marketplace will tend to be the profit maximizers.

This view provides an apparent synthesis of maximizing and evolutionary theories of the firm. The distinction between the theories is not so stark as it might seem.

In contrast, many organization theorists point out that evolutionary equilibrium is unlikely ever to be achieved. As technology and tastes change over time, so does the behaviour that will maximize profits. Without a fixed target, a firm's behaviour will continually evolve (generally toward profit maximization) but will never reach an equilibrium. The target refuses to stay put.

Foreign investment

When takeovers involve a domestic firm being taken over by a foreign firm, a further consideration is added: How much should we worry about the nationality of the owners of firms that operate in our country? This question arises not only when foreign takeovers occur, but also when a domestic firm *merges* with a foreign firm. It pertains more generally to all **foreign direct investment (FDI)**—that is, investment which gives foreign owners control over the behaviour of firms in which the investment is made. In Canada's case, FDI gives foreign owners control over the decisions of producers located in Canada (just as Canadian FDI made abroad gives Canadian owners control over the decisions of producers located in foreign countries). In contrast, the other major category of foreign investment, called **portfolio investment,** involves no control. Major components of portfolio investment are foreign holdings of government and private-sector bonds. Portfolio investment does not usually arouse the popular concerns that are associated with FDI. The latter often causes great concern, whether it is the formation of a new foreign-owned firm in Canada, new investment by an existing foreign-owned firm (*greenfield* investment), or a takeover of a Canadian-owned firm by a foreign-owned firm (*brownfield* investment).

In the past, the major form of foreign investment was greenfield investment, and it is still important, for instance, in the establishment of Japanese transplant automobile factories in North America. In the last decade or so, more and more FDI has taken the form of mergers or acquisitions of domestically-owned firms by foreign-owned firms. Large companies have deemed it necessary to have a physical presence in each of what are called the triad set of countries: Canada and the United States; Japan and Southeast Asia; and the countries of Western Europe. Developing that presence is usually done through takeovers and mergers rather than by greenfield investment. More and more stand-alone companies found it hard to compete in the globalizing marketplace, so they welcomed mergers with firms operating throughout the triad.

For example, in 1991, 22 percent of the mergers in the United States involved at least one foreign-owned company, while the comparable figure in Canada was 73 percent. There are two interesting things about these figures. First, these figures are historically high for both countries—the participation of foreign-owned firms in mergers was significantly less 20 years earlier; this reflects the trend toward increasing globalization. Second, the much smaller size of the Canadian economy explains why, in a globalizing world, a higher proportion of Canadian than American mergers will involve foreign firms. Both figures illustrate the key development of the past two decades that much FDI took the form of international mergers as transnational corporations sought to position themselves in the markets of the world's major economies.

ATTITUDES TOWARD FOREIGN INVESTMENT

Foreign investment has long been a major factor in world development. The residents of newly settled areas, such as North and South America in the seventeenth, eighteenth, and nineteenth centuries, could not hope to generate enough savings to finance the rapid development of their vast potential. Investment funds were required in large amounts to build *infrastructure* (such as roads, dams, city halls, post offices, and bridges), *private productive facilities* (such as factories, machines, and offices), and *housing* both for rental and for ownership. In the first instance, the economic growth of all such countries was financed largely by foreign investment.

As these economies grew, they produced larger and larger flows of their own domestic saving. This saving financed an increasing proportion of domestic investment, helped to buy back much of the foreign-owned assets in their country, and provided a flow of foreign investment going to other, newer countries. This was the pattern in the United States, which was a net importer of capital from abroad until the early part of the twentieth century but became, as the century advanced, a net exporter of capital.[2]

The same pattern has been observed in Canada, but it has not yet gone as far as in the United States. This is due mainly to Canada's smaller size in relation to the investment needed to exploit its huge resources. Canada has always been a recipient of a great deal of foreign investment. As the Canadian economy grew, however, the flow of domestic saving increased. This increase in domestic saving led to an increasing proportion of new investment in Canada being financed by domestic rather than by imported capital. It also led to an increasing Canadian investment abroad as successful Canadian firms expanded into foreign markets and private Canadian investors added foreign investments to their asset portfolios.

Table 14-1 shows the stock of foreign direct investment in Canada (and the stock of Canada's direct investment abroad) as a share of the flow of Canadian GDP since 1960. As the table shows, the importance of foreign ownership in Canada has declined significantly since 1960. In 1960, the value of foreign-owned assets was about 35 percent of GDP, whereas by 1994 foreigners owned assets in Canada worth only 20 percent of Canadian GDP. Thus over the past 35 years, the Canadian economy has grown more quickly than has foreign ownership of domestic assets. Note also the increasing importance of Canada's ownership of assets located in foreign countries. In 1960, the value of foreign-located assets owned by Canadians amounted to only 5 per-

---

[2]In the 1980s the pattern was reversed, with the United States once again becoming a net importer of capital. By 1990, it was home to more foreign capital than any other country in the world.

TABLE 14-1
Foreign Direct Investment in Canada and Canadian Direct Investment Abroad, 1960–1994

Year	Foreign Direct Investment as a percentage of Canadian GDP	Canadian Direct Investment Abroad as a percentage of Canadian GDP
1960	34.5	6.3
1970	30.8	7.0
1980	20.9	8.7
1990	19.6	13.7
1994	19.7	16.7

Expressed in terms of the size of the Canadian economy, foreign direct investment in Canada has been declining and Canadian direct investment abroad has been increasing. The numbers shown are the value of the *stocks* of foreign-owned assets in Canada (or Canadian-owned assets abroad) divided by the *flow* of Canadian GDP.

(*Source:* Statistics Canada, 67–202)

cent of GDP, but by 1994 the value of Canadian direct investment abroad was almost 17 percent of GDP. Thus over the past 35 years, Canadian direct investment abroad has grown much more quickly than the Canadian economy.

World Attitudes to Foreign Investment

World attitudes toward foreign investment have been fairly tolerant throughout most of the period since the Industrial Revolution. Most people saw such investment as a benign force leading to more rapid growth, both in total output and in output per person, than could be financed through domestic savings alone.

In the late 1950s and the 1960s, many countries became more hostile to foreign investment. The change in attitude was partly the result of the growth of what was then called the *multinational enterprise,* now called the *transnational corporation (TNC).* These are firms that have locations in more than one (and often many) countries. A domestic firm may engage in international trade by selling in many countries; a transnational corporation has production facilities in many countries. In the 1960s, the vast majority of the world's TNCs were U.S.-owned.

In the 1950s and 1960s, the rise of TNCs was seen in many parts of the world as an ominous development. People correctly perceived that TNCs would make it more difficult for individual countries to

maintain economic policies that differed from those of their trading partners. For example, TNCs have some ability, through internal accounting, to shift costs to areas where local tax laws permit the greatest cost write-offs and to shift profits to areas where profit taxes are lowest. They can also often shift research and development (R&D) to where tax advantages or subsidies are largest and then make the results of this R&D available throughout their entire organization—which often means throughout the entire world.

These powers imply an inevitable weakening of the power of the individual state. It also provides a pressing reason for the creation of larger political units such as the European Union (EU) to provide the political scope necessary to exercise some control over TNCs.

In the 1960s, the rise of TNCs also aroused worldwide concern over what was perceived as U.S. economic imperialism. Because many of the most successful early TNCs were U.S.-owned, many observers in other countries feared the spread of U.S. economic dominance and cultural influence. Influential books in Europe decried the growth of U.S. economic and cultural imperialism and urged that TNCs be kept out as a defense. Today, with North American firms often on the defensive against Japanese and European TNCs, the fear of U.S. dominance seems but a quaint reminder of the human tendency to think that whatever is happening now will persist forever.

TNCs have become increasingly important over the years and now account for the majority of international trade and foreign investment. Indeed, much international trade is between different units of the same TNC (intra-TNC trade). Also, the typical organization of a TNC has undergone changes. The typical form in earlier times was a highly centralized firm. Today, with the demands for specialized products carefully tailored to the specific needs of each country and with the ability to produce small runs of each product variation efficiently thanks to computer-assisted production, internationally decentralized organizations are becoming increasingly prevalent.

By the 1980s, world attitudes toward TNCs had become tolerant again. Several developments were responsible for this softening of attitudes. First, it was clear to industrial nations that TNCs were here to stay. As world trade became more and more globalized under the impact of the communication and computer revolutions, TNCs became increasingly important until it became apparent that no advanced country could do without them. Second, less-developed countries came to the same realization and put out a welcome mat. As the executive director of the United Nations centre on TNCs said:[3]

> The 1980s have witnessed major changes in the world production system, with TNCs being the principal forces shaping the future of technological innovation. At the same time, a more pragmatic and businesslike relationship between host governments and TNCs has emerged within the past decade. Many developing countries, burdened by debt and economic stagnation, have liberalized their policies towards TNCs while these corporations have displayed greater sensitivity to the development and economic goals of host countries. The era of confrontation has receded and been replaced by a practical search for a meaningful and mutually beneficial accommodation of interests.

Canadian Attitudes to Foreign Investment

Official Canadian views have matched these swings in world views. Until the 1960s, Canada welcomed foreign investment as a means to achieving economic growth that would have been impossible had it been required to rely on domestic saving alone. Then, in the 1960s, suspicion of foreign (particularly American) investment grew. This resulted in the formation of the Foreign Investment Review Agency (FIRA) in the 1970s. This agency had the right to screen all new foreign direct investment coming into Canada. It turned down about 5 percent of the applications that it reviewed—quite a high rejection rate by international standards. It imposed requirements with respect to domestic production and exports on many of the investments that it did accept. Its presence also discouraged some unknown number of other firms from applying in the first place, making its overall effect in limiting foreign investment in the country hard to discern.

In line with the change in world opinion toward TNCs in the 1980s, the Canadian government re-

placed FIRA with an organization called Investment Canada (which has since been replaced by the Investment Review Division within Industry Canada). With the demise of FIRA, Canadian officials announced that Canada once again welcomed foreign investment. Although the Canadian government still has the power to review foreign takeovers of Canadian firms, it has turned down no applications in the past dozen years. It has, however, insisted on some conditions before approving some deals. For example, when the Canadian laser company Lumonics was taken over by the Japanese conglomerate Sumatoma (because Lumonics could not raise sufficient capital in Canada), Investment Canada insisted on a number of assurances designed to keep the creative activities of Lumonics located in Canada.

In the Canada-U.S. Free Trade Agreement (FTA) which began in 1989, Canada agreed to raise the threshold of review of U.S. takeovers of Canadian firms from a firm size of $5 million to $150 million. Critics decried this reduction in ability to screen foreign takeovers of Canadian firms. Supporters pointed out, first, that fully 80 percent of nonfinancial capital in Canada was located in firms larger than $150 million and so was still subject to review and, second, that in return for this Canadian concession, the United States had in effect exempted Canadian firms wishing to operate in that country from any review that the United States might subsequently initiate.

FDI IN CANADA: FACTS AND DEBATES

Canada is still heavily reliant on foreign direct investment. During 1994, Canada received an inflow of foreign direct investment equal to $8 billion; by the end of that year, foreigners owned a total of $148 billion worth of plant, buildings, and equipment physically located in Canada. To put this number in perspective, (see Table 14-1) this value represented just under 20 percent of the *flow* of Canadian GDP in 1994.

Canada is not just a recipient of foreign direct investment; Canadian firms are also very active investors in foreign countries. During 1994, Canada made $9.1 billion worth of new foreign direct investment; by the end of that year, Canadians owned a total of $125.2 billion worth of physical capital lo-

[3]United Nations Centre on Transnational Corporations, *Transnational Corporations in World Development: Trends and Prospects* (New York: United Nations, 1988).

cated abroad (a value equal to almost 17 percent of Canadian GDP in 1994).

Not surprisingly—given Canada's proximity to the United States—there is a great deal of foreign investment which crosses the 49th parallel. Canada is the largest single host country for U.S. foreign investment. By the end of 1993, the accumulated stock of U.S. investment in Canada was $95 billion—about 68 percent of total FDI in Canada. The United States once accounted for over 75 percent of the stock of all foreign direct investment in Canada, but this share has been gradually declining for many years.

Many people are surprised to learn of the amount of Canadian direct investment made in the United States. Canadian foreign direct investment in the United States totaled $65 billion by the end of 1993 (about 52 percent of Canada's total direct investment abroad). The gap between the two countries' holdings in each other's investment has been steadily narrowing since 1975. In recent years, Canadian TNCs have been far more aggressive investors in the United States than vice versa. As a result, Canadian direct investment in the United States grew by over 800 percent in the period 1977–1993, while U.S. direct investment in Canada grew by only about 250 percent over the same period. If present trends continue, Canadian investors will own as much of the U.S. capital stock as U.S. investors own of the Canadian capital stock shortly after the start of the twenty-first century.

Potential Benefits of Foreign Investment

By and large, but with some notable exceptions, economists have been skeptical of the view that Canada loses by foreign investment. Among the benefits attributed to foreign investment are these:

- More total investment than could be possible if all investment had to be financed by domestic saving, hence more domestic production than could otherwise be achieved

- A higher rate of growth due to a more rapid rise in the capital available for each worker

- Participation in the world's division of labour as brought about by TNCs

- Transfer of superior technology and superior management and labour practices

- Higher wages through use of best-practice technology

The first two listed advantages are important in countries, such as Canada, where domestic saving is insufficient to finance the domestic investment needed to produce a high rate of economic growth.

The third point is key in today's globalized world. The growth of global production and globalized competition, with its attendant growth of the TNCs, means that many individual firms are developing a presence over the entire trading world. If ownership of TNCs is spread evenly over several major trading countries, no single country can expect to own all of the capital in the TNCs that are operating within its borders. So if Canada is to own substantial investment in other countries, it must expect the TNCs of other countries to own substantial investments within Canada.

The fourth point concerns the transfer of new technology related to new products and new production processes. These are developed at home by Canadian firms and are then used at home as well as being taken to foreign countries. They are also developed in foreign countries and then used there as well as being brought to Canada. Just as most economists see foreign trade as mutually beneficial, most see foreign direct investment (FDI) as mutually beneficial to the countries owning and receiving the investment. Where Canadian firms have superior technology, they can gain by using it to produce *wherever* it can be profitably employed. If foreign countries have superior technology, Canada gains when this technology is brought to Canada to provide income, employment, and new knowledge. For example, the Japanese technology of lean production, which proved superior to the older assembly-line techniques, was to a significant extent transferred to Canada through the operation of the so-called Japanese transplant automobile factories. As these techniques became more widely appreciated within Canada, their use spread more rapidly to Canadian-owned firms.

The more that best-practice technology is diffused throughout the world, the higher world production is and the larger are the benefits to trading among nations. As technological know-how has spread, world income and the volume of trade have risen greatly. Countries that take part in this trade have seen both their exports and their imports rising.

Today, trade and investment tend to go together, so that a rising volume of foreign trade brings with it a rising volume of FDI. Generally, both inward- and outward-bound FDI are part of the globalizing of competition, technology diffusion, and trade from which all trading nations tend to gain.

The fifth point concerns the high wages that are generally paid by firms using the best-practice technology. Normally, labour that is employed in firms that use less up-to-date technological processes earn lower wages than labour that is employed in firms using the most productive techniques. Generally, when TNCs come to a less-developed country bringing advanced technology, wages rise (though they do not always achieve the levels of advanced countries because the productivity of labour is held down by other characteristics of the country, such as poor infrastructure). This is clear when one looks at less-developed countries whose technology is well below the state of the art, but it is also true in advanced countries. This is the point that Harvard's Robert Reich makes when he argues that the location of TNCs is more important than their ownership. According to Reich, having TNCs located in one's country using the most productive techniques that produce the highest-valued products and pay the highest wages is more important than who owns these firms.

Alleged Costs of Foreign Investment

Among the alleged costs of foreign direct investment are:

- Profits earned by foreigners rather than domestic owners
- Loss of control over resource development
- Loss of control over one's own economy
- Loss of good managerial and research jobs to foreign locations favoured by TNCs.

We consider each of these in turn.

Loss of Profits to Foreigners.   Insofar as the industries are competitive, profits are merely normal returns on capital. If foreigners provide capital that domestic sources cannot or will not provide, they get only the normal return. Employment, wages, and many other benefits stay in Canada.

More recently, however, economists have been interested in the pure profits that accompany innovations in oligopolistic industries. If innovating firms can earn large profits, these profits accrue to the firms' owners. In this case, ownership matters. This is not, however, an argument for locating Canadian-owned enterprises in Canada and keeping foreign enterprises out. What matters is the *share* of those innovating enterprises that is owned domestically. Where they operate does not matter. Indeed, to maximize the profits that the Canadian owners earn from their firms' innovations, the firms should use their new technology everywhere in the world where it is profitable to do so. If Canadian firms lose out to foreign TNCs and own a shrinking share of these innovating enterprises, Canadian income will fall relative to foreign income. But it does not matter *where* that competition occurs. The result is the same whether these Canadian firms lose market share in foreign markets or in the Canadian market.

Loss of Control over Domestic Resources.   All industries in Canada are subject to Canadian law. For example, Canada can regulate the rate of resource extraction in oil and gas and impose that regulation equally on Canadian- and foreign-owned firms operating within Canada. It can also have tough environmental laws and others that impose requirements on all firms operating within Canada.

However, TNCs do pose a serious problem called *extraterritoriality*. This occurs when the laws of a TNC's home country are extended to cover the activities of the TNC in other countries. The United States, however, has championed the principle of extraterritoriality by sometimes trying to make U.S. multinationals that operate in other countries follow U.S. laws rather than host-country laws. Thus, for example, if the United States has prohibitions against trading with Cuba (or, as it did not so long ago, with China), it tries to apply these laws not only to foreign TNCs operating within the United States but also to U.S. TNCs operating in such foreign countries as Canada and Britain. Host countries have resisted these attempts by the United States to extend its legal jurisdiction beyond its own borders, and the issue remains unresolved.

Many people worried that the Canada-U.S. Free Trade Agreement (FTA) which began in 1989, and the NAFTA which followed it, would erode Canadian sovereignty with respect to control over TNCs. Defenders of the FTA argued that such concerns were based on a misunderstanding of the principle of "national treatment," which allows Canada and the United States each to impose its own requirements on firms operating within its borders. These requirements may differ between the two countries; all that is required by national treatment is that foreign and domestic firms be treated equally *within any one country*. The only thing neither country can do is use its laws to discriminate by applying tougher laws to foreign-owned than to domestically-owned firms. So the FTA and NAFTA would appear to have introduced no new reason why foreign investment should limit Canada's ability to control its economy and its environment as it wishes.

Loss of Key Activities. Some industries are located in a country by virtue of natural advantages. For example, Canadian natural gas must be extracted in Canada, and Canadian lumber must be cut in Canada. Thus the gas and lumber industries are firmly rooted in Canada as long as supplies of these important natural resources exist. Other industries—high-tech ones are important examples—are much more flexible. They can be moved among countries to wherever the economic climate and economic policies are most favourable to them. The key characteristic of these industries is that they are knowledge-intensive. When head offices determine the location of R&D and other knowledge-intensive activities, they make decisions that influence the course of a country's economic development. They could conceivably direct the types of production with the highest values to their home countries and keep lower-value production, which produces lower wages, in host countries. But insofar as they are profit maximizers, they will choose the most profitable location, whether it be domestic or foreign.

A similar issue relates to what are called *key industries*. Some observers believe that certain industries have important *spillovers* to the rest of the economy. Keeping these key industries at home will favourably affect the value of economic activity elsewhere in the economy. If a foreign TNC takes over one of these key industries, it may relocate the industry to its own country, thereby harming the economy of the original country. Shipbuilding and steel production were thought to be key industries in the 1960s, and many people believe that automobiles and such high-tech industries as high-definition television and computers are key industries today.

These are important and unresolved issues. No one is sure how important these possibilities are. Furthermore, it is not easy to see what practical policy measures should be recommended if these possibilities were shown to be significant.

What Could Be Done?

Suppose we conclude—when all aspects of the issue are considered—that foreign investment is harmful for Canada. What could be done?

It would be impractical to prohibit all, or even most, foreign investment. First, this would greatly reduce the amount of capital available in Canada, with adverse effects on Canadian economic growth. Second, this would deny Canada's participation in the large segment of international trade that is dominated by TNCs, most of which cannot be owned by Canadians. For a small trading nation such as Canada, with over 35 percent of its GDP generated by exports, that would be a serious matter.

Given the volume of Canadian savings, the most that could be done would be to redirect foreign investment from some industries into others. This would be done by discouraging foreign investment in some key industries, hoping both that Canadian investment would flow into these industries and that foreign investment would fill in the gaps where the Canadian investment would otherwise have gone. For such a policy to be successful, bureaucrats must be able to discern the areas where it is advantageous to prevent foreign investment, Canadian capital must flow into these areas, and foreign capital must fill the gaps created by the reallocation of Canadian investment. Such a policy is full of risks, of which the following are merely illustrative.

First, because Canadian investment did not flow into the designated activities in the first place, there is a risk that it may not do so after the restrictions are imposed. Second, there is a risk that the activities will be transferred abroad if foreign TNCs are prevented from engaging in them in Canada. This is particularly likely where a foreign takeover of a Canadian firm is designed to make it a part of a large international organization with the linkages necessary for the firm's success. In this case, the substitution is not of Canadian-owned for foreign-owned activity in Canada but rather of foreign-located for Canadian-located activity. Third, politicians and administrators must be able to identify and promote those activities that are best held in Canadian ownership. Large firms, such as Canadian Pacific, Air

Canada, and Noranda, are the ones that would cause the most political problems if they were taken over by foreigners. Unfortunately, these most visible and best-known companies are not necessarily the ones with the greatest potential payoff from restricting foreign ownership, since they are likely to be only normally profitable. If there is a case to hold ownership at home, it is likely to be stronger for small and midsize industries that are not yet household names but are at the forefront of industrial development. Yet it is not clear that these are the industries that the political process would hold at home if foreign investment were once again to be seriously controlled.

Conclusion

Throughout most of the world, the debate about the value of foreign investment is not as heated as it was a decade or two ago. Most countries have come to accept that foreign investment contributes to their economic growth. There is an awareness of how easy it is to kill the goose that lays the golden eggs by adopting attitudes and passing laws that drive TNCs to relocate elsewhere. It is also accepted that TNCs play a key part in today's globalized economy. Because most TNCs can no longer be owned by any one single country, all countries that play a major part in the globalized economy must have substantial presences of foreign-owned TNCs within their boundaries.

There is debate about the need to encourage domestic ownership of certain key industries and about the need to control the activities of TNCs within one country by such means as requiring local R&D expenditure.

The prevailing view among economists during the 1980s and early 1990s has been that foreign investment is generally beneficial and that it should be subject to only a minimum of constraints. According to this view, TNCs are profit maximizers who will locate activities where it is most profitable to do so rather than hold them in their home country as a matter of course. In that case, the market activities of TNCs will produce the most efficient international allocation of resources and the highest possible living standards, both at home and in host countries. Furthermore, according to this view, the international economy with globalized competition is so complex and sophisticated that intervention to regulate investment is all too likely to do more harm than good.

Critics are not so sure. They advocate controls to hold certain key industries under domestic ownership and certain key activities, such as R&D, in home locations.

SUMMARY

A. THE ORGANIZATION OF FIRMS

- The firm is the economic unit that produces and sells commodities. The definition of the firm used in economics abstracts from real-life differences in the size and form of the organization of firms.
- The single proprietorship, the partnership, and the corporation are the major forms of business organization in Canada today. The corporation is by far the most common wherever large-scale production is required. The corporation is recognized as a legal entity; the liability of its owners (shareholders) is limited to the amount of money that they have invested in the organization. Corporate ownership is readily transferred by the sale of shares of the company's stock in securities markets.
- Firms can raise money through equity financing or debt financing. A firm's owners provide equity capital both when they purchase newly-issued shares and when the firm reinvests its profits. The firm obtains debt financing from creditors either by borrowing from financial institutions or by selling bonds to the public.

B. THE GOALS OF MODERN FIRMS

- Principal-agent theory gives support to the idea that corporate managers do not always operate in the best interests of the stockholders; that is, the managers may pursue their own interests rather than simply maximizing profits. Sales maximization is an example of such a pursuit.
- In the market for corporate control, would-be buyers of firms deal with would-be sellers (in friendly takeovers and mergers) as well as with reluctant sellers (in hostile takeovers). Buyers who believe that they can

operate a firm more profitably than can its present management can afford to pay more than the present market value of the firm's equities to acquire it. The possibility of such purchases provides an incentive for current managers to come close to maximizing the firm's profits and encourages their replacement by new buyers when they do not.

- Even if individual firms do not always maximize profits, it is possible that the industry will be characterized by behaviour that is approximately profit maximizing. The reason is that the firms that come closest to maximizing profits will prosper and grow while those further away from profit maximization will shrink or fail altogether.

C. FOREIGN INVESTMENT

- Foreign investment has played a large part in helping less-developed countries to develop over the past few centuries. In their time, Canada and the United States were less developed than the United Kingdom and some other European countries and were the recipients of large amounts of foreign investment that flowed from Europe to the New World.

- As the countries of the New World grew, they were able to generate an increasing flow of domestic saving, which reduced their need for foreign investment, repatriated some old foreign investment, and provided a flow of investment to newer, less-developed countries.

- The growth of transnational corporations means that no country can hope to own all of the capital that is devoted to the production of internationally traded commodities within its borders. TNCs are a major means by which technologies that are developed in one country are transferred to other countries. TNCs also have the power to avoid many national policies by shifting profits, costs, R&D, production, and investment around the world in response to relative incentives in different countries. This reduces the effectiveness of many national policies designed to give advantages to the initiating country.

- Although there is debate in Canada about the benefits and costs of foreign investment, such investment could not be dispensed with in today's world of globalized production and competition.

KEY CONCEPTS

Single proprietorship, partnership, and corporation
Advantages of the corporation
Debt and equity financing

Principal-agent theory
Sales maximization
Satisficing behaviour
Mergers, takeovers, and buyouts

Transnational corporations
Foreign direct investment

DISCUSSION QUESTIONS

1. In light of principal-agent theory, why might dentists and attorneys be required to subscribe to professional codes of ethics that prevent (or at least limit) their ability to sell unneeded services to their clients? Why do we not see similar codes of ethics for automobile mechanics?

2. Comment on these lead lines of recent newspaper stories.

   a. "Critic calls takeovers and mergers fiscal roulette that does nothing to contribute to Canadian national income."

   b. "The candidate called on Canadians to take back their country by ending all foreign ownership."

   c. "Union leaders worry that concern over Quebec separation may cause exodus of foreign investment from Canada."

3. Assume that each of the following assertions is factually correct. Taken together, what would they tell you about the prediction that big business is increasing its control of the North American economy?

   a. The share of total manufacturing assets owned by the 100 largest corporations has been rising over the past 25 years.

   b. The number of new firms begun each year has increased over the past 25 years.

   c. The share of manufacturing in total production has been decreasing for 40 years.

   d. Profits as a percentage of national income are no higher now than half a century ago.

4. In his now-famous article "Who Is Us?" Robert Reich criticizes U.S. policy for giving assistance to domestically-owned rather than domestically-located TNCs.

Why, he asks, should a domestically-owned firm get R&D assistance for research done in Taiwan to produce goods in Singapore that is denied to a Japanese-owned firm doing research on the West Coast to develop new products to be produced in the Midwest? Who gains the benefits from subsidies provided by governments (and paid for by taxpayers) to each of these types of firms?

5. "Our list prices are really set by our accounting department: They add a fixed markup to their best estimates of fully accounted cost and send these to the operating divisions. Managers of these divisions may not change those prices without permission of the board of directors, which is seldom given. Operating divisions may, however, provide special discounts if necessary to stay competitive." Does this testimony by the president of a leading manufacturing company suggest that his firm is a profit maximizer?

6. The leading automobile tire manufacturers sell original-equipment tires to automobile manufacturers at a price below the average total cost of all the tires they make and sell. This happens year after year. Is this consistent with profit-maximizing behaviour in the short run? In the long run? If it is not consistent, what does it show? Do original-equipment tires compete with replacement tires?

PART FIVE

THE MARKETS FOR FACTORS OF PRODUCTION

Why do university professors typically get paid more than elementary-school teachers? Why does an acre of land outside Kamloops rent for less than an acre of land in downtown Vancouver? Are governments successful in their attempts to equalize income across the various Canadian regions or in their attempts to equalize the earnings of people in different occupations? What are the effects of legislating a minimum wage? What do unions do? Is there discrimination in the labour market and, if so, what can be done about it? Should we be alarmed at the overall trend in Canada (and other countries) toward fewer manufacturing jobs but more service jobs? What is the connection between the interest rate and firms' investment in physical capital? What determines the interest rate? These are the sort of questions you will be able to answer after reading the next three chapters.

In Chapter 15, you are introduced to the way economists think about markets for *factors of production*. Not surprisingly, demand and supply play a key role. You will see several reasons for *factor-price differentials*. It is here that you will learn why the acre of land in Kamloops rents for less than the one in Vancouver. You will also see the importance of *factor mobility*, and why this mobility can thwart government efforts to reduce income inequality across regions.

Chapter 16 examines labour markets in detail. You will see how *working conditions* and *human capital* can combine to explain why some workers get paid more than others. You will learn about the effects of *legislated minimum wages*, and about the objectives of *labour unions*. You will also examine the important issue of *discrimination* in labour markets, and you will learn about government policies to redress it. Finally, you will see whether the decline of the manufacturing sector (and the rise of the service sector) is necessarily a bad thing.

Chapter 17 begins by discussing the market for *physical capital*. You will see why firms choose to buy less capital when the *interest rate* rises (and more when the interest rate falls). You will learn how the *equilibrium* interest rate is determined, and how it is affected by changes in technology. The chapter then goes on to discuss the pricing of *nonrenewable resources*, such as oil, natural gas, or minerals. You will learn how the market system works as a *conservation mechanism*—the idea that rising prices of nonrenewable resources encourage the conservation of these scarce resources.

CHAPTER 15

FACTOR PRICING AND FACTOR MOBILITY

Most people spend a considerable amount of their time working. Some of those people are fortunate enough to earn good wages, and thus have good incomes which enable them to afford some of the "good things in life." Others are not so fortunate, and earn only low wages (or are unable to find jobs at all). What determines the wages that individuals earn? What explains why professors usually get paid more than high-school teachers, or why doctors get paid more than nurses? Labour is not the only factor of production, of course. Physical capital is also important, as are land and natural resources. What determines the payments that these factors earn? Why does an acre of farm land in Northern Saskatchewan rent for far less than an acre of land in downtown Toronto? Not surprisingly, understanding why different factors of production earn different payments requires us to understand both demand-side and supply-side aspects of the relevant factor markets.

In this chapter we examine the issue of factor pricing and the closely related issue of factor mobility. Understanding what determines the payments to different factors of production will help us to understand the overall distribution of income in the economy, which is our first topic.

INCOME DISTRIBUTION AND FACTOR PRICING

The founders of Classical economics, Adam Smith (1723–1790) and David Ricardo (1772–1823), were concerned with the distribution of income among what were then the three great social classes: workers, capitalists, and landowners. They defined three factors of production as labour, capital, and land. The return to each factor was treated as the income of the respective social class.

Smith and Ricardo were interested in what determined the income of each class relative to the total national income. Their theories predicted that as society progressed, landlords would become relatively better off and capitalists would become relatively worse off. Karl Marx (1818–1883) had a different theory which predicted that as growth occurred, capitalists would become relatively better off and workers would become relatively worse off (until the whole capitalist system collapsed).

TABLE 15-1
Functional Distribution of National Income in Canada, 1994

Type of Income	Billions of Dollars	Percentage of Total
Employee Compensation	410.3	72.4
Corporate Profits	57.4	10.1
Proprietor's Income (including rent)	43.0	7.6
Interest	56.4	9.9
Total	567.1	100.0

Total income is classified here according to the nature of the factor service that earned the income. Although these data show that employee compensation accounts for over 72 percent of national income, this does not mean that workers and their families receive only that proportion of national income. Many households will have income in more than one category listed in the table.
(*Source:* Statistics Canada, 13-001.)

These nineteenth-century debates focused on what is now called the **functional distribution of income,** defined as the distribution of total income among the major factors of production. Table 15-1 presents data for the functional distribution of income in Canada in 1994.

Although functional distribution categories (wages, rent, profits) pervade current statistics, modern economists have shifted their emphasis to another way of looking at differences in incomes, called the **size distribution of income.** This refers to the distribution of income among different households without reference to the source of the income or the "social" class of the household. Tables 15-2 and 15-3 show that there is substantial inequality in the distribution of income across families, but that the system of government taxes and transfers are effective in reducing the extent of this inequality.

Inequality in the distribution of income is shown graphically in Figure 15-1, which displays the information contained in the second column of Table 15-3. This curve of income distribution, called a **Lorenz curve,** shows how much of total income is accounted for by given proportions of the nation's households. If every household had the same income, then the Lorenz curve would lie exactly along the diagonal. The farther the curve bends away from the diagonal, the less equal the distribution of income. The curve shows, for example, that in 1993 the bottom 20 percent of all Canadian households received 7.7 percent of all after-tax income.

TABLE 15-2
After-Tax Incomes of Canadian Families, 1993

Income Category	Percentage of families
Less than $9,999	2.1
$10,000–$19,999	11.8
$20,000–$29,999	18.5
$30,000–$39,999	19.2
$40,000–$49,999	16.7
$50,000–$59,999	12.0
$60,000 and over	19.7

Although average family after-tax income in 1993 was just under $40,000, many families received much less than this, and some received a great deal more. While almost 20 percent of Canadian families had very comfortable incomes of more than $60,000, 14 percent had to subsist on incomes below $20,000.

(*Source:* Statistics Canada, 13-210.)

Today, most economists devote more attention to the size distribution of income than to the functional distribution. After all, some capitalists (such as the owners of small retail stores) are in the lower part of the income scale, and some wage earners (such as professional athletes) are at the upper end of the income scale. Moreover, if someone is poor, it matters little whether that person is a landowner or a worker.

TABLE 15-3
Inequality in Family Income Distribution, 1993

Family Income Rank	Percentage of Aggregate Income	
	Before taxes and transfers	After taxes and transfers
Lowest fifth	6.4	7.7
Second fifth	12.0	13.2
Middle fifth	17.6	18.1
Fourth fifth	24.1	23.8
Highest fifth	39.9	37.2

The distribution of income is unequal before and after taxes. The first column shows the inequality of income produced by market forces. The second column shows that the Canadian system of taxes and transfers reduced income inequalities to some extent. The distribution of income is more equal in the second column because the share of total income going to the lowest three income groups increased, while the share going to the highest two groups decreased.

(*Source:* Statistics Canada, 13-207 and 13-210.)

To understand the size distribution of income, we must first study how individual incomes are determined. Superficial explanations of differences in income, such as "People earn according to their ability," are clearly inadequate. Incomes are distributed much more unequally than any *measured* index of ability, be it IQ, physical strength, or typing skill. The best professional sports players may only score twice as many points as the average players, but their salary is many times more than the average salary. Something other than simple ability is at work here. However, if answers that are couched in terms of ability are easily refuted, so are answers such as "It's all a matter of luck" or "It's just the system." In this chapter, we look beyond such superficial explanations.

FACTOR PRICING

In this chapter, we confine ourselves to goods and factor markets that are perfectly competitive. This means that individual firms are price takers in both markets. They face a given price for the product they produce, and that price is both their average revenue and their marginal revenue. Similarly, they face a given price of each factor that they buy, and that price is both the average cost and the marginal cost of the factor.

Dealing first with firms that are price takers in product and factor markets allows us to study the principles of factor-price determination in the simplest context. Once these are understood, it is relatively easy to allow for monopolistic elements in either or both types of markets. This is done in Chapter 16.

The income that a factor earns depends on the price charged for its services and on the quantity that is employed. To determine factor incomes, therefore, we need to ask how markets determine these prices and quantities. To anticipate, the answer is that factor prices and quantities are determined in just the same way as the prices and quantities of goods—by the interaction of demand and supply. What is new about factor pricing arises from the *determinants* of factor demands and factor supplies.

THE LINK BETWEEN OUTPUT AND INPUT DECISIONS

In Chapters 8 and 9, we saw how firms' costs varied with their outputs and how they could achieve cost

FIGURE 15-1
A Lorenz Curve of Family Income in Canada, 1993

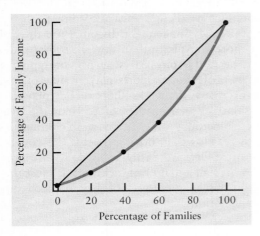

The size of the shaded area between the Lorenz curve and the diagonal is a measure of the inequality of income distribution. If there were complete income equality, the bottom 20 percent of income receivers would receive 20 percent of the income, and so forth, and the Lorenz curve would coincide with the diagonal line. Because the lowest 20 percent receive less than 8 percent of the income, the Lorenz curve lies below the diagonal line. The extent to which it bends away from the straight line indicates the amount of inequality in the distribution of income. This Lorenz curve graphs the data from the second column in Table 15-3.

minimization by finding the least-cost combination of factors to produce any given output. In Chapter 10, we saw that firms in perfect competition decided how much to produce by equating their marginal costs to given market prices. We also saw how the market supply curve interacted in each product's market with the market demand curve of consumers. This interaction determines the market price as well as the quantity that is produced and consumed.

These events in goods markets have implications for factor markets. The decisions of firms on how much to produce and how to produce it imply specific demands for various quantities of the factors of production. These demands, together with the supplies of the factors of production (which are determined by the owners of the factors), come together in factor markets. Together they determine the quantities of the various factors of production that are employed, their prices, and the incomes earned by their owners.

The foregoing discussion shows that there is a close relationship between the production and pricing of the goods and services produced by firms on the one hand and the pricing, employment, and incomes earned by the factors of production they hire on the other hand. They are two aspects of a single set of economic activities relating to the production of goods and services and the allocation of the nation's resources among their various possible uses. This discussion provides a brief introduction to one of the great insights of economics:

When demand and supply interact to determine the allocation of resources among various lines of production, they also determine the incomes of the factors that are used in producing the goods.

The rest of this chapter is an elaboration of this important theme. We first study the demand for factors, then their supply, and finally how demand and supply come together to determine factor prices and quantities.

THE DEMAND FOR FACTORS

Firms require the services of land, labour, capital, and natural resources to be used as inputs. Firms also use as inputs the products of other firms, such as steel, legal services, and electricity.

If we investigate the production of these produced inputs, we will find that they, too, are made by using land, labour, capital, natural resources, and other produced inputs. If we continue following through the chain of products used as inputs, we can account for all of the economy's output in terms of inputs of the basic factors of production—land, labour, capital, and natural resources. The theory of factor pricing applies to *all* inputs used by a firm. The theory of distribution explains the division of total national income among the owners of the basic factors: land, labour, capital, and natural resources. It also explains the division of income between the *different types* of labour (such as highly skilled or less-skilled workers) and the different types of other factors (such as arable land and poor land, or new capital equipment and obsolete capital equipment).

Firms require inputs not for their own sake but as a means to produce goods and services. For example, the demand for computer programmers and technicians is growing as more and more computers are used. The demand for carpenters and building materials rises and falls as the amount of housing construction rises and falls. The demand for any input is therefore *derived from the demand* for the goods and services that it helps to produce; for this reason, the demand for a factor of production is said to be a **derived demand.**

Derived demand provides a link between the markets for output and the markets for inputs.

THE FIRM'S MARGINAL DECISION ON FACTOR USE

What determines whether an individual firm will choose to hire one extra worker, or whether the same firm will decide to use one extra machine, or an extra kilowatt-hour of electricity? Since we are considering whether the firm will use one *extra unit* of some factor, we refer to this as the firm's *marginal decision* on factor use.

We start by deriving a famous relation that holds for every factor employed by profit-maximizing firms. In Chapter 10, we established the rules for the maximization of a firm's profits in the short run. When one factor is fixed and another is variable, the profit-maximizing firm increases its output until the last unit produced adds just as much to cost as to revenue, that is, until marginal cost equals marginal revenue. Another way of stating that the firm maximizes profits is to say that the firm will increase production up to the point at which the last unit of the variable factor employed adds just as much to revenue as it does to cost.

The addition to total cost resulting from employing one more unit of a factor is that factor's price. (Recall that the firm is assumed to buy its factors in competitive markets.) So if one more worker is hired at a wage of $15 per hour, the addition to the firm's costs is $15. The amount that a unit of a variable factor adds to revenue is the amount that the unit adds to total output multiplied by the change in revenue caused by selling an extra unit of output.

In Chapter 8, we introduced the concept of *marginal product*—the amount by which output increased when the variable factor was increased by one unit. When dealing with factor markets, economists use the term **marginal physical product (MPP)** to avoid confusion with the revenue concepts that they also need to use. The change in revenue caused

by selling one extra unit of output is just the price of the output, *P* (because the firm is a price taker in the market for its output). The resulting amount, which is *MPP* × *P*, is called the factor's **marginal revenue product (MRP).**[29] For example, if the variable factor's marginal physical product is 2 units per hour and the price of a unit of output is $7.50, the factor's marginal revenue product is $15 ($7.50 × 2).

We can now restate the condition for a firm to be maximizing its profits in two ways. First:

$$\begin{matrix} \text{Marginal} & & \text{Marginal} \\ \text{Cost of the} & = & \text{Revenue Product} \\ \text{Factor} & & \text{of the Factor} \end{matrix} \qquad [1]$$

Because the firm is a price taker in both its input and output markets, we can restate Equation 1 by noting that the left-hand side is just the price of a unit of the variable factor, which we call *w*, and the right-hand side is the factor's marginal physical product, multiplied by the price at which the output is sold. In words, this gives us

$$\begin{matrix} \text{Price of} & & \text{Factor's Marginal} \\ \text{a Unit of} & = & \text{Physical Product} \\ \text{the Factor} & & \text{times its Price} \end{matrix} \qquad [2a]$$

Expressed in symbols, this is

$$w = MPP \times P \qquad [2b]$$

To check your understanding of Equation 2, consider an example. Suppose that the factor is available to the firm at a cost of $10 a unit (*w* = $10). Suppose also that employing another unit of the factor adds 3 units to output (*MPP* = 3). Suppose further that output is sold for $5 a unit (*P* = $5). Thus the additional unit of the factor adds $15 to the firm's revenue and $10 to its costs. Hiring one more unit of the factor brings in $5 more than it costs. *The firm will take on more of the factor whenever its marginal revenue product exceeds its price.*

Now assume, however, that the last unit of the factor taken on by the firm has a marginal physical product of 1 unit of output—it adds only one extra unit to output—and so adds only $5 to revenue. Clearly, the firm can increase profits by cutting back on its use of the factor because laying off 1 unit reduces revenues by $5 while reducing costs by $10. *The firm will lay off units of the factor whenever its marginal revenue product is less than its price.*

Finally, assume that another unit of the factor taken on or laid off changes revenue by $10. Now the firm cannot increase its profits by altering its employment of the variable factor in either direction.

The firm cannot increase its profits by altering employment of the factor whenever the factor's marginal revenue product equals its price.

This example illustrates what was said earlier, and we are doing nothing that is essentially new—instead, we are merely looking at the firm's profit-maximizing behaviour from the point of view of its inputs rather than its output. In Chapters 10 and 11, we saw the firm varying its output until the marginal cost of producing another unit was equal to the marginal revenue derived from selling that unit. Now we see the same profit-maximizing behaviour in terms of the firm's varying its inputs until the marginal cost of another unit of input is just equal to the revenue derived from selling that unit's marginal product.

THE FIRM'S DEMAND CURVE FOR A FACTOR

We now know what determines the quantity of a variable factor a firm will buy when facing some specific price of the factor and some specific price of its output. Next we wish to derive the firm's *entire* demand curve for a factor, which tells us how much of the factor the firm will buy at *each* price.

To derive a firm's demand curve for a factor, we start by considering the right-hand side of Equation 2b, which tells us that the factor's marginal revenue product is composed of a physical component and a value component. We examine these two separate components in turn.

The Physical Component of *MRP*: *MPP*

As the quantity of the variable factor changes, output will change. The hypothesis of diminishing returns, first discussed in Chapter 8, predicts what will happen: As the firm adds further units of the variable factor to a given quantity of the fixed factor, the additions to output will eventually get smaller and smaller. In other words, the factor's marginal physical product declines. This is illustrated in part (i) of Figure 15-2. The negative slope of the *MPP* curve reflects the operation of the law of diminishing returns: Each unit of labour adds less to total output than the previous unit.

The Value Component of *MRP*: *MR*

To convert the marginal physical product curve of Figure 15-2(i) into a curve showing the marginal rev-

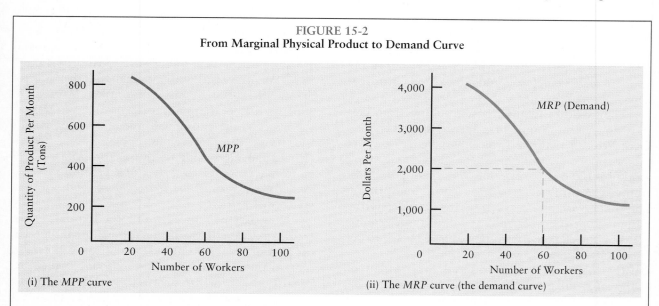

FIGURE 15-2
From Marginal Physical Product to Demand Curve

(i) The *MPP* curve

(ii) The *MRP* curve (the demand curve)

Each additional unit of the factor employed adds a certain amount to total product, as shown in part (i), and hence a certain amount to total revenue, as shown in part (ii). This determines the amount of the factor that firms will demand at each price.

enue product of the variable factor, we need to know the dollar value of the extra physical product. As long as the firm sells its output in a competitive market, the dollar value of *one extra* unit of output (marginal revenue) is simply the market price of the product. In this case, the marginal revenue product of the factor is simply the marginal physical product multiplied by the market price of output.

Part (ii) of Figure 15-2 shows a marginal revenue product curve for labour on the assumption that the firm sells its product in a competitive market at a price of $5 per unit. This curve shows—for each level of total employment of the factor—how much would be added to revenue by employing one more unit of the factor. Thus, the *MRP* curve represents $MPP \times MR$ for each additional unit of the factor. Since the *MR* for a firm in perfect competition is simply equal to price, the *MRP* curve has the same shape as the *MPP* curve.

Note, however, that if the firm were not perfectly competitive, then *MR* would not be equal to price. If *MR* declines as output increases (as it does whenever the firm is not a price taker), then the *MRP* curve will be steeper than the *MPP* curve; this is because the increase in output produced by the extra unit of the factor leads to a fall in the price of the product.

From *MRP* to the Demand Curve

Equation 2a states that the profit-maximizing firm will employ additional units of the factor up to the point at which the *MRP* equals the price of the factor. For example, in Figure 15-2, if the price of the variable factor were $2,000 per month, the profit-maximizing firm would employ 60 workers. (There is no point in employing a sixty-first because that would add less than $2,000 to revenue but a full $2,000 to costs.) So the profit-maximizing firm hires the quantity of the variable factor that equates the marginal revenue product with the price of the variable factor. Thus the curve that relates the quantity of the variable factor employed to its *MRP* is also the curve that relates the quantity of the variable factor the firm wishes to employ to its price.

The *MRP* curve of the variable factor is the firm's (derived) demand curve for that variable factor.

ELASTICITY OF FACTOR DEMAND

The elasticity of demand for a factor measures the *degree* of the response of the quantity demanded to a

change in its price. The preceding sections have explained the *direction* of the response; that is, that quantity demanded is negatively related to price. But you should not be surprised to hear that the magnitude of the response depends on the strength of various effects. For example, the extent of diminishing returns to labour, and the ability of the firm to substitute between labour and other factors of production, will both affect the firm's elasticity of demand for labour. This section presents the four principles of derived demand that come from the work of the English economist Alfred Marshall (1842–1924).

Diminishing Returns

The first influence on the slope of the demand curve for a factor is the diminishing marginal productivity of that factor. If marginal productivity declines rapidly as more of a variable factor is employed, a fall in the factor's price will not induce many more units to be employed. Conversely, if marginal productivity falls only slowly as more of a variable factor is employed, there will be a large increase in quantity demanded as price falls.

For example, both labour and fertilizers are used by farmers who produce vegetables for sale in nearby cities. For many crops, additional doses of fertilizers add significant amounts to yields over quite a wide range of fertilizer use. Although the marginal product of fertilizer does decline, it does so rather slowly as more and more fertilizer is used. In contrast, although certain amounts of labour are needed for planting, weeding, and harvesting, there is only a small range over which additional labour can be used productively. The marginal product of labour, although high for the first units, declines rapidly as more and more labour is used. Under these circumstances, such farmers will have a more elastic demand for fertilizer than for labour.

Substitution Between Factors

In the long run, all factors are variable. If one factor's price rises, firms will try to substitute relatively cheaper factors for it. For this reason, the slope of the demand curve for a factor is influenced by the ease with which other factors can be substituted for the factor whose price has changed.

The ease of substitution depends on the substitutes that are available and on the technical conditions of production. It is often possible to vary factor proportions in surprising ways. For example, in automobile manufacturing and in building construction, glass and steel can be substituted for each other simply by varying the dimensions of the windows. Another example is that construction materials can be substituted for maintenance labour in the case of most durable consumer goods. This is done by making the product more or less durable and more or less subject to breakdowns by using more or less expensive materials in its construction.

Such substitutions are not the end of the story. Plant and equipment are being replaced continually, which allows more or less capital-intensive methods to be built into new plants in response to changes in factor prices. Similarly, engines that use less gasoline per kilometre tend to be developed when the price of gasoline rises severely.

Importance of the Factor

Other things being equal, the larger the fraction of the total costs of producing some commodity that are made up of payments to a particular factor, the greater the elasticity of demand for that factor.

To see this, suppose that wages account for 50 percent of the costs of producing a good and raw materials account for 15 percent. A 10 percent rise in the price of labour raises the cost of producing the commodity by 5 percent (10 percent of 50 percent), but a 10 percent rise in the price of raw materials raises the cost of the commodity by only 1.5 percent (10 percent of 15 percent). The larger the increase in the cost of production, the larger the shift in the commodity's supply curve and hence the larger the decreases in quantities demanded of both the commodity and the factors used to produce it.

Elasticity of Demand for the Output

Other things being equal, the more elastic is the demand for the commodity that the factor is used to produce, the more elastic is the demand for the factor.

If an increase in the price of the commodity causes a large decrease in the quantity demanded—that is, if the demand for the commodity is highly elastic—there will be a large decrease in the quantity of a factor needed to produce it in response to a rise in the factor's price. However, if an increase in the price of a commodity causes only a small decrease in the quantity demanded—that is, if the demand for the commodity is inelastic—there will be only a small decrease in the quantity of the factor required in response to a rise in its price.

In Extension 15-1, the forces affecting the elasticity of the derived demand curves that have just been discussed are related more specifically to the market for the industry's output.

THE SUPPLY OF FACTORS

When we consider the supply of any factor of production, we can consider supply at three different levels of aggregation:

- the amount supplied to the economy as a whole

- the amount supplied to a particular use (such as a particular industry or occupation)

- the amount supplied to a particular user (such as a particular firm)

The elasticity of supply of a factor will normally be different at each of these levels of aggregation. This is because the amount of factor mobility is very different at these different levels of aggregation; a given factor of production is often very mobile between firms within a given industry, less mobile between different industries, and almost completely immobile from the perspective of the entire economy. As an example, an electrician may be very mobile between industries within a given city, reasonably mobile between provinces, but it may be very difficult for that electrician to move to another country to find a job. In this section, we examine the relationship between factor mobility and the supply of factors of production. We start with the highest level of aggregation, the supply of each factor to the economy as a whole.

THE TOTAL SUPPLY OF FACTORS

At any one time, the total supply of each factor of production is given. For example, in each country, the labour force is of a certain size, so much arable land is available, and there is a given supply of discovered petroleum. However, these supplies can and do change in response to both economic and noneconomic forces. Sometimes the change is very gradual, as when a climatic change slowly turns arable land into desert or when medical advances re-

EXTENSION 15-1

MARSHALL'S PRINCIPLES OF DERIVED DEMAND

The great English economist Alfred Marshall (1842–1924) referred to the two propositions derived here as the principles of **derived demand**.

1. The larger the proportion of total costs accounted for by a factor, the more elastic the demand for it.

Consider the figure on the left. The demand curve for the industry's product is D and, *given the factor's original price,* the industry supply curve is S_0. Equilibrium is at E_0 with output at q_0.

Suppose that the factor's price then falls. If the factor accounts for a small part of the industry's total costs, each firm's marginal cost curve shifts downward by only a small amount. So also does the industry supply curve, as illustrated by the supply curve S_1. Output expands only a small amount to q_1, which implies only a small increase in the quantity of the factor demanded.

If the factor accounts for a large part of the industry's total costs, each firm's marginal cost curve shifts downward a great deal. So also does the indus-

try supply curve, as illustrated by the curve S_2. Output expands to q_2, which implies a large increase in the quantity of the factor demanded.

2. The more elastic the demand curve for the product made by a factor, the more elastic the demand for the factor.

Now consider the figure on the right. The original demand and supply curves for the industry's product intersect at E_0 to produce an industry output of q_0. A fall in the price of a factor causes the industry supply curve to shift downward to S_1.

When the demand curve is relatively inelastic, as shown by the curve D_i, industry output increases by only a small amount, to q_1. The quantity of the factor demanded only increases by a correspondingly small amount.

When the demand curve is relatively elastic, as shown by the curve D_e, industry output increases by a large amount to q_2. The quantity of the factor demanded then increases by a correspondingly large amount.

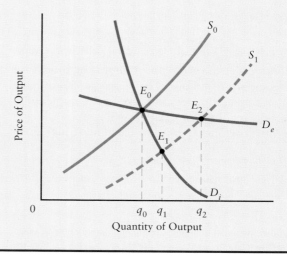

duce the rate of infant mortality and hence increase the rate of population growth, thereby eventually increasing the supply of adult labour. Sometimes the changes can be quite rapid, as when a boom in busi-

ness activity brings retired persons back into the labour force or a rise in the price of agricultural produce encourages the draining of marshes to add to the supply of farmland.

The Total Supply of Capital

The supply of capital in a country consists of the stock of existing machines, plants, and equipment.[1] Capital is a manufactured factor of production, and its total supply is in no sense fixed, although it changes only slowly. Each year, the stock of capital goods is diminished by the amount that becomes physically or economically obsolete and is increased by the amount that is newly produced. The difference between these is the net addition to (or net subtraction from) the capital stock. On balance, the trend has been for the capital stock to grow from decade to decade over the past few centuries. We will consider the determinants of investment in capital in Chapter 17.

The Total Supply of Land

The total area of dry land in a country is almost completely fixed, but the supply of *fertile* land is not fixed.[2] Considerable care and effort are required to sustain the productive power of land. If farmers earn low incomes, they may not provide the necessary care, and the land's fertility may be destroyed within a short time. In contrast, high earnings from farming may provide the incentive to increase the supply of arable land by irrigation and other forms of reclamation.

The Total Supply of Labour

The number of people willing to work is called the labour force; the total number of hours they are willing to work is called the *supply of effort* or, more simply, the **supply of labour.** The supply of labour depends on three influences: the size of the population, the proportion of the population willing to work, and the number of hours worked by each individual. Each of these is partly influenced by economic forces.

Population.   The population of a country varies over time, and these variations are influenced to some extent by economic forces. There is some evidence, for example, that the birthrate and the net immigration rate (immigration minus emigration) are higher in good times than in bad.

Labour-Force Participation.   The proportion of the total population that is willing to work is called the *labour-force participation rate*. We can also define participation rates for subgroups, such as women or youths. Participation rates vary in response to many influences, including changes in attitudes and tastes. The enormous rise in female participation rates in the past four decades is one example. Another is a lowering of the retirement age, which has the effect of reducing the overall labour-force participation rate.

Forces other than tastes also play a role in determining the labour-force participation rate. For example, a rise in the demand for labour, and an accompanying rise in the wage, will lead to an increase in the proportion of the population willing to work. More married women and elderly people enter the labour force when the demand for labour is high. For the same reasons, the labour force tends to decline when earnings and employment opportunities decline.[3]

Hours Worked.   The wage rate not only influences the number of *people* in the labour force, but it is also a major determinant of the number of *hours* worked for each person. When workers sell their leisure services to employers, they are trading leisure for income. By giving up leisure in order to work, they obtain income with which to buy goods. They can therefore be thought of as trading leisure for goods.

A rise in the wage implies a change in the relative price of goods and leisure. Goods become cheaper relative to leisure because each hour worked buys more goods than before. Or, looked at the other way around, an increase in the wage means that leisure becomes more expensive relative to goods, because each hour of leisure consumed is at the cost of more goods forgone.

---

[1]Recall the distinction between *financial capital* (the money that a firm raises to carry on its business) and *physical capital* (the assets of the firm like buildings and equipment). In this chapter, whenever we use the term "capital" we are referring to physical capital.
[2]Although natural resources are often included with land as a single factor of production, they have so many important special characteristics that it is sometimes worthwhile treating them as a separate factor. Some of the issues involved with pricing natural resources are discussed in Chapter 17.

[3]Economists sometimes refer to the decline in labour-force participation in bad economic times when there are few job opportunities as the *discouraged-worker effect*. When there is a temporary decline in family income, perhaps because one member of the family loses a job in a recession, the number of family members seeking market work may increase; this is known as the *added-worker effect*. Generally, the discouraged-worker effect is larger than the added-worker effect during recessions; the labour-force participation rate declines during recessions and increases during periods of economic recovery.

It is not necessarily the case, however, that an increase in the wage increases the amount of hours worked. This is because an increase in the wage generates both income and substitution effects (see Chapter 7), and these effects typically work in opposite directions. As the wage rises, the substitution effect leads the individual to consume more goods and less leisure because leisure is now relatively more expensive (in terms of foregone goods). The income effect of a higher wage, however, leads the individual to consume more goods *and* more leisure. Since the income and substitution effects work in the same direction for the consumption of goods, we can be sure that a rise in the wage rate will lead to a rise in goods consumed. However, because the two effects work in the opposite direction for leisure, the following is true:

A rise in the wage rate leads to less leisure being consumed (more hours worked) when the substitution effect is the dominant force and to more leisure consumed (fewer hours worked) when the income effect is the dominant force.

Much of the long-run evidence suggests that as real hourly wage rates rise for the economy as a whole, people wish to *reduce* the number of hours they work, indicating that the income effects of wage increases dominate the substitution effects. Extension 15-2 provides a more detailed treatment of these two effects using indifference curves. (Recall the Appendix to Chapter 7.)

THE SUPPLY OF FACTORS TO A PARTICULAR USE

Most factors have many uses. A given piece of land can be used to grow any one of several crops, or it can be subdivided for a housing development. A computer programmer living in the Ottawa valley can work for one of several firms, for the government, or for Carleton University. A lathe can be used to make many different products, and it requires no adaptation when it is turned for one use or another.

One industry or occupation can attract a factor away from another industry or occupation, even though the total supply of that factor may be fixed. Thus a factor's elasticity of supply to a particular use is larger than its elasticity of supply to the entire economy.

Factor Mobility

When considering the supply of a factor for a particular use, the most important concept is **factor mobility**. A factor that shifts easily between uses in response to small changes in incentives is said to be *mobile*. Its supply to any one of its uses will be elastic because a small increase in the price offered will attract many units of the factor from other uses. A factor that does not shift easily from one use to another, even in response to large changes in remuneration, is said to be *immobile*. It will be in inelastic supply in any one of its uses because even a large increase in the price offered will attract only a small inflow from other uses. Often a factor may be immobile in the short run but mobile in the long run.

An important key to factor mobility is time: The longer the time interval, the easier it is for a factor to convert from one use to another.

Consider the factor mobility among particular uses of each of the three key factors of production.

Capital. Some kinds of capital equipment—lathes, trucks, and computers, for example—can be shifted readily among uses; many others are comparatively unshiftable. A great deal of machinery is quite specific: Once built, it must be used for the purpose for which it was designed, or it cannot be used at all. Indeed, it is the immobility of much fixed capital equipment that makes the exit of firms from declining industries the slow and difficult process described in Chapter 10.

In the long run, however, capital is highly mobile. When capital goods wear out, a firm may simply replace them with identical goods, or it may exercise other options. It may buy a newly designed machine to produce the same goods, or it may buy machines to produce totally different goods. Such decisions lead to changes in the long-run allocation of a country's stock of capital among various uses.

Land. Land, which is physically the least mobile of factors, is one of the *most mobile* in an economic sense. Consider agricultural land. In a given year, one crop can be harvested and a totally different crop can be planted. A farm on the outskirts of a growing city can be sold for subdivision and development on short notice. Once land is built on, its mobility is much reduced. A site on which a hotel has been built can be converted into a warehouse site, but it takes a large differential in the value of land use to make that transfer worthwhile because the hotel must be torn down.

EXTENSION 15-2

THE SUPPLY OF LABOUR

The discussion in the text can be formalized for readers who have studied indifference curves in the appendix to Chapter 7. The key proposition is this:

Because a change in the wage rate has an income effect and a substitution effect that work in opposite directions, the supply curve of labour may have a positive or a negative slope.

Part (i) of the figure plots leisure on the horizontal axis and the consumption of goods (measured in dollars) on the vertical axis. The budget line always starts at 24, indicating that all individuals are endowed with 24 hours a day that they may either consume as leisure or trade for goods by working.

At the original wage rate, the individual could obtain q_a of goods by working 24 hours (i.e., the hourly wage rate is $q_a/24$). The outcome is at point E_0, where the individual consumes l_0 of leisure and works $24 - l_0$ hours in return for q_0 of goods.

The wage rate now rises so that q_b becomes available if 24 hours are worked (i.e., the hourly wage rate rises to $q_b/24$). The individual now chooses point E_1, where the consumption of leisure

falls to l_1 and the individual works $24 - l_1$ hours in return for a consumption of q_1 of goods. The rise in wages increases hours worked.

The hourly wage rate now rises further to $q_c/24$, and the individual chooses point E_2. Consumption of leisure rises to l_2, and $24 - l_2$ hours are worked in return for an increased consumption of q_2 of goods. This time, therefore, the rise in the wage rate lowers hours worked.

Part (ii) of the figure shows the same behaviour as in part (i), using a supply curve. It plots the number of hours worked against the wage rate. At wage rates of up to $\underline{w}$, the individual is not in the labour force, for no work is offered. As the wage rate rises from $\underline{w}$ to w^*, more and more hours are worked, so the supply curve of effort has the normal positive slope. The wage rates that result in E_0 and E_1 in part (i) of the figure lie in this range. Above w^*, the quantity of effort falls as wages rise so that the supply curve has a negative slope. This latter case is often referred to as a *backward-bending supply curve of labour*. The wage that gives rise to point E_2 in part (i) lies in this range.

(i) Indifference curves

(ii) A supply curve of effort

Although land is highly mobile among alternative uses, it is completely immobile as far as location is concerned. There is only so much land within a given distance of the center of any city, and no increase in the price paid can induce further land to be located within that distance. This locational immobility has important consequences, including high prices for desirable locations and the tendency to build tall buildings to economize on the use of scarce land, as in the centre of large cities.

Labour.   Labour is unique as a factor of production in that the supply of the service often requires the physical presence of the person who supplies it.[4]

Absentee landlords, while continuing to live in the place of their choice, can obtain income from land that is located in remote parts of the world. Investment can be shifted from iron mines in South Africa to mines in Labrador while the owners commute between Calgary and Hawaii. However, when a worker who is employed by a firm producing men's ties in Montreal decides instead to supply his or her labour services to a firm producing women's shoes in Winnipeg, the worker must physically travel to Winnipeg. This has an important consequence.

Because of the need for labour's physical presence when its services are provided for the production of many commodities, nonmonetary considerations are much more important for the supply of labour than for other factors of production.

People may be satisfied with or frustrated by the kind of work that they do, where they do it, the people with whom they do it, and the social status of their occupations. Because these considerations influence their decisions about what they will do with their labour services, they will not always move just because they could earn a higher wage.

Nevertheless, labour does move among industries, occupations, and areas in response to changes in the signals provided by wages and opportunities for employment. The ease with which movement occurs depends on many forces. For example, it is

not difficult for a secretary to shift from one company to another in order to take a job in Red Deer, Alberta, instead of Regina, Saskatchewan, but it can be difficult for a secretary to become an editor, a model, a machinist, or a doctor within a short period of time. Workers who lack ability, training, or inclination find certain kinds of mobility difficult or impossible.

Some barriers to movement may be virtually insurmountable once a person's training has been completed. It may be impossible for a farmer to become a surgeon or for a truck driver to become a professional athlete, even if the relative wage rates change greatly. However, the children of farmers, doctors, truck drivers, and athletes, when they are deciding how much education or training to obtain, are not nearly as limited in their choices as their parents, who have already completed their education and are settled in their occupations.

In any given year, some people enter the labour force directly from school, and others leave it through retirement or death. The turnover in the labour force owing to these causes is 3 or 4 percent per year. Over a period of 10 years, the allocation of labour can change dramatically merely by directing new entrants to jobs other than the ones that were left vacant by workers who left the labour force.

The role of education in helping new entrants to adapt to available jobs is important. In a society in which education is provided to all, it is possible to achieve large increases in the supply of any needed labour skill within a decade or so. These issues are discussed at greater length in the first part of Chapter 16.

The labour force as a whole is mobile, even though many individual members in it are not.

THE SUPPLY OF FACTORS TO A PARTICULAR FIRM

Most firms usually employ a small proportion of the total supply of each factor that they use. As a result, they can usually obtain their factors at the going market price. This is true both in the case of less-skilled workers and in the case of highly skilled workers. For example, a firm of management consultants can usually augment its clerical staff by placing an ad in the local newspaper and paying the going rate for clerks. A university which is hoping to expand its economics department can similarly place

---

[4]Labour must be physically present if it is helping in the direct production of most goods, such as automobiles, and of some services, such as haircuts. In other cases, however, labour services, such as consulting, design of a product, or writing advertising copy, can be supplied at a distance and its product communicated to the purchaser by such means as phone, fax, or mail.

an ad in *The Economist* or in a professional journal; it would also find itself paying the going rate for economics professors. In neither case will the employer's hiring actions affect the rate of pay earned by clerks (or professors) in its area.

Most firms are price takers in factor markets.

THE OPERATION OF FACTOR MARKETS

Once you have mastered the basic analysis of demand and supply in Chapters 4 through 6, the determination of the price, quantity, and income of a factor in a single market poses no new problems. Figure 15-3 shows a competitive market for a factor where the intersection of the demand and the supply curve determine the factor's price and the quantity of it that is employed. The price times quantity is the factor's total income, and that amount, divided by the

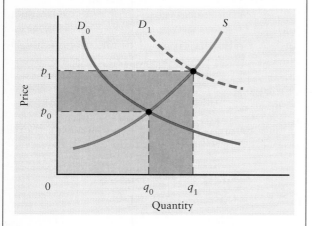

FIGURE 15-3
The Determination of Factor Price and Income in a Competitive Factor Market

In competitive factor markets, demand and supply determine factor prices, quantities of factors used, and factor incomes. With demand and supply curves D_0 and S, the price of the factor will be p_0 and the quantity employed will be q_0. The total income earned by the factor is the light gray shaded area. A shift in demand from D_0 to D_1 raises equilibrium price and quantity to p_1 and q_1, respectively. The income earned by the factor rises by an amount equal to the dark gray shaded area.

total income earned by all factors in the economy, represents that factor's share of the nation's total income.

In this section, we explore three issues relating to factor pricing. First, what explains the differences in payments received by different units of the same factor? For example, why do some workers get paid more than others? Second, what is the effectiveness of policies designed to reduce these differences? For example, can policies that promote "pay equity" eliminate these differences? Finally, we explore the important concept of *economic rent*.

DIFFERENTIALS IN FACTOR PRICES

Why is it that airline pilots typically get paid more than auto mechanics? Why does an acre of land in downtown Calgary rent for much more than an acre of land 150 kilometres away in the Crowsnest Pass? Do such differences in factor payments reflect some aspect of the factor markets that is not functioning properly, or are such *factor-price differentials* to be expected in well-functioning markets?

If every labourer were the same, if all benefits were monetary, and if workers moved freely among markets, the price of labour would tend to be the same in all uses. Workers would move from low-priced jobs to high-priced ones. The quantity of labour supplied would diminish in occupations in which wages were low, and the resulting labour shortage would tend to force those wages up; the quantity of labour supplied would increase in occupations in which wages were high, and the resulting surplus would force wages down. The movement would continue until there were no further incentives to change occupations—that is, until wages were equalized in all uses.

In fact, however, wage differentials commonly occur. These differentials may be divided into two distinct types: those that exist only temporarily and those that persist in long-term equilibrium.

As it is with labour, so it is with other factors of production. If all units of any factor of production were identical and moved freely among markets, all units would receive the same remuneration in equilibrium. In fact, however, different units of any one factor receive different payments.

Temporary Differentials

Some factor-price differentials reflect temporary disturbances. They are brought about by circumstances such as the growth of one industry and the decline of another. The differentials themselves lead to reallocation of factors, and such reallocations in turn act to eliminate the differentials.

Consider the effect on factor prices of a rise in the demand for air transport and a decline in the demand for rail transport. The airline industry's demand for factors increases while the railroad industry's demand for factors decreases. Relative factor prices will go up in airlines and down in railroads. The differential in factor prices causes a net movement of factors away from the railroad industry and toward the airline industry, and this movement causes the differentials to lessen and eventually to disappear. How long this process takes will depend on how easily factors can be reallocated from one industry to the other—that is, on the degree of factor mobility.

Equilibrium Differentials

Some factor-price differentials persist without generating any forces that eliminate them. These *equilibrium differentials* can be explained by intrinsic differences in the factors themselves and, for labour, by differences in the cost of acquiring skills and by different nonmonetary advantages of different occupations.

Intrinsic Differences. If various units of a factor have different characteristics, the price that is paid may differ among these units. If dexterity is required to accomplish a task, manually dexterous workers will earn more than less dexterous workers. If land is to be used for agricultural purposes, highly fertile land will earn more than poor land. These differences will persist even in long-run equilibrium.

Acquired Differences. If the fertility of land can be increased by costly methods, then more fertile land must command a higher price than less fertile land. If it did not, landowners would not incur the costs of improving fertility. The same holds true for labour since it is costly to acquire most skills. For example, a mechanic must train for some time, and unless the earnings of mechanics remain sufficiently above what can be earned in less skilled occupations, people will not incur the cost of training.

Nonmonetary Advantages. Whenever working conditions differ among various uses for a single factor, that factor will earn different equilibrium amounts in its various uses. The difference between a test pilot's wage and a chauffeur's wage is only partly a matter of skill; the rest is compensation to the

worker for facing the higher risk of testing new planes as compared to driving a car. If both were paid the same, there would be an excess supply of chauffeurs and a shortage of test pilots.

Academic researchers commonly earn less than they could earn in the world of commerce and industry because of the substantial nonmonetary advantages of academic employment. If chemists were paid the same in both sectors, many chemists would prefer academic to industrial jobs. Excess demand for industrial chemists and excess supply of academic chemists would then force chemists' wages up in industry and down in academia until the two types of jobs seemed equally attractive on balance.

The same forces account for equilibrium differences in regional earnings of otherwise identical factors. People who work in remote logging or mining areas are paid more than people who do jobs requiring similar skills in large cities. Without higher pay, not enough people would be willing to work at sometimes dangerous jobs in unattractive or remote locations. Similarly, because many people prefer living in the Maritimes to living in the Yukon, equilibrium wages in comparable occupations are lower in the Maritimes than in the Yukon.

Differentials and Factor Mobility: Equalizing Net Advantage

The distinction between temporary and equilibrium differentials is closely linked to factor mobility.

Temporary differentials lead to, and are eroded by, factor movements; equilibrium differentials are not eliminated by factor mobility.

The behaviour that causes the erosion of disequilibrium differentials is summarized in the hypothesis of the *maximization of net advantage:* The owners of factors of production will allocate those factors to uses that maximize the net advantages to themselves, taking both monetary and nonmonetary rewards into consideration. If net advantages were higher in occupation A than in occupation B, factors would move from B to A. The increased supply in A and the lower supply in B would drive factor earnings down in A and up in B until net advantages would be equalized, after which no further movement would occur. This analysis gives rise to the prediction of *equal net advantage:* In equilibrium, units of each kind of factor of production will be allocated among alternative possible uses in such a way that the net advantages in all uses are equalized.

Although nonmonetary advantages are important in explaining differences in levels of pay for labour in different occupations, they tend to be quite stable over time. As a result, monetary advantages, which vary with market conditions, lead to *changes* in net advantage.

A change in the relative price of a factor between two uses will change the net advantages of the uses. It will lead to a shift of some units of that factor to the use for which relative price has increased.

This implies an upward-sloping supply curve for a factor in any particular use. When the price of a factor rises in that use, more will be supplied to that use. This factor supply curve (like all supply curves) can also *shift* in response to changes in other variables. For example, an improvement in the safety record in a particular occupation improves the attractiveness of that occupation and thus shifts to the right the labour-supply curve to that occupation. We examine some of the consequences of this in Chapter 19.

POLICY ISSUES

The distinction between temporary and equilibrium factor-price differentials raises an important consideration for policy. Trade unions, governments, and other bodies often have explicit policies about earnings differentials, sometimes seeking to eliminate them in the name of equity. The success of such policies depends to a great extent on the kind of differential that is being attacked. One general lesson here is the following: Policies that attempt to eliminate *equilibrium* differentials will encounter severe difficulties. Here are two examples.

Pay Equity

Recent government legislation has sought to require *equal pay for work of equal value,* or **pay equity**. Such policy is designed to eliminate the wage differentials that exist between workers *in different jobs* but who are deemed to have approximately the same skills and responsibilities. For example, a policy of pay equity might require that a nurse with 10 years of experience receive the same salary as a teacher with 10 years of experience. Whatever the social value of such laws, they run into trouble whenever they require equal pay for jobs that have different nonmonetary advantages.

To illustrate the nature of the problem encountered by such legislation, consider the following example. Suppose that two jobs demand equal skills, training, and everything else that is taken into account when deciding what constitutes work of equal value but that, in a city with an extreme climate, one is an outside job and the other is an inside job. If legislation requires equal pay for both jobs, there will be a shortage of people who are willing to work outside and an excess of people who want to work inside. Employers will seek ways to attract outside workers. Higher pensions, shorter hours, longer holidays, overtime paid for but not worked, and better working conditions may be offered. If these are allowed, they will achieve the desired result but will defeat the original purpose of equalizing the monetary benefits of the inside and outside jobs; they will also cut down on the number of outside workers that employers will hire because the total cost of an outside worker to an employer will have risen. If the jobs are unionized or if the government prevents such "cheating," the shortage of workers for outside jobs will remain.

In Chapter 16, we discuss the effects of race and sex discrimination on wage differentials. Although these effects can be important, it remains true that many factor-price differentials are a natural market consequence of supply and demand conditions that have nothing to do with inequitable treatment of different groups in the society. Generally, mobility of factors tends to establish factor prices at which temporary differentials are eliminated but equilibrium differentials are stabilized.

Policies that seek to eliminate factor-price differentials without consideration of what causes them or how they affect the supply of the factor often have perverse results.

Regional Income Equalization

Canada's various regions differ markedly in their wealth. For example, the oil resources in Alberta have contributed considerably to that province's wealth over the past several decades; in contrast, the dramatic decline of the Atlantic fishery over the past decade has been one contributing factor to falling real incomes in the Atlantic provinces, especially

Newfoundland. Over the years, the federal government has developed several policies designed to reduce regional differences in per capita incomes. (In Chapter 20 we will see that such regional disparities are part of the motivation behind Canada's program of *equalization payments*.) The problems that these policies encounter are most easily seen by asking if it would be possible to equalize per capita incomes and unemployment rates across the provinces. The answer to this question is almost certainly no—at least when we consider the kinds of policy tools likely to be available to any foreseeable Canadian government. The reason is because as long as provinces differ in their nonmonetary attractiveness, there will be equilibrium differences in their per capita incomes and/or unemployment rates. And, as we saw above, trying to eliminate *equilibrium* factor-price differentials is problematic.

To illustrate the problem in this context, consider the following example. Suppose that Province A—despite strong physical, climatic, and social attractions—has a set of natural endowments that will not produce as high an income per person employed as Province B.[5] Suppose also that because of migration costs, cultural and language differences, climatic advantages, or other local amenities, many people choose to live in Province A even though they earn lower incomes there. In short, living in Province A has nonmonetary advantages over living in Province B. Markets can adjust to such regional differences in two basic ways; one way when wages are flexible, and another when wages are inflexible.

Flexible Wages.   If wages and prices are flexible, real wages and incomes will fall in Province A for the kinds of workers who are in excess supply. The falling real wages will give the province an advantage in new lines of production. Real wages will continue to fall until everyone who is willing to stay in Province A at the lower wage has a job and those who are not have migrated. In long-run equilibrium, Province A is a low-wage, low-income province, but it has no special unemployment problem. Those who do not value Province A's amenities as much as

they value the higher incomes to be earned in Province B, or who are subject to lower migration costs, will have left. What the price system does is equalize total advantages. It does not equalize factor payments, because the nonmonetary advantages of living in Province A exceed those of living in Province B.

Inflexible Wages.   The second possibility arises when wages are *not* totally flexible. Minimum-wage laws, national unions, and nationwide pay scales for the federal civil service put substantial restraints on possible interprovincial wage differentials. People who prefer Province A remain there, yet wages do not fall to create a wage incentive to employ more people in A or for those people to move to B. Instead, unemployment rates in A rise until (1) the extra uncertainty of finding a job and (2) the lower lifetime income expectations because of bouts of unemployment just balance both the nonmonetary advantages that Province A enjoys over Province B and the costs of moving from A to B. In long-run equilibrium, those who are willing to stay in spite of the higher unemployment remain, and the others leave.

Suppose now that the government of Province A attempts to battle against the high unemployment in its region by introducing some labour-market policies. Could policies close the unemployment gap between the two provinces? In these circumstances, market restrictions (such as laws that require the employment of local labour only) and labour-market policies (such as employment subsidies) will not reduce the unemployment *rate* in Province A, although they will increase the *level* of employment. As new jobs are created in Province A, the rate of emigration slows so that the rate of unemployment is unchanged. The local supply rises as fast as the local demand for labour, and the unemployment rate is left unchanged. This is because in the long run, A's unemployment rate must remain sufficiently above B's to balance the nonmonetary advantages that A enjoys over B.

The foregoing argument does not imply that we should ignore regions that have lower incomes or higher unemployment rates. However, it is important to realize that if the differential is an *equilibrium* phenomenon, no amount of policy intervention will remove it. If the policies continue to be strengthened as long as these differentials in unemployment persist, expenditures will continue to rise, but the ultimate goal of equalization will continue to prove elusive.

---

[5]Deficiencies in economic opportunities in a particular province might arise for many reasons: an inadequate resource base; technological backwardness; slow growth in demand for one region's products; or rapid natural growth of the labour force.

Some Evidence of Labour Mobility in Canada

This chapter has emphasized the importance of factor mobility. In particular, in the previous examples policy interventions to eliminate equilibrium differentials were thwarted *because of the mobility of labour*. In the first case, the requirement that outside jobs earned the same wage as inside jobs induced workers to reduce their supply of labour to the outside job and to increase their supply of labour to the inside job. This is labour mobility across jobs. In the second example, the policy designed to reduce the unemployment gap between two regions induced workers to move into the high-unemployment region, thereby leaving the unemployment rate in that region unchanged. This is labour mobilty across regions.

But does this kind of labour mobility really take place? The answer is yes. Table 15-4 shows some data on the amount of net migration between Canadian provinces and territories from 1970 to 1992. The first column shows the net migration between provinces for the year 1992 in particular. The second column shows the cumulative net flow from 1970 to 1992.

Over the 22-year period, there was a net migration of over 800,000 individuals between the provinces. But even this large number understates the actual amount of interregional labour mobility, for three reasons. First, these data do not include individuals who emigrated from Canada or who arrived to Canada from foreign countries. Second, the data do not include individuals who moved from one location in a region to another location within the same region. For example, an individual who moves from Lethbridge in Southern Alberta to Grand Prairie in Northern Alberta does not show up in this table. These two problems suggest that both the data from 1992 and the cumulative data for 1970–1992 understate the true amount of labour mobility. The third reason applies to the cumulative data, but less so to the annual data. The cumulative data does not show the migration that "reverses itself" during the period. For example, the many individuals who moved from Ontario to Alberta in the mid 1970s, and then returned to Ontario in the mid 1980s, do not show up in the cumulative data, but would show up in the annual data. Partly for this reason, the migration numbers for 1992 are much more than one-twenty-second of the migration numbers for the entire 1970–1992 period.

TABLE 15-4
Net Canadian Interregional Migration

Region	Net Change	Cumulative Net Change
	(number of individuals)	
	1992	1970–1992
Newfoundland	− 3,626	− 63,265
P.E.I.	504	1,711
Nova Scotia	− 2,132	3,444
New Brunswick	− 1,890	− 3,526
Quebec	− 15,497	− 429,820
Ontario	− 2,956	156,059
Manitoba	− 6,513	− 129,821
Saskatchewan	− 8,472	− 168,679
Alberta	− 1,278	185,342
British Columbia	41,240	454,140
Yukon/N.W.T.	620	− 5,585
Net Total Movers	42,364	800,696

The past few decades have seen significant migration of individuals between Canadian regions. In the 1970–1992 period, a cumulative net flow of 429,820 people left Quebec and settled in some other Canadian province or territory; in contrast, a cumulative net flow of 454,140 people arrived in B.C. from other Canadian regions. The numbers in the table sum to zero because each person who emigrates from one province also immigrates to another. The total number of movers is the total amount of emigration (or immigration). For the three reasons given in the text, these numbers understate the actual amount of interregional labour mobility in Canada.

(*Source:* Richard Chaykowski, *Modern Labour Economics,* HarperCollins 1994.)

For these three reasons, even the relatively large amount of labour mobility suggested by Table 15-4 understates the actual amount of interregional labour mobility in Canada.

ECONOMIC RENT

One of the most important concepts in economics is that of *economic rent*.

A factor must earn a certain amount in its present use to prevent it from moving to another use—Alfred Marshall called this amount the factor's *transfer earnings*. If there were no nonmonetary advantages in alternative uses, the factor would have to earn its opportunity cost (what it could earn elsewhere) to prevent it from moving elsewhere. This is usually true for capital and land. Labour, however, gains important nonmonetary advantages in various jobs, and it must earn in one use enough to equate the two jobs' total advantages, both monetary and nonmonetary.

Any excess that a factor earns over the minimum amount needed to keep it at its present use is called its **economic rent.** Economic rent is analogous to economic profit as a surplus over the opportunity cost of capital. The concept of economic rent is crucial in predicting the effects that changes in earnings have on the movement of factors among alternative uses. However, the terminology is confusing because economic rent is often called simply *rent*, which can

of course also mean the price paid to hire something, such as a machine, a piece of land, or an apartment. How the same term came to be used for these two very different concepts is explained in Extension 15-3.

How Much of Factor Earnings is Rent?

In most cases, economic rent makes up part of the actual earnings of a factor of production. The distinction is most easily seen, however, by examining

---

E X T E N S I O N   **15-3**

Origin of the term "economic rent"

In the early nineteenth century, there was a public debate about the high price of wheat in England. The price was causing great hardship because bread was a primary source of food for the working class. Some people argued that wheat had a high price because landlords were charging high rents to tenant farmers. In short, it was argued that the price of wheat was high because the rents of agricultural land were high. Some of those who held this view advocated restricting the rents that landlords could charge.

David Ricardo (1772–1823), a great British economist who was one of the originators of Classical economics, argued that the situation was exactly the reverse. The price of wheat was high, he said, because there was a shortage, caused by the Napoleonic Wars. Because wheat was profitable to produce, there was keen competition among farmers to obtain land on which to grow wheat. This competition in turn forced up the rental price of wheat land. Ricardo advocated removing the existing tariff on wheat so that imported wheat could come into the country, thereby increasing its supply in England and lowering both the price of wheat and the rent that could be charged for the land on which it was grown.

The essentials of Ricardo's argument were these: The supply of land was fixed. Land was regarded as having only one use, the growing of wheat. Nothing had to be paid to prevent land from transferring to a use other than growing wheat because it had no other

use. No landowner would leave land idle as long as some return could be obtained by renting it out. Therefore, all the payment to land, that is, rent in the ordinary sense of the word, was a surplus over and above what was necessary to keep it in its present use.

Given a fixed supply of land, the price of land depended on the demand for land, which depended in turn on the demand for wheat (i.e., the demand for land was *derived from* the demand for wheat). *Rent,* the term for the payment for the use of land, thus became the term for a surplus payment to a factor over and above what was necessary to keep it in its present use.

Later, two facts were realized. First, land often had alternative uses, and, from the point of view of any one use, part of the payment made to land would necessarily have to be paid to keep it in that use. Second, factors of production other than land also often earned a surplus over and above what was necessary to keep them in their present use. Television stars and great athletes, for example, are in short and fairly fixed supply, and their potential earnings in other occupations often are quite moderate. However, because there is a huge demand for their services as television stars or athletes, they may receive payments greatly in excess of what is needed to keep them from transferring to other occupations. This surplus is now called *economic rent,* whether the factor is land, labour, or a piece of capital equipment.

FIGURE 15-4
The Determination of Rent in Factor Payments

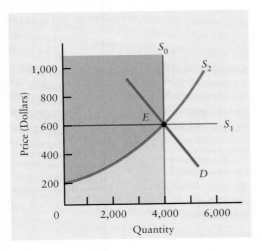

The amount of rent in factor payments depends on the shape of the supply curve. A single demand curve is shown with three different supply curves. In each case, the competitive equilibrium price is $600, and 4,000 units of the factor are hired. The total payment ($2.4 million) is represented by the entire shaded area.

When the supply curve is vertical (S_0), the whole payment is economic rent because a decrease in price would not lead any units of the factor to move elsewhere.

When the supply curve is horizontal (S_1), none of the payment is rent because even a small decrease in price offered would lead all units of the factor to move elsewhere.

When the supply curve is positively sloped (S_2), part of the payment is rent. As shown by the height of the supply curve, at a price of $600, the 4,000th unit of the factor is receiving just enough to persuade it to offer its services in this market, but the 2,000th unit, for example, is earning well above what it requires to stay in this market. The aggregate of economic rents is shown by the red shaded area, whereas the aggregate of what must be paid to keep all 4,000 units in this market is shown by the entire shaded area.

two extreme cases. In one, everything a factor earns is rent; in the other, none is rent.

The possibilities are illustrated in Figure 15-4. When the supply curve is perfectly inelastic (vertical), the same quantity is supplied, whatever the price. Evidently, the quantity supplied does not de-

crease, no matter how low the price goes. This indicates that the factor has no alternative use, and thus requires no minimum payment to keep it in its present use. In this case, the whole of the payment is economic rent. The price actually paid allocates the fixed supply to whoever is most willing to pay for it.

When the supply curve is perfectly elastic (horizontal), none of the price paid is economic rent. If any lower price is offered, nothing whatsoever will be supplied since all units of the factor will transfer to some other use.

The more usual situation is that of an upward-sloping supply curve. A rise in the factor's price serves the allocative function of attracting more units of the factor into the market in question, but the same rise provides additional economic rent to all units of the factor that are *already employed*. We know that the extra pay that is going to the units already employed is economic rent because the owners of these units were willing to supply them at the lower price. The general result for a positively sloped supply curve is stated as follows.

If the demand for a factor in any of its uses rises relative to the supply available to that use, its price will rise in that use. This will serve the allocative function of attracting additional units into that use. It will also increase the economic rent to all units of the factor already in that use.

Various Perspectives on Economic Rent

The proportion of a given factor payment that is economic rent varies from situation to situation. We cannot point to a factor of production and assert that some fixed fraction of its income is always its economic rent. The proportion of its earnings that is rent depends on the alternatives that are open to it.

Focus first on a narrowly defined use of a given factor, say, its use by a particular firm. From that firm's point of view, the factor will be highly mobile, as it could readily move to another firm in the same industry. The firm must pay the going wage or risk losing that factor. Thus from the perspective of the single firm, a large proportion of the payment made to a factor is needed to prevent it from transferring to another use.

Focus now on a more broadly defined use, for example, the factor's use in an entire industry. From the industry's point of view, the factor is less mobile because it would be more difficult for it to gain employment quickly outside the industry. From the perspective of the particular *industry* (rather than the specific *firm* within the industry), a larger proportion of the payment to a factor is economic rent.

From the even more general perspective of a particular *occupation,* mobility is likely to be even less, and the proportion of the factor payment that is economic rent is likely to be more. It may be easier, for example, for a carpenter to move from the construction industry to the furniture industry than to retrain to be a computer operator.

As the perspective moves from a narrowly defined use of a factor to a broadly defined use of a factor, the mobility of the factor decreases; as mobility decreases, the share of the factor payment that is economic rent increases.

Consider how this applies to the often controversial large salaries that are received by some highly specialized types of labourers, such as recording stars and professional athletes. These performers have a style and a talent that cannot be duplicated, whatever the training. The earnings that they receive are mostly economic rent from the viewpoint of the occupation: These performers generally enjoy their occupations and would pursue them for much less than the high remuneration that they actually receive. For example, Shaquille O'Neal would probably choose basketball over other alternatives even at a much lower salary. However, because of O'Neal's amazing skills as a basketball player, most NBA teams would pay handsomely to have him on their rosters, and he is able to command a high salary from the team he does play for. From the perspective of the individual firm, the Orlando Magic, most of O'Neal's salary is required to keep him from switching to another team and hence is not economic rent. From the point of view of the basketball "industry," however, much of his salary is economic rent.

Notice also that O'Neal's salary is largely determined by the demand for his services. The supply is perfectly inelastic—no one else possesses his particular combination of skills. So the market-clearing price is determined by the position of the demand curve. This is generally the case with economic rent—supply is fixed, so price is determined by demand.

A FINAL WORD

This chapter has examined the operation of factor markets. You should now be able to answer the questions that we posed in the opening paragraph. Here are some of the key points for two of those questions.

What explains why professors usually get paid more than high-school teachers? Part of the answer surely lies in the fact that to be a university professor typically requires nine years of university education (four for the bachelor's degree plus five for the completion of the doctorate) whereas to be a teacher usually requires only four or five years. Since that extra education is costly and time-consuming, it is not surprising that fewer people are willing to become university professors than teachers. This lower supply for professors, other things equal, leads to a higher wage.

Why does an acre of farm land in Northern Saskatchewan rent for far less than an acre of land in downtown Toronto? To answer this, just think about the alternative uses for the farm land, and compare them to the alternative uses for the acre in downtown Toronto. The acre of farm land has very few alternative uses. Or, more correctly, it has many alternative uses, but there is little demand to use that particular piece of land to build a skyscraper, shopping mall, or baseball stadium. But one acre of land in downtown Toronto has many alternative uses—there always seems to be demand for additional space for parking garages, office buildings, shopping malls, and many other things. Since the piece of farm land in Saskatchewan must stay where it is, its rental price is determined by demand. Since there is little demand for the land, its rental price is low. Similarly, the land in downtown Toronto cannot move anywhere, and so its rental price is determined by demand. And since there is lots of demand for an acre in downtown Toronto, its rental price is high.

Having learned about factor markets in general, we are now ready to examine some specific factor markets. In Chapter 16, we examine some details about labour markets, such as minimum wages, discrimination, and labour unions. In Chapter 17, we examine the pricing of physical capital and of nonre-

SUMMARY

A. INCOME DISTRIBUTION AND FACTOR PRICING

- The functional distribution of income refers to the shares of total national income going to each of the major factors of production; it focuses on sources of income. The size distribution of income refers to the shares of total national income going to various groups of households; it focuses only on the amount of income, not its source.
- The income of a factor of production is composed of two elements: the price paid per unit of the factor and the quantity of the factor used. The determination of factor prices and quantities is an application of the same price theory that is used to determine product prices and quantities.

B. THE DEMAND FOR FACTORS

- The firm's decisions on how much to produce and how to produce it imply demands for factors of production, which are said to be derived from the demand for goods that they are used to produce.
- A profit-maximizing firm will hire units of a factor until the last unit adds as much to cost as it does to revenue. This means that the marginal cost of the factor would be equated with that factor's marginal revenue product. Marginal revenue product is equal to the marginal physical product multiplied by the revenue associated with the sale of another unit of output (i.e., marginal revenue).
- When the firm is a price taker in input markets, the marginal cost of the factor is its price per unit. When the firm sells its output in a competitive market, the marginal revenue product is the factor's marginal physical product multiplied by the market price of the output.
- A price-taking firm's demand for a factor is negatively sloped because the law of diminishing returns implies that the marginal physical product of a factor declines as more of that factor is employed (with other inputs held constant).
- The industry's demand for a factor will be more elastic (a) the faster the marginal physical product of the factor declines as more of the factor is used, (b) the easier it is to substitute one factor for another, (c) the larger the proportion of total variable costs accounted for by the cost of the factor in question, and (d) the more elastic the demand for the good that the factor helps to produce.

C. THE SUPPLY OF FACTORS

- The total supply of each factor is fixed at any moment but varies over time. The supply of labour depends on the size of the population, the participation rate, and hours worked.
- A rise in the wage rate has a substitution effect, which tends to induce more work, and an income effect, which tends to induce less work (more leisure consumed).
- The supply of a factor to a particular industry or occupation is more elastic than its supply to the whole economy because one industry can bid units away from other industries. The elasticity of supply to a particular use depends on factor mobility, which tends to be greater the longer the time allowed for a reaction to take place.

D. THE OPERATION OF FACTOR MARKETS

- Factor-price differentials often occur in competitive markets. Temporary differentials in the earnings of different units of factors of production induce factor movements that eventually remove the differentials. Equilibrium differentials reflect differences among units of factors as well as nonmonetary benefits of different jobs; they can persist indefinitely.
- Equal net advantage is a theory of the allocation of the total supply of factors to particular uses. Owners of factors will choose the use that produces the greatest net advantage, allowing for monetary and nonmonetary advantages of a particular employment. In so doing, they will cause temporary factor price differentials to be eliminated.
- Some amount must be paid to a factor to prevent it from transferring to another use. This amount is the factor's transfer earnings. Economic rent is the difference between that amount and a factor's actual earnings. Whenever the supply curve is positively sloped, part of the total pay going to a factor is needed to prevent it from transferring to another use, and part of it is rent. The proportion of each depends on the mobility of the factor. The more narrowly defined the use, the larger the fraction that is transfer earnings and the smaller the fraction that is economic rent.

KEY CONCEPTS

Functional distribution and size distribution of income
Derived demand for a factor
Marginal physical product
Marginal revenue product

The determinants of elasticity of factor demand
Factor mobility
Temporary versus equilibrium factor-price differentials

Equal net advantage
Transfer earnings
Economic rent

DISCUSSION QUESTIONS

1. Other things being equal, how would you expect each of the following events to affect the size distribution of after-tax income? Do any lead to clear predictions about the functional distribution of income?

   a. An increase in unemployment
   b. Rapid population growth in an already crowded city
   c. An increase in food prices relative to other prices
   d. An increase in social insurance benefits and taxes
   e. Elimination of the personal income-tax exemption for interest earned within an RRSP.

2. Consider the effects on the overall level of income inequality of each of the following situations.

   a. Increasing participation of women in the labour force as many women shift from work in the home to full-time jobs in the workplace
   b. Increasing use by fruit growers of migrant workers who are in the country on temporary visas
   c. Increasing numbers of minority group members studying law and medicine
   d. Cuts in the rates of income tax, together with the elimination of some personal income tax deductions

3. How much of the following payments for factor services is likely to be economic rent?

   a. The $750 per month that a landlord receives for an apartment leased to students
   b. The salary of the Canadian Prime Minister
   c. The large annual income of recording stars such as Rod Stewart, Céline Dion, and Bryan Adams
   d. The salary of a window cleaner who says, "It's dangerous and dirty work, but it beats driving a truck."

4. Which of the following are temporary differentials and which are equilibrium differentials in factor prices?

   a. Differences in earnings of football coaches and wrestling coaches

   b. A "bonus for signing on" offered by a construction company seeking carpenters in a tight labour market
   c. Differences in monthly rent charged for three-bedroom houses in different parts of the same metropolitan area
   d. Higher prices per square foot of condominium space in Vancouver compared with Halifax

5. A labour dispute has broken out at a university between the faculty and the university's board of governors. One of the issues is the faculty's complaint that summer school teaching salaries are below the regional average and hence too low. The trustees argue that considering that they have more professors asking to teach summer school at the current pay than they have courses for these faculty to teach, the pay is adequate. Comment.

6. Jim Kelly, quarterback for the Buffalo Bills, is paid many millions of dollars a year to play football. However, Kent Hull, the starting center, is paid only a few hundred thousand dollars per year, even though without Hull's efforts, Kelly would not be able to pass the ball. What can explain these differences in pay, despite the fact that in a team sport such as football, both players' efforts are arguably of "equal value"?

7. The demands listed here have been increasing rapidly in recent years. What derived demands would you predict have also risen sharply? Where will the extra factors of production that are demanded be drawn from?

   a. Demand for natural gas
   b. Demand for medical services
   c. Demand for international and interregional travel

8. Consider the large-scale substitution of jumbo jets, each of which has a seating capacity of about 350, for jets with a seating capacity of about 125. What kinds of labour service would you predict will experience an increase in demand, and what kinds will experience a decrease? Under what conditions would airplane pi-

lots (as a group) be made better off economically by virtue of this substitution?

9. A recent *Wall Street Journal* article asks, "Why do baseball players earn millions of dollars a year for their negligible contribution to society while major contributors—such as schoolteachers, policemen, firemen, and ambulance drivers—earn barely enough to survive?" Can you offer an answer based on what was discussed in this Chapter?

10. For most of the years in the past two decades, the unemployment rate in the province of Quebec has been higher than the Canadian average. It has also been higher than the unemployment rate in next-door Ontario. Given that there are almost no legal restrictions on the flow of labour across Canadian provincial boundaries, provide an explanation for how such a gap in unemployment rates can persist for so long.

CHAPTER 16

LABOUR MARKETS

The competitive theory of factor-price determination, presented in Chapter 15, tells us a great deal about factor prices, factor movements, and the distribution of income. In this chapter, we apply this theory to the most important of factor markets, the labour market. In the process, we extend the theory to cover situations in which suppliers and demanders of labour have some market power in the labour market, and are thus not price takers. We also examine the effects of legislated minimum wages, the role of labour unions, and the effects of employers' discrimination between different types of workers. The chapter closes with a discussion of the often-heard claim that Canada and other developed countries have been gaining "bad jobs" at the expense of "good jobs."

LABOUR MARKETS AND WAGE DIFFERENTIALS

We observed in Chapter 15 that the need for most workers to be physically present when their labour services are used differentiates labour from other factors of production. As a result, nonmonetary considerations, such as location of employment and other working conditions, are more important in the labour market than in markets for other factors of production.

Considerations other than material advantage also enter the relationship between employer and employee, for it is a relationship that involves loyalty, fairness, appreciation, and justice along with paycheques and productivity. It is also a relationship that may involve both actual and perceived discrimination on the basis of such things as gender, race, and age. The performance of labour markets will be affected by all of these noneconomic considerations and more.

Labour unions, employers' associations, collective bargaining, and government intervention in wage determination are important features of labour markets. They influence wages and working conditions and affect the levels of employment and unemployment in many industries. This means that the basic theory of factor-price determination from Chapter 15 must be augmented before it can be applied to the full range of problems concerning the determination of wages.

CONDITIONS FOR A SINGLE WAGE

All workers would receive the same wage if the following conditions held.

- All jobs had the same working conditions
- All workers were identical
- Labour markets were perfectly competitive

If these three conditions were satisfied, then everyone would earn the same wage in equilibrium and that wage would be equal to the marginal revenue product of labour. In reality, however, wages vary enormously. Some people work full time and are in poverty; others are able to live very well on what they earn from working. Generally, the more education and experience a worker has, the higher are his or her wages. Given equal education and experience, women on average earn less than men. In the United States, blacks on average earn less than similarly-educated whites. Workers in highly unionized industries tend to get paid more than workers with similar skills and experience in nonunionized industries. Such differentials arise because workers are not all identical, jobs are not all identical, and because many important noncompetitive forces operate in labour markets. We now look more systematically at the reasons why different types of labour earn different wages.

WAGE DIFFERENTIALS IN COMPETITIVE MARKETS

Where there are many employers (buyers) and many workers (sellers), there is a competitive labour market of the kind discussed in Chapter 15. Under competitive conditions, the wage rate and level of employment are set by supply and demand. No worker or group of workers, and no firm or group of firms, is able to affect the market wage. In practice, there are many kinds of workers and many kinds of jobs, even within individual industries or occupations. When considering these, we can think of a series of related labour markets rather than a single national market. In competitive equilibrium, we can distinguish several major sources of wage differentials.

Working Conditions

Given identical skills, those working under relatively onerous or risky conditions earn more than those working in pleasant or safe conditions. For example, construction workers who work the "high iron," assembling the frames for skyscrapers, are paid more than workers who do similar work at ground level. The reason is simple: Risk and unpleasantness reduce the supply of labour, thus raising the wage above what it would otherwise be. Another example is that a university professor who teaches at a "big-name" university might earn less than he would earn doing exactly the same job at a less well-known university. Again, the reason is simple: The nonmonetary advantages of being on staff at a famous university increase the supply of labour and reduce the wages relative to those at the less famous universities. Different working conditions in different jobs thus lead to wage differentials—these are *equilibrium* differentials as discussed in Chapter 15.

In competitive labour markets, supply and demand set the equilibrium wage, but the wage will differ according to the nonmonetary aspects of the job.

Luck

Large incomes will be earned by people who have scarce skills that cannot be taught and that are highly valued—for example, the physical ability to be an NBA basketball player. In this case, the combination of a small and inelastic supply and a large enough demand of the relevant kind of labour cause the market-clearing wage to be high. There are also less extreme cases. Some people are endowed with the ability to make others feel good—they make superior salespersons and therapists. Some people enjoy working hard more than others; they are thus more valuable on the job and often get paid more. All of these are also equilibrium differentials in the sense discussed in Chapter 15.

Inherited skills, which are mostly beyond the individual's control, can have important effects on the ability to earn income.

Human Capital

A machine is physical capital. It requires an investment of time and money to create it, and once created, it yields valuable services over a long time. In the same way, labour skills require an investment of time and money to acquire, and once acquired, they yield an increased income to their owner over a long time. Since investment in labour skills is similar to investment in physical capital, acquired skills are called **human capital.** The supply of some particular skill increases when more people find it worthwhile to acquire the necessary human capital; the supply decreases when fewer do so. The more costly it is to acquire the skill required for a particular job, the higher its pay must be to attract people to train for it.

The stock of skills acquired by individual workers is called human capital; investment in human capital is usually costly, and the return is usually in terms of higher labour productivity and hence higher earning power.

The two main ways in which human capital is acquired are through formal education and through on-the-job training.

Formal Education. Compulsory education is an attempt to provide some minimum human capital for all citizens. Some people, either through luck in the school they attend or through their own efforts, profit more from their early education than others. They acquire more human capital than their less fortunate contemporaries. Subsequent income differentials reflect these differences in human capital acquired in the early stages of education.

Those who decide to stay in school beyond the years of compulsory education are deciding to invest voluntarily in acquiring further human capital. The (opportunity) cost is measured by the income that could have been earned if the person had entered the labour force immediately, plus any out-of-pocket costs for such items as tuition fees and equipment. The return is measured by the higher income earned when a better job is obtained. (Recall Application 1-1 in Chapter 1.)

If the demand for labour with more human capital rises, the earnings of such labour will rise. This will raise the expected return to those currently deciding whether to make the investment themselves. If the demand for labour with low amounts of human capital falls, the earnings of such persons will fall. This lowers the opportunity costs of staying on in school and acquiring more capital because the earnings forgone by not going to work are reduced. A rise in unemployment will also lower the costs because the probability of earning a steady income will be reduced, and this will reduce the expected loss from not entering the labour force early.

Market forces adjust the overall costs and benefits of acquiring human capital, and individuals respond according to their varying personal assessments of costs and benefits.

The evidence suggests that in most advanced industrialized countries the demand for people with a college or university education has been rising relative to the demand for those without post-secondary education. Thus the wages for highly educated people have been rising relative to the wages of less-educated people. For example, Table 16-1 shows how the real returns to higher education changed for Canadian men and women from 1984 to 1992. For every year shown in the table, the real earnings for college graduates are significantly higher than for those with only

TABLE 16-1
Real Returns to Education for Full-Year, Full-Time Workers, 1984–1992

Year	Real Mean Earnings, Men Aged 35–44 Years		Real Mean Earnings, Women Aged 35–44 Years	
	High School	College	High School	College
1984	$29,858	$45,396	$18,656	$32,455
1986	28,902	46,296	18,455	34,174
1988	30,780	45,642	17,818	32,988
1990	29,140	46,221	20,589	33,469
1992	30,307	46,884	20,582	35,140

Real earnings for college graduates have been rising relative to real earnings for those with only high-school diplomas. The data show for various years the real earnings (in 1986 dollars) for men and women with different levels of education. Real earnings for high-school graduates were roughly constant from 1984 to 1992, whereas real earnings for college graduates have increased by between 3 percent (for men) and 8 percent (for women). Note also that there is a considerable difference in any given year between the real earnings for men and women.

(*Source:* Statistics Canada, *Earnings of Men and Women,* 13-217.)

a high-school diploma. Furthermore, the earnings for college graduates increased by between 3 and 8 percent over that period (for men and women, respectively), but remained roughly constant for those with only a high-school education. Thus the *relative earnings* of more highly educated workers increased over this period.

The evidence also suggests that more people stay on to complete more education when times are bad than when times are good. The reason is that the opportunity cost of education, measured in terms of expected earnings forgone, is lower when unemployment rates are high and earnings are depressed than when unemployment rates are low and earnings are buoyant.

In the long run, decisions to acquire human capital help to erode differentials in income. Market signals change the costs and benefits of acquiring human capital in such specific forms as skill in electronics, accountancy, law, or medicine. By reacting to these signals, young people help to increase the supplies of high-income workers and reduce the supplies of low-income workers, thereby eroding the differentials that exist at a given time.

Of course, people's ability to acquire human capital is limited by their innate abilities and their past experiences. Those with below-average cognitive abilities are unlikely to become computer programmers. Those handicapped by inadequate elementary and high school education will find it difficult to become highly skilled technicians. (A few dedicated and highly intelligent people may manage to do so later in life, but for most, the handicaps of bad early training are too great to overcome.)

On-the-Job Education. Differentials according to age are readily observable in most firms and occupations. To a significant extent, these differentials are a response to human capital acquired on the job.

Acquiring this type of human capital is important in creating rising wages for employees and for making firms competitive. Evidence suggests that people who miss on-the-job training early in life are handicapped relative to others throughout much of their later working careers. This makes prolonged unemployment early in one's potential working career more serious than just the wages lost at the time. It also appears that different countries' firms have different practices with respect to investing in their employees' human capital. For example, Japanese auto companies operating in North America spend substantially more on employee training than do the North American auto companies. To some extent, this is because the Japanese methods of flexible manufacturing (discussed in Application 9-2 in Chapter 9) require more worker flexibility and training than do the North American mass-production methods.

Gender and Race

Crude statistics show that incomes vary by race and gender. (Indeed, referring again to Table 16-1, it is clear that for every year in the table, and for either of the two education levels shown, the average real earnings for men exceeds that for women.) More detailed studies suggest that a significant part of these differences can be explained by such considerations as the amount of human capital acquired through both formal education and on-the-job experience. When all such explanations are taken into account, however, differentials that are consistent with discrimination based on race and sex seem to remain. We discuss discrimination in some detail later in this chapter.

WAGE DIFFERENTIALS IN NONCOMPETITIVE MARKETS

So far we have examined four broad explanations for why wage differentials exist in competitive labour markets. Another explanation for wage differentials is that the labour market may *not* be competitive. In Chapters 10 through 12, we distinguished different *structures* for the markets in which firms sell their outputs. The inputs that firms use are also bought in markets that can have different structures. Although some markets are perfectly competitive, many show elements of market power on either the demand or the supply side.

To study the influence of different labour market structures on wages, we consider the case of an industry that employs identical workers for only one kind of job. In this way, we eliminate the possibility that any wage differentials are caused by differences between workers or differences between jobs—we thus highlight the role of market structure.

We examine two general cases. The first is when workers get together in a group and exercise some market power over setting the wage. The second is when the firm does not have to compete with other firms to hire workers. We examine these cases in turn.

Monopoly: A Union in a Competitive Market

For the purposes of our discussion of labour markets, a **union** (or *trade union* or *labour union*) is an association that is authorized to represent workers in negotiations with their employers. We examine unions in greater detail later in this chapter. For now we take the simple view that when workers are represented by a labour union, there is essentially only a single supplier of labour.

Suppose that a union enters a competitive labour market to represent all of the workers. As the single seller of labour for many buyers, the union is a monopolist, and it can establish a wage below which no one will work, thus changing the supply curve of labour. The industry can hire as many units of labour as are prepared to work at the

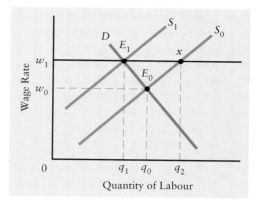

FIGURE 16-1
Effect on Wages of Union Entry in a Competitive Labour Market

A union can raise the wages of people who continue to be employed but only by reducing the number of people employed. The competitive equilibrium is at E_0, the wage is w_0, and employment is q_0. If a union enters this market and sets a wage of w_1, a new equilibrium will be established at E_1. The supply curve has become $w_1 x S_0$. At the new wage w_1, employment will be q_1, and there will be $q_1 q_2$ workers who would like to work but whom the industry will not hire. The decrease in employment due to the wage increase is $q_1 q_0$.

The wage w_1 can be achieved without generating a pool of persons who are seeking but unable to find work. To do so, the union must restrict entry into the occupation and thus shift the supply curve to the left to S_1. Employment will again be q_1.

This figure can also be used to illustrate the effect of the government imposing a minimum wage of w_1 on the market where the competitive equilibrium is at E_0. The q_1 workers who remain employed benefit by the wage increase. The $q_1 q_0$ workers who lose their jobs in this industry suffer to the extent that they fail to find new jobs at a wage of w_0 or more.

union wage but no one at a lower wage. Thus the industry (and each firm) faces a supply curve that is horizontal at the level of the union wage up to the maximum quantity of labour that is willing to work at that wage.

If the union uses its monopoly power, it will negotiate a wage above the competitive level. This situation is shown in Figure 16-1, in which the intersection of this horizontal supply curve and the demand curve establishes a higher wage rate and a lower level of employment than the competitive equilibrium.

There will be some workers who would like to obtain work in the industry or occupation but cannot. A conflict of interest has been created between serving the interests of the union's employed and unemployed members.

An alternative way to achieve the higher wage is to shift the supply curve to the left. The union may do this by restricting entry into the occupation by methods such as lengthening the required period of apprenticeship and reducing openings for trainees. Alternatively, the union may shift the supply curve by persuading the government to impose restrictive licensing or certification requirements on people who wish to work.

Raising wages by restricting entry is not limited to unions, of course. It occurs, for example, with many professional groups, including doctors. Because professional standards have long been regarded as necessary to protect the public from incompetent practitioners, doctors have found it publicly acceptable to control supply by limiting entry into their profession. Physicians' incomes are among the highest of any profession partly because of barriers to entry, including the difficulties of getting into an approved medical school, the high costs of setting up new medical schools, and various certification requirements applying to students, schools, and practitioners.

Monopsony: A Single Buyer in the Market

A **monopsony** is a market in which there is only one buyer; monopsony is to the buying side of the market what monopoly is to the selling side. Although cases of monopsony are not very common, it does sometimes arise. Monopsony sometimes occurs in small towns which contain only one industry and often only one large plant or mine. For example, the towns of Iroquois Falls in Ontario and Pine Falls in Manitoba are small towns where the principal employer is a single firm (Abitibi Price) which operates a newsprint plant. Although both towns provide alternative sources of employment in retailing and service establishments, the large industrial employer has some monopsony power over the local labour market. In other cases, local labour markets may contain only a few large industrial employers. Individually, each has substantial market power, and if they all act together, either explicitly or tacitly, they can behave as if they were a single monopsonist. Our analysis applies whenever employers have substantial monopsony power, but for concreteness, we consider a case

in which the few firms operating in one labour market form an employers' hiring association in order to act as a single buying unit. We therefore refer to a single monopsonist.

Monopsonistic Labour Markets in the Absence of Unions. Suppose that there are many potential workers and that they are not members of a union. The monopsonist can offer any wage rate that it chooses, and the workers must either accept employment at that rate or find a different job.

Suppose that the monopsonist decides to hire some specific quantity of labour. The labour supply curve shows the wage that it must offer. To the monopsonist, this wage is the *average cost curve* of labour. In deciding how much labour to hire, however, the monopsonist is interested in the *marginal cost* of hiring additional workers. The monopsonist wants to know how much its total costs will increase as it takes on additional units of labour.

Whenever the supply curve of labour slopes upward, the marginal cost of employing extra units will exceed the average cost. It exceeds the wage paid (the average cost) because the increased wage rate necessary to attract an extra worker must also be paid to *everyone already employed.* [30]

For example, assume that 100 workers are employed at $8.00 per hour and that to attract an extra worker, the wage must be raised to $8.01 per hour. The marginal cost of the 101st worker is not the $8.01 per hour paid to the worker but $9.01 per hour—made up of the extra 1 cent per hour paid to the 100 existing workers and $8.01 paid to the new worker. Thus the marginal cost is $9.01 whereas the average cost is $8.01.[1]

The profit-maximizing monopsonist will hire labour up to the point at which the marginal cost just equals the amount that the firm is willing to pay for an additional unit of labour. That amount is determined by labour's marginal revenue product and is shown by the demand curve illustrated in Figure 16-2.

Monopsonistic conditions in a labour market will result in a lower level of employment and a lower wage

---

[1]This marginal cost of hiring an extra worker must not be confused with the marginal cost of *producing an extra unit of output.* Suppose that the extra worker in the example increased total output by 3 units. Because the worker adds $9.01 to cost and 3 units to output, the marginal cost of producing 1 extra unit of output is 9.01/3, which is approximately $3.00.

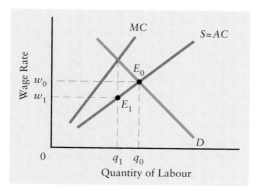

FIGURE 16-2
Monopsony in a Labour Market

A **monopsonist lowers both the wage rate and employment below their competitive levels.** D and S are the competitive demand and supply curves, respectively. In competition, equilibrium is at E_0, the wage rate is w_0, and the quantity of labour hired is q_0. The marginal cost of labour *(MC)* to the monopsonist is above the average cost. The monopsonistic firm will maximize profits at E_1. It will hire only q_1 units of labour. At q_1, the marginal cost of the last worker is just equal to the amount that the worker adds to the firm's revenue, as shown by the demand curve. The wage that must be paid to get q_1 workers is only w_1

rate than would exist when labour is purchased under competitive conditions.

The intuitive explanation is that the monopsonistic employer is aware that by trying to purchase more, it is responsible for driving up the wage. It will therefore stop short of the point that is reached when the wages are negotiated by many separate firms, no one of which can exert a significant influence on the wage rate.

Bilateral Monopoly: A Union in a Monopsonistic Market. Suppose that the workers in this industry organize themselves under a single union so that the monopsonistic employer's organization now faces a monopoly union. This situation is often referred to as one of *bilateral monopoly* since both sides of the market have considerable market power. In this case, the two sides will settle the wage through a process known as *collective bargaining.* The outcome of this bargaining process will depend on each side's objective and on the skill that each has in bargaining for its objective. We have seen that left to itself, the employer's organization will set the monopsonistic wage shown in Figure 16-2. To un-

derstand the possible outcomes for the wage after the monopoly union enters the market, let us ask what the union would do if it had the power to set the wage unilaterally. The result will give us insight into the union's objectives in the actual collective bargaining that does occur.

Suppose then that the union can set a wage below which its members will not work. Here, just as in the case of a wage-setting union in a competitive market, the union presents the employer with a horizontal supply curve (up to the maximum number of workers who will accept work at the union wage). As demonstrated in Figure 16-3, if the union sets the wage above the monopsony wage but below the competitive wage, the union can raise wages *and employment* above the monopsonistic level.

However, the union may not be content merely to neutralize the monopsonist's power. It may choose to raise wages further above the competitive level. If it does, the outcome will be similar to that shown in Figure 16-1. If the wage is raised above the competitive level, the employer will no longer wish to hire all the labour that is offered at that wage. The amount of employment will fall, and unemployment will develop. This is also shown in Figure 16-3. Notice, however, that the union can raise wages substantially above the competitive level before employment falls to a level as low as it was in the preunion monopsonistic situation.

We now know that the employers would like to set the monopsonistic wage (w_1) while the union would like a wage *no less than* the competitive wage (w_0). The union may target for a still higher wage, depending on how it trades off employment losses against wage gains. If the union is happy with an amount of employment as low as would occur at the monopsonistic wage, it could target for a wage substantially higher than the competitive wage.

Simple demand and supply analysis can take us no further. The actual outcome will, as we have already observed, depend on such other things as what target wage the two sides actually set for themselves, their relative bargaining skills, how each side assesses the costs of concessions, and how serious a strike would be for each. We discuss unions in more detail in the next section of this chapter.

LEGISLATED MINIMUM WAGES

We have examined wage differentials arising in competitive and noncompetitive labour markets.

FIGURE 16-3
Effects of Union Entry in a Monopsonistic Labour Market

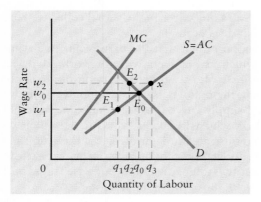

By presenting a monopsonistic employer with a fixed wage, the union can raise both wages and employment over the monopsonistic level. The monopsony position before the union enters is at E_1 (from Figure 16-2), with a wage rate of w_1 and q_1 workers hired. A union now enters and sets the wage at w_0. The supply curve of labour becomes $w_0 E_0 S$, and wages and employment rise to their competitive levels of w_0 and q_0 without creating a pool of unemployed workers. If the wage is raised further, say, to w_2, the supply curve will become $w_2 x S$, the quantity of employment will fall below the competitive level to q_2, and a pool of unsuccessful job applicants of $q_2 q_3$ will develop.

This figure can also be used to illustrate the effect of the government imposing a minimum wage of w_0 or w_2 on a monopsonistic labour market where the equilibrium wage was initially w_1.

Government policy can also affect observed wage differentials by legislating minimum wages. We explore this possibility now.

Governments in Canada and many other countries legislate specific **minimum wages,** which define the lowest wage rates that may legally be paid. In Canada, industries under federal jurisdiction—such as airlines, trucking, and railways—are subject to the Canadian Labour Code, which in 1995 had a minimum wage of $4.00 per hour. Most Canadian workers, however, are employed in industries covered by provincial legislation. In 1995, the provincial minimum wages ranged from $4.75 per hour in Newfoundland and Prince Edward Island to $7.00 per hour in British Columbia and parts of the Northwest Territories.

For a large proportion of all employment covered by the law, the minimum wage is below the actual market wage, and thus in such cases the minimum wage is *not binding.* Some workers, however, are employed in industries in which the free-market wage would be below the legal minimum, and so the legislated minimum wage is *binding.* It is in these cases only where the effects of minimum wages are of interest.

Although legislated minimum wages are now an accepted part of the labour scene in Canada and many other industrialized countries, economists are often sceptical about the benefits from such a policy. To the extent that the minimum wages are binding, they clearly raise the wages of employed workers. However, as our analysis in Chapter 6 indicated, a binding price floor in a competitive market leads to a market surplus of the product—in this case, an excess supply of labour, or unemployment. Thus a policy which legislates minimum wages is likely to benefit some workers only by hurting others.

The problem is more complicated than the analysis of Chapter 6 would suggest, however, both because not all labour markets are competitive and because minimum-wage laws do not cover all employment. Moreover, those groups in the labour force that tend to have the lowest wages, such as youth and minorities, are affected more than the average worker.

Employment Effects of a Minimum Wage

Suppose that minimum-wage laws apply uniformly to all occupations. The occupations and the industries in which minimum wages are binding will be the lowest paying in the country; they usually involve unskilled or semiskilled labour. In most of them, the workers are not members of unions. Thus the situations in which minimum wages are likely to be binding include competitive labour markets and those in which employers exercise monopsony power. The effects on employment are different in the two cases.

Competitive Labour Markets. The consequences for employment of a binding minimum wage are unambiguous when the labour market is competitive. By raising the wage that employers must pay, minimum-wage legislation leads to a reduction in the quantity of labour that is demanded and an increase in the quantity of labour that is supplied. As a result, the actual level of employment falls, and unemployment is generated. This situation is exactly analogous to the one that arises when a union succeeds in setting a wage above the competitive equilibrium wage, as illustrated in Figure 16-1. The excess supply of labour at the minimum wage also creates incentives for people to evade the law by working "under the table" below the legal minimum wage.

Monopsonistic Labour Markets.   The minimum-wage law can simultaneously increase both wages and employment in monopsonistic labour markets. The circumstances in which this can occur are the same as those in which a union facing a monopsonistic employer is able to increase both the wage and the level of employment, as shown in Figure 16-3. Of course, if the minimum wage is raised above the competitive wage, employment will start to fall, as in the union case. When it is set at the competitive level, however, the minimum wage can protect workers against monopsony power *and* lead to increases in employment.

Evidence on the Effects of Minimum Wages

Empirical research on the effects of minimum-wage laws reflects these mixed theoretical predictions. There is some evidence that people who keep their jobs gain when the minimum wage is raised. There is some evidence that some groups suffer a decline in employment consistent with raising the wage in a fairly competitive market. At other times and places, there is evidence that both wages earned and employment rise when the minimum wage rises, consistent with monopsonistic labour markets.

Employment Effects.   Several Canadian studies have examined the relationship between minimum wages and employment (or unemployment). Though the studies differ in their approaches and data used, there is a broad concensus that minimum wages decrease the level of employment (and raise unemployment), particularly for low-wage groups such as women and teenagers. In this sense, the Canadian results confirm the theoretical predictions of the effects of minimum wages in competitive labour markets.

Some recent research in the United States, however, has produced quite different results. David Card and Alan Krueger, both of Princeton University, traced the effects of minimum-wage increases in California during 1988 and New Jersey during 1992 and found that substantial rises in these states' minimum wages not only increased wages but were also associated with small employment gains for teenagers. Card and Krueger argue that these findings are inconsistent with a competitive labour market and thus take the results as evidence in support of the view that firms have some monopsony power in the labour market.

The Card and Krueger results have not been widely accepted, however. One criticism relates to the quality of their data. Another relates to the short span of time covered by their study. The argument is that firms will not immediately reduce the level of employment in response to an increase in the minimum wage—they will instead choose *not to replace* workers who leave their jobs in the natural process of "turnover" that occurs in labour markets. Thus it is not surprising to see few employment losses (or slight gains) when examining the labour market immediately before and immediately after the change in legislation. Proponents of this view argue that the total employment effects of minimum wages can only be detected by examining the data over longer periods of time.[2]

Distributional Effects.   The primary concern in research about minimum wages has been the effect on the total level of employment. A related issue, however, is how the effects of a legislated minimum wage are *distributed* over the labour force. Professors Charles Beach and Michael Shannon have recently examined this distributional issue by analysing the effects of a proposed change in the Ontario minimum wage, from $5.40 per hour to $6.75 per hour.[3] They showed that approximately 20 percent of all Ontario workers would be affected by the increase. Of those workers affected, 62 percent were women, 59 percent were under the age of 25, and 66 percent had no more than a high-school education. These findings confirm the idea that the effects of legislated minimum wages are more likely to fall on low-wage workers than on high-wage workers. Beach and Shannon also showed that the proposed increase in minimum wages would generate a reduction of employment of about 80,000 jobs, a reduction of approximately 1.3 percent.

---

[2]See, for example, "The Effects of Minimum Wages in the Canadian Labour Market: 1975–1993," by Michael Baker, Dwayne Benjamin and Shuchita Stanger, University of Toronto, mimeo, 1994.

[3]Michael Shannon and Charles Beach, "Distributional Employment Effects of Ontario Minimum-Wage Proposals: A Microdata Approach," *Canadian Public Policy XXI,* 284–303.

THE PUZZLE OF INTERINDUSTRY WAGE DIFFERENTIALS IN CANADA

Differences in wages across industries have been observed for as long as information on wages has been collected. But only in the past decade or so have economists looked closely at the wage differentials in an attempt to understand whether they could be explained by differences in skills, differences in jobs, or differences in market structure. In Canada, a recent study published by Surendra Gera and Gilles Grenier shows the extent of these wage differentials in 1986. Their approach follows closely that of two American economists who have explored the same issue (and found broadly similar results) in the United States.*

The table shows results from their study for selected industries; for each industry, the number in the table shows the amount by which wages in that industry are above or below the average wage across all industries. These numbers are referred to as the industry's *wage premium,* and reflect the differences in wages across industries *that cannot be explained* by differences in such factors as the worker's education, years of experience, age, gender, marital status, occupation, region of country, or union status. The challenge is to explain such wage premia.

COMPETITIVE WAGE DIFFERENTIALS

Following our discussion in the text, three possible explanations of these wage differentials are consistent with the labour market being competitive.

The first possibility is that these observed wage differentials for 1986 may reflect temporary shifts in the pattern of labour demand or supply across industries. If wages are slow to adjust to such shifts, or if labour is slow to move between industries, then such

shifts could indeed lead to differentials. For example, a large increase in the demand for labour in the forestry industry that occurs together with a large decline in the demand for labour in the textiles industry, could account for some of the data in the table. To address this possible explanation, Gera and Grenier examine Canadian census data for 1970, 1980, and 1985. They find that the pattern of interindustry wage differentials is very similar across these three periods, suggesting that the observed wage differentials are not simply temporary phenomena.

The second possibility is that the wage differentials can actually be explained by differences in the quality of the workers, but many of these differences are not observable to the economist when conducting such a study. For example, we are not able to observe whether a worker is "highly motivated," "innovative," or "a good problem solver." But many of these characteristics *are* observable to potential employers, either by watching the individual work for a short period of time, or by asking previous employers who know the worker. To examine this explanation, Gera and Grenier examine the group of individuals in their sample that move from a job in one industry to a job in a different industry. For example, if high wages to a particular worker in the Tobacco industry are due to that worker's unobserved skills, then when that worker switches to the Clothing industry, the high wage should persist. But Gera and Grenier find the opposite. A worker that moves from a high-wage industry to a low-wage industry tends to suffer a fall in wage; similarly, a worker that moves from a low-wage industry to a high-wage industry tends to experience a rise in the wage. This suggests that the observed wage differentials are not due mainly to unobserved labour quality.

The final possible explanation consistent with a competitive labour market is that the observed wage differentials reflect different characteristics of the *jobs.* Thus, maybe the jobs in the high-wage industries are less pleasant jobs—longer hours, less job security, less safe—than those in the low-wage industries. Gera and Grenier offer two pieces of evidence

---

*S. Gera and G. Grenier, "Interindustry Wage Differentials and Efficiency Wages: Some Canadian Evidence," *Canadian Journal of Economics,* 1994. A. Krueger and L. Summers, "Efficiency Wages and the Interindustry Wage Structure," *Econometrica,* 1988.

against this explanation. First, they note that workers in *similar occupations* receive very different wages in different industries, and it is difficult to believe that working conditions for, say, a clerk are very different in the Tobacco industry than in the Textiles industry. Second, if the observed wage differentials just reflect different job characteristics, then in competitive equilibrium workers are indifferent between (pleasant) jobs in the low-wage industries and (unpleasant) jobs in the high-wage industries. But this is hard to reconcile with the observation that workers appear to quit jobs in the high-wage industries much less frequently than they quit jobs in the low-wage industries. In other words, workers *appear* to view the high-wage jobs as valuable relative to the low-wage jobs. This, of course, suggests that the observed wage differentials are reflecting more than just differences in working conditions.

OTHER EXPLANATIONS?

Maybe the explanation for these observed wage differentials lies in a noncompetitive market structure. Perhaps unions have a large presence in some industries and little or no presence in others. When Gera and Grenier examine this possibility, they find that the interindustry wage differentials are just as marked among unionized workers as they are among nonunionized workers.

If the observed wage differentials across Canadian industries cannot be explained by considering different characterstics of the workers, jobs, or market structures, then what is the explanation? One explanation that is starting to attract considerable attention among economists is based on the theory of *efficiency wages*. According to this theory, firms in even a competitive labour market *pay more than the competitive wage* to their workers. The reason firms do this is that they perceive that a higher wage will make their workers more productive. Since workers are receiving more than is required to attract their services, they are earning *economic rents*. The fact that workers are receiving rents, in turn, explains why they are reluctant to leave these good jobs—and thus their quit rates from such jobs are low.

Though the efficiency-wage theory offers one possible explanation for why some workers might earn rents, it does not directly offer an explanation for why these rents might be different across industries. In order for the efficiency-wage theory to explain the observed interindustry wage differentials, it must explain why firms' incentives to pay higher wages are greater in some industries than in others. So far, proponents of the theory have not come up with convincing reasons.

The efficiency-wage theory is still young and still generates considerable disagreement among economists. But there is little debate that there exist significant wage differentials across industries, even after taking account of observable characteristics of workers and jobs. As more data become available, perhaps we will find better explanations for the interindustry wage differentials that do exist.

1986 Industry Wage Premia in Canada
(percentage above average wage)

Tobacco Products	33.4
Mineral Fuels	25.5
Forestry	18.9
Electric Power, Gas, and Water Utilities	14.4
Paper and Allied Products	12.0
Communications	10.5
Rubber and Plastics	7.1
Transportation Equipment	7.0
Wholesale Trade	3.8
Electrical Products	2.6
Education and Related Services	−1.0
Health and Welfare	−3.1
Food and Beverages	−3.5
Insurance and Real Estate Agencies	−4.1
Clothing	−8.1
Fishing and Trapping	−9.5
Personal Services	−16.7
Retail Trade	−11.1
Textiles	−19.0
Accommodation and Food Services	−20.3

Economists have not reached a definitive conclusion regarding the desirabilty or the effects of legislated minimum wages. Given its mixed economic effects, support for and opposition to the minimum wage might be understood as arising largely from political and sociological motives. Organized labour has consistently pressed for a broad, relatively high minimum wage. There is some economic reason for this, in that there is evidence that the minimum wage "trickles up" to higher-wage workers, both unionized and not. Arguably, however, the support dates back to the 1930s, when organized labour was still fighting for its position in North American society. Enactment of a minimum wage was then a great political victory, and the minimum wage still has symbolic significance.

A FINAL WORD

We have examined several explanations for why some workers get paid more than others. The explanations include differences in workers' educations and skills, differences in job characteristics, and differences in the structure of the various labour markets. But this apparent abundance of explanations should not lead you to believe that economists understand *all* wage differentials that are observed in the labour market. Recent studies, both in Canada and in the United States, have revealed significant differences in wages across industries that appear to defy explanations based on the sort of arguments we have examined. Application 16-1 discusses the puzzle of interindustry wage differentials in Canada.

TABLE 16-2
Union Membership in Canada, Selected Years, 1921–1992

Year	Total (thousands)	Percent of Labour Force
1921	313	9.4
1931	311	7.5
1941	462	10.3
1951	1,029	19.7
1962	1,423	21.5
1972	2,388	27.6
1982	3,617	30.4
1992	4,089	29.7

Union membership in Canada grew steadily from the 1920s until peaking in the early 1980s; it has dropped slightly since then.

(*Source:* Richard Chaykowski, *Modern Labour Economics,* HarperCollins 1994.)

LABOUR UNIONS

Unions currently represent fewer than 30 percent of workers in Canada. Of those workers employed in the public sector, however, approximately 80 percent are unionized. Table 16-2 shows how union membership has changed in Canada over the past several decades. Table 16-3 shows unionization rates by industry in 1990. As is clear from the table, unionization is most common in the public and educational sectors, and least common in agriculture, finance, and business services.

There is considerable variation across countries in the degree of unionization. In 1988, Canada's unionization rate (expressed as a share of the non-agricultural labour force) was 36.5 percent. This was far below the unionization rates in Sweden (96 percent), Italy (62.7 percent) and Australia (53 percent), but considerably more than the United States (16 percent) and France (12 percent).

Despite the relatively low degree of unionization among Canada's private-sector workers, unions have

TABLE 16-3
Unionization Rates by Industry, 1990

Industry	Membership as Percentage of Paid Workers
Agriculture	1.8
Forestry	58.8
Fishing & Trapping	33.4
Mining	28.4
Manufacturing	36.7
Construction	59.6
Transportation, Communication and other utilities	54.8
Trade	11.6
Finance, Real Estate and Insurance	3.5
Services	
Business	3.1
Educational	77.0
Health and Social	50.8
Other	11.6
Public Administration	80.6
Total	34.7

There is considerable variation across industries of the extent of unionization. The public sector and the educational services sector are the most unionized; agriculture, finance, and business services are the least unionized.

(*Source:* Richard Chaykowski, *Modern Labour Economics,* HarperCollins 1994.)

a considerable influence in the private sector. One reason is the impact that union wage contracts have on other labour markets. When, for example, the Canadian Auto Workers negotiate a new contract with an automobile producer in Oshawa, its provisions set a pattern that directly or indirectly affects other labour markets, both in Ontario and in other provinces. A second reason is the major leadership role that unions have played in the past 50 years in the development of labour market practices and in lobbying for legislation that applies to all workers.

In this section, we discuss the process of *collective bargaining* and, in particular, examine the inherent conflict that unions face between striving for higher wages or for increased employment. Extension 16-1 examines the historical development of labour unions in Canada.

COLLECTIVE BARGAINING

The process by which unions and employers (or their representatives) arrive at and enforce their agreements is known as **collective bargaining**. This process has an important difference from the theoretical models with which we began this chapter. In those models, we assumed that the union had the power to set the wage unilaterally; the employer then decided how much labour to hire. In real-world collective bargaining, however, the firm and union typically bargain over the wage. There is usually a substantial range over which an agreement can be reached, and the actual result in particular cases will depend on the strengths of the two bargaining parties and on the skill of their negotiators.[4]

Wages Versus Employment

Unions seek many goals when they bargain with management. They may push for higher wages, higher fringe benefits, more stable employment, or less onerous working conditions. Whatever their specific goals, unless they face a monopsonist across the

bargaining table, they must deal with a fundamental dilemma.

There is an inherent conflict between the level of wages and the size of the union itself.

The more successful a union is in raising wages, the more management will attempt to reduce the size of its work force, substituting capital for labour. This will lead to lower union membership. However, if the union does not provide some wage improvement for its members, they will have little incentive to stay around.

The Union Wage Premium

Despite the costs to unions (i.e., reduced membership) of pushing for higher wages, there is clear evidence in Canada of a *union wage premium*—that is, a higher wage attributed only to the union status of the job. It is not an easy task to measure this wage premium, however, because it is not appropriate simply to compare the average wage of unionized workers with the average wage of non–unionized workers. After all, unions may occur mainly in industries where workers have higher skills or where working conditions are less pleasant. And we know from the first section of this chapter that differences in skills or working conditions can lead to wage differentials. Economists have therefore been forced to use complicated statistical techniques to identify this union wage premium. The consensus of these studies appears to be that the union wage premium in Canada is somewhere between 10 and 25 percent—that is, unionized workers with a particular set of skills in particular types of jobs get paid 10 to 25 percent more than *otherwise identical workers* that are not members of unions.

There is also evidence that the size of this union wage premium differs across industries. Given that workers in different industries and with different occupations are often represented by different unions, this cross-industry difference in the union wage premium may simply reflect the differences in unions' preferences for higher wages versus higher employment.

UNION RESPONSES TO CHANGING CONDITIONS

A union that, through the bargaining process, pushes the wage above the competitive level is making a

---

[4]In terms of Figure 16-3, it may be that the firm wants the wage to be w_1 and the union wants the wage to be w_2. Depending on each side's market power, and on their bargaining tactics, the final agreed-upon wage may be anywhere in between. Note that while real-world collective bargaining has the firm and union bargaining over the wage, it is typically the case that the firm retains the "right to manage"—meaning that the firm can decide how much labour it wants to employ at the bargained wage.

EXTENSION 16-1

THE DEVELOPMENT OF UNIONS IN CANADA

Early Canadian unionization was strongly dominated by the influence of international unions, which had their headquarters and an overwhelming proportion of their membership outside Canada. The creation of Canadian locals of American unions began in the 1860s, and by 1911, the earliest date for which figures are available, 90 percent of Canadian workers who were union members belonged to international unions.

During the first half of the twentieth century, there was strong pressure, first, toward a single national federation, and second, to achieve autonomy from American unions. The issues became intertwined when conflicts in the United States arose between craft and industrial unions. Until the 1930s, *craft unions*—which cover persons in a particular occupation—were the characteristic form of collective action in the United States. In Canada, meanwhile, trade unionists were attracted to the principle of *industrial unions* that embraced unskilled workers as well as skilled craftsmen in one industry such as steel making.

Because of the impossibility of establishing bargaining strength by controlling the supply of unskilled workers, the rise of industrial unionism in Canada was associated with political action as an alternative means of improving the lot of the membership. In general, social and political reform were given much more emphasis by Canadian unionists than by their American counterparts. Political action here extended to the support for social democratic political parties: first, the Cooperative Commonwealth Federation (CCF), established in 1932, and later its successor, the New Democratic Party (NDP), formed in 1961.

The late Senator Eugene Forsey, a former director of research for the Canadian Labour Congress, viewed the unification of the bulk of Canadian unions under the CLC in 1956 as the beginning of virtual autonomy for Canadian locals from their U.S. head offices—the CLC has guidelines for the conduct of international unions operating in Canada. Throughout the postwar period, the percentage of total Canadian union membership represented by international unions fell: In the mid 1950s, it was about 70 percent, and by the mid 1990s, it was just over 30 percent.

One factor in the increased share of national unions is the growth of membership in the two unions representing government workers, the Canadian Union of Public Employees and the Public Service Alliance. Another major component of non-international union membership has arisen out of the distinct aspirations of French-Canadian workers. More recently, the formation of the Canadian Auto Workers, independent of the American Auto Workers, represented a significant further reduction of membership in international unions.

Rapid gains in union membership in Canada occurred in the years during World War II. This led to pressure for the rights of workers to organize and to elect an exclusive bargaining agent. These rights were established by provisions of the Wartime Labour Relations Regulations Act of 1944.

Government intervention in industrial disputes in Canada has a history dating back to the early years of the twentieth century. The earliest legislation applied only to public utilities and coal mining. It provided that before a strike or a lockout could be initiated, the parties were required to submit any dispute to a conciliation board. This system of compulsory conciliation and compulsory delay in work stoppage was extended to a much larger segment of the economy under special emergency powers adopted by the government of Canada during World War II. In the postwar period, jurisdiction over labour policy reverted to the provinces, but the principles established have been carried over into provincial legislation.

---

choice of higher wages for some workers and unemployment for others. Should the union strive to maximize the earnings of the group that remains employed? If it does, some of its members will lose their jobs, and the union's membership will decline.

Should it instead maximize the welfare of its present members? Or should it seek to expand employment opportunities (perhaps by a low-wage policy) so that the union membership grows? Different unions decide these questions differently.

Severe strains developed between Canadian and American members of international unions as a result of different views of how to respond to the difficult economic conditions of the 1980s. Two key differences typified a range of differences in attitudes.

American unions were willing to reopen contracts and accept wage cuts when the alternative seemed to be plant closures or company liquidations. They were also willing to consider schemes designed to move away from the traditional pattern where wages are relatively stable over the business cycle while employment does most of the adjusting to fluctuating demand. The alternative is to have wages vary more over the cycle in order to maintain a more stable employment pattern. One way of doing this is to move toward the Japanese arrangement whereby wages are to some extent linked to profits.

Canadian unions have been more inclined to stick with traditional approaches. First, they argue that contracts should not be reopened before they expire. Even if the agreed wages threaten to cause plant closures, the sanctity of the contract is a more important principle than the saving of specific jobs. Second, profit sharing is often viewed as selling out to the bosses. Canadian unions believe that the traditional system should be maintained, in which wages are stable over the cycle and most of the adjustment to variations in demand occurs through variations in employment.

The Canadian Automobile Workers (CAW) eventually split with the United Automobile Workers (UAW) over these and related issues. A separate Canadian union was set up, and its different approach to bargaining soon became apparent.

Since the breakaway, the CAW has been significantly more hostile to changes in work organization than the UAW has been. The CAW's National Policy Statement issued in October 1989 explicitly rejected such innovations as flexible job classifications and supervisor-worker interchanges that appear to have contributed greatly to productivity in the Japanese automobile industry. Because the North American automobile industry is under immense challenges from Japanese and other foreign producers, this statement seemed to many observers to be an open invitation to automobile firms to invest in the United States rather than Canada. However, the policy statement and the actual policies adopted by the CAW differed: Faced, for example, with the real possibility of the closure of a major GM plant in Ste. Thérèse, Québec, the union was considerably more flexible about agreeing to a number of changes in work arrangements than its policy statement would have suggested.

DISCRIMINATION IN LABOUR MARKETS

The economic effects of discrimination against minorities and women take many forms. Labour market discrimination does not wholly explain, but surely contributes to, lower wages and higher unemployment rates for those discriminated against. Both lower wages and greater unemployment lead to lower incomes for the workers involved.

Discrimination may also have powerful indirect effects on attitudes toward the workplace and toward society. It affects not only the workers discriminated against but also their children, whose ability, aspirations, and willingness to undertake the education and training required to succeed may be adversely affected. Indeed, it may change their definition of success. There are many subtle ways in which discrimination can become part of the way in which a society functions, and these can be as important in their effects as overt (and now generally illegal) direct discrimination.

The problems of race discrimination and gender discrimination differ, but there are similarities as well. It is helpful to look first at how both kinds of discrimination lead to important economic effects.

A MODEL OF LABOUR-MARKET DISCRIMINATION

To isolate the effects of discrimination, we begin by building a simplified picture of a nondiscriminating labour market and then introduce discrimination between two sets of equally qualified workers. The discussion here is phrased in terms of males and females but the analysis applies equally well to any situation in which workers are distinguished on grounds *other than* their ability, such as race or skin colour, citizenship, religion, or political beliefs.

Suppose that half of the people are male and the other half are female. Each group has the same proportion who are educated to various levels, identical distributions of talent, and so on. Suppose also that there are two occupations. Occupation E (*elite*) requires people of above-average education and skills, and occupation O (*ordinary*) can use anyone. Finally, suppose that the nonmonetary aspects of the two occupations are the same.

In the absence of discrimination, the labour markets that we are studying are competitive. The theory of competitive factor markets that we have developed suggests that the wages in E occupations will be bid up above those in O occupations in order that the E jobs attract the workers of above-average skills. Men and women of above-average skill will take the E jobs, while the others, both men and women, will have no choice but to seek O jobs. Because skills are equally distributed, each occupation will employ one-half men and one-half women.

Now suppose that discrimination enters in an extreme form. All E occupations are hereafter open only to men, but O occupations are open to either men or women. The immediate effect is to reduce by 50 percent the supply of job candidates for E oc-

cupations; candidates must now be *both* men and above average. The discrimination also increases the supply of applicants for O jobs by 50 percent; this group now includes all women and the below-average men.

Wage Level Effects

Suppose that labour is perfectly mobile among occupations, that everyone seeks the best job that he or she is eligible for, and that wage rates are free to vary so as to equate supply and demand. The analysis is shown in Figure 16-4. Wages rise in E occupations and fall in O occupations. The take-home pay of people in O occupations falls, and the O group is now approximately two-thirds women.

Discrimination, by changing supply, can decrease the wages and incomes of a group that is discriminated against.

FIGURE 16-4
Economic Discrimination: wage Level Effects

(i) Elite market (E)

(ii) Ordinary market (O)

If market E discriminates against one group and market O does not, the supply curve will shift to the left in E and to the right in O. Market E requires above-average skills, while market O requires only ordinary skills. When there is no discrimination, demand and supply are D_E and S_E in market E and D_O and S_O in market O. Initially, the wage rate is w_0 and employment is q_0 in each market. (w_0 in market E will be higher than w_0 in market O because the workers in E have higher skills than those in O.) When all women are barred from E occupations, the supply curve shifts to S'_E, and the wage earned by the remaining workers, all of whom are men, rises to w_1. Women put out of work in the E occupations now seek work in the O occupations. The resulting shift in the supply curve to S'_O brings down the wage to w_2 in the O occupations. Because all women are in O occupations, they have a lower wage rate than many men. The average male wage is higher than the average female wage.

Discrimination also hurts members of the favoured group who cannot obtain E jobs.

In the longer run, further changes may occur. Notice that total employment in the E jobs falls. Employers may find ways to use slightly below average labour and thus lure the next best qualified men out of O occupations. Although this will raise O wages slightly, it will also make these occupations increasingly "female occupations." If discrimination has been in effect for a sufficient length of time, women will learn that it does not pay to acquire above-average skills. Regardless of ability, women are forced by discrimination to work in unskilled jobs.

Now suppose that a long-standing discriminatory policy is reversed. Because they will have responded to discrimination by acquiring fewer skills than men, many women will be locked into the O occupations, at least for a time. Moreover, if both men and women come to expect that women will have less education than men, employers will tend to look for men to fill the E jobs. This will reinforce the belief of women that education does not pay. Such subtle discrimination can persist for a very long time, making the supply of women to O jobs higher than it would be in the absence of discrimination, thereby depressing the wages of women and below-average men.

Employment Effects

For a number of reasons, labour-market discrimination may have adverse employment effects that are even more important than the effects on wages. Labour is not perfectly mobile, wages are not perfectly flexible downward, and not everyone who is denied employment in an E occupation for which he or she is trained and qualified will be willing to take a "demeaning" O job. We continue the graphical example in Figure 16-5.

If wages do not fall to the market-clearing level, possibly because of minimum-wage laws, the increase in the supply of labour to O occupations will cause excess supply, which will result in unemployment in O occupations. Because women dominate these occupations, women will bear the brunt of the extra unemployment, as illustrated in Figure 16-5(i).

A similar result will occur if labour is not fully mobile between occupations. For example, many of the O jobs might be in places to which the women are unable or unwilling to move. (Discrimination in housing markets may be one reason for this.) See Figure 16-5(ii). Potential O workers who cannot move to places where jobs are available become unemployed or withdraw from the labour force. Quite apart from any discrimination, long-term technological changes tend to decrease the demand for less skilled labour of the kind that is required in O occupations. Occupation O then becomes increasingly oversupplied. This possibility is outlined in Figure 16-5(iii).

The kind of discrimination that we have considered in our model is extreme. It is similar to the South African apartheid system that was dismantled in the 1980s and 1990s, in which blacks were excluded by law from prestigious and high-paying occupations. In Canada and the United States, labour-market discrimination against a specific group usually occurs in somewhat less obvious ways. First, it may be difficult (but not impossible, as in our model) for members of the group to get employment in certain jobs. Second, members of groups subject to discrimination may receive lower pay for a given kind of work than members of groups not subject to discrimination.

Indeed, the first type of discrimination may encourage the second type. How might this happen? First, if discrimination makes it difficult for a qualified woman to get a good job, she may be more willing to accept such a job even if the pay and working conditions are poorer than those given to men in the same job. Even under relatively unfavourable terms, the job will still be better than the alternative (an O job). Second, employers who are seeking to fill E jobs and who have no taste for discrimination will nonetheless be able to hire qualified women at wages that, although higher than O wages, are lower than E wages for men. As long as there is some discrimination of the first type (in the extreme, apartheid), there will be pressures coming from both the supply and the demand sides of the labour market for discrimination of the second type.

Can Discrimination Exist in Equilibrium?

We have seen that in the absence of discrimination, competitive labour markets will tend to equalize the wages of the two groups, men and women in our example above. (Note in Figure 16-4 that wages in E jobs are higher than those in O jobs because workers in E jobs—both men and women—have higher skills

FIGURE 16-5
Economic Discrimination: Employment Effects

(i) Wage rigidities (or minimum wage)

(ii) Immobile labour (or withdrawal from labour force)

(iii) Declining demand

Increasing supply or decreasing demand in occupations in which the people discriminated against are the major sources of labour can increase unemployment. In each part of the diagram, the curves D_0 and S_0 are those from part (ii) of Figure 16-4; they show the market for O workers after the discriminatory policies are put into effect. Equilibrium is at E_1. In each case, the wage w_2 would clear the market and provide employment of q_2.

In part (i), if the wage rate cannot fall below w_3, perhaps because of a legislated minimum wage, employment will fall to q_3, and unemployment will occur in the amount shown by the arrows.

In part (ii), if some of the potential workers in the O occupations are unable or unwilling to take employment in O jobs, the supply curve will not be S_0' but S_0''. Equilibrium will be at E_3. Although O wages will rise somewhat to w_3, employment will be only q_3, and a number of workers, shown by the arrows, will not be employed. Whether they are recorded as "unemployed" or as having withdrawn from the labour force will depend on the official definitions.

In part (iii), if demand is declining in O occupations over time, say, from D_0 to D_0', either wages and employment will fall to the new equilibrium E_4 with w_4 and q_4, or wages will be maintained but employment will fall to q_3. The arrows illustrate the latter case, where the fall in employment is $q_3 q_2$.

than workers in O jobs.) Some economists go further than this and argue that under perfect competition, discrimination *cannot be sustained in equilibrium,* and thus if it exists at all it must only be a temporary phenomenon. This theory, most forcefully propounded by Thomas Sowell of the Hoover Institution and Nobel Laureate Gary Becker of the University of Chicago, works like this: Employers of workers in E jobs who pay high wages (w_1) can increase their profits if they hire qualified women at any lower wage. If women have the same distribution of qualifications as men (as they do in our model above), under discrimination there will be plenty of workers who will be willing to work in E jobs at any wage that is greater than the low wage level in the O market (w_2)—much less than the going wage for men. If some employers take advantage of this opportunity, there will be competitive pressure that, all other things being equal, works against the

maintenance of discrimination. As firms who hire qualified women at wages below w_1 (but above w_2) earn profits, they will grow, and other firms will have to imitate them or go out of business. Eventually, the discrimination will disappear in competitive equilibrium.

This argument shows the important pressures that act against discrimination in competitive markets. However, the proposition that competitive equilibrium is completely inconsistent with the practice of discrimination fails to take into account a number of important phenomena. One of these is the indirect effect of discrimination on both the acquisition of skills and on the expectations of employers. There may also be direct market effects. For example, prejudiced workers may be less productive if women are treated as equals in the workplace. Another example—though perhaps a bit extreme in this context—is that prejudiced customers may refrain from buying the products of firms that employ women in E occupations. (A less extreme example is that some customers in southern U.S. states may boycott firms that employ blacks in service jobs.) In these cases, it is customers and workers whose prejudices matter, and employers may thus have powerful economic incentives to discriminate, even if they have no prejudice of their own.

In any event, the history of both race and sex discrimination in Canada, the United States, and elsewhere suggests that however strong are the competitive forces working against discrimination in the labour market, they are not strong enough to *eliminate* it.

MALE-FEMALE WAGE DIFFERENTIALS IN CANADA

The model of labour-market discrimination that we have discussed helps us to think about discrimination that may occur in actual labour markets. We discuss briefly the male-female wage differential in Canada, and how much of this differential can be attributed to discrimination.

There is no doubt that some discrimination does occur. For example, psychologists have conducted many studies that suggest a bias against women that could easily lead to discriminatory pay differences. In one experiment, university department heads were given identical files, one with a male name and the other with a female name. They were 10 percent more likely to select the male for a job offer than the female with the identical resume. In another experiment, *female* college students were asked to rank paintings on a scale from 1 to 10. The same picture consistently got a higher rating when it had a male name attached than when it was ascribed to a female artist.

How does this discrimination translate into different labour-market performance of men versus women? Despite obvious gains that women have made in the labour market over the past few decades, the average earned income of females in the labour force is well below that of males of similar ages. The female-to-male earnings ratio has risen slightly from approximately 0.59 in 1960 to about 0.70 in 1995. The persistence of the remaining salary gap for females is due to a combination of causes in addition to straightforward discrimination: Women are still underrepresented in high-status occupations, proportionately fewer women than men reach higher-paying jobs in the occupations in which both

work, and those who do reach higher-paying jobs do so more slowly.

Most empirical studies of male-female wage differentials show that a considerable portion of the difference between men's and women's wages is due to differences in such objective considerations as educational requirements and years of experience in the work force and on the job. When all such factors have been taken into account, however, there remains a "residual" that is consistent with some direct sex discrimination.

Discrimination Within Occupations. To what extent do differences in pay levels of men and women within an occupation reflect direct discrimination against women? To what extent do they reflect other sex-linked characteristics, the most important of which is the persistent difference in lifetime patterns of labour-force participation? The evidence shows that, on average, women have fewer years of work experience than men of the same age. The average working female is less mobile occupationally and geographically than her male counterpart. These facts reflect, at least in part, *labour-market attachment*. For example, many women withdraw from the labour force or work only part time in order to have and raise children.

The causes of gender differences in labour-market attachment have attracted attention from both social psychologists and economists. There is some evidence that *sex-role socialization* is an important factor. To the extent that women and men are socialized to accept the view that women should be the primary caretakers of young children, some social scientists argue that differences in labour-market attachment arise from a form of indirect discrimination. However important this may be, it arises from differences in the way in which boys and girls are raised, not from the direct behaviour of the labour market.

The extent of direct discrimination within an occupation may be measured by comparing the pay status of groups with similar characteristics. Studies of the sources of male-female pay differences in Canada have found that between one-third and one-half of the differences in earnings can be explained by differences in education, work experience, and labour-market attachment.[5] Analysts attribute the remaining one-half to two-thirds of the male-female pay differentials to direct sex discrimination.

---

[5]Much of this literature is summarized in University of Toronto economist Morley Gunderson's "Male-Female Wage Differentials and Policy Responses," *Journal of Economic Literature* 27, 1989.

Interoccupational Discrimination. For many years, women were refused admission to (or were discouraged from seeking entry into) certain occupations; for example, women were urged into nursing rather than medicine, social work rather than law, and secretarial schools rather than managerial training programs. The result of this is called *occupational segregation*. Similarly, girls were raised in a culture in which their education seemed less important than that of their brothers or in which they were trained to think of themselves as potential homemakers and were thus less likely to acquire the skills for many high-paying occupations that were wholly within their capabilities. This is a form of sex-role socialization.

Differences in pay among occupations reflect, as we have seen, differences in supply and demand, including nonmonetary considerations. Might they not also reflect discrimination, if one occupation is predominantly female and the other predominantly male? This is certainly possible, and a number of studies have shown that such an effect exists; that is, if one uses the characteristics of workers (education, training, experience, etc.) to explain their wages, the fraction of female workers in the occupation has a significant negative effect. Moreover, this effect exists for both men and women. Men (and women) who work in predominantly female occupations are paid less than men (and women) with the same training and experience in predominantly male occupations. For this reason, many have urged that attention be paid to interoccupational pay differences under the general term *pay equity*. Determining how much observed differences reflect discrimination is extremely difficult, because so many different considerations affect the pay levels of, say, firefighters and librarians.

GOVERNMENT POLICIES TO REDRESS DISCRIMINATION

Governments have long had policies to eliminate discrimination between men and women *doing the same job*. Such policies require that a man and a woman doing a job with the same job description must receive the same pay. These policies are relatively easy to administer, as long as it is easy to identify that two individuals are indeed doing the same job (i.e., same hours, same factory, same health risk, etc.).

A much harder case arises when an attempt is made to remove alleged discrimination *between jobs*. If one job is staffed primarily with women and another primarily with men (such as nurses and firefighters), do differences between the wages paid in the two jobs represent differences in market conditions, or are they due to discrimination?

Much of the persistence of male-female pay differentials results from wages in male-dominated occupations exceeding those in female-dominated ones. As a way of eliminating these differentials, the federal government and many of the provinces have enacted legislation that mandates wage adjustments to eliminate disparities between jobs of "comparable worth" or "equal value."

Pay-equity policy relies on a job evaluation program that measures the *intrinsic value* of different occupations. In practice, this involves assigning "worth points" to various attributes of a given job (typically effort, initiative, skill, training, responsibility, and conditions of work). These points can then be summed to obtain a "total job score"; comparing scores for different jobs allows a comparison of their intrinsic values. Pay equity then requires that two jobs judged to be of equal value receive equal pay.

Needless to say, pay-equity policies have been controversial. Supporters argue that they do not go far enough and that significant differentials will persist even after full implementation. Critics argue that the evaluation schemes are often arbitrary and always imperfect. Simple schemes are easy to administer but give poorer results; more complex schemes are, in principle, more accurate but harder to administer. Implementation problems such as definition of an establishment, determination of criteria to include in the evaluation program and the weights to assign to them, and definition of gender dominance plague most schemes currently in place.

Economists are often concerned that the policies fail to distinguish between temporary and equilibrium differentials as stressed in Chapter 15. They fear that misguided attempts to eliminate equilibrium differentials will lead to the emergence of excess demand in some occupations and excess supply in others, with associated efficiency costs for the economy.

Supporters of pay-equity policy often argue that job evaluation and comparison play an important role in any big firm's employment policy, implicitly and often explicitly. Hence, they argue, pay-equity legislation merely formalizes in law procedures that already play an important role in labour markets. Economists point out, however, that market-oriented job evaluation policies of individual firms, whether explicit or implicit, have the major advantage of reacting quickly to market forces. Such evaluations are only a guideline to determining wages. If changes occur to make previously determined evaluations no longer consistent with market balance, and surpluses or shortages arise, firms will respond quickly by altering their guidelines and changing relative wages. Legislated comparisons determining wages may cause shortages or surpluses to persist for long periods of time.

Professor Roberta Robb of Brock University identifies three potential costs of pay-equity legislation: economic efficiency losses (including allocation distortions and implementation costs), private costs of employers (including higher wages for some female employees and administration costs), and private costs of employees (including adverse employment effects for females). Potential benefits include increased productivity of females (resulting from the incentive effects of increased earnings) and a reduced male-female wage differential. The latter is viewed as a benefit in its own right, and it has been suggested that current legislation may succeed in reducing the male-female earnings differential by about 10 percentage points (out of a total differential in 1995 of about 30 percentage points).[6]

Is pay-equity policy "progressive pragmatism," as one supporter put it, or is it "a profoundly flawed concept," as a critic pronounced? The answer will depend on the magnitude of the resource misallocation caused by setting relative wages through a system that does not attempt to balance demand and supply and on one's view of whether this lost efficiency is a price worth paying in the name of equity. As Professor Robb concludes, "This kind of legislation is likely to have a very significant impact on individual perceptions of what women's jobs are worth. This result is clearly important if one believes that part of the role of this policy is to break the cycle of systematically undervaluing women's jobs."

---

[6]Roberta Robb, "The Costs and Benefits of Canadian Pay Equity Policy," in Richard Chaykowski, ed. *Pay Equity Legislation* (Kingston, Ont.: Queen's University Industrial Relations Centre, 1990).

THE "GOOD JOBS–BAD JOBS" DEBATE

We saw in Chapter 1 (see Figure 1-5) how the composition of Canadian employment has changed dramatically over the past century. Similar changes have also occurred in the United States and in many other industrialized countries. This changing composition of the labour force has led to some concerns in recent years. The specific change which has received considerable attention in Canada and elsewhere is the decline in the share of total employment in the manufacturing sector since the Second World War, and the simultaneous increase in the share of total employment in the service sector.

Some people fear that productivity is lower and the opportunities for growth are much more limited in some service industries than in goods-producing industries. They argue that the possibilities for using more capital per unit of labour employed, which raises labour productivity, are less in the service sector than in the manufacturing sector. Another concern is that many of the "good jobs" in the manufacturing sector appear to have been replaced by "bad jobs" in the service sector, where such "bad jobs" are characterized by low pay and little job security.

Should these dramatic changes in the composition of employment worry us? Is there something undesirable about the fact that fewer Canadian workers are now producing manufactured goods than forty years ago? Or that more Canadian workers are working in the service sector than forty years ago? Are the good jobs in Canada being replaced by bad jobs? This final section of the chapter addresses this issue.

FOUR OBSERVATIONS

There are four reasons why the decline in the manufacturing sector may not necessarily reflect anything "wrong" with the economy. First, we need to keep a sense of perspective about the emergence of low-paying service jobs. As is apparent in Figure 1-5, the trend toward services has been going on for over a century. Yet real income per hour worked has been rising throughout this period (recall Figure 1-4); as a nation, we are getting wealthier, not poorer. Further, the size distribution of income has not changed dramatically over this period, so the increased wealth has been experienced by individuals in *all* income classes.

Second, to a considerable extent, the decrease in the share of manufacturing in total employment is a result of that sector's dynamism. More and more manufactured goods have been produced by fewer and fewer workers, leaving more workers to produce services. This movement is analogous to the one out of agriculture earlier in the century (see Figure 1-5 again). At the turn of the century, nearly 50 percent of the Canadian labour force worked on farms. Today that number is less than 5 percent, yet they produce more total output than did the 50 percent in 1900. This movement away from agricultural employment freed workers to move into manufacturing, raising our living standards and transforming our way of life. In like manner, the movement away from manufacturing is freeing workers to move into services, and by replacing the grimy blue-collar jobs of the smokestack industries with more pleasant white-collar jobs in the service industries, it will once again transform our way of life.

Third, to a considerable extent, the decrease in the share of manufacturing in total employment also follows from consumers' tastes. Just as consumers in the first half of the century did not want to go on consuming more and more food products as their incomes rose, today's consumers do not wish to spend all of their additional income on manufactured products. Households have chosen to spend a high proportion of their increased incomes on services, thus creating employment opportunities in that sector. This simply reflects the fact that many products of the service sector—like restaurant meals, hotel stays, and airline flights—are products which have a high income elasticity of demand. Thus as the income of the average Canadian household increases, so too does that household's demand for these products of the service sector.

Finally, it is easy to underestimate the scope for quality, quantity, and productivity increases in services. As one example of productivity increases, consider your ability to make an automatic cash withdrawal from your bank account in Truro, Nova Scotia, while you are on vacation in Brazil. Now compare that to the apprehension your parents faced twenty years ago when they had to get to the bank before 3:00 pm on a Friday afternoon to make sure that they had enough cash for the weekend. As another example, note that since 1950, output per full-time worker has grown about *twice as fast* in the communication industry as it has in manufacturing.

CONTINUING CHANGE

The service sector is changing quickly. There has been some trend toward the mass-production techniques that provided much of the basis for productivity growth in the goods sector earlier in this century. This should increase productivity further. Services are also becoming globalized, so international trade will provide more opportunity for specialization and, hence, increased productivity. Also, much of the recent growth in demand for services comes as an input into goods-producing industries—either indirectly in the form of bundling sales with, say, maintenance contracts, or directly through productivity-enhancing management skills, inventory control methods, and the like. These contribute to the value added of the goods sector and hence to real national income.

It is also the case that many quality improvements in services go unrecorded. Today's hotel room is vastly more comfortable than a hotel room of 40 years ago, yet this quality improvement does not show up in our national income statistics. Measuring such technological improvements is even more difficult when they take the form of entirely new products. Airline transportation, telecommunication, fast-food chains, and financial services are prominent examples. The resulting increase in output is not always properly captured in our existing statistics.

It is easy to become concerned when looking at the official statistics, which show low wages earned in some service jobs. Indeed, the shift in employment toward services is, like most changes that hit the economy, a mixed blessing. It entails a significant increase in the number of "bad" service-sector jobs with low pay or low job security. Further, such transitions often generate temporary unemployment as workers get laid off from a contracting manufacturing sector and only slowly find jobs in the expanding service sector. Such transitions suggest a role for government policy to maintain the income of those workers temporarily unemployed (we discuss unemployment insurance and other income-support programs in Chapter 20). However, if we focus on the *overall economy*, and consider the growth in the real living standards of the *average* Canadian household, we are reminded that average real income has continued to rise, not only throughout the shift from agriculture to manufacturing, but also throughout the shift from manufacturing to services. There is little reason to think that the continued growth of the service sector will stand in the way of this slow but steady improvement in Canadians' living standards.

SUMMARY

A. LABOUR MARKETS AND WAGE DIFFERENTIALS

- In a competitive labour market, wages are set by the forces of supply and demand. Differences in wages will arise because some skills are more valued than others, because some jobs are more onerous than others, because of varying amounts of human capital, and because of discrimination based on such factors as gender and race.
- A union entering a competitive market acts as a monopolist and can raise wages, but only at the cost of reducing employment and creating a pool of unemployed who would like to work at the going wage rate but are unable to find employment in that market.
- A monopsonistic employer entering a competitive labour market will reduce both the wage and the level of employment.
- A union in a monopsonistic labour market—a case of bilateral monopoly—may increase both employment and wages relative to the pure monopsony outcome. If the union sets wages above the competitive level, however, it will create a pool of workers who are unable to get the jobs that they want at the going wage.
- Governments set some wages above their competitive levels by passing minimum-wage laws. In competitive labour markets, these laws raise the incomes of many employees, and cause unemployment for some of those with the lowest levels of skills. In monopsonistic labour markets, a legislated minimum wage (as long as it is not too high) can raise both wages and employment.

B. LABOUR UNIONS

- Labour unions seek many goals when they bargain with management. They may push for higher wages, higher fringe benefits, more stable employment, or less onerous working conditions. Whatever their specific goals, unless they face a monopsonist across the

bargaining table, they must recognize the inherent conflict between the level of wages and the size of the union itself.
- Despite the costs to unions (i.e., reduced membership) of pushing for higher wages, there is clear evidence in Canada of a union wage premium. The union wage premium in Canada is somewhere between 10 and 25 percent—that is, unionized workers with a particular set of skills in particular types of jobs get paid 10 to 25 percent more than otherwise identical workers that are not members of unions.

C. DISCRIMINATION IN LABOUR MARKETS

- Discrimination has played an important role in labour markets, as it has in other aspects of life in Canada, the United States, and other industrialized countries. Direct discrimination affects wages and employment opportunities in part by limiting labour supply in the best-paying occupations and by increasing it in less attractive occupations.
- Some economists take the view that under perfect competition, discrimination cannot be sustained in equilibrium. This view is based on the argument that if some employers discriminate against certain types of workers, then this represents an opportunity for other employers. By taking advantage of this opportunity, those other employers create competitive pressure that works against the maintenance of discrimination.

D. THE "GOOD JOBS–BAD JOBS" DEBATE

- The past few decades have witnessed an increase in the share of total employment in the service sector and a decline in the share of employment in manufacturing. Some people are concerned that "good" manufacturing jobs are being replaced by "bad" service jobs.

- There are four reasons why the decline of the manufacturing sector is *not* necessarily a problem.

  1. Real disposable income per employed person has continued to rise throughout this period of decline in manufacturing employment.
  2. The decline in manufacturing employment is partly a result of the dynamism of that sector.

  3. Some of the decline in manufacturing reflects consumers' increased desires for services as their real income grows.
  4. It is easy to underestimate the importance of productivity improvements in the service sector. This is partly because the output of services is sometimes very hard to measure.

KEY CONCEPTS

Wage differentials in competitive labour markets
Labour unions as monopolists
Single employer as monopsonist
Effects of legislated minimum wages

Collective bargaining
Union goals: wages versus employment
Union wage premium
Effects of discrimination on wages and employment

Direct and indirect discrimination
"Comparable worth" and "pay equity"
"Good jobs" vs. "bad jobs"
Growth of the service sector

DISCUSSION QUESTIONS

1. "Because firms' demand curves for labour are downward-sloping, raising the minimum wage must reduce employment." Why is this statement wrong? When would raising the minimum wage reduce employment, and when might it increase employment?

2. Interpret the following statements or practices in terms of the subject matter of this chapter.

   a. A requirement that one must pass an English-language proficiency test to be a carpenter in Vancouver
   b. A statement by an official of a textile workers' union in New England (U.S.): "Until we have organized the southern [U.S.] textile industry, we will be unable to earn a decent wage in New England."
   c. A statement by an official of a steel-workers union in Hamilton: "Things are getting rough in our locals because the youngsters have different views about wages than the old-timers."

3. "The great increase in the number of women entering the labour force for the first time means that relatively more women than men earn beginning salaries. It is therefore not evidence of discrimination that the average wage earned by females is less than that earned by males." Discuss.

4. During the late 1980s and early 1990s, North American industry underwent an apparent restructuring that saw the elimination of many middle-management jobs. As a result, a relatively large group of work-

ers in their forties and fifties were thrown back into the job market. Many of these people had difficulty finding new work and attributed this problem to age discrimination. What are some factors *other than prejudice* that could place such workers at a competitive disadvantage relative to their younger counterparts?

5. Physicians are among the highest-paid of workers. However, in addition to a bachelor's degree, would-be physicians must attend four years of medical school, three years of residency, and up to seven additional years of residency for some specialists. How does this change your perception with respect to how much physicians are paid? What additional information would you need to determine whether physicians' real pay is higher than that of other professionals?

6. This chapter discusses several supply-side origins of discrimination in the labour market. Recall from Chapter 15 that the demand for a factor of production is equal to that factor's marginal revenue product. In light of this, can you identify any sources of discrimination that originate on the demand side of the labour market? Discuss how these forces would lead to discrimination.

7. The United States Supreme Court recently ruled on a case in which a company had a policy of prohibiting women of childbearing age from working in jobs where they would be exposed to lead, which has been shown to be damaging to fetal development. The company argued that the policy simply protected its employees.

The plaintiffs in the case, women who had been excluded from these relatively high-paying jobs, argued that the policy was discriminatory. What do you think?

8. In considering the distributional impact of a higher minimum wage, economists have grown increasingly concerned about the composition of the population working at the minimum wage. For example, one commentator suggested, "Much of the gain from a higher minimum wage would go to surfboards and stereos—not into rent and baby formula." In what respects would we expect to see different behavioural responses to changes in the minimum wage when the affected population is largely teenagers working for discretionary income or adults who are the primary earners in their families?

9. Former U.S. President Ronald Reagan stated that the minimum wage "has caused more misery and unemployment than anything since the Great Depression." What evidence would we need to support or refute Reagan's statement?

10. "One can judge the presence or absence of discrimination by looking at the proportion of the population in different occupations." Does such information help? Does it suffice? Consider each of the following examples. Relative to their numbers in the total population, there are

a. Too many blacks and too few Jews among professional athletes
b. Too few male secretaries
c. Too few female judges
d. Too few female prison guards
e. Too few male school teachers

11. "Equal pay for work of equal value" is a commonly held goal, but "equal value" is hard to define. What would be the consequences of legislation that enforces equal pay for what turns out to be work of unequal value?

12. One critic of pay-equity legislation argues that it confuses "value determined *at the margin* by supply and demand" with a "job evaluator's concept of the *average* value of the inputs required to do the job." Reread the discussion of the paradox of value in Chapter 7, and then comment on this criticism of pay-equity legislation.

CAPITAL AND NONRENEWABLE RESOURCES

In this chapter, we discuss capital and nonrenewable resources. These are similar factors of production in that each is a stock of valuable things that gets used up in the process of producing goods and services. They are also similar in that the optimal level of capital used by firms and the optimal level of extraction of a nonrenewable resource depend on the interest rate. They are different in that capital can be replaced, whereas nonrenewable resources cannot. A new machine can always be built to replace one that wears out, but a barrel of petroleum used represents a permanent reduction in the total stock of petroleum in the world—no more can be created to replace what has been used.

Resources that can be replaced, either through human effort, as with machines, or through natural reproduction, as with trees, humans, or fish, are called renewable resources. Resources that cannot be renewed, as with fossil fuels or minerals, are called nonrenewable resources or exhaustible resources.

CAPITAL AND THE INTEREST RATE

Capital is a produced factor of production. The nation's capital stock consists of all produced goods that are used in the production of other goods and services. Factories, machines, tools, computers, roads, bridges, and railroads are but a few of the many examples.

We begin our study of capital by exploring an important complication that arises because factors of production are durable—a machine lasts for years, a labourer for a lifetime, and land more or less forever. It is convenient to think of a factor's lifetime as being divided into the shorter periods that we refer to as *production periods* or *rental periods*. The present time is the current period. Future time is one, two, three, and so on, periods hence.

The durability of factors makes it necessary to distinguish between the factor itself and the *flow of services* that it provides in a given production period. For example, we can rent a piece of land for use over some period of time, or we can buy the land outright. This distinction is just a particular instance of the general distinction between flows and stocks that we first encountered in Chapter 4.

Although what follows applies to any durable factor, applications to capital are of most importance, so we limit the discussion to capital. Extension 17-1 discusses some of these issues as they apply to labour.

TWO PRICES OF CAPITAL

If a firm hires a piece of capital equipment for use over some period of time—for example, one truck

---

EXTENSION 17-1

THE RENTAL AND PURCHASE PRICE OF LABOUR

If you wish to farm a piece of land, you can buy it yourself, or you can rent it for a specific period of time. If you want to set up a small business, you can buy your office and equipment, or you can rent them. The same is true for all capital and all land; a firm often has the option of buying or renting.

Exactly the same would be true for labour if we lived in a slave society. You could buy a slave to be your assistant, or you could rent the services either of someone else's slave or of a free person. Fortunately, slavery is illegal throughout most of today's world. As a result, the labour markets that we know deal only in the *services* of labour; we do not go to a labour market to buy a worker, only to hire his or her services.

You can, however, hire the services of a labourer for a long period of time. In professional sports, multiyear contracts are common, and 10-year contracts are not unknown. The late Herbert von Karajan was made conductor for life of the Berlin Philharmonic Orchestra. Publishers sometimes tie up their authors in multibook contracts, and movie and television production firms often sign up their actors on long-term contracts. In all cases of such *personal services contracts,* the person is not a slave, and his or her personal rights and liberties are protected by law. The purchaser of the long-term contract is nonetheless buying ownership of the factor's *services* for an extended period of time. The price of the contract will reflect the person's expected earnings over the contract's lifetime. If the contract is transferable, the owner can sell these services for a lump sum or rent them out for some period. As with land and capital goods, the price paid for this stock of labour services depends on the expected rental prices over the contract period.

for one month—it pays a price for the privilege of using that piece of capital equipment. If the firm buys the truck outright, it pays a different (and higher) price for the purchase. Consider each of these prices in turn.

Rental Price

The *rental price of capital* is the amount that a firm pays to obtain the services of a capital good for a given period of time. The rental price of one week's use of a piece of capital is analogous to the weekly wage rate that is the price of hiring the services of labour.

Just as a profit-maximizing firm operating in a competitive labour market continues to hire labour until its marginal revenue product (*MRP*) equals the wage, so will the firm go on hiring capital until its *MRP* equals its rental price, which we call *r*. Because in a competitive market each firm faces the same market-determined rental price, and each hires capital until *MRP* equals *r*, it follows that each profit-maximizing firm will have the same *MRP* of capital.

A capital good may also be used by the firm that owns it. In this case, the firm does not pay out any rental fee. However, the rental price is the amount that the firm could charge if it leased its capital to another firm. The rental price is thus the *opportunity cost* to the firm of using the capital good itself. This rental price is the *implicit* price that reflects the value to the firm of the services of its own capital that it uses during the current production period.

Whether the firm pays the rental price explicitly or calculates it as an implicit cost of using its own capital, the rental price of a capital good over the current production period is equal to its marginal revenue product.

Purchase Price

The price that a firm pays to buy a capital good is called the *purchase price of capital*. When a firm buys a capital good outright, it obtains the use of the good's services over the whole of that good's lifetime. What the capital good will contribute to the firm is a flow that is equal to the marginal revenue product of the capital good's services over its lifetime. The price that the firm is willing to pay for the capital good, naturally enough, is related to the total value that it places now on this stream of *expected* receipts to be received over future time periods. The term *expected* emphasizes that the firm is usually uncertain about

the prices at which it will be able to sell its outputs in the future.

In order to compute the value that the firm places on receiving a future stream of benefits (the *MRP* of the capital good), we must examine the concept of *present value*. The following discussion proceeds under the simplifying assumption that the firm knows the future *MRP*s. This allows us to develop the central insights about *present value* without dealing with the complications arising from uncertainty.

THE PRESENT VALUE OF FUTURE RETURNS

Consider the stream of future income that is provided by a capital good. How much is that stream worth *now*? How much would someone be willing to pay now to buy the right to receive that flow of future payments? The answer is called the good's *present value*. In general, present value (*PV*) refers to the value now of one or more payments to be received in the future.

The Present Value of a Single Future Payment

One Period in the Future. To learn how to find the present value, we start with the simplest possible case. How much would a firm be prepared to pay now to purchase a capital good that will produce a marginal revenue product (*MRP*) of $100 in one year's time, after which time the capital good will be useless? One way to answer this question is to ask a somewhat *opposite* question: How much would the firm have to lend now in order to have $100 a year from now? Suppose for the moment that the interest rate is 5 percent, which means that $1.00 invested today will be worth $1.05 in one year's time.[1]

If we use *PV* to stand for this unknown amount, we can write $PV \times (1.05) = \$100$. Thus $PV = \$100/1.05 = \$95.24$. This tells us that the present value of $100, receivable in one year's time, is $95.24 when the interest rate is 5 percent. Anyone who lends out $95.24 for one year at 5 percent interest will receive $95.24 back plus $4.76 in interest, which makes $100 in total. When we calculate this present value, the interest rate is used to *discount* (reduce to its present value) the $100 to be received in one year's time. The maximum price that a firm would be willing to pay for this capital good is

---

[1]The analysis in the rest of this chapter assumes *annual* compounding of interest.

$95.24 (assuming that the interest rate relevant to the firm is 5 percent).

To see why, let us start by assuming that firms are offered the capital good at some other price. Suppose that the good is offered at $98. If, instead of paying this amount for the capital good, a firm lends its $98 out at 5 percent interest, it would have at the end of one year more than the $100 that the capital good will produce. (At 5 percent interest, $98 yields $4.90 in interest, which, together with the principal, makes $102.90.) Clearly, no profit-maximizing firm would pay $98—or, by the same reasoning, any sum in excess of $95.24—for the capital good. It could do better by using its funds in other ways.

Now suppose that the good is offered for sale at $90. A firm could borrow $90 to buy the capital good and would pay $4.50 in interest on its loan. At the end of the year, the good yields $100. When this is used to repay the $90 loan and the $4.50 in interest, $5.50 is left as profit to the firm. Clearly, it would be worthwhile for a profit-maximizing firm to buy the good at a price of $90 or, by the same argument, at any price less than $95.24.

The actual present value that we have calculated depended on our assuming that the interest rate is 5 percent. What if the interest rate is 7 percent? At that interest rate, the present value of the $100 receivable in one year's time would be $100/1.07 = $93.46.

These examples are easy to generalize. In both cases, we have found the present value by dividing the sum that is receivable in the future by 1 plus the rate of interest.[2] In general, if the interest rate is i per year, then the present value of the MRP (in dollars) received one year hence is

$$PV = MRP/(1 + i) \qquad [1]$$

Several Periods in the Future. Now we know how to calculate the present value of a single sum that is receivable one year hence. The next step is to ask what would happen if the sum were receivable at a later date. For example, what is the present value of $100 to be received *two* years hence when the interest rate is 5 percent? This is $100/[(1.05)(1.05)] = $90.70. We can check this by seeing what would happen if $90.70 were lent out for two years. In the first year, the loan would earn interest of

(0.05)($90.70) = $4.54, and hence after one year, the firm would receive $95.24. In the second year, the interest would be earned on this entire amount; interest earned in the second year would equal (0.05)($95.24) = $4.76. Hence, in two years the firm would have $100.

In general, the present value of MRP dollars received t years in the future when the interest rate is i per year is

$$PV = MRP/(1 + i)^t \qquad [2]$$

All that this formula does is discount the sum MRP by the interest rate, repeatedly, once for each of the t periods that must pass until the sum becomes available. If we look at the formula, we see that the higher is i or t, the higher is the whole term $(1 + i)^t$. This term, however, appears in the denominator, so PV is *negatively* related to both i and t.

The formula $PV = MRP/(1 + i)^t$ shows that the present value of a given sum payable in the future will be smaller the more distant the payment date and the higher the rate of interest.

The Present Value of a Stream of Payments

Now consider the present value of a stream of receipts that continues indefinitely. Indeed, this is essentially the question that we are interested in when examining the firm's decision to purchase a capital good since that capital good will typically generate a stream of benefits long into the future. At first glance, the PV in this case might seem very high because the total amount received grows without reaching any limit as time passes. The preceding section suggests, however, that people will not value the far-distant payments very highly.

To find the PV of $100 a year, payable forever, we ask: How much would you have to invest now, at an interest rate of i percent per year, to obtain $100 each year in interest earnings? This is simply $i \times PV$ = $100, where i is the interest rate and PV the sum required. Dividing through by i shows the present value of the stream of $100 a year forever:

$$PV = \$100/i \qquad [3]$$

For example, if the interest rate is 10 percent, the present value would be $1,000. This merely says that $1,000 invested at 10 percent yields $100 per year

---

[2] In this type of formula, the interest rate i is expressed as a decimal fraction where, for example, 7 percent is expressed as 0.07, so that $1 + i$ equals 1.07.

forever. Notice that, as in the preceding sections, PV is negatively related to the rate of interest: The higher the interest rate, the lower the present value of the stream of future payments.

Conclusions

From the foregoing discussion we can put together three important propositions about the rental and purchase prices of capital.

1. The rental price of capital paid in each period is the flow of net receipts that the capital good is expected to produce during that period—that is, the marginal revenue product of the capital good.

2. The maximum purchase price that a firm would pay for a capital good is the discounted present value of the flow of net receipts (rental values) that the good is expected to produce over its lifetime.

3. The maximum purchase price that a firm would pay for a capital good is positively associated with its rental price and negatively associated with both the interest rate and the amount of time that the owner must wait for payments to accrue.

THE FIRM'S DECISION

An individual firm faces a given interest rate and a given purchase price of capital goods. The firm can vary the quantity of capital that it employs, and as a result, the marginal revenue product of its capital varies. The law of diminishing returns tells us that the more capital the firm uses, the lower its MRP.

The Decision to Purchase a Unit of Capital

Consider a firm that is deciding whether or not to add to its capital stock and facing an interest rate of i at which it can borrow or lend money. The first thing the firm has to do is to estimate the expected marginal revenue product of the new piece of capital over its lifetime. Then it discounts this at the interest rate of i per year to find the present value of the stream of receipts the machine will generate. Having computed the PV of the stream of $MRPs$, the firm then compares this PV with the purchase price of the capital good. If the purchase price is less than the PV, then the firm buys the capital good; if PV is less than the purchase price, the firm will not buy the capital good.

Consider the following simple example. Suppose that a machine has an MRP of $1,000 each period—that is, by buying this machine the firm can produce and sell an extra $1,000 worth of output each period. Suppose further that the machine lasts for 3 periods—after that, the machine is completely worn out and worth nothing. Finally, suppose the interest rate is 10 percent per year. The PV of this stream of $MRPs$ is then equal to

$$PV = \$1,000 + \$1,000/(1 + 0.10) + \$1,000/(1 + 0.10)^2 = \$2,735.53.$$

The present value, by its construction, tells us how much any flow of future receipts is worth now. If the firm can buy the machine for less than its PV—that is, for any amount less than $2,735.53—then this machine is a good buy. If it must pay more, the machine is not worth its price.

It is always worthwhile for a firm to buy another unit of capital whenever the present value of the stream of future $MRPs$ that the capital provides exceeds its purchase price.

The Firm's Optimal Capital Stock

Because the MRP declines as the firm's capital stock rises, the firm will go on adding to its stock of capital until the *present value* of the flow of $MRPs$ generated by the *last unit* added is equal to the purchase price of that unit.

The profit-maximizing capital stock of the firm is such that the present value of the flow of $MRPs$ that is provided by the marginal unit of capital is equal to its purchase price.

Now suppose the firm has achieved its profit-maximizing stock of capital. What would then lead the firm to wish to increase that stock? Given the price of the machines, anything that increases the present value of the flow of income that the machines produce will have that effect. Two things will do this. First, the $MRPs$ of the capital may rise. That would happen if technological changes make capital more productive so that each unit produces more than before. (This possibility is dealt with later in the chapter.) Second, the interest rate may fall, causing an increase in the *present value* of any given stream of future $MRPs$. For example, suppose that next

FIGURE 17-1
The Firm's Demand for Capital

The lower the rate of interest, the larger is the firm's desired capital stock. The lower the interest rate, the higher is the present value of any given stream of marginal revenue products and hence the more capital that the firm will wish to use.

year's *MRP* is $1,000. This has a *PV* of $909.09 when the interest rate is 10 percent and $952.38 when the interest rate falls to 5 percent.

So when the interest rate falls, the firm will wish to add to its capital stock. It will go on doing so until the decline in the *MRP*s of successive additions to its capital stock, according to the law of diminishing returns, reduces the present value of the *MRP* at the new lower rate of interest to the purchase price of the capital.

The size of a firm's desired capital stock increases when the rate of interest falls, and it decreases when the rate of interest rises.

This relationship is shown in Figure 17-1. It can be thought of as the firm's demand curve for capital plotted against the interest rate. It shows how the desired stock of capital varies with the interest rate. (It is sometimes called the **marginal efficiency of capital curve.**)

One final comment about the firm's decision. We have shown that changes in the interest rate lead to changes in the firm's desired capital stock. When you go on to study *macroeconomics*, however, you will learn that the presence of *inflation* forces economists to make a distinction between the *real* interest rate and the *nominal* interest rate. All of our discussion here has been about the real interest rate. See Extension 17-2 for a more detailed discussion of inflation and interest rates.

THE EQUILIBRIUM INTEREST RATE

The analysis that we used for a single firm in the previous section also applies for the entire economy. This is because the aggregate or total demand for capital goods is simply the sum of all the individual firms' demands. Thus the higher is the market interest rate, the lower will be the total quantity of capital goods demanded. Also, changes in technology which make each unit of capital more productive lead to an increase in the total demand for capital goods.

The important difference between the analysis of a single firm and the analysis of the entire economy is that whereas any individual firm takes the market interest rate as given, the interest rate is determined *in equilibrium* for the economy as a whole. This is exactly analogous to each competitive firm taking the product price as given, whereas the product's price is determined *in equilibrium* in the market as a whole.

Short-Run Equilibrium

In the short run, the *economy's* capital stock is given. Though any given firm can change its own capital stock relatively easily—by buying or selling capital goods to or from other firms—the economy as a whole can adjust its capital stock only slowly. To reduce the aggregate capital stock, firms must allow their capital goods to wear out, or *depreciate;* to increase the aggregate capital stock, new capital goods must be built, some of which—buildings, bridges, etc.—take a considerable time to complete.

Figure 17-2 shows the economy's fixed short-run supply of capital as well as the total demand for capital goods, which is negatively related to the interest rate. Since the aggregate capital stock is fixed in the short run, equilibrium is achieved through changes in the interest rate, as opposed to changes in the level of capital.

For the economy as a whole, the condition that the present value of the *MRP*s should equal the price of capital goods determines the equilibrium interest rate.

EXTENSION 17-2

INFLATION AND INTEREST RATES

Inflation means the prices of all goods in the economy are rising. More correctly, it means that the prices of goods are rising on *average*—some prices may be rising and others may be falling, but if there is inflation then the price of the average good is rising. Economists refer to the average price of all goods as the *price level*. When the price level is rising, inflation is positive; if prices are rising at a rate of 5 percent per year, we say that the rate of inflation is 5 percent. When the price level is falling, inflation is negative. If prices are falling at a rate of 2 percent per year, we say that the rate of inflation is −2 percent.

REAL AND NOMINAL INTEREST RATES

In the presence of inflation, it becomes very important to distinguish between the **real interest rate** and the **nominal interest rate.** The nominal interest rate is measured simply in dollars paid. If you pay me $7 interest for a $100 loan for one year, the nominal interest rate is 7 percent.

Consider further my one-year loan to you of $100 at the nominal rate of 7 percent. The real rate that I earn depends on what happens to the price level during the course of the year. If the price level remains constant over the year, then the real rate that I earn is also 7 percent. This is because I can buy 7 percent more real goods and services with the $107 that you repay me than with the $100 that I lent you. However, if the price level were to rise by 7 percent during the

year, the real rate would be zero because the $107 you repay me will buy exactly the same quantity of real goods as did the $100 I gave up. If I were unlucky enough to have lent money at a nominal rate of 7 percent in a year in which prices rose by 10 percent, the real rate would be −3 percent. The real rate of interest concerns the ratio of the purchasing power of the money returned to the purchasing power of the money borrowed, and it will be different from the nominal rate whenever inflation is not zero.

The real interest rate is the difference between the nominal interest rate and the rate of inflation.

If lenders and borrowers are concerned with the real costs measured in terms of purchasing power, the nominal interest rate will be set at the real rate they require plus an amount to cover any expected rate of inflation. Consider a one-year loan that is meant to earn a real return to the lender of 3 percent. If the expected rate of inflation is zero, the nominal interest rate for the loan will also be 3 percent. If, however, a 10 percent inflation is expected, the nominal interest rate will have to be set at 13 percent in order that the real return be 3 percent.

To provide a given expected real rate of interest the nominal interest rate will have to be set at the desired real rate of interest plus the expected rate of inflation.

This point is often overlooked, and as a result people are surprised at the high nominal interest rates that exist during periods of high inflation. But it is the

Let us see how this comes about. If the price of capital is less than the present value of its stream of future *MRPs,* it would be worthwhile for all firms to borrow money to invest in capital. For the economy as a whole, however, the stock of capital cannot change quickly, so the effect of this demand for borrowing would be to push up the interest rate until the present value of the *MRPs* equals the price of a unit of capital goods. Conversely, if the price of capital is above its present value, no one would

wish to borrow money to invest in capital, and the rate of interest would fall. This is illustrated in Figure 17-2.[3]

---

[3]In the macroeconomics part of this textbook, we see that if prices are inflexible in the short run, then actions taken by the central bank can also affect the interest rate. For now, we continue our assumption that all prices (for goods and factors) rise or fall quickly to clear markets, so that the short-run equilibrium interest rate is determined only by the economy's marginal product of capital.

real interest rate that matters more to borrowers and lenders. Inflation is currently quite low in Canada (below 2 percent in 1997), but it has not always been that way. For example, in 1981 the rate of inflation was 12.4 percent and the nominal interest rate to prime borrowers was an unprecedented 19.3 percent! The real interest rate was then 6.9 percent. By 1993, the rate of inflation had fallen to 1.8 percent and the nominal rate to prime borrowers had fallen to 5.9 percent; the real rate was then 4.1 percent.

UNEXPECTED INFLATION

If an inflation is fully expected, the nominal interest rate can be set to give any desired real interest rate. Problems arise, however, when the inflation rate changes unexpectedly. Consider, for example, a loan contract in which the parties wish to carry a 3 percent real rate of interest. If a 7 percent inflation rate is expected, the nominal interest rate will be set at 10 percent. But what if the inflationary expectations turn out to be wrong? If the inflation rate ends up being only 4 percent, the real interest rate will be 6 percent. If, on the other hand, the inflation rate is 12 percent, the real interest rate will be −2 percent; the lender, even after paying the interest on the loan, will give back less purchasing power at the end of the period than he or she borrowed at the beginning.

Unexpected changes in the rate of inflation cause the real rate of interest on contracts already drawn up to vary in unexpected ways. An unexpected fall in the inflation rate is beneficial to lenders; an unexpected rise is beneficial to borrowers.

Such unexpected changes in inflation have happened in Canada. In the mid 1970s, for example, the massive increase in the world price of oil, driven by the actions of the OPEC oil cartel, contributed to a sudden increase in the rate of inflation. During these years, the real interest rate was actually negative—reflecting the fact that actual inflation was much greater than people had expected.

BACK TO CAPITAL

In this chapter, we have examined the firm's decision to buy capital stock, and we emphasized the importance of the interest rate to this decision. Though we did not say it explicitly in the text, all of our discussion about the interest rate was about the *real* interest rate. Thus the central conclusion about the firm's decision can be restated more accurately: *The size of the firm's desired capital stock increases when the real interest rate falls, and it decreases when the real interest rate rises.*

When you go on to study *macroeconomics*, in Chapters 21–38 of this book, you will learn more about what causes inflation, and thus what forces us to make the distinction between real and nominal interest rates. For now, however, keep in mind that in this chapter we are supposing that there is no inflation, so real and nominal interest rates are the same.

Changing Capital and Technology

In the long run, the economy's capital stock is free to change, but technology is constant. If capital is accumulated over time, then the *MRP* will fall, and the equilibrium interest rate will also fall. Conversely, the aggregate capital stock is allowed to wear out, then the *MRP* will rise and so will the equilibrium interest rate. This is shown in Figure 17-2, where the aggregate capital stock changes between K_0 and K_1, holding the demand for capital goods constant.

In the very-long run, technology changes. As a result, the capital stock becomes more productive as the old, obsolete capital is replaced by newer, more efficient capital. This shifts the *MRP* curve outward, which tends to increase the equilibrium interest rate associated with any particular size of the capital stock. In contrast, the accumulation of capital moves the economy downward to the right along any given *MRP* curve, and that tends to lower the interest rate associated with any one *MRP* curve. The net effect

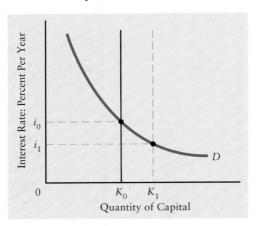

FIGURE 17-2
The Equilibrium Interest Rate

In the short run, the interest rate fluctuates to equate the demand and supply of capital; in the long run, the interest rate falls as more capital is accumulated. The economy's desired capital stock is negatively related to the interest rate, as shown by the curve D. In the short run, the aggregate capital stock is given. When the capital stock is K_0, the equilibrium interest rate is i_0. Above that rate firms will not want to hold all of the available capital; below that rate firms will want to borrow and add to their capital. In the long run, as the capital stock grows to K_1, the equilibrium interest rate falls to i_1.

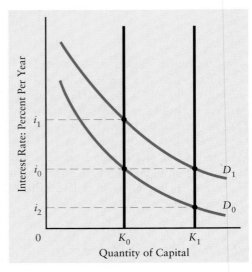

FIGURE 17-3
The Effect of Changing Technology and Capital Stock

Technological changes which increase the marginal product of capital, and changes in the capital stock itself, have opposite effects on the equilibrium interest rate. The original capital stock is K_0 and the original technology gives rise to the demand for capital given by D_0. Thus, the equilibrium interest rate is i_0. Technological changes which increase the marginal product of capital shift the demand curve to D_1 and, with a constant capital stock, would increase the interest rate to i_1. Alternatively, an increase in the capital stock to K_1, holding technology constant, lowers the interest rate to i_2. If technology improves *and* the capital stock increases, then the interest rate could rise or fall. In the figure, the two effects exactly offset each other so that the interest rate is unchanged at i_0.

on the interest rate of both of these changes may be to raise it, to lower it, or to leave it unchanged, as shown in Figure 17-3.

In almost all industrialized countries, there have been enormous increases in the aggregate capital stock over the past century. Yet, there *have not* been large decreases in the interest rate over the same period. This fact is explained easily by examining Figure 17-3. Technological change has improved the marginal productivity of capital goods and has thus led to increases in the aggregate demand for capital. This fact, taken alone, would lead to increases in the equilibrium interest rate. Working in the other direction, however, is the continual accumulation of capital, which tends to push down the equilibrium interest rate. The observation that the aggregate capital stock has increased dramatically, combined with the absence of a clear trend in the interest rate, suggests that these forces are offsetting each other more-or-less equally. The very-long-run effects of changing technology, combined with a growing capital stock, are studied further in Chapter 33.

NONRENEWABLE RESOURCES

So far, we have discussed the pricing of factors, such as labour and capital, that can be replaced as they wear out. As older people leave the labour force because of retirement or death, young persons, seeking their first jobs, enter. As an existing piece of capital equipment is retired because of depreciation or obsolescence, it is replaced by a new piece of equipment. Such resources are called **renewable resources**.

We now consider factors of production that are available in fixed amounts. For each such factor, the total stock is given, and every unit that is used today permanently reduces the stock that is available for future use. Such a factor is called a **nonrenewable resource** or an *exhaustible resource*.

In practice, few, if any, resources are completely nonrenewable. Although there is only a fixed stock of oil, coal, or iron ore that is known to exist at any given time, new discoveries add to the known stock, and extraction subtracts from it. It is, however, possible to imagine exhausting all of the world's supplies of oil, natural gas, or coal. In this sense, they are nonrenewable resources.

THE EXTRACTION RATE OF A RESOURCE

To focus on the basic issues, it is easiest to think of a resource that is completely nonrenewable. Suppose for the moment that all of the petroleum in existence has been discovered so that every unit that is used permanently diminishes the available stock by 1 unit.

Suppose that many firms own the land that contains the oil supply. They have invested money in discovering the oil, drilling wells, and laying pipelines. Their current extraction costs are virtually zero; all they have to do is turn their taps on, and the oil flows at any desired rate to the oil markets.[4]

Profit-Maximizing Firms

What should each firm do? It could extract all of its oil in a great binge of production this year, or it could save the resource for some future rainy day and produce nothing this year. In practice, it is likely to adopt some intermediate policy, producing and selling some oil this year and holding stocks of it in the ground for extraction in future years. But *how much* should it extract this year and *how much* should it carry over for future years? What will the decision imply for the price of oil over the years?

The firms that own land with petroleum underneath it are holding a valuable resource. Holding it, however, has an opportunity cost: It could have been extracted and sold this year, yielding revenue to the firms in the same year. A firm will be willing to leave the resource in the ground only if it earns a return equal to what it can earn in alternative investments. This alternative return is measured by the interest rate. To see why, consider two cases.

First, suppose that the price of oil is expected to rise by less than the interest rate. For example, suppose the interest rate is 10 percent per year but the price of oil is expected to increase by only 5 percent per year. Oil extracted and sold now will in this case have a higher value than oil left in the ground, since revenues from current sales could be earning 10 percent in a bank account. Firms will therefore extract more oil this year. Because the demand curve for oil has a negative slope, raising the extraction rate will lower this year's price. Production will rise, and the current price will fall until the expected price rise between this year and next year is equal to the interest rate.[5] The firms will then be indifferent between producing another barrel this year and holding it for production next year.

Second, suppose that the price is expected to rise by more than the interest rate. Firms will in this case prefer to leave more in the ground, where they earn a higher return than could be earned by selling the oil this year and investing the proceeds at the current interest rate. Thus firms will cut their rate of production for this year, which will raise this year's price. When the current price has risen so that the gap between the current price and next year's expected price is equal to the interest rate, firms will value equally a barrel of oil extracted and one left in the ground.

In a perfectly competitive industry for a nonrenewable resource, the equilibrium occurs when the last unit currently produced earns just as much for each firm as it would if it had been left in the ground for future sales.

To illustrate these important relations, suppose that next year's price is expected to be $1.05 and that the rate of interest is 5 percent. First, suppose that

---

[4]It is, of course, a simplification of any real case to assume that current production costs are actually zero. The assumption, however, is not too far from reality in the case of such a resource as oil, where the fixed costs of discovery, extraction, and distribution account for the bulk of total costs. When extraction costs are nonzero, all statements about prices in the text refer to the margin by which price exceeds the current cost of extraction.

[5]The discussion is simplified by assuming next year's expected price to be given. The decision to produce more this year may also affect next year's price. If the total supplies are small, next year's expected price may rise. The argument proceeds exactly as in the text, except that the equilibrium gap between two prices is achieved by the present price falling and the expected future price rising rather than by having next year's expected price remaining constant and all the adjustment coming through this year's price.

the current price is $1.04 per barrel. It clearly pays to produce more now because the $1.04 that is earned by selling a barrel now can be invested to yield approximately $1.09 ($1.04 × 1.05), which is more than the $1.05 that the oil would be worth in a year's time if it is left in the ground. Second, suppose that the current price is $.90 cents per barrel. Now it pays to reduce production because oil left in the ground will be worth 16.66 percent more next year [(1.05/0.90) × 100]. Extracting it this year and investing the money will produce a gain of only 5 percent. Finally, let the current price be $1.00. Now oil producers make the same amount of money whether they leave $1.00 worth of oil in the ground to be worth $1.05 next year or they sell the oil for $1.00 this year and invest the proceeds at 5 percent interest.

Market Pricing

What we have established so far determines the *rate of increase* of prices over time: If stocks are given and unchanging, prices should rise over time at a rate equal to the rate of interest. But what about the *level* of prices? Will they start low and rise to only moderate levels over the next few years, or will they start high and then rise to even higher levels? The answer depends on the total stock of the resource that is available (and, where some new discoveries are possible, on the expected additions to that stock in the future). The scarcer the resource relative to the demand for it, the higher its market price at the outset.

A resource's price tends to rise over time at a rate equal to the rate of interest; the current price will depend on the resource's scarcity relative to current demand.

Socially Optimal Behaviour: Hotelling's Rule

Petroleum is a scarce resource, and the value to consumers of one more barrel produced now is the price that they would be willing to pay for it, which is the current $1.00 market price of the oil. If the oil is extracted this year and the proceeds are invested at the rate of interest (5 percent), they will produce $1.05 worth of valuable goods next year. If that barrel of oil is not produced this year and is left in the ground for extraction next year, its value to consumers at that time will be next year's price of oil. It is not socially optimal, therefore, to leave the oil in the ground unless it will be worth at least $1.05 to consumers next year. More generally, society obtains in-

creases in the value of what is available for consumption by conserving units of a nonrenewable resource only if the price of the units is expected to rise at a rate that is at least as high as the interest rate.

This answer to the question "How much of a nonrenewable resource should be consumed now?" was provided many years ago by the U.S. economist Harold Hotelling. His answer—now referred to as **Hotelling's Rule**—is very simple, yet it specifically determines the optimal pattern of prices over the years. It is interesting that the answer applies to *all* nonrenewable resources. It does not matter whether there is a large or a small demand or whether that demand is elastic or inelastic. In all cases the answer is the same:

The rate of extraction of any nonrenewable resource should be such that its price increases at a rate equal to the interest rate.

For example, if the rate of interest is 4 percent, the price of the resource should be rising 4 percent per year. If it is rising by more, there is too much current extraction; if it is rising by less, there is not enough current extraction. We have already seen that this is the rate of extraction that will be produced by a competitive industry.

The Rate of Extraction

Hotelling's Rule does not tell us exactly how many barrels of oil should be extracted each year. Instead, it only tells us that the year's extraction rate *should be such that* the market price rises at a rate equal to the interest rate. What then should the actual extraction rate be if the competitive market fulfills Hotelling's Rule for optimal extraction rates? The answer to this question *does* depend on market conditions. Specifically, it depends on the position and the slope of the demand curve. If the quantity demanded at all prices is small, the rate of extraction will be small. The larger the quantity demanded at each price, the higher the rate of extraction will tend to be.

Now consider the influence of the demand elasticity. A highly inelastic demand curve suggests that there are few substitutes and that purchasers are prepared to pay large sums rather than do without the resource. This will produce a relatively even rate of extraction, with small reductions in each period being sufficient to drive up the price at the required rate. A relatively elastic demand curve suggests that people can easily find substitutes once the price rises.

FIGURE 17-4
The Extraction Rate for a Nonrenewable Resource

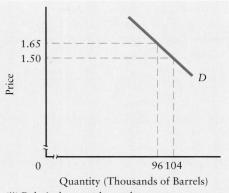

(i) Relatively flat demand curve

(ii) Relatively steep demand curve

The shape of the demand curve determines the extraction pattern over time. In the example in this figure, the interest rate is assumed to be 10 percent, and there is a fixed supply of 200,000 barrels of oil that can be extracted from the ground at zero variable cost. (All costs are fixed costs.) The oil is available for extraction either in the current period or in the next period, after which it spoils.

In part (i) of the figure, the demand curve is relatively flat. The two conditions—that the whole supply be used over two periods and that the price rise by 10 percent between the two periods—dictate that the quantities be 120,000 barrels in the first period, with a price of $1.00 per barrel, and 80,000 in the second period, with a price of $1.10 per barrel.

In part (ii), the demand curve is rather steep. The same two conditions now dictate that the quantities be 104,000 barrels in the first period, with a price of $1.50 per barrel, and 96,000 barrels in the second period, with a price of $1.65 per barrel.

This will encourage a great deal of consumption now and a rapidly diminishing amount over future years because large reductions in consumption are needed to drive the price up at the required rate.

Figure 17-4 illustrates this working of the price mechanism with a simple example in which the whole stock of oil must be consumed in only two periods, this year and next year. The general point is this:

The more inelastic the demand curve, the more even the rate of extraction (and hence the rate of use) will be over the years; the more elastic the demand curve, the more uneven the rate of extraction will be over the years.

An elastic demand curve will lead to large consumption now and a rapid fall in consumption over the years. An inelastic demand curve will lead to lower consumption now and a less rapid fall in consumption over the years.

Rents to Natural Resources

The incomes earned by the owners of petroleum are rents in the sense defined in Chapter 15: The owners would be willing to produce the oil at any price that covers the direct costs of extraction, which in this example is zero.[6] Although these incomes serve no function in getting the product produced, since any nonzero price would do that, they do fulfill the important function of determining the extraction rate, and hence the use of the resource, *over time.* As we have seen, the pattern of prices determines the use of the resource and hence the amount of resources allocated to its production *over time.*

CONSERVATION THROUGH THE PRICE SYSTEM

In this discussion, we see the price system playing its now familiar role of coordinator. By following private profit incentives, firms are led to conserve the resource in a manner that is consistent with society's needs.

The Role of Rising Prices

From society's viewpoint, the optimal extraction pattern of a nonrenewable resource occurs when its

---

[6]In real cases, the direct cost of extracting the resource is positive, and the rent is the income earned above that amount.

price rises each year at a rate equal to the interest rate. If the price is prevented from rising, the resource is depleted much too fast. The rising price fulfills a number of useful functions.

First, the rising price encourages conservation. As the resource becomes scarcer and its price rises, users will be motivated to be more and more economical in its use. Uses with low yields may be abandoned altogether, and uses with high yields will be pursued only as long as their value at the margin is enough to compensate for the high price.

Second, the rising price encourages the discovery of new sources of supply—at least in cases in which the world supply is not totally fixed and already known.

Third, the rising price encourages innovation. New products that will do the same job may be developed, as well as new processes that use alternative resources.

How Might the Price System Fail?

We now examine three basic ways in which the price system might fail to produce the optimal rate of resource extraction. First, private owners may not have sufficient information to determine the optimal extraction rate. Second, deficiencies in property rights may result in firms' having incentives to extract the resource too fast. Third, markets may not correctly reflect social values. We look at examples of each of these and ask if they justify government intervention.[7]

Ignorance. Private owners might not have enough knowledge to arrive at the best estimate of the rate at which prices will rise. If they do not know the world stocks of their commodity and the current extraction rate, they may be unable to estimate the rate of the price rise and thus will not know when to raise or lower their current rates of extraction. For example, if all firms think that prices will rise only slowly in the future, but prices actually end up rising quickly, they will all produce too much now and conserve too little for future periods.

In this situation, however, there is no reason to think that the government could do any better, unless it has access to some special knowledge that private

firms do not possess. If it does have such knowledge, the government can make it public; further intervention is unnecessary if a competitive industry is maximizing profits on the basis of the best information available to it. In practice, what knowledge does exist about both the proven reserves of nonrenewable resources and their current extraction rates is usually freely and openly available.

Inadequate Property Rights. Some nonrenewable resources have the characteristics of what is called *common property*. Such property cannot be exclusively owned and controlled by one person or firm. For example, one person's oil-bearing land may be adjacent to another person's, and the underground supplies may be interconnected. In such a case, if one firm holds off producing now, the oil may end up being extracted by the neighbour. In such cases, which are sometimes encountered with petroleum, there is a tendency for a firm to extract the resource too fast because a firm's oil that has been left in the ground may not be available to that firm at a future date. (Similar issues arise with any common-property resource such as fishing grounds—we examine this further in Chapter 18.)

What is being described here is a problem of *inadequate property rights*. Because the resource will be worth more in total value when it is exploited at the optimal extraction rate than when small firms exploit it too quickly, there will be an incentive for individual owners to combine until each self-contained source of supply is owned by only one firm. After that, the problem of overexploitation will no longer arise. Government ownership is not necessary to achieve this result. What is needed, at most, is intervention to ensure that markets can work to provide the optimal size of individual units so that proper extraction management can be applied by the private owners.

Political uncertainty can be another source of inadequate property rights. For example, the owners of the resource may fear that a future election or a revolution will establish a government that will confiscate their property. They will then be motivated to exploit the resource too quickly, on the grounds that certain revenue now is more valuable than uncertain revenue in the future. The current rate of extraction will tend to increase until the expected rate of price rise exceeds the interest rate by a sufficient margin to compensate for the risks of future confiscation of supplies left in the ground.

Unequal Market and Social Values. In a competitive world, the market interest rate indicates the

---

[7]This discussion partly anticipates the analysis in Part 6, which investigates market successes and market failures in more general terms.

rate at which it is optimal to discount the future. Society's investments are beneficial if they earn at least the market rate of return; they are not beneficial if they earn less (because the resources could be used in other ways to produce more value to consumers). In certain circumstances, however, the government may have reasons to adopt a different rate of discount. It is then said that the *social rate of discount*—the discount rate that is appropriate to the society as a whole—differs from the private rate, as indicated by the market rate of interest. In such circumstances, there is reason for the government to intervene to alter the rate at which the private firms would exploit the resource.

Critics are often ready to assume that profit-hungry producers will despoil most exhaustible resources by using them up too quickly. They argue for government intervention to conserve the resource by slowing its rate of extraction. Yet unless the social rate of discount is below the private rate, there is no clear social gain in investing by holding resources in the ground where they will yield only, say, a 2 percent return when perhaps 5 percent can be gained on other investments.

Because governments must worry about their short-term popularity and their chances of reelection, there is no presumption that government intervention will slow the rate of extraction even if the social discount rate exceeds the private rate. Instead, governments might extract resources faster than market forces alone would.

ACTUAL PRICE MOVEMENTS

Many nonrenewable resources do not seem to have the steadily rising prices predicted by Hotelling's Rule. The price of oil, having been raised artificially by the OPEC cartel in the 1970s, returned in the late 1980s to an inflation-adjusted level that was not far from where it was in 1970. Indeed, it has since been held somewhat above that price only insofar as the producing countries have succeeded in intermittently enforcing some output restrictions. The price of coal has not soared; nor has the price of iron ore. In many cases, the reason lies in the discovery of new supplies, which have prevented the total known stocks of many resources from being depleted. In the case of petroleum, for example, the ratio of known reserves to one year's consumption is no lower now than it was two or even four decades ago. Furthermore, most industry experts believe that

large quantities of undiscovered oil exist under both the land and the sea.

In other cases, the invention of new substitute products has reduced the demand for some of these resources and has thus prevented prices from rising as quickly as they otherwise would have. For example, plastics have replaced metals in many uses, and fiber optics have replaced copper wire in many types of message transmission.

In yet other cases, the reason is to be found in government pricing policy. An important example of this type is the use of nonrenewable water for irrigation in much of the United States. Though vast underground reserves of water lie in aquifers beneath many areas of the United States, they are being used up at a rate that will exhaust them in a matter of decades. The water is often supplied by government water authorities at a price that covers only a small part of total cost and that does not rise steadily to reflect the dwindling stocks. Current U.S. water policy will have strong effects on Canada, which controls a large *renewable* supply of fresh water from rivers and lakes.

Such a constant-price policy for *any* nonrenewable resource creates three characteristic problems. First, the resource will be exhausted much faster than if the price were to rise over time. With a given demand, a constant price will lead to a constant rate of extraction to meet the quantity demanded at that price until the resource is completely exhausted. Second, since the price is not allowed to rise, no signals go out to induce conservation, innovation, and exploration. Third, when the supply of the resource is finally exhausted, the adjustment will have to come all at once. If the price had risen steadily each year under free-market conditions, adjustment would have taken place little by little each year. The controlled price, however, gives no signal of the ever-diminishing stock of the resource until all at once the supplies run out. The required adjustment will then be much more painful than it would have been if it had been spread over time in response to steadily rising prices.

When governments intervene to keep the price of a nonrenewable resource below its free-market value, the current users of the resource are essentially obtaining a subsidy from future users, who, if the policy continues, will have to make many adjustments abruptly while paying much higher prices for the resource.

SUMMARY

A. CAPITAL AND THE INTEREST RATE

- Because capital goods are durable, it is necessary to distinguish between the stock of capital goods and the flow of services provided by them and thus between their purchase price and their rental price. The rental price is the amount that is paid to obtain the flow of services that a capital good provides for a given period. The purchase price is the amount that is paid to acquire ownership of the capital.
- The linkage between the rental price and the purchase price relies on the ability to assign a present value to future returns. The present value of a future payment will be lower when the payment is more distant and the interest rate is higher.
- An individual firm will invest in capital goods as long as the present value of the stream of future net returns that is provided by another unit of capital exceeds its purchase price. For a single firm and for the economy as a whole, the profit-maximizing size of the capital stock varies negatively with the rate of interest.
- Whereas individual firms take the market interest rate as given, the interest rate is determined in equilibrium for the economy as a whole. Long-run increases in the aggregate capital stock, holding technology constant, lead to reductions in the equilibrium interest rate. Changes in technology which increase the marginal product of capital lead to increases in the equilibrium interest rate.

B. NONRENEWABLE RESOURCES

- The socially optimal rate of extraction for a nonrenewable resource occurs when its price rises at a rate equal to the rate of interest. This is Hotelling's Rule. This rate of price increase is also the rate that will be established by profit-maximizing firms in a competitive industry.
- Resources for which the demand is highly elastic will have a high rate of extraction in the near future and a fairly rapid falloff over time. Resources for which the demand is highly inelastic will have a lower rate of extraction in the near future and a smaller falloff over time.
- Rising prices act as a conservation device by rationing consumption over time according to people's preferences. As prices rise, conservation, discovery of new sources of supply, and innovation to reduce demand are all encouraged.
- The price system can fail to produce optimal results if (a) people lack the necessary knowledge, (b) property rights are inadequate to protect supplies left for future use by their owners, or (c) the social rate of discount differs significantly from the market rate.
- Controlling the price of an exhaustible resource at a constant level speeds up the rate of extraction and removes the price incentives to react to its growing scarcity.

KEY CONCEPTS

Rental price and purchase price of capital
Present value

Marginal efficiency of capital
The interest rate and the capital stock
The equilibrium interest rate

Hotelling's Rule
The role of rising prices of exhaustible resources

DISCUSSION QUESTIONS

1. Suppose you are offered, free of charge, one from each of the following pairs of assets. What considerations would determine your choice?

   a. A perpetuity that pays $20,000 per year forever or an annuity that pays $100,000 per year for five years

   b. An oil-drilling company that earned $100,000 after corporate taxes last year or Canadian government bonds that paid $100,000 in interest last year

   c. A 1 percent share in a new company that has invested $10 million in a new cosmetic that is thought to appeal to middle-income women or a $100,000 bond that has been issued by the same company

2. How would you go about evaluating the present value of each of the following?

   a. The existing reserves of a relatively small oil company
   b. The total world reserves of an exhaustible natural resource with a known completely fixed supply
   c. A long-term bond, issued by a very unstable third-world government, that promises to pay the bearer $1,000 per year forever
   d. A lottery ticket that your neighbour bought for $10, which was one of 1 million tickets sold for a drawing to be held in one year's time that will pay $2 million to the single winner

3. Can you think of any resources that are renewable if they are exploited at one rate and nonrenewable if they are exploited at other, higher rates?

4. Some Canadians opposed the 1989 Free Trade Agreement (FTA) between Canada and the United States because they wished to prohibit the export of Canadian oil and natural gas to the U.S. and instead to save it for use by future generations of Canadians. What would have been the economic gains and losses resulting from following the courses of action advocated by these people?

5. Outline some of the main events that would follow if no further significant discoveries of oil were ever made after 1997.

6. Your parents argue that it makes more sense for you to take taxis and, on occasion, to rent a car while you are at school because you will be spending most of your time in the library and your need for a car should be minimal. Make an argument based on the rental price of transportation (not on the other advantages of having the car) that it may be cheaper for you to buy a car for use while you are at school.

7. It is possible to rent a movie such as *Casablanca* for 24 hours for $3. Alternatively, you can buy the tape for about $20. How many times would you need to plan on viewing the movie to justify purchasing it? How would the interest rate and interval between viewings affect your calculations? How would the transactions costs of going to the video rental store affect your calculations?

8. There are many examples of resources that are technically renewable—such as the stock of old-growth forests—but may not be replenished within your lifetime if the current stock is depleted. Explain how you would expect the market to price such resources.

9. Species that are on the verge of extinction—beluga whales, African elephants, mountain gorillas, and the California condor—might be classified as nonrenewable resources; once they disappear, there will be no regeneration. Does the market create appropriate incentives to ensure that extinction will not occur?

10. Why would Americans be interested in gaining control over Canadian water supplies in the future? Why would the Canadian government have resisted granting such control in the text of the Canada-U.S. Free Trade Agreement?

PART SIX

GOVERNMENT POLICY IN THE MARKET ECONOMY

When is there a role for government to intervene in the market economy? Is government action necessary to reduce sulphur dioxide emissions, or can the market economy handle that problem itself? Why doesn't the private sector provide things like national defense? Why do some people believe that government actions to improve equity in the economy almost surely reduce efficiency? Is government action needed to ensure that workers have safe workplaces, or will firms find it in their own interests to have safe working conditions? How does the Canadian government raise the money it needs to finance its expenditures, and on what does the Canadian government spend? What is the financial relationship between the federal government and the various provincial governments, and how has this relationship affected the design and operation of Canada's social programs? These are the sort of questions you will be able to answer after reading the next three chapters.

Chapter 18 examines the case for free markets. You will see the reasons why economists often argue in favour of free markets and against government intervention. You will then explore the case for government intervention which is based on the concept of a *market failure*—a situation in which the free market fails to produce the socially desirable outcome. It is here that you will see that the free market typically cannot be relied upon to solve the problem of pollution; you will also learn why the private sector does not provide national defense. You will then learn about the process of government intervention, and about the reasons why there are *government failures*.

In Chapter 19 you are introduced to the economics of pollution. You will learn about the *rationale for regulating pollution* and about the various methods of pollution control that have been tried. You will learn about *tradable pollution permits*—the most recent (and most controversial) method for dealing with pollution. The chapter then examines government regulation for health and safety. One of the key points made in this chapter is that firms often can be counted on to provide adequate safety for their workers; one exception, however, is when there is *imperfect information* about the dangers in the workplace.

Chapter 20 then examines the taxation and expenditure patterns of Canadian governments. You will learn about the Canadian tax system, and about how to evaluate a tax system from the standpoints of both efficiency and equity. You will learn about the concept of *fiscal federalism*, upon which many Canadian programs are based. You will then examine the programs which make up Canadian social policy, and you will learn about the continuing pressures to reform these programs.

CHAPTER 18

BENEFITS AND COSTS OF GOVERNMENT INTERVENTION

There are two extreme views of the Canadian economy. In one, Canada is a stronghold of free enterprise, with millions of people in a mad and brutal race for the almighty dollar. In the other, Canadian business people, workers, and consumers are seen as strangling slowly in a web of red tape spun by the spider of government regulation. Neither of these extreme views is accurate.

Many aspects of economic life in Canada are determined by the free-market system. Private preferences, expressed through private markets and influencing private profit-seeking enterprises, determine much of what is produced, how it is produced, and the incomes of productive factors. But even casual observation makes it clear that public policies and public decisions also play a large role in the economic life of the Canadian populace. Laws restrict what people and firms may do, and taxes and subsidies influence their choices. Much public expenditure is not market determined, and this influences the distribution of the national product. Canada's economy, like all others, is a mixed economy.

The general case for some reliance on free markets is that allowing decentralized decision making is more desirable than having all economic decisions made by a centralized planning body. Indeed, much of the political upheaval in Eastern Europe in the past decade arose from the weak performance of planned economies. (Recall Application 1-2 in Chapter 1.)

The general case for some public intervention is that almost no one wants to let markets decide everything about our economic affairs. Most people's moral and practical sense argues for some state intervention to mitigate the disastrous results that the market deals out to some. Most people believe that there are areas in which markets do not function well and in which state intervention can improve the general social good. Indeed, even when there is maximum reliance on the market economy, government is needed to enforce contracts and prevent theft. For such reasons, there is no known economy in which the people have opted for complete free-market determination of all economic matters and against any kind of government intervention.

The operative choice today is not between an unhampered free-market economy and a fully centralized command economy. It is rather the choice of *which mix* of markets and government intervention best suits people's hopes and needs. Although all

economies are mixed, the mixture varies greatly among them and over time. Whether the existing mixture could be improved—and, if so, how—is debated continually and is a major political issue. But even the most passionate advocates of free markets agree that government must provide for enforcement of the rules under which private firms and persons make contracts. Without well-defined property rights, the enforcement of contracts, and a reasonable assurance that goods and services will not be stolen, market economies cannot function. In the modern mixed economy, however, government does a great deal more than act as a "traffic cop" for the private sector.

In this chapter, we discuss the role of the government in market-based economies, making the case both for and against government intervention. In the following two chapters, we look at the principal types of intervention in more detail. Before turning to the cases for and against government intervention in market economies, it is useful to briefly review the fundamental function of markets—coordinating the decisions of large numbers of decentralized private decision makers.

HOW MARKETS COORDINATE

Any economy consists of thousands upon thousands of individual markets. There are markets for agricultural goods, for manufactured goods, and for consumers' services; there are markets for intermediate goods such as steel and lumber, which are outputs of some industries and inputs of others; there are markets for raw materials such as iron ore, trees, bauxite, and copper; there are markets for land and for thousands of different types of labour; there are markets in which money is borrowed and in which securities are sold.

COORDINATION: SIGNALS AND RESPONSES

An economy is not, however, a series of markets functioning in isolation—it is an interlocking system in which events in one market affect tens of thousands of others. Any change, such as an increase in demand for a particular product, requires many further changes and adjustments. Should the quantity produced change? If it should, by how much and by what means? Any change in the output of one product will generally require changes in other markets. Someone or something must decide what is to be produced, how, and by whom, and what is to be consumed and by whom.

The essential characteristic of the market system is that its coordination occurs in an unplanned and decentralized way. Millions of people make millions of independent decisions concerning production and consumption every day. Most of these decisions are not motivated by a desire to contribute to the social good or to make the whole economy work well; instead, these decisions are motivated by the fairly immediate considerations of self-interest. The price system coordinates these decentralized decisions, making the whole system fit together and respond to the wishes of individual consumers and producers.

The basic insight into how a market system works is that decentralized decision makers, acting in their own interests, respond to such *signals* as the prices of what they buy and sell. Economists have long emphasized the signaling feature of free-market prices. When a commodity becomes scarce, its free-market price rises. Firms and households that use the commodity are led to economize on it and to look for alternatives. Firms that produce it are led to produce more of it. How the price system informs these decisions has been examined at many places in this book.

THE ROLE OF PROFITS AND LOSSES

If prices are the signals to which firms and consumers respond, economic profits may be thought of as the engine that drives the economy. Except when there is monopoly or oligopoly (in which cases entry barriers might allow profits to exist in the long run) economic profits and losses are symptoms that a market is not in long-run equilibrium. Economic profits or losses represent the underlying motivation behind the economy's response to change.

A rise in demand for a commodity or a fall in production costs creates profits for that commodity's producers. Profits make an industry attractive to new investment. They signal that there are too few resources allocated to that industry. In search of these profits, more resources enter the industry, increasing output and driving down price until profits

are driven to zero. A fall in demand or a rise in production costs creates losses. Losses reveal that too many resources are allocated to the industry. Resources will leave the industry until those left behind are no longer suffering losses.

The importance of profits and losses is that they set in motion forces that tend to move the economy toward a new equilibrium.

Individual households and firms respond to common signals according to their own best interests. Yet these individuals and firms are decentralized—there is nothing intentionally coordinated about their actions. However, when a shortage of some product causes its price to rise, individual buyers begin to reduce the quantities that they demand and individual firms begin to increase the quantities that they supply. As a result, the shortage begins to lessen. As it does, price begins to come back down, and profits are reduced. These signals in turn are seen and responded to by firms and households. Eventually, when the shortage has been eliminated, there are no profits to attract further increases in supply. The chain of adjustments to the original shortage is completed.

Notice that in the sequence of signal-response-signal-response, no single individual has to foresee at the outset the final price and quantity, nor does any government agency have to specify who will increase production and who will decrease consumption. Some firms respond to the signals for more output by increasing production, and they keep on increasing production until it is no longer profitable to do so. Some buyers withdraw from the market when they think that prices are too high, perhaps to return when (in their view) prices become more reasonable. Households and firms, responding to market signals, not to the orders of government bureaucrats, determine who will increase production and who will limit consumption. No one is forced to do something against his or her best judgment. Voluntary responses collectively produce the end result.

Because the economy is adjusting to shocks continuously, a snapshot of the economy at any given moment reveals substantial positive profits in some industries and substantial losses in others. A snapshot at any other moment will also reveal profits and losses, but their locations will be different.

The price system, like an "invisible hand" (Adam Smith's famous phrase), coordinates the responses of individual decision makers who seek only their own self-interests. Because they respond to signals that reflect market conditions, their responses are coordinated without any conscious planning.

Notice that the price system coordinates responses even to prices that are set by monopolistic producers or pegged by government controls. The process of signal-response-signal-response occurs in a price system even when the prices have not been determined in freely competitive markets. The details of the outcomes will be somewhat different under monopoly and oligopoly than with competition, but when market signals change, the responses will usually be in the same direction. Although monopoly and government controls usually lead to allocative inefficiency (recall our discussion in Chapter 13), they do not prevent the tendency of prices to rise when things are scarce, nor do they stop the tendency for producers to minimize costs. It is these reactions that are at the heart of a price system's ability to coordinate economic behaviour.

THE CASE FOR FREE MARKETS

In presenting the case for free-market economies, economists have used two quite different approaches. The first of these may be characterized as the "formal defense," and is based on the concept of allocative efficiency, introduced in Chapter 13. The essence of the formal defense of free-market economies is that if all markets are perfectly competitive, and if governments allow all prices to be determined by demand and supply, then resources will be allocated in the *optimal* manner. That is, prices will equal marginal cost for all products and thus the economy will be allocatively efficient—it would be impossible to make any individual better off without at the same time making somebody else worse off.

The other defense of free markets—what might be called the "informal defense"—is at least as old as Adam Smith and is meant to apply to market economies whether or not they are perfectly competitive. It is based on the theme that markets are a very effective mechanism for coordinating the decisions of decentralized decision makers. The informal defense is intuitive in that it is not laid out in equations representing a formal model of an economy, but it does follow from some hard reasoning, and it has been subjected to much intellectual probing.

This informal defense of free markets is based on four central arguments, which we examine in turn.

1. Free markets are flexible and provide automatic coordination of the actions of decentralized decision makers.

2. The pursuit of profits which is central to free markets provides a stimulus to innovation and economic growth.

3. Free markets are self-correcting so that situations of disequilibrium are only temporary.

4. Free markets permit a decentralization of economic power.

FLEXIBLE AND AUTOMATIC COORDINATION

Defenders of the market economy argue that, compared with the alternatives, the decentralized market system is more flexible and leaves more scope for adaptation to change at any moment in time and for quicker adjustment over time.

Suppose, for example, that the price of oil rises. One household might prefer to respond by maintaining a high temperature in its house and economizing on its driving; another household might do the reverse. A third household might give up air-conditioning instead. This flexibility can be contrasted with centralized control, which would force the same pattern on everyone, say, by fixing the price, by rationing heating oil and gasoline, by regulating permitted temperatures, and by limiting air-conditioning to days when the temperature exceeded 27°C.

Furthermore, as conditions continue to change, prices in a market economy will continue to change, and decentralized decision makers can react continually. In contrast, government quotas, allocations, and rationing schemes are much more difficult to adjust. As a result, there are likely to be shortages and surpluses before adjustments are made. One great value of the market is that it provides automatic signals *as a situation develops* so that not all of the consequences of an economic change have to be anticipated and allowed for by a body of central planners. Millions of adaptations to millions of changes in tens of thousands of markets are required every year, and it would be a herculean task to anticipate and plan for them all.

A market system allows for coordination *without anyone needing to understand how the whole system works.* As Professor Thomas Schelling put it:

> The dairy farmer doesn't need to know how many people eat butter and how far away they are, how many other people raise cows, how many babies drink milk, or whether more money is spent on beer or milk. What he needs to know is the prices of different feeds, the characteristics of different cows, the different prices . . . for milk . . . , the relative cost of hired labor and electrical machinery, and what his net earnings might be if he sold his cows and raised pigs instead.[1]

It is, of course, an enormous advantage that all the producers and consumers of a country collectively can make the system operate without any one of them, much less all of them, having to understand how it works. (Such a lack of knowledge becomes a disadvantage, however, when people have to vote on schemes for interfering with market allocation.)

STIMULUS TO INNOVATION AND GROWTH

Technology, tastes, and resource availability are changing all the time, in all economies. Thirty years ago, there was no such thing as a personal computer or a digital watch. Front-wheel drive was a curiosity in North America. Students carried their books in briefcases or in canvas bags that were anything but waterproof. Manuscripts only existed as hard copy, not as electronic files in a computer. To change one word in a manuscript, one usually had to retype an entire page. Videocassettes did not exist, nor did compact discs.

Digital watches, personal computers, front-wheel drive cars and compact discs are all products that were invented or developed by individuals or firms in pursuit of profits. An entrepreneur who correctly "reads" the market and perceives that there may be a demand for some product will be inclined to develop it.

The next 20 years will also surely see changes great and small. Changes in technology may make an

idea that is not practical today practical five years from now. New products and techniques will be devised to adapt to shortages, gluts, and changes in consumer demands and to exploit new opportunities made available by new technologies. Fibre optics, for example, is likely to change radically the nature of communication, permitting widespread availability of inexpensive, two-way video transmission.

In a market economy, individuals risk their time and money in the hope of earning profits. While many fail, some succeed. New products and processes appear and disappear. Some are fads or have little impact; others become items of major significance. The market system works by trial and error to sort them out and allocates resources to what prove to be successful innovations.

In contrast, planners in more centralized systems have to guess which innovations will be productive and which goods will be strongly demanded. Centrally planned effort may achieve wonders by permitting a massive effort in a chosen direction, but central planners also may guess incorrectly about the direction and put too many eggs in the wrong basket or reject as unpromising something that will turn out to be vital. Perhaps the biggest failure of centrally planned economies was their inability to encourage the experimentation and innovation that has proved to be the driving force behind long-run growth in advanced market economies. It is striking that the last decade has seen most centrally planned economies abandon their system in favour of a price system in one fell swoop while the only remaining large planned economy, China, is increasing the role of markets in most aspects of its economy.

SELF-CORRECTION OF DISEQUILIBRIUM

Equilibrium of the economic system is continually disrupted by change. If the economy did not "pursue" equilibrium, its behaviour in equilibrium would be of little interest. An important characteristic of the price system is its ability to set in motion forces that tend to correct disequilibrium.

To review the advantages of the price system in this respect, imagine operating without a market mechanism. Suppose that planning boards make all market decisions. The Planning Board for Men's Clothing somehow learns that pleated shirts are all the rage in neighbouring countries. It orders a certain

---

[1]Schelling, T.C. *Microeconomics and Macro Behavior* (New York: Norton, 1978).

proportion of clothing factories to make pleated shirts instead of the traditional men's dress shirt. Conceivably, the quantities of pleated shirts and traditional shirts produced could be just right, given shoppers' preferences. But what if the Board guesses wrong and orders the production of too many traditional shirts and not enough pleated shirts? Long lines would appear at pleated-shirt counters, while mountains of traditional shirts would pile up. Once the Board sees the lines for pleated shirts, it could order a change in quantities produced. Meanwhile, it could store the extra traditional shirts for another season or ship them to a country with different tastes.

Such a system can correct an initial mistake, but it may prove inefficient in doing so. It may use a lot of resources in planning and administration that could instead be used to produce commodities. Further, many consumers may be greatly inconvenienced if the Board is slow to correct its error. In such a system, the members of the Board may have no incentive to admit and correct a mistake quickly. Indeed, if the authorities do not like pleated shirts, the Board may get credit for having stopped the craze before it went too far!

In contrast, suppose that in a market system, a similar misestimation of the demand for pleated shirts and traditional shirts is made by firms in the men's clothing industry. Lines develop at pleated-shirt counters, and inventories of traditional shirts accumulate. Stores raise the prices of pleated shirts and at the same time lower them for traditional shirts. Consumers could then get bargains by buying traditional shirts. Pleated-shirt manufacturers could earn profits by raising prices and running extra shifts to increase production. Some traditional-shirt producers would be motivated to shift production quickly to pleated shirts and to make traditional shirts more attractive to buyers by cutting prices. Unlike the planning board, the producers in a market system would be motivated to correct their initial mistakes as quickly as possible. Those who were slowest to adjust would lose the most money and might even be forced out of business.

DECENTRALIZATION OF POWER

Another important part of the case for a market economy is that it tends to decentralize power and thus requires less coercion of individuals than any other type of economy. Of course, even though markets tend to diffuse power, they do not do so completely; large firms and large unions clearly have and exercise substantial economic power.

Though the market power of large corporations and unions is not negligible, it tends to be constrained both by the competition of other large entities and by the emergence of new products and firms. This is the process of creative destruction that was described by Joseph Schumpeter (see Application 11-1 in Chapter 11). In any case, say defenders of the free market, even such aggregations of private power are far less substantial than government power.

Governments must coerce if markets are not allowed to allocate people to jobs and commodities to consumers. Not only will such coercion be regarded as arbitrary (especially by those who do not like the results), but the power creates major opportunities for bribery, corruption, and allocation according to the tastes of the central administrators. If, at the going prices and wages, there are not enough apartments or coveted jobs to go around, the bureaucrats can allocate some to those who pay the largest bribe, some to those with religious beliefs, hairstyles, or political views that they like, and only the rest to those whose names come up on the waiting list.

This line of reasoning has been articulated forcefully by the Nobel laureate and conservative economist Milton Friedman, who was for many years a professor of economics at the University of Chicago. Friedman argues that economic freedom—the ability to allocate resources through private markets—is essential to the maintenance of political freedom.[2] Many other economists and social theorists have challenged this proposition.

THE CASE FOR GOVERNMENT INTERVENTION

Free markets do all of the good things that we have just discussed; yet there are many circumstances in which the free market does not produce the most desirable outcomes. When this happens, economists say that markets have *failed*. The case for intervening

[2]Milton Friedman, *Capitalism and Freedom* (Chicago: The University of Chicago Press: 1982).

in free markets turns in large part on identifying the conditions that lead to **market failure.** Much of the following discussion is devoted to this task.

Care must be taken when using the expression *market failure* because the word *failure* may convey the wrong impression. Market failure does not mean that nothing good has happened—but rather that the *best attainable outcome* has not been achieved.

The concept of a market failure is used to apply to two quite different sets of circumstances. One is the failure of the market system to achieve efficiency in the allocation of society's resources. The other is the failure of the market system to serve social goals other than allocative efficiency, such as a desirable distribution of income or the preservation of value systems. We treat each in turn.

Four broad types of phenomena lead to a failure of allocative efficiency: *monopoly power, externalities, public goods,* and *information asymmetries.* Recall that allocative efficiency requires that the marginal cost for society of producing each good equals the marginal benefit to society of that good. In each of these four cases, the free market does not generate an allocatively efficient outcome because the marginal benefit to society does not equal the marginal cost to society.

MONOPOLY POWER

As we discussed in Chapter 11, firms that face downward-sloping demand curves will maximize profits at an output where price exceeds marginal cost, leading to allocative inefficiency. Although some market power is maintained through artificial barriers to entry, such power can also arise naturally because in some industries the least costly way to produce a good or a service is to have few producers relative to the size of the market. The standard government remedies are competition policy and regulation, which, as discussed in Chapter 13, present problems of their own.

EXTERNALITIES

Recall that in order for the economy to be allocatively efficient, price must equal marginal cost for all products. But whose costs are relevant here? Firms that are maximizing their *own* profits are interested only in their own costs of production—they are not interested in any costs that their actions might impose on others. An **externality** occurs whenever actions taken by firms or consumers impose costs or confer benefits on *others that are not involved in the transaction.* When you smoke a cigarette in a restaurant, you might impose costs on others present; when you cut your lawn early on a weekend morning you might impose costs on sleeping neighbours. Externalities are also called *third-party effects* because parties other than the two primary participants in the transaction (the buyer and the seller) are affected.

Private and Social Costs

The foregoing discussion suggests the importance of the distinction between *private cost* and *social cost.* **Private cost** measures the best alternative use of the resource available to the private decision maker. **Social cost** includes the private cost (since the decision maker is a member of society) but also includes the best use of all resources available to society.

In general, discrepancies between private cost and social cost occur when there are externalities. The presence of externalities, even when all markets are perfectly competitive, leads to allocatively inefficient outcomes.

Private producers and consumers make their decisions about production and consumption based on private marginal cost and market price. When they neglect to take into account the social costs involved in the transaction, they arrive at an outcome where the market price does not reflect *social cost,* and thus allocative efficiency is not achieved. This is shown in Figure 18-1.

Externalities arise in many different ways, and they may be harmful or beneficial to the third parties. When they are harmful they are called *negative externalities;* when they are beneficial, they are called *positive externalities.* Here are two examples.

Consider the case of a firm whose production process for steel generates harmful smoke as a byproduct. Individuals who live and work near the firm bear real costs due to the firm's production. In addition to the disutility of enduring the smoke and of any adverse health effects, they may be forced to invest in air conditioners so that they can keep the noxious fumes out of their homes. When the firm makes its decision concerning how much steel to produce, it ignores these costs that it imposes on other people. This is a negative externality. In this case, because the firm ignores those parts of social cost that are not its own private cost, the firm will produce too much steel relative to what is allocatively efficient.

FIGURE 18-1
Private and Social Cost

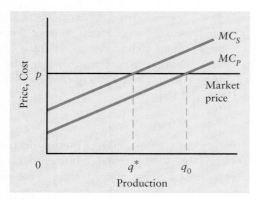

A competitive firm will produce output to the point where its private marginal cost equals the market price. In this case, every unit of output produced imposes *external costs,* equal to the distance between MC_P (private marginal cost) and MC_S (social marginal cost).

The profit-maximizing competitive firm chooses to produce q_0, the output where price equals private marginal cost. If the full social cost of production were taken into account, only q^* would be produced. Notice that for each unit of output between q^* and q_0, the cost incurred by society exceeds the value to consumers, which is given by the market price. Thus in this example, the profit-maximizing firms end up producing *too much* of the good compared to what is allocatively efficient (q^*).

Now consider what happens when an individual renovates her home and thus improves its external appearance. Such improvements enhance the neighbours' view and the value of their property. Yet the individual renovator ignores the benefits that her actions have on the neighbours. This is a positive externality. In this case, because the renovator ignores those parts of **social benefits** that are not her own private benefits, there will be too little home renovation done relative to what is allocatively efficient.

Externalities, whether adverse or beneficial to the third parties, cause market outcomes to be inefficient because they cause marginal social benefit to differ from marginal social cost.

In those cases where the production of a good generates *negative* externalities, private producers will produce too much of the good relative to what is allocatively efficient. This is because the private producer ignores the costs imposed on the rest of society. In those cases where the production of a good generates *positive* externalities, private producers will produce too little of the good relative to what is allocatively efficient. This is because the private producer ignores the benefits conferred on the rest of society.

The Importance of Property Rights

Economist and Nobel laureate Ronald Coase has argued that when property rights are well defined (e.g., the law is clear on whether a polluter has rights to determine the emissions from a smokestack), third parties will be able to negotiate with the producers of externalities in order to ensure that the producers take all relevant valuations of their behaviour into account. In such cases, externalities would not be a source of market failure because social marginal cost and social marginal benefit would be included in the supply and demand curves of the parties engaged in the externality-producing activity. Since social marginal cost and social marginal benefit would then be equalized, the free market would generate the allocatively efficient outcome.

An example will help to clarify this important idea—known as the **Coase Theorem.** Suppose there is a paper mill that dumps toxic waste in a nearby river and there is a privately owned beach resort on the shore of the river downstream from the paper mill. Suppose further that for every ton of paper produced there is an accompanying barrel of toxic waste dumped in the river, and this imposes a $100 cost on the downstream resort owner. The social marginal cost of paper production is thus $100 more than the private marginal cost of paper production.

Coase's insight is that *as long as property rights are well defined,* this situation need not result in allocative inefficiency. For example, if the owners of the paper mill also owned the river, then they would clearly have the "right" to dump their toxic waste there. However, the downstream resort owner would be prepared to pay $100 for every ton of paper that the paper mill *did not produce.* The paper mill would therefore face an incentive to reduce the output of paper. Indeed, since the paper mill would gain $100 for each ton *not produced,* the paper mill's private marginal cost of production would equal the social marginal cost of production. The market outcome would therefore be allocatively efficient.

Note, however, that the efficient result does not depend on ownership over the river being given to the paper mill. Perhaps the most striking part of the Coase Theorem is that the allocatively efficient outcome is also achieved if the resort owner were awarded ownership over the river. To see this, note that if the resort owner owned the river, then he could force the paper mill to pay for the right to dump toxic waste in the river. If the resort owner charged the paper mill $100 per barrel of waste dumped in the river, then the paper mill would be forced to recognize the costs that its activities incur on the rest of society. That is, the paper mill's private marginal cost would now equal the social marginal cost, and hence the market outcome would be allocatively efficient.

The practical application of the Coase Theorem depends in large part on the *number* of third parties affected. In cases where there is only one (or a few), as in the example above, it is quite plausible that careful definition of property rights would be sufficient to permit private markets to deal efficiently with the externality. Where there are millions of third parties affected, however, as often is the case with air pollution in urban areas, it is hard to see how the negotiations could proceed except with government acting on behalf of the third parties. Another example is where the externalities cross international boundaries. The smokestack industries of the U.S. industrial midwest are commonly thought to be responsible for the problems of acid rain in Canada and New England. It is difficult to believe that any practical definition of property rights could eliminate the effects of these externalities.

Thus since many externalities in real-world economies will have large numbers of third parties involved, it seems reasonable to conclude that many externalities will indeed lead to allocative inefficiency and thus provide a motivation for government intervention.

PUBLIC GOODS

Public goods are sometimes called *collective consumption goods* because many people can consume them simultaneously. The total cost of providing public goods therefore does not necessarily increase as the number of consumers increases. Public goods also have a property that makes it difficult to exclude somebody from using them. The classic case of a public good is national defense. Adding to the population of Canada does not diminish the extent to which each Canadian citizen is defended by a given size and quality of armed forces. Nor would it be possible to exclude any one individual from consuming the benefits of national defense.

Information is also a public good. Suppose a certain food additive causes cancer. The cost of discovering this needs to be borne only once. The information is then of value to everyone who might have used the additive, and the cost of making the information available to one more consumer is essentially zero. Furthermore, once the information of the newly discovered carcinogen is available, it is impossible to prevent people from using that information. Other public goods include lighthouses, weather forecasts (a type of information), the provision of clean air, streetlighting, public parks, and outdoor band concerts.

All of these examples raise what is called the *free-rider problem,* which follows from the fact that it is difficult to prevent people from using public goods once they are produced. The private market will generally not produce efficient amounts of the public good because once the good is produced, it is impractical (or impossible) to make people pay for its use. Indeed, free markets may fail to produce public goods at all. The obvious remedy in these cases is for the government to provide the good, financed from its tax revenues.

How much of a public good should the government provide? It should provide up to the point where the *sum of everyone's individual valuations* of the good is just equal to the marginal cost of providing the good. To see why we must add up everyone's marginal valuation, consider a simple example. Suppose that Andy, Bibbi, Carol, and Dick are all thinking of renting a video. Watching the video will be a collective consumption good for the four of them because the cost will be the same no matter how many of them decide to watch. Suppose that each honestly expresses his or her value of watching the tape. Say it is worth $1.00 to Andy, $2.00 each to Bibbi and Carol, and 50 cents to Dick. If the rental charge for the tape is $5.50 or less, it is worth renting because the total value to all four consumers will be at least equal to the cost.

This example also illustrates the free-rider problem. If the cost of renting the tape is only $3.00, everyone will have an incentive to understate the value that they place on watching the tape, hoping to get the others to pay for their "free ride."

Sometimes it is possible to eliminate the free-rider problem by charging a fee for using a public good. In our example, the videotape rental would have been covered if the group decided to charge each member of the group $1.00 to watch the video. Doing this, however, would have been inefficient. Dick, who would be willing to pay 50 cents to see the video, would be excluded. The marginal benefit from letting Dick see the video is 50 cents, and the marginal cost is zero. It is plainly inefficient to exclude him because 50 cents worth of value is forgone, at no cost, when he is excluded.

Parks, roads, and bridges often are financed through fees or tolls that lead to *inefficient exclusion*. Exclusion in these cases is inefficient for exactly the same reason that it was inefficient to exclude Dick from watching the video. Efficiency requires that social marginal cost be equal to social marginal benefit. For a road with little or no traffic, the marginal cost of use is very close to zero. Charging a toll that pays for construction of a road excludes users who value its use at more than the marginal cost of their using it but less than the toll.

Even where getting around the free-rider problem is technically possible, doing so is usually inefficient. As in cases in which the private market would not produce a public good at all, the obvious remedy is government provision.

Efficient provision of public goods requires that consumers pay the marginal cost of their consumption—zero. Private markets will never provide goods at a price of zero and thus will always underprovide public goods.

An important example of a problem which is related both to public goods and to externalities—the overfishing of the world's oceans—is discussed in Application 18-1.

ASYMMETRIC INFORMATION

The role of information in the economy has received increasing attention from economists in recent years. Information is, of course, a valuable commodity, and markets for information and expertise are well developed, as every college student is aware. Markets for expertise are conceptually identical to markets for any other valuable service. They can pose special problems, however. One of these we have already discussed: Information is often a public good and thus will tend to be underproduced by a free market because once the information is known to anyone, it is extremely cheap to make it available to others.

Even where information is not a public good, markets for expertise are prone to market failure. The reason for this is that one party to a transaction can often take advantage of special knowledge in ways that change the nature of the transaction itself. The two important sources of market failure that arise when privately held information is bought and sold are *moral hazard* and *adverse selection*.

Moral Hazard

In general, **moral hazard** exists when one party to a transaction has both the *incentive* and the *ability* to shift costs onto the other party. Moral hazard problems often arise from insurance contracts. The classic example is the homeowner who does not bother to shovel snow from his walk because he knows that his insurance will cover the cost if the mail carrier should fall and break a leg. The costs of the homeowner's lax behaviour will be borne largely by others, including the mail carrier and the insurance company. Individuals and firms who are insured against loss will often take less care to prevent that loss than they would in the absence of insurance. They do so because they do not bear all of the marginal cost imposed by the risk, while they do bear all of the marginal cost of taking action to reduce the risk.

As in all of the cases of market failure that we have considered, the failure arises because the marginal private benefit of an action is not equal to the marginal social cost of that action. The existence of insurance markets, which ideally merely spread existing risk, will also increase the total amount of risk present because of moral hazard.

Insurance is not the only context in which moral hazard problems arise. Another example is professional services. Suppose that you ask a dentist whether your teeth are healthy or a lawyer whether you need legal assistance. The dentist and the lawyer both face moral hazard in that they both have a financial interest in giving you answers that will encourage you to buy their services, and it is difficult for you to find out if their advice is good advice. A similar situation occurs when you ask your mechanic what is wrong with your engine. In all of these cases, one party to the transaction has special knowledge that he or she could use to change the nature of the transaction in his or her favour. As long as the auto mechanic is merely selling her expertise in repairing cars, there is no problem, but when she uses her expertise to persuade the consumer to demand more repairs than are warranted, there is a moral hazard problem. Codes of professional ethics and licensing and certification practices, both governmental and private, are reactions to concerns about this kind of moral hazard.

Adverse Selection

Closely related to moral hazard is the problem of **adverse selection**—the tendency of people who are most at risk to buy the most insurance. A person who is

APPLICATION 18-1

OVERFISHING AND THE TRAGEDY OF THE COMMONS

In March 1995, the Spanish fishing trawler *Estai* was fishing off the coast of Newfoundland just outside of Canada's 200-nautical-mile "economic zone" when a Canadian fisheries-protection vessel fired across its bow and then forced it into harbour in St. John's. The European Union, of which Spain is a member, accused Canada of piracy. Canada in turn accused Spain of overfishing and of depleting the value of Canada's turbot fishery.

This was an unusually dramatic event in the Canadian fishing industry, but it revealed problems and frustrations that have been present for many years. The problem of Canada's fisheries (and other countries' fisheries as well) has two sources. The first relates to the special public-good nature of the fishery; the second relates to technological advance. Each of these has given rise to overfishing by both Canadian and foreign fishing fleets off of Newfoundland (and of almost all other fisheries in the world).

COMMON-PROPERTY RESOURCE

The North Atlantic fishery represents a special kind of public good. Fish are obviously mobile and cannot be confined to international boundaries. Thus even if Canada has a well-defined 200-mile limit, there is nothing preventing the "Canadian fish" from being caught outside of the limit by fishing fleets from other countries. The same problem has also led to disputes in the Pacific salmon fishery when U.S. fishing fleets in U.S. or international waters catch the salmon that are returning to spawn in Canada's rivers. A resource which everyone has access to—like the fish in international waters—is known as a *common-property resource*.

The public-good nature of the fishery illustrates an important example of an externality. The externality is that fishermen catching fish today deplete the stock of fish available both for other fishermen and for future generations. Thus they impose costs on other potential users of the resource. Since their private marginal cost of catching fish is less than the social marginal cost of catching fish, the free market will result in overuse of the fishery—that is, too many fish being caught.

A 1994 article in *The Economist* captured the problem succinctly:

A fisherman who tries to conserve stock by leaving fish in the sea has no reason for thinking that he will gain by his investment: the fish he has spared, or their offspring, will probably be caught by someone else. On the contrary, if he catches more fish now he will be the richer for it. Although there will be fewer fish next year, the cost will not be borne by him alone, but spread over the entire fleet. Without regulation, in other words, fisherman have an incentive to overfish.*

TECHNOLOGICAL ADVANCE

Technological advance exacerbates the fundamental problem stemming from the public-good nature of the fishery. With technological advancements and the growth of the fishing fleets, fisherman have caught more fish than are naturally replenished, leading to serious declines in the stocks of many species. Many observers argue that the only way to make commercial fishing in the North Atlantic viable in the twenty-first century is to stop fishing entirely until the fish population increases. Indeed, Canada closed the entire Newfoundland cod fishery in 1993 so that cod stocks could replenish themselves. In 1994, the multinational Northwest Atlantic Fisheries Organization set the allowable yearly catch of turbot to only 27,000 tonnes, less than half of the normal catch only a few years earlier. Not surprisingly, shutting down the fishery in this way imposes considerable hardship on those that earn their living either from fishing or processing the fish products.

GENERAL PRINCIPLE

The result of overfishing in the North Atlantic is just one example of what is known as "the tragedy of the commons," which refers to the tragic results from having unregulated access to a common-property resource. Another example is that ranchers who are given unlimited access to public grazing land will overgraze and thus deplete the value of that resource. In both cases, appropriate regulation will lead to a more efficient allocation of resources than would occur in an unregulated free market. Such regulation would require that users of the resource are forced to pay the costs that their actions impose on future users of the resource.

---

* "The Tragedy of the Oceans," *The Economist*, March 19, 1994.

suffering from a heart condition may seek to increase his life insurance coverage by purchasing as much additional coverage as is available without a medical examination. People who buy insurance almost always know more about themselves as individual insurance risks than do their insurance companies. The company can try to limit the variation in risk by requiring physical examinations (for life or health insurance) and by setting up broad categories based on variables, such as age and occupation, over which actuarial risk is known to vary. The rate charged is then different across categories and is based on the average risk in each category, but there will always be much variability of risk *within* any one category.

People who know that they are well above the average risk for their category are offered a bargain and will be led to take out more car, health, life, or fire insurance than they otherwise would. Their insurance premiums will also not cover the full expected cost of the risk that they are insuring against. Once again, their private cost is less than social cost. On the other side, someone who knows that she is at low risk and pays a higher price than the amount warranted by her risk is motivated to take out less insurance than she otherwise would. In this case, her private cost is more than the social cost.

In both cases, resources are allocated inefficiently because the marginal private benefit of the action (taking out insurance) is not equal to the social cost.

More generally, whenever either party to a transaction lacks information that the other party has or is deceived by claims made by the other party, market results will tend to be changed, and such changes may lead to inefficiency. Economically (but not legally), it is but a small step from such unequal knowledge to outright fraud. The arsonist who buys fire insurance before setting a building on fire and the business person with fire insurance who decides that a fire is preferable to bankruptcy are extreme examples of moral hazard.

Asymmetric information is involved in many other situations of market failure. The *principal-agent problem,* which we discussed in Chapter 14, is one example. In its classic form, the firm's managers act as agents for the stockholders, who are the legal principals of the firm. The managers are much better informed than the principals are about what they do and what they can do. Indeed, the managers are hired for their special expertise. Given that it is expensive for the shareholders (principals) to monitor what the managers (agents) do, the managers have latitude to pursue goals other than maximizing the firm's profits. The private costs and benefits of their actions will thus be different from the social costs and benefits, with the usual consequences for the allocative efficiency of the market system.

A second example of market failure due to asymmetric information is the apparent overdiscounting of the prices of used cars because of the buyer's risk of acquiring a "lemon." See the discussion of this problem in Application 18-2.

FAILURE TO ACHIEVE SOCIAL GOALS

We have examined four general ways in which free markets may fail to produce allocatively efficient outcomes. But suppose that the market *did* generate the allocatively efficient outcome. That is, suppose that all markets were perfectly competitive and that there were no problems of externalities, public goods or asymmetric information. In such an extreme world, does the achievement of allocative efficiency mean that the free-market outcome is desirable? The answer, in general, is no.

It should not be surprising that even when the free-market system generates an allocatively efficient outcome, it may not always achieve broader social goals. Some of these goals (for example, the desire for an "equitable" income distribution) are basically economic. Some, especially notions that people in a given society should have shared values, such as patriotism or a belief in basic human rights, are clearly not economic. In either set of cases, however, markets are not very effective, precisely because the goods in question are not of the kind that can be exchanged in decentralized transactions. (Indeed, if we stretch the definition a bit, these are public goods, and we have seen that markets tend to underproduce such goods.)

Income Distribution

An important characteristic of a market economy is the *distribution of income* that it determines. People whose services are in heavy demand relative to supply, such as good television anchors and outstanding hockey players, earn large incomes, whereas people whose services are not in heavy demand relative to supply, such as doctorates in classics and high-school graduates without work experience, earn much less.

The distribution of income produced by the market can be looked at in the long run or in the short run. In the long run, in an efficiently operating free-market economy, similar efforts of work or invest-

APPLICATION 18-2

USED-CAR PRICES: THE "LEMONS" PROBLEM

It is common for people to regard the large loss of value of a new car in the first year of its life as a sign that consumers are overly style-conscious and will always pay a big premium for the latest in anything. Professor George Akerlof of the University of California at Berkeley suggests a different explanation based on the proposition that the flow of services expected from a one-year-old car that is *purchased on the used-car market* will be lower than those expected from an *average* one-year-old car on the road. Consider his theory.

Any particular model year of automobiles will include a certain proportion of "lemons"—cars that have one or more serious defects. Purchasers of new cars of a certain year and model take a chance on their car turning out to be a lemon. Those who are unlucky and get a lemon are more likely to resell their car than those who are lucky and get a quality car. Hence in the used-car market, there will be a disproportionately large number of lemons for sale. (Also, not all cars are driven in the same manner; those that are driven for long dis-

tances or under bad conditions are much more likely to be traded in or sold as used cars than those that are driven on good roads and for moderate distances.)

Thus buyers of used cars are right to be on the lookout for low-quality cars, while salespeople are quick to invent reasons for the high quality of the cars they are selling ("It was owned by a little old lady who drove it only on Sundays"). Because it is difficult to identify a lemon or a badly treated used car before buying it, the purchaser is prepared to buy a used car only at a price that is low enough to offset the increased probability that it is of poor quality.

This is a rational consumer response to uncertainty and may explain why one-year-old cars typically sell for a discount that is much larger than can be explained by the physical depreciation that occurs in one year in the *average* car of that model. The large discount reflects the lower services that the purchaser can expect from a used car because of the higher probability that it will be a lemon.

---

ment by similar people will tend to be similarly rewarded everywhere in the economy. Of course, dissimilar people, or people in dissimilar jobs, will be dissimilarly rewarded. (Recall our discussion of equilibrium factor-price differentials in Chapter 15.)

In the short run, however, similar people making similar efforts may be dissimilarly rewarded. People in declining industries, areas, and occupations suffer the "punishment" of low earnings through no fault of their own. Those in expanding sectors earn the "reward" of high earnings through no extra effort or talent of their own. But these differentials are likely to be temporary, eliminated by the mobility of workers across industries, occupations, or regions.

These rewards and punishments serve the important function in decentralized decision making of motivating people to adapt. The advantage of such a system is that individuals can make their own decisions about how to alter their behaviour when mar-

ket conditions change; the disadvantage is that temporary rewards and punishments are dealt out as a result of changes in market conditions that are beyond the control of the affected individuals.

Moreover, even equilibrium differences in income may seem unfair. A free-market system rewards certain groups and penalizes others. Because the workings of the market may be stern, even cruel, society often chooses to intervene. Should heads of households be forced to bear the full burden of their misfortune if, through no fault of their own, they lose their jobs? Even if they lose their jobs through their own fault, should they and their families have to bear the whole burden, which may include starvation? Should the ill and the aged be thrown on the mercy of their families? What if they have no families? Both private charities and a great many government policies are concerned with modifying the distribution of income that results from such things as where one starts, how able one is, how lucky one is, and how one fares in the labour market.

We might all agree that it is desirable to have a more equal distribution of income than the one generated by the free market. We would probably also agree that the pursuit of allocative efficiency is a good thing. It is important to understand, however, that the goal of a more equitable distribution of income invariably conflicts with the goal of allocative efficiency. To understand why this is so, see Extension 18-1 which discusses Arthur Okun's famous analogy of the "leaky bucket."

Preferences for Public Provision

Police protection and justice could in principle be provided by private-market mechanisms. Security guards, private detectives, and bodyguards all provide police-like protection. Privately hired arbitrators, "hired guns," and vigilantes of the Old West represent private ways of obtaining "justice." Yet the members of society may believe that a public police force is *preferable* to a private one and that public justice is preferable to justice for hire. The question of the boundary between public and private provision of any number of goods and services became an important topic of debate during the 1980s, and the debate shows no sign of waning. In Canada, the United States and Western Europe, the issue is framed as *privatization*. In the formerly Socialist countries of Eastern Europe, the disposition of much of the productive capacity of entire countries is currently under dispute. In all of these cases, part of the debate is about the magnitude of the efficiency gains that could be realized by private organization, and part is about less tangible issues, such as changes in the nature and distribution of goods and services that may take place when production is shifted from one sector to the other.

Protecting Individuals from Others

People can use and even abuse other people for economic gain in ways that the members of society find offensive. Child labour laws and minimum standards of working conditions are responses to such actions. Yet direct abuse is not the only example of this kind of market failure. In an unhindered free market, the adults in a household would usually decide how much education to buy for their children. Selfish parents might buy no education, while egalitarian parents might buy the same education for all of their children, regardless of their abilities. The rest of society may want to interfere in these choices, both to protect the child of the selfish parent and to ensure that some of the scarce educational resources are distributed according to the ability and the willingness to use them rather than according to a family's wealth. All households are forced to provide a minimum of education for their children, and a number of inducements are offered—through public universities, scholarships, and other means—for talented children to consume more education than they or their parents might choose if they had to pay the entire cost themselves.

Paternalism

Members of society, acting through government, often seek to protect adult (and presumably responsible) individuals, not from others, but from themselves. Laws prohibiting the use of addictive drugs and laws prescribing the installation and use of seat belts are intended primarily to protect individuals from their own ignorance or shortsightedness. This kind of interference in the free choices of individuals is called **paternalism**. Whether such actions reflect the wishes of the majority in the society or whether they reflect the actions of overbearing governments, there is no doubt that the market will not provide this kind of protection. Buyers do not buy what they do not want, and sellers have no motive to provide it.

Social Obligations

In a free-market system, if you can pay another person to do things for you, you may do so. If you persuade someone else to clean your house in return for $35, presumably both parties to the transaction are better off (otherwise neither of you would have voluntarily conducted the transaction). Normally, society does not interfere with people's ability to negotiate mutually advantageous contracts.

Most people do not feel this way, however, about activities that are regarded as social obligations. For example, when military service is compulsory, contracts similar to the one between you and a housekeeper could also be negotiated. Some persons faced with the obligation to do military service could no doubt pay enough to persuade others to do their military service for them.[3] By exactly the same argument as we just used, we can presume that both par-

---

[3]During the U.S. Civil War, it was common practice for a man to avoid the draft by hiring a substitute to serve in his place.

EXTENSION 18-1

ARTHUR OKUN'S "LEAKY BUCKET"

Economists recognize that government actions can affect both the allocation of resources and the distribution of income. Resource allocation is easier to talk about simply because economists have developed precise definitions of *efficient* and *inefficient* allocations. Distribution is more difficult because we cannot talk about *better* or *worse* distributions of income without introducing normative considerations. (Recall the important distinction between *positive* and *normative* statements discussed in Chapter 2.) Partly because of this, much of economics concerns efficiency and neglects the effects on the distribution of income. Many disagreements about economic and social policy can be understood in terms of differences in emphasis on efficiency and distribution. Distribution, of course, is often more important as a political matter because distribution (especially one's own share) is what people care about most, not the overall efficiency with which the economy is operating.

Moreover, to the extent that society chooses to redistribute income, it is generally the case that allocative efficiency will be reduced. Arthur Okun (1928–1980)—a noted economist at Yale University—developed the image of a "leaky bucket" to illustrate this problem. Suppose we have a well-supplied reservoir of water and we wish to get some water to a household that is not able to come to the reservoir. The only vessel available for transporting the water is a leaky bucket; it works, in that water is deliverable to the intended location, but it works at a cost, in that some of the water is lost on the trip. Thus to get a litre of water to its destination, more than a litre of water has to be removed from the reservoir. It may be possible to design better or worse buckets, but all of them will leak somewhat (if only via evaporation of water from the surface).

The analogy to an economy is this: The act of redistribution (carrying the water) reduces the total value of goods and services available to the economy (by the amount of water that leaks on the trip). Getting a dollar to the poor reduces the resources available to everyone else by more than a dollar. This means that pursuing social goals—like the redistribution of income—conflicts with the goal of allocative efficiency.

Why is the bucket always leaky? Because there is no way to redistribute income without changing the incentives that private households and firms face. Generally, a program that takes from the rich and gives to the poor will reduce the incentives of both the rich and the poor to produce income. A policy of subsidizing goods that are deemed to be important, such as food, shelter, or oil, will cause the market prices of those goods to be lower than marginal costs, implying that resources used to produce those goods could be used to produce goods of higher value elsewhere in the economy. (This is the basic efficiency argument that we first discussed in Chapter 13.)

Measuring the efficiency costs of redistribution is an important area of economic research. Most economists would agree that programs that directly redistribute income are more efficient (per dollar of resources made available to a given income group) than programs that subsidize the prices of specific commodities. One reason for this is that price subsidies apply even when high-income households purchase the commodities in question.

Redistribution virtually always entails some efficiency cost, and price subsidies are generally less efficient than direct income transfers. However, this does *not* imply that such programs should not be undertaken. (That buckets leak surely does not imply that they should not be used to transport water, given that we want to transport water and that the buckets we have are the best available tools.) Whatever the social policy regarding redistribution of income, economics has an important role to play in measuring the efficiency costs and distributional consequences of different programs of redistribution. Put another way, it has useful things to say about the design and deployment of buckets.

ties will be better off if they are allowed to negotiate such a trade. Yet such contracts are usually prohibited by law. They are prohibited because there are values to be considered other than those that can be expressed in a market. In times when it is necessary, military service by all healthy males is usually held to be a duty that is independent of an individual's tastes, wealth, influence, or social position. It is felt that everyone *ought* to do this service, and exchanges between willing traders are prohibited.

Military service is not the only example of a social obligation. Citizens cannot buy their way out of jury duty or legally sell their voting rights to others, even though in many cases they could find willing trading partners.

We have discussed how the free market may fail to achieve social goals that members of society deem to be desirable. This discussion suggests the following general principle:

Even if the price system generated allocatively efficient outcomes, members of a society may not wish to rely solely on the market if they have social goals that they wish to achieve. Furthermore, there is generally a trade off between allocative efficiency and the achievement of these social goals.

GOVERNMENT INTERVENTION

Private collective action can sometimes remedy the failures of private individual action. For example, private charities can help the poor, volunteer fire departments can fight fires, or insurance companies can guard against adverse selection by more careful classification of clients. However, by far the most common remedy for market failure is government intervention.

Since markets sometimes *do* fail, there is a potential scope for governments to intervene in beneficial ways. Whether government intervention is warranted in any particular case depends both on the magnitude of the market failure that the intervention is designed to correct and on the costs of the government action itself.

The benefits of some types of government intervention (e.g., the advantages of having a publicly provided justice system) are both difficult to quantify and potentially very large. Further, government intervention often imposes difficulties of its own. For many types of government activity, however, *benefit-cost analysis,* devel-

oped by economists to consider the consequences of economic projects undertaken by governments, can be helpful in considering the general question of when governments ought to intervene and to what extent.

The idea behind **benefit-cost analysis** is simple: Add up the (opportunity) costs of a given policy, then add up the benefits, and implement the policy if the benefits outweigh the costs. In practice, however, benefit-cost analysis is usually quite difficult for three reasons. First, it may be difficult to ascertain what will happen when an action is undertaken. Second, many government actions involve costs and benefits that will occur only in the distant future. The evaluation of future events raises both technical and normative problems for the analyst. Third, some benefits and costs (e.g., the benefits of prohibiting actions that would harm members of an endangered species of animal) are very difficult to quantify. Indeed, many people would argue that they cannot be and should not be quantified, as they involve values that are not commensurate with money. The practice then is to use benefit-cost analysis to measure the things that can be measured and to be sure that the things that cannot be measured are not ignored when collective decisions are made. By narrowing the range of things that must be determined by informal judgment, benefit-cost analysis can still play a useful role.

In this chapter, we have been working toward a benefit-cost analysis of government intervention. We have made a general case against it (free markets are great economizers on information and coordination costs). We have made a general case for it (free markets will fail to produce allocative efficiency when there are public goods, externalities, or information asymmetries and may also not achieve social goals). We now turn to the more specific questions of what governments do when they intervene, what the costs of government intervention are, and under which circumstances government interventions may fail to improve on even imperfect private markets.

THE TOOLS OF GOVERNMENT INTERVENTION

The legal power of governments to intervene in the workings of the economy is limited only by the Charter of Rights (as interpreted by the courts), the willingness of legislatures to pass laws, and the willingness of the government to enforce them. There are numerous ways in which one or another level of government can prevent, alter, complement, or replace the workings of the unrestricted market economy.

Public Provision. National defense, the criminal justice system, public schools, the highway system, air traffic control, and national parks are all examples of goods or services that are directly provided by governments in Canada. Public provision is the most obvious remedy for market failure to provide public goods, but it is also often used in the interest of redistribution (e.g., hospitals) and other social goals (e.g., public schools). We shall consider public spending in detail in Chapter 20.

Redistribution and Social Insurance Programs. Taxes and spending are often used to provide a distribution of income that is different from that generated by the private market. Government transfer programs affect the distribution of income in this way. We examine the distributive effects of the Canadian tax system in Chapter 20.

Regulation. Government regulations are public rules that apply to private behaviour. In Chapter 13, we saw that governments regulate private markets to limit monopoly power. In Chapter 19, we will focus on regulations designed to deal with environmental quality and with workplace safety. Among other things, government regulations prohibit minors from consuming alcohol, require that children attend school, penalize racial discrimination in housing and labour markets, and require that new automobiles have passive passenger restraints. Government regulation is used to deal with all of the sources of market failure that we have discussed in this chapter; it applies at some level to virtually all spheres of modern economic life.

Structuring Incentives. Almost all government actions, including the kinds we have discussed here, change the incentives that consumers and firms face. If the government provides a park, people will have a weakened incentive to own large plots of land of their own. Fixing minimum or maximum prices (as we saw in the discussion of rent control and agriculture in Chapter 6) affects privately chosen levels of output.

The government can adjust the tax system to provide subsidies to some kinds of behaviour and penalties to others. In the United States, for example, deductible mortgage interest makes owned housing relatively more attractive than other assets that a person might purchase. In Canada, tax exemptions for contributions to Registered Retirement Saving Plans (RRSPs) may lead individuals to increase their total

saving. Such tax treatment sends the household different signals from those sent by the free market. Scholarships to students to become nurses or teachers may offset barriers to mobility into those occupations. Fines and criminal penalties for breaking the law are another part of the incentive structure. By providing direct or indirect fines or subsidies, the government can (in principle) correct externalities, induce private production of public goods, change the income distribution, and encourage behaviour that is deemed socially desirable. However, as we shall see, interventions of this kind are not always successful, and they often do as much (or more) harm than good.

THE COSTS OF GOVERNMENT INTERVENTION

Consider the following argument: The market system is working imperfectly; government has the legal means to improve the situation; therefore, the public interest will be served by government intervention.

This appealing argument is deficient because it neglects three important considerations. First, government intervention is itself costly since it uses scarce resources; for this reason alone, not every market failure is worth correcting because the intervention itself may use up more resources than are being wasted in the (inefficient) free-market outcome. Second, government intervention may be imperfect. Just as markets sometimes succeed and sometimes fail, so government interventions sometimes succeed and sometimes fail. Third, deciding what governments are to do and how they are to do it is also costly and intrinsically imperfect. These are among the messages that can be drawn from a relatively new speciality in economics and political science, called *social choice theory*. Extension 18-2 provides an example of the problems that can arise when social choices are made on the basis of majority rule.

For the remainder of the discussion in this section, note that the *benefit* of government intervention is the value of the market failures that the intervention will correct. Imagine that such a failure has been identified and evaluated. The question at hand, then, is whether the benefits of the intervention will exceed the costs.

Large potential benefits do not necessarily justify government intervention, nor do large potential costs necessarily make it unwise. What matters is the balance between benefits and costs.

EXTENSION 18-2

ARROW'S IMPOSSIBILITY THEOREM

Nobel laureate Kenneth Arrow from Stanford University has shown that it is generally impossible to construct a set of rules for making social choices that is at once comprehensive, democratic, efficient, and consistent. Arrow's theorem has led to decades of work on the part of economists, philosophers, and political scientists, who have tried to find conditions under which democracy can be expected to yield efficient (or otherwise favoured) allocations of resources. The news is generally not good. Unless individual preferences or their distribution in the population meet fairly unlikely criteria, either democracy or efficiency must be sacrificed in the design of social choice mechanisms.

The Arrow theorem can be illustrated by a simple case, depicted in the following table.

Density of Trees	Voter		
	A	B	C
Sparse (1)	3	1	2
Medium (2)	1	2	3
Thick (3)	2	3	1

Imagine that we have a society that consists of three voters who are choosing how many trees to plant in the local park. The three possibilities are as follows: (1) Plant very few trees in one corner. This would make the park suitable for Frisbee and soccer but not for walks in the woods. (2) Plant trees in moderate density throughout the park. In this case, the park would be nice for playing tag and jogging but not usable for most sports. (3) Plant trees densely everywhere. This would make the park a pleasant place to get away from it all (for whatever reasons) but not a good place to jog. Voter A loves jogging, hates Frisbee, and likes walking in the woods. His ranking of the alternatives is 2–3–1. Voter B likes the wide open spaces. His ranking is 1–2–3. Voter C likes to play Frisbee, likes solitude even more, and has little taste for a park that provides neither. Her ranking is 3–1–2.

Suppose that the electorate gets to choose between alternatives that are presented two at a time. What does majority rule do? It depends on which two alternatives are presented. In a choice of 1 versus 2, 1 wins, getting votes from B and C. When the choice is between 2 and 3, 2 wins, getting votes from A and B. When 3 is pitted against 1, 3 wins with the support of A and C. Thus the social choice mechanism of majority rule is *inconsistent*. It tells us that 1 is preferred to 2, 2 is preferred to 3, and 3 is preferred to 1. There is no way to make a choice without arbitrarily (i.e., undemocratically) choosing which set of alternatives to offer the electorate.

There are several different costs of government intervention. We divide these costs into two categories—*direct resource costs* and *indirect costs*.

Direct Resource Costs

Government intervention uses real resources that could be used elsewhere. Civil servants must be paid. Paper, photocopying, and other trappings of bureaucracy; the steel in the navy's ships; the fuel for the army's tanks; and the pilot of the Prime Minister's jet all have valuable alternative uses. The same is true of the accountants who administer the social security system, the economists who are employed by the Bureau of Competition Policy, and of the educators who retrain displaced workers.

Similarly, when government inspectors visit plants to monitor compliance with federally imposed standards of health, industrial safety, or environmental protection, they are imposing costs on the public in the form of their salaries and expenses. When regulatory bodies develop rules, hold hearings, write opinions, or have their staff prepare research reports, they are incurring costs. The costs of the judges, clerks, and court reporters who hear, transcribe, and review the evidence are likewise costs imposed by government regulation. All these activities use valuable resources that could have provided very different goods and services.

All forms of government intervention use real resources and hence impose direct costs.

This type of cost is fairly easy to identify, as it almost always involves expenditure of public funds. Other costs of intervention are less apparent but no less real.

Indirect Costs

Most government interventions in the economy impose some costs on firms and households. The nature and the size of the extra costs borne by firms and households vary with the type of intervention. A few examples will illustrate what is involved.

Changes in Costs of Production.   Government safety and emission standards for automobiles have raised the costs of both producing and operating cars. These costs are much greater than the direct budgetary costs of administering the regulations. Taxes used to finance the provision of public goods must be paid by producers and consumers and often increase the cost of producing or selling goods and services. Less direct, but also important, is the possibility that some kinds of regulation deter potential innovation because the innovation might not be approved by the regulators. This, too, could increase the costs of production in the long run.

Costs of Compliance.   Government regulation and supervision generates a flood of reporting and related activities that are often referred to collectively as *red tape*. The number of hours of business time devoted to understanding, reporting, and contesting regulatory provisions is enormous. Pay Equity, occupational safety, and environmental control have all increased the size of nonproduction payrolls. The legal costs alone of a major corporation sometimes can run into tens or hundreds of millions of dollars per year. While all this provides lots of employment for lawyers and economic experts, it is costly because there are other tasks these professionals could do that would add more to the production of consumer goods and services.

Households also bear compliance costs directly. A recent study found that the time and money cost of filling out individual income-tax returns was about 8 percent of the total revenue that is collected. In addition to costs of compliance, there are costs borne as firms and households try to avoid regulation. There

will be a substantial incentive to find loopholes in regulations. Resources that could be used elsewhere will be devoted by the regulated to the search for such loopholes and then, in turn, by the regulators to counteracting such evasion.

Rent Seeking.   A different kind of problem arises from the mere existence of government and its potential to use its tools in ways that affect the distribution of economic resources. This phenomenon has been dubbed **rent seeking** by economists because private firms, households, and business groups will use their political influence to seek economic rents from the government. These valuable rents can come in the form of favourable regulations, direct subsidies, and profitable contracts. Democratic governments are especially vulnerable to manipulation of this kind because they respond to well articulated interests of all sorts.

Rent seeking is endemic to mixed economies. Because of the many things that governments are called on to do, they have the power to act in ways that transfer resources among private entities. Because they are democratic, they are responsive to public pressures of various kinds. If a government's behaviour can be influenced, whether by voting, campaign contributions, lobbying, or bribes, real resources will be used in trying to influence government behaviour.

THE CAUSES OF GOVERNMENT FAILURE

Our conceptual benefit-cost analysis of government intervention is almost complete. First, we identify each market failure. Then we make our best estimate of the benefits of a government intervention designed to correct that failure—in most cases, the best that we can do is less than the maximum potential benefit. Then we calculate the costs of the government intervention, as outlined in the preceding section. If the benefits exceed the costs, the intervention is warranted. Unfortunately, things are never this simple. For one thing, as we have already noted, many of the benefits of government intervention are extremely difficult to quantify. Even in the easy cases, however, where the benefits and the direct costs of intervention can be measured and the indirect costs are unimportant, governments, like private markets, are imperfect. Often they will fail, in the same sense that markets do, to achieve their potential.

The reason for government failure is not that public-sector employees are less able, honest, or virtuous than people who work in the private sector. Rather, the causes of government failure are inherent in government institutions, just as the causes of market failure stem from the nature of markets. Importantly, some government failure is an inescapable cost of democratic decision making.

Inefficient Public Choices

At the core of most people's idea of democracy is that each citizen's vote should have the same weight. One of the insights of social choice theory is that resource allocation, based on the principle of one vote per person will generally be inefficient because it fails to take into account the *intensity of preferences.* Consider three farmers, A, B, and C, who are contemplating building access roads. Suppose that the road to A's farm is worth $7,000 to A and that the road to B's farm is worth $7,000 to B. (C's farm is on the main road, which already exists.) Suppose that under the taxing rules currently in effect, each road would cost A, B, and C $2,000 each. It is plainly efficient to build both roads because each generates net benefits of $1,000 ($7,000 gross benefits to farmers A and B less $6,000 total cost). But each road would be defeated 2-1 in a simple majority vote. (B and C would vote against A's road; A and C would vote against B's road.)

Now suppose that we allow A and B to make a deal: "I will vote for your road if you will vote for mine." Although such deals are often decried by political commentators, the deal enhances efficiency: Both roads now get 2–1 majorities, and both roads get built. However, such deals can just as easily reduce efficiency. If the gross value of each road were $5,000 instead of $7,000, and farmers A and B again make their deal, each road will still command a 2–1 majority, but building the roads will now be inefficient. (The gross value of each road is now only $5,000, but the cost is still $6,000.) A and B will be using democracy to appropriate resources from C while reducing economic efficiency.

Special Interests

The case in the preceding paragraph can be interpreted in a different way. Instead of being the third farmer, C might be all of the other voters in the country. Instead of bearing one-third of the costs, A and B each might bear only a small portion of the costs. To the extent that A and B are able to forcefully articulate the benefits that they would derive from the roads, they may be able to use democracy to appropriate resources from taxpayers in general. Much of the concern with the power of "special interests" stems from the fact that the institutions of representative democracy tend to be responsive to benefits (or costs) that focus on particular, identifiable, and articulate groups. Often costs that are borne diffusely by taxpayers or voters in general are hardly noticed.

This potential bias applies to regulations as well as to direct government provisions. Chapter 13 discussed a number of cases in which economic regulations are used to benefit the affected industry. Similarly, as we saw in Chapter 6, rent control can be interpreted, at least in part, as benefiting existing tenants at the expense of future potential tenants; the latter group tends to have no political power at all.

Governments as Monopolists

Governments face the same problems of cost minimization that private firms do but often operate in an environment where they are monopoly producers without stockholders. Large governments (provinces, big cities, the federal government) face all of the organizational problems faced by large corporations. They tend to use relatively rigid rules and hence to respond slowly to change. Building codes are an example of this type of problem. Most local governments have detailed requirements regarding the materials that must go into a new house, factory, or office. When technology changes, the codes often lag behind. For example, plastic pipe, which is cheaper and easier to use than steel pipe, was prohibited by building codes for decades after its use became efficient. Similarly, much antipollution regulation specifies the type of control equipment that must be employed. Changes in technology may make a regulation inefficient, but the regulation may stay in place for some time.

Like those of large private enterprises, a government's "organization chart" will often be out of date. For example, for most of this century the Canadian government has regulated freight rates charged by railroads. With the advent of buses and trucks, the government should have turned to developing a healthy *transportation system.* Yet for years, the imposed rate structure favoured the railroads. The same kind of problem—a misclassification of the relevant economic issue—might well have arisen when the purchasing division in a large corporation, which used typewriters exclusively, was confronted with modern word-processing technology. In the private sector, market forces often push the corporation into revising its view of the problem at hand, whereas there is ordinarily no market mechanism to force governments to use relatively efficient rules of thumb and organizational structures. Put in the language of Chapter 14, the scope for satisficing governments to depart from optimal behaviour is generally greater than that for satisficing firms. Put another way, much government failure arises precisely because governments do not have competitors and are not constrained by the "bottom line."

Principal-Agent Problems in Government

Governments face the same kinds of principal-agent problems that firms do, but the problem in the case of governments can be more serious for two reasons. First, the possibility of a hostile takeover, although quite powerful as applied to elected officials (they can be removed from office), is very weak as applied to bureaucracies. Second, the principal in the case of government is all of its citizens, and this group will generally be unable to agree on what government *should* do. Stockholders can all agree that the firm should maximize profits. Citizens who vote, by contrast, are not expected to agree on any simple mission for their elected representatives. This lack of agreement makes it that much more difficult for the agents to serve their principals and that much easier for agents who do not perform well to get away with it.

HOW MUCH SHOULD GOVERNMENT INTERVENE?

The theoretical principles for determining the optimal amount of government intervention are individually accepted by almost everyone. What they add up to, however, is more controversial. Moreover, the issue is often framed ideologically. Those on the "right wing" tend to compare heavy-handed government with a hypothetical and perfectly operating competitive market. In contrast, those on the "left wing" tend to compare hypothetical and ideal government intervention with a laissez-faire economy rife with market failures.

Evaluating the costs and the benefits of government intervention requires a comparison of the private economic system as it is working (not as it might work ideally) with the pattern of government intervention as it is likely to perform (not as it might perform ideally).

The cases that we have made for and against government intervention are both valid, depending on time, place, and the values that are brought to bear. At this point, we turn to the issue of what government actually does, something that will perhaps illuminate the question of what it ought to do. In Chapter 13, we discussed government action that is designed to affect monopoly and competition. In the next two chapters, we will discuss in some detail three other important types of intervention in the Canadian economy today: environmental and safety regulation, taxation, and public spending.

SUMMARY

A. HOW MARKETS COORDINATE

- The various markets in the economy are coordinated in an unplanned, decentralized way by the price system. Profits and losses play a key role in achieving a coordinated market response. Changes in prices and profits, resulting from emerging scarcities and surpluses, lead to responses by consumers and producers. Such responses tend to correct the shortages and surpluses as well as to change the market signals of prices and profits.
- Important features of a market economy include voluntary responses to market signals, the limited informa-

tion required by any individual, and the fact that coordination will occur under any market structure.

B. THE CASE FOR FREE MARKETS

- The case for free markets can be made in two different ways. The "formal defense" is based on the concept of allocative efficiency. This was the basis for the appeal of competitive markets as discussed in Chapter 13.
- The "informal defense" of free markets is not specifically based on the idea of allocative efficiency, and thus applies to market structures other than just perfect

competition. The informal defense of free markets is based on four central arguments:

1. Free markets are flexible and provide automatic co-ordination of the actions of decentralized decision makers.
2. The pursuit of profits which is central to free markets provides a stimulus to innovation and economic growth.
3. Free markets are self-correcting so that situations of disequilibrium are only temporary.
4. Free markets permit a decentralization of economic power.

C. THE CASE FOR GOVERNMENT INTERVENTION

- Markets do not always work perfectly. Dissatisfaction with market results often leads to government intervention. Five main sources of market failure are

  1. monopoly
  2. externalities
  3. public goods
  4. information asymmetries
  5. failure to achieve social goals

- Pollution is an example of an externality. A producer who pollutes the air or water does not pay the social cost of the pollution and is therefore not motivated to avoid the costs. Private producers will therefore produce too much pollution relative to what is allocatively efficient.

- National defense is an example of a public good (or collective consumption good). Markets fail to produce public goods because the benefits of such goods are available to people whether they pay for them or not.

- Information asymmetries cause market failure when one party to a transaction is able to use personal expertise to manipulate the transaction in his or her own favour. Moral hazard, adverse selection, and principal-agent problems are all consequences of information asymmetries.

- Changing the distribution of income is one of the roles for government intervention that members of a society may desire. Others include values that are placed on public provision for its own sake, on protection of individuals from themselves or from others, and on recognition of social obligations.

D. GOVERNMENT INTERVENTION

- Microeconomic policy concerns activities of the government that alter the unrestricted workings of the free-market system in order to affect either the allocation of resources or the distribution of income. Major tools of microeconomic policy include (a) public provision, (b) redistribution, (c) regulation, and (d) structuring incentives. (The first two are the subject of Chapter 20.) Regulation can take various forms. Incentives can be structured in a number of ways, including the use of fines, subsidies, taxes, and effluent charges (which are discussed in Chapter 19).

- The costs and benefits of government intervention must be considered in deciding whether, when, and how much intervention is appropriate. Among the costs are the direct costs that are incurred by the government, the costs that are imposed on the parties who are regulated, directly and indirectly, and the costs that are imposed on third parties. These costs are seldom negligible and are often large.

- The possibility of government failure must be balanced against the potential benefits of removing market failure. It is neither possible nor efficient to correct all market failure; neither is it always efficient to do nothing.

KEY CONCEPTS

Market coordination	Coase theorem	Benefits and costs of government intervention
Differences between private and social valuations	Public goods	Rent seeking
Market failure	Information asymmetries	Government failure
Externalities	Moral hazard and adverse selection	
	Benefit-cost analysis	

1. Should the free market be allowed to determine the price for the following, or should government intervene? Defend your choice for each.

   a. Transit fares
   b. Garbage collection
   c. Postal delivery of newspapers and magazines
   d. Fire protection for churches
   e. Ice cream

2. The following activities have known harmful effects. In each case, identify any divergence between social and private costs.

   a. Cigarette smoking
   b. Driving a car at the speed limit of 100 km per hour
   c. Private ownership of guns
   d. Drilling for offshore oil

3. The size of commercial fishing fleets has fallen markedly in recent years. Suppose there are many boats engaged in fishing a given area. Use the idea of externalities to show that each boat can be expected to fish more than the socially optimal amount.

4. Suppose the facts asserted here are true. Should they trigger government intervention? If so, what policy alternatives are available?

   a. The proportion of total national income taken up in medical and hospital costs in Canada has been rising more rapidly than in any other country (except the United States).
   b. The cost of an average one-family house in Vancouver is now about $300,000—an amount that is out of the reach of most people.
   c. Cigarette smoking reduces the smoker's life expectancy by eight years.
   d. Saccharin in large doses has been found to cause cancer in mice.

5. Consider the possible beneficial and adverse effects of each of the following forms of government intervention.

   a. Charging motorists a tax for driving in the downtown areas of large cities and using the revenues to provide peripheral parking and shuttle buses

   b. Prohibiting juries from awarding large malpractice judgments against doctors
   c. Mandating no-fault automobile insurance, in which the automobile owner's insurance company is responsible for damage to his or her vehicle no matter who causes the accident
   d. Requiring that automobile manufacturers rather than tire manufactures warrant the tires on cars that they sell

6. The president of Goodyear Tire and Rubber Company complained that government regulation had imposed $30 million per year in "unproductive costs" on his company, as listed here. How would one determine whether these costs were "productive" or "unproductive?"

   a. Environmental regulation, $17 million
   b. Occupational safety and health, $7 million
   c. Motor vehicle safety, $3 million
   d. Personnel and administration, $3 million

7. Your local government almost certainly provides a police department, a fire department, and a public library. What are the market imperfections, if any, that each of these seeks to correct? Which of these are closest to being public goods? Which are furthest?

8. Suppose that for $100, a laboratory can accurately assess a person's probability of developing a fairly rare disease that is costly to treat. What would be the likely effects of such a test on health insurance markets?

9. What market failures do public support of higher education seek to remedy? How would you go about evaluating whether the benefits of this support outweigh the costs?

10. What government failure might be involved when professional organizations encourage a provincial government to stiffen the requirements necessary to be licensed to practice a profession? What market failure might such requirements correct? How would you weigh arguments for and against stiffening the requirements?

CHAPTER 19

ENVIRONMENTAL AND SAFETY REGULATION

In almost everything we do, we are subject to some form of government regulation. The system of criminal law regulates our interactions with people and property. Local zoning ordinances regulate the ways in which the land that we own may be used. Insurance commissions must approve both the insurance contracts that we sign and the rates that we are charged. Regulatory commissions set rates for electricity, natural gas, local telephone service, and a host of other goods and services. Seat belts, brake lights, turn signals, air bags, internal door panels, bumpers, and catalytic converters are all subjects of regulation in just one industry. The number of electrical outlets per room, the material used for plumbing, and the spacing of the vertical supports in an interior wall are usually dictated by local building codes. The list goes on and on. A good case can be made that various governments in Canada have more effect on the economy through regulation than through taxing and spending.

In Chapter 18, we identified a number of types of market failure that might be addressed by government policy. Regulation of economic activity is used to address each of them. Market failure arising from natural monopoly has led to public regulation, as discussed in Chapter 13. *Externalities,* especially the negative externalities of industrial pollution, are the motivation for environmental regulation, a major topic of this chapter.

Regulation of advertising and much health and safety regulation are designed to deal with market failures arising from *information asymmetries.*

There is no easy way for a consumer to know whether the paint on a child's toy can cause lead poisoning, so a government body regulates the market for children's toys. Occupational licensing is defended on the same grounds; in most provinces, professionals as different as barbers and psychiatrists must undergo specified courses of training before they are allowed to ply their trades. The idea is to prevent "just anyone" from claiming and abusing alleged expertise.

Information about a professional's training is a *public good*: Once the information is available to one consumer, it can be made available to all very cheaply. Occupational licensing is a way to produce this public good—in the form of the familiar diploma that hangs on the wall of the barbershop, physician's office, or repair garage.

Regulations can also be used to change the *distribution of income*. This is the purpose of such regulations as rent controls, minimum wages, and agricultural supply-management policies. Finally, the laws and regulations that enforce private contracts are pure public goods that are essential to the operation of a market economy. Without reliably enforceable contracts, many transactions would be so risky that they would not take place.

The principal topic of this chapter is **social regulation**. Social regulation does not mean the regulation of social behaviour such as the clothes we wear or the words we use. Rather, it is the regulation of economic behaviour to advance social goals in circumstances in which neither competition nor economic regulation can be expected to do the job.

In this chapter, we consider both the market failures that social regulation addresses and the effectiveness and costs of different kinds of regulation in correcting these market failures. We start by extending the analysis of negative externalities in Chapter 18 to the problem of environmental pollution.

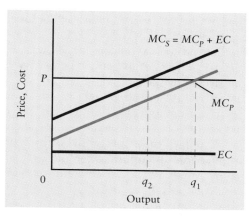

FIGURE 19-1
Pollution Externalities

Internalizing an externality can correct market failure. The private marginal cost curve MC_P is the conventional marginal cost for a firm that is producing output in a competitive market. The external cost curve EC depicts marginal cost that the firm's production imposes on people other than its owners, employees, and customers. Because the firm is maximizing profits, it will ignore EC and produce output q_1, where the market price p equals private marginal cost. Adding EC and MC_P yields social marginal cost, MC_S. The socially optimal level of output is q_2, where price is equal to MC_S.

Suppose that the firm is required to pay a tax of $\$EC$ per unit of output. Its MC_P curve will now become the MC_S curve. The externality will be *internalized*, and the profit-maximizing firm will be motivated to reduce its output to the socially optimal level, q_2. It does this because with the tax added to its private marginal cost, q_2 is the profit-maximizing level of output.

THE ECONOMICS OF POLLUTION CONTROL

Pollution is a negative externality. As a consequence of producing or consuming goods and services, "bads" are produced as well. Steel plants produce smoke in addition to steel. Farms produce chemical runoff as well as food. Households produce human waste and garbage as they consume goods and services. In all of these cases, the technology of production and consumption automatically generates pollution. Indeed, there are few human endeavors that do not have negative pollution externalities.

THE ECONOMIC RATIONALE FOR REGULATING POLLUTION

When firms use resources that they do not regard as scarce, they fail to consider the cost of those resources. This is a characteristic of most examples of pollution, including the case that is illustrated in Figure 19-1. When a paper mill produces pulp for the world's newspapers, more people are affected than its suppliers, employees, and customers. Its water-discharged effluent hurts the fishing boats that ply nearby waters, and its smog makes many resort areas less attractive, thereby reducing the tourist revenues that local motel operators and boat renters can expect. The profit-maximizing paper mill neglects these external effects of its actions because its profits are not affected by them.

Allocative efficiency requires that the price (the value that consumers place on the marginal unit of output) be just equal to the marginal social cost (the value of resources that society gives up to produce the marginal unit of output). When there are harmful externalities, marginal *social* cost and marginal *private* cost (the cost born by the producer) will diverge, because the firm is not charged for its contamination of the water.

By producing where price equals marginal private cost and thereby ignoring the externality, the firm is maximizing profits but producing too much output. The price that consumers pay just covers the marginal private cost but does not pay for the external damage. The *social benefit* of the last unit of output (the market price) is less than the social cost (marginal private cost plus the social cost imposed by the externality). Reducing output by 1 unit would reduce both social benefit and social cost but would reduce social cost by more because social cost is larger. Reducing output by 1 unit would save economic resources and increase allocative efficiency.

Making the firm bear the entire social cost of its production is called **internalizing** the externality. This will cause it to produce at a lower output. Indeed, at the optimal output, where the externality is completely internalized, consumer prices would just cover all of the marginal *social* cost of production—marginal private cost plus the externality. We would have the familiar condition for allocative efficiency that marginal benefits to consumers are just equal to the marginal cost of producing these benefits. The difference here is that some of the marginal social cost takes the form of an externality.

As an example, suppose that Great Cabinets Inc. produces kitchen cabinets and that residue from painting the cabinets is washed into a stream that runs beside the plant. The stream is part of the municipal water supply, which is treated at a water purification plant before it is sent into people's homes. Suppose that each cabinet produced increases the cost of running the water treatment plant by $1. In terms of the previous analysis, the external cost is $1 per cabinet, and thus the social cost per cabinet is exactly $1 above the private cost per cabinet—that is, social marginal cost exceeds private marginal cost by $1.

In practice, the external cost is often quite difficult to measure. This is especially so in the case of air pollution, where the damage is often spread over hundreds of thousands of square kilometres and can have real but small effects on millions of people. Another difficulty arises because the cost that is imposed by pollution will generally depend on the mechanisms that are used to undo the damage that it causes. Pollution-control mechanisms are themselves costly, and their costs must also be counted as part of the social cost of pollution. Nevertheless, the basic analysis of Figure 19-1 applies to these more difficult cases.

The socially optimal level of output is at the quantity where all marginal costs, private plus external, equal the marginal benefit to society.

Notice that the optimal level of output is not the level at which there is no pollution. Rather, it is the level at which the beneficiaries of pollution (the consumers and producers of Great Cabinets' kitchen cabinets, in our example) are just willing to pay the marginal social cost that is imposed by the pollution.

Unregulated markets will generally produce excessive amounts of environmental damage. Zero environmental damage, however, is neither technologically possible nor economically efficient.

POLLUTION CONTROL IN THEORY AND PRACTICE

The economics of determining how much pollution to prohibit, and therefore how much to allow, is summarized in Figure 19-2, which depicts the benefits and costs of pollution control. The analysis might be thought of as applying, say, to water pollution in a specific watershed. It is drawn from the perspective of a public authority that has been charged with maximizing social welfare.

Note that the figure is drawn in terms of the amount of pollution that is prevented (or abated) rather than in terms of the total amount of pollution. This is because pollution *abatement* (rather than pollution) is a "good" of economic value, and we are used to applying the concepts of supply and demand for goods with positive values. If no pollution is

FIGURE 19-2
The Optimal Amount of Pollution Abatement

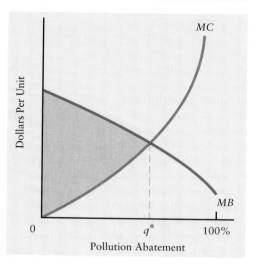

The optimal amount of pollution abatement occurs where the marginal cost of reducing pollution is just equal to the marginal benefits from doing so. *MB* represent the marginal benefit that is achieved by pollution prevention in some activity. *MC* represents the marginal cost of preventing pollution; it rises sharply as more and more pollution is eliminated. The optimal level of pollution control is q^*, where $MB = MC$. *Notice that not all pollution is eliminated.* For each unit up to q^*, the marginal benefit derived from pollution abatement exceeds the marginal cost. The total net benefit from the optimal amount of pollution abatement is given by the shaded area—the sum of the difference between marginal benefit and marginal cost at each level of abatement. Any further reductions in pollution beyond q^* would add more to costs than to benefits.

abated, the watershed will be subjected to the amount of pollution that would occur in an unregulated market. The greater the amount of pollution prevented, the smaller the amount of pollution that remains.

The marginal cost of preventing pollution is likely to be small at low levels of abatement but to rise steeply after some point. This is the upward-sloping line shown in Figure 19-2. There are two reasons for believing that this shape is generally accurate. First is the familiar logic behind increasing marginal costs. For each firm that pollutes, there will be some antipollution measures that can be taken fairly easily, so the first portion of pollution reduction will be cheap relative to later portions. In addi-

tion, it is likely that pollution reduction of any degree will be easier for some firms than for others. New facilities are likely to run cleaner than old ones, for example. Reducing pollution from a factory that was designed in the era of environmental concern may be much easier than obtaining similar reductions from an older factory. After some point, however, the easy fixes are exhausted, and the marginal cost of reducing pollution further rises steeply.

The downward-sloping curve in Figure 19-2 is the "demand" for pollution abatement, and reflects the marginal benefit of pollution reduction. The curve slopes downward for much the same reason that the typical demand curve slopes downward. Starting at any nonlethal level of pollution, people will derive some benefit from reducing the level of pollution, but the marginal benefit from a given amount of reduction will be lower, the lower the level of pollution. Put another way, in a very dirty environment, a little cleanliness will be much prized, but in a very clean environment, a little more cleanliness will be of only small additional value.

The optimal amount of pollution reduction occurs where the marginal benefit is equal to the marginal cost—where "supply" and "demand" in Figure 19-2 intersect. In trying to reach this optimum, the pollution control authority faces three serious problems.

First, although Figure 19-2 looks like a supply-demand diagram, we have already seen that the private sector will not by itself create a market in pollution control. Hence the government must intervene in private-sector markets if the optimal level of control shown in Figure 19-2 is to be attained.

The second problem is that the optimal level of pollution abatement is not easily known because the marginal benefit and the marginal cost curves shown in Figure 19-2 are not usually observable. In practice, the government can only estimate these curves, and accurate estimates are often difficult to obtain, especially when the technology of pollution control is changing rapidly and the health consequences of various pollutants (e.g., chemicals that are new to the marketplace) are not known.

The third problem is that the available techniques for regulating pollution are themselves imperfect. Even when the optimal level of pollution control is known, there are both technical and legal impediments to achieving that level through regulation.

In what follows we examine three different types of policies designed to bring about the optimal amount of pollution abatement (or the optimal amount of pollution). These are *direct controls, emissions taxes,* and *tradable emissions permits.*

Direct Controls

Direct control is the form of environmental regulation that is used most often. Automobile emissions standards are direct controls that are familiar to most of us. The standards must be met by all new cars that are sold in Canada. They require that emissions per kilometre of a number of noxious chemicals and other pollutants be less than certain specified amounts. The standards are the same no matter where the car is driven. The marginal benefit of reducing carbon monoxide emissions in rural Saskatchewan, where there is relatively little air pollution, is certainly much less than the marginal benefit in Montreal, where there is already a good deal of carbon monoxide in the air. Yet the standard is the same in both places.

Direct controls also often require that specific techniques be used to reduce pollution. For example, coal-fired electric plants were sometimes required to use devices called "scrubbers" to reduce sulfur dioxide emissions, even in cases where other techniques could have achieved the same level of pollution abatement at lower cost.

Another form of direct control is the simple prohibition of certain polluting behaviours. For example, many cities and towns prohibit the private burning of leaves and other trash because of the air pollution problem that the burning would cause. A number of communities have banned the use of wood stoves. Similarly, the government gradually reduced the amount of lead allowed in leaded gasoline and then eliminated leaded gasoline altogether.

Problems with Direct Controls. Direct controls are likely to be economically inefficient; in most cases, more pollution could be abated at the same economic cost as that imposed by direct controls. Suppose that pollution of a given waterway is to be reduced by a certain amount. Regulators will typically apportion the required reduction among all of the polluters according to some roughly equitable criterion. The regulators might require that every polluter reduce its pollution by the same percentage. Alternatively, every polluter might be required to install a certain type of control device or to ensure that each litre of water that is dumped into the watershed

meets certain quality criteria. Although any of these rules might seem reasonable, each of them will be inefficient *except in the extreme case where all polluters face identical pollution abatement costs.*

To see this, consider two firms that face different costs of pollution abatement, as depicted in Figure 19-3. Suppose that Firm A's marginal cost of pollution abatement is everywhere below Firm B's. Such a circumstance is quite likely when one recalls that pollution comes from many different industries. It may be easy for one industry to cut back on the amount that it uses of some pollutant; in another industry, the pollutant may be an integral part of the production process. The most efficient way to reduce pollution would be to have Firm A cut back on its pollution until the marginal cost of further reductions is just equal to Firm B's marginal cost of reducing its first (and cheapest to forgo) unit of pollution. Once their marginal costs of reducing pollution are equalized, *further* reductions in pollution will be efficient only if this equality is maintained. To see this, suppose that the marginal costs of abatement are different for the two firms. By reallocating some pollution abatement from the high-marginal-cost firm to the low-cost firm, total pollution abatement could be kept constant while the real resources used to abate pollution would be reduced. Alternatively, one could hold the resource cost constant and increase the amount of abatement.

Direct pollution controls are usually inefficient in that they do not minimize the cost of a given amount of pollution abatement. This implies that they also do not abate the most pollution possible for a given cost.

When direct controls require that firms adopt specific techniques of pollution abatement, a second type of inefficiency arises. Regulations of this kind tend to change only slowly: The regulators will often mandate today's best techniques tomorrow, even if something more effective has come along.

Both of these sources of inefficiency in direct controls are examples of *government failure,* discussed in Chapter 18. In both cases, the government does not do as well as it could in pursuing its important social objectives. In terms of Figure 19-2, government failure would add to the marginal cost of pollution reduction. Thus the less efficient the method used to control pollution the lower the opti-

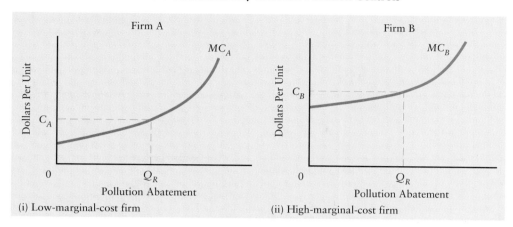

FIGURE 19-3
The Potential Inefficiency of Direct Pollution Controls

Requiring equal amounts of pollution abatement from different polluters is inefficient when the different polluters have different technologies of pollution abatement. Firm A is able to reduce its emissions according to the marginal cost curve MC_A. Firm B, which operates at the same scale but in a different kind of factory, has a higher marginal cost of abatement, MC_B. Suppose that a regulatory authority requires that the two firms reduce pollution by the same amount, Q_R. Firm A will have a marginal cost of pollution abatement of C_A, whereas firm B's marginal cost will be C_B, which is larger than C_A.

To see that this outcome is inefficient, consider what happens if firm A reduces its pollution (increases its pollution abatement) by 1 unit while firm B increases its pollution by 1 unit. Total pollution remains the same, but total costs fall. Firm A incurs added costs of C_A, and firm B saves a greater amount, C_B. Because the total amount of pollution is unchanged, the total social cost of pollution and pollution abatement is lower.

mal amount of pollution abatement and hence the higher the optimal level of pollution.

A final problem that arises with direct controls in practice is that they are expensive to monitor and to enforce. The regulatory agency has to check, factory by factory, farm by farm, how many pollutants of what kinds are being emitted. It then also needs a mechanism for penalizing offenders. Accurate monitoring of all potential sources of pollution requires a level of resources that is much greater than has ever been made available to the relevant regulatory agencies. Moreover, the existing system of fines and penalties, in the view of many critics, is not nearly harsh enough to have much effect. A potential polluter, required to limit emissions of a pollutant to so many kilograms or litres per day, will take into account the cost of meeting the standard, the probability of being caught, and the severity of the penalty before deciding how to behave. If the chances of being caught and the penalties for being caught are small, the direct controls may have little effect.

Monitoring and enforcement of direct pollution controls is costly, and this reduces the effectiveness of the controls.

Emissions Taxes

An alternative method of pollution control is to levy a tax on emissions at the source. The great advantage of such a procedure is that it internalizes the pollution externality so that decentralized decisions can lead to allocatively efficient outcomes. Again, suppose that Firm A can reduce emissions cheaply, while it is more expensive for Firm B to reduce emissions. If all firms are required to pay a tax of t for each unit of pollution they produce, then t is equal to the marginal benefit of pollution reduction. The goal of profit maximization will then lead firms to reduce emissions to the point where the marginal cost of further reduction is just equal to t. This means that Firm A will reduce emissions much more than Firm B and that both will then have the same

FIGURE 19-4
A Tax on Pollution

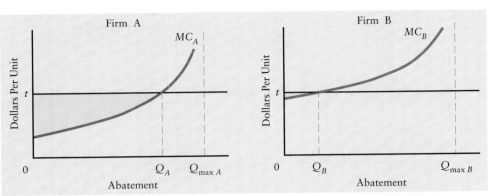

Taxes on pollution can lead to efficient pollution abatement. As in Figure 19-3, firm A faces a lower marginal cost of pollution abatement than does firm B. Suppose that the regulatory authority imposes a tax of t dollars per unit of pollution. Since each firm must then pay t dollars for each unit of pollution it produces, t can be viewed as the firm's marginal benefit of pollution abatement—for each unit of pollution it *does not produce* it avoids paying taxes equal to t.

Firm A will choose to reduce its pollution by Q_A. Up to this point, the tax saved by reducing pollution exceeds the marginal cost of reducing pollution. If firm A chooses not to reduce pollution at all, it would pay $t \times Q_{maxA}$ in pollution taxes, where Q_{maxA} is the firm's total pollution if it does nothing to prevent pollution. By abating its pollution by Q_A, firm A saves an amount that is given by the shaded area in the panel on the left.

Firm B chooses to abate only a small amount of pollution, Q_B. Any further abatement would require that the firm incur costs along MC_B, which would be greater than the benefits of taxes saved.

marginal cost of further abatement, which is required for allocative efficiency. This is illustrated in Figure 19-4.

Note that if the regulatory agency is able to obtain a good estimate of the marginal damage that is done by pollution, it could set the tax rate just equal to that amount. In such a case, polluters would be forced by the tax to internalize the full pollution externality. A second great advantage of using emissions taxes is that they do not require that regulators specify anything about *how* polluters should abate pollution. Rather, polluters themselves can be left to find the most efficient abatement techniques. The profit motive will lead them to do so because they will want to avoid paying the tax.

Emissions taxes can, in principle, perfectly internalize pollution externalities so that profit-maximizing firms will produce the allocatively efficient amount of pollution abatement. Furthermore, unlike direct controls, emissions taxes minimize the total cost of a given amount of pollution abatement.

Application 19-1 discusses a simple type of pollution tax that is becoming quite common in many U.S. cities—charging for household garbage by the bag.

Problems With Emissions Taxes. Emissions taxes can work only if it is possible to measure emissions accurately. For some kinds of pollution-creating activities, this does not pose much of a problem, but for many other types of pollution, good measuring devices that can be installed at reasonable cost do not exist. Obviously, in these cases, emissions taxes cannot work, and direct controls are the only feasible approach.

When there is good reason to prohibit a pollutant altogether, direct controls are obviously better than taxes. Municipal bans on the burning of leaves fall in this category, as do the occasional emergency bans on some kinds of pollution that are invoked during an air pollution crisis in cities such as Los Angeles and Vancouver.

Another problem with emissions taxes involves setting the tax rate. Ideally, the regulatory agency

CHARGING FOR GARBAGE BY THE BAG

One of the most common forms of pollution is household garbage. The economic theory of pollution externalities discussed in the text suggests that a tax on household trash should reduce the volume of pollution. In a number of communities in the United States, per-bag charges on household garbage have led to reductions in the amount of trash generated. The waste that is not going into the costly bags is going into compost heaps and into recycling. Communities vary in the way that charges are assessed and in the degree of support that they provide for alternative uses of waste. Typically, the municipal garbage trucks will only pick up trash if the trash bag (or other type of garbage) carries a special sticker. The stickers are sold by the municipal authorities; the fewer a household uses, the less money it spends on having its trash picked up. Fees of $1 to $2 per bag are not uncommon. In one U.S. community (High Bridge, New Jersey), a fee of $1.25 per bag has led to a 25 percent reduction in the volume of garbage.

The externality in this case is the use of landfills. Especially in the more populated areas of the United States, landfills for solid waste are becoming scarce and, consequently, expensive. By charging residents something for use of the landfill, alternative means of dealing with waste are encouraged, and a solid waste facility of given size can last longer.

Even in this case, the problem of finding the optimal charge per bag of garbage poses serious technical difficulties. There are also enforcement problems: Rather than pay the charge, some households will illegally dump their trash, adding to environmental damage. However, the pollution itself is very easy to measure, and it is plain that the optimum charge is greater than zero.

---

would obtain an estimate of the marginal social damage caused per unit of each pollutant and set the tax equal to this amount. This would perfectly internalize the pollution externality. However, the information that is needed to determine the marginal social damage curve shown in Figure 19-1 is often difficult to obtain. If society is currently far away from the optimum, it may be very difficult to estimate what the marginal social damage will be at the optimum. If the regulatory agency sets the tax rate too high, too many resources will be devoted to pollution control (the outcome will be beyond q^* in Figure 19-2). If the tax is set too low, there will be too much pollution. In many practical cases, regulators may have a much better idea of the acceptable level of pollution than of the tax rate that would lead to that result. Further, when the technology of pollution abatement changes, the tax rate would have to change as well, and governments are often very slow to adjust tax rates.

A potentially serious problem with emissions taxes is that information necessary to determine the optimal tax rate is often unavailable.

Tradable Emissions Permits

One great advantage of direct controls is that the regulators can set the standards to limit the total quantity of pollution in a given geographical area. This can be done without knowing the details of either the marginal benefit or the marginal cost curve in Figure 19-2. The great advantage of emissions taxes is that they allow for decentralized decision making, providing firms with an incentive to internalize the negative externality of pollution. **Tradable emissions permits** can combine both of these advantages and thus have the potential for being superior to either direct controls or emissions taxes.

In Figure 19-3, we noted that direct pollution controls would generally be inefficient because the marginal cost curves for pollution abatement would vary across firms. Tradable permits can solve this problem. To see this, we must first figure out how much pollution to allow. This involves reformulating the regulator's problem. Start with the same conditions as those in Figure 19-3, and permit each firm to pollute exactly the same amount as would be allowed by the direct controls in Figure 19-3. Now suppose that the firms are allowed to buy and to sell tradable emissions permits which are simply "rights to pollute." Trades among firms will lead to discovery of the lowest-cost means of achieving the permitted level of pollution.

To see how the outcome is changed in the presence of tradable emissions permits, note that at the initial allowed amounts of pollution (Q_R), the marginal cost of pollution for Firm A is lower than that for Firm B. Firm B would be willing to pay up to C_B for the right to pollute 1 more unit, and Firm A would be willing to sell that right for any amount that exceeded C_B. Notice that if such a trade were made, the total amount of pollution would be unchanged, the total cost of abating pollution would fall (by $C_B - C_A$), and both firms would be at least as well off as before. We would thus have a clear efficiency improvement. No one is made worse off, and at least one party is made better off.

Once the firms are allowed to exchange rights to pollute, they will do so until their marginal abatement costs are equalized. At this point, there is no further gain from trading permits. Notice that the new outcome is identical to that depicted in Figure 19-4, with the equilibrium price of an emissions permit just equal to the emissions tax shown in that figure. However, with tradable permits, regulators do not need to calculate the optimal pollution tax. Given the permitted quantity of pollution, the market in permits will calculate the equivalent to the tax through the voluntary trades of firms.

Tradable emissions permits can be used to achieve the same allocation of resources as would occur with emissions taxes, with much less information required of the regulatory authorities.

One problem with both pollution taxes and tradable permits is more political than economic, but it is certainly important in explaining why such policies are so rare. Opponents of tradable permits often argue that by providing permits, rather than simply outlawing pollution above some amount, the government is condoning crimes against society. Direct controls, according to this argument, have much greater normative force because they say that violating the standards is simply wrong. Emissions taxes and markets for pollution make violating the standards just one more element of cost for the firm to consider as it pursues its private goals.

Most economists find arguments of this kind unpersuasive. An absolute ban on pollution is impossible, and in choosing how much pollution to allow, society must trade pollution abatement against other valuable things. Economic analysis has a good deal to say about how a society might minimize the cost of *any* degree of pollution abatement or maximize the amount of pollution abated for any given cost that the society is willing to bear.

Problems with Tradable Emissions Permits. Tradable permits pose formidable problems of implementation. Some of these involve technical difficulties in measuring pollution and in designing mechanisms to ensure that firms and households comply with regulations (some of these problems also exist for emissions permits). Furthermore, the potential efficiency gains arising from tradable permits cannot be realized if regulatory agencies are prone to change the rules under which trades may take place. This has been a problem in the past, but it is a problem that can be corrected.

Although they have been seriously discussed in Canada, most experimentation with tradable pollution permits has so far been conducted in the United States. The U.S. Environmental Protection Agency and a number of state regulatory agencies have allowed limited trading of emissions permits for the past two decades. One study that examined the most important of these programs estimated that they had saved as much as $12 billion in the cost of pollution control, with approximately the same result for environmental quality as the costlier direct controls that

_____
[1]Robert W. Hahn, "Economic Prescriptions for Environmental Problems", *Journal of Economic Perspectives* 3 (Spring 1989): 95–115.

A MARKET FOR SO₂ EMISSIONS IN THE UNITED STATES

In 1991, the Chicago Board of Trade, which oversees the most important commodity market in the United States, voted to create a market in rights to emit sulfur dioxide (SO_2). The Board's decision can be traced directly to the U.S. Clean Air Act of 1990, which adopted a market approach to dealing with the problem of acid rain.

Coal-burning electric power plants are the major cause of acid rain. They emit sulfur dioxide through their tall smokestacks, and the sulfur dioxide, which stays in the air for two to five days, becomes acidic when it combines with moisture. Two to five days in the atmosphere, with prevailing winds from the southwest, turns Ohio Valley and Midwest emissions into a Canadian and New England pollution problem. Acid rain (and snow) harms the ability of lakes to sustain aquatic life and damages agricultural crops, forests, and even buildings.

The U.S. Clean Air Act of 1990 sets targets for sulfur dioxide emissions and implements those targets by issuing a fixed number of "permits to pollute." The total number of permits is fixed such that by the year 2000, emissions will be less than half the 1980 level. After 2000, the allowed emissions will be sharply reduced again. Most of the permits will be allocated to plants based on the

plants' fuel use between 1985 and 1987. Thus the largest plants will get the most permits, but virtually all "dirty" plants will be required to reduce their emissions substantially.

Once firms have their permits in hand, they may use them or sell them as they please. Of course, for the new system to be effective, the level of emissions must be measured. All utilities subject to the new law were required to install continuous monitoring equipment by 1992. If a firm pollutes without a permit, it is subject to a $2,000 fine for each ton of excess emissions and must make up the overpollution by underpolluting by the same amount in the future.

No one yet knows what the market price of the emissions permits will be. And there is every reason to believe that it will not be constant over time. As technology for operating power plants with reduced sulfur dioxide emissions improves, the price of both the technology and the permits will surely fall. As a result, utilities will face interesting choices. On the one hand, they may choose to buy permits early and wait for improvements in technology. On the other, if they adopt emissions-reducing technology early, they could sell their permits and pocket the proceeds.

---

they replaced.[1] Application 19-2 discusses how the U.S. Clean Air Act of 1990 has created a national market in tradable permits for sulfur dioxide, the major cause of acid rain.

Governmental creation of a market in "bads" may become one of the most promising strategies for efficiently overcoming the market failure that leads to environmental pollution.

Despite the view held by most economists that market-based schemes—such as emissions taxes or tradable emissions permits—are both efficient and

practical ways of regulating pollution in a market economy, many people remain unconvinced. Extension 19-1 examines why.

REGULATION FOR HEALTH AND SAFETY

The federal government (through the Department of Consumer and Corporate Affairs) approves the marketing of both prescription and nonprescription drugs

RESISTANCE TO MARKET-BASED ENVIRONMENTAL POLICIES

Despite the many advantages that can be identified for market-based approaches to environmental protection, such approaches encounter considerable resistance from firms, members of the public, and environmentalists. Why?

PRODUCERS

1. *Some firms object to the costs that they are asked to pay in terms of emissions taxes or the purchase prices of emissions permits.* However, there is no reason why payments to government under any market-based scheme need to be an unjustified "tax grab." Emissions taxes need not be in excess of the costs imposed on society by the industry's activities. If government uses the introduction of a market-based scheme to raise general revenue—and thus levies emissions taxes in excess of the costs generated by the pollution—firms can oppose the extra tax burden without opposing the market-based scheme itself.

2. *The introduction of market-based measures may signal the end of a free ride that producers have been taking at society's expense.* If the firms in an industry were bearing none of the cost of its pollution, almost any antipollution scheme will impose a burden on them—but only to the extent of forcing them to bear the costs of their own activities. The difference between using direct controls and the market-based solution, however, is that the former will cost the average firm in the industry more than the market solution. (This just reflects the fact that direct controls are generally less efficient than emissions taxes or emissions permits.)

3. *Under market-based schemes (rather than direct controls), many firms feel a sense of unfairness because their competitors continue polluting while they must clean up.* Their complaints ignore the fact that those firms that continue to pollute have paid for the right to do so, either by paying effluent taxes or by buying pollution rights, and that the complaining firm could do the same if it wished (it does not do so because cleaning up is cheaper for it than paying to pollute, as the competitors are doing).

This points to a key issue in assessing market-based solutions: Such solutions must not be judged relative to a "no action" policy. Given a government's decision to reduce pollution, the market solution must be compared with other alternatives *that lower pollution by the same amount.* When this is done, much of the opposition from producers fades away.

THE PUBLIC

1. *Some members of the public have a moral opposition to selling anyone the right to pollute.* Since it involves human survival, dealing in rights to pollute seems evil to many people. This view makes difficult

in Canada. The National Transportation Agency requires that automobiles have brake lights and seat belts. Consumer and Corporate Affairs can remove dangerous goods from the marketplace. It can also set standards for product safety, such as requiring "dead man" controls that automatically stop engines in lawn mowers when the operator lets go of the handle. It also regulates "truth in advertising." The Workers' Compensation Board is broadly responsible for health and safety in the workplace. It sets detailed standards designed to reduce workers' exposure to injury and to health risks, such as asbestos.

What all of these examples have in common is that the market failure they address is in the market for information. A consumer will generally have difficulty determining if a cold remedy has dangerous side effects, what the effect of brake lights is on the chances of having an accident, or how likely a child's pajamas are to catch fire. An individual worker may be in no position to assess the risks of working with a the rational evaluation of alternative plans for dealing with a serious social problem.

2. *Opposition to the outcome where those who have the highest costs of cleaning up continue to pollute while those with the lowest costs do the cleaning up.* Morality may dictate to many observers that the biggest polluters should do the cleaning up. Economists cannot show this reaction to be wrong; they can only point out the cost in terms of higher prices, lower employment, unnecessary resource use, and less overall pollution abatement that follow from adopting such a position.

ENVIRONMENTALISTS

1. *Many environmentalists are sceptical about the efficiency and desirability of markets.* Some do not understand economists' reasoning as to why markets can be, and often are, efficient mechanisms for allocating scarce resources. Others understand the economists' case but reject it, although few complete the argument by trying to demonstrate that direct government controls will be more effective.

2. *Many environmentalists do not like the use of self-interest incentives to solve what they would regard as "social" rather than "economic" issues.* Economists who point to the voluminous evidence of the importance of self-interest incentives are often accused of ignoring higher motives such as social duty, self-sacrifice, and compassion. Although such motives are absent from the simple theories that try to explain the everyday behaviour of buyers and sellers, economists since Adam Smith have been aware that these higher motives often do exert strong influences on human behaviour.

Such higher motives are very powerful at some times and in some situations, but they do not govern many people's behaviour in the course of day-to-day living. If we want to understand how people behave in the aftermath of a flood, or an earthquake, or a war, we need motives in addition to self-interest; if we want to understand how people behave day after day in their buying and selling, we need little other than a theory of the self-interested responses to market incentives. Since control of the environment requires influencing the mass of small decisions, as well as a few large ones, the appeal to self-interest is the only currently known way to induce the required behaviour through voluntary actions.

3. *Some environmentalists have the view that resources such as clean air and pure water are above mere monetary calculation and should thus be treated in special ways.* The economist can point out that the use of this view to justify departing from market-based solutions ensures that measured material living standards will be lowered. If that is the understood and accepted price of regarding resources as special entities, then so be it!

given machine and may not be able to find out easily whether there are toxic chemicals in the workplace.

HEALTH AND SAFETY INFORMATION AS A PUBLIC GOOD

In Chapter 18, we saw that information is likely to be underproduced in private markets because many kinds of information are *public goods.* Once the flammability of different materials that are used in children's pajamas is known, making the information available to interested parents can be done at negligible marginal cost. A private firm that develops the information would be unable to recoup its investment. Thus unless the government intervenes, product information would tend to be either unavailable or available only at inefficiently high prices. Most economists would agree that information about safety in the workplace and product safety is a public good; this provides a rationale for the government either to produce such information or to require that private firms produce it.[2]

Is Good Information Enough?

In practice, most health and safety regulation goes well beyond the simple provision of information. Rather, firms are required to meet standards of workplace and product safety. Many economists have argued that, given good information, private markets will ensure efficient levels of workplace safety. To evaluate this argument, we present here a very simple example of what might happen if there were no legislated standards but everyone had accurate information about safety risks.

Consider a worker who can take a job at either Firm A or Firm B. Suppose that the worker knows that accidents at Firm A will lead the typical worker to miss two weeks of work per year, whereas the average time lost to injury at firm B is one week per year. No compensation is paid for the time spent at home due to injury. To keep the example simple, suppose also that lost pay is the only cost of accidents that is borne by workers. Equilibrium in the labour market can occur only if workers at Firm A have a higher wage than workers at Firm B. Suppose that full-time work at both firms is 50 weeks per year. Workers at Firm A can expect to be laid up and unable to work for an average of one week per year more than those at Firm B. They will thus require a wage that is 50/49 times the wage paid to workers at Firm B (assuming that they get no pleasure from spending a week at home in bed).

The result in this example that the wage at the less-safe Firm A is higher than the wage at the more-safe Firm B is simply an application of the idea of equilibrium wage differentials, first introduced in Chapter 15.

---

[2]People who do not agree would rely on the legal system to compel private producers and employers to develop the information. If someone is hurt by an unsafe product, the person can sue the manufacturer for damages. If the manufacturer has provided accurate information about the risks inherent in using the product, such as warning labels on medicines, the consumer's chance of winning the lawsuit is much reduced. Thus the manufacturer has an interest in developing accurate information. A similar case can be made regarding worker health and safety. In practice, however, many lawsuits of this kind are defended on the grounds that manufacturers had no knowledge of or reason to be concerned about their products' hazards. That such defenses often succeed suggests that there is an incentive to fail to develop relevant information about health and safety.

Notice that in this example, all that is required for equilibrium to occur is that the workers know the probability of accidents at each firm and that markets respond to conditions of demand and supply. No government standard needs to be set. Rather, workers who work at the firm that is less safe will demand a compensating wage differential in order to work there. Thus the greater the chance of an accident at work, the higher the wages that a firm must pay. This is illustrated by the upward-sloping curve shown in Figure 19-5. From the perspective of the employer, the curve represents the marginal wage cost (per worker) of *increasing* the probability of accidents. As accidents become more likely (moving along the horizontal axis), the firm must pay higher wages to attract workers.

The firm also has a marginal benefit of increasing the probability of accidents. That is, if improving work-place safety requires an expenditure of real resources (such as improved lighting or more frequent clean-up), then *increasing* the probability of accidents is associated with a *saving* of real resources, and this saving of resources is the marginal benefit to the firm. Since the costs of making marginal improvements in work-place safety are higher when the workplace is already quite safe, the marginal benefit of *less safety* is higher when the workplace is less safe. Thus the firm's marginal benefit curve in Figure 19-5 is downward sloping.

In equilibrium, firms will choose a level of safety such that the savings in nonwage costs of reducing safety a little bit is just equal to the increase in the wages that the firm would have to pay. Notice that the optimal rate of accidents, much like the optimal level of pollution, is not zero. Rather, it depends on the cost of reducing the level of accidents.

In the simplified world of Figure 19-5, there is no need for safety standards; if workers are perfectly informed about the risk of accidents (and about the costs that they would bear when accidents occur) and firms minimize costs, the private market will generate the allocatively efficient solution. This argument also can be extended to product safety, given the strong assumption that consumers are perfectly informed about the risks inherent in consuming the products that they buy.

With perfect information, private markets will produce allocatively efficient levels of occupational and product safety.

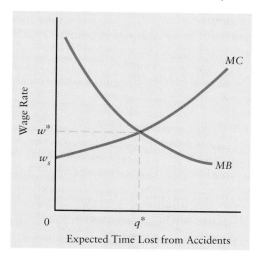

FIGURE 19-5
The Market for Occupational Safety

Competition in the labour market can induce firms to provide workplace safety. Suppose that a perfectly safe workplace would have to pay a wage of only w_s. As the expected time lost because of accidents increases, the required wage rises to compensate workers for the risk of injury. The curve that shows the higher wages is labeled *MC* because it gives the marginal cost to the firm per worker of letting the workplace become less safe.

The marginal benefit to the firm of reducing safety is given by the *MB* curve, which shows the savings per worker that the firm can obtain by reducing safety-related expenditures. At the axis, time that is lost through accidents is zero; the workplace is perfectly safe. The *MB* curve starts very high because the cost of making an already very safe workplace perfectly safe is likely to be very high. Thus reducing safety by a small amount from perfect safety would sharply reduce the firm's costs.

Where the two curves intersect, the marginal cost of making the workplace safer is just equal to the marginal benefit from doing so. To the left of q^*, reducing safety in the workplace saves *MB* and costs only *MC*.

Given that the *MC* curve is derived from the preferences of workers who are well informed about workplace risks, the market solution of q^* and w^* will be cost-minimizing for the firm and allocatively efficient.

A Role for Government

There are two main arguments for government intervention to promote health and safety. One relies on the presence of *imperfect information*. The other is based on *paternalism*.

Imperfect Information. Perfect information may be impossible to obtain or to evaluate. Our example of Firm A and Firm B could work quite well for, say, an experienced machinist who is comparing two machine shops. Such a worker will have a good sense of what can be expected on the shop floor and may be able to estimate the chances of injury quite accurately. If the government requires all firms to publish their accident histories every year, the worker can make an informed choice. Such a choice may be impossible, however, when the cause of harm in the workplace is a chemical that might cause cancer. Evaluation of carcinogens often takes many years; there is likely to be uncertainty in the medical literature; and it is very likely that the typical worker will have a difficult time interpreting the information, even if it is made easily available.

Information about safety risks in offices is also unlikely to be available, at least in some cases. Most white-collar workers have no idea what their buildings are made of, how quickly the buildings would burn, or what kind of emergency lighting would be available in case of a fire. Further, it would not be easy for them to decode the blueprints of different buildings to make informed choices about fire safety.

Similar problems arise with product safety. The typical automobile driver is not able to make informed choices about the benefits of collapsing steering columns, reinforced door panels, or antilock braking systems. A complete maintenance report on each airplane that you fly on would probably be of little help to you in assessing the safety of the airplane. Less dramatically, it would be prohibitively expensive for the government to develop accident data for every consumer product and then to let consumers sift through the information as they decided what to buy.

Safety standards can free workers and consumers from attempting difficult calculations that they are ill-equipped to make. When information is costly or impossible to process, standards can enhance efficiency.

Paternalism. One of the most cost-effective regulations in existence involves collapsing steering columns in automobiles. (The idea is that in the event of a front-end collision, the steering column breaks rather than impaling the driver.) According to one estimate, the protection afforded by the collapsing steering column saves about 1,300 lives per year at a total cost of $188.5 million—this implies a cost *per saved life* of $145,000. On pure efficiency grounds, matters might be further improved if automobile manufacturers offered the collapsing steering column as an option and were required to provide data on the hazards of noncollapsing steering columns. Only very ardent proponents of laissez faire would argue for such a policy.

Another safety regulation requires that children's sleepwear meet a nonflammability standard. (The standard requires that the fabric not burst into flame when it is lit.) This regulation is less cost-effective than the requirement of collapsing steering columns. The cost per life saved is estimated to be about $1.9 million. Still, few people would wish to permit parents to choose flammable pajamas at somewhat lower cost. It is hard to think of a government regulation that is more literally paternalistic!

HEALTH AND SAFETY REGULATION IN PRACTICE

In Chapter 18, we noted that even when there is market failure, the case for government intervention is weakened by the possibility of government failure. Perhaps the most widely cited examples of government failure arise in the area of health and safety regulation. A notorious example of (temporary) regulatory failure is the short-lived ban on saccharin. Saccharin was banned when huge doses were shown to cause cancer in rats. When the required doses were seen to exceed anything humans were likely to take, the ban was lifted.

Assessing the risk that a product will cause cancer can be extremely difficult, and scientists' estimates of the risk often changes with new information. For example, dioxin, which was once believed to be among the most toxic of substances produced by industry, is now widely believed to be much less dangerous. At the same time, many scientists are coming to believe that electric blankets may increase the risk of cancer. Uncertainty about the actual risks engendered by the use of different products greatly increases the difficulty of health and safety regulation and increases the economic cost of regulation as well. If regulatory standards and rules could be expected to stay fixed, businesses could plan and act accordingly. However, new scientific evidence often leads to changes in regulation, which can require that firms change their techniques and their products, adding to the average cost of doing business. There is no obvious solution to this problem.

As with pollution, health and safety regulators often take an engineering approach to their task. Rather than specifying a particular outcome or providing incentives for increased safety, they mandate that certain kinds of equipment be used to perform certain functions. For example, government regulation requires that handrails be of a certain height and a certain distance from the wall, and have supports of specified spacing and diameter.

In principle, the case for the engineering approach may be stronger for safety regulation than it is for pollution control because the alternative of a "safety tax" is generally not feasible. Unfortunately, the problems inherent in all engineering standards—that they may become obsolete and that they may be much more effective in some settings than in others—remain. To the extent possible, efficiency dictates that standards be expressed in terms of *required performance* rather than *required design and materials*. The reason for this is that it provides an incentive for firms to find inexpensive ways of meeting the standards, thereby reducing the cost of complying with them.

BENEFIT-COST ANALYSIS OF SOCIAL REGULATION

The social purpose of health, safety, and pollution regulation is obvious. No one wants unsafe products, hazardous workplaces, and ugly or dangerous environments. However, even for as wealthy a society as Canada in the 1990s, the goals of health, safety, and a clean environment cannot be absolute ones. There is no such thing as a completely safe workplace or product; it is impossible to establish that a prescription drug can never be harmful, and it is difficult to think of any human activity that does not generate some amount of pollution. Given that these problems will always be with us to some degree, the relevant question is, *To what degree?* Economics can help provide an answer by evaluating costs as well as benefits—a recurring theme of this chapter and this book.

For economic efficiency, environmental, health, and safety risks should be reduced to the point where the marginal social cost of further reduction is just equal to the marginal social benefit of further reduction.

Many critics of the economic approach to social regulation rightly point out that these costs and benefits are often very difficult to measure. True as this may be in certain cases, the logic of the benefit-cost criterion still holds. Thus unless public policies attempt to equate marginal benefits and marginal costs, scarce social resources will be wasted and we will get fewer positive results than could be obtained from the resources that are used.

Cost-effectiveness analysis is a procedure that is much easier to perform than cost-benefit analysis. In cost-effectiveness analysis, the analyst holds constant the *outputs* of a policy and looks for the cheapest (most cost-effective) way of pursuing those outputs. Such analysis is particularly useful when it is difficult to measure the value of outputs. A prominent example involves the cost of saving lives. We do not presume to put a dollar value on a human life. Cost-effectiveness analysis, however, tells us that in designing programs to save human lives, we should implement programs that do so at lowest cost first. If we do not, we will be wasting resources that could be devoted to saving lives and thus will be saving fewer lives than we could.

A study of regulations designed to save lives reveals an extraordinary range in the cost per life saved of actual and proposed regulations. The most cost-effective is the collapsing steering column, at $145,000 per life. The least cost-effective regulation in place at the time of the study involved the use of DES in cattle feed and was calculated at $190 million per life saved, over 1,000 times as much.[3] We do not need to put a specific value on human life to know that there are thousands of ways to spend $190 million and save more than one life. Consider, for example, the hiring of crossing guards who would work during rush hours, policing the most traveled street corners that do not have crossing guards. Assuming a salary of $19,000 per year per guard (which is a part-time job), 10,000 such guards could be hired per year. They would surely save more than one life. Moreover, researchers have identified numerous examples in which the cost of life-saving interventions is nearly zero; examples include windshields with adhesive bonding rather than rubber gaskets, elimination of flammable fabrics in children's sleepwear, and immunization of children for measles, mumps, and rubella. At the other end of the spectrum, however, a number of interventions such as radionuclide emission control at coal-fired indus-

trial boilers, sickle-cell screening for all newborns, and control of benzene emission at rubber tire manufacturing plants are estimated to cost more than $1 million per life-year saved.[4]

The rationale for seeking efficiency in social regulation comes from the same source as the rationale for seeking efficiency in other areas. The more efficiently the goals of social regulation are pursued, the more resources will be available to pursue other things of value, and the more benefits can be achieved for any given amount of resource use.

REGULATORY REFORM

Growing concerns about a variety of perceived problems with Canada's regulatory structure—including obsolescence in the face of rapid changes in technology and world markets, significant compliance costs, and inefficiencies in the regulatory process—have led to a number of developments in Canada.[5] (There have been similar developments in the United States, Europe, and Japan.) We have already encountered the deregulation trend in Chapter 13 in the context of competition policy, but the current debate and trend concerning regulation of the economy extends beyond the direct regulation of industry.

Several years ago, the now-disbanded Economic Council of Canada published two major reports of the regulatory process, and included a number of specific recommendations. In one report, the Council proposed that an extensive consultative process be part of any major government attempt at regulatory change, that any major new regulatory proposals be subjected to formal benefit-cost analysis, and that the government review existing regulations and operations of regulatory agencies on a regular basis.

In the other report, the Council made proposals that touched on a wide range of regulated activities—trucking, airlines, telecommunications, agriculture, occupational health and safety, and the environment. The general thrust of its proposals was to "streamline the regulatory process and where possible to reduce the extent of regulation." Increased

---

[3]John F. Morral III, "A Review of the Record", *Regulation*, November–December 1986, pp. 25–34.

[4]Tammy Tengs et al., "Five-Hundred Life-saving Interventions and Their Cost-effectiveness", self-published manuscript, 1994.

[5]This section draws on the discussion by Professor John Strick of the University of Windsor, *The Economics of Government Regulation. Theory and Canadian Practice* (Toronto: Thompson, 1990).

competition and increased application of market forces and financial incentives were also stressed.

In the mid 1980s, the Canadian government took up this theme of regulatory reform and announced its Regulatory Reform Strategy. Although it did not endorse comprehensive deregulation, the government committed itself not only to limit the proliferation of new regulations but also "to 'regulate smarter' through greater efficiency, greater accountability, and greater sensitivity to those affected by federal regulations." The strategy invoked a number of principles, including

- Recognition of the importance of markets

- Continued use of regulation to achieve social and economic objectives

- Use of benefit-cost analysis to screen new initiatives

- Increased public access and participation in the process

Many of the new procedures found their way into practice, and regulatory hearings have become a regular part of the public policy landscape. Whether the new procedures have in fact met the stated objectives is not yet clear; many critics argue that the new processes, though open, are inefficient. For example, the hearings that finally ended Bell Canada's monopoly on long-distance phone service lasted over 18 months and cost close to $100 million.

Most economists would support the principles of the Regulatory Reform Strategy. Even if it is fully adopted, however, difficult social choices and difficult technical problems, of both measurement and program design, will remain. Moreover, when health, life, and safety are at stake, there are many who will never be comfortable with the results of decentralized decision making, no matter how well-informed the parties to private transactions may be. The desire to protect people from the negative consequences of their actions extends well beyond an interest in internalizing externalities or providing efficient levels of information.

Economic analysis can help society to examine the costs and the consequences of social regulation. Most important, it can help regulators to achieve desired consequences at minimum cost and thus reduce the level of government failure. It can help us to decide *how best* to intervene in the interest of health and safety, but it cannot tell us *how much* we should intervene.

SUMMARY

A. THE ECONOMICS OF POLLUTION CONTROL

- Almost all economic activity is subject to at least some government regulation. Government regulation, of some form or another, is used to deal with every type of market failure—public goods, externalities, natural monopoly problems, information asymmetries, and social values.

- Economic regulation typically refers to the regulation of natural monopoly, which was discussed in Chapter 13. Social regulation is the regulation of economic behaviour to advance social goals where neither competition nor economic regulation can be expected to do the job.

- Most pollution problems can be analyzed as negative externalities. Polluting firms and households going about their daily business do harm to the environment and fail to take account of the costs that they impose on others.

- The allocatively efficient level of pollution in any activity is generally not zero; it is the level where the marginal cost of further pollution reduction is just equal to the marginal damage done by a unit of pollution. If a firm or a household faces incentives that cause it to internalize fully the costs that pollution imposes, it will choose the allocatively efficient level of pollution.

- Pollution can be regulated either directly or indirectly. Direct controls are used most often. Direct controls are often inefficient because they require that all polluters meet the same standard regardless of the benefits and costs of doing so. Indirect controls, such as taxes on emissions, are more efficient; ideally, they cause firms to internalize perfectly the pollution externality. Tradable emissions permits could have the same effect as taxes without requiring regulators to know as much about the technology of pollution abatement.

B. REGULATION FOR HEALTH AND SAFETY

- Health and safety regulation covers workplace health and safety and product safety. Some economists have argued that regulation of this kind is unnecessary because if people are well informed about health and safety risks, the level of resources devoted to safety and health will be allocatively efficient.

- Information about health and safety risks is often difficult to obtain or to evaluate. Society may also choose not to permit people to face certain kinds of risks. In either of these cases, health and safety regulation addresses a real market failure. Government failure is common in the areas of health and safety regulation.

C. BENEFIT-COST ANALYSIS OF SOCIAL REFULATION

- Cost-effectiveness analysis is a method of evaluating regulations when the benefits are hard to measure. It is particularly helpful for evaluating regulations that are designed to save lives, where the most cost-effective regulation is the one that saves the most lives per dollar of cost.
- Increased use of benefit-cost and cost-effectiveness analysis could reduce the social costs imposed by social regulation. Alternatively, holding social cost constant, it could increase the benefits from social regulation.

KEY CONCEPTS

Costs and benefits of pollution abatement
The efficient level of pollution

Direct pollution controls
Emissions taxes and tradable emissions permits

Regulatory failure
Cost-effectiveness analysis
Regulatory reform

DISCUSSION QUESTIONS

1. Many occupations are licensed, either by governments or by professional organizations (such as provincial engineering associations, which are run by professional engineers). Are economists licensed? Should they be? Why or why not?

2. "Pollution is wrong. When a corporation pollutes, it commits assault on the citizens of the country, and it should be punished." Comment on this statement in light of the discussion in this chapter.

3. Assume that the following statements are true. What do they imply about the argument that health and safety regulations are necessary to promote economic efficiency?

   a. Welders who work on the upper stories of unfinished skyscrapers are paid more than welders who work only indoors.
   b. Following a commercial airplane crash, the stock market value of the airline company tends to fall.
   c. Within a city, housing of a given structural quality tends to sell for less, the greater the health risk posed by air quality in the neighbourhood.
   d. For decades, asbestos was widely used as insulation. Installers of asbestos insulation routinely

breathed asbestos fibre in concentrations that are now known to be potentially lethal. For some years, asbestos producers were aware that asbestos was dangerous but did not share this information with installers.
   e. Until the mid 1980s, the upholstery in airline seats emitted lethal fumes when the seats were burning.

4. Consider the following (alleged) facts about pollution control and indicate what influence they might have on policy determination.

   a. The cost of meeting government pollution requirements is about $300 per person per year.
   b. More than one-third of the world's known oil supplies lie under the ocean floor, and there is no known blowout-proof method of recovery.
   c. Sulfur-removal requirements and strip-mining regulations have led to the tripling of the cost of a ton of coal used in generating electricity.
   d. Every million dollars that is spent on pollution control creates 47 new jobs in the economy.

5. Suppose you were given the job of drafting a law to regulate water pollution over the entire length of some river.

a. How would you determine how much total pollution to permit?

b. What control mechanism would you use to regulate emissions into the river? Why?

c. Would you impose the same rules on cities as on farms?

d. Would your answer to a, b, or c depend on the quality of information that would be available to you? How and why?

6. Under current regulations, cleaning up all known toxic waste sites in the United States would cost between $300 billion and $700 billion. Yet according to the *New York Times*, "Virtually all of the risk to human health, most analysts agree, could be eliminated for a tiny fraction of these sums." The same article notes that many experts argue that once dangerous sites are identified, "the cleanup should be carefully aimed at saving lives rather than restoring land to preindustrial condition." In one site, the former goal could be achieved for $71,000; the latter would cost over $13 million. How would you frame a benefit-cost analysis of different strategies for cleaning up toxic waste?

7. The text presents several values of regulation per human life saved, ranging from $145,000 to $190 million. What do you think is the value of a statistical human life? Are there ever circumstances in which we would be willing to trade one group's lives for another's lives—or for another's comfort?

8. The federal government has imposed many regulations aimed at reducing the pollution which is generated by driving. The more familiar regulations are direct—catalytic converters, fuel efficiency, and the like. Given the discussion in the chapter, why do you think the government opted for such direct controls? Can you think of any indirect controls currently in use to reduce automobile pollution?

9. The federal government has a very rigorous approval process for all drugs introduced into the Canadian market. Drug makers are required to demonstrate safety and effectiveness through a process of animal and human trials that can take as long as 10 years. Is it efficient to have the same approval process for all drugs? Explain your answer.

CHAPTER 20

TAXATION AND PUBLIC EXPENDITURE

PUBLIC VERSUS PRIVATE SECTOR
SCOPE OF GOVERNMENT ACTIVITY
EQUITY AND EFFICIENCY
EVOLUTION OF POLICY

In Chapter 19, we saw some of the reasons why the scope of government is so extensive. Taxation is needed to raise money for public spending, and it can also play a policy role in its own right. Taxes can affect the distribution of income—some people get taxed more than others. Moreover, by taxing some activities heavily and others lightly or not at all, the tax system can influence the allocation of resources. In some cases, tax policy is carefully designed with such effects in mind; in other cases, the effects are unintentional by-products of policies pursued for other purposes.

By far the largest item on which Canadian governments spend—both federally and provincially—is on social programs. For the past few years, Canada's social programs have been under significant pressure for reform, the pressure coming both from the governments' tight fiscal situation and from an overall desire to reconstruct the social programs in ways that will be both more efficient and more fair. Coincident with these pressures to reform Canada's social programs has been pressure for the devolution of power from the federal government to the provincial governments.

In this chapter, we examine the various sources of government tax revenues and the various types of government expenditures. We ask how taxation and public expenditure affect the allocation of resources and the distribution of income, and to what extent they are effective tools of public policy. We begin with a discussion of taxation in Canada. We then examine the basis on which one would evaluate a tax system, emphasizing the distinction between equity and efficiency. The types of public expenditures in Canada are then examined along with the important concept of "fiscal federalism." The five pillars of Canadian social policy are then described, as are some of the current pressures for reform of social programs. Finally, we conclude this chapter with a discussion of evaluating the overall role of government.

TAXATION IN CANADA

There is a bewildering array of taxes in Canada today. These are levied at the federal, provincial, and local levels. Some are highly visible, such as income taxes and the Goods and Services Tax (GST). Others are all but invisible to most people because they do not show up on income tax forms or on receipts for purchases. For example, there are special taxes levied on the sales of alcohol, cigarettes, and gasoline, but these taxes are levied directly on the producers (rather than the retailers) of these goods. People and firms are taxed on what they earn, on what they spend, and on what they own. Not only are taxes numerous, but taken together they raise a tremendous amount of revenue. Canada is not alone in the significance of government taxation. Table 20-1 shows for several countries in 1993 the total tax revenues as a fraction of Gross Domestic Product. At the top of the list is Denmark, which collects taxes equal to 50 percent of GDP; at the bottom is Turkey, collecting only 23 percent of GDP in tax revenue. Canada lies roughly in the middle, with total tax revenue equal to 36 percent of GDP.

SOME DEFINITIONS

Before discussing some details about the Canadian tax system, we examine two general concepts—*tax expenditures,* and the *progressivity* of taxes.

Tax Expenditures

Sometimes taxes are used in ways that are similar to spending programs. For example, one way to deal with polluted rivers is to spend public funds to clean them up. An alternative, as we saw in Chapter 19, is to use taxes to penalize polluters or to give tax concessions to firms that install pollution-abating devices. Tax concessions that seek to induce market responses are called **tax expenditures**—tax revenue forgone to achieve purposes that the government believes are desirable.

The difference between a tax expenditure and an ordinary budgetary expenditure is that a tax expenditure represents *a reduction in tax revenue* whereas an ordinary expenditure represents *an increase in spending.* Because tax expenditures represent foregone earnings for the government, they are considerably less visible than actual budgetary expenditures. They therefore usually receive little scrutiny from Parliament or the public. But this does not mean that they are small or unimportant. On the contrary, tax expenditures are very significant in the current Canadian economy. Table 20-2 gives some examples of federal personal income tax expenditures. As is clear from the table, specific tax expenditures range in value from a few million to many billion dollars per year.

TABLE 20-1
International Comparison of Government Tax Revenues, 1993

Country	Total Tax Revenue as Percent of GDP
Denmark	50.0
Sweden	49.5
Netherlands	48.2
Finland	46.8
Norway	45.8
Belgium	45.7
France	44.0
Austria	43.4
Italy	43.2
Germany	39.7
Ireland	37.1
Canada	36.1
New Zealand	35.6
Spain	34.7
United Kingdom	34.4
Switzerland	32.5
Iceland	32.2
Portugal	31.1
United States	30.0
Japan	29.4[a]
Turkey	22.7

Canada lies roughly in the middle of other developed countries in terms of total tax revenue as a share of GDP. The figures reflect total tax revenues by all levels of government, including mandatory contributions to public pension plans. Of those countries shown in the table, Denmark has the highest tax burden, at 50 percent of GDP; Turkey has the lowest, at under 23 percent of GDP.

[a]Data for Japan is for 1992.

(*Source*: David Perry, "Fiscal Figures", *Canadian Tax Journal* 1994.)

TABLE 20-2
Some Federal Personal Income Tax Expenditures for 1992

Nature of Tax Expenditure	Millions of Dollars
Nontaxation of lottery and gambling winnings	900
Deductions for clergy residence	50
Tuition fee credit	155
Northern residents deduction	235
Investment tax credit	58
Nontaxation of employer-paid health and dental benefits	1,125
Nontaxation of employer-paid premiums for life insurance	160
Deductions for contributions to RRSPs	3,685
Nontaxation of investment income inside RRSPs	2,755
Deductions for contributions to employer-sponsored pension plans	4,990
Nontaxation of investment income inside employer-sponsored pension plans	7,690
Nontaxation of capital gains on principal residences	8,955
Charitable donations credit	865
Child-care expense deductions	315
Subtotal	31,938
Other personal income-tax expenditures	32,121
Total personal income-tax expenditures	64,059

There is a wide variety of tax expenditures, ranging in size from a few million dollars to several billion dollars per year. The table shows some selected personal income tax expenditures for the federal government. Each number represents tax revenue that is not earned due to the presence of some exemption or deduction in the federal personal income-tax system. For example, if the federal government did not permit tuition fees to be tax deductible, its personal income-tax revenues in 1992 would have been $155 million higher. Note that the total excludes tax expenditures that arise out of federal-provincial tax-sharing arrangements.

(*Source: Government of Canada Tax Expenditures*, December 1994.)

Progressivity

When the government taxes one group in society more heavily than it taxes another, it influences the distribution of income. The effect of taxes on the distribution of income can be summarized in terms of *progressivity*. A **progressive tax** takes a larger percentage of income from high-income people than it does from low-income people. A **proportional tax** takes amounts of money from people in direct proportion to their income—for example, every individual pays 10 percent of their income in taxes. A **regressive tax** takes a larger percentage of income from people the lower their income.

Note that the progressivity or regressivity of a tax is expressed in terms of *shares* of income rather than absolute dollar amounts. So, a tax which collects $1000 from each individual clearly collects the same dollar amount from everybody, though it collects a higher share of income from low-income people than from higher-income people. A tax of this type—often called a **poll tax** or a *lump-sum tax*—is therefore a regressive tax.

Since a progressive tax takes a larger share of income from high-income people than it does from low-income people, progressive taxes reduce the inequality

TABLE 20-3
Taxes as a Percentage of Canadian GDP and Their Division Among Levels of Government, 1992

	Taxes as Percentage of GDP	Percentage of Taxes Divided	
		Federal	Provincial/Local
Personal income taxes	15.0	62.8	37.2
Corporate income taxes	2.0	65.0	35.0
Property taxes	4.0	—	100.0
General sales taxes	5.2	47.9	52.1
Excise taxes (fuel, alcohol, and cigarettes)	2.1	46.4	53.6
Import duties	0.6	100.0	—
Health and social insurance levies	3.6	62.6	37.4
Other taxes	2.3	15.8	84.2
Total Taxes	34.8		

Taxes on personal income raise the most revenue, two thirds of which goes to the federal government. The first column shows the percentage of Canadian GDP taken by various taxes. The next two columns show the percentage division of the revenues from each tax going to each level of government.

(*Source: The National Finances 1994*, The Canadian Tax Foundation.)

of income. A regressive tax increases the inequality of income.

THE CANADIAN TAX SYSTEM

Taxes are collected by the federal government, by each of the provinces, and by thousands of cities, townships, and villages. The federal government collects about as much revenue as all other governments put together. The provinces, in turn, collect about four times as much as local governments. The federal government gets over 50 percent of its revenues from taxes paid directly by individuals and corporations and over 20 percent from taxes collected on the sale of goods and services (mainly the GST). The provinces get just over 40 percent from income taxes and about 35 percent from sales taxes.[1] The municipalities rely almost exclusively on property taxes for their tax revenues. The diversity and yield of various taxes are shown in Table 20-3.

Personal Income Taxes

Personal income taxes are paid directly to the government by individuals. The amount of tax any individual pays is the result of a fairly complicated series of calculations. All types of income are included in

what is called total income, although certain types of income qualify for total or partial exemption. Then a number of allowable deductions are subtracted from total income to determine taxable income. Once taxable income is calculated, the amount of tax payable is then calculated by applying different tax rates to different levels of income. There are three federal personal income tax rates, each applying within what is called a tax bracket. In 1996, the three **tax brackets** were roughly $0–$28,000, $28,000–$56,000, and greater than $56,000. The federal tax rates in these brackets were 17 percent, 26 percent, and 29 percent, respectively.

To see how this system of differential tax rates and tax brackets operates, consider an individual who has a taxable income of $70,000. To the federal government, she pays at a rate of 17 percent on the first $28,000 ($4,760), at a rate of 26 percent on the next $28,000 ($7,280), and at a rate of 29 percent on all income *above* $56,000 (0.29 × $14,000 = $4,060). Her total federal income tax payable is thus equal to $16,100.

Average Versus Marginal Tax Rates. This brings us to the important distinction between an individual's *average tax rate* and *marginal tax rate*. The **average tax rate** paid by a taxpayer is his or her total income tax payment divided by total income. In the previous example, the average tax rate is 23 percent ($16,100/$70,000 = 0.23). The taxpayer's **marginal tax rate** is the amount of tax he or she would pay on

---

[1]Each of the lower levels of government also receives revenue in the form of transfers from more senior governments. We examine such transfer payments shortly.

an additional dollar of income—for this individual, 29 percent since she is in the highest tax bracket.

Provincial Taxation.   The three federal personal income-tax rates do not represent the complete taxation of personal income in Canada, for two reasons. First, both the federal and many provincial governments have added more progressivity to the personal income tax by levying surcharges that kick in at various higher levels of income.

Second, the provincial governments also tax personal income. Quebec runs its own income-tax system, whereas the other nine provinces simply use the federal tax base (and federally distributed tax forms) and essentially "top up" federal taxes. Except for Quebec, taxpayers pay a single amount to Revenue Canada, which then distributes the total between the federal government and each province according to the amount collected from residents of that province.

Table 20-4 shows the marginal income-tax rates paid by a single taxpayer at various income levels and in each province. The figures vary across provinces because different provincial rates are added onto the common federal rate. Average tax rates rise continually with income as more and more income becomes subject to the top marginal tax rate. Currently in most provinces an average tax rate of 40 percent is reached when income is about $100,000. As can be seen from the table, the combined marginal tax rate rises as income rises; this rising marginal tax rate contributes to the progressivity of the income tax system.

The 1987 Reforms.   Many of the elements of the current personal income tax system date from a major federal reform which occurred in 1987. The theme of that reform was to broaden the tax base by eliminating a number of exemptions and deductions and to lower marginal tax rates. The new system also reduced the number of tax brackets from ten to the current three.

Although the changes introduced in 1987 were substantial and were intended to be part of a comprehensive reform of the tax system, the personal income-tax system continues to change. A special levy has been introduced on high-income earners, intended to "claw back" social benefits such as family allowances. Also, both federal and provincial governments have introduced temporary surtaxes on medium and high incomes to help deal with growing fiscal deficits. As of 1995, these surtaxes had pushed the top marginal rate above 50 percent in all provinces except Alberta.

The 1987 reforms simpified the income-tax system, removed loopholes and broadened the tax base. The subsequent levying of surtaxes, however, made the tax system more complex and significantly increased the top marginal tax rates. These developments run counter to the principles that guided the 1987 reforms. They also raise the question of how high tax rates can become without causing major shrinkages in the tax base as some people emigrate, some move to the underground economy, and some choose leisure over work.

TABLE 20-4

Combined Marginal Personal Income Tax Rates for a Single Taxpayer in Selected Provinces, 1994

Province	Taxable Income				
	$10,000	$25,000	$50,000	$75,000	$100,000
Newfoundland	25.6	27.6	44.7	51.3	51.3
PEI	24.1	26.1	42.3	48.6	50.3
Nova Scotia	24.1	26.1	42.3	52.0	53.8
New Brunswick	24.8	26.8	43.4	49.9	51.4
Quebec	30.1	36.2	48.2	52.9	52.9
Ontario	42.4	25.8	41.9	53.2	53.2
Manitoba	27.9	26.9	44.3	50.4	50.4
Saskatchewan	30.5	27.5	45.5	51.9	51.9
Alberta	26.2	24.3	40.1	46.1	46.1
British Columbia	22.9	24.9	40.4	51.1	54.2

Tax rates vary across provinces due to different provincial add-ons and surtaxes. These rates, which include federal and provincial surtaxes, have been creeping up over the last few years. By 1994, the combined maximum marginal rate exceeded 50 percent in all but one province (Alberta) and approached 55 percent in some.

(*Source: The National Finances 1994*, Canadian Tax Foundation.)

Corporate Taxes

The federal corporate income tax is, for practical purposes, a flat-rate tax on profits as defined by the taxing authorities—which includes the return on capital as well as economic profits. In 1995, the rate was 28 percent.

As with the personal income tax, the 1987 reforms not only lowered tax rates but also broadened the tax base, and on the whole, the changes tended to raise taxes paid by corporations. The broadening of the tax base was accomplished primarily by eliminating tax concessions, called investment tax credits, that had been used to encourage investment.

Recently the British Columbia government instituted a corporate wealth tax. This is an annual levy on the value of each firm's assets. It is paid whether the firm makes profits or losses. Such corporate wealth taxes are almost unknown in other industrialized countries, and their introduction in British Columbia was bitterly criticized by the business community and would-be foreign investors, especially from Southeast Asia.

Excise and Sales Taxes

An excise tax is levied on a particular commodity. In many countries, commodities such as tobacco, alcohol, and gasoline are singled out for high rates of excise taxation. Because these commodities usually account for a much greater proportion of the expenditure of lower-income than higher-income groups, the excise taxes on them are regressive.

A sales tax applies to the sale of all or most goods and services. All provinces except Alberta impose a retail sales tax. Such a tax is mildly regressive, because poorer families tend to spend a larger proportion of their incomes than richer families. For example, suppose there is a 7 percent comprehensive sales tax. A family that earns $25,000 per year and saves nothing will pay 7 percent of its income on sales taxes; a family that earns $70,000 per year and saves $10,000 will pay 6 percent.

Both excise and sales taxes are often referred to as "indirect" taxes to contrast them with income taxes, which are levied directly on the income of individuals or firms.

The Goods and Services Tax. Since 1991, Canada has had a country-wide tax which applies at the same rate (7 percent) to the sale of all goods and services (with a few exceptions, such as basic groceries). The Goods and Services Tax (GST) was intro- duced—despite enormous political controversy—for a number of reasons. First, it followed the modern trend in taxing expenditure rather than income. One problem with taxing income is that interest earnings from accumulated savings get counted as income and thus get taxed. Income taxes therefore discourage saving by lowering the after-tax rate of return to saving. In contrast, the GST only applies to the value of expenditure. Since the GST does not tax income (and therefore does not tax interest income) it does not discourage saving.

Second, the GST does not distort the relative prices of goods and services because it is applied at the same rate to all goods and services; in contrast, the old Manufacturers Sales Tax (MST) which the GST replaced applied only to goods and thus raised the price of goods relative to services. Third, it followed the trend in almost all other developed nations (except the United States), which levy similar taxes; they are called *value added taxes* (VAT) in Europe.

In practice, the GST works by taxing a firm on the gross value of its output and then allowing a tax credit equal to the taxes paid on the inputs that were produced by other firms. Effectively, this taxes each firm's contribution to the value of final output—its value added. The result is the same as if each good and service bore a 7 percent tax when it was sold to its final user. An example of the operation of the GST for the case of the stages leading from the mining of iron ore to the manufacture of a washing machine is illustrated in Figure 20-1.

As is clear from the figure, the GST is a *multistage* tax, applying at each stage of the production process. One advantage of using a multistage tax is that it reduces *tax cascading*, which is the term used to describe the fact that under the MST some commodities effectively got taxed more than once. For example, consider again the case of the washing machine in Figure 20-1. If sales taxes were levied on all transactions, with no offsetting tax credits applied to inputs in the manufacturing process, the ore would be taxed three times: when it was sold to the steel maker, when the steel was sold to the appliance manufacturer, and when the appliance was sold to the consumer. Similarly, the steel would be taxed twice. The GST eliminates this cascading. Once the tax on the ore is collected when it is sold to the steel maker, its value is not taxed again, since further purchasers are given a tax credit for the tax embodied in their purchases.

The elimination of tax cascading is especially important when considering investment and international trade. When a firm invests in a new machine

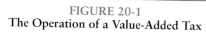

FIGURE 20-1
The Operation of a Value-Added Tax

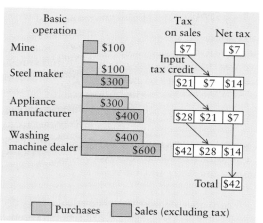

A tax on value added is the same as a tax on the value of total output produced by a firm with a credit allowed for the tax paid to other firms from which it has purchased produced inputs. The example is for the stages involved as iron ore is mined and then sold to a steel maker, the steel then sold to an appliance manufacturer, and the washing machine sold to a retailer and then to a consumer. The example makes the simplifying assumption that no produced inputs are used in the mining operation (so that the value of the iron ore is all value added); at all further stages, however, the use of produced inputs makes the firm's value added less than the value of final output at that stage. The steel maker's value added is $200, and its tax is thus $14; $21 on the total value of its output less the $7 credit on the taxes already paid by the mine on the value of the iron ore. Total taxes paid equal $42, which is 7 percent of the $600 value of the final product; each firm pays 7 percent of its share in creating that $600 value.

or builds a new plant, many of its purchases will be subject to sales tax. Under a single-stage tax, this is the end of the story, and the sales tax clearly raises the cost of investment to the firm. With a multistage tax, the firm gets a credit for the taxes already paid on its purchases of goods and machines. This reduces the cost of investment to the firm.

In spite of its being an improvement over the MST, the GST proved to be extremely unpopular, partly because most Canadians were unaware of the MST, and its deficiencies. Unlike provincial sales taxes, the MST was "invisible"; it was applied before the retail transaction, and hence its presence was hidden in retail selling prices. Much of the opposition to the GST came from small business, farmers, fisher-

men, and professionals, who feared the burden of record keeping and paperwork that such a complicated system entails. Others feared that once the GST was introduced, governments could easily raise more revenue by increasing the GST rate.

Being a tax applied to expenditure rather than income, the GST taken alone would be mildly regressive, because the proportion of income saved, and hence not taxed, rises with income. This characteristic was avoided by exempting food and, more importantly, giving low- and middle-income people a refundable tax credit, which for the poor exceeds the value of GST that they would pay even if they spent all of their incomes on taxable commodities.

Property Taxes

The property tax is the most important Canadian tax that is based on wealth, and it an important source of revenue for municipalities. It is different from any other important tax because it is not related directly to a current transaction. In contrast, income taxes are levied on the current payment to a factor of production (income) and sales taxes are levied on the value of a currently purchased good or service.

Taxing the value of existing property creates two problems. First, someone has to assess what the property is worth. Because the assessment is only an estimate, it is always subject to challenge. Second, sometimes owners of valuable property have low *incomes* (though considerable wealth) and thus have difficulty paying the tax.

The progressivity of the property tax has been studied extensively. It is obvious that the rich typically live in more expensive houses than the poor, and thus pay more in property taxes. But this does not mean that the rich pay more property taxes *as a fraction of their income* than the poor. Thus it is not readily apparent that property taxes are progressive. Indeed, most studies have shown that the proportion of income spent on housing tends to decrease with income. This suggests, therefore, that the property tax tends to be mildly regressive in its overall effect.

EVALUATING THE TAX SYSTEM

To evaluate the *tax system* (as opposed to a specific tax within the system), the important question is this: Holding constant the amount of revenue to be raised, what makes one tax system better or worse than another? Economists deal with this question by considering two aspects of taxation—equity and efficiency. We deal with equity first.

TAXATION AND EQUITY

Debate about income distribution and tax policy usually involves the important but hard-to-define concepts of *equality* and *equity*.

Equality Versus Equity

To tax everyone *equally* can mean several things. It might mean that everyone should pay the same amount—as would be the case with a lump-sum tax. But this would clearly be much harder on the unemployed worker than on the heiress. It might mean that everyone should pay the same proportion of income—say, a flat 20 percent, whether rich or poor, living alone or supporting eight children, healthy or suffering from a costly-to-treat disease. It might mean that each should pay an amount of tax such that everyone's income after taxes is the same—which would remove any incentive to earn an above-average income. Or it might mean none of these things.

Unlike equality, *equity* (or fairness) is a normative concept; what one group thinks is fair may seem outrageous to another. Two principles can be helpful in assessing equity in taxation: equity according to *ability to pay,* and equity according to *benefits received.*

The Ability-to-Pay Principle. Most people view an equitable tax system as being based on people's ability to pay taxes. In considering equity that is based on ability to pay, two concepts need to be distinguished.

Vertical equity concerns equity *across* income groups; it focuses on comparisons between individuals or families with different levels of income. The concept of vertical equity is central to discussions of the progressivity of taxation. Proponents of progressive taxation argue as follows. First, taxes should be based on ability to pay. Second, the greater one's income, the greater the percentage of income that is available for goods and services beyond the bare necessities. It follows, therefore, that the greater one's income, the greater the proportion of income that is available to pay taxes. Thus an ability-to-pay standard of vertical equity requires progressive taxation.

Horizontal equity concerns equity *within* a given income group; it is concerned with establishing just who should be considered equal to whom in terms of ability to pay taxes. Two households with the same income may have different numbers of children to support. One of the households may have greater dental expenses, leaving less for life's necessities and for taxes. One of the households may incur expenses that are necessary for earning income (e.g., requirements to buy uniforms or to pay union dues). There is no objective way to decide how much these and similar factors affect the ability to pay taxes. In practice, the income-tax law makes some allowance for factors that create differences in ability to pay by permitting taxpayers to exempt some of their income from tax. However, the corrections are rough at best.

The Benefit Principle. According to the benefit principle, taxes should be paid in proportion to the benefits that taxpayers derive from public expenditure.[2] From this perspective, the ideal taxes are *user charges,* such as those that would be charged if private firms provided the government services.

The benefit principle is the basis for the gasoline tax, since gasoline usage is closely related to the services obtained from using public roads. There is also a special airline ticket excise tax that is used for airport operations, air traffic control, and airport security. Although there are other examples, especially at the local level, the benefit principle has historically played only a minor role in the design of the Canadian tax system. But its use is growing in Canada and elsewhere as governments seek new ways to finance many of their expenditures.

How Progressive Is the Canadian Tax System?

Although most public controversy over tax equity stresses the progressivity or regressivity of particular taxes, what matters in the end is the overall progressivity of the *entire tax system.* For a modern government to raise sufficient funds, many taxes must be used. We have already discussed personal and corporate income taxes, excise and provincial sales taxes, the Canada-wide GST, and municipal property taxes. Not all of them are equally progressive in design and each one has its own loopholes and anomalies. So, how high-, middle- and low-income people are taxed relative to each other depends on how the entire tax system impacts on each group.

---

[2]It is difficult to see how the benefit principle could be applied to many of the most important categories of government spending. Who gets how much benefit from national defense or from interest on the public debt? It is even more difficult to imagine applying the benefit principle to programs that redistribute income.

Assessing how the entire tax system affects the distribution of income is complicated by two factors. First, the progressivity of the system depends on the mix of the different taxes. Federal taxes tend to be somewhat progressive; the progressivity of the income-tax system and the use of a low-income tax credit more than offset the regressivity of the federal GST. Provincial and municipal governments rely heavily on property and sales taxes and thus have tax systems that are probably slightly regressive.

Second, income from different sources is taxed at different rates. For example, in the federal personal income tax, income from royalties on oil wells is taxed less than income from royalties on books, and profits from sales of assets (capital gains) are taxed less than wages and salaries. To evaluate progressivity, therefore, one needs to know the way in which different *levels* of income are related with different *sources* of income. For example, is wage income more important than capital-gain income for high-income people *relative to* low-income people?

Many economists have concluded that the Canadian tax system has very little overall effect on the distribution of income, except for very low- and very high-income persons. The tax system tends to be roughly proportional for middle-income classes and mildly progressive for low- and high-income persons. Thus the overall tax system is essentially redistributing income from high-income people to low-income people, and doing very little redistribution among the middle-income people. (Look back to Table 15-3 in Chapter 15 to see the pre-tax and post-tax distribution of family income in Canada. That table shows that income is essentially redistributed from the richest one-fifth of the families to the poorest two-fifths of the families, leaving the middle-income families largely unaffected.) Mainly what it is doing therefore is raising revenue to finance government spending rather than effecting major income redistributions.

TAXATION AND EFFICIENCY

The tax system influences the allocation of resources by altering such things as the relative prices of various goods and factors and the relative profitability of various industries.

Although it is theoretically possible to design a neutral tax system—one that leaves all relative prices unchanged—the conditions are too complex to be met in practice. As a result, any actual tax system, including Canada's, does alter the allocation of resources. The taxes change the relationship between prices and marginal costs and shift consumption and production toward goods and services that are taxed relatively lightly and away from those that are taxed more heavily. Usually, this alteration of free-market outcomes causes allocative inefficiency. In a world without taxes (and without other market imperfections), prices would equal marginal costs, and society's resources could be allocated efficiently.

Of course, in a world without taxes, there would be other problems—it would be impossible to pay for any government programs or public goods desired by society. In practise, then, the relevant objective for tax policy is to design a tax system that minimizes inefficiency, *holding constant the amount of revenue to be raised*. In designing such a tax system, a natural place to start would be with taxes that both raise revenue and enhance efficiency. An example of such a tax is the emissions tax that we discussed in Chapter 19. When taxes are imposed on negative externalities, marginal social benefit is moved closer to marginal social cost, *and* government revenue is raised. Unfortunately, such taxes cannot raise nearly enough revenue to finance all of government expenditure.

The Burdens of Taxation

In the absence of externalities, a tax normally does two things. It takes money from the taxpayers, and it changes their behaviour. Taxpayers are typically made worse off by both. Economists call the revenue collected the **direct burden** of the tax. The additional cost that result from the induced changes in behaviour is called the **excess burden.**

The excess burden of a tax is the amount of money that the taxpayers would have to be given, over and above the tax paid, in order to be just as well off as they would be without the tax. The excess burden reflects the allocative inefficiency of the tax.

An example will illustrate this important distinction. Suppose that your provincial government imposes a $2 excise tax on the purchase of compact discs. Suppose further that you are a serious music lover and that this tax does not change your quantity demanded of CDs—that is, your demand for them is perfectly inelastic and hence you continue to buy your usual five CDs per month. In this case, you pay $10 in taxes per month, and you therefore have to reduce your consumption of other goods by $10 per month.

In this special case, the burden on you is not reflected by the change in your consumption of CDs (because there is no change), but rather by the change in your overall purchasing power. That is, if you were to be given an additional $10 a month in income, you would be exactly as well off as you were before the tax was imposed. Thus the total burden on you is equal to the direct burden, $10 a month; there is no excess burden of this tax. The absence of any excess burden from this tax is just another way of saying that there is no allocative inefficiency; the cost of raising $10 a month for the province is just the $10 a month that you pay in taxes. In this case, the tax is *purely* a redistribution of resources from you to the government.

Now suppose that a friend of yours is also a music lover but is not quite so dedicated. The tax leads her to cut back on her consumption of CDs from two per month to none. In this case, your friend pays no taxes and therefore experiences no reduction in her overall purchasing power. The direct burden of the tax is therefore zero. However, your friend *is* worse off as a result of this tax—she has given up the satisfaction that she would have derived from two new CDs per month. She would have to be given some amount of money greater than zero (exactly her consumer surplus from buying two untaxed CDs per month) in order to make her as well off as she was before the tax was imposed. In this case, the direct burden is zero (because no tax is paid) but there *is* an excess burden. The excess burden is equal to her loss in consumer surplus from the CDs that she no longer enjoys.

When a tax is imposed, some people behave like the music buff and do not change their consumption of the taxed good at all, others cease consuming the taxed good altogether, and most simply reduce their consumption. There will be an excess burden for those in the latter two groups. This means that the revenue collected will understate the total cost to taxpayers of generating that revenue. Since our exercise in judging the efficiency of a tax system is to hold constant the total revenue raised, and thus to hold constant the direct burden generated by the tax system, *an efficient tax system will be one that minimizes the amount of excess burden.*

As the example above shows, the excess burden is minimized when taxes are imposed on goods with the lowest price elasticities of demand; the extreme case is illustrated by the music fan, whose price elasticity of demand is zero. A good with perfectly inelastic demand (one that has a vertical de-

mand curve) can be taxed with no excess burden at all. Unfortunately, many of life's necessities (such as food) have very price inelastic demand curves, so a tax system that taxed only goods that had inelastic demand curves would prove to be very regressive. This example illustrates an important general point:

Efficiency and equity are often competing goals in the design of tax systems. Improving efficiency often reduces equity; improving equity often reduces efficiency.

Supply-Side Effects of Taxation

In principle, income taxes can be so high that reducing the tax rate would actually *increase* tax revenue. This is the idea behind the **Laffer curve** shown in Figure 20-2. Its essential feature is that income tax revenues reach a maximum at some income tax rate well below 100 percent.

The reasoning behind the general shape of the Laffer curve is as follows. At a zero tax rate, no revenue would be collected. As rates are raised above zero, some revenue will be gained. But as rates approach 100 percent, revenue will again fall to zero because no one will bother to earn income if they

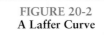

FIGURE 20-2
A Laffer Curve

Increases in tax rates beyond some level will decrease rather than increase tax revenues. The curve relates the government's tax revenue to the tax rate. As drawn, revenue reaches a maximum level of R_0 at the tax rate r_0. If the tax rate were r_1, then *reducing* it to r_0 would increase the government's tax revenue from R_1 to R_0.

know that it must all be paid to the government in taxes. It follows that there must be *some* tax rate, greater than zero and less than 100 percent, at which tax revenue reaches a maximum. Tax rates above that revenue-maximizing rate will actually generate less tax revenue.

The shape of the Laffer curve can be better understood by thinking about the income and the substitution effects of an increase in the tax rate. An increase in the income tax rate makes each additional dollar earned less valuable to the individual and this leads the individual to earn less income by working less hard—this is the substitution effect of the increase in the tax rate. But the increase in the tax rate also produces an income effect—by lowering after-tax income, the individual is led to consume less leisure and work harder, thus earning more income. Which effect dominates as tax rates rise? In general, we don't know. Individuals may choose to earn less or they may choose to earn more as tax rates increase. But since individuals will choose to earn *no income* when tax rates are 100 percent, we know that as tax rates continue to rise higher and higher toward 100 percent, the substitution effect eventually dominates.

Figure 20-2 is drawn under the assumption that there is a steady increase in tax revenue as tax rates rise to r_0, and a steady decrease in tax revenues as tax rates continue to rise toward 100 percent. This particular shape—with a single peak in tax revenues—is not necessary. It is possible that as the tax rate rises from zero to 100 percent, the income and substitution effects combine to produce a tax-revenue curve that has many peaks; this would be unusual but it is not impossible. But this is largely beside the point. The key point is that there is *some* tax rate like r_0 that maximizes total tax revenue. And as long as this is true, then tax rates both above and below r_0 will raise less tax revenue than is raised at r_0.

Just where this maximum occurs—whether at average tax rates closer to 40 or to 70 percent—is currently unknown for either corporate or personal income taxes. Also, there will be a separate Laffer curve for each type of tax. The curve does, however, provide an important warning: Governments cannot increase their tax revenues to any desired level simply by increasing their tax rates. Sooner or later, further increases in the rates will reduce economic activity so much that total tax revenues will fall.

A PROPOSAL TO INCREASE EQUITY AND EFFICIENCY

We saw above that most people's view of an equitable tax system is based on the notion of progressivity. Furthermore, the evidence seems to suggest that the Canadian tax system is roughly proportional for middle-income people and only mildy progressive for high-income and low-income people. This explains why many people would probably be in favour of an increase in the progressivity of the Canadian tax system.

On the other hand, we have also discussed some of the efficiency losses associated with taxation. In particular, the Laffer curve illustrates the important income-reducing effects of taxation—the higher is the tax rate on income, the less incentive individuals have to earn an extra dollar of income. It is important to note here that the disincentive effects from taxation relate to the *marginal tax rate* rather than the average tax rate; your decision to work an *extra* hour depends on the rate at which that *extra*—or marginal—income would be taxed. Concern over these disincentive effects of taxation have lead many people to support reforms in the tax system that reduce marginal income tax rates. Indeed, many of the 1987 reforms that we referred to above were driven by these concerns.[3]

Can more progressivity and lower marginal tax rates be achieved simultaneously? It would appear that there is some trade off between the two goals, especially since we saw in Table 20-4 that it is marginal tax rates *rising with income* which generates much of the progressivity of the Canadian tax system. Many economists, however, have proposed a major reform to the income tax system which combines the benefits of a progressive tax system with *constant* marginal income tax rates. For a more detailed discussion of such a proposal—the Negative Income Tax—see Application 20-1.

---

[3]Such concern over high marginal tax rates has led some people to accept the roughly proportional nature of the tax system, but to look to the system of government *expenditures* to give progressivity to the *entire range* of government activity.

THE NEGATIVE INCOME TAX

A tax is negative when the government pays the taxpayer rather than the other way around. The so-called **negative income tax (NIT)** is designed to increase progressivity by making taxes negative at very low incomes. Such a tax would extend progressivity to the very lowest incomes, and thus help to combat poverty. Furthermore, the NIT achieves its progressivity *without* a schedule of marginal income-tax rates that rise with income, and thus potentially avoids some of the extreme supply-side effects that are caused by very high marginal tax rates.

Many versions of the NIT have been proposed; the one described here illustrates the basic idea. The underlying principle is that a family of a given size should be *guaranteed* a minimum annual income. The tax system must be designed, however, to guarantee this income without eliminating the household's incentive to be self-supporting.

As an example (illustrated in the figure), consider a system in which each household is guaranteed a minimum annual income of $10,000 and the marginal tax rate is 40 percent. Money can be thought of as flowing in two directions; the government gives every household $10,000, and then every household remits 40 percent of any *earned* income back to the government. The *break-even* level of income in this example is $25,000. All households earning less than $25,000 pay *negative* taxes overall; they receive more money from the government than they remit in taxes. Households earning exactly $25,000 pay no taxes—their $10,000 from the government exactly equals the taxes they remit to the government on their earned income. All households earning more than $25,000 pay more than $10,000 in taxes and so they are paying *positive* taxes overall.

The figure shows the operation of this scheme by relating earned income on the horizontal axis to after-tax income on the vertical axis. The 45° line shows what after-tax income would be if there were no taxes. The heavy line shows the operation of the negative income tax. It starts at the guaranteed annual income of $10,000, rises by 60 cents for every one dollar increase in earned income, and crosses the 45° line at the break-even level of income, $25,000. The vertical distance between the two lines shows the net transfers between the household and the government: Below the break-even level, the government makes a net transfer to the household; above the break-even level, the household makes a net transfer to the government.

Note that the NIT is a progressive tax, despite the *constant* marginal income tax rate. To see this, note that a household's *average* tax rate is equal to the total taxes paid divided by total earned income. If I_E is earned income, then the average tax rate is

PUBLIC EXPENDITURE IN CANADA

In recent years, spending by the consolidated public sector—which includes federal, provincial, and municipal governments—has equaled about 45 percent of Canadian GDP. Table 20-5 gives the distribution of consolidated government spending across a number of major *functions*. As can be seen, health care, education, and social welfare are the largest items; collectively, they make up half the total. Spending on transportation and communication makes up 4.6 percent of the total. Interest on the public debt—a category of spending that has received considerable attention in recent years—represents 18.2 percent of total expenditure. The remaining

27 percent covers everything else, from police protection and sanitation to general administration of government and scientific research. About 40 percent of combined public expenditure is made by the federal government.

TYPES OF GOVERNMENT EXPENDITURE

Table 20-6 classifies federal and provincial government expenditure by type. For each level of government, total expenditures are equal to the sum of program expenditures and debt service payments; program expenditures include purchases of goods and services and various transfer payments.

Figure 20-3 shows the changing importance of different types of federal government spending.

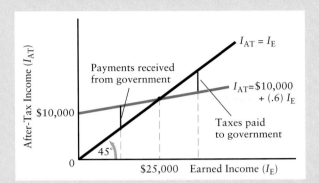

$$\text{Average Tax Rate} = \frac{(0.40) \times I_E - \$10,000}{I_E}$$

$$= (0.40) - \frac{\$10,000}{I_E}$$

Thus the average tax rate for the household rises as earned income rises, but the average tax rate is *always less* than the marginal tax rate (40 percent). That the average tax rate rises with earned income means that higher-income households pay a larger fraction of their income in taxes than is paid by lower-income households—that is, the negative income tax is progressive. For example, a household with earned income of $30,000 would pay total taxes of $2,000 ($12,000 − $10,000), for an average tax rate of 6.67 percent. A household with earned income of $60,000 would pay total taxes of $14,000 ($24,000 − $10,000), for an average tax rate of 23.3 percent.

Supporters of the negative income tax believe that it would be an effective tool for reducing poverty. The NIT provides a minimum level of income as a matter of right, not of charity, and it does so without removing the work incentives for people who are eligible for payments; every dollar earned adds to the after-tax income of the family.

One step toward the NIT was taken with the 1987 reforms to the personal income tax. In those reforms, many personal *exemptions* were replaced with *tax credits*. An exemption reduces an individual's tax base relative to earned income, whereas a tax credit reduces taxes payable by the amount of the credit. At present, however, the tax credit is not *refundable*—this means that the credit can be used to reduce taxes payable to zero, but *cannot* be used to reduce taxes payable to a negative number. Thus if an individual has taxes payable equal to $5,000 and then receives a $6000 tax credit, total taxes payable fall only to zero—any remaining credit ($1,000) cannot be claimed back from the government. If the tax credit were fully *refundable*, however, someone whose taxes on earned income were less than the tax credit would receive the difference from the government. This would be a negative income tax. Many advocates of the NIT argue that the government should take the next step of making the personal tax credits fully refundable, thus bringing the Canadian personal income tax system closer to the pure negative income tax.

Federal government purchases of goods and services have been declining steadily over the past forty years. In the early 1950s, roughly 50 percent of federal spending was purchases of goods and services; by 1995, the share was below 20 percent. In contrast, federal transfers to individuals have been gradually increasing, from about 20 percent of federal spending in the early 1950s to about 35 percent in 1995.

Two other spending categories of federal spending are shown in Figure 20-3. First, the federal government makes transfers to provincial and municipal governments (which we explore in detail later in this chapter). These transfers increased steadily from 5 percent of federal spending in the early 1950s to a high of 25 percent in 1971. Since then, these transfers have fallen to about 18 percent of federal spend-

ing, where they are now. The final category of federal spending, which has received considerable attention in the past decade, is the payments made to service the outstanding stock of government debt—these are called *debt service* payments. In the mid 1950s, debt service amounted to about 10 percent of federal spending. But with the arrival of large budget deficits beginning in the early 1970s, the stock of debt began increasing quickly, pushing debt service payments up to about 28 percent of federal spending in 1990. Over the past few years, however, there has been a modest decline in the share of federal spending devoted to debt service (though there has been an increase in the share of provincial government spending on debt service). This recent decline in the share of federal spending on debt service

TABLE 20-5
Expenditures of Combined Governments by Function, 1994

Category	Expenditures (billions of dollars)	Percentage of total	Average annual rate of growth 1984–1994 (%)
Health	47.8	13.5	7.3
Social services	85.6	24.1	7.8
Education	44.4	12.5	6.1
Interest on public debt	64.7	18.2	8.6
Transportation & Communication	16.3	4.6	3.4
All other	95.8	27.1	4.6
Total	354.6	100.0	6.4

Health, social services, and debt service charges were the fastest growing categories of combined government expenditure from 1984 to 1994. The table shows combined expenditures for federal, provincial, and municipal governments. The category "All other" includes sanitation and waste removal, natural resources, general government, police and fire protection, recreation, and cultural activities.

(*Source:* Statistics Canada, CANSIM database.)

has been due largely to a reduction in interest rates since the early 1990s, despite the continued rise in the stock of debt until the mid 1990s.

Provision of Goods and Services

As Table 20-6 indicates, about 20 percent of federal and 30 percent of provincial government spending is for the purchase of goods and services. Among these are defense, transportation facilities, education, and municipal services. In these activities, the government acts in much the same way a firm acts, using factors of production to produce outputs. By and large, these are outputs of public goods, goods with strong externalities, or services whose benefits are not marketable. Public-opinion polls show that the majority of Canadians support public provision of such services as basic education, hospital care, and medical care. Nonetheless, rising costs of such services are becoming a serious problem, forcing the various governments to re-think the level of government provision that is deemed to be appropriate.

Transfer payments

Transfer payments are defined as payments that do not arise out of the production or sale of goods and services. They include welfare, unemployment insurance,

TABLE 20-6
Federal and Provincial Expenditures by Type, 1993

	Federal		Provincial	
	billion $	percentage of total	billion $	percentage of total
Purchases of goods and services	33.3	19.9	49.7	30.3
Transfers to persons	56.6	33.8	34.6	21.1
Transfers to businesses	4.7	2.8	5.7	3.4
Transfers to other levels of government	31.2	18.6	50.9	31.0
Other transfers	3.4	2.0	0.8	0.5
Interest on public debt	38.3	22.9	22.4	13.7
Total	167.5	100.0	164.1	100.0

Purchases of goods and services constitute about 20 percent of federal government expenditures and about 30 percent of provincial government expenditures. The table shows total expenditures by type for the federal and provincial governments. Transfer payments constitute the majority of expenditures. For the federal government, transfers to persons plus interest on the debt account for about 57 percent of its total expenditures, while transfers to governments (mostly the provinces) account for another 20 percent. For the provinces, transfers to municipalities account for 32 percent of total expenditures (excluding hospitals).

(*Source:* Statistics Canada, 13-001.)

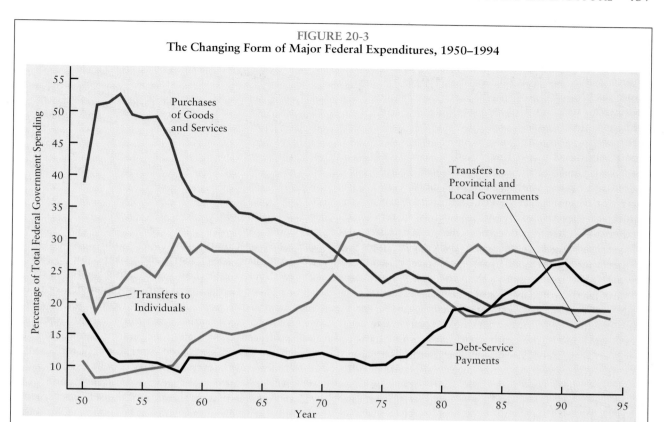

FIGURE 20-3
The Changing Form of Major Federal Expenditures, 1950–1994

Federal purchases of goods and services have declined dramatically in importance over the past 45 years, whereas debt-service payments have increased in importance. Transfers to individuals have gradually increased from about 20 percent of federal spending in the 1950s to about 35 percent today. Transfer payments to provinces are currently around 18 percent of federal spending.

(Source: Statistics Canada, *National Income and Expenditure Accounts)*

and Canada Pension Plan (CPP) payments, and intergovernmental transfers—that is, transfers from one level of government to another. Transfers are also made by provincial and municipal governments.

Although federal government purchases of goods and services are large (about $35 billion in 1995), they have remained roughly constant in *real* terms since the early 1960s. They have been overtaken by transfer payments as the largest form of federal government expenditure.

FISCAL FEDERALISM

Canada is a federal state with governing powers divided between the central authority and the ten provinces and three territories. Municipalities provide a third level of government, whose powers are determined by the provincial legislatures. Understanding the fiscal interaction of the various levels of govern-

ment is central to understanding the nature of government expenditure in Canada. In this section, we examine the concept of *fiscal federalism;* in the next section we examine how fiscal federalism affects the operation of Canada's social programs.

The Logic of Fiscal Federalism

The essence of fiscal federalism is the recognition that Canada is a country with many different fiscal authorities (federal, provincial, and municipal governments) that need a certain amount of coordination to be responsive to the needs and desires of the citizens—who are free to move from one area to another. We discuss four motivations for fiscal federalism: *revenue sources versus revenue needs; geographic externalities; regional preferences; and administrative efficiency.*

Revenue Sources Versus Revenue Needs. One obvious fact about Canada is that the provinces vary in population and income and thus correspondingly vary in the size of their tax bases. For example, Prince Edward Island has only a few hundred thousand residents and thus has a much smaller tax base than does Ontario, with roughly 9 million residents. Recall from Chapter 18 that one of the roles of government is the provision of public goods. It is easy to imagine that some public goods—especially those which require considerable fixed costs—are much easier to provide in the richer provinces than in the poorer ones. For example, each province has its own system of provincial laws, courts, and judges. Some amount of the cost of operating such a system is a fixed cost—a cost that does not change as the *size* of the system changes. In this case, the cost *per person* of operating the provincial court system in a large province like Ontario is less than the cost *per person* in a smaller province like Prince Edward Island.

So why don't we just let some provinces have many public goods and others have fewer? The answer is that one of the guiding principles in Canada's system of fiscal federalism is that individuals should have approximately the same access to public goods *no matter where they live*. This is an especially important principle when the public good in question is something as important as the legal system.

Since revenue sources do not always match revenue needs at each level, and since there are typically significant fixed costs associated with the provision of public goods, *intergovernmental transfers* are required (as shown in Table 20-6). This is the underlying motivation behind Canada's system of equalization payments, which transfers resources from the richer provinces to the poorer ones. We examine this shortly.

Geographic Extent of Externalities. Because the government of a province or a municipality is unlikely to be responsive to the needs of citizens outside its jurisdiction, public services that involve *geographic spillovers* may not be provided adequately unless responsibility for them is delegated to a higher level of government. For example, national defense is normally delegated to the central government for this reason. Control of pollution is another obvious case, since contamination of air and water often literally spills over provincial and municipal boundaries. At the other extreme is fire protection. If fire protection is to be effective, it is necessary that there be fire stations serving small geographic areas. Accordingly, responsibility for fire stations lies with municipal governments.

Regional Differences in Preferences. The delegation of some functions to lower levels of government may provide a political process that is more responsive to regional differences in preferences for public versus private goods. Some people may prefer to live in communities with higher-quality schools and police protection, and they may be prepared to pay the high taxes required. Others may prefer lower taxes and lower levels of services. Another important issue at the local level is the extent to which industry should be attracted in order to broaden the property tax base; individual valuations of the social costs in terms of aesthetic or environmental effects are bound to differ, and different local governments will develop different policies in this regard.

There may also be different preferences regarding the redistribution of income. An important activity of government is the redistribution of income by taxing the relatively well-off and channeling the funds to citizens in need by means of transfer payments. Both the federal and the provincial governments actively pursue redistributive policies within their jurisdictions. The differences in the marginal income-tax rates which we saw in Table 20-4 presumably reflect such differences in preferences across provinces.

Administrative Efficiency. Administrative efficiency requires that duplication of the services provided at different levels of government be minimized and that related programs be coordinated. On the revenue side, it is desirable that a particular tax be collected by only one level of government. This consideration has led to the negotiation of federal-provincial tax agreements that provide for efficient tax collection and revenue sharing.

The foregoing discussion suggests two central ideas for a system of fiscal federalism to be effective. First, the various fiscal authorities need to be *coordinated*, at least in the sense that there are well-defined responsibilties. Thus national defense is the sole responsibility of the federal government whereas fire protection is the sole responsibility of municipal governments. In the absence of such coordination, there would be a considerable waste of resources as the various fiscal authorities duplicated tasks.

The second central idea is that an effective system of fiscal federalism needs a mechanism to make *intergovernmental transfers*. This is especially true if there are considerable fixed costs involved in the provision of public goods. We explore the types of Canadian intergovernmental transfers in detail in the next subsection.

Intergovernmental Transfers

The scope and nature of intergovernmental grants have changed dramatically over the years. Measured in constant 1994 dollars, federal transfers to provincial governments expanded from $1.38 billion in 1950 to over $30 billion in 1994. This represented an increase from 6.8 percent to 19 percent of federal revenues; for the provincial governments, federal transfers as a share of their revenues increased, on average, from 20 percent to over 35 percent.

Over the past few years, the system of intergovernmental transfers in Canada has undergone substantial reform. One major part of this reform was the creation in 1996 of the *Canada Health and Social Transfer (CHST)*. Before examining the CHST it is useful to examine briefly the system of intergovernmental transfers in place immediately preceding this reform. Four central programs comprised the system of intergovernmental transfers until 1996: *equalization payments, revenue sharing, Established Programs Financing (EPF)*, and *Canada Assistance Plan (CAP)*. The equalization and revenue-sharing programs exist today; the EPF and CAP ended with the creation of the CHST in 1996.

Equalization Payments.   With the object of ensuring that citizens in all regions of the country have access to a reasonable level of public services, **equalization payments** are made out of federal government general revenues to provinces with below-average tax capacity. Though this is not explicitly a revenue-sharing program (provinces with above-average tax capacity do not pay in), the richer provinces (typically British Columbia, Alberta, and Ontario) are, in effect, transfering resources via the federal government to the poorer provinces. The equalization payments are calculated by a complicated formula that involves, at last count, 29 revenue sources.

Equalization payments are a relatively new phenomenon in Canada, but they have exhibited rapid growth. From their inception with the 1957 Tax-Sharing Act to the time of the 1977 Fiscal Arrangements Act to their formal inclusion in the Constitution Act of 1982, they have expanded considerably. Equalization payments for the 1992–1993 fiscal year were $307 per person, making a total of about $9 billion.

Revenue Sharing. Since the 1940s, most provinces have maintained **tax-rental arrangements,** whereby the federal government collects income taxes and makes a per capita payment to the provinces for that right. In 1995, with the exception of the Quebec personal income tax and the Ontario and Quebec corporate levies, all income taxes in Canada were collected by the federal government.

Outside Quebec, the provincial income tax is calculated as a percentage of the federal tax payable at rates determined by the individual provinces. Federal income-tax rates are set at levels that allow substantial "tax room" to the provinces. That is, by keeping the federal income-tax rates relatively low (17 percent, 26 percent, or 29 percent), the provinces can still raise considerable revenue by taxing income (without extreme supply-side effects such as those discussed in Figure 20-2). A similar arrangement applies to the corporate income tax. The effect of these measures can be thought of in terms of the "value of tax points." Tax points reflect the taxes levied by the provinces, collected by the federal government, and then returned to the provinces as a transfer.

Established Programs Financing (EPF).   Until 1996, federal financing of health care and postsecondary education was referred to as *established programs financing* (to indicate that the existence of these programs was not conditional on federal involvement). Because federal contributions were independent of the costs of the programs, the federal government could control its own contribution. The provinces benefited from such autonomy, for they were not constrained by narrowly defined federal program conditions. In the early 1990s, transfers for EPF (cash plus tax points) made up over one half of the total federal transfers to provinces.

Canada Assistance Plan (CAP).   Under this program, which also ended in the 1996 reforms, the federal government paid half of the costs of the provincial welfare programs, including half the associated administrative costs. Uniformity of the various provincial welfare programs was not a requirement. The provinces could design and administer their own programs but then only needed to meet one-half of the cost themselves. These programs also covered road building, vocational schools, and assistance to needy seniors, the disabled, and unemployed persons not eligible for unemployment insurance.

National Standards

Although it is common to hear people talk as if the federal-provincial transfers established *national standards* for the provision of health care or education, neither the CAP nor the EPF actually had such standards. Support levels under the Canada Assistance Plan varied widely across provinces, reflecting the fact the the CAP was simply a way of sharing the costs of *provincially* designed and administered programs. No conditions were set in relation to the transfers linked to postsecondary education. In health care, the only national standards were general principles such as portability among provinces and universality. No federal authority could complain about an alleged inadequacy in some province's health care system. The only rule was that whatever was provided by a province must be universally available within that province.[4]

Financial Cutbacks

As we said above, the system of intergovernmental transfers was in the midst of major reform as recently as the spring of 1996. Thus the four programs just described do not describe the *current* system of transfers—they describe the system that was in place from the mid 1970s to the spring of 1996. To understand the pressure for the most recent reforms, we have to go back to the mid 1970s.

In every year since the mid 1970s, the federal government has had a budget deficit. By the mid 1980s, the annual deficit had reached $30 billion and was projected to rise even further. Furthermore, the stock of debt (the accumulated past deficits) had reached the point where debt-service payments were becoming onerous, and were placing severe constraints on the government's plans for program spending. In that atmosphere of fiscal concern, the federal government began to look for every possible avenue of expenditure reduction. Not surprisingly, the intergovernmental transfer system came under close scrutiny.

Financial cutbacks affected all major areas of the system. A ceiling was placed on equalization payments so that they could not grow faster than the GDP. In 1987, the ceiling began to have an effect, reducing equalization payments by about $3 billion from what they otherwise would have been over the next three years.

The EPF programs were first "capped" in 1983. The growth in EPF transfers (cash plus tax points) was reduced successively from the rate of GDP growth to GDP growth minus first one, then two, then three percentage points. Finally in 1989–1990, the EPF transfers were fixed in nominal dollar terms. The CAP was also "capped." Beginning in 1990, the rule was that payments under the CAP to provinces *not receiving equalization payments* (typically the "rich" provinces

of B.C., Alberta, and Ontario) could not increase by more than 5 percent per year. This was a particularly severe blow to Ontario, which lost $1.1 billion of CAP payments in the 1991–1992 fiscal year alone.

Writing in 1993, Queen's University professor Peter Leslie said:

> It is quite clear that the present pattern of fiscal arrangements cannot be sustained for long. They are already set to self-destruct. The problem is most obvious in the case of EPF. As the federal government's cash contribution to health care and postsecondary education dwindles, its ability to exercise any policy influence in these areas will also disappear. Opinions on the subject will vary on whether the removal is desirable or not. However, there is no doubt that when it happens—as it will if EPF is allowed to phase itself out—a major feature of Canadian federalism will be phased out with it.[5]

Professor Leslie's prediction that the fiscal arrangements in place in 1993 could not be sustained for long turned out to be true. The tight financial position in which the federal government found itself in the early 1990s forced changes in the size and the nature of federal transfer payments to provinces. In its budget of 1995, the federal government announced the creation of the *Canada Health and Social Transfer (CHST)* to be implemented in spring of 1996. The CHST is a "block transfer" that rolls together the transfers previously made under the Established Program Financing (EPF) and Canada Assistance Plan (CAP). With the new CHST, the federal government gives a lump sum to each province (depending on the number of residents) which the provincial government can then use to fund post-secondary education, health care, and income-support programs.

There are benefits to both federal and provincial governments with the CHST. The federal government now focusses on a single lump-sum transfer to the province. The provincial governments, though still receiving considerable transfers from the federal government, have much more freedom in how that money is spent—the CHST is money with "no strings attached." As the new CHST settles into place, and the federal government decides on the appropriate size of lump-sum transfer to make under the CHST, there will inevitably be an effect on the nature and generosity of

---

[4]In recent years, the federal government has threatened to remove funding to those provinces permitting physicians to "extra bill" for health services. The federal government has interpreted such extra billing as a movement away from universality and toward a two-tier health system.

---

[5]Peter Leslie, "The Fiscal Crisis of Canadian Federalism", in *A Partnership in Trouble*, C. D. Howe Institute (Toronto, 1993).

provincially designed social programs. It is to the various social programs in Canada that we now turn.

CANADIAN SOCIAL POLICY

Canada has a wide variety of social programs, from unemployment insurance and the Canada Pension Plan to the systems of publicly provided health care and heavily subsidized post-secondary education. Canadian governments—both federal and provincial—have been urged to reexamine and redesign these programs with the twin objectives of improving the benefits delivered to the intended beneficiaries and reducing costs wherever possible. In the midst of such reform-minded governments, it is not surprising that controversies over Canada's social programs have been major news items in recent years. Indeed, these contoversies will likely continue well into the future.

Given the concern over government budget deficits in the past 15 years, it is natural that such a large category of spending should come under scrutiny. Assessing program effectiveness and evaluating proposals for the reform of Canada's social policies are not, however, simple matters. One-line evaluations, such as "Nothing needs to be changed" or "The whole system needs to be swept away," are too simplistic but all too common.

THE BASIC SETTING

Spending by all levels of government on social programs has grown dramatically over the past 40 years. Table 20-5 shows that in 1994 combined government expenditures on health, education, and social services equalled $178 billion, just over 50 percent of total government expenditures. In addition to the upward trend in spending on social programs, there has been a steady increase in the relative importance of spending by the provincial governments; their share of spending on social programs has grown from just over 5 percent in 1950 to about 25 percent in 1995.

The Variety of Social Programs

Some social programs are universal, in the sense that they pay benefits to anyone meeting only such minimal requirements as age or residence. These are referred to as **demogrants**. Other programs are selective, in the sense that they pay benefits only to people who qualify by meeting specific conditions, such as by having young children or being unemployed. When these conditions are related to the individual's

income, the term **income-tested** (or *income-related*) **benefits** is used. Some benefits are taxable, so that the after-tax benefits decline as income rises; others are not taxable, so after-tax benefits are independent of income. Some benefits are expenditure programs (including direct transfers to persons), while others are delivered through the tax system in the form of tax expenditures (see Table 20-2 for some examples). Some programs are administered by the federal government, some by the provincial governments, and still others by the municipalities.

The Federal-Provincial Perspective

Canada's constitution originally granted all authority in social policy to the provinces. As social policy became increasingly important, agreements between the two levels of government gave the federal government responsibility for a large amount of social spending. In some cases, this involves direct federal spending, as with the Old Age Security (OAS) program, and in other cases it involves transferring funds to the provincial governments, as with the Canada Health and Social Transfer (CHST). Thus some federal payments to provinces are distributed directly to individuals; others are used by the provinces to finance various expenditures.

Understanding Canada's social programs, therefore, requires an understanding of federal-provincial relations, together with recognizing some of the important differences across regions. We make four points in this regard.

Federal Transfers. As we have already observed, a large amount of federal spending is in the form of transfer payments to the provinces. Though some transfer payments are nominally earmarked for specific purposes, the provinces are not required to match their spending changes in these areas to changes in federal transfers received. In recent years, growth in provincial spending in these areas, particularly education, has often been less than the growth in transfers from the federal government. Hence to analyse the efficacy of social programs in these areas, it is not sufficient to focus only on federal transfers. Further, since provinces typically allocate over 60 percent of their spending to social policy, any dramatic change in provincial spending would also represent a significant change in total national spending.

Regional Pressures. Canada's regional pressures play a major role in shaping federal-provincial fiscal relations. Equalization payments, discussed in the previous section, are relevant here. Although they are not considered part of federal social spending, they are a transfer to the provinces whose explicit purpose is to compensate for any shortfall in the fiscal capacity of the relatively poorer provinces to provide a minimum level of government services.

Financial Cutbacks. Under intense pressure over the past decade to reduce its budget deficit, the federal government has been capping, and sometimes reducing, its transfers to the provinces. The extent of these changes is such that the whole concept of fiscal federalism is being eroded and may slowly disappear. As the federal contributions are reduced, provincial autonomy is increased. Some see this as a major loss of national commonality, others as an important and beneficial step toward much-needed decentralization.

The Need for Coordination. Since the multitude of federal and provincial social programs overlap in their effects, any program change made by one level of government will have one effect if it is offset by the other level and another effect if it is not offset. For example, when in its 1985 budget the federal government enriched the child tax credit to increase the after-tax income of very poor families with children, a number of provinces reacted by cutting back on their welfare programs. In those provinces, benefits delivered to the poor were not changed in aggregate, but the burden of financing those benefits was shifted to the federal government, and the distribution of benefits was shifted from families without children to those with children.

These observations suggest an important lesson relating to the potential reform of Canada's social programs:

Reform of Canadian social policy is more effective when changes are coordinated and sweeping rather than piecemeal. The inherent difficulties of such coordination are aggravated by Canada's adversarial political system and by the often stormy nature of federal-provincial relations in Canada.

We first wrote the above colour passage in 1987, and events since then only serve to underline the central message. Every independent body that has studied Canadian social policy has called for major reforms to allow the system to continue to do its job at a cost the tax system can bear; every attempt at reform by the federal government (first Conservative, then Liberal) has met with strong resistance from the opposition parties and the provinces.

FIVE PILLARS OF CANADIAN SOCIAL POLICY

We now turn to a brief description of the five pillars of Canadian social policy: education, health care, income support, unemployment insurance, and retirement benefits. Each of these pillars, at various points in recent years, have been the focus of attention as financially strapped governments have explored new ways to provide what many perceive as vital social services.

Education and Training

Public education, one of the earliest types of social expenditure in Canada, remains one of the most important. It has been supplemented over the years by numerous other programs aimed at developing human resources.

Basic Education. Primary and secondary schools teach literacy and numeracy. These basic skills are needed in order to acquire further marketable skills. Canada has one of the world's highest per capita expenditures on basic education, yet Canadian students do relatively poorly on international comparisons that use standardized tests. Studies show that many Canadian adults (some estimates say as many as one-quarter) are functional illiterates—people who cannot comprehend simple written instructions well enough to carry them out. One educational target should be to reduce illiteracy and innumeracy, deficiencies that are lifetime handicaps.

Basic education is supplemented by further education and training. This occurs in technical schools, colleges and universities, as well as in the workplace. At the beginning of the 1990s, the federal government operated about a dozen nonuniversity job creation and training programs, enrolling nearly half a million people and costing nearly $2 billion. Although few doubt that these schemes are of great value, the critics have noted many deficiencies in the programs and recommended major changes.

Postsecondary Education. Postsecondary education is a provincial responsibility in Canada. As discussed earlier in this chapter, until 1996 the federal government made large payments to the provinces for postsecondary education as part of Established Programs Financing (EPF)—in the early 1990s the annual transfer for post secondary education was about $1.5 billion. Since 1996, federal transfers for postsecondary education have been contained in the Canada Health and Social Transfer (CHST).

In Canada, all universities are public institutions, and university education is heavily subsidized by government, with tuition fees accounting for only about 15 percent of total costs. Two arguments can be advanced for subsidizing higher education; one is an efficiency argument, and the other concerns equity. The efficiency argument is based on the claim that there are positive externalities from higher education—that is, that the country as a whole benefits when a student receives higher education. In many cases these externalities cannot be internalized by the students receiving the education, so, left to their own maximizing decisions, students who had to pay the whole cost of their education would choose less than is socially optimal. The equity argument is that if students were forced to pay anything like the full cost of the services they receive, a university education would become prohibitively expensive to low- and even middle-income families. Government subsidies help provide training according to ability rather than according to income.

Arguments to reduce the subsidy to higher education, and thus to finance a larger fraction of the costs of running universities from tuition fees, start with the observation that the value of many kinds of education is internalized and recaptured in higher incomes earned by the recipients later in their life. This is particularly true of professional training in such fields as law, medicine, dentistry, management, and computer science. Yet students in these fields typically pay a smaller part of their real education costs than students in the arts, where the argument for externalities is greatest. Also, subsidized education does represent a significant income transfer from taxpayers to students, even though the average taxpayer may have a lower income than the average student can expect to earn in the future.

People who worry about the equity issue in this context often argue for a system of student loans (which currently exist in Canada), whereby more of the cost of education would be recouped from the students themselves later in their lifetimes. People opposed to loans argue, among other things, that loans will discourage children in lower-income families from continuing on to higher education because, from the vantage point of their family's current low income, the liability to be taken on by the student will seem enormous.

Health Care

Taking federal and provincial payments into account, Canada's public health-care system is the country's single most expensive social program. In 1994, government expenditures on health care accounted for about 7.5 percent of Canadian GDP; private spending on health care brought total (private plus public) expenditures up to 10.1 percent of GDP. This is the second highest proportion of GDP so devoted in all the advanced industrial countries. The annual cost of the part of health care that is paid for by government amounted in that year to over $2,500 for every man, woman, and child in the country. It has also been rising rapidly in recent years.

"Cost containment" in the health-care sector has become a priority for most provincial governments and the debate currently rages over what reforms are practicable and acceptable. Hospital and bed closures, and growing queues for non-critical treatments, are part of the daily news. Most observers agree that some type of expenditure-controlling reform is urgently needed. Unfortunately, agreement stops here.

Fee for Service.   One major possibility of cost containment is to move away from the present system of "fee for service." In the system used in most of Canada, the physician and the hospital charge a prescribed fee for each service that is performed. Since under any provincial health scheme, the doctor's and hospital's collection rate is 100 percent, there is no reason for the provider of health services to economize on those services. Indeed, much research shows that the rate of elective surgery—operations that are not necessary for survival but may be useful—rises with the ratio of physicians to the population. In areas where there are many physicians, the typical physician has time on his or her hands, and the rate of elective surgery goes up. In areas where doctors are in short supply, much less elective surgery is performed.

This illustrates a general point. The case for the free market is strongest when consumers are the best judges of their own needs. The case for market efficiency is greatly weakened when suppliers, such as physicians, can influence the demand for the product they supply. Thus in the many cases where judgment is needed to decide among several courses of action, all of which have something to recommend them, the evidence is that doctors often create their own demand. This does not imply dishonesty on the part of doctors, merely that where judgment calls must be made, the amount of spare time available to doctors will influence their decisions.

Health Maintenance Organizations.   Health maintenance organizations (HMOs) provide a possi-

---

EXTENSION 20-1

POVERTY IN CANADA

What is poverty, and whom does it affect? One definition says that one lives in poverty if one is poorer than most of one's fellow citizens. Since there will always be a bottom 10 percent of any income distribution who are poorer than the remaining 90 percent, poverty in this sense will always be with us. If a completely relative definition is not very revealing, neither is an unchanging absolute definition. The living standards of Canadians who are today regarded as poor would have looked more than adequate to Canadians of 100 years ago and would look princely to citizens of many countries even today.

To meet both of these concerns, economists define poverty as some given level of income, rather than just in relative terms, but they also recognize that as average living standards rise over time, so will our ideas of what constitutes poverty.

Statistics Canada defines the **poverty line** as the level of income at which a household spends on average more than 54.7 percent of its income on the three basic necessities of food, shelter, and clothing. For a family of four, the Canadian poverty line in 1994 ranged from $21,472 in rural areas to $31,071 in the largest cities. Although $30,000 may buy enough food, shelter, and clothing for a family of four to get by, it does not provide enough money for the full range of commodities that most of us take for granted, such as having a refrigerator, a TV set that works, constant hot water, and an occasional night out for dinner or a movie. Many of the poor are understandably upset that they are outsiders looking in on the comfortable way of life shown in ads and on television.

WHO ARE THE POOR?

According to the criterion just outlined, 13.5 percent of Canadian families were living in poverty in 1994.

There are poor among all ages, races, and educational levels, employed as well as unemployed. Yet some groups have much higher incidences of poverty than others. For example, the table shows that you are more likely to be poor if you live in Quebec, if you are a member of a large family, or if you live in a large city.

But poverty is by no means restricted to these groups. More than half the poor families live in urban areas, live in Ontario and the western provinces, have no more than one child, and are headed by persons of working age. Furthermore, about one quarter of those in poverty work full time (the so-called working poor), and over half work at least part time. These facts help to dispose of two superficial caricatures: the slothful father who feigns a disability because he is too lazy to do an honest day's work and the family with so many children that an ordinary decent wage is spread so thin that the entire household is reduced to poverty. Individual households that come close to these extremes can be found, but most poor households do not.

CAN ECONOMIC GROWTH SOLVE THE PROBLEM?

Between 1969 and 1994, the proportion of Canadians living in poverty fell by 35 percent. In part this reflected a variety of government initiatives of the sort discussed in this chapter. But in large mea-

---

ble way around this problem. Large hospitals and large groups of doctors work on what is called a *capitation* basis. This means that the HMO is paid an annual fee for each person registered with it. Since payment is on a per capita basis rather than on a services-rendered basis, there is no incentive to prescribe more care than is needed. Furthermore, to the extent that an individual registers with the same HMO for several years, there is little incentive for the HMO to scimp on necessary services, because scimping today (by ignoring a problem, for example) may

mean that much more is spent in the future (to correct the problem after it has gotten worse). Thus one big advantage of HMOs is that each HMO has the incentive to keep its clients healthly *and* to keep costs down. The HMO at Sault Ste. Marie, pioneered by the steelworkers' union and their employers, was an early and successful Canadian example of such an organization.

The Alberta Reforms. One of the hot spots for debate over reform of the health-care system in recent years has been Alberta. In the early 1990s, sure, it resulted from the growth in average income, which has always been the greatest source of relief from poverty.

It would be a mistake, however, to expect growth to eliminate all poverty. The source of today's poverty problem is no longer low average income but particular groups who are left behind in the general rise in living standards caused by economic growth. It is little consolation—indeed, it must add to the gall—that they are poor in an increasingly affluent society.

There is no single answer to the question of what causes poverty in the midst of plenty. It is partly a result of mental and physical handicaps, partly of low motivation, partly of the raw deal that fate gives to some, partly the result of changing market conditions when industries and occupations can no longer prosper, partly a result of unwillingness or inability to invest in the kind of human capital that does pay off in the long run, and partly the result of the market's valuing the particular abilities an individual does have at such a low price that even in good health and with full-time employment the income that can be earned leaves that person below the poverty line.

Just as there is no single reason for poverty, there is no single cure. Many of the social programs outlined in this chapter attempt to get at various causes. If poverty has fallen over the decades in Canada, the two main reasons are economic growth and social programs that seek to provide assistance for those who cannot help themselves and to assist those who can to learn to do so.

Incidence of Poverty Among Canadian Families by Selected Characteristics, 1994

Characteristics	Percentage of families falling below the poverty line
All families	13.5
Place of residence	
Metropolitan	16.0
Other urban	12.3
Rural	9.2
Region	
Atlantic	14.4
Quebec	16.4
Ontario	11.7
Prairies	13.2
British Columbia	12.6
Number of children under 16 years of age	
0	9.0
1	20.1
2	16.4
3 or more	24.5
Age of head of family	
Under 25	44.4
25–54	13.5
55–64	13.0
65 and over	7.1
Sex of head of family	
Male	9.7
Female	40.9
Employment status of head of family	
In labour force	9.7
Not in labour force	23.6

Source: Statistics Canada, 13-207.

Premier Ralph Klein brought health care in Alberta onto the centre stage of policy reform. Regional health boards were established in the hope that decentralized decisions concerning resource allocation would be superior to those made by a centralized provincial health ministry. Each health board decides which hospitals in its region will remain open and which will close, which will have emergency wards and which will not, which will conduct heart transplants and which will not. The regional health boards receive their funds directly from the provincial government and disperse the money according to its plans for health care in the region.

Not surprisingly, there have been competing views on the value of the Alberta reforms. Many people associated with the provision of health care (e.g., doctors and nurses) were opposed to the rationalization and consolidation of hospital services, not least because some of them lost their jobs. On the other hand, many people across the province viewed the reforms as a sensible slimming of a social program that had become too fat over the years. By early 1996, the basic designs of the system were in place; but it will take a few years before a complete evaluation of the reforms is possible.

Income Support Programs

Canada has various programs that provide assistance for people in financial need—these programs constitute what is often called the "social safety net." The overriding objective of this safety net is to reduce poverty. Though nothing like the serious problem it was in Canada's past and still is in many other countries, poverty remains a matter of real concern to Canadian policy makers. One cause for concern is that most of the poverty that can be eliminated by economic growth may have already been eliminated, implying that much of the remaining poverty may represent the "hard core" that will persist no matter how wealthy the society (on average) becomes and can only be alleviated by active public policy. See Extension 20-1 for a more detailed discussion of poverty in Canada.

The variety of income-support programs can be divided into three groups. The first is designed to provide income assistance to those individuals whose incomes are deemed to be too low to provide an adequate standard of living. The second is designed to assist specifically those individuals who are in financial need because of temporary job loss—unemployment insurance. The third is designed to provide income assistance specifically to the elderly. In this subsection, we examine the first group. The next two subsections discuss unemployment insurance and elderly benefits, respectively.

Social Assistance.   Social assistance for individuals below retirement age, usually called *welfare*, is mainly a provincial responsibility in Canada. The details of the programs vary considerably across the provinces even though they are partly financed by transfers received from the federal government. Until 1996, the federal government contributed (under the CAP) to the provincial welfare programs. Until 1990, the federal contribution was equal to one-half of the cost of the program, but starting in 1990 the higher-income provinces had the federal government's contribution limited to an increase of 5 percent per year. In 1996, the federal government initiated the Canada Health and Social Transfer (CHST) which folded together transfers previously made under the EPF and CAP into a single lump-sum transfer (based on the number of residents in the province). The changes in the form of federal funding have put strong pressures on the provincial governments to al-

ter their systems—for better or worse. This is especially true of the CHST—since the cost of the welfare program is no longer directly shared with the federal government, each provincial government has an increased incentive to reduce costs.

Suggested reforms to social assistance take two main forms. First, most economists advocate reforms of the tax-and-transfer system in an effort to reduce what are called *poverty traps*. **Poverty traps,** which are common, occur whenever the tax-and-transfer system results in individuals having very little incentive to increase their pre-tax income (by accepting a job, for example) because such an increase in their pre-tax income would make them ineligible for some benefits (such as welfare) and might even make them worse off overall. The presence of such poverty traps reflects a tax-and-transfer system that has been modified in many small steps over many years, the result of which is a plethora of programs often working at cross purposes. The elimination of such poverty traps requires that the tax-and-transfer system be examined in its entirety rather than on a piecemeal basis.

The second type of reform is designed to provide positive incentives to self-help by increasing benefits for recipients who accept work or training for work. A related (and quite contentious) proposal is referred to as *workfare*—the idea that welfare recipients should be required to put in some sort of work in order to be eligible for welfare benefits.[6]

Child Benefits.   The support system for families with children has been evolving quite rapidly over the years. Prior to the last change in 1993, the system was a combination of universal family allowance payments and tax credits. In 1993, universality was eliminated. A Child Tax Benefit is now paid according to the number of children in the family and varies according to family income, reaching zero at an income of $60,000.

The reforms to the child benefits system no doubt points the direction to be taken by many other welfare reforms to come. Indeed, it is probable that no part of the system has settled into its final new shape. Further changes can be expected until the whole system of social expenditures has been rethought from top to bottom.

---

[6]For a wide-ranging discussion of the issues involved in workfare, see John Richards and William Watson (eds.), *Helping the Poor: A Qualified Case for Workfare*, C. D. Howe Institute (Social Policy Challenge No. 5), Toronto, 1995.

Unemployment Insurance

Unemployment insurance (UI) is the single most costly program administered by the federal government, accounting for over $17.5 billion of payments in 1993–1994. Just looking at the federal *spending* on UI, however, is misleading because the program is more-or-less self financing, at least over the duration of the average business cycle (5–6 years). Employers and employees remit UI premiums to the government equal to a small percentage of wages and salaries— these premiums then finance the UI payments to unemployed workers who qualify for the benefits. In boom times, when there is little unemployment, the UI premiums exceed the UI benefits; in times of high unemployment, the benefits exceed the premiums.[7]

Originally instituted in 1940 as an insurance scheme against temporary bouts of unemployment, it was extended in scope and generosity by changes instituted in the 1970s. Many studies of the UI system over the last decade have concluded that the system has become overburdened by being used for too many, often conflicting objectives. It should, they argued, be returned to its prime objective of providing insurance against temporary bouts of involuntary unemployment, and other schemes should be used to achieve other objectives. Supporters of the system have fiercely resisted all suggested changes.

UI gives incentives to remain in seasonal jobs and in areas with poor employment prospects and to take UI-financed holidays. Saying that the UI system encourages behaviour that increases unemployment and reduces regional mobility does not say that the unemployed themselves are responsible for the "abuses" of the system that lead to these results. The responsibility lies with the people who designed the incentives and those who strive to preserve them. It is they who can alter the system to make it deliver the intended benefits with fewer incentives for undesired behaviour.

A number of changes have been made during the 1990s. Some respond to the criticisms noted above. For example, rules for qualifying to receive benefits have been tightened, and extended coverage and additional assistance provided for individuals attending approved training courses. Other changes worked in the opposite direction, by expanding coverage into areas some critics had argued were better handled outside of the UI program (for example, expanded parental and sickness benefits).

Retirement Benefits

Canada's present youthful age structure may make us think we are richer as a nation than we actually are. When only a small fraction of the population is retired, it is easy to be generous to them, because the burden is spread over so many working persons. However, generous schemes may become difficult to honour when a large proportion of the population is retired, as it will be early in the twenty-first century. Over the coming decades, a larger and larger fraction of Canadians will be retired, and the working people who will be directly or indirectly supporting the retired will constitute a smaller and smaller fraction of the population.

There are essentially three components of the system of benefits for the elderly. These are the Canada Pension Plan (CPP), retirement income support programs such as Old Age Security (OAS) and Guaranteed Income Supplement (GIS), and tax-assisted saving plans.

The Canada Pension Plan (CPP).   The CPP provides a basic level of retirement income for all Canadians who have contributed to it over their working lives. (A separate but similar scheme exists in Quebec, the Quebec Pension Plan or QPP.) Unlike some private programs, the pension provided by the CPP is portable—changing jobs does not cause any loss of eligibility.

The most important concern about the CPP is that it subsidizes the generation currently receiving pensions. Contribution rates were very low when these people were young, and as a result they will receive pensions more than five times as large as what their contributions would actually have bought. This makes the plan a very good deal for those presently retired, but it means that any increase in future benefits will have to be paid for on top of the existing subsidy to those already retired. To make the scheme self-supporting, the government would have to more than double the CPP contribution rates over the next twenty years.

Such proposed increases in the contribution rates (with no scheduled increases in the benefits), however, make the Canada Pension Plan a "poor investment" for the current younger generations, because the rate of return that the young will effectively earn on their contributions will be less than what they could earn on alternative investments. This situation naturally leads

---

[7]In 1996, the name of the program was formally changed to Employment Insurance (EI). In this textbook, however, we continue to use the acronym "UI" because of its familiarity.

to calls for a complete overhaul—and perhaps even the elimination—of the current system of public pensions.[8]

Retirement Income Support Programs. The existing public benefits system for the elderly is in many ways analogous to the child benefits system. There are three parts to the system. First, a universal benefit called the Old Age Security (OAS) program, acts much like the family allowance. Under the OAS program, the government sends out monthly benefit cheques to each Canadian over the qualifying age of 65. Since 1989, however, OAS payments to relatively wealthy individuals have been recaptured by means of a tax "clawback."

Second, in calculating the personal nonrefundable tax credit, provisions available to the elderly serve to reduce their taxes payable. These include a credit available to anyone 65 or older and a pension income credit that offsets the taxes due on the first $1,000 of pension income.

Third, an income-tested program, called the Guaranteed Income Supplement (GIS), provides benefits targeted to the low-income elderly. (In some provinces this is supplemented by further targeted assistance.) The GIS provides for most of the progressivity that arises in the elderly benefits system.

Tax-Assisted Saving Plans. The CPP, OAS, and GIS are programs which involve direct spending on the part of the government. But the government has also introduced programs that require no direct government spending but instead rely on *tax expenditures* (i.e., tax reductions). These tax expenditures are designed to provide incentives for individuals to save more for their retirement. There are essentially two types of programs. The first is through Registered Retirement Savings Plans (RRSPs) and the second is through employer-sponsored Registered Pension Plans (RPPs).

RRSPs provide an incentive for individuals to provide for their own retirement, either because they are not covered by a company plan or because they wish to supplement their company plan. Funds contributed are deductible from taxable income but become fully taxable when they are withdrawn. It is thus a tax deferral plan, and as such it is more valuable the higher one's current taxable income and the lower one's expected future income.

Individuals without RRSPs may still receive some tax assistance for saving if their employer has a Registered Pension Plan. In this case, contributions to the company pension plan (which are often mandatory and are withdrawn directly from the regular paycheque) are tax deductible in a manner similar to an RRSP contribution.

The program of RRSPs and RPPs does not require direct expenditures from either the federal or provincial governments, but because of the tax-deductability of contributions, these plans represent a significant amount of foregone tax revenue. From Table 20-2, the total tax expenditures associated with RRSPs and RPPs in 1992 was $13.6 billion, and this is for the federal government only. The combined federal and provincial tax expenditures would be approximately $20 billion for 1992.

A FINAL WORD

We have seen that Canada's social policy is made up of a complex system of benefits and tax expenditures. While there is no doubt that many of its goals are achieved, there is also no doubt that the system is under increasing pressure for a massive and integrated set of reforms. As the problems of large government deficits continue, many who support the system argue that it must be reformed to become more focused on those in need. They argue that, failing such reform, across-the-board massive reductions may be forced on governments who are being pressed by unsustainably high levels of debt to make major cuts in their deficits.

Reforming the system, however, is unpopular. When the Ontario government in 1995 reduced welfare payments in that province by 22 percent, there was public outcry. When Alberta instituted its reforms of the health-care system in 1994–1995, there was public outcry. When the federal government in 1995–1996 proposed changes to the unemployment insurance system, especially to reduce the generosity of the program to seasonal workers, there was public outcry.

It is no surprise that reform is unpopular. People who run the risk of losing some net benefits tend to be very vocal and to find ready political champions. Other opponents of reform fear that any changes will begin a process of eroding the whole social policy system, which many regard as one of Canada's outstanding accomplishments. It remains to be seen whether any Canadian government will attempt a major and comprehensive overhaul of the system—an overhaul that many observers feel would make the system fairer, less costly, yet more effective, but

---

[8]See, for example, William Robson, *Putting Some Gold in the Golden Years: Fixing the Canada Pension Plan,* C. D. Howe Institute, Commentary No. 76, January 1996.

which others feel would be the beginning of the end of Canada as a "caring society."

Evaluating the role of government

Almost everyone would agree that the government has a major role to play in the economy because of the many sources of possible market failure. Yet there is no consensus that the present level and role of government intervention is the correct one.

PUBLIC VERSUS PRIVATE SECTOR

When the government raises money by taxation and spends it on an activity, it increases the spending of the public sector and decreases that of the private sector. Since the public sector and the private sector spend on different things, the government is changing the allocation of resources. Is that good or bad? How do we know if the country has the "right" balance between the public and private sectors? Should there be more schools and fewer houses or more houses and fewer schools?

For all goods that are produced and sold on the market, consumers' demand has a significant influence on the relative prices and quantities produced and thus on the allocation of the nation's resources. But no market provides relative prices for private houses versus public schools; thus, the choice between allowing money to be spent in the private sector and allowing it to be spent for public goods is a matter to be decided by Parliament and other legislative bodies.

John Kenneth Galbraith's bestseller, *The Affluent Society*, proclaimed that a correct assignment of marginal utilities would show them to be higher for an extra dollar's worth of public parks, clean water, and education than for an extra dollar's worth of television sets, shampoo, or automobiles. In Galbraith's view, the political process often fails to translate preferences for public goods into effective action; thus more resources are devoted to the private sector and fewer to the public sector than would be the case if the political mechanism were as effective as the market.

The alternative view has many supporters, who agree with Nobel Laureate James Buchanan that society has already reached a point where the value of the *marginal* dollar spent by government is less than the value of that dollar left in the hands of households or firms. These people argue that because bureaucrats are spending other people's money, they care very little about a few million or billion dollars here or there. They have only a weak sense of the opportunity cost of public expenditure and, thus, tend to spend beyond the point where marginal benefits equal marginal costs.

SCOPE OF GOVERNMENT ACTIVITY

One of the most difficult problems for the student of the Canadian economic system is to maintain the appropriate perspective about the scope of government activity in the market economy. On the one hand, there are literally tens of thousands of laws, regulations, and policies that affect firms and households. Many people believe that a general reduction in the role of government—fewer regulations as well as fewer crown corporations—is both possible and desirable. On the other hand, private decision makers still have an enormous amount of discretion about what they do and how they do it.

One pitfall is to become so impressed (or obsessed) with the many ways in which government activity impinges on the individual that one fails to see that these only make changes—sometimes large, but often small—in market signals in a system that basically leaves individuals free to make their own decisions. It is in the private sector that most individuals choose their occupations, earn their living, spend their incomes, and live their lives. In this sector too, firms are formed, choose products, live, grow, and sometimes die.

A different pitfall is to fail to see that a significant share of the taxes paid by the private sector is used to buy goods and services that add to the welfare of individuals. By and large, the public sector complements the private sector, doing things the private sector would leave undone or would do differently. For example, Canadians pay taxes which are used to finance expenditures on health and education. But certainly Canadians would continue to use hospitals and attend schools even if the various levels of government did not provide these goods, and instead left more money in peoples' pockets. Thus in many cases the government is levying taxes to raise money to finance goods that people would have purchased anyway. To recognize that we often benefit directly from public expenditure in no way denies that there is often waste, and sometimes worse, in public expenditure.

Yet another pitfall is failing to recognize that the public and private sectors compete in the sense that both make claims on the resources of the economy. Government activities are not without opportunity costs, except in those very rare circumstances in which they use resources that have no alternative use.

EQUITY AND EFFICIENCY

A related pitfall is to believe that the government's alleged inability to improve efficiency also implies an inability to improve equity. Throughout the world, governments are placing more reliance on markets in order to improve allocative efficiency and prospects for growth. Accepting the market for efficiency reasons does not, however, require accepting an increase in the hardships borne by the poor. Promoting social justice through government interventions directed at equity is compatible with promoting allocative efficiency, provided that appropriate means are carefully chosen.

EVOLUTION OF POLICY

Public policies in operation at any time are not the result of a single master plan that specifies precisely where and how the public sector shall seek to complement or interfere with the workings of the market mechanism. Rather, as individual problems arise, governments attempt to meet them by passing appropriate legislation to deal with the problem. These laws stay on the books, and some become obsolete and unenforceable. This is generally true of systems of law.

Many anomalies exist in our economic policies; for example, laws designed to support the incomes of small farmers have created some agricultural millionaires, and commissions created to ensure competition between firms often end up creating and protecting monopolies. Neither individual policies nor whole programs are above criticism.

In a society that elects its policy makers at regular intervals, however, the majority view on the amount and type of government intervention that is desirable will have some considerable influence on the amount of intervention that actually occurs. Fundamentally, a free-market system is retained because it is valued for its lack of coercion and its ability to do much of the allocating of society's resources better than any known alternative. But we are not mesmerized by it; we feel free to intervene in pursuit of a better world in which to live. We also recognize, however, that sometimes intervention has proved ineffective or even counterproductive.

SUMMARY

A. TAXATION IN CANADA

- Although the main purpose of the tax system is to raise revenue, tax policy is potentially a powerful device for income redistribution because the progressivity of different kinds of taxes varies greatly. An important part of the Canadian tax system is based on tax expenditures—provisions in the tax law that provide favourable tax treatment for certain economic behaviour.
- The most important taxes in Canada are the personal income tax, the corporate income tax, excise and sales taxes (including the nation-wide GST), and property taxes.

B. EVALUATING THE TAX SYSTEM

- Evaluating the tax system involves evaluating the efficiency and progressivity of the entire system, rather than of individual taxes within the system. For a given amount of revenue to be raised, efficiency and progressivity can be altered by changing the mix of the various taxes used.
- The total Canadian tax structure is roughly proportional, except for very low-income and very high-income groups (where it is mildly progressive).
- There are potentially important supply-side effects of taxation, as represented by a Laffer curve. A rise in the tax rate initially raises total tax revenue; after some point, however, further increases in the tax rate eliminate the incentive to produce taxable income, and so total tax revenue falls. Governments thus cannot always raise tax revenues by raising tax rates.

C. PUBLIC EXPENDITURE IN CANADA

- A large part of public expenditure is for the provision of goods and services. Other types of expenditures, including subsidies, transfer payments to individuals, and intergovernmental transfers, have increased sharply from the 1950s.

- Fiscal federalism is the idea that the various fiscal authorities should be coordinated in their spending plans and should have a mechanism for transfers between the various levels of government. Understanding the relationship between the federal government and the various provincial governments is of utmost importance in understanding many of Canada's most important government spending programs.

D. CANADIAN SOCIAL POLICY

- The five pillars of Canadian social policy are:

  1. Education
  2. Health care
  3. Income support programs (welfare and child benefits)
  4. Unemployment insurance
  5. Retirement benefits (CPP, GIS, OAS, and tax-assisted saving plans)

- Canadian governments have been urged to reexamine and redesign most social programs with the twin goals of improving their ability to deliver benefits and reducing costs.

E. EVALUATING THE ROLE OF GOVERNMENT

- When evaluating the overall role of government in the economy, we should keep four basic issues in mind:

  1. What is the appropriate mix between public goods and private goods?
  2. Much government activity is directed to providing goods and services that add directly to the welfare of the private sector (health and education, for example).
  3. The alleged inability of the government to improve the efficiency of the economy does not necessarily mean that it is also unable to improve equity.
  4. We should continually reevaluate existing programs; some that were needed in the past may no longer be needed; others may have unintended and undesirable side effects.

KEY CONCEPTS

Tax expenditures
Progressive, proportional, and regressive taxes

Vertical and horizontal equity
Laffer curve
Transfer payments to individuals

Fiscal federalism
Intergovernmental transfers
Canadian social policy

DISCUSSION QUESTIONS

1. The Canadian taxpayer faces dozens of different taxes with different incidences, different progressivities, and different methods of collection. Discuss the case for and against a single taxing authority that would share the revenue with all levels of government. Why don't governments use a single tax source with the desired amount of progressivity built into it?

2. Consider a change in the tax law that lowers every taxpayer's marginal tax rate, with the maximum rate dropping from 50 percent to 33 percent, but with an increase in the tax base that leaves total tax revenue unchanged.

   a. Is it possible that everyone's average tax rate will fall?
   b. Is it possible that everyone's tax bill will fall?
   c. Suppose that charitable contributions to universities and colleges are tax deductible under the original tax law but not under the revised one. Would you predict that such contributions would increase, decrease, or remain the same?
   d. If such contributions are fully deductible under both the original and revised tax laws, would the amount of such contributions be expected to increase, decrease, or remain the same?
   e. Consider now taxpayers whose marginal tax rate falls from 50 percent to 33 percent and whose tax bills are less after the revision. Repeat the question in d.

3. Until recently in Canada, each individual had a lifetime $100,000 exemption for capital gains income, and subsequent capital gains were taxed at three-quarters the rates applicable to other income. Who were the likely beneficiaries of this policy? What were the likely effects on the distribution of income and the allocation of resources? Can you think of both equity and efficiency arguments supporting the elimination of such an exemption?

4. "Taxes on tobacco and alcohol are nearly perfect taxes. They raise lots of revenue and discourage smoking and drinking." In this statement, to what extent are the two effects inconsistent? How is the incidence of an excise tax related to the extent to which it discourages use of the product?

5. Suppose that it is agreed to spend $1 billion in programs to provide the poor with housing, better clothing, more food, and better health services.

   a. Argue the case for and against assistance of this kind rather than giving the money to the poor to spend as they think best.

   b. Should federal transfers to the provinces be conditional grants or grants with no strings attached? Is this the same issue raised in *a* or is it a different one?

6. Medical and health costs were 4.5 percent of GDP in 1950 and over 10 percent in 1993. Is 10 percent necessarily too much? Is it necessarily a sign that we are providing better health care? How might an economist think about what is the right percentage of GDP to devote to medical care?

7. Is the tax deduction allowed for RRSPs progressive or regressive (or neither)?

PART SEVEN

AN INTRODUCTION TO MACROECONOMICS

What is macroeconomics all about? What do we mean when we talk about national income, and what is the difference (if any) between national income and national output? What is unemployment, and why does it appear to be such a problem? Is it possible to eliminate unemployment entirely? How about inflation? What do we mean by inflation, and what causes it? What are interest rates, and how are they related to inflation? Is it just a coincidence that periods of high inflation are also periods of high interest rates? What is the exchange rate, and how is this related to Canada's trade balance with the rest of the world? These are the sorts of questions that dominate macroeconomics and that you will be introduced to in the next two chapters.

Chapter 21 introduces you to the issues that make up the study of macroeconomics. All of the major issues that are discussed in Chapters 23 through 38 are introduced in this overview chapter. One of the central themes of this chapter (and of macroeconomics itself) is the distinction between *trends* and *cycles*. This reflects a distinction between the short run—in which our focus is on the cyclical fluctuations in macroeconomic variables—and the long run—in which our primary focus is on the trends in those same variables.

Chapter 22 examines the measurement of key macroeconomic variables, with the emphasis on the measure of *national income*, known as *Gross Domestic Product (GDP)*. One of the key points of this chapter is that the value of national income is the same as the value of *national output* as well as the value of *national expenditure*. This provides us with three different ways of measuring national income, all of which must give us the same answer! We then go on to examine the important distinction between *real* and *nominal* national income. This distinction helps to explain why measured national income can rise even when no more goods are being produced (the answer has something to do with inflation). Finally, we examine some of the things that national income *does not measure*. Illegal activities, nonmarket activities, and economic "bads" are just some of the omissions from measures of national income. A final key point of the chapter is that measures of national income such as GDP are very poor measures of some things, but they are actually quite good measures of what they are designed to measure.

CHAPTER 21

WHAT MACROECONOMICS IS ALL ABOUT

Turn on the evening news, and you will likely hear talk of unemployment, inflation, recession, international competitiveness, and economic growth. Almost everyone cares about the economy. Workers are anxious to avoid the unemployment that comes with recessions, to protect themselves against the hazards of inflation, and to share in the rising income that is brought about by economic growth. Firms are concerned about how inflation, recession, and foreign competition affect their profits. Few things are more likely to bring a change of government than bad economic performance.

Macroeconomics is the study of how the economy behaves in broad outline without dwelling on much of its interesting but sometimes confusing detail. As was noted in Chapter 3, macroeconomics is largely concerned with the behaviour of economic *aggregates*, such as total consumption, total investment, total exports, and the average price of all goods and services. These aggregates result from activities in many different markets and from the behaviour of different decision makers in households, governments, and firms. In contrast, *microeconomics* deals with the behaviour of individual markets, such as those for wheat, coal, or strawberries, and with the detailed behaviour of individual decision makers, such as firms and households.

In macroeconomics, we add the value of wheat, compact discs, restaurant meals, and appendectomies to the value of all other goods and services produced and study the movement of *aggregate national product*. We also average the prices of all commodities and discuss the *price level* for the entire economy. We know perfectly well that an economy that produces much wheat and few automobiles is different from one that produces many automobiles but little wheat. We also know that an economy with cheap wheat and expensive cars is different from one with cheap cars and expensive wheat. Studying aggregates alone may cause us to miss these important differences, but it focuses our attention on some important issues for the economy as a whole.

In return for losing sight of some valuable detail, studying aggregates allows us to view the big picture. In macroeconomics, we look at the broad range of opportunities and difficulties facing the economy as a whole. When national product rises, the output of most commodities and the incomes of most people usually rise with it. When the price level rises, virtually everyone in the economy is forced to make adjustments. When the unemployment rate rises, workers are put at an increased risk of losing their jobs and suffering reductions in their incomes. These movements in economic aggregates are strongly associated with the economic concerns of most individuals: the health of the industries in which they work and the prices of the goods that they purchase. This association is why macroeconomic aggregates get

airtime on the evening news, and it is one important reason why we study macroeconomics.

Major macroeconomic issues

The most important macroeconomic issues can be divided into two broad categories—the causes of long-term economic growth, and the size and sources of short-term business cycles. Broad government policies, such as monetary policy and fiscal policy, typically make an appearance in both discussions.

Economic Growth. As we saw in Chapter 1, both total output and output per person have risen for many decades in most industrial countries. These long-term trends have meant rising average living standards. Since the early 1970s, however, average living standards have grown less rapidly than during the preceding decades of the twentieth century. Although long-term growth gets less play on the evening news than the current inflation rate or unemployment rate, it has considerably more importance for a society's prospects and constraints from decade to decade and generation to generation. What caused the slowdown in worldwide growth rates that began in the 1970s?

A second set of questions regarding economic growth involves government policy. Can governments do anything to promote economic growth? Do some government policies, directed to quite different goals, have unintended consequences on the long-term rate of economic growth? What is the connection between the monetary policy conducted by the Bank of Canada and the rate of growth of the Canadian economy? Does the adherence to a low-inflation policy have any effects on the growth rate? Or is long-term economic growth more-or-less independent of monetary policy? The government *budget deficit* also enters into the discussion of economic growth. Many economists believe that when governments spend more than they raise in tax revenue—and thus have a budget deficit—the need for borrowing drives up interest rates and curtails investment by the private sector. Such reductions in investment imply a reduced stock of resources for future production, and thus a reduction in economic growth. Do all government budget deficits reduce future growth, or does it depend on the nature of the government expenditure? Or do budget deficits have no effect at all on the economy's future ability to produce?

Business Cycles.   The economy tends to move in a series of ups and downs, called *business cycles,* rather than in a steady pattern. Why did the greatest economic depression in the twentieth century occur in the 1930s, when almost one-fifth of the Canadian labour force was out of work and massive unemployment plagued all major industrial countries? Why were the 25 years following World War II a period of sustained economic growth, with only minor interruptions caused by modest recessions? Why did the early 1980s see the onset of the worst worldwide recession since the 1930s? What fueled the recovery of the mid 1980s? Why did it falter at the end of the decade? Why did the economy fail to grow in 1990 and 1991 and then improve only slowly in the years immediately following?

Understanding business cycles requires an understanding of inflation and recession. Why, during the 1970s and early 1980s, did inflation in many advanced Western nations reach levels never seen before in peacetime? In the mid 1970s, when inflation crept up to about 5 percent, concern was so great that the Canadian government introduced a major program of wage and price controls, designed to reduce inflation. Yet, by the mid 1980s, after inflation had peaked at around 13 percent, the government was claiming credit for having *reduced* inflation to about 5 percent!

Earlier in the century, alternating bouts of inflationary boom and deflationary recession caused many headaches for policymakers. Booms still tend to be accompanied by inflationary pressures, but it can no longer be assumed that recession will bring deflation. Why were the recessions of the 1970s and early 1980s accompanied not only by their familiar companion, high unemployment, but also by an unexpected fellow traveler, rapid inflation? Will **stagflation**—the coexistence of high unemployment and high inflation—return? Or will the relatively low inflation rates of the first half of the 1990s persist?

Government budget deficits also enter the discussion of business cycles. Some economists think that in recessionary years, the government ought to increase its spending (and lower its tax rates) in an effort to stimulate economic activity (and do the opposite when the economy is booming). Indeed, several government policies, from income taxation to unemployment insurance, are actually designed to mitigate the short-term fluctuations in national income. Other economists believe that the government cannot successfully "fine-tune" the economy by spending and taxing because our knowledge of how the economy works is very imperfect and also because such policies tend to be very imprecise.

KEY MACROECONOMIC PHENOMENA

The current macroeconomic state of the nation can be fairly completely described by total output and output per person, the rate of growth of output and output per person, employment and the unemployment rate, the inflation rate, the interest rate, the exchange rate, and the balance of trade. In this chapter, we discuss each of these variables, with an emphasis on why and how they matter for economic welfare. Here and in Chapter 22 we also explain how the key macroeconomic variables are measured. The remainder of this book is largely about the causes and consequences of changes in each of these variables, the many ways in which they interact, and the effect they have on the well-being of Canadians.

OUTPUT AND INCOME

The most comprehensive measure of a nation's overall level of economic activity is the value of its total production of goods and services, called *national product.*

One of the most important ideas in economics is that the production of output generates income.

For the nation as a whole, all of the value that is produced must ultimately belong to someone in the form of an income claim on that value. For example, if a firm produces $100 worth of ice cream, then that $100 must ultimately represent income for the firm's workers, the firm's suppliers of material inputs, or the firm's owners. Thus the national product is *by definition* equal to the total income claims generated by the production of goods and services. In short, when we study national product, we are also studying national income. Figure 21-1 depicts national income and expenditure as a circular flow.

There are several related measures of a nation's total output and total income. Their various definitions, and the relationships among them, are discussed in detail in the next chapter. In this chapter, we

FIGURE 21-1
The Circular Flow of Expenditure and Income

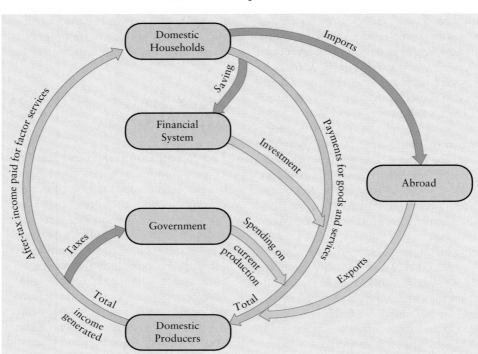

The circular flow of income and product implies that national income is equal to national product. Consider first only the red lines. In this case, the flow would be a simple circle from households to producers and back to households, and the result that national income equals national product would be obvious. Now add the blue and green lines. The blue lines represent *injections* to the circular flow (exports, investment, and government purchases) while the green lines represent *withdrawals* from the circular flow (imports, saving, and taxes). Injections and withdrawals complicate the picture but do not change the basic result: Domestic production creates a claim on the value of that production. When all of the claims are added up, they must be equal to the value of all of the production.

use the generic term *national income* to refer to both the value of total output and the value of the income claims generated by the production of that output.

Aggregating Total Output

To measure total output, quantities of a variety of goods are *aggregated*. To construct such totals, we add up the *values* of the different products. We cannot add tons of steel to loaves of bread, but we can add the money value of steel production to the money value of bread production. Hence by multiplying the physical output of a good by its price per unit and then summing this value for each good produced in a nation, we can calculate the quantity of total output *measured in dollars*.

Real and Nominal Values

The total that was just described gives the *money value* of national output, usually called **nominal national income**. A change in this measure can be caused by a change in either the physical quantities or the prices on which it is based. To determine the extent to which any change is due to quantities or to prices, economists calculate **real national income**. This measures the value of individual outputs not at current prices but at a set of prices that prevailed in some base period that was chosen for this purpose.

Nominal national income is often referred to as *money national income* or *current-dollar national income*. Real national income is often called *con-*

stant-dollar national income. Denoted by the symbol *Y*, real national income tells us the value of current output measured at constant prices—the sum of the quantities valued at prices that prevailed in the base period. Since prices are held constant when computing real national income, changes in real national income reflect *only* changes in quantities. Comparing real national incomes of different years therefore provides a measure of the change in real output that has occurred during the intervening period.

Since our interest is primarily in the *real* output of goods and services, we shall use the terms *national income* and *national output* to refer to *real national income* unless otherwise specified. (An example, illustrating the important distinction between real national income and nominal national income, is given in Extension 22-3 in the next chapter.)

National Income: The Historical Experience

One of the most commonly used measures of national income is called *gross domestic product (GDP)*. Since GDP can be measured in either real or nominal terms, we focus here on real GDP. The details of its calculation will be discussed in Chapter 22.

Part (i) of Figure 21-2 shows real national income produced by the Canadian economy since 1930; part (ii) shows its annual percentage change for the same period. The GDP series in part (i) shows two kinds of movement. The major movement is a positive trend that increased real output by over 550 percent since the end of the Second World War. Because the trend has generally been upward throughout Canadian economic history, it is referred to as *economic growth*. Long-term growth in real national income is reflected in the upward trend in real GDP.

A second feature of the real GDP series is short-term fluctuations around the trend, often described as cyclical fluctuations. Overall growth so dominates the real GDP series that the fluctuations are hardly visible in part (i) of Figure 21-2. However, as can be seen in part (ii), the growth of GDP has never been smooth. In most years, GDP increases, but in 1954, 1981, and 1991, the rate of growth of GDP fell below zero, meaning that GDP actually decreased in those years.

The **business cycle** refers to the continual ebb and flow of business activity that occurs around the long-term trend after seasonal adjustments have been

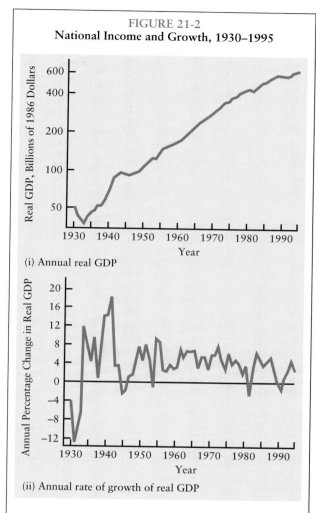

FIGURE 21-2
National Income and Growth, 1930–1995

(i) Annual real GDP

(ii) Annual rate of growth of real GDP

Real GDP measures the quantity of total output produced by the nation's economy over the period of a year. Fluctuations in the annual rate of growth of real GDP reflect cyclical changes in the level of activity in the economy. Real GDP is plotted in part (i) in semilog form, where equal vertical distances represent equal percentage changes. (See the Appendix to Chapter 2.) Real GDP has risen steadily since the early 1930s, with only a few interruptions. This demonstrates the growth of the Canadian economy. Short-term fluctuations are obscured by the long-term growth trend in part (i) but are highlighted in part (ii). The growth rate fluctuates considerably from year to year. The long-term upward trend of real GDP shows up in part (i) because most of the observations in part (ii) are positive. (Data prior to 1947 are based on GNP, thereafter on GDP, which is now the standard measure of real national income.)

(*Sources:* M. C. Urquhart, ed., *Historical Statistics of Canada;* Department of Finance, *Economic Reference Tables,* August 1995.)

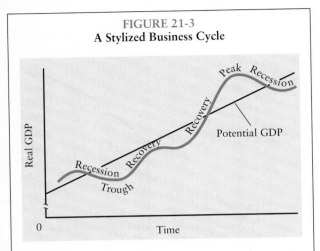

FIGURE 21-3
A Stylized Business Cycle

Although the phases of business fluctuations are described by several commonly used terms, no two cycles are the same. Starting from a lower turning point, real output goes through a phase of recovery, or expansion; reaches an upper turning point (a peak); and then enters a period of recession. Cycles differ from one another in the severity of their troughs and peaks and in the speed with which one phase follows another. Sometimes the entire rising half of the cycle is loosely referred to as a *boom,* and the entire falling half as a *slump.*

made.[1] Such cyclical fluctuations can be seen in many economic series; in particular, they are obvious from the continual oscillations in the growth rate of GDP that we see in Figure 21-2(ii).

Although recurrent fluctuations in economic activity are neither smooth nor regular, a vocabulary has developed to denote their different stages. Figure 21-3 shows stylized cycles that illustrate some useful terms. It is important to realize that no two business cycles are exactly the same. There are variations in duration and magnitude. Some expansions are long and drawn out, like the one that began in 1983 and ended in 1990. Others come to an end before high employment of labour and industrial capacity is reached. Nonetheless, fluctuations are systematic enough that it still seems useful to identify common

factors in the four phases, which are outlined in Extension 21-1.

Potential Income and the Output Gap

Actual national income represents what the economy *actually* produces. An important related concept is *potential* national income, which measures what the economy could produce if all resources—land, labour, and productive capacity—were employed at their normal levels of utilization. This concept is usually referred to as **potential income** (but is sometimes called *full-employment income*).[2] We give it the symbol Y^* to distinguish it from actual national income, indicated by Y.

The **output gap** (sometimes called the *GDP gap*) measures the difference between potential national income and what is actually produced, as measured by current GDP. The gap is calculated by subtracting potential national income from actual income ($Y - Y^*$). The output gap is thus positive when actual income exceeds potential income and it is negative when actual income is less than potential income.

When potential income is greater than actual income, the gap measures the market value of goods and services that *could have been produced* if the economy's resources had been fully employed, but that actually went unproduced. The goods and services that are not produced when the economy is operating below Y^* are permanently lost to the economy. Because these losses occur when employable resources are not used, they are often called the *deadweight loss* of unemployed resources. When the economy is operating below its potential level of output—that is, when Y is less than Y^*—there is a **recessionary gap**.

In booms, actual national income *exceeds* potential income. Actual GDP can exceed potential income because potential income is defined for a *normal rate of utilization* of factors of production, and there are many ways in which these normal rates can be exceeded temporarily. Labour may work longer hours than normal; factories may operate an extra shift or

---

[1]When economists analyze monthly or quarterly data, they usually make a *seasonal adjustment* to remove the fluctuations due to the regular seasonal pattern in the data. For example, logging activity is typically much higher in the summer than the winter, whereas sales of fuel oil is much greater in the winter than the summer.

[2]The words *real* and *actual* have similar meanings in everyday usage. When measuring national income, however, their meanings are quite distinct. *Real* national income is distinguished from *nominal* national income; and *actual* national income is distinguished from *potential* national income. The latter both refer to *real* measures of national income.

EXTENSION 21-1

THE TERMINOLOGY OF BUSINESS CYCLES

TROUGH

A trough is characterized by unemployed resources and a level of output that is low in relation to the economy's capacity to produce. There is thus a substantial amount of unused productive capacity. Business profits are low; for some individual companies, they are negative. Confidence about economic prospects in the immediate future is lacking, and, as a result, many firms are unwilling to risk making new investments.

RECOVERY

The characteristics of a recovery, or expansion, are many: Run-down equipment is replaced; employment, income, and consumer spending all begin to rise; and expectations become more favourable as a result of increases in production, sales, and profits. Investments that once seemed risky may be undertaken as the climate of business opinion starts to change from one of pessimism to one of optimism. Production can be increased with relative ease merely by reemploying the existing unused capacity and unemployed labour.

PEAK

A peak is the top of a cycle. At the peak, existing capacity is used to a high degree; labour shortages may develop, particularly in categories of key skills; and shortages of essential raw materials are likely. As shortages develop in more and more markets, a situation of general excess demand develops. Costs rise, but because prices rise also, business remains profitable.

RECESSION

A **recession,** or contraction, is a downturn in economic activity. Common usage defines a recession as a fall in the real GDP for two successive quarters. Demand falls off, and, as a result, production and employment also fall. As employment falls, so do households' incomes. Profits drop, and some firms encounter financial difficulties. Investments that looked profitable with the expectation of continually rising demand now appear unprofitable. It may not even be worth replacing capital goods as they wear out because unused capacity is increasing steadily. In historical discussions, a recession that is deep and long-lasting is often called a **depression.**

BOOMS AND SLUMPS

These terms are nontechnical but descriptive. The entire falling half of the cycle is often called a *slump,* and the entire rising half is often called a *boom.*

---

delay closing for routine repairs and maintenance. Although these expedients are only temporary, they are effective in the short term. When actual GDP exceeds potential GDP, there is often upward pressure on prices. Thus when Y exceeds Y^*, we say there is an **inflationary gap.**

When actual income is less than potential income, there is said to be a recessionary gap. When actual income exceeds potential income, there is said to be an inflationary gap.

Figure 21-4(i) shows potential income for the years since 1970. The upward trend reflects the growth in the productive capacity of the Canadian economy over this period. The figure also shows actual national income (reproduced from Figure 21-2), which has kept approximately in step with potential income. The distance between the two, which is the GDP gap, is plotted in part (ii) of Figure 21-4. Fluctuations in economic activity are apparent from fluctuations in the size of the gap. The deadweight loss from unemployed resources over any time span is indicated by the overall amount of the gap over that time span. It is shown in part (ii) of Figure 21-4 by the shaded area between the curve and the zero line, which represents the equality of actual output with potential output.

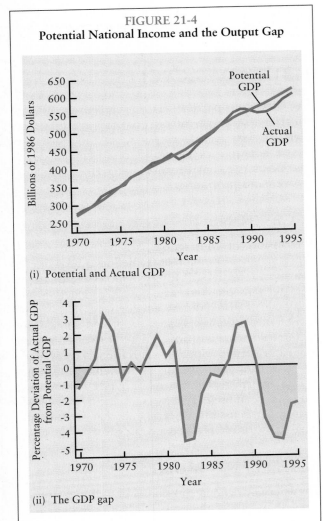

FIGURE 21-4
Potential National Income and the Output Gap

(i) Potential and Actual GDP

(ii) The GDP gap

Potential and actual GDP both display an upward trend. The output gap measures the difference between an economy's potential output and its actual output; the gap is expressed here as a percentage of potential output. Since 1970, potential and actual GDP have more than doubled. The distance between the two is the output gap, which shows clearly the cyclical behaviour of the economy. Shaded regions in figure (ii) show recessionary gaps.

(*Source:* Bank of Canada)

Why National Income Matters

National income is an important measure of economic performance in both the short run and the long run. Short-run movements in the business cycle receive the most attention in politics and in the press, but most economists agree that long-term growth, the rate of change of *potential GDP,* is in many ways the more important of the two.

Short-Term Fluctuations.   Recessions are associated with unemployment and lost output. When actual GDP is below potential GDP, economic waste and human suffering result from the failure to use the economy's resources (including its human resources) at their normal intensity of use.

Booms, although associated with high employment and high output, can bring problems of their own. When actual GDP exceeds potential GDP, inflationary pressure usually ensues, causing serious concern for any government that is committed to keeping the inflation rate low.

Long-Term Growth.   The long-run trend in real national income per capita is the principal determinant of improvements in a society's overall standard of living. When income per person grows, each generation can expect, on average, to be substantially better off than preceding ones. For example, if real income per capita grows at the relatively modest rate of 1.5 percent per year, the average person's lifetime income will be about *twice* that of his or her grandparents.

In the long run, national income per person can grow for two reasons. One is growth in the amount of output produced per hour of work. It is this growth, the growth of *labour productivity,* that has generally eliminated the low living standards that prevailed at the start of the Industrial Revolution. A second source of growth in per capita income arises from changes in the amount of labour (that is, the total hours of work) supplied by a given population. If people work more hours, they will produce more output. The difference between these two sources of growth is important. When productivity increases, more output is obtained for a given amount of effort. When total hours worked increase, more output is obtained by using more resources. Income rises, but the amount of time that people have to devote to life's pleasures falls.

In Canada, much of the growth in per capita income during the past three decades was due to increases in the number of hours worked per person of working age. A relatively small part of that growth, compared to the trend of the rest of the century, could be attributed to growth in labour productivity. This slowdown in productivity growth has created new interest in the sources of economic growth, a subject that is one of the major themes in our discussion of macroeconomics.

Finally, it is important to remember that although economic growth makes people better off *on average,* it does not necessarily make *every* individual better off. This is because the benefits of growth do not typically fall evenly on all members of the population. For example, if growth involves significant changes in the structure of the economy, such as a shift away from agriculture and toward manufacturing (as happened in the first part of this century), then these changes may actually hurt some people for extended periods of time.

Income Doesn't Measure Well-Being.   Finally, bear in mind that national income is far from a perfect measure of economic well-being, in part because it fails to measure many important things such as leisure time and household production (i.e., the output *within* the home that is not traded in markets). For example, suppose that a person can increase the value of output by $100, but only by decreasing her leisure by an amount that is worth *more* to her than $100 (that is, she would be prepared to pay more than $100 to have that extra leisure time). In this case, the leisure-reducing increase in national income actually represents a *reduction* overall well-being. Chapter 22 contains a detailed discussion of how economists measure national income and an evaluation of the strengths and weaknesses of those measures.

EMPLOYMENT, UNEMPLOYMENT, AND THE LABOUR FORCE

National income and *employment* are closely related. If more is to be produced, either more workers must be used in production, or existing workers must produce more. The first change means a rise in employment; the second means a rise in output per person employed, which, as we have seen, is called a rise in *labour productivity.* In the short run, when the productive capacity of the economy (potential GDP) is fixed, the only way to produce more output is to employ more workers. Increases in productivity are a major source of economic growth, but they occur only over longer periods of time.

Employment denotes the number of adult workers (defined in Canada as workers aged 15 and over) who hold jobs. **Unemployment** denotes the number of adult workers who are not employed but who are actively searching for a job. The **labour force** is the total number of people who are either employed or unemployed. The **unemployment rate** is equal to the number of unemployed people expressed as a fraction of the labour force—it represents the fraction of people wanting jobs who do not currently have one.

$$\text{Unemployment Rate} = \frac{\text{number of people unemployed}}{\text{number of people in the labour force}} \times 100 \text{ percent}$$

The level of unemployment in Canada is estimated from the Labour Force Survey conducted each month by Statistics Canada. Persons who are currently without a job but who say they have searched actively for one during the sample period are recorded as unemployed. The total number of estimated unemployed is then expressed as a percentage of the labour force (employed plus unemployed) to obtain the figure for the unemployment rate. Extension 21-2 discusses some difficulties in the measurement of unemployment.

Frictional, Structural, and Cyclical Unemployment

When the economy is at potential GDP, we call the level of employment *full employment* or, sometimes, *high employment.* Whichever term is used, it is important to understand that there will generally be unemployment even when the economy is at potential GDP. There are two main reasons why this is so.

First, there is a constant turnover of individuals in given jobs and a constant change in job opportunities. New members enter the workforce; some people quit their jobs; others are fired. It may take some time for these people to find jobs. So at any point in time, there is unemployment due to the normal turnover of labour. Such unemployment is called **frictional unemployment.**

Second, because the economy is constantly changing and adapting, at any moment there will always be some mismatch between the characteristics of the labour force and the characteristics of the available jobs. This is a mismatch between the *structure* of the supplies of labour and the *structure* of the demands for labour. The mismatch may occur, for example, because labour does not have the skills that are in demand or because labour is not in the part of the country where the demand is located.

EXTENSION 21-2

PROBLEMS IN MEASURING UNEMPLOYMENT

No measurement of unemployment is completely accurate. The unemployment figures that are calculated by Statistics Canada, however, have a number of shortcomings that reveal much about the concept of unemployment itself.

Measured unemployment may overstate or understate the number of people who are involuntarily unemployed. On the one hand, measured unemployment overstates true unemployment by including some people who are voluntarily out of work. For example, unemployment insurance provides protection against genuine hardship, but it also induces some people to stay out of work to collect unemployment benefits for as long as the benefits last. Such people have, in fact, voluntarily withdrawn from the labour force, although to remain eligible for unemployment payments they must make a show of looking for a job by registering at the local unemployment service office. Such people are usually included in the ranks of the unemployed because, for fear of losing their benefits, they tell the person who surveys them that they are actively looking for a job.

On the other hand, the measured figure understates involuntary unemployment by omitting some people who would accept a job if one were available but who did not actively look for one during the week in which the data were collected. For example, people who have not found jobs after searching for a long time may become discouraged and stop seeking work. Such people have withdrawn voluntarily from the labour force and will not be recorded as unemployed. They are, however, unemployed in the sense that they would willingly accept a job if one were available. People in this category are referred to as *discouraged workers*. They have withdrawn from the labour market because they believe that they cannot find a job under current conditions.

In addition, there are part-time unemployed people. If some people are working six hours instead of eight hours per day because there is insufficient demand for the product that they help to make, these workers are suffering 25 percent unemployment even though none of them are reported as unemployed. Twenty-five percent of that group's potential labour resources are going unused. Involuntary part-time work is a major source of unemployment of labour resources that is not reflected in the overall unemployment figures that are reported in the press.

The official figures for unemployment are useful, particularly because they tell us the *direction* of changes in unemployment. It is unlikely, for example, that the official unemployment figures will be rising when "real" unemployment is actually falling. For the reasons that we have just discussed, however, they can at times give under- or over-estimates of the total number of persons who would be genuinely willing to work if they were offered a job at the going rate of pay.

Unemployment that occurs because of a mismatch between the characteristics of the supply of labour and the demand for labour, even when the overall demand for labour is equal to the overall supply, is called **structural unemployment.**

Even when the economy is said to be at full employment, some unemployment exists due to natural turnover in the labour market and to mismatch between firms and workers.

Full employment is said to occur when the only existing unemployment is frictional and structural. When this is the case, factors of production are being used at their normal intensity, and the economy is at potential GDP. At less than full employment, other types of unemployment are present as well. One major reason for lapses from full employment lies in the business cycle. During recessions, unemployment rises above the minimum avoidable amount of frictional and structural unemployment. This excess amount is called **cyclical unemployment** (or, sometimes, *deficient-demand unemployment*).

The measured unemployment rate when the economy is at full employment (that is, at potential output) is often called the **natural rate of unemployment** or the **NAIRU**.[3] Although estimates of this rate are difficult to obtain, they provide a useful benchmark against which to gauge the current performance of the economy, as measured by the actual unemployment rate. Estimates indicate that the NAIRU rose throughout the 1970s, from around 5.5 percent to a high of around 8 percent in the early 1980s, and it has now fallen to around 7 percent. (We will discuss the reasons for these changes in Chapter 31.)

Unemployment: The Historical Experience

Figure 21-5(i) shows the trends in the labour force, employment, and unemployment since 1930. Despite booms and slumps, employment has grown roughly in line with the growth in the labour force and in the total population. In the 1980s, however, the labour force and employment grew faster than the total population in response to the maturing of the "baby boom" generation and the increasing participation of women in the labour force.

Although the long-term growth trend dominates the employment data, Figure 21-5(ii) shows that the short-term fluctuations in the unemployment rate have been quite marked. The unemployment rate has been as low as 1.4 percent in 1944 and as high as 19.3 percent in 1933; in the period after World War II, the unemployment rate fell as low as 3.4 percent in 1956 and rose as high as 12.6 percent in 1982. The high unemployment rate of the Great Depression in the early 1930s tends to dwarf the fluctuations in unemployment that have occurred since then. Nonetheless, the fluctuations in unemployment in recent decades have been neither minor nor unimportant.

Unemployment can rise either because employment falls or because the labour force expands (or both). In recent decades, the number of people entering the labour force has invariably exceeded the

FIGURE 21-5
Labour Force, Employment, and Unemployment, 1930–1995

(i) Labour force, employment, and unemployment

(ii) Unemployment rate

The labour force and employment have grown since the 1930s with only a few interruptions. The unemployment rate responds to the cyclical behaviour of the economy. The labour force and the level of employment in Canada have both more than tripled since 1930. Booms are associated with a low unemployment rate and slumps with a high unemployment rate. The Great Depression of the 1930s produced record unemployment figures for an entire decade. Most recently, unemployment rose during the recessions of the early 1980s and the early 1990s.

(Sources: M. C. Urquhart, ed., Historical Statistics of Canada; Department of Finance, Economic Reference Tables, August 1995.)

---

[3]This is an acronym for the Nonaccelerating Inflation Rate of Unemployment; its relationship with potential GDP is discussed in Chapter 30.

number leaving it. The resulting increase in the labour force has meant that unemployment has sometimes grown even in periods when employment was also growing.

Why Unemployment Matters

The social and political significance of the unemployment rate is enormous. The government is blamed when it is high and takes credit when it is low. Few macroeconomic policies are planned without some consideration of how they will affect unemployment. No other summary statistic, with the possible exception of the inflation rate, carries such weight as a source of both formal and informal policy concern as the percentage of the labour force that is unemployed.

Unemployment involves economic waste and human suffering. The economic waste is obvious. Human effort is the least durable of economic commodities. If a fully employed economy has 15 million people who are willing to work in 1996, their services must either be used in 1996 or wasted. When the services of only 13.5 million are used because 10 percent of the labour force is unemployed, one year's potential output of 1.5 million workers is lost forever. In an economy in which there is not enough output to meet everyone's needs, such a waste of potential output seems pointless and possibly tragic.

Severe hardship can be caused by prolonged periods of unemployment. A person's spirit can be broken by a long period of desiring work but being unable to find it. Research has shown that crime, mental illness, and general social unrest tend to be positively associated with unemployment. The loss of income associated with unemployment can and does push people into poverty.

In the not-so-distant past, only personal savings, private charity, or help from friends and relatives stood between the unemployed and starvation. Today, welfare and unemployment insurance have created a safety net, particularly when unemployment is for short periods, as is often the case. However, when an economic slump lasts long enough, as in the early 1980s and the early 1990s, people begin to exhaust their unemployment insurance and must fall back on savings, welfare, or charity.

INFLATION AND THE PRICE LEVEL

Everyone knows what inflation is, though they might not be able to define it precisely. Most people complain about its effects when the inflation rate is high and worry that it is just around the corner when the inflation rate is low. Inflation means that prices in general are going up—not just the price of gasoline, jeans, or burritos, but the prices of almost everything.

To study inflation, economists use two concepts. The first is the **price level,** which refers to the average level of all prices in the economy and is given by the symbol P. The second is the rate of **inflation,** which is the rate at which the price level (P) is rising.

To measure the average price level, economists construct a *price index*, which averages the prices of various commodities according to how important they are. The best-known price index in Canada is the **Consumer Price Index (CPI),** which measures the average cost of the goods and services that are bought by the average Canadian household. Extension 21-3 shows how a price index such as the CPI is constructed.

The CPI expresses the price level at any time in relation to what a given bundle of commodities cost in a base period. The base period in use in 1995 was 1986, for which the average value of the index is set to 100. Thus when we read that the CPI for January 1995 had a value of 131.9 we know that a bundle of goods and services that cost $100 during 1986 would cost $131.90 to purchase in January 1995. Generally, price indexes compare the cost of a given bundle of goods and services purchased at different times.

The CPI is designed to measure changes in the cost of living for the average household in Canada. Because it is based on consumption for the average household, it does not measure accurately the change in the cost of living for *each and every* household. Rich, poor, young, old, single, married, urban, and rural households typically consume goods in different proportions. An increase in air fares, for example, will raise the cost of living of a frequent traveler but not affect that of a nontraveling household.

The more an individual household's consumption pattern conforms to that of the typical pattern used to create a price index, the better the index will reflect changes in that household's cost of living.

By allowing us to compare the general price level at different times, a price index such as the CPI also allows us to measure the rate of inflation. For example, the value of the CPI in January 1995 was 131.9 and in January 1996 was 135.2. The *rate of inflation*

EXTENSION 21-3

HOW THE CONSUMER PRICE INDEX IS CONSTRUCTED

Although the details are somewhat more complicated, the basic idea behind the Consumer Price Index is straightforward, as is illustrated by the following hypothetical example.

Suppose we wish to discover what was happening to the overall cost of living for typical students at a university. A survey of student behaviour in 1987 shows that the average student at the university consumed only three goods—pizza, coffee, and photocopying—and spent a total of $200 a month on these items, as shown in Table 1.

TABLE 1
Expenditure Behaviour in 1987

Product	Price	Quantity per Month	Expenditure per Month
Photocopying	$0.10 per sheet	140 sheets	$14.00
Pizza	8.00 per pizza	15 pizzas	120.00
Coffee	0.75 per cup	88 cups	66.00
Total expenditure			200.00

By 1997, the price of photocopying has increased to 12 cents per copy, the price of pizza has fallen to $7.90, and the price of coffee has increased to 90 cents. What has happened to the cost of living? In order to find out, we calculate the cost of purchasing the 1987 bundle of goods at the prices that prevailed in 1997, as shown in Table 2.

TABLE 2
Expenditure Behaviour in 1997

Product	Price	Quantity per Month	Expenditure per Month
Photocopying	$0.12 per sheet	140 sheets	$16.80
Pizza	7.90 per pizza	15 pizzas	118.50
Coffee	0.90 per cup	88 cups	79.20
Total expenditure			214.50

The total expenditure required to purchase the bundle of goods that cost $200.00 in 1987 has risen to $214.50. The increase in required expenditure is $14.50, which is a 7.25 percent increase over the original $200.00.

If we define 1987 as the *base year* for the "student price index" and assign an index value of 100 to the cost of the average student's expenditure in that year, the value of the index in 1997 is 107.25. This means that goods and services which cost $100.00 in the base year cost $107.25 in 1997, exactly what is implied by Table 2.

The Consumer Price Index, as constructed by Statistics Canada, is built on exactly the same principles as the preceding example. In the case of the CPI, many thousands of consumers are surveyed, and the prices of thousands of products are monitored, but the basic method is the same:

1. Survey the consumption behaviour of consumers.

2. Calculate the cost of the goods and services purchased by the average consumer in the year in which the original survey was done. Define this as the *base period* of the index.

3. Calculate the cost of purchasing the same bundle of goods and services in other years.

4. Divide the result of step 3 (in each year) by the result of step 2, and multiply by 100. The result is the value of the CPI for each year.

For example, in January 1995 the CPI in Canada was 131.9 on a base of 1986 (the period in which the original survey was done). This means that the price level had risen by 31.9 percent in the preceding 9 years.

The CPI is not a perfect measure of the cost of living because it does not account for quality improvements or for the tendency of consumers to purchase more of things whose prices fall (and less of things whose prices rise). Thus from time to time the underlying survey of consumer expenditure must be updated in order to keep up with changes in consumption patterns.

during that one-year period, expressed in percentage terms, is equal to the change in the price level divided by the initial price level, times 100:

$$\text{Rate of Inflation} = \frac{135.2 - 131.9}{131.9} \times 100 \text{ percent}$$

$$= 2.50 \text{ percent}$$

When time periods are not exactly one year apart, changes in price levels are usually converted to annual rates, the average year-to-year percentage change in prices over the period measured. For example, in January 1995 the CPI was 131.9, and in April 1995 it was 133.1. During the three months separating January and April, the CPI rose by 0.9 percent. If the CPI continued to grow at 0.9 percent every three months for a whole year, the percentage increase over the year would be 3.64. Thus we say that over the period from January 1995 to April 1995, the CPI was growing at an *annual rate* of 3.64 percent.[4] [31]

Inflation: The Historical Experience

Figure 21-6 shows the CPI and the inflation rate (measured by the annual rate of change in the CPI) from 1930 to 1995. What can we learn from Figure 21-6? First, we learn that the price level is constantly changing. Second, we learn that in only 2 years since the end of World War II did the price level fall; in all other years, the inflation rate was positive. The cumulative effect of this sequence of small but repeated price increases is quite dramatic: By 1995, the price level was roughly 12 times what it was in 1930.

Third, we learn that although the long-term upward trend stands out when we look at the price level, the short-term fluctuations stand out when we look at the inflation rate. The sharp year-to-year swings in the inflation rate have sometimes been dramatic. The increase in the inflation rate into double-digit levels in 1974, and again in 1979, were associated with major shocks to the world prices of oil and foodstuffs, and the declines in inflation that followed were delayed responses to major recessions. (Note that even when the inflation rate *falls*, as it did in the early 1990s, for example, the price level continues to rise as long as inflation remains *positive*.)

---

[4]Notice that 3.64 is slightly more than 0.90 × 4. The reason for this is that the growth rate of 0.90 percent per quarter is *compounded* when the annual rate is calculated.

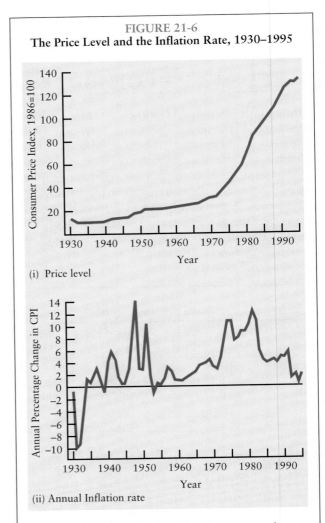

FIGURE 21-6
The Price Level and the Inflation Rate, 1930–1995

(i) Price level

(ii) Annual Inflation rate

The trend in the price level has been upward over the past half century. The rate of inflation has varied from −10 percent to +14 percent since 1930. The data are for the Consumer Price Index from 1930 to 1995, with the value in 1986 equal to 100.

(*Sources*: M. C. Urquhart, ed., *Historical Statistics of Canada*; Department of Finance, *Economic Reference Tables*, August 1995.)

Why Inflation Matters

Money is the universal yardstick in our economy. This does not mean that we care only about money—it means simply that we measure *economic values* in terms of money, and we use money to conduct our economic affairs. Things as diverse as wages, bank balances, the value of a house, and a university's endowment are all stated in terms of money. We value money, however, not for itself but for what we can purchase with it. The terms **purchasing power of money** and *real value of money* refer to the amount of goods and services that can be purchased with a given amount of money. A change in the price level affects us because it changes the real value of money.

The purchasing power of money is negatively related to the price level.

For example, if the price level doubles, a dollar will buy only half as much, whereas if the price level halves, a dollar will buy twice as much. Figure 21-6 shows that inflation has reduced the purchasing power of money over each of the last six decades.

If inflation reduces the real value of a given sum of money, it also reduces the real value of anything else whose price is *fixed* in money terms. Thus the real value of a money wage, a savings account, or the balance that is owed on a student loan is reduced by inflation.

The real effects of inflation depend to a great extent on whether or not the inflation comes as a surprise.

A Fully Anticipated Inflation. It is possible to imagine an inflation that has no real effects. What is required for this to happen is, first, that everyone who is making any sort of financial arrangement knows what the inflation rate will be over the life of the contract and, second, that *all* financial contracts be written to incorporate the expected inflation. In this case, the real value of the financial obligations will not change when the price level changes. The real behaviour of the economy would then be exactly the same with and without inflation.

If all financial contracts are written to incorporate a fully anticipated inflation, then such an inflation will have no real effects.

For example, suppose that both sides of a wage contract agree that wages should go up by 3 percent in real terms. If the inflation rate is expected to be zero, they would agree to a 3 percent increase in money wages. If 10 percent inflation is expected, however, they would agree to a 13 percent increase in money wages. Ten percent would be needed to maintain the purchasing power of the money wages that would be paid, and 3 percent would be needed to bring about the desired increase in purchasing power.

As another example, a loan contract would specify that the amount repaid on the loan be increased over the amount borrowed by the rate of inflation. Thus if $100 is borrowed and the price level rises by 10 percent, $110 would have to be returned (quite apart from any interest that might be paid on the loan). This would ensure that the real value of what is borrowed stays equal to the real value of what is repaid.

Taxes would also have to be adjusted (as would public pensions, life insurance benefits, income-support payments, etc.). For example, the personal exemption on the income tax (the amount of income that each person can exempt from taxation) would have to be increased by 10 percent to keep the real value of the exemption constant, given a 10 percent inflation rate.

The result of all this would be a 10 percent increase in everyone's money incomes and money assets combined with a 10 percent increase in all money prices and all money liabilities. Nothing real would have changed. People's higher money incomes would buy the same amount of goods as before, and the real value of their assets and liabilities would be unchanged.[5]

An Unanticipated Inflation. At the opposite extreme from a fully anticipated inflation is a completely unanticipated inflation. No one sees it coming; no one is prepared to offset its consequences. The real value of all contracts that are specified in nominal terms will change unexpectedly. Who will gain and who will lose?

An unexpected inflation benefits anyone who has an obligation to pay out money and harms anyone who is entitled to receive money.

For example, consider a wage contract that specifies a wage increase of 3 percent on the assumption that the price level will remain constant. Both employers and employees expect that the purchasing power of wages paid will rise by 3 percent as a result of the new contract. Now assume, however, that the price level unexpectedly rises by 10 percent over the life of the wage contract. The combination of the 10 percent inflation and the 3 percent increase in money

---

[5]For those readers who have studied microeconomics, this is an illustration of the point that *only relative prices matter* for the allocation of resources. If all prices rise by 10 percent, or by any other uniform percentage, relative prices are unchanged.

wages implies a reduction in the purchasing power of wages of 7 percent. Employers gain because their wage payments represent a smaller part of the value of their output than they had expected. Workers lose because their wages represent a smaller receipt of purchasing power than they had expected.

People who have borrowed money will pay back a smaller real amount than they borrowed. By the same token, people who have lent money will receive back a smaller real amount than they lent. Say that Greg lends Helen enough money to buy an expensive sports car, and the price level subsequently doubles. When Helen pays back the money that she borrowed, Greg finds himself with only one-half of the amount now required to buy the car.

Wage earners and lenders will be able to adjust to the new price level when they make new contracts, but some people will be locked in to their old money contracts for the rest of their lives. The extreme case is suffered by those who live on fixed money incomes. For example, pensions that are provided by the private sector often promise to pay a certain number of dollars per year for life. On retirement, this sum may look adequate, even generous. Twenty years later, however, inflation may have reduced its purchasing power to the poverty level. A family that retired on a fixed money income in 1970 would have found the purchasing power of that income reduced year by year until in 1995, it would have had only 23 percent of its original value. To understand the impact of this, imagine being told that for every dollar that you now spend, only 23 cents can be spent in the future.

Intermediate Cases.   There are several reasons why virtually all real inflations fall somewhere between the two extremes (fully anticipated or complete surprise) that we have just discussed.

First, the inflation rate is usually variable and seldom foreseen exactly, even though its general course may be anticipated. Thus the actual rate will sometimes be higher than expected—to the benefit of those who have contracted to pay money. At other times the inflation rate will be lower than expected—to the benefit of those who have contracted to receive money. Given the lack of certainty, different people will have different expectations.

Because it is hard to forecast accurately, inflation adds to the uncertainties of economic life. Highly variable inflation rates cause great uncertainty.

Second, even if the inflation rate is accurately anticipated, all adjustments to it cannot occur at the same speed. As a result, inflation redistributes income, and it does so in a haphazard way. People whose money incomes rise more slowly than prices will lose; those whose money incomes keep ahead of the inflation will gain.

Third, even if the inflation rate is anticipated, the full set of institutions that would be needed for everyone to avoid its consequences do not exist. For example, many private pension plans are stated in money terms and employees have little choice but to take the only plan that their employers make available to them. Thus even when inflation is predicted, some people will wind up living on fixed nominal incomes and thus will see their real incomes erode over time.

Fourth, much of the tax system is defined in nominal money terms, causing its effects to vary with the price level. For example, machinery and equipment owned by businesses wear out with use. The tax code allows for this by permitting firms to deduct *depreciation allowances* from their income for tax purposes. The depreciation allowances are calculated as a certain fraction of the original purchase price of the machinery or equipment. If there has been rapid inflation, the allowed depreciation may be much less than the real depreciation. This makes capital more expensive for firms and tends to reduce investment (and, as we shall see, economic growth) in the economy.

Indexation.   Some of the real effects of inflation can be avoided by indexing. **Indexation** means linking the payments that are made under the terms of a contract to changes in the price level. For example, a retirement pension might pay the beneficiary $15,000 per year starting in 1995, and it might specify that the amount paid will increase each year in proportion to the increase in the CPI. Thus if the CPI rises by 10 percent between 1995 and 1996, the pension that is payable in 1996 would rise by 10 percent, to $16,500. If the CPI rose only 5 percent, the pension would also rise by 5 percent, to $15,750. In either case, indexing would hold the real purchasing power of the pension constant.

Indexing is potentially valuable as a defense against unforeseen changes in the price level, as a method of reducing uncertainty, and as a way of adapting institutions so that contracts can be made in real terms. In practice, however, indexing is used relatively little in Canada. Most of the tax code is not indexed, and the vast majority of contracts are written in nominal terms, putting them at risk for the consequences of unanticipated inflation.

THE INTEREST RATE

If a bank or credit union lends you money, it will usually ask you to agree to a schedule for repayment. Furthermore, it will charge you **interest** for the privilege of borrowing the money. If, for example, you are lent $1,000 today, repayable in one year's time, you may also be asked to pay $10 per month in interest. This makes $120 in interest over the year, which can be expressed as an interest rate of 12 percent per annum.

The **interest rate** is the price that is paid to borrow money for a stated period of time and is expressed as a percentage amount per dollar borrowed. For example, an interest rate of 12 percent per year means that the borrower must pay 12 cents per year for every dollar that is borrowed. (Unless explicitly indicated otherwise, interest rates are almost invariably expressed as the amount of interest per dollar per year.)

There are many interest rates. A bank will lend money to an industrial customer at a lower rate than it will lend money to you—there is a lower risk of not being repaid. The rate charged on a loan that is not to be repaid for a long time will usually differ from the rate on a loan that is to be repaid quickly.

When economists speak of "the" interest rate, they mean a rate that is typical of all the various interest rates in the economy. Dealing with one interest rate suppresses much interesting detail. However, interest rates commonly move together, at least for major changes, so following the movement of one rate allows us to consider changes in the general level of interest rates. The *prime interest rate,* the rate that banks charge to their best business customers, is an interest rate which attracts much attention because when the prime rate changes, most other rates change in the same direction. Another high-profile interest rate is the *bank rate,* the interest rate that the Bank of Canada (Canada's central bank) charges on short-term loans to commercial banks.

Interest Rates and Inflation

How does inflation affect interest rates? To begin developing an answer, imagine that your friend lends you $100 and that the loan is repayable in one year.

The amount that you pay her for making this loan, measured in money terms, is the **nominal interest rate.** If you pay her $108 in one year's time, $100 will be repayment of the amount of the loan (which is called the *principal*) and $8 will be payment of the interest. In this case, the nominal interest rate is 8 percent $((8/100) \times 100$ percent$)$.

How much purchasing power has your friend gained or lost by making this loan? As we have already noted in our discussion of the consequences of inflation, the answer will depend on what happens to the price level during the year. Intuitively, the more the price level rises, the worse your friend will do and the better the transaction will be for you. This result occurs because the more the price level rises, the less valuable are the dollars that you use to repay the loan. The **real interest rate** measures the *real* return on a loan, in terms of purchasing power.

If the price level remains constant over the year, the real rate of interest that your friend earns would also be 8 percent, because she can buy 8 percent more goods and services with the $108 that you repay her than with the $100 that she lent you. However, if the price level rises by 8 percent, the real rate of interest would be zero because the $108 that you repay her buys the same quantity of goods as the $100 that she originally gave up. If she is unlucky enough to lend money at 8 percent in a year in which prices rise by 10 percent, the real rate of interest that she earns is −2 percent. The repayment of principal and nominal interest of 8 percent will purchase 2 percent less in goods and services than the original loan.

If lenders and borrowers are concerned with real costs, measured in terms of purchasing power, the nominal rate of interest will be set at the real rate to which they agree as a return on their money *plus* an amount to cover any expected rate of inflation. Consider a one-year loan that is meant to earn a real return to the lender of 5 percent. If the expected rate of inflation is zero, the nominal interest rate set for the loan will be 5 percent. If 10 percent inflation is expected, the nominal interest rate will be 15 percent.

To provide a given expected real rate of interest, the nominal interest rate must be set at the desired real rate of interest plus the expected annual rate of inflation.

Because they often overlook this point, many people are surprised at the high nominal rates of interest that exist during periods of high inflation. For example, when the nominal interest rates rose drastically in 1980, many commentators expressed shock at the unbearably high rates. Most of them failed to notice that with inflation running at about 12 percent, an interest rate of 15 percent represented a real rate of only 3 percent. Had the Bank of Canada given in to the pressure to hold interest rates to the more "reasonable" level of 10 percent, it would have been imposing a *negative* real rate of interest. The purchasing power that lenders would get back, including interest, would be less than the purchasing power of the amount originally lent.

The burden of borrowing depends on the real, not the nominal, rate of interest.

For example, a nominal interest rate of 8 percent combined with a 2 percent rate of inflation is a much greater real burden on borrowers than a nominal rate of 16 percent combined with a 14 percent rate of inflation.

Figure 21-7 shows the nominal and real interest rate paid on short-term government borrowing since 1950. Interest rates were high and volatile during the early part of the 1980s. During the latter part of the 1980s, rates fell somewhat and became somewhat less variable. In the early 1990s, both real and nominal interest rates fell.

Why Interest Rates Matter

As we shall see in Chapter 23, real interest rates help to determine the amount of investment. High real interest rates make borrowing costly, and there is less real investment than when interest rates are low. But less investment today implies less productive capacity in the future. Thus real interest rates, through their effect on investment, affect long-term growth and *future* living standards. Changes in investment can also cause swings in the business cycle. A slowdown in investment can trigger a slump; conversely, when investment increases sharply, GDP generally follows. Thus through their effect on investment, real interest rates also affect employment and output in the short run. Changes in interest rates also affect the standard of living of retirees whose pensions are derived from interest-bearing assets.

THE INTERNATIONAL ECONOMY

The two important indicators of the Canadian position in the international economy are the *exchange*

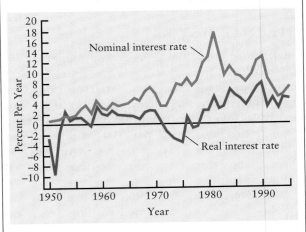

FIGURE 21-7
Real and Nominal Interest Rates, 1950–1995

Inflation over the past four decades has meant that the real interest rate has always been less than the nominal interest rate. The data for the nominal interest rate show the average rate on three-month treasury bills in each year since 1950. The real interest rate is calculated as the nominal interest rate minus the actual rate of inflation over the same period. For the most part, the real interest rate has been below 4 percent for the past four decades. Through much of the 1970s, the real interest rate was negative, indicating that the inflation rate exceeded the nominal interest rate. The 1980s saw real interest rates rise as high as 8 percent. Since then, real rates have declined again to levels that are closer to the long-term historical average.

(*Source: Bank of Canada Review,* various issues.)

rate, which measures the external value of the dollar, and the *balance of payments,* which records all transactions between Canada and the rest of the world.

The Exchange Rate

If you are going on a holiday to France, you will need French francs to pay for your purchases. Many of the larger banks, as well as any foreign exchange office, will make the necessary exchange of currencies for you; they will sell you francs in return for your Canadian dollars. If you get 4 francs for each dollar that you give up, the two currencies are trading at a rate of 1 dollar = 4 francs or, expressed another way, 1 franc = 0.25 dollar.

As our example shows, the exchange rate can be defined either as dollars per franc or francs per dollar. In this book we adopt the convention of defining the **exchange rate** between the Canadian dollar and any foreign currency as the number of Canadian dollars required to purchase one unit of foreign currency. For example, on October 4, 1995, 1 Canadian dollar was worth 3.6873 French francs; expressed the other way, 1 French franc was worth 0.2712 Canadian dollars. The exchange rate on that day was therefore equal to 0.2712, telling us that it took just over 27 Canadian cents to purchase one French franc.

The exchange rate is the number of Canadian dollars required to purchase one unit of foreign currency.[6]

The term **foreign exchange** refers to foreign currencies or claims to foreign currencies, such as bank deposits, cheques, and promissory notes, that are payable in foreign money. The **foreign exchange market** is the market where foreign exchange is traded—at a price expressed by the exchange rate.

Internal Versus External Value of the Dollar

The value of the dollar can be looked at in two ways. The **internal value of the dollar** refers to its power to purchase goods in domestic markets. We have already seen that the internal value of the dollar is reflected by the price level—specifically, increases in the price level reduce the internal value of the dollar (and decreases in the price level increase the internal value of the dollar).

The **external value of the dollar** refers to its power to purchase foreign currencies. This is reflected by the exchange rate. A rise in the exchange rate means that it takes *more* Canadian dollars to purchase one unit of foreign currency—this is a *reduction* in the external value of the dollar and is referred to as a **depreciation** of the Canadian dollar. Conversely, a fall in the exchange rate means that it takes *fewer* Canadian dollars to purchase one unit of foreign currency—this is an *increase* in the external

value of the dollar and is referred to as an **appreciation** of the dollar.

A rise in the exchange rate reflects a depreciation of the Canadian dollar; a fall in the exchange rate reflects an appreciation of the Canadian dollar.

Understanding exchange rates, appreciations, depreciations, and changes in the external value of the dollar is difficult. (Many students appear to have difficulties even after studying economics for three years!) But it is important to get these concepts straight in your mind. Extension 21-4 presents the basic definitions and interpretations one more time, and uses the example of the Canadian-U.S. exchange rate.

Figure 21-8 shows two measures of the Canadian exchange rate for the period since 1970. The first is the Canadian-dollar price of one U.S. dollar; the second is an index of the weighted-average Canadian-dollar price of the currencies of a group of major industrial countries, called the G10. Since the United States is Canada's largest trading partner, the U.S. dollar gets a large weight in this index, and so the two series move closely together.

For the first half of the 1970s, the external value of the Canadian dollar was relatively stable, fluctuating only modestly and showing no clear trend. From 1976 through 1986, however, the Canadian dollar depreciated sharply, by roughly 40 percent over that ten-year period. This depreciation in the Canadian dollar is reflected by a rise in the exchange rate. During this period, therefore, the external value of the Canadian dollar was *falling*. From 1986 through the early 1990s, the Canadian dollar appreciated, shown as a reduction in both measures of the exchange rate. During this period, the external value of the Canadian dollar was *rising*. By 1992, the external value of the Canadian dollar had returned approximately to where it was in 1980.

The substantial appreciation of the Canadian dollar between 1986 and 1992 was a major point of controversy in Canada. John Crow, then Governor of the Bank of Canada, argued that the strengthening of the Canadian dollar was a necessary part of the economy's adjustment in the fight against inflation; others, notably those involved in Canada's export sectors, argued that the dollar's appreciation was a substantial cause of declining Canadian competitiveness in international markets. This important debate will be explored in more detail in Chapter 38, when we examine the nature of macroeconomic policy in an open economy.

---

[6]Some economists use a reverse definition of the exchange rate—the number of units of foreign currency that can be purchased by one Canadian dollar. It is up to the student, then, to examine carefully the definition that is being used by a particular writer or speaker. We define the exchange rate as the number of Canadian dollars required to purchase one unit of foreign currency because this measure emphasizes that foreign currency, like any other good or service, has a price. In this case, the price has a special name—the exchange rate.

EXTENSION 21-4

THE EXCHANGE RATE AND THE EXTERNAL VALUE OF THE CANADIAN DOLLAR

To illustrate these important relations, we concentrate on the rates that are most familiar to all of us, those between the Canadian dollar and the U.S. dollar. Recall once again the critical definitions.

The exchange rate is the number of Canadian dollars required to buy one U.S. dollar. The external value of the Canadian dollar is its power to purchase U.S. currency.

Thus a rise in the Canada-U.S. exchange rate is a *reduction* in the external value of the Canadian dollar. A fall in the exchange rate is an *increase* in the external value of the Canadian dollar.

Consider an example. Suppose you are told that the cost of one U.S. dollar is 1.32 Canadian dollars. In this case, the exchange rate is 1.32. But what is the external value of the Canadian dollar? What we know is

$$1 \text{ U.S. dollar} = 1.32 \text{ Canadian dollars}$$

Dividing through by 1.32 tells us that

$$\frac{1 \text{ U.S. dollar}}{1.32} = 1 \text{ Canadian dollar}$$

which, doing the division, is

$$0.758 \text{ U.S. dollar} = 1 \text{ Canadian dollar, or}$$

$$75.8 \text{ U.S. cents} = 1 \text{ Canadian dollar}$$

This shows that the exchange rate and the external value of the currency are the reciprocals of each other. It follows that they move in opposite directions. Thus when the exchange rate rises, the external value of the Canadian dollar falls—this is called a *depreciation* of the Canadian dollar. Conversely, when the exchange rate falls, the external value of the Canadian dollar rises—this is called an *appreciation* of the Canadian dollar.

Now suppose you go into your bank to discover that the exchange rate has increased to 1.36. This tells you that you now have to pay 1.36 Canadian dollars for each U.S. dollar you buy. It is clear that the Canadian dollar is now less valuable, since you have to pay more of them to buy each U.S. dollar. To see this, calculate the external value of the Canadian dollar as 1/1.36 = 0.735. So one Canadian dollar is now worth only 73.5 U.S. cents.

It may sound confusing that a fall in the external value of the Canadian dollar is shown by a rise in the exchange rate, while a rise in the external value of the Canadian dollar is shown by a fall in the exchange rate. This, however, is no more confusing than the definition of the *internal* value of the dollar. Recall that when all Canadian prices go up, the internal value of the Canadian dollar goes down (and when all prices fall, the internal value of the Canadian dollar rises).

All you need to remember is that the exchange rate tells us how many Canadian dollars are needed to buy one U.S. dollar, and the higher that number, the less each Canadian dollar is worth.

The Balance of Payments

To know what is happening to the course of international trade and international capital movements, governments keep an account of the transactions among countries. These accounts are called the **balance-of-payments accounts.** They record all international payments that are made for the buying and selling of both goods and services, as well as financial assets such as as stocks and bonds.

Figure 21-9 shows one part of the balance of payments that is most often at the centre of controversy—the balance of trade.[7] This balance, also called net exports, is the difference between the value of Canadian exports and the value of Canadian imports. As we can see from Figure 21-9, Canadian ex-

---

[7]The trade balance that one hears about on the evening news is often the *merchandise* trade balance, which counts only trade in tangible goods, but excludes trade in services such as engineering or legal services. There is no economic rationale for treating goods differently from services, and in this book, unless otherwise specified, when we refer to the balance of trade we mean the balance on both goods and services.

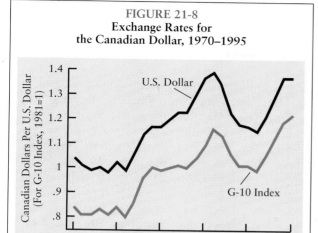

FIGURE 21-8
**Exchange Rates for
the Canadian Dollar, 1970–1995**

The exchange rate rose—the Canadian dollar depreciated—steadily from the mid 1970s through the mid 1980s. From 1986 to 1992, the Canadian dollar appreciated; since 1992, the dollar has been depreciating. The black line shows the Canada-U.S. exchange rate, defined as the Canadian-dollar price of one U.S. dollar. The coloured line shows the Canadian dollar exchange rate in terms of ten major industrialized countries. It is expressed as an index, with the 1981 value set equal to 100. Since the United States is Canada's largest trading partner, the two exchange rates move closely together.

(*Source:* Department of Finance, *Economic Reference Tables*, August 1995.)

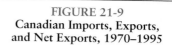

FIGURE 21-9
**Canadian Imports, Exports,
and Net Exports, 1970–1995**

Though imports and exports have increased dramatically over the past 25 years, the trade balance has remained roughly in balance. The nominal values of imports and exports rose steadily over the past few decades, due to price increases and quantity increases. The sharp recession that Canada experienced in the early 1980s was accompanied by a reduction in imports; the subsequent recovery was spurred in part by a sharp increase in exports. Thus the trade balance moved into a surplus position in the early and mid 1980s. The trade balance moved to a deficit position in the early 1990s, due to a sharp reduction in exports caused in part by a significant recession in the United States.

(*Source:* Department of Finance, *Economic Reference Tables*, August 1995.)

ports and imports have increased fairly closely in step with each other over the past twenty-five years. The trade balance has thus had mild fluctuations over the years, but has stayed at or near a roughly balanced position.

As we shall see in later chapters, a negative balance of trade (imports exceeding exports), which is also called a *trade deficit*, is not necessarily undesirable. Nor is a *trade surplus* necessarily desirable. But the long-discredited doctrine of *merchantilism* (which we examine in Chapter 37) which holds that trade surpluses are desirable still has some supporters. During the 1980s, for example, many U.S. commentators expressed the fear that the large U.S. trade deficit—especially the large *bilateral* deficits with Canada and Japan—was undesirable, and reflected a reduction in the ability of U.S. industry to compete against stiffening foreign competition. Others argued that there was nothing in principle undesirable about

the U.S. trade deficit, and that its underlying cause was the large U.S. government budget deficit that existed throughout the 1980s.

In Part 11 of this textbook, we explore in detail the reasons for international trade and the benefits that trade brings. At that time, we will be better able to interpret the data shown in Figure 21-9.

TRENDS VERSUS CYCLES

Our study of macroeconomics will enable us to understand how and why the price level, national income, employment, and the exchange rate change over time. In undertaking that study, we will find it useful to emphasize a distinction that has been made repeatedly in this chapter—the distinction between *cycles* and *trends*. Both are crucial to understanding the economy and evaluating its ability to provide goods, services, and opportunities.

TRENDS

The study of economic trends is the study of the economy over extended periods of time. Here we are concerned primarily with understanding the sources of long-term growth and the development of public policies that affect economic growth. Recent economic history has made the study of trends especially important. From the end of World War II until the late 1960s, output per hour of work in Canada grew at a rate of about 4 percent per year. Since 1973, it has grown at a rate of about 1.05 percent per year. The rate for the 1980s was slightly lower, the 1990s somewhat higher. These differences matter: With productivity growing at 3 percent per year, living standards double in 23 years. At an annual growth of 1.05 percent per year, living standards double in 66 years. The trend in productivity and the trend in potential GDP that is determined by productivity growth and population growth are the key objects of study for the long term.

In studying long-term trends, we will simplify our task by ignoring deviations from trend.

For trend analysis, this simplification does not cost us much because over the long haul, actual GDP moves quite closely with potential GDP. And over long time periods, we are most interested in the evolution of the economy's capacity (that is, its potential).

CYCLES

Although trends greatly affect economic welfare over the long haul, at any given time what matters more is how the economy is doing relative to its *current* potential. To examine this, we study business cycles, shorter-term fluctuations away from trend growth. These fluctuations are important: When the economy is operating below its potential, there is generally unemployment, with its accompanying human suffering and economic waste. When the economy is operating above its potential, there are threats of inflation, with its accompanying economic distortions and, as we shall see, policy problems.

Changes in productivity and in the labour force dominate the long-term trends of output and employment, but productivity and the labour force generally change only slowly.

Our study of short-term movements in the economy is simplified by treating the labour force and productivity (and thus potential income) as constant.

Under these assumptions, a rise in output generally means a rise in employment and a fall in unemployment: Output is positively associated with employment and negatively associated with unemployment. Taking productivity and the labour force as constant not only greatly simplifies our discussion but also reasonably approximates reality when we are dealing with the short-term behaviour

---

SUMMARY

A. MAJOR MACROECONOMIC ISSUES

- Macroeconomics examines the behaviour of such broad aggregates and averages as the price level, national income, potential national income, the output or GDP gap, employment, unemployment, the exchange rate, and the balance of payments.
- The most important macroeconomic issues can be divided into two broad categories—the causes of long-term economic growth, and the size and sources of short-term business cycles. Broad government policies,

such as monetary policy and fiscal policy, typically make an appearance in both discussions.

B. KEY MACROECONOMIC PHENOMENA

- The value of the total production of goods and services in a nation is called its national product. Because production of output generates income in the form of claims on that output, the total is also referred to as national income. One of the most commonly used measures of national income is gross domestic product (GDP).

- Nominal national income evaluates output in current prices. Real national income evaluates output in constant base-period prices. Changes in real national income reflect changes in quantities of output produced.
- Potential real national income measures the capacity of the economy to produce goods and services when factors of production are employed at their normal intensity of use. The GDP gap is the difference between actual and potential national income.
- Fluctuations of national income around its potential level are associated with the business cycle. Recoveries pass through peaks and turn into recessions, which in turn pass through troughs to become recoveries. Although these movements are systematic rather than random, they are by no means predictably regular.
- The unemployment rate is the percentage of the labour force not employed but actively searching for a job. The labour force and employment have both grown steadily for the past half century. The unemployment rate fluctuates considerably from year to year. Unemployment imposes serious costs on the economy in the form of economic waste and human suffering.
- The average price level is measured by a price index, which measures the cost of a set of goods in one year relative to their cost in an (arbitrary) base year. The price level has displayed a continual upward trend since 1930. The inflation rate measures the rate of change of the price level. Although it fluctuates considerably, the inflation rate has been consistently positive.
- Nominal and real interest rates are also important macroeconomic variables. The interest rate is the price that is paid to borrow money for a stated period and is expressed as a percentage amount per dollar borrowed. The nominal interest rate is this price expressed in money terms; the real interest rate is this price expressed in terms of goods or purchasing power.
- The exchange rate is the number of Canadian dollars needed to purchase one unit of foreign currency. A rise in the exchange rate is a reduction in the external value of the Canadian dollar. The balance of payments is a record of all international transactions made by Canadian firms, households, and governments.

C. TRENDS VERSUS CYCLES

- The dominant historical trends of the economy are growth of the price level, real output, and employment over the long term. This growth has never been entirely smooth; there have always been fluctuations in the price level, output, and unemployment around their trend growth rates. The study of growth is simplified by ignoring these fluctuations and focusing on the broad trends.
- The study of the fluctuations is simplified by assuming that the labour force, productivity, and productive capacity (that is, potential income) do not change during the period being analyzed.

KEY CONCEPTS

National product and national income
Real and nominal national income
Potential and actual national income
The output gap
Employment, unemployment, and the labour force

Full employment
Frictional, structural, and cyclical unemployment
The price level and the rate of inflation
The effects of anticipated and unanticipated inflation

Real and nominal interest rates
The exchange rate
Depreciation and appreciation of the Canadian dollar
The balance of payments
Cycles and trends

DISCUSSION QUESTIONS

1. Classify as microeconomic or macroeconomic (or both) the issues that are raised in the following newspaper headlines.

    a. "Lettuce crop spoils as strike hits B.C. lettuce producers"

    b. "Analysts fear rekindling of inflation as economy recovers toward full employment"

    c. "Index of industrial production falls by 4 points"

    d. "Price of bus rides soars in Centresville as city council withdraws transport subsidy"

e. "Fall in the unemployment rate signals beginning of the end of the recession in the Edmonton area"

f. "New computer technology brings falling prices and growing sales of microcomputers"

g. "Rising costs of imported raw materials cause most Canadian manufacturers to raise prices"

2. Explain carefully what has happened to the CPI to justify each of the following newspaper headlines.

a. "Prices on the rise again after a year of stability"

b. "Inflation increases for three successive months"

c. "Finance Minister pleased at moderation in inflation rate"

d. "Cost-of-living increases devastating pensioners"

e. "Union leader warns that inflation is stabilizing at a disturbingly high level"

3. A leading financial newspaper ran the following headline in 1995: "Stocks Sink Amid Signs of Slow Growth in Economy, New Inflation; Dollar Weak." Must rising inflation, a weaker dollar, and slow growth necessarily represent bad news to all market participants? Can you think of situations where any of these events would be welcomed by some people?

4. It is common knowledge that the unemployment rate varies greatly from country to country. Even between democracies there are sometimes vast differences in the unemployment rates. Can you suggest some reasons for these sometimes wide discrepancies?

5. Most of the films on the list of the 10 largest all-time moneymakers are of recent vintage. Does this mean that the most successful films are the most recent ones?

6. Evaluate the following statements about unemployment.

a. "Unemployment is a personal tragedy and a national waste."

b. "No one needs to be unemployed these days; just look at the Help Wanted ads in the newspapers and the signs in the stores."

c. "Unemployment insurance is a boondoggle for the lazy and unnecessary for the industrious."

7. How could you make a sure profit in a year in which the interest rate was 10 percent and you *knew* that the inflation rate was going to be 15 percent?

8. Use a recent edition of the *Bank of Canada Review* to discover the real interest rate in the latest year for which figures are available.

9. A friend's grandmother has government bonds as her only means of support. Explain to her why she cannot regard all of the interest that she receives as current income. (Hint: What will happen to her ability to purchase real goods and services each year if she does treat all of her interest receipts as current income and spends all of it each year?)

10. If you thought that the inflation rate was going to be 10 percent next year, why should you be unwilling to lend money at 5 percent interest? Say that 5 percent was all you could get and you had money that you did not want to spend for a year. Would you do better just to hold the money? What could you do that would be better than lending your money at 5 percent?

11. Consider a 10-year period over which output per worker falls, but per capita GDP increases. How can this happen?

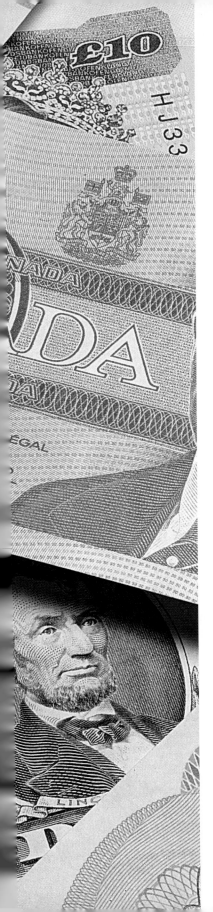

CHAPTER 22

THE MEASUREMENT OF NATIONAL INCOME AND PRODUCT

To understand the macroeconomic events that were outlined in Chapter 21, we need to look in some detail at the measurement and interpretation of variables relating to national output and national income. Indeed, this is a general rule of all economics and all science: Before using any data, it is essential to understand how those data are developed and what they measure.

NATIONAL OUTPUT AND VALUE ADDED

The central topic of macroeconomics is the overall level of economic activity—output and the income that is generated by its production. We start by asking what we mean by output.

It may seem strange to ask what we mean by output. Surely the town bakery knows what it produces, and if General Motors does not know its own output, what does it know? If each firm knows the value of its total output, the national income statisticians simply have to add up each separate output value to get the nation's output—or is that really all?

The reason that obtaining a total for the nation's output is not quite that simple is that one firm's output is often another firm's input. The local baker uses flour that is the output of the flour milling company, and the flour milling company, in turn, uses wheat that is the farmer's output. What is true for bread is true for most commodities.

Production occurs in stages: Some firms produce outputs that are used as inputs by other firms, and these other firms in turn produce outputs that are used as inputs by yet other firms.

If we merely added up the market values of all outputs of all firms, we would obtain a total greatly in excess of the value of the economy's actual output.

Consider the baker as an example. If we added the total value of the sales of the wheat farmer, the flour mill, and the baker, we would be counting the value of the wheat three times, the value of the milled flour twice, and the value of the bread once.

The error that would arise in estimating the nation's output by adding all sales of all firms is called **double counting.** "Multiple counting" would be a better term because if we added up the values of all sales, the same output would be counted every time that it was sold by one firm to another.

The problem of double counting could in principle be solved by distinguishing between two types of output. **Intermediate products** are outputs of some firms that are used as inputs by other firms. **Final goods** are products that are not used as inputs by other firms, at least not in the period of time under consideration. The term **final demand** refers to the purchase of final goods for consumption, for investment (including inventory accumulation), for use by governments, and for export.

If the sales of firms could be readily disaggregated into sales for final demand and sales for further processing by other firms, measuring total output would be straightforward. It would equal the value of all final goods produced by firms, excluding all intermediate products. However, when Stelco sells steel to the Ford Motor Company, it does not care, and usually does not know, whether the steel is for final use (say, construction of a warehouse that will not be sold by Ford) or for use as part of an automobile that will be sold again. Even in our earlier example of bread, a bakery cannot be sure that its sales are for final use, for the bread may be further "processed" by a restaurant prior to its final sale to a customer. In general, it is extremely difficult if not impossible to successfully distinguish final from intermediate goods. The problem of double counting must therefore be resolved in some other manner.

To avoid double counting, statisticians use the important concept of **value added.** Each firm's value added is the value of its output minus the value of the inputs that it purchases from other firms (and which were in turn the outputs of those other firms). Thus a steel mill's value added is the value of the steel it produces minus the value of the ore that it buys from the mining company, the value of the electricity and fuel oil that it uses, and the values of all other inputs that it buys from other firms. A bakery's value added is the value of the baking products that it produces minus the value of the flour and other inputs that it buys from other firms.

Note that a firm's value added equals the value of output minus the value of *inputs purchased from other firms.* Payments to factors of production, such as labour income or profits, are not purchases from other firms, and hence are not subtracted from the value of output when computing value added. Indeed, since the total value of output is simply the sum of materials inputs plus payments to factors of production, value added is exactly equal to the sum of factor payments.[1]

Value added avoids the statistical problem of double counting; it is the correct measure of each firm's contribution to total output, the amount of market value that is produced by that firm.

---

[1]We are ignoring here the role of indirect taxes, such as provincial sales taxes or the Goods and Services Tax (GST). Such taxes are included in the market value of a firm's output, but these taxes are remitted to the government and do not represent a payment to a factor of production.

EXTENSION 22-1

VALUE ADDED THROUGH STAGES OF PRODUCTION

Because the output of one firm often becomes the input of other firms, the total value of goods sold by all firms greatly exceeds the value of the output of final products. This general principle is illustrated by a simple example in which firm R starts from scratch and produces goods (raw materials) valued at $100; the firm's value added is $100. Firm I purchases raw materials valued at $100 and produces semimanufactured goods that it sells for $130. Its value added is $30, because the value of the goods is increased by $30 as a result of the firm's activities. Firm F purchases the semi-manufactured (intermediate) goods for $130, works them into a finished state, and sells the final products for $180. Firm F's value added is $50. The value of the final goods, $180, is found either by counting only the sales of firm F or by taking the sum of the values added by each firm. This value is much smaller than the $410 that we would obtain if we merely added up the market value of the commodities sold by each firm.

Transactions at Three Different Stages of Production

	Firm R	Firm I	Firm F	All firms	
A. Purchases from other firms	$ 0	$100	$130	$230	Total interfirm sales
B. Purchases of factors of production (wages, rent, interest, profits)	100	30	50	180	Total value added
A + B = value of product	$100	$130	$180	$410	Total value of all sales

The firm's value added is the *net value* of its output. It is this net value that is the firm's true contribution to the nation's total output, representing the firm's own efforts that add to the value of what it takes in as inputs. The concept of value added is further illustrated in Extension 22-1. In this simple example, as in all more complex cases, the value of the nation's total output is obtained by summing all the individual values added.

The sum of all values added in an economy is a measure of the economy's total output. This measure of total output is called *gross domestic product (GDP)*. It is a measure of all final output that is produced by all productive activity in the economy.

NATIONAL INCOME ACCOUNTING: THE BASICS

The measures of national income and national product that are used in Canada derive from an accounting system called the National Income and Expenditure Accounts (NIEA). The accounts, produced by Statistics Canada, provide us with a framework for analyzing the generation of national income. The National Income and Expenditure Accounts are not simply collections of economic data. They have a logical structure, based on the simple yet important idea that whenever money is spent on national product, it generates an equivalent amount of national income.

Look again at Figure 21-1 which shows the circular flow of expenditure and income. The right half of the figure focuses on expenditure to purchase the nation's output in product markets, and the left half focuses on factor markets through which the receipts of producers are distributed to factors of production.

The circular flow of income suggests three different ways of measuring national income. The first is simply to add up the value of all goods and services produced in the economy. This requires the concept of value added, which we discussed in the previous section. The remaining two approaches correspond to the two halves of the circular flow of income. One approach is to add up the total flow of expenditure on domestic output; the other is to add up the total flow of income generated by the flow of domestic production. All three measures yield the same total, which is called **gross domestic product (GDP)**. When it is calculated by adding up the total value added in the economy, it is called *GDP by value added*. When it is calculated by adding up total expenditure for each of the main components of final output, the result is called *GDP on the expenditure side*. When it is calculated by adding up all the incomes generated by the act of production, it is called *GDP on the income side*.

The conventions of double-entry bookkeeping require that all value produced must be accounted for by a claim that someone has to that value. Thus the two values calculated from the income and the expenditure sides are identical conceptually and differ in practice only because of errors of measurement. Any discrepancy arising from such errors is then reconciled so that one common total is given as *the* measure of GDP. Both calculations are of interest, however, because each gives a different and useful breakdown. Also, having two independent ways of measuring the same quantity, in this case the sum of values added in the economy, provides a useful check on statistical procedures and on unavoidable errors in measurement.

GDP FROM THE EXPENDITURE SIDE

GDP for a given year is calculated from the expenditure side by adding up the expenditures *needed to purchase* the final output produced in that year. Total expenditure on final output is the sum of four broad categories of expenditure: consumption, investment, government, and net exports. In the following chapters, we will discuss in considerable detail the causes and consequences of movements in each of these four expenditure categories. Here we define what they are and how they are measured. Throughout, it is important to remember that these four categories of expenditure are exhaustive—they are *defined* in such a way that all expenditure on final output falls into one of the four categories.

Consumption Expenditure

Consumption expenditure includes expenditure on all goods and services produced and sold to their final users during the year. It includes services, such as haircuts, dental care, and legal advice; non-

durable goods, such as fresh vegetables, clothing, cut flowers, and fresh meat; and durable goods, such as cars, television sets, and air conditioners. We denote actual measured consumption expenditure by the symbol C_a.

Investment Expenditure

Investment expenditure is expenditure on the production of goods not for present consumption, including inventories, capital goods such as factories, machines and warehouses, and residential housing. Such goods are called **investment goods.**

Inventories. Almost all firms hold stocks of their inputs and their own outputs. These stocks are called **inventories.** Inventories of inputs and unfinished materials allow firms to maintain a steady stream of production despite short-term fluctuations in the deliveries of inputs bought from other firms. Inventories of outputs allow firms to meet orders despite temporary fluctuations in the rate of production or sales.

Inventories are an investment by the firm, since the firm has paid for the goods but has not sold them yet. An accumulation of inventories counts as current investment because it represents goods produced but not used for current consumption. The drawing down of inventories, often called *decumulation,* counts as disinvestment because it represents a reduction in the stock of finished goods that are available to be sold.

Additions to inventories are a part of the economy's production of investment goods. These goods are included in the national income accounts at market value, which includes the wages and other costs that the firm incurred in producing them and the profit that the firm will make when they are sold. Thus in the case of inventories of a firm's own output, the expenditure approach measures what will have to be spent to purchase the inventories when they are sold rather than what has so far been spent to produce them.

Plant and Equipment. All production of goods and services uses capital goods, which are manufactured aids to production, such as tools, machines, and factory buildings. The economy's total quantity of capital goods is called the **capital stock.** Creating new capital goods is an act of investment and is called *business fixed investment*, often shortened to **fixed investment.**

Residential Investment. A house or an apartment building is a durable asset that yields its utility over a long period of time. This meets the definition of investment that we gave earlier, so housing construction—the building of a *new* house—is counted as investment expenditure rather than as consumption expenditure. However, when a household purchases a house from a builder or from another household, an existing asset is simply transferred, and the transaction is not part of national income. Only when a new house is built does it appear as residential investment in the national accounts.

Gross and Net Investment. The total investment that occurs in the economy is called **gross investment.** Gross investment is divided into two parts: replacement investment and net investment. **Replacement investment** is the amount of investment that just maintains the level of existing capital stock; it is called the **capital consumption allowance** or simply **depreciation.** Gross investment minus replacement investment is **net investment.** Positive net investment increases the economy's total stock of capital, whereas replacement investment simply keeps the existing stock intact by replacing what has been used up.

All of gross investment is included in the calculation of national income. This is because all investment goods are part of the nation's total current output, and their production creates income whether the goods produced are a part of net investment or are merely replacement investment. Actual total investment expenditure is denoted by the symbol I_a.

Government Purchases of Goods and Services

When governments provide goods and services that households want, such as highways and air-traffic control, it is clear that they are adding to the sum total of valuable output in the same way as do private firms that produce trucks and airplanes that use the highways and air lanes. With other government activities, the case may not seem so clear. Should expenditures by the federal government to send peacekeepers overseas, or to pay a civil servant to refile papers from a now-defunct department, be regarded as contributions to national income?

National income statisticians do not speculate about such matters. Instead they include all **government purchases** of goods and services as part of national income. (Government expenditure on investment goods is included as government purchases rather than investment expenditure.) Just as the national product includes the outputs of both gin and Bibles, it also includes coast-guard ships and the up-keep of parks, along with the services of RCMP officers and members of parliament. Actual government purchases of goods and services is denoted G_a.

Cost Versus Market Value. Government output is typically valued at cost rather than at market value. In many cases, there is really no choice. What, for example, is the market value of the services of a court of law? No one knows. We do know, however, what it costs the government to provide these services, so we value them at their cost of production.

Although valuing at cost is the only possible way to measure many government activities, it does have one curious consequence. If due to an increase in productivity, one civil servant now does what two used to do and the displaced worker shifts to the private sector, the government's contribution to national income will register a decline. Conversely, if two workers now do what one worker used to do, the government's contribution will rise. Both changes could occur even though what the government actually does has not changed. This is an inevitable but curious consequence of measuring the value of the government's output by the cost of the factors, mainly labour, that are used to produce it.

Government Purchases Versus Government Expenditure. It is important to recognize that only government *purchases* of currently produced goods and services are included as part of GDP. A great deal of government expenditure does *not* count as part of GDP. For example, when the government makes payments to a retired person through the Canada Pension Plan, it is not purchasing any currently produced goods or services from the retiree. The payment itself does not add to total output. The same is true of payments for unemployment insurance, welfare, and interest on the national debt (which transfers income from taxpayers to holders of government bonds). All these are examples of **transfer payments,** which are government expenditures that are not made in return for currently produced goods and services. They are not a part of expenditure on the nation's total output and are therefore not included in GDP.[2]

---

[2] Of course, the recipients of transfer payments often choose to spend their money on consumption. Such expenditure then counts as consumption, and thus as part of GDP, in the same way as any other consumption expenditure.

Hence when we refer to government purchases as part of national income (using the symbol G_a) we include all government purchases of currently produced goods and services, and we *exclude* all government transfer payments.

Net Exports

The fourth category of aggregate expenditure arises from foreign trade. How do imports and exports influence national income? **Imports** are domestic expenditure on foreign-produced goods and services, whereas **exports** are foreign expenditure on domestically produced goods and services.

Imports.   A country's national income is the total value of final commodities produced in that country. If you buy a car that was made in Japan, only a small part of that value will represent expenditure on Canadian production. Some of it represents payment for the services of the Canadian dealers and for transportation; the rest is the output of Japanese firms and expenditure on Japanese products. If you take your next vacation in Italy, much of your expenditure will be on goods and services produced in Italy and thus will contribute to Italian GDP rather than to Canadian GDP.

Similarly, when a Canadian firm makes an investment expenditure on a U.S.-produced machine tool that was made partly with imported raw materials, only part of the expenditure is on Canadian production; the rest is expenditure on production by the countries that are supplying the raw materials. The same is true for government expenditure on such things as roads and dams; some of the expenditure is for imported materials, and only part of it is for domestically produced goods and services.

Consumption, investment, and government expenditures all have an import content. To arrive at total expenditure on Canadian products, we need to subtract from total Canadian expenditure any expenditure on imports, which is given the symbol IM_a.

Exports.   If Canadian firms sell goods to German households, the goods are a part of German consumption expenditure but also constitute expenditure on Canadian output. Indeed, all goods and services that are produced in Canada and sold to foreigners must be counted as part of Canadian production and income; they are produced in Canada, and they create incomes for the Canadian residents who produce them. They are not purchased by Canadian residents, however, so they are not included as part

TABLE 22-1
Components of GDP from the Expenditure Side, 1994

Category	Billions of Dollars	Percent of GDP
Consumption	$ 452.9	60.4
Government purchases	150.8	20.1
Investment	142.0	18.9
Net exports	5.6	0.7
Statistical discrepancy	−1.2	−0.2
Total	750.1	100.0

GDP measured from the expenditure side of the national accounts gives the size of the major components of aggregate expenditure. Consumption was by far the largest expenditure category, equal to almost two-thirds of GDP. In 1994, as in most years for Canada, net exports were positive. (*Source:* Statistics Canada, *National Income and Expenditure Accounts*, 13–001.)

of C_a, I_a, or G_a. Therefore, to arrive at the total value of expenditure on Canadian domestic product, it is necessary to add in the value of Canadian exports of goods and services. Actual exports are denoted X_a.

It is customary to group actual imports and actual exports together as **net exports.** Net exports are defined as total exports minus total imports ($X_a − IM_a$), which we will also denote NX_a. When the value of Canadian exports exceeds the value of Canadian imports, the net export term is positive. When the value of imports exceeds the value of exports, the net export term is negative.

Total Expenditures

Gross domestic product measured from the expenditure side is equal to the sum of the four expenditure categories that we have just discussed. In terms of a simple equation, we have

$$GDP = C_a + I_a + G_a + (X_a − IM_a)$$

GDP, calculated from the expenditure side, is the sum of consumption, investment, government, and net export expenditures.

These data are shown in Table 22-1 for Canada in 1994.

GDP FROM THE INCOME SIDE

The production of a nation's output generates income. Labour must be employed, land must be rented, and capital must be used. The calculation of GDP from the income side involves adding up factor incomes and other claims on the value of output until all of that value is accounted for. We have already noted that because all value produced must be owned by someone, the value of production must equal the value of income claims generated by that production.

Factor Payments

National income accountants distinguish four main components of factor incomes: wages, rent, interest, and profits.[3]

Wages.   Wages and salaries (which national income accountants call *compensation to employees* but which are usually just called *wages*) are the payment for the services of labour. Wages include take-home pay, taxes withheld, unemployment insurance contributions, pension fund contributions, and other fringe benefits. In total, wages represent the part of the value of production that is attributable to labour.

Rent.   Rent is the payment for the services of land and other factors that are rented. For the purposes of national income accounting, homeowners are viewed as renting accommodations from themselves. The amount of rent in the GDP thus includes payments for rented housing plus "imputed rent" for the use of owner-occupied housing. This allows national income measures to reflect the value of all housing services used in the current accounting period, whether or not the housing is owned by its user.

Interest.   Interest includes interest that is earned on bank deposits, interest that is earned on loans to firms, and miscellaneous other investment income (but excludes interest income generated from loans to Canadian governments).

Profits.   Some profits are paid out as **dividends** to owners of firms; the rest are retained for use by firms. The former are called *distributed profits,* and the latter are called *undistributed profits* or *retained earnings.* Both distributed and undistributed profits are included in the calculation of GDP. For accounting purposes, total profits are reported in two separate categories—corporate profits and incomes of unincorporated businesses (mainly small businesses, farmers, partnerships, and professionals).

Profits and interest together represent the payment for the use of capital—interest for borrowed capital and profits for capital contributed by the owners of firms.

Nonfactor Payments

Some payments for goods and services do not create direct claims by factors of production. Put another way, every time a consumer spends $10 on some item, it is typically the case that less than $10 is generated as income for factors of production. This is because of indirect taxes and depreciation.

Indirect Taxes.   An important claim on the market value of output arises out of indirect taxes, which are taxes on the production and sale of goods and services. In Canada, the most important indirect taxes are provincial retail sales taxes which differ across provinces, and the federal Goods and Services Tax (GST) which is uniform across all provinces.

For example, if a good's market price of $10.00 includes 50 cents in sales taxes, only $9.50 is available as income to factors of production. Fifty cents worth of market value represents some government's claim on that value. When adding up income claims to determine GDP, it is therefore necessary to include the portion of the total market value of output that is the government's claim exercised through its taxes on goods and services.

Subsidies.   It is also necessary to subtract government subsidies on goods and services, since these payments allow incomes to *exceed* the market value of output. Suppose that a municipal bus company spends $150,000 producing bus rides and covers its costs by selling $140,000 in fares and obtaining a $10,000 subsidy from the local government. The total income that the company will generate from its production is $150,000, but the total market value of its output is only $140,000, with the difference made up by the subsidy. To get from total income to the market value of its total output, we must subtract the amount of the subsidy.

Net Domestic Product.   Adding indirect taxes to the four components of factor incomes and subtracting subsidies gives **net domestic product.** Taxes and subsidies are often combined into a single term, called *indirect taxes net of subsidies.*

---

[3]The concepts of wages, rent, interest, and profits that are used when measuring macroeconomic variables do not correspond exactly to the concepts with the same names that are used in microeconomics, but the details of the differences need not detain us.

Net domestic product equals the sum of wages, rent, interest, profits, and indirect taxes net of subsidies.

Depreciation. Another component on the income side arises from the distinction between net and gross investment. One claim on the value of final output is depreciation, or capital consumption allowance.

Depreciation is the value of capital that has been used up in the process of producing final output. It is part of gross profits, but because it is needed to compensate for capital used up in the process of production, it is not part of net profits. Hence depreciation is not income earned by any factor of production. Rather, it is value that must be reinvested just to maintain the existing stock of capital equipment.

Total Product

Adding depreciation to net domestic product gives *gross domestic product.*

From the income side, GDP is the sum of the factor incomes that are generated in the process of producing final output *plus* indirect taxes net of subsidies *plus* depreciation.

The various components of the income side of the GDP in the Canadian economy in 1994 are shown in Table 22-2. Note that one of the terms in the table (and in Table 22-1) is called *statistical discrepancy;* this is a "fudge factor" to make sure that the independent measures of income and product come to the same total. Statistical discrepancy is a clear indication that national income and product accounting is not an error-free science. Although national income and the value of national product are conceptually identical, in practice both are measured with error.

Extension 22-2 provides a further discussion of the way in which arbitrary classification decisions, inherent in any accounting scheme, affect measures of national income and national product.

NATIONAL INCOME ACCOUNTING: SOME EXTRA ISSUES

Now that we have examined the basics of national income accounting, we are ready to explore some

TABLE 22-2
Components of GDP from the Income Side, 1994

Category	Billions of Dollars	Percent of GDP
Wages, salaries and supplementary income	$ 410.3	54.7
Interest and miscellaneous investment income	56.4	7.5
Business income (including net income of farmers and unincorporated businesses)	95.6	12.8
Capital consumption allowance	93.0	12.4
Indirect taxes less subsidies	93.7	12.5
Statistical discrepancy	1.1	0.1
Total	750.1	100.0

GDP measured from the income side of the national accounts gives the size of the major components of the income that is generated by producing the nation's output. The largest category, equal to about 55 percent of income, is compensation to employees, which includes wages and salaries and other benefits. The capital consumption allowance (depreciation) is the part of the earnings of businesses that is needed to replace capital used up during the year. This amounts to over 10 percent of GDP. *(Source:* Statistics Canada, *National Income and Expenditure Accounts,* 13–001.)

more detailed issues. We discuss the distinction between GDP and the related concept of gross national product (GNP), the important difference between real and nominal GDP, and some simple measures for productivity.

GDP AND GNP

A measure of national output closely related to GDP is **gross national product (GNP).** The difference between GDP and GNP is the difference between *income produced* and *income received.* GDP measures the total output *produced in Canada* and the total income generated as a result of that production. GNP measures the total amount of income *received by Canadian residents,* no matter *where* that income was generated. How can GDP differ from GNP? GDP differs from GNP for two reasons.

First, some Canadian production creates factor income for foreigners. For example, the profit generated by the Toyota factory in Cambridge, Ontario is income generated from production in Canada (part of GDP). But some part of this profit is sent outside of Canada to the foreign shareholders of

EXTENSION 22-2

ARBITRARY DECISIONS IN NATIONAL INCOME ACCOUNTING

National income accounting practices contain many arbitrary decisions. Goods that are finished and held in inventories are valued at market value, thereby anticipating their sale, even though the actual sales price may not be known. In the case of a Ford in a dealer's showroom, this practice may be justified because the *value* of this Ford is perhaps virtually the same as that of an identical Ford that has just been sold to a customer. However, what is the correct market value of a half-finished house or an unfinished novel? Accountants arbitrarily treat goods in process at cost (rather than at market value) if the goods are being made by firms. They ignore completely the value of the novel in progress. The arbitrary nature of these decisions is inevitable: Because people must arrive at some practical compromise between consistent definitions and measurable magnitudes, any decision will be somewhat arbitrary.

The definition of final goods provides further examples. Business investment expenditures are treated as final products, as are all government purchases. However, intermediate goods purchased by businesses for further processing are not treated as final products. Hence when a firm buys a machine or a truck, the purchase is treated as a final good, but when it buys a ton of steel, the steel is treated as a raw material that will be used as an input into the firm's production process. If the steel sits in inventory, however, it is regarded as a business investment and thus *is* a final good.

Such arbitrary decisions surely affect the size of measured GDP. Does it matter? The surprising answer, for many purposes, is no. In any case, it is wrong to believe that just because a statistical measure falls short of perfection (as all statistical measures do), it is useless. Crude measures often give estimates to the right order of magnitude, and substantial improvements in sophistication may make only trivial improvements in these estimates.

In the third century, for example, the Alexandrian astronomer Eratosthenes measured the angle of the sun at Alexandria at the moment that it was directly overhead 800 km south at Aswan, and he used this angle to calculate the circumference of the earth to within 15 percent of the distance as measured today by the most advanced measuring devices. For the knowledge he wanted—the approximate size of the earth—his measurement was satisfactory, even though it would have been disastrously inadequate for launching a modern earth satellite.

Absolute figures mean something in general terms, although they cannot be taken seriously to the last dollar. In 1994, Canadian GDP was measured as $750.1 billion. It is certain that the market value of all production in Canada in that year was neither $100 billion nor $2,000 billion, but it might well have been $700 billion or $800 billion had different measures been defined with different arbitrary decisions built in.

International and intertemporal comparisons, though tricky, may be meaningful if they are based on measures that contain roughly the same arbitrary decisions. Canadian per capita GDP is about three times the Spanish per capita GDP and is a little less than U.S. per capita GDP. Other measures might differ, but it is unlikely that any measure would reveal the Spanish per capita GDP to be higher than Canada's, or Canada's to be significantly above that of the United States. Canadian real GDP has grown at about 4 percent per year (on average) since the end of the Second World War; it is unlikely that a different measure of output would indicate either a 2 percent or 10 percent growth rate.

Toyota, and this part of the profit is not part of GNP. (Note that the wages earned by the Canadian workers in the Cambridge plant count as both GDP and GNP.)

Second, many Canadian residents earn income as a result of foreign investments and factor services sold abroad. Income accruing to Canadian residents from activities undertaken abroad is part of GNP but is not part of GDP. For example, when Newbridge Networks, a high-tech communications firm based in Ottawa, earns profits from its production plant in Wales, those profits are returned to the Canadian owners of the firm. This represents income to Canadians (part of GNP) even though the production does not take place in Canada (not part of GDP).

The relative sizes of GDP and GNP depend primarily on the balance between income from Canadian investments abroad and income from foreign investments in Canada. For most of Canada's history, Canada has been a net debtor country. This means that the value of foreign-based assets owned by Canadian residents is less than the value of Canadian-based assets owned by foreigners. As a result, the foreign-generated income received by Canadian residents is less than the Canadian-generated income going to foreigners. This makes Canadian GNP less than Canadian GDP. In 1994, when Canadian GDP was equal to $750.1 billion, Canadian GNP was $723.8 billion—a difference of $26.3 billion, or 3.5 percent of GDP.

Which Measure Is Better?

In Canada, the gap between GDP and GNP has been roughly constant when expressed in percentage terms—that is, GNP has typically been slightly less than GDP by three or four percent. This simply reflects the fact that Canada is a net debtor country and thus in order to pay the Canadian-generated incomes to the foreign asset owners requires that some of the value of domestic production be remitted abroad.

GDP is superior to GNP as a measure of domestic economic activity. GNP is superior to GDP as a measure of the economic well-being of domestic residents.

If you want to know how easy it will be to find a job or whether factories are working double shifts or whether new buildings are going up right and left, look to changes in the GDP. By its definition, it is the GDP that tells us how much is being produced within a nation's borders. To know how much income is available to the residents of a country, however, one should look at the GNP, which counts income earned abroad and subtracts

out income produced at home that accrues to residents of other nations. Thus the GNP is a better measure of the economic welfare of a country's residents.

Disposable Personal Income

Both GDP and GNP are important measures of overall economic activity and of national income. Most important to consumers, however, is **disposable personal income,** the part of national income that is available to households to spend or to save. The easiest way to calculate disposable personal income is to subtract from GNP the parts of the GNP that are not available to households. Hence we must subtract capital consumption allowances, taxes net of subsidies, retained earnings, and interest paid to institutions. However, having subtracted taxes, we need to add back in transfer payments made to households. In 1994, disposable income was $497.4 billion, which represented 66 percent of GDP.

Disposable personal income is GNP minus any part of it that is not actually paid to households minus personal income taxes paid by households plus transfer payments received by households.

REAL AND NOMINAL MEASURES

In Chapter 21, we distinguished between real and nominal measures of national income and output. When we add up money values of outputs, expenditures, or incomes, we end up with what are called *nominal values.* Nominal GDP increased by 68.7 percent between 1984 and 1994. If we want to compare *real* GDP in 1994 to that in 1984, we need to determine how much of that 68.7 percent nominal increase was due to increases in prices and how much was due to increases in quantities produced. Although there are many possible ways of doing this, the underlying principle is always the same: The value of output, expenditure, and income in each period is computed using a common set of *constant base-period prices.* When this is done, real output, expenditure, or income is measured in *constant dollars.*

Total GDP that is valued at current prices is a nominal measure, often called *nominal national in-*

come. GDP that is valued at constant base-period prices is a real measure, referred to as *real national income.*

Any change in nominal GDP reflects the combined effects of changes in quantities and changes in prices. However, when real income is measured over different periods by using a common set of base-period prices, changes in real income reflect only changes in quantities.

The Implicit GDP Deflator

If nominal and real GDP change by different amounts over a given time period, then prices must have changed over that period. Comparing what has happened to nominal and real GDP over the same period implies the existence of a price index measuring the change in prices over that period. We say "implies" because no price index is used in calculating either real or nominal GDP. However, an index can be inferred by comparing these two values. Such an index is called an implicit price index or an implicit deflator. It is defined as follows:

Implicit GDP Deflator =

$$\frac{\text{GDP at current prices}}{\text{GDP at base-period prices}} \times 100$$

The **implicit GDP deflator** is the most comprehensive available index of the price level because it covers all the goods and services that are produced by the entire economy. Implicit deflators use the current year's bundle of production to compare the current year's prices with those prevailing in the base period. The GDP deflator was 31.7 percent higher in 1994 than in 1984. This means that in 1994, it cost 31.7 percent more to produce the goods and services than it would have cost to produce the same goods and services in 1984. Extension 22-3 illustrates the calculation of real and nominal GDP and an implicit deflator for a simple hypothetical economy that produces only wheat and steel.

As we said above, a change in nominal national income can be split into a change due to prices and a change due to quantities. For example, in 1994, Canadian nominal GDP was 68.7 percent higher than in 1984. This increase was due to a 31.7 percent increase in prices and a 28 percent increase in

real GDP.[4] Table 22-3 gives nominal and real income and the implicit deflator for selected years since 1950.

TOTAL OUTPUT, PER CAPITA OUTPUT, AND PRODUCTIVITY

The rise in real GDP during this century has had two main causes:

1. an increase in the amounts of land, labour, and capital used in production; and,

2. an increase in the amount of output produced *per unit of input.*

In other words, more inputs have been used, and each input has become more productive. Although it is useful to measure total output for some purposes, such as assessing the total size of a particular economy, for other purposes, such as studying changes in overall living standards, it is better to use output per person, which is called **per capita output.** Per capita GDP gives a measure of how much output there is on average for each person in the country.

An even better way of assessing overall living standards is to consider measures of *productivity.* For example, GDP divided by the number of *employed* persons tells us the average output per employed worker. This is one measure of *labour productivity.* GDP divided by the total number of hours worked measures output per hour of labour input and provides a second measure of labour productivity.

Until recently, it did not much matter whether we looked at changes in per capita output or

---

[4]For large percentage changes in price and quantity, the nominal percentage change is not exactly equal to the sum of the price and the quantity changes; generally, the relationship is multiplicative. In this case, prices and quantities are respectively 1.317 and 1.28 times their original values. This makes nominal GDP $(1.317) \times (1.28) = 1.68$ times its original value, which is an increase of 68 percent. For small percentage changes, the sum is a very good approximation of the multiplicative change. If prices grow by 2 percent and quantities by 3 percent, the nominal change is $(1.02) \times (1.03) = 1.0506$, which is very close to 1.05. [31].

EXTENSION 22-3

CALCULATION OF NOMINAL AND REAL NATIONAL INCOME

To see what is involved in calculating nominal national income, real national income, and the implicit deflator, an example may be helpful. Consider a simple hypothetical economy that produces only two commodities, wheat and steel. Table 1 gives the basic data for output and prices in the economy for two years.

TABLE 1
Data for a Hypothetical Economy

	Quantity produced		Prices	
	Wheat (bushels)	Steel (tonnes)	Wheat (dollars/bushel)	Steel (dollars/tonnes)
Year 1	100	20	10	50
Year 2	110	16	12	55

Table 2 shows nominal national income, calculated by adding the money values of wheat output and of steel output for each year. In year 1, the value of both wheat and steel production was $1,000, so nominal income was $2,000. In year 2, wheat output rose to $1,320, and steel output fell to $880. Since the rise in value of wheat was greater than the fall in value of steel, nominal income rose by $200.

TABLE 2
Calculation of Nominal National Income

Year 1: $(100 \times 10) + (20 \times 50) = \$2,000$
Year 2: $(110 \times 12) + (16 \times 55) = \$2,200$

Table 3 shows real national income, calculated by valuing output in each year *by year 2 prices*; that is, year 2 becomes the base year for weighting purposes.

In year 2, wheat output rose, but steel output fell. Using year 2 prices, the value of the fall in steel output between years 1 and 2 exceeded the value of the rise in wheat output, and real national income fell.

TABLE 3
Calculation of Real National Income Using Year 2 Prices

Year 1: $(100 \times 12) + (20 \times 55) = \$2,300$
Year 2: $(110 \times 12) + (16 \times 55) = \$2,200$

In Table 4, the ratio of nominal to real national income is calculated for each year and multiplied by 100. This ratio implicitly measures the change in prices over the period in question and is called the *implicit GDP deflator* or *implicit price index*. The implicit deflator shows that the price level increased by 15 percent between year 1 and year 2.

TABLE 4
Calculation of the Implicit GDP Deflator

Year 1: $(2,000/2,300) \times 100 = 86.96$
Year 2: $(2,200/2,200) \times 100 = 100.00$

In Table 4, we used year 2 as the base year for comparison purposes, but we could have used year 1. The implicit deflator would then have been 100 in year 1 and 115 in year 2, and the increase in price level would still have been 15 percent. Or the base year could be some earlier year. No matter what year is picked as the year in which the index had a value of 100, however, the change in the implicit GDP deflator between year 1 and year 2 is 15 percent.

changes in labour productivity because the growth in per capita output was largely due to growth in labour productivity. Thus per capita output and labour productivity moved closely together. Since the mid 1970s, however, we have had a different explanation for the continued rise in per capita output. The growth of labour productivity slowed, and

the increases in per capita output were thus explained by an increase in the fraction of the population that chose to work (the *labour-force participation rate*).

This divergence between the growth of per capita output and the growth of labour productivity means that the increases in output per capita over-

TABLE 22-3
Nominal and Real GDP in Canada, Selected Years Since 1950 (billions of dollars)

Year	Nominal GDP (current prices)	Real GDP (1986 prices)	Implicit GDP Deflator
1950	19.1	104.8	18.2
1955	29.3	134.9	21.7
1960	39.4	164.1	24.0
1965	57.5	216.8	26.5
1970	89.1	271.4	32.8
1975	171.5	350.1	49.0
1980	309.9	424.5	73.0
1986	505.7	505.7	100.0
1990	669.5	565.2	118.4
1994	750.1	597.9	125.4

Nominal GDP tells us about the money value of output; real GDP tells us about change in physical output. Nominal GDP gives the total value of output in any year, valued at the selling prices of that year. Real GDP gives the total value of output in any year, *valued at prices from some base year*, in this case 1986. The comparison of real and nominal GDP implicitly defines a price index, changes in which reveal changes in the (average) prices of goods produced domestically. Note that in 1986, nominal GDP equals real GDP (measured in 1986 prices) and thus the implicit GDP deflator equals 100.

(*Source:* Statistics Canada, *National Income and Expenditure Accounts*, 13–001.)

state increases in economic welfare. When output grows while inputs stay constant, the average person will be unambiguously better off. However, when output grows because more people are working longer hours, the average person may be no better off than before.

Changes in overall living standards are better measured by changes in productivity than by changes in per capita output.

OMISSIONS FROM MEASURED NATIONAL INCOME

National income as measured in the National Income and Expenditure Accounts provides an excellent measure of the flow of economic activity in organized markets in a given year. But much economic activity takes place outside of the markets that the national income accountants survey. Although these activities are not typically included in the measure of GDP, they nevertheless use real resources and satisfy real wants and needs.

Illegal Activities

GDP does not measure illegal activities, even though many of them are ordinary business activities that produce goods and services sold on the market and that generate factor incomes. Many forms of illegal gambling, prostitution, and drug trade come into this category. To gain an accurate measure of the total demand for factors of production, of total marketable output, or of total incomes generated, we should include these activities, whether or not we as individuals approve of them. The omission of illegal activities is no trivial matter: The drug trade alone is a multibillion-dollar business.[5]

Unreported Activities

A significant omission from the measured GDP is the so-called underground economy. The transactions that occur in the underground economy are perfectly legal in themselves; the only illegality involved is that such transactions are not reported for tax purposes. One example of this is the carpenter who repairs a leak in your roof and takes payment in cash or in kind to avoid taxation. Because such transactions go unreported, they are omitted from GDP.

The growth of the underground economy is facilitated by the rising importance of services in the nation's total output. It is much easier for a carpenter to pass unnoticed by government authorities than it is for a manufacturing establishment. Estimates of the value of income earned in the underground economy run from 2 percent to 15 per-

---

[5]Some illegal activities do get included in national income measures, although they are generally misclassified by industry. The income is included because people sometimes report their earnings from illicit activities as part of their earnings from legal activities. They do this to avoid the fate of Al Capone, the famous Chicago gangster in the 1920s and 1930s, who, having avoided conviction on many counts, was finally caught for tax evasion.

cent of GDP. In some countries, the figures are even higher. The Italian underground economy, for example, has been estimated at close to 25 percent of that country's GDP.

Nonmarket Activities

If a homeowner hires a firm to do some landscaping, the value of the landscaping enters into GDP; if the homeowner does the landscaping herself, the value of the landscaping is omitted from GDP. Other nonmarket activities include the services of homemakers, any do-it-yourself activity, and voluntary work such as canvassing for a political party, helping to run a volunteer day-care centre, or leading a scout troop. All of these activities add to economic welfare, and all use economic resources. Yet none of them are included in official measures of national income and product.

Compared to developing countries, the nonmarket sector in most advanced industrial economies is relatively small, although much household maintenance, education, and child care is performed at home. The omissions become very misleading when national income measures are used to compare living standards in structurally different economies. Generally, the nonmarket sector of the economy is larger in rural than in urban settings and in less developed than in more developed economies. Be cautious, then, when interpreting data from a country with a very different climate and culture. When you hear that the per capita GDP of Nigeria is about $1,200 per year (compared to about $26,000 in Canada), you should not imagine having to live in Canada on that income.

One extremely important nonmarket activity is leisure itself. If an attorney voluntarily chooses to reduce her time at work from 2,400 hours to 2,200 hours per year, measured national income will fall by the attorney's wage rate times 200 hours. Yet the value to the attorney of the 200 hours of new leisure which is enjoyed outside of the marketplace must exceed the lost wages (otherwise she would choose to work the extra 200 hours), so total economic welfare must rise rather than fall. Until recently, one of the most important ways in which economic growth benefited people was by permitting increased amounts of leisure. Because the time off is not marketed, its value does not show up in measures of national income.

Economic Bads

When an electric power plant sends sulfur dioxide into the atmosphere, leading to acid rain and environmental damage, the value of the electricity sold is included as part of GDP, but the value of the damage done by the acid rain is not deducted. Similarly, the gasoline that we use in our cars is part of national income, but the damage done by burning that gasoline is not deducted. To the extent that economic growth brings with it increases in pollution, congestion, and other disamenities of modern living, national income measures will overstate the value of the growth. They measure the increased economic output and income, but they fail to deduct for the increased "bads" that generally accompany economic growth.

Do the Omissions Matter?

GDP does a reasonably good job of measuring the flow of goods and services through the market sector of the economy. Usually, an increase in GDP implies greater opportunities for employment for households that sell their labour services in the market. Unless the importance of unmeasured economic activity changes rapidly, *changes* in GDP will probably do a satisfactory job of measuring *changes* in economic activity and economic opportunities. However, when the task at hand is measurement of the overall flow of goods and services available to satisfy people's wants, regardless of the source of the goods and services, then the omissions that we have discussed become undesirable and potentially serious. Still, in the relatively short term, changes in GDP will usually be good measure of the direction, if not the exact magnitude, of changes in economic welfare. Extension 22-4 examines further why GDP may be especially unsuitable as a measure of economic welfare when considering the economy over very long periods of time.

EXTENSION 22-4

GDP AND ECONOMIC GROWTH*

GDP is not a very good indicator of the long-term growth in welfare that accompanies long-term economic growth. The reason is that so many of the major benefits that growth provides are imperfectly measured or not measured at all by GDP. This can be dramatically illustrated by looking at some of the most important changes that accompanied the first Industrial Revolution.

1. In early eighteenth-century Europe, average life expectancy was around 30 years; in France, one in five children were dead by the end of the first year of life, and 50 percent of registered children were dead by age 10! Life expectancy rose dramatically after the Industrial Revolution.

2. Industrialization reduced famine and hunger. Not only did the average food intake rise, its year-to-year variation fell. It is of little consolation to a peasant that the average food consumption is above the subsistence level over the decades if fluctuations in harvests periodically drive it below the subsistence level, thus causing starvation.

3. Technological changes that accompanied the Industrial Revolution virtually eliminated many terrible diseases that had been common until that time, such as plague, tuberculosis, cholera, dysentery, smallpox, and leprosy.

4. The urbanization that accompanied industrialization increased literacy and education and broadened experience. Before then, poverty and a rural, peasant existence, with little or no com-munication between the village and the outside world, tended to be associated with superstition and very narrow experience.

5. Privacy became possible when people moved from the peasant dwelling, where the entire family lived, ate, and slept in one room, to multi-room urban sites.

6. The introduction of a market economy greatly increased the mobility of persons among jobs. In the rural societies, there were few options for employment, and customary behaviour—doing what one's parents did—dominated job selection.

7. The Industrial Revolution was based on mass production of goods sold mainly to low- and middle-income people. These changed the quality of consumption. For example, instead of wooden clogs, people adopted leather shoes; instead of rough, homespun cloth, people had factory-made shirts and skirts; instead of mud floors and thatched roofs, people had wooden floors and rain-proof roofs; instead of all living in one room, parents had a room separate from their children. These things may seem trivial to us today, but they changed the way of life of ordinary people.

Throughout the late eighteenth century and all of the nineteenth century, a succession of new products continued to alter the way ordinary people lived until, by the mid-twentieth century, the ordinary working person had a structurally different way of life from his or her counterpart in the mid-eighteenth century. Statistics, however, are the same if a doubling of GDP takes the form of twice as much of the same, or of new things that enhance the quality of life. The effect on living standards is, however, much greater when new commodities replace older ones rather than just more of the same becoming available.

*This box draws on material in: J. Blum, *Our Forgotten Past: Seven Centuries of Life on the Land*, (London: Thames and Hudson, 1982); F. Braudel, *Structures of Everyday Life, 15th–18th Century* (New York: Harper and Row, 1981); and N. Rosenberg and L. E. Birdzell, Jr., *How the West Grew Rich* (New York: Basic Books, 1986).

SUMMARY

A. NATIONAL OUTPUT AND VALUE ADDED

- Each firm's contribution to total output is equal to its value added, which is the gross value of the firm's output minus the value of all intermediate goods and services—that is, the outputs of other firms—that it uses. The sum of all the values added produced in an economy is the economy's total output, which is called gross domestic product (GDP).

B. NATIONAL INCOME ACCOUNTING: THE BASICS

- Gross domestic product (GDP) can be calculated from the expenditure side, from the income side, or as the sum of values added in the economy. The expenditure side gives the total value of expenditures required to purchase the nation's output, and the income side gives the total value of income claims generated by the production of that output. By standard accounting conventions, these three aggregations define the same total.

- From the expenditure side of the national accounts,

$$GDP = C_a + I_a + G_a + (X_a - IM_a)$$

C_a comprises consumption expenditures of households. I_a is investment in plant and equipment, residential construction, and inventory accumulation. G_a is government purchases of goods and services. $(X_a - IM_a)$ represents net exports.

- GDP measured from the income side adds up all claims to the market value of production. Wages, rent, interest, profits, depreciation (or capital consumption allowance), and indirect taxes net of subsidies are the major categories.

C. NATIONAL INCOME ACCOUNTING: SOME EXTRA ISSUES

- GDP measures the value of production that is located in Canada, and gross national product (GNP) measures income accruing to Canadian residents. The difference is due to the balance between Canadian claims to incomes that are generated abroad and foreign claims to incomes that are generated in Canada. Throughout Canada's history, GNP has been slightly less than GDP.

- Real measures of national income are calculated to reflect changes in real quantities. Nominal measures of national income are calculated to reflect changes in both prices and quantities. Any change in nominal income can be split into a change in quantities and a change in prices. Appropriate comparisons of nominal and real measures yield implicit deflators.

- Economists frequently use measures of GDP, GDP per capita, and various measures of labour productivity such as GDP per employed worker or GDP per hour worked. Changes in overall living standards are better reflected by changes in productivity than by changes in GDP per capita.

- GDP and related measures of national income must be interpreted with their limitations in mind. GDP excludes production resulting from activities that are illegal, that take place in the underground economy, or that do not pass through markets. Hence GDP does not measure everything that contributes to (or detracts from) human welfare.

- Notwithstanding its limitations, GDP remains a useful measure of the total economic activity that passes through the nation's markets. Recorded *changes* in GDP will generally do an accurate job of measuring *changes* in economic activity and economic opportunities.

KEY CONCEPTS

Intermediate and final goods
Value added
GDP as the sum of all values added
GDP from the expenditure side

GDP from the income side
GNP versus GDP
Disposable income
Implicit GDP deflator

Per capita GDP and labour productivity
The significance of omissions from measured national income

DISCUSSION QUESTIONS

1. If Canada and the United States were to join together as a single country, what would be the effect on their total GDP (assuming that output in each country is unaffected)? Would any of the components in their GDPs change significantly?

2. In 1986, Statistics Canada switched from reporting national income in terms of GNP to reporting it in terms of GDP. How do these two measures differ? Do you think GDP is a better or worse measure of national income than GNP? Does your answer depend on the purpose the measure is being used for?

3. Residents of some Canadian cities have recently become concerned about the growing proportion of their local real estate that is being bought up by foreign residents. What is the effect of this transfer of ownership on Canadian GDP and GNP?

4. "Every time you rent a U-Haul, build a patio, grow a vegetable, fix your own car, cook a meal, develop your own film, sew a dress, or raise a child, you are performing a productive act, even though these activities are not reflected in the gross domestic product." To what extent are each of these things "productive acts"? Are any of them included in GDP? If they are excluded, does the exclusion matter?

5. In measuring GDP from the expenditure side, which of the following expenditures are included, and within which category?

   a. Expenditures on automobiles by consumers and by firms
   b. Expenditures on food and lodging by tourists and by businesspeople on expense accounts
   c. Expenditures on new machinery by foreign-owned firms in Canada
   d. The purchase of one corporation by another corporation
   e. Increases and decreases in business inventories
   f. Purchase of a second-hand automobile

6. What would be the effect of the following events on the measured value of Canada's real GDP? Speculate on the effects of each event on the true well-being of Canadians.

   a. Destruction of thousands of homes by flood water
   b. Complete cessation of all imports from Europe
   c. An increase in the amount of acid rain that falls
   d. An increase in the amount of spending on devices that reduce pollution at a major hydroelectricity plant
   e. Reduction in the standard work week from 40 hours to 30 hours
   f. Hiring of all welfare recipients as government employees

7. A recent United Nations study concluded that Canada is the best country in which to live—that Canada has the best "quality of life." In view of the fact that Canada does not have the highest per capita real GDP in the world, explain how it can be ranked as the "best"?

8. There is now a good deal of scientific evidence that the burning of fossil fuels is causing general "global warming," which may pose considerable long-term risk to economic and social well-being. In the current national accounts, value added in the production and use of fossil fuel adds to the GDP. What does this suggest about GDP as a measure of economic welfare?

9. One way of estimating the size of the underground economy is to see the amount of cash Canadians are carrying relative to the total value of GDP. Why would a rapid rise in the ratio of cash held by the public to GDP indicate a rise in the underground economy? Can you offer an explanation for why this ratio has risen steadily since the introduction of the GST in 1991?

10. A company's wages and salaries are part of its value added. Suppose, however, that the cleaning and machinery maintenance that its own employees used to do are now contracted out to specialist firms who come in to do the same work more cheaply. What happens to the value added when a company follows this recent trend of "contracting out"?

PART EIGHT

NATIONAL INCOME AND FISCAL POLICY

What determines the level of national income in the economy? Why, in the midst of a recession, does the government sometimes attempt to increase national income by spending a few billion dollars? During other recessions our elected leaders implore us to "go out and spend." Can such increased spending end a recession? If so, why does this work? At other times, when the economy has been growing quickly for several years, the government may be worried that any further spending will tend to increase prices. What determines when an increase in spending leads to an increase in national income and when it just leads to an increase in prices? What is the essence of the difference between the short run and the long run in macroeconomics? These are the sorts of questions you will be able to answer after reading the next four chapters.

Chapters 23 and 24 examine the determination of national income under the assumption that *the price level is held constant*. Chapter 23 introduces you to the simplest possible model of the macro economy. This model explains how *equilibrium national income* is determined. The key to understanding this model involves understanding the essential distinction between *desired expenditure* and *actual expenditure*. One of the results from this simple model is reflected by the *multiplier*—that a $1 billion increase in desired expenditure will end up increasing equilibrium national income by more than $1 billion.

Chapter 24 extends this simple model by adding a government sector and international trade. This is your introduction to *fiscal policy;* it is also the first time you see the relationship between the *exchange rate* and a country's *exports* and *imports*. Surprisingly, this more complicated model works in exactly the same way as the simple one. The distinction between *desired expenditure* and *actual expenditure* is still there, the meaning of *equilibrium* is unchanged, and the *multiplier* still makes its appearance. (But it can never hurt to see these concepts a second time!)

Chapters 25 and 26 remove the assumption of the fixed price level. In Chapter 25 we make the distinction between the demand side and the supply side of the economy—we introduce the important concepts of *aggregate demand* and *aggregate supply*. We then examine what is called *macroeconomic equilibrium*—the simultaneous determination of the equilibrium level of national income and the equilibrium price level.

Chapter 26 examines the behaviour of the economy in the long run—when the price level is free to adjust to *excess demand* or *excess supply* in the economy as a whole. You are introduced to the concepts of *potential output* and the *output gap*. The chapter ends with a detailed discussion of fiscal policy in the short run and in the long run. (Many of these issues will resurface in Chapter 32 when we examine government debt and deficits.)

CHAPTER 23

NATIONAL INCOME AND AGGREGATE EXPENDITURE I: CONSUMPTION AND INVESTMENT

THE MULTIPLIER
Definition
The Size of the Simple Multiplier

In Chapters 21 and 22, we encountered a number of important macroeconomic variables. We described how they are measured and how they have behaved over the past several decades. We now turn to a more detailed study of what *causes* these variables to behave as they do. In particular, we study the forces that determine national income and the price level.

National income and the price level are determined simultaneously. To understand how they are determined, it is easier first to study them one at a time. So in this chapter and the next, we simplify matters by studying the determination of national income *under the assumption that the price level is constant*. The simplified analysis that we explore now will be an important step toward understanding how prices and incomes are determined together, which is the subject of Chapters 25 and 26.

Our ability to explain the behaviour of national income depends on our understanding of what determines the amount that households and firms spend and why they change their spending. For this reason, we begin with an examination of the expenditure decisions of households and firms.

DESIRED VERSUS ACTUAL EXPENDITURE

In Chapter 22, we discussed how national income statisticians divide *actual* GDP, calculated from the expenditure side, into its components: consumption, investment, government purchases, and net exports.

In this chapter and the next, we are concerned with a different concept. It is variously called *desired, planned,* or *intended* expenditure. Of course, all people would like to spend virtually unlimited amounts, if only they had the resources. Desired expenditure does not refer, however, to what people would like to do under imaginary circumstances; it refers to what people want to spend out of the resources that are at their command. The *actual* values of the various categories of expenditure are indicated by C_a, I_a, G_a, and $(X_a - IM_a)$. We use the same letters without the subscript "*a*" to indicate the *desired* expenditure in the same categories: C, I, G, and $(X - IM)$.

Everyone makes expenditure decisions. Fortunately, it is unnecessary for our purposes to look at each of the millions of such individual decisions. Instead, it is sufficient to consider four main groups of decision makers: domestic households, firms, governments, and foreign purchasers of domestically produced commodities. The *actual* purchases made by these four groups account for the four main categories of expenditure that we studied in Chapter 22: consumption, investment, government purchases, and net exports. Their *desired* expenditures, made up of desired consumption, desired investment, desired government purchases, and desired exports, account for total desired expenditure. Because many of the goods and services desired by each group will have an import content, we subtract expenditure on imports. The result is total desired expenditure on domestically produced goods and services, called desired aggregate expenditure, or more simply **aggregate expenditure (AE)**:

$$AE = C + I + G + (X - IM)$$

Desired expenditure need not equal actual expenditure, either in total or in any individual category. For example, firms may not plan to invest in inventory accumulation this year but may do so unintentionally. If they produce goods to meet estimated sales but sales are unexpectedly low, the unsold goods that pile up on their shelves are undesired, and unintended, inventory accumulation. In this case, actual investment expenditure, I_a, will exceed desired investment expenditure, I.

National income accounts measure *actual* expenditures in each of the four categories of consumption, investment, government, and net exports. National income theory deals with *desired* expenditures in each of these four categories.

Though the distinction between *desired* and *actual* expenditure should by now be clear, readers may be wondering why this distinction is so important. The significance of this distinction will be made clear in the next section where we discuss the concept of *equilibrium national income* which involves the relationship between desired and actual expenditure. For now, however, the remainder of this section examines more fully the various components of desired expenditure.

Autonomous Versus Induced Expenditure

In what follows, it will be useful to distinguish between *autonomous* and *induced* expenditure.

Components of aggregate expenditure that do *not* depend on national income are called **autonomous expenditures.** Autonomous expenditures can and do change, but such changes do not occur systematically in response to changes in national income. Components of aggregate expenditure that *do* change in response to changes in national income are called **induced expenditures.** As we will see, the induced response of aggregate expenditure to a change in national income plays a key role in the determination of equilibrium national income.

A Very Simple Model

To develop a theory of national income determination, we need to examine the determinants of each component of desired aggregate expenditure. In this chapter, we focus on desired consumption and desired investment. Consumption is the largest single component of aggregate expenditure, and as we will see, it provides the single most important link between desired aggregate expenditure and national income. Investment is national income that is not used either for current consumption or by governments, and it is an important determinant of potential income in the future.

We will discuss net exports and government expenditure in detail in Chapter 24. These two components of aggregate expenditure are essential to understanding how national income is determined and are important in their own right. However, our purpose here is to develop the simplest model of a national economy that can show how desired expenditure and actual national income are determined together.

The basic structure of the model is most easily seen if things are kept as simple as possible. For this reason, we consider a **closed economy,** an economy that has no international trade. This economy also has no government and a constant price level. Although this is about as simple as an economy can get, it allows us to discover the principles of national income and expenditure determination that apply directly to the more complex models that we study in subsequent chapters.

DESIRED CONSUMPTION EXPENDITURE

We are now ready to study the determinants of desired expenditure flows. We start with consumption.

Households can do one of two things with their disposable income: spend it on consumption or save it. **Saving** is all disposable income that is not consumed.

By definition, there are only two possible uses of disposable income—consumption or saving. So when the household decides how much to put to one use, it has automatically decided how much to put to the other use.

What determines the division between the amount that households decide to consume and the amount they decide to save? The factors that influence this decision are summarized in the consumption function and the saving function.

The Consumption Function

The **consumption function** relates the total desired consumption expenditure of all households to the factors that determine it. It is, as we shall see, one of the central relationships in macroeconomics.

Although we are ultimately interested in the relationship between consumption and national income, the underlying behaviour of households depends on the income that they actually have to spend, which is called their *disposable income.* Under the simplifying assumptions that we have made in this chapter, there are no taxes. All income that is generated by households is received by households. Therefore, disposable income, which we denote by Y_D, is equal to national income, Y. (Later in our discussion, Y and Y_D will diverge because taxes are a part of national income that is not at the disposal of households.)

It is not surprising that a household's expenditure is related to the amount of income that it has at its disposal. However, there is more than one way in which this relationship could work. To see what is involved, consider two quite different households.

The first household is headed by the proverbial prodigal son. This short-sighted household spends everything it receives and puts nothing aside for a rainy day. When some overtime work results in a large paycheque, the members of the household go on a binge. When it is hard to find work during periods of slack demand, the household's paycheque is small and its members cut their expenditures correspondingly. This household's monthly expenditure is thus directly linked to each month's take-home pay, that is, its current disposable income.

The second household is headed by a prudent planner. Its members think about the future as much as the present and make plans that stretch over their lifetimes. They put money aside for retirement and for the occasional rainy day when disposable income may fall temporarily—they know that they must expect alternating bouts of good and bad times. They also know that they will need to spend extra money while the family is being raised and educated and that their income will probably be highest later in life when the children have left home and the parents have finally reached the peaks of their personal careers. This household may borrow to meet higher expenses earlier in life, paying back out of the higher income that the household expects to attain later in life. A temporary, unexpected windfall of income may be saved. A temporary, unexpected shortfall may be cushioned by spending some of the accumulated savings that were put aside for just such a rainy day. In short, this household's current expenditure will be closely related to its expected *lifetime income*. Fluctuations in its *current income* will have little effect on its current expenditure, unless such fluctuations also cause the household to change its expectations of lifetime income, as would be the case, for example, if an unexpected promotion came along.

John Maynard Keynes (1883–1946), the famous English economist who developed much of the basic theory of macroeconomics—and gave his name to Keynesian economics—inhabited his theory with short-sighted households. For them, current consumption expenditure depended only on current income. To this day, a consumption function based on this assumption is called a *Keynesian consumption function*.

Later, two U.S. economists, Franco Modigliani and Milton Friedman, both of whom were subsequently awarded Nobel Prizes in economics, analyzed the behaviour of prudent households. Their theories, which Modigliani called the *life-cycle theory* and Friedman called the *permanent-income theory*, explain some observed consumer behaviour that cannot be explained by the Keynesian consumption function.

Despite the sharp distinction we have drawn between the short-sighted household and the prudent-planning household, the differences between the theories of Keynes, on the one hand, and Friedman and Modigliani, on the other, are not as great as it might seem at first sight. To see why this is so, let us return to our two imaginary households and see why their actual behaviour may not be quite so divergent as we first described.

Even the short-sighted household may be able to do some smoothing of expenditures in the face of income fluctuations. Most households have some money in the bank and some ability to borrow, even if it is just from friends and relatives. As a result, every income fluctuation need not be matched by an equivalent expenditure fluctuation.

In contrast, although the prudent household wants to smooth its pattern of consumption completely, it may not have the borrowing capacity to do so. Its bank may not be willing to lend money for consumption when the security consists of nothing more than the *expectation* that the household's income will be much higher in later years. This may mean that the household's consumption expenditure fluctuates with its current income more than it would wish.

This suggests that the consumption expenditure of both types of households will fluctuate to some extent with their current disposable incomes and to some extent with their expectations of future disposable income. Moreover, in any economy there will be households of both types, both spendthrifts and planners, and aggregate consumption will be determined by a mix of the two types. As we develop our basic theory, we will often find it useful to make the simplifying assumption that consumption expenditure is determined primarily by current disposable income. That is, we will often use a Keynesian consumption function in the basic theory and then indicate how things change when we allow for more sophisticated theories of consumer spending.

The consumption function describes the relationship between consumption and the variables that influence it; in the simplest theory, consumption is determined primarily by current disposable income.

When a household's income is zero, it will still consume some minimal amount (via begging, borrowing, or drawing down savings). This level of consumption expenditure is *autonomous* because it persists even when there is no income. The higher a household's income, the more it will want to consume. This part of consumption is *induced*; that is, it varies with disposable income and hence, in our simple model, with national income.

Consider the schedule relating disposable income to desired consumption expenditure for a hypothetical economy that appears in the first two columns of Table 23-1. In this example, autonomous consump-

TABLE 23-1
The Calculation of Average Propensity to Consume (APC)
and Marginal Propensity to Consume (MPC)
(billions of dollars)

Disposable Income (Y_D)	Desired Consumption (C)	$APC = C/Y_D$	ΔY_D (Change in Y_D)	ΔC (Change in C)	$MPC = \Delta C/\Delta Y_D$
0	10	—			
10	18	1.800	10	8	0.8
40	42	1.050	30	24	0.8
50	50	1.000	10	8	0.8
100	90	0.900	50	40	0.8
150	130	0.867	50	40	0.8
175	150	0.857	25	20	0.8
200	170	0.850	25	20	0.8
300	250	0.833	100	80	0.8

APC measures the proportion of disposable income that households desire to spend on consumption; *MPC* measures the proportion of any increment to disposable income that households desire to spend on consumption. The data are hypothetical. We call the level of income at which desired consumption equals disposable income the break-even level; in this example it is $50 billion. *APC*, calculated in the third column, exceeds one—that is, consumption exceeds income—below the break-even level. Above the break-even level, *APC* is less than one. It is negatively related to income at all levels of income. The last three columns are set between the rows of the first three columns to indicate that they refer to changes in the levels of income and consumption. *MPC*, calculated in the last column, equals 0.80 at all levels of Y_D. This indicates that in this example 80 cents of every additional dollar of disposable income is spent on consumption, and 20 cents is saved.

tion expenditure is $10 billion, whereas induced consumption expenditure is 80 percent of disposable income (for every $1 increase in disposable income, there is an 80 cent increase in consumption). In what follows, we use this hypothetical example to illustrate the various properties of the consumption function.

Average and Marginal Propensities to Consume. To discuss the consumption function concisely, economists use two technical expressions.

The **average propensity to consume (APC)** is total consumption expenditure divided by total disposable income:

$$APC = C/Y_D$$

The third column of Table 23-1 shows the *APC* calculated from the data in the table. Note that *APC* falls as disposable income rises.

The **marginal propensity to consume (MPC)** relates the *change* in desired consumption to the *change* in disposable income that brought it about. *MPC* is the change in desired consumption divided by the change in disposable income:

$$MPC = \Delta C/\Delta Y_D,$$

where the Greek letter Δ, delta, means "a change in." The last column of Table 23-1 shows the *MPC* that corresponds to the data in the table. Note that by construction in this example, the *MPC* is constant. [32]

The Slope of the Consumption Function. Part (i) of Figure 23-1 shows a graph of the consumption function, derived by plotting consumption against income using data from the first two columns of Table 23-1. The consumption function has a slope of $\Delta C/\Delta Y_D$, which is, by definition, the marginal propensity to consume. The positive slope of the consumption function shows that the *MPC* is positive; increases in income lead to increases in consumption expenditure.

Using the concepts of the average and marginal propensities to consume, we can summarize the properties of the consumption function as follows:

1. There is a break-even level of income at which *APC* equals one. Below this level, *APC* is greater than one; above it, *APC* is less than one.

2. *MPC* is greater than zero but less than one for all levels of income.

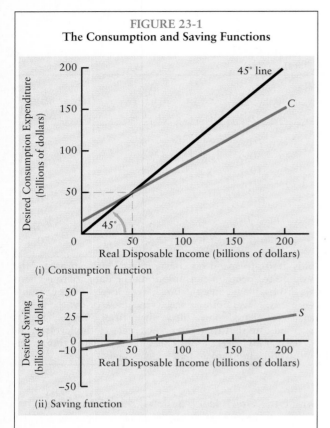

FIGURE 23-1
The Consumption and Saving Functions

(i) Consumption function

(ii) Saving function

Both consumption and saving rise as disposable income rises. Line C in part (i) relates desired consumption expenditure to disposable income by using the data from Table 23-1. The consumption function cuts the 45° line at the break-even level of disposable income, $50 billion in this case. Note that the level of autonomous consumption is $10 billion.

Saving is all disposable income that is not spent on consumption ($S = Y_D - C$). The relationship between desired saving and disposable income is derived in Table 23-2, and it is shown in part (ii) by line S. The vertical distance between C and the 45° line in part (i) is by definition the height of S in part (ii); that is, any given level of disposable income must be either consumed or saved. Note that the level of autonomous saving is −$10 billion.

TABLE 23-2
Consumption and Saving Schedules
(billions of dollars)

Disposable Income	Desired Consumption	Desired Saving
0	10	−10
10	18	−8
40	42	−2
50	50	0
100	90	10
150	130	20
175	150	25
200	170	30
300	250	50

Saving and consumption account for all household disposable income. The first two columns repeat the data from Table 23-1. The third column, desired saving, is disposable income minus desired consumption. Consumption and saving both increase steadily as disposable income rises. In this example, the break-even level of disposable income is $50 billion, and so desired saving is zero at this point.

The 45° line is a useful reference line. In part (i) of Figure 23-1, it helps to locate the break-even level of income at which consumption expenditure equals disposable income. The consumption function cuts the 45° line at the break-even level of income—in this instance, $50 billion. (The 45° line is steeper than the consumption function because the *MPC* is less than one.)

The Saving Function

Households decide how much to consume and how much to save. As we have said, this is only a single decision—how to divide disposable income between consumption and saving. It follows that once we know the dependence of consumption on disposable income, we automatically know the dependence of saving on disposable income. This is illustrated in Table 23-2.

There are two saving concepts that are exactly parallel to the consumption concepts of *APC* and *MPC*. The **average propensity to save (APS)** is the proportion of disposable income that households want to save, derived by dividing total desired saving by total disposable income:

$$APS = S/Y_D$$

The **marginal propensity to save (MPS)** relates the change in desired saving to the change in disposable income that brought it about:

The 45° Line. Figure 23-1(i) contains a line that is constructed by connecting all points where desired consumption (measured on the vertical axis) equals disposable income (measured on the horizontal axis). Because both axes are given in the same units, this line has a positive slope equal to one; that is, it forms an angle of 45° with the axes. The line is therefore called the **45° line.**

$$MPS = \Delta S/\Delta Y_D$$

There is a simple relationship between the saving and the consumption propensities. APC and APS must sum to one, and so must MPC and MPS. Because all disposable income is either spent or saved, it follows that the fractions of income consumed and saved must account for all income ($APC + APS = 1$). It also follows that the fractions of any *increment* to income consumed and saved must account for all of that increment ($MPC + MPS = 1$). [33]

Calculations from Table 23-2 will allow you to confirm these relationships in the case of the example given. MPC is 0.80 and MPS is 0.20 at all levels of income, while, for example, at an income of $200 billion, APC is 0.85 and APS is 0.15. Figure 23-1(ii) shows the saving function given in Table 23-2. At the break-even level of income, where desired consumption equals disposable income, desired saving is zero. The slope of the saving function, $\Delta S/\Delta Y_D$, is equal to the MPC.

Wealth and the Consumption Function

We have been analyzing the Keynesian consumption function—where consumption expenditure depends only on current disposable income. But this extreme depiction of consumption behaviour can easily be combined with the more recent life-cycle and permanent-income theories of consumption. According to these theories, households save to accumulate wealth that they can use during their retirement or during periods of unexpectedly low income. Suppose that there is an unexpected rise in wealth—say because a household receives an inheritance. This means that less of current disposable income needs to be saved for the future, and it will tend to cause a larger fraction of disposable income to be spent on consumption and a smaller fraction to be saved. Hence the consumption function will be shifted upward and the saving function downward, as shown in Figure 23-2. A fall in wealth increases the incentive to save in order to restore wealth. This shifts the consumption function downward and the saving function upward.

Consumption and Disposable Income in Canada

We have devoted considerable time and space to discussing the consumption function, and we have said that this relationship between desired consumption and disposable income is of central importance in the determination of national income. It is worthwhile,

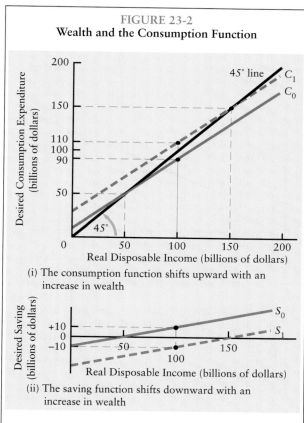

FIGURE 23-2
Wealth and the Consumption Function

(i) The consumption function shifts upward with an increase in wealth

(ii) The saving function shifts downward with an increase in wealth

Changes in wealth shift the consumption function. In part (i), line C_0 reproduces the consumption function from Figure 23-1(i). An increase in wealth raises desired consumption at each level of disposable income, thus shifting the consumption function up to C_1. In the figure, the consumption function shifts up by $20 billion, so with disposable income of $100 billion, for example, desired consumption rises from $90 billion to $110 billion.

The saving function in part (ii) shifts down by $20 billion, from S_0 to S_1. Thus, for example, at a disposable income of $100 billion, desired saving falls from $10 billion to −$10 billion.

therefore, to take a brief look at actual data to see if such a relationship appears to exist in Canada.

Figure 23-3 plots real per capita consumption expenditure against real per capita disposable income for Canada from 1970 to 1994. The straight line drawn through the data points is the straight line which shows the single "best fit" in the relationship between consumption and disposable income. According to the simple model we have been discussing, the consumption function should have a positive vertical intercept (consumption would be

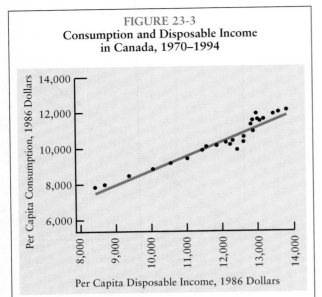

FIGURE 23-3
Consumption and Disposable Income in Canada, 1970–1994

The Canadian data suggest a consumption function with a positive marginal propensity to consume that is less than one. The figure plots real per capita consumption on the vertical axis and real per capita disposable income on the horizontal axis. Each point corresponds to the data from one year. The straight line is the line which shows the single "best fit" in the relationship between consumption and income. The slope of this best-fit line is 0.81, suggesting that a $100 increase in disposable income is associated with an $81 increase in consumption. Though it is not shown in the figure, the vertical intercept of the best-fit line is $736, indicating that consumption would be positive even if disposable income were zero.

(*Source:* Department of Finance, *Economic Reference Tables,* August 1995.)

positive if disposable income were zero) and should have a slope of less than one. This relationship is indeed suggested by the data.

Keep in mind that when we simply plot the data as in Figure 23-3, we are not accounting for changes in those variables which could *shift* the consumption function. Failure to account for such changes means that the true marginal propensity to consume is not necessarily well represented by the slope of the best fit line. A precise estimate of the marginal propensity to consume therefore requires more complicated statistical techniques. (You will learn about the appropriate estimation methods if you go on to study econometrics.) In the mean time, however, Figure 23-3 does give us a rough estimate of the consumption function. It suggests that

the theoretical consumption function we have been discussing is indeed broadly supported by a first glance at the Canadian data.

DESIRED INVESTMENT EXPENDITURE

Investment expenditure is the most volatile component of GDP, and changes in investment expenditure are strongly associated with economic fluctuations. For example, the Great Depression witnessed a dramatic fall in investment. Total investment in Canada fell from almost double the amount that was needed to replace the capital goods that were being used up in the process of producing GDP in 1929 to less than one-sixth the amount that was needed just to keep the stock of capital intact. Less dramatically, at the trough of the recession that occurred in the early 1990s, investment expenditure was 10 percent less than what it had been only three years earlier, at the previous business-cycle peak.

What explains such fluctuations in investment? Here we examine three important determinants of aggregate investment expenditure—the real interest rate, changes in sales, and business confidence.

Investment and the Real Interest Rate

The real interest rate represents the real cost of borrowing money for investment purposes. Other things being equal, therefore, a rise in the real interest rate reduces the amount of desired investment expenditure. This relationship is most easily seen if we separate investment into three components: inventory accumulation, residential housing, and business fixed investment.

Inventories.   Changes in inventories represent only a small percentage of private investment in a typical year, but the average size of such changes is not an adequate measure of their importance. Since they are one of the more volatile elements of total investment, they have a major influence on fluctuations in investment expenditure.

When a firm ties up funds in inventories, those same funds cannot be used elsewhere to earn income. As an alternative to holding inventories, the firm could lend the money out at the going rate of interest. Hence the higher the real rate of interest, the higher the opportunity cost of holding an inventory of a given size; the higher that opportunity cost, the smaller the inventories that will be desired.

Residential Housing Construction.   Expenditure on residential housing is also volatile. Because expenditures for housing construction are both large and variable, they exert a major impact on the economy.

Most houses are purchased with money that is borrowed by means of mortgages. Interest on the borrowed money typically accounts for over one-half of the purchaser's annual mortgage payments; the remainder is repayment of the original loan, called the *principal*. Because interest payments are such a large part of mortgage payments, variations in interest rates exert a substantial effect on the demand for housing.

The importance of interest rates was borne out by experiences from 1978 to 1982, when mortgage rates rose from less than 11 percent to 18 percent and housing starts fell from 228,000 in 1978 to 126,000 in 1982. (Because inflation fell from 1980, the increased nominal interest rates also meant increased real rates.) The construction industry itself and its major suppliers, such as the cement and lumber industries, felt the blow of a dramatic fall in demand. Conversely, during the mid 1980s, interest rates fell sharply, and there was a boom in the demand for new housing; that boom persisted until late 1988, when interest rates started to rise again.

Plant and Equipment.   Investment in plant and equipment is the largest component of domestic investment. Over one-half is financed by firms' retained profits (profits that are not paid out to shareholders). This means that current profits are an important determinant of investment.

The rate of interest is also a major determinant of investment in plant and equipment. When interest rates are high, it is expensive for firms' to borrow funds that can be used for fixed investment. At the same time, firms with cash on hand can earn high returns on interest-earning assets, again making fixed investment a less attractive alternative. Thus high real interest rates lead to reduced investment in plant and equipment, and low real interest rates increase such investment. (We discuss these issues in more detail in Chapter 28).

The real interest rate reflects the opportunity cost associated with investment, whether it is investment in inventories, residential housing, or plant and equipment. The higher the real interest rate, the higher the opportunity cost of investment, and thus the lower the amount of desired investment.

Investment and Changes in Sales

Studies show that the stock of inventories tends to rise as production and sales rise. Because the size of inventories is related to the level of sales, the *change* in inventories (which is current investment) is related to the *change* in the level of sales.

A firm may decide to hold inventories of 10 percent of its sales. If sales are $100,000, it will wish to hold inventories of $10,000. If sales increase to $110,000, it will want to hold inventories of $11,000. Over the period during which its stock of inventories is being increased, there will be a total of $1,000 of new inventory investment.

The higher the level of production and sales, the larger the desired stock of inventories. This means that changes in the rate of production and sales cause temporary bouts of investment (or disinvestment) in inventories.

Changes in sales have similar effects on investment in plant and equipment. For example, if there is a general increase in consumers' demand for products that is expected to persist and that cannot be met by existing capacity, investment in new plant and equipment will be needed. Once the new plants have been built and put into operation, however, the rate of new investment will fall.

This further illustrates an important characteristic of investment that we have encountered already in the case of inventories:

If the desired stock of capital goods increases, there will be an investment boom that will last as long as the new capital is being produced.

However, if nothing else changes, and even if business conditions continue to look rosy enough to justify the increased stock of capital, investment in new plant and equipment will cease once the larger capital stock is achieved.

Investment and Business Confidence

Investment takes time. When a firm invests, it increases its future capacity to produce output. If the new output can be sold profitably, the investment will prove to be a good one. If the new output does not generate profits, the investment will have been a bad one. When an investment is undertaken, the firm does not know if it will turn out well or badly—it is betting on a favourable future that cannot be known with certainty.

When firms expect good times ahead, they will want to invest so as to reap future profits. When they expect bad times ahead, they will not invest because, given their expectations, there will be no payoff to doing so.

Investment depends in part on firms' forecasts of the future state of the economy.

Investment as Autonomous Expenditure

We have seen that investment is influenced by many things, and a complete discussion of the determination of national income is not possible without including all of these factors.

For the moment, however, our goal is to build the *simplest* model of the aggregate economy in which we can examine the interaction of actual national income and desired aggregate expenditure. To build this simple model, we begin by treating investment as *autonomous,* meaning only that it is uninfluenced by changes in national income. This allows us to study first how national income is determined when there is an unchanged amount of desired investment expenditure and, second, how changes in the amount of desired investment cause changes in national income.

In later chapters, we will complicate this simple model by making investment into an induced expenditure flow by linking changes in national income to changes in investment via induced changes in interest rates. For now, however, we simply assume that desired investment is a constant which does not vary with changes in national income.

THE AGGREGATE EXPENDITURE FUNCTION

The aggregate expenditure function relates the level of desired real expenditure to the level of real income. Generally, total desired expenditure on the nation's output is the sum of desired consumption, investment, government, and net export expenditures. In the simplified economy of this chapter, in which there is no government and no international trade, aggregate expenditure is just equal to $C + I$.

$$AE = C + I$$

Table 23-3 shows how the AE function can be calculated, given the consumption function in Table 23-1 and a constant level of desired investment of $25 billion. In this specific case, all of investment ex-

TABLE 23-3
Desired Aggregate Expenditure
(billions of dollars)

National Income (Y)	Desired Consumption Expenditure (C = 10 + 0.8 × Y)	Desired Investment Expenditure (I = 25)	Desired Aggregate Expenditure (AE = C + I)
10	18	25	43
40	42	25	67
50	50	25	75
100	90	25	115
150	130	25	155
175	150	25	175
200	170	25	195
300	250	25	275
400	330	25	355

In a simple economy with no government and no international trade, desired aggregate expenditure is the sum of desired consumption and desired investment. In this table, government and net exports are assumed to be zero, desired investment is assumed to be constant at $25 billion, and desired consumption is based on the hypothetical data given in Table 23-1. The autonomous components of desired aggregate expenditure are desired investment and the constant term in desired consumption expenditure. The induced component is the second term in desired consumption expenditure (0.8 × Y).

penditure is autonomous, as is the $10 billion of consumption that would be desired if national income were equal to zero. Total autonomous expenditure is therefore $35 billion—induced expenditure is just equal to induced consumption, which is equal to the *MPC* times disposable income $(0.8 \times Y_D)$. Furthermore, since our simple model has no government and no taxes, disposable income, Y_D, is equal to national income, Y. Hence desired aggregate expenditure, whether thought of as $C + I$ or as autonomous plus induced expenditure, can be written as:

$$AE = \$35 \text{ billion} + 0.8 \times Y$$

This aggregate expenditure function is illustrated in Figure 23-4.

The Propensity to Spend Out of National Income

The fraction of any increment to national income that people desire to spend on purchasing domestic output is called the economy's **marginal propensity to spend.** The marginal propensity to spend is measured

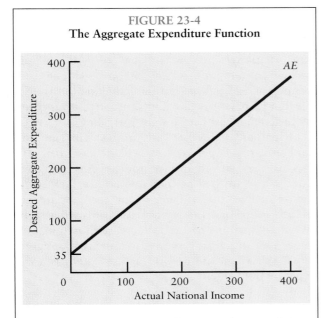

FIGURE 23-4
The Aggregate Expenditure Function

The aggregate expenditure function relates total desired expenditure to actual national income. The curve AE in the figure plots the data from the first and last columns of Table 23-3. Its intercept, which in this case is $35 billion, shows the sum of autonomous consumption and autonomous investment. Its slope, which in this case is 0.8, is equal to the marginal propensity to spend.

by the change in desired aggregate expenditure divided by the change in national income, or $\Delta AE/\Delta Y$, the slope of the aggregate expenditure function. In this book, we will denote the marginal propensity to spend by the symbol z, which will typically be a number greater than zero and less than one.

Similarly, the **marginal propensity not to spend** is the fraction of any increment to national income that does *not* add to desired aggregate expenditure. This is denoted $1 - z$; if z is the part of a dollar of incremental income that is spent, $1 - z$ is the part that is not spent.

More fully, these terms would be called the marginal propensity to spend on *national income* and the marginal propensity not to spend on *national income*. The marginal propensity not to spend $(1 - z)$ is often referred to as the *marginal propensity to withdraw*, since not spending part of income amounts to a withdrawal from the circular flow of income (see Figure 21-1).

In the example given in Table 23-3, z, the marginal propensity to spend, is 0.8. If national income

increases by a dollar, 80 cents will go into increased spending; 20 cents will go into increased saving and will not be spent.

The marginal propensity to spend, which we have just defined, should not be confused with the marginal propensity to consume, which we defined earlier in the chapter.

The marginal propensity to spend is the amount of extra total expenditure induced when national income rises by $1, whereas the marginal propensity to consume is the amount of extra consumption expenditure induced when households' disposable income rises by $1.

In the simple model of this chapter, the marginal propensity to spend is equal to the marginal propensity to consume, and the marginal propensity not to spend is equal to the marginal propensity to save. In later chapters, when we add government and international trade, the marginal propensity to spend differs from the marginal propensity to consume. Both here and in later chapters, it is the more general measures z and $1 - z$ that are important for determining equilibrium national income.

EQUILIBRIUM NATIONAL INCOME

We are now ready to see what determines the *equilibrium* level of national income. When something is in equilibrium, there is no tendency for it to change; forces are acting on it, but they balance out, and the net result is no change. Any conditions that are required for something to be in equilibrium are called its *equilibrium conditions*. We will see that the distinction between *desired* and *actual* is central to the equilibrium conditions for national income.

EQUILIBRIUM: DESIRED EXPENDITURE EQUALS ACTUAL OUTPUT

Table 23-4 illustrates the determination of equilibrium national income for our simple hypothetical economy. Suppose that firms are producing a final output of $100 billion, and thus national income is

TABLE 23-4
Equilibrium National Income
(billions of dollars)

National Income (Y)	Desired Aggregate Expenditure ($AE = C + I$)	Effect
10	43	Pressure
40	67	on income
50	75	to rise
100	115	↓
150	155	↓
175	175	Equilibrium income
200	195	↑
300	275	↑
400	355	Pressure on income to fall

National income is in equilibrium where aggregate desired expenditure equals actual national income. The data are from Table 23-3.

$100 billion. According to the table, at this level of income, aggregate desired expenditure is $115 billion. If firms persist in producing a current output of only $100 billion in the face of an aggregate desired expenditure of $115 billion, one of two things must happen.[1]

One possibility is that households, firms, and governments will be unable to spend the extra $15 billion that they would like to spend, so lines or waiting lists of unsatisfied customers will appear. These will send a signal to firms that they can increase their sales if they increase their production. When the firms increase production, national income rises. Of course, the individual firms are interested only in their own sales and profits, but their individual actions have as their inevitable consequence an increase in GDP.

Another possibility is that all spenders will spend everything that they wanted to spend. Then, however, expenditure will exceed current output, which can happen only when some expenditure plans are fulfilled by purchasing inventories of goods that were produced in the past. In our example, the fulfilment of plans to purchase $115 billion worth of commodities in the face of a current output of only $100 bil-

lion will reduce inventories by $15 billion. As long as inventories last, more goods can be sold than are currently being produced. (Notice that in this example, actual national income is equal to $100 billion. Desired consumption is $90 billion and desired investment is $25 billion, but the reduction of inventories of $15 billion is unplanned negative investment; hence actual investment is only $10 billion.)

Eventually, however, inventories will run out. But before this happens, firms will increase their outputs as they see their inventories being depleted. Extra sales can then be made without a further depletion of inventories. Once again, the consequence of each individual firm's behaviour, in search of its own individual profits, is an increase in national income. Thus the final response to an excess of aggregate desired expenditure over actual output is a rise in national income.

At any level of national income at which aggregate desired expenditure exceeds actual output, there will be pressure for national income to rise.

Next consider the $400 billion level of national income in Table 23-4. At this level, desired expenditure on domestically produced goods is only $355 billion. If firms persist in producing $400 billion worth of goods, $45 billion worth must remain unsold. Therefore, inventories must rise. However, firms will not allow inventories of unsold goods to rise indefinitely; sooner or later, they will reduce the level of output to the level of sales. When they do, national income will fall.

At any level of income for which aggregate desired expenditure is less than actual output, there will be pressure for national income to fall.

Finally, look at the national income level of $175 billion in Table 23-4. At this level, and only at this level, aggregate desired expenditure is equal to actual national income. Purchasers can fulfill their spending plans without causing inventories to change. There is no incentive for firms to alter output. Because everyone wishes to purchase an amount equal to what is being produced, output and income will remain steady; they are in equilibrium.

The equilibrium level of national income occurs where aggregate desired expenditure equals actual total output.

---

[1]Actually, there are three possibilities, but one involves a rise in the prices of goods. In this chapter, however, we have ruled this out by assumption. This possibility will be explored in detail in Chapters 25 and 26.

This conclusion is quite general and does not depend on the numbers that are used in the specific example. Extension 23-2 and the Appendix to Chapter 24 show this by giving more general derivations of equilibrium national income.

EQUILIBRIUM: DESIRED SAVING EQUALS DESIRED INVESTMENT

We have just seen that equilibrium national income occurs where desired aggregate expenditure equals actual total output. The same equilibrium can also be described as the level of national income where *desired saving equals desired investment*.

The saving-investment formulation of the model is useful because it adds perspective on how equilibrium national income is determined. Later in this book, the saving-investment formulation will illuminate a key issue in economic policy—the influence of macroeconomic policy on economic growth. Since investment adds to an economy's stock of productive resources, investment is often the only way for new and better technologies to be introduced to the workplace. In the long run, the level of a country's saving, through its effect on investment, can exert an important influence on economic growth. We are not yet ready to explore this important point, but when we are, the saving-investment balance will be an important part of the story. For now, our goal is to show that the equilibrium level of national income can be examined in terms of saving and investment.

Withdrawals and Injections

Before using this approach, we need to recall the concepts of withdrawals and injections from the circular flow of income, as shown in Figure 21-1. The circular flow of income refers to the flows of income and expenditure between domestic households and domestic firms. Domestic households spend by buying the output of domestic firms, and domestic firms spend by buying factor services from domestic households.

Injections add to this basic flow of expenditure. In this chapter, we have only one injection, investment expenditure. It occurs when firms spend money to buy the outputs of other firms in the form of capital goods, inventories, and residential housing. It is an injection because it represents earnings of firms that do not arise from *households'* spending.

Withdrawals subtract from the basic flow between domestic households and domestic firms. In this chapter, there is only one withdrawal, domestic saving. This is income received by domestic households that is *not* passed on to firms in return for goods purchased from them. The act of saving withdraws expenditure from the circular flow.

Equilibrium Income

Table 23-5 repeats data from Table 23-4, with two columns added: desired saving (which is disposable income minus desired consumption) and investment. Careful examination of this table reveals an important point: *The difference between desired invest-*

TABLE 23-5
The Saving-Investment Balance

National Income (Y)	Desired Aggregate Expenditure ($AE = C + I$)	Desired Consumption ($C = 10 + 0.8 \times Y$)	Desired Saving ($S = Y - C$)	Desired Investment (I)
10	43	18	−8	25
40	67	42	−2	25
100	115	90	10	25
175	175	150	25	25
200	195	170	30	25
300	275	250	50	25
400	355	330	70	25

National income is in equilibrium where desired saving is equal to desired investment. The data for Y, AE, and I are from Table 23-3. The data for desired saving are from Table 23-2.

ment and desired saving is exactly equal to the difference between desired aggregate expenditure and actual national income.

Suppose that national income is $100 billion. At that level of income, desired saving will be $10 billion ($100 billion less $90 billion of desired consumption). Desired investment will be $25 billion. When national income is $100 billion, therefore, desired investment will exceed desired saving by $15 billion. Note that this excess of investment over saving is exactly equal to the excess of desired aggregate expenditure over national income. When Y is $100 billion, desired saving of $10 billion implies desired consumption of $90 billion. Added to autonomous investment of $25 billion, this means that desired aggregate expenditure is $115 billion, which is $15 billion greater than actual national income.

Now suppose that national income is $400 billion. Desired saving is $70 billion, and desired investment is $25 billion—desired investment is less than desired saving by $45 billion. But it is also true that desired aggregate expenditure equals $330 billion of desired consumption plus $25 billion of desired investment, making a total of $355 for desired aggregate expenditure. Thus desired aggregate expenditure is $45 billion less than national income (when national income equals $400 billion).

In the simple model of this chapter, with no government and no international trade, the difference between desired saving and desired investment is exactly the same as the difference between national income and desired aggregate expenditure at every level of national income.

Finally, notice that at the equilibrium level of national income, $175 billion, desired saving and desired investment are equal, at $25 billion.

In the simple model of this chapter, the economy is in equilibrium when desired investment equals desired saving.

EQUILIBRIUM ILLUSTRATED

Figure 23-5 shows the determination of the equilibrium level of national income. The line labeled *AE*

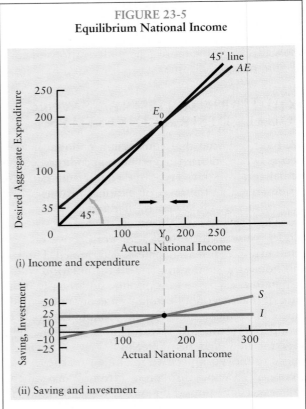

FIGURE 23-5
Equilibrium National Income

(i) Income and expenditure

(ii) Saving and investment

Equilibrium national income is that level of national income where desired aggregate expenditure equals actual national income. If actual national income is below Y_0 in panel (i), desired aggregate expenditure will exceed national income, and production will rise. This is shown by the arrow to the left of Y_0. If national income is above Y_0, desired aggregate expenditure will be less than national income, and production will fall. This is shown by the arrow to the right of Y_0. Only when national income is equal to Y_0 will desired aggregate expenditure equal actual national income.

Panel (ii) shows desired saving and desired investment on the same scale as panel (i). Equilibrium national income occurs where desired saving equals desired investment. The vertical distance between saving and investment is exactly the same as the vertical distance in part (i) between *AE* and the 45° line.

graphs the aggregate expenditure function that is given by the first and last columns of Table 23-3 and also shown in Table 23-4. The 45° line (*AE* = *Y*) graphs the equilibrium condition that aggregate desired expenditure equals actual national income. Because, in equilibrium, the variables measured on the two axes must be equal, the line showing this equality is a 45° line. Anywhere along that line, the value of desired aggregate expenditure, which is measured on the vertical axis, is equal to the value of actual national income, which is measured on the horizontal axis.[2]

Graphically, equilibrium occurs at the level of income at which the desired aggregate expenditure line intersects the 45° line. This is the level of income where desired expenditure is just equal to actual national income and hence is just sufficient to purchase total final output.

Exactly the same equilibrium is illustrated in part (ii) of the figure, but in terms of the saving-investment balance. The line labeled S is equal to aggregate saving. In an economy without government and without international trade, the case we are studying here, aggregate saving is equal to $Y - C$, the difference between national income and consumption. The line labeled I is investment, in this case assumed to be constant at all levels of income.

Notice that the vertical distance between S and I is exactly equal to the distance between the 45° line and AE. When desired investment exceeds actual desired saving, desired aggregate expenditure exceeds national income by the same amount. When desired investment is less than desired saving, desired aggregate expenditure is less than actual national income by the same amount.

Now we have explained the equilibrium level of national income that arises at a *given price level*. In the next section, we will study the forces that cause equilibrium income to change, maintaining the assumption of a given price level. In this setting, we will see that shifts in desired consumption and in-

vestment expenditure can cause major swings in national income.

CHANGES IN EQUILIBRIUM NATIONAL INCOME

Because the AE function plays a central role in determining equilibrium national income, you should not be surprised to hear that *shifts* in the AE function are central to explaining why national income changes. To understand this influence, we must recall an important distinction first encountered in Chapter 4—the distinction between *shifts of* a curve and *movements along* a curve.

Suppose that desired aggregate expenditure rises. This may be a response to a change in national income, or it may be the result of an increased desire to spend *at each level* of national income. A change in national income causes a *movement along* the aggregate expenditure function. An increased desire to spend at each level of national income causes a *shift of* the aggregate expenditure function. Figure 23-6 illustrates this important distinction.

SHIFTS OF THE AGGREGATE EXPENDITURE FUNCTION

For any specific aggregate expenditure function, there is a unique level of equilibrium national income. If the aggregate expenditure function shifts, the equilibrium will be disturbed, and national income will change. Hence if we wish to find the causes of changes in national income, we must understand the causes of shifts in the AE function.

The aggregate expenditure function shifts when one of its components shifts, that is, when there is a shift in the consumption function, in desired investment expenditure, in desired government purchases, or in desired net exports. In this chapter, we consider only shifts in the consumption function and in desired investment expenditure.

Upward Shifts in Expenditure Functions

What will happen if households permanently increase their desired levels of consumption spending at each level of disposable income, or if the expec-

---

[2]Because it turns up in many different guises, the 45° line can cause a bit of confusion until one gets used to it. The main thing to remember is that it can be used whenever the variables plotted on the two axes are measured in the same units, such as dollars, and are plotted on the same scale. In that case, equal distances on the two axes measure the same amounts. For example, one cm may correspond to $1,000 on each axis. In such circumstances, the 45° line joins all points where the values of the two variables are the same. In Figures 23-1 and 23-2, the 45° line shows all points where desired consumption expenditure equals real disposable income because these are the two variables that are plotted, one on each axis. In Figure 23-5 and all those that follow it, the 45° line shows all points at which desired aggregate expenditure equals actual national income because those are the variables that are measured on the two axes of these figures.

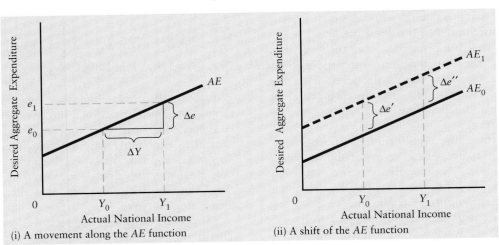

FIGURE 23-6
Movements Along and Shifts of the *AE* Function

(i) A movement along the *AE* function

(ii) A shift of the *AE* function

A movement along the aggregate expenditure function occurs in response to a change in national income; a shift of the *AE* function indicates a different level of desired expenditure at each level of national income. In part (i), a change in income of ΔY, from Y_0 to Y_1, changes desired expenditure by Δe, from e_0 to e_1. In part (ii), a shift in the *AE* function from AE_0 to AE_1 raises the amount of expenditure associated with each level of national income. At Y_0, for example, desired aggregate expenditure is increased by $\Delta e'$; at Y_1, it is increased by $\Delta e''$. (If the *AE* function line shifts parallel to itself, then $\Delta e' = \Delta e''$.)

tation of higher future sales causes domestic auto makers to increase their rate of annual investment? (In considering these questions, remember that we are dealing with continuous flows measured as so much per period of time. A permanent upward shift in any expenditure function means that the desired expenditure associated with each level of national income rises to, and stays at, a higher amount.)

Because any such increase in autonomous expenditure shifts the entire aggregate expenditure function upward, the same analysis applies to each of the changes mentioned. Two types of shift in *AE* occur. First, if the same addition to expenditure occurs at all levels of income, the *AE* curve shifts parallel to itself, as shown in part (i) of Figure 23-7. Second, if there is a change in the propensity to spend out of national income, the slope of the *AE* curve changes, as shown in part (ii) of Figure 23-7. (Recall that the slope of the *AE* curve is z, the marginal propensity to spend.) A change such as the one illustrated would occur if consumers decided to spend more of every dollar of disposable income.

Figure 23-7 shows that an upward shift in the aggregate expenditure function increases equilibrium national income. After the shift in the *AE* curve, income is no longer in equilibrium at its original level because at that level, desired expenditure exceeds actual national income. Equilibrium national income now occurs at the higher level indicated by the intersection of the new *AE* curve with the 45° line.

Shifts in the Saving and Investment Functions

We saw earlier that in equilibrium, desired aggregate expenditure is equal to actual national income and desired saving is equal to desired investment. When the aggregate expenditure function shifts and equilibrium income changes, this equality must still hold true at the new equilibrium.

Consider the case of a shift in the aggregate expenditure function that is caused by a shift in the consumption function. As we discussed earlier (see Figure 23-2), when the consumption function shifts, the saving function shifts as well, and by an equal

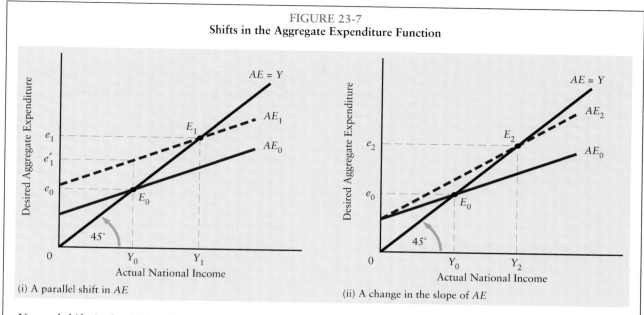

FIGURE 23-7
Shifts in the Aggregate Expenditure Function

(i) A parallel shift in *AE*

(ii) A change in the slope of *AE*

Upward shifts in the *AE* function increase equilibrium income; downward shifts decrease equilibrium income. In parts (i) and (ii), the *AE* function is initially AE_0 with national income Y_0.

In part (i), a parallel upward shift in the *AE* curve from AE_0 to AE_1 means that desired expenditure has increased by the same amount at each level of national income. For example, at Y_0, desired expenditure rises from e_0 to e_1' and therefore exceeds national income. Equilibrium is reached at E_1, where income is Y_1 and expenditure is e_1. The increase in desired expenditure from e_1' to e_1, represented by a movement along AE_1, is an induced response to the increase in income from Y_0 to Y_1.

In part (ii), a nonparallel upward shift in the *AE* curve, say, from AE_0 to AE_2, means that the marginal propensity to spend has increased. This leads to an increase in equilibrium national income. Equilibrium is reached at E_2, where the new level of expenditure e_2 is equal to income Y_2. Again, the initial shift in the *AE* curve induces a movement along the new *AE* curve.

and opposite amount. This is true because consumption and saving always adds up to disposable income. Hence if the consumption function shifts up by some amount at every level of income, the saving function *must* shift down by exactly the same amount.

Figure 23-8(i) shows a downward shift in the saving function (corresponding to an upward shift in the consumption function). Equilibrium national income occurs where desired saving equals desired investment. With desired investment fixed, a downward shift in the saving function leads to an *increase* in equilibrium national income. This is just as it should be; a downward shift in the saving function implies an upward shift in the consumption and aggregate expenditure functions.

In Figure 23-8(ii), the same increase in equilibrium national income is shown as arising from an upward

shift in the investment function. Such a change might take place, for example, in response to a fall in real interest rates or an increase in business confidence.

Notice that although the change in equilibrium income is the same in both parts of Figure 23-8, the composition of GDP is not. When the saving function shifts downward, investment is unchanged in the new equilibrium—remember, I is constant. With Y up and I constant, consumption must have risen. In contrast, when the investment function shifts upward, saving, consumption, and investment are all higher at the new level of income. (The higher levels of saving and investment can be seen directly in the figure. The higher level of consumption is inferred from the fact that income has risen, the marginal propensity to consume is positive, and the consumption function has not shifted.)

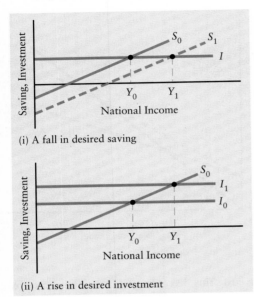

FIGURE 23-8
Shifts in Desired Saving and Investment

(i) A fall in desired saving

(ii) A rise in desired investment

Upward shifts in investment and downward shifts in saving both increase equilibrium income but lead to different compositions of national product. Panel (i) shows a downward shift in desired saving (the equivalent of an upward shift in desired consumption). National income increases from Y_0 to Y_1.

In panel (ii), the economy starts at the same initial equilibrium (Y_0) and ends at the same equilibrium income (Y_1). The economy in panel (ii) differs from that in panel (i), however. At Y_1, the economy in panel (ii) has higher saving and investment than in panel (i). This implies that in the future, the panel (ii) economy will have greater productive resources in the form of a larger capital stock.

Downward Shifts in Expenditure Functions

What happens to national income if there is a decrease in the amount of consumption or investment expenditure desired at each level of income? These changes shift the aggregate expenditure function downward. A constant reduction in desired expenditure at all levels of income shifts AE parallel to itself. A fall in the marginal propensity to spend out of national income reduces the slope of the AE function. When we use the saving-investment relation, we must note that a downward shift in the consumption function implies an upward shift in

the saving function, reducing the equilibrium level of income.

The Results Restated

We have derived two important general propositions of the elementary theory of national income.

1. A rise in the amount of desired aggregate expenditure that is associated with each level of national income will increase equilibrium national income.

2. A fall in the amount of desired aggregate expenditure that is associated with each level of national income will lower equilibrium national income.

THE MULTIPLIER

We have learned how to predict the direction of the changes in national income that occur in response to various shifts in the aggregate expenditure function. We would like also to predict the *magnitude* of these changes.

Economists need to know the *size* of the effects of changes in expenditures. During a recession, the government sometimes takes measures to stimulate the economy. If these measures have a larger effect than estimated, demand may rise too much, and full employment may be reached while demand is still rising. This outcome will have an inflationary effect on the economy. If the government overestimates the impact of its measures, the recession will persist longer than necessary. In this case, there is a danger that the policy will be discredited as ineffective, even though the correct diagnosis is that too little of the right thing was done.

Definition

A measure of the magnitude of changes in income is provided by the *multiplier*. We have just seen that a shift in the aggregate expenditure curve will cause a change in equilibrium national income. Such a shift could be caused by a change in any autonomous component of aggregate expenditure, such as an increase or a decrease in investment. An increase in desired aggregate expenditure increases equilibrium national income by a multiple of the initial increase in autonomous expenditure.

The multiplier is the change in national income divided by the change in autonomous expenditure that brought it about.

Why the Multiplier is Greater than One. What will happen to national income if MacMillan Bloedel spends $300 million per year on new paper mills? Initially, the construction of the paper mills will create $300 million worth of new national income and a corresponding amount of income for households and firms on which the initial $300 million is spent, but this is not the end of the story. The increase in national income of $300 million will cause an increase in disposable income, which will cause an induced rise in consumption expenditure.

Electricians, masons, and carpenters—who gain new income directly from the building of the paper mills—will spend some of it on food, clothing, entertainment, cars, television sets, and other commodities. When output expands to meet this demand, new incomes will be created for workers and firms in these industries. When they, in turn, spend their newly earned incomes, output will rise further. More income will be created, and more expenditure will be induced. Indeed, at this stage, we might wonder whether the increases in income will ever come to an end. To deal with this concern, we need to consider the multiplier in somewhat more precise terms.

The Simple Multiplier Defined.   Consider an increase in autonomous expenditure of ΔA, which might be, say, $1 billion per year. Remember that ΔA stands for *any* increase in autonomous expenditure; this could be an increase in investment or in the autonomous component of consumption. The new autonomous expenditure shifts the aggregate expenditure function upward by that amount. National income is no longer in equilibrium at its original level because desired aggregate expenditure now exceeds actual income. Equilibrium is restored by a *movement along* the new AE curve.

The **simple multiplier** measures the change in equilibrium national income that occurs in response to a change in autonomous expenditure *at a constant price level*. We refer to it as "simple" because we have simplified the situation by assuming that the price level is fixed. Figure 23-9 illustrates

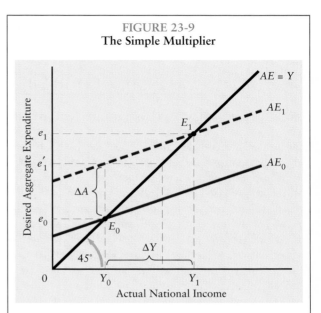

FIGURE 23-9
The Simple Multiplier

An increase in the autonomous component of desired aggregate expenditure increases equilibrium national income by a multiple of the initial increase. The initial equilibrium is at E_0, where AE_0 intersects the 45° line. At this point, desired expenditure, e_0, is equal to national income, Y_0. An increase in autonomous expenditure of ΔA then shifts the desired expenditure function upward to AE_1. If national income stays at Y_0, desired expenditure rises to e_1'. Because this level of desired expenditure is greater than national income, national income will rise.

Equilibrium occurs when income rises to Y_1. Here desired expenditure, e_1, equals national income, Y_1. The increase in desired expenditure from e_1' to e_1 represents the induced increase in expenditure. It is the amount by which the overall increase in national income, ΔY, exceeds the initial increase in autonomous expenditure, ΔA. Because ΔY is greater than ΔA, the simple multiplier is greater than one $(\Delta Y / \Delta A > 1)$.

the simple multiplier and makes clear that it is greater than one. Extension 23-1 provides a numerical example.

The Size of the Simple Multiplier

The size of the simple multiplier depends on the slope of the *AE* function—that is, on the marginal

EXTENSION 23-1

THE MULTIPLIER: A NUMERICAL EXAMPLE

Consider an economy that has a marginal propensity to spend out of national income of 0.80. Suppose that autonomous expenditure increases by $1 billion per year, because a large corporation spends an extra $1 billion per year on new factories. National income initially rises by $1 billion, but that is not the end of it. The factors of production that received the first $1 billion spend $800 million. This second round of spending generates $800 million of new income. This new income, in turn, induces $640 million of third-round spending, and so it continues, with each successive round of new income generating 80 percent as much in new expenditure. Each additional round of expenditure creates new income and yet another round of expenditure.

The table carries the process through 10 rounds. Students with sufficient patience (and no faith in mathematics) may compute as many rounds in the process as they wish; they will find that the sum of the rounds of expenditures approaches a limit of $5 billion, which is five times the initial increase in expenditure. [34]

The graph of the cumulative expenditure increases shows how quickly this limit is approached. The multiplier is thus 5, given that the marginal propensity to spend is 0.8. Had the marginal propensity to spend been lower, say, 0.667, the process would have been similar, but it would have approached a limit of three instead of five times the initial increase in expenditure.

Round of spending	Increase in Expenditure (millions of dollars)	Cumulative Total (millions of dollars)
1 (initial increase)	1,000	1,000
2	800	1,800
3	640	2,440
4	512	2,952
5	409.6	3,361.6
6	327.7	3,689.3
7	262.1	3,951.4
8	209.7	4,161.1
9	167.8	4,328.9
10	134.2	4,463.1
11 to 20 combined	479.3	4,942.4
All others	57.6	5,000.0

propensity to spend, z. This is illustrated in Figure 23-10.

A high marginal propensity to spend means a steep *AE* curve. The expenditure induced by any initial increase in income is large, with the result that the final rise in income is correspondingly large. By contrast, a low marginal propensity to spend means a relatively flat *AE* curve. The expenditure induced by the initial increase in income is small, and the final rise in income is not much larger than the initial rise in autonomous expenditure that brought it about.

The larger the marginal propensity to spend, the steeper the aggregate expenditure function and the larger the multiplier.

The precise value of the simple multiplier can be derived by using elementary algebra. (The derivation is given in Extension 23-2.) The result is that the simple multiplier, which we call K, is

$$\text{Simple Multiplier} = K = \frac{\Delta Y}{\Delta A} = \frac{1}{1 - z}$$

FIGURE 23-10
The Size of the Simple Multiplier

(i) Flat *AE*, multiplier equal to one

(ii) Intermediate case

(iii) Steep *AE*, multiplier large

The larger the marginal propensity to spend out of national income (z), the steeper is the AE curve and the larger is the multiplier. In each part of the figure, the initial aggregate expenditure function is AE_0, equilibrium is at E_0, with income Y_0. The AE curve then shifts upward to AE_1 as a result of an increase in autonomous expenditure of ΔA. ΔA is the same in each part. The new equilibrium is at E_1.

In part (i), the AE function is horizontal, indicating a marginal propensity to spend of zero ($z = 0$). The change in equilibrium income ΔY is only the increase in autonomous expenditure because there is no induced expenditure by the people who receive the initial increase in income. The simple multiplier is then equal to one, its minimum possible value.

In part (ii), the AE curve slopes upward but is still relatively flat (z is low). The increase in equilibrium national income to Y_2 is only slightly greater than the increase in autonomous expenditure that brought it about.

In part (iii), the AE function is quite steep (z is high). Now the increase in equilibrium income to Y_3 is much larger than the increase in autonomous expenditure that brought it about. The simple multiplier is quite large.

where z is the marginal propensity to spend out of national income. (As we have seen, z is the slope of the aggregate expenditure function.)

As we saw earlier, the term $1 - z$ stands for the marginal propensity *not* to spend out of national income. For example, if 80 cents of every dollar of new national income is spent ($z = 0.8$), 20 cents is the amount not spent. The value of the multiplier is then calculated as $K = 1/0.2 = 5$.

The simple multiplier equals the reciprocal of the marginal propensity not to spend.

From this we see that, if $1 - z$ is small (that is, if z is large), the multiplier will be large (because extra income induces a lot of extra spending). What if $1 - z$ is large? The largest possible value of $1 - z$ is one, which arises when z equals zero, indicating that none of any additional national income is spent. In this case, the multiplier itself has a value of one; the increase in equilibrium national income is confined to the initial increase in autonomous expenditure. There are no induced additional effects on spending,

so national income increases only by the original increase in autonomous expenditure.

To estimate the size of the multiplier in an actual economy, we need to estimate the value of the marginal propensity not to spend out of national income in that economy, that is, $1 - z$. Evidence suggests that the Canadian value is much larger than the 0.2 that we used in our example, in large part because there are a number of withdrawals from the circular flow of income that we have not yet included in our model of the economy. In addition to saving, which we have discussed, these withdrawals include income taxes and import expenditures. For the Canadian economy in the 1990s, this leads to a realistic estimate of around 0.7 for $1 - z$. Hence the simple multiplier is closer to 1.5 than to 5, as in the example.

The simple multiplier is a useful starting point for understanding the effects of changes in autonomous expenditures on equilibrium national income; however, as we shall see in subsequent chapters, many complications will arise which make the story more complex.

EXTENSION 23-2

THE MULTIPLIER: AN ALGEBRAIC APPROACH

Basic algebra is all that is needed to derive the exact expression for the multiplier. Readers who feel at home with algebra may want to follow this derivation. Others can skip it and rely on the graphical and numerical arguments that have been given in the text.

First, we derive the equation for the *AE* curve. Desired aggregate expenditure can be decomposed into autonomous expenditure and induced expenditure. In the simple model of this chapter, autonomous expenditure is just equal to investment plus autonomous consumption. Induced expenditure is just equal to induced consumption.

Hence we can write

$$AE = z \times Y + A \qquad [1]$$

where *A* is autonomous expenditure and $z \times Y$ is induced expenditure, *z* being the marginal propensity to spend out of national income.* In the simple model of this chapter, with no government and no international trade, *z* is equal to the marginal propensity to consume.

Now we write the equation of the 45° line,

$$AE = Y \qquad [2]$$

_____
*When we add imports and government in the next chapter, induced expenditure will include induced imports, and *A* will include government spending and exports. The derivation here is quite general, however. All that matters is that desired aggregate expenditure can be divided into one class of expenditure that varies with income and another class that does not.

which states the equilibrium condition that desired aggregate expenditure equals actual national income. Equations 1 and 2 are two equations with two unknowns, *AE* and *Y*. To solve them, we substitute Equation 1 into Equation 2 to obtain

$$Y = z \times Y + A \qquad [3]$$

Equation 3 can be easily solved to get *Y* expressed in terms of *A* and *z*. The solution is

$$Y = \frac{A}{1 - z} \qquad [4]$$

Equation 4 tells us the equilibrium value of *Y* in terms of autonomous expenditures (*A*) and the marginal propensity not to spend out of national income $(1 - z)$. Now consider a \$1 increase in *A*. The expression $Y = A/(1 - z)$ tells us that if *A* changes by one dollar, the change in *Y* will be $1/(1 - z)$ dollars. Generally, for a change in autonomous spending of ΔA, the change in *Y* will be

$$\Delta Y = \frac{\Delta A}{1 - z} \qquad [5]$$

Dividing through by ΔA gives the value of the multiplier, which we designate by *K*:

$$K = \frac{\Delta Y}{\Delta A} = \frac{1}{1 - z} \qquad [6]$$

SUMMARY

A. DESIRED VERSUS ACTUAL EXPENDITURE

- Desired aggregate expenditure includes desired consumption, desired investment, desired government purchases, plus desired net exports. It is the amount that economic agents want to spend on purchasing the national product. In this chapter, we consider only consumption and investment.

- The relationship between disposable income and consumption is called the consumption function. The constant term in the consumption function is autonomous expenditure. The part of consumption that responds to income is called induced expenditure.

- A change in disposable income leads to a change in desired consumption and desired saving. The responsiveness of these changes is measured by the marginal propensity to consume (*MPC*) and the marginal propensity to save (*MPS*), which are both positive and sum to one, indicating that all disposable income is either consumed or saved.

- A change in wealth tends to cause a change in the allocation of disposable income between consumption and saving. Consumption is positively related to wealth, whereas saving is negatively related to wealth.

- Investment depends, among other things, on real interest rates, changes in sales, and business confidence. In our simplest model of the economy, investment is treated as an autonomous expenditure.

B. EQUILIBRIUM NATIONAL INCOME

- Equilibrium national income is defined as that level of national income where desired aggregate expenditure equals actual national income. At incomes above equilibrium, desired expenditure falls short of national income, and production will sooner or later be curtailed. At incomes below equilibrium, desired expenditure exceeds national income, and production will sooner or later be increased.

- In a closed economy with no government, an alternative definition of equilibrium national income is that level of national income where desired saving equals desired investment.

- Equilibrium national income is represented graphically by the point at which the aggregate expenditure curve cuts the 45° line—that is, where desired aggregate expenditure equals total output. This is the same level of income at which the saving function intersects the investment function.

C. CHANGES IN EQUILIBRIUM NATIONAL INCOME

- Equilibrium national income is increased by a rise in either the desired consumption or the desired investment expenditure that is associated with each level of the national income. Equilibrium national income is reduced by a fall in these desired expenditures.

- The magnitude of the effect on national income of shifts in autonomous expenditure is given by the multiplier. It is defined as $K = \Delta Y / \Delta A$, where ΔA is the change in autonomous expenditure.

- The simple multiplier is the multiplier when the price level is constant. It is equal to $1/(1 - z)$, where z is the marginal propensity to spend out of national income. Thus, the larger is z, the larger is the multiplier. It is a basic prediction of national income theory that the simple multiplier, relating \$1 increase in spending on domestic output to the resulting increase in national income, is greater than one.

KEY CONCEPTS

Desired versus actual expenditure
The consumption function
Average and marginal propensities to consume
Average and marginal propensities to save
The aggregate expenditure function

Marginal propensities to spend and not to spend
Equilibrium national income
Saving-investment balance
Shifts of and movements along expenditure curves

Effect on national income of changes in desired expenditures
The simple multiplier
The size of the multiplier and slope of the *AE* curve

DISCUSSION QUESTIONS

1. Relate the following newspaper headlines to shifts in the *C, S, I* and *AE* functions and to changes in equilibrium national income.

   a. "Revival of consumer confidence leads to increased spending."
   b. "High mortgage rates discourage new house purchases."

   c. "Concern over future leads to a reduction in inventories."
   d. "Accelerated depreciation allowances in the new federal budget sets off boom on equipment purchases."

2. Interpret each of the following statements either in terms of the shape of the consumption function or the values of *MPC* and *APC*.

a. "Tom Green has lost his job, and his family is existing on its past savings."

b. "The Grimsby household is so rich that they used all the extra income they earned this year to invest in a wildcat oil-drilling venture."

c. "The inflation has made the Schultzes feel so poor that they are adding an extra $100 a week to their account at the savings bank."

d. "The last stock market crash led young Ross to cancel two planned trips abroad, even though his job as a broker was never at risk."

3. Why might an individual's marginal propensity to consume be higher in the long run than in the short run? Why might it be lower? Is it possible for an individual's average propensity to consume to be greater than one in the short run? In the long run? Can a country's average propensity to consume be greater than one in the short run? In the long run?

4. What relationship holds along the 45° line between total desired expenditures and total income? In determining equilibrium graphically, are we restricted to choosing identical vertical and horizontal scales?

5. Explain carefully why national income changes when desired aggregate expenditure does not equal national income. Sketch scenarios that fit the cases of too much and too little desired expenditure.

6. Explain why a sudden, unexpected fall in consumer expenditure would initially cause an increase in investment expenditure by firms.

7. The "Paradox of Thrift" is a famous idea connected with the type of model that we have developed in this chapter (and we will discuss it in detail in later chapters). The basic idea is that if every household in the economy tries to increase its level of autonomous saving, they will end up saving no more than they were initially (hence the paradox), but the level of national income will be lower. Using the model of this chapter, explain how an increase in desired saving would reduce equilibrium income and lead to no change in aggregate saving.

8. Explain in terms of the aggregate expenditure function what is being described by the following newspaper headline: "Auto sales soar as economy booms."

9. "The concept of an equilibrium level of national income is useless because the economy is never in equilibrium. If it ever got there, no economist would recognize it anyway." Comment on this statement.

10. In Figure 23-5, the equilibrium level of national income is $175 billion. Suppose that actual national income is less than $175 billion. What is the relationship between *desired* aggregate expenditure and *actual* aggregate expenditure in this situation? What explains the difference between the two? Now consider a situation where actual national income exceeds $175 billion, and answer the same two questions.

11. In the simple model of this chapter, aggregate investment was assumed to be autonomous. The simple multiplier was $K = 1/(1 - z)$, where z was the marginal propensity to spend. With autonomous investment, the marginal propensity to spend is simply the marginal propensity to consume. Now suppose that investment is *not* completely autonomous. That is, suppose that $I = \bar{I} + mY$, where $\bar{I}$ is autonomous investment and m is the "marginal propensity to invest" ($m > 0$). Explain how this modification to the simple model changes the simple multiplier.

CHAPTER 24

NATIONAL INCOME AND AGGREGATE EXPENDITURE II: AN OPEN ECONOMY WITH GOVERNMENT

In Chapter 23, we developed a simplified model of national income determination in a closed economy with fixed prices. The economy that we live in and wish to study is both more interesting and more complicated. Unlike the economy of Chapter 23, it has a government (in fact, several levels of government), and it engages in foreign trade. In this chapter, we add a government and a foreign sector to our simple model. In Chapters 25 and 26, we will expand the model further to explain the determination of the price level.

Adding the government sector to the model allows us to study *fiscal policy,* the ability of the government to use its taxing and spending powers to affect the level of national income. Fortunately, the key elements of last chapter's theory of income determination are unchanged even after incorporating government and the foreign sector. The most important of these are restated here.

1. Desired aggregate expenditure can be divided into autonomous expenditure and induced expenditure. Induced expenditure is expenditure that depends on the level of national income.

2. Equilibrium national income occurs where desired aggregate expenditure equals actual national income. Graphically, this is where the aggregate expenditure function intersects the 45° line.

3. The simple multiplier measures the change in equilibrium national income that takes place in response to a unit change in autonomous domestic expenditure (with the price level held constant).

INTRODUCING GOVERNMENT

Government spending and taxing policies affect equilibrium national income in two important ways. First, government purchases are part of autonomous expenditure. Second, in deriving disposable income, taxes must be subtracted from national income, and government transfer payments must be added. Because disposable income determines consumption expenditure, the relationship between desired consumption and national income becomes somewhat more complicated when a government is added.

A government's **fiscal policy** is defined by its plans for taxes and spending. These influence the size of national income in both the short and the long run. Our discussion of fiscal policy begins in this chapter; we go into more detail in Chapter 26 and again in Chapter 32.

GOVERNMENT SPENDING

In Chapter 22, we distinguished between government *purchases of goods and services* and government *transfer payments.* The distinction bears repeating here. Government purchases are part of GDP. When the government hires a bureaucrat, buys a paper clip, or purchases fuel for the armed forces, it is adding directly to the demands for the economy's current output of goods and services. Hence desired government purchases, G, are part of aggregate desired expenditure. For now, we assume that the government simply chooses a level of desired purchases and is able to spend that amount. Later we will look at the determinants of desired government purchases in more detail.

The other part of government spending, transfer payments, also affects desired aggregate expenditure, but only indirectly. Consider welfare or unemployment-insurance payments, for example. These government expenditures place no demand on the nation's production of goods and services. However, when recipients spend some of these payments on consumption, their expenditure is part of aggregate expenditure. Thus government transfer payments do affect aggregate expenditure but only through the effect that these payments have on *disposable* income. An increase in transfer payments increases disposable income, and an increase in disposable income increases desired consumption expenditure—via the consumption function.

TAX REVENUES

Tax revenues may be thought of as negative transfer payments in their effect on desired aggregate expenditure. Tax payments reduce disposable income relative to national income; transfers raise disposable income relative to national income. For the purpose of calculating the effect of government policy on desired consumption expenditure, it is the net effect of the two that matters.

We define **net taxes** as total tax revenue received by the government minus total transfer payments made by the government, and we denote it as T. (For convenience, when we use the term "taxes," we will mean "net taxes" unless we explicitly state otherwise.) Because transfer payments are smaller than total tax revenues, net tax revenues are positive. This helps to make disposable personal income substantially less than national income. (It was about 67 percent of GDP in 1995.)

THE BUDGET BALANCE AND PUBLIC SAVING

The **budget balance** is the difference between total government revenue and total government expenditure; equivalently, it equals net tax revenue minus government purchases, $T - G$. When revenues exceed expenditures, the government is said to be running a **budget surplus.** When expenditures exceed revenues, as they have for over two decades in the federal government, the government is said to be running a **budget deficit.**[1] When the two amounts are equal, the government has a **balanced budget.**

In the simple model of Chapter 23, all saving was private since we had no government in the model. Here we define **private saving** as the difference between disposable income and consumption expenditure, or the amount that households choose to save. But governments can save as well. Consider the circular flow diagram, Figure 21-1. Net taxes, like household saving, are a withdrawal from the flow of expenditure. Government purchases, like household consumption, are an injection into the flow of expenditure. When government tax revenues exceed government spending, government is withdrawing more from the spending stream than it is adding. Put another way, the amount of national output used by the government, through purchases of goods and services, is less than the amount of national income accruing to the government in the form of tax revenue. Hence when the government runs a budget surplus, it is consuming less than its "income." The government is therefore saving.

Similarly, when the government runs a budget deficit, it is dissaving. It is spending more of national

[1]When the government runs a budget deficit, it must borrow the excess of spending over revenues. It does this by issuing and selling *government bonds*. When the government runs a surplus, it uses the excess revenue to purchase outstanding government bonds. The stock of outstanding bonds is termed the *national debt*. Deficits and the national debt are the principal topics of Chapter 32.

TABLE 24-1
The Public Saving (Budget Surplus) Function
(billions of dollars)

National Income (Y)	Government Purchases (G)	Net Taxes ($T = 0.1 \times Y$)	Public Saving ($T - G$)
50	17	5	−12
100	17	10	−7
175	17	17.5	0.5
200	17	20	3
300	17	30	13
400	17	40	23

Desired public saving, which is just equal to the planned budget surplus, is negative at low levels of national income and becomes positive at sufficiently high levels of national income. The table shows that the size of the budget surplus (which is the same thing as public saving) increases with national income, given a constant set of expenditure and taxing rules. As national income rises, public saving rises by the income-tax rate times the change in national income. Thus when national income rises by $100 billion, public saving rises by $10 billion.

income than it receives in net taxes. In this case, its "income" is less than its expenditure. **Public saving** is equal to government revenues less government spending ($T - G$).

When government runs a budget surplus, public saving is positive; when government runs a budget deficit, public saving is negative.

The Public Saving Function

In this chapter, we treat government purchases of goods and services as autonomous—that is, the level of government purchases does not depend on the level of national income. The government decides on how much it wishes to spend and holds to these plans whatever the level of national income. We also treat *tax rates* as autonomous. The government sets its tax rates and does not vary them as national income varies. This, however, implies that *tax revenues* are induced. As national income rises, a tax system with given rates will yield more revenue. For example, when income rises, people will pay more income tax in total even though income tax *rates* are unchanged.

Table 24-1 and Figure 24-1 illustrate these assumptions with a specific example using hypothetical data. They show desired public saving when desired government purchases (G) are constant at $17

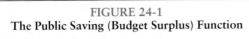

FIGURE 24-1
The Public Saving (Budget Surplus) Function

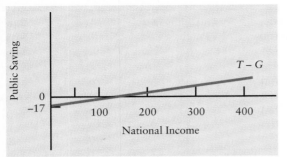

Public saving increases as national income increases. The figure plots the $T - G$ column from Table 24-1. Notice that the slope of the public saving function is equal to the income-tax rate of 0.1.

Hence G and T in the national income accounts measure purchases by all governments and net taxes collected by all governments.

INTRODUCING NET EXPORTS

Foreign trade accounts for about 30 percent of national income in Canada. Canada imports all kinds of goods and services, from French wine and Peruvian anchovies, to Swiss financial and American architectural services. Canada also exports a variety of goods and services, including timber, nickel, automobiles, engineering services, computer software, and commuter jets. U.S.-Canadian trade is the largest two-way flow of trade between any two countries in the world today.

THE NET EXPORT FUNCTION

Exports depend on spending decisions made by foreign households that purchase Canadian goods and services. Typically, therefore, exports will not change as a result of changes in Canadian national income. They are autonomous expenditure from the point of view of Canadian national income.

Imports, however, depend on the spending decisions of Canadian households. All categories of expenditure have an import content; Canadian-made cars, for example, use large quantities of imported components in their manufacture. Hence imports rise when the other categories of expenditure rise. Because consumption rises with income, imports of foreign-produced consumption goods and materials that go into the production of domestically produced consumption goods also rise with income.

There is a positive relationship between desired imports and national income. Since exports are autonomous with respect to national income, this means that desired net exports (exports minus desired imports) are negatively related to national income.

This negative relationship between net exports and national income is called the *net export function*. Data for a hypothetical economy with constant exports and with imports that are 10 percent of national income are given in Table 24-2 and illustrated in Figure 24-2. In this example, exports form the au-

billion and net taxes are equal to 10 percent of national income. Notice that public saving (which is exactly equal to the government budget surplus) increases with national income. This relationship occurs because net tax revenues rise with income but, by assumption, government purchases do not. The slope of the public saving function (which can also be called the *budget surplus function*) is just equal to the income tax rate. The position of the budget surplus function is determined by fiscal policy, as we discuss later in this chapter.

PROVINCIAL AND MUNICIPAL GOVERNMENTS

Most of our discussion of government spending and taxing is focused on the federal government, which generally has more discretion over its fiscal policy than do provincial and municipal governments. However, it is important to remember that the Canadian provincial and municipal governments account for *more* purchases of goods and services than does the federal government. The federal government raises about the same amount of tax revenue as do the provincial and municipal governments combined, but spends much more of its revenues on transfer payments.

When measuring the overall contribution of the public sector to aggregate expenditure and to national saving, all levels of government must be included.

TABLE 24-2
A Net Export Schedule
(billions of dollars)

National Income (Y)	Exports (X)	Imports (IM = 0.1 × Y)	Net Exports
100	24	10	14
200	24	20	4
240	24	24	0
300	24	30	−6
400	24	40	−16
500	24	50	−26

Net exports fall as national income rises. The data are hypothetical. They assume that exports are constant and that imports are 10 percent of national income. In this case, net exports are positive at low levels of national income and negative at high levels of national income.

tonomous component and imports the induced component of the desired net export function.[2]

SHIFTS IN THE NET EXPORT FUNCTION

The net export function relates net exports (X − IM), which we also denote NX, to national income. It is drawn under the assumption that everything affecting net exports, except domestic national income, remains constant. The major factors that must be held constant are foreign national income, domestic and foreign prices, and the exchange rate. A change in any of these factors will affect the amount of net exports that will occur at each level of Canadian national income and hence will shift the net export function.

Notice that anything that affects Canadian exports will change the values in the export column in Table 24-2 and so will shift the net export function parallel to itself, upward if exports increase and downward if exports decrease. Also notice that anything that affects the *proportion of income* that Canadian consumers wish to spend on imports will change the values in the import column in Table 24-2 and thus will change the *slope* of the net export function.

[2]The formulation in the table implicitly assumes that all imports are for final consumption; imports rise when income rises, but imports do not change when other categories of autonomous expenditure change. This simplification will prove useful in our development of the determination of equilibrium income but does not affect the essentials of the theory.

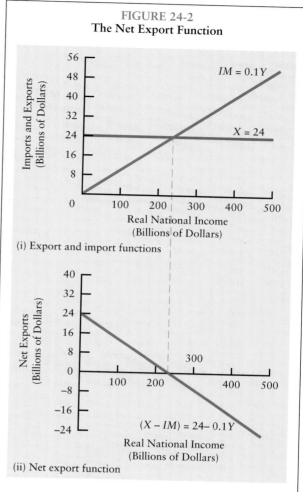

FIGURE 24-2
The Net Export Function

(i) Export and import functions

(ii) Net export function

Net exports, defined as the difference between exports and imports, are inversely related to the level of national income. In part (i), exports are constant at $24 billion while imports rise with national income. Therefore, net exports, shown in part (ii), decline with national income. The figure plots the data from Table 24-2.

Foreign Income

An increase in foreign income, other things being equal, will lead to an increase in the quantity of Canadian goods demanded by foreign countries—that is, to an increase in Canadian exports. The increase is in the constant X of the net export function, causing NX to shift upward, parallel to its original position. A fall in foreign income leads to a parallel downward shift in the net export function.

Relative International Prices

Any change in the prices of Canadian goods relative to those of foreign goods will cause both imports and exports to change. This will shift the net export function.

Consider first a rise in Canadian prices relative to those in foreign countries. The increase in Canadian prices means that foreigners now see Canadian goods as more expensive relative both to goods produced in their own country and to goods imported from countries other than Canada. As a result, the value of Canadian exports will fall.[3] Similarly, Canadians will see imports from foreign countries become cheaper relative to the prices of Canadian-made goods. As a result, they will shift their expenditures more toward foreign goods and away from domestic goods. The combination of these two effects is that the net export function shifts downward and changes its slope, as shown in Figure 24-3.

Now consider the opposite case of a fall in Canadian prices relative to prices of foreign-made goods. The decline in Canadian prices means that Canadian exports now look cheaper in foreign markets relative both to foreign goods and to goods imported from countries other than Canada. As a result, Canadian exports rise. Similarly, the same change in relative prices—Canadian-made goods become cheaper relative to foreign-made goods—causes Canadian imports to fall. Thus the net export function shifts upward and changes its slope, as shown in Figure 24-3.

To apply these results, we need only note things that will cause relative international prices to change. The two important causes are international differences in inflation rates and changes in exchange rates.

Different Inflation Rates.   Canadian prices will rise relative to foreign prices if Canada's inflation rate is higher than the inflation rates in other major trading countries. Conversely, Canadian prices will fall relative to foreign prices if Canada's inflation rate is lower than the rates in other major trading countries.

Changes in the Exchange Rate.   Now consider changes in the exchange rate. A fall in the external value of the Canadian dollar (a *depreciation* of the Canadian dollar) means that foreigners must pay less

---

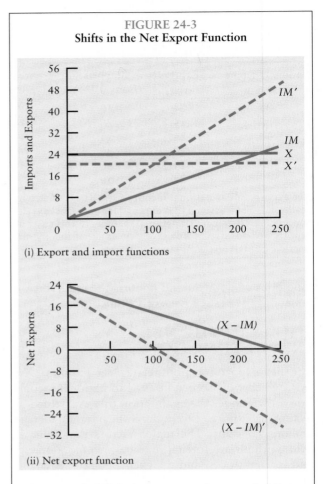

FIGURE 24-3
Shifts in the Net Export Function

(i) Export and import functions

(ii) Net export function

An upward shift in imports or a downward shift in exports shifts the net export function downward. A rise in Canadian prices relative to foreign prices, or a rise in the external value of the Canadian dollar, lowers exports from X to X' and raises the import function from IM to IM'. This shifts the net export function downward from (X − IM) to (X − IM)'. Starting from the primed functions, a fall in Canadian prices relative to foreign prices, or a fall in the external value of the Canadian dollar, raises exports to X and lowers the import function to IM, thus raising the net export function to (X − IM).

---

of their money to buy one Canadian dollar, and Canadian residents must pay more Canadian dollars to buy a unit of any foreign currency. As a result, the price of foreign goods in terms of Canadian dollars rises, and the price of Canadian goods in terms of foreign currency falls. This reduction in the relative price of Canadian goods will cause a shift in expen-

---

[3] This assumes that the demand for Canadian goods in international markets has a price elasticity greater than one. We make this assumption, which is generally believed to be true, throughout this book.

diture away from foreign goods and toward Canadian goods. Canadian residents will import less at each level of Canadian national income, and foreigners will buy more Canadian exports. The net export function thus shifts upward.

A rise in the external value of the Canadian dollar (an *appreciation* of the Canadian dollar) has the opposite effect: It causes a fall in exports and a rise in imports, shifting the net export function downward.

Because calculations involving exchange rates can be confusing, an example may help. First, suppose that one Canadian dollar is worth 80 Japanese yen (¥) on the foreign exchange market. A Japanese must pay ¥80 to buy one Canadian dollar, and a Canadian must pay $1 to buy ¥80. Next, let the external value of the Canadian dollar fall to ¥60. Now a Japanese need only pay ¥60 to get one Canadian dollar, and Canadian goods and services will look cheaper to the Japanese buyer. In contrast, a Canadian must now pay $1.33 to get ¥80 (80/60 = 1.33), and Japanese goods and services will look more expensive to the Canadian.

The results of this important chain of reasoning are as follows:

1. Canadian prices rise relative to foreign prices if either the Canadian inflation rate exceeds the rate in other major trading countries or if the Canadian dollar appreciates on the foreign exchange market. This discourages exports and encourages imports, causing the net export function to shift downward.

2. Canadian prices fall relative to foreign prices if either the Canadian inflation rate is less than the rates in other major trading countries or if the Canadian dollar depreciates on the foreign exchange market. This encourages exports and discourages imports, causing the net export function to shift upward.

One final word of caution regarding prices, exchange rates, and net exports. It is important to keep in mind that the simple model in this chapter *takes the price level and the exchange rate as given*—they are exogenous variables in this chapter. In the actual economy, of course, they are very much endogenous variables. We discuss the determination of the price level in Chapters 25 and 26 (where we still take the exchange rate as given) and the determination of the exchange rate in Chapters 37 and 38. In a more complete model of the economy, in which prices and ex-

change rates are determined endogenously, the relationship between prices, exchange rates and net exports is not as simple as what we have discussed here. For now, however, we continue to take the price level and exchange rate as given, and thus we can consider how changes in these variables affect net exports and equilibrium national income.

Equilibrium national income

As in Chapter 23, we will determine equilibrium national income by finding the level of national income where desired aggregate expenditure is equal to actual national income. The addition of government and net exports changes the calculations that we must make but does not alter the basic principles that are involved.

DESIRED CONSUMPTION AND NATIONAL INCOME

Our theory of national income determination requires that we relate each of the components of aggregate expenditure to the level of national income. When there are taxes, the relationship between consumption and national income involves both the relationship between consumption and disposable income and the relationship, via taxes, between disposable income and national income.

Continuing the example begun earlier, suppose that disposable income is always 90 percent of national income—that is, desired net taxes (T) is given by the function $T = 0.1 \times Y$. This means that whatever the relationship between C and Y_D, we can always substitute $0.9Y$ for Y_D. Hence if changes in consumption were always 80 percent of changes in Y_D (i.e., an *MPC* out of disposable income equal to 0.8), changes in consumption would always be 72 percent (80 percent of 90 percent) of changes in Y. [35]

Table 24-3 illustrates how we can write desired consumption as a function of Y as well as of Y_D. We can then derive the response of consumption to changes in Y by determining the proportion of any change in *national income* that goes to a change in desired consumption.

The response of consumption to changes in national income ($\Delta C/\Delta Y$) is equal to the marginal propensity to consume out of disposable income ($\Delta C/\Delta Y_D$) mul-

TABLE 24-3

Consumption as a Function of Disposable Income and National Income

(billions of dollars)

(1) National Income (Y)	(2) Disposable Income $(Y_D = 0.9 \times Y)$	(3) Desired Consumption $(C = 10 + 0.8Y \times_D)$
0	0	10
100	90	82
200	180	154
300	270	226
400	360	298
500	450	370

If desired consumption depends on disposable income, which in turn depends on national income, desired consumption can be written as a function of either income concept. The data are hypothetical. Column 2 shows deductions of 10 percent of any level of national income to arrive at disposable income. Deductions of 10 percent of Y imply that the remaining 90 percent of Y becomes disposable income. Column 3 shows consumption as $10 billion (the autonomous component) plus 80 percent of disposable income.

By relating columns 2 and 3, one sees the relationship between consumption and disposable income. By relating columns 1 and 3, one sees the relationship between consumption and national income. In this example, the change in consumption in response to a change in *disposable* income (i.e., the *MPC*) is 0.8, and the change in consumption in response to a change in *national* income is 0.72.

tiplied by the fraction of national income that becomes disposable income $(\Delta Y_D/\Delta Y)$.

We now have a function that shows how desired consumption expenditure varies as national income varies, including the effects of taxes and transfer payments. This function is part of the aggregate expenditure function.

THE AGGREGATE EXPENDITURE FUNCTION

As in Chapter 23, in order to determine equilibrium national income, we define the **aggregate expenditure (AE) function**:

$$AE = C + I + G + NX$$

Table 24-4 illustrates the calculation of the aggregate expenditure function. It shows a schedule of desired expenditure for each of the components of aggregate expenditure, and it shows desired *aggregate* expenditure at each level of national income. Figure 24-4 shows this aggregate expenditure function in graphical form.

The Marginal Propensity to Spend

As in Chapter 23, the slope of the aggregate expenditure function is the *marginal propensity to spend* on national income (z). With the addition of taxes and net exports, however, the marginal propensity to

TABLE 24-4

The Aggregate Expenditure Function

(billions of dollars)

National Income (Y)	Desired Consumption Expenditure $(C = 10 + 0.72 \times Y)$	Desired Investment Expenditure $(I = 25)$	Desired Government Expenditure $(G = 17)$	Desired Net Export Expenditure $(X - IM = 24 - 0.1 \times Y)$	Desired Aggregate Expenditure $(AE = C + I + G + X - IM)$
0	10	25	17	24	76
50	46	25	17	19	107
100	82	25	17	14	138
200	154	25	17	4	200
300	226	25	17	−6	262
400	298	25	17	−16	324
500	370	25	17	−26	386

The aggregate expenditure function is the sum of desired consumption, investment, government purchases, and net export expenditures. The table is based on the hypothetical data given in Tables 24-1, 24-2, and 24-3. The autonomous components of desired aggregate expenditure are desired investment, desired government purchases, desired export expenditures, and the constant term in desired consumption expenditure. These sum to $76 billion in the given example. The induced components are the second term in desired consumption expenditure ($0.72 \times Y$) and desired imports ($-0.1 \times Y$).

The response of consumption to a change in national income is 0.72, calculated as the product of the marginal propensity to consume (0.8) times the fraction of national income that becomes disposable income (0.9). The response of desired aggregate expenditure to a change in national income, $\Delta AE/\Delta Y$, is 0.62. For example, as national income rises from $400 billion to $500 billion, desired aggregate expenditure increases from $324 billion to $386 billion. Thus $\Delta AE/\Delta Y = 62/100 = 0.62$.

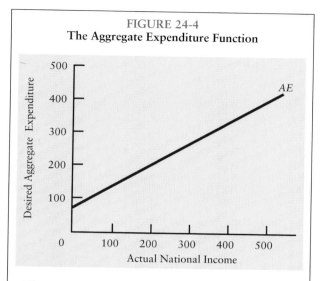

FIGURE 24-4
The Aggregate Expenditure Function

The aggregate expenditure function relates total desired expenditure to actual national income. The *AE* curve in the figure plots the data from the first and last columns of Table 24-4. Its intercept shows $76 billion of autonomous expenditure. Its slope is the marginal propensity to spend (which, according to the calculations in Table 24-4, is 0.62 in this case).

spend is no longer simply equal to the marginal propensity to consume.

Suppose that the economy produces $1 of extra income and that the response to this is governed by the relationships in Tables 24-1 and 24-2. Because 10 cents is collected by the government as net taxes, 90 cents becomes disposable income, and 80 percent of this amount (72 cents) is spent on consumption while the other 20 percent (18 cents) is saved. However, 10 cents of all expenditure goes to imports, so expenditure on domestic goods, that is, aggregate expenditure, rises by only 62 cents (72 − 10). Hence z, the marginal propensity to spend, is 0.62. What is not spent on domestic output includes the 10 cents in taxes, the 18 cents of disposable income that is saved, and the 10 cents of import expenditure, for a total of 38 cents. Hence the marginal propensity *not* to spend, $1 - z$, is $1 - 0.62 = 0.38$.

DETERMINING EQUILIBRIUM NATIONAL INCOME

The logic of national income determination in this chapter's hypothetical economy is exactly the same as in the simpler economy studied in Chapter 23. In this chapter, we have added two new components of aggregate expenditure, G and $(X - IM)$. The calculation of desired consumption expenditure is also more complicated; taxes must be subtracted from national income in order to determine disposable income. However, *equilibrium national income is still the level of national income at which desired aggregate expenditure equals actual national income.*

The aggregate expenditure function can be used directly to determine equilibrium national income. In Table 24-4, the equilibrium is $200 billion. When national income is equal to $200 billion, it is also equal to desired aggregate expenditure.

Suppose that national income is less than its equilibrium amount. The forces leading back to equilibrium are exactly the same as those described in Chapter 23. When households, firms, foreign demanders, and governments try to spend at their desired amounts, they will try to purchase more goods and services than the economy is currently producing. Hence some of the desired expenditure must either be frustrated or take the form of purchases of inventories of goods that were produced in the past. As firms see that they are (or could be) selling more than they are producing, they will increase production, thereby increasing the level of national income.

The opposite sequence of events occurs when national income is greater than the level of aggregate expenditure desired at that income. Now the total of desired household consumption, business investment, government purchases, and net foreign demand on the economy's production is less than national output. Firms will notice that they are unable to sell all of their output. Their inventories will be rising, and they will not permit this to happen indefinitely. They will seek to reduce the level of output until it equals the level of sales, and national income will fall.

Finally, when national income is equal to desired aggregate expenditure ($200 billion in Table 24-4), there is no pressure for output to change. Desired consumption, investment, government purchases, and net exports just add up to national product. Firms are producing exactly the quantity of goods and services that purchasers want to use, given the level of income.

Figure 24-5 illustrates the determination of equilibrium and the behaviour of the economy when it is not in equilibrium. The line labeled *AE* is simply the aggregate expenditure function shown in Figure 24-4. Recall that *AE* is a depiction of the behaviour of desired purchases in the economy. It shows how much national product people wish to purchase at each level of national income.

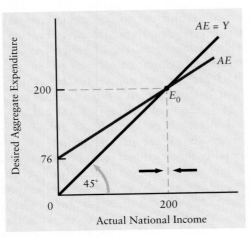

FIGURE 24-5
Equilibrium National Income

Equilibrium national income occurs at E_0, where the desired aggregate expenditure line intersects the 45° line. The aggregate expenditure line is taken from Figure 24-4; autonomous expenditure is $76 billion and the slope of AE is 0.62. If actual national income is below $200 billion, desired aggregate expenditure will exceed national income, and production will rise. If actual national income is above $200 billion, desired aggregate expenditure will be less than national income, and production will fall. Only when actual national income is $200 billion will desired aggregate expenditure equal actual national income.

The line labeled $AE = Y$ (the 45° line) depicts the equilibrium condition that desired aggregate expenditure be equal to actual national income. Any point on this line *could* be an equilibrium, but only one is. Equilibrium occurs where behaviour (as depicted by the AE function) is consistent with equilibrium (as depicted by $AE = Y$). At the equilibrium level of income, desired expenditure is just equal to national income and is therefore just sufficient to purchase total national output.

THE AUGMENTED SAVING-INVESTMENT APPROACH

In the closed-economy model of Chapter 23, we saw an alternative way of stating the equilibrium condition for national income: At the equilibrium level of income, desired saving equals desired investment. Adding government and international trade changes the precise form that this condition takes, but not the

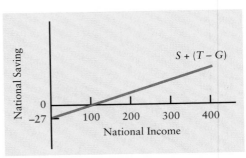

FIGURE 24-6
The National Saving Function

National saving is the sum of private saving and public (government) saving. The figure shows the national saving function for the data given in Tables 24-1 and 24-3. Desired private saving is equal to disposable income minus desired consumption. Public saving is the government's planned budget surplus.

central underlying principle. Now instead of equilibrium being characterized by saving equals investment, equilibrium will be characterized by *national saving* equal to *national asset formation*. We define these new terms in turn.

National Saving

National saving is the sum of private and public saving, $S + (T - G)$. Private saving (S) is the part of disposable income that is not used for current consumption. Public saving $(T - G)$ is the part of government revenue that is not spent by governments. Between them, households and governments account for all claims to national income. Thus the sum of what households and governments save accounts for all national saving.

The national saving function is illustrated in Figure 24-6. The slope of this function is the sum of the slopes of its two parts, private saving and public saving. In the example that we have been using throughout this chapter, the income-tax rate, t, is 0.1. So when national income rises by $1, public saving $(T - G)$ rises by 10 cents (recall that G is assumed to be autonomous and so does not change when national income changes). The remaining 90 cents is added to disposable income. From this 90-cent $(1 - t)$ increase in disposable income, private saving is increased by the marginal propensity to save (MPS), which is equal to 0.2 in our example. The total increase in saving per marginal dollar of national income is therefore $t + MPS(1 - t)$, or $0.1 + (0.2 \times 0.9) = 0.28$. This is the slope of the national saving function.

Consider a simple example. Let national income rise by $1 billion. With a 10 percent tax rate, net government tax revenue rises by $100 million. Because government spending does not change, net government saving $(T - G)$ also rises by $100 million. After taxes are paid, the other $900 million accrues to households as their disposable income. They spend $720 million and save the remaining $180 million. Thus total national saving rises by the $100 million of new government saving and the $180 million of new household saving, for a total of $280 million. The slope of the national saving function is the $280 million rise in saving divided by the $1000 million ($1 billion) rise in income that induced the extra saving. The resulting value is 0.28.

National Asset Formation

In Chapter 23, all of national output was either consumption or investment goods. All income that was received by households was either consumed or saved. So the saving of households, which was income not spent on consumption, was the counterpart of the economy's investment—output not used for current consumption but instead used for capital goods, inventories, and residential housing. Thus in the closed economy of Chapter 23—and indeed in any closed economy—the only way that the economy can accumulate assets for future use is to devote some part of national product to investment, which in equilibrium must be financed by saving.

In an open economy, however, it is possible to accumulate assets in a different form—as net claims on foreigners. And net exports are central to determining the rate at which a country acquires claims on foreigners.

Investment and net exports thus have a great deal in common: They are the two uses of national product that do not meet the domestic economy's current public or private demands. Investment, by definition, is product that will yield services in the future rather than in the present. Plainly, an economy that invests is adding to its assets.

To demonstrate that net exports also lead to asset accumulation, we must go through a number of steps. First, we note that net exports are the difference between what an economy produces and what it uses for consumption, investment, and govern-

ment. In a closed economy, there are no net exports. All of national income is produced at home for use at home. Now consider an economy whose net exports are positive. Its national income exceeds its domestic uses of national income. It is producing more than it is using, with the difference sold abroad. Similarly, an economy that has negative net exports is using (for consumption, investment, and government purchases) more than it is producing, with the difference purchased from abroad.

What happens when a country produces more or less than it uses? Here the analogy to an individual is instructive. Suppose that you spend more than you earn and that you borrow money to cover the difference. You consequently go into debt because there is no other way to cover your spending. Now suppose that you earn more than you spend. As a result, you inevitably acquire assets (or reduce your debts). When you earn more than you spend and do nothing with the balance, you end up holding cash. If you put the money into a bank, you have a bank balance; if you buy stocks or bonds with money, you hold the stocks or bonds. Try as you might, if we rule out gifts, spending more than you earn reduces your net asset position, and earning more than you spend increases your net asset position.

This simple idea can be extended to the national level because a nation's balances between expenditure and income are simply the total of what individual citizens do. If a nation's firms, households, and governments sell more to other countries than they buy from them (X exceeds IM), that nation *must accumulate foreign assets*. These assets could be in the form of foreign currency, balances in foreign banks, foreign stocks and bonds, or even foreign lands and factories.

Conversely, if the nation's firms, households, and governments spend more abroad than they earn by selling abroad (IM exceeds X), the nation *must incur foreign liabilities* (or run down foreign assets.) To finance the excess of imports over exports, funds must come from somewhere. Since they are not earned by selling current output, they must be raised by transferring assets to foreigners. This means that a new liability is generated domestically, in the form of domestic assets held by foreigners. Again, these could be bank balances, stocks, and bonds or titles to factories and farms.

Net exports result in the accumulation of income-earning assets for the exporting country. Hence net

TABLE 24-5
National Saving and National Asset Formation
(billions of dollars)

National Income (Y)	Desired National Saving (S + T − G)	Desired National Asset Formation (I + X − IM)	Saving Minus Asset Formation (S + T − G) − (I + X − IM)
0	−27	49	−76
100	1	39	−38
200	29	29	0
300	57	19	38
400	85	9	76

Desired national saving and desired national asset formation are equal at the equilibrium level of national income. The data are taken from Table 24-4, which shows that desired aggregate expenditure equals national income at $200 billion, the equilibrium for this hypothetical economy. Note that here desired national saving and desired national asset formation are also equal when national income is $200 billion. Note also that the last column, which displays the difference between desired national saving and desired national asset formation, is the same as the difference between aggregate expenditure and national income in Table 24-4.

exports are like investment in the sense that they generate future income for the exporting country.

The balance between exports and imports over time determines whether a country is a debtor or a creditor nation internationally. A country with positive net exports accumulates foreign assets and therefore adds to its position as a creditor. A country with negative net exports accumulates foreign liabilities and therefore adds to its position as a debtor.[4] Each year, the net export position alters the country's net creditor or debtor position. Whether it is in total a creditor or a debtor depends on the sum of all past net export positions. A country that has been a net importer over time will be an overall debtor; a country that has been an overall net exporter over time will be a net creditor.

Net exports and domestic investment are the two ways that a country can accumulate assets that will generate income in the future. We define their sum as *national asset formation.*

In a closed economy, **national asset formation** is just equal to investment. In an open economy, however, we must add net assets accumulated abroad (equal to payments for positive net exports) or subtract net domestic assets accumulated by foreigners (equal to negative net exports) in order to calculate the extent to which the domestic economy is accumulating assets worldwide.

[4]In Chapter 37, we will see that things are not quite so simple. The one-to-one relationship between net exports and international asset or liability accumulation presented here requires that all other items on what is called the current account in the international balance of payments be zero.

Equilibrium and Disequilibrium

Table 24-5 shows planned national saving according to the aggregate expenditure function given in Table 24-4. Private saving is disposable income less desired consumption. Public saving is tax revenue, equal to $0.1Y$ in our examples, less government purchases. The third column of Table 24-5 shows the sum of planned investment and net exports, or national asset formation.

Pick any level of national income, and compare Tables 24-4 and 24-5. The amount by which desired aggregate expenditure differs from national income in Table 24-4 will be exactly the same as the amount by which desired national asset formation differs from desired national saving in Table 24-5. When national income exceeds desired aggregate expenditure by a given amount, desired national saving exceeds desired national asset formation by the same amount. When national income is less than desired aggregate expenditure, desired national saving falls short of desired national asset formation.

When desired national saving is just equal to desired national asset formation, national income is at its equilibrium level, and desired aggregate expenditure is also equal to actual national income.

Why do these relationships hold? The easiest way to see what is going on is to look at the circular flow of income and product in Figure 21-1. There are three leakages between the income that households receive and the output that firms produce. These are taxes, saving, and import purchases. Each is a way that households can use their income without spending it directly on the domestic economy's production. There are also three injections of demand that come from sources other than households: government purchases, investment, and exports. In each of these cases, expenditure is used to satisfy purchasers other than domestic households.

Suppose that desired leakages exceed desired injections. In this case, more expenditure will be withdrawn from the circular flow than is added to it. Hence desired aggregate expenditure on output will be less than national income, leading to a fall in national income. Similarly, if desired leakages are less than desired injections, desired aggregate expenditure will exceed national income, leading to a rise in national income.

Equilibrium requires that the desired leakages from the income flow just equal the desired injections. In this case, aggregate expenditure will just equal national income, the defining condition for equilibrium. We can write this condition as an equation, with the sum of all leakages $(S + T + IM)$ equal to the sum of all injections $(G + I + X)$:

$$S + T + IM = G + I + X$$

From here we can establish the equality of national saving with national asset formation directly by subtracting imports and government purchases from both sides of the equation. Subtracting IM and G from both sides of this equation yields

$$S + (T - G) = I + (X - IM)$$

In words, national saving equals national asset formation.

Figure 24-7 shows the determination of equilibrium income using the concepts of national saving and national asset formation. The national saving function is taken from Figure 24-6. The national asset formation function is the sum of desired investment and desired net exports. It is negatively sloped because net exports decline when national income rises; the magnitude of its slope is determined by the marginal propensity to import. Equilibrium occurs at the level of national income where national saving (the part of national income that the private and public sectors desire to set aside for the future) is just equal to national asset formation (the part of national product that is not used to satisfy current consumption and government purchases of goods and services).

The vertical difference between the AE function and the 45° line ($AE = Y$) in Figure 24-5 is just equal

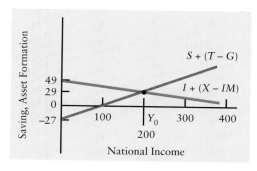

FIGURE 24-7
National Saving and National Asset Formation

The economy is in equilibrium at Y_0, where desired national saving, $(S + T - G)$, equals desired national asset formation, $(I + X - M)$. To the left of Y_0, desired national asset formation exceeds desired national saving. This implies that desired aggregate expenditure exceeds national income. Firms will respond to the imbalance by producing more, moving the economy toward equilibrium. To the right of Y_0, desired national asset formation is less than desired national saving, and aggregate expenditure is less than national income. Firms will reduce output to avoid accumulating excess inventories, and the economy will move toward equilibrium.

to the vertical difference between the desired national asset formation function and the desired national saving function in Figure 24-7. The level of equilibrium income in the two figures is the same, as both are representations of exactly the same model of income determination.

CHANGES IN AGGREGATE EXPENDITURE AND NATIONAL INCOME

Changes in any of the components of desired aggregate expenditure will cause changes in equilibrium national income. In Chapter 23, we investigated the consequences of shifts in the consumption function and in the investment function. Here we take a first look at fiscal policy—the effects of government spending and taxes. We also consider shifts in the net export function. First, we take account of the fact that the simple multiplier is reduced by the presence of taxes and imports.

THE MULTIPLIER WITH TAXES AND IMPORTS

In Chapter 23, we saw that the *simple multiplier,* the amount by which equilibrium national income changes when autonomous expenditure changes by a dollar, was equal to $1/(1 - z)$, where z is the marginal propensity to spend out of national income. In the simple model of Chapter 23, with no government and no international trade, z is simply the marginal propensity to consume out of disposable income. But in the more complex model of this chapter, in which we have added government and net exports, the marginal propensity to spend out of national income is slightly more complicated. The central point here is that the presence of imports and income taxes reduces the marginal propensity to spend out of national income and thus reduces the value of the simple multiplier.

To see this, note that in Chapter 23 the marginal propensity to spend was equal to 0.8 and the multiplier was therefore equal to 5. In the example that we have developed in this chapter, with a marginal propensity to import of 0.1 and an income-tax rate of 0.1, the marginal propensity to spend is 0.62. Ten percent of a $1 increase in autonomous spending goes to taxes, leaving 90 cents of disposable income. With a marginal propensity to consume of 0.8, 72 cents is spent. Of this, 10 cents is spent on imports, leaving a total of 62 cents to be spent on domestically produced consumption goods. Hence $1 - z$ is 0.38, and the simple multiplier is $1/0.38 = 2.63$.

Dealing with the numbers in a specific example is sometimes confusing, and it is useful to think more generally about why the presence of imports and income taxes reduces the value of the simple multiplier. The basic reason is that with taxes and imports both increasing in response to an increase in national income, every incremental increase in national income generates more leakages from the flow of expenditure than would be the case in the simpler world with no taxes and no imports. Thus as national income increases, there is less induced expenditure *on the domestic economy* and thus the overall change in equilibrium national income is lower.

The higher is the marginal propensity to import, the lower is the simple multiplier. The higher is the income-tax rate, the lower is the simple multiplier.

NET EXPORTS

Earlier in this chapter, we discussed the determinants of net exports and of shifts in the net export function. As with the other elements of desired aggregate expenditure, if the net export function shifts upward, equilibrium national income will rise; if the net export function shifts downward, equilibrium national income will fall.

Autonomous Net Exports

Net exports have both an autonomous component and an induced component. Generally, exports themselves are autonomous with respect to domestic national income. Foreign demand for Canadian goods and services depends on foreign income, on foreign and Canadian prices, and on the exchange rate, but it does not depend on Canadian income. Export demand could also change because of a change in tastes. Suppose that foreign consumers develop a taste for Canadian-made furniture and desire to consume $1 billion more per year of these goods than they had in the past. The net export function (and the aggregate expenditure function) will shift up by $1 billion, and equilibrium national income will increase by $1 billion times the multiplier.

Induced Net Exports

The Canadian demand for imports depends, in part, on Canadian income. The greater is domestic income, the greater will be Canadian demand for goods and services in general, including those produced abroad. Because imports are subtracted from exports to obtain net exports ($NX = X - IM$), the marginal propensity to import, m, is subtracted in obtaining the marginal propensity to spend, z. Hence the greater the marginal propensity to import, the lower the marginal propensity to spend, and the lower the multiplier, $1/(1 - z)$.

FISCAL POLICY

Fiscal policy involves the use of government spending and tax policies to influence total desired expenditure so as to change the equilibrium level of national income. Typically, until recently the goal of the government has been to dampen the fluctuations in national income that are caused by factors beyond its control, such as changes in foreign demand for

Canadian goods and changes in the world prices of commodities, such as oil, coffee, paper, or copper.[5]

Because government purchases increase aggregate desired expenditure and taxation decreases it, the *directions* of the required changes in spending and taxation are generally easy to determine once we know the direction of the desired change in national income. But the *timing, magnitude,* and *mixture* of the changes are more difficult issues.

Any policy that attempts to stabilize national income at or near any desired level (usually potential national income) is called **stabilization policy**. Here we deal only with the basic ideas of stabilization through fiscal policy. In Chapters 26 and 32, we return to discuss some of its complications after we have developed the required theory.

The basic idea of stabilization policy follows from what we have already learned. A reduction in tax rates or an increase in government purchases shifts the *AE* curve upward, causing an increase in equilibrium national income. An increase in tax rates or a decrease in government purchases shifts the *AE* curve downward, causing a decrease in equilibrium income.

If the government has some target level of national income, it can try to use its taxes and expenditures as instruments to push the economy toward that target. First, suppose that the economy is in a serious recession and the government would like to increase national income. The appropriate fiscal tools are to raise expenditures or to lower tax rates (or both). Second, suppose that the economy is "overheated." In the next two chapters, we will study what this means in detail. In the meantime, we observe that an overheated economy has such a high level of national income that shortages are pushing up prices and causing inflation. Without worrying too much about the details right now, just suppose that the current level of national income is higher than the target income that the government deems appropriate. What should the government do? The fiscal tools at its command are to lower government expenditure and to raise tax rates, both of which have a depressing effect on national income.

Let us look in a little more detail at how this occurs.

Changes in Government Purchases

Suppose the government decides to reduce its purchases of all consulting services, saving $100 million per year in spending. Planned government purchases (G) would fall by $100 million at every level of income, shifting *AE* downward by the same amount. How much would equilibrium income change? This can be calculated using the multiplier. Government purchases are part of autonomous expenditure, so a *change* in government purchases of ΔG will lead to a *change* in equilibrium national income equal to the multiplier times ΔG. In this example, equilibrium income will fall by $100 million times the simple multiplier.

Increases in government purchases would have the opposite effect. If the government were to spend $1 billion on new highways, equilibrium national income would rise by $1 billion times the simple multiplier.

Changes in Tax Rates

If tax rates change, the relationship between disposable income and national income changes. As a result, the relationship between desired consumption expenditure and national income also changes. For any given level of national income, there will be a different level of disposable income and hence a different level of consumption. Consequently, a change in tax rates will also cause a change in z, the marginal propensity to spend out of national income.

Consider a decrease in tax rates. If the government decreases its rate of income tax so that it collects 5 cents less out of every dollar of national income, disposable income rises in relation to national income. Hence consumption also rises at every level of national income. This results in a (nonparallel) upward shift of the *AE* curve, that is, an increase in the slope of the curve, as shown in Figure 24-8. The result of this shift will be a rise in equilibrium national income, also shown in Figure 24-8.

A rise in tax rates has the opposite effect. A rise in tax rates causes a decrease in disposable income, and hence consumption expenditure, at each level of national income. This results in a (nonparallel) downward shift of the *AE* curve and decreases the level of equilibrium national income.

Balanced Budget Changes

Another policy available to the government is to make a *balanced budget change* by altering spending

---

[5]As we discuss in detail in Chapter 32, in recent years the high level of government debt has limited the government's ability to dampen these cyclical fluctuations.

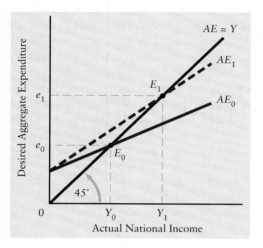

FIGURE 24-8
The Effect of Changing the Tax Rate

Changing the tax rate changes equilibrium income by changing the slope of the AE curve. A reduction in tax rates rotates the AE curve from AE_0 to AE_1. The new curve has a steeper slope because the lower tax rate withdraws a smaller amount of national income from the desired consumption flow. Equilibrium income rises from Y_0 to Y_1 because at every level of national income, desired consumption, and hence aggregate expenditure, is higher.

If we take AE_1 and Y_1 to be the initial equilibrium, an increase in tax rates will reduce the slope of the AE curve, thereby reducing equilibrium income, as shown by AE_0 and Y_0.

and taxes equally. Say the government increases tax rates enough to raise an extra $1 billion that it then uses to purchase goods and services. Aggregate expenditure would remain unchanged if, and only if, the $1 billion that the government takes from the private sector in higher taxes would otherwise have been entirely spent by that sector. If so, the government's policy would reduce private expenditure by $1 billion and raise its own spending by $1 billion. Aggregate expenditure, and hence national income, would remain unchanged.

But this is not the usual case. When an extra $1 billion in taxes is taken away from households, the reduction in spending on domestically produced goods is less than $1 billion. If the marginal propensity to consume out of disposable income is, say, 0.8, consumption expenditure will fall by only $800 million. If the government spends the entire $1 billion on domestically produced goods, aggregate expenditure will increase by $200 million. In this case, the

balanced budget increase in government expenditure has an expansionary effect because it shifts the aggregate expenditure function upward.

In the simple model of national income determination, a balanced budget increase in government expenditure will have a mild expansionary effect on national income, and a balanced budget decrease will have a mild contractionary effect.

The **balanced budget multiplier** measures these effects. It is the change in income divided by the balanced budget change in government expenditure that brought it about. If the extra $1 billion of spending and taxes causes national income to rise by $800 million, the balanced budget multiplier is 0.8; if income rises by only $200 million, it is 0.2.

Now compare the sizes of the multipliers for a balanced budget and a deficit-financed increase in government spending. (When expenditure is increased with no corresponding increase in tax rates, we say it is deficit financed.) With a deficit-financed increase in expenditure, there is no increase in tax rates and hence no resulting decrease in consumption expenditure to offset the increase in government expenditure. With a balanced budget increase in expenditure, however, the offsetting increase in tax rates and decrease in consumption does occur. Consequently, the balanced budget multiplier is much lower than the multiplier that relates the change in income to an increase in government expenditure with tax rates constant.

LIMITATIONS OF THE INCOME-EXPENDITURE APPROACH

In this and the preceding chapter, we have discussed the determination of the four categories of aggregate expenditure and seen how they simultaneously determine equilibrium national income. The basic approach is the same no matter how many categories are considered. An algebraic exposition of the model is presented in the appendix to this chapter.

The simple income-expenditure model of the economy that we have explored is based on two central concepts.

Equilibrium National Income. The equilibrium level of national income is that level where *desired* aggregate expenditure equals *actual* national income. If actual national income exceeds desired expenditure, then the unintended accumulation of inventories eventually leads firms to reduce production—national income falls. If actual national income is less than desired expenditure, then the unintended running-down of inventories eventually leads firms to increase production—national income rises.

The Multiplier. The multiplier measures the change in equilibrium national income that results from a change in the *autonomous* part of desired aggregate expenditure. The multiplier is equal to $1/(1 - z)$, where z is the marginal propensity to spend out of national income. In the model of Chapter 23, in which there is no government and no international trade, z is simply the marginal propensity to consume out of disposable income. The addition of government and net exports to the model reduces the value of z, and thus reduces the value of the simple multiplier.

It is important to keep in mind that the income-expenditure model that we have examined is constructed *for a given price level*—that is, the price level is assumed to be exogenous to the model. Moreover, by constructing a model with a given price level, we have been (implicitly) making another important assumption about the economy. The fact that equilibrium income depends only on the amount of desired expenditure (and not, for example, on firms' technical abilities to produce output) *assumes that the economy has a significant amount of unemployed resources.* Only in the presence of unemployed resources will firms be prepared to provide more output—at unchanged prices—simply because there has been an increase in *desired* expenditure. In contrast, if all resources in the economy were fully employed, an autonomous increase in desired aggregate expenditure would not cause an increase in output with an unchanged price level. In such circumstances, the increase in desired expenditure would typically cause both an increase in national income and an increase in prices.

The assumptions of a fixed price level and unemployed resources imply that the equilibrium level of national income is determined by the *demand side* of the economy. In this case, we say that output is *demand determined.*

The simple income-expenditure model of national income determination is constructed for a given price level. This reflects the related assumption that the economy has unemployed resources, which then means that national income is demand determined.

In the following chapters, we augment the income-expenditure model by making the price level endogenous to the model. We do this by considering the *supply side* of the economy—that is, those things that influence firms' abilities to produce output, such as technology and factor prices. When we consider the demand side and the supply side of the economy simultaneously, we will see that changes in desired aggregate expenditure usually cause both prices and real national income to change. This is why the simple multiplier, derived under the assumption that prices do not change, is too simple.

Nonetheless, there are three ways in which the simple income-expenditure models of Chapters 23 and 24 remain useful, even when the price level does change. First, the simple multiplier will continue to be a valuable starting place in calculating actual changes in national income in response to changes in autonomous expenditure. Second, no matter what the price level may be, the components of desired aggregate expenditure add up to national income *in equilibrium*. Third, no matter what the price level may be, equilibrium requires that desired national saving be equal to desired national asset formation. This last point will be especially important when we consider the determinants of national income and prices in the long run.

SUMMARY

A. INTRODUCING GOVERNMENT

- Government spending is part of autonomous aggregate expenditure. Taxes minus transfer payments are called net taxes and affect aggregate expenditure indirectly. Taxes reduce disposable income, whereas transfers increase disposable income. Disposable income in turn determines desired consumption, according to the consumption function.

- The budget balance is defined as government revenues minus government expenditures, $(T - G)$. When $(T - G)$ is positive, there is a budget surplus; when $(T - G)$ is negative, there is a budget deficit.

- When there is a budget surplus, there is positive public saving because the government is using less national product than the amount of income that it is withdrawing from the circular flow of income. When there is a budget deficit, public saving is negative.

B. INTRODUCING NET EXPORTS

- Exports are foreign purchases of Canadian goods, and thus do not depend on Canadian national income. Desired imports increase as national income increases. Hence net exports decrease as national income increases.
- An increase in domestic prices (with foreign prices held constant) leads foreigners and Canadians to purchase fewer Canadian goods and to purchase more foreign goods. This causes the net export function to shift down. A fall in domestic prices (with foreign prices held constant) has the opposite effect.
- A rise in the exchange rate (a depreciation of the Canadian dollar) implies that Canadian goods are now cheaper relative to foreign goods. This leads to a rise in exports and a fall in imports, shifting the net export function up. A fall in the exchange rate (an appreciation of the Canadian dollar) has the opposite effect.

C. EQUILIBRIUM NATIONAL INCOME

- As in Chapter 23, national income is in equilibrium when desired aggregate expenditure equals actual national income. The equilibrium condition is

$$Y = AE, \quad \text{where } AE = C + I + G + (X - IM)$$

- The sum of investment and net exports is called *national asset formation* because investment and net exports represent the two ways in which national income that is not used in the current year can be used to generate future national income. At the equilibrium level of national income, desired national saving is just equal to national asset formation:

$$S + (T - G) = I + (X - IM)$$

D. CHANGES IN AGGREGATE EXPENDITURE AND NATIONAL INCOME

- The presence of taxes and net exports reduces the value of the simple multiplier. The reason is that with taxes and imports both increasing in response to an increase in national income, every increase in national income generates more leakages from the flow of expenditure.
- An increase in government purchases shifts up the *AE* function and thus increases the equilibrium level of national income. An increase in the income-tax rate makes the *AE* function rotate downward and thus reduces the equilibrium level of national income.
- An increase in exports can be caused by either an increase in foreign demand for Canadian goods, a fall in the Canadian price level, or a depreciation of the Canadian dollar. An increase in exports shifts the *AE* function up and increases the equilibrium level of national income.

E. LESSONS AND LIMITATIONS OF THE INCOME-EXPENDITURE APPROACH

- The simple income-expenditure model of national income determination is constructed for a given price level. That prices are assumed not to change in response to an increase in desired expenditure reflects the underlying assumption that the economy has unemployed resources. This implies that national income is demand determined.
- In later chapters when we consider the demand side and the supply side of the economy simultaneously, we will see that changes in desired aggregate expenditure usually cause both prices and real national income to change. This is why the simple multiplier, derived under the assumption that prices do not change, is too simple.

KEY CONCEPTS

Taxes and net taxes
The budget balance
The public saving (budget surplus) function
The net export function

National saving
National asset formation
Calculation of the simple multiplier in an open economy with government

Fiscal policy and equilibrium income
The balanced budget multiplier

DISCUSSION QUESTIONS

1. State the implied impact on the *AE* curve (and hence on equilibrium national income) that relates to each of the following headlines.

   a. "Minister takes an axe to the Armed Forces."
   b. "Russia agrees to buy more Canadian wheat."
   c. "Major Canadian companies expected to cut capital outlays."
   d. "Finance Minister increases personal income-tax rates."
   e. "U.S. imposes import restrictions on Canadian lumber."

2. Massive and growing public debt has forced the federal and most provincial governments to try to reduce their budget deficits irrespective of the state of the economy. What fiscal measures would reduce their deficits? Why might a reduction of 10 percent in government expenditure accomplish much less than a 10 percent decrease in the deficit, at least in the first instance?

3. It is typical for the federal government's forecasts of its own budget deficit to be less than the forecasts made by private-sector economists. Much of the discrepancy seems to be accounted for by assumptions about the state of the economy over the coming year. How do assumptions about the economy affect estimates of the budget deficit?

4. During the recession of 1990–1991, net exports fell. Is this consistent with Canadian imports depending on Canadian income while Canadian exports are autonomous? Is it consistent with Canadian exports being autonomous because they depend on U.S. income? (Approximately 75 percent of Canadian exports go to the United States). What do you think happened to U.S. income?

5. The government allows contributions to Registered Retirement Saving Plans (RRSPs) to be deducted from gross income when calculating taxable income. What is the likely effect of this on personal saving?

6. Many U.S. state governments are prohibited by law from running budget deficits. Compare this with Canadian provincial governments. What effect do such laws in the United States and their absence in Canada have on the shape of the government budget surplus functions in the two countries?

7. Classify each of the following government activities as either government purchases or transfers.

   a. Welfare payments for the poor
   b. Payments to teachers in public schools
   c. Payments to teachers at military colleges
   d. Payments on account of hospital and medical care
   e. Public Health Service vaccination programs

8. As discussed in this chapter, whenever desired leakages equal desired injections, national income equals desired aggregate expenditure and thus the economy is in equilibrium. If net exports equal zero, and the government has a balanced budget, it follows that desired saving must equal desired investment. What is the relationship between saving and investment if trade remains balanced but the government decides to run a deficit? Can you explain intuitively why this makes sense?

9. The trade deficit that the United States has with Japan has received much attention over the last 15 years. Given an economy in equilibrium, what is the relationship between saving and investment if the government budget remains balanced but there exists a trade deficit? What additional role must foreigners play in this situation? Can you explain why this situation is viewed by many Americans as troublesome? Do you agree with them?

10. In Chapter 21 we examined how national income was *measured*. Using the expenditure approach, we showed that GDP is always equal to the sum of consumption, investment, government purchases, and net exports. In Chapters 23 and 24 we examined the *determination* of national income. We showed that equilibrium national income occurs when actual national income equals the sum of desired consumption, investment, government purchases, and net exports. Does this mean that national income is always at its equilibrium level? Explain the important difference between "actual" and "desired" expenditures.

APPENDIX TO CHAPTER 24

An Albegraic Exposition of the Income-Expenditure Model

We start with the definition of desired aggregate expenditure:

$$AE = C + I + G + (X - IM) \qquad [1]$$

For each component of AE, we write down a behavioural function.

$$C = a + bY_D \quad (consumption\ function) \qquad [2]$$

$$I = I_0 \quad (autonomous\ investment) \qquad [3]$$

$$G = G_0 \quad (autonomous\ government\ purchases) \quad [4]$$

$$X = X_0 \quad (autonomous\ exports) \qquad [5]$$

$$IM = mY \quad (imports) \qquad [6]$$

where a is autonomous consumption spending, b is the marginal propensity to consume, and m is the marginal propensity to import. Obviously, the "behavioural" functions for investment, government purchases, and exports are very simple: These are all assumed to be independent of the level of national income.

Before deriving aggregate expenditure, we need to determine the relationship between national income (Y) and disposable income (Y_D), because it is Y_D that determines desired consumption expenditure. Y_D is defined as income after net taxes. In Chapter 24 we examined a very simple linear income tax of the form $T = tY$. More generally, we might imagine autonomous net taxes T_0 and induced net taxes tY, so the tax function is given by:

$$T = T_0 + tY \qquad [7]$$

Taxes must be subtracted from national income to obtain disposable income:

$$Y_D = Y - T_0 - tY = Y(1 - t) - T_0 \qquad [8]$$

Substituting Equation 8 into the consumption function allows us to write consumption as a function of national income.

$$C = a - bT_0 + b(1 - t)Y \qquad [9]$$

Notice that autonomous consumption now has two parts, a and $-bT_0$, where the latter term is the effect of autonomous taxes on consumption.

Now we can add up all of the components of desired aggregate expenditure, substituting Equations 3, 4, 5, 6, and 9 into Equation 1:

$$AE = a - bT_0 + b(1 - t)Y + I_0 + G_0 + X_0 - mY \quad [10]$$

Equation 10 is the aggregate expenditure function which shows desired aggregate expenditure as a function of actual national income.

In equilibrium, desired aggregate expenditure must equal actual national income:

$$AE = Y \qquad [11]$$

Equation 11 is the equilibrium condition for the income-expenditure model. It is the equation of the 45° line in the figures in this chapter.

To solve for the equilibrium level of national income, we want to solve for the level of Y which satisfies both equations 10 and 11. That is, solve for the level of Y which is determined by the intersection of the AE curve and the 45° line. Substitute equation 11 into 10:

$$Y = a - bT_0 + b(1 - t)Y + I_0 + G_0 + X_0 - mY \quad [12]$$

Group all the terms in Y on the right-hand side, and subtract them from both sides:

$$Y = Y[b(1 - t) - m] + a - bT_0 + I_0 + G_0 + X_0 \quad [13]$$

$$Y - Y[b(1 - t) - m] = a - bT_0 + I_0 + G_0 + X_0 \quad [14]$$

Notice that $[b(1 - t) - m]$ is exactly the marginal propensity to spend out of national income, defined earlier as z. When national income goes up by a dollar, only $1 - t$ dollars go into disposable income, and only b of that gets spent on consumption.

Additionally, m gets spent on imports, which are not expenditure on domestic national income. Hence $[b(1 - t) - m]$ gets spent on domestic output.

Substituting z for $[b(1 - t) - m]$ and solving Equation 14 for equilibrium Y yields

$$Y = \frac{a - bT_0 + I_0 + G_0 + X_0}{1 - z} \qquad [15]$$

Notice that the numerator of Equation 15 is total autonomous expenditure, A (see Extension 23-2). Hence Equation 15 can be rewritten as

$$Y = \frac{A}{1 - z} \qquad [16]$$

Notice also that if autonomous expenditure rises by some amount ΔA, Y will rise by $\Delta A/(1 - z)$. So the simple multiplier is $1/(1 - z)$.

THE ALGEBRA ILLUSTRATED

The numerical example that was carried through Chapters 23 and 24 can be used to illustrate the preceding exposition. In that example, the behavioural equations are:

$$C = 10 + 0.8Y_D \qquad [17]$$

$$I = 25 \qquad [18]$$

$$G = 17 \qquad [19]$$

$$X - IM = 24 - 0.1Y \qquad [20]$$

$$T = 0.1Y \qquad [21]$$

T_0 is 0, so, from Equation 8, disposable income is given by $Y(1 - t) = 0.9Y$. Substituting this into Equation 17 yields

$$C = 10 + 0.72Y$$

as in Equation 9.

Now, recalling that in equilibrium $AE = Y$, we add up all of the components of AE and set the sum equal to Y, as in Equation 12:

$$Y = 10 + 0.72Y + 25 + 17 + 24 - 0.1Y \quad [22]$$

Collecting terms yields

$$Y = 76 + 0.62Y$$

Subtracting $0.62Y$ from both sides gives

$$0.38Y = 76$$

and dividing through by 0.38, we have

$$Y = \frac{76}{0.38} = 200$$

This can also be derived by using Equation 16. Autonomous expenditure is 76, and z, the marginal propensity to spend out of national income, is 0.62. Hence $(1 - z)$ is 0.38. Thus from Equation 16, equilibrium income is $76/(0.38) = 200$, which is exactly the equilibrium we obtained in Table 24-4.

CHAPTER 25

NATIONAL INCOME AND THE PRICE LEVEL IN THE SHORT RUN

In Chapters 23 and 24, we developed a model of income determination in an economy with a constant price level. Of course, in any real economy, prices are changing more or less all the time. On the supply side of the economy, the prices of imported materials used by firms and households change frequently and sometimes dramatically, as when oil prices soared during 1973–1974 and 1979–1980 in response to the actions of the OPEC oil cartel. On the demand side of the economy, a boom in the United States—as happened in the early 1980s following a reduction in income taxes—increases the demand for Canadian exports. A large enough increase will cause prices to rise as the Canadian economy reaches full capacity and inflationary pressures build up.

544

Virtually all shocks to the economy affect *both* national income *and* the price level; that is, they have both real and nominal effects, at least initially. To understand why this happens, we need to drop the assumption that the price level is constant and then develop some further tools, called the *aggregate demand curve* and the *aggregate supply curve*.

We make the transition to a variable price level in three steps. First, we study the consequences for national income of *exogenous* changes in the price level—changes that happen for reasons that are not explained by our model of the economy. Since the focus of the analysis is on how changes in the price level affect desired aggregate expenditure, this analysis amounts to examining the *demand side* of the economy. Second, we examine the *supply side* of the economy by exploring the relationship between the price level, the prices of factor inputs, and the level of output firms would like to supply. Finally, we examine the concept of *macroeconomic equilibrium* which combines both the demand and supply sides of the economy to simultaneously determine the price level and national income.

THE DEMAND SIDE OF THE ECONOMY

What happens to equilibrium national income when the price level changes for some exogenous reason, such as a rise in the price of imported raw materials? To find out, we need to understand how the change affects desired aggregate expenditure. This requires use of the *AE* curve that we developed in the previous two chapters.

SHIFTS IN THE AE CURVE

There is one key result that we need to establish: A rise in the price level shifts the aggregate expenditure curve downward, and a fall in the price level shifts it upward. In other words, the price level and desired aggregate expenditure are negatively related to each other. A major part of the explanation lies with how the change in the price level affects desired consumption expenditure and desired net exports.[1]

Changes in Consumption

One link between a change in the price level and changes in desired consumption is provided by wealth. We first consider the link between the price level and wealth, and then the link between wealth and consumption.

Much of the private sector's total wealth is held in the form of assets with a fixed nominal money value. One obvious example is money itself—cash and bank deposits. Other examples include many kinds of debt, such as treasury bills and corporate bonds.[2] When a bill or a bond matures, the owner is repaid a stated sum of money. What that money can buy—its real value—depends on the price level. The higher the price level, the less the given sum of money can purchase. For this reason, a rise in the domestic price level lowers the real value of all assets that are denominated in money units. How does this affect individuals?

The holder of a bond has loaned money to the issuer of the bond. When the real value of the asset falls, the holder's wealth is reduced. The issuer's wealth, however, is increased by an exactly offsetting amount. This is because the face value of the bond represents less purchasing power as a result of the rise in the price level. The issuer, who has to repay the bond, will part with less purchasing power to do so and hence has more wealth.

When the price level changes, holders of assets denominated in money terms will see their wealth go in the opposite direction of the change in the price level, while the wealth of those who issued the same assets will move in the same direction as the change in the price level.

Inside Assets.   An *inside asset* is one that is issued by an individual or a firm in the private sector and also held by someone in the private sector. It is called an inside asset because both the owner and the issuer of the asset are inside the domestic private sector. For inside assets, a rise in the price level lowers the real wealth of a bondholder but raises the real wealth of the bond issuer. With inside assets, therefore, the wealth changes are exactly offsetting. A rise

---

[1]The effect on investment expenditure is also important, and it works in the same direction as the change in consumption and net exports. This is discussed in Chapter 28.

[2]These and other credit instruments are discussed later in this book. In the meantime, all you need to know is that a bill is evidence of a short-term loan, typically of one year or less to maturity, and a bond is evidence of a longer-term loan that may run for up to 30 years.

in the price level lowers the real wealth of the person who owns any asset that is denominated in money, but it raises the real wealth of the person who must redeem the asset.

Outside Assets.   An *outside asset* is one that is held by someone inside the domestic private sector but issued by some entity outside of that sector. It is called an outside asset because the issuer of the asset is outside the domestic private sector. The single most important example of an outside asset is a government bond or treasury bill held by domestic firms or residents. A rise in the price level lowers the wealth of the holders of outside assets but, unlike the case for inside assets, there are no offsetting private-sector wealth changes for the issuers because the issuers are not part of the domestic private sector. It follows that a change in the price level *does* cause a change in net private wealth held in outside assets. A rise in the price level lowers the real wealth of holders of these assets.[3]

A change in the price level causes no net change in the wealth of the private sector with respect to inside assets, but it does cause a change with respect to outside assets because the issuers are not in the domestic private sector.

The second link in the chain running from changes in the price level to changes in desired consumption is provided by the relationship between wealth and consumption that we stressed in Chapter 23. Whenever households suffer a decrease in their wealth, they increase their saving so as to restore their wealth to the level that they desire for such purposes as retirement. An increase in desired saving, of course, implies a reduction in desired consumption. Conversely, whenever households get an increase in their wealth, they reduce their saving and consume more, causing an upward shift in the consumption function.

A rise in the domestic price level lowers private-sector wealth; this leads to a fall in desired consumption, and this in turn implies a downward shift in the aggregate expenditure curve. A fall in the domestic price level leads to a rise in wealth and desired consumption and thus to an upward shift in the aggregate expenditure curve.

We have concentrated here on the direct effect of the change in wealth on desired consumption expenditure. There is also an indirect effect that operates through the interest rate. Although this effect is potentially very powerful, we cannot study it until we have studied the macroeconomic role of money and interest rates. Further discussion of this point must therefore be postponed until Chapter 28.

Changes in Net Exports

When the domestic price level rises, Canadian goods become more expensive relative to foreign goods. As we saw in Chapter 24, this change in relative prices causes Canadian consumers to reduce their purchases of Canadian-made goods, which have now become relatively more expensive, and to increase their purchases of foreign goods, which have now become relatively less expensive. At the same time, consumers in other countries reduce their purchases of the now relatively more expensive Canadian-made goods. We saw in Chapter 24 that these changes can be summarized as a downward shift in the net export function.

A rise in the domestic price level shifts the net export function downward, which means a downward shift in the aggregate expenditure curve. A fall in the domestic price level shifts the net export function and hence the aggregate expenditure curve upward.

The common sense of these changes is that if Canadian goods and services become more expensive, less of them are being bought by foreigners, so total desired expenditure on Canadian output falls. If Canadian goods and services become cheaper, more will be bought, and total desired expenditure on them will rise.[4]

---

[3]If the issuer of the outside asset is the domestic government, then the change in wealth of the domestic private sector is exactly offset by the change in wealth of the domestic government. Any change in wealth of the government, however, is ultimately made up by domestic citizens through changes in taxes. For example, taxpayers must pay taxes to service the national debt, and when a rise in the price level lowers its real value, it also lowers the real value of future tax liabilities by exactly the same amount. In this chapter, however, we are assuming that taxpayers do not include in their wealth calculations the real value of *future* tax liabilities. This amounts to focusing only on the change in private-sector wealth and ignoring the offsetting change in the wealth of the government. We examine this issue in detail in Chapter 32.

[4]This assumes that the price elasticity of demand for traded goods exceeds one.

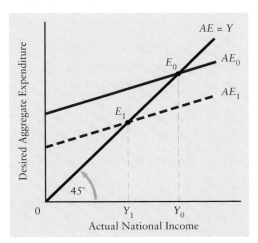

FIGURE 25-1
Aggregate Expenditure and the Price Level

Changes in the price level cause the *AE* curve to shift and thus cause equilibrium national income to change. At the initial price level, the *AE* curve is given by the solid line AE_0, and hence equilibrium national income is Y_0. An increase in the price level reduces desired aggregate expenditure and thus causes the *AE* curve to shift downward to the dashed line, AE_1. As a result, equilibrium national income falls to Y_1.

Starting with the dashed line, AE_1, a fall in the price level increases desired aggregate expenditure, shifting the *AE* curve up to AE_0 and raising equilibrium national income to Y_0.

CHANGES IN EQUILIBRIUM INCOME

Because it causes downward shifts in both the net export function and the consumption function, an exogenous rise in the price level causes a downward shift in the aggregate desired expenditure curve, as shown in Figure 25-1. This figure also allows us to reconfirm what we already know from Chapters 23 and 24: When the *AE* curve shifts downward, the equilibrium level of national income falls.

Now suppose that there is a fall in the price level. Because this is simply the opposite of the case that we have just studied, we can summarize the two key effects briefly. First, Canadian goods become relatively cheaper internationally, so net exports rise. Second, the purchasing power of some existing assets (outside assets) that are denominated in money terms is increased, so households spend more. The resulting increase in desired expenditure on Canadian

goods causes the *AE* curve to shift upward and hence raises equilibrium national income. This is also shown in Figure 25-1.

THE AGGREGATE DEMAND CURVE

We now know from the behaviour underlying the aggregate expenditure function that the price level and real equilibrium national income are negatively related to each other; that is, an exogenous change in the price level changes equilibrium national income in the opposite direction. This negative relationship can be shown in an important new concept, the *aggregate demand curve.*

Recall that the *AE* curve relates actual national income to desired aggregate expenditure for a given price level, plotting income on the horizontal axis. The **aggregate demand (AD) curve** relates equilibrium national income to the price level, again plotting national income on the horizontal axis. Because the horizontal axes of both the *AE* and *AD* curves measure actual national income, the two curves can be placed one above the other so that the level of national income on each can be compared directly. This is shown in Figure 25-2.

Now let us see how the *AD* curve is derived. Given a value of the price level, equilibrium national income is determined in part (i) of Figure 25-2 at the point where the *AE* curve crosses the 45° line. In part (ii) of Figure 25-2, the combination of the equilibrium level of national income and the corresponding value of the price level is plotted, giving one point on the *AD* curve.

When the price level changes, the *AE* curve shifts, for the reasons just seen. The new position of the *AE* curve gives rise to a new equilibrium level of national income that is associated with the new price level. This determines a second point on the *AD* curve, as shown in part (ii) of Figure 25-2. Note that because the *AD* curve relates equilibrium national income to the price level, changes in the price level that cause *shifts in* the *AE* curve cause *movements along* the *AD* curve. A movement along the *AD* curve thus traces out the response of equilibrium income to a change in the price level.

The aggregate demand curve shows for each price level the associated level of national income for which aggregate desired expenditure equals actual national income.

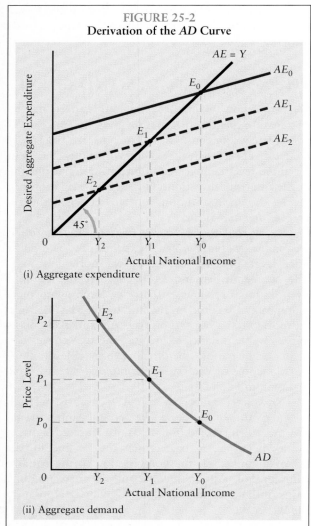

FIGURE 25-2
Derivation of the AD Curve

(i) Aggregate expenditure

(ii) Aggregate demand

Equilibrium income is determined by the AE curve for each given price level; the level of equilibrium income and its associated price level are then plotted to yield a point on the AD curve. When the price level is P_0, the AE curve is AE_0, and hence equilibrium national income is Y_0, as shown in part (i). Plotting Y_0 against P_0 yields the point E_0 on the AD curve in part (ii).

An increase in the price level to P_1 causes AE_0 to shift downward to AE_1 and causes equilibrium national income to fall to Y_1. Plotting this new level of national income against the higher price level yields a second point, E_1, on the AD curve. A further increase in the price level to P_2 causes the AE curve to shift downward to AE_2, and thus causes equilibrium national income to fall to Y_2. Plotting P_2 and Y_2 yields a third point, E_2, on the AD curve.

Thus a change in the price level causes a shift in the AE curve but a movement along the AD curve.

The Slope of the AD Curve

Figure 25-2 provides us with sufficient information to establish that the AD curve is negatively sloped.

1. A rise in the price level causes the AE curve to shift downward and hence leads to a movement upward and to the left along the AD curve, reflecting a fall in the equilibrium level of national income.

2. A fall in the price level causes the AE curve to shift upward and hence leads to a movement downward and to the right along the AD curve, reflecting a rise in the equilibrium level of national income.

In Chapter 4, we saw that demand curves for individual goods such as carrots and automobiles are downward sloping. However, the reasons for the negative slope of the AD curve are very different from the reasons for the negative slope of individual demand curves used in microeconomics. Let us explore why this is the case.

If we assume that we can obtain a negatively sloping aggregate demand curve in the same manner that we derived negatively sloping individual market demand curves, we would be committing what is called *the fallacy of composition:* assuming that what is correct for the parts must be correct for the whole.

Consider a simple example of the fallacy. An art collector can go into the market and add to her private collection of nineteenth-century French paintings provided only that she has enough money. However, the fact that any one person can do this does not mean that everyone could do so simultaneously. The world's stock of nineteenth-century French paintings is fixed. All of us together cannot do what any one of us with enough money can do.

How does the fallacy of composition relate to demand curves? An individual demand curve describes a situation in which the price of one commodity changes *while the prices of all other commodities and consumers' money incomes are constant.* Such an individual demand curve is negatively sloped for two reasons. First, as the price of the commodity rises, each consumer's given money income will buy a smaller *total* amount of goods, so a smaller quantity of each commodity will be bought, other things being equal. Second, as the price of the commodity rises, consumers buy less of that commodity and more of the now relatively cheaper substitutes.

The first reason has no application to the aggregate demand curve, which relates the total demand for all output to the price level. All prices and total output are changing as we move along the *AD* curve. Because the value of output determines income, consumers' money incomes will also be changing along this curve.

The second reason does apply to the aggregate demand curve, but only in a limited way. A rise in the price level entails a rise in *all* domestic commodity prices. Hence there is no incentive to substitute among domestic commodities whose prices do not change relative to each other. However, it does give rise, as we saw earlier in this chapter, to some substitution between domestic and foreign products. Domestic goods and services rise in price relative to imported goods and services, and the switch in expenditure will lower desired aggregate expenditure on domestic output and hence will lower equilibrium national income.

Points off the *AD* Curve

The *AD* curve depicts combinations of national income and the price level such that aggregate desired expenditure equals actual output. These points are said to be *consistent* with expenditure decisions.

The national income given by any point on the aggregate demand curve is such that if that level of output is produced, aggregate desired expenditure at the given price level will exactly equal the output.

Points to the left of the *AD* curve show combinations of national income and the price level that cause aggregate desired expenditure to exceed output. There is thus pressure for income to rise because firms could sell more than current output. Points to the right of the *AD* curve show combinations of national income and the price level for which aggregate desired expenditure is less than current income. There is thus pressure for income to fall because firms will not be able to sell all of their current output. These relationships are illustrated in Figure 25-3.

Shifts in the *AD* Curve

Because the *AD* curve plots equilibrium national income as a function of the price level, anything that alters equilibrium national income *at a given price*

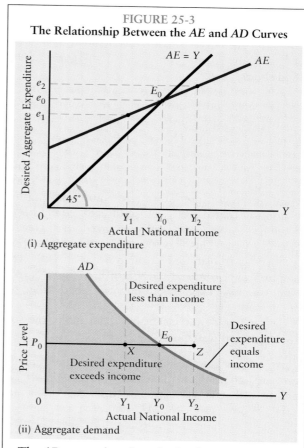

FIGURE 25-3
The Relationship Between the *AE* and *AD* Curves

(i) Aggregate expenditure

(ii) Aggregate demand

The *AD* curve plots the price level against the level of national income consistent with expenditure decisions at that price level. With the price level P_0, equilibrium national income is Y_0, shown by the intersection of *AE* and the 45° line at E_0 in part (i) and by the point E_0 on the *AD* curve in part (ii).

With the price level constant at P_0, consider a level of national income of Y_1. In part (i), if national income were equal to Y_1, desired aggregate expenditure would be e_1. Hence Y_1 is not an equilibrium level of national income when the price level is P_0, and the combination (P_0, Y_1) is not a point on the *AD* curve, as shown by point X.

Now consider a level of national income of Y_2. In part (i), if national income were equal to Y_2, desired aggregate expenditure would be e_2. Hence Y_2 is not an equilibrium level of national income when the price level is P_0, and the combination (P_0, Y_2) is not a point on the *AD* curve in part (ii), as shown by point Z.

Repeating the same analysis for each given price level tells us that for all points to the left of the *AD* curve, income is tending to rise because desired expenditure exceeds income, whereas for all points to the right of the *AD* curve, income is tending to fall because desired aggregate expenditure is less than income.

level must shift the *AD* curve. In other words, any change—other than a change in the price level—that causes the AE curve to shift will also cause the *AD* curve to shift. Such a shift is called an **aggregate demand shock.**

For example, in the early 1980s, changes in the U.S. tax laws led to an increase in the amount of consumption expenditure associated with each level of national income. This was an expansionary demand shock that shifted the U.S. *AD* curve to the right. It spilled over into Canada in terms of a shift in Canada's net export function. Increased U.S. expenditure on consumption meant more expenditure on imports that directly and indirectly entered into consumption. So Canada also received an aggregate demand shock. This was ultimately due to U.S. policy but was transmitted through a rise in U.S. consumption expenditure to a rise in U.S. imports to a rise in Canada's exports and then to Canadian aggregate demand.

Using our new concepts, we can make the following general statement:

A rise in the amount of desired consumption, investment, government purchases, or net export expenditure that is associated with each level of national income shifts the *AD* curve to the right. A fall in any of these expenditures shifts the *AD* curve to the left.

The Simple Multiplier and the *AD* Curve

We saw in Chapters 23 and 24 that the simple multiplier measures the magnitude of the change in equilibrium national income in response to a change in autonomous expenditure when the price level is held constant. It follows that this multiplier gives the magnitude of the *horizontal shift* in the *AD* curve in response to a change in autonomous expenditure. This is shown in Figure 25-4.

The simple multiplier measures the horizontal shift in the *AD* curve in response to a change in autonomous expenditure.

If the price level remains constant and firms are willing to supply everything that is demanded at that price level, the simple multiplier will also show the change in equilibrium income that will occur in response to a change in autonomous expenditure.

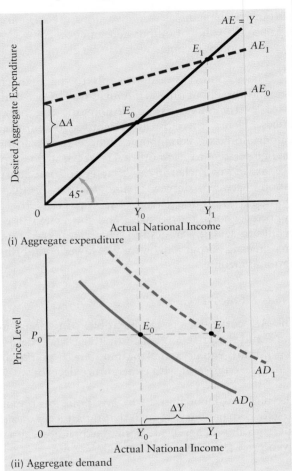

FIGURE 25-4

The Simple Multiplier and Shifts in the *AD* Curve

(i) Aggregate expenditure

(ii) Aggregate demand

A change in autonomous expenditure changes equilibrium national income for any given price level, and the simple multiplier measures the resulting horizontal shift in the aggregate demand curve. The original desired expenditure curve is AE_0 in part (i). Equilibrium is at E_0, with national income Y_0 at price level P_0. This yields point E_0 on the curve AD_0 in part (ii).

The AE curve in part (i) then shifts upward from AE_0 to AE_1, due to an increase in autonomous expenditure of ΔA. Equilibrium income now rises to Y_1, with the price level still constant at P_0. Thus the *AD* curve in part (ii) shifts to the right to point E_1, indicating the higher equilibrium income Y_1 associated with the same price level P_0. The magnitude of the shift, ΔY, is equal to the simple multiplier times ΔA.

A fall in autonomous expenditure can be analyzed by reversing these steps, starting with the dashed curves and moving to the solid ones.

THE SUPPLY SIDE OF THE ECONOMY

So far, we have explained how the equilibrium level of national income is determined *when the price level is taken as given* and how that equilibrium changes as the price level is changed exogenously. We are now ready to take an important further step: adding an *explanation* for the behaviour of the price level. To do this, we need to take account of the supply decisions of firms.

THE AGGREGATE SUPPLY CURVE

Aggregate supply refers to the total output of goods and services that firms wish to produce, assuming that they can sell all that they wish to sell. Aggregate supply thus depends on the decisions of firms to use workers and other inputs to produce goods and services to sell to households, governments, and other firms, as well as for export.

An **aggregate supply curve** relates aggregate supply to the price level. It is necessary to define two types of such curves. The **short-run aggregate supply (SRAS) curve** relates the price level to the quantity that firms would like to produce and sell *on the assumption that the prices of all factors of production remain constant.* The **long-run aggregate supply (LRAS) curve**, which we will define more fully in the next chapter, relates the price level to desired sales after the economy has fully adjusted to that price level. For the remainder of this chapter, we confine our attention to the *SRAS* curve.

The Slope of the *SRAS* Curve

To study the slope of the *SRAS* curve, we need to see how costs are related to output and then how prices and output are related.

Costs and Output.   Suppose that firms wish to increase their output above current levels. What will this do to their costs per unit of output—usually called their **unit costs?** The short-run aggregate supply curve is drawn on the assumption that the prices of all factors of production remain constant. This does not, however, mean that unit costs will be constant. As output increases, less efficient standby plants may have to be used, and less efficient workers may have to be hired, while existing workers may have to be paid overtime rates for additional work. For these and other similar reasons, unit costs will tend to rise as output rises, even when input prices are constant. (Readers who have studied microeconomics will recognize the law of diminishing returns as one reason why costs rise in the short run as firms squeeze more output out of a fixed quantity of capital equipment.)

Prices and Output.   To consider the relationship between price and output, we need to consider firms that sell in two distinct types of markets: those in which firms are *price takers* and those in which firms are *price setters*.

Some industries, including those that produce most basic industrial materials and some energy products, contain many individual firms. In these cases, each one is too small to influence the market price, which is set by the overall forces of demand and supply. Each firm must accept whatever price is set on the open market and adjust its output to that price. Such firms are said to be *price takers* and *quantity adjusters*. When the market price changes, these firms will react by altering their level of production.

Because their unit costs rise with output, price-taking firms will produce more only if price rises and will produce less if price falls.

Many other industries, including most of those that produce manufactured products, contain so few firms that each can influence the market price of its product. Most such firms sell products that differ from one another, although all are similar enough to be thought of as a single product produced by one industry. For example, no two kinds of automobiles are the same, but all automobiles are sufficiently alike that we have no trouble talking about the automobile industry and its product, automobiles. In such cases, each firm must quote a price at which it is prepared to sell each of its products; that is, the firm is a *price setter*. If the demand for the output of price-setting firms increases sufficiently to take their outputs into the range in which their unit costs rise (e.g., because overtime is worked and standby plants are brought into production), these firms will not increase their outputs unless they can pass at least some of these extra costs on through higher prices. When demand falls, they will reduce output, and competition among them will tend to cause a reduction in prices whenever their unit costs fall.

Price-setting firms will increase their prices when they expand output into the range in which unit costs are rising.

This is the basic behaviour of firms in response to the changes in demand and prices when factor prices are constant, and it explains the slope of the *SRAS* curve, such as the one shown in Figure 25-5.

The actions of both price-taking and price-setting firms cause the price level and the aggregate supply of output to be positively related; the graphical expression of this relationship is the positively sloped short-run aggregate supply curve.

As we will see later in this chapter, the shape of the short-run aggregate supply curve will be crucial for determining how the effect of an aggregate demand shock is divided between a change in the price level and a change in real national income. Extension 25-1 contains more detail on the shape of the *SRAS* curve.

Shifts in the *SRAS* Curve

Shifts in the *SRAS* curve, which are shown in Figure 25-5, are called **aggregate supply shocks.** Two sources of aggregate supply shocks are of particular importance: changes in the price of inputs and increases in productivity.

Changes in Input Prices. Factor prices are held constant along the *SRAS* curve, and when they change, the curve shifts. If factor prices rise, firms will find the profitability of their current production reduced. For any given level of output to be produced, an increase in the price level will be required. If prices do not rise, firms will react by decreasing production. For the economy as a whole, this means that there will be less output supplied at each price level than before the increase in factor prices. Or, to put it another way, there will be a higher price level for each level of output than before the increase in factor prices. So if factor prices rise, the SRAS curve shifts upward (or to the left). This is a decrease in aggregate supply.

Similarly, a fall in factor prices causes the *SRAS* curve to shift downward (or to the right). This increase in aggregate supply means that more will be produced and offered for sale at each price level.

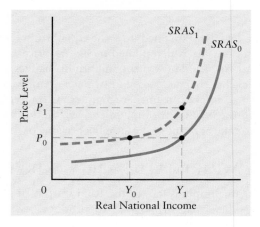

FIGURE 25-5
The Short-Run Aggregate Supply Curve

The *SRAS* curve is upward sloping, indicating that firms will only supply more aggregate output when there is an increase in the price level. The positive slope of the *SRAS* curve shows that with the prices of labour and other inputs given, the supply of output and the price level are positively related. Thus on the dashed *SRAS* curve, a rise in the price level from P_0 to P_1 is associated with a rise in the quantity of total output supplied from Y_0 to Y_1.

Notice that the slope of each *SRAS* curve is fairly flat at low levels of income and very steep at higher levels. Extension 25-1 provides a detailed explanation of this characteristic shape. Briefly, at low levels of income, where there is excess capacity in the economy, output can be increased with little change in cost. As the economy approaches potential income, it becomes very difficult to increase real output without pushing up costs.

A shift to the left of the *SRAS* curve reflects a decrease in supply; a shift to the right reflects an increase in supply. Starting from (P_0, Y_1) on $SRAS_0$, suppose that there is an increase in input prices. At price level P_0, only Y_0 would be produced. Alternatively, to get output Y_1 would require a rise to price level P_1. The new supply curve is $SRAS_1$, which may be viewed as being above and to the left of $SRAS_0$. An increase in supply, caused, say, by a decrease in input prices, would shift the *SRAS* curve downward and to the right, from $SRAS_1$ to $SRAS_0$.

Increases in Productivity. If labour productivity rises, meaning that each worker can produce more, the unit costs of production will fall (for given wages). Lower costs generally lead to lower prices. Competing firms cut prices in attempts to raise their market shares, and the net result of such

More on the Shape of the *SRAS* Curve

The *SRAS* curve relates the price level to the quantity of output that producers are willing to sell. Notice two things about the shape of the *SRAS* curve that is reproduced in Figure 25-5: It has a positive slope, and the slope increases as output rises.

POSITIVE SLOPE

The most obvious feature of the *SRAS* curve is its positive slope, indicating that a higher price level is associated with a greater supply of real output, other things being equal. Because the prices of all of the factors of production are being held constant along the *SRAS* curve, why is the curve not horizontal, indicating that firms would be willing to supply as much output as might be demanded with no increase in the price level?

The answer is that even though *input prices* are constant, *unit costs of production* eventually rise as output increases. Higher prices for increasing output—rising short-run aggregate supply—is necessary to compensate firms for rising costs.

The preceding paragraph addresses this question: What has to happen to the price level if national output increases, with the price of factors of production remaining constant? Alternatively, one could ask, What will happen to firms' willingness to supply output if product prices rise with no increase in factor prices? Production becomes more profitable, and because firms are interested in making profits, they will usually produce more.* Consequently, when the price level of final output rises *while factor prices are held constant,* firms are

*Readers who have studied microeconomics can understand this in terms of perfectly competitive firms facing higher prices and thus expanding output along their marginal cost curves until marginal cost is once again equal to price.

motivated to increase their output. This is true for the individual firm and also for firms in the aggregate. This increase in the amount produced leads to a positive slope of the *SRAS* curve.

Thus whether we look at how the price level will respond in the short run to increases in output or how the level of output will respond to an increase in the price level with input prices being held constant, we find that the *SRAS* curve has a positive slope.

INCREASING SLOPE

A less obvious but in many ways more important property of a typical *SRAS* curve is that its slope *increases* as output rises. It is rather flat for low levels of output and rather steep for high levels. Why? When output is low (below potential output), firms typically have unused capacity—some plant and equipment are idle. When firms have unused capacity, only a small increase in the price of their output may be needed to induce them to expand production—at least up to normal capacity.

Once output is pushed far beyond normal capacity, however, unit costs tend to rise quite rapidly. Many higher-cost expedients may have to be adopted. Standby capacity, overtime, and extra shifts may have to be used. Such expedients raise the cost of producing a unit of output. These higher-cost methods will not be used unless the selling price of the output has risen enough to cover them. The further that output is expanded beyond normal capacity, the more rapidly unit costs rise and hence the larger is the rise in price that is needed to induce firms to increase output even further.

This increasing slope is sometimes called the *first important asymmetry* in the behaviour of aggregate supply. (The second, *sticky wages,* will be discussed in Chapter 26.)

competition is that the fall in production costs is accompanied by a fall in prices. Because the same output is sold at a lower price, this causes a downward shift in the *SRAS* curve. This shift is an increase in aggregate supply, as illustrated in Figure 25-5.

A rightward shift in the *SRAS* curve, brought about, for example, by an increase in productivity with no increase in factor prices, means that firms will be willing to supply more output with no increase in the price level. This result has been the object of many government policies that seek to encourage increases in productivity.

A change in either factor prices or productivity will shift the *SRAS* curve because any given output will be supplied at a different price level than previously. An increase in factor prices or a decrease in productivity shifts the *SRAS* curve to the left; an increase in productivity or a decrease in factor prices shifts it to the right.

MACROECONOMIC EQUILIBRIUM

We have now reached our objective: We are ready to see how both real national income and the price level are simultaneously determined by the interaction of aggregate demand and aggregate supply.

The equilibrium values of national output and the price level occur at the intersection of the *AD* and *SRAS* curves, as shown by the pair Y_0 and P_0 that arise at point E_0 in Figure 25-6. We describe the combination of national income and price level that is on both the *AD* and *SRAS* curves as a *macroeconomic equilibrium,* and its determination in Figure 25-6 should be studied carefully at this point.

To see why the point (Y_0, P_0) is the only macroeconomic equilibrium, first consider what Figure 25-6 shows would happen if the price level were below P_0. At this lower price level, the desired output of firms, as given by the *SRAS* curve, is less than desired aggregate expenditure at that level of output. The excess desired aggregate expenditure will cause prices to be bid up, and national income will increase along the *SRAS* curve. Hence there can be no macroeconomic equilibrium when the price level is below P_0.

Similarly, Figure 25-6 shows that when the price level is above P_0, the behaviour underlying the *SRAS* and *AD* curves is not consistent. In this case, producers will wish to supply more than the level of output that is demanded at that price level. If firms were to produce their desired levels of output, desired expenditure would not be large enough to purchase everything that would be produced.

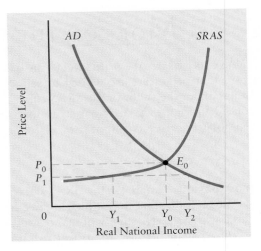

FIGURE 25-6
Macroeconomic Equilibrium

Macroeconomic equilibrium occurs at the intersection of the *AD* and *SRAS* curves and determines the equilibrium values for national income and the price level. Given the *AD* and *SRAS* curves in the figure, macroeconomic equilibrium occurs at E_0, with national income equal to Y_0 and the price level equal to P_0.

If the price level were equal to P_1, the desired output of firms, given by the *SRAS* curve, would be Y_1. However, at P_1, the level of output that is consistent with expenditure decisions, given by the *AD* curve, would be Y_2, which is greater than Y_1. Hence when the price level is less than P_0, the desired output of firms will be less than the level of national income that is consistent with expenditure decisions. This causes upward pressure on the price level.

Similarly, for any price level above P_0, the desired output of firms, given by the *SRAS* curve, would exceed the level of output that is consistent with expenditure decisions, given by the *AD* curve. This causes downward pressure on the price level.

The only price level where the supply decisions of firms are consistent with desired expenditure is at macroeconomic equilibrium. At P_0, firms wish to produce Y_0. When they do so, they generate a national income of Y_0; when income is Y_0, decision makers wish to spend exactly Y_0, thereby purchasing the nation's output. Hence all decisions are consistent with each other.

Only at the combination of national income and price level given by the intersection of the *SRAS* and *AD* curves are demand behaviour and supply behaviour consistent.

Macroeconomic equilibrium thus requires that two conditions be satisfied. The first is familiar to us because it comes from Chapters 23 and 24: At the prevailing price level, desired aggregate expenditure must be equal to actual national income, which means that households are just willing to buy all that is produced. The *AD* curve is constructed in such a way that this condition holds everywhere on it. The second requirement for equilibrium is introduced by consideration of aggregate supply: At the prevailing price level, firms must wish to produce the prevailing level of national income, no more and no less. This condition is fulfilled everywhere on the *SRAS* curve. Only where the two curves intersect are both conditions fulfilled simultaneously.

CHANGES IN THE MACROECONOMIC EQUILIBRIUM

The aggregate demand and aggregate supply curves now can be used to understand how various shocks to the economy change both national income and the price level.

As indicated earlier, a shift in the *AD* curve is called an aggregate demand shock. A rightward shift in the *AD* curve is an increase in aggregate demand; it means that at all price levels, expenditure decisions will now be consistent with a higher level of real national income. Similarly, a leftward shift in the *AD* curve is a decrease in aggregate demand; it means that at all price levels, expenditure decisions will now be consistent with a lower level of real national income.

Also as indicated earlier, a shift in the *SRAS* curve is called an aggregate supply shock. A rightward shift in the *SRAS* curve is an increase in aggregate supply; at any given price level, more real national income will be supplied. A leftward shift in the *SRAS* curve is a decrease in aggregate supply; at any given price level, less real national income will be supplied.

What happens to real national income and to the price level when one of the aggregate curves shifts?

A shift in either the *AD* or the *SRAS* curve leads to changes in the equilibrium values of the price level and real national income.

Extension 25-2 deals with the special case of a perfectly elastic (horizontal) *SRAS* curve. In that case, the aggregate supply curve determines the price level by itself, and the aggregate demand curve then determines real national income by itself. In this special case, we say that output is *demand determined*.

AGGREGATE DEMAND SHOCKS

Figure 25-7 shows the effects of an increase in aggregate demand. This increase could have occurred because of, say, increased investment or government purchases, or perhaps a depreciation of the Canadian dollar leading to a rise in net exports. Whatever the cause, the increase in aggregate demand means that more national output is demanded at any given price level. As is shown in the figure, following an increase in aggregate demand, both the price level and real national income rise. Conversely, a decrease in demand causes both the price level and real national income to fall.

Aggregate demand shocks cause the price level and real national income to change in the same direction; both rise with an increase in aggregate demand, and both fall with a decrease in aggregate demand.

An aggregate demand shock means that there is a shift in the *AD* curve (for example, from AD_0 to AD_1 in Figure 25-7). Adjustment to the new equilibrium following an aggregate demand shock involves a movement along the *SRAS* curve (for example, from point E_0 to point E_1).

The Multiplier When the Price Level Varies

We saw earlier in this chapter that the simple multiplier (which was examined in detail in Chapters 23 and 24) gives the extent of the horizontal shift in the *AD* curve in response to a change in autonomous expenditure. If the price level remains constant and firms are willing to supply all that is demanded at the existing price level, the simple multiplier gives the increase in equilibrium national income.

Now that we can use aggregate demand and aggregate supply curves, we can answer a more interesting question: What happens in the more usual

THE KEYNESIAN *SRAS* CURVE

In this box, we consider an extreme version of the *SRAS* curve that is horizontal over some range of national income. It is called the *Keynesian short-run aggregate supply curve,* after John Maynard Keynes (1883–1946), who in his famous book *The General Theory of Employment, Interest and Money* (1936) pioneered the study of the behaviour of economies under conditions of high unemployment. Despite its name, this curve does not describe Keynes' own views on the behaviour of the price level. It is instead the version of aggregate supply used by many of Keynes' followers in their early attempts to express Keynes' work in a formal model—something Keynes himself did not do.

The behaviour that gives rise to the Keynesian *SRAS* curve can be described as follows. When real national income is below potential national income, individual firms are operating at less than normal-capacity output, and they hold their prices constant at the level that would maximize profits if production were at normal capacity. They then respond to demand variations below that capacity by altering output. In other words, they will supply whatever they can sell at their existing prices as long as they are producing below their normal capacity. In this case, we say that output is *demand determined.**

---
*The evidence is strong that many firms do behave like this in the short run. One possible explanation for this is that changing prices frequently is too costly, so firms set the best possible (profit-maximizing) prices when output is at normal capacity and then do not change prices in the face of short-term fluctuations in demand.

Under these circumstances, the economy has a horizontal aggregate supply curve, indicating that any output up to potential output will be supplied at the going price level. The amount that is actually produced is then determined by the position of the aggregate demand curve, as shown in the figure. Thus we say that real national income is *demand determined.* If demand rises enough so that firms are trying to squeeze more than normal output out of their plants, their costs will rise, and so will their prices. Hence the horizontal Keynesian *SRAS* curve applies only to national incomes below potential income.

---

case in which the aggregate supply curve slopes upward? In this case, a rise in national income caused by an increase in aggregate demand will be associated with a rise in the price level (as the economy moves up an upward-sloping aggregate supply curve). However, as we saw in Figure 25-2, a rise in the price level (by reducing net exports and by lowering the real value of household wealth) shifts the

AE curve downward, which lowers equilibrium national income, other things being equal. These conflicting forces—which appears quite complicated—can be easily understood by using aggregate demand and aggregate supply curves.

As can be seen in Figure 25-7, when the *SRAS* curve is positively sloped, the change in national income that has been caused by a change in au-

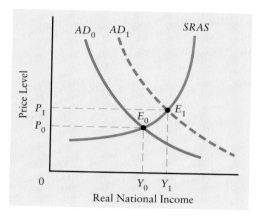

FIGURE 25-7
Aggregate Demand Shocks

Shifts in aggregate demand cause the price level and real national income to move in the same direction. An increase in aggregate demand shifts the *AD* curve to the right, say, from AD_0 to AD_1. Macroeconomic equilibrium moves from E_0 to E_1. The price level rises from P_0 to P_1, and real national income rises from Y_0 to Y_1, reflecting a movement along the *SRAS* curve.

tonomous expenditure is no longer equal to the size of the horizontal shift in the *AD* curve. A rightward shift of the *AD* curve causes the price level to rise, which in turn causes the rise in national income to be less than the horizontal shift of the *AD* curve. Part of the expansionary impact of an increase in demand is dissipated by a rise in the price level, and only part is transmitted to a rise in real output. Of course, an increase in output does occur, so a multiplier may still be calculated, but its value is not the same as that of the simple multiplier.

When the *SRAS* curve is upward sloping, the multiplier is smaller than the simple multiplier.

Why is the multiplier smaller when the *SRAS* curve is positively sloped? The answer lies in the behaviour that is summarized by the *AE* curve. To understand this, it is useful to think of the final change in national income as occurring in two stages, as shown in Figure 25-8.

First, with prices remaining constant, an increase in autonomous expenditure (e.g., investment) shifts the *AE* curve upward (from AE_0 to

FIGURE 25-8
The *AE* Curve and the Multiplier When the Price Level Varies

(i) Aggregate expenditure

(ii) Aggregate demand

An increase in autonomous expenditure causes the *AE* curve to shift upward, but the rise in the price level causes it to shift part of the way down again. Hence the multiplier effect on income is smaller than when the price level is constant. Originally, equilibrium is at point E_0 in both part (i) and part (ii). Desired aggregate expenditure then shifts by ΔA to AE_1', shifting the aggregate demand curve to AD_1. These shifts are shown by arrow 1 in both parts. The amount Y_0Y_1' is the change called for by the simple multiplier, which holds prices constant at P_0.

Instead, however, the shift in the *AD* curve raises the price level to P_1 because the *SRAS* curve is positively sloped. The rise in the price level shifts the aggregate expenditure curve down to AE_1, as shown by arrow 2 in part (i). This is shown as a movement along the *AD* curve, as indicated by arrow 2 in part (ii). The new equilibrium is thus at E_1. The amount Y_0Y_1 is ΔY, the actual increase in real income. The multiplier, adjusted for the effect of the price increase, is the ratio $\Delta Y/\Delta A$ in part (i).

FIGURE 25-9
The Effects of Increases in Aggregate Demand

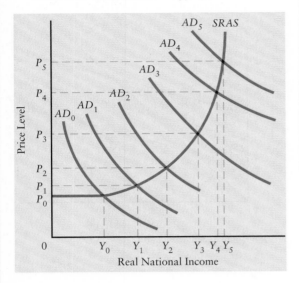

The effect of increases in aggregate demand is divided between increases in real income and increases in prices, depending on the slope of the *SRAS* curve. Because of the increasing slope of the *SRAS* curve, increases in aggregate demand up to AD_0 have virtually no impact on the price level. When aggregate demand increases from AD_0 to AD_1, there is a relatively small increase in the price level, from P_0 to P_1, and a relatively large increase in output, from Y_0 to Y_1. Successive further increases bring larger price increases and relatively smaller output increases. By the time aggregate demand is at AD_4 or AD_5, virtually all of the effect is on the price level.

AE_1') and therefore shifts the *AD* curve to the right. This is shown by a shift upward of the *AE* curve in part (i) of the figure and a shift to the right of the *AD* curve in part (ii). The horizontal shift in the *AD* curve is measured by the simple multiplier, but this cannot be the final equilibrium position because firms are unwilling to produce enough to satisfy the extra demand at the existing price level. The final equilibrium must be a point on the *SRAS* curve.

Second, we take account of the rise in the price level that occurs because of the positive slope of the *SRAS* curve. As we have seen, a rise in the price level, via its effect on net exports and on wealth, leads to a downward shift in the *AE* curve (from AE_1' to AE_1).

This second shift of the *AE* curve partly counteracts the initial rise in national income and so reduces the size of the multiplier. The second stage shows up as a downward shift of the *AE* curve in part (i) of Figure 25-8 and a movement upward and to the left along the new *AD* curve in part (ii).

The Importance of the Shape of the *SRAS* Curve

We have now seen that the shape of the *SRAS* curve has important implications for how the effects of an aggregate demand shock are divided between changes in real national income and changes in the price level. Figure 25-9 highlights this by considering *AD* shocks in the presence of an *SRAS* curve that exhibits three distinct ranges.

Over the *flat* range, from 0 to Y_0, any change in aggregate demand leads to no change in prices and, as seen earlier, a response of output equal to that predicted by the simple multiplier. In this case, output is said to be *demand determined* (see Extension 25-1).

Over the *intermediate* range, along which the *SRAS* curve is positively sloped, from Y_0 to Y_4, a shift in the *AD* curve gives rise to appreciable changes in both real income and the price level. As we saw earlier in this chapter, the change in the price level means that real income will change by less in response to a change in autonomous expenditure than it would if the price level were constant.

Over the *steep* range, for output above Y_4, very little more can be produced, however large the demand is. This range deals with an economy near its capacity constraints. Any change in aggregate demand leads to a sharp change in the price level and to little change in real national income. The multiplier in this case is nearly zero.

Reconciliation with Previous Analysis

One of the central points of this chapter is that changes in aggregate demand (caused by shifts in the *AE* function) typically lead to changes in *both* the price level and the level of real national income. Furthermore, with a steep enough *SRAS* curve, such aggregate demand shocks will result in no change in real national income, but only a change in the price level. How do we reconcile this possibility with the analysis of Chapters 23 and 24, where shifts in *AE al-ways* change national income? The answer is that each *AE* curve is drawn on the assumption that there

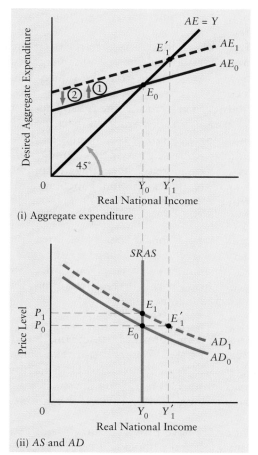

FIGURE 25-10
Demand Shocks When the *SRAS* Curve is Vertical

(i) Aggregate expenditure

(ii) *AS* and *AD*

If the *SRAS* curve is vertical, the effect of an increase in autonomous expenditure is solely a rise in the price level. An increase in autonomous expenditure shifts the *AE* curve upward from AE_0 to AE_1, as shown by arrow 1 in part (i). Given the initial price level P_0, equilibrium would shift from E_0 to E_1' and real national income would rise from Y_0 to Y_1'. However, the price level does not remain constant. This is shown by the *SRAS* curve in part (ii). Instead, the price level rises to P_1. This causes the *AE* curve to shift back down all the way to AE_0, as shown by arrow 2 in part (i), and equilibrium income stays at Y_0. In part (ii), the new equilibrium is at E_1 with income at Y_0, which is associated with the new price level, P_1.

shifts the *AE* curve downward, offsetting some of its initial rise.

This interaction is seen most easily if we study the extreme case, shown in Figure 25-10, in which the *SRAS* curve is vertical. An increase in autonomous expenditure shifts the *AE* curve upward, thus raising the amount demanded. However, a vertical *SRAS* curve means that output cannot be expanded to satisfy the increased demand. Instead, the extra demand merely forces prices up, and as prices rise, the *AE* curve shifts downward again. The rise in prices continues until the *AE* curve is back to where it started. Thus the rise in prices offsets the expansionary effect of the original shift and consequently leaves both real aggregate expenditure and equilibrium real income unchanged.

The discussion of Figures 25-9 and 25-10 illustrates a general proposition:

The effect of any given shift in aggregate demand will be divided between a change in real output and a change in the price level, depending on the conditions of aggregate supply. The steeper the *SRAS* curve, the greater the price effect and the smaller the output effect.

For reasons discussed in Extensions 25-1 and 25-2, many economists think that the *SRAS* curve is shaped like that in Figure 25-9, that is, relatively flat for low levels of income and becoming steeper as the level of national income increases. This shape of the *SRAS* curve implies that at low levels of national income (well below potential), shifts in aggregate demand primarily affect output and at high levels of national income (above potential), shifts in aggregate demand primarily affect prices.

Of course, as we have noted already, treating wages and other factor prices as constant is appropriate only when the time period under consideration is short. Hence the *SRAS* curve is used only to analyze short-run, or *impact*, effects. In the next chapter, we will see what happens in the long run when factor prices respond to changes in national income and the price level. First, however, our analysis of the short run needs to be rounded out with a discussion of aggregate supply shocks.

AGGREGATE SUPPLY SHOCKS

A decrease in aggregate supply is shown by a shift to the left in the *SRAS* curve and means that less na-

is a constant price level. A rise in *AE* shifts the *AD* curve to the right. However, a steep *SRAS* curve means that the price level rises significantly, and this

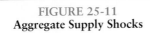

FIGURE 25-11
Aggregate Supply Shocks

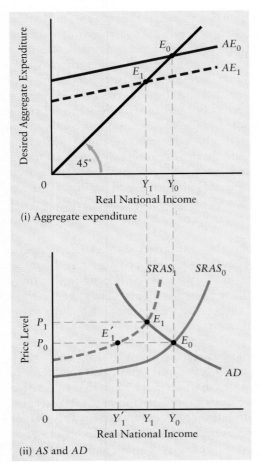

(i) Aggregate expenditure

(ii) AS and AD

Aggregate supply shocks cause the price level and real national income to move in opposite directions. The original equilibrium is at E_0, with national income of Y_0 appearing in both parts of the figure. The price level is P_0 in part (ii), and at that price level, the desired aggregate expenditure curve is AE_0 in part (i).

An aggregate supply shock now shifts the *SRAS* curve in part (ii) to $SRAS_1$. At the original price level of P_0, firms are now only willing to supply Y_1'. The fall in supply, with no corresponding fall in demand, causes a shortage that leads to a rise in the price level. The new equilibrium is reached at E_1, where the *AD* curve intersects $SRAS_1$. At the new and higher equilibrium price level of P_1, the *AE* curve has fallen to AE_1, as shown in part (i), which is consistent with equilibrium national income of Y_1.

tional output will be supplied at any given price level. An increase in aggregate supply is shown by a shift to the right in the *SRAS* curve and means that more national output will be supplied at any given price level.

Figure 25-11 illustrates the effects on the price level and real national income of aggregate supply shocks. As can be seen from the figure, following the decrease in aggregate supply, the price level rises and real national income falls. This combination of events is called *stagflation,* a term derived by combining *stagnation* (sometimes used to mean less than full employment) and *inflation.* Conversely, an increase in aggregate supply leads to an increase in real national income and a decrease in the price level.

Aggregate supply shocks cause the price level and real national income to change in opposite directions. With an increase in supply, the price level falls and income rises; with a decrease in supply, the price level rises and income falls.

An aggregate supply shock means that there is a shift in the *SRAS* curve (for example, from $SRAS_0$ to $SRAS_1$ in Figure 25-11). Adjustment to the new equilibrium following the shock involves a movement along the *AD* curve (for example, from E_0 to E_1).

Oil prices have provided three major examples of aggregate supply shocks in recent decades. The economy is especially responsive to changes in the market for oil because in addition to being used to produce energy, oil is an input into plastics and many other materials that are widely used in the economy. Massive increases in oil prices during 1973–1974 and 1979–1980 caused leftward shifts in the *SRAS* curve. National income fell while the price level rose—stagflation. During the mid 1980s, oil prices fell substantially. This shifted the *SRAS* curve to the right, increasing national income and putting downward pressure on the price level.

We can see now how a rightward shift in the *SRAS* curve, which is brought about by an increase in productivity or a fall in input prices, raises real national income and lowers the price level.

SUMMARY

A. THE DEMAND SIDE OF THE ECONOMY

- The *AE* curve shows desired aggregate expenditure for each level of income at a particular price level. Its intersection with the 45° line determines equilibrium national income for that price level, on the assumption that firms will produce everything that they can sell at the going price level. Equilibrium income thus occurs where desired aggregate expenditure equals actual national income. A change in the price level causes a shift in the *AE* curve: upward when the price level falls and downward when the price level rises. This leads to a new equilibrium level of national income.

- The *AD* curve plots the equilibrium level of national income that corresponds to each possible price level. A change in equilibrium national income following a change in the price level is shown by a movement along the *AD* curve.

- A rise in the price level lowers exports and lowers consumers' spending (because it decreases consumers' wealth). Both of these changes lower equilibrium national income (by shifting the *AE* curve downward) and cause the *AD* curve to have a negative slope.

- The *AD* curve shifts horizontally when any element of autonomous expenditure changes, and the simple multiplier measures the magnitude of the shift. This multiplier also measures the size of the change in real equilibrium national income when the price level remains constant and firms produce everything that is demanded at that price level.

B. THE SUPPLY SIDE OF THE ECONOMY

- The short-run aggregate supply *(SRAS)* curve, drawn for given factor prices, is positively sloped because unit costs rise with increasing output and because rising product prices make it profitable to increase output.

- An increase in productivity or a decrease in factor prices shifts the *SRAS* curve to the right. This is an increase in aggregate supply. A decrease in productivity or an increase in factor prices shifts the *SRAS* curve to the left. This is a decrease in aggregate supply.

C. MACROECONOMIC EQUILIBRIUM

- Macroeconomic equilibrium refers to equilibrium values of national income and the price level, as determined by the intersection of the *AD* and *SRAS* curves. Shifts in the *AD* and *SRAS* curves, called aggregate demand shocks and aggregate supply shocks, change the equilibrium values of national income and the price level.

D. CHANGES IN THE MACROECONOMIC EQUILIBRIUM

- When the *SRAS* curve is upward sloping, an aggregate demand shock causes the price level and national income to move in the same direction. The division of the effects between a change in national income and a change in the price level depends on the shape of the *SRAS* curve. When the *SRAS* curve is flat, shifts in the *AD* curve primarily affect real national income. When the *SRAS* curve is steep, shifts in the *AD* curve primarily affect the price level.

- An aggregate supply shock moves equilibrium national income along the *AD* curve, causing the price level and national income to move in opposite directions. A leftward shift in the *SRAS* curve causes stagflation—rising prices and falling national income. A rightward shift causes an increase in real national income and a fall in the price level.

KEY CONCEPTS

Inside and outside assets
Effects of an exogenous change in the price level
Relationship between the *AE* and *AD* curves

Negative slope of the *AD* curve
Positive slope of the *SRAS* curve
Macroeconomic equilibrium
Aggregate demand shocks

The multiplier when the price level varies
Aggregate supply shocks
Stagflation

DISCUSSION QUESTIONS

1. Indicate whether each of the following events is either the cause or the consequence of a shift in aggregate demand or supply. If it is a cause, what do you predict will be the effect on the price level and on real national income?

   a. After the recession of the early 1990s, national income increased with little change in the price level.
   b. OPEC raised oil prices in 1980.
   c. In the early 1970s, Canada experienced a rapid inflation under conditions of approximately full employment.
   d. In France in 1981, income and employment continued to fall while the price level was relatively stable.
   e. The end of the Cold War led to large decreases in defense spending in many countries.
   f. Canadian exports rise in response to a falling external value of the Canadian dollar in the early 1990s.
   g. Most provinces raised their personal income-tax rates in the 1990s.
   h. Inflationary pressures recede during the recession of 1990–1992.
   i. The federal government takes measures to reduce its budget deficit.

2. Explain the following as consequences of shifts in either the aggregate demand curve or the aggregate supply curve (or both). Pay attention to the initial position before each shift occurred.

   a. Output and employment rise while prices hold steady.
   b. Prices soar, but employment and output hold steady.
   c. Inflation accelerates even as the recession in business activity deepens.

3. In 1979 and 1980, the British government greatly reduced income taxes but restored the lost government revenue by raising excise and sales taxes. This led to a short burst of extra inflation and a fall in output. Explain this in terms of shifts in the aggregate demand or aggregate supply curves (or both).

4. What would happen to employment and income if, in an attempt to lower Canadian unemployment, the federal government increased import barriers? What would happen if all countries did the same?

5. Show the effects on the price level and output of income-tax cuts that make people work more in an economy that is on the steep portion of its SRAS curve.

6. Following are the combinations of output and price level given by GDP and the CPI, respectively, for some recent years. Treat each pair as if it is the intersection of an AD and an SRAS curve. Plot these data. Then think about the possible shifts in the AD or SRAS curves that could have caused them. Is it possible to know what the underlying shifts are? Why or why not?

Year	CPI (1986 = 100)	GDP (billions of 1986 dollars)
1986	100.0	506
1987	104.4	527
1988	108.6	553
1989	114.0	566
1990	119.5	563
1991	126.2	553
1992	128.1	559
1993	130.4	572
1994	130.7	598
1995	132.2	626

7. A survey of private economic forecasters in 1995 showed that the consensus economic outlook for 1996 was cautiously optimistic—most thought that real growth would remain roughly constant and unemployment would fall slightly, while inflation would increase somewhat. Explain what factors underlying the AD and SRAS curves would give rise to such a forecast. In retrospect, how accurate were these forecasts? What happened to the underlying determinants to cause actual events to differ from the forecasts?

CHAPTER 26

NATIONAL INCOME AND THE PRICE LEVEL IN THE LONG RUN

Every worker knows that the best time to ask for a raise is during a boom, and that it is difficult to get significant wage increases during a recession. Every businessperson knows that the cost of many materials tends to rise rapidly during business expansions and to fall—often dramatically—during recessions. In short, factor prices change with economic conditions, and we need to allow for these effects. It is high time, therefore, to go beyond the assumption of fixed factor prices that we used to study the initial effects of aggregate demand and aggregate supply shocks in Chapter 25. To do this, we need to see what happens in a longer-term setting, when changes in national income *induce* changes in factor prices.

INDUCED CHANGES IN FACTOR PRICES

We must begin by reconsidering two key concepts that we first encountered in Chapter 21—potential income and the output gap.

POTENTIAL INCOME AND THE OUTPUT GAP

Recall that *potential income* is the total output that can be produced when all productive resources—labour and capital equipment in particular—are being used at their *normal rates of utilization.* When a

nation's actual national income diverges from its potential income, the difference is called the output gap (or GDP gap). (See Figure 21-4.)

Although growth in potential income has powerful effects from one decade to the next, its change from one *year* to the next is small enough to be ignored when studying the year-to-year behaviour of national income and the price level. Therefore, in this discussion we continue with the convention, first adopted in Chapter 21, of ignoring the small changes in potential income caused by year-to-year changes in productivity. This means that variations in the output gap are determined solely by variations in *actual* national income around a constant level of *potential* national income.

Figure 26-1 shows actual national income being determined by the intersection of the *AD* and *SRAS* curves. Potential income is constant, and it is shown by identical vertical lines in the two parts of the figure. In part (i), the *AD* and *SRAS* curves intersect to produce an equilibrium national income that falls short of potential income. The result is called a *recessionary gap* because recessions are often characterized as having actual income below potential in-

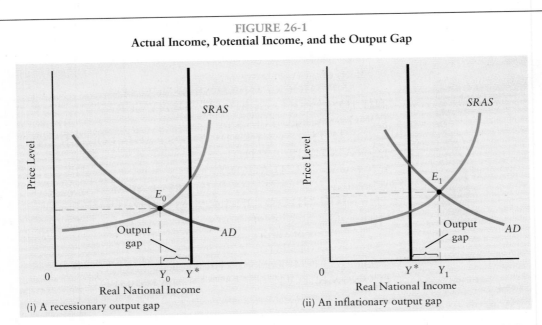

FIGURE 26-1
Actual Income, Potential Income, and the Output Gap

(i) A recessionary output gap

(ii) An inflationary output gap

The output gap is the difference between potential national income, Y*, and actual national income, Y. Potential income is shown by the vertical line at Y*. A recessionary gap, shown in panel (i), occurs when potential national income is greater than actual national income. An inflationary gap, shown in panel (ii), occurs when actual national income is greater than potential national income.

come. In part (ii), the *AD* and *SRAS* curves intersect to produce an equilibrium national income that exceeds potential income, resulting in what is called an *inflationary gap*. The way in which an inflationary output gap puts upward pressure on prices will become clear in the ensuing discussion.

FACTOR PRICES AND THE OUTPUT GAP

The output gap provides a convenient measure of the pressure of demand on factor prices. When national income is high relative to potential income, demand for factors will also be high. When national income is low relative to potential income, demand for factors will be correspondingly low. This relationship is true of all factors. The discussion that follows is simplified, however, by focusing on one key factor, labour, and on its price, the wage rate.

When there is an inflationary gap, actual income exceeds potential, and the demand for labour services will be relatively high. When there is a recessionary gap, actual income is below potential, and the demand for labour services will be relatively low.

Each of these situations has implications for wages. Before turning to a detailed analysis, we first consider a benchmark for the behaviour of wages. Earlier we referred to average costs per unit of output as *unit costs;* to focus on labour costs, we now use average wage costs per unit of output, which we refer to as *unit labour costs.*

Upward and Downward Wage Pressures

In this section, we consider the *upward* and *downward* pressures on wages that are associated with various output gaps. Inflationary gaps exert upward pressure on wages, and recessionary gaps exert downward pressure on wages. To what do the upward and downward pressures relate? One answer would be that upward pressure means that wages will rise, and downward pressure means that wages will fall. However, most workers and firms start from the assumption that, other things being equal, workers will get the benefit of increases in their own productivity by receiving higher wages. Hence when national income is at its potential level, so that there are neither upward nor downward pressures on wages caused by output gaps, wages will tend to be

rising at the same rate that productivity is rising.[1] When wages and productivity change proportionately, *unit labour costs* remain unchanged. For example, if each worker produces 4 percent more per hour and also earns 4 percent more per hour, unit labour costs will remain constant. This, then, is the benchmark:

When there is neither excess demand nor excess supply in the labour market, wages will tend to be rising at the same rate as labour productivity; as a result, unit labour costs will remain constant.

Note that with unit labour costs remaining constant, there is no pressure coming from the labour market for the *SRAS* curve to shift and hence no pressure for the price level to rise or to fall.

In comparison with this benchmark, upward pressure on wages means that there is pressure for wages to rise faster than productivity is rising. Consequently, unit labour costs will also be rising. For example, if wages rise by 8 percent while productivity rises by only 4 percent, unit labour costs will be rising by about 4 percent. In this case, the *SRAS* curve will be shifting to the left, reflecting upward pressure on wages coming from the labour market. It is too much of a mouthful to say every time that wages are rising at a faster rate than productivity is rising, so we use the shorthand expression *wages are rising faster than productivity.*

Downward pressure on wages means that there is pressure for wages to rise more slowly than productivity is rising. When this occurs, unit labour costs will be falling. For example, if productivity rises by 4 percent while wages rise by only 2 percent, unit labour costs will be falling by about 2 percent. In this case, the *SRAS* curve will be shifting to the right, reflecting downward pressure on wages coming from the labour market. It is too much of a

---

[1]Ongoing inflation would also influence the normal pattern of wage changes. Wage contracts often allow for changes in prices that are expected to occur during the life of the contract. (Of course, if wages rise merely to keep pace with product prices, there is no effect on unit labour costs; labour cost per dollar's worth of output will be constant.) For now we make the simplifying assumption that the price level is expected to be constant; hence changes in money wages are also expected to be changes in real wages. The distinction between changes in money wages and real wages and the important role played by expectations of price level changes will be discussed in Chapter 30.

mouthful to say every time that wages are rising at a slower rate than the rate at which productivity is rising, so again we use the shorthand expression *wages are rising more slowly than productivity.*

Output Above Potential

Sometimes the *AD* and *SRAS* curves intersect where actual output exceeds potential, as illustrated in part (ii) of Figure 26-1. Firms are producing beyond their normal capacity output, so there is an unusually large demand for all factor inputs, including labour. Labour shortages will emerge in some industries and among many groups of workers. Firms will try to bid workers away from other firms in order to maintain the high levels of output and sales made possible by the boom conditions.

As a result of these tight labour-market conditions, workers will find that they have considerable bargaining power with their employers, and they will put upward pressure on wages relative to productivity. Firms, recognizing that demand for their goods is strong, will be anxious to maintain a high level of output. To prevent their workers from either striking or quitting and moving to other employers, firms will be willing to accede to some of these upward pressures.

The boom that is associated with an inflationary gap generates a set of conditions—high profits for firms and unusually large demand for labour—that causes wages to rise faster than productivity (and thus for unit labour costs to rise).

Output Below Potential

Sometimes the *AD* and *SRAS* curves intersect where actual output is less than potential, as illustrated in part (i) of Figure 26-1. In this situation, firms are producing below their normal-capacity output, so there is an unusually low demand for all factor inputs, including labour. The general conditions in the market for labour will be the opposite of those that occur when actual output exceeds potential. There will be labour surpluses in some industries and among some groups of workers. Firms will have below-normal sales and will not only resist upward pressures on wages but also tend to offer wage increases below productivity increases and may even seek reductions in wages.

The slump that is associated with a recessionary gap generates a set of conditions—low profits for firms and low demand for labour—that causes wages to rise more slowly than productivity (and thus for unit labour costs to fall).

Adjustment Asymmetry

At this stage, we encounter an important asymmetry in the economy's aggregate supply behaviour.[2] Boom conditions (an inflationary gap), along with severe labour shortages, cause wages, unit labour costs, and the price level to rise rapidly. When there is a large excess demand for labour, wage (and price) increases often run well ahead of productivity increases. Wages might be rising by 10 percent, while productivity might be rising at only 2 percent. Under such conditions, unit labour costs will be rising rapidly.

The experience of many developed economies suggests, however, that the downward pressures on wages during slumps (recessionary gaps) often do not operate as quickly as the upward pressures during booms. Even in quite severe recessions, when the price level is fairly stable, wages may continue to rise, although their rate of increase tends to fall below that of productivity. For example, productivity might be rising at 2 percent per year while wages are rising at 1 percent. In this case, unit labour costs are falling, but only by 1 percent per year, so the rightward shift in the *SRAS* curve and the downward pressure on the price level are correspondingly slight. Wages do sometimes fall, reducing unit labour costs even more, but the reduction in unit labour costs in times of the deepest recession has never been as fast as the increases that have occurred during several of the strongest booms.

Both upward and downward adjustments to unit labour costs do occur, but there are differences in the speed at which they typically operate. Booms can cause unit labour costs to rise very rapidly; recessions usually cause unit labour costs to fall only slowly.

In Chapters 30 and 31, we explore the consequences of this asymmetry for the relationship between unemployment and inflation, which is one of the most important relationships in macroeconomics.

---

[2]This is the second asymmetry in aggregate supply that we have encountered. The first involves the changing slope of the *SRAS* curve, discussed in Extension 25-1.

Inflationary and Recessionary Gaps

Now it should be clear why the output gaps are named as they are. When actual national income exceeds potential national income, there will normally be rising unit costs, and the *SRAS* curve will be shifting upward. This will in turn push the price level up. Indeed, the most obvious event accompanying these conditions is likely to be significant inflation. The larger the excess of actual income over potential income, the greater the inflationary pressure. The term *inflationary gap* emphasizes this salient feature when output exceeds potential output.

When actual output is less than potential output, as we have seen, there will be unemployment of labour and other productive resources. Unit labour costs will fall only slowly, leading to a slow downward shift in the *SRAS* curve. Hence the price level will be falling only slowly, so that *unemployment* will be the output gap's most obvious result. The term *recessionary gap* emphasizes this salient feature that high rates of unemployment occur when actual output falls short of potential output.

The induced effects of output gaps on unit labour costs and the consequent shifts in the *SRAS* curve play an important role in our analysis of the long-run consequences of aggregate demand shocks, to which we now turn.

THE EFFECTS OF AGGREGATE DEMAND SHOCKS

We can now extend our study to cover the longer-run consequences of aggregate demand shocks, incorporating changes in factor prices. We need to examine the effects of aggregate demand shocks on factor prices for expansionary and for contractionary shocks separately because the behaviour of unit costs is not symmetrical for the two cases.

EXPANSIONARY *AD* SHOCKS

Suppose that the economy starts with a stable price level at full employment so that actual income equals potential income, as shown by the initial equilibrium in part (i) of Figure 26-2. Now suppose that this situation is disturbed by an increase in autonomous ex-

penditure, perhaps caused by an upturn in business confidence and a resulting boom in investment spending. Figure 26-2(i) shows the effects of this aggregate demand shock in raising both the price level and national income. The aggregate demand curve shifts from AD_0 to AD_1, and actual national income rises above potential income. There is an inflationary gap.

We have seen that an inflationary gap leads to increases in wages, which cause unit costs to rise. The *SRAS* curve shifts to the left as firms respond to the higher input costs by increasing their output prices. For this reason, the initial increases in the price level and in real national income shown in Figure 26-2 (i) are *not* the final effects of the aggregate demand shock. As seen in part (ii) of the figure, the upward shift of the *SRAS* curve causes a further rise in the price level, but this time the price rise is associated with a fall in output.

The cost increases (and the consequent upward shifts of the *SRAS* curve) continue until the inflationary gap has been removed, that is, until in part (ii) income returns to Y^*, its potential level. Only then is there no abnormal demand for labour, and only then do wages and unit costs, and hence the *SRAS* curve, stabilize.

This important expansionary demand-shock sequence can be summarized as follows:

1. Starting from full employment, a rise in aggregate demand raises the price level and raises income above its potential level as the economy expands along a given *SRAS* curve.

2. The expansion of income beyond its normal capacity level puts pressure on factor markets; factor prices begin to increase faster than productivity, shifting the *SRAS* curve upward, such that prices are higher at every level of output.

3. The shift of the *SRAS* curve causes national income to fall along the new *AD* curve. This process continues as long as actual income exceeds potential income; actual income eventually falls back to its potential level. However, the price level is now higher than it was after the initial impact of the increased aggregate demand, but inflation will have come to a halt.

The ability to get more output and income from the economy than its underlying potential output (as

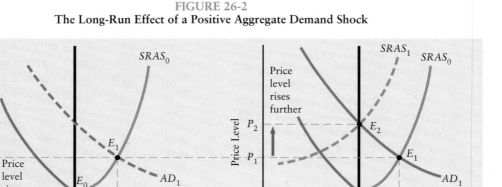

FIGURE 26-2
The Long-Run Effect of a Positive Aggregate Demand Shock

(i) Autonomous increase in aggregate demand

(ii) Induced shift in aggregate supply

A rightward shift of the *AD* curve first raises prices and output along the *SRAS* curve. It then induces a shift of the *SRAS* curve that further raises prices but lowers output along the new *AD* curve. In part (i), the economy is in equilibrium at E_0, at its level of potential output, Y^*, and price level P_0. The *AD* curve then shifts from AD_0 to AD_1. This moves equilibrium to E_1, with income Y_1, and price level P_1, and opens up an inflationary gap of Y^*Y_1.

In part (ii), the inflationary gap results in an increase in wages and other input costs, shifting the *SRAS* curve leftward. As this happens, income falls and the price level rises along AD_1. Eventually, when the *SRAS* curve has shifted to $SRAS_1$, income is back to Y^* and the inflationary gap has been eliminated. However, the price level has risen to P_2. The long-run result of the aggregate demand shock is therefore a higher price level with no change in real national income.

in point 2) is only a short-term possibility. National income greater than Y^* sets into motion inflationary pressures that tend to push national income back to Y^*.

An adjustment mechanism eventually eliminates any boom caused by a one-time demand shock by returning output to its potential level and thereby removing the inflationary gap.

CONTRACTIONARY *AD* SHOCKS

Let us return to that fortunate economy with full employment and stable prices. It appears again in part (i) of Figure 26-3, which is similar to part (i) of Figure 26-2. Now assume that there is a *decline* in aggregate demand. This negative aggregate demand shock might be a reduction in investment expenditure, or perhaps a decline in the world demand for Canadian exports of lumber or computer software.

The first effects of the decline are a fall in output and some downward adjustment of prices, as shown

in part (i) of the figure. As output falls, unemployment rises. The difference between potential output and actual output is the recessionary gap that is shown in Figure 26-3.

Flexible Wages

What would happen if severe unemployment caused wage rates to fall rapidly? Suppose that with productivity rising by 1 percent per year, wages fell by 4 percent. Unit costs would then *fall* by 5 percent, causing a rightward shift of the *SRAS* curve. As shown in part (ii) of Figure 26-3, the economy would move along its fixed *AD* curve, with falling prices and rising output, until full employment was restored at potential national income Y^*. We conclude that if wages were to fall rapidly whenever there was unemployment, the resulting shift in the *SRAS* curve would restore full employment.

Flexible wages that fall rapidly during periods of unemployment provide an automatic adjustment mech-

FIGURE 26-3
The Long-Run Effect of a Negative Aggregate Demand Shock

A leftward shift of the *AD* curve first lowers the price level and output along the *SRAS* curve and then induces a (slow) shift of the *SRAS* curve that further lowers prices but raises output along the new *AD* curve. In part (i), the economy is in equilibrium at E_0, at its level of potential output, Y^*, and price level P_0. The *AD* curve then shifts to AD_1, moving equilibrium to E_1, with income Y_1 and price level P_1, and opens up a recessionary gap of Y_1Y^*.

Part (ii) shows the adjustment back to full employment that occurs from the supply side of the economy. The fall in wages shifts the *SRAS* curve to the right. Real national income rises, and the price level falls further along the new *AD* curve. Eventually, the *SRAS* curve reaches $SRAS_1$, with equilibrium at E_2. The price level stabilizes at P_2 when income returns to Y^*, closing the recessionary gap.

anism that pushes the economy back toward full employment whenever output is below potential.

Extension 26-1 takes up the interesting case of how the adjustment mechanism might work if the aggregate demand shock were anticipated in advance. This might happen, for example, when the government announces its intention to change its expenditure or taxation plans at some point in the future.

Sticky Wages

Boom conditions, along with severe labour shortages, do cause wages to rise rapidly, shifting the *SRAS* curve upward. However, as we noted earlier when we encountered the second asymmetry of aggregate supply behaviour, the experience of many economies suggests that wages typically do not fall rapidly in response to recessionary gaps and their accompanying unemployment. It is sometimes said that wages are "sticky" in the downward direction. This does not mean that wages never fall. In recessions, wages often rise more slowly than productivity and some wages actually do fall. But the gap between wage changes and productivity changes is typically quite small during recessions. This means that unit labour costs will fall only slowly. This in turn means that the downward shifts in the *SRAS* curve occur slowly, and the adjustment mechanism that depends on these shifts will act sluggishly.

The weakness of the adjustment mechanism does not mean that slumps must always be prolonged. Rather, this weakness means that speedy recovery back to full employment must be generated mainly from the demand side. If the economy is to avoid a lengthy period of recession or stagnation, the force leading to recovery usually must be a rightward shift of the *AD* curve rather than a downward drift of the *SRAS* curve. The possibility that government *stabilization policy* might accomplish such a rightward shift in the *AD* curve is an important and contentious issue in macroeconomics, one that we will return to often throughout the remainder of this book.

ANTICIPATED DEMAND SHOCKS

Suppose that the increase in aggregate demand that is illustrated in Figure 26-2 was widely anticipated well before it occurred. For example, an approaching election might lead to the widespread belief that the government will stimulate the economy in order to improve its chances of reelection.

Further suppose that most employers and employees believe that one of the effects of demand stimulation will be inflation. Workers might press for wage increases to prevent the purchasing power of their earnings from being eroded by the coming price increases. Firms would believe that demand for their products was likely to rise, enabling them to raise their selling prices. They might therefore be persuaded to grant wage increases now and pass these on to consumers in terms of higher prices.

A demand stimulus that is widely expected to occur and whose inflationary effects are widely understood could lead to upward pressure on wages, even without the presence of an inflationary gap.

If this were to occur, the leftward shift in the *SRAS* curve that is depicted in part (ii) of Figure 26-2 could occur quickly, perhaps accompanying, or even preceding, the rightward shift in the *AD* curve in part (i). Given *perfect* anticipation of the effects of the demand stimulus and *full* adjustment to it in advance, the equilibrium would go straight from E_0 to E_2. The intermediate position, E_1, with its accompanying inflationary gap (with national income in ex-cess of potential income), would be completely by-passed.

A similar story might be told for an anticipated fall in aggregate demand. The effects of an unanticipated fall are shown in the two parts of Figure 26-3. However, if the fall were widely anticipated and its effects were generally understood, firms might reduce their wage offers, and workers might accept the decreases because they expect prices to fall as well. In this case, it is conceivable that the economy could bypass the recessionary stage and go straight to a lower price level at an unchanged level of real national income.

This possibility, that anticipated demand shocks might have no effect on real national income, plays a key role in some important controversies concerning the effectiveness of government policies. We shall study these in detail in Chapters 30 and 31.

In the meantime, we may notice that the complete absence of real effects in the transitionary period, with the only change being in the price level, requires that everyone has full knowledge both of the exact amount of the stimulus that the government will induce and of the new equilibrium values of the relevant prices and wages. In other words, everyone knows what the new equilibrium will be and goes directly to it. Generally, however, people do not have perfect knowledge and foresight, so there are some temporary real effects until the final equilibrium set of wages and prices is reached.

The *SRAS* curve shifts to the left fairly rapidly when national income exceeds Y^*, but it shifts to the right only slowly when national income is less than Y^*. This is because wages tend to be upwardly flexible but downwardly sticky.

Effects of the Asymmetry

The difference in speed of adjustment is a consequence of the important asymmetry in the behaviour of aggregate supply that was noted earlier in this chapter. This asymmetry helps to explain two key facts about our economy. First, unemployment can persist for quite long periods without causing decreases in unit costs and prices of sufficient magnitude to remove the unemployment. Second, booms, along with labour shortages and production beyond normal capacity, do not persist for long periods without causing increases in unit costs and the price level.

DEMAND SHOCKS AND BUSINESS CYCLES

Aggregate demand shocks are a major source of fluctuations in actual national income around potential income. As we have seen, an expansionary demand shock, starting from a position of full employment, will lead to an increase in output and prices, followed by a fall in output accompanied by a further increase in prices as the adjustment mechanism restores the economy to equilibrium. Depending on the nature and magnitude of the shock, the adjustment will take many months, often a year or two.

Suppose that the government increases spending on roads or that economic growth in Europe leads to an increase in demand for Canadian exports. No matter what the source of growth in demand, the economy will not respond instantaneously. In many industries, it takes weeks or months or even longer to bring new or mothballed capacity into production and to hire and train new workers. The multiplier process itself also takes time as households and firms respond to the change in income that results from an initial increase in autonomous spending.

Because of these lags in the economy's response, changes in demand give rise to changes in output that are spread out over a substantial period of time. An increase in demand may lead to a gradual increase in output that lasts several months. Then, as output does change, the adjustment mechanism comes into play—as an inflationary gap opens up, wages and costs start to rise, shifting the *SRAS* curve to the left.

Thus a once-and-for-all positive demand shock (beginning from a position of full employment) gives rise to a *cyclical* output response, with *Y* first rising because of the rightward shift in the *AD* curve and then falling because of the leftward shift in the *SRAS* curve. A negative demand shock is likely to play out even more slowly because of the asymmetry of response. Again, however, the behaviour of output will be cyclical: Starting from potential output, *Y* will fall over a period of time because of a leftward shift in the *AD* curve and then rise slowly as the adjustment mechanism shifts *SRAS* to the right.

Each major component of aggregate expenditure (consumption, investment, net exports, and government purchases) is subject to continual random shifts, which are sometimes large enough to disturb the economy significantly. Adjustment lags convert such shifts into cyclical fluctuations in national income.

THE LONG-RUN AGGREGATE SUPPLY CURVE

The adjustment mechanism leads us to an important concept: the **long-run aggregate supply** (*LRAS*) curve. This curve relates the price level to real national income after wage rates and all other input costs have been fully adjusted to eliminate any unemployment or overall labour shortages.[3]

Once all the adjustments that are required have occurred, any excess demand or excess supply of labour will have been eliminated. In other words, full employment will prevail, and output will be at its potential level, Y^*. It follows that the aggregate supply curve becomes a vertical line at Y^*, as shown in Figure 26-4. It is a vertical line because the total amount of goods that the economy produces when all factors are used at their normal rate of utilization does not vary with the price level. If the price level were to rise *and wages and all other factor prices were to rise by the same proportion,* the desired output of firms would remain at Y^*. The *LRAS* curve is sometimes called the *classical aggregate supply curve* because the Classical economists were mainly concerned with the behaviour of the economy in long-run equilibrium.[4]

Notice that the vertical *LRAS* curve does not represent the same thing as the vertical portion of the *SRAS* curve (see Figure 25-9). Over the vertical range of the *SRAS* curve, the economy is at its utmost limit of productive capacity, when no more output can be squeezed out under any circumstances. In contrast, the vertical shape of the *LRAS* curve is due to the workings of an adjustment mechanism that brings the economy back to its potential output, even though output may differ from potential for considerable periods of time. It is called the long-run aggregate supply curve because it describes what happens as a result of adjustments that take a substantial amount of time.

---

[3]Readers who have studied microeconomics will notice that this use of the term *long run* is different from its meaning in microeconomics. Note, however, the key similarity is that the long run has more flexibility for adjustment than has the short run.

[4]The Classical school of economic thought began with Adam Smith (1723–1790) and was developed through the work of David Ricardo (1772–1823), Thomas Malthus (1766–1834) and John Stuart Mill (1806–1873). These economists emphasized the long-run behaviour of the economy. Beginning in the middle of the nineteenth century, Neoclassical economists devoted much time and effort to studying short-term fluctuations. *The General Theory of Employment, Interest and Money* (1936), written by John Maynard Keynes (1883–1946), was in a long tradition of the study of short-term fluctuations. Where Keynes differed from the neoclassical economists was in approaching the issues from a macroeconomic perspective that emphasized fluctuations in real expenditure flows. Each of the economists mentioned in this footnote, along with several others, are discussed in more detail in the timeline at the back of the book.

Along the *LRAS* curve, all the prices of all outputs and all inputs have been fully adjusted to eliminate any excess demands or supplies. Proportionate changes in money wages and the price level (which, by definition, will leave real wages unaltered) will also leave equilibrium employment and total output unchanged. In the next section, we will ask what does change when we move from one point on the *LRAS* curve to another.

LONG-RUN EQUILIBRIUM

Figure 26-4 shows the equilibrium output and the price level as they are determined by the intersection of the *AD* curve and the vertical *LRAS* curve. Because the *LRAS* curve is vertical, shifts in aggregate demand change the price level but not the level of equilibrium output, as shown in part (i). By contrast, a shift in aggregate supply changes both output and the price level, as shown in part (ii). For example, a rightward shift of the *LRAS* curve increases national income and leads to a fall in the price level.

In the long run, total output is determined solely by conditions of aggregate supply, and the role of aggregate demand is only to determine the price level.

What does change when the economy moves from one point on the *LRAS* curve, such as E_0 in part (i) of Figure 26-4, to another point, such as E_1? Although *total output* and *total desired expenditure* do not change, their *compositions* do change. The higher the price level, the lower the level of household wealth (for a given nominal stock of assets) and hence of consumption. (Recall from Chapter 23 that the lower the level of wealth the lower the level of consumption.) Also, the higher the price level, the lower are exports and the higher are imports and hence the lower the level of net exports.

Suppose that the economy starts at an equilibrium point on the *SRAS* curve and an increase in government expenditure then creates an inflationary gap. Money wages and the price level rise until the gap is removed. At the new long-run equilibrium, the higher level of government spending is exactly offset by lower consumption and net exports, leaving total output unchanged. To see this, recall from the national income accounting in Chapter 22 that national income is the sum of actual consumption, investment, government purchases and net exports. When one of these components changes, but the overall level of national income is constant, there

FIGURE 26-4
Long-Run Equilibrium and Aggregate Supply

(i) A rise in aggregate demand

(ii) A rise in long-run aggregate supply

Because the *LRAS* curve is vertical, aggregate supply determines the long-run equilibrium value of national income at Y^*. Given Y^*, aggregate demand determines the long-run equilibrium value of the price level. In both parts of the figure, the initial long-run equilibrium is at E_0, so the price level is P_0 and national income is Y_0^*.

In part (i), a shift in the *AD* curve from AD_0 to AD_1, with the *LRAS* curve remaining unchanged, moves the long-run equilibrium from E_0 to E_1. This raises the price level from P_0 to P_1 but leaves national income unchanged at Y_0^* in the long run.

In part (ii), a shift in the *LRAS* curve from $LRAS_0$ to $LRAS_1$, with the aggregate demand curve remaining constant at AD_0, moves the long-run equilibrium from E_0 to E_2. This raises national income from Y_0^* to Y_1^* and lowers the price level from P_0 to P_2.

must be an offsetting change in one of the other components. Thus the increase in government purchases in long-run equilibrium simply forces a reduction in the other components of aggregate demand.

A similar analysis holds for an increase in some component of aggregate demand—say investment. At the new long-run equilibrium, the higher level of investment spending will be exactly offset by lower consumption spending and net exports. In such circumstances, it is often said that the increased autonomous expenditure, whether by the government or private investors, has "crowded out" an equivalent amount of induced expenditure (in the form of reduced consumption and net exports).

The vertical *LRAS* curve shows that given full adjustment of input prices, potential income, Y^*, is compatible with any price level, although its composition among consumption, investment, government, and net exports may vary at different price levels.

In Chapter 28, we will discover a special type of aggregate demand shock which has *no real effects,* so that not only are total income and total expenditure the same at all points on the *LRAS* curve, but the composition of national product among *C, I, G,* and *NX* is also unchanged.

NATIONAL INCOME IN THE SHORT AND LONG RUN

We have now identified two distinct equilibrium conditions for the economy.

1. In the short run, the economy is in equilibrium at the level of income and prices where the *SRAS* curve intersects the *AD* curve.

2. In the long run, the economy is in equilibrium at potential income, the position of the vertical *LRAS* curve. The price level is determined where the *AD* curve intersects the *LRAS* curve.

The position of the *LRAS* curve is at Y^*, which is determined by past economic growth. Since in the long run, output equals Y^*, it follows that economic growth explains long-run movements in output. In contrast, deviations of actual output from potential output—output gaps—are short-run phenomena and are generally associated with *business cycles.* Changes in total real output may therefore take place due either to long-term growth or to the business cycle.

This suggests a need to distinguish three ways in which *Y* can increase. The first two relate to short-

run changes in *Y;* the third is a long-run change in *Y.* These are illustrated in Figure 26-5.

Increases in Aggregate Demand. As shown in part (i) of Figure 26-5, an increase in aggregate demand will yield a one-time increase in real *Y.* If that increase occurs when there is a recessionary gap (a shift from AD_0 to AD_1), it pushes *Y* toward potential income and thus short-circuits the working of the automatic adjustment mechanism that eventually would have achieved the same outcome by depressing wages and other costs. (The operation of this adjustment mechanism is discussed in detail earlier in this chapter.)

If the demand shock pushes *Y* beyond potential income (a shift from AD_1 to AD_2), the rise in *Y* above potential income will be only temporary; the inflationary gap will cause wages and other costs to rise, shifting the *SRAS* curve to the left. This drives *Y* back toward potential so that the only lasting effect is on the price level.

Temporary Increases in Aggregate Supply. Increases in aggregate supply will also lead to a temporary increase in *Y.* Part (ii) of Figure 26-5 shows the effects of a temporary increase in aggregate supply. This will shift the *SRAS* curve to the right but will have no effect on the *LRAS* curve and hence on potential income. The shock will thus cause *Y* to rise relative to potential, but the increase will be soon reversed—in this case, possibly even before any significant impact on wages and other costs can be detected.

Permanent Increases in Aggregate Supply. Part (iii) of Figure 26-5 shows the effects of permanent increases in aggregate supply that shift the *LRAS* curve. We can think of a few possible explanations for such a shift. For example, a once-and-for-all change in a labour-market policy that reduces the level of structural unemployment will lead to a one-time rightward shift in the *LRAS* curve. Another example might be a one-time improvement in the education system which makes workers more productive, shifting the *LRAS* curve to the right. Recurring changes such as population growth, capital accumulation, or ongoing improvements in productivity cause a continual rightward shift in the *LRAS* curve, giving rise to a continual increase in the level of potential output.

Increases in aggregate demand or temporary increases in aggregate supply can increase national income in the short run, but not in the long run. Only

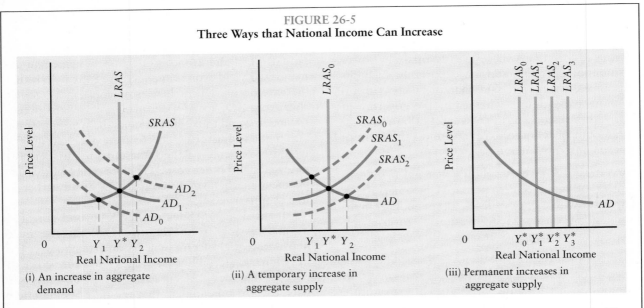

FIGURE 26-5
Three Ways that National Income Can Increase

(i) An increase in aggregate demand

(ii) A temporary increase in aggregate supply

(iii) Permanent increases in aggregate supply

National income will increase in response to an increase in aggregate demand or an increase in aggregate supply. The increase will be permanent if the *LRAS* curve shifts, but if the *LRAS* curve does not shift, any divergence of Y from potential will only be temporary; the output gap that is created will set in motion the wage adjustments that we studied earlier in this chapter. In the cases shown in parts (i) and (ii), any increase in GDP beyond potential is temporary because in the absence of any additional shocks, the inflationary gap will cause wages and other factor prices to rise; this will cause the *SRAS* curve to shift upward and hence cause national income to converge to Y^*.

In part (iii), the *LRAS* curve shifts to the right, causing potential income to increase. Whether or not actual income increases immediately depends on what happens to the *AD* and *SRAS* curves. Because in the absence of other shocks, actual income eventually converges to potential income, a rightward shift in the *LRAS* curve eventually leads to an increase in actual income. If the shift in the *LRAS* curve is recurring, national income will grow continually.

permanent increases in aggregate supply can lead to permanent increases in national income.

ECONOMIC GROWTH

A gradual but continual rise in potential output, or what we have called *economic growth,* is the main source of improvements in living standards over the long term.

Eliminating a severe recessionary gap will cause a once-and-for-all increase in national income of perhaps 4 percent. However, a growth rate of 3 percent per year raises national income by 10 percent in 3 years, *doubles* it in 24 years, and *quadruples* it in 48 years.

In any given year, the position of the *LRAS* curve is at potential income, Y^*. The long run to which the *LRAS* curve refers is thus one in which the resources available to the economy do not change but in which all markets reach equilibrium. Economic growth

moves the *LRAS* curve to the right, year by year. Here there is no long run in which everything settles down because growth is a continuing process. Rather, the movement in *LRAS* is a continuing movement in Y^*.

In Chapter 33, we present a detailed discussion of the determinants of long-term economic growth and of polices that can affect economic growth.

CYCLICAL FLUCTUATIONS

Figure 26-5 allows us to distinguish the causes of trend growth in potential output, which is the gradual rightward shifting of the *LRAS* curve, from the causes of cyclical fluctuations, which are shifts in the *AD* and *SRAS* curves. These shifts are in turn caused by changes in a variety of factors, including interest rates, exchange rates, consumer and business confidence, and government policy. Although the resulting

FIGURE 26-6
Canadian Business Activity Since 1925

Cyclical ups and downs have dominated the short-term behaviour of the Canadian economy. This chart is constructed by selecting one index of general economic activity (real GDP), fitting a trend line to it, and plotting the deviations of the index from its trend value. It clearly shows the tendency for an economy to fluctuate. Major booms and slumps are unmistakable.

(*Source:* Authors' calculations based on GDP data in Department of Finance, *Economic Reference Tables*, August 1995)

deviations of actual from potential output are described as temporary, recall that the automatic adjustment mechanism may work so slowly that the deviations can persist for some time, perhaps several years.

Figure 26-6 shows graphically the extent to which cycles in national income have been the norm in Canada over the past 75 years. Figure 26-7 shows three different economic series. Each of these, as well as dozens of others that we might have studied, tells us something about the general variability of the economy. Some move more than others, and no two move exactly together; yet all exhibit a cyclical pattern, and they tend to move approximately together.

FISCAL POLICY AND THE BUSINESS CYCLE

In Chapter 24, we briefly introduced the basic concepts of fiscal stabilization policy, which attempts to stabilize national income at or near some desired level

(usually potential national income). In the remainder of this chapter, we look into taxing and spending as tools of fiscal stabilization policy. We will return to the subject in more detail in Chapter 32, after we have discussed money and the banking system.

Because government expenditure increases aggregate demand and taxation decreases it, the *direction* of the required changes in spending and taxation is generally easy to determine once we know the direction of the desired change in national income. However, the *timing, magnitude,* and *mixture* of the changes are more difficult issues.

There is no doubt that the government can exert a major influence on national income. Prime examples are the massive increases in military spending during major wars. Canadian federal expenditure during World War II rose from 12.2 percent of GDP in 1939 to 41.8 percent in 1944. At the same time, the unemployment rate fell from 11.4 percent to 1.4 percent. Economists agree that the increase in government spending helped to bring about the rise in income and the associated fall in unemployment. Similar experiences occurred during the rearmament of most European countries before or just following the outbreak of World War II in 1939, in the United States after it entered the war in December 1941, and also during the Vietnam War in the late 1960s and early 1970s.

When used appropriately, fiscal policy can be an important tool for stabilizing the economy. In the heyday of fiscal policy, from about 1945 to about 1970, many economists were convinced that the economy could be stabilized adequately just by varying the size of the government's taxes and expenditures. That day is past. Today, most economists are aware of the many limitations of fiscal policy.

THE BASIC THEORY OF FISCAL STABILIZATION

A reduction in tax rates or an increase in government expenditure will shift the *AD* curve to the right, causing an increase in Y. An increase in tax rates or a cut in government expenditure will shift the *AD* curve to the left, causing a decrease in Y.

How Fiscal Stabilization Works

A more detailed look at how fiscal stabilization works will provide a useful review. It will also help

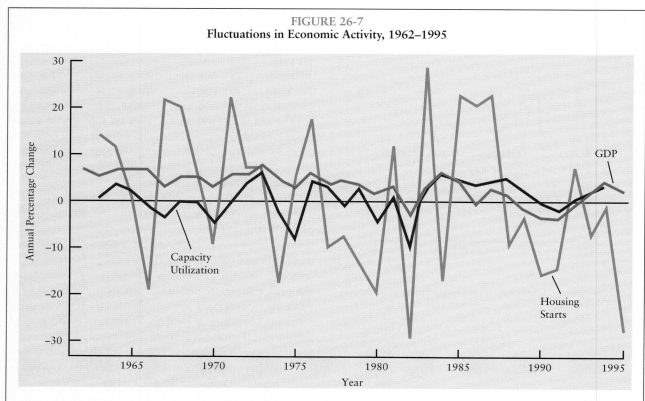

FIGURE 26-7
Fluctuations in Economic Activity, 1962–1995

Fluctuations follow similar, but by no means identical, paths for various measures of economic activity. Fluctuations are easily seen in these three series—the annual percentage changes in real GDP, annual housing starts, and the capacity utilization rate in manufacturing.

(Source: Department of Finance, Economic Reference Tables, August 1995.)

to show some of the complications that arise in making fiscal policy.

A Recessionary Gap. The closing of a recessionary gap is illustrated in Figure 26-8. There are two possible ways in which the gap may be closed. First, the recessionary gap may eventually drive wages and other factor prices down enough to shift the *SRAS* curve to the right and thereby reinstate full employment and potential income (at a lower price level). The evidence, however, is that this process takes a substantial period of time.

Second, the *AD* curve could shift to the right, restoring the economy to full employment and potential income (at a higher price level). The government can cause such a shift by using expansionary fiscal policy (or, as we shall see in Chapter 28, expansionary monetary policy). The advantage of using fiscal policy is that it may substantially shorten what would otherwise be a long recession. One disadvantage is that the use of fiscal policy may stimulate the economy just before private-sector spending recovers on its own. As a result, the economy may overshoot its potential output, and an inflationary gap may open up. In this case, fiscal policy that is intended to promote economic stability can actually cause instability.

An Inflationary Gap. Figure 26-9 shows the ways in which an inflationary gap can be closed. First, wages and other factor prices may be pushed upward by the excess demand. The *SRAS* curve will therefore shift to the left, eventually closing the gap, reducing income to its potential level, and raising the price level. Second, the *AD* curve can shift to the left, restoring equilibrium *Y*. The government, by raising taxes or cutting spending, can induce such a shift, reducing aggregate demand sufficiently to close the inflationary gap. The advantage of this approach is that it avoids the inflationary increase in prices that accompanies the first method. One disadvantage is that if private-sector expenditures fall due to natural

FIGURE 26-8
The Closing of a Recessionary Gap

(i) A recessionary gap closed by a rightward shift in *SRAS*.

(ii) A recessionary gap closed by a rightward shift in *AD*.

A recessionary gap may be closed by a (slow) rightward shift of the *SRAS* curve, a natural revival of private-sector demand, or a fiscal-policy-induced increase in aggregate demand. Initially, equilibrium is at E_0, with national income at Y_0 and the price level at P_0. The recessionary gap is Y_0Y^*.

As shown in part (i), the gap might be removed by a shift in the *SRAS* curve to $SRAS_1$. The shift in the *SRAS* curve causes a movement down and to the right along AD_0 to a new equilibrium at E_1, achieving potential income Y^* and lowering the price level to P_1.

As shown in part (ii), the gap might also be removed by a shift of the *AD* curve to AD_1. The shift in the *AD* curve causes a movement up and to the right along $SRAS_0$. This movement shifts the equilibrium to E_2, raising income to Y^* and the price level to P_2.

causes, national income may be pushed below potential, thus opening up a recessionary gap.

A Key Proposition. This discussion suggests that in circumstances in which the automatic adjustment mechanisms—upward wage adjustments during booms and downward adjustments during slumps—either fail to operate quickly enough or give rise to undesirable side effects such as rising prices, there is a potential stabilizing role for fiscal policy.

The Paradox of Thrift

The theory of national income determination predicts that an increase in national saving will shift the *AD* curve to the left and hence *reduce* the equilibrium level of income in the short run. The contrary case, a general decrease in thrift and increase in expenditure, shifts the *AD* curve to the right and hence increases national income in the short run. Thus frugality on the part of individuals, which may seem to be prudent behaviour for each individual taken separately, ends up reducing short-run national income and is bad for the economy as a whole. This prediction is known as the *paradox of thrift*.[5]

The policy implication of this prediction is that a major and persistent recession can be battled by encouraging governments, firms, and households to spend more, *not* to save more. In times of unemployment and recession, frugality will only make things worse. This prediction goes directly against the idea that we should tighten our belts when times are

---

[5]The prediction is not a true paradox but rather a straightforward implication of the theory of income determination. The view that leads to the "paradox" is based on the *fallacy of composition*—the belief that what is true for the parts is necessarily true for the whole.

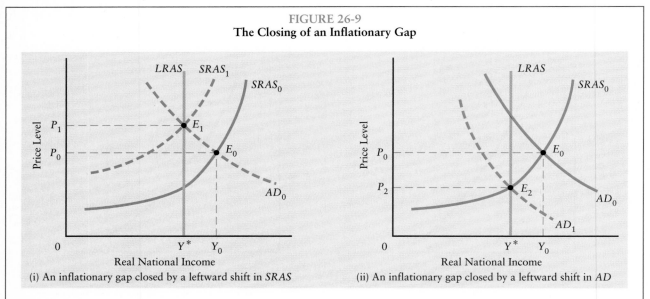

FIGURE 26-9
The Closing of an Inflationary Gap

(i) An inflationary gap closed by a leftward shift in *SRAS*

(ii) An inflationary gap closed by a leftward shift in *AD*

An inflationary gap may be removed by a leftward shift of the *SRAS* curve, a reduction in private-sector demand, or a policy-induced reduction in aggregate demand. Initially, equilibrium is at E_0, with national income at Y_0 and the price level at P_0. The inflationary gap is Y^*Y_0.

As shown in part (i), the gap might be removed by a shift in the *SRAS* curve to $SRAS_1$. The shift in the *SRAS* curve causes a movement up and to the left along AD_0. This movement establishes a new equilibrium at E_1, reducing income to its potential level Y^* and raising the price level to P_1.

As shown in part (ii), the gap might also be removed by a shift in the *AD* curve to AD_1. The shift in the *AD* curve causes a movement down and to the left along $SRAS_0$. This movement shifts the equilibrium to E_2, lowering income to Y^* and the price level to P_2.

tough. The notion that it is not only possible but even *desirable* to spend one's way out of a recession touches a sensitive point with people raised on the belief that success is based on hard work and frugality and not on prodigality; as a result, the idea often arouses great hostility.

Applications.   As is discussed in Application 26-1, the implications of the paradox of thrift were not generally understood during the Great Depression of the 1930s. Most governments, faced with depression-induced reductions in tax revenues, reduced their expenditures to balance their budgets. As a result, many economists argue that the fiscal policies at the time actually made things worse. When Milton Friedman (many years later) said, "We are all Keynesians now," he was referring (among other things) to the general acceptance of the view that the government's budget is much more than just the revenue and expenditure statement of a very large organization. Whether we like it or not, the sheer size of the government's budget inevitably makes it a powerful tool for influencing the economy.

Limitations.   The paradox of thrift concentrates on shifts in aggregate demand that have been caused by changes in saving (and hence spending) behaviour. That is why it applies only in the short run, when the *AD* curve plays an important role in the determination of national income.

In the long run, however, the paradox of thrift does not apply. Remember that in the long run, aggregate demand is *not* the determinant of national income—only the position of the *LRAS* curve determines long-run national income. In the long run, the more people and governments save, the larger is the supply of funds available for investment. And the more people invest, the greater is the growth of potential income. Increased potential income causes the *LRAS* curve to shift to the right. These longer-term effects were discussed briefly earlier in this chapter and are taken up in detail in Chapter 33 in the discussion of economic growth.

The paradox of thrift—the idea that an increase in saving reduces the level of national income—is only

APPLICATION 26-1

FISCAL POLICY AND THE GREAT DEPRESSION

Failure to understand the implication of the paradox of thrift led many countries to adopt disastrous policies during the Great Depression. In addition, failure to understand the role of built-in stabilizers has led many observers to conclude, erroneously, that fiscal expansion was tried in the Great Depression but failed. Let us see how these two misperceptions are related.

THE PARADOX OF THRIFT IN ACTION

In 1932, during the worst recession in recorded history, Canadian Prime Minister R. B. Bennett said, "We are now faced with the real crisis in the history of Canada. To maintain our credit we must practice the most rigid economy and not spend a single cent." His government that year brought down a budget based on the principle of trying to balance revenues and expenditures, and it included *increases* in tax rates.

In the same year, Franklin Roosevelt was elected U.S. president on a platform of fighting the Great Depression with government policies. In his inaugural address he urged, "Our great primary task is to put people to work. . . . [This task] can be helped by insistence that the federal, state, and local governments act forthwith on the demand that their costs be drastically reduced. . . . There must be a strict supervision of all banking and credits and investments."

Across the Atlantic, King George V told the British House of Commons in 1931, "The present condition of the national finances, in the opinion of His Majesty's ministers, calls for the imposition of additional taxation and for the effecting of economies in public expenditure."

As the paradox of thrift predicts, these policies tended to worsen, rather than cure, the depression.

INTERPRETING THE DEFICIT IN THE 1930S

Government deficits did increase in the 1930s, but they were not the result of a program of deficit-financed public expenditure. Rather, they were the result of the fall in tax yields, brought about by the fall in national income as the economy sank into depression. The various governments did not advocate programs of massive deficit-financed spending to shift the *AD* curve to the right. Instead, they hoped that a small amount of government spending plus numerous policies designed to stabilize prices and to restore confidence would lead to a recovery of private investment expenditure that would substantially shift the *AD* curve. To have expected a massive revival of private investment expenditure as a result of the puny increase in aggregate demand that was instituted by the federal government now seems hopelessly naive.

When we judge these policies from the viewpoint of modern multiplier theory, their failure is no mystery. Indeed, Professor E. Cary Brown of MIT, after a careful study, concluded, "Fiscal policy seems to have been an unsuccessful recovery device in the 'thirties—not because it did not work, but because it was not tried."

The performance of the Canadian and U.S. economies from 1930 to 1945 is well explained by national income theory. It is clear that the governments did not effectively use fiscal measures to stabilize their economies. War cured the Depression because war demands made acceptable a level of government expenditure sufficient to remove the recessionary gap. Had the Canadian and American administrations been able to do the same, it might have ended the waste of the Great Depression many years sooner.

true in the short run when the level of aggregate demand is relevant for determining national income. In the long run, a larger amount of saving increases investment and thus increases the level of potential income.

Automatic Stabilizers

In Chapter 24, we introduced the *budget surplus function* (the function showing how the government's budget surplus changes as national income changes). The *discretionary* fiscal policy that we have been discussing in this chapter involves *shifts* in the budget surplus function. Expansionary policies, whether they involve increases in purchases or decreases in net taxes, reduce the budget surplus (increase the deficit) at every level of national income, shifting the *AD* curve to the right. Contractionary policies increase the surplus (reduce the deficit) at every level of income, shifting the *AD* curve to the left.

Even when the government does not attempt to stabilize the economy via discretionary fiscal policy, the upward slope of the budget surplus function means that there are fiscal effects that cause the budget to act as an "automatic stabilizer" for the economy.

The budget surplus increases as income increases because tax revenues rise and some transfer payments, especially unemployment insurance, fall. Thus net taxes move in the same direction as national income. (Unless there are changes in policy, government purchases are generally unaffected by cyclical movements in the economy.) With **procyclical** net tax revenues, disposable income moves in the same direction as national income but does not move by as much. The government keeps a share of the increased national income when national income rises. When national income falls, the fall in net taxes makes disposable income fall by less.

In Chapter 24, for example, we assumed that the net income tax rate was 10 percent of national income. This implies that a $1 rise in autonomous spending would increase disposable income by only 90 cents, dampening the multiplier effect of the initial increase. Generally, the wedge that income taxes place between national income and disposable income reduces the marginal propensity to spend out of national income, thereby reducing the size of the multiplier. The lower the multiplier, the less equilibrium national income will tend to change for a given change in autonomous expenditure. The effect is to stabilize the economy, reducing the fluctuations in national income that are caused by changes in autonomous expenditure. Because no policies need to be changed to achieve this result, the properties of the government budget that cause the multiplier to be reduced are called **automatic fiscal stabilizers**.

Limitations of Discretionary Fiscal Policy

According to the foregoing discussion, returning the economy to full employment would simply be a mat-

ter of cutting taxes and raising government spending, in some combination. Why did so many economists believe that such policies would be "as likely to harm as help"? Part of the answer is that the execution of discretionary fiscal policy is anything but simple.[6]

Lags.   To change fiscal policy requires making changes in taxes and government expenditures. The changes must be agreed on by the cabinet and passed by parliament. The political stakes in such changes are generally very large; taxes and spending are called "bread-and-butter issues" precisely because they affect the economic well-being of almost everyone. So even if economists agreed that the economy would be helped by, say, a tax cut, politicians would likely spend a good deal of time debating *whose* taxes should be cut and by *how much*. The delay between the initial recognition of a recessionary or inflationary gap and the enactment of legislation to change fiscal policy is called a **decision lag.**

Once policy changes are agreed on, there is still an **execution lag,** adding time between the enactment and the implementation of the change. Furthermore, once policies are in place, it will usually take still more time for their economic consequences to be felt. Because of these lags, it is quite possible that by the time a given policy decision has any impact on the economy, circumstances will have changed such that the policy is no longer appropriate. Figure 26-10 illustrates the problems that arise when the expansionary effects of fiscal policy are felt at the same time as private-sector spending has recovered enough to create full employment.

Temporary Versus Permanent Policy Changes. To make matters even more frustrating, tax measures that are known to be temporary are generally less effective than measures that are expected to be permanent. If households know that a given tax cut will last only a year, they may recognize that the effect on their long-run consumption possibilities is small and may adjust their short-run consumption relatively little. Thus the more closely household consumption expenditure is related to lifetime income rather than to current income, the smaller will be the effects on current consumption of tax changes that are known to be of short duration.

The Role of Discretionary Fiscal Policy.   All of these difficulties suggest that attempts to use discre-

---

[6]Another part of the answer has to do with the long-term consequences of budget deficits. This subject is taken up in Chapter 32. Also, as we shall see in Chapter 38, international considerations may reduce fiscal policy's effectiveness as a stabilization tool.

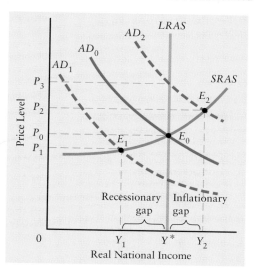

FIGURE 26-10
Effects of Fiscal Policies That Are Not Reversed

Fiscal policies that are initially appropriate may become inappropriate when private expenditure shifts. The normal position of the aggregate demand curve is assumed to be AD_0, leaving income normally at Y^* and the price level at P_0. Suppose that a slump in private investment shifts aggregate demand to AD_1, lowering national income to Y_1 and causing a recessionary gap of Y_1Y^*.

The government now introduces fiscal expansion to restore aggregate demand to AD_0 and national income to Y^*. Suppose that private investment then recovers, raising aggregate demand to AD_2. If fiscal policy can be quickly reversed, aggregate demand can be returned to AD_0 and income stabilized at Y^*. If the policy is not quickly reversed, equilibrium will be at E_2 and an inflationary gap Y^*Y_2 will open up. This gap will cause wages to rise and thus shift the $SRAS$ curve leftward and eventually restore Y^* at price level P_3.

Now suppose that starting from equilibrium E_0, a persistent investment boom takes AD_0 to AD_2. To stop the price level from rising in the face of the newly opened inflationary gap, the government introduces fiscal restraint, thereby shifting aggregate demand back to AD_0. Further assume, however, that the investment boom then comes to a halt so that the aggregate demand curve shifts downward to AD_1. Unless the fiscal policy can be rapidly reversed, a recessionary gap will open up, and equilibrium income will fall to Y_1.

tionary fiscal policy to "fine tune" the economy are fraught with difficulties. **Fine tuning** refers to the use of fiscal (and monetary) policy to offset virtually all fluctuations in private-sector spending so as to hold national income at or near its potential level at all times. However, neither economic nor political science has yet advanced far enough to allow policymakers to undo the consequences of every aggregate demand shock. Nevertheless, many economists would still argue that when a recessionary gap is large enough and persists for long enough, *gross tuning* may be appropriate. **Gross tuning** refers to the occasional use of fiscal and monetary policy to remove large and persistent output gaps. Advocates of gross tuning hold that fiscal policy can and should be used to return the economy to full employment when an output gap is large and has persisted for a long time. Other economists believe that fiscal policy should not be used for economic stabilization under any circumstances. Rather, they would argue, tax and spending behaviour should be the outcome of public choices regarding the long-term size and financing of the public sector and should not be altered for short-term considerations. We return to these debates in Chapter 32.

ECONOMIC POLICY, STABILITY, AND GROWTH

The desirability of using fiscal policy to stabilize the economy depends a great deal on the speed with which the economy's own adjustment mechanism returns the economy to potential income. If the adjustment mechanism works very quickly, there is little value to discretionary fiscal policy. If the adjustment mechanism works slowly, however, there may well be a role for policies that can be used to shift aggregate demand. Fiscal policy is one; monetary policy, which we take up in the next three chapters, is another. Only when we have completed our study of the way in which money and monetary institutions fit into the overall macroeconomy can we fully outline the choices available to governments that wish to stabilize their economies.

Stabilization policy will generally have consequences for economic growth—for the rightward shifting of the $LRAS$ curve over time. In an economy at or near potential income, the more expansive is its fiscal policy, the lower will be national saving and national asset formation and, consequently, the lower will be future economic growth. Of course, if the economy would otherwise stay in recession for a period of years, the gain in output in the near term may outweigh the longer-term consequences of a smaller stock of assets at full employment. (After all—and this was part of Keynes's message—the state of the world at full employment is not very interesting to members of a society who are a long way from it.)

Stability, growth, and the effect of economic policy on both are among the key subjects of this book.

With the tools that we have developed so far, we can begin to see how they fit together. Once we add a better understanding of money and monetary policy, presented in the next three chapters, we will be able to complete the story.

SUMMARY

A. INDUCED CHANGES IN FACTOR PRICES

- Potential income is treated as given and is represented by a vertical line at Y^*. The output gap is equal to the horizontal distance between Y^* and the actual level of income, Y, as determined by the intersection of the AD and $SRAS$ curves.
- An inflationary gap means that Y is greater than Y^*, and hence demand in the labour market is relatively high. As a result, wages rise faster than productivity, causing unit costs to rise. The $SRAS$ curve shifts leftward, and the price level rises.
- A recessionary gap means that Y is less than Y^*, and hence demand in the labour market is relatively low. Although there is some resulting tendency for wages to fall relative to productivity, asymmetrical behaviour means that the strength of this force will be much weaker than is the case with an inflationary gap. Unit costs will fall only slowly, so the output gap will persist for some time.

B. THE EFFECTS OF AGGREGATE DEMAND SHOCKS

- Beginning from a position of full employment, an expansionary demand shock creates an inflationary gap. It causes wages to rise faster than productivity. Unit costs rise, shifting the $SRAS$ curve to the left and resulting in a higher level of prices, with output eventually falling back to its potential level.
- Beginning from a position of full employment, a contractionary demand shock creates a recessionary gap. Because factor prices tend to be sticky downwards, the automatic adjustment process tends to be slow, and a recessionary gap tends to persist for some time.
- Demand shocks are an important source of business cycles. As a shock works its way through the economy and the adjustment mechanism comes into play, Y will often exhibit a cyclical pattern.
- The long-run aggregate supply ($LRAS$) curve relates the price level and national income after all wages and other input prices have been adjusted fully to long-run equilibrium. The $LRAS$ curve is vertical at the level of potential income, Y^*. Because the $LRAS$ curve is vertical, output in the long run is determined by the position of the $LRAS$ curve, and the only long-run role of the AD curve is to determine the price level. Economic growth determines the position of the $LRAS$ curve.

C. NATIONAL INCOME IN THE SHORT AND LONG RUN

- In the short run, macroeconomic equilibrium is determined by the intersection of the AD and $SRAS$ curves. In the long run, the economy is in equilibrium when national income is equal to potential income—the economy is therefore on the $LRAS$ curve. In the long run, the price level is determined by the intersection of the AD and $LRAS$ curves.
- Increases in aggregate demand or temporary increases in aggregate supply can increase national income in the short run, but not in the long run. Only permanent increases in aggregate supply can lead to permanent increases in national income.

D. FISCAL POLICY AND THE BUSINESS CYCLE

- In principle, fiscal policy can be used to stabilize output at or near potential output. To remove a recessionary gap, governments can shift AD to the right by cutting taxes and increasing spending. To remove an inflationary gap, governments can pursue the opposite policies.
- In the short run, increases in desired saving on the part of firms, households, and governments leads to further reductions in Y and may lead to reductions in actual saving. This phenomenon is often called the paradox of thrift. In the long run, the paradox of thrift does not apply, and increased thrift will lead to increased asset accumulation and economic growth.
- Because government tax and transfer programs tend to reduce the size of the multiplier, they act as automatic stabilizers. When national income changes, in either di-

rection, disposable income changes by less because of taxes and transfers.

- Discretionary fiscal policy is subject to decision lags and execution lags that limit its ability to take effect quickly. Some economists argue that these limitations are so severe that fiscal policy should never be used for stabilization because it will end up increasing instability. Others argue that the automatic adjustment mechanism works

so slowly that fiscal policy can play an important role in stabilizing the economy.

- Fiscal policy has very different effects in the short and long run. The same fiscal policies (reduced taxes and increased spending) that stimulate the economy in the short run will, if pursued at full employment, reduce national saving, asset formation, and economic growth in the long run.

KEY CONCEPTS

The output gap and factor prices
Inflationary and recessionary gaps
Asymmetry of wage adjustment: flexible and sticky wages

Wages, productivity, and unit costs
The long-run aggregate supply (*LRAS*) curve
Economic stabilization

Decision lags and execution lags
Sources of long-run growth
Automatic stabilizers
Fine tuning and gross tuning

DISCUSSION QUESTIONS

1. Discuss the following two statements in terms of short- and long-run aggregate supply curves.

   a. "Starting from a full-employment equilibrium, an increase in government spending can produce more output and employment at the cost of a once-and-for-all rise in the price level."

   b. "Increased spending can never lead to a permanent increase in output above its full-employment level."

2. Identify the effects of each of the following events on the *SRAS* curve and the *LRAS* curve.

   a. Increases in the prices of imported raw materials that are used in key manufacturing industries

   b. Increases in the prices of imported consumption goods such as coffee or bananas

   c. Increased restrictions on pollution emissions in an attempt to combat acid rain

   d. Projections of increased federal government deficits over the next five years

   e. An improvement in business confidence leading to an investment boom

   f. An increase in the labour-force participation rate of key sectors of the population

3. Interpret each of the following news items in terms of *AD* and *SRAS* curves. (Assume that the statements are correct for the purposes of drawing your curves.)

   a. "Management representative says union wage demands are irresponsible in the face of current high unemployment rates."

   b. "Government spokesman says that although the recovery is expected to be vigorous, it will witness only modest reductions in the unemployment rate."

   c. "Wage increases have failed to keep up with inflation during the current boom."

   d. "Innovations in microelectronic technology will lead to an increase in both national output and unemployment."

4. Explain the logic behind the following newspaper headline: "More growth seen as cure for inflation."

5. Politicians are sometimes accused of adopting policies that bring "short-term gain at the cost of long-term pain," whereas statesmen offer "short-term pain to buy long-term gain." What policies that shift aggregate demand or aggregate supply curves might come under one or the other of these descriptions?

6. About 30 percent of Canadian income is generated through exports, three-quarters of which are to the United States. Why do Canadians worry that, economically, "when the United States gets a cold, Canada may get pneumonia"? Why does Canada often experience "export-led recoveries" from severe recessions?

7. If downward flexibility of money wages would allow the automatic adjustment mechanism to eliminate recessionary gaps quickly, why do workers usually resist wage cuts during times of economic slump?

8. Because different economic series behave differently, does it make sense to talk about "the" business cycle?

Predict the comparative behaviour of the following pairs of series in relation to fluctuations in GDP, then check your predictions against the facts for the past decade.

a. Purchases of food and purchases of consumer durables
b. Tax receipts and bankruptcies
c. Unemployment and birthrates
d. Employment in Hamilton and in Vancouver

9. Which of the following would be built-in stabilizers?

a. Unemployment insurance payments
b. Cost-of-living escalators in government contracts and pensions
c. Income taxes
d. Free university tuition for unemployed workers after six months of unemployment, provided that they are under 30 years old and have had five or more years of full-time work experience since high school

10. In his first inaugural address, U.S. President Franklin D. Roosevelt expounded the doctrine of "sound finance"—that the government's budget should always be balanced. During his term, however, government spending rose faster than taxes, and budget deficits resulted. How would the effectiveness of the New Deal on employment have been different if Roosevelt had been successful in keeping the budget balanced throughout his first term?

PART NINE

MONEY, BANKING, AND MONETARY POLICY

What is money, and where does it come from? Must all money bear the signature of the Governor of the Bank of Canada? If so, what did we do before the Bank of Canada existed? Was there no money then? Is the amount of money in the Canadian economy equal only to the actual value of bills and coins in circulation, or do accounts at commercial banks matter? If bank accounts matter, does this mean that commercial banks can "create" money? Why do households and firms hold money? And why do they decide to hold less when interest rates are higher? What determines the level of interest rates in the economy? Does the Bank of Canada "control" interest rates, or are these rates determined by market forces? Or is the truth somewhere in between? How does the Bank of Canada conduct its monetary policy? These are the sorts of questions you will be able to answer after reading the next three chapters.

Chapter 27 traces the development of money, from the use of *barter* in ancient economies to *deposit money* that is so important today. You will then learn about the Canadian banking system, from the *commercial banks* to the Bank of Canada, Canada's *central bank*. The idea of *money creation* will then be examined, and you will see that commercial banks do indeed "create" money. Finally, you will be introduced to several formal measures of the Canadian *money supply*.

Chapter 28 begins by discussing the *demand for money*. Here you will learn the various reasons why households and firms hold money, and you will learn why the level of interest rates is so important in these decisions. The concept of *monetary equilibrium* is then examined, and it is here that you will see the Bank of Canada's role in determining interest rates. You will also see how changes in the Bank of Canada's policy can affect interest rates, aggregate expenditure, and eventually national income and the price level.

In Chapter 29 we focus on *monetary policy*. You will learn some of the details of how the Bank of Canada's actions influence the commercial banking system. The Bank's *policy variables*, *policy instruments*, and *policy targets* will all be discussed, and it is here that you will confront the *lags* and *uncertainty* that make the conduct of monetary policy so difficult. You will then be presented with a brief review of the past 25 years of monetary policy in Canada. This discussion will help to put together the lessons learned throughout this part of the book.

CHAPTER 27

THE NATURE OF MONEY AND MONETARY INSTITUTIONS

DEFINITIONS OF THE MONEY SUPPLY
NEAR MONEY AND MONEY SUBSTITUTES
CHOOSING A MEASURE
THE ROLE OF THE BANK OF CANADA

In the next three chapters, we examine the significance of money in market economies. The role of money may seem obvious—money is what people use to buy things. Yet as we shall see, increasing the world's money supply would not make the average person better off. Although money allows those who have it to buy someone else's output, the total amount of goods and services available for everyone to buy depends on the total output produced, not on the total amount of money that people possess. In the terminology of Chapter 26, an increase in the quantity of money will not increase the level of potential national income, Y^*. Still, without money, modern economies could not function, and most economists would agree that the quantity of money, although it cannot affect Y^*, can and does affect short-run movements in national income.

THEORETICAL PERSPECTIVES ON MONEY

Theories on the role of money in a market economy have been evolving for several centuries.

THE CLASSICAL VIEW

In the eighteenth and nineteenth centuries, economists articulated the independence of Y^* from monetary factors in terms of an economic theory that distinguished sharply between the "real sector" of the economy and the "monetary sector" of the economy. This approach led to a view of the economy that is now referred to as the *Classical dichotomy*.

According to the **Classical dichotomy,** the allocation of resources, and hence the determination of real national income, is determined only by the real sector of the economy. It is *relative prices,* including the level of wages relative to the price of commodities, that matter for this process. Early economists argued that the price *level* is determined in the monetary sector of the economy. If the quantity of money were doubled, other things being equal, the

prices of all commodities and money income would also double. Relative prices would remain unchanged, and the real sector of the economy would be unaffected.

According to the Classical economists, the allocation of resources—and the determination of real national income—depends only on relative prices. An increase in the money supply leads to a proportionate increase in all money prices, with no change in the allocation of resources or the level of real national income.

The doctrine that the quantity of money influences the level of money prices but has no effect on the real part of the economy is called the **neutrality of money.** Because early economists believed that the most important questions—How much does the economy produce? What share of it does each group in the society get?—were answered in the real sector, they spoke of money as a "veil" behind which occurred the real events that affected material well-being.

THE MODERN VIEW

Most modern economists still accept the insights of the Classical economists that relative prices are the major determinant of the allocation of resources and that the quantity of money has a lot to do with determining the absolute level of prices. They accept the neutrality of money in the long run when all the forces causing change have fully worked themselves out. However, they do not accept the neutrality of money when the economy is adjusting to the various forces that cause it to change—that is, when the economy is not in a state of long-run equilibrium. Consequently, they reject the Classical dichotomy as a description of the economy in the short run.

The view that the neutrality of money holds in the long run leads modern economists to stress the strong link between money and the price level, especially over long periods of time. In Chapter 21, we discussed the price level and inflation, and we presented some evidence from Canada's experience over the past half century or so. Figure 27-1 gives a longer-run perspective. It shows the course of wholesale prices in Canada over the past 100 years. There are two things that stand out in figure 27-1. First, the dramatic reduction in prices from 1920 to 1930. Second, the more-or-less uninterrupted increase in prices since 1930.

FIGURE 27-1
An Index of Wholesale Prices in Canada,
1895–1995

Persistent peacetime inflation is only a recent problem in Canada. Before 1930, prices in Canada went through periods of dramatic increase as well as dramatic decrease. From the time of World War II to the present, the price level has more-or-less consistently increased. Note: This is a semilog graph.

(Source: Statistics Canada, *Industrial Price Index,* 62–011.)

Although admittedly a long time, even 100 years may still not be enough to give us a clear perspective of very-long-term price fluctuations. Figure 27-2 shows the course of the price level in southern England over seven centuries. It shows that there was an overall inflationary trend but that it was by no means spread evenly over the centuries.

THE NATURE OF MONEY

Economists agree that money affects the price level in the long run and both the price level and the level of real income in the short run. But what exactly is money? In this section, we describe the functions of money and briefly outline its history.

WHAT IS MONEY?

In economics, **money** has usually been defined as any generally accepted medium of exchange. A **medium of exchange** is anything that will be widely accepted in a society in exchange for goods and services. Although its medium-of-exchange role is perhaps its most important one, money also acts as a *store of value* and as a *unit of account*. Different kinds of money vary in the

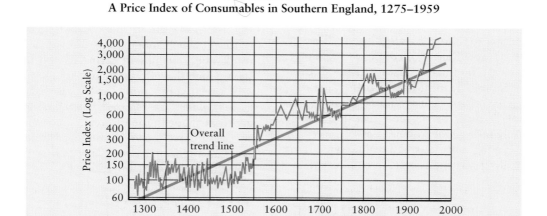

FIGURE 27-2
A Price Index of Consumables in Southern England, 1275–1959

Over the past seven centuries, long periods of stable prices have alternated with long periods of rising prices. This remarkable graph shows an index of the prices of food, clothing, and fuel in southern England from 1275 through 1959. The trend line shows that the average change in prices over the whole period was 0.5 percent per year. The graph also shows that even the perspective of a century can be misleading because long periods of stable or gently falling prices tended to alternate with long periods of rising prices.

(Source: Lloyd's Bank Review, October 1960.)

degree of efficiency with which they fulfill these functions. As we shall see, the *money supply* is measured by using different definitions for different purposes.

Money as a Medium of Exchange

If there were no money, goods would have to be exchanged by **barter** (one good being swapped directly for another). We discussed this cumbersome system in Chapter 3. The major difficulty with **barter** is that each transaction requires a *double coincidence of wants:* anyone who specialized in producing one commodity would have to spend a great deal of time searching for satisfactory transactions. For example, the barber who needs his sink repaired would have to find a plumber who wants a haircut. Or the engineer who wants to buy some bread would need to find a baker that needs some engineering services. In a world of many different goods and many different people, the effort required to make transactions would be extreme.

The use of money as a medium of exchange alleviates this problem. People can sell their output for money and then use the money to buy what they wish from others.

The double coincidence of wants is unnecessary when a medium of exchange is used.

By facilitating transactions, money makes possible the benefits of specialization and the division of labour, which in turn contribute to the efficiency of the economic system. It is not without justification that money has been called one of the great inventions contributing to human freedom and well-being.

To serve as an efficient medium of exchange, money must have a number of characteristics. It must be readily acceptable. It must have a high value relative to its weight (otherwise it would be a nuisance to carry around). It must be divisible, because money that comes only in large denominations is useless for transactions having only a small value. Finally, it must be difficult, if not impossible, to counterfeit.

Money as a Store of Value

Money is a convenient way to store purchasing power; goods may be sold today for money and the money may then may be stored until it is needed for some future purchase. To be a satisfactory store of value, however, money must have a relatively stable value. A rise in the price level is also a decrease in the purchasing power of money. When the price level is stable, the purchasing power of a given sum of money is also stable; when the price level is highly variable, this is not so, and the usefulness of money as a store of value is undermined. Over the past two decades, inflation in Canada has been high enough and variable enough to diminish money's usefulness as a store of value. However, the Canadian experience in this respect is modest compared to that in some other countries; the severe German hyperinflation of the early 1920s is discussed in Application 27-1.

Money as a Unit of Account

Money may also be used purely for accounting purposes without having a physical existence of its own. For instance, a government store in a truly communist society might say that everyone had so many "dollars" to use each month. Goods could then be assigned prices and each consumer's purchases recorded, the consumer being allowed to buy until the allocated supply of dollars was exhausted. These dollars need have no existence other than as entries in the store's books, yet they would serve as a perfectly satisfactory unit of account.

Whether they could also serve as a medium of exchange between individuals depends on whether the store would agree to transfer dollar credits from one customer to another at the customer's request. Banks will transfer dollars credited to deposits in this way, and thus a bank deposit can serve as both a unit of account and a medium of exchange. Notice that the use of *dollars* in this context suggests a further sense in which money is a unit of account. People think about values in terms of the monetary unit with which they are familiar.

A related function of money is that it can be used as a *standard of deferred payments*. Payments that are to be made in the future, on account of debts and so on, are reckoned in money. Money's ability to serve as a *unit of account over time* in this manner is much diminished by inflation.

THE ORIGINS OF MONEY

The origins of money go far back in antiquity. Most primitive tribes are known to have made some use of it.

Metallic Money

All sorts of commodities have been used as money at one time or another, but gold and silver proved to

APPLICATION 27-1

HYPERINFLATION

Can the price level ever rise so rapidly that money loses its usefulness either as a medium of exchange or as a store of value? The answer appears to be that occasionally this does happen. Inflation rates of 50, 100, 200 percent, or more per year have occurred year after year and have proved to be manageable as people adjust their contracts in real terms. Although there are strains and side effects, the evidence shows such situations to be possible without causing money to become useless.

Does this mean that there is no reason to fear that rapid inflation will turn into hyperinflation that will destroy the value of money completely? The historical record is not entirely reassuring. In a number of instances, prices rose at an ever-accelerating rate until a nation's money ceased to be a satisfactory store of value, even for the short period between receipt and expenditure, and hence ceased also to be useful as a medium of exchange.

The index of wholesale prices in Germany during and after World War I is given in the table. The index shows that a good purchased for one 100-mark note in July 1923 would have cost *10 million* 100-mark notes only four months later! Although Germany had experienced substantial inflation during World War I, averaging more than 30 percent per year, the immediate postwar years of 1920 and 1921 gave no sign of explosive inflation. Indeed, prices were relatively stable until 1922 and 1923 when they exploded. On November 15, 1923, the German mark was officially repudiated, its value wholly destroyed. How could this happen?

When inflation becomes so rapid that people lose confidence in the purchasing power of their currency, they rush to spend it. People who have goods become increasingly reluctant to accept the rapidly depreciating money in exchange. The rush to spend money accelerates the increase in prices until people finally become unwilling to accept money on any terms. What was once money ceases to be money.

The price system can then be restored only by repudiation of the old monetary unit and its replacement by a new unit. This destroys the value of monetary savings and of all contracts specified in terms of the old monetary unit.

About a dozen hyperinflations in world history have been documented, among them the collapse of the continental during the American Revolution in 1776, the ruble during the Russian Revolution in 1917, the drachma during and after the German occupation of Greece in World War II, the pengö in Hungary in 1945 and 1946, and the Chinese national currency from 1946 to 1948. Every one of these hyperinflations was accompanied by great increases in the money supply; new money was printed to give governments purchasing power that they could not or would not obtain by taxation. Further, every one occurred in the midst of a major political upheaval in which grave doubts existed about the stability and the future of the government itself.

Is hyperinflation likely in the absence of civil war, revolution, or collapse of the government? Most economists think not. Further, it is clear that high inflation rates over a period of time do not mean the inevitable or even likely onset of hyperinflation, however serious the distributive and social effects of such rates may be.

Date	German Wholesale Price Index (1913 = 1)
January 1913	1
January 1920	13
January 1921	14
January 1922	37
July 1922	101
January 1923	2,785
July 1923	74,800
August 1923	944,000
September 1923	23,900,000
October 1923	7,096,000,000
November 1923*	750,000,000,000

*The mark was repudiated on November 15, 1923.

have great advantages. They were precious because their supplies were relatively limited, and they were in constant demand by the wealthy for ornament and decoration. Hence these metals tended to have high and stable prices. Further, they were easily recognized, they were divisible into extremely small units, and they did not easily wear out. Thus precious metals came to circulate as money and to be used in many transactions.

Before the invention of coins, it was necessary to carry the metals in bulk. When a purchase was made, the requisite quantity of the metal was carefully weighed on a scale. The invention of coinage eliminated the need to weigh the metal at each transaction, but it created an important role for an authority, usually a monarch, who made the coins and affixed his or her seal, guaranteeing the amount of precious metal that the coin contained. This was clearly a great convenience, as long as traders knew that they could accept the coin at its "face value." The face value was nothing more than a statement that a certain weight of metal was contained therein.

However, coins often could not be taken at their face value. The practice of clipping a thin slice off the edge of the coin and keeping the valuable metal became common. This, of course, served to undermine the acceptability of coins, even if they were stamped. To get around this problem, the idea arose of minting the coins with a rough edge. The absence of the rough edge would immediately indicate that the coin had been clipped. This practice, called *milling*, survives on some coins as an interesting anachronism to remind us that there were days when the market value of the metal in the coin was equal to the face value of the coin.

Not to be outdone by the cunning of their subjects, some rulers were quick to seize the chance of getting something for nothing. The power to mint placed rulers in a position to work a very profitable fraud. They often used some suitable occasion—a marriage, an anniversary, an alliance—to remint the coinage. Subjects would be ordered to bring their coins in to the mint to be melted down and coined afresh with a new stamp. Between the melting down and the recoining, however, the rulers had only to toss some further inexpensive base metal in with the molten gold. This *debasing* of the coinage allowed the ruler to earn a handsome profit by minting more new coins than the number of old

ones collected, and putting the extras in the royal vault.

The result of debasement was inflation. The subjects had the same number of coins as before and hence could demand the same quantity of goods. When rulers paid their bills, however, the recipients of the extra coins could be expected to spend them. This caused a net increase in demand, which in turn bid up prices. Thus debasing of the coinage was a common cause of increases in prices.

It was the experience of such inflations that led early economists to stress the link between the quantity of money and the price level.

Gresham's Law.   The early experience of currency debasement led to the observation known as **Gresham's law**, after Sir Thomas Gresham (1519–1579), an adviser to the Elizabethan court, who coined the phrase "bad money drives out good."

When Queen Elizabeth I came to the throne of England in the middle of the sixteenth century, the coinage had been severely debased. Seeking to help trade, Elizabeth minted new coins that contained their full face value in gold. However, as fast as she fed these new coins into circulation, they disappeared. Why?

Suppose that you possessed one of these new coins and one of the old ones, each with the same face value, and had to make a purchase. What would you do? You would use the debased coin to make the purchase and keep the undebased one; you part with less gold that way. Suppose that you wanted to obtain a certain amount of gold bullion by melting down the gold coins (as was frequently done). Which coins would you use? You would use new, undebased coins because you would part with less face value that way (it would take more of the debased coins than the new coins to get a given amount of gold bullion). The debased coins (bad money) would thus remain in circulation, and the undebased coins (good money) would disappear—the "bad" money would drive out the "good" money.

Gresham's insights have proved helpful in explaining the experience of a number of modern high-inflation economies. For example, in the 1970s, inflation in Chile raised the value of the metallic content in coins above their face value. Coins quickly disappeared from circulation as private citizens sold them to entrepreneurs who melted them down for their metal. Only paper currency remained in circulation and was used even for tiny transactions such as purchasing a pack of matches.

Gresham's law is one reason why modern coins, unlike their historical counterparts, are merely tokens that contain a metallic value that is only a small fraction of their face value.

Paper Money

The next important step in the history of money was the evolution of paper currency. Artisans who worked with gold required secure safes, and the public began to deposit gold with such goldsmiths for safekeeping. Goldsmiths would give their depositors receipts promising to hand over the gold on demand. When a depositor wished to make a large purchase, he could go to his goldsmith, reclaim some of his gold, and hand it over to the seller of the goods. If the seller had no immediate need for the gold, he would carry it back to the goldsmith for safekeeping.

If people knew the goldsmith to be reliable, there was no need to go through the cumbersome and risky business of physically transferring the gold. The buyer needed only to transfer the goldsmith's receipt to the seller, who would accept it as long as they were confident that the goldsmith would pay over the gold whenever it was needed. If the seller wished to buy a good from a third party, who also knew the goldsmith to be reliable, this transaction could also be effected by passing the goldsmith's receipt from the buyer to the seller. The convenience of using pieces of paper instead of gold should be obvious.

When it first came into being, paper money represented a promise to pay so much gold on demand. In this case, the promise was made first by goldsmiths and later by banks. Such paper money was *backed* by precious metal and was *convertible on demand* into this metal. In the nineteenth century, private banks commonly issued paper money, called **bank notes,** nominally convertible into gold. As with the goldsmiths, each bank issued its own notes, and these notes were convertible into gold at the issuing bank. Thus in the nineteenth century, bank notes from many different banks circulated side by side, each of them being backed by gold at the bank that issued them.

Fractionally Backed Paper Money. Early on, many goldsmiths and banks discovered that it was not necessary to keep one ounce of gold in the vaults for every claim to one ounce circulating as paper money. This is because at any one time, some of the bank's customers would be withdrawing gold, others would be depositing it, and most would be trading in the bank's paper notes without any need or desire to convert them into gold. As a result, the bank was able to issue more money redeemable in gold than the amount of gold that it held in its vaults. This was good business because the money could be invested profitably in interest-earning loans to households and firms. To this day, banks have many more claims outstanding against them than they actually have in reserves available to pay those claims. We say that the currency issued in such a situation is *fractionally backed* by the reserves.

The major problem with a fractionally backed convertible currency was maintaining its convertibility into the precious metal behind it. The imprudent bank that issued too much paper money would find itself unable to redeem its currency in gold when the demand for gold was even slightly higher than usual. It would then have to suspend payments, and all holders of its notes would suddenly find that the notes were worthless. The prudent bank that kept a reasonable relationship between its note issues and its gold reserves would find that it could meet a normal range of demand for gold without any trouble.

If, for whatever reason, the public lost confidence in the banks and demanded redemption of its currency *en masse*, the banks would be unable to honour their pledges. The history of nineteenth- and early-twentieth-century banking on both sides of the Atlantic is full of examples of banks that were ruined by "panics," or sudden runs on their gold reserves. When this happened, the banks' depositors and the holders of their notes would find themselves with worthless pieces of paper.

Fiat Money

As time went on, currency (notes and coins) issued by private banks became less common, and central banks took control of the currency. In time, *only* central banks were permitted to issue currency. Originally, the central banks issued currency that was fully convertible into gold. In those days, gold would be brought to the central bank, which would issue currency in the form of "gold certificates" that asserted that the gold was available on demand. The gold supply thus set some upper limit on the amount of currency.

However, central banks, like private banks before them, could issue more currency than they had in gold because in normal times only a small fraction of the outstanding currency was presented for payment at any one time. Thus even though the need to maintain convertibility into gold put an upper limit on note issuance, central banks had substantial discretionary control over the quantity of currency outstanding.

During the period between the world wars, almost all of the countries of the world abandoned the gold standard; their currencies were thus no longer convertible into gold. Money that is not convertible by law into anything valuable derives its value from its acceptability in exchange. Such **fiat money** is widely acceptable because it is declared by government order, or *fiat*, to be legal tender. **Legal tender** is anything that by law must be accepted when offered either for the purchase of goods or services or to discharge a debt.

Today, a few countries preserve the fiction that their currency is backed by gold, but no country allows its currency to be converted into gold on demand. Gold backing for Canadian currency was eliminated in 1940, although note issues continued to carry the traditional statement "will pay to the bearer on demand" until 1954. Today's Bank of Canada notes simply say, "This note is legal tender." It is, in other words, fiat money pure and simple.

Many people are disturbed to learn that present-day paper money is neither backed by nor convertible into anything more valuable—that it consists of nothing but pieces of paper whose value derives from common acceptance and from confidence that it will continue to be accepted in the future. Many people believe that their money should be more "substantial" than this. Yet money is, in fact, nothing more than pieces of paper.

If fiat money is acceptable, it is a medium of exchange. If its purchasing power remains stable, it is a satisfactory store of value. If both of these things are true, it serves as a satisfactory unit of account. Today, almost all currency is fiat money.

MODERN MONEY: DEPOSIT MONEY

Early in the twentieth century, private banks lost the authority to issue bank notes, and this authority was reserved for central banks (which we discuss shortly). Yet as we shall see, they did not lose the power to create *deposit money*. (A number of terms that will be encountered as we discuss modern money and the institutions related to it are discussed in Extension 27-1.)

Today's bank customers frequently deposit coins and paper money with the banks for safekeeping, just as in former times they deposited gold. Such a deposit is recorded as a credit to the customer's account. A customer who wishes to pay a debt may come to the bank and claim the money in dollars and then pay the money to other persons who may themselves redeposit the money in a bank.

As with gold transfers, this is a tedious procedure. It is more convenient to have the bank transfer claims to money on deposit. As soon as cheques, which are written instructions to the bank to make a transfer, became widely accepted in payment for commodities and debts, bank deposits became a form of money called *deposit money*. **Deposit money** is defined as money held by the public in the form of deposits in commercial banks that can be withdrawn on demand. Such deposits are called *demand deposits*. Cheques, unlike bank notes, do not circulate freely from hand to hand; hence cheques themselves are not currency. However, a balance in a demand deposit *is* money; the cheque transfers money from one person to another. Because cheques are easily drawn and deposited and are relatively safe from theft, they are widely used. In recent years, the development of debit cards has taken the place of cheques for many transactions. The use of debit cards instantly (electronically) transfers funds from the bank account of the purchaser to the bank account of the seller—it is thus the same as a cheque, only faster.

Thus when commercial banks lost the right to issue notes of their own, the form of bank money changed, but the substance did not. Today, banks have money in their vaults (or on deposit with the central banks), just as they always did. Once it was gold; today it is the legal tender of the times—fiat money. It is true today, just as in the past, that most of the bank's customers are content to pay their bills by passing among themselves the bank's promises to pay money on demand. Only a small proportion of the transactions made by the bank's customers are made in cash.

Bank deposits are money. Today, just as in the past, banks can create money by issuing more promises to pay (deposits) than they have cash reserves available to pay out.

THE CANADIAN BANKING SYSTEM

Many types of institutions make up a modern banking system such as exists in Canada today. The **central bank** is the government-owned and government-operated institution that serves to control the banking system. Through it, the government's monetary policy is conducted. In Canada, the central bank is the Bank of Canada, often just called the Bank.

Financial intermediaries are privately owned institutions that serve the general public. They are called *intermediaries* because they stand between savers, from whom they accept deposits, and investors, to whom they make loans. For many years, government regulations created a sharp distinction among the various types of financial intermediaries by limiting the types of transactions that each could engage in. The past two decades have seen a sweeping deregulation of the financial system so that many of these traditional distinctions no longer apply. In this book, when we speak of *commercial banks,* we use that term to extend to all financial intermediaries that create deposit money, including trust companies and credit unions.

THE BANK OF CANADA

All advanced free-market economies have, in addition to commercial banks, a central bank. Many of the world's early central banks were private, profit-making institutions that provided services to ordinary banks. Their importance, however, caused them to develop close ties with government. Central banks soon became instruments of the government, though not all of them were publicly owned. The Bank of England (the "Old Lady of Threadneedle Street"), one of the world's oldest and most famous central banks, began to operate as the central bank of England in the seventeenth century, but it was not formally taken over by the government until 1947.

The similarities in the functions performed and the tools used by the world's central banks are much more important than the differences in their organiza-tion. Although our attention is given to the operations of the Bank of Canada, its basic functions are similar to those of the Bank of England, the Bank of Greece, or the Federal Reserve System in the United States.

Organization of the Bank of Canada

The Bank of Canada commenced operations on March 11, 1935. It is a publicly owned corporation; all profits accruing from its operations are remitted to the Government of Canada. The responsibility for the Bank's affairs rests with a board of directors composed of the governor, the senior deputy governor, the deputy minister of finance, and 12 directors. The governor is appointed by the directors, with the approval of the federal cabinet, for a seven-year term. Since the Bank's inception, there have been six governors:

- Graham Towers (1935–54)
- James Coyne (1955–61)
- Louis Rasminsky (1961–73)
- Gerald Bouey (1973–87)
- John Crow (1987–94)
- Gordon Thiessen (1994–)

The organization of the Bank of Canada is designed to keep the operation of monetary policy free from day-to-day political influence. Thus the Bank is not responsible to Parliament for its day-to-day behaviour in the way that the Department of Finance is for the operation of fiscal policy. In this sense, the Bank of Canada has considerable autonomy in the way it carries out monetary policy. Despite this considerable autonomy, however, the Bank of Canada is not completely independent. The *ultimate* responsibility for the Bank's actions rest with the government, since it is the government which must answer to Parliament. This system is known as "joint responsibility," and it dates back to 1967.

Under the system of joint responsibility, the governor of the Bank and the minister of finance consult regularly. In the case of fundamental disagreement over policy, the minister of finance has the option of issuing an explicit *directive* to the governor. In such a case (which has not happened since the inception of joint responsibility), the governor would simply carry out the minister's directive (or resign), and the

---

EXTENSION 27-1

TERMINOLOGY OF A MODERN FINANCIAL SYSTEM

Throughout this and subsequent chapters, we will encounter many different types of financial assets, or *securities*. One important distinction is between equity and debt.

Equity refers to assets such as stocks or shares that represent evidence of partial ownership of a firm and hence provide a claim on the earnings of that firm; the return on equity depends on the performance of the firm. Equity is also often called *real capital*, or just *capital*; unless the context makes it clear, care must be taken to distinguish between use of the term real capital to refer to the actual plant, equipment, and machinery that constitute a firm's physical assets and use of the term to refer to the financial assets that represent a claim on the firm's earnings.

Debt refers to assets issued by firms and governments that promise to pay a specified rate of interest over a specified period of time. Unless the firm in question goes bankrupt and cannot meet its obligations, the return on debt does not depend on the earnings of the firm—the interest must be paid whether the firm is profitable or not and thus represents a prior claim on the firm's earnings before any payment to equity holders is made.

Most debt instruments, often called **bonds,** promise to pay a stated sum of money as interest each year and to repay the principal (often called the *face value* or the *redemption value*) of the bond at some future maturity date, often many years distant. The time until the maturity date is called the **term to maturity,** or simply the **term,** of the bond. Some bonds, called *perpetuities*, pay interest forever and never repay the principal.

Very-short-term bonds that promise a single payment (combining interest and principal) are called *money-market instruments* and include **treasury bills** (short-term government bonds), certificates of deposit (CDs), banker's acceptances, and commercial paper. The price paid for one of these instruments is less than the amount that the instrument pays on maturity, and the difference is called the *discount*. For example, the government issues three- and six-month treasury bills each week that are priced on a discount basis. The difference between the purchase price and the payment on maturity represents the interest on the bill.

A key feature of most financial assets is that their ownership is transferable, and hence they can

---

responsibility for monetary policy would rest with the government. In the absence of such a directive, however, responsibility for monetary policy rests with the governor of the Bank.

The system of joint responsibility keeps the conduct of monetary policy free from day-to-day political influence while ensuring that the government retains ultimate responsibility for monetary policy.

This system was motivated by the so-called "Coyne Affair" in 1961. James Coyne, then governor of the Bank of Canada, disagreed with the minister of finance over the conduct of monetary policy and was eventually forced to resign. Louis Rasminsky then accepted the position as governor of the Bank on the condition that the Bank of Canada

Act be modified to incorporate the idea of joint responsibility. The Bank of Canada Act was so amended in 1967.[1]

Basic Functions of the Bank

A central bank serves four main functions: as a banker for private banks, as a bank for the government, as the regulator of the nation's money supply, and as a supporter of financial markets. The first three functions are revealed by a study of Table 27-1, which shows the balance sheet of the Bank of Canada.

---

[1]For a discussion of the early history of the Bank of Canada, see George Watts, *The Bank of Canada: Origins and Early History* (Carleton University Press, 1993).

be bought and sold in financial markets. As with anything else that is bought and sold, the price of financial assets fluctuates in response to shifts in supply and demand. In the next chapter we will look more carefully at the determination of the price of financial assets. In particular, we will examine the relationship between the price paid for an asset and the *yield* it earns. To anticipate that discussion, we will see that when the price of an asset that promises to pay a certain income stream in the future changes, the yield on that asset changes in the opposite direction. *The more one pays to obtain a claim on a given income stream, the lower the yield on one's investment, and vice versa.*

One important characteristic of financial assets is their *riskiness*, which refers to the possibility that the future payments will not be made in full or at all. Typically, investors are thought to be risk-averse, meaning that the riskier an asset is, the higher is the yield it will have to offer to induce investors to buy it.

Another important characteristic of financial assets is their *liquidity*, which refers to their usefulness as a ready means of payment. Money can always be used as a means of payment and hence is a perfectly liquid asset. Other financial assets can be sold in the market and hence are convertible into cash, so they appear to be just as liquid as money. However, the markets for some assets are such that they cannot always be instantly sold, or at least not at anything other than a "bargain-basement" price (often called the *liquidation value*); to receive the price that is justified by the asset's risk and return, some time and expense must be incurred.

A bank deposit that allows the depositor to write cheques is, from this perspective, just one very-short-term and highly liquid asset, and hence it is often called *deposit money*. (Although most deposits do earn some interest, they are of such a short term that fluctuations in interest rates do not influence their value.)

When a commercial bank receives a deposit, the deposit increases the assets and liabilities shown on the bank's balance sheet by the same amount. It creates an obligation on the part of the bank (a liability) in that it must stand ready to turn the funds over to the depositor. Thus it is common to speak of a bank's *deposit liabilities*.

Banker to the Chartered Banks. The central bank accepts deposits from the chartered banks and will, on order, transfer them to the account of another bank. In this way, the central bank provides the chartered banks with the equivalent of a chequing account and with a means of settling debts to other banks. The deposits of the chartered banks with the Bank of Canada—also called *reserves*—appear in Table 27-1. In December 1995, the banks had $518 million on reserve at the Bank of Canada. Notice that the cash reserves of the chartered banks deposited with the central bank are liabilities of the central bank, because it promises to pay them on demand.

Historically, one of the earliest services provided by central banks was that of "lender of last resort" to the banking system. Central banks would lend money to private banks that had sound investments (such as government securities and safe loans to individuals) but were in urgent need of cash. If such banks could not obtain ready cash, they might be forced into insolvency, because they could not meet the demands of their depositors, in spite of their being basically sound. Today's central banks continue to be lenders of last resort.

U.S. commercial banks borrow extensively from the Federal Reserve System (the U.S. central bank) in order to maintain their reserves, but the corresponding institutional arrangement that Canadian banks use is less direct. Rather than relying on direct loans from the Bank of Canada, the chartered banks meet their immediate cash requirements by varying the amount of *day-to-day loans* they make available to a group of investment dealers who carry inventories of government of Canada securi-

TABLE 27-1

Assets and Liabilities of the Bank of Canada, December 1995
(millions of dollars)

Assets		Liabilities	
Government of Canada securities	23,364	Notes in circulation	28,778
Advances to banks	545	Government of Canada deposits	18
Foreign-currency assets	548	Deposits of banks (reserves)	518
Other assets	5,743	Foreign-currency liabilities	185
		Other liabilities and capital	701
Total	30,200	Total	30,200

The balance sheet of the Bank of Canada shows that it serves as banker to the commercial banks and to the Government of Canada and as issuer of our currency; it also suggests the Bank's role as regulator of money markets and the money supply. The principal liabilities of the Bank are the basis of the money supply. Bank of Canada notes are currency, and the deposits of the commercial banks give them the reserves they need to create deposit money. The Bank's holdings of Government of Canada securities arise from its operations designed to regulate the money supply and financial markets.

(*Source: Bank of Canada Review*, Winter 1995–96.)

ties. A chartered bank that has an immediate need for cash will sell some of its holdings of government securities to these investment dealers. These dealers can then obtain financing from the Bank of Canada under what is called *purchase and resale agreement (PRA)*—they can sell securities to the Bank of Canada and agree to buy them back at a later date. The result is the same as if the banks had borrowed from the Bank of Canada directly.

Thus when the chartered banks reduce their day-to-day loans (sell government securities to the private investment dealers), they induce an increase in the Bank of Canada's holdings of government securities under PRA. In terms of the balance sheet shown in Table 27-1, this indirect method of borrowing means that some of the $23.4 billion of government securities are actually held under PRA and thus are effectively loans to the chartered banks. (So the $545 million as advances to banks understates the total value of outstanding loans to the banks.)

Banker to the Federal Government. Governments, too, need to hold their funds in an account into which they can make deposits and on which they can write cheques. The government of Canada keeps its chequing deposits at the Bank of Canada, replenishing them from much larger accounts kept at the chartered banks. In December 1995 the federal government had $18 million in deposits at the Bank of Canada.

When the government requires more money than it collects in taxes, it needs to borrow, and it does so by issuing government securities (short-term treasury bills or longer-term bonds). Most are sold directly to the public, but occasionally the government raises

funds by selling securities to the central bank which "buys" them by crediting the government's account with a deposit for the amount of the purchase. In December 1995, the Bank of Canada held $23.4 billion in government of Canada securities. These securities are an interest-earning asset for the Bank of Canada but a liability for the government. (Indeed, it is largely by earning interest on these securities that the Bank of Canada earns a profit every year—a profit that is eventually remitted to the government.)

We will see in Chapter 29 that the Bank's holdings of government securities and its control over the location of government deposits (switching them between the central bank and the commercial banks) are the primary tools for the conduct of monetary policy.

Regulator of the Money Supply. One of the most important functions of a central bank is to regulate the *money supply*. Though we have not yet defined the money supply precisely—and there are several different definitions of "the" money supply that we will encounter—we will see that most measures of the money supply include currency plus deposits held at commercial banks. From Table 27-1, it is clear that the overwhelming proportion of a central bank's liabilities (its promises to pay) are either currency (notes and coins) or the reserves of the chartered banks. These reserves, in turn, underlie the deposits of households and firms—in exactly the same way that the nineteenth century goldsmith's holdings of gold underlay its issue of notes.

Thus by changing its liabilities (currency plus reserves), the Bank of Canada can change the money supply. The Bank of Canada can change the levels of its assets and liabilities in many ways, and as its liabilities rise and fall, so does the money supply. In Chapter 29, we will explore in detail how this happens and how the Bank uses this ability to conduct monetary policy.

Regulator and Supporter of Money Markets. Central banks usually assume a major responsibility to support the country's financial system and to prevent serious disruption by wide-scale panic and resulting bank failures. Various institutions are in the business of borrowing on a short-term basis and lending on a long-term basis. To some extent, the chartered banks do this when they take in deposits and lend money for various terms. But trust and mortgage loan companies are the major institutions for this kind of transaction. They receive deposits from the public and lend the money on long-term mortgages.

Large, unanticipated increases in interest rates tend to squeeze these institutions. The average rate they earn on their investments rises only slowly as old contracts mature and new ones are made, but they must either pay higher rates to hold on to their deposits or accept wide-scale withdrawals that could easily bring about insolvency. To prevent such financial disasters, central banks often buy and sell government bonds either to slow the rate of change in interest rates or to narrow the range over which the rates are allowed to fluctuate.

Conflicts Among Functions.   The several functions of the Bank of Canada are not always compatible. For example, in pursuit of an anti-inflationary policy, the Bank may cause a temporary rise in interest rates. The resulting squeeze makes life uncomfortable for banks and other financial institutions and makes borrowing expensive for the government. If the Bank of Canada chooses to ease those problems, say, by lending money to chartered banks, it is relaxing its anti-inflationary policy.

The Bank must strive to balance conflicting objectives. We discuss a number of aspects of this conflict in Chapter 29. However, at this stage, we note that many critics think that the Bank does not always succeed in finding the right balance between its conflicting objectives.

COMMERCIAL BANKS IN CANADA

All Canadian banks owned in the private sector, that is, all banks except the Bank of Canada, are referred to as **commercial banks.** The Canadian banking system is controlled by the provisions of the Bank Act,

first passed in 1935 and revised several times since. Under the Bank Act, charters can be granted to financial institutions to operate as banks, and until 1980, there were only a few chartered banks, most of which were very large and each of which operated under identical regulatory provisions.

The 1980 revisions to the Bank Act allowed foreign banks to commence operations in Canada, although it severely limited the scale and scope of their activity. Subsequent revisions have removed some of these restrictions and made it easier to obtain new banking charters, but the revisions have maintained the distinction between these newer institutions and banks operating under what are essentially the pre-1980 provisions of the Bank Act. The original provisions, in slightly modified form, are now known as Schedule A of the Bank Act; the foreign banks and the new, smaller domestic banks operate under Schedules B and C. The term *chartered banks* is usually reserved for the Schedule A banks.

The chartered banks have common attributes: They hold deposits for their customers; they permit certain deposits to be transferred by cheque from an individual account to other accounts held in any bank branch in the country; they make loans to households and firms; they invest in government securities.

Banks are not the only financial institutions in the country. Many other privately owned, profit-seeking institutions, such as trust companies and credit unions, accept savings deposits and grant loans for specific purposes. Finance companies make loans to households for practically any purpose—sometimes at very high interest rates. Department stores and credit-card companies will extend credit so that purchases can be made on a buy-now, pay-later basis.

The commercial banks are subject to federal regulations and until recently were required to hold reserves with the Bank of Canada against their deposit liabilities. Other institutions do not face reserve requirements, but most are subject to various federal and provincial regulations concerning ownership and control and the types of financial activities they are allowed to engage in. Thus there are differences among all types of financial institutions, not just between banks and others.

The chartered banks have historically been such a stable and dominant group that the terms *chartered banks* and *banking system* have been considered virtually synonymous. However, some events over the past 15 years may serve to break this identification. First, there have been dramatic changes in

EXTENSION 27-2

THE GLOBALIZATION OF FINANCIAL MARKETS

Technological innovations in communication and the desire to avoid onerous government regulations have led to a globalization of the financial service industry over the past two decades. Computers, satellite communication systems, reliable telephones with direct worldwide dialing, electronic mail, and fax machines—all coming into widespread use only within the past decade—have put people in instantaneous contact anywhere in the world.

As a result of these new technologies, borrowers and lenders can learn about market conditions and then move their funds instantly in search of the best loan rates. Large firms need transaction balances only while banks in their area are open. Once banks close for the day in each centre, the firms will not need these balances until tomorrow's reopening; hence the funds can be moved to another market, where they are used until it closes. They are then moved to yet another market. Funds are thus free to move from London to New York to Tokyo and back to London on a daily rotation. This is a degree of global sophistication that was inconceivable before the advent of the computer, when international communication was much slower and costlier than it now is. To facilitate the movement in and out of various national currencies, increasing amounts of bank deposits are denominated in foreign rather than domestic currencies.

One of the first developments in this movement toward globalization was the growth of the foreign-currency markets in Europe in the 1960s. Initially, the main currency involved was the U.S. dollar, which is why *Eurodollar* markets were the first to develop. Today, the *Eurobond* market is an international market where bonds of various types, denominated in various national currencies, are issued and sold to customers located throughout the world. The customers are mainly public corporations, international organizations, and multinational enterprises. The *Eurocurrency* market is a market for short-term bank deposits and bank loans denominated in various currencies.

The original attraction of the Eurodollar market was the freedom from the restrictions placed by the Federal Reserve (the U.S. central bank) on American commercial banks. By operating in offshore markets, banks were able to cut unit costs by dealing in large volumes at the wholesale level. They could then offer rates that were higher for lenders and lower for borrowers than those prevailing in the United States.

The progressive worldwide lifting of interest rate ceilings and other capital market restrictions that oc-

the makeup of the chartered banks—in 1985, two relatively new regionally based chartered banks failed, and since then, banks have merged in two instances and two Canadian banks were taken over by foreign banks. Second, the federal government and several provincial governments proposed extensive changes in regulations, including the abolition of reserve requirements for the chartered banks, that would further blur the distinction between the chartered banks and other financial institutions. Third, there have been sweeping changes internationally in the structure and functioning of financial markets; some of these developments are discussed further in Extension 27-2.

Interbank Activities

Chartered banks have a number of interbank cooperative relationships. For example, banks often share loans. Even the biggest bank cannot meet all the credit needs of a giant corporation, and often a group of banks will offer a "pool loan," agreeing on common terms and dividing the loan up into manageable segments.

Another form of interbank cooperation is the bank credit card. Visa and MasterCard are the two most widely used credit cards, and each is operated by a group of banks.

Probably the most important form of interbank cooperation is cheque clearing and collection. Bank curred in the 1980s led to a further globalization of financial markets. Although this removed some of the original reasons for their growth, the Euromarkets prospered. First, they allowed banks to avoid the remaining domestic regulations. Second, the advantage of having an international market dealing in many different national currencies was sufficient to sustain the markets.

The increasing sophistication of information transfer also led to a breakdown of the high degree of specialization that had characterized financial markets in earlier decades. When information was difficult to obtain and analyze, an efficient division of labour called for a host of specialist institutions, each with expertise in a narrow range of transactions. As a result of the new developments in communication technology, economies of large scale led to the integration of various financial operations within one firm. For example, in many countries, banks have moved into the markets where securities are traded, while many security-trading firms have begun to offer a range of banking services. As the scale of such integrated firms increases, they find it easier to extend their operations geographically as well as functionally.

It has often been difficult for government regulations to keep up with these rapid changes.

Governments that relaxed their regulations first in face of the evolving realities often allowed their financial institutions to gain important advantages in international competition. The British government has been quick to react to these developments, and as a result, London has retained its strong position in the international financial world. The Canadian government also reacted relatively quickly by allowing banks to expand their functions into areas formerly barred to them and by allowing foreign banks increased access to the Canadian market. In contrast, the U.S. government has been slow to adapt. For example, it still limits interstate banking and prevents U.S. banks from extending their operations beyond the ones traditionally reserved for banks. As a result, U.S. banks have lost out heavily to European and Japanese banks.

The kinds of government intervention into domestic capital markets and government control over international capital flows that characterized the 1950s and 1960s are no longer possible. International markets are just too sophisticated. Globalization is here to stay, and by removing domestic restrictions and exchange controls, governments in advanced countries are simply bowing to the inevitable.

deposits are an effective medium of exchange only because banks accept each other's cheques. If a depositor in the Bank of Montreal writes a cheque to someone who deposits it in the Toronto Dominion Bank, the Bank of Montreal now owes money to the Toronto Dominion Bank. This creates a need for the banks to present cheques to each other for payment.

Millions of such transactions take place in the course of a day, and they result in an enormous sorting and bookkeeping job. Multibank systems make use of a **clearing house** where interbank debts are settled. At the end of the day, all the cheques drawn by the Bank of Montreal's customers and deposited in the Toronto Dominion Bank are totaled and set against the total of all the cheques drawn by the Toronto Dominion's customers and deposited in the Bank of Montreal. It is necessary only to settle the difference between the two sums. The actual cheques are passed through the clearing house back to the bank on which they were drawn. Both banks are then able to adjust the individual accounts by a set of book entries. A flow of cash between banks is necessary only when there is a net transfer of cash from the customers of one bank to those of another. This flow of cash is accompanied by a daily transfer of deposits held by the chartered banks with the Bank of Canada.

Banks as Profit Seekers

Banks are private firms that seek to make profits in the same sense as firms making neckties or bicycles. A chartered bank provides a variety of services to its customers: a safe place to store money, the convenience of demand deposits that can be transferred by personal cheque, a safe and convenient place to earn a modest but guaranteed return on savings, and often financial advice and estate-management services. The bank earns some revenue by charging for these services, but such fees are a small part of the bank's total earnings. The largest part (typically about five-sixths) of a bank's earnings is derived from the bank's ability to invest profitably the funds placed with it.

Table 27-2 is the combined balance sheet of the chartered banks in Canada. The bulk of a bank's liabilities are deposits owed to its depositors. The principal assets of a bank are the *securities* it owns (including government bonds), which pay interest or dividends, and the *loans* it makes to individuals and to businesses. A bank loan is a liability to the borrower (who must pay it back) but an asset to the bank. The bank expects not only to have the loan repaid but also to receive interest that more than compensates for the paperwork involved and the risk of nonpayment.

Banks attract deposits by paying interest to depositors and by providing them with services such as clearing cheques, automatic-teller machines, debit cards, and the provision of regular monthly statements. Banks earn profits by lending and investing money deposited with them for more than they pay their depositors in terms of interest and other services provided.

Competition for Deposits

Competition for deposits is active among banks and between banks and other financial institutions. Financial deregulation, which removed restrictions on the activities of various financial institutions, has contributed to this competition. Interest paid on deposits, special high-interest certificates of deposit (CDs), advertising, personal solicitation of accounts, giveaway programs for new deposits to existing accounts, and improved services are all forms of competition for funds. Among the special services are payroll-accounting and pension-accounting schemes for corporate customers. Banks also establish locked deposit-boxes in which retail customers of large companies send their payments, with the bank then crediting them to the company's account. All of these services are costly to the bank, but they serve as inducements for customers to make deposits.

RESERVES

All bankers would as a matter of convenience and prudence keep sufficient cash on hand to be able to meet depositors' day-to-day requirements for cash. However, just as the goldsmiths of long ago discovered that only a fraction of the gold they held was

---

TABLE 27-2
Consolidated Balance Sheet of the Canadian Chartered Banks, October 1995
(millions of dollars)

Assets		Liabilities	
Reserves (including deposits with Bank of Canada)	4,068	Demand deposits	34,943
Government of Canada securities	83,189	Savings deposits	295,093
Mortgage and nonmortgage loans	413,108	Time deposits	90,928
Canadian securities (corporate and provincial		Government of Canada deposits	8,381
and municipal governments)	37,109	Foreign-currency liabilities	310,817
Foreign-currency assets	296,456	Shareholder's equity	43,356
Other assets	68,778	Other liabilities	119,190
Total	902,708	Total	902,708

Reserves are only a tiny fraction of deposit liabilities. If all the commercial banks' customers who held demand deposits tried to withdraw them in cash, the banks could not meet this demand without liquidating about $30 billion of other assets. This would be impossible without assistance from the Bank of Canada.

(Source: Bank of Canada Review, Winter 1995–1996.)

ever withdrawn at any given time, and just as banks of long ago discovered that only a small fraction of convertible bank notes was actually converted, so too have modern banks known that only a small fraction of their deposits will be withdrawn in cash at any one time.

The reserves needed to assure that depositors can withdraw their deposits on demand will be quite small in normal times.

In abnormal times, however, nothing short of 100 percent would do the job if the commercial banking system had to stand alone. When a few bank failures cause a general loss of confidence in banks' ability to redeem their deposits, the results can be devastating. Until relatively recently, such an event—or even the rumor of it—could lead to a "run" on banks as depositors rushed to withdraw their money. Faced with such a panic, banks would have to close until they had borrowed enough funds or sold enough assets to meet the demand or until the demand subsided. However, banks could not instantly turn their loans into cash because the borrowers would have the money tied up in such things as real estate or business enterprises. Neither could the banks obtain cash by selling their securities to the public because payments would be made by cheques, which would not provide cash to pay off depositors.

The difficulty of providing sufficient reserves to meet abnormal situations can be alleviated by the central bank. Because it controls the supply of bank reserves, the central bank can provide all the reserves that are needed to meet any abnormal situation. It can do this in two ways. First, it can lend reserves directly to commercial banks on the security of assets that are sound but not easy to liquidate quickly, such as interest-earning residential or commercial mortgages. Second, it can enter the open market and buy all the securities that commercial banks need to sell. Once the public finds that deposits can be turned into cash, the panic will usually subside, and any further drain of cash out of banks will cease.

The possibility of panic withdrawals is also greatly diminished by the provision of deposit insurance, provided in Canada by the Canada Deposit Insurance Corporation (CDIC), a crown corporation. The CDIC guarantees that depositors will get their money back even if a bank fails completely. Most depositors will not withdraw their money as

long as they are certain they can get it when they need it. Although deposit insurance confers a number of benefits on the operation of the financial system, it has also been subject to considerable criticism in recent years. This is explored in more detail in Extension 27-3.

Target Reserves

We have seen that commercial banks hold reserves in order to meet temporary cash drains that arise when a bank's payments exceed its receipts. Receipts occur when the bank's customers deposit either cash or cheques drawn on other banks; payments are required either when cheques drawn by the bank's customers are deposited in other banks or when customers make cash withdrawals. A bank with no access to reserves will be unable to meet even a temporary cash drain and will be forced to suspend payments. This is something that banks must avoid at almost any cost, so that banking panics can be avoided.

A bank's **reserve ratio** is the fraction of its deposit liabilities that it actually holds as reserves, either as cash or as deposits with the central bank. A bank's **target reserve ratio** is the fraction of its deposits it *wishes* to hold as reserves.

In the past, legislation contained in the Bank Act required the chartered banks to hold reserves. These requirements were thought necessary to ensure the stability of the banking system. The reserves that the Bank Act required the banks to hold were called **required reserves.** Starting in the early 1980s, however, Canadian banks argued that the legal requirement to hold some of their assets as non-interest-bearing reserves placed them at a disadvantage relative to their competitors that were not subject to such requirements. The competitors included both foreign commercial banks and Canadian nonbank financial institutions, such as trust companies and credit unions. Globalization of financial markets had brought domestic financial institutions into direct competition with foreign ones, and continuing deregulation of financial markets had enhanced the competition between banks and nonbank financial institutions. After much deliberation, the government responded to these complaints by phasing out all legal reserve requirements early in the 1990s.

We can imagine two situations under a regime of zero required reserves. In the first, the commercial banks are on their own (the situation before

EXTENSION 27-3

DEPOSIT INSURANCE AND THE FINANCIAL SYSTEM

Deposit insurance, provided in Canada by the government-owned Canada Deposit Insurance Corporation (CDIC), assures depositors that their funds are secure whatever the fate of their deposit institution. This is a great boon for depositors, but experience has shown that it is a double-edged sword.

On the one hand, deposit insurance provides security to depositors. This is a good thing in itself. It also helps to stabilize the economy in times of financial distress by preventing large losses of wealth when financial institutions fail.

On the other hand, deposit insurance creates an incentive for financial intermediaries to pursue riskier investments than they would if depositors had to worry about losing their deposits should the institution fail.* Because of deposit insurance, depositors have no reason to select deposit institutions according to the riskiness of their investments. They are free instead to select the institution that pays the highest interest without worrying about the associated risk.

Deposit insurance is thus an example of an important class of government institutions that create situations whereby "heads the private investor wins, tails the taxpayer loses." Financial institutions take in depositors' insured funds; if the owners place them in risky ventures that pay off, the owners get the profits; if the owners place the funds in ventures that fail often enough to bring down the whole insti-

---
*Readers who have studied microeconomics will recognize this incentive as an example of *moral hazard*.

tution, the taxpayers must meet the bill by repaying those who provided the capital (the depositors). Canadian financial institutions have occasionally failed, including two western banks in the mid 1980s. When those institutions went under, depositors were repaid by the CDIC. Although the legal ceiling on deposit insurance was $60,000, deposits in excess of that amount were also repaid, using taxpayer money. This created the precedent that ceilings on deposit insurance were not to be taken seriously. Any amount would be likely to be repaid. Hence, no investor need worry about the financial probity of the investments made by the institutions in which his or her money was deposited.

Two types of reforms are possible. One type would keep deposit insurance and provide the necessary accompanying regulations; the other would take deregulation to its logical conclusion of ending deposit insurance.

The implications of deposit insurance for the investment behaviour of financial intermediaries suggest that if deposit insurance is to be maintained, other regulations concerning capital requirements and investment standards need to be applied. In addition, the deposit insurance system might be reformed in order to relate the cost of insurance for a particular institution to the risks implied by that institution's asset position.

Many economists believe that if deregulation of financial institutions is regarded as desirable, it should be accompanied by a removal of deposit insurance, so that the people who use the funds will be accountable to those who provide them.

---

central banks were instituted). They can count on no other institution to help them in time of need. In this case, the target reserves needed to meet any normal cash drain would be a significant fraction of the bank's total liabilities—indeed, nothing short of 100 percent reserves would guarantee solvency in the face of a major run by the bank's depositors.

In the second situation, a central bank is present, to come to the commercial banks' assistance when they are caught short of reserves due to a temporary adverse payments balance. Now the banks can carry less reserves than in the first situation. How few reserves they will carry will depend on the cost of getting assistance from the central bank when they are caught short of reserves. This is the system the Bank of Canada now operates. The commercial banks have no required reserves but they must worry about running out of reserves because the support given them by the Bank of Canada comes at a substantial cost (the Bank of Canada charges interest on its loans to the commercial banks).

Look again at Table 27-2. Notice that the banking system's cash reserves of just over $4 billion are less than one-half of 1 percent of its liabilities of over $900 billion. If the holders of even 5 percent of its deposits demanded cash, the banks would have been unable to meet the demand without outside help. Reserves can be as low as they are because the banks know that the Bank of Canada will help them out in time of temporary need. The Canadian banking system is thus a **fractional-reserve system,** with commercial banks holding reserves—either as cash or as deposits at the Bank of Canada—of much less than 100 percent of their deposits.

In Chapter 29 we will study how the Bank of Canada can influence the money supply under a zero required reserve system after we have examined how the money supply is itself determined. Our analysis of the money supply process is based on the following behaviour of the chartered banks:

Commercial banks strive to maintain some target ratio of reserves to deposits. In the past, this target ratio was legally imposed; today, it is determined by the banks themselves.

Any reserves in excess of target reserves are called **excess reserves.** All that matters for what follows is that there is some target reserve ratio, no matter how small.

MONEY CREATION BY THE BANKING SYSTEM

We noted before that the *money supply* refers to both currency and deposits at financial institutions. The fractional-reserve system provides the leverage that permits chartered banks and other financial institutions to create new deposits, and thus to create new money. The process is important, so it is worth examining in some detail.

TABLE 27-3 The Initial Balance Sheet of Incidental Bank and Trust (IB&T)			
Assets		Liabilities	
Cash and other reserves	200	Deposits	1,000
Loans	900	Capital	100
	1,100		1,100

IB&T has a reserve of 20 percent of its deposit liabilities. The commercial bank earns money by finding profitable investments for much of the money deposited with it. In this balance sheet, loans are its earning assets.

SOME SIMPLIFYING ASSUMPTIONS

To focus on the essential aspects of how banks create money, suppose that banks can invest in only one kind of asset, loans, and that there is only one kind of deposit, a demand deposit.

Two other assumptions are provisional. When we have developed the basic ideas concerning the banks' creation of money, these assumptions will be relaxed.

1. *Fixed reserve ratio.* We assume that all banks have the same target reserve ratio which does not change. In our numerical illustration, we will assume that the target reserve ratio is 20 percent (0.20); that is, for every $5 of deposits the banks wish to hold $1 in cash reserves. Thus we are assuming that all banks want to invest any reserves that they have in excess of their target reserves. This implies that they always believe that there are safe investments—loans, in our example—to be made when they have excess reserves.

2. *No cash drain from the banking system.* We also assume that the public holds a fixed amount of currency in circulation. This means that any transfers of funds between individuals will not cause changes in the total amount of currency available for the banks to hold as reserves. Changes in the money supply will consequently take the form of changes in deposits held at the commercial banks.

THE CREATION OF DEPOSIT MONEY

The balance sheet of a hypothetical commercial bank is shown in Table 27-3. Incidental Bank and Trust

(IB&T) has assets of $200 of reserves, held partly as cash on hand and partly as deposits with the central bank, and $900 of loans outstanding to its customers. Its liabilities are $100 to investors who contributed capital to start the bank and $1,000 to current depositors. The bank's ratio of reserves to deposits is 0.20 (200/1,000), exactly equal to its target reserve ratio.

New Deposits

In what follows, we are interested in knowing how the commercial banking system can "create money" when confronted with a new deposit. But what do we mean by a new deposit? By "new," we mean a deposit of cash that is new to the *commercial banking system*. There are three examples. First, an individual might immigrate to Canada and bring cash with them. When that cash is deposited into a commercial bank, it constitutes a new deposit to the (Canadian) banking system. A second example is an individual that had some cash stashed under his bed (or in a safe-deposit box) and who has now decided to deposit it into an account at a commercial bank. The final example is perhaps the most interesting, but is also the most complicated. If the Bank of Canada were to purchase a government security from an individual or from a firm, it would purchase that asset with a cheque drawn on the Bank of Canada. When the individual or firm deposits the cheque with their commercial bank, it would be a new deposit to the commercial banking system.

The important point to keep in mind here is that the *source* of the new deposit is irrelevant to the process of money creation by the commercial banks. In the discussion that follows, we use the example of the Bank of Canada buying government securities from firms or households as a way of generating a new deposit, but this is not central. We use this example because, as we shall see in Chapter 29, this is in fact an important way that the Bank of Canada conducts its monetary policy. But the general process of money creation that we are about to describe applies to *any* new deposit.

A Single New Deposit

Suppose that the Bank of Canada buys $100 worth of securities on the open market. It issues a cheque to the seller, and that individual or firm opens an account with IB&T and deposits the $100 cheque.

TABLE 27-4
IB&T's Balance Sheet Immediately After a New Deposit of $100

Assets		Liabilities	
Cash and other reserves	300	Deposits	1,100
Loans	900	Capital	100
	1,200		1,200

The deposit raises deposit liabilities and cash assets by the same amount. Because both cash and deposits rise by $100, the reserve ratio, formerly 0.20, increases to 0.27. The bank has more cash than it needs to provide a 20 percent reserve against its deposit liabilities.

This is a wholly new deposit for the commercial bank, and it results in a revised balance sheet (Table 27-4). As a result of the new deposit, IB&T's cash assets and deposit liabilities have both increased by $100. More important, IB&T's ratio of reserves to deposits has increased from 0.20 to 0.27 (300/1,100). The bank now has $80 in excess reserves; with $1,100 in deposits, its target reserves are only $220.

IB&T can now lend the $80 in excess reserves that it is holding. Table 27-5 shows the position after this has been done and after the proceeds of the loan have been withdrawn to be deposited to the account of a customer of another bank. IB&T once again has a 20 percent reserve ratio.

So far, of the $100 initial deposit at IB&T, $20 is held by IB&T as reserves against the deposit and $80 has been lent out in the system. As a result, other banks have received new deposits of $80 stemming

TABLE 27-5
IB&T's Balance Sheet After a New Loan and Cash Drain of $80

Assets		Liabilities	
Cash and other reserves	220	Deposits	1,100
Loans	980	Capital	100
	1,200		1,200

IB&T lends its surplus cash and suffers a cash drain. The bank keeps $20 as a reserve against the initial new deposit of $100. It lends $80 to a customer, who writes a cheque to someone who deals with another bank. When the cheque is cleared, IB&T suffers an $80 cash drain. Comparing Tables 27-3 and 27-5 shows that the bank has increased its deposit liabilities by the $100 initially deposited and has increased its assets by $20 of cash reserves and $80 of new loans. It has also restored its reserve ratio of 0.20.

TABLE 27-6
Changes in the Balance Sheets of Second-Generation Banks

Assets		Liabilities	
Cash and other reserves	+16	Deposits	+80
Loans	+64		
	+80		+80

Second-generation banks receive cash deposits and expand loans. The second-generation banks gain new deposits of $80 as a result of the loan granted by IB&T, which is used to make payments to customers of the second-generation banks. These banks keep 20 percent of the cash that they acquire as their reserve against the new deposit, and they can make new loans using the other 80 percent. When the customers who borrowed the money make payments to the customers of third-generation banks, a cash drain occurs.

from the loans made by IB&T; persons receiving payment from those who borrowed the $80 from IB&T will have deposited those payments in their own banks.[2]

The banks that receive deposits from the proceeds of IB&T's loan are sometimes called *next-generation banks* or, more specifically according to the situation, *second-generation, third-generation,* and so on. In this case, the second-generation banks receive new deposits of $80, and when the cheques clear, they have new reserves of $80. Because they desire to hold only $16 in additional reserves to support the new deposits, they have $64 of excess reserves. They now increase their loans by $64. After this money has been spent by the borrowers and has been deposited in other, third-generation banks, the balance sheets of the second-generation banks will have changed, as in Table 27-6.

The third-generation banks now find themselves with $64.00 of new deposits. Against these they want to hold only $12.80 in cash, so they have excess reserves of $51.20 that they can immediately lend out. Thus there begins a long sequence of new deposits, new loans, new deposits, and new loans. These stages are shown in Table 27-7. The series in the table should look familiar, for it is the same convergent process that we saw when we were dealing with the simple multiplier in Chapter 23.

TABLE 27-7
The Sequence of Loans and Deposits After a Single New Deposit of $100

Bank	New Deposits	New Loans	Addition to Reserves
IB&T	$100.00	$80.00	$20.00
2nd-generation bank	80.00	64.00	16.00
3rd-generation bank	64.00	51.20	12.80
4th-generation bank	51.20	40.96	10.24
5th-generation bank	40.96	32.77	8.19
6th-generation bank	32.77	26.22	6.55
7th-generation bank	26.22	20.98	5.24
8th-generation bank	20.98	16.78	4.20
9th-generation bank	16.78	13.42	3.36
10th-generation bank	13.42	10.74	2.68
Total for first 10 generations	446.33	357.07	89.26
All remaining generations	53.67	42.93	10.74
Total for banking system	500.00	400.00	100.00

The banking system as a whole can create deposit money whenever it receives new deposits. The table shows the process of the creation of deposit money on the assumptions that all the loans made by one set of banks end up as deposits in another set of banks (the next-generation banks), that the target reserve ratio (v) is 0.20, and that banks always lend out any excess reserves. Although each bank suffers a cash drain whenever it grants a new loan, the system as a whole does not, and in a series of steps it increases deposit money by $1/v$, which, in this example, is five times the amount of any increase in reserves that it obtains.

The banking system has created new deposits and thus new money, although each banker can honestly say, "All I did was invest my excess reserves. I can do no more than manage wisely the money that I receive." At the end of the process that is depicted in Table 27-7, the change in the combined balance sheets of the entire banking system is shown in Table 27-8.

If v is the reserve ratio, the ultimate effect on the deposits of the banking system of a new deposit will be $1/v$ times the new deposit.[3] [36]

Many New Deposits

A more realistic picture of deposit creation is one in which new deposits accrue simultaneously to all commercial banks, perhaps because of changes in the

---

[2]Note that even though the *banking system* suffers no cash drain (i.e., all the money that has been lent out is returned to the banking system as deposits), IB&T does suffer a cash drain (i.e., most of the $80 goes to other banks and is not redeposited at IB&T).

[3]The "multiple expansion of deposits" that has just been worked through applies in reverse to a withdrawal of funds. Deposits of the banking system will fall by $1/v$ times any amount withdrawn from one bank and not redeposited at another.

TABLE 27-8
**Change in the Combined Balance Sheets
of All the Banks in the System Following
the Multiple Expansion of Deposits**

Assets		Liabilities	
Cash and other reserves	+100	Deposits	+500
Loans	+400		
	+500		+500

The reserve ratio is returned to 0.20. The entire initial deposit of $100 ends up as reserves of the banking system. Therefore, deposits rise by (1/0.2) times the initial deposit, that is, by $500.

Bank of Canada's monetary policy. For example, suppose that a community contains 10 banks of equal size and that as a result of a purchase by the Bank of Canada of $1,000 worth of securities, each receives new deposits of $100 in cash. Now each bank is in the position shown in Table 27-4, and each can begin to expand deposits based on the $100 of excess reserves. (Each bank does this by granting loans to customers.)

Because each bank does one-tenth of the total banking business, an average of 90 percent of any newly created deposit will find its way into other banks as the customer pays other people in the community by cheque. This will represent a cash drain from the lending bank to the other banks. However, roughly 10 percent of each new deposit created by every other bank should find its way into any particular bank. All banks receive new cash, and all begin creating deposits simultaneously.

The expansion can go on, with each bank watching its own ratio of cash reserves to deposits, expanding deposits as long as the ratio exceeds 1:5 and ceasing when it reaches that figure. The process will come to a halt when each bank has created $400 in additional deposits, so that for each initial $100 cash deposit, there is now $500 in deposits backed by $100 in cash. In the absence of a cash drain from the banking system, the total change in deposits is given by

$$\text{Change in Deposits} = \frac{\text{Change in Reserves}}{\text{Reserve Ratio}}$$

The general rule, if there is no cash drain from the banking system, is that a banking system with a reserve ratio of v can change its deposits by $1/v$ times any change in reserves.

EXCESS RESERVES AND CASH DRAINS

The two simplifying assumptions that were made earlier can now be relaxed.

Excess Reserves

If banks do not choose to invest their excess reserves, the multiple expansion that we discussed will not occur. Go back to Table 27-4. If IB&T had been content to hold 27 percent in reserves, it might well have done nothing more. Other things being equal, banks will choose to invest their excess reserves because of the profit motive, but there may be times when they believe that the risk is too great. It is one thing to be offered a good rate of interest on a loan, but if the borrower defaults on the payment of interest and principal, the bank will be the loser. Similarly, if the bank expects interest rates to rise in the future, it may hold off making loans now so that it will have reserves available to make more profitable loans after the interest rate has risen.

Deposit creation does not happen automatically; it depends on the decisions of bankers. If banks do not choose to use their excess reserves to expand their investments, there will not be an expansion of deposits.

Recall that we have said that the money *supply* includes both currency and bank deposits. What we have just seen is that the behaviour of commercial banks is central to the process of deposit creation. It follows that the money supply is thus at least partly determined by the commercial banks—in response, for example, to changes in national income and interest rates. However, the *upper limit* of deposit creation is determined by the banks' target reserve ratio and by the reserves available to the banks (from the central bank), both of which are influenced by the Bank of Canada.

Cash Drain

Suppose that firms and households find it convenient to keep a fixed *fraction* of their money holding in cash (say, 5 percent) instead of a fixed *number* of dollars. In that case, an extra $100 in money supply will not all stay in the banking system—only $95 will remain on deposit, and the rest will be added to currency in circulation. In such a situation, any multiple expansion of bank deposits will be accompa-

TABLE 27-9
Change in the Combined Balance Sheets of All the Banks in the System Following the Multiple Expansion of Deposits with a Cash Drain

Assets		Liabilities	
Cash and other reserves	+80	Deposits	+400
Loans	+320		
	+400		+400

The reserve ratio is 0.20, and cash drain is 0.05. Only $80 of the initial deposit of $100 ends up as reserves of the banking system. Deposits therefore rise by (1/0.2) times the $80, that is, by $400. The cash drain ($20) is 5 percent of the increase in deposits ($400).

nied by a cash drain to the public that will reduce the maximum expansion below what it was when the public was content to hold all its new money as bank deposits.

The story of deposit creation when all banks receive new deposits and there is a cash drain to the public happens as follows. Each bank starts creating deposits and suffers no significant cash drain to other banks. However, because 5 percent of newly created deposits is now withdrawn to be held as cash, each bank suffers a cash drain to the public. The expansion continues, each bank watching its own ratio of cash reserves to deposits, expanding deposits as long as the ratio exceeds 1:5 and ceasing when it reaches that figure. Because the expansion is accompanied by a cash drain, it will come to a halt with a smaller deposit expansion than in the case of no cash drain.[4]

Table 27-9 shows the consolidated balance sheets of the banking system after the deposit expansion, arising from a new deposit of $100 when there is a cash drain. As shown, because there is a cash drain of $20, reserves rise by only $80 and deposits rise by only $400.

THE MONEY SUPPLY

Several times in this chapter we have mentioned the *money supply* without ever defining it precisely. But

now that you are familiar with the balance sheets of the Bank of Canada and the commercial banking system, and are comfortable with the idea of deposit creation by the commercial banks, we are ready to be more precise about what we mean by the money supply.

The total stock of money in the economy at any moment is called the **money supply** or the **supply of money.** Economists use several alternative definitions for the money supply, most of which are regularly reported in the *Bank of Canada Review*—a quarterly publication of the Bank of Canada. Each definition of the money supply includes the amount of currency in circulation *plus* some types of deposit liabilities of the financial institutions. The different definitions vary only by which deposit liabilities are included. We begin by looking at the different kinds of deposits.

KINDS OF DEPOSITS

Over the past 20 years or so, banks have evolved a bewildering array of different types of deposits. From our point of view, the most important distinction is between deposits that can be transferred by cheque, called "chequable," and those that cannot, called "nonchequable." Chequable deposits are media of exchange; nonchequable ones are not.

Until recently, the distinction lay between *demand deposits,* which earned little or no interest but were chequable, and *savings deposits,* which earned a higher interest return but were nonchequable.

Today, however, it is so easy to transfer funds from accounts that are technically nonchequable to other accounts that are chequable that the distinction becomes quite blurred. The deposit that is genuinely tied up for a period of time now takes the form of a **term deposit,** which has a specified withdrawal date, a minimum of 30 days into the future, and which pays a much reduced interest rate in the event of early withdrawal. Term and other nonchequable deposits pay significantly higher interest rates than do chequable deposits.

Nonbank financial institutions such as brokerage firms now offer **money market mutual funds** and **money market deposit accounts.** These accounts earn high interest and are chequable, although some are

---

[4]It can be shown algebraically that the percentage of cash drain must be added to the reserve ratio to determine the maximum possible expansion of deposits. [37]

subject to minimum withdrawal restrictions and others to prior notice of withdrawal.

The long-standing distinction between money and other highly liquid assets used to be that, narrowly defined, money was a medium of exchange that did not earn interest, whereas other liquid assets earned interest but were not media of exchange. Today, this distinction has almost completely broken down.

DEFINITIONS OF THE MONEY SUPPLY

Different definitions of the money supply include different types of deposits. The narrowly defined money supply, called **M1,** includes currency and deposits that are themselves usable as media of exchange (such as chequable deposits). A broader definition, **M2,** includes M1 plus savings accounts at the chartered banks. A still broader measure, **M2+,** includes M2 plus the deposits held at the financial institutions that are *not* chartered banks, such as trust companies and credit unions.

M1 concentrates on the medium-of-exchange function of money. M2 and M2+ contain assets that serve the temporary store-of-value function and are in practice quickly convertible into a medium of exchange at a known price ($1 on deposit in a savings account is always convertible into a $1 demand deposit or $1 in cash). Table 27-10 shows the principal elements in these definitions of the money supply. The details of the differences are not important at this stage; what matters is that, broadly defined, money comprises a spectrum of closely related financial assets that their holders regard as highly substitutable for each other.

NEAR MONEY AND MONEY SUBSTITUTES

Over the past two centuries, what has been accepted by the public as money has expanded from gold and silver coins to include bank notes and bank deposits subject to transfer by cheque. Until recently, most economists would have agreed that money stopped at that point. No such agreement exists today, and an important debate centres on the definition of money appropriate to present circumstances.

TABLE 27-10	
Three Measures of the Money Supply in Canada, October 1995	
(millions of dollars)	
Currency	25,999
+ Demand deposits	33,792
= **M1**	**59,791**
+ Personal saving deposits and nonpersonal notice deposits	322,105
= **M2**	**381,896**
+ Deposits at trust and mortgage loan companies, credit unions, and caisses populaires	153,875
+ Money market mutual funds and deposits at other institutions	77,613
= **M2+**	**613,384**

The three widely used measures of the money supply are M1, M2, and M2+. The narrowest definition, M1, concentrates on what can be used directly as media of exchange, and thus includes only currency and demand deposits. The broader definitions then add in deposits that serve the store-of-value function but can be readily converted to a medium of exchange. M2 is thus M1 plus saving deposits. M2+ is M2 plus deposits at the nonbank financial institutions. *(Source: Bank of Canada Review, Winter 1995–1996.)*

The problem of deciding what constitutes money arises because some assets may provide relatively poor ways to meet the store-of-value function whereas others may perform poorly as media of exchange. For example, during times of high inflation, currency may serve well as a medium of exchange but poorly as a store of value (because the rising price level erodes the purchasing power of cash). In contrast, heavy gold bars may serve well as a store of value but poorly as a medium of exchange (both because they are heavy and difficult to divide into small units).

If we concentrate only on the medium-of-exchange function of money, money certainly consists of the assets included in M1, and most economists would argue that it extends to those included in M2 and M2+. Some of these assets that are effective media of exchange, however, are poor stores of value because they earn little or no interest. Assets that earn higher interest—like term deposits—will do a better job of meeting the store-of-value function than will currency or demand deposits. At the same time, however, these other assets are less capable of fulfilling the medium-of-exchange function.

Assets that fulfill adequately the store-of-value function and are readily converted into a medium of exchange but are not themselves a medium of exchange are sometimes called **near money**. Deposits at a trust company are a characteristic form of near money. When you have such a deposit, you know exactly how much purchasing power you hold (at current prices), and, given modern banking practices, you can turn your deposit into a medium of exchange—cash or a chequing deposit—at a moment's notice. Furthermore, your deposit will earn some interest during the period that you hold it.

Why then does everybody not keep his or her money in such deposits instead of in demand deposits or currency? The answer is that the inconvenience of continually shifting money back and forth may outweigh the interest that can be earned. One week's interest on $100 (at 10 percent per year) is only about 20 cents, not enough to cover car fare to the bank or the cost of mailing a letter. For money that will be needed soon, it would hardly pay to shift it to a term deposit.

In general, whether it pays to convert cash or chequable deposits into higher interest-earning term deposits for a given period will depend on the inconvenience and other transactions costs of shifting funds and on the amount of interest that can be earned.

Things that serve as temporary media of exchange but are not a store of value are sometimes called **money substitutes**. Credit cards are a prime example. With a credit card, many transactions can be made without either cash or a cheque. The evidence of credit, the credit slip you sign and hand over to the store, is not money, because it cannot be used to make other transactions. The credit card serves the short-run function of a medium of exchange by allowing you to make purchases, even though you have no cash or bank deposit currently in your possession. But this is only temporary; money remains the final medium of exchange for these transactions when the credit account is settled.

CHOOSING A MEASURE

Since the eighteenth century, economists have known that the amount of money in circulation is an important economic variable. As theories became more carefully specified in the nineteenth and early twentieth centuries, they included a variable called the "money supply." But for theories to be useful (and especially for the predictions to be testable), we must be able to identify real-world counterparts of these theoretical variables.

What is included in the definition of money has changed and will continue to change over time. New monetary assets are continually being developed to serve some, if not all, the functions of money, and they are more or less readily convertible into money. There is no single, timeless definition of money and what is only near money or a money substitute. Indeed, as we have seen, our monetary authorities use several definitions of money, and these definitions change from year to year.

For the purposes of this book, we will focus on the medium-of-exchange function of money and hence define it to include currency plus deposits that can be withdrawn or transferred on very short notice.

THE ROLE OF THE BANK OF CANADA

In this chapter, we have seen that the commercial banking system, when confronted with a new deposit, can create a multiple expansion of bank deposits. This shows how the reserves of the banking system are systematically related to the money supply. We have also seen a glimpse of how the Bank of Canada can affect the reserves of the banking system—we will see in Chapter 29 that the Bank of Canada has almost complete control over these reserves. Thus the Bank of Canada controls reserves, and the commercial banking system turns those reserves into bank deposits.

This is the basis for the view taken throughout the remainder of this book that the Bank of Canada controls the money supply. In the next two chapters, we examine how the Bank uses this power to conduct monetary policy, and how monetary policy affects interest rates, national income, and the price level.

SUMMARY

A. THEORETICAL PERSPECTIVES ON MONEY

- Early economists regarded the economy as being divided into a real sector and a monetary sector. The real sector is concerned with production, allocation of resources, and distribution of income, determined by relative prices. The level of prices at which all transactions take place is determined by the monetary sector, that is, by the demand for and supply of money. With the demand for money being constant, an increase in the money supply would cause all equilibrium money prices to increase, but relative prices, and hence everything in the real sector, would be left unaffected.

- Today, most economists do not hold the view that changes in the money supply will only affect the price level, except as a description of the economy in long-run equilibrium. Most economists believe that changes in the supply of money have important short-run effects on real national income, employment, and unemployment.

B. THE NATURE OF MONEY

- Traditionally in economics, money has referred to any generally accepted medium of exchange. A number of functions of money may, however, be distinguished. Generally, money acts as a medium of exchange, a store of value, and a unit of account.

- Money arose because of the inconvenience of barter, and it developed in stages from precious metal to metal coinage to paper money convertible to precious metal to token coinage and paper money fractionally backed by precious metals to fiat money and to deposit money. Societies have shown great sophistication in developing monetary instruments to meet their needs.

C. THE CANADIAN BANKING SYSTEM

- The banking system in Canada consists of two main elements: the Bank of Canada (which is the central bank) and the commercial banks. The Bank of Canada is a publicly owned corporation that is responsible for the day-to-day conduct of monetary policy. Though the Bank has considerable autonomy in its policy decisions, ultimate responsibility for monetary policy resides with the government.

- Commercial banks are profit-seeking institutions that allow their customers to transfer demand deposits from one bank to another by means of cheques. They create money as a by-product of their commercial operations by making or liquidating loans and various other investments.

D. MONEY CREATION BY THE BANKING SYSTEM

- Because most customers are content to pay by cheque or debit card rather than with cash, banks need only small reserves to back their deposit liabilities. It is this *fractional-reserve* aspect of the banking system that enables commercial banks to create deposit money.

- When the banking system receives a new cash deposit, it can create new deposits to some multiple of this amount. The amount of new deposits created depends on the banks' target reserve ratio, the amount of cash drain to the public, and whether the banks choose to hold excess reserves.

E. THE MONEY SUPPLY

- The money supply—the stock of money in an economy at a specific moment—can be defined in various ways. M1, the narrowest definition, includes currency and chequable deposits. M2 includes M1 plus savings deposits and smaller term deposits. M2+ includes M2 plus deposits at non-bank financial institutions and money market mutual funds.

- Near money includes interest-earning assets that are convertible into money on a dollar-for-dollar basis but that are not currently included in the definition of money. Money substitutes are things such as credit cards that temporarily serve as a medium of exchange but are not money.

KEY CONCEPTS

The real and monetary sectors of the economy

Medium of exchange, store of value, and unit of account

Fully backed, fractionally backed, and fiat money

The banking system and the Bank of Canada

Target reserve ratio and excess reserves

The creation of deposit money

Demand and term deposits

The money supply

Near money and money substitutes

DISCUSSION QUESTIONS

1. "The love of money is the root of all evil" (I Timothy 6:10). If a nation were to become a theocracy in which money was illegal, would you expect the level of national income to be affected? How about the productivity of labour?

2. Consider each of the following with respect to its potential use as a medium of exchange, a store of value, and a unit of account. Which would you think might be regarded as money?

   a. A $100 Bank of Canada note
   b. An American Express charge card
   c. A painting by Picasso
   d. An interest-bearing savings account
   e. A treasury bill payable in three months
   f. A savings account with a trust company in London, Ontario
   g. One share of General Motors stock

3. When the Austrian government minted a new 1,000-schilling gold coin, worth $78 at face value, the 2.5-cm-diameter coin came into great demand among jewelers and coin collectors. By law, the number of such coins to be minted each year was limited. Lines of people eager to get the coins formed outside the government mint and local banks. "There is exceptional interest in the new coin," said a Viennese banker. "It's a numismatic hit and a financial success." However, it has disappeared from circulation. Explain why.

4. A Canadian who receives a U.S. coin has the option of spending it at face value or taking it to the bank and converting it to Canadian money at the going rate of exchange. When the rate of exchange was near par (in the early 1970s), so that $1 Canadian was within 3 cents of $1 U.S., U.S. and Canadian coins circulated side by side, exchanged at face value. Use Gresham's law to predict which coinage disappeared from circulation in Canada when the Canadian dollar fell to 75 cents U.S. Why did a 3-cent differential not produce this result?

5. During hyperinflations in several foreign countries after World War II, American cigarettes were sometimes used in place of money. What made them suitable?

6. Suppose that on January 1, 1996, a household had $100,000, which it wished to hold for use one year later. Calculate, using library sources, which of the following would have been the best store of value over that period. Will the best store of value over that

period necessarily be the best over the next 24 months?

   a. The (Canadian) dollar
   b. Stocks whose prices moved with the Toronto Stock Exchange (TSE) 300
   c. An Ontario Hydro 11.75 percent bond coming due in 2005
   d. Gold
   e. Silver

7. If all depositors tried to turn their deposits into cash at once, they would find that there are not sufficient reserves in the system to allow all of them to do this at the same time. Why then do we not still have panicky runs on the banks? Would it be better for the Bank of Canada to impose a 100 percent reserve requirement? What effect would such a reserve requirement have on the banking system's ability to create money? Would it preclude any possibility of a panic?

8. Compared to a few years ago, credit and bank cards are used extensively today to facilitate purchase of goods and services all over the world. Does this distort the true measure of money in the economy? Should credit and bank cards be incorporated in the definitions of M1 or M2?

9. An older gentleman was recently overheard speaking with his granddaughter. "I don't understand why the banks are offering so many different types of accounts. It's too confusing. Why not return to the good old days when you either had a chequing account or a savings account?" Can you answer him? What effect does the proliferation of different types of savings accounts have on the measures of money in the economy?

10. As we become more firmly entrenched in the information age, some people advocate eliminating Bank of Canada notes (and coins). Instead, everyone would be issued a "cash flow" card that would be accepted at all businesses. People would still be allowed to write cheques (for birthday cards and ballpark donations, etc.), but on presentation of the cheque, the amount of the cheque could be deducted from the cheque writer's cash flow card account by any business. Would this drastically alter the banking system? Would the banks necessarily have money available to lend? Would there be a need for reserve deposits? What kinds of social problems could arise?

11. What would be the effect on the money supply of each of the following?

    a. Declining public confidence in banks
    b. Banks' desire to increase their reserve ratios
    c. Increased use of credit cards
    d. Transfer of deposits from chartered banks to other financial institutions

28

THE ROLE OF MONEY IN MACROECONOMICS

In Chapter 27, we saw how commercial banks lend their excess reserves to create bank deposits. The banking system transforms a given amount of reserves into the nation's money supply. We concluded that chapter by saying that because the Bank of Canada can control the reserves in the banking system, the Bank of Canada effectively *controls* the nation's money supply. What we have not yet discussed, however, is how the Bank of Canada controls the reserves of the banking system. We leave that discussion until the next chapter when we discuss the details of monetary policy. For now, just think of the supply of money as being determined by the Bank of Canada.

In this chapter, we focus on how money affects the economy. To understand the role of money, we need to discuss the interaction of money supply and money demand. To examine the nature of money demand, we begin by examining how households decide to divide their total holdings of assets between money and interest-earning assets (which we call "bonds"). Once that is done, we put money supply and money demand together to examine *monetary equilibrium*. Only then can we ask how changes in the supply of money or in the demand for money affect the economy—interest rates, national income, and the price level.

We begin with a discussion of financial assets and interest rates. This material is essential to understand how households decide to divide their total assets between money and interest-earning bonds and is therefore needed to understand the demand for money.

UNDERSTANDING FINANCIAL ASSETS

At any moment, households have a stock of wealth that they hold in many forms. Some of it is money in the bank or in the wallet, some may be in treasury bills and bonds, and some may be in stocks and shares.[1]

To simplify our discussion, we will group wealth into just two categories, which we will call "money" and "bonds." By money we mean all assets that serve as a medium of exchange—that is, paper money, coins, and deposits on which cheques can be drawn. By bonds we mean all other forms of wealth; this includes interest-earning financial assets and claims on real capital. This simplification can take us quite a long way because it serves to emphasize the important distinction between interest-earning and non-interest-earning assets. For some issues, however, it is necessary to treat debt and claims on capital as distinct assets, in which case at least three categories—money, debt (bonds), and equity (stocks)—are used. For our purposes however, we continue with the simple division of wealth into either "money" or "bonds."

THE RATE OF INTEREST AND PRESENT VALUE

Recall from Extension 27-1 that a bond is a financial asset that promises to make one or more specified payments at specified dates in the future. The **present value** *(PV)* of any asset refers to the value now of the future payments to which the asset represents a claim.

Present value depends on the rate of interest because when we calculate present value, the interest rate is used to *discount* the future payments. This relationship between the rate of interest and present value can be seen by considering two extreme examples.

A Single Payment One Year Hence

We start with the simplest case. How much would someone be prepared to pay *now* to purchase a bond that will return a single payment of $100 in one year's time?

Suppose that the interest rate is 5 percent, which means that $1.00 invested today will be worth $1.05 in one year's time. Now ask how much someone would have to lend out in order to have $100 a year from now. If we use PV to stand for this unknown amount, we can write $PV \times (1.05) = \$100$. Thus $PV = \$100/1.05 = \$95.24$.[2] This tells us that the present value of a $100 receivable in one year's time is $95.24; anyone who lends out $95.24 for one year at 5 percent interest will get back the $95.24 plus $4.76 in interest, which makes $100.

What if the interest rate had been 7 percent? At that interest rate, the present value of the $100 receivable in one year's time would be $100/1.07 = $93.46, which is less than the present value when the interest rate was 5 percent.

A Perpetuity

Now consider another extreme case—a perpetuity that promises to pay $100 per year to its holder *forever*. The present value of the perpetuity depends on how much $100 per year is worth, and this again depends on the rate of interest.

A bond that will produce a stream of income of $100 per year forever is worth $1,000 at 10 percent

---

[1]At this time, you may find it helpful to review the discussion of the various types of financial assets in Extension 27-1.

[2]Notice that in this type of formula, the interest rate is expressed as a decimal fraction where, for example, 5 percent is expressed as 0.05, so $1 + i$ equals 1.05.

interest because $1,000 invested at 10 percent per year will yield $100 interest per year forever. However, the same bond is worth $2,000 when the interest rate is 5 percent per year because it takes $2,000 invested at 5 percent per year to yield $100 interest per year.

A General Statement

Similar relations apply to bonds that are more complicated than single payments but that are not perpetuities. Although in such cases the calculation of present value is more complicated, the same negative relationship between the interest rate and present value still holds.

The present value of any asset that yields a given stream of money over time is negatively related to the interest rate.

Further details on the calculation of present value are given in Extension 28-1.

PRESENT VALUE AND MARKET PRICE

Present value is important because it establishes the market price for an asset.

The present value of an asset is also the amount that someone would be willing to pay now to secure the right to the future stream of payments conferred by ownership of the asset.

To see this, let us return to our example of a bond that promises to pay $100 one year hence. When the interest rate is 5 percent, the present value is $95.24. To see why this is the maximum that anyone would pay for this bond, suppose that some sellers offer to sell the bond at some other price, say, $98. If, instead of paying this amount for the bond, a potential buyer lends its $98 out at 5 percent interest, it would have at the end of one year more than the $100 that the bond will produce. (At 5 percent interest, $98 yields $4.90 in interest, which when added to the principal makes $102.90.) Clearly, no well-informed individual would pay $98—or, by the same reasoning, any sum in excess of $95.24—for the bond.

Now suppose that the bond is offered for sale at a price less than $95.24, say, $90. A potential buyer could borrow $90 to buy the bond and would pay $4.50 in interest on the loan. At the end of the year, the bond yields $100. When this is used to repay the

$90 loan and the $4.50 in interest, $5.50 is left as profit. Clearly, it would be worthwhile for someone to buy the bond at the price of $90 or, by the same argument, at any price less than $95.24.

This discussion should make clear that the present value of an asset determines its market price. If the market price of any asset is greater than the present value of the income stream that it produces, no one will want to buy it, and this excess supply will push down the market price. If the market value is below its present value, there will be a rush to buy it, and this excess demand will push up the market price. These facts lead to the following conclusion:

In a free market, the equilibrium price of any asset will be the present value of the income stream that it produces.

THE RATE OF INTEREST AND THE MARKET PRICE

The foregoing discussion leads us to three important propositions. The first two stress the negative relationship between interest rates and asset prices:

1. If the rate of interest falls, the value of an asset producing a given income stream will rise.

2. A rise in the market price of an asset producing a given income stream is equivalent to a decrease in the rate of interest earned by the asset.

The first proposition is illustrated by the following example. When the interest rate is 8 percent, you would have to pay $92.59 now for a bond promising to pay you $100 one year from now ($92.59 × 1.08 = $100). When the interest rate is 12 percent, you would have to pay $89.29 for the same bond ($89.29 × 1.12 = $100).

The second proposition is illustrated as follows. If you buy for $89.29 a bond which promises to pay $100 one year from now, then your asset will earn a 12 percent rate of return. But if you must pay $92.59 for the same bond, the rate of return will be only 8 percent.

The third proposition focuses on the term to maturity of the bond:

3. The sooner the maturity date of a bond, the less the bond's value will change with a change in the rate of interest.

EXTENSION 28-1

CALCULATING PRESENT VALUE

An asset held now will generate returns in the future. What that stream of future income is worth now is called the asset's *present value (PV)*. In general, present value refers to the value *now* of one or more payments to be received in the future.

This box provides some details concerning the calculation of present value that will prove helpful for understanding the material in the text. If you have studied microeconomics first, some of this material will be familiar from Chapter 17.

THE PRESENT VALUE OF A SINGLE FUTURE PAYMENT

One Period Hence. The numerical examples given in the text are easy to generalize. In calculating the present value of a payment one year hence, we divided the sum that is receivable in the future by 1 plus the rate of interest. In general, the present value of R dollars one year hence at an interest rate of *i* per year is

$$PV = \frac{R}{(1 + i)}$$

Several Periods Hence. What happens to our calculation if the bond still offers a single future payment but the payment is receivable at a date later than one year from now? For example, what is the present value of $100 to be received *two* years hence

if the interest rate is 5 percent? This is $100/(1.05 × 1.05) = $90.70. We can check this by seeing what would happen if $90.70 were lent out for two years. In the first year, the loan would earn interest of 0.05 × $90.70 = $4.54, and hence after one year, the lender would receive $95.24. In the second year, the interest would be earned on this entire amount; interest earned in the second year would thus equal 0.05 × $95.24 = $4.76. So in two years, the lender would have $100. (Payment of interest in the second year on the interest income earned in the first year is called *compound interest*.)

In general, the present value of R dollars after *t* years at *i* percent is

$$PV = \frac{R}{(1 + i)^t}$$

This formula simply discounts the sum R by the interest rate *i* repeatedly—once for each of the *t* periods that pass until the sum becomes available. If we look at the formula, we see that the higher is *i* or *t*, the higher is the whole term $(1 + i)^t$. This term, however, appears in the denominator, indicating that *PV* is *negatively* related to both *i* and *t*. (Try manipulating the formula yourself with different numbers to see that this is the case.)

The formula $PV = R/(1 + i)^t$ shows that the present value of a given sum payable in the future will be

---

To see this, consider an extreme case. The present value of a bond that is redeemable for $1,000 in one week's time will be very close to $1,000 no matter what the interest rate is. Its value will not change much, even if the rate of interest leaps from 5 percent to 10 percent during that week. Note that the interest-earning assets included in our definition of money are so short term that their values remain unchanged when the interest rate changes.

As a second example, consider two bonds, one that promises to pay $100 next year and one that promises to pay $100 in 10 years. A rise in the interest rate from 8 to 12 percent will lower the value of

$100 payable in one year's time by 3.6 percent, but it will lower the value of $100 payable in 10 years' time by 37.9 percent.[3]

---

[3]The example assumes annual compounding. The first case is calculated from the numbers of the previous example: (92.58 − 89.29)/92.58 = 0.036 or 3.6 percent. The 10-year case uses the formula

$$\text{Present value} = \frac{\text{Principal}}{(1 + i)^t}$$

which gives $46.30 at 8 percent and $28.75 at 12 percent. The percentage fall in value is thus (46.30 − 28.75)/46.30 = 0.379 or 37.9 percent.

smaller the more distant the payment date and the higher the rate of interest.

THE PRESENT VALUE OF A SEQUENCE OF PAYMENTS

Suppose now that we wish to calculate the present value of a bond that promises a sequence of payments for a given number of periods. Let R_1, R_2, R_3, and so on represent the payment promised after period 1, period 2, period 3, and so on, and let the last period for which a payment is promised be period T.

The present value of a bond that produces a sequence of payments is just the sum of the present values of each of the payments.

If we also suppose that the interest rate remains constant at i percent, the present value of the bond can be written as follows:

$$PV = \frac{R_1}{1 + i} + \frac{R_2}{(1 + i)^2} + \frac{R_3}{(1 + i)^3} + \dots + \frac{R_T}{(1 + i)^T}$$

THE PRESENT VALUE OF A PERPETUAL STREAM OF PAYMENTS

Now, assuming an interest rate of 10 percent, consider the value that a buyer would place on a $100 perpetuity—that is, on a bond that produces a stream of payments of $100 a year *forever*. To find the present value of $100 payable every year in the future, we ask how much money would have to be invested now at an interest rate of 10 percent per year to obtain $100 every year in the future. This present value is simply $0.1 \times PV = \$100$, where PV is the sum required. In other words, $PV = \$100/0.1 = \$1,000$. This tells us that $1,000 invested at 10 percent interest forever would yield a constant stream of income of $100 per year; put the other way around, when the interest rate is 10 percent, the present value of $100 per year forever is $1,000.

To generalize for any interest rate, we merely write i for the interest rate and R for the revenue to be received each year. Now we wish to find the amount PV that, invested at i, will yield R per year forever. This is $i \times PV = R$, or

$$PV = \frac{R}{i}$$

Here, as before, PV is related to the rate of interest: The higher the interest rate, the less the present value of any stream of future receipts, and hence the lower the price that anyone would be prepared to pay to purchase the bond.

THE DEMAND FOR MONEY

The amount of wealth that everyone in the economy wishes to hold in the form of money balances is called the **demand for money**. Because households are choosing how to divide their given stock of wealth between money and bonds, it follows that if we know the demand for money, we also know the demand for bonds. With a *given level of wealth*, a rise in the demand for money necessarily implies a fall in the demand for bonds—for a given amount of wealth, if people wish to hold $1 billion more money, they must wish to hold $1 billion less of bonds. It also follows that if households are content with the fraction of their wealth they are holding in the form of money, they must also be content with the fraction of their wealth they are holding in the form of bonds.

When we say that on some particular date the quantity of money demanded was $375 billion, we mean that on that date the public wished to hold money balances that totaled $375 billion. But why do firms and households wish to hold money balances at all? There is a cost to holding any money balance because the money could have been used to purchase bonds, which earn higher interest than money.

The opportunity cost of holding any money balance is the extra interest that could have been earned if the money had been used instead to purchase bonds.

The opportunity cost of holding money is equal to the nominal rate of interest. Recall from Chapter 21 the distinction between real and nominal interest rates caused by the presence of inflation. However, because in this chapter we make the simplifying assumption that there is no ongoing inflation, the nominal and real rates of interest are the same; both are measured by the market rate of interest.

Clearly, money will be held only when it provides services that are valued at least as highly as the opportunity cost of holding it. Three important services that are provided by money balances give rise to three motives for holding money: the *transactions*, *precautionary*, and *speculative* motives. We examine each of these in detail.

THE TRANSACTIONS MOTIVE

Most transactions require money. Money passes from households to firms to pay for the goods and services produced by firms; money passes from firms to households to pay for the factor services supplied by households to firms. Money balances that are held to finance such flows are called **transactions balances.**

In an imaginary world in which the receipts and disbursements of households and firms were perfectly synchronized, it would be unnecessary to hold transactions balances. If every time a household spent $10 it received $10 as part payment of its income, no transactions balances would be needed. In the real world, however, receipts and disbursements are not perfectly synchronized.

Consider the balances that are held because of wage payments. Suppose, for purposes of illustration, that firms pay wages every Friday and that households spend all their wages on the purchase of goods and services, with the expenditure spread out evenly over the week. On Friday morning, firms must therefore hold balances equal to the weekly wage bill; on Friday afternoon, households will hold these balances.

Over the week, households' balances will be drawn down as a result of purchasing goods and ser-

vices. Over the same period, the balances held by firms will build up as a result of selling goods and services until, on the following Friday morning, firms will again have amassed balances equal to the wage bill that must be met that day.

What determines the size of the transactions balances to be held? It is clear that in our example total transactions balances vary with the value of the wage bill. If the wage bill doubles for any reason, the transactions balances held by firms and households for this purpose will also double. As it is with wages, so it is with all other transactions: The size of the balances held is positively related to the value of the transactions.

Next we ask how the total value of transactions is related to national income. Because there is a double-counting problem, which we first discussed in Chapter 22, the value of all transactions exceeds the value of the economy's final output. When the miller buys wheat from the farmer and when the baker buys flour from the miller, both are transactions against which money balances must be held, although only the value added at each stage is part of national income (rather than the total value of the product at each stage).

There is a positive relationship between transactions and national income. That is, a rise in national income leads to a rise in the total value of transactions and hence to an associated rise in the demand for transactions balances. This allows us to relate transactions balances to national income. [38]

The transactions motive arises because payments and receipts are not synchronized. The larger the value of national income, the more transactions are made and thus the larger will be the value of transactions balances.

THE PRECAUTIONARY MOTIVE

Many goods and services are sold on credit. The seller can never be certain when payment will be made, and the buyer can never be certain of the day of delivery and hence when payment will fall due. As a precaution against cash crises, when receipts are abnormally low or disbursements are abnormally high, firms and households carry money balances. **Precautionary balances** provide a cushion against uncertainty about the timing of cash flows. The larger are such balances, the greater is the protection against running out of money because of temporary fluctuations in cash flows.

The seriousness of the risk of a cash crisis depends on the costs of being caught without sufficient money balances. A firm is unlikely to be pushed into insolvency, but it may incur considerable costs if it is forced to borrow money at high interest rates to meet a temporary cash crisis.

The protection provided by a given quantity of precautionary balances depends on the volume of payments and receipts. A $100 precautionary balance provides a large cushion for a household whose volume of payments per month is $800 and a small cushion for a firm whose monthly volume is $25,000. For firms, fluctuations of the sort that create the need for precautionary balances tend to vary directly with the size of the firm's cash flow. To provide the same degree of protection as the value of transactions rises, more money is necessary. Since the value of transactions rises with national income, this implies that precautionary balances need to be higher when national income is higher.

The precautionary motive arises because households and firms are uncertain about the degree to which payments and receipts will be synchronized. Precautionary balances rise when national income rises.

THE SPECULATIVE MOTIVE

Firms and households hold some money to provide a hedge against the uncertainty inherent in fluctuating prices of other financial assets. Money balances held for this purpose are called **speculative balances**. This motive was first analyzed by John Maynard Keynes, and the classic modern analysis was made by Professor James Tobin of Yale University, the 1981 Nobel laureate in Economics.

When a household or a firm holds money balances, it forgoes the extra interest income that it could earn if it held bonds instead. However, market interest rates fluctuate, and so do the market prices of existing bonds (their present values depend on the interest rate). Because their prices fluctuate, bonds are a risky asset. Many households and firms do not like risk; they are said to be *risk-averse*.[4]

In choosing between holding money or holding bonds, wealth holders must balance the extra inter-

est income that they could earn by holding bonds against the risk that bonds carry. At one extreme, if a household or a firm holds all its wealth in the form of bonds, it earns extra interest on its entire wealth, but it also exposes its entire wealth to the risk of changes in the price of bonds. At the other extreme, if the household or firm holds all its wealth in the form of money, it earns less interest income, but it does not face the risk of unexpected changes in the price of bonds. Wealth holders usually do not take either extreme position. They hold part of their wealth as money and part of it as bonds—that is, they *diversify* their holdings.

The Influence of Wealth

Suppose that Ms. B. Smart elects to diversify her wealth by holding 5 percent of her wealth in money and the other 95 percent in bonds. If her wealth is $50,000, her demand for money will be $2,500. If her wealth increases to $60,000, her demand for money will rise to $3,000.

Although an individual's wealth may rise or fall rapidly, the total wealth of a society changes only slowly. For the analysis of short-term fluctuations in national income, the effects of changes in wealth are fairly small, and we shall ignore them for the present. Over the long term, however, variations in wealth can have a major effect on the demand for money.

The Influence of Interest Rates

Wealth that is held as cash or deposits earns little or no interest; hence the reduction in risk involved in holding money carries a cost in terms of forgone interest earnings. The speculative motive leads households and firms to add to their money holdings until the reduction in risk obtained by the last dollar added is just balanced (in each wealth holder's view) by the cost in terms of the interest forgone on that dollar.

When the rate of interest falls, the opportunity cost of holding money falls. This leads to more money being held both for the precautionary motive (to reduce risks caused by uncertainty about the flows of payments and receipts) and for the speculative motive (to reduce risks associated with fluctuations in the market price of bonds). When the rate of interest rises, the cost of holding money rises. This leads to less money being held for speculative and precautionary motives.

[4]A person is said to be risk averse when he or she prefers to receive a particular sum of money—say X dollars—*with certainty* to an uncertain sum of money which has the *expected value* equal to X dollars.

The speculative motive implies that the demand for money varies positively with wealth and negatively with the rate of interest.

REAL AND NOMINAL MONEY BALANCES

In referring to the demand for money, it is important to distinguish real from nominal values. Real values are measured in purchasing power units; nominal values are measured in money units.

First, consider the demand for money in real terms. This demand is the number of units of purchasing power that the public wishes to hold in the form of money balances. For example, in an imaginary one-product wheat economy, this would be measured by the number of bushels of wheat that could be purchased with the money balances held. In a more complex economy, it could be measured in terms of the number of "baskets of goods" represented by a price index, such as the Consumer Price Index, that could be purchased with the money balances held. When we speak of the demand for money in real terms, we speak of the amount demanded in constant dollars:

The real demand for money is the nominal quantity demanded divided by the price level.

For example, in the decade from 1984 to 1994, the *nominal* quantity of M1 balances held in Canada nearly doubled, from $28.9 billion to $57.3 billion. Over the same period, however, the price level, as measured by the CPI, rose from 92.4 to 130.7—an increase of 41.5 percent. Such increases in the price level imply that the increase in *real* money balances was less than the increase in nominal money balances. Expressed in constant 1984 dollars, *real* M1 increased from $28.9 billion to about $40.5 billion, an increase of 40.1 percent.

Our discussion has identified three fundamental determinants of the demand for real money balances—real national income, real wealth, and the interest rate. Notice that the real demand for money depends on, among other things, real national income; it is not influenced by the price level.

Now suppose that with the interest rate, real wealth, and real national income being held constant, the price level were to double. Because the demand for *real* money balances would be unchanged, the demand for *nominal* balances would have to double. If the public previously demanded $30 billion in nominal money balances, it will now demand $60 billion. The money balance of $60 billion at the new, higher price level represents exactly the same purchasing power as $30 billion at the old price level.

Other things being equal, the nominal demand for money balances varies in proportion to the price level; when the price level doubles, desired nominal money balances also double.

TOTAL DEMAND FOR MONEY

The preceding few pages have discussed the three motives for households and firms to hold money—the transactions motive, the precautionary motive, and the speculative motive. Together, these make up the total demand for money. But it is important to keep in mind that these three motives are not "visible" in any way—it is not possible to say that an individual, for example, is holding this amount of money for transactions purposes and that amount for precautionary purposes. All we can observe is that an individual is holding a given amount of money, and we view each of the three motives as being partially responsible for that individual's behaviour.

Figure 28-1 summarizes the influences of national income, the nominal rate of interest, and the price level—the three variables that account for most of the short-term variations in the nominal quantity of money demanded. The function relating money demanded to the rate of interest is often called the **liquidity preference (LP) function.** (It is also known as the *demand for money function.*)

MONETARY FORCES AND NATIONAL INCOME

We are now in a position to examine the relationship between money, on the one hand, and the equilibrium values of national income and the price level, on the other. The first step in explaining this relationship is a new one: the link between *monetary equilibrium* and aggregate demand. The second is familiar from earlier chapters: the effects of shifts in aggregate demand on equilibrium values of national income and the price level.

Before we introduce the concept of monetary equilibrium, let us briefly review what we have learned about money supply (in the previous chapter) and money demand (in this chapter).

The money supply is a stock. It is so many billions of dollars *at a point in time*—it is *not* a flow of so much per unit of time. (This important distinction between

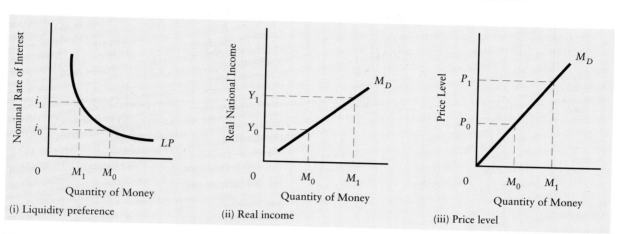

FIGURE 28-1

The Demand for Money as a Function of Interest Rates, Income, and the Price Level

(i) Liquidity preference

(ii) Real income

(iii) Price level

The quantity of money demanded varies negatively with the nominal rate of interest and positively with both real national income and the price level. In part (i), the demand for money is shown varying negatively with the nominal interest rate along the liquidity preference function. When the interest rate rises from i_0 to i_1, households and firms reduce the quantity of money demanded from M_0 to M_1.

In part (ii), the demand for money varies positively with national income. When national income rises from Y_0 to Y_1, households and firms increase the quantity of money demanded from M_0 to M_1.

In part (iii), the demand for money varies in proportion to the price level (hence the line is a ray from the origin). When the price level doubles from P_0 to P_1, households and firms double the quantity of money demanded from M_0 to M_1.

stocks and flows was examined in Extension 4-1.) In October 1995, the supply of money as measured by M2 was approximately $382 billion (see Table 27-10). We saw in Chapter 27 that the money supply is a measure of currency plus bank deposits, and we saw that commercial banks create deposits, but only within limits set by their reserves. Because the reserves of the banking system are under the control of the Bank of Canada, ultimate control of the money supply is also in the hands of the Bank. As we said above, in this chapter we simply assume that the money supply can be controlled by the Bank of Canada, although, as we shall see in Chapter 29, that control is actually imperfect.

Money demand is also a stock—at a given point in time, firms and households would like to hold some amount of their assets in the form of money. The amount of money they would like to hold depends on real national income, interest rates, and the price level.

MONETARY EQUILIBRIUM AND AGGREGATE DEMAND

Monetary equilibrium occurs when the demand for money equals the supply of money. In Chapter 4,

we saw that in a competitive market for some commodity the price will adjust so as to establish equilibrium—where quantity demanded equals quantity supplied. In the market for money, the interest rate is that "price" which adjusts to bring about equilibrium.

In this section we first examine how the demand for money and the supply of money interact to determine the interest rate—this is the *liquidity preference theory of interest*. We then examine how "shocks" in the money market—changes in either the demand for or the supply of money—feed through to affect aggregate demand. This is the *transmission mechanism*.

The Liquidity Preference Theory of Interest

Figure 28-2 shows how the interest rate will change to equate the demand for money with its supply. When a single household or firm finds that it has less money than it wishes to hold, it can sell some bonds and add the proceeds to its money holdings. This transaction simply redistributes given supplies of bonds and money among individuals; it does not change the total supply of either money or bonds.

FIGURE 28-2
The Liquidity Preference Theory of Interest

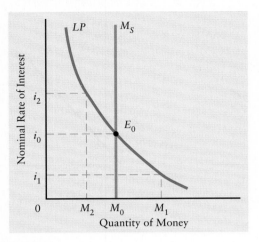

The interest rate rises when there is an excess demand for money and falls when there is an excess supply of money. The fixed quantity of money M_0 is shown by the completely inelastic supply curve M_S. The demand for money is given by LP; its negative slope indicates that a fall in the rate of interest causes the quantity of money demanded to increase. Monetary equilibrium is at E_0, with a rate of interest of i_0.

If the interest rate is i_1, there will be an excess demand for money of $M_0 M_1$. Bonds will be offered for sale in an attempt to increase money holdings. This will force the rate of interest up to i_0 (the price of bonds falls), at which point the quantity of money demanded is equal to the fixed available quantity of M_0. If the interest rate is i_2, there will be an excess supply of money $M_2 M_0$. Bonds will be demanded in return for excess money balances. This will force the rate of interest down to i_0 (the price of bonds rises), at which point the quantity of money demanded is equal to the fixed supply of M_0.

Now suppose that all of the firms and households in the economy have excess demands for money balances. They all try to sell bonds to add to their money balances, but what one person can do, all persons cannot do simultaneously. At any moment, the economy's total supply of money and bonds is fixed; there is just so much money, and there are just so many bonds in existence. If everyone tries to sell bonds, there will be no one to buy them, and this excess supply of bonds will cause their price to fall.

We saw earlier that a fall in the price of bonds means a rise in the rate of interest. As the interest rate rises, people economize on money balances because the opportunity cost of holding such balances is rising. This is what we saw in Figure 28-1(i), where the quantity of money demanded falls along the liquidity preference curve in response to a rise in the rate of interest. Eventually, the interest rate will rise enough that people will no longer be trying to add to their money balances by selling bonds. At that point, there is no longer an excess supply of bonds, and the interest rate will stop rising. The demand for money again equals the supply.

Suppose now that firms and households hold larger money balances than they would like. A single household or firm would simply purchase bonds with its excess balances. However, just as in the previous example, what one household or firm can do, all cannot do simultaneously. At any moment, the total quantity of bonds is fixed, so everyone cannot simultaneously add to personal bond holdings. When all households enter the bond market and try to purchase bonds with unwanted money balances, they bid up the price of existing bonds, and the interest rate falls. Hence households and firms become willing to hold larger quantities of money; that is, the quantity of money demanded increases along the liquidity preference curve in response to a fall in the rate of interest. The interest rate falls until firms and households stop trying to convert bonds into money. In other words, it continues until everyone is content to hold the existing supply of money and bonds.

Monetary equilibrium occurs when the rate of interest is such that the quantity of money demanded equals the quantity of money supplied.

The determination of the interest rate depicted in Figure 28-2 is often called the *liquidity preference theory of interest*. This name reflects the fact that a demand to hold money (rather than bonds) is a demand for the more liquid of the two assets—a preference for liquidity. Due to the emphasis on the firms' and households' decision to hold bonds versus money—which is essentially a portfolio decision—this theory is also sometimes called the *portfolio balance theory*.

As we shall see, a monetary disturbance or shock—a change in either the demand for money or the supply of money—will lead to a change in the interest rate. However, as we saw in Chapter 23, changes in the interest rate lead to changes in desired aggregate expenditure, especially investment expenditure. Here, then, is a link between monetary factors and real expenditure flows.

The Transmission Mechanism

The mechanism by which changes in the demand for and supply of money affect aggregate demand is called the **transmission mechanism**. The transmission mechanism operates in three stages: The first is the link between monetary equilibrium and the interest rate, the second is the link between the interest rate and investment expenditure, and the third is the link between investment expenditure and aggregate demand. For purposes of this discussion, we assume there is no inflation. This assumption implies that real and nominal interest rates are the same.

From Monetary Disturbances to Changes in the Interest Rate. The interest rate will change if the equilibrium depicted in Figure 28-2 is disturbed by a change in either the supply of money or the demand for money. For example, as shown in Figure 28-3(i), an increase in the supply of money, with an unchanged

liquidity preference function, will give rise to an excess supply of money at the original interest rate. As we have seen, an excess supply of money leads firms and households to attempt to buy bonds, thus driving up the price of bonds and pushing down the interest rate. As also shown in Figure 28-3(i), a decrease in the supply of money will cause the interest rate to rise.

As shown in Figure 28-3(ii), an increase in the demand for money, with an unchanged supply of money, will give rise to an excess demand for money at the original interest rate. Firms and households try to acquire more money by selling their holdings of bonds. This drives down the price of bonds and pushes up the interest rate. As also shown in part (ii) of Figure 28-3, a decrease in the demand for money will cause the interest rate to fall.

Monetary disturbances, which can arise from changes in either the demand for or the supply of money, cause changes in the interest rate.

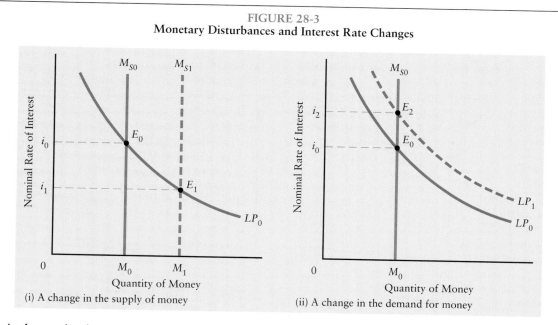

FIGURE 28-3
Monetary Disturbances and Interest Rate Changes

(i) A change in the supply of money

(ii) A change in the demand for money

Shifts in the supply of money or in the demand for money cause the equilibrium interest rate to change. In both parts of the figure, the money supply is shown by the vertical curve M_{S0}, and the demand for money is shown by the negatively sloped curve LP_0. The initial monetary equilibrium is at E_0, with corresponding interest rate i_0.

In part (i), an increase in the money supply causes the money supply curve to shift to the right, from M_{S0} to M_{S1}. The new equilibrium is at E_1, where the interest rate is i_1. Starting at E_1, with M_{S1} and i_1, it can be seen that a decrease in the money supply to M_{S0} leads to an increase in the interest rate from i_1 to i_0.

In part (ii), an increase in the demand for money causes the LP curve to shift to the right from LP_0 to LP_1. The new monetary equilibrium occurs at E_2, and the new equilibrium interest rate is i_2. Starting at E_2, we see that a decrease in the demand for money from LP_1 to LP_0 leads to a decrease in the interest rate from i_2 to i_0.

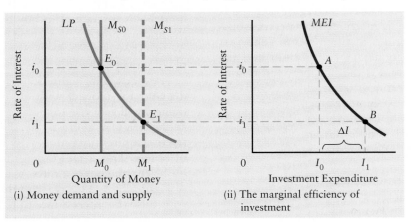

FIGURE 28-4
The Effects of Changes in the Money Supply on Investment Expenditure

Increases in the money supply reduce the rate of interest and increase desired investment expenditure. Equilibrium in the money market, in panel (i), is at E_0, with a quantity of money of M_0 (shown by the inelastic money supply curve M_{S0}), and an interest rate of i_0. The corresponding level of investment expenditure is I_0 (point A) in panel (ii). The Bank of Canada then increases the money supply to M_1 (shown by the money supply curve M_{S1}). This lowers the rate of interest to i_1 and increases investment expenditure by ΔI to I_1 (point B). A reduction in the money supply from M_1 to M_0 raises interest rates from i_1 to i_0 and lowers investment expenditure by ΔI, from I_1 to I_0.

From Changes in the Interest Rate to Shifts in Aggregate Expenditure. The second link in the transmission mechanism relates interest rates to desired aggregate expenditure. We saw in Chapter 23 that investment, which includes expenditure on inventory accumulation, residential construction, and business fixed investment, responds to changes in the real rate of interest. Other things being equal, a decrease in the real rate of interest makes borrowing cheaper and generates new investment expenditure.[5] This negative relationship between investment and the rate of interest is called the **marginal efficiency of investment (MEI) function.**

The first two links in the transmission mechanism are shown in Figure 28-4. We concentrate for the moment on changes in the money supply, although, as we have seen already, the process can also be set in motion by changes in the demand for money. In part (i), we see that a change in the money supply causes the rate of interest to change in the opposite direction. In part (ii), we see that a change in the interest rate causes the level of investment expenditure to change in the opposite direction. Therefore, changes in the money supply cause investment expenditure to change in the same direction.

An increase in the money supply leads to a fall in the interest rate and an increase in investment expenditure. A decrease in the money supply leads to a rise in the interest rate and a decrease in investment expenditure.

From Shifts in Aggregate Expenditure to Shifts in Aggregate Demand. Now that we see how monetary disturbances lead to shifts in desired aggregate expenditure, we are back on familiar ground. In Chapter 25, we saw that a shift in the aggregate expenditure curve (caused by something *other than* a change in the price level) leads to a shift in the *AD* curve. This is shown again in Figure 28-5.

A change in the money supply, by causing a change in desired investment expenditure and hence a shift in the *AE* curve, causes the *AD* curve to shift.

[5]In Chapter 23, we saw that purchases of durable consumer goods also respond to changes in the real interest rate. In this chapter, we concentrate on investment expenditure, which may be taken to stand for all interest-sensitive expenditure, and we maintain our simplifying assumption that inflation is zero so that the real and nominal interest rates are equal.

FIGURE 28-5
The Effects of Changes in the Money Supply on Aggregate Demand

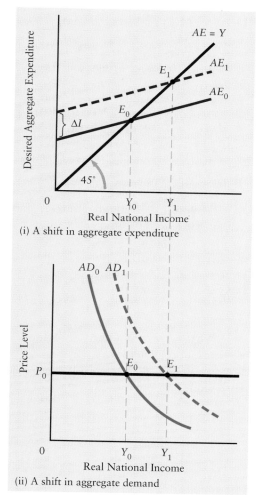

(i) A shift in aggregate expenditure

(ii) A shift in aggregate demand

Changes in the money supply cause shifts in the aggregate expenditure and aggregate demand functions. In Figure 28-4, an increase in the money supply increased desired investment expenditure by ΔI. In part (i) of this figure, the aggregate expenditure function shifts up by ΔI (which is the same as ΔI in Figure 28-4), from AE_0 to AE_1. At the fixed price level P_0, equilibrium income rises from Y_0 to Y_1, as shown by the horizontal shift in the aggregate demand curve from AD_0 to AD_1 in part (ii).

When the supply of money falls (from M_{S1} to M_{S0} in Figure 28-4), investment falls by ΔI, thereby shifting aggregate expenditure from AE_1 to AE_0. At the fixed price level P_0, this shifts the AD curve to the left and reduces equilibrium income from Y_1 to Y_0.

An increase in the money supply causes an increase in investment expenditure and therefore an increase in aggregate demand. A decrease in the money supply causes a decrease in investment expenditure and therefore a decrease in aggregate demand.

The transmission mechanism connects monetary forces and real expenditure flows. It works from a change in the demand for or the supply of money to a change in bond prices and interest rates, to a change in investment expenditure, to a shift in the aggregate demand curve.

This is illustrated in Figure 28-6 for the case of an expansionary monetary shock—that is, a shift in money

FIGURE 28-6
Transmission Mechanism for an Expansionary Monetary Shock

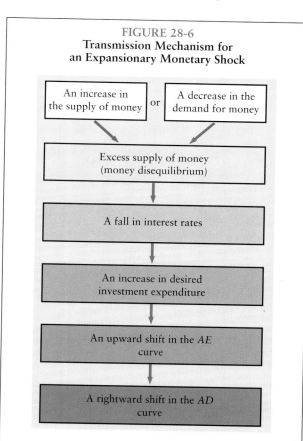

An increase in the supply of money or a decrease in the demand for money leads to an increase in aggregate demand. The excess supply of money following an expansionary monetary disturbance leads to a fall in the interest rate and an increase in investment. This causes an upward shift in the AE curve and thus a rightward shift in the AD curve.

THE OPEN ECONOMY TRANSMISSION MECHANISM*

The text focuses on the interest rate as the channel through which the effects of changes in the money supply are transmitted to the economy. However, the openness of the economy to international trade and to the flows of financial capital means that two additional complications must be allowed for. First, the effects of monetary contraction or expansion are weakened because Canadian interest rates are closely linked to interest rates in the rest of the world; this restricts the scope for domestic interest rates to change in response to changes in the money supply. Second, there is an added channel through which the effects of monetary policy are transmitted to real aggregate demand. This is through changes in the external value of the Canadian dollar.

THE LINK BETWEEN INTEREST RATES AND THE EXTERNAL VALUE OF THE DOLLAR

Suppose the Bank of Canada decides to reduce the supply of money in Canada. This has the effect of raising Canadian interest rates relative to those in other countries. These high Canadian interest rates make Canadian interest-earning assets attractive relative to similar assets available in other countries, and thus the demand for Canadian assets will rise, both by Canadians and by foreigners. Furthermore, to purchase these assets, foreigners need to buy Canadian dollars—this demand for Canadian dollars on the foreign exchange market will increase the external value of the Canadian dollar (the Canadian dollar will *appreciate*).

An increase in the money supply which reduces Canadian interest rates will have the opposite effect on the external value of the Canadian dollar. The lower Canadian interest rates make foreign interest-earning assets more attractive than Canadian ones. Canadians will want to purchase foreign assets, and foreigners will be less eager to purchase Canadian assets. Foreigners will demand fewer Canadian dollars, and people in Canada will be selling more dollars to obtain the foreign currencies required to purchase higher-yielding foreign assets. This will reduce the external value of the Canadian dollar (the Canadian dollar will *depreciate*.)

Other things being equal, the higher are Canadian interest rates, the higher will be the external value of the dollar. The lower are Canadian interest rates, the lower will be the external value of the dollar.†

This *positive* relationship between interest rates and the external value of the dollar is often featured in newspaper and television discussions. For example, an increase in the external value of the Canadian

---

*This box addresses issues that will be discussed in much more detail in Chapters 37 and 38. It can be omitted now without any loss of continuity.

†Specifically, we are holding constant all things other than the interest rate which influence the public's demand for Canadian assets, such as the public perception of risk associated with Canadian assets. We are therefore considering changes in interest rates that are caused only by changes in money supply rather than by changes in money demand. When the demand for assets changes, it is possible to get the reverse relationship between interest rates and the external value of the dollar. For example, immediately prior to the Quebec referendum in October 1995, the political uncertainty in Canada led many foreigners to sell off their holdings of Canadian interest-earning assets. This reduction in the demand for those assets led to a fall in their price and a rise in interest rates. Furthermore, as these foreigners sold their Canadian dollars for foreign currencies, there was a *reduction* in the external value of the dollar.

---

demand or in money supply that tends to reduce interest rates and increase aggregate demand. Details on how the transmission mechanism is modified in an open economy are presented in Extension 28-2.

(Extension 28-2 is advanced material and can be skipped now without any loss of continuity. This material will also be covered in detail in Chapter 38 where we examine macroeconomic policy in open economies.)

dollar, say from 74 cents U.S. to 76 cents U.S., might be the result of actions taken by the U.S. Federal Reserve Board to increase the U.S. money supply. Such a monetary expansion in the United States lowers U.S. interest rates and thus makes Canadian interest-earning assets relatively more attractive. This increases the demand for Canadian assets and so generates an increase in demand for the Canadian dollar, leading to a rise in its external value.

THE TRANSMISSION MECHANISM

Now that you understand the relationship between interest rates and the external value of the dollar, consider the entire transmission mechanism in an open economy. To begin, suppose that the Bank of Canada increases the Canadian money supply. The initial effects will be exactly the same as in the closed economy analyzed in the text. The excess supply of money leads firms and households to attempt to buy bonds. Ths will cause Canadian interest rates to fall.

It is at this point that open economy forces come into play. As Canadian interest rates fall, foreigners and Canadian citizens will start to sell Canadian assets to purchase foreign assets that now earn interest rates higher than those prevailing in Canada. Because people are selling Canadian-dollar assets, the fall in Canadian interest rates is mitigated. In this way, Canadian interest rates are constrained by those abroad; the availability of interest-earning assets in foreign currencies that investors consider substitutes for Canadian securities implies that Canadian interest rates do not move as much in response to changes in the money supply as they would in a closed economy. People who have sold their Canadian-dollar assets will now wish to sell Canadian dollars to buy foreign currency, which they will then use to purchase foreign assets. This reduces the external value of the Canadian dollar.

How are these changes in the interest rate and the external value of the dollar transmitted into changes in the level of economic activity? The reduced response of interest rates to monetary policy implies less effect, for a given change in the money supply, on interest-sensitive expenditures. However, the induced changes in the external value of the dollar add a new channel by which monetary policy is transmitted to the economy. As we saw in Chapter 24, a reduction in the external value of the Canadian dollar, other things being equal, makes Canadian-produced goods more competitive on world markets and thus increases exports and decreases imports.

Because an increase in the money supply leads to a reduction in the external value of the dollar, it stimulates net exports and thereby raises aggregate demand. Similarly, a decrease in the money supply will lower aggregate demand because it leads to an increase in the external value of the dollar and hence to a fall in net exports.

In a closed economy, monetary policy operates through changes in the interest rate influencing desired investment expenditure as well as any interest-sensitive consumption expenditures; in an open economy, that channel is weakened, but the effects on aggregate demand are reinforced through the effects of changes in the exchange rate on net exports. Though the channels are different, the ability of monetary policy to affect national income remains. In the rest of this chapter, we maintain the closed-economy analysis for simplicity; we return to the open-economy issues in Chapters 37 and 38.

AGGREGATE DEMAND, THE PRICE LEVEL, AND NATIONAL INCOME

We have just seen that a change in the money supply shifts the aggregate demand curve. If we want to know what it does to real national income and to the price level, we need to know the slope of the aggregate supply curve. This step, which is

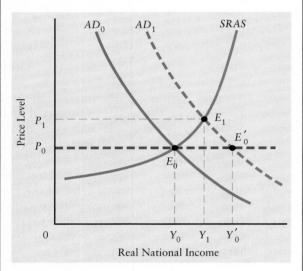

FIGURE 28-7
The Effects of Changes in the Money Supply

A change in the money supply leads to a change in national income that is smaller than the horizontal shift in the *AD* curve. An increase in the money supply causes the *AD* curve to shift to the right, from AD_0 to AD_1. With the price level being held constant, national income would rise from Y_0 to Y'_0. With the upward-sloping *SRAS* curve, income rises only to Y_1 while the price level rises as well—to P_1.

familiar from earlier chapters, is reviewed in Figure 28-7.[6]

The key result is that the increase in equilibrium real income is less than the horizontal shift in the *AD* curve. This is true because part of this shift is dissipated by a rise in the price level: Because the *AD* curve is negatively sloped, the rise in the price level means that the rise in real output is smaller than the horizontal shift of the *AD* curve. (If you draw the graph, you will see that if the *AD* curve were vertical, the rise in the price level would not diminish the effect on real output; real output would rise by an

amount equal to the horizontal shift of the *AD* curve.)

Another Look at the Slope of the *AD* Curve

We can now use the transmission mechanism to add to the explanation (given in Chapter 25) of the negative slope of the *AD* curve—that is, to explain why equilibrium national income is negatively related to the price level. In Chapter 25, when we explained the negative slope of the *AD* curve, we mentioned two reasons: the wealth effect and the substitution of domestic for foreign goods. But there is also a third, indirect effect operating through interest rates. And we are now in a position to understand this indirect effect.

The essential feature of this indirect effect is that a rise in the price level raises the money value of transactions. This leads to an increased demand for money, which brings the transmission mechanism into play. People try to sell bonds to add to their money balances; but, collectively, all they succeed in doing is forcing up the interest rate. The rise in the interest rate then reduces desired investment expenditure and so reduces equilibrium national income.

This effect is important because, empirically, the interest rate is the most important link between monetary factors and real expenditure flows. This reason for the negative slope of the *AD* curve is discussed in more detail in the appendix to this chapter.

More on the Adjustment Mechanism

In Chapter 26, we saw that there is an adjustment mechanism in the economy that eventually stops any inflation caused by a one-time demand shock. As shown in part (ii) of Figure 26-2, this mechanism operates by the increase in price causing a movement up and to the left along the *AD* curve, thus returning output to its potential level and removing the inflationary gap.

In this chapter, we introduced an additional reason for the *AD* curve to be negatively sloped. The transmission mechanism implies that a rise in the price level leads to a rise in interest rates and a fall in investment expenditure. This additional effect reinforces the adjustment mechanism. An increase in the price level following a demand shock still leads to a movement up and to the left along the *AD* curve; in

---

[6]Because the demand for money in general will depend on the level of national income, as shown in Figure 28-1(ii), our analysis at this stage is incomplete. The induced change in equilibrium national income will lead to a shift in the liquidity preference function in Figure 28-2. For simplicity, we assume for now that the demand for money function does not shift in response to a change in national income.

the expanded model of this chapter, some of the reduction in aggregate expenditure is now accounted for by a fall in investment.

We can now restate the basic proposition from Chapter 26 *and identify an important qualification:*

A sufficiently large rise in the price level will eliminate any inflationary gap, *provided that the nominal money supply remains constant.*

The adjustment operates through the transmission mechanism linking money to the price level. This mechanism is the reason that the price level and the money supply have been linked for so long in economics; it is also the reason for the qualification about the money supply remaining constant. Many things can cause the price level to rise for some time. Yet whatever the reason for the rise, unless the money supply is expanded, the increase in the price level sets up forces that will remove the initial inflationary gap and so bring inflation caused by excess aggregate demand to a halt.

Frustration of the Adjustment Mechanism. The self-correcting mechanism for removing an inflationary gap can be frustrated indefinitely if the money supply is increased at the same rate that prices are rising. Suppose that the price level is rising by 10 percent per year under the pressure of a large inflationary gap. Demand for nominal money balances will also be rising by about 10 percent per year. Now suppose that the Bank of Canada increases the money supply by 10 percent per year. No excess demand for money will develop because the extra money needed to meet the rising demand will be forthcoming. The interest rate will not rise, and the inflationary gap will not be reduced on this account. This process is analyzed in Figure 28-8.

If the money supply increases at the same rate as the price level rises, the real money supply and hence the real interest rate will remain constant, and the adjustment mechanism will be frustrated.

Inflation is said to be *validated* when the money supply is increased as fast as the price level, frustrating the adjustment mechanism. Validated inflation can go on indefinitely, although, as we shall see in Chapter 30, not at a constant rate.

A Recessionary Gap. In principle, the adjustment mechanism will also operate to eliminate a re-

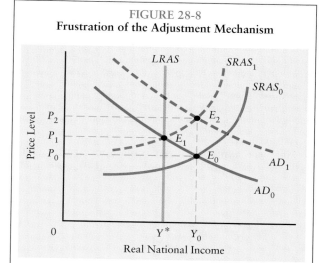

FIGURE 28-8
Frustration of the Adjustment Mechanism

An inflationary gap can persist indefinitely if the money supply increases as fast as the price level. Suppose that the economy is at E_0, with income Y_0 and price level P_0. Because potential income is Y^*, there is an inflationary gap of Y^*Y_0. The price level now rises, which tends to shift the economy upward along any given AD curve, thereby tending to reduce aggregate demand. However, the Bank of Canada increases the money supply so that the AD curve shifts outward, thereby tending to increase aggregate demand. If the two forces just balance each other, by the time the price level has risen to P_2, the curve will have shifted to AD_1, leaving the inflationary gap unchanged, with equilibrium at E_2.

cessionary gap. If the recessionary gap were to lead to a fall in wages and other factor prices, the $SRAS$ curve would shift to the right, causing the price level to fall and national income to rise. However, as we saw in Chapter 26, many economists argue that wages are slow to fall in the face of a recessionary gap. (This was referred to as the second asymmetry of aggregate supply.) In this circumstance, the adjustment mechanism will not be effective in causing national income to return quickly to its potential level. This is one reason why many economists argue that aggregate demand should be stimulated in the face of a persistent recessionary gap, either through fiscal policy, which we studied in Chapter 26, or through monetary policy. However, this view is challenged by other economists; we will study this debate in Chapter 29.

THE STRENGTH OF MONETARY FORCES

How much will a given change in the money supply cause national income to change? Because a change in the money supply affects national income by causing the *AD* curve to shift, we know from the analysis developed earlier in this chapter (which in turn built on that in Chapter 26) that it is important to distinguish between the effects on national income in the long run and in the short run.

LONG-RUN EFFECTS ON NATIONAL INCOME

We have seen that the adjustment mechanism operates to ensure that regardless of the size of the money supply, real national income eventually converges to its potential level. The operation of this adjustment mechanism following an increase in the money supply is illustrated in Figure 28-9.

Although a change in the money supply causes the *AD* curve to shift, it has no effect on the level of national income in the long run.

Figure 28-9, which essentially reproduces the analysis of part (i) of Figure 26-4, also shows that the only long-run effect of a shift in the *AD* curve following a change in the money supply is a change in the price level. This result is often referred to as the *neutrality of money,* as discussed at the beginning of Chapter 27.

SHORT-RUN EFFECTS ON NATIONAL INCOME

We now focus on the effects of a change in the money supply on the short-run equilibrium level of national income. As shown in Figure 28-8, this will depend on both aggregate demand and aggregate supply.

The Role of Aggregate Demand

The size of the shift in the *AD* curve in response to an increase in the money supply depends on the size of the increase in investment expenditure that is stimulated. This in turn depends on the strength of

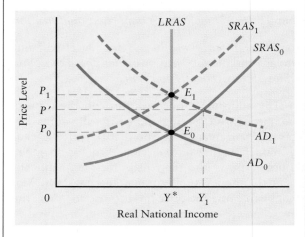

FIGURE 28-9
The Long-Run Effect of an Increase in the Money Supply

An increase in the money supply leads to a rightward shift in the *AD* curve, but because it has no effect on potential income, in the long run it has no effect on national income and results only in a change in the price level. The economy is initially in equilibrium at E_0, with price level P_0 and real national income Y^*. An increase in the money supply causes the *AD* curve to shift rightward from AD_0 to AD_1. National income rises to Y_1, and the price level rises to P'. The inflationary gap of Y^*Y_1 sets the adjustment mechanism in action, driving up wages and causing the *SRAS* curve to shift up and to the left. The process comes to a halt when national income has returned to its potential level, Y^*, thus eliminating the inflationary gap, and the price level has increased to P_1.

the two key linkages that make up the transmission mechanism.

The first consideration is how much interest rates fall in response to an increase in the money supply. Interest rates must fall to induce households and firms to hold the increased amount of money. The more interest sensitive the demand for money (i.e., the flatter is the *LP* curve), the less interest rates must fall.

The second consideration is how much investment expenditure increases in response to the fall in interest rates. Desired investment expenditure increases in response to a fall in the interest rate. The more interest sensitive desired investment expenditure (i.e., the flatter is the *MEI* curve), the greater the response will be.

It follows that the size of the shift of the *AD* curve in response to a change in the money supply

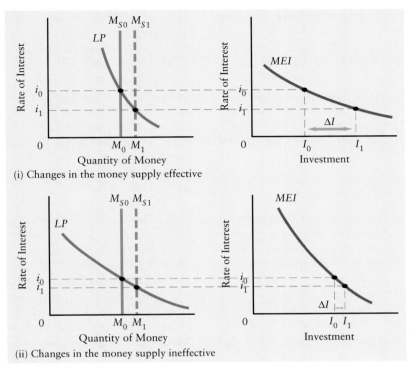

The strength of the effect of a change in the money supply on investment and hence on aggregate demand depends on the interest elasticity of both the demand for money and desired investment expenditure. Initially in parts (i) and (ii), the money supply is M_{S0}, and the economy has an interest rate of i_0 and investment expenditure of I_0. The central bank then expands the money supply from M_{S0} to M_{S1}. The rate of interest thus falls from i_0 to i_1, as shown in each of the left panels. This causes an increase in investment expenditure of ΔI, from I_0 to I_1, as shown in each of the right panels.

In part (i), the demand for money is highly interest-inelastic, so the increase in the money supply leads to a large fall in the interest rate. Further, desired investment expenditure is highly interest-elastic, so the large fall in interest rates also leads to a large increase in investment expenditure. Hence, in this case, the change in the money supply will be very effective in stimulating aggregate demand. This corresponds to the view held by the so-called *Monetarists*.

In part (ii), the demand for money is more interest-elastic, so the increase in the money supply leads to only a small fall in the interest rate. Further, desired investment expenditure is interest-inelastic, so the small fall in interest rates leads to only a small increase in investment expenditure. Hence, in this case, the change in the money supply will be less effective in stimulating aggregate demand. This corresponds to the view held by some so-called *Keynesians*.

depends on the shapes of the demand for money and marginal efficiency of investment curves. The influence of the shapes of the two curves is shown in Figure 28-10 and may be summarized as follows:

1. The steeper (less interest-sensitive) the *LP* function, the greater the effect on interest rates of a given change in the money supply.

2. The flatter (more interest-sensitive) the *MEI* function, the greater the effect on investment expenditure a change in the interest rate will have and hence the larger will be the shift in the *AD* curve.

The combination that produces the largest shift in the *AD* curve for a given change in the money supply is a steep *LP* function and a flat

MEI function. This combination is illustrated in Figure 28-10(i). It accords with the view that monetary policy is relatively effective as a means of influencing the economy—a view associated with the so-called **Monetarists.** The combination that produces the smallest shift in the *AD* curve is a flat *LP* function and a steep *MEI* function. This combination is illustrated in Figure 28-10(ii). It accords with the view that monetary policy is relatively ineffective—a view associated with some so-called **Keynesians.** (We will encounter the differences between Monetarists and Keynesians again in Chapter 29.)

The Role of Aggregate Supply

As we saw in Chapters 25 and 26, the response of real national income and the price level to any given shift in the *AD* curve depends on the behaviour of aggregate supply. Two aspects of this behaviour are relevant.

    The Slope of the *SRAS* Curve. As you will recall from Chapter 25, the steeper the *SRAS* curve, the larger the change in the price level and the smaller the change in real national income following a given shift in the *AD* curve. Many economists think that when the level of real national income is near or above its capacity level, the *SRAS* curve is very steep.

When the economy is operating near or above its capacity level of output, increases in aggregate demand (including those caused by increases in the money supply) will lead to small increases in real national income but will have a substantial effect on the price level.

    Shifts in the *SRAS* Curve. You may also recall, in this case from Chapter 26, that shifts in the *SRAS* curve can offset the expansionary effects of an increase in aggregate demand. However, many economists think that such offsetting shifts in the *SRAS* curve can occur even without the emergence of an inflationary gap if the *AD* shock was caused by an increase in the money supply that was *anticipated*. (This view is related to the views discussed in Extension 26-1, where we examined the possibility that *expectations effects* can cause the *SRAS* curve to shift in anticipation of a shift in the *AD* curve.)

    Figure 28-9 can also be used to illustrate the case of an increase in the money supply that is perfectly anticipated by workers and employers alike. The monetary disturbance shifts the *AD* curve rightward. Workers, knowing that the prices of goods that they buy are going to rise, demand increases in wages to compensate. Employers, knowing that the price of their output is going to rise, grant the wage increases. Thus the *SRAS* curve immediately shifts leftward; this expectations effect means that the adjustment mechanism operates very quickly, thus reducing the effect of a monetary disturbance on real national income.

    How far does the *SRAS* curve shift in anticipation of a future shock? In the extreme case where there is no disagreement about the extent or the implications of the initial monetary disturbance and no contractual or institutional forces that would cause wages to adjust slowly to changes in the economy, wages would rise immediately to offset the price increase completely. Real wages would thus remain unchanged, as would real output. Hence the *SRAS* curve must shift enough to completely offset the expansionary effects on real national income, as shown in the figure.

It is conceivable that in the case of a perfectly anticipated monetary disturbance, all the effects fall immediately on money wages and prices, and none fall on real wages or real national output.

    Of course, most monetary disturbances are, at best, imperfectly foreseen, and typically there is considerable uncertainty about the exact nature and implications of any particular disturbance. Further, responses take time. Hence an outcome in which the effects on real national income are completely offset is extreme, and any monetary disturbance can be expected to have at least some temporary effects. However, the expectations effects complicate the analysis of monetary disturbances and create problems for economists who are trying to understand the implications of current monetary events or to advise governments on the use of monetary policy. We will encounter this issue repeatedly in the next few chapters as we study monetary policy and other macroeconomic problems and controversies.

S U M M A R Y

A. UNDERSTANDING FINANCIAL ASSETS

- For simplicity, we divide all forms of wealth into "money," which is a medium of exchange, and "bonds," which earn a higher interest return than money and can be turned into money by being sold at a price that is determined on the open market.
- The price of bonds varies negatively with the rate of interest—a rise in the interest rate lowers the prices of all bonds. The longer its term to maturity, the greater the change in the price of a bond for a given change in the interest rate.

B. THE DEMAND FOR MONEY

- The opportunity cost of holding money (rather than bonds) is the interest earnings that are foregone—the interest that would have been earned had bonds been held instead of money.
- Despite the opportunity cost of holding money, households and firms hold money for three reasons—the transactions, precautionary, and speculative motives. Taken together, they have the effect of making the demand for money vary positively with real national income, the price level, and wealth and negatively with the nominal rate of interest. The nominal demand for money varies proportionally with the price level.
- The liquidity preference (LP) function is the relationship between money demand and the nominal interest rate (holding real income and the price level constant).

C. MONETARY FORCES AND NATIONAL INCOME

- The supply of money is a stock—it is equal to so many billions of dollars at a point in time. The value of money balances that the public wishes to hold is called the demand for money. It is also a stock—measured as so many billions of dollars at a point in time.
- The interest rate is determined by the interaction of the demand for money and the supply of money. An excess demand for money balances leads people to sell bonds. This pushes the price of bonds down and the interest rate up. An excess supply of money balances leads people to buy bonds. This pushes the price of bonds up and the rate of interest down. Monetary equilibrium is established when people are willing to hold the fixed stock of money (and therefore bonds) at the current rate of interest.
- With a given rate of inflation (in this chapter we maintained the assumption of zero inflation), changes in the nominal interest rate translate into changes in the real interest rate. A change in the real interest rate causes desired investment to change along the marginal efficiency of investment (MEI) function. This shifts the aggregate desired expenditure function and causes equilibrium national income to change. This means that the aggregate demand curve shifts.
- The link between money and aggregate demand is known as the transmission mechanism. A decrease in the supply of money raises interest rates, reduces desired investment expenditure, and thus reduces aggregate demand. An increase in the supply of money lowers interest rates, increases desired investment expenditure, and thus increases aggregate demand.
- The negatively sloped aggregate demand curve indicates that the higher the price level, the lower the equilibrium national income. The explanation lies in part with the effect of money on the adjustment mechanism: Other things being equal, the higher the price level, the higher the demand for money and the rate of interest, the lower the aggregate expenditure function, and thus the lower the equilibrium income.
- The adjustment mechanism that causes the aggregate demand curve to have a negative slope means that a sufficiently large rise in the price level will eliminate any inflationary gap. However, this mechanism can be frustrated if the Bank of Canada validates the price rise by increasing the money supply.

D. THE STRENGTH OF MONETARY FORCES

- Changes in the money supply affect national income via shifts in the AD curve. But such changes do not affect potential output. Hence changes in the money supply can affect output in the short run but not in the long run.
- The steeper the LP curve and the flatter the MEI curve, the greater the effect on aggregate demand of a given change in the money supply. The steeper the SRAS curve or the faster wages adjust, the smaller the transitory effect on national income of a given shift in the AD curve.
- If the change in the money supply were widely anticipated and its effects understood, the SRAS curve might shift very quickly so as to reduce any effects on national income.

KEY CONCEPTS

Interest rates and bond prices

The transactions, precautionary, and speculative motives for holding money

The liquidity preference *(LP)* function

Monetary equilibrium

The transmission mechanism

The marginal efficiency of investment *(MEI)* function

Money and the adjustment mechanism

The strength of monetary forces

Keynesians and Monetarists

DISCUSSION QUESTIONS

1. "Central banker says using monetary policy to lower interest rates now would only cause inflation to rise and lead to higher interest rates in the future." Explain how this might be so.

2. The liquidity preference theory of interest that we examined in this chapter predicts that an increase in the money supply will lead to a reduction in interest rates. Now consider the following headline from the *Wall Street Journal:* "Bond prices pressed downward by news of M1's sharp rise, economy's rebound." Does this contradict the theory? What would be the effect on bond prices (or interest rates) of the rise in M1 alone (without the economy's rebound)? What would be the effect on bond prices of only the rebound in the economy (without the change in M1)?

3. Historically, construction of new houses has been one of the most interest-sensitive categories of aggregate expenditure. Recently, the financial press have carried a number of stories suggesting that because of financial deregulation and innovations in housing finance, this interest sensitivity has apparently decreased. If this is true, what are the implications for monetary policy?

4. What motives do you think explain the following holdings?

   a. Currency and coins in the cash register of the local supermarket at the start of each working day
   b. Money to meet Stelco's bi-weekly payroll deposited in the local bank
   c. Term deposits that mature after one's retirement
   d. Government bonds held by private individuals

5. In 1989, economists Christina Romer and David Romer (currently of the University of California, Berkeley) produced a study of post–World War II policies of the U.S. Federal Reserve Board (the central bank in the United States). They examined six episodes in which the Fed tightened monetary policy to reduce inflation and found that each time, following the tightening of monetary policy, the unemployment rate rose sharply and industrial production fell. Further, they estimated that these effects persist, so that unemployment is at its peak 2½ years after the policy is initiated, and "there is only a limited tendency for economic activity to return to its previous path subsequently." Interpret these results in terms of the theoretical framework developed in this chapter.

6. Suppose that you alone know that the Bank of Canada is going to engage in policies that will decrease the money supply sharply, starting next month. How might you make speculative profits by purchases or sales of bonds now?

7. What would happen if, starting from a situation of a 10 percent rate of inflation and of monetary expansion, the Bank of Canada cut the rate of monetary expansion to 5 percent?

8. Trace the full sequence of events by which the adjustment mechanism would work if, in the face of a constant money supply, workers and firms insisted on actions that raised prices continually at a rate of 10 percent per year. "Sooner or later in this situation, something would have to give." What possible things could "give"? What would be the consequence of each "giving"?

9. Discuss the precautionary, speculative, and transaction motives for the demand for money in light of the continuing demand for "hard currency" (such as the U.S. dollar, the German mark, or the Japanese Yen), in Russia and elsewhere.

10. Explain why the effect of a change in the supply of money on aggregate demand depends crucially on the interest-elasticity of money demand and on the interest-elasticity of desired investment expenditure. Discuss two conditions under which a change in the money supply would have absolutely no effect on aggregate demand.

APPENDIX TO CHAPTER 28

The Slope of the Aggregate Demand Curve

The *AD* curve relates the price level to the equilibrium level of real national income. Its negative slope means that the higher the price level, the lower the equilibrium national income. In Chapter 25 we explained the slope of the aggregate demand curve by arguing that a change in the price level changed the wealth of firms and households (by changing the real value of *outside assets*). We also argued that a change in the price level changed the prices of Canadian goods relative to foreign goods, and so affected net exports. What we *did not say* in Chapter 25, however, is that a third reason for a negatively sloped *AD* curve is due to the monetary transmission mechanism. We omitted this argument then for the simple reason that we had not yet introduced the concepts of money, money demand, and money supply. But we now have the tools in hand to do this.

Let us look at the transmission mechanism in detail. Although the argument contains nothing new, it does require that you follow carefully through several steps.

We start with an initial equilibrium position, corresponding to a given price level P_0, shown by the 0 subscripts in the two figures. Figure 28A-1, which reproduces the relationships depicted in

---

FIGURE 28A-1
Changes in the Price Level: Interest Rates and Investment

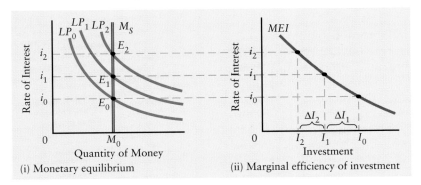

(i) Monetary equilibrium

(ii) Marginal efficiency of investment

Changes in the price level influence the demand for money and hence cause the level of interest rates and desired investment spending to change. In part (i), the money supply is fixed at M_0. Initially, money demand is given by LP_0, equilibrium is at E_0, and the interest rate is i_0. Given that interest rate, desired investment spending is I_0, as shown in part (ii) by the *MEI* schedule.

An increase in the price level causes an increase in the demand for money, and hence the *LP* curve shifts upward to LP_1. Equilibrium is at E_1, the interest rate rises to i_1, and desired investment spending falls by ΔI_1 to I_1. A further increase in the price level causes a further increase in the demand for money, to LP_2. Equilibrium is at E_2, the interest rate rises to i_2, and desired investment spending falls by ΔI_2 to I_2.

Figure 28-4, shows the determination of the interest rate by the conditions of monetary equilibrium in part (i); that in turn determines the level of desired investment spending by the marginal efficiency of investment schedule in part (ii). Figure 28A-2, which reproduces the relationships depicted in Figure 28-5, shows the AE curve, drawn for that level of investment spending, and the determination of equilibrium national income in part (i); that level of national income is then plotted against the price level to give point A on the AD curve in part (ii).

A rise in the price level raises the money value of transactions and increases the quantity of nominal money demanded at each possible value of the interest rate. As a result, the liquidity preference function shifts upward, raising the equilibrium interest rate and reducing the level of desired investment expenditure, as shown in Figure 28A-1. The reduction in investment spending in turn causes the AE curve to shift downward, leading to a reduction in the equilibrium level of national income, as shown in part (i) of Figure 28A-2. The combination of the higher price level and the lower equilibrium level of national income can be plotted as another point, say, point B, on the AD curve in part (ii).

Changes in the price level lead to changes in the interest rate and hence in desired aggregate expenditure and the equilibrium level of national income; other things being equal, the higher the price level, the lower the equilibrium level of national income.

The negative relationship between the price level and equilibrium real income shown by the AD curve occurs because, other things being equal, a rise in the price level raises the quantity of money demanded. Note the qualification "other things being equal." It is important for this process that the nominal money *supply* remain constant. The adjustment mechanism operates because the demand for money increases when the price level rises whereas the money supply remains constant. The attempt to add to money balances by selling bonds is what drives the interest rate up and reduces desired expenditure, thereby reducing equilibrium national income. (This argument is conducted in terms of the nominal supply of and demand for money. Arguing in terms of the real demand and supply of money leads to identical results.) [39]

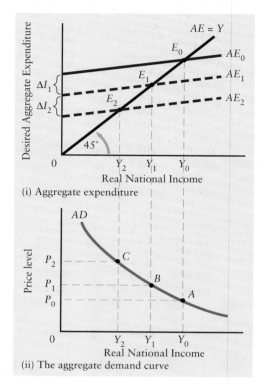

FIGURE 28A-2
Changes in the Price Level:
Aggregate Expenditure and National Income

(i) Aggregate expenditure

(ii) The aggregate demand curve

Changes in the price level lead to changes in desired aggregate expenditure and hence in the equilibrium level of national income. Equilibrium national income is determined in part (i). At a given initial price level—hence with an initial level of desired investment spending of I_0 from Figure 28A-1—desired aggregate expenditure is shown by AE_0. Equilibrium is at E_0, and equilibrium national income is Y_0. In part (ii), Y_0 is plotted against P_0 to give point A on the AD curve.

An increase in the price level causes a decrease of ΔI_1 in the level of desired investment spending, as determined in Figure 28A-1 and shown in part (i) here. Thus the AE curve shifts down to AE_1. Equilibrium is at E_1, and equilibrium national income falls to Y_1. In part (ii), the higher price level P_1 is plotted against the lower equilibrium level of income Y_1 as point B on the AD curve.

A further increase in the price level causes a further decrease of ΔI_2 in desired investment spending, as determined in Figure 28A-1 and shown in part (i) here. Thus the AE curve shifts downward to AE_2. Equilibrium is at E_2, and equilibrium national income falls to Y_2. In part (ii), the higher price level P_2 is plotted against the lower equilibrium level of income Y_2 as point C on the AD curve.

MONETARY POLICY IN CANADA

In the previous two chapters, we saw how money supply and money demand interact to determine interest rates. Further, we saw how monetary disturbances—changes in either the demand for money or the supply of money—affect interest rates, desired aggregate expenditure and thus the level of national income.

We also saw how commercial banks, through the process of making loans and new deposits, are able to affect the money supply. But there is still one important piece missing from our analysis. Though we discussed some of the functions of the Bank of Canada in Chapter 27, we have not yet examined how the

Bank of Canada sets the level of reserves in the commercial banking system. And it is these reserves which form the basis of commercial-bank lending. Thus until we have examined the operations of the Bank of Canada in more detail, we do not have a full picture of the determinants of the money supply.

In this chapter, we examine the operations of the Bank of Canada—in particular, how it sets the level of reserves in the banking system, and thus how it affects the money supply. We are then in a position to explore how the Bank conducts its **monetary policy.**

THE BANK OF CANADA'S CONTROL OVER THE MONEY SUPPLY

Deposit money is the most important part of the money supply. Demand (chequable) deposits at the chartered banks account for about 60 percent of M1, the narrowest definition of money, and for over 25 percent of M2, the broader measure. As we have seen, the ability of banks to create such deposit money depends on their reserves. These reserves, in turn, are determined by the Bank of Canada. Thus the ability of the central bank to affect the money supply is critically related to its ability to determine the reserves of the commercial banking system.

In the following sections, we shall discuss two ways in which the Bank of Canada alters the reserves of the banking system and hence influences the money supply. In Chapter 27, we identified the *target reserve ratio* of the commercial banks as the ratio of reserves they wished to hold relative to their deposit liabilities. At this stage of our discussion of the money supply, we suppose that the target reserve ratio is constant.

OPEN-MARKET OPERATIONS

One important tool that the Bank of Canada uses for influencing the supply of money is the purchase or sale of government securities on the open market. These actions are known as **open-market operations.** Just as there are stock markets, there are active and well-organized markets for government securities. Anyone, including you, the Toronto Dominion Bank, Ford Motor Company, or the Bank of Canada can enter this market to buy or sell negotiable government securities at whatever price supply and demand establishes. But there is an important difference between the purchase and sale of government securities

among members of the private sector and *between the central bank and the private sector.* As we shall see, whenever the Bank of Canada is involved in either the purchase or sale of government securities, the reserves of the entire banking system are altered, and this affects the money supply.

At the start of 1996, the Bank of Canada held about $23 billion in government securities. In a typical year, the Bank of Canada may make a *net* addition of $1–2 billion to these holdings. During the year, however, its *gross* purchases and sales of government securities on the open market amount to many times this amount. What is the effect of these open-market purchases and sales?

Open-Market Purchases

When the Bank of Canada buys a treasury bill or a bond from a household or a firm, it pays for the bond with a cheque drawn on itself and payable to the seller. The seller deposits this cheque in a commercial bank, which then presents the cheque to the Bank of Canada for payment. The Bank of Canada then makes a book entry, increasing the deposit of the commercial bank at the central bank, which adds to the commercial bank's reserves.

Table 29-1 shows the changes in the balance sheets of the several parties involved in a Bank of Canada purchase of $100,000 in government securities from a household. At the end of these transactions, the central bank has acquired a new asset in the form of a security and a new liability in the form of a deposit by the commercial bank. The seller has reduced its security holdings and increased its deposits. The commercial bank has increased its deposit liabilities and its reserves by the amount of the transaction. Typically, when the Bank of Canada buys securities on the open market, the entire banking system gains new reserves.

Given a constant target reserve ratio, after the transactions shown in Table 29-1 are completed, the commercial banks have excess reserves—that is, reserves over and above those needed to maintain their target reserve ratio. To see this, simply note that deposits and reserves have increased by the same amount ($100,000 in this case). So as long as the target reserve ratio is less than 100 percent (and it would typically be only a tiny fraction of that), there are now excess reserves. Thus the commercial banks are in a position to expand their loans and deposits.

When the central bank buys securities on the open market, the reserves of the commercial banks are in-

TABLE 29-1
Balance Sheet Changes Caused by an Open-Market Purchase from a Household
(thousands of dollars)

Private households

Assets		Liabilities
Bonds	−100	No change
Deposits	+100	

Commercial banks

Assets		Liabilities	
Reserves	+100	Demand deposits	+100

Central bank

Assets		Liabilities	
Bonds	+100	Chartered bank deposits	+100

An open-market purchase by the Bank from the private sector increases bank reserves and thus, through an expansion of bank lending, increases the money supply. When the Bank of Canada buys a $100,000 bond from a household, the household gains money and gives up a bond. The commercial banks gain a new deposit of $100,000 and thus new reserves of $100,000. Commercial banks can now engage in a multiple expansion of deposit money of the sort analyzed in Chapter 27.

creased. These banks can then expand deposits, thereby increasing the money supply.

Open-Market Sales

When the Bank of Canada sells a security to a household or firm, it receives in return the buyer's cheque drawn against a deposit in a bank. The Bank of Canada presents the cheque to the commercial bank for payment. Payment is made by a book entry that reduces the bank's deposit at the central bank, and hence reduces its reserves.

The changes in this case are the opposite of those shown in Table 29-1. The central bank has reduced its assets by the value of the security it sold and reduced its deposit liabilities to the banks. The household or firm has increased its holdings of securities and reduced its deposit with a commercial bank. The commercial bank has reduced its deposit liability to the household or firm and reduced its reserves (on deposit with the central bank) by the same amount. In each case, the asset change is balanced by a liability change.

Given a constant target reserve ratio, the commercial bank finds that by suffering an equal reduc-

tion in its reserves and its deposit liabilities, its actual ratio of reserves to deposits falls below its target ratio. Banks whose actual reserve ratios are pushed below their target ratios will take steps to restore their reserve ratios. The necessary reduction in deposits can be accomplished by not granting new loans when old ones are repaid or by selling (liquidating) existing investments.

When the central bank sells securities on the open market, the reserves of the commercial banks are decreased. These banks must in turn contract deposits, thereby decreasing the money supply.

Although the process just described reflects the mechanics of an open-market sale by the Bank of Canada, it does not fully capture some of the subtleties involved in the Bank's selling of securities. For example, how is the Bank sure that it can always find a willing buyer? Or every time the Bank successfully sells government securities and thus decreases the reserves of the banking system, is this necessarily a "contractionary" monetary policy? These issues are examined in Extension 29-1.

SHIFTING GOVERNMENT DEPOSITS

In addition to open-market operations, the Bank of Canada has a second general method for changing the level of reserves in the banking system. As the government's *fiscal agent,* the Bank of Canada manages a large amount of government funds. It maintains government accounts on its own books, into which funds are deposited and from which funds are withdrawn. In addition, it manages some government accounts with the chartered banks. Alterations in the amount held in these accounts will affect the reserves of the chartered banks. The process of shifting government accounts from the Bank of Canada to the chartered banks (or in the other direction) is referred to as *cash management.*

Cash management—the shifting of government deposits between the Bank of Canada and the chartered banks—is a major tool used by the Bank of Canada in its day-to-day operations.

When the Bank of Canada transfers government deposits, it influences the reserves of the banking system relative to its target level of reserves, thereby inducing an expansion or contraction of commercial-bank lending and thus an expansion or contraction

---

EXTENSION 29-1

OPEN-MARKET SALES AND "CONTRACTIONARY" MONETARY POLICY

This box looks at two additional issues that arise whenever the Bank of Canada conducts an open-market sale of government securities (which reduces the reserves of the banking system and is thus called a *contractionary monetary policy*).

CAN THE BANK OF CANADA ALWAYS FIND BUYERS FOR SECURITIES?

One way in which the Bank pursues a contractionary monetary policy is to sell government securities, thus reducing the reserves available to the banking system. What if the public does not wish to buy the securities that the Bank wishes to sell? Can the Bank force them to do so?

The answer is that there is always a price at which the public will buy. The Bank must be prepared in its open market operations to lower the price of securities as far as necessary in order to sell them. This fall in price is, as we have seen, the same thing as an increase in the interest rate. If the Bank wishes to pursue a contractionary policy by selling government securities, it will have to accept that interest rates must rise.

DO RESERVES AND THE MONEY SUPPLY ACTUALLY FALL?

In every year since 1950, real GDP growth and inflation have ensured that nominal national income has risen. As a result, the demand for money has grown. In every year in the period, the nominal money supply has grown, reflecting the Bank's decision to supply additional reserves to the banking system to meet the growing demand for money. Does this mean that the Bank has never followed a contractionary monetary policy?

The answer is no. When real income growth and inflation result in a continually growing nominal national income, the stance of monetary policy depends upon the rate at which the money supply is allowed to grow *relative to the rate of growth of the demand for money.* A contractionary monetary policy occurs when the growth in the money supply is held below the rate of growth in the demand for money; it does not require a fall in the absolute size of the money supply.

For example, if nominal national income and the demand for money are both growing at 4 percent per year, the Bank of Canada can follow a contractionary policy if it limits the rate of growth of reserves and the money supply to 2 percent. This would create an excess demand for money, causing interest rates to rise. The higher interest rates, in turn, would feed through the transmission mechanism to slow the growth in spending and, hence, slow the growth in real income or inflation, or both.

---

of the money supply. Suppose, for example, that the Bank of Canada were to transfer $100,000 from the government's account at the Bank to the government's account with a chartered bank. The transactions involved are illustrated in Table 29-2. From the government's view, nothing substantial has changed, since its deposits with one financial institution will have fallen, but its deposits with another have risen by the same amount. However, the chartered bank in question will find that its deposit liabilities and re-serves will each have risen by $100,000, and hence its ratio of reserves to deposits will have risen. With an unchanged target reserve ratio, the bank will have excess reserves. As with the situation following a Bank of Canada purchase of government securities on the open market, the chartered bank will wish to loan out some of its excess reserves, thus setting in motion an expansion of deposits.

A transfer of government deposits from the chartered banks to the Bank of Canada has the op-

TABLE 29-2
Balance Sheet Changes Caused by a Transfer of Government Deposits from the Bank of Canada to a Chartered Bank
(thousands of dollars)

Chartered bank			
Assets		Liabilities	
Reserves	+100	Government deposits	+100

Bank of Canada			
Assets		Liabilities	
		Government deposits	−100
		Chartered bank deposits	+100

A transfer of government deposits from the Bank of Canada to a chartered bank increases bank reserves and thus, through an expansion of bank lending, increases the money supply. When the Bank of Canada transfers $100,000 of government deposits to a chartered bank, the chartered bank's account with the Bank of Canada is credited with a deposit of $100,000. Thus the decrease in the Bank of Canada's deposit liabilities to the government is exactly balanced by the increase in its deposit liabilities to the chartered bank. The chartered bank's increase in its deposit liabilities to the government is balanced by the increase in its reserves on deposit with the Bank of Canada. Since its deposits and its reserves have increased by the same amount, it has excess reserves and the potential is created for multiple expansion of deposit money as analyzed in Chapter 27.

posite effect. The reserves and deposit liabilities of the banking system fall by the same amount, thus driving the actual reserve ratio below the target reserve ratio. Banks will now have insufficient reserves and will begin to call in existing loans and stop making new ones, setting in motion a process of deposit contraction.

When government deposits are transferred between the Bank of Canada and the chartered banks, the reserves of the chartered banks are changed. Such changes in reserves, through the expansion or contraction of lending, lead to changes in the money supply.

EFFECTS ON THE MONEY SUPPLY

Recall from Table 27-2 that the Bank of Canada holds government securities among its assets and government deposits among its liabilities. Either

through open-market operations or switching these government deposits, the Bank can significantly change the reserves of the commercial banks.

Open-market operations and control of government deposits give the Bank of Canada potent weapons for affecting the size of commercial-bank reserves and thus for affecting the money supply.

Though the details of an open-market operation differ from the details of switching government deposits, both actions have the same basic result: They change the reserves of the banking system, and this change in reserves then gets transformed, through commercial-bank lending, into changes in the money supply. In the remainder of this chapter, we focus on the Bank's control of reserves, ignoring the precise way in which these reserves are altered.

MONETARY POLICY WITH ZERO REQUIRED RESERVES

In many countries, commercial banks are *required* to hold some fraction of their deposit liabilities in reserves, either in their own vaults or as deposits at the central bank. In the past, Canadian banks faced such requirements as well, but these were eliminated in the early 1990s.

As we observed in Chapter 27, even without requirements to hold reserves, banks would still choose to hold quite large reserves if they did not have a central bank to fall back on, for the simple reason that there is considerable uncertainty over how many customers will enter the bank on any given day wanting the value of their deposits in cash. Today, however, in the absence of reserve requirements, the commercial banks know that as long as their balance sheets show them to be solvent, the Bank of Canada will provide them with whatever liquidity they require.

Borrowing from the central bank is not free, however. When commercial banks borrow from the Bank of Canada, they are charged interest on their loan—the interest rate they are charged is called the **bank rate.** The bank rate changes quite frequently and draws considerable public attention when it does. See Application 29-1 for some detailed information about how the bank rate is determined.

The current Canadian policy of "zero required reserves" is really a policy that requires the banks to

MONETARY POLICY AND THE BANK RATE

When commercial banks find it necessary to borrow funds temporarily from the Bank of Canada—such as when their reserves at the Bank are negative (overdrawn)—they are charged an interest rate on their loan. The **bank rate** is the interest rate at which the Bank of Canada makes loans to the commercial banks.

Commercial banks in need of temporary financing are not forced to borrow from the Bank of Canada, however. They can also borrow from each other or from investment dealers. The interest rate for these loans, which are often overnight (or just a few days), is called the **overnight rate.**

A higher bank rate (or a higher overnight rate) induces the commercial banks to hold more reserves in view of the higher cost of borrowing they would have to incur if they should suffer a loss of cash and are forced to seek a loan either from the Bank or from the overnight market. Thus, other things equal, an increase in the bank rate increases the target reserve ratio of the commercial banks and thus reduces the amount by which a given level of reserves in the banking system can be expanded into bank deposits.

THE SETTING OF THE BANK RATE

But where does the bank rate come from? The determination of the bank rate has changed considerably over the past twenty years.

Prior to March 1980, the bank rate was simply set by the Bank of Canada. Changes in the rate were widely interpreted as a signal of changes in the stance of monetary policy, which would cause market interest rates to move quickly in the same direction. In March 1980, the bank rate became a market-determined rate. From March 1980 to 1996, the bank rate was set automatically at a premium of one quarter of a percentage point over the average rate determined in the weekly auction of 3-month treasury bills.

Beginning in 1996, the bank rate lost its connection to the average yield on 3-month treasury bills and reverted to being a rate set by the Bank of Canada. The bank rate is now set at the upper end of a range that the Bank of Canada announces as its *desired* range for the overnight rate. By moving this range (which is one-half of a percentage point wide) up or down, the Bank signals to the financial markets where it would like the overnight rate to be.

If the overnight rate does not move quickly into the Bank's desired range, the Bank takes action to change the overnight rate. It does this by changing the reserves in the banking system. An increase in reserves (through either an open-market purchase or a switch of government deposits toward the commercial banks) puts commercial banks in the position of having excess reserves. As they try to lend these funds on the overnight market, the overnight rate falls. A decrease in reserves (through either an open-market sale or a switch of government deposits away from the commercial banks) puts commercial banks in the position of having deficient reserves. As they try to borrow funds in the overnight market, the overnight rate rises.

As we will see in Application 29-2, the Bank of Canada uses its primary "instrument" of changes in banks' reserves to affect the overnight rate, with the goal of changing its "intermediate target" of other interest rates (and the exchange rate), so as to achieve its desired path of national income and the price level.

have zero (or positive) reserves on *average* over a four-week averaging period. Thus if a commercial bank has a negative balance of $10 million for one day (covered by a loan from the Bank of Canada), they are required to balance that shortfall with positive reserves of $10 million on some other day during the four-week averaging period. Given this legal requirement to have *nonnegative average reserves,* the true cost of borrowing from the Bank of Canada ends up being *twice* the bank rate. The first cost arises because any cash drain that a bank cannot meet from its own reserves must be covered by a loan from the Bank of Canada, which charges the bank rate. The second cost then arises from the non-negative legal reserve requirement. When the commercial bank holds the positive reserves (to balance out the negative reserves), it loses the interest it could have earned by lending them out. So the interest cost is incurred twice, once when money is borrowed to cover the cash drain and once when zero-interest earning reserves are held to offset the negative reserves implied by that borrowing.

As a result, commercial banks target to hold some positive level of reserves that will make the return on the last dollar loaned out equal to the benefit of the last dollar added to reserves. This benefit depends on two things. The first is the probability of running out of reserves, which is negatively related to the size of reserves. The second is the penalty of having to borrow from the Bank of Canada to cover a deficiency of reserves, which is twice the bank rate times the amount borrowed.

Monetary policy now works in the same way as described in the earlier sections. When the Bank of Canada buys government securities in the open market, the commercial banks find themselves with excess reserves. They will expand their loans until the excess reserves drain away. When the Bank sells government securities, the commercial banks find themselves short of reserves and hence suffer increased risk of being forced to borrow reserves from the Bank. They will cut down on their loans in an attempt to restore their reserves.

A REVIEW OF THE TRANSMISSION MECHANISM

We have now seen how the Bank of Canada can alter the money supply: The Bank of Canada, through its open-market operations or the switching of government deposits, changes the reserves of the banking system. The commercial banks, facing a different level of reserves, then alter their loans and deposits to change the money supply. Before turning to a more detailed discussion of the policy choices faced by the Bank, we briefly review the analysis in Chapter 28 of the effects of changes in the money supply on the economy—this is a review of the *transmission mechanism*.

Suppose that initially the economy is in equilibrium at less than potential income. The Bank of Canada then increases the reserves of the banking system (either through an open-market purchase or by switching government deposits toward the chartered banks). This leads to an increase in the money supply and thus a fall in interest rates. As a result, there is an increase in desired investment expenditure, which in turn shifts the aggregate demand curve rightward, thus raising equilibrium national income. This process is shown in Figures 28-4 and 28-5 in Chapter 28.

When the Bank of Canada reduces the reserves of the banking system (either through an open-market sale or by switching government deposits away from the chartered banks), the money supply falls and interest rates rise. The increased interest rate causes a reduction in investment expenditure. This in turn shifts the aggregate demand curve leftward and lowers equilibrium income.

Thus monetary policy works through the transmission mechanism to shift the aggregate demand curve and thus to change equilibrium national income. An increase in the money supply is an expansionary monetary policy; a decrease in the money supply is a contractionary monetary policy. As a result, changes in the money supply will cause real national income and the price level to change in the same direction, as shown in Figure 28-7 in Chapter 28.

POLICY VARIABLES AND POLICY INSTRUMENTS

The Bank conducts monetary policy to influence real national income and the price level. These ultimate objectives of the Bank's policy are called **policy variables.** The variables that it *directly* controls to achieve these objectives are called its **policy instruments.** The Bank also has **intermediate targets,** which are neither the ultimate objective of policy nor are they under the direct control of the Bank. Intermediate targets nevertheless play a key role in the execution of monetary policy; their importance lies in their close relationship to policy variables.

POLICY VARIABLES

The Bank of Canada's twin policy variables are real national income and the price level. Recall from

FIGURE 29-1
Monetary Policy and Macroeconomic Equilibrium

$M_D = M_S$; determines equilibrium i	$\rightarrow$	$I = MEI(i)$; determines AD	$\rightarrow$	$AD = SRAS$; determines equilibrium P and Y
(i) Monetary equilibrium		(ii) Determination of aggregate demand		(iii) Macroeconomic equilibrium

Monetary policy influences aggregate demand through the transmission mechanism; macroeconomic equilibrium then determines the price level and the level of real output. Monetary equilibrium requires that the interest rate be such that money supply equal the quantity of money demanded. Changes in the money market give rise to changes in the interest rate and hence, via the transmission mechanism, to changes in desired aggregate expenditure. Aggregate demand and short-run aggregate supply then determine the price level P and the level of real national income Y.

Chapter 28 that monetary policy operates by influencing aggregate demand; the resulting link between the Bank's monetary actions and the determination of the price level and real national income is summarized in Figure 29-1.

Short Run: Nominal National Income

We also saw in Chapter 28 that the short-run effects of a shift in the AD curve are divided between the price level and real output in a manner determined by the slope of the $SRAS$ curve. However, the Bank has no control over this slope. Thus although the Bank cares about the separate reactions of the price level and of real output, there is little that it can do in the short run to control them independently. For any price level response that is achieved, the real output consequence must be accepted. Alternatively, for any real output response that is achieved, the price level consequence must be accepted.

Monetary policy is therefore not capable of pushing the price level (P) and real national income (Y) toward independently determined targets simultaneously. For this reason, central banks often focus on nominal national income (PY) as the target for monetary policy in the short run.

Long Run: The Price Level

We have seen that in the long run, when the level of wages is fully adjusted to the price level, the $LRAS$ curve is vertical. This implies that the only long-run impact of monetary policy will be on the price level. For this reason, central banks often focus on the price level (or the rate of change in the price level—

the rate of inflation) as the long-run target for monetary policy.

POLICY INSTRUMENTS

Having selected its policy variables and formulated targets for their behaviour, the Bank of Canada must decide how to achieve these targets. Because the Bank can control neither income nor the price level directly, it must employ its *policy instruments*, which it does control directly, to influence aggregate demand in the desired manner.

The instruments used by the Bank of Canada to conduct monetary policy are open-market operations and switching government deposits at the chartered banks. These are the ways the Bank changes the reserves of the banking system.

Open-market operations and the switching of government deposits change the reserves of the banking system. These reserves, together with the currency in circulation, make up the Bank of Canada's liabilities (see Tables 27-1 and 27-2 in Chapter 27). Chartered bank reserves are held on deposit with the Bank of Canada, and are the Bank's liability because they can be redeemed on demand. The Bank's monetary liabilities, as we saw in Chapter 27, form the *base* on which chartered banks can expand and create deposits. For this reason, the Bank's liabilities are often referred to as the *monetary base*. Therefore, we say that the Bank's policy instrument is the monetary base. It is this monetary base that the Bank is changing when it conducts open-market operations or when it switches government deposits.

INTERMEDIATE TARGETS

Major changes in the direction or method of monetary policy are typically made only infrequently. Decisions regarding the implementation of policy must, however, be made almost daily. Given the values that the Bank of Canada wishes its policy variables to take on, and given the current state of the economy, are increases or decreases in the monetary base called for? How big an increase, or how big a decrease? Such questions must be answered continually in the Bank's day-to-day operations.

Daily information about the policy variables, however, is rarely available. Inflation and unemployment rates are available only on a monthly basis and with a considerable lag. National income figures are available even less frequently; they appear on a quarterly basis. Thus the policy makers do not know exactly what is happening to the policy variables when they make their daily decisions regarding the Bank's policy instruments.

How, then, does the Bank of Canada make decisions? Central banks have typically used *intermediate targets* to guide them when implementing monetary policy in the very-short run. To serve as an intermediate target, a variable must satisfy two criteria. First, information about it must be available on a frequent basis, daily if possible. Second, its movements must be closely correlated with those of the policy variable, so that changes in it can reasonably be expected to indicate that the policy variable is also changing (or will do so in the near future).

Consistency of Intermediate Targets

The two most commonly used intermediate targets have been the money supply and the interest rate. However, these two variables are not independent of each other; recall that the liquidity preference function relates the quantity of money demanded to the rate of interest. This relationship and its implications for the Bank's choice of intermediate targets are reviewed in Figure 29-2.

The Bank of Canada cannot expect to be able to use its control of the monetary base to influence both the interest rate and the money supply independently.

It is therefore important that the Bank not choose a target for one that is inconsistent with the other. By the same token, because the two are closely related, it might appear not to matter much which

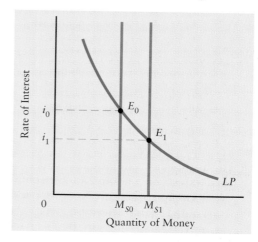

FIGURE 29-2
Alternative Intermediate Targets

For a given liquidity preference function, the Bank of Canada cannot choose independent targets for the money supply and the interest rate. The money supply is determined by the Bank of Canada. The liquidity preference function relates the interest rate to the quantity of money demanded by firms and households. Monetary equilibrium then determines the interest rate.

If the Bank chooses a target of M_{S0} for the money supply, it must accept the interest rate of i_0. If it then decides to increase the money supply to M_{S1}, it must accept the lower interest rate of i_1.

If the Bank chooses a target of i_0 for the interest rate, it must accept the money supply of M_{S0}. If it then decides to reduce the interest rate to i_1, it must accept the higher money supply of M_{S1}.

one is used. For example, if the Bank wishes to remove an inflationary gap by reducing aggregate demand, it will sell government securities and thus drive their prices down and interest rates up. These open-market sales will also reduce the monetary base and thus contract the money supply. It is largely immaterial whether the Bank seeks to force interest rates up or to contract the money supply; doing one accomplishes the other. Similarly, driving interest rates down by means of open-market purchases of government securities will tend to expand the money supply as the public gains money in return for the securities that it sells to the Bank.

Despite what we have just said, whether the Bank uses interest rates or the money supply as its intermediate target can have some important effects in the short run.

Choice of Intermediate Targets

Over the years, there has been controversy over the intermediate target that the Bank should rely on most. In the earlier part of the postwar period, many central banks relied mainly on interest rates.

Many economists criticized the use of interest rates as an intermediate target. These economists pointed out that since interest rates tended to vary directly with the business cycle, rising on the upswing and falling on the downswing, it was difficult for the central bank to determine the impact of its monetary policy by observing the interest rate alone. They cited historical examples in which central banks wished to restrain a boom and were convinced that they were doing so because interest rates were rising sharply, only to later determine that it was the boom itself that was driving up the demand for money and thus driving up interest rates. During such periods, the money supply grew substantially, so that contrary to the signals from the rising interest rate, monetary policy had been stimulative—resulting in a cumulative inflationary impact.

These criticisms, and the experience with focusing on interest rates, led to changes in intermediate targets.

In the 1970s, the Bank of Canada focused on the money supply as its intermediate target.

At the outset, the measure that was used for this purpose was the narrowly defined money supply, M1. However, it soon became clear that problems also arose when the Bank focused exclusively on M1 as its intermediate target.

To understand the problems associated with focusing on a single measure of the money supply, note that changes in the money supply are reliable indicators of the direction of monetary policy *only if the demand for money is stable.* However, the demand for money can be unstable for two reasons. First, the demand for *any particular monetary aggregate* can change quite substantially as firms and households *substitute* one type of financial asset for another. For example, households might reduce their deposits in chequing accounts and increase their deposits in saving accounts. This would be a reduction in M1 but, because M2 includes both chequing and saving deposits, there would be no change in M2. But if the Bank is only monitoring M1, then this reduction in the money supply (as defined by M1) suggests that monetary policy is becoming tighter. In fact, however, all that is happening is a substitution of one type of asset for another. The Bank's response to the problems caused by shifts of this type was again to change its intermediate targets.

In the early 1980s, dissatisfaction with M1 as an intermediate target led the Bank of Canada to monitor several monetary aggregates rather than just one.

Even the monitoring of several different monetary aggregates does not solve the problem of the instability of money demand. There are times when the current state of monetary policy needs to be gauged by measures other than money supply magnitudes, and interest rates can provide valuable additional information.

For example, during the last half of the 1970s, slow growth in all measures of the money supply suggested (to those who were monitoring only the money supply) that monetary policy was fairly tight. However, decreases in the demand for money that were not fully recognized at the time meant that the money supply was growing quite rapidly *relative to demand,* and hence monetary policy was much more expansionary than was thought at the time. More attention to interest rates would have given an important signal of this, because throughout this period interest rates were quite low. Figure 29-3 illustrates the general lesson.

Changes in the demand for money imply that the stance of monetary policy cannot be judged only by looking at measures of the money supply. In such cases, interest rates provide additional information about monetary policy.

Since the early 1990s, the Bank of Canada has chosen to focus more on interest rates than on measures of the money supply. It has formalized this procedure by creating what it calls the *Monetary Conditions Index* (MCI) as its primary intermediate target. The MCI is an index that reflects both changes in short-term interest rates (such as the interest rate on 90-day corporate bonds) and changes in the external value of the dollar. The inclusion of the exchange rate in the intermediate target reflects the fact that the transmission mechanism in an open economy works not only through domestic interest rates, but also through the exchange rate. (We will see more about monetary policy in open economies in Chapter 38.)

FIGURE 29-3
**Intermediate Targets When the Demand
for Money Shifts**

**Shifts in the liquidity preference function change the
relationship between the money supply and the interest rate.** The demand for money is initially given
by the LP function, LP_0. It then shifts to the left to
the dashed LP function, LP_1—this is a reduction in
the demand for money.

Suppose that, following the shift in the LP function, the money supply falls from M_{S0} to M_{S1} and so
the interest rate falls from i_0 to i_1. If the Bank were
to focus on the fall in the money supply (and did not
recognize the reduction in money demand), it would
conclude that monetary policy had tightened. But if
it focused on the fall in the interest rate (and did not
recognize the reduction in money demand), it would
conclude that monetary policy had loosened.

Since the combination of demand and supply
shifts led to a reduction in the interest rate, the truth
is that money supply fell by less than money demand. From the discussion in Extension 29-1, this
reduction in money supply would *not* be viewed as a
contractionary monetary policy. Indeed, given the
reduction in money demand, the *smaller* reduction
in money supply would be viewed as an *expansionary* monetary policy.

To see how the exchange rate enters the transmission mechanism, consider a reduction in reserves by the Bank of Canada. This reduces the
money supply, pushes up domestic interest rates
and reduces desired investment expenditure. But
these high Canadian interest rates in turn induce
foreigners to purchase high-yield Canadian bonds

and thus increase their demand for Canadian dollars. The resulting appreciation of the Canadian
dollar then reduces foreigners' demand for
Canadian exports of goods and services. The contractionary monetary policy thus reduces aggregate
demand for two reasons: it reduces desired investment expenditure (the interest rate effect) and it reduces exports (the exchange rate effect). This "dou-
ble-barrelled" transmission mechanism is what
motivates the Bank of Canada to use the MCI,
rather than the interest rate alone, as its primary
intermediate target.

Since the early 1990s, the Bank of Canada has used
the Monetary Conditions Index as an intermediate
target. The MCI contains information which reflects
the open-economy nature of Canada's monetary
transmission mechanism.

The Bank uses its policy instrument—the control
of bank reserves—to set the MCI at a level that it believes is consistent with its primary long-run policy
variable, the price level. See Application 29-2 for a
more detailed discussion of how the Bank uses the
MCI in its conduct of monetary policy. (This is optional material and can be omitted without loss of
continuity.)

LAGS IN THE CONDUCT
OF MONETARY POLICY

In Chapter 28 we encountered one difference between two groups of macroeconomists involved in a
debate that was prominent in the 1960s and 1970s.
Monetarists argued that monetary policy was potentially very powerful in the sense that a given change
in the money supply would lead to a substantial
change in aggregate demand, whereas **Keynesians**
were associated with the view that monetary policy
was much less powerful.

This debate had some of its roots in differing interpretations of the causes of the Great Depression,
especially as it occurred in the United States amidst a
large number of commercial-bank failures. Now that
you better understand the role of central banks and
commercial banks in the determination of the money
supply, this debate can be well understood. One interesting part of the debate is why Canada and the

THE MONETARY CONDITIONS INDEX AS AN INTERMEDIATE TARGET*

Because monetary policy in an open economy works through changes in both the interest rate and the exchange rate, the Bank of Canada, since the early 1990s, has closely monitored what it calls the *Monetary Conditions Index (MCI)*. The MCI is an index that reflects changes in short-term interest rates (typically the 90-day rate on corporate bonds) and the exchange rate. The Bank uses its policy instruments—changes in bank reserves—to alter the MCI so that it is consistent with the Bank's longer-term inflation goals. In this box, we explain the MCI and how the Bank uses it to conduct its monetary policy.

THE MONETARY CONDITIONS INDEX

Suppose that we let i be the short-term interest rate and e be the exchange rate. Recall from Chapter 21 that e is defined as the number of Canadian dollars required to purchase one unit of foreign currency, so an increase in e is a depreciation of the Canadian dollar. Further, let i_B and e_B be the values taken by i and e in some arbitrary base year (the Bank currently uses

---

*This box draws on the discussion in Charles Freedman, "The Role of Monetary Conditions and the Monetary Conditions Index in the Conduct of Policy," *Bank of Canada Review*, Autumn 1995.

1987 as the base year), and let i and e be the current values of i and e. The MCI is then defined to be

$$MCI = (i - i_B) - \theta(e - e_B)$$

where θ is a positive parameter (which we discuss in a moment).

An increase in the MCI is referred to as a "tightening" of monetary conditions. This is because a rise in MCI reduces aggregate demand; an increase in i reduces desired investment expenditure whereas a reduction in e reduces net exports. The parameter θ is used to convert changes in the exchange rate into "equivalent" changes in the interest rate. The Bank uses θ = one-third; the economists at the Bank have estimated that a 1 percentage point rise in the interest rate reduces aggregate demand by approximately the same amount as a 3 percent fall in the exchange rate.

To make sure you understand why the MCI can be used to reflect the stance of monetary policy, consider what would happen if the Bank engineered a monetary contraction. The Bank reduces reserves to the banking system and this reduces the money supply. For given money demand, the reduction in money supply pushes up interest rates. The MCI therefore rises. But that is not the end of the story—not in an open economy. The high interest rates on Canadian bonds then attract foreign purchasers, who must buy Canadian dollars in order to pur-

---

the United Kingdom had collapses in economic activity similar in magnitude to that in the United States even though they did not suffer the same banking crisis. See Application 29-3 for more on this interesting debate.

However, the debate between the Monetarists and the Keynesians involved more than just the *size* of the effect of a change in the money supply on national income; it also focused on the question of whether active use of monetary policy in an attempt to stabilize output and the price level was likely to be

successful, or whether it would instead lead to an increase in fluctuations in those variables. This aspect of the debate centres on the role of *lags*.

EXECUTION LAGS

Experience has shown that lags in the operation of policy can cause stabilization policy to be destabilizing. In Chapter 26, we discussed how decision and implementation lags might limit the extent to which chase these high-yield bonds. The increase in demand for the Canadian dollar leads to an appreciation, which is a fall in the exchange rate. As *e* falls, MCI rises further.

A rise in MCI therefore reflects a tightening of monetary conditions whereas a fall in MCI reflects a loosening of monetary conditions. See the figure for the path of the MCI since 1980.

HOW THE BANK USES THE MCI

Now that you know how to think about changes in the MCI, let's examine how the Bank uses this as an intermediate target to pursue its policy goals. As we will see later in this chapter, the Bank of Canada in 1991 announced formal *inflation-control targets.* Suppose that the Bank's target is to keep inflation between 1 and 3 percent (this was in fact the Bank's goal until the end of 1998). Given this long-term inflation target, how is the MCI used as an intermediate target?

The economists at the Bank use complex statistical methods to estimate the relationship between the MCI, real nominal income, world commodity prices, foreign demand, and inflation. Given this estimated relationship, and the Bank's predictions of what will occur over the next 1–2 years, the Bank then arrives at an estimate of the level of the *current* MCI that is consistent with its inflation target *6–8 quarters in the future.*

Given this desired level of the MCI, the Bank then uses its policy instrument (changes in reserves) to alter the MCI so that it is consistent with the desired level.

After the Bank has adjusted its policy instruments to get the MCI to its desired level, it must continue to monitor the economy, both within Canada and in the rest of the world. As new information becomes available, and as unforeseen events occur, the Bank revises its estimate of where the current MCI ought to be in order to reach the inflation target 6–8 quarters in the future.

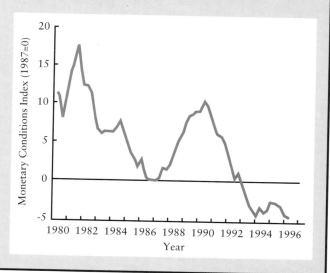

active use of fiscal policy can be relied upon to stabilize the economy. Although both of these sources of lags are much less relevant for monetary policy, the full effects of monetary policy nevertheless occur only after quite long time lags. *Execution lags,* lags that occur after the decision has been made to implement the policy, can have important implications for the conduct of monetary policy.

There are four reasons why monetary policy—changes in the reserves of the banking system—does not affect the economy instantly.

Deposit Creation Takes Time.   Open-market operations or the switching of government deposits affect the reserves of the banks. This process takes place more-or-less instantly. But the full increase in the money supply occurs only when the commercial banks have granted enough new loans and made enough investments to expand the money supply by the full amount that is possible by existing reserve ratios. This process can take quite a long time.

Switching Between Assets Takes Time. Dividing all assets into just two categories, money

TWO VIEWS ON THE ROLE OF MONEY IN THE GREAT DEPRESSION*

In most peoples' minds, the Great Depression began with the stock market crash of October 1929. In the United States, Canada, and Europe, the decline in economic activity over the next four years was massive. From 1929 to 1933, real output fell by roughly 25 percent, one quarter of the labour force was unemployed by 1933, the price level fell by over 25 percent, and businesses failed on a massive scale. In the six decades that have followed, no recession has come close to the Great Depression in terms of reduced economic activity, business failures or unemployment.

The Great Depression has naturally attracted the attention of economists and, especially in the United States, these few years of experience has served as a kind of "retrospective laboratory" in which they have tried to test their theories.

THE BASIC FACTS

The stock market crash of 1929, and other factors associated with a moderate downswing in business activity during the late 1920s, caused the U.S. public

(firms and households) to wish to hold more cash and less demand deposits. The banking system, however, could not meet this increased demand for liquidity without help from the Federal Reserve System (the U.S. central bank). As we saw in Chapter 27, because of the fractional-reserve banking system, commercial banks are never able to satisfy from their own reserves a large and sudden demand for cash— their reserves are always only a very small fraction of total deposits.

The Fed had been set up to provide just such emergency assistance to commercial banks that were basically sound but were unable to meet sudden demands by depositors to withdraw cash. However, the Fed refused to extend the necessary help, and successive waves of bank failures followed as a direct result. During each wave, hundreds of banks failed, ruining many depositors and thereby worsening an already severe depression. In the second half of 1931, almost 2,000 U.S. banks were forced to suspend operations. One consequence of this was a sharp drop in the money supply; by 1933, 33 percent less money (M2) was in circulation than in 1929.

COMPETING EXPLANATIONS

To Monetarists, these facts seem decisive: To them, the fall in the money supply was clearly the major cause of the fall in output and employment that occurred during the Great Depression. Monetarists see

*For a discussion of these two views, and some attempts to discriminate between them, see Peter Temin, *Did Monetary Forces Cause the Great Depression?* (New York: Norton, 1976). For the classic statement of the Monetarist view, see Milton Friedman and Anna Schwartz, *A Monetary History of the United States 1867–1960* (Princeton: Princeton University Press, 1963).

and bonds, is useful for showing the underlying forces at work in determining the demand for money. In fact, however, there is a whole series of assets, including currency and demand deposits, term deposits, treasury bills, short-term bonds, long-term bonds, and equities. When households find themselves with larger money balances than they require,

a chain of substitution occurs, and households try to hold less money and more interest-earning assets. These adjustments can take considerable time to work out.

Changes in Investment Take Time.   A change in the money supply leads to a change in the interest rate. This, in turn, affects interest-sensitive expendithe Great Depression as perhaps the single best piece of evidence of the strength of monetary forces, and the single best lesson of the importance of monetary policy. In their view, the increased cash drain which led to the massive monetary contraction could have been prevented had the Federal Reserve quickly increased the level of reserves in the commercial banking system. In this case, the rise in the monetary base would have offset the increase in the cash drain, so that the money supply (currency plus bank deposits) could be maintained.

Keynesians argue that the fundamental cause of the Great Depression was a reduction in autonomous expenditure. They cite a large decline in housing construction (in response to a glut of housing) and a reduction in consumption driven largely by pessimism caused by the stock market crash. Although Keynesians accept the argument that the Fed's behavior was perverse, and exacerbated an already bad situation, they do not attribute a pivotal role to the Fed or to the money supply. Indeed, they see the fall in the money supply as a *result* of the decline in economic activity (through a reduced demand for loans and thus reduced bank lending) rather than as its cause.

LESSONS FROM CANADA'S EXPERIENCE

Canada can be used as a "control" in this retrospective laboratory, for the simple reason that Canada

had broadly the same magnitude of economic collapse as did the United States, but it *did not* have the same magnitude of bank failures. Unfortunately, Canada's experience is not able to resolve the disagreement—both sides of the debate offer explanations of Canada's experience that is consistent with their central arguments.

Keynesians look to Canada's experience to support their view that money was not central to the cause of the economic collapse in the United States. They point out that in Canada, where the central bank came to the aid of the banking system, bank failures were trivial during the Great Depression, and as a consequence, the money supply did not shrink drastically as it did in the United States. Thus their argument is that since Canada and the U.K. did not escape the Great Depression, but they *did* escape the collapse in the money supply, then money must not have been the central cause of the U.S. economic collapse.

Monetarists accept the point that Canada did not have a massive reduction in the money supply, but they argue that the economic contraction in the United States (which *was* caused by the collapse in the money supply) spilled over into Canada, largely through a dramatic reduction in demand for Canadian goods. This implies a large decline in autonomous export expenditure for Canada, and thus a decline in Canadian national income. Thus this view is essentially that money in the United States could have been an important contributor to the economic decline in Canada.

---

tures. But it takes time for new investment plans to be drawn up, approved, and put into effect. It may take a year or more before the full increase in investment expenditure occurs in response to a fall in interest rates.

The Multiplier Process Takes Time. Changes in investment expenditures brought about by

changes in the interest rate set off the multiplier process that increases national income. This, too, takes some time to work out.

Furthermore, although the end result is fairly predictable, the speed with which the entire expansionary or contractionary process works itself out can vary in ways that are hard to predict. So though the effects of monetary policy might be reasonably straightforward to predict, the timing of those effects is difficult to predict.

Monetary policy is capable of exerting expansionary and contractionary forces on the economy, but it operates with a time lag that is long and variable.

IMPLICATIONS OF EXECUTION LAGS

To see the significance of execution lags for the conduct of monetary policy, consider a simple example. To begin, suppose that the lag is known to be exactly 18 months. If on December 1, the Bank of Canada decides that the economy needs a stimulus, it can increase the reserves of the banking system within the day and the money supply can then begin to increase. By the end of the year a significant increase may be registered.

However, because the full effects of this policy take time to work out, the policy may prove to be destabilizing. By the next autumn, a substantial inflationary gap may have developed because of cyclical forces unrelated to the Bank's monetary policy. However, the effects of the monetary expansion that was initiated nine months earlier are just beginning to be felt, so an expansionary monetary stimulus is adding to the existing inflationary gap.

If the Bank now applies the monetary brakes by contracting the money supply, the full effects of this move will not be felt for another 18 months. By that time, a contraction may have already set in because of the natural cyclical forces of the economy. If this is so, the delayed effects of the monetary policy may turn a minor downturn into a major recession.

The long execution lag of monetary policy makes monetary fine-tuning difficult; the policy may have a destabilizing effect.

We supposed in this example that the execution lag was known with certainty to be 18 months. In this case, it could be built into the Bank's calculations. But the fact that the lag is actually highly variable makes this nearly impossible. Of course, when a persistent gap has existed and is predicted to continue for a long time, monetary policy may be stabilizing even when its effects occur after a long time lag.

A MONETARY RULE?

Monetarists have persistently criticized the Bank for fine-tuning, and the poor record of monetary policy as a short-run stabilizer has lent force to their criticisms. Monetarists in Canada typically argue that:

- monetary policy is a potent force of expansionary and contractionary pressures;

- monetary policy works with long and variable lags;

- the Bank is given to sudden and sharp reversals of its policy stance.

Given these three premises, Monetarists have concluded that monetary policy has sometimes had a destabilizing effect on the economy, the policy itself accentuating rather than dampening the economy's natural cyclical swings.

Monetarists argue from this position that the stability of the economy would be much improved if the Bank *stopped trying to stabilize it.* What then should the Bank do? Because growth of population and of productivity leads to a rising level of real output, Monetarists think the Bank ought to expand the money supply year in and year out at a constant rate that is equal to the rate of growth of real income. When the growth rate shows signs of long-term change, the Bank can adjust its rate of monetary expansion. It should not, however, alter this rate with a view to stabilizing the economy against short-term fluctuations.

Many other economists disagree with the Monetarists' position against fine tuning. They argue that an appropriate monetary policy of fine tuning can, *in principle,* reduce cyclical fluctuations below what they would be under a constant-rate rule. Monetarists respond, however, by arguing that the experience of the 1970s shows that whatever may be true of the *best conceivable* monetary policy, the Bank's *actual* policy made cyclical fluctuations larger than they would have been under a constant-rate rule. They argue that attempts to use monetary policy to fine-tune the economy inevitably are fraught with dangers.

There is another argument against a constant-rate rule, however. Recent experience has shown that the demand for money sometimes can shift quite substantially. A stable money supply rule in the face of demand instability guarantees monetary shocks, rather than monetary stability (recall Figure 29-3). This undermines confidence in the appropriateness of a monetary rule. The daunting challenge that faces central banks in this situation is to offset such shifts in the demand for money while not overreacting and thereby destabilizing the economy.

25 YEARS OF CANADIAN MONETARY POLICY

This section describes a few key episodes in recent Canadian monetary history. This is not done to teach history for its own sake, but because the lessons of past experience and past policy mistakes, interpreted through the filter of economic theory, provide our best hope for improving our policy performance in the future.

Throughout the 1950s and 1960s, the Bank of Canada used interest rates as its main intermediate target. Although it was frequently difficult to judge the stance of monetary policy by observing interest rates, in some instances the stance was clear. For example, there is little doubt that monetary policy was contractionary in 1968 and 1969, when the Bank tried to insulate Canada from rising U.S. inflation.[1] There is also little doubt that monetary policy was quite expansionary in the early 1970s. In 1974, Canadian inflation was close to the double-digit level *before* the first OPEC shock that sent oil prices, and then the general price level, soaring.

By the mid 1970s there was a wide consensus that using interest rates as the main intermediate target was inappropriate, and central banks around the world began to focus instead on monetary aggregates.

MONETARY GRADUALISM: 1975–1980

In 1975, the Bank of Canada announced its policy of "monetary gradualism." This involved gradually re-ducing the rate of growth of the narrowly defined money supply (M1) in an effort to reduce the inflation rate slowly. A target range for money supply growth was publicly announced and periodically revised downward.

The Bank was quite successful at keeping actual money growth inside the target range, although there was considerable movement within that range. But after some reduction during the early periods of gradualism, the inflation rate accelerated, and by the end of the decade, it was not far below the rate prevailing when the policy was introduced in 1975. Why didn't the slow growth rate of M1 reduce inflation? The explanation was as follows:

The monetary restraint sought through gradual reduction in the rate of growth of the money supply was offset by reductions in the demand for money.

These reductions in money demand resulted from a series of spectacular institutional changes induced by the high inflation rate. The changes showed just how adaptive financial systems can be to changes in the needs of their users and in the information and technology available to them. Firms learned how to reduce their M1 balances by careful cash management and were often able to lend their operating balance on an overnight basis, thus earning interest on funds that would otherwise have been idle. Banks introduced automatic transfer systems, where money could be held in interest-earning accounts and transferred to chequing accounts only when needed. As a result of such changes, the private-sector demand for M1 balances often fell faster than the supply was being restricted by the bank. Thus M1 control did not always create the desired conditions of tight money.

In 1982, the Bank of Canada formally abandoned monetary targeting, although it remained committed to trying to control the economy through aggregate demand. It stated, however, that no observed relation between M1 or any other monetary magnitude, on the one hand, and national income, on the other hand, was stable enough to make complete reliance on monetary aggregates useful.

---

[1] The attempt was frustrated by the Bank's commitment to a fixed exchange rate between the Canadian dollar and the U.S. dollar. As we shall see in Chapters 37 and 38, monetary policy cannot simultaneously control the money supply and the exchange rate.

FIGURE 29-4
Short-Term Interest Rates, Canada and the United States, 1979–1996

Canadian interest rates have been highly variable over the period shown. They increased with the rising inflation from 1980 to mid 1981. They then fell as inflation fell through most of the 1980s. Starting in 1988, the rates rose steadily under the impact of the Bank of Canada's anti-inflation policy. Then as the inflation rate tumbled in mid 1992, interest rates, which began to decline in 1990, finally in 1993 reached levels lower than had been seen since the 1960s. These low interest rates continued (with some ups and downs) through to the middle of 1996.

Historically, Canadian interest rates have usually been higher than U.S. rates, the margin typically being between 1½ and 2½ percentage points. In the late 1980s the Bank's anti-inflation policy, which was not matched in the United States by the Fed, drove the differential to unprecedented heights, reaching over 5 percentage points at the end of 1990. This rising differential between 1988 and 1990 contributed, through an inflow of foreign financial capital, to an appreciation of the Canadian dollar which reduced the competitiveness of Canadian exports.

MONETARY STRINGENCY: 1981–1983

The early 1980s saw an extremely restrictive monetary policy, with interest rates rising to unprecedented levels; the rate on 90-day government treasury bills reached over 18 percent, as shown in Figure 29-4. Over a period of 18 months, inflation

fell from around 10 percent to around 4 percent. The cost was a very severe recession.

In 1980, the Canadian and the U.S. central banks had embarked on a policy of monetary restraint aimed at fighting inflation. Interest rates rose, helping to choke off the recovery that had just started. The subsequent rise in rates in early 1982 fed the downturn and helped make it the most serious recession since the 1930s.

These high interest rates, and the recession they wrought, were more severe than might have been expected from the relatively moderate slowdown in the rate of growth of the money supply induced by the central banks.

An unanticipated surge in the demand for money led to a much tighter monetary policy than the Bank had intended.

This unplanned tight monetary policy did not occur because money supply targets were missed, but because money demand rose. (This was the opposite of the shift in the demand for money that disrupted Canadian monetary gradualism in the 1970s.) By June 1982, M1 was back in its target range. The serious weakness in the economy and the "room for monetary ease" created by the return of M1 to its target range led to a loosening of monetary policy in the second half of 1982.

ECONOMIC RECOVERY: 1983–1987

In early 1983, a sustained recovery began, and by mid 1987, national income had moved back toward potential. Much of the growth was centred in the export-oriented manufacturing industries in Ontario and Quebec. The first four years of the recovery saw cumulative output growth of 15.7 percent.

The main challenge for monetary policy in this period was to create sufficient liquidity to accommodate the recovery without triggering a return to the high inflation rates that prevailed at the start of the decade.

In other words, the Bank of Canada had to increase the money supply to *accommodate* the recovery-induced increase in money demand *without* increasing the money supply so much that it refueled inflationary pressures.

In spite of much debate and uncertainty, the Bank handled this so-called "reentry" problem quite well. The Bank allowed a short but rapid burst of growth in the nominal money supply, thus generating the desired increase in real money balances. Once the new level of real balances was achieved, money growth was cut back to a rate consistent with low inflation, allowing for the underlying rate of growth in real income. The trick with this policy was that to avoid triggering expectations of renewed inflation, the Bank had to generate a one-shot increase in the *level* of the money supply without creating the impression that it was raising the long-term *rate of growth* of the money supply.

In late 1983 and early 1984, when growth in monetary aggregates first started to surge, many voiced the fear that the Bank was being overly expansionary and was risking a return to higher inflation. As the reentry problem came to be more widely understood and as inflationary pressures failed to reemerge, these criticisms subsided, and the consensus appeared to be that the Bank had done a commendable job of handling the reentry problem.

RISING INFLATION: 1987–1991

By mid 1987, many observers began to worry that Canadian policy makers were too complacent in accepting the 4 percent range that Canadian inflation had settled into. Further, there was concern that inflationary pressures were starting to build—monetary aggregates were growing quickly, real output growth was strong, unemployment was falling, and an inflationary gap was opening.

In 1987, many economists argued that if monetary policy was not tightened, Canada would experience gradually increasing inflation until once again a severe monetary restriction would be necessary.

Inflation slowly crept upward. A monetary restriction designed to reduce inflation would obviously impose costs in the form of lower output and higher unemployment. Was the Bank prepared to inflict such costs, especially given that Canada had emerged from a deep recession only five years earlier?

In January 1988, Bank of Canada Governor John Crow announced that monetary policy would henceforth be less guided by short-term stabilization issues and more guided by the goal of long-term "price stability." Specifically, he said that "monetary policy should be conducted so as to achieve a pace of monetary expansion that promotes stability in the value of money. This means pursuing a policy aimed at achieving and maintaining stable prices."[2]

This explicit adoption of price stability as the Bank's only target set off a heated debate about the appropriate stance for monetary policy. The debate was fueled by Crow's decision to give a high profile to his policy by repeatedly articulating and defending it in speeches and public appearances. Some critics said that price stability was unobtainable. Others said the costs of reaching it would be too large in terms of several years of recessionary gaps. Supporters said that the long-term gains from having a stable price level with a secure and certain value of money would exceed the costs of getting there.

Despite the Bank's explicit policy of "price stability," the actual inflation rate increased slightly in the years immediately following John Crow's policy announcement, from about 4 percent in 1987 to just over 5 percent in 1990.

The controversy reached new heights when in 1990 the country (and much of the world) entered a sustained recession. Maintaining the policy of tight money with high interest rates seemed perverse to many when the economy was already suffering from too little aggregate demand to sustain potential output.

Furthermore, the high Canadian interest rates attracted foreign funds. Foreigners who wished to buy Canadian bonds needed Canadian dollars, and their demands led to an appreciation of the Canadian dollar. This increased the price of Canadian exports while reducing the price of Canadian imports, putting Canadian export and import-competing industries at a competitive disadvantage, and further increasing the unemployment that had been generated by the worldwide recession.

In spite of heavy political pressure to lower interest rates, and of criticism from many economists who might have supported a move toward price sta-

bility in less depressed times, the Bank stood by its tight monetary policy. Indeed, in 1991, it formally announced *inflation-control targets* for the next several years. Beginning in 1992, inflation was to lie within the 3–5 percent range, with the range falling to 2–4 percent by 1993 and to 1–3 percent by the end of 1995.

The result of this commitment to tight money was an unprecedented differential between Canadian and U.S. interest rates (see Figure 29-4), and a high value of the Canadian dollar, which temporarily hurt the international competitiveness of Canadian goods.

THE DRIVE FOR PRICE STABILITY: 1992-?

As a result of the tight monetary policy of the Bank, the inflation rate eventually fell, from about 5 percent in 1990 to less than 2 percent in 1992. For 1993 and 1994, inflation hovered around 2 percent. Furthermore, short-term nominal interest rates fell from a high of 12 percent in 1990 to about 6 percent by the end of 1993. The differential between Canadian and U.S. rates also fell. Figure 29-4 tells the story in detail.

Much of the little inflation that did occur in early 1993 was beyond the Bank's reach, since it came in the government sector, being due to rises in prices resulting from rising taxes on goods and services as well as price rises in regulated industries.

Clearly, the Bank had succeeded in coming close to its target of price stability. Controversy continued, however, on two issues. First, was the result worth the price of a deeper, possibly more prolonged recession than might have occurred if the Bank had been willing to accept 3–4 percent inflation? Second, would the low inflation rate be sustainable once the recovery took the economy back toward potential income? If the inflation rate were to rise to 4 percent during the post-1993 recovery, then the verdict might well be that the cost of temporarily reducing the rate to about 1 percent was not worth the transitory gains.

The debate over the Bank's disinflation policy became centered on Governor John Crow, especially during the federal election campaign of 1993. Some called for the nonrenewal of John

[2]John W. Crow, "The Work of Canadian Monetary Policy," speech given at the University of Alberta, January 18, 1988; reprinted in *Bank of Canada Review*, February 1988.

Crow's term as Governor (which would end in 1994), and his replacement with someone more concerned with the costs of disinflation. Others argued that the Bank's policy of "price stability" under the stewardship of John Crow was the right policy for the times, and that the long-run benefits of low inflation would be worth the costs required to achieve it.[3]

In 1994, the minister of finance appointed Gordon Thiessen, the former deputy governor of the Bank, to be the new governor. With some irony, the minister of finance, whose party had been severe critics of Crow's policy while they were in opposition, affirmed the previous monetary policy of the Bank and urged the new governor to maintain the hard-won low inflation rate. The new governor also affirmed the policy of price stability, and extended the formal inflation target, then in the 1–3 percent range, to the end of 1998.

Throughout most of 1994 and 1995, the rate of inflation continued to hover between 1 and 2 percent. The main challenge for the Bank in the next few years was to keep inflation low while at the same time encouraging the economy to progress through what was viewed as a fragile economic recovery. Excessive stimulation of the economy would lead to the rise of inflation which would sacrifice the hard-won gains achieved only a few years earlier. On

---

[3]For a very readable account of Canadian monetary policy from 1988 to 1993, see William Robson and David Laidler, *The Great Canadian Disinflation* (Toronto: C. D. Howe Institute, 1993).

the other hand, insufficient stimulation would itself be an obstacle to economic recovery.

THE LESSONS

The study of the past 25 years of monetary policy provides a number of important lessons that, if properly understood, should help to guide policy in the future. First, the economy is too complex in its behaviour for a simple money supply rule to provide the best monetary policy. Second, monetary policy can alter between being restrictive and expansive for reasons that are related to shifts in the private sector's demand for money and that are not related to the Bank's monetary policy. Third, to judge the stance of current monetary policy, the Bank needs to monitor a number of variables, including the various measures of the money supply, real and nominal interest rates, and the exchange rate. Fourth, contrary to what was once widely believed, monetary policy is an extremely potent tool for influencing aggregate demand. It may be difficult to predict in advance how fast and how strongly a given policy will operate, but if the Bank is prepared to be restrictive enough, it can reduce the inflation rate to low levels. There is room for debate about whether the result is worth the cost, but there should be no debate about the ability of the Bank to operate a very restrictive or a very expansionary monetary policy, and hence to alter the inflation rate over a wide range of values.

SUMMARY

A. THE BANK OF CANADA'S CONTROL OVER THE MONEY SUPPLY

- The major tool the Bank of Canada uses to control the supply of money is control of reserves of the commercial banking system through open-market operations and by switching government deposits between itself and the chartered banks. Purchases of bonds on the

open market or switching government deposits toward the chartered banks increases the reserves of the banking system. Sales on the open market or withdrawing government deposits away from the chartered banks reduces bank reserves.

- The Bank of Canada now operates a system of zero required reserves, which means that each commercial bank's reserves must average to zero (or a positive amount) over a four-week averaging period.

- Commercial banks wish to hold some positive reserves, because if they are forced by inadequate reserves to borrow from the Bank of Canada, they pay a price through direct interest costs and forgone interest earnings that is twice the bank rate.

B. POLICY VARIABLES AND POLICY INSTRUMENTS

- The Bank's policy variables are national income and the rate of inflation. To influence these, the Bank works through policy instruments that it can control and that will in turn influence its policy variables. Intermediate targets are used to guide decisions about policy instruments.
- When it sets the reserves of the banking system, the Bank must choose between the interest rate and the money supply as the intermediate target.
- To reduce national income, the Bank reduces bank reserves, driving up the interest rate, and shifting the aggregate demand curve to the left. To increase national income, the Bank increases reserves, driving down the interest rate, and shifting the aggregate demand curve to the right.

C. LAGS IN THE CONDUCT OF MONETARY POLICY

- Though the Bank can change the reserves of the banking system more-or-less instantly, it takes time for this change in reserves to be transformed into a change in bank deposits and thus a change in the money supply.
- Once interest rates change in response to a change in the money supply, it takes time for firms and households to change their expenditure. Even once those new plans are carried out, it takes time for the multiplier process to work its way through the economy, eventually increasing equilibrium national income.
- Not only is there a significant lag from when bank reserves are changed to when national income changes, but this time lag is itself uncertain. Monetary policy is thus said to work with "long and variable lags."
- The existence of such long and variable lags have led some economists to argue that the Bank of Canada should not use monetary policy in an attempt to stabilize national income. They argue that attempts to stabilize will in fact be destabilizing, and advocate the use of a monetary rule whereby bank reserves are increased at a more-or-less constant rate.

- Others argue that such a monetary rule would be undesirable, especially since experience shows that the demand for money is unstable. They argue that the Bank of Canada could *in principle* reduce fluctuations in national income by responding to sudden changes in money demand.

D. 25 YEARS OF CANADIAN MONETARY POLICY

- During the late 1970s, the Bank of Canada adopted a policy of "monetary gradualism" which was aimed at gradually reducing the rate of growth of the narrowly defined money supply, M1. Changes in the demand for money during this time undermined the usefulness of this approach.
- In the early 1980s, the Bank of Canada embarked on a policy of extremely tight money to reduce inflation. This policy contributed to the severity of the recession.
- A sustained economic recovery occurred from 1983 to 1987. The main challenge for monetary policy during this time was to create sufficient liquidity to accommodate the recovery without triggering a return to the high inflation rates that prevailed at the start of the decade.
- In 1988, when inflation was between 4 and 5 percent, the Bank of Canada announced that monetary policy would no longer be guided by short-term stabilization and instead would be guided by the long-term goal of "price stability." By 1992, the Bank's tight money policy had reduced inflation to below 2 percent.
- Controversy concerned two issues. First, was the cost in terms of lost output, heavy unemployment and a temporary reduction in international competitiveness worth the benefit in terms of long-term stable currency? Second, could the low inflation rate be sustained?
- This controversy was partly responsible for the 1994 change in the Bank of Canada's Governor, from John Crow to Gordon Thiessen. Despite this administrative change, the stated policy of price stability continued. By early 1996, the rate of inflation had been hovering around 2 percent for about four years.
- One lesson for the experience of monetary policy is that the stance of monetary policy depends on fluctuations in both the demand for and the supply of money. Although the Bank can exert a strong influence on money supply, it has less control over money demand. For this reason, monetary policy cannot be reduced to any simple rule.

KEY CONCEPTS

Open-market operations
Shifting government deposits
The bank rate
Policy variables

Policy instruments
Intermediate targets
The Monetary Conditions Index
  (MCI)

Variability of monetary policy
Monetary rules
Lags in the effect of monetary policy
Shifts in the demand for money

DISCUSSION QUESTIONS

1. During the recovery of the Canadian economy from 1983 to 1985, two different views were often expressed. Some analysts said that adherence to a long-run constant growth rate rule for monetary aggregates was particularly important, lest inflationary expectations be rekindled by an overly fast rate of monetary expansion. Others said that encouraging the recovery required a temporary burst of monetary expansion. Discuss these two views.

2. The U.S. Federal Reserve Board runs a facility in Culpeper, Virginia, that costs $1.8 million per year to maintain and to guard against robbery. Inside this "Culpeper switch," a dugout in the side of a mountain, the government has hidden $4 billion in new currency for the purpose, it says, of "providing a hedge against any nuclear attack that would wipe out the nation's money supply." Comment on the sense of this policy.

3. Describe the chief weapons of monetary policy available to the Bank of Canada, and indicate whether—and if so, how—they might be used for the following purposes:

   a. To create a mild tightening of bank credit
   b. To signal that the Bank of Canada favours a sharp curtailment of bank lending
   c. To permit an expansion of bank credit with existing reserves
   d. To supply banks and the public with a temporary increase of currency for Christmas shopping

4. It is often said that an expansionary monetary policy is like "pushing on a string." What is meant by this statement? How does this contrast with a contractionary monetary policy?

5. In what situations might the following pairs of objectives come into conflict?

   a. Lowering the cost of government finance and using monetary policy to change aggregate demand
   b. Ending a deep recession and maintaining a currently achieved target for monetary growth
   c. Maintaining stable interest rates and controlling inflation
   d. Stimulating the economy and supporting the value of the dollar on foreign exchange markets

6. In 1988, the Bank of Canada announced that it was committed to achieving "price stability," but it did not commit itself to a particular target growth rate for any monetary aggregate that would be consistent with achieving its price stability target. Why do you think it failed to make such a commitment?

7. In 1993, with 11 percent unemployment, a slow recovery just underway and inflation in the 1 to 2 percent range, the Bank permitted a rapid expansion of M1. Was this inflationary? Why might the Bank have adopted this policy? What is meant by the "reentry" problem?

8. In late 1993, the new Liberal minister of finance was being urged by some economists to reappoint Bank of Canada governor John Crow when his current term was set to expire in early 1994. Economists from the banking community predicted that not appointing Crow would hurt the government's credibility on anti-inflation policy, leading to a sharp rise in Canadian interest rates that would cost the government extra billions in serving its massive national debt. As it turned out, the minister of finance replaced John Crow with Gordon Thiessen. Was there any discernible effect on Canadian interest rates? If so, how long did it appear to last? If there wasn't, provide one possible explanation.

9. Suppose that the Bank of Canada increases the reserves of the banking system by $100 million. Using

the Bank of Canada's balance sheet, explain the difference between an open-market purchase of $100 million and a switch of government deposits of $100 million. Do these two actions have different implications for the eventual change in the money supply?

10. The term "moral suasion" is generally used to describe attempts by the Bank of Canada to enlist the cooperation of private financial institutions in the pursuit of some objective of monetary policy. In a country such as Canada, where there are only a few banks, the central bank can easily communicate its view to the chartered banks. Using the balance sheets of the Bank of Canada and the commercial banking system, explain how an attempt by the Bank of Canada to persuade commercial banks to increase their lending would affect bank reserves and total bank deposits.

PART TEN

MACROECONOMIC PROBLEMS AND POLICIES

What causes sustained inflation? Why does the Bank of Canada appear to believe that an important part of reducing *actual* inflation is to reduce peoples' *expectations* of inflation? What do we mean by the "natural" rate of unemployment, and how does this differ from cyclical unemployment? Do labour-market policies such as unemployment insurance affect the natural rate? What is the connection between the government budget deficit and the stock of government debt? Do government budget deficits raise interest rates, or do they have little or no effect on key macroeconomic variables? What are the key determinants of economic growth? Can the market be left to its own to provide growth, or are government policies to encourage growth necessary? What explains the different rates of economic growth in developed versus developing countries? These are the sorts of questions you will be able to answer after reading the next five chapters.

This part of the book contains five chapters on key macroeconomic issues. The chapters may be read in any order and each one may be read independently of the others. Chapter 30 discusses the causes of *inflation*. You will see the important distinction between *cyclical* inflation and *sustained* inflation. You will learn about the Bank of Canada's role in maintaining a sustained inflation, as well as its role in ending one. It is there that you will understand why peoples' *expectations* about inflation are so important to the inflation process itself.

In Chapter 31 we discuss unemployment. Two different theories of *cyclical* unemployment are considered—*New Classical* and *New Keynesian*. You then learn about the natural rate of unemployment—often called the *Nonaccelerating Inflation Rate of Unemployment* (NAIRU). You will see what determines the NAIRU and why several labour-market policies have the unintended consequence of increasing the NAIRU.

Chapter 32 returns you to the issues of fiscal policy, examining in detail government deficits and government debt. You will learn how to judge the *stance* of fiscal policy, as well as the important connection between government deficits and *national saving*. You will understand in what situations government deficits raise interest rates, and what happens as a result.

Chapters 33 and 34 examine economic growth. Chapter 33 emphasizes the theory of economic growth, discussing some established theories based on *capital accumulation* as well as some more recent theories based on *endogenous technical change* and *increasing returns*. Chapter 34 then examines the issue of economic growth in the *developing economies* and examines why some countries have had such slow rates of growth. You will then learn some of the recent views about what policies these countries might implement to improve their growth rates.

CHAPTER 30

INFLATION

If you look again at Figure 21-6 in Chapter 21, you will see that inflation remained relatively low for 20 years following World War II. The only exceptions were the "bubbles" immediately following World War II and during the Korean War in the early 1950s. Starting in the late 1960s, the inflation rate slowly rose, reaching the double-digit range by the mid 1970s. It fell only slightly during the late 1970s, in spite of a concerted anti-inflationary policy, and rose again to the double-digit level in 1980. It remained quite high during the recession of 1981–1982, fell dramatically to 4 percent in 1983, and remained near that figure through 1987. Although this was an improvement over the double-digit inflation rates experienced earlier, 4 percent was, historically, a high inflation rate to be experienced at the end of a serious recession.

During the latter half of 1988, after several years of a vigorous economic recovery, the inflation rate crept up to over 5 percent, where it stayed through 1989 and the early part of 1990. The Bank of Canada's attempt to reduce inflation—first back to the 4 percent level and then down to below 2 percent—caused renewed controversy about the methods, the costs, and the benefits of fighting inflation. By mid 1996, inflation was between 1 and 2 percent. At that time, the Bank of Canada's monetary policy, as we saw in the last chapter, was attempting the fine balancing act between encouraging a fragile recovery and risking a rekindling of inflationary pressures.

In Chapter 21, we briefly examined the costs of inflation, and that discussion should be reread at this time. Recall that there we examined the costs of inflation, but we did not discuss the costs of *reducing* inflation. And as we shall see in this chapter, the costs associated with reducing inflation play an important part in the conduct of monetary policy.

We now turn to the subject of inflation in more detail. What causes inflation? What are the costs of reducing it? Can inflation be prevented from rising into the double-digit range again? Can inflation ever be eliminated altogether?

CAUSES AND CONSEQUENCES OF INFLATION

An *inflationary shock* is anything that tends to increase the price level; a *deflationary shock* is anything that tends to decrease it. We start by making three important distinctions concerning these shocks.

1. Inflations or deflations that are caused by shifts in aggregate demand—which are referred to as *demand shocks*—must be distinguished from inflations or deflations that are caused by shifts in aggregate supply—which are referred to as *supply shocks*.

2. Isolated, once-and-for-all shocks must be distinguished from repeated shocks. The former cause temporary bouts of inflation as the price level moves from one equilibrium level to another. The latter cause continuous, or sustained, inflation.

3. Increases in the price level that occur even though the money supply is constant must be distinguished from those that take place when the money supply is increasing. When an increase in the money supply accompanies inflationary shocks, the resulting inflation is said to be *validated* by the monetary expansion.

In this book, we use the term **inflation** as it is commonly used in ordinary speech to mean any rise in the price level. We then make the distinction between once-and-for-all and continuing rises in the price level by referring to temporary or once-and-for-all inflation on the one hand and to continuing or sustained inflation on the other.[1]

We first studied inflationary shocks in Chapter 26. There it was enough to say that an inflationary gap implies excess demand for labour, low unemployment, upward pressure on wages, and hence an upward-shifting *SRAS* curve. Understanding the forces that cause wage rates to change, and knowing when these changes do and do not cause the *SRAS* curve to shift, are keys to understanding inflation.

WHY WAGES CHANGE

We saw in Chapter 26 that increases in wage rates do not necessarily cause unit costs to rise because these costs depend on the relationship between the price of labour and labour productivity (i.e., output per unit of labour input). For example, if wage rates and productivity both rise by 3 percent, each unit of labour costs 3 percent more but also produces 3 percent more. As a result, labour costs *per unit of output* remain unchanged. What matters then is the re-

---

[1]Some economists reserve the term *inflation* for sustained changes in the price level, using other words, such as *a rise in the price level*, to refer to once-and-for-all changes. As long as one understands the distinction, the choice of words is not important.

lationship between changes in money wages and changes in productivity. As in earlier chapters, we use the expression "changes in money wages relative to productivity" to refer to *the percentage change in money wages minus the percentage change in productivity;* the result measures the change in unit labour costs.

Two of the main forces that can cause unit labour costs to change systematically are the demand for labour and expectations of future inflation.[2] Much of what we say in the case of labour demand is a recapitulation of material first presented in Chapter 26, but the points are important enough to bear repeating.

Labour Demand and the NAIRU

In Chapter 26, we stated three propositions about how changes in money wages relative to productivity were influenced by the relationship between aggregate demand and aggregate supply:

1. The excess demand for labour that is associated with an inflationary gap puts upward pressure on money wages relative to productivity. Money wages rise more rapidly than productivity is rising.

2. The excess supply of labour associated with a recessionary gap puts downward pressure on money wages relative to productivity. Money wages rise more slowly than productivity is rising (and money wages may even fall).

3. The absence of either an inflationary or a recessionary gap means that demand forces do not exert any pressure on money wages either to rise or to fall relative to productivity.

We saw in Chapter 21 that when current national income is equal to its potential level (Y^*), the unemployment rate is said to be equal to the NAIRU, which stands for the *nonaccelerating inflation rate of*

---

[2]Changes in wages relative to productivity may be affected by other forces that are associated with neither excess demand nor expectations of inflation, such as government guidelines, union power, and employers' optimism. Because there are many such forces that tend to act independently of one another, they may be regarded as random shocks. Although they may occasionally have significant effects in any one year, over a longer period of time, positive shocks in some years will tend to be offset by negative shocks in other years so that in total they contribute little to the long-term trend of the price level. For this reason, they can be ignored in an introductory study.

TABLE 30-1
The Characteristics of Various Output Gaps

Actual Income = Y
Potential Income = Y^*
Actual Unemployment Rate = U
NAIRU = U^*
$\dot{X}$ = rate of change of X

Recessionary Gaps	Potential Income	Inflationary Gaps
$Y < Y^*$	$Y = Y^*$	$Y > Y^*$
$U > U^*$	$U = U^*$	$U < U^*$
$\dot{W} < \dot{g}$	$\dot{W} = \dot{g}$	$\dot{W} > \dot{g}$
$\dot{c} < 0$	$\dot{c} = 0$	$\dot{c} > 0$

Unit costs fall during recessionary gaps and rise during inflationary gaps. During a recessionary gap, income is less than potential, the unemployment rate exceeds the NAIRU (U^*), money wages rise at a lower rate (indicated by $\dot{W}$) than productivity (indicated by $\dot{g}$) does, and the change in unit costs (indicated by $\dot{c}$) is negative—unit costs fall.

During an inflationary gap, income exceeds potential, the unemployment rate is less than the NAIRU, money wages rise at a faster rate than productivity, and unit costs rise.

---

unemployment. The use of this particular name will be explained later in this chapter. Another name sometimes used in place of NAIRU is the *natural rate of unemployment,* but NAIRU is now the more common usage. We designate NAIRU by the symbol U^*.

The NAIRU is not zero. Instead, even when output equals potential output, there may be a substantial amount of *frictional* and *structural* unemployment caused, for example, by the movement of people between jobs or between regions. When national income exceeds potential income ($Y > Y^*$), the unemployment rate will be less than the NAIRU ($U < U^*$). When national income is less than potential income ($Y < Y^*$), the unemployment rate will exceed the NAIRU ($U > U^*$).

We have seen that wages and unit costs react to various pressures of demand. These demand pressures can now be stated either in terms of the relationship between actual and potential income or in terms of the relationship between the actual unemployment rate and the NAIRU. This is done in Table 30-1. When output exceeds potential (and unemployment is less than U^*), there is an inflationary gap which is characterized by excess demand for labour; wages and unit costs tend to rise. Conversely, when output is less than potential (and unemployment exceeds U^*), there is a recessionary gap which is characterized by excess supply of labour; wages and unit costs tend to fall.

EXTENSION 30-1

THE PHILLIPS CURVE AND THE SHIFTING *SRAS* CURVE

In the early 1950s, Professor A. W. Phillips of the London School of Economics was conducting pioneering research on macroeconomic policy. In his early models, he related the rate of inflation to the difference between actual and potential income, Y^*. Later he investigated the empirical underpinnings of this equation by studying the relationship between the rate of increase of wages and the level of unemployment. He studied these variables because unemployment data were available as far back as the mid-nineteenth century, whereas very little data on output gaps were available when he did his empirical work. In 1958, he reported that a stable relationship had existed between these two variables for 100 years in the United Kingdom. This relationship came to be known as the Phillips curve. The **Phillips curve** provided an explanation, rooted in empirical observation, of the speed with which wage changes shifted the *SRAS* curve by changing unit labour costs.

The original Phillips curve related wage changes to the level of unemployment. But we can express the same information in a slightly different way. Note that unemployment and output gaps are negatively related—a recessionary gap is associated with high unemployment, and an inflationary gap is associated with low unemployment. We

can therefore create another Phillips curve which plots wage changes against output (rather than against unemployment). Both figures show the same information.

Inflationary gaps (which correspond to low unemployment rates) are associated with *increases* in wages relative to productivity, and recessionary gaps (which correspond to high unemployment rates) are associated with *decreases* in wages relative to productivity. (For simplicity, we assume zero productivity growth in this box.)

The Phillips curve must be clearly distinguished from the *SRAS* curve. The *SRAS* curve has the price level on the vertical axis, whereas the Phillips curve has the *rate of wage inflation* on the vertical axis. Therefore, the Phillips curve tells us how fast the *SRAS* curve is shifting when actual income does not equal potential income.

Only when $Y = Y^*$ is the *SRAS* curve not shifting because of demand pressures. Aggregate demand for labour then equals aggregate supply; the only unemployment is thus frictional and structural. There is then neither upward nor downward pressure on wages. Hence the Phillips curve cuts the axis at potential income Y^* and at the corresponding level of unemployment U^*. This is how Phillips drew his curve.

The relationship between the excess demand or supply of labour, the unemployment rate and the rate of change of wages is shown by what is called a *Phillips curve*. Extension 30-1 discusses the Phillips curve and how this relates to the short-run aggregate supply curve.

Expectational Forces

A second force that can influence wages is *expectations* of future inflation. Suppose that both employers and employees expect 4 percent inflation next year. Workers will start negotiations from a base of a 4 percent increase in money wages, which would

hold their *real wages* constant. Firms may also be inclined to begin bargaining by conceding at least a 4 percent increase in money wages relative to productivity because they expect that the prices at which they sell their products will rise by 4 percent. *Starting from that base,* workers will attempt to obtain some desired increase in their real wages. At this point, such factors as profits and bargaining power become important.

The expectation of some specific inflation rate creates pressure for wages to rise by that rate relative to productivity and hence for unit costs to rise at that rate.

The Phillips curve soon became famous. It provided a link between national income models and labour markets. This link allowed macroeconomists to drop the uncomfortable assumption, which they had often been forced to use in many of their earlier formal models, that money wages were rigidly fixed and neither rose nor fell as national income varied. By relating money wages to national income, the Phillips curve determines (in conjunction with productivity changes) the speed at which the SRAS curve shifts.

Consider, for example, the situation shown in Figure 30-2, where the level of income determined by the AD and SRAS curves is Y_1. Plotting Y_1 on the Phillips curve in part (i) of the figure in this box tells us that wage costs will be rising at $\dot{W}_1$. The SRAS curve in Figure 30-2 will be shifting upward by that amount. The same information can be seen in part (ii) of the figure in this box, where a national income of Y_1 in part (ii) corresponds to unemployment of U_1 in part (i).

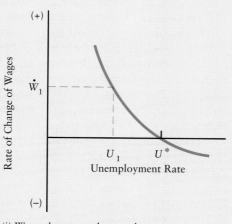

(i) Wage changes and unemployment

(ii) Wage changes and output

The key point is that money wages can be rising relative to productivity even if no inflationary gap is present. As long as people expect prices to rise, their behaviour will put upward pressure on money wages, causing unit costs to rise, thus shifting the SRAS curve upward.

The Formation of Expectations

The foregoing discussion suggests that the manner in which people form their expectations about the future course of inflation may have an important effect on that inflation. Generally, we can distinguish two main patterns: One is to look backward at past expe-

rience; the other is to look at current circumstances for a clue as to what may happen in the near future.

The first type of expectations are called *backward-looking*. People look at the past in order to predict what will happen in the future. The simplest possible form of such expectations is to expect the past to be repeated in the future. According to this view, if inflation has been 10 percent over the past year, people will expect it to be 10 percent next year. This expectation, however, is quite naive. Everyone knows that the inflation rate does change, and therefore the past cannot be a perfectly accurate guide to the future.

A less naive version would have people revise their expectations in light of the mistakes that they made in estimating inflation in the past. For example, if you thought that this year's inflation rate was going to be 10 percent but it turned out to be only 6 percent, you might revise your estimate of next year's rate down somewhat from 10 percent. Perhaps you might not go all the way to 6 percent; you might split the difference and estimate next year's rate to be 8 percent.

These are just simple illustrations of the many ways in which people can base their predictions of the future on the immediate past.

Backward-looking expectations tend to change slowly because some time must pass before a change in the actual rate of inflation provides enough past experience to cause expectations to adjust.

The second main type of expectations are those that look to current conditions to estimate what is likely to happen in the future. One version of this type assumes that people look to the government's current macroeconomic policy to form their expectations of future inflation. They are assumed to understand how the economy works, and they form their expectations by predicting the outcome of the policies now being followed. In an obvious sense, such expectations are *forward-looking*.

A strong version of forward-looking expectations is called **rational expectations.** Rational expectations are not necessarily always correct; rather, the *rational expectations hypothesis* assumes that people make the best possible use of all the available information, which implies that they will not continue to make persistent, systematic errors in forming their expectations. Thus if the economic system about which they are forming expectations remains stable, their expectations will be correct *on average*. Sometimes next year's inflation rate will turn out to be above what people expected it to be; at other times, it will turn out to be below what people expected it to be. On average over many years, however, the actual rate will not, according to the rational expectations theory, be consistently under- or overestimated.

Rational expectations have the effect of speeding up the adjustment of expectations. Instead of being based on past inflation rates, expected inflation is based on the anticipation of the outcome of existing and expected economic conditions and government policies.

Assuming that expectations are solely backward-looking seems overly naive. People do look ahead and assess future possibilities rather than just blindly reacting to what has gone before. Yet the assumption of "fully rational" forward-looking expectations that predict the expected inflation rate correctly, or nearly correctly, much of the time requires that workers and firms have a degree of understanding about the effects of government policy on inflation that few economists would claim to have.

Of course, people will not make the same error of consistently underpredicting (or overpredicting) the inflation rate for decades, but evidence suggests that they can do so for substantial periods, especially when they do not fully understand the causes of current inflation. Every past period of inflation has led to intense debate among economists about its causes, cures, and probable future course. If professional economists are uncertain, it would be surprising if wage and price setters made correct predictions on average over any short period of time.

Many observers suspect that the process of wage setting combines forward-looking behaviour with expectations based on the experience of the recent past. Depending on the circumstances, expectations will sometimes tend to rely more on past experience and at other times more on present events whose effects are expected to influence the future.

The importance of rational expectations in the study of macroeconomics is reflected by the fact that the economist most closely associated with the development of the idea, Robert E. Lucas Jr. of the University of Chicago, was awarded the Nobel Prize in 1995 for his work in this area.

Overall Effect

The foregoing discussion suggests that we can think of changes in money wages as being the result of two different basic forces:

$$\text{Change in money wages} = \text{demand effect} + \text{expectational effect}$$

It is important to realize that what happens to wages is the net effect of both of these forces. Consider two examples.

First, suppose that, with productivity unchanged, both labour and management expect 3 percent inflation next year and are willing on this account to allow money wages to increase by 3 percent. Doing so would leave the relationship between wages and other prices unaltered. Suppose as well that at the current level of national income there is a significant inflationary gap with an associated labour shortage. The demand pressure causes wages to rise by an additional 2 percentage points. The final outcome is that wages rise by 5 percent, the net effect of a 3 percent increase due to expected inflation and a 2 percent increase due to demand forces.

For the second example, assume again that with productivity constant, expected inflation is 3 percent, but that this time there is a recessionary gap at the current level of national income. The associated heavy unemployment exerts downward pressure on wage bargains. Hence the demand effect now works to moderate wage increases, say, to the extent of 2 percentage points. Wages rise by 1 percent, the net effect of a 3 percent increase due to expected inflation and a 2 percent decrease due to demand forces.

FROM WAGES TO THE *SRAS* CURVE

We established in Chapter 25 that shifts in the *SRAS* curve depend on what happens to unit costs. (Recall that for movements along a given *SRAS* curve, wage rates and other input prices are constant.) We have just seen that inflationary gaps and expectations of future inflation put pressure on wage rates to rise relative to productivity and hence cause the *SRAS* curve to shift upward. Recessionary gaps and expectations of future deflation put pressure on wage rates to fall relative to productivity and hence cause the *SRAS* curve to shift downward. What happens to the *SRAS* curve in any one year is the net effect of these two forces.

The net effect of the two forces acting on unit costs—demand and inflation expectations—determines what happens to the *SRAS* curve.

We are now ready to examine the causes and consequences of inflationary shocks. We begin with an economy in long-run equilibrium: The price level is stable, and national income is at its potential level, Y^*. We then study the economy as it is buffeted by different types of shocks. Figure 30-1 provides a guide to the various cases that we will consider; it should be used as a reference as the discussion proceeds.

DEMAND INFLATION

Inflation that is caused by general excess demand in the markets for final output and for factors of pro-

duction is variously called *demand-shock inflation, demand-pull inflation,* or simply **demand inflation.** Demand inflation occurs when a rightward shift in the aggregate demand curve causes equilibrium income to exceed Y^*. The initial shift in the *AD* curve could have been caused by a reduction in taxes, by an increase in such autonomous expenditure items as investment, government, and net exports, or by an increase in the money supply. (As we saw in Chapter 28, an increase in the money supply works through the transmission mechanism—lower interest rates, and increased investment expenditure—to shift the *AD* curve to the right.)

Major demand-shock inflations occurred in Canada during and after World Wars I and II. In these cases, large increases in government expenditure without fully offsetting increases in taxes led to general excess demand. Demand inflations also occurred in the early 1970s and early 1980s, but we shall see that these inflations were exacerbated by severe supply shocks. More generally, demand inflation sometimes occurs at the end of a strong peacetime upswing, as rising output causes excess demand to develop simultaneously in the markets for labour, intermediate goods, and final output.

To begin our study of demand inflation, suppose that an initial equilibrium is disturbed by a rightward shift in the aggregate demand curve. This shift causes the price level and output to rise, summarized under "Initial effects" of a demand shock in Figure 30-1. It is important next to distinguish between the case in which the Bank of Canada validates the demand shock and the case in which it does not.

No Monetary Validation. The case of no monetary validation is summarized as Case 1 in Figure 30-1. Because the initial rise in *AD* takes output above the full-employment level, an inflationary gap opens up. The pressure of excess demand soon causes wages to rise relative to productivity, shifting the *SRAS* curve upward and to the left. As long as the Bank of Canada holds the money supply constant, the rise in the price level moves the economy upward and to the left along the fixed new *AD* curve, reducing the inflationary gap. Eventually, the gap is eliminated, and equilibrium is established at a higher but stable price level, with income at its potential level. In this case, the initial period of inflation is followed by further inflation that lasts only until the new equilibrium is reached.

FIGURE 30-1
The Effects of Inflationary Shocks

Initial shock	Initial effects	Alternative possibilities		Final effects
Demand Shock (AD curve shifts rightward)	P rises Y rises above Y^* (inflationary gap) SRAS curve starts to shift upwards	Isolated shock Not validated →		**Case 1** P rises further and then stabilizes Y falls back to Y^*
		Sustained shock Validated →		**Case 2** P rises continuously Y remains above Y^*
Supply Shock (SRAS curve shifts leftward)	P rises Y falls below Y^* (recessionary gap)	Isolated shock	Not validated →	**Case 3** P falls back to initial level Y rises back to Y^*
			Validated →	**Case 4** P rises further and then stabilizes Y rises back to Y^*
		Repeated shock Validated →		**Case 5** P continues to rise Y remains at, or below, Y^*

Demand and supply shocks have different final effects, depending on whether or not they are isolated or sustained and are validated or nonvalidated. This figure summarizes the analysis of each of the five cases given in the text. It should be referred to after reading the text discussion of each of the cases. All comparisons assume that income is initially at its potential level and that the price level is stable.

The initial effects of a positive demand shock are to raise national income and the price level. If the shock is isolated, the price level continues to rise until income falls back to its potential level (case 1). If the shock is sustained and validated the price level continues to rise while income stays above its potential level (case 2).

The initial effects of an adverse supply shock are to raise the price level but to reduce national income. Once the shock is over, income will return to its potential level, with a lowered price level if there is no validation (case 3) and with a higher price level if there is validation (case 4). If the shock is sustained and validated, the price level can continue to rise with or without a persistent recessionary gap (case 5).

Monetary Validation. Suppose that after the demand shock has created an inflationary gap, the Bank of Canada increases the money supply whenever output starts to fall. This case takes us beyond our discussions in earlier chapters. It is analyzed in Figure 30-2, and its results are summarized as Case 2 in Figure 30-1.

Two forces are now brought into play. Spurred by the inflationary gap, the increases in wages relative to productivity cause the SRAS curve to shift to the left. Fueled by the expansionary monetary policy, however, the AD curve shifts to the right. As a result of both of these shifts, the price level rises, but national income need not fall. Indeed, if the shift in the AD curve exactly offsets the shift in the SRAS curve, national income and the inflationary gap will remain constant.

Validation of an initial demand shock turns what would have been transitory inflation into sustained inflation fueled by monetary expansion. The subsequent shifts in the AD curve that perpetuate the inflation are caused by continuing increases in the money supply.

SUPPLY INFLATION

Any rise in the price level originating from increases in costs that are *not caused by excess demand* in the

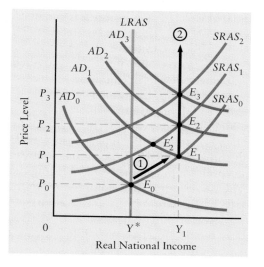

FIGURE 30-2
A Validated Demand-Shock Inflation

Monetary validation of a positive demand shock causes the _AD_ curve to shift further to the right, offsetting the leftward shift in the _SRAS_ curve and thereby leaving an inflationary gap despite the ever-rising price level. An initial demand shock shifts equilibrium from E_0 to E_1, taking income to Y_1 and the price level to P_1. The resulting inflationary gap then causes the _SRAS_ curve to shift to the left. This time, however, the Bank of Canada validates the demand shock by increasing the money supply. As the money supply is increased, the _AD_ curve shifts to the right. By the time the aggregate supply curve has reached $SRAS_1$, the aggregate demand curve has reached AD_2. Now instead of being at E_2', equilibrium is at E_2. Income remains constant at Y_1 leaving the inflationary gap constant while the price level rises to P_2.

The persistent inflationary gap continues to push the _SRAS_ curve to the left, while the continued monetary validation continues to push the _AD_ curve to the right. As long as this monetary validation continues, the economy moves along the vertical path of arrow 2.

markets for factors of production is variously called _supply-shock inflation, cost-push inflation_ or more simply **supply inflation.**

An example of a supply shock is a rise in the costs of imported raw materials or a rise in domestic wage costs per unit of output. The rise in wage costs may occur, as we saw earlier, because of generally held expectations of future inflation. If both employers and employees expect inflation, money wages are

likely to rise in relation to productivity in anticipation of that inflation.

These shocks cause the _SRAS_ curve to shift upward. They may or may not also shift the _LRAS_ curve. Suppose that the shock takes the form of a large increase in money wages relative to productivity. This shock will raise costs of production, and hence the price level needed to sustain any given output will be higher. As a result, the _SRAS_ curve will shift upward. However, this price change will not affect the economy's capacity to produce output when all resources are fully employed at normal levels of capacity. This type of shock, called a _nominal shock_, tends to leave the economy's potential income unchanged and therefore does not shift the _LRAS_ curve.

Now suppose, in contrast, that the shock comes in the form of rising prices of energy and other raw materials brought about because more and more labour and capital are needed to produce a given output from depleting stocks. This is an example of a _real shock_. Firms are not just paying more money for the same inputs and outputs; instead, more real inputs are required to produce the same domestic outputs. Shocks of this sort reduce the economy's capacity to produce—potential output is reduced, causing the _LRAS_ curve to shift to the left. (Other real supply-side shocks, such as improvements in technology, shift the _LRAS_ and the _SRAS_ curves to the right. We consider such shocks in Chapter 33 when we examine economic growth.)

Adverse aggregate supply shocks always shift the _SRAS_ curve to the left; if they are real shocks, they will also tend to shift the _LRAS_ curve to the left.

In the following discussion, we deal with supply-side shocks that shift the _SRAS_ curve to the left but leave the _LRAS_ curve unchanged.[3]

The initial effects of any adverse supply shock are that the equilibrium price level rises while equilibrium output falls. The rise in the price level shows up as a temporary burst of inflation. These effects were first discussed in Chapter 25. Although we now wish to go beyond that earlier discussion,

---

[3]Other cases can be handled easily by shifting the _LRAS_ curve to the left. In such cases, when the analysis in the text tells us that the long-run position is restored, it will not be at its preshock level of income but rather at a lower one that is consistent with the new leftward-shifted _LRAS_ curve.

FIGURE 30-3
Supply Shocks With and Without Monetary Validation

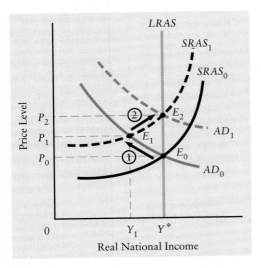

Adverse supply shocks initially raise prices while lowering income. An adverse supply shock causes the *SRAS* curve to shift leftward from $SRAS_0$ to $SRAS_1$, as shown by arrow 1. Equilibrium is established at E_1. If there is no monetary validation, the *SRAS* curve shifts slowly back to the right, to $SRAS_0$. If there is monetary validation, the *AD* curve shifts from AD_0 to AD_1, as shown by arrow 2. This reestablishes full-employment equilibrium at E_2 but with a higher price level, P_2.

we will begin by repeating it in Figure 30-3, which compares the original equilibrium with the equilibrium after the supply shock. (Figure 30-1 summarizes these results as the initial effects of a supply shock.)

What happens next depends both on whether the shock is an isolated event or one of a series of recurring shocks and on how the Bank of Canada reacts. If the Bank responds by increasing the money supply, it validates the supply shock; if it holds the money supply constant, the shock is not validated.

Isolated Supply Shocks

Suppose that the leftward shift in the *SRAS* curve is an isolated event, perhaps caused by a once-and-for-all increase in the cost of imported raw materials. An example of this type of shock is the OPEC-induced increase in the world price of oil in 1974 (which we dis-

cuss shortly). How does monetary policy affect the economy's response to such an isolated supply shock?

No Monetary Validation.   The possibility of a nonvalidated isolated supply shock is summarized as Case 3 under "Final effects" in Figure 30-1. The leftward shift in the *SRAS* curve in Figure 30-3 causes the price level to rise and pushes income below its full-employment level, opening up a recessionary gap. Pressure mounts for money wages and other factor costs to fall relative to productivity.

As long as money wages rise less rapidly than productivity is rising, unit costs will fall. Consequently, the *SRAS* curve shifts rightward, increasing equilibrium income while reducing the price level. The *SRAS* curve will continue to shift, stopping only when national income is returned to its potential level. If potential income is unaffected by the shock, the *SRAS* curve will shift back to its initial position ($SRAS_0$ in Figure 30-3). Equilibrium income is returned to Y^*, and the price level is returned to its initial value of P_0. Thus the period of inflation accompanying the original supply shock is eventually followed by a period of *deflation* (negative inflation) that continues until long-run equilibrium is reestablished at the intersection of the AD_0 and *LRAS* curves.

A major concern in this case is the speed of the adjustment, which in earlier chapters we referred to as the second asymmetry of aggregate supply. If unit labour costs do not fall rapidly in the face of excess supply in the labour market, the adjustment back to full employment can take a very long time. For example, suppose that the original shock raised prices and money costs by 10 percent. To reverse this shock, unit costs must fall by 10 percent. If money wages stayed constant while productivity increased by 2 percent each year, it would take nearly five years to complete the adjustment.

Whenever unit costs fall only slowly in the face of excess supply, the recovery to full employment after a nonvalidated adverse supply shock will take a long time.

Concern that such a lengthy adjustment will occur is the motive that often lies behind the strong pressure on the Bank of Canada to validate adverse supply shocks.

Monetary Validation.   Now let us see what happens if the money supply is changed in response to an isolated supply shock. Suppose that the monetary authorities decide to validate the supply shock because they believe that relying on cost deflation to restore full employment would force the economy to suffer an extended slump. The monetary validation shifts the aggregate demand curve to the right and causes both the price level and output to *rise*. As the recessionary gap is eliminated, the price level rises further, rather than falling back to its original value as it did when the supply shock was not validated. These effects are also illustrated in Figure 30-3, and they are summarized under Case 4 in Figure 30-1.

Monetary validation of an isolated adverse supply shock causes the initial rise in the price level to be followed by a further rise, resulting in a higher price level than would occur if the recessionary gap were relied on to reduce costs and prices.

The most dramatic example of an isolated supply-shock inflation came in the wake of the first OPEC oil-price shock. In 1974, the countries who were members of the Organization of Petroleum Exporting Countries (OPEC) agreed to restrict output. Their action caused a dramatic increase in the prices of petroleum and many petroleum-related products such as fertilizer and chemicals. The resulting increase in industrial costs shifted *SRAS* curves upward in all industrial countries. At this time, the Bank of Canada validated the supply shock with large increases in the money supply, whereas the Fed (the U.S. central bank) did not. As the theory predicts, Canada experienced a large increase in its price level but almost no recession, and the United States experienced a much smaller increase in its price level but a severe recession.

Repeated Supply Shocks

Now suppose that the economy is buffeted by a series of repeated supply shocks. One example would be a repeated rise in the prices of all imported raw materials and energy products for several years in succession. A second example could come from wages in the case studied earlier, where persistent expectations of continued inflation cause wages to rise period by period. Because it turns out to be important to our later analysis, we take the second case, in which wages rise relative to productivity because both employers and employees expect further inflation. This rise in wages shifts the *SRAS* curve upward.

No Monetary Validation. Suppose that the Bank of Canada does not validate these repeated supply shocks and instead holds the money supply

constant. The initial effect of the leftward shift in the *SRAS* curve is to open up a recessionary gap, as shown by arrow 1 in Figure 30-3. If wages continue to rise, subjecting the economy to further supply shocks, prices continue to rise and output continues to fall. Eventually, the trade off between higher wages and unemployment will become obvious to everyone. On the one hand, workers will realize that higher wages come at the cost of falling employment, and they will cease pressing for wage increases. On the other hand, employers will realize that they cannot simply pass on increased wages in the form of increased prices without suffering further decreases in sales, and they will become less willing to grant such increases in wages even if they expect inflation to continue for some time. Thus a nonvalidated supply-shock inflation is self-limiting because the rising recessionary gap that it causes tends to restrain further wage increases.

Because repeated nonvalidated supply shocks must come to an end, their results are identical to those of a single, isolated supply shock. Whether the recessionary position shown by E_1 in Figure 30-3 is the result of a single, isolated supply shock or of a series of repeated shocks, the end result is the same: The price level is higher and national income is lower than in the economy's initial, preshock equilibrium.

What happens next is also just a repeat of what we have already studied for an isolated shock. When the persistent unemployment eventually erodes inflationary expectations, wages will fall relative to productivity, thus reversing the supply shock. Eventually, full employment will be restored, and the price level will return to its original value. This is Case 3 in Figure 30-1.

Repeated and nonvalidated adverse supply shocks caused by expectations of future inflation have natural correctives created by the increasing recessionary gap. But these correctives may take a long time to operate, and hence a wage-cost push can cause long and sustained stagflation, combining inflation with rising unemployment.

Monetary Validation. Now suppose that the Bank of Canada validates the initial supply shock with an increase in the money supply, thereby shifting the aggregate demand curve to the right, as shown in Figure 30-4.

In the new full-employment equilibrium, both money wages and prices have risen. Workers are no better off than they were originally, although those

FIGURE 30-4
Monetary Validation of a Repeated Supply Shock

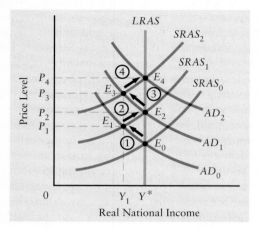

Monetary validation of a repeated supply shock causes continuous inflation in the absence of excess demand. The initial equilibrium is at E_0. An adverse supply shock then takes equilibrium to E_1. This is the stagflation phase of rising prices and falling output; it is indicated by arrow 1.

The Bank of Canada then validates the supply shock by increasing the money supply, taking the AD curve to AD_1 and equilibrium to E_2. This is the expansionary phase of rising prices and output (arrow 2).

A second supply shock, followed by monetary validation, takes equilibrium to E_3 (arrow 3) and then to E_4 (arrow 4). As long as the supply shocks and monetary validation continue, inflation continues.

who remained in their jobs were temporarily better off in the transition after wages had risen (taking equilibrium to E_1 in Figure 30-4) but before the price level had risen (taking equilibrium to E_2). The rise in wages has been offset by a rise in prices.

There is no reason for employers and employees to expect that the inflation will stop here. Insofar as expectations are backward-looking, people have the experience of past inflation to go on. Insofar as expectations are forward-looking, there is no reason for people to see current monetary policy as stopping inflation unless, first, the Bank of Canada emphasizes that what it has just done is a once-and-for-all monetary validation and, second, the Bank is believed by wage and price setters.

The stage is now set for wages and prices to rise further when the economy is hit with another supply shock. If the Bank of Canada again validates the

shock with an appropriate increase in the money supply, full employment is restored, but at the cost of a further round of inflation. If this process goes on repeatedly, it causes a continual supply-shock inflation. The wage-cost push tends to cause stagflation, with rising prices and falling output. Monetary validation tends to reinforce the rise in prices but to offset the fall in output. The results are summarized as Case 5 in Figure 30-1.

Two things are required for this type of supply-shock inflation to be sustained over a long time. First, continued increases in money wages must occur, even in the absence of excess demand for labour and goods. In some countries, powerful unions can cause such increases, but most economists believe that this is not a real possibility in Canada today. What can cause continued wage increases today, however, is expectations of continued inflation. As discussed earlier, if everyone expects 3 percent inflation, workers may ask for a 3 percent increase in money wages just to hold their own against the expected inflation, and employers may grant the increases, expecting to be able to pass the extra costs on through increased prices. The result is *self-fulfilling expectations*. Because everyone anticipates the inflation rate, their actions in expectation of that rate bring that rate about.

Second, the Bank of Canada must validate the resulting inflation by increasing the money supply, thereby preventing the unemployment that would otherwise occur. The process set up by this sequence of wage-cost increases and monetary validation is often called a *wage-price spiral*.

Is Monetary Validation of Supply Shocks Desirable?

Once started, a wage-price spiral can be halted only if the Bank of Canada stops validating the supply shocks that are causing the inflation. But the longer it waits to do so, the more firmly held will be the *expectations that it will continue* its policy of validating the shocks. These entrenched expectations may cause wages to continue rising even after validation has ceased. Because employers expect prices to rise, they go on granting wage increases. If expectations are entrenched firmly enough, the wage push can continue for quite some time, in spite of the downward pressure caused by the rising unemployment associated with the growing recessionary gap.

Because of this possibility, many economists argue that the wage-price spiral should not be allowed to begin. One way to ensure that it does not begin is to refuse to validate any supply shock whatsoever.

To some economists, caution dictates that no supply shock should ever be validated, lest a wage-price spiral be created. Other economists are willing to risk validating obviously isolated shocks in order to avoid the significant, though transitory, recessions that otherwise accompany them.

INFLATION AS A MONETARY PHENOMENON

A long-standing debate among economists concerns the extent to which inflation is a monetary phenomenon. Does it have purely monetary causes—changes in the demand or the supply of money? Does it have purely monetary consequences—only the price level is affected? One slogan that states an extreme position on this issue was popularized many years ago by Milton Friedman: "Inflation is *everywhere* and *always* a monetary phenomenon." To consider these issues, let us summarize what we have learned already. First, look at the *causes* of inflation:

- *Cause 1:* On the demand side, anything that shifts the *AD* curve to the right will cause the price level to rise. This includes such expenditure changes as increases in desired consumption, investment, government purchases, or net exports. Such inflation can continue for some time without being validated by increases in the money supply (of course, the initial shift in the *AD* curve could also have been caused by an increase in the money supply).

- *Cause 2:* On the supply side, anything that increases the costs of production will shift the *SRAS* curve to the left and cause the price level to rise. Such inflation can continue for some time without being validated by increases in the money supply.

- *Cause 3:* Unless monetary expansion occurs, the increases in the price level must eventually come to a halt.

The first two points provide the sense in which, looking at causes, a temporary burst of inflation need not be a monetary phenomenon. It need not have monetary causes, and it need not be accompanied by monetary expansion. The third point provides the sense in which, looking at causes, *sustained* inflation *must* be a monetary phenomenon. If a rise in prices is to continue indefinitely, it must be accompanied by continuing increases in the money supply. This is true regardless of the cause that set the inflation in motion. Of course, something that cannot continue indefinitely might continue for a very long time, so there is still plenty of room for disagreement over the mix of monetary and nonmonetary causes in any observed inflation.

Second, let us summarize the *consequences* of inflation, assuming that actual national income was initially at its potential level.

- *Consequence 1:* In the short run, demand-shock inflation tends to be accompanied by an *increase* in national income above its potential level.

- *Consequence 2:* In the short run, supply-shock inflation tends to be accompanied by a *decrease* in national income below its potential level.

- *Consequence 3:* When all costs and prices are adjusted *fully* (so that the relevant aggregate supply curve is the *LRAS* curve), shifts in either the *AD* or *SRAS* curve leave national income unchanged and affect only the price level.

The first two points provide a sense in which, looking at consequences, inflation is not, in the short run, a purely monetary phenomenon. The third point provides the sense in which, looking at consequences, inflation is a purely monetary phenomenon from the point of view of long-run equilibrium.

There is still plenty of room for debate, however, on how long the short run will last. Most economists believe that the short run can be long enough for inflation to have major real effects. Indeed, if inflation is sustained, many of its real effects may persist indefinitely. For example, distortions caused by many aspects of the tax system being defined in nominal rather than real terms will persist as long as inflation continues, even if it proceeds at a steady and fully expected rate.

We have now reached three important conclusions:

- *Conclusion 1:* Without monetary validation, aggregate-demand shocks cause temporary bursts of inflation that are accompanied by inflationary gaps. The gaps are removed as rising costs push the *SRAS* curve to the left, returning national income to its potential level, but at a higher price level.

- *Conclusion 2:* Without monetary validation, aggregate-supply shocks cause temporary bursts of inflation that are accompanied by recessionary gaps. The gaps are removed as real wages fall relative to productivity, restoring equilibrium at potential income and at the initial price level.

- *Conclusion 3:* With continuing validation, inflation initiated by either aggregate-supply or aggregate-demand shocks can continue indefinitely; an ever-increasing money supply is necessary for sustained inflation.

SUSTAINED INFLATION

Why has the Canadian economy undergone several periods of sustained inflation—sometimes rapid, as in the 1970s and early 1980s, and sometimes more gradual, as in the late 1980s and early 1990s? Can sustained inflation continue indefinitely at a more or less constant rate? What are the costs and benefits of reducing or eliminating sustained inflation?

ACCELERATING INFLATION

To study one of the most serious problems associated with sustained inflation, we take up the story where we left it at the end of the section discussing the monetary validation of a demand-shock inflation. When the Bank of Canada engages in such validation, the *AD* and *SRAS* curves will both be shifting upward, allowing the price level to rise with no necessary reduction in the inflationary gap. This is the situation shown in Figure 30-2.

What now happens to the rate of inflation is predicted by the **acceleration hypothesis,** which holds that when the central bank engages in whatever rate of monetary expansion is needed to hold the inflationary gap constant, the actual inflation rate will *accelerate.* The Bank of Canada may start by validating 3 percent inflation, but soon 3 percent will become 4 percent, and if the Bank insists on validating 4 percent, the rate will become 5 percent, and so on without limit, until the Bank finally stops its validation.

There are several steps in the reasoning behind this hypothesis. The first concerns the development of inflationary expectations.

Expectational Effects

To illustrate the importance of expectations in accelerating inflation, suppose that the inflationary gap shown in Figure 30-2 creates sufficient excess demand to push up wages 2 percent per year faster than productivity is rising. As a result, unit costs and hence the *SRAS* curve will also tend to be rising at 2 percent per year.

When inflation has persisted for some time, however, people will come to expect that the monetary validation, and hence inflation, will continue. Once this happens, the expectation of 2 percent inflation will tend to push up wages and unit costs by that amount *in addition to* the demand pressure. As the demand effect on wages is augmented by the expectational effect, the *SRAS* curve will begin to shift upward more rapidly. When expectations are for a 2 percent inflation and demand pressure is also pushing wages up by 2 percent, the overall effect will be a 4 percent increase in wages, unit costs, and the *SRAS* curve. Sooner or later, however, 4 percent inflation will come to be expected, and the expectational effect will rise to 4 percent. This, added to the demand component, will create an inflation rate of 6 percent. And so this cycle will go on. As long as there is a demand effect arising from an inflationary gap and as long as actual inflation is equal to the demand effect plus the expectational effect, the inflation rate cannot stay constant because expectations will always be revised upward toward the actual inflation rate.

Our discussion about the importance of *both* excess demand and inflation expectations in determining the actual inflation rate suggests that we can decompose the actual inflation rate into the amount due to demand inflation and the amount due to expectations:

Actual Inflation	=	Demand Inflation	+	Expected Inflation

From this simple relationship, it is clear that if we have *any* demand inflation, then expected inflation cannot equal actual inflation. Instead, expected inflation must be less than actual inflation by the amount of the demand inflation. Hence it is not possible to find a steady inflation rate in which expectations are fulfilled *in the presence of an inflationary gap.* Correct expectations means that expected inflation equals actual inflation, and this implies that demand inflation must be zero.

More Rapid Monetary Validation Required

The second step in the argument is that if the Bank of Canada still wishes to hold the level of output constant, it must increase the rate at which the money supply is growing. This action is necessary because to hold national income constant, the *AD* curve must be shifted at an increasingly rapid pace to offset the increasingly rapid shifts in the *SRAS* curve, which are driven by the continually rising rate of expected inflation.

An Increasing Rate of Inflation

The third step in the argument is that the rate of inflation must now be increasing because of the increasingly rapid upward shifts in both the *AD* and *SRAS* curves. The rise in the actual inflation rate will in turn cause an increase in the expected inflation rate. This will then cause the actual inflation rate to increase, which will in turn increase the expected inflation rate, and so on. The net result is a *continually increasing rate of inflation.* (Now we see the reason for the name NAIRU. At any level of unemployment less than the NAIRU, national income is above Y*, and the inflation rate tends to accelerate. So the NAIRU is the lowest level of unemployment consistent with a *nonaccelerating* rate of inflation.)

The tendency for inflation to accelerate is discussed further in Extension 30-2, which examines how expected inflation affects the position of the Phillips curve.

According to the acceleration hypothesis, as long as an inflationary gap persists, expectations of inflation will be rising, which will lead to increases in the actual rate of inflation.

A SUSTAINED RATE OF INFLATION

The discussion of accelerating inflation implies that sustained inflation at a constant rate is possible only when national income is at its potential level, so that there is no demand component to inflation. In that case, all inflation is expectational. If the inflation is fully expected, the actual and the expected rates must be equal. Provided that there is no demand component, inflation can go on forever at a constant rate, validated by a constant rate of monetary expansion.

The simple equation from above can be used to explain why a constant rate of inflation that persists must be a purely expectational inflation. Recall that actual inflation is the sum of expected and demand inflation. If the actual rate of inflation is to be constant, then households' and firms' expectations will come to equal the actual inflation rate. But if actual and expected inflation are equal, then demand inflation must be zero. And demand inflation can be zero only at potential income, where there is neither an inflationary nor a deflationary gap. The case of constant inflation is considered in more detail in Extension 30-3.

ENDING A SUSTAINED INFLATION

An economy may be undergoing sustained inflation in either of two situations. First, national income may exceed its potential, producing an inflationary gap, with the resulting demand inflation fully validated by the Bank of Canada. Such a situation is shown in Figure 30-2. Second, there may be a validated pure expectational inflation with national income equal to its potential (and thus no inflationary or recessionary gap).

Costs of Reducing Inflation

In either situation, reducing the rate of inflation takes time and involves major costs. The technique is for the Bank of Canada to stop validating the inflation. It does this by lowering the rate of growth of the money supply below the rate of growth of money demand, thus creating an excess demand for money. This action forces up interest rates and lowers real aggregate demand, reducing any existing inflationary gap. We will soon see that it is usually necessary for the Bank to go further, creating a substantial recessionary gap that persists until the inflation is eliminated.

The process involves many costs. The recessionary gap hurts all who suffer in recessions, including the unemployed workers and the owners of firms who lose profits and risk bankruptcy. Unemployed resources mean lost output and hence lower real national income than would otherwise be produced. The temporary rise in interest rates hurts borrowers, including people with mortgages and firms with large loans. Among these groups who are most ex-

THE PHILLIPS CURVE AND ACCELERATING INFLATION

As discussed in Extension 30-1, Phillips was interested in studying the short-run behaviour of an economy subjected to cyclical fluctuations. In the years following Phillips's study, however, some economists treated the Phillips curve as establishing a long-term trade off between inflation and unemployment.

Suppose the government stabilizes income at Y_1 (and hence the unemployment rate at U_1), as shown in the accompanying figures. To do this, it must validate the ensuing wage inflation, which is indicated by $\dot{W}_1$ in the figure. The government thus seems to be able to choose among particular combinations of inflation and unemployment, with lower levels of unemployment being attained at the cost of higher rates of inflation (by moving leftward along the solid curve in part (i) of the figure).

In the 1960s, Phillips curves were fitted to the data for many countries, and governments made decisions about where they wished to be on the trade off between inflation and unemployment. Then in the late 1960s, in country after country, the rate of wage and price inflation associated with any given

(i) Wage changes and unemployment

(ii) Wage changes and output

posed and may lose their wealth are young households with large mortgages and small firms that have taken on large debts to finance expansions.

Reducing sustained inflation is thus a classic case of a policy that brings short-term pain for long-term gain. Inevitably, the question arises: Are the future benefits worth the immediate costs?

Reducing sustained inflation quickly incurs high costs for a short period of time; reducing it slowly incurs lower costs but for a longer period of time.

The process of reducing sustained inflation can be divided into three phases. In the first phase, the monetary validation is removed. In the second phase,

the monetary validation has stopped, but the economy still suffers from declining output and rising prices—stagflation. In the final phase, the economy experiences both increasing output and increasing prices, but the inflation then comes to an end. We now examine these three phases in detail.

Phase 1: Removing Monetary Validation

The first phase consists of slowing the rate of monetary expansion, thereby slowing the rate at which the AD curve is shifting upward. The simplest case is when the Bank of Canada adopts a "cold-turkey approach" in which the rate of monetary expansion is level of unemployment began to rise. Instead of being stable, the Phillips curves began to shift upward. The explanation lay primarily in a shifting relationship between the pressure of demand and wage increases due to *inflationary* expectations, as discussed in the text.

It was gradually understood that the original Phillips curve concerned only the influence of demand and left out inflationary expectations. This omission proved important and unfortunate. An increase in expected inflation shows up as an upward shift in the original Phillips curve that was drawn in Extension 30-1. The importance of expectations can be shown by drawing what is called an **expectations-augmented Phillips curve,** as shown here. The heights of the Phillips curves above the axis at Y^* and at U^* show the expected inflation rate. These distances represent the amount that wages will rise when neither excess demand nor excess supply pressures are being felt in labour markets. The actual wage increase is shown by the augmented curve, with the increase in wages exceeding expected inflation whenever $Y > Y^*$ ($U < U^*$) and falling short of expected inflation whenever $Y < Y^*$ ($U > U^*$).

The simple Phillips curve shows the demand component of inflation when expected inflation is zero. The expectations-augmented Phillips curve shows the demand component of inflation plus the expected rate of inflation.

Now we can see what was wrong with the idea of a stable inflation-unemployment trade off. Targeting a particular income Y_1 or unemployment U_1 in the figures is fine as long as no inflation *is expected*. But getting to Y_1 or U_1 itself requires some inflation ($\dot{W}_1$). And once this rate of inflation comes to be expected, people will demand that much just to hold their own. The Phillips curve will shift upward to the position shown in the figures. Now there is inflation $\dot{W}_2$ because of the combined effects of expectations and excess demand. However, this higher rate is above the expected rate ($\dot{W}_1$). Once this higher rate comes to be expected, the Phillips curve will shift upward once again.

As a result of the combination of excess-demand inflation and expectational inflation, the inflation rate associated with any given positive output gap ($Y > Y^*$ or $U < U^*$) rises over time. This is the phenomenon of accelerating inflation that is discussed in the text.

The shifts in the Phillips curve are such that most economists agree that in the long run, when inflationary expectations have fully adjusted to actual inflation, there is no trade off between inflation and unemployment. That is, they believe that the long-run Phillips curve is a vertical line at the NAIRU.

cut to zero so that the upward shift in the AD curve is halted abruptly. This implies a large and rapid increase in both nominal and real interest rates.

At this point, a controversy often breaks out—as it did in the early 1980s and early 1990s—over the effects that the increase in interest rates has on inflation. One group will point out that the rise in the interest rate increases business costs and that passing on the extra costs through higher prices adds to inflation. They will condemn the Bank's tight monetary policy as inflationary. A second group will argue that the rising interest rate signifies a slowdown in the rate of monetary expansion, without which inflation cannot be curbed.

The first group is correct in pointing out that the rise in interest rates may cause a one-time increase in the price level. The rise in interest costs may shift the *SRAS* curve upward, just as a rise in wage costs does. This rise in interest costs, however, has only a *one-time effect* on the price level. The first group is wrong, therefore, in asserting that the Bank's policy of driving up interest rates is contributing to a long-term increase in the rate of inflation.

The second group is correct in saying that the rise in the interest rate is a necessary part of an anti-inflationary policy. As long as the price level continues to rise, the rise in the interest rate reduces desired aggregate expenditure, thus reducing

---

EXTENSION 30-3

CONSTANT INFLATION

When national income is at its potential level, there is neither an inflationary nor a recessionary gap. In this case, there is no demand effect operating on wage changes. Leaving random shocks aside, the only force operating on wages is expectations. Suppose that both workers and employers expect 4 percent inflation and that employers are prepared to raise wages by 4 percent per year to keep wages in line with everything else. Wages will rise by 4 percent per year, and the SRAS curve will shift upward by that amount each year. If the Bank of Canada validates the resulting inflation, the AD curve will also shift upward by that amount.

Real National Income

This case is illustrated in the accompanying figure. Expectations of a constant rate of inflation cause wages, unit costs, and the SRAS curve to shift upward at a uniform rate from $SRAS_0$ to $SRAS_1$ to $SRAS_2$ and so on. Monetary validation is causing the

AD curve to shift upward at the same time from AD_0 to AD_1 to AD_2 and so on. As a result, national income remains at Y^*, with unemployment at the NAIRU and a steady inflation rate that takes the price level from P_0 to P_1 to P_2 and so on. Equilibrium follows the arrow from E_0 to E_1 to E_2 and so on. In this situation, wage costs are rising due to expectations of inflation, and these expectations are being fulfilled.

Steady inflation at potential income results when the rate of monetary growth, the rate of wage increase, and the expected rate of inflation are all consistent with the actual inflation rate.

The key point about pure expectational inflation at a constant rate is that there is no demand effect operating on wage bargains. Wages rise at the expected rate of inflation, just enough to preserve the existing relationship between wages and all other prices. The labour shortages that accompany an inflationary gap are absent, as are the labour surpluses that accompany a recessionary gap.

If all forces worked precisely as described in the simple theoretical model, steady inflation would occur only when income was exactly at its potential level. In practice, however, stable inflation rates also seem to be compatible with modest recessionary gaps.

In such circumstances, there is a tendency for wages to fall (relative to productivity), forcing the SRAS curve downward. However, the negative demand effect of a recessionary gap seems to be weak. Thus when the gap is relatively small, the demand effect may be swamped by the expectational effect and random shocks so that an approximately stable inflation rate is the net result.

---

equilibrium national income by moving leftward along a fixed AD curve.

Now suppose that the Bank resists the pleas to hold down interest rates. It continues with its no-validation policy (a monetary contraction). The AD curve stops shifting, but under the combined influence of the present inflationary gap and expectations

of continued inflation, wages continue to rise. Hence the SRAS curve continues to shift upward. Eventually, the inflationary gap will be removed, as shown in part (i) of Figure 30-5.

If demand were the only influence on wages, that would be the end of the story. At $Y = Y^*$, there would be no upward demand pressure on wages and

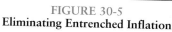

FIGURE 30-5
Eliminating Entrenched Inflation

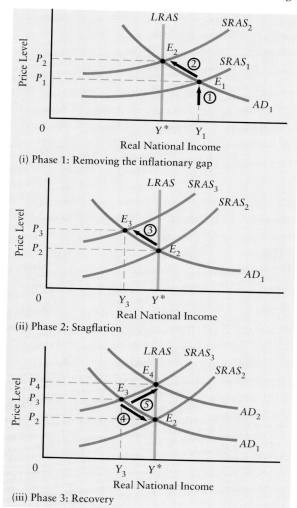

(i) Phase 1: Removing the inflationary gap

(ii) Phase 2: Stagflation

(iii) Phase 3: Recovery

(i) Phase 1: The elimination of entrenched inflation begins with a demand contraction to remove the inflationary gap. The initial position is one where fully validated inflation is taking the economy along the path shown by arrow 1. When the curves reach $SRAS_1$ and AD_1, the Bank stops expanding the money supply, thus stabilizing aggregate demand at AD_1. Wages continue to rise, taking the SRAS curve leftward. The economy moves along arrow 2, with income falling and the price level rising. When aggregate supply reaches $SRAS_2$, the inflationary gap is removed, income is Y^*, and the price level is P_2.

(ii) Phase 2: Expectations and wage momentum lead to stagflation, with falling output and continuing inflation. The economy moves along the path shown by arrow 3. The driving force is now the SRAS curve, which continues to shift because inflationary expectations cause wages to continue rising. The recessionary gap grows as income falls. Inflation continues, but at a diminishing rate. If wages stop rising when income has reached Y_3 and the price level has reached P_3, the stagflation phase is over, with equilibrium at E_3.

(iii) Phase 3: After expectations are reversed, recovery takes income to Y^*, and the price level is stabilized. There are two possible scenarios for recovery. In the first, the recessionary gap causes wages to fall (slowly), taking the SRAS curve back to $SRAS_2$ (slowly), as shown by arrow 4. The economy retraces the path originally followed in part (ii) back to E_2. In the second scenario, the Bank increases the money supply sufficiently to shift the AD curve to AD_2. The economy then moves along the path shown by arrow 5. This restores potential income at the cost of further temporary inflation that takes the price level to P_4. Full employment and a stable price level are now achieved.

other costs. Unit costs would stop rising, the *SRAS* curve would be stabilized, and the economy would remain at full employment with a stable price level.[4]

Phase 2: Stagflation

Governments around the world have often wished that things were really so simple. However, wages

depend not only on current excess demand but also on inflationary expectations. Once inflationary expectations have been established, it is not always easy to get people to revise them downward, even in the face of announced changes in monetary policies. Hence the *SRAS* curve continues to shift upward, causing the price level to continue to rise and income to fall. This is phase 2, shown in part (ii) of Figure 30-5.

Expectations can cause inflation to persist even after its original causes have been removed. What was initially a demand and expectational inflation due to an inflationary gap becomes a pure expectational inflation.

---

[4]If the economy began with a purely expectational inflation with national income at or below full employment, what we call phase 2 would be the first phase. However, the rest of the story is the same whether the starting point is demand inflation or pure expectational inflation.

The ease with which the Bank of Canada can end such an inflation, and the costs of doing so, both depend on how easy it is to change these expectations of continued inflation. This change is more difficult to the extent that expectations are backward-looking and easier to the extent that expectations are forward-looking.

To the extent that people look mainly to past inflation rates to determine their expectations of the future, they will be slow to change their expectations. As the actual inflation rate falls below the expected rate, a long time will be required for the downward adjustment to take place. The longer a given rate has persisted, the more firmly will expectations that the rate will persist be built into people's behaviour. An inflation that has persisted long enough to create firmly established expectations that it will continue is sometimes called an *entrenched inflation.*

To the extent that expectations are adjusted to current events, people will take notice of the Bank's changed behaviour and revise their expectations of future inflation downward in the light of the new monetary policy. If people fully understand the Bank's policies as soon as they are implemented, if they have full confidence that the Bank will stick to its policies, if they know exactly how much time will be required for the Bank's policies to have effect, and if they adjust their expectations exactly in line with this knowledge, there is little need for any recessionary gap to develop. Once the inflationary gap has been removed, expectations will immediately be revised downward, so there will then be no pressure on unit costs to rise because of either demand or expectational forces. In Figure 30-5, Y would not fall below Y^* because the $SRAS$ curve would stop shifting upward at $SRAS_2$. The inflation will be eliminated at almost no cost.

How long inflation persists after the inflationary gap has been removed depends on how quickly expectations of continued inflation are revised downward. This revision will be faster the more expectations are based on a clear understanding of the Bank of Canada's current policies, the stronger the belief is that these policies will be adhered to in the future, and the better the public's knowledge is of how the economy will react to the anti-inflationary policies.

When the $SRAS$ curve does continue to shift upward, causing Y to fall below Y^*, the emerging recessionary gap has two effects. First, unemployment is rising; hence the demand influence on wages becomes negative. Second, as the recession deepens and monetary restraint continues, people revise their expectations of inflation downward. When they have no further expectations of inflation, there are no further increases in wages relative to productivity, and the $SRAS$ curve stops shifting. The stagflation phase is over. Inflation has come to a halt, but a large recessionary gap now exists. At this point, nominal interest rates will fall because they no longer need to include an inflationary premium. Furthermore, the Bank can allow real interest rates to fall, as it no longer wishes to exert contractionary pressure on the economy.

As we note later in this chapter, the evidence from the Canadian economy is that phase 2 can be accompanied by large recessionary gaps and significant amounts of lost output before inflation is checked.

Phase 3: Recovery

The final phase is the return to full employment. When the economy comes to rest at the end of the stagflation, the situation is exactly the same as when the economy is hit by an isolated supply shock (see Figure 30-3). The move back to full employment can be accomplished in either of two ways. First, the recessionary gap can be relied on to reduce unit costs, thereby shifting the $SRAS$ curve downward, reducing prices but increasing national income. Second, the money supply can be increased to shift the AD curve upward, increasing both prices and national income. These two possibilities are illustrated in part (iii) of Figure 30-5.

Some economists worry about relying on the $SRAS$ curve to shift downward to return to economy to potential output. Their concern is primarily that it will take too long for prices and wages to fall sufficiently to shift the $SRAS$ curve—though output will eventually return to potential, the long adjustment period will be characterized by high unemployment. These economists have a preference for a monetary expansion to get the economy back to full employment.

Other economists worry about a temporary burst of monetary expansion because they fear that expectations of inflation may be rekindled when the Bank increases the money supply. This is the *reentry problem* that we discussed in Chapter 29: the Bank could increase output through a monetary expansion but too large an expansion might fuel inflation expectations. And if inflationary expectations *are* revived, the Bank will then be faced with a tough decision—either it must let another recession develop to break these new inflationary expectations, or it must validate the inflation to reduce unemployment. In the latter case, the Bank is back where it started, with validated inflation on its hands—and diminished credibility.

INFLATION POLICY IN CANADA

In this chapter's final section, we continue the discussion of Canadian inflation policy that we began in Chapter 29. As with previous chapters, we are not covering history for its own sake, but for two specific reasons. First, a discussion of some recent history lets us practice using the new tools we have developed in this chapter. These new tools will make our understanding of Canadian inflation more complete. Second, we study the lessons of the past because the past experience can shed considerable light on current policy issues. We begin our study with the inflation of the 1970s. See Figure 30-6 for the time path of the annual inflation rate in Canada since the late 1960s. In the discussion that follows, it will be useful to refer back to Figure 30-6 frequently.

The early 1970s witnessed quite expansionary fiscal and monetary policies. The money supply was expanded rapidly, and an inflationary gap opened up as national income exceeded potential income. As a result, inflation began to rise. Expansion continued until early 1974, and inflation rose throughout that period. Then a worldwide recession began, and Canada did not escape its effects. As a recessionary gap began to open up, the normal expectation was that inflation would diminish. Just then, however, the first OPEC shock hit. The prices of oil and other petroleum products soared. This supply shock sent inflation into the double-digit range. The result was stagflation.

THE RISE OF INFLATION: 1975–1980

Rather than viewing the stagflation as the result of rising oil prices, Canadian policy makers interpreted the stagflation as accelerating wage-push inflation in a time of world recession. Having failed in an attempt to secure agreement of labour in a voluntary

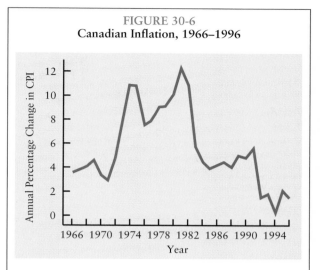

FIGURE 30-6
Canadian Inflation, 1966–1996

Canada's recent experience with inflation is varied. From about 4 percent in the late 1960s, inflation rose dramatically to a high of 13 percent in 1980–1981. It then fell to about 4 percent by 1984. It hovered between 4 and 5 percent for the next few years, eventually creeping up to 6 percent in 1989. It then fell to about 2 percent by 1992 and then hovered between 1 and 2 percent for the next four years. Inflation in this figure is measured as the annual percentage change in the Consumer Price Index (all items).

(Sources: Department of Finance, Economic Reference Tables, August 1995; Bank of Canada Review.)

incomes policy, the government decided to impose **wage and price controls.** An Anti-Inflation Board was set up and given power to control wages and prices for 3 years. At roughly the same time, the Bank of Canada adopted the policy of "monetary gradualism" (discussed in Chapter 29) by announcing its intention to gradually reduce the rate of growth of the money supply.

Whether by accident or by design, the two policies made a coherent package. The monetary policy was meant to reduce the speed with which the *AD* curve was shifting upward. Wage-price controls were meant to reduce the speed with which the *SRAS* curve was shifting upward. If the upward rush of the two curves could be slowed at the same rate, the inflation rate could be reduced without having to endure the stagflation phase (phase 2 in Figure 30-5), which occurs when the rise of the *AD* curve rising more slowly than the *SRAS* curve.

INCOMES POLICIES

In the past, some economists have recommended the use of **incomes policies** as an anti-inflationary device. There is a wide range of such policy measures. Voluntary guidelines for wage and price increases can be set, as they were in the United States under the Kennedy administration in the 1960s. The government may consult labour and business leaders with a view to moderating their wage demands and price hikes, as has often been done in European countries. More drastically, compulsory controls may be imposed on wage, price, and profit increases. A proposal commonly made in the 1970s and early 1980s was for a **tax-related incomes policy (TIP)**, which would operate through the tax system to provide penalties for "excessive" wage and price hikes and rewards for moderate ones.

Incomes policies might be used for three quite distinct purposes: (1) to suppress demand inflation, (2) to break expectational inflation, and (3) to control permanent wage-cost push inflation. We discuss the first two purposes in this box and the third in the text.

DEMAND INFLATION

One reason that incomes policies have a bad reputation throughout the world is that they have often

been used, as they were in the United States during Richard Nixon's presidency (1968–1974), in an attempt to stop demand inflation. If nothing is done to eliminate the primary cause of the inflationary gap, however, the wage-and-price controls will not be permanently effective. They may prevent prices from rising while they are in effect, but once the controls are removed, the continued excess demand will cause prices to begin rising once again.

The conclusion that using incomes policy in an attempt to control demand inflation will be ineffective (while the cost in terms of social stress and economic disruption can be enormous) is borne out not only by the U.S. experience of the early 1970s but by the experience of Britain and a number of other European countries as well.

EXPECTATIONAL INFLATION

When entrenched inflation exists, incomes policies may help to break expectations. If successful, incomes policies will greatly reduce the stagflation phase. This could happen if, once Phase 1 is over and the inflationary gap has been eliminated, incomes policies were used to stop wages and prices from rising because of the expectational effect. The *SRAS* curve would not continue to shift upward and

At first, all seemed to go well. The inflation rate fell in successive years starting in 1975. Then in 1979 and in 1980, a new setback appeared in the form of a substantial supply shock. The cause was another large increase in the world price of oil, due to a second round of OPEC output restrictions. There were also a series of *AD* shocks caused by a continual decline in the demand for M1 balances due to the monetary innovations discussed in Chapter 28. The result was that money became more plentiful *relative to demand*. Thus instead of operating its intended contractionary monetary policy, the Bank was presiding over an expansionary policy. (This experience was discussed in the section on monetary

gradualism in Chapter 29.) So there was both a positive *AD* shock and a negative *SRAS* shock (both curves shifted upwards). As a result, the 1980 inflation rate became once again as high as it had been just before wage and price controls were introduced.

As we have noted earlier, the propositions that a loose monetary policy stimulates the economy and leads to inflation and that a tight monetary policy does the opposite remained valid. The key conclusions illustrated by the failure of monetary gradualism in the 1970s are that demand-side measures can be offset by unfavourable supply-side shocks and that it is not always possible to identify a tight or loose policy solely by the rate of growth of the money supply.

thereby open up a recessionary gap. Once expectations have adjusted to the new anti-inflationary monetary policy and to the existing stable price level, the controls could be removed. Phase 2 in Figure 30-5 would have been eliminated, leaving the economy with stable prices and full employment without having had to suffer the prolonged recession typical of Phase 2.

The sequence of events seems almost too good to be true. The stagflation phase is eliminated, and the economy goes directly from Phase 1, with an inflationary gap, to the final equilibrium at Y^*. If such a policy had been tried, as many advocated during the early 1980s, *and if it had worked,* the recession of the early 1980s, with all of its consequent unemployment and lost output, could possibly have been avoided.

Controls were used in Canada when an Anti-Inflation Board (the AIB) formed part of a package to counter the double-digit inflation of the 1974–1975 period. Detailed studies by several Canadian economists have shown that the AIB probably reduced the rate of inflation by about 2 percentage points. It did this by helping to break generally held expectations that the inflation would not respond rapidly to monetary restraint. This means that it helped to shorten, even if not to eliminate, the recessionary Phase 2.

WHAT CAN WE CONCLUDE?

Opponents of incomes policies believe that the costs of using incomes policies will exceed the alleged benefits. First, they argue that the benefits, in terms of shortening the stagflation phase, would be small, because the policies would not be wholly successful in restraining wage and price increases. Second, they argue that the costs, in terms of direct administrative burdens and indirect frustration of the workings of the price system, would be large.

Although most international experience is with incomes policies used in futile attempts to control demand inflation, the evidence regarding the costs of using such policies may be relevant, even in those cases where the objective is not so clearly futile. The evidence suggests that when prices are set by government administrators rather than market forces, the allocation of resources becomes increasingly arbitrary, with serious consequences for the efficient working of the economic system. There is nothing in theory or evidence, however, to conclusively rule out the possibility that a short period of incomes policy, combined with a severely restrictive monetary policy, may shorten Phase 2 sufficiently to make the benefits of a smaller loss of output exceed the costs of temporarily distorting the pattern of wages and prices.

THE FALL OF INFLATION: 1981–1988

By the beginning of the 1980s, rapid inflation seemed firmly entrenched, and a major controversy arose over how to reduce it. Most people agreed on the goal of returning to a much lower inflation rate, but there was disagreement as to the means of achieving that goal.

Some economists advocated breaking the entrenched inflation with monetary restraint in the manner analyzed earlier in this chapter. Since they felt that there would be a short Phase 2, they were willing to rely exclusively on monetary policy to

bring about the transition from a high to a low inflationary environment.

Other economists agreed that a low rate of monetary growth was a necessary condition for returning to a low rate of inflation. However, because they felt that Phase 2 would be long—some talked in terms of 5 to 10 years—they were reluctant to use monetary policy *alone* during the transition. As a result, these economists advocated using wage and price controls once again in conjunction with a restrictive monetary policy. Such controls, which are an example of a broader class of policies, called *incomes policies,* are further discussed in Application 30-1.

The Reduction of Inflation: 1981–1984

In 1981, with inflation above 12 percent, the Bank of Canada chose to follow the United States in adopting a highly restrictive monetary policy. A serious recession eventually moderated wage and price increases. When it came, the fall in inflation was dramatic: from a peak of 12 percent in mid 1981 to around 5 percent by early 1984 (see Figure 30-6). By 1984, the restrictive monetary policy had thus succeeded in reducing inflation to a level not seen since the early 1960s. But the sharp reduction in inflation had also contributed to a major recession with all its attendant costs, including unemployment, lost output, business bankruptcies, and foreclosed mortgages.

The results came out somewhere between the extremes that had been predicted. Thus as so often happens with great debates, neither the extreme pessimists nor the extreme optimists were right—the truth lay somewhere in between. Whatever the reasons, during the early 1980s, inflation fell faster than many economists had expected, but the slump was deeper and more prolonged than many others had expected.

Stable Inflation: 1985–1988

For several years following 1984, the Canadian inflation rate stabilized at around 4 percent, and it was a time of low inflation in the world as a whole. There was no reason for the inflation rate to rise, since there was no inflationary gap in the Canadian economy. Indeed, since there was actually a *recessionary gap* during this period, the actual inflation seemed to be purely expectational: People expected a 4 percent inflation rate, and the Bank validated that inflation rate through a continued monetary expansion. Thus inflation persisted at a rate of about 4 percent.

But since there was a recessionary gap during this period, why did inflation not fall further? The answer here seems to be that the weak demand forces that work toward deceleration when there is excess supply were swamped by the forces of expectational inflation and random shocks.

TOWARD PRICE STABILITY: 1988–1996

In 1988, a long period of expansion was bringing Canadian national income close to its potential level.

From hovering around 4 percent between 1983 and 1987, the inflation rate began to creep upward, exceeding 5 percent in 1989 and reaching 6 percent for a few months in 1990 (see Figure 30-6).

As we discussed in Chapter 29, the Bank of Canada in 1988, under the leadership of Governor John Crow, announced that monetary policy would no longer be guided by short-term stabilization issues and instead would be guided by the long-term goal of price stability. This important shift in policy indicated that henceforth the Bank of Canada would be prepared to fight inflation while more-or-less ignoring the short-term pain that such battles would produce.

Thus in 1988 and 1989, fearing an erosion of its hard-won gains in reducing inflation earlier in the decade, the Bank of Canada reacted by adopting a restrictive monetary policy. Interest rates were driven up, and as discussed in Chapter 29, the Canadian dollar appreciated, putting tradeable-goods producers under heavy competitive pressure. The country's economic expansion proved remarkably resilient. The inflationary gap and the high inflation rate persisted for over a year, in spite of very high interest rates and a strong Canadian dollar. Finally, by the middle of 1990, the inflation rate began to fall significantly. By autumn, it had returned to the 4 percent plateau from which it had accelerated two years earlier. The Bank, however, persisted in its tight policy.

Recession and Tight Money: 1990–1992

By late 1990, the economy was clearly into a recession and many who supported the Bank's long-term policy of price stability nonetheless called for a little fine tuning to offset some of the short-term pain associated with monetary restraint. They felt that the Bank could mitigate the recession by easing up on its tight monetary policy, returning to it once the next recovery had begun. The Bank responded by reiterating the policy of driving the inflation rate close to zero over a period of a few years. The Bank, therefore, ignored the growing recessionary gap and continued its tight monetary policy.

As a way of formalizing the Bank's shift in policy away from short-term stabilization and toward long-term price stability, the Bank of Canada and the federal department of finance announced in

1991 a series of *inflation-control targets*. Beginning in 1992, the Bank would aim at having the rate of inflation in the 3–5 percent range. The target range declined gradually so that by the end of 1995 it was 1–3 percent.

This policy sparked enormous controversy. Some critics felt that the costs of reducing the inflation rate below 4 percent would be excessive. They preferred to have the economy adjust to that rate rather than undergo the costs of reducing the rate to 2 percent, let alone to zero. Other critics, while accepting price stability as the ultimate goal, argued that the policy should not be pursued when the economy was already in the midst of a serious recession.

Supporters pointed out that 4 percent inflation cut the purchasing power of money in half in about 18 years and that 4 percent was a high inflation rate by historical standards. They therefore argued that price stability was the best long-run goal. To the critics who said, "yes, but not now," the supporters replied that reducing entrenched inflation is always costly, and there will always be strong arguments for not incurring these costs at present. They felt that the commitment to price stability must be honoured and the costs accepted, since the longer that attempt was postponed the greater would be the costs of finally reducing inflation. The reason why the costs might grow over time is that inflationary expectations might become more firmly entrenched and the Bank's commitment to price stability less and less credible. For both these reasons, the longer the attempt was postponed, the more severe the recession that would have to be endured to finally get the inflation rate close to zero.

In the event, the Bank stuck to its policy despite strong criticism from most politicians, many businesspersons, and quite a few economists. The recession was indeed severe. Canadian interest rates stayed well above U.S. rates, and the Canadian dollar remained high on foreign exchange markets, putting Canadian exporters at a competitive disadvantage. However, the inflation rate responded as theory predicts, and by the end of 1992, *below the bottom* of the formal target range. The Bank was able to declare victory against inflation, at least for the time being. Monetary policy was then eased somewhat, causing interest rates and the external value of Canadian dollar to fall.

Recovery and Low Inflation: 1993–1996

The subsequent economic recovery was considered to be a fragile one, at least for 1991 and 1992. Many people blamed the Bank for the deep recession that Canada suffered, and much of the disagreement over the Bank's policy became focused on the Governor, John Crow. In the federal election campaign in the fall of 1993, the opposition Liberals were under considerable pressure to promise the replacement of Governor Crow when his term of appointment ended, which was due early in 1994. In contrast, many economists argued that the hard-won battle against inflation was largely over and the costs of achieving low inflation were in the past. Thus to replace Governor Crow might send a signal that the Bank was no longer committed to keeping inflation low. According to this view, the replacement of Governor Crow might fuel expectations of future inflation which could set off another wage-price spiral.

Early in 1994, the minister of finance in the newly elected Liberal government announced that Gordon Thiessen, former deputy governor under John Crow, would be the new governor of the Bank of Canada. At the same time, both the finance minister and Mr. Thiessen affirmed the recent monetary policy of the Bank and announced that the formal inflation targets of 1–3 percent would continue until the end of 1998, at which point they would be reevaluated. So political considerations dictated a change in the governor while economic considerations dictated no change in monetary policy.

By 1993 and 1994 economic growth had picked up considerably, even though the unemployment rate seemed to decline only slowly. The Bank's main challenge during this period of recovery was to provide enough growth in the money supply to allow a healthy recovery while at the same time not expanding so much that inflationary pressures would build. Throughout 1995 and 1996 the rate of inflation was well within the established 1–3 percent target range (see Figure 30-6).

IS PRICE STABILITY POSSIBLE IN THE LONG TERM?

The Bank's zero-inflation policy rekindled a debate that had recurred at various times in the past:

Is full employment compatible with a stable price level?

As long as the *SRAS* curve shifts only because of demand and expectational (plus random shock) effects, as we assumed earlier in this chapter, the answer is yes, full employment *is* compatible with stable prices. What worries some observers, however, is the possibility of a cost push that pushes wages up faster than productivity, once the fear of unemployment is reduced by the continued achievement of potential income. As far back as the 1940s, many economists were worried that once the government was committed to maintaining full employment, much of the discipline of the market would be removed from wage bargains. The scramble of every group trying to get ahead of every other group would lead to wage-cost push inflation. The commitment to full employment would then lead to validating increases in the money supply: a wage-price spiral would follow.

There is evidence that something like this has happened periodically over the past 40 years in Britain and in many of the countries of continental Europe. Most economists are more sceptical that it has been a serious force in the United States, while the Canadian case is less clear. Some observers still worry that full employment and a low, stable inflation rate may in the end prove incompatible in Canada.

Some economists follow this line of reasoning and argue that although zero inflation may be achieved for short periods of time, there will always be a tendency for the price level to rise when the economy remains at or near its potential income. They argue that a positive inflation rate in the 3–5 percent range should be accepted by the Bank as the inevitable price of achieving "full employment." They argue further that a sustained commitment to stable prices will condemn the economy to operate on average well below its level of potential income. They believe that at or even near potential income, wage-push inflation becomes strong. As inflation begins to develop, the Bank will quickly adopt a contractionary monetary policy that will cut off expansions before they are fully developed. They believe that the only way to reconcile high employment with zero inflation is by using some form of the incomes policies discussed in Application 30-1.

Those who support the zero inflation policy argue as follows. The best way to ensure that the two objectives of stable prices and full employment can be obtained most of the time is for governments to make clear that a stable price level, rather than full employment, is their overriding commitment; whenever the two come into short-run conflict, price stability will be given priority over full employment. They argue that once this message has been accepted by the public, there will be two benefits. First, wage-cost push inflation may not occur, even at full employment. Second, incipient inflation of the supply- or demand-shock variety will be easy to quell with only minor recessions, because inflationary expectations will never have a chance to become strongly entrenched. In this environment, major policy-induced recessions would not be required to control an outbreak of inflation. Paradoxically, by abandoning its full-employment commitment, the government might make the maintenance of something close to full employment much more likely.

CONCLUSION

Throughout the history of economics, inflation has been recognized as a harmful phenomenon. This view was given renewed strength as a result of the worldwide experiences of high inflation rates since the 1960s. The resolve is there, at least in advanced industrial countries, to prevent another outbreak of rapid inflation and, should one occur for reasons of unavoidable supply-side shocks, to prevent it from continuing long enough to become firmly entrenched in people's expectations.

It is clear from experience that reducing the inflation rate by any significant amount usually has costs in terms of reduced output and increased unemployment. It is also clear from past policy debates that every time the Bank undertakes to do this, controversy will break out, whatever the current inflation rate. One side will argue that any reduction in the inflation rate is too costly and the other side will argue that these consequences must be accepted as the price of keeping some control over the inflation rate. Otherwise, the rate would slowly ratchet up under the impacts of supply- and demand-side shocks that the Bank was never allowed to counter because of fear of the short-run costs of doing so.

A. CAUSES AND CONSEQUENCES OF INFLATION

- Sustained price inflation will be accompanied by closely related growth in wages and other factor costs such that the *SRAS* curve is shifting upward. Factors that influence shifts in the *SRAS* curve can be divided into two main components: demand and expectations. Random supply-side shocks will also exert an influence.

- The influence of demand can be expressed in terms of inflationary and recessionary gaps, which relate national income to potential income, or in terms of the difference between the actual rate of unemployment and the NAIRU.

- With constant productivity, expectations of inflation tend to cause wage settlements that preserve the expected real wage and hence lead to nominal wage increases equal to the expected price-level increases. Expectations can be based on past experience of inflation or on expectations of the outcome of current economic policies (or both).

- The initial effects of inflationary demand shocks (upward shifts in the *AD* curve) are a rise in the price level and a rise in national income. If the inflation is unvalidated, income returns to its potential level while the price level rises further (as the *SRAS* curve shifts upward). Monetary validation allows demand inflation to proceed without reducing the inflationary gap (*AD* curve continues to shift upward). If the Bank of Canada validates continuing demand inflation, seeking to hold the inflationary gap constant, the actual rate of inflation will tend to accelerate.

- The initial effects of inflationary supply shocks are a rise in the price level and a fall in national income (upward shift in the *SRAS* curve). If inflation is unvalidated, national income will slowly return to its potential level as the price level slowly falls to its preshock level (*SRAS* curve slowly shifts down). Monetary validation allows sustained cost-push inflation to continue in spite of a persistent recessionary gap (*AD* curve shifts up with monetary validation).

B. SUSTAINED INFLATION

- If the Bank of Canada wishes to end a sustained inflation, it must reduce the rate of monetary expansion.

This reduction will raise interest rates and reduce aggregate desired expenditure, eventually eliminating any inflationary gap. Although the rise in interest rates may cause a one-time upward shift in the *SRAS* curve, the rise is a necessary part of an anti-inflationary policy that slows the rate of growth of the money supply, thereby stopping the outward shift of the *AD* curve.

- The process of ending a sustained inflation can be divided into three phases. Phase 1 consists of ending monetary validation and allowing the upward shift in the *SRAS* curve to remove any inflationary gap that does exist. In Phase 2, a recessionary gap develops as expectations of further inflation cause the *SRAS* curve to continue to shift upward even after the inflationary gap is removed. In Phase 3, the economy returns to full employment, sometimes aided by a one-time monetary expansion that raises the *AD* curve to the level consistent with potential income at the present price level.

C. INFLATION POLICY IN CANADA

- In the early 1980s, inflation peaked at around 13 percent. The Bank of Canada followed the United States in pursuing a tight-money policy. In Canada, inflation fell to around 4 percent by 1984, but the recession Canada experienced in the early 1980s was severe. During the next four years amidst a healthy economic recovery, inflation hovered between 4 and 5 percent, then toward the end of the recovery it crept up until reaching over 5 percent in 1989.

- In 1988, the Bank of Canada announced an important shift in policy. Henceforth, monetary policy would no longer be guided by short-term stabilization issues and instead would be guided by the long-term goal of price stability. As a means of formalizing this shift in policy, the Bank and the federal department of finance announced a series of inflation-control targets, beginning in the 3–5 percent range for 1992 and falling to the 1–3 percent range by the end of 1995. The 1–3 percent range has been extended through 1998.

- The Bank's policy of reducing inflation below 4–5 percent sparked considerable controversy. Despite the controversy, however, the Bank stuck to its policy and lowered inflation to roughly 2 percent by 1992. For the next four years, inflation hovered between 1 and 2 percent.

KEY CONCEPTS

Temporary and sustained inflation
Rational expectations
Monetary validation of demand and
   supply shocks

Expectational inflation
The NAIRU
Accelerating inflation
Ending sustained inflation

Wage and price controls
Monetary gradualism (1975–1980)
Inflation in the 1980s and 1990s
Inflation-control targets

DISCUSSION QUESTIONS

1. On what source or sources of inflation do the following statements focus attention?

   a. "Rapid growth in M2 raises fears of renewed inflation."

   b. "Wage bargains currently being negotiated in several key industries by strong British unions may cause British inflation to accelerate."

   c. "Americans have become so accustomed to 4 percent inflation that it would be difficult for the Fed to induce the transition to 1 percent inflation."

   d. "As the Canadian recovery continued, inflationary pressures seemed to be building up across the country."

   e. "Heavy borrowing by the German government to finance investment in the former East Germany fuels inflation, causing the Bundesbank (the German central bank) to push up interest rates in response."

2. It has been estimated that reducing inflation by 1 percentage point in the early 1980s required a 4-percentage-point reduction of national income for one year. Use *AD* and *SRAS* curves to show why this might be so. Why might the cost in terms of lost income vary from one inflationary period to another? Are there reasons to think that the cost might be higher the longer inflation has persisted? What might the Bank of Canada do to reduce the cost?

3. Use the *Bank of Canada Review* to plot the rate of inflation and the level of unemployment since 1981. Is there any obvious relationship between reductions in inflation and temporary rises in unemployment? (Note: Although looking at the data is always instructive, important relationships between two variables are often not revealed by simple inspection because many influencing forces are usually changing at once and because causes take time to bring their full effects.)

4. When the persistent worldwide inflation of the early 1980s was brought under control, the economies of many industrial countries came to rest with a relatively low inflation rate and high unemployment.

People who feared the outbreak of inflation opposed even a temporary increase in the rate of monetary expansion. Use aggregate demand and aggregate supply analysis to show why some people felt that a *temporary* burst of monetary expansion might bring increases in employment without increases in inflation.

5. What theory or theories of inflation are suggested by each of the following quotations?

   a. A Canadian newspaper headline in 1986: "February producer prices steady—fall in energy costs largest in six years."

   b. A newspaper editorial in Manchester, England: "If American unions were as strong as those in Britain, America's inflationary experience would have been as disastrous as Britain's."

   c. A study issued in 1980 by the Worldwatch Institute: "The nation's spiraling inflation reflects a global depletion of physical resources and therefore cannot be cured by traditional fiscal and monetary tools." Has the prediction in this quotation been borne out since then?

   d. An article in *The Economist:* "Oil price collapse will reduce today's inflation rate."

   e. A Canadian newspaper article in October 1990: "The combination of the Kuwaiti crisis and an emerging recession is a sure recipe for worldwide stagflation."

   f. A U.S. newspaper headline in May 1992: "Fed's move to cut interest rates spurs concerns about renewed inflation."

6. Discuss the apparent conflict between the following views. Can you suggest how they might be reconciled using aggregate demand and aggregate supply analysis?

   a. "A rise in interest rates is deflationary, because ending entrenched inflation with a tight monetary policy usually requires that interest rates rise steeply."

   b. "A rise in interest rates is inflationary, because interest is a major business cost and, as with other costs, a rise in interest will be passed on by firms in the form of higher prices."

7. Whatever its initiating causes, inflation cannot persist indefinitely unless it is validated by increases in the money supply. Why is this so? Does it not imply that control of inflation is merely a matter of not allowing the money supply to rise faster than the rate of increase of real national income?

8. When Gordon Thiessen was appointed the new Governor of the Bank of Canada early in 1994, he was quick to reaffirm the past tight-money policy of the Bank. He also continued the formal 1–3 percent inflation targets until the end of 1998. Describe what would have been the likely effect on inflation expectations if Mr. Thiessen had instead announced that past Bank policy had been too tight, and that the inflation target should be raised to the 2–4 percent range. What would this have done to the *SRAS* curve?

9. In January 1991, the federal government introduced the Goods and Services Tax (GST). If you were to suppose that the GST was a *new* tax (in fact, it replaced an existing tax), what would be the effect on the *SRAS* curve? Is the introduction of the GST (or an increase in its rate) inflationary? Does it increase inflation permanently?

10. In April of 1996, at a time when U.S. GDP was approximately equal to potential, a story in *The Globe and Mail* reported that the release of strong employment-growth data for the United States led to a plunge in prices on the U.S. stock market. Explain the following points related to this story:

   a. Explain why high employment growth would lead people to expect the U.S. central bank to tighten their monetary policy.
   b. Explain why a tighter monetary policy would lead to higher U.S. interest rates.
   c. Explain why higher U.S. interest rates would lead to lower prices of U.S. stocks.
   d. How would you expect this announcement to affect Canada? (At the time, there was still a recessionary gap in Canada.)

CHAPTER 31

UNEMPLOYMENT

When national income changes, the levels of employment and unemployment change as well. Figure 21-5 in Chapter 21 shows the course of unemployment in Canada over the past several decades. It is clear from that figure that the unemployment rate follows a cyclical path, rising during periods of recession and falling in periods of business expansion. In addition, at least over the past thirty years or so, the unemployment rate appears to have an upward trend. What are the sources of these cyclical fluctuations? What are the sources of the upward trend?

In macroeconomics, we distinguish between the NAIRU, which you will recall is the rate of unemployment that occurs when national income is at its potential (Y^*), and the rate of *cyclical* unemployment, which is the unemployment associated with fluctuations of national income around its potential. The unemployed are people who are without jobs and are actively searching for jobs. The unemployed are sometimes measured as the *number* of persons and sometimes as a *rate*, expressed as a percentage of the total labour force.

After a preliminary look at Canada's recent experience with employment and unemployment, we study cyclical unemployment, why it exists, and why the adjustment mechanism often takes so long to make it disappear. Then we consider the NAIRU in much more detail, asking such questions as these: What types of unemployment make up the NAIRU? Why does the NAIRU change? Are government policies partly (and perhaps unintentionally) responsible for increases in the NAIRU? Can government policy do anything to reduce the NAIRU?

EMPLOYMENT AND UNEMPLOYMENT IN CANADA

Considered over the long term, the most striking features revealed by Figure 21-5(i) are trend increases in both total employment and the total labour force. Over the decades, the pace of creation of new jobs has been roughly equal to growth in the number of potential workers. In the roughly 20 years since 1976, employment and the labour force have both increased by approximately 50 percent.

Less obvious in Figure 21-5(i), but more clear in Figure 21-5(ii), are the substantial year-to-year fluctuations in the unemployment rate. There is also some indication that the unemployment rate, aside from these short-term fluctuations, has been slowly increasing over the past thirty years. For example, at the peak of the business cycle in 1973, the unemployment rate was roughly 5 percent; by the business-cycle peak in 1989, the unemployment rate was above 7 percent.

Over the span of many years, increases in the labour force are more-or-less matched by increases in employment. But from year to year the unemployment rate fluctuates because changes in the labour force are not exactly matched by changes in employment.

CHANGES IN TOTAL EMPLOYMENT

The level of employment in Canada has increased dramatically over the past few decades. In 1956, there were approximately 5 million Canadians employed. By 1976, the number was 9.7 million, and by 1996 total employment was just under 14 million.

On the supply side, the labour force has expanded virtually every year since the end of World War II. The causes have included a rising population, which boosts entry into the labour force of people born 15 to 25 years previously; increased labour force participation by various groups, especially women; and net immigration of working-age persons.

On the demand side, many existing jobs are eliminated every year, and many new jobs are created. Economic growth causes some sectors of the economy to decline and others to expand. Jobs are lost in the sectors that are contracting and created in sectors that are expanding. Furthermore, even in stable industries, many firms disappear and many new ones are set up. The net increase in employment is the difference between all the jobs that are lost and all those that are created.

In most years, enough new jobs have been created both to replace old jobs that have been eliminated and to provide jobs for the increased numbers of people in the labour force. The result has been a net increase in employment in almost all years.

In mild recessions, often called "growth recessions," the unemployment rate increases because the net creation of new jobs, though positive, falls below the net increase in the size of the labour force. Only in relatively severe recessions does the actual level of employment fall.

CHANGES IN UNEMPLOYMENT

In the early 1980s, worldwide unemployment rose to high levels. The unemployment rate remained high in many advanced industrial countries and only began to come down, and even then very slowly, during the latter half of the decade. Canadian experience reflected these international developments rather closely. From a high of 11.9 percent in 1983, the Canadian unemployment rate fell to 7.5 percent in 1989, a point that many economists think is very close to the Canadian NAIRU. With the onset of another recession in the early 1990s, the unemployment rate then rose through 1990 and 1991, reaching 11.3 percent by 1992. Over the next several years, during an economic recovery, it fell only slowly. By early in 1997, the unemployment rate was still about 9.5 percent.

GROSS FLOWS IN THE LABOUR MARKET

We have said that many existing jobs are eliminated every year, as industries contract and firms either shrink or close down altogether. Similarly, new jobs are continually being created, as other industries expand and new firms are born. The focus on the labour market, however, tends to be on the overall level of employment and unemployment rather than on the amount of job creation and job destruction. This focus can often lead us to the conclusion that few changes are occurring in the labour market when in fact the truth is exactly the opposite.

For example, the overall unemployment rate in Canada fell from 10.4 percent of the labour force in 1994 to 9.5 percent in 1995. This change represented an increase in the level of employment of 214,000 persons combined with an increase in the labour force of 96,000 persons. Thus not only did employment increase enough to accommodate the expanded labour force, but it also accounted for a reduction in the level of unemployment by 118,000 persons.

This decline in unemployment by 118,000 persons—a reduction in the unemployment rate of only nine-tenths of a percentage point—would be mistakenly interpreted by many as reflecting only a small level of job creation activity in the economy. But this number conceals what is actually a very active labour market with very large amounts of both *gross job creation* and *gross job destruction*. In each of the months of 1995, approximately 200,000 people left unemployment and became employed. At the same time, however, about 190,000 persons per month were leaving jobs and becoming unemployed. Over the year, the total flows out of unemployment ex-

ceeded the total flows into unemployment. This accounts for the *net* reduction in unemployment of 118,000 people.

By looking at the *gross flows* in the labour market, we are able to see economic activity that is hidden when we just look at the overall level of employment and unemployment (which is determined by *net* flows). Indeed, these gross flows are typically so large that they dwarf the net flows. Gross job creation in 1995 was approximately 2.4 million whereas gross job destruction was approximately 2.3 million. The difference, a mere 118,000 people, is the overall reduction in unemployment.

See Application 31-1 for more discussion of the gross flows in the Canadian labour market, and how these gross-flows data can be used to compute the average length of unemployment spells.

CONSEQUENCES OF UNEMPLOYMENT

Economists view unemployment as a social "bad" just as they view output as a social "good." But this does not mean that *all* unemployment is bad, just as we know that all output is not good (e.g., pollution). Indeed, we will see later in this chapter that some unemployment is probably socially desirable as it reflects the necessary time spent searching to make appropriate matches between firms and workers. Generally, however, unemployment—a factor of production sitting idle rather than producing valuable output—is viewed as "bad."

We examine two costs of unemployment. The first is reflected by the loss in output. The second is the harm done to the individuals who are unemployed.

Lost Output

Every person counted as unemployed is willing and able to work but unable to find a job. Hence the unemployed are valuable resources whose contribution to producing output is wasted. The output counterpart of unemployment is the recessionary gap—output that is not produced. According to an empirical relation sometimes called *Okun's law*—named for the economist Arthur Okun (1928–1980)—for every percentage point that unemployment rises above the NAIRU, output falls by about 2.5 percentage points below potential output. In a world of scarcity with many unsatisfied wants, this loss represents a serious waste of resources.

Personal Costs

Being unemployed, even for substantial periods of time, is no longer the disaster that it once was. But this does not mean there are no problems associated with unemployment. The effects of long-term high unemployment, in terms of the disillusioned who have given up trying to make it within the system and who contribute to social unrest, should be a matter of serious concern to the "haves" as well as the "have-nots." The loss of self-esteem and the dislocation of families that often result from situations of prolonged unemployment are genuine tragedies.

The general case for concern about high unemployment has been eloquently put by Princeton economist Alan Blinder:

> A high-pressure economy provides opportunities, facilitates structural change, encourages inventiveness and innovation, *and* opens doors for society's underdogs. . . . All these promote the social cohesion and economic progress that make democratic mixed capitalism such a wonderful system when it works well. A low-pressure economy slams the doors shut, breeds a bunker mentality that resists change, stifles productivity growth, and fosters both inequality and mean-spirited public policy. All this makes reducing high unemployment a political, economic, and moral challenge of the highest order.[1]

KINDS OF UNEMPLOYMENT

For purposes of study, the unemployed are classified in various ways. They can be grouped by personal characteristics, such as age, sex, degree of skill or education, or ethnic group. They can also be classified by geographical location, occupation, duration of unemployment, or reasons for unemployment.

In this chapter, we are concerned mainly with the reasons for unemployment. Although it is not always possible to say why a particular person does not have a job, it is often possible to gain some idea of the total number of people unemployed for each major cause.

In Chapter 21, we noted that the recorded figures for unemployment may significantly understate or overstate the numbers of people who are actually willing to work at the existing wages. Overstatement arises because the measured figure for unemployment includes people who are not interested in work but say they are interested in order to collect unemployment benefits. Understatement arises because people who would like to work but have ceased to believe that suitable jobs are available voluntarily withdraw from the labour force. Although these people are not measured in the survey of unemployment (which requires that people actively look for work), they are unemployed in the sense that they would accept a job if one were available at going wage rates. People in this category are referred to as **discouraged workers.** They have voluntarily withdrawn from the labour market not because they do not want to work but because they believe that they cannot find a job under current labour-market conditions.

In Chapter 21, we also distinguished three types of unemployment: *cyclical*, *frictional*, and *structural*. Both frictional and structural unemployment exist even when national income is at its potential level, and hence there is neither a recessionary gap nor an inflationary gap. Together these two types of unemployment make up the NAIRU. We first study cyclical unemployment and then the two components of the NAIRU.

CYCLICAL UNEMPLOYMENT

As we saw in Chapter 21, the term *cyclical unemployment* refers to unemployment that occurs whenever national income is below potential income. This is a recessionary gap. Cyclical unemployment can be measured as the difference between the number of persons currently employed and the number of persons who would be employed at potential income.

When cyclical unemployment is zero, the number of unfilled jobs currently available is equal to the number of persons unemployed.

In this situation, all existing unemployment is either structural or frictional, and the rate of unemployment is the NAIRU.

People who are cyclically unemployed are normally presumed to be suffering **involuntary unemployment** in that they are willing to work at the going wage rate but jobs are not available. The persistence of cyclical unemployment poses a challenge to economic theory.

[1]A. S. Blinder, "The Challenge of High Unemployment," *American Economic Review* 78 (1988), 2:1.

APPLICATION 31-1

STOCKS AND FLOWS IN THE CANADIAN LABOUR MARKET

In most reports about changes in unemployment, both in Canada and abroad, emphasis is typically on the changes in the *stock* of unemployment—that is, on the number of people who are unemployed at a particular point in time. But as we said in the text, the focus on the stock of unemployment can often hide much activity in the labour market—activity that is revealed by looking at *gross flows* in the labour market.

WHAT ARE LABOUR-MARKET FLOWS?

In the accompanying figure, there are three series of data shown for Canada from 1976 to 1992. (All have been smoothed to remove the very significant seasonal fluctuations.) The top line is the stock of unemployment—the actual *number* of people unemployed at a specific point in time (it is not the unemployment *rate*). During the severe recession of the early 1980s, unemployment peaked at approximately 1.5 million people, and then fell during the recovery until 1989. With the onset of the next recession in 1990–1991, unemployment rose again, exceeding 1.5 million in early 1992.

The two lower lines in the figure show *gross flows* in the labour market. The dark line shows the *monthly* flow into unemployment. This flow into unemployment represents either:

- workers losing their jobs through layoffs or plant closure; or

- workers quitting their jobs to search for a different job; or

- new entrants to the labour force searching for a job.

Note that the monthly flow into unemployment varies between 300,000 and 500,000 *per month* and

also tends to rise and fall together with the overall stock of unemployment. The light line shows the monthly flow out of unemployment. This outflow represents either:

- unemployed individuals finding new jobs; or

- unemployed individuals becoming discouraged and leaving the labour force.

Note that the monthly flow out of unemployment is roughly the same size as the monthly inflow (300,000–500,000 per month).

THE CONNECTION BETWEEN STOCKS AND FLOWS

What is the connection between the flows and the stocks in the labour market? Whenever the flows into unemployment exceed the flows out of unemployment, the stock of unemployment rises. This is seen clearly, for example, during 1981 and 1982. For these two years, the inflow exceeds the outflow by an average of about 25,000 individuals *per month,* and so over the two-year period the stock of unemployment rises by about 600,000 workers (24 months × 25,000 workers per month). Similarly, whenever the flows out of unemployment exceed the flows into unemployment, the stock of unemployment falls. This is evident during the recovery in the mid and late 1980s.

USEFULNESS OF FLOWS DATA

There are two reasons why looking at flows can be very useful when thinking about the labour market. First, they show the tremendous amount of activity in the labour market even though the stock of unemployment may not be changing. For example, throughout the year 1983, the stock of unemployment in Canada was roughly constant at 1.4 million persons. But during those 12 months, roughly 500,000 persons *per month* either became unemployed or ceased being unemployed. This reflects the massive amount of regular turnover that exists in the Canadian labour market—turnover that is the essence of what we call in this chapter *frictional unemployment*.

The second reason why looking at flows is useful is that the relationship between the flows and the stock can tell us something about the amount of time the average unemployed person spends unemployed. If U_s is the stock of unemployment, and U_o is the monthly outflow from unemployment, then one simple estimate of the average duration of an unemployment spell is

$$\text{Average duration of unemployment spell} = \frac{U_s}{U_o}$$

To see this, consider the situation in 1989, at the most recent peak of the business cycle. At that time, the stock of unemployment was approximately 1 million people and the outflow from unemployment was at a rate of approximately 400,000 persons per month. Thus the average unemployed person in 1989 could expect to leave unemployment in about 2½ months (1,000,000 people/400,000 people per month = 2.5 months). In contrast, by early 1992, at the depth of the subsequent recession, the expected duration of an unemployment spell was over 3½ months (1,600,000/450,000 = 3.6).

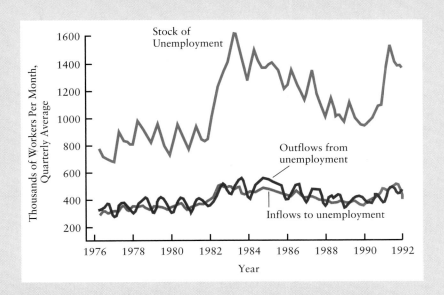

To see what is involved in this challenge, suppose that aggregate demand is fluctuating, causing national income to fluctuate around its potential level. This fluctuation will cause the demand for labour in each of the economy's labour markets to fluctuate as well, rising in booms and falling in slumps. If all of the labour markets had fully flexible wage rates, wages would fluctuate to keep quantity demanded in each individual market equal to quantity supplied in that market. We would observe cyclical fluctuations in employment and in the wage rate but no changes in unemployment. Again, if labour markets had fully flexible wage rates, in recessions the demand for labour would fall, and wage rates would fall as well. On the one hand, some people would withdraw from the labour force, being unwilling to work at the lower wage. On the other hand, firms would cut the number they employ by less than they would have if the wage rate had not changed. The labour market would then reach equilibrium at a lower wage and a lower level of employment but with no involuntary unemployment. In booms the demand for labour would rise, causing the wage rate to rise. This would attract more workers into the labour force while reducing the quantity of labour demanded by firms below what it would have been if wage rates had not changed.

Employment and the labour force would be procyclical (rising in booms and falling in slumps), but there would be no significant amounts of involuntary unemployment. The behaviour just outlined is shown for a typical labour market in Figure 31-1.

The hypothetical situation that we have just described is not what we actually observe. Instead, we see cyclical fluctuations not only in employment but also in unemployment. Furthermore, the changes in wage rates that do occur are insufficient to equate demand and supply, as is shown in Figure 31-2. Unemployment exceeds the NAIRU in slumps and is

FIGURE 31-1
Employment and Wages in a Single Competitive Labour Market

(i) Demand shifts

(ii) Supply shifts

In a perfectly competitive labour market, real wages and employment fluctuate in the same direction when demand fluctuates and in opposite directions when supply fluctuates; in both cases, there is no involuntary unemployment. The figure shows a single perfectly competitive market for one type of labour. In part (i), the demand curves D_1, D_2, and D_0 are the demands for this market when there is a slump, when there is a boom, and when aggregate income is at its potential level. As demand rises from D_1 to D_0 to D_2, real wages rise from w_1 to w_0 to w_2, and employment rises from L_1 to L_0 to L_2. At no time, however, is there any involuntary unemployment.

In part (ii), the supply of labour fluctuates from S_1 to S_0 to S_2, and wages fluctuate from w_1 to w_0 to w_2. In this case, wages fall when employment rises, and vice versa, but again there is no involuntary unemployment.

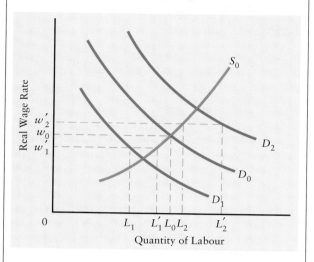

FIGURE 31-2
Unemployment in a Single Labour Market with Sticky Wages

When the wage rate does not change enough to equate quantity demanded and quantity supplied at all times, there will be unemployment in slumps and labour shortages in booms. When demand is at its normal level D_0, the market is cleared with wage rate w_0, employment is L_0, and there is no unemployment. In a recession, demand falls to D_1, but the wage only falls to w_1'. As a result, L_1 of labour is demanded and L_1' is supplied. Employment is determined by the quantity demanded at L_1. The remainder of the supply for which there is no demand, L_1L_1', is unemployed. In a boom, demand rises to D_2, but the wage rate rises only to w_2'. As a result, the quantity demanded is L_2', whereas only L_2 is supplied. Employment rises to L_2, which is the amount supplied. The rest of the demand cannot be satisfied, making excess demand for labour of L_2L_2'.

below it in booms. Although wages do tend to vary over the cycle, the fluctuations are not sufficient to remove all cyclical variations in unemployment. Why is this so?

Two types of explanation have been advanced over the years. The line of explanation that we consider first is associated with what is called **New Classical economics.** The explanation assumes that labour markets are always in equilibrium in the sense that quantity demanded is continually equated with quantity supplied.

NEW CLASSICAL THEORIES[2]

One New Classical explanation of cyclical fluctuations in employment assumes that they are caused by fluctuations in the willingness of people to supply their labour, as shown in part (ii) of Figure 31-1. If the supply curves of labour fluctuate cyclically (supply increases during booms and falls during slumps) this will lead to cyclical variations in employment. This explanation of cyclical behaviour in the labour market has two problems. First, the wage will tend to rise in slumps and fall in booms, which is not what we observe. Second, there will still be no systematic cyclical *unemployment* because labour markets always clear, leaving everyone who wishes to work actually working. Supply-induced fluctuations in employment form part of the basis of what is called real business cycle theory, which is discussed in Extension 31-1.

A second line of explanation lies in errors on the part of workers and employers in predicting the course of the price level over the business cycle. To see the argument, start by supposing that all of the economy's markets are in equilibrium, that there is full employment, that prices are stable, and that the actual and expected rates of inflation are zero. Now suppose the government increases the money supply by 5 percent. People find themselves with unwanted money balances, which they seek to spend. For simplicity, suppose that the increased money supply leads to an increase in desired expenditure on all commodities; the demand for each commodity shifts to the right, and all prices, being competitively determined, rise. Individual decision makers see their selling prices go up and mistakenly interpret the increase as a rise in their own relative price. The reason is that they expect the overall inflation rate to be zero. Firms will produce more, and workers will work more; both groups think they are getting an increased *relative* price for what they sell. Thus total output and employment rise.

When both groups eventually realize that their own relative prices are in fact unchanged, output and employment fall back to their initial levels. The

[2]The source of the label "New Classical" is that many of the arguments put forward by this group of economists are essentially more detailed and precise versions of arguments that would have been very familiar to the Classical economists, from Adam Smith and David Ricardo to Alfred Marshall.

EXTENSION 31-1

REAL BUSINESS CYCLE THEORY

Real business cycle (RBC) theory attempts to explain cyclical fluctuations in the context of models in which wages and prices are flexible and markets always clear. This is in sharp contrast to the Keynesian and New Keynesian models we have discussed in this book in which business cycles arise largely because wages and prices are slow to adjust and thus markets do not always clear. In such models, if wages and prices were able to adjust instantly to all shocks, then output would always be equal to potential output—there would never be inflationary or recessionary gaps. Thus the flexibility of wages and prices is an important distinguishing feature between RBC models and New Keynesian models.

KEY PROPOSITIONS AND CRITICISMS

The view of the business cycle found in RBC models is that short-run fluctuations in national income are caused by fluctuations in the vertical *LRAS* curve. In this view, unemployment is always equal to the NAIRU, and it is the NAIRU itself that fluctuates.

The explanation of cyclical fluctuations that arises in real business cycle models is based on the role of supply shocks originating from sources such as oil price changes, technical progress, and changes in tastes.

The RBC approach is controversial. The major claims in favour of it include the following:

1. It has been able to explain the recent behaviour of the economy quite well statistically, while downplaying the role for aggregate demand fluctuations in the business cycle.

2. It suggests that an integrated approach to understanding cycles and growth may be appropriate, as both reflect forces that affect the LRAS curve. The distinction it makes is that some shocks are temporary (and hence have cyclical effects) whereas others are permanent (and therefore affect the economy's growth).

3. It provides valuable insights into how shocks, regardless of their origin, spread over time to the different sectors of the economy. By abstracting from monetary issues, it is possible to address more details concerning technology and household choice involving intertemporal trade offs between consumption, labour supply, and leisure.

4. It has focused on integrating the explanation of a number of facts that other approaches have ig-

---

extra output and employment occur only while people are being fooled. When they realize that *all* prices have increased by 5 percent, they revert to their initial behaviour. The only difference is that now the price level is 5 percent higher, leaving relative prices unchanged.

A similar argument shows that an unanticipated decrease in the money supply would cause output to fall below its full-employment level.

New Classical explanations assume that labour markets clear, and then they look for reasons why employment fluctuates. They imply, therefore, that people who are not working have voluntarily withdrawn

from the labour market for one reason or another; there is no involuntary unemployment.

NEW KEYNESIAN THEORIES[3]

Many economists find the New Classical explanations implausible. They believe that people correctly read market signals but react in ways that do not cause markets to clear at all times. These econo-

---

[3]The source of the label "New Keynesian" is that many of the arguments put forward by these economists are closely related to some of the ideas put forward by John Maynard Keynes in *The General Theory of Employment, Interest and Money* (1936).

nored, such as seasonal and cyclical fluctuations, consumption varying less than output over the business cycle, and procyclical movements of hours worked and of average labour productivity.

Critics of the RBC approach focus on some implausible results, express concern about its assumed underlying behaviour, and argue that the phenomena mentioned in point 4 have already been given satisfactory explanations. More important, they are sceptical about a model in which monetary issues are completely ignored. For example, they point out that RBC models are unable to provide insights into the correlation between money and output that is at the heart of the traditional macro model. Furthermore, RBC models are unable to provide insights into empirical regularities involving nominal variables, such as prices that apparently vary less than quantities and nominal prices that vary procyclically.

POLICY IMPLICATIONS

Because the RBC approach gives no role to aggregate demand in influencing business cycles, it provides no role for stabilization operating through monetary and fiscal policies. Indeed, the models predict that the use of such demand-management policies can be *harmful*.

The basis for this prediction is the proposition in RBC models that cycles represent *efficient* responses to the shocks that are hitting the economy. Policymakers may mistakenly interpret cyclical fluctuations as deviations from full employment that are caused by fluctuations in aggregate demand. The policymakers may try to stabilize output and thereby distort the maximizing decisions made by households and firms. This distortion will in turn cause the responses to the real shocks (as opposed to nominal, monetary shocks) to be inefficient.

Although a minority of economists espouse these models as complete or even reasonable descriptions of the business cycle, and hence only a minority take seriously the strict implications for policy, many accept the view that real disturbances can play an important role in business cycles. Moreover, since the RBC approach emphasizes the importance of markets always clearing in response to changes in technology or other shocks, many economists that view RBC models as a poor description of the economy in the short run believe that many of the insights from the RBC approach are very useful when thinking about the behaviour of the economy in the long run.

mists—who refer to themselves as New Keynesians—believe that many people who are recorded as unemployed are involuntarily unemployed in the sense that *they would accept an offer of work in jobs for which they are trained, at the going wage rate, if such an offer were made.* These economists concentrate their efforts on explaining why wages do not fluctuate in labour markets so as to eliminate involuntary unemployment.

Theories that attempt to explain involuntary unemployment examine the forces that determine how quickly wages in actual labour markets respond to changes in economic conditions. If wages do not respond quickly to shifts in supply and demand, quantity supplied and quantity demanded may *not* be equated for extended periods of time. Labour markets will then display unemployment during recessions and excess demand during booms. This is shown for one typical labour market in Figure 31-2.

These theories start with the everyday observation that wage rates do not change every time demand or supply shifts. When unemployed workers are looking for jobs, they do not knock on employers' doors and offer to work at lower wages than are being paid to current workers; instead, they answer want ads and hope to get the jobs offered but are often disappointed. Nor do employers, seeing an excess of applicants for the few jobs that are available, go to the current workers and reduce their wages until there is no one who is looking for a job; instead, they pick and choose until they fill their needs and then hang a sign saying "No Help Wanted."[4]

Long-Term Employment Relationships

One set of theories explains the familiar observations made in the preceding paragraph as results of the advantages to both workers and employers of relatively long-term and stable employment relationships. Workers want job security in the face of fluctuating demand. Employers want workers who understand the firm's organization, production, and marketing plans. Under these circumstances, both parties care about things in addition to the wage rate, and wages become somewhat insensitive to fluctuations in current economic conditions. Wages are, in effect, regular payments to workers over an extended employment relationship rather than a device for fine-tuning the current supplies and demands for labour. Given this situation, the tendency is for employers to "smooth out" the income of employees by paying a steady money wage and letting profits and employment fluctuate to absorb the effects of temporary increases and decreases in demand for the firm's product.

A number of labour-market institutions work to achieve these results. For example, many long-term contracts provide for a schedule of money wages over a period of several years. Similarly, fringe benefits, such as pensions and health care, tend to bind workers to particular employers. Another example is pay that rises with years of service. This helps to bind the employee to the company, whereas seniority rules for layoffs bind the employer to the long-term worker.

These things tend to be the glue that leads to long-term employment, despite the known fact that the output attributable to workers rises rapidly as they gain experience, reaches a peak, and then falls off as their age advances. Under gradually rising wages, workers tend to get less than the value of the output that they produce at earlier ages and more as they near retirement (the relevant output concept here is the value of labour's marginal product). But over a span of many years they are paid, on average, the value of their output to the firm, just as microeconomic theory predicts (see Chapter 16). Between the impact of wages that rise with employee age and the impact of dismissal during recessions in ascending order of seniority, employers and employees are held to each other, allowing payment of a more or less steady wage in spite of fluctuating economic circumstances.

Thus in labour markets in which long-term relationships are important (and this is the case in many labour markets), the wage rate does not fluctuate to continuously clear the market. Wages are written over what has been called the long-term "economic climate" rather than the short-term "economic weather." Because wages are thus insulated from short-term fluctuations in demand, any market clearing that occurs does so through fluctuations in the volume of employment rather than in wages. Of course, wages must respond to permanent shifts in market conditions—for example, the permanent and unexpected decline in the demand for the output of a particular industry.

To see the importance of long-term employment relationships in the Canadian economy, note that in January 1996, the regular (monthly) *Labour Force Survey* found that among full-time workers, the average time spent with the same employer—what is referred to as *job tenure*—was just under nine years. Further, 56 percent of those workers surveyed had been at their employer for six years or longer. Only 16 percent of those surveyed reported being at their employers for less than one year.

Efficiency Wages

The idea of **efficiency wages** forms the core of another strand of New Keynesian thinking about why wages do not readily fall in response to excess supply in labour markets. For any of a number of reasons, employers may find that they get more output per dollar of wages paid (i.e., a more *efficient* workforce) when they pay labour somewhat more than the minimum amount that would induce workers to work for them.

Suppose that it is costly for employers to monitor workers' performance on the job, so that some workers will be able to shirk duties with a low

---

[4]This observation concerns cyclical variations in the demand for labour. It does not conflict with the different observation that when firms get into long-term competitive trouble, workers sometimes reopen contracts and agree to wage cuts in order to save the firm and their jobs.

probability of being caught.[5] Given prevailing labour-market institutions, it is generally impossible for employers to levy fines on employees for shirking on the job. The employees could just leave their jobs rather than pay the fines. Further, if the workers can easily find new jobs that are just as good, firing is not much of a threat. However, if there is a group of potential employees who are currently unemployed and would like to work at the going wage, the threat of firing workers in order to discipline them is much enhanced. Under these conditions, employees who are fired will be made worse off by being fired precisely because it is difficult to find work at the going wage.

Efficiency-wage theory says that firms may find it advantageous to pay high enough wages so that working is a clearly superior alternative to being laid off. This will improve the quality of workers' output without firms' having to spend heavily to monitor workers' performance.

Several economists have observed that workers who believe that they are well treated work harder than those who believe that they are treated badly. This gives a reason for paying an efficiency wage—provided that the increased output from treating workers well covers the increased cost of doing so.

A variant of efficiency wage theory seeks to explain why firms do not cut wages during recessions. If workers feel unfairly treated when their wages are reduced, wage reductions (at least in response to moderate recessions) may cost firms more (in lost output from unhappy employees) than they save in reduced wages.[6] If so, real wages may not fall rapidly enough to eliminate cyclical unemployment.

The basic message of New Keynesian theories of unemployment is that competitive labour markets cannot be relied on to eliminate unemployment by equating current demand for labour with current supply.

As a result, unemployment will rise and fall as the demand for labour rises and falls over the cycle.

THE NAIRU

We now turn to a consideration of the NAIRU, which, as we have seen, is composed of frictional and structural unemployment. Our interest is in how the NAIRU changes over time and in the extent that economic policy can affect the NAIRU.

FRICTIONAL UNEMPLOYMENT

As we saw in Chapter 21, *frictional unemployment* results from the normal turnover of labour. An important source of frictional unemployment is young people who enter the labour force and look for jobs. Another source is people who leave their jobs. Some may quit because they are dissatisfied with the type of work or their working conditions; others may be fired. Whatever the reason, they must search for new jobs, which takes time. Persons who are unemployed while searching for jobs are said to be frictionally unemployed or in **search unemployment.**

The normal turnover of labour would cause frictional unemployment to persist, even if the economy were at potential income.

How voluntary is frictional unemployment? Some of it is clearly voluntary. For example, a worker may know of an available job but may not accept it so she can search for a better one. An extreme New Classical view regards *all* frictional unemployment as voluntary. Critics of that view argue that many frictionally unemployed workers are involuntarily unemployed because they lost their jobs through no fault of their own (e.g., their factories may have closed down) and have not yet located specific jobs that they know to be available *somewhere* for which they believe they are qualified.

Extension 31-2, which discusses search unemployment in more detail, shows that the distinction between voluntary and involuntary unemployment is not always as clear as it might at first seem.

STRUCTURAL UNEMPLOYMENT

Structural adjustments can cause unemployment. When the pattern of demand for goods changes, the

SEARCH UNEMPLOYMENT

Frictional unemployment is *involuntary* if the job seeker has not yet found a job for which his or her training and experience are suitable. Frictional unemployment is *voluntary* if the unemployed person is aware of available jobs for which he or she is suited but is searching for better options. But how should we classify an unemployed person who refuses to accept a job at a lower skill level than the one for which she is qualified? What if she turns down a job for which she is trained because she hopes to get a higher wage offer for a similar job from another employer?

In one sense, people in search unemployment are voluntarily unemployed because they could almost always find some job; in another sense, they are involuntarily unemployed because they have not yet succeeded in finding the job for which they feel they are suited at a rate of pay that they believe is attainable.

Workers do not have perfect knowledge of all available jobs and rates of pay, and they may be able to gain information only by searching the market.

Facing this uncertainty, it may be sensible for them to refuse a first job offer, for the offer may prove to be a poor one in light of further market information. Too much search—for example, holding off while being supported by others in the hope of finding a job better than a job for which one is really suited—is an economic waste. Thus search unemployment is a gray area: Some of it is useful, and some of it is wasteful.

It is socially desirable for there to be sufficient search unemployment to give unemployed people time to find an available job that makes the best use of their skills.

How long it pays for people to remain in search unemployment depends on the economic costs of being unemployed. By lowering the costs of being unemployed, unemployment insurance tends to increase the amount of search unemployment. This may or may not increase economic efficiency, depending on whether or not it induces people to search beyond the point at which they acquire new and valuable information about the labour market.

---

pattern of the demand for labour changes. Until labour adjusts fully, *structural unemployment* develops. Such unemployment may be defined as unemployment caused by a mismatch between the structure of the labour force—in terms of skills, occupations, industries, or geographical locations—and the structure of the demand for labour.

Natural Causes

Changes that accompany economic growth shift the structure of the demand for labour. Demand rises in such expanding areas as British Columbia's lower mainland or Ontario's Ottawa valley and falls in declining areas such as Newfoundland and parts of Quebec. Demand rises for workers with certain skills, such as computer programming and electronics engineering, and falls for workers with other skills, such as stenography, assembly line work, and

middle management. According to a 1992 federal government report, "A gradual but significant shift toward high-skilled jobs has taken place. The evolutionary shift toward service-sector employment and the restructuring within all industries in response to technological change has favoured workers with more years of schooling." To meet changing demands, the structure of the labour force must change. Some existing workers can retrain and some new entrants can acquire fresh skills, but the transition is often difficult, especially for already experienced workers whose skills become economically obsolete. Structural unemployment occurs when such adjustments are slow enough that severe pockets of unemployment develop in areas, industries, and occupations in which the demand for labour is falling faster than the supply.

One of the more dramatic recent structural changes in the economy has been in the organization of the firm. Manufacturing firms used to be organized much like an army, with a pyramidal command structure. Most key strategic decisions were made near the top and lesser ones concerning implementation at lower levels. This structure required an array of middle-level managers who passed information upward to the top level and downward to the production level and who made various secondary decisions themselves. Recent changes, pioneered among Japanese firms and facilitated by the use of computers, have led to a much looser organization with much more local autonomy among the subsections of the firm. As a result, large numbers of middle managers' jobs have been made redundant. They find themselves on the labour market at middle age and with many of their skills rendered obsolete.[7]

Increases in international competition can have effects similar to those of economic growth and change. As the geographical distribution of world production changes, so does the composition of production and of labour demand in any one country. Labour adapts to such shifts by changing jobs, skills, and locations, but until the transition is complete, structural unemployment exists.

Structural unemployment will increase if there is either an increase in the pace at which the structure of the demand for labour is changing or a decrease in the pace at which labour is adapting to these changes.

Policy Causes

Government policies can influence the speed with which labour markets adapt to changes. Some countries, such as the United Kingdom and Canada, have adopted policies that *discourage* movement among regions, industries, and occupations. These policies (which may be desirable for other reasons) tend to *raise* structural unemployment rather than lower it. Other countries, such as Sweden, have done the reverse and have encouraged workers to adapt to change. Partly for this reason, Sweden's unemploy-

ment rates were well below the European and North American norms during the 1980s.

Policies that discourage firms from replacing labour with machines may protect employment over the short term. However, if such policies lead to the decline of an industry because it cannot compete effectively with innovative foreign competitors, more serious structural unemployment can result in the long run.

Minimum-wage laws can cause structural unemployment by pricing low-skilled labour out of the market. As explained in Chapter 16, minimum-wage laws have two effects when they are imposed on competitive markets: They reduce employment of the unskilled, and they raise the wages of the unskilled who retain their jobs. In most of the Canadian provinces today, however, minimum wages are low enough that they probably have little effect on wage rates and employment.

Unemployment insurance (UI) also contributes to structural unemployment, for at least two reasons. First, the Canadian UI system ties workers' benefits to the regional unemployment rate in such a way that unemployed workers can collect UI benefits for more weeks in regions where unemployment is high than where it is low. The UI system therefore encourages unemployed workers to remain in high-unemployment regions rather than encouraging them to move to regions where employment prospects are more favourable.

Second, workers are only eligible for unemployment insurance if they have worked for a given number of weeks in the previous year—this is known as the *entrance requirement*. In some cases, however, these entrance requirements are very low (10–12 weeks) and thus seasonal workers are encouraged to work for a few months and then collect UI and wait for the next season, rather than finding other jobs during the off season.

Is Structural Unemployment Voluntary?

According to the New Classical view, all structural unemployment is voluntary. Suppose that there is an excess supply of skilled auto workers and an excess demand for unskilled dishwashers. If an unemployed auto worker does not take one of the available jobs as a dishwasher, he is voluntarily deciding to stay unemployed in the hope of finding a job that uses his skills.

---

[7]These changes are discussed in detail in a number of books, including R. Reich, *The Work of Nations* (New York: Knopf, 1991), and J. Womack, D. Jones, and D. Roos, *The Machine That Changed the World* (New York: Macmillan, 1990), both of which can be read without an in-depth knowledge of economic theory.

Critics reply, "But what if it is the other way around?" What if, as is often the case, there is an excess supply of unskilled workers and an excess demand for those with skills? The unemployed dishwasher cannot get a job as a computer programmer; his skills do not equip him for this. This mismatching between the skills of those unemployed and the skills required by the available jobs cannot easily be removed by individual actions of the unemployed dishwashers, nor can it be blamed on their union, for they have none.

THE FRICTIONAL-STRUCTURAL DISTINCTION

As with many distinctions, the one between frictional and structural unemployment becomes blurred at the margin. In a sense, structural unemployment is really long-term frictional unemployment. Consider, for example, what would happen if there was an increase in world demand for Canadian-made car parts but at the same time a decline in world demand for Canadian-assembled cars. This change would require labour to move from one sector (the car-assembly sector) to another (the car-parts manufacturing sector). If the reallocation were to occur quickly, we would call the unemployment *frictional;* if the reallocation were to occur slowly, we call the unemployment *structural.*

The major characteristic of both frictional and structural unemployment is that there are as many unfilled vacancies as there are unemployed persons.

In the case of pure frictional unemployment, the job vacancy and the searcher are matched—the only problem is that the searcher has not yet located the vacancy. In the case of structural unemployment, the job vacancy and the searcher are mismatched in one or more relevant characteristics, such as occupation, industry, location, or skill requirements.

In practice, structural and frictional unemployment cannot be separated. But the two of them, taken together, *can* be separated from cyclical unemployment. Specifically, when national income is at its potential level, the *only* unemployment (by definition) is the NAIRU, which comprises frictional and structural unemployment. For example, as of early 1996, the most recent year for which national income was equal to potential income was 1989. In 1989, the unemployment rate was 7.5 percent, and

thus the NAIRU was also 7.5 percent. By late in 1996, the unemployment rate was 10 percent. To the extent that the underlying causes of frictions and structural change in the economy were unchanged between 1990 and 1996, we could conclude that in 1996, 2½ percentage points of actual unemployment was due to cyclical factors and the rest due to frictional and structural factors.

WHY DOES THE NAIRU CHANGE?

We have noted that structural unemployment can increase because the pace of change accelerates or the pace of adjustment to change slows down. An increase in the rate of growth, for example, usually speeds up the rate at which the structure of the demand for labour is changing. The adaptation of labour to the changing structure of demand may be slowed by such diverse factors as a decline in education and new regulations that make it harder for workers in a given occupation to take new jobs in other areas or occupations. Any of these changes will cause the NAIRU to rise. Changes in the opposite direction will cause the NAIRU to fall.

Demographic Changes

Because people usually try several jobs before settling into one for a longer period of time, young or inexperienced workers have higher unemployment rates than experienced workers. The proportion of inexperienced workers in the labour force rose significantly as the baby boom generation of the 1950s entered the labour force in the 1970s and 1980s, along with an unprecedented number of women who elected to work outside the home. It is estimated that these demographic changes added nearly a percentage point to the NAIRU. Because birthrates were low in the 1960s and a further increase in the percentage of women entering the labour force is unlikely, some demographically induced fall in this type of unemployment has been occurring recently and will continue through the 1990s.

Although the NAIRU, and youth unemployment in particular, should fall as the baby boom generation continues to age, many observers worry about the long-term consequences for some individuals. Learning through on-the-job experience is a critical part of developing marketable labour skills, and people who suffered prolonged unemployment during their teens and twenties have been denied that experience early in their working careers. Some of these workers may have little option later in life but to take temporary jobs at low pay and with little future job security.

The large increase in female participation rates and the related increase in the number of households with more than one income earner have also affected the NAIRU. In 1950, only 30 percent of women 20 years and older were in the labour force. By 1976, the figure was 41.3 percent and by 1996 the number was over 57 percent. When both husband and wife work, it is possible for one to support both while the other looks for "a really good job" rather than accepting the first job offer that comes along. This can increase recorded unemployment while not necessarily inflicting hardship on the people involved.

See Table 31-1 for the different unemployment rates for various groups in the Canadian labour force in 1996.

Wage and Price Rigidity

Some research suggests that the speed with which wages and prices adjust to changing market conditions may have slowed in the 1970s and 1980s. Anything that slows the speed of adjustment to the economy's ever-changing conditions will create a larger pool of structural unemployment. The decline of unions and the willingness of many workers to accept wage cuts when their employers get into serious difficulties may increase wage flexibility in the future—particularly compared with many European countries, where wage structures are relatively insensitive to shorter-term fluctuations in business conditions. If so, this should reduce the NAIRU.

Hysteresis

Recent models of unemployment show that the size of the NAIRU can be influenced by the size of the actual current rate of unemployment.[8] Such models get their name from the Greek word *hysteresis,* meaning "lagged effect."

One mechanism that can lead to hysteresis in labour markets has already been noted. It arises from the importance of experience and on-the-job training. Suppose that a period of recession causes a sig-

---

[8]See, for example, O. Blanchard and L. Summers, "Hysteresis and the European Unemployment Problem," *NBER Macroeconomics Annual* (1986): 15–78.

TABLE 31-1
Unemployment Rates for Various Groups, January 1996
(Percent of the Labour force)

Unemployment Rates by Sex and Age	
Males 15 and over	10.0
Males 15–24 years	17.8
Males 25 and over	8.5
Females 15 and over	9.0
Females 15–24 years	14.0
Females 25 and over	8.0
Unemployment Rates by Education Level	
0–8 years of school	18.3
Some secondary education	16.8
High school graduates	10.4
Post-secondary diploma	9.1
University Degree	4.9
Unemployment Rates by Province	
British Columbia	9.2
Alberta	7.6
Saskatchewan	7.1
Manitoba	8.3
Ontario	8.9
Quebec	10.9
New Brunswick	11.6
Nova Scotia	11.3
PEI	13.9
Newfoundland	19.6

Unemployment is unevenly spread among different groups in the labour force. In January 1996, when the overall Canadian unemployment rate was 9.6 percent, various groups in the labour force had very different unemployment rates.

(*Source:* Statistics Canada, 71–001).

---

nificant group of new entrants to the labour force to encounter unusual difficulty obtaining their first jobs. As a result, the unlucky group will be slow to acquire the important skills that workers generally learn in their first jobs. When demand increases again, this group of workers will be at a disadvantage relative to workers with normal histories of experience, and the unlucky group may have unemployment rates that will be higher than average. Hence the NAIRU will be higher than it would have been had there been no recession.

Another force that can cause such effects is emphasized by commentators in Western Europe, which has a heavily unionized labour force. In times of high unemployment, people who are currently employed ("insiders") may use their bargaining power to ensure that their own status is maintained and prevent new entrants to the labour force ("outsiders") from competing effectively. In an *insider-outsider model* of this type, a period of prolonged, high unemployment—whatever its initial cause—will tend to become "locked in." If outsiders are denied access to the labour market, their unemployment will fail to exert downward pressure on wages, and the NAIRU will tend to rise.

In some countries in Western Europe, there is evidence that hysteresis may be quite important. For Canada, however, the empirical importance of hysteresis has not yet been established.[9]

Increasing Structural Change

The amount of resources being moved between industries and regions increased in the mid 1970s and appears to be carrying on through the 1980s and 1990s. In part, this is the result of the increasing integration of the Canadian economy with the rest of the world and the globalization of world markets. Most economists would argue that this integration has been beneficial overall, for reasons we discuss in Chapters 35 and 36. One less fortunate consequence, however, is that Canadian labour markets are increasingly affected by changes in demand and supply conditions anywhere in the world—changes that require adjustments throughout the world's trading nations. Although evidence is difficult to obtain, some observers argue that the increasing pace and the changing nature of technological change since the mid 1970s has contributed to an increase in the level of structural unemployment.

Some points of caution concerning policies directed at structural unemployment and other consequences of structural change are given in Application 31-2.

Policy and Labour-Market Flexibility

We mentioned briefly above how policies can affect structural unemployment and thus affect the NAIRU. It is worthwhile emphasizing again the important role that government policy can have on the NAIRU.

Our discussion in the previous several pages suggests that one important cause of unemployment—in very general terms—is *inflexibility* in the labour market. If wages are inflexible, then shocks to labour demand can cause unemployment. If workers are unable or unwilling to move between regions or between industries, then changes in the structure of the economy can cause unemployment. If it is costly for firms to hire workers, then firms will find other ways of increasing output (such as switching to more capital-intensive methods of production). In general, since the economy is always being buffeted by shocks of one sort or another, the more inflexibility there is in the labour market, the higher unemployment will be.

This suggests a general point about the effect of government policy on the NAIRU:

Any government policy that reduces labour-market flexibility is likely to increase the NAIRU.

We discuss two examples.

The first example is unemployment insurance (UI). UI provides income support to eligible unemployed workers and thus reduces the costs to the worker of being unemployed. This will typically lead the worker to search longer for a new job and thus increase the unemployment rate. As we suggested in Extension 31-2, this may be desirable since by reducing the cost of unemployment the worker is able to conduct a thorough search for a job that is an appropriate match for his or her specific skills. On the other hand, if the UI system is so generous that workers have little incentive to accept reasonable jobs—instead holding out for the "perfect" job— then the increase in unemployment generated by the UI system may be undesirable.

In general, however, the basic message should be clear. The more generous is the unemployment insurance system, the less motivated unemployed workers will be to quickly accept a new job. This reduction in labour-market flexibility will increase the NAIRU.

The second example concerns policies designed to increase job security for workers. In most western European countries, firms that lay off workers are required either to give several months notice before doing so or, in lieu of such notice, are required to make severance payments equal to several months worth of pay. In Italy, for example, a worker who has been with the firm for ten years is guaranteed either 20 months notice before termination or a severance payment equal to 20 months worth of pay.

[9]For one review of the Canadian evidence, see Stephen Poloz, "The Causes of Unemployment in Canada: A Review of the Evidence", Bank of Canada Working Paper 94–11.

Such job-security provisions dramatically reduce the flexibility of firms. But this inflexibility on the part of the firms is passed on to workers. Any policy that forces the firm to incur such large costs for laying off workers will surely lead the same firm to be very hesitant about hiring workers in the first place. Given this reduction in labour market flexibility, such policies are likely to increase the NAIRU.

Such mandated job security is relatively rare in Canada and the United States. This contributes to the general belief among economists that North American labour markets are much more flexible than those in Europe. Many economists see this as the most important explanation for why unemployment rates in Canada and the United States are significantly below the unemployment rates in Europe, and have been for the past fifteen years.

Future Outlook

Certain factors may work to reduce the NAIRU in the future. First, the proportion of youths and women newly entering the labour force has diminished as the baby boom generation ages and the female participation rate has stabilized. Second, to the extent that structural change has increased the NAIRU, there is no reason to expect the rate of structural change to increase further; hence there may be little or no future effect on the NAIRU. Conversely, structural unemployment could rise if the demand for unskilled workers declines fast enough as a result of ongoing technological change. This could lead to increased structural unemployment among the young, the unskilled, and those with only high school educations.

Reducing Unemployment

Other things being equal, all governments would like to reduce unemployment. The questions are "Can it be done?" and "If so, at what cost?"

CYCLICAL UNEMPLOYMENT

We do not need to say much more about cyclical unemployment because its control is the subject of stabilization policy, which we have studied in several earlier chapters. A major recession that occurs because of natural causes can be countered by monetary and fiscal policies to reduce cyclical unemployment.

There is room for debate, however, about *how much* the government can and should do in this respect. Advocates of stabilization policy call for expansionary fiscal and monetary policies to reduce such gaps, at least when they last for sustained periods of time. Advocates of a hands-off approach say that normal market adjustments can be relied on to remove such gaps and that government policy, no matter how well intentioned, will only make things worse. They call for setting simple rules for monetary and fiscal policy that would make discretionary stabilization policy impossible. This matter was discussed in detail at the end of Chapter 26.

Whatever may be argued in principle, policymakers have not yet agreed to abandon such stabilization measures in practice. However, the persistent slump that beset the Canadian economy in 1990–1992 was the first since the Second World War that was not countered by monetary and fiscal policy designed to provide stimulus for the recovery phase. On the fiscal side, government deficits that had persisted over booms and slumps had led to such an accumulation of government debt that the policy of long-term debt reduction took precedence over short-term stabilization policy. On the monetary side, the Bank of Canada had adopted long-term price stability as its overriding policy goal and abandoned any attempt at short-term stabilization.

FRICTIONAL UNEMPLOYMENT

The turnover that causes frictional unemployment is an inevitable part of the functioning of the economy. Some frictional unemployment is a natural part of the learning process for young workers. New entrants to the labour force (many of which are young) have to try several jobs to see which is most suitable, and that leads to a high turnover rate among the young and hence high frictional unemployment.

To the extent that frictional unemployment is caused by ignorance regarding where the appropriate jobs are, increasing the knowledge of workers about market opportunities may help. But such measures have a cost, and that cost has to be balanced against the benefits.

Unemployment insurance is one method of helping people cope with unemployment. It has reduced

INDUSTRIAL CHANGE: AN ECONOMIST'S CAUTIONARY TALE*

The audience hushed as the members of the government's investigating commission filed into the room. The chief forecasting wizard began his report: "I have identified beyond reasonable doubt the underlying trends now operating," he declared to the expectant audience. "The nation's leading industry, industry X, is in a state of decline. From its current position of employing close to 50 percent of our work force, it will, within the duration of one lifetime, employ only 3 percent."

"Over 40 percent of the nation's jobs destroyed within one lifetime!" proclaimed the newspapers headlines.

"Where can new jobs possibly come from at so rapid a pace?" asked a labour leader.

"The government must protect industry X; we just cannot let all these jobs go down the tubes," argued an employer.

"Perhaps we should identify and promote new 'sunrise industries,'" said a senior bureaucrat. Indeed, it had been widely believed that a new high-tech product, product Z, would become the wave of a future new transportation revolution. A call went out for subsidies and tax breaks to back its development.

*Copyright 1984 by R. G. Lipsey and D. D. Purvis. Reprinted and adapted by permission of the *Financial Post*.

"Is there any hope that the private sector might provide the new jobs?" someone asked.

"Possibly," said a junior economist, more out of desperation than hope, "the new product Y that is being produced by a few people in backyard sheds might grow to be a significant employer."

He was immediately pounced on by a pride of self-proclaimed realistic thinkers. "Product Y! It's noisy, it's smelly, and it's a plaything for the rich. Surely *it* will never provide significant employment."

All of the salient economic facts in the above tale are true. The country was Canada. The year was 1900. Industry X, the employer of close to 50 percent of the work force, was agriculture. Product Z, the sunrise industry, was the large, powered, lighter-than-air craft known as the zeppelin. Product Y, the scorned plaything of the rich, was the automobile.

The decline of some traditional industries is always a cause for concern. Some of them are suffering a temporary decline, and some are declining permanently. In either event, the hardships on those losing their jobs are severe. The tale just told has a serious message. Here are a few of the lessons that can be gained from comparing the Canadian economy in 1900 and in 1996.

First, the economy is constantly changing. Indeed, the motto of any market economy could be, "Nothing is permanent." New products appear continually; others disappear. At the early stage of a new product, total demand is low, costs of produc-

significantly the human costs of the bouts with unemployment that are inevitable in a changing society. Nothing, however, is without cost. Although unemployment insurance alleviates the suffering caused by some kinds of unemployment, it can itself contribute to unemployment in that it encourages search unemployment, as we have already observed.

Supporters of unemployment insurance emphasize its benefits. Critics emphasize its costs. As with any policy, a rational assessment of the value of un-

employment insurance requires a balancing of its undoubted benefits against its undoubted costs. Many Canadians believe that when this calculation is made, the benefits greatly exceed the costs, although many also recognize the scope for reform of certain aspects of the program.

Many provisions have been added over the years to the unemployment insurance scheme to focus it more on people in general need and to reduce its effect of raising the unemployment rate. For example, tion are high, and many small firms are each trying to get ahead of their competitors by finding the twist that appeals to consumers or finding the technique that slashes costs. Sometimes new products never get beyond that phase; they prove to be passing fads. Others, however, become items of mass consumption.

Successful firms in growing industries buy up, merge with, or otherwise eliminate their less successful rivals. Simultaneously, their costs fall, owing to scale economies. Competition drives prices down along with costs. Eventually, at the mature stage, a few giant firms often control the industry. They become large, conspicuous, and important parts of the nation's economy. Sooner or later, new products arise to erode the position of the established giants. Demand falls off, and unemployment occurs as the few firms run into financial difficulties.

A large, sick, declining industry may look like an insoluble economic problem and be a source of national concern. At any moment, however, firms can be found in all phases, from small firms in new industries to giant firms in declining industries. Large, declining industries are as much a natural part of a healthy, changing economy as large, stable industries and small, growing ones.

Second, the policy of shoring up the declining industries of the 1990s could be just as destructive to our living standards as the policy of protecting the agricultural sector from decline in 1900 would have been. (Policies that ease the human cost of the adjustment are not, however, in this category.)

Third, to tell where the new employment will come from requires the kind of crystal ball that our young economist would have needed in 1900 to stick by his wild guess of identifying the new plaything of the rich as the massive automobile industry 30 years later. Economists are continually being asked, "Where will the new employment come from?" The answer "We don't know" is *wrongly* taken to mean it won't come. In the past, the new jobs *have* come, and we see no new, identifiable forces that would prevent their coming in the future. For example, in the course of the current recovery, many people gaining employment are starting in *new* jobs—jobs with firms and in locations that did not exist or would not have been predicted even five years ago.

Fourth, "picking winners" and backing them with government policy is a likely way to waste public funds and inhibit the development of the real winners. People risking their own money and diversifying risks over many ventures are probably a better route to employment creation than governments that risk taxpayers' money, mesmerized by fads and fashion.

Fifth, the industrial policy that is needed is one that is generally supportive of innovation and risk taking rather than one that supports specific industries and specific products.

workers must be actively seeking employment in order to be eligible for UI. Also, beginning in April 1993, workers who voluntarily quit their jobs (without cause) are not eligible to collect UI. Finally, a system of *experience rating* has recently been proposed to distribute the costs more in proportion to the benefits. In the absence of experience rating all firms pay the same UI tax; this implicitly subsidizes those firms who create the most unemployment and taxes most heavily those firms who create the least unemployment. Under experience rating, firms with histories of sizable layoffs pay more than those with better layoff records.

STRUCTURAL UNEMPLOYMENT

The reallocation of labour among occupations, industries, skill categories, and regions that gives rise to structural unemployment is an inevitable part of a market economy. There are two basic approaches to reducing structural unemployment: Try to arrest the changes that the economy experiences or accept the changes and try to speed up the adjustments. Throughout history, labour and management have advocated both approaches and governments have tried them both.

Resisting Change

Since the beginning of the Industrial Revolution, workers have often resisted the introduction of new techniques to replace the older techniques at which they were skilled. This is understandable. New techniques often destroy the value of the knowledge and experience of workers skilled in the displaced techniques. Older workers may not even get a chance to start over with the new technique. Employers may prefer to hire younger persons who will learn the new skills faster than older workers who are set in their ways of thinking. From society's point of view, new techniques are beneficial because they are a major source of economic growth. From the point of view of the workers they displace, new techniques can be an unmitigated disaster.

Over the long term, policies that subsidize employment in declining industries run into increasing difficulties. Agreements to hire unneeded workers raise costs and can hasten the decline of an industry threatened by competitive products. An industry that is declining because of economic change becomes an increasingly large burden on the public purse as economic forces become less and less favourable to its success. Sooner or later, public support is withdrawn, followed by a precipitous decline.

In assessing these remedies for structural unemployment, it is important to realize that although they are not viable in the long run for the entire economy, they may be the best alternatives for the affected workers during their lifetimes.

There is often a genuine conflict between the private interest of workers threatened by structural unemployment, whose interests lie in preserving existing jobs, and the social interest served by economic growth, which raises living standards.

Aiding Adjustments to Change

Another general approach to dealing with structural change is to accept the decline of specific industries

and the loss of specific jobs that go with it and to try to reduce the cost of adjustment for the workers affected. A number of policies have been introduced in Canada to ease the adjustment to changing economic conditions.

One such policy is publicly subsidized education and retraining schemes. The public involvement is motivated largely by imperfections in capital markets that make it difficult for workers to borrow funds for education, training or retraining. A major component of labour-market policies is a system of loans and subsidies for higher education. Between 1960 and 1990, university enrollment rose from 107,000 to 514,000, and community college enrollment increased from 50,000 to 315,000. Over the same period, the number of persons undertaking technical training increased from fewer than 5,000 to over 350,000, partly under the stimulus of the Adult Occupational Training Act of 1967.

Another such policy is motivated by the lack of good information about current and future job prospects. Policies to improve the flow of information include the creation of job banks and information centres and initial steps toward a nationwide computerized information system called Jobscan. Job-creation programs, especially those aimed at getting young people their first job, are also major labour-market policies aimed at reducing structural unemployment.

As global economic competition becomes more and more severe and as new knowledge-driven methods of production spread, the ability to adjust to economic change will become increasingly important. Countries that succeed in the global marketplace, while also managing to maintain humane social welfare systems, will be those that best learn how to co-operate with change. This will mean avoiding economic policies that inhibit change while adopting social policies that reduce the human cost of adjusting to change. This is an enormous challenge for future Canadian economic and social policies.

CONCLUSION

Over the years, unemployment has been regarded in many different ways. Harsh critics see it as proof that the market system is badly flawed. Reformers regard it as a necessary evil of the market system and a suitable object for government policy to reduce its incidence and its harmful effects. Others see it as overblown in importance and believe that it does not reflect any real inability of workers to obtain jobs if they really want to work.

Most government policy has followed a middle route. Fiscal and monetary policies have sought to reduce at least the most persistent of recessionary gaps, and a host of labour-market policies have sought to reduce the incidence of frictional and structural unemployment. Such social policies as unemployment insurance have sought to reduce the sting of unemployment for the many who were thought to suffer from it for reasons beyond their control.

SUMMARY

A. EMPLOYMENT AND UNEMPLOYMENT IN CANADA

- Canadian employment and the Canadian labour force have increased along a strong upward trend throughout all of this century. The unemployment rate has fluctuated significantly; over the past thirty years it has also shown an upward trend.
- Looking only at the level of employment or unemployment in the economy can hide a tremendous amount of activity in the labour market as individuals flow from unemployment to employment or from employment to unemployment. In recent years in Canada, approximately 200,000 people *per month* flow between employment and unemployment. This level of gross flows reflects the turnover which is a normal part of any labour market.
- Looking at causes, it is useful to distinguish among several kinds of unemployment: cyclical unemployment, which is caused by too low a level of aggregate demand; frictional unemployment, which is caused by the length of time it takes to find a first job and to move from job to job as a result of normal labour turnover; and structural unemployment, which is caused by the need to reallocate resources among occupations, regions, and industries as the structure of demands and supplies change.
- Together, frictional unemployment and structural unemployment make up the NAIRU, which is then expressed as a percentage of the total labour force. The actual unemployment rate is equal to the NAIRU when national income is equal to potential income.

B. CYCLICAL UNEMPLOYMENT

- There is a long-standing debate among economists regarding the causes of cyclical unemployment.

- New Classical theories look to explanations that allow the labour market to be cleared continuously. Such theories can explain cyclical variations in employment but do not predict a large group of workers who would like to work at the going wage rates but for whom jobs are not available.
- New Keynesian theories have focused on the long-term nature of employer-worker relationships in which wages tend to respond only a little, and employment tends to respond a lot, to changes in the demand and supply of labour. More recent New Keynesian theories have examined the possibility that it may be efficient for employers to pay wages that are above the level that would clear the labour market (efficiency wages).

C. THE NAIRU

- The NAIRU will always be positive because it takes time for labour to move between jobs both in normal turnover (frictional unemployment) and in response to changes in the structure of the demand for labour (structural unemployment).
- Because different workers have different sets of skills and because different firms require workers with different sets of skills, some unemployment—resulting from workers searching for appropriate job matches with employers—is socially desirable.
- Anything that increases the rate of turnover in the labour market, or the pace of structural change in the economy, will likely increase the NAIRU.
- Government policies that reduce labour-market flexibility are likely to increase the NAIRU. Unemployment insurance, though reducing the human suffering associated with unemployment, also increases the NAIRU by encouraging workers to continue searching for an appropriate job. Policies that mandate job security, which are very common in western Europe, increase the costs

to firms of laying off workers. This makes them reluctant to hire workers in the first place and thus increases the NAIRU.

D. REDUCING UNEMPLOYMENT

- Cyclical unemployment can be reduced by raising aggregate demand. Frictional and structural unemployment can be reduced by making it easier to move between jobs, by slowing down the rate of change in the economy, and by raising the cost of staying unemployed (e.g., by reducing unemployment insurance benefits).

- However, in a growing, changing economy populated by people who wish to change jobs for many reasons, it is neither possible nor desirable to reduce unemployment to zero.

KEY CONCEPTS

Gross flows in the labour market
Cyclical unemployment
Frictional unemployment
Structural unemployment

Long-term employment relationships
Efficiency wages
Hysteresis
The components of the NAIRU

Determinants of the size of the NAIRU
Policies to reduce the NAIRU
Labour-market flexibility

DISCUSSION QUESTIONS

1. Interpret the following statements from newspapers in terms of types of unemployment.

   a. "Recession hits local factory; 2,000 laid off."
   b. "When they raised the minimum wage, I just could not afford to keep all of these retired policemen on my payroll as security guards," says the owner of a local shopping center.
   c. "Of course, I could take a job as a dishwasher, but I'm trying to find something that makes use of my high school training," says a local teenager in our survey of the unemployed.
   d. "Retraining is the best reaction to the increased use of robots."
   e. "Uneven upturn: Signs of recovery in Alberta, but Ontario is still in recession."

2. Discuss the following views. Is it possible that both views are right? Explain.

   a. "Canadian workers should resist automation, which is destroying their jobs," says a labour leader.
   b. "Given the fierce foreign competition faced by Canadian firms, it's a case of automate or die," says an industrialist.

3. "No one needs to be out of work if he or she really wants a job; just look at the Help Wanted signs in many fast-food businesses and retail shops." Does the existence of the unfilled vacancies suggested in the quotation imply that there need be no cyclical unemployment as long as workers are not excessively fussy about the kinds of jobs they will take?

4. Take another look at Table 31-1. What reasons can you suggest to explain why unemployment rates stay persistently above average for youths and below average for males over 25? Can you offer an explanation for why the unemployment rate in Quebec has been above the Canadian average for the past 20 years?

5. It is often argued that the true unemployment figure for Canada is much higher than the officially reported figure. What are possible sources of "hidden unemployment"? On the other side, are there reasons for expecting some exaggeration of the number of people who are reported as unemployed? Would the relative strength of these opposing forces change over the course of the business cycle? What would you expect if a short recession turned into a long and deep depression?

6. At a time when the Canadian unemployment rate stood at close to 12 percent, the press reported: "Skilled labour shortages plague many firms—newspaper ads often draw few qualified workers; wages and overtime are up." What type of unemployment does this suggest is important?

7. What differences in approach toward the problem of unemployment are suggested by the following facts?

a. In the 1960s and 1970s, Britain spent billions of dollars on subsidizing firms that would otherwise have gone out of business in order to protect the jobs of the employees.

b. Sweden has been a pioneer in spending large sums to retrain and to relocate displaced workers.

8. Comment on the following statements from a recent federal government report.

a. "Service workers are less likely than manufacturing workers to become unemployed during an economic downturn."

b. "Workers with more classroom education often possess knowledge that is more general and can be applied to a variety of jobs."

c. "Low-skilled workers are more likely to work only part time and are more frequently unemployed."

d. "Some economists have proposed that training be linked directly to the UI program."

e. "Another option . . . currently being tested . . . offers UI recipients . . . their benefit entitlement on a lump-sum payment as seed capital once they have started their own business."

9. Is it possible to say which type of unemployment is involved in each case cited in question 8? Can you suggest reasons that might account for statements made about unemployment? What do you think about those statements that suggest policy changes?

10. In the 1993 election campaign, the Liberals promised to create many new jobs by having the federal, provincial, and municipal governments combine to spend $6 billion on infrastructure. Given that the economy was in the middle of a recovery in 1993–1995, do you think it is more likely that these new government expenditures would "create" jobs in the economy, or more likely that existing jobs would be redistributed between various sectors? Explain your position.

CHAPTER 32

GOVERNMENT DEBT AND DEFICITS

No single measure associated with the government has been the focus of more attention and controversy—in the media, on the political campaign trails, and in coffee shops across the country—as the size of the government budget deficit. Strongly worded views about the potential effects of government budget deficits are easy to come by, whether they come from political parties, special interest groups, think tanks, or academics. One extreme view is that the deficit is a time bomb ticking away, threatening the prosperity of all Canadians. The opposite extreme view is that the only real danger posed by budget deficits is from drastic policy changes introduced by those obsessed with deficit reduction.

Canada's current large stock of government debt has its origins in the onset of large budget deficits which began in the early 1970s. By the mid 1980s, the Conservative government headed by Brian Mulroney brought the issues of the federal deficit and debt to the fore of public attention. By the early 1990s, focus had shifted toward the large budget deficits of the provincial governments, especially those of Ontario and Quebec. Only a few years later, however, when most provinces had undertaken serious deficit-reduction policies, attention once again focused on the federal government. The Liberals, elected in 1993 and headed by Jean Chrétien, were committed to making substantial cuts in government spending as a means of bringing the federal government's budget deficit down to 3 percent of GDP by the 1996–1997 fiscal year. This policy was controversial. Some argued that the government was not doing enough to reduce the deficit; others argued that the government's plans to reduce expenditures (and services) were both unnecessary and undesirable.

In this chapter, we examine the issues surrounding government budget deficits and the accumulation of government debt. In the first section, we introduce the simple arithmetic of deficits and debt and then describe the recent history of government deficits and debt in Canada. The next section discusses three important analytical issues about debt and deficits. With these issues in mind, we then examine the potential effects of government deficits on the economy. The final section examines some proposed policies to deal with government deficits.

Deficits and debt: facts and definitions

To understand the significance of budget deficits, it is first necessary to understand the government's budget constraint. This is the simple relationship between the government's expenditures, its tax revenues, and its borrowing.

THE GOVERNMENT'S BUDGET CONSTRAINT

Just like any individual, government expenditures must either be financed by income or by borrowing. The difference between individuals and governments, however, is that governments typically do not earn income by selling products or labour services; instead, they earn income by levying taxes. Thus all government expenditure must be financed either by tax revenues or by borrowing. This is illustrated by the following simple equation, which is called the government's *budget constraint*:

$$\begin{matrix} \text{Government} \\ \text{Expenditure} \end{matrix} = \begin{matrix} \text{Tax} \\ \text{Revenue} \end{matrix} + \text{Borrowing}$$

There are three broad components to government expenditures. The first is the government's purchases of goods and services, G. The second is transfers to individuals or firms, such as unemployment insurance or industrial subsidies, denoted TR. The third component is interest payments on the outstanding stock of debt. This is referred to as **debt-service payments**, denoted $i \times D$, where i is the interest rate and D is the stock of government debt. If we let T represent the government's tax revenues, we can rewrite the government's budget constraint as

$$G + TR + i \times D = T + \text{Borrowing}$$

or, subtracting T from both sides,

$$(G + TR + i \times D) - T = \text{Borrowing}$$

All this equation says is that any excess of total government spending over tax revenues must be financed by government borrowing.

The government's annual **budget deficit** is the excess of total government expenditure over total tax revenues in a given year.[1] From the budget constraint above, this annual deficit is exactly the same as the

---

[1]The government has another (small) source of revenue that we have ignored here—the income earned from government-owned enterprises. We ignore this only to simplify the presentation of the essential arguments.

amount borrowed by the government during the year. Since the government borrows by selling bonds to lenders, borrowing by the government increases the government's outstanding stock of debt. Thus since D is the outstanding stock of government debt, ΔD is the *change* in the stock of debt during the course of the year. The budget deficit can therefore be written as

$$\text{Budget Deficit} = \Delta D = (G + TR + i \times D) - T$$

The government's annual budget deficit is the excess of total expenditure over total tax revenues in a given year. It is also equal to the change in the stock of government debt during the year.

Notice two points about budget deficits. First, a change in the size of the deficit requires a change in the level of expenditures *relative* to the level of tax revenues. For a given level of tax revenues, a smaller deficit can only come about through a reduction in government expenditures; conversely, for a given level of expenditures, a smaller deficit requires an increase in tax revenues. Second, since the deficit is equal to the amount of new government borrowing, the stock of government debt will rise whenever the budget deficit is positive. Even a drastic reduction in the size of the annual budget deficit is therefore not sufficient to reduce the outstanding stock of government debt; the stock of debt will only fall if the budget deficit becomes *negative*. In this case, there is said to be a **budget surplus.**

A deficit increases the stock of debt; a surplus reduces it.

The Primary Budget Deficit

The total level of government expenditure comprises purchases of goods and services (G), transfer payments (TR), and debt-service payments $(i \times D)$. Since at any point in time the outstanding stock of government debt—determined by *past* government borrowing—cannot be influenced by current government policy, the debt-service component of total expenditures is beyond the control of the government. In contrast, the other components of the government's budget are said to be *discretionary* be-

cause the government can choose to change the levels of G, TR or T. To capture the part of the total deficit which is attributable to discretionary expenditures and revenues, we define the government's **primary budget deficit** as the difference between the total budget deficit and the debt-service payments:

$$\begin{array}{ccc}
\text{Primary} & \text{Total} & \text{Debt-Service} \\
\text{Budget Deficit} & = \text{Budget Deficit} & - \text{Payments}
\end{array}$$
$$= (G + TR + i \times D - T) - i \times D$$
$$= (G + TR) - T$$

Thus we see that the primary budget deficit is equal to the amount by which government purchases plus transfer payments exceeds total tax revenues.

The government's primary budget deficit shows the extent to which tax revenues are able to finance the *discretionary* part of total expenditure. Another name for discretionary expenditure, the portion denoted $(G + TR)$, is the government's *program spending*. It is possible that the government has an overall budget deficit but a *primary* budget surplus, indicating that tax revenues more than cover program spending but are insufficient to fully cover debt-service payments as well. For example, in the 1996–1997 fiscal year, the federal government had an overall budget deficit of approximately $25 billion while debt-service payments were approximately $42 billion. There was thus a primary budget *surplus* in that year of about $17 billion—that is, total tax revenues exceeded program expenditures by $17 billion.

The primary budget deficit is the difference between the overall budget deficit and the level of debt-service payments. In recent years, the federal government has run an overall budget deficit but a primary budget surplus, indicating that tax revenues were more than sufficient to cover program expenditures.

For a diagrammatic illustration of the government's budget constraint, and of the distinction between overall budget deficits and primary budget deficits, see Figure 32-1. This distinction between overall and primary budget deficits becomes very important when we examine changes in the debt-to-GDP ratio later in the chapter.

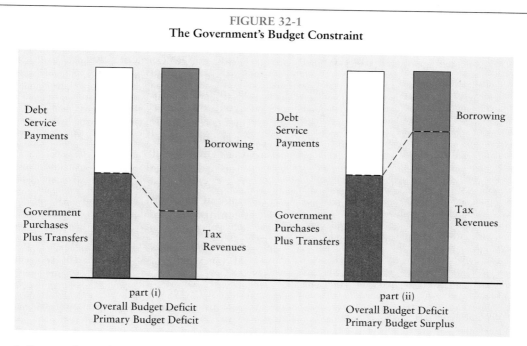

FIGURE 32-1
The Government's Budget Constraint

The sum of all expenditures by government must be financed either by tax collection or by borrowing. The deficit is the difference between total expenditures and total tax collection; it is also equal to the total level of borrowing. In both parts, the government's budget constraint is illustrated by the fact that the two bars are the same height, showing that total expenditures must be equal to tax revenues plus borrowing. In both parts there is an overall budget deficit because tax revenues are not sufficient to finance total expenditures (and so there is positive borrowing). In part (i), taxes are not even enough to cover government purchases and transfers, and so there is a primary budget deficit. In part (ii), taxes are more than enough to cover government purchases and transfers, and so there is a primary budget surplus (even though there is an overall budget deficit).

GOVERNMENT DEFICITS AND DEBT IN CANADA

Federal Government Deficits and Debt

In a growing economy, many macroeconomic variables such as the levels of government expenditure and tax revenue tend also to grow. As a result, rather than looking at the absolute size of the government deficit or debt, we should examine government debt and deficits in relation to the overall size of the economy. Some budget deficits that would be unmanageable in a small economy like New Zealand might be quite acceptable for a larger economy like Canada, and trivial for a huge economy like the United States. Similarly, a government budget deficit that seemed crushing in Canada in 1897 might appear trivial in 1997 because the size of the

Canadian economy is many times larger now than it was then.

The relatively recent emergence of large federal budget deficits is shown in Figure 32-2. The top panel shows total federal spending and total federal tax revenues as percentages of GDP. The bottom panel shows the total federal deficit as a percentage of GDP. Persistent deficits began in the mid 1970s. From 1975 to 1980, federal expenditures were a relatively constant fraction of GDP, while federal tax revenues fell sharply. This is the basis for the view that discretionary tax cuts introduced in the 1970s were initially responsible for rapid growth in the deficit. A contrary view holds that it was the failure to restrain government spending in the face of the tax cuts that was responsible for the escalation of the deficit.

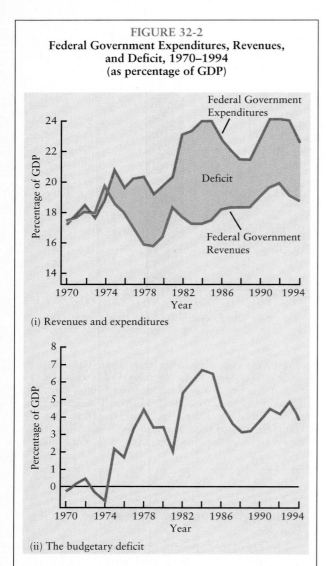

FIGURE 32-2
Federal Government Expenditures, Revenues, and Deficit, 1970–1994
(as percentage of GDP)

(i) Revenues and expenditures

(ii) The budgetary deficit

The federal budget has been in deficit every year since 1975. It is currently equal to roughly 3 percent of GDP. The graphs in part (i) show expenditures and revenues of the federal government, both as a percentage of GDP. The difference is the federal deficit, shown in part (ii).

(*Source: Economic Reference Tables*, Department of Finance, August 1995).

The substantial increase in the budget deficit in the early 1980s reflects the combined effects of the severe recession in 1982, some mild discretionary fiscal expansion, and increased interest payments on the government's debt. This last element was due in part to the higher real interest rates in the early

1980s and the accumulation of the deficits in the late 1970s which added to the stock of government debt. After reaching a peak of about 7 percent of GDP in 1984, the government's budget deficit fell steadily as a share of GDP until 1988. The effects of a strong economic recovery in the late 1980s, combined with active measures on the part of the federal government, resulted in a reduction in the deficit. By 1989, at the beginning of a significant economic downturn, the deficit was just over 3 percent of GDP. The recession of 1991 again pushed up the deficit, but by then the large stock of federal government debt (which we will see shortly) made the federal government reluctant to let the deficit rise considerably. As a result, by 1993, two years into a slow economic recovery, the federal budget deficit had increased only to about 5 percent of GDP. As the recovery progressed further, and the federal government continued its policy of reducing the deficit, the deficit fell until reaching roughly 3 percent of GDP in the 1996–1997 fiscal year.

Figure 32-3 shows the path of Canadian federal government net debt since 1926.[2] At the beginning of the Second World War, the stock of federal debt was equal to about 40 percent of GDP. The enormous increase in the debt-to-GDP ratio over the next five years reflects wartime borrowing used to finance military expenditures. From 1945 to 1975, however, there was a continual decline in the debt-to-GDP ratio. Not only was the economy growing very quickly over this period, but the federal government in the post-war years typically ran significant budget surpluses. By 1975 the federal debt was only 14 percent of GDP. The large and persistent budget deficits beginning in the mid 1970s, however, combined with a general slowdown in the rate of economic growth to produce a significant upward trend in the debt-to-GDP ratio. With only a brief slowdown in the rate of growth of the debt-to-GDP ratio in the late 1980s, reflecting primarily the booming economy at that time, the ratio climbed steadily for the next 20 years.

[2]Note that when computing its net debt the government does not include its non-financial assets such as buildings, roads, or national parks; nor does it include its "unfunded liabilities," such as its future commitments through the public pension system. The government's net debt is therefore equal to the (net) amount of its bonds currently held by its creditors.

FIGURE 32-3

FIGURE 32-3
Federal Government Net Debt as Percentage of GDP, 1926–1995

After falling for 30 years after the Second World War, the stock of federal government debt has increased markedly as a share of GDP. The stock of federal debt, after rising to exceed 100 percent of GDP during the Second World War, fell steadily to 14 percent by 1975. Since then, the continual annual budget deficits (see Figure 32-2) have increased the debt-to-GDP ratio considerably.

(Source: Statistics Canada, *CANSIM* database*).*

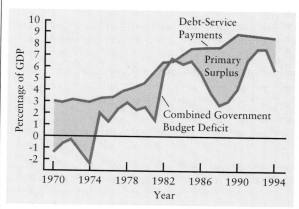

FIGURE 32-4
Budget Deficit and Debt-Service Payments for Combined Federal and Provincial Governments, 1970–1994

Debt-service payments for the combined federal and provincial governments have increased from 3 percent of GDP in 1970 to approximately 9 percent of GDP today. The difference between the overall budget deficit and the debt-service payments is the primary budget deficit. In almost every year, the combined government ran a primary budget surplus.

(Source: Economic Reference Tables, Department of Finance, August 1995*).*

Provincial Government Deficits and Debt

Canada is relatively special among developed countries in the sense that its provincial governments are responsible for a significant fraction of total government borrowing. In many countries, sizable regional governments either do not exist, as in New Zealand, or are often required to run balanced budgets, as is the case for about two thirds of the fifty U.S. states. In contrast, the size of Canadian provincial governments—measured by their spending and taxing powers relative to that of the federal government—means that an examination of government debt in Canada would not be complete without paying attention to the provincial governments' debt.

For the provincial governments combined, the stock of provincial-government net debt was more-or-less constant at about 4 percent of GDP from 1970 to 1982. This implies that the provincial governments were running budget deficits during this period, but these deficits were small enough so that the stock of provincial debt grew at the same rate as

the overall economy. In the early 1980s, however, things changed dramatically. The large run-up of provincial deficits from 1982 through 1993 led to a significant increase in the provincial debt-to-GDP ratio, from about 4 percent in the early 1980s to approximately 20 percent in 1993. Beginning approximately in 1993, however, many provinces undertook significant deficit-reduction policies. By 1996, several provinces had either balanced budgets or small surpluses. Ontario and Quebec were slower off the mark than the other provinces but have also moved in the same direction. Thus by 1996 the rise of the combined provincial debt-to-GDP ratio had slowed considerably.

Debt-Service Payments

To see how the rising stock of government debt affects the annual government expenditures, Figure 32-4 shows the debt-service payments for the federal and provincial governments combined. In 1970, when combined government debt was about 24 percent of GDP, the annual debt-service requirements were just over 3 percent of GDP. By 1995 the debt-service requirements had increased to about 9 percent of GDP. One way to put this in perspective is to examine the debt-service payments relative to the size of the combined government budget. In 1995, combined federal and provincial government debt-service payments amounted to about 22 percent of total government revenues. Thus out of every dollar raised in revenues by the combined federal and provincial governments in 1995, approximately 22 cents went to service the stock of government debt.[3]

In addition to showing debt-service payments, Figure 32-4 also shows the overall budget deficit for the combined federal and provincial governments. As we noted earlier, the difference between the budget deficit and the debt-service payments shows the *primary* budget deficit or surplus. Years in which the overall budget deficit is less than the debt-service payments are periods in which total tax revenues are more than adequate to cover total program spending—that is, there is a primary budget *surplus*. As is clear from the figure, the combined governments have had primary budget surpluses in almost every year since 1970. Note the cyclical pattern in the primary surplus, falling sharply in the recessions of the early 1980s and early 1990s (as tax revenues fall in the recessions) and rising sharply in the recoveries of the mid 1980s and the mid 1990s (as tax revenues rise in recoveries).

An International Perspective

To give some indication of how Canada's government debt compares with that of other developed nations, Figure 32-5 shows the consolidated government debt in each of the G7 countries in 1995, expressed as a share of GDP. These figures show the combined net debt positions of all levels of government. As is clear from the figure, Canada's government debt is second in size only to that of Italy, which in 1995 had a debt-to-GDP ratio just under 110 percent. Canada's debt-to-GDP ratio for the

consolidated government sector was 66 percent in 1995. The next highest debt-to-GDP ratio is in the United States, which at 51 percent is fully 15 percentage points below Canada's.

DEFICITS AND DEBT: SOME ANALYTICAL ISSUES

In the next section we discuss some potential effects of budget deficits on the aggregate economy. Before doing this, however, some basic analytical issues must be examined: deficits and the stance of fiscal policy; changes in the debt-to-GDP ratio; and the relationship between government deficits and national saving.

THE STANCE OF FISCAL POLICY

In Chapter 24 we examined some basic issues surrounding **fiscal policy,** which is the use of government spending and tax polices to alter national income. We argued there that changes in expenditure and taxation normally lead to changes in the government's budget deficit or surplus. It is thus tempting to view changes in the government's budget deficit as the result of changes in fiscal policy. For example, we could interpret an increase in the deficit as indicating an expansionary fiscal policy, since the rise in the deficit is associated with either an increase in government expenditures or a reduction in tax revenue (or both).

The problem with this interpretation is that it fails to recognize that only some changes in the deficit are due to discretionary changes in the government's expenditure or taxation policies. Other changes have nothing to do with explicit changes in policy, but instead are the result of changes in the level of economic activity that are outside the influence of government policy. If our goal is to judge the stance of fiscal policy, however, it is only the changes in the deficit *caused by changes in policy* that are relevant.

The Budget Deficit Function

To see why the budget deficit can rise or fall in the absence of changes in policy, recall the equation defining the government's budget deficit. Since gov-

---

[3]Since the combined governments had a budget deficit in 1995, total government tax revenues were less than total government expenditures. Thus debt-service payments represented a smaller fraction of total expenditure than of total revenue. In 1995, approximately 19 cents of every dollar *spent* by the federal or and provincial governments was spent to service the government debt.

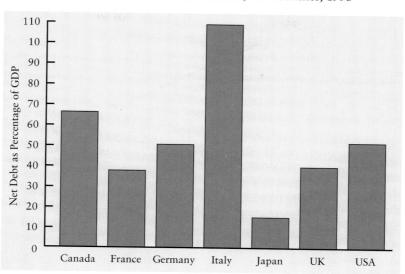

FIGURE 32-5
Consolidated Government Net Debt, G7 Countries, 1995

Canada's government debt is high by the standards of the richest countries. The data shown here are for all levels of government combined.
(Source: OECD Economic Outlook, December 1995.)

ernment transfers are payments by the government to the private sector, and taxes are payments made by the private sector to the government, it is convenient to rewrite the government's budget deficit by combining taxes and transfers to get

$$\text{Budget Deficit} = (G + i \times D) - (T - TR)$$

where the second term is government taxes net of transfers. The key point now is that the level of taxes and transfers typically depend on the level of national income, even with unchanged policy. For example, as income rises the level of revenue raised through income taxation also rises. Furthermore, as national income rises there are typically fewer transfers (such as welfare or unemployment insurance) made to the private sector. Thus $(T - TR)$ increases when national income increases. In contrast, the level of government purchases and debt-service payments can be viewed as more-or-less independent of the level of national income, at least over short periods of time. This implies that with no changes in expenditure or taxation policies, the budget deficit will tend to increase in recessions and fall in booms. That

is, as national income rises, the government's budget deficit falls.

For a given spending and taxing policy, the budget deficit rises when national income falls.

Figure 32-6 plots this basic relationship which is called the **budget deficit function.** Part (i) of the figure plots the budget deficit against the level of national income, *Y*. When the government determines its expenditure and taxation polices, it determines the *position* of the budget deficit function; a more expansionary fiscal policy shifts the budget deficit function up whereas a more contractionary fiscal policy shifts the budget deficit function down. In contrast, a change in the level of national income in the absence of any policy change will represent a *movement along* the budget deficit function. Thus for a given set of policies, the budget deficit will decrease when *Y* rises and increase when *Y* falls. Similarly, for a given level of national income, an expansionary fiscal policy shifts the function up and increases the budget deficit; a contractionary fiscal policy shifts the function down and reduces the budget deficit.

FIGURE 32-6
The Budget Deficit Function and Cyclical Adjustment

(i) The budget deficit function

(ii) Change in the measured deficit

(iii) Change in the cyclically adjusted deficit

The budget deficit can change either because of a change in fiscal policy or because of a change in national income. Parts (i) and (ii) illustrate the same budget deficit function, showing that the budget deficit declines (budget surplus rises) as national income rises. The budget deficit function is labelled B.

Part (ii) defines the cyclically adjusted deficit (CAD) as the budget balance that would exist if national income were equal to potential income Y^*. In the example, the CAD is a deficit. At a sufficiently high income Y_0, the actual budget would be in surplus by an amount S_0. At incomes lower than Y^*, such as Y_1, the actual budget would be in deficit by D', more than the amount of the CAD. Throughout the curve in part (ii), fiscal policy is unchanged. The deficit (and surplus) changes only because national income changes.

Part (iii) shows how the actual deficit (or surplus) might move in a different direction from the CAD. Suppose that the economy starts at Y_0, with fiscal policy given by B_0. If fiscal policy is made more restrictive, through some combination of higher taxes and lower government purchases, the budget balance will now behave according to B_1. At the same time, if income should fall to Y_1, the budget surplus of S will turn into a deficit of D'. By looking at the actual budget balance, one would see the budget move from surplus to deficit, suggesting, incorrectly, that the fiscal policy had become more stimulative of the economy. Focusing on the CAD, however, the level of budget balance at Y^* makes it clear that B_1 is more restrictive than B_0—the CAD is smaller at Y^* (and at every level of income) with the fiscal policy given by B_1—than that given by B_0.

Fiscal policy determines the position of the budget deficit function.

The Cyclically Adjusted Deficit

Given the problem of using the budget deficit to gauge the stance of fiscal policy, economists define the **cyclically adjusted deficit (CAD)** as the budget deficit that would exist with the current set of policies if national income were equal to potential income, Y^*. This is also called the *structural budget deficit* or the *full-employment budget deficit*. This is shown in parts (ii) and (iii) of Figure 32-6. Fixing the level of income at which the deficit is computed removes the possibility that changes in the deficit reflect changes in the level of national income. Thus all *changes in the cyclically adjusted deficit reflect changes in the stance of fiscal policy,* because they come only from shifts in the budget deficit function.

Figure 32-7 shows one estimate of the cyclically adjusted deficit in Canada, and plots it together with the actual budget deficit. Both are expressed as percentages of GDP and represent the combined budget deficits of all levels of government. Unlike the actual budget deficit, which can be precisely measured, the cyclically adjusted deficit can only be estimated. The reason is that its value depends on the value of potential income, Y^*, which itself is not directly observable and hence must be estimated. Note from Figure 32-7 that the actual deficit is larger than the cyclically adjusted deficit during time of recessionary gaps such as 1981–1985 and 1990–1995. This simply reflects that during these periods actual income is less than potential income and thus actual tax revenues are *less than they would be if output were equal to potential.* Conversely, the actual budget deficit is less than the cyclically adjusted deficit during periods of inflationary gaps, such as 1978–1981 and 1985–1990. This reflects that during these peri-

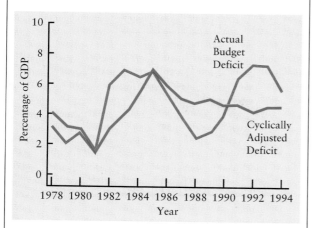

FIGURE 32-7
**The Actual and Cyclically Adjusted Deficit
in Canada, 1978–1994**

The difference between the actual budget deficit and
the cyclically adjusted budget deficit reveals the level
of output compared to potential. The changes in the
cyclically adjusted deficit show changes in the stance
of fiscal policy. The actual budget deficit is above the
cyclically adjusted budget deficit when output is below
potential; the actual deficit is less than the cyclically
adjusted deficit when output is above potential. An increase in the cyclically adjusted deficit reveals a fiscal
expansion; a decrease reveals a fiscal contraction.

(Source: Economic Reference Tables, Department of
Finance, August 1995; and *OECD Economic Outlook,*
December 1995.)

ods actual income is greater than potential and thus
tax revenues are *greater than they would be if output
were equal to potential.* In those years where the actual deficit is equal to the cyclically adjusted deficit,
such as 1981, 1985, and 1990, national income is
equal to potential.

The stance of fiscal policy is shown by the
changes in the cyclically adjusted deficit. For example,
the dramatic rise in the cyclically adjusted deficit from
1981 to 1985 reveals a considerable fiscal expansion;
the decline from 1985 through 1988 reveals a fiscal
contraction. From 1989 to 1994, the path of the cyclically adjusted deficit suggests that the stance of fiscal
policy has not changed appreciably, despite the 5 percentage point increase in the actual budget deficit.

The stance of fiscal policy—that is, whether fiscal
policy is expansionary or contractionary—is determined by changes in the cyclically adjusted deficit.

THE DEBT-TO-GDP RATIO

We argued above that in order to gauge the importance of government deficits and debt they should be
considered relative to the size of the economy. Public
debate, however, is often couched in terms of the absolute size of the budget deficit. Here we examine the
link between the overall budget deficit, the primary
budget deficit, and changes in the debt-to-GDP ratio.

Changes in the Debt-to-GDP Ratio

With a little work, it is possible to write a simple expression that relates the government's primary budget
deficit to the change in the debt-to-GDP ratio. The algebra required to derive this expression, however, is a
little complicated. Those students who want to see
the derivation in full can refer to Extension 32-1. For
now, however, we simply state the following simple
equation:

$$\Delta d = x + (r - g) \times d$$

where d is the debt-to-GDP ratio, x is the government's *primary* budget deficit as a percentage of
GDP, r is the real interest rate, g is the growth rate of
real GDP, and Δd is the *change* in the debt-to-GDP
ratio.

This simple equation shows that there are two
distinct forces which tend to increase the debt-to-
GDP ratio. We simply mention them now, and then
discuss them in greater detail. First, if the real interest rate exceeds the growth rate of real GDP (if r exceeds g), then the debt-to-GDP ratio will rise (that is,
Δd will be positive). Second, if the government has a
primary budget deficit (if x is positive) then the debt-
to-GDP ratio will rise.

There are two important points that are not generally recognized in many discussions of government
debt and deficits, and discussing these points will
help to develop the intuition surrounding this simple
equation.

The Importance of Real Interest Rates. The
first point is that it is the real interest rate, and not
the nominal interest rate, that is important for determining the changes in the debt-to-GDP ratio. Many
commentators argue that high nominal interest rates
are largely responsible for increasing the government's debt-service requirements and thus pushing
up the deficit and debt. But this view is only partly

┌─────────────────────────────────┐
│   E X T E N S I O N   3 2 - 1   │
└─────────────────────────────────┘

CHANGES IN THE DEBT-TO-GDP RATIO

This box derives the simple equation in the text describing the change in the debt-to-GDP ratio. Let d be the debt-to-GDP ratio and let Δd be the amount by which d changes annually. Since d is a ratio, its change over time depends on the change in the numerator relative to the change in the denominator. That is, the debt-to-GDP ratio will increase if the stock of debt grows more quickly than GDP; it will decrease if the stock of debt grows less quickly than GDP. Representing the *percentage change* in d as $\Delta d/d$, we have*

$$\frac{\Delta d}{d} = \frac{\Delta D}{D} - \frac{\Delta \text{GDP}}{\text{GDP}}$$

Now think about each of these terms separately. As you will recall from the first section of this chapter, the change in the stock of debt, ΔD, is equal to the amount of new government borrowing—that is, it is equal to the budget deficit. From the government's budget constraint, this is equal to $(G + TR + i \times D - T)$. The second term in the equation above is the growth rate of GDP. Note that the growth rate of GDP depends on both the rate of growth of real output and the rate of inflation. If we let g be the rate of

growth of *real* GDP and Π be the rate of inflation, then $g + \Pi$ is the growth rate of (nominal) GDP. We therefore rewrite the expression above to get

$$\frac{\Delta d}{d} = \frac{G + TR - T + i \times D}{D} - (g + \Pi)$$

Now we multiply both sides by d to get an expression for the absolute change in the debt-to-GDP ratio:

$$\Delta d = \frac{G + TR - T + i \times D}{D} \times d - (g + \Pi) \times d$$

But noting that d is equal to D/GDP, it follows that d/D is 1/GDP. Our equation can thus be simplified to be

$$\Delta d = \frac{G + TR - T + i \times D}{\text{GDP}} - (g + \Pi) \times d$$

Now recall that $(G + TR - T)$ is the primary budget deficit. Let x be this primary budget deficit *as a percentage of GDP* and express the debt-service payments also as a percentage of GDP. This gives

$$\Delta d = x + i \times d - (g + \Pi) \times d$$

Finally, recall that the real interest rate is equal to the nominal interest rate minus the rate of inflation,

$$r = i - \Pi$$

We thus combine terms to get

$$\Delta d = x + (r - g \times d)$$

which is the equation shown in the text.

---

*For any variable X which is equal to the ratio of two other variables, Y/Z, the percentage change in X is very well approximated by the percentage change in Y minus the percentage change in Z. The lower are the rates of change of Y and Z, the better is this approximation.

correct. While it is true that it is the nominal interest rate which determines how a given stock of debt will accumulate over time, this view misses the point that it is the accumulation of the *real* stock of debt which matters in terms of the government's *real* financial liabilities. And as we saw in Chapter 30 when we discussed inflation, high nominal interest rates are often associated with high inflation. Thus while high nominal interest rates increase the debt-service requirements, the accompanying high inflation reduces the real value of the government's debt. The accumulation of the government's stock of *real* debt therefore

depends on the difference between the nominal interest rate and the rate of inflation. This difference is simply the real interest rate, r. It follows, therefore, that changes in the debt-to-GDP ratio depend on the difference between the growth rate of the real stock of debt, r, and the growth rate of real GDP, g.

The Role of the Primary Deficit. The second point is that if our focus is to be on the debt-to-GDP ratio, rather than on the absolute size of the debt, then tracking the behaviour of the overall budget deficit may be misleading. The reason is that *it is possible to reduce the debt-to-GDP ratio even* *though the overall budget deficit may never be eliminated,* and thus even though the absolute size of the debt continues to increase. To see this, suppose for simplicity that $r = g$ and so the second term in the equation above is zero. Further, suppose that the government is running a small primary surplus, so that total tax revenues more than cover program spending. In this case, the primary surplus (x is negative) implies that the debt-to-GDP ratio is *falling;* but it is entirely possible that the overall budget deficit is positive, revealing simply that the debt-service payments exceed the primary surplus.

Stabilizing the Debt-to-GDP Ratio

One final point comes from this equation. Suppose the government's goal is to prevent further increases in the debt-to-GDP ratio. To do this it must maintain certain relationships between the primary deficit, the debt-to-GDP ratio, and the values of r and g. For example, if the real interest rate exceeds the growth rate of real GDP—a reasonable description of the Canadian economy over the past two decades—then a government with a positive stock of outstanding debt *must* run a primary surplus in order to stabilize the debt-to-GDP ratio. Furthermore, the larger is the real interest rate relative to the growth rate of GDP, the larger is the primary surplus required to stabilize the debt-to-GDP ratio.

To see this, let x^* be the value of the primary budget deficit which is consistent with a stable debt-to-GDP ratio—that is, x^* is the value of x such that Δd equals zero. From our equation above, setting Δd equal to zero results in

$$x^* = -(r - g) \times d$$

This shows the basic point that if the debt-to-GDP ratio is being pushed up by a real interest rate which exceeds the real growth rate of GDP, then a stable debt-to-GDP ratio is only possible with a value of x which is negative—that is, a primary budget surplus.

If the real interest rate exceeds the growth rate of real GDP, then stabilizing the debt-to-GDP ratio requires that the government run a primary budget surplus.

For an illustration of this central point, consider some of the numbers facing the federal minister of finance at the time of the March 1996 budget. The real interest rate on government debt was about 6 percent while the real growth rate of the economy was about 2 percent. Given the existing debt-to-GDP ratio of about 0.70, this implied a value of x^* equal to $-(0.06 - 0.02) \times (0.70) = -0.028$. Thus the federal government would have had to run a primary surplus of about 2.8 percent of GDP in order to keep the debt-to-GDP ratio from increasing further. (In fact, their actual primary surplus in 1996 was only about 1.5 percent of GDP—not large enough to immediately stabilize the debt-to-GDP ratio.)

GOVERNMENT DEFICITS AND NATIONAL SAVING

As we will see in the next section, the effects of government deficits on key macroeconomic variables depend in large part on the relationship between government deficits and national saving. We therefore examine this important issue now.

Defining Terms

As we saw in Chapter 23, private saving is the difference between disposable income and consumption. And as we saw in Chapter 24, government saving is the difference between government tax revenues and government expenditures. That is, government saving is equal to the government budget surplus. National saving is the sum of government saving and private saving:

National Saving	=	Private Saving	+	Government Saving

Since government saving is equal to the government's budget surplus, it follows that an increase in the government's budget *deficit* is a *reduction* in government saving.

National Saving	=	Private Saving	−	Government Budget Deficit

The effect of budget deficits on the level of national saving thus depends on the link between budget deficits and private saving. For example, suppose that the government budget deficit increases by $1 billion. If this *reduction* in government saving leads to an *increase* in private saving by exactly $1 billion, there will be no change in national saving. On the other hand, if private saving rises by less than $1 billion, national saving will fall as a result of the increase in the budget deficit.

But what is the link between the government deficit and the level of private saving? The answer lies in recognizing that government deficits represent *deferred liabilities for taxpayers*. At the beginning of this chapter when we said that all government expenditures must be financed either through taxes or borrowing, we could equivalently have said that all expenditures must be financed either through current taxes or future taxes (current borrowing). This reflects the simple fact that government expenditure must be paid for; either it is paid for by current tax payments, or the liability is passed on to future taxpayers. The cost of passing the tax liability on to future taxpayers is the interest that must be paid on the debt incurred to finance the expenditure. The link between government deficits and private saving then rests on the extent to which the current population of taxpayers recognizes the requirement for higher future taxes when the government increases its current borrowing.

Government debt is a postponed tax liability, and the interest paid on that debt is the cost of postponing the liability.

Ricardian Equivalence

The link between government deficits and private saving is associated with the idea of **Ricardian Equivalence,** named after the Classical economist David Ricardo (1772–1823), and recently brought back to prominence among modern-day economists through the work of Robert Barro, currently at Harvard University. The central proposition of Ricardian Equivalence is that consumers recognize government borrowing as a future tax liability and thus they view taxes as *equivalent* to government borrowing in terms of the effect on their own wealth. Therefore, a reduction in taxes and a rise in borrowing (or the reverse case) does not affect the wealth of the private sector and thus does not affect their consumption behaviour.

An example will help you to understand the basic idea of Ricardian Equivalence. Suppose that the government decides to reduce current taxes by $1 billion *with unchanged government expenditures,* and thus decides to increase its current borrowing by $1 billion. If current taxpayers recognize that an increase in government borrowing of $1 billion today represents an increase in their future taxes of $1 bil-

lion (plus interest), then the current generation of taxpayers will not feel any more or less wealthy as a result of the reduction in current taxes, and consequently will not change their level of current expenditure on goods and services. But if their consumption is unchanged and their disposable income is higher by $1 billion, then their current saving must increase by the full amount of the reduction in government saving. Thus *"Ricardian" consumers faced with a change in taxes will change their saving to exactly offset the change in government saving.*

Now suppose that current taxpayers do perceive an increase in their wealth when their current taxes are reduced. There are several reasons why this might be so. One possibility is that individuals might be short-sighted and thus tend to place more emphasis on current tax reductions than on tax increases in the possibly distant future. Another possibility is that there may be a great deal of uncertainty about the government's future spending plans so that it is unclear whether the current tax reduction will be offset by future tax increases or matched by future expenditure reductions. Whatever the reason, suppose that the current generation *feels wealthier* as a result of the reduction in current taxes. We then expect them to increase their current expenditures on goods and services. As a result of the higher expenditures, private saving of such "non-Ricardian" individuals will therefore increase by less than the reduction in government saving, leading to an overall reduction in national saving.

"Ricardian" consumers will not feel wealthier as a result of the government borrowing because they recognize the increase in their future tax liabilities. "Non-Ricardian" consumers do not recognize this future liability and thus feel wealthier when the government borrows.

The degree to which taxpayers recognize the future tax liabilities associated with government deficits is ultimately an empirical question. Most evidence suggests that Ricardian Equivalence does not hold completely and hence suggests a negative relationship between government deficits and national saving. That is, the evidence suggests that an increase in government borrowing by $1 billion will be associated with an increase in private saving by less than $1 billion and thus a fall in national saving.

THE EFFECTS OF GOVERNMENT DEBT AND DEFICITS

The previous two sections have explained what government budget deficits are and how different measures of the budget deficit are related to the accumulation of government debt. We now ask the question: Why should we care about government budget deficits? In particular, we examine the propositions that government deficits "crowd out" private economic activity, that government debt harms future generations, and that government debt hampers the conduct of economic policy.

DO DEFICITS CROWD OUT PRIVATE ACTIVITY?

We first examine the important idea of *crowding out*—the idea that an increase in government activity may force a reduction in the level of private activity. We consider the cases of closed and open economies separately.

Investment in Closed Economies

In a closed economy, the amount of national saving is exactly equal to the amount of domestic investment; after all, the only way that a closed economy can save is to accumulate physical capital. Suppose that in a closed economy there is an increase in government borrowing brought about by a reduction in taxes. What is the effect on domestic investment of the resulting increase in the government's budget deficit? As we saw in the previous section, the answer to this question depends on the degree to which taxpayers are Ricardian—that is, on the degree to which current taxpayers recognize that today's deficit must be financed by higher future taxes. If taxpayers are not purely Ricardian, then private saving will rise by less than the fall in government saving. This implies a net decrease in the supply of national saving. The resulting excess demand for funds will put upward pressure on the domestic real interest rate. As the real interest rate increases, moreover, those components of aggregate demand that are sensitive to the interest rate—investment in particular—

will fall. This is the **crowding out** of domestic investment; it is shown in Figure 32-8.

If government borrowing to finance the deficit drives up the interest rate, some private investment will be crowded out.

Net Exports in Open Economies

The effect of budget deficits in an open economy is a little different, though the story is very similar. The issues surrounding open economies will be dealt with in greater detail in Chapters 37 and 38, but the broad outlines of the story can be laid out now. Consider once again the possibility that the Canadian government reduces taxes and thus increases its deficit. Furthermore, suppose that taxpayers are not purely Ricardian so that private saving rises by less than the fall in government saving. What is the effect of such a fall in national saving in an open economy like Canada? As domestic real interest rates rise in Canada, foreigners are attracted to the higher-yield Canadian assets and thus foreign financial capital flows into Canada. But since Canadian dollars are required in order to buy Canadian interest-earning assets, this capital inflow increases the demand for Canadian dollars and thus increases the external value of the Canadian dollar (the Canadian dollar appreciates).

This appreciation makes Canadian goods more expensive relative to foreign goods, inducing an increase in imports and a reduction in exports. Canada's net exports therefore fall. In an open economy like Canada, therefore, a rise in the government deficit leads to an appreciation in the currency and to a crowding out of net exports.

In an open economy like Canada's, instead of driving up interest rates sufficiently to crowd out private investment, the government budget deficit tends to attract foreign financial capital, appreciate the Canadian dollar, and crowd out net exports.

The Long-Term Burden of the Debt

We have just argued that in a closed economy, a rise in the government deficit will push up interest rates and crowd out domestic investment, whereas in an open economy a rise in the government deficit will push up the external value of the currency and

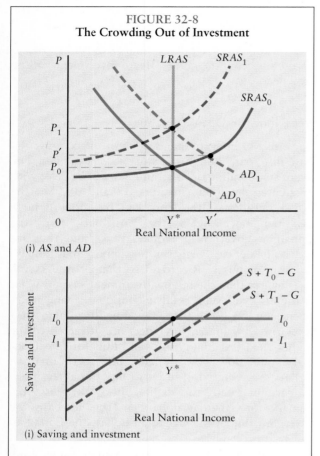

FIGURE 32-8
The Crowding Out of Investment

(i) *AS* and *AD*

(i) *Saving and investment*

For a closed economy whose income equals potential income, an increase in the budget deficit will cause a reduction in national saving and investment. Consider a closed economy that is in long-run equilibrium at Y^* and P_0 in part (i). The same position is shown in part (ii) as saving equal to investment at Y^* and I_0. Suppose that the government reduces its taxes from T_0 to T_1, thus increasing the budget deficit. This raises desired aggregate expenditure (and lowers desired national saving) at all levels of income. In part (i), the new short-run equilibrium is at Y' and P'. Assuming that the demand shock is not validated by monetary expansion, the adjustment mechanism will eventually cause factor prices to rise, shifting the *SRAS* curve from $SRAS_0$ to $SRAS_1$. The new long-run equilibrium will be at Y^* and P_1.

The effect of this change on saving and investment can be seen in part (ii). At the new long-run equilibrium, real income is unchanged at Y^*, but the price level is higher. This implies that the demand for money will have increased, causing a rise in interest rates. These higher interest rates will reduce desired investment expenditure, shown in the figure as a reduction from I_0 to I_1.

crowd out net exports. Despite the apparent differences in these two effects, they both imply a *long-term burden of government debt*.

A Closed Economy.   The overall effect of the increase in the government deficit in a closed economy is a rise in the real interest rate and a fall in the level of domestic investment. But less current investment means that there will be a lower stock of physical capital in the future, and thus a reduced ability to produce goods and services in the future. This reduction in future production possibilities, which implies lower consumption levels for future generations, is the long-term burden of the debt.

An Open Economy.   The overall effect of the increase in the government deficit in an open economy is an appreciation of the currency and a reduction in net exports. Recall from Chapter 24, however, that such a reduction in net exports implies a reduction in the country's *national asset formation*. This in turn increases the need for the domestic economy to make interest payments to foreigners in the future. Thus in an open economy, an increase in the government budget deficit does not lead to a reduction in the domestic capital stock—it leads instead to an increase in the stock of debt that the country as a whole owes to foreigners. So instead of having a lower future capital stock as a result of the government's budget deficit, the country has an unchanged capital stock but less of it is owned by domestic residents. This reduces the domestic residents' future stream of income because payments must be paid to the foreign owners of the domestic capital stock. This reduction in the future stream of income for domestic residents is the long-term burden of the public debt in an open economy.

DOES GOVERNMENT DEBT HARM FUTURE GENERATIONS?

In both open and closed economies there is a long-term burden associated with government debt. In a closed economy, government deficits crowd out private investment and thereby reduce the future capital stock; in an open economy, government deficits crowd out net exports and increase a country's net foreign indebtedness. In both cases, there is less output available for consumption by future generations of domestic residents. This reveals an important aspect of the costs associated with government debt and deficits:

Government borrowing generates a redistribution of resources away from future generations toward the current generation.

After all, the government deficits are being used to finance goods and services which are provided to the current generation, but which will be financed by taxes levied on future generations.

This last sentence suggests that current government deficits are always financing goods and services which are provided to the current generation. But is this really true? Some government spending is on goods and services that will continue to be used well into the future. For example, if the government increases its current borrowing to finance the building of a bridge or the expansion of a highway, future generations will receive some of the benefits of this government spending. And given that future generations will reap the benefits of some of these projects, it may be regarded as appropriate that future generations should also pay some of the taxes required to finance such projects.

Whether current government deficits impose a burden on future generations thus depends on the nature of the government goods and services being financed by the deficit. At one extreme, the government borrowing may finance a project that generates a return only to future generations, and thus the future generations may not be made worse off by today's budget deficit. An example might be the government financing long-term medical research projects that generate a return only in the distant future. At the other extreme, the government deficit may finance some government program which benefits only the current generation, and thus the future generations are inappropriately saddled with the future tax bill. An example might be the government financing a world's fair such as Expo '67 in Montreal or Expo '86 in Vancouver.

The concern that deficits may be inappropriately placing a financial burden on future generations has led some economists to advocate the idea of *capital budgeting* by the government. Under this scheme, the government would essentially classify all of its expenditures as either *consumption* or *investment*; the former would be spending which mostly benefits the current generation while the latter would be spending which mostly benefits future generations.

With capital budgeting, government deficits could be used to minimize the undesirable redistribu-

tions of income between generations. For example, the government might be committed to borrowing no more in any given year than the expenditures classified as investments. In this way, future generations would receive benefits from current government spending which are approximately equivalent to the future taxes they will pay.

A system of capital budgeting in government seems unlikely in Canada's near future. Without such a system, however, it will be difficult to prevent the redistribution of income away from future generations that is caused by government budget deficits.

DOES GOVERNMENT DEBT HAMPER ECONOMIC POLICY?

The costs imposed on future generations by government debt are very real. Unfortunately, the fact that these costs sometimes occur in the very distant future often leads us to ignore their importance. But there are other costs associated with the presence of government debt that are more immediately apparent. In particular, government debt may make the conduct of monetary and fiscal policy more difficult.

Monetary Policy

Recall that the long-term *goal* of monetary policy is to influence the rate of inflation, and that the Bank of Canada's primary *instrument* is its control over the rate of growth of the money supply. In our discussion of government deficits, we are then naturally led to examine the link between government budget deficits and the rate of inflation. In Chapter 30 we saw that sustained inflation was only possible when the Bank of Canada permitted a sustained growth in the money supply. In Chapter 29 we saw that the Bank of Canada increases the supply of money by purchasing government bonds in the open market (an open-market purchase)—that is, by lending to the government. This would appear to suggest that government deficits cause inflation.

Note, however, that when the government operates a budget deficit and is thus borrowing funds, it can borrow from households or firms in the private sector, it can borrow from foreigners, or it can borrow from the Bank of Canada. But not all of these are the same in terms of the effect on the money supply. As we saw in Chapter 29, changes in the Bank's balance sheet are central to changes in the money supply.

And when the government borrows from either the private sector or from foreigners, there is no change in the Bank's balance sheet, and thus no change in the money supply. In contrast, if the government borrows from the Bank of Canada (an open-market purchase by the Bank), this increases the Bank's assets (government securities) and similarly increases the Bank's liabilities (currency). Thus *it is only when the government borrows from the Bank of Canada that budget deficits increase the money supply.*

To summarize the foregoing argument, unless the central bank finances some of the budget deficit, there is no necessary link between budget deficits and *sustained* inflation. In this sense, there is a separation between budget deficits (fiscal policy) and inflation (monetary policy).[4]

Deficits financed by the continual creation of new money cause sustained inflation; deficits financed by private-sector borrowing do not.

This last point suggests that the *independence of the central bank* from the government determines the strength of the link between government deficits and inflation. For example, if the government were able to force the central bank to finance some fraction of government deficits—referred to as *monetizing the deficit*—then government deficits would clearly lead to the creation of money and eventual inflation. On the other hand, a central bank that is sufficiently independent from the fiscal arm of the government is free to set the money supply to pursue its inflation objectives, independent of the size of the budget deficit.

Though budget deficits need not be inflationary, their accumulated value over many years—the stock of government debt—can still make monetary policy more difficult. To see how a large stock of government debt can hamper the conduct of monetary policy, consider a country that has a high debt-to-GDP ratio and that has a real interest rate above the growth rate of GDP. As we saw previously, the debt-to-GDP ratio will continue to grow in this situation unless the government starts running significant primary budget *surpluses*. But such primary surpluses require either increases in taxation or reductions in program spending, both of which are politically unpopular. If such primary surpluses look unlikely to be achieved in the near future, both foreign and domestic creditors may come to expect that the government will put pressure on the central bank to monetize an increasing portion of its deficit. Any ensuing inflation would thus erode the real value of the outstanding government debt, lowering the real value of the bonds held by creditors. Such fears of future debt monetization will lead to expectations of future inflation and thus will put upward pressure on nominal interest rates and on some prices and wages. Thus even in the absence of any actions by the central bank to increase the rate of growth of the money supply, a large government debt may lead to the *expectation* of future inflation, thus hampering the task of the central bank in keeping inflation and inflationary expectations low.

In December 1995, the Governor of the Bank of Canada, Gordon Thiessen, appeared before the House of Commons Standing Committee on Public Accounts. His comments to that committee expressed this view that high levels of government debt generate concerns on the part of creditors.

> . . . We would probably all agree . . . that our society needs to sort out its views about acceptable levels of taxation and the size of government, and those views can influence the amount of debt our society can afford to carry. However, when you reach a high debt-to-GDP ratio, what is sustainable is also very much influenced by the willingness of investors in financial markets to hold your debt.
>
> I do not mean to imply that financial markets might suddenly decide to stop lending to Canadian governments. What happens, as recent experience has shown, is that at very high levels of debt, there may be an increasing nervousness among lenders so that they would only continue to hold Canadian government debt at much higher interest rates.[5]

---

[4]Note the emphasis here on *sustained* inflation. Even if the Bank of Canada does not change the money supply, an increase in government purchases or a reduction in taxation (both of which increase the budget deficit) will shift the *AD* curve to the right and thus increase the price level. As prices rise, the *SRAS* curve will then shift up. Thus a budget deficit can cause a one-time increase in the price level, but unless the Bank of Canada increases the rate of growth of the money supply, it will not cause a sustained inflation.

---

[5]Comments by Gordon Thiessen in the *Bank of Canada Review,* Winter 1995–1996.

Fiscal Policy

In Chapter 24 we saw that fiscal policy could potentially be used to stabilize aggregate demand and thereby stabilize national income. For example, in a recession the government might reduce tax rates or increase spending to stimulate aggregate demand; in a booming economy, the government might reduce spending or increase tax rates to prevent the economy from overheating. Thus running cyclically-adjusted budget deficits in recessions and cyclically-adjusted budget surpluses in booms is one obvious way of implementing *counter-cyclical fiscal policy*.

How does the presence of government debt affect the government's ability to conduct such counter-cyclical fiscal policy? Perhaps the easiest way to answer this question is to recall the equation which describes the change in the debt-to-GDP ratio:

$$\Delta d = x + (r - g) \times d$$

This shows that the size of the *change* in the debt-to-GDP ratio depends on the *level* of the debt-to-GDP ratio. For example, if the real interest rate exceeds the growth rate of real GDP, so that $r - g$ is positive, then the increase in the debt-to-GDP ratio (Δd) will be higher if d is already high than if it is low (for any given value of x).

With this in mind, consider the dilemma faced during a recession by a government that is considering the costs and benefits of an expansionary fiscal policy. On the one hand, the short-run benefits in terms of stabilizing the level of national income seem clear; on the other hand, the same government may be wary of taking actions which lead to large increases in the debt-to-GDP ratio.

If the stock of outstanding government debt is small relative to the size of the economy, then the government has a great deal of flexibility in conducting counter-cyclical fiscal policy. The small value of d implies that d will be rising only slowly in the absence of a primary deficit. Thus there may well be room for the government to increase the primary deficit—either by increasing program spending or reducing tax rates—without generating a large increase in the debt-to-GDP ratio. But the government has significantly less flexibility when the stock of outstanding government debt is already very large. In this case, the high value of d means that even in the absence of a primary budget deficit, d will be increasing quickly. Thus any increase in the primary deficit brought about by the counter-cyclical fiscal policy runs the danger of generating increases in the debt-to-GDP ratio which may be viewed by creditors as unsustainable.

The idea that a large and rising stock of government debt could "tie the hands" of the government in times when it would otherwise want to conduct counter-cyclical fiscal policy was brought to the fore of Canadian economic policy by the late Douglas Purvis of Queen's University (and a coauthor on this textbook for many years). Purvis, and his colleague Neil Bruce, argued in the mid 1980s that Canadian government deficits must be brought under control quickly so that the debt would not accumulate to the point where the government would have no room left for fiscal stabilization policy. Their warnings were not heeded. Between the time of their warnings and the onset of the next recession in 1990, the federal government had added roughly $200 billion to the stock of debt and, predictably, the government felt unable to use discretionary fiscal policy to reduce some of the effects of the recession.

PROPOSALS TO DEAL WITH BUDGET DEFICITS

As we have seen in this chapter, government budget deficits contribute to aggregate demand and thus have the potential to be used as an integral part of a fiscal policy designed to stabilize national income. However, we have also seen that government budget deficits crowd out private economic activity and impose a long-term burden, either through a reduced stock of physical capital or through greater foreign indebtedness. A trade off therefore appears to exist between the desirable short-run stabilizing role of deficits and the undesirable long-run costs of government debt. This trade off has been the source of constant debate. Here we examine some possible solutions.

Before examining some proposals for dealing with deficits, however, note that not everyone agrees that government deficits and debt represent a problem. Some economists take the view that Ricardian equivalence *does* hold and thus budget deficits do not lead to a crowding out of investment or net exports and thus there is no long-term burden associated with the public debt. Other economists accept the view that sufficiently high deficits and debt can indeed represent a problem,

TWO MYTHS ABOUT GOVERNMENT DEBT

There are two common misconceptions about government debt. These misconceptions often form the basis for arguments suggesting that government debt—even at a high level—does not present a serious problem (or does not represent a problem at all). You may recognize both of these arguments from discussions that often appear in the media.

GOVERNMENT DEBT IS NOT A PROBLEM: WE JUST OWE IT TO OURSELVES

One view that government debt presents no problem is based on the argument that government debt simply represents borrowing by all of us (taxpayers) from some of us (bondholders) and thus does not present a problem for the economy as whole. There are four points which should be addressed when confronted with this worry-free attitude about government debt.

First, the claim that government debt simply represents borrowing by Canadians from Canadians is factually incorrect. A considerable fraction of federal government debt is actually held by foreigners—by early 1996 about 25 percent was held abroad. This means that every year some of the taxes raised domestically are used to service the debt held by foreigners.

Second, even if it were the case that all Canadian government debt were held by Canadians, the debt would still create a problem. We saw above that in a closed economy (in which all government debt is certainly held domestically) an increase in government borrowing crowds out domestic investment and thus creates a long-term burden by reducing the productive potential of the economy. In an open economy, *even if all of the government debt is held by Canadians*, the govern-

ment borrowing still crowds out net exports and creates a long-term burden which takes the form of greater foreign indebtedness of the economy as a whole. As we saw above, the only situation in which there is no long-term burden from the government debt is if domestic taxpayers are purely Ricardian, but there is little evidence to support this extreme view.

Third, we saw in the text how the presence of large amounts of government debt has the potential to hamper the conduct of monetary and fiscal policy. If the central bank's job of keeping inflation low and stable is made more difficult by the existence of government debt, then this cost should not be overlooked. In addition, if the presence of large government debt reduces the government's ability to stabilize some of the short-run fluctuations in national income through counter-cyclical fiscal policy, then this cost also should not be ignored.

Finally, the government debt represents borrowing by *all* Canadians from *some* Canadians (and some foreigners). The interest payments on the debt thus represent a redistribution of income away from Canadian taxpayers in general toward Canadian (and foreign) bondholders. To the extent that the typical Canadian bondholder is wealthier than the typical Canadian taxpayer, this redistribution of income may be viewed as undesirable.

GOVERNMENT DEBT SHOULD BE HELD ONLY BY CANADIANS

One might think upon reading the previous arguments that if we were able to ignore for the moment the long-term burden of the debt and the hampering of economic policy that is caused by the debt, it would be preferable if Canadian governments could somehow restrict their borrowing so that only

but argue that Canada's current debt-to-GDP ratio, at about 70 percent, is not high enough to cause concern.

Though these debates might be reasonable, there are some *unreasonable* arguments for why we

should not worry about government debt and deficits. Extension 32-2 explores two myths about government debt that are often heard in public debate. One myth is that government debt is not a problem because "we just owe it to ourselves." The

Canadian residents held Canadian government debt. In this case, at least the interest payments on the debt would then remain within the country rather than enriching some foreign creditors. This view has led to the proposal that the federal government issue new debt to Canadians and use the proceeds of this borrowing to redeem existing debt held by foreigners. By so doing, the fraction of government debt held by Canadians would be increased and the fraction held by foreigners decreased. Advocates of this proposal argue that the result would be higher Canadian income in the long run as fewer interest payments are sent to foreign creditors.

Proponents of this view fail to recognize the importance of an *integrated* world capital market and the fact that government bonds are only one type of asset held by creditors. Suppose that the federal government issued $1 billion of new "Canadians-only" bonds to Canadians and used the proceeds to redeem an equal amount of existing foreign-held federal government debt. There are two questions which must be addressed: (1) What would make Canadians buy such bonds?; and (2) What would happen to the country's net foreign indebtedness as a result? We deal with these two issues in turn.

In order to convince Canadians to buy $1 billion worth of these new bonds, these same Canadians must somehow be convinced to divert $1 billion from some other use. For example, they could give up $1 billion worth of consumption to buy these bonds or they could sell $1 billion worth of their holdings of private corporate bonds to buy these new government bonds. In the first case, the reduction in consumption implies an increase in private saving. But it is difficult to see why Canadians would be prepared to increase their private saving simply in response to a change in the ownership of the federal government debt. One thing that might convince

Canadians to increase their saving is if these new bonds offered a rate of return greater than other assets available on the market. But in this case, it is hard to see how the federal government can improve its fiscal position by issuing new high-interest-rate bonds to raise funds used to redeem lower-interest-rate bonds.

Suppose, then, that these new "Canadians-only" bonds are *not* successful in increasing the amount of total private saving. Instead, the issuance of these bonds simply leads some Canadians to sell $1 billion of their holdings of private corporate debt so that they can hold the new bonds. The government then takes the $1 billion raised by the selling of the new bonds and redeems $1 billion worth of foreign-held debt. The total amount of government debt is unchanged, but less of the total debt is held by foreigners. The story does not end there, however. Recall that Canadians were only able to buy these new bonds by selling off some of their current holdings of private corporate debt. These private corporate borrowers are now forced to raise funds from other sources, and since there is an unchanged pool of national saving, they are forced to borrow from foreigners. So total private corporate debt is unchanged, but *more* of it is held by foreigners. Thus while it is true that the federal government has $1 billion less foreign-held debt, the private sector has $1 billion *more* foreign-held debt. And though the government will now be making fewer interest payments to foreign creditors, the Canadian economy as a whole—the private plus public sectors—will be making the same interest payments to foreigners as before. Thus the issuing of "Canadians-only" bonds and the reduction in foreign-held government debt, has no effect on the stream of income available to domestic residents.

other myth is that Canada is better off if a given amount of government debt is held by Canadians rather than by foreigners.

We now go on to examine some proposals for dealing with government budget deficits.

ANNUALLY BALANCED BUDGETS

Much current rhetoric of fiscal restraint calls for the government budget to be balanced every year. In the United States, the Gramm-Rudman-Hollings bill, passed in 1985, mandated expenditure cuts in order to balance the budget by 1993. That it failed to do so reflects a great deal of disagreement within the U.S. Congress over the costs and benefits associated with balanced budgets. There remains, however, considerable support by leading members of the U.S. Congress for an amendment to the U.S. Constitution which would require the federal government to balance its budget on an annual basis.

Though there has clearly been a significant move toward deficit reduction in Canada over the past few years, both federally and among the provinces, there has been little emphasis placed on the idea that governments should be constrained to balance their budgets *every year*.

Balancing the budget on an annual basis would be extremely difficult to achieve. The reason is that a significant portion of the government budget is beyond the short-term control of the government, and a further large amount is hard to change quickly. For example, the entire debt-service component of government expenditures is determined by past borrowing and thus cannot be altered by the current government. In addition, as we saw in our discussion of the cyclically adjusted deficit, changes in national income that are beyond the control of the government lead to significant changes in tax revenues (and transfer payments) and thus generate significant changes in the budget deficit.

Even if it were possible for the government to perfectly control its path of spending and revenues on a year-to-year basis, it would probably be *undesirable* to balance the budget every year. We saw above that government tax revenues tend to fall in recessions and rise in booms. In contrast, the level of government expenditure is more-or-less independent of the level of national income. As a result, fiscal policy contains a built-in stabilizer; in recessions, the increase in the budget deficit stimulates aggregate demand whereas in booms the budget surplus reduces aggregate demand. But things would be very different with an annually balanced budget. With a balanced budget, government expenditures would be *forced* to adjust to the changing level of tax revenues. In a recession, when tax revenues naturally decline, a balanced budget would require either a *reduction* in government expenditures or an *increase* in tax rates, thus generating a major *destabilizing* force on national income. Similarly, as tax revenues natu-

rally rise in an economic boom, the balanced budget would require either an increase in government expenditures or a reduction in taxes, thus risking an overheating of the economy.

An annually balanced budget would accentuate the swings in national income.

CYCLICALLY BALANCED BUDGETS

One alternative to the extreme policy of requiring an annually balanced budget is to require that the government budget be balanced over the course of a full economic cycle, as shown in Figure 32-9. Budget deficits would be permitted in recessions as long as they were matched by surpluses in booms. In this way, the built-in stabilizers could still perform their important role, but there would be no persistent build-up of government debt. In principle, this is a desirable treatment of the trade off between the short-run benefits of deficits and the long-run costs of debt.

Despite its appeal, the idea of cyclically balanced budgets has its problems as well. Perhaps the most important problem with a cyclically balanced budget is an operational one. In order to have a law which requires the budget to be balanced over the cycle, it is necessary to be able to *define* the cycle unambiguously. But there will always be disagreement about what stage of the cycle the economy is currently in, and thus there will be disagreement as to whether the current government should be increasing or reducing its deficit. Compounding this problem is the fact that politicians will have a stake in the identification of the cycle. Those who favour increased deficits will argue that this year is an unusually bad year and thus an increase in the deficit is justified; deficit "hawks," in contrast, will always tend to find this year to be unusually good, and thus a time to run budget surpluses.

Though a budget balanced over the course of the business cycle is in principle a desirable way of reconciling short-term stabilization with long-term prudence, the business cycle may not be well enough defined to make this policy operational.

A second problem is largely political. Suppose that one government runs large deficits for a few years and then gets replaced in an election. Would the succeeding government then be bound to run budget surpluses? What one government commits itself to in one year does not necessarily restrict what it (or its successor) does in the next year. It is this problem which leads many in the U.S. to suggest a Constitutional Amendment to deal with deficits; once the Constitution is altered, any government is bound by it until, through a very lengthy process, it is changed again.

ALLOWING FOR GROWTH

A further problem with any policy that requires a balanced budget—whether over one year or over the business cycle—is that the emphasis is naturally on the overall budget deficit. But as we saw earlier in this chapter, what determines the change in the debt-to-GDP ratio is the growth of the debt *relative* to the growth of the economy. With a growing economy, it is possible to have positive overall budget deficits (i.e., a growing debt) and still have a falling debt-to-GDP ratio. To the extent that the debt-to-GDP ratio is the relevant gauge of a country's debt problem, this suggests that focus should be placed on the debt-to-GDP ratio rather than on the budget deficit directly.

Some economists view a stable (or falling) debt-to-GDP ratio as the appropriate indicator of fiscal prudence. This permits a deficit such that the stock of debt grows no faster than GDP.

One example of this point was evident in the federal budgets of 1995 and 1996. The minister of finance, Paul Martin, announced a series of expenditure cuts designed to bring the budget deficit in the 1996–1997 fiscal year down to about $25 billion, or about 3 percent of GDP. Some opposition members in the House complained that Martin appeared to have no plan designed to *eliminate* the deficit, but appeared instead to be satisfied with a deficit that was declining.

To see that Martin's plan was essentially designed to stabilize the debt-to-GDP ratio (rather than to eliminate the deficit), note that a constant debt-to-GDP ratio requires that the debt grow at the same rate as GDP. Recall that the deficit is the change in the stock of debt and so the *growth rate* of the debt is therefore given by the ratio of the deficit to the debt. The growth rate of nominal GDP is $\Pi + g$, where recall that Π is the rate of inflation and g is the growth rate of real GDP. Thus a

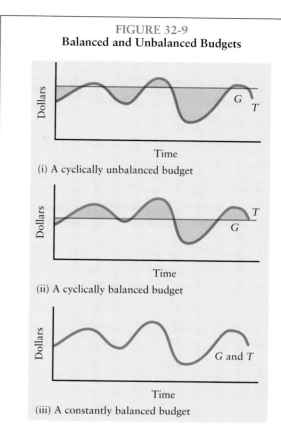

FIGURE 32-9
Balanced and Unbalanced Budgets

(i) A cyclically unbalanced budget

(ii) A cyclically balanced budget

(iii) A constantly balanced budget

An annually balanced budget is a destabilizer; a cyclically balanced budget is a stabilizer. The flow of tax receipts (net of transfers) T is shown varying over the business cycle; in parts (i) and (ii), government expenditure G is shown at a constant rate.

In part (i), deficits (red areas) are common and surpluses (green areas) are rare because the average level of expenditure exceeds the average level of taxes. Such a policy will tend to stabilize the economy against cyclical fluctuations, but public saving is negative, on average. This has been the characteristic Canadian budgetary position for several decades.

In part (ii), government expenditure has been reduced until it is approximately equal to the average level of tax receipts. The budget is now balanced cyclically. The policy still tends to stabilize the economy against cyclical fluctuations because of deficits in slumps and surpluses in booms. However, public saving is higher than in part (i).

In part (iii), a balanced budget has been imposed. Deficits have been prevented, but government expenditure now varies over the business cycle, which tends to destabilize the economy by accentuating the cyclical swings in aggregate expenditure.

constant debt-to-GDP ratio requires deficit/debt = $(\Pi + g)$, or

$$\text{Deficit} = (\Pi + g) \times \text{Debt}$$

Expressed in terms of percentages of GDP, a constant debt-to-GDP ratio therefore requires

$$\text{Deficit/GDP} = (\Pi + g) \times (\text{Debt/GDP})$$

As of 1995–1996, the federal debt-to-GDP ratio was about 70 percent (see Figure 32-3). A reasonable forecast of future long-term real GDP growth was about 2.5 percent and for inflation a long-run forecast of about 2 percent seemed realistic. Thus the size of the overall budget deficit (as a share of GDP) required to stabilize the debt-to-GDP ratio was about $(0.02 + 0.025) \times (0.7) = 0.0315$, or just over 3 percent GDP.

THE POLITICAL ECONOMY OF DEFICITS AND DEBT

Almost all economists accept the view that if the debt got so large that it could not be serviced without either putting a crushing burden on taxpayers or forcing the government to create new money to service it, there would be serious problems. However, many think that we are still a long way from that point.

This does not mean that the deficit (and the debt) is nothing to worry about. As we have seen, persistent deficits at high employment reduce national saving and asset formation and thus reduce the growth of national income over time. Aside from a fairly small minority who believe that deficits have no effect on the economy at all, most economists agree that the large deficits of recent years, and in prospect for the foreseeable future, will reduce economic growth relative to what it would otherwise be. Why then are the deficits such a difficult political problem?

Reducing the deficit involves, in some combination, increasing taxes and reducing transfer payments (thereby reducing private consumption) and cutting government purchases (thereby reducing government provision of goods and services). Either one of these actions will immediately reduce the economic well-being of some of the population, whether it be of taxpayers generally or beneficiaries of government spending generally. In exchange for enduring a current reduction in standard of living, people are told that their incomes in the future will be higher. Although, as we shall see in the next chapter, it may take a considerable amount of time before such a sacrifice of current living standards is outweighed by the higher growth.

Because the payoff from increased national saving takes so long to materialize, not everyone will benefit from the change. For one thing, the older a taxpayer is, the less likely that he or she will benefit at all, and the less the total benefit accruing to that taxpayer is likely to be. Moreover, the real incomes of many households in Canada have barely grown at all for more than a decade. This makes households generally unwilling to accept a reduction in their standard of living, even if the long-term payoff would be very high.

Virtually all politicians and virtually all voters say that the deficit is a serious national problem. Yet as a practical matter, politicians who raise taxes and cut spending often find themselves unemployed. The deficit, for all that it is decried on television, in the media, and by the person on the street, has broad political support. To date, it has also had the overwhelming support of the voters. Nobody likes the deficit, but almost everybody seems to like it better than the alternative.

SUMMARY

A. DEFICITS AND DEBT: FACTS AND DEFINITIONS

- The government's budget deficit is equal to total government expenditure minus total government revenue. Since the government must borrow to finance any shortfall in its revenues, the annual deficit is equal to the increase in the stock of government debt during the course of a year. Whenever the deficit is positive, the stock of government debt is growing.

- The primary budget deficit is equal to the excess of the government's program spending over total tax revenues. The difference between the total budget deficit and the primary deficit is the debt-service payments.

- In 1975, the Canadian federal government net debt was 14 percent of GDP. Large and persistent budget deficits beginning in the 1970s increased the stock of debt so that by 1996 the federal government net debt was equal to about 70 percent of GDP. Large deficits by the provinces beginning in 1982 increased the provincial debt-to-GDP ratio from 5 percent in 1982 to about 20 percent in 1996. For the combined federal and provincial governments, annual debt-service payments amount to about 9 percent of GDP.

B. DEFICITS AND DEBT: SOME ANALYTICAL ISSUES

- Since taxes (net of transfers) tend to rise when national income rises, the overall budget deficit tends to rise during recessions and fall during booms. This makes the budget deficit a poor measure of the stance of fiscal policy.
- The cyclically adjusted deficit is the budget deficit that would exist with the current set of fiscal policies if national income were equal to potential income. Changes in the cyclically adjusted deficit reflect changes in the stance of fiscal policy.
- The change in the debt-to-GDP ratio from one year to the next is given by

$$\Delta d = x + (r - g) \times d$$

where d is the debt-to-GDP ratio, x is the primary deficit as a percentage of GDP, r is the real interest rate and g is the growth rate of real GDP. Changes in the debt-to-GDP ratio therefore depend on the real interest rate, the growth rate of real GDP, and the size of the primary budget deficit.

- Reductions in the debt-to-GDP ratio are possible even though the overall budget deficit is not eliminated. For a given real interest rate and rate of growth of real GDP, a larger primary budget surplus implies a smaller increase in the debt-to-GDP ratio. If r exceeds g, then a primary surplus is required to stabilize the debt-to-GDP ratio.

- National saving equals government saving plus private saving. An increase in the government budget deficit represents a fall in government saving. The link between budget deficits and private saving depends on the extent to which taxpayers recognize the future tax liabilities associated with current government deficits. When taxpayers are purely Ricardian, any change in government saving is exactly offset by an equal and opposite change in private saving, leaving national saving unchanged. Available evidence suggests that an increase in the government's budget deficit will not be fully offset by an increase in private saving and thus will decrease national saving.

C. THE EFFECTS OF GOVERNMENT DEBT AND DEFICITS

- In a closed economy, an increase in the budget deficit leads to a reduction in national saving and a rise in real interest rates. This reduces the amount of investment and leads to a long-term decline in the domestic capital stock.
- In an open economy, an increase in the budget deficit initially pushes up real interest rates. But this attracts foreign financial capital which drives up the external value of the currency. As the currency appreciates, there is a reduction in net exports. The capital inflow implies an increase in the country's net foreign indebtedness.
- In either open or closed economies, the long-term burden of government debt is a redistribution of resources away from future generations and toward current generations.
- A large debt-to-GDP ratio may lead creditors to expect increases in inflation, as the government attempts to finance deficits through the creation of money. Such increases in inflationary expectations hamper the conduct of monetary policy.
- A large debt-to-GDP ratio also limits the extent to which the government can conduct counter-cyclical fiscal policy without risking large increases in the debt-to-GDP ratio which may be viewed by creditors as unsustainable.

D. PROPOSALS TO DEAL WITH BUDGET DEFICITS

- Since tax revenues (net of transfers) naturally rise as national income increases, a policy to balance the budget on an annual basis forces either expenditures to rise or tax rates to fall during booms. This produces destabilizing fiscal policy.
- Cyclically balanced budgets, in principle, permit the short-run benefits of deficits to be realized without incurring the long-run costs of debt. Implementation of this policy is very difficult, however, since the identification of the business cycle is very controversial.
- In a growing economy, it is more sensible to focus on changes in the debt-to-GDP ratio than on balancing the budget over some horizon.

KEY CONCEPTS

Government's budget constraint
Primary budget deficit
The relationship between deficits and the national debt
Debt-service payments

Debt-to-GDP ratio
National, government, and private saving
Ricardian equivalence
Crowding out of investment

Crowding out of net exports
Long-term burden of the debt
Cyclically balanced budget

DISCUSSION QUESTIONS

1. In 1990, the Canadian economy slid into a recession, while the deficit and, in particular, debt-service payments continued at record levels. The first development led many people to call for fiscal stimulus, while the second development led to calls for fiscal restraint. Explain the basis for each view.

2. Evaluate each of the following proposals to "control the deficit" in order to avoid the long-run burden of the debt.

   a. Maintain a zero cyclically adjusted deficit.
   b. Keep the debt-to-GDP ratio constant.
   c. Limit government borrowing in each year to some fixed percentage of national income in that year.

3. One of the problems with the idea of an annually balanced budget is that it results in a *procyclical* fiscal policy. Consider instead the idea of balancing the budget deficit over a specified number of years. Suppose, for example, that governments were forced to balance the budget over a 7-year cycle, so that deficits in early years would have to be matched by surpluses in later years. Do you see any problems with this policy?

4. Judith Maxwell, former chairperson of the now disbanded Economic Council of Canada, warned in 1991 that "when interest rates are higher than the economic growth rate, the ratio of debt to GDP acquires dangerous upward momentum." Discuss why this is so. Does the current Canadian situation reflect this combination?

5. What problems for budgetary control are posed by the fact that economic forecasting is imperfect? How might these problems be minimized?

6. In the federal budget of 1995, the minister of finance announced some significant expenditure reductions which would reduce the deficit. In the budget of 1996, he announced no new expenditure cuts yet still predicted the deficit to fall. Using Figure 32-7, explain how these statements by the minister of finance should be interpreted.

7. In the past few years, the governor of the Bank of Canada, Gordon Thiessen, has expressed concern about the persistent government deficit and the growing level of debt in the economy. Why should this concern him? Explain how a high level of debt may make the conduct of monetary policy more difficult.

8. In 1989, the U.S. Congressional Budget Office director, Robert Reischaner, said: "We have a long way to go before the [government budget] deficit is brought down to a level where Americans should feel comfortable." Arguing that the borrowing caused by the deficit erodes living standards for future generations, "How well do you want your children and grandchildren to live?" he asked. Explain why he seems to think that current government borrowing harms future generations? Can you think of a situation in which deficits do not harm future generations?

9. What will well-informed taxpayers do in each of the following situations after the government decides to spend an additional sum for one period?

   a. Both the government and the taxpayers wish to pay now.
   b. Both wish to postpone payment.
   c. The government wishes to postpone but taxpayers want to pay now.
   d. The government wants to pay now but taxpayers wish to postpone payment.

10. Explain why attempts to ensure that Canadian government debt is held by Canadians (rather than foreigners) are unlikely to change the net foreign indebtedness of the country as a whole. Would such a change affect government tax revenues?

ECONOMIC GROWTH

Economic growth is the single most powerful engine for generating long-term increases in living standards. What happens to our material living standards over time depends primarily on the growth in national income (as measured, for example, by the GDP) in relation to the growth in population—that is, it depends on the growth of real *per capita* GDP. This does not mean that growth in real Canadian per capita GDP necessarily makes *everybody* in Canada better off. But it does mean that the *average* standard of living is higher.

But what determines the growth rate of per capita GDP in Canada? Is this something that is beyond our control, or are there some government policies that could stimulate economic growth? If there are, what are the costs of such policies, and are the benefits worth the costs?

In this chapter we examine this important issue of economic growth beginning with some basic concepts and then moving on to explore the costs and benefits of growth. The remainder of the chapter then examines various theories of economic growth, an area in which much new research is being done. Finally, we examine the idea that there may be *limits to growth*.

THE NATURE OF ECONOMIC GROWTH

We saw in Chapter 1 that in the first seven decades of the twentieth century, per capita GDP rose steadily. As a result, most residents of most countries in the industrialized world have become materially better off decade by decade, and children have typically been substantially better off than their parents were at the same age. Beginning in the mid 1970s, however, the engine of growth faltered. Growth rates fell, though they remained positive. Although we still live in a very wealthy society, many observers speak of the end of the dream that each generation can expect to be much better off than its predecessors. The change in attitudes and perceptions brought about in the minds of ordinary, middle-class Canadians by the mere slowdown of rapid growth shows how important a part that steady growth had played in people's minds and hearts over the decades of the twentieth century.

THREE WAYS OF INCREASING GDP

In earlier chapters, we outlined the effects of shifts in aggregate demand and aggregate supply. Economic growth concerns sustained shifts in long-run aggregate supply; hence many of the points made in earlier chapters in the context of one-time shifts bear repeating in this new context.

Figure 33-1 illustrates some important causes of rising national income. If there is a recessionary gap, policies that increase aggregate demand will yield a once-and-for-all increase in national income. Once potential income is achieved, however, further increases in aggregate demand yield only transitory increases in real income but lasting increases in the price level.

Policies that reduce structural or frictional unemployment can also increase the employed labour force and thus increase potential income. The resulting increase in income might not be very large, but some social benefits would result from the reduction in unemployment, especially in the reduction of long-term unemployment that occurs when people are trapped in declining areas, industries, or occupations. The increase in national income, however, is once and for all as the total number of unemployed falls to a new, lower level. Similar results come from measures that increase economic efficiency. A once-and-for-all increase in potential output occurs as a given employed labour force works more efficiently.

Over the long run, the main cause of rising national income is **economic growth**—the increase in potential income due to changes in factor supplies (labour and capital) and in the productivity of factors (output per unit of factor input). The removal of a serious recessionary gap or the elimination of all structural and frictional unemployment might cause a once-and-for-all increase in national income by, at the very most, 5 to 10 percent. However, a growth rate of 3 percent per year raises potential income by 10 percent in three years, *doubles* it in about 24 years, and *quadruples* it in 48 years. Even a 1 percent growth rate doubles potential income over one normal lifetime of about 70 years.

Growth is a much more powerful method of raising living standards than the removal of recessionary gaps, structural unemployment, or inefficiencies because growth can go on indefinitely.

Table 33-1 illustrates the cumulative effect of what you might think are very small differences in

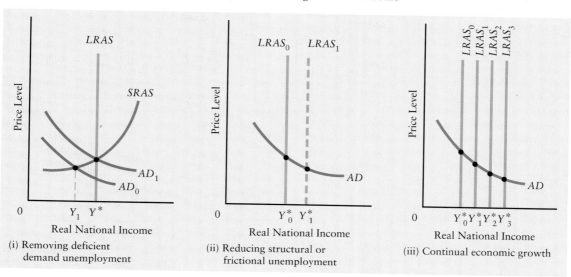

FIGURE 33-1
Three Ways of Increasing National Income

A once-and-for-all increase in national income can be obtained by raising aggregate demand to remove a recessionary gap or by shifting the *LRAS* curve, say, by cutting structural or frictional unemployment. Continual increases in national income are possible through continued economic growth, which shifts the *LRAS* curve. In part (i), with the aggregate demand curve at AD_0, there is a recessionary gap of Y_1Y^*. An increase in aggregate demand from AD_0 to AD_1 achieves a once-and-for-all increase in national income from Y_1 to Y^*.

In part (ii), potential output rises from Y_0^* to Y_1^* due to measures that reduce structural or frictional unemployment. The *LRAS* curve shifts from $LRAS_0$ to $LRAS_1$ because people who were formerly unemployed due to having the wrong skills or being in the wrong place are now better suited for employment.

In part (iii), increases in factor supplies and productivity lead to increases in potential income. This *continually* shifts the long-run aggregate supply curve outward. In successive periods, it moves from $LRAS_0$ to $LRAS_3$, taking potential income from Y_0^* to Y_1^* to Y_2^*, and so on, as long as growth continues.

TABLE 33-1
The Cumulative Effect of Economic Growth

	Rate of Growth per Year				
Year	1%	2%	3%	5%	7%
0	100	100	100	100	100
10	111	122	135	165	201
30	135	182	246	448	817
50	165	272	448	1,218	3,312
70	201	406	817	3,312	13,429
100	272	739	2,009	14,841	109,660

Small differences in growth rates make enormous differences in levels of potential national income over a few decades. Let potential national income be 100 in year 0. At a rate of growth of 3 percent per year, it will be 135 in 10 years, 448 after 50 years, and over 2,000 in a century. The compounding of sustained rates of growth is a powerful force.

growth rates. Notice that if one country grows faster than another, the gap in their respective living standards will widen progressively. If, for example, countries A and B start from the same level of income and if country A grows at 3 percent per year while country B grows at 2 percent per year, A's per capita income will be twice B's in 72 years. You may not think that it matters much whether the economy grows at 2 percent or 3 percent per year, but your children and grandchildren certainly will. [40]

EFFICIENCY, EQUITY, AND ECONOMIC GROWTH

Observing that sustained economic growth is the most important force for raising living standards over the long term in no way implies the unimportance of policies designed to increase economic efficiency or to redistribute income in the pursuit of greater equity.

Reducing Inefficiency

If, at any moment in time, national income could be increased by removing certain inefficiencies in the economy, such gains would be valuable. After all, as long as scarcity exists (and it always does), any increase in national income is welcome. Furthermore, inefficiencies may themselves act to reduce the growth rate. For example, government subsidies to failing firms that may be criticized on grounds of productive and allocative efficiency may also lower growth rates by reducing the incentive to innovate.

Improving Equity

Economic growth has made the poor vastly better off than they would have been if they had lived 100 years ago. Yet that is little consolation when they see that they cannot afford many things that are currently available to citizens with higher incomes. After all, people compare themselves with others in their own society, not with their counterparts at other times or in other places. Because people care about relative differences among individuals, governments continue to have policies to redistribute income and to make such basic services as education and health care available to all people, regardless of their ability to pay for them.

Interrelationships Among the Goals

Economists once assumed that the goals of improving equity, increasing economic efficiency, and ensuring growth could each be treated independently. But it is now understood that equity, efficiency, and economic growth are interrelated.[1] For example, policies that create extreme allocative inefficiencies by subsidizing failing firms can alter the allocation of resources in such a way that adversely affects the growth rate. Or policies that redistribute income to the poor in ways that provide large disincentives to work may also adversely affect economic growth. It

follows that policies designed to reduce inefficiencies or improve equity should be examined carefully for any effects that they may have on economic growth, and policies designed to affect growth need to be examined for their effects on economic efficiency and income distribution. A policy that reduces growth may be a bad bargain, even if it increases the immediate efficiency of the economy or creates a more equitable distribution of income. Similarly, a policy that increases growth may be a bad bargain if it only achieves that higher growth by misallocating resources or by redistributing income in ways that are deemed to be undesirable.

To see this, consider a simple example. Consider a hypothetical redistributive policy that raises the share of GDP going to poorer people by 5 percent but lowers the rate of economic growth from 2 to 1 percent. After 10 years, the people who gained from the policy would be no better off than if they had not received the redistribution of income while the growth rate had remained at 2 percent (and, of course, everyone who did not gain from the redistribution would be worse off from the outset). After 20 years, those who had gained from the redistribution would have 5 percent more of a national income that was 12 percent smaller than it would have been if the growth rate had remained at 2 percent.

Of course, not all redistribution policies have unfavourable effects on the growth rate. Some may have no effect, and others—by raising the health and educational standards of workers in general—may raise the growth rate.

BENEFITS AND COSTS OF ECONOMIC GROWTH

We start by looking at the benefits of growth, and then we consider the costs. Applications 33-1 and 33-2 outline some of the commonly heard popular arguments on both sides of the growth debate.

BENEFITS OF GROWTH

Growth and Living Standards

We have already observed that over the long term, economic growth is the primary engine for raising general living standards. For all who share in it, growth is a powerful weapon against poverty. A family that is earning $25,000 today can expect an in-

---

[1]Recall in Chapter 18 that we discussed Arthur Okun's example of a leaky bucket to demonstrate the notion that policies designed to redistribute income inevitably lead to inefficiencies.

APPLICATION 33-1

AN OPEN LETTER TO THE ORDINARY CITIZEN FROM A SUPPORTER OF THE "GROWTH IS GOOD" SCHOOL

Dear Ordinary Citizen:

You live in the world's first civilization that is devoted principally to satisfying *your* needs rather than those of a privileged minority. Past civilizations have always been based on leisure and high consumption for a tiny upper class, a reasonable living standard for a small middle class, and hard work with little more than subsistence consumption for the great mass of people.

The continuing Industrial Revolution is based on mass-produced goods for you, the ordinary citizen. It ushered in a period of sustained economic growth that has dramatically raised consumption standards of ordinary citizens. Reflect on a few examples: travel, live and recorded music, art, good food, universal literacy, inexpensive books, and a genuine chance to be educated. Most important, there is leisure to provide time and energy to enjoy these and thousands of other products of the modern industrial economy.

Would any ordinary family seriously prefer to go back to the world of 150 or 500 years ago in its same *relative* social and economic position? Surely the answer is no. However, for those with incomes in the top 1 or 2 percent of the income distribution, economic growth has destroyed much of their privileged consumption position. They must now vie with the masses when they visit the world's beauty spots and be annoyed, while lounging on the terrace of a palatial mansion, by the sound of charter flights carrying ordinary people to inexpensive holidays in far places. Many of the rich complain bitterly about the loss of exclusive rights to luxury consumption, and it is not surprising that they find their intellectual apologists.

Whether they know it or not, the antigrowth economists are not the social revolutionaries that they think they are. They say that growth has produced pollution and wasteful consumption of all kinds of frivolous products that add nothing to human happiness. However, the democratic solution to pollution is not to go back to the time when so few people consume luxuries that pollution is trivial but rather to learn to control the pollution that mass consumption tends to create.

It is only through further growth that the average citizen can enjoy consumption standards (of travel, culture, medical and health care, and so on) now available only to people in the top 25 percent of the income distribution—which includes the intellectuals who earn large royalties from the books they write in which they denounce growth. If you think that extra income confers little real benefit, just ask those in the top 25 percent to trade incomes with average citizens.

Ordinary citizens, do not be deceived by disguised elitist doctrines. Remember that the very rich and the elite have much to gain by stopping growth and even more by rolling it back, but you have everything to gain by letting it go forward.

Onward!

A. N. Optimist

---

come of about $30,500 within 10 years (in constant dollars) if it shares in a 2 percent growth rate, $37,000 if the rate is 4 percent.

A family often finds that an increase in its income can lead to changes in the pattern of its consumption—that extra money buys important amenities of life and also allows them to save more for the future.

Similarly, economic growth that raises average income may change the whole society's consumption patterns. Not only do expanding markets in a rapidly growing country make it profitable to produce more cars, but the government is led to construct more highways and to provide more recreational areas for its newly affluent and mobile population.

APPLICATION 33-2

AN OPEN LETTER TO THE ORDINARY CITIZEN FROM A SUPPORTER OF THE "GROWTH IS BAD" SCHOOL

Dear Ordinary Citizen:

You live in a world that is being despoiled by a mindless search for ever-higher levels of material consumption at the cost of all other values. Once upon a time, men and women knew how to enjoy creative work and to derive satisfaction from simple activities. Today, the ordinary worker is a mindless cog in an assembly line that turns out more and more goods that the advertisers must work overtime to persuade the worker to consume.

Statisticians count the increasing flow of material output as a triumph of modern civilization. You arise from your electric-blanketed bed, clean your teeth with an electric toothbrush, open a can of the sad remnants of a once-proud orange with an electric can opener, and eat your bread baked from super-refined and chemically refortified flour; you climb into your car to sit in vast traffic jams on exhaust-polluted highways.

Television commercials tell you that by consuming more, you are happier, but happiness lies not in increasing consumption but in increasing the ratio of *satisfaction of wants* to *total wants*. Because the more you consume, the more the advertisers persuade you that you want to consume, you are almost certainly less happy than the average citizen in a small town in 1900, whom we can visualize sitting on the family porch, sipping lemonade, and enjoying the antics of the children as they jump rope using pieces of old clothesline.

Today, the landscape is dotted with endless factories that produce the plastic trivia of the modern industrial society. They drown you in a cloud of noise, air, and water pollution. The countryside is despoiled by strip mines, petroleum refineries, acid rain, and dangerous nuclear power plants, producing energy that is devoured insatiably by modern factories and motor vehicles. Worse, our precious heritage of natural resources is being rapidly depleted.

Now is the time to stop this madness. We must stabilize production, reduce pollution, conserve our natural resources, and seek justice through a more equitable distribution of existing total income.

A long time ago, Thomas Malthus taught us that if we do not limit population voluntarily, nature will do it for us in a cruel and savage manner. Today, the same is true of output: If we do not halt its growth voluntarily, the halt will be imposed on us by a disastrous increase in pollution and a rapid exhaustion of natural resources.

Citizens, awake! Shake off the worship of growth, learn to enjoy the bounty that is yours already, and reject the endless, self-defeating search for increased happiness through ever-increasing consumption.

Upward!

I. Realvalues

One illustration of the basic point that patterns of demand change as a country becomes wealthier is to note the different attitudes toward environmental protection in rich and poor countries. In developing countries, most of the resources of the country are devoted to providing basic requirements of life such as food, shelter, and clothing. These countries typically do not have the "luxury" of being concerned about environmental degradation. Some may view this as short-sighted, but the fact is that the concerns associated with hunger *today* are much more urgent than the concerns associated with *future* environmental problems. In contrast, richer countries are wealthy enough that they can easily provide the basic requirements of life and thus they have the luxury of being able to devote significant resources to environmental protection.

The transformation of the lifestyle of ordinary workers in advanced industrial nations between 1870 and 1970 provides a notable example of the escape from poverty that growth makes possible. Much of the concern today over economic problems facing Canadian families stems from the decline of growth that occurred after 1970. Partly because growth has slowed and partly because the distribution of income has changed unfavourably to them, many working families have seen their income fail to grow for two decades.

Growth and Income Redistribution

Not everyone benefits equally from growth. Many of the poorest are not even in the labour force and hence are unlikely to share in the higher wages that, along with profits, are the primary means by which the gains from growth are distributed. For this reason, even in a growing economy, redistribution policies will be needed if poverty is to be reduced.

A rapid growth rate makes the alleviation of poverty easier politically. If existing income is to be redistributed, someone's standard of living will actually have to be lowered. However, when there is economic growth and when the increment in income is redistributed (through government intervention), it is possible to reduce income inequalities without actually having to lower anyone's income. It is much easier for a rapidly growing economy to be generous toward its less fortunate citizens—or neighbours—than it is for a static economy.

COSTS OF GROWTH

Other things being equal, most people would probably regard a fast rate of growth as preferable to a slow one. However, we know that other things are seldom equal.

The Opportunity Cost of Growth

In a world of scarcity, almost nothing is free. Growth requires heavy investment of resources in capital goods, as well as in activities such as education. Often these investments yield no immediate return in terms of goods and services for consumption; thus they imply that sacrifices have been made by the current generation of consumers.

Growth, which promises more goods tomorrow, is achieved by consuming fewer goods today. For the economy as a whole, this sacrifice of current consumption is the primary cost of growth.

An example will suggest the magnitude of this cost. Suppose that a hypothetical economy has full employment and is experiencing growth in real GDP at the rate of 2 percent per year. Its citizens consume 85 percent of the GDP and invest 15 percent. They know that if they immediately decrease their consumption to 77 percent of GDP, they will produce more capital and thus shift at once to a 3 percent growth rate. The new rate can be maintained as long as they keep saving and investing 23 percent of the national income. Should they do it?

Table 33-2 illustrates the choice in terms of time paths of consumption. Using the assumed figures, it takes ten years for the actual amount of consumption to catch up to what it would have been had no reallocation been made. In the intervening 10 years, a good deal of consumption is lost, and the cumulative losses in consumption must be made up before society can really be said to have broken even. It takes an *additional* 9 years before total consumption over the whole period is as large as it would have been if the economy had remained on the 2 percent path. [41]

Over a longer period, however, the payoff from the growth policy becomes enormous. Forty years on, the national income in the more rapidly growing economy is 35 percent higher than in the slower-growing economy. The total difference in consumption over those 40 years has become three times the annual amount of consumption in the faster-growing society at year 40.

Social and Personal Costs of Growth

A growing economy is also a changing economy. Part of growth is accounted for by existing firms expanding and producing more output, hiring more workers, and using more equipment and intermediate goods. But another part of growth is accounted for by existing firms being overtaken and made obsolete by new firms, by old products being made obsolete by new products, and by existing workers being made obsolete by new workers.

TABLE 33-2
The Opportunity Cost of Growth

Year	(1) Level of Consumption at a 2 Percent Growth Rate	(2) Level of Consumption at a 3 Percent Growth Rate	(3) Cumulative Gain (Loss) in Consumption
0	85.0	77.0	(8.0)
1	86.7	79.3	(15.4)
2	88.5	81.8	(22.1)
3	90.3	84.2	(28.2)
4	92.1	86.8	(33.5)
5	93.9	89.5	(37.9)
6	95.8	92.9	(40.8)
7	97.8	95.0	(43.6)
8	99.7	97.9	(45.4)
9	101.8	100.9	(46.3)
10	103.8	103.9	(46.2)
15	114.7	120.8	(28.6)
20	126.8	140.3	19.6
30	154.9	189.4	251.0
40	189.2	255.6	745.9

Transferring resources from consumption to investment lowers current consumption but raises future consumption. The example assumes that income in year 0 is 100 and that consumption of 85 percent of national income is possible with a 2 percent growth rate. It is further assumed that to achieve a 3 percent growth rate, consumption must fall to 77 percent of income. A shift from column 1 to column 2 decreases consumption for ten years but increases it thereafter. The cumulative effect on consumption is shown in column 3; the gains eventually become very large.

The process of innovation that is central to economic growth renders some machines obsolete and also leaves some people partly obsolete.

No matter how well trained workers are at age 25, in another 25 years many will find that their skills are at least partly obsolete. A rapid growth rate usually requires rapid adjustments, which can cause much upset and misery to the people who are affected by it.

It is often argued that costs of this kind are a small price to pay for the great benefits that growth can bring. Even if this is true in the aggregate, these personal costs are borne very unevenly. Indeed, many of the people for whom growth is most costly (in terms of lost jobs) share least in the fruits that growth brings.

ESTABLISHED THEORIES OF ECONOMIC GROWTH

In this section, we study some of the established theories that seek to explain economic growth. These ideas have been around for many years and form the basis of the way most economists think about economic growth. In the next section we examine some of the newer theories of growth. That such new theories exist (and continue to be produced every year) reveals that economists view the subject of economic growth as an exciting topic of economic research. Ideas are changing rapidly as both theoretical and empirical research expands our knowledge of the growth process.

To help you keep these various theories of growth clear in your own mind, we begin with a simple taxonomy of the fundamental determinants of growth.

We know that output is produced by combining the services of various factors of production such as labour, capital, and land. Furthermore, we know that the current state of our knowledge—or technology—limits our ability to get more and more output from a given set of factors of production. It follows, therefore, that we can account for growth in output (GDP) by increases in the *amount* of available factors of production, increases in the *quality* of the available factors of production, or increases in the state of *technology* which determines how much output we are able to get from a given set of factors of production.

The four fundamental determinants of growth of total output are:

1. *Growth in the labour force.* This may be caused by growth in population or by increases in the fraction of the population that chooses to participate in the labour force.

2. *Growth in human capital.* Human capital is the term economists use to refer to the set of skills that workers have. Thus human capital can increase either through formal education or on-the-job experience.

3. *Growth in physical capital.* The stock of physical capital (such as factories, machines, transportation and communications facilities) increases only through the process of investment.

4. *Technological improvement.* This may be brought about by innovation that introduces new products, new ways of producing existing products, and new forms of business organization.

The various theories of economic growth that we explore in the remainder of this section can be viewed as theories of these different sources of growth. For example, some theories emphasize the role of increases in labour and physical capital in explaining growth; others emphasize the role of increases in human capital; still others emphasize the importance of technological improvements.

Before turning to explore these different theories of economic growth, however, we have one last thing to do. In Chapters 23 and 24 we encountered the idea that an increase in desired saving would actually lead to a *reduction* in equilibrium income. Yet here we seem to be suggesting that an increase in saving (which finances an increase in investment) is one of the important determinants for *increasing* output. So before we go on to examine the different theories of economic growth, we must first understand the relationship between saving, investment, and economic growth.

SAVING, INVESTMENT, AND GROWTH

Both saving and investment affect the level and rate of growth of real national income. To understand their influence, it is critical to distinguish between their short-run and long-run effects.

Short-Run and Long-Run Effects of Investment

The theory of income determination that we studied in Chapters 23 through 26 is a short-run theory. It takes potential income as constant and concentrates on the effects of shifts in aggregate demand brought about by changes in various types of desired expenditure, including investment. These shifts cause actual national income to fluctuate around a given potential income. This short-term viewpoint is the focus of Figure 33-1(i).

In the long run, by adding to the nation's capital stock, investment raises potential income. This effect is shown by the continuing shift of the *LRAS* curve in Figure 33-1(iii).

The theory of economic growth is a long-run theory. It concentrates on the effects of investment in raising potential national income and ignores short-run fluctuations of actual national income around potential income.

The contrast between the short- and long-run aspects of investment is worth emphasizing. In the short run, any activity that puts income into people's hands will raise aggregate demand. Thus the short-run effect on national income is the same whether a firm spends by hiring workers to dig holes (and then hires more workers to refill them) or it spends by building a new factory. But the long-run growth of potential income is affected only by the part of spending that *adds to a nation's productive capacity*—by the new factory but not by the refilled hole.

Similar observations hold for government purchases of goods and services. Any increase in purchases will add to aggregate demand and raise national income if there are unemployed resources, but only some expenditures increase *potential* income. Although public investment expenditure on such things as roads and health may increase potential national income, expenditure that shores up a declining industry in order to create employment may have an adverse effect on growth of potential income. The latter expenditure may prevent the reallocation of resources in response to shifts both in the pattern of world demand and in the country's comparative advantage. Thus in the long run, the country's capacity to produce commodities that are demanded on world markets may be diminished.

Short-Run and Long-Run Effects of Saving

As we saw in Chapters 23 and 24, the short-run effect of an increase in saving is to reduce aggregate demand. If households or governments elect to save more, they must (by definition) decide to spend less. The resulting downward shift in the aggregate expenditure function lowers aggregate demand and thus lowers equilibrium national income.

Over the longer term, however, higher national saving is necessary for higher investment. Firms usually reinvest their own saving, and the saving of households passes to firms, either directly through the purchase of stocks and bonds or indirectly through financial intermediaries. In the long run, the higher the level of national saving, the higher the level of investment—and, due to the accumulation of more and better capital equipment, the higher the level of investment, the higher the level of real income.

In the long run, there is no paradox of thrift; societies with high rates of national saving have high investment rates and, other things being equal, high growth rates of real income.

Notice that the discussion refers to national saving: what the government saves or dissaves plus what the private sector saves. The amount of national saving available for private-sector investment is equal to private saving plus the government's budget surplus (or minus the government's budget deficit):

National Saving	=	Private Saving	+	Government Budget Surplus

This expression tells us that if the government's total expenditures exceed its tax revenues (and thus it has a budget deficit), it diminishes the flow of saving available to finance private investment. In contrast, if the government's total expenditures are less than its tax revenues (and thus it has a budget surplus), it adds to the flow of national saving.

Saving and Growth in Industrialized Countries

We said above that countries with high rates of national saving are also countries with high rates of investment and thus high rates of real GDP growth. To provide evidence in support of this claim, Figure 33-2 shows data from the G7 countries (Japan, Germany, France, Italy, Canada, the United States, and the United Kingdom) from the decades of the 1960s, 1970s, and 1980s. Each point in the figure corresponds to a country-decade combination; each shows the annual average national saving rate (as a percentage of GDP) for that country-decade plotted against the annual average growth rate in real per capita GDP. What is clear from the figure is a strong positive relationship between national saving rates and growth rates, exactly as suggested by our discussion above.

NEOCLASSICAL GROWTH THEORY

Recall the four fundamental sources of economic growth that we discussed at the beginning of this section. Much of what is referred to as *neoclassical*

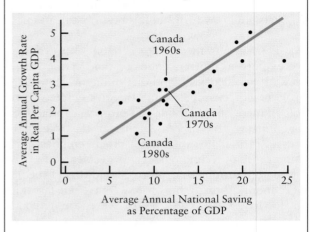

FIGURE 33-2
Cross-Country National Saving and Growth Rates

There is a strong positive relationship between a country's national saving rate (as a percentage of GDP) and its growth rate of real per capita GDP. Each point represents a country-decade combination. For each of the G7 countries, the annual averages for national saving rates and per capita growth rates are computed for the decades of the 1960s, 1970s, and 1980s. The line shows the "line of best fit" between the growth rates and the saving rates. Countries with high saving rates tend to be countries with high investment rates and thus high rates of economic growth.

(*Source:* Jose De Gregario, International Monetary Fund, Working Paper #93–31.)

growth theory is based on the idea that these four forces of economic growth can be connected by what is called the **aggregate production function**. This is an expression for the relation between the total amounts of labour (*L*) and physical capital (*K*) employed, the quality of labour's human capital (*H*), the state of technology (*T*), and the nation's total level of output (GDP). The aggregate production function can be expressed as:

$$GDP = F_T (L, K, H)$$

It is an *aggregate* production function because it relates the economy's *total* output to the *total* amount of the factors that are used to produce that output.[2]

---

[2]Natural resources (including land, forests, mineral deposits, etc.) are also important inputs to the production process. We leave them out of this discussion only for simplicity.

TABLE 33-3
Diminishing Returns Illustrated

(1) Units of Fixed Factor	(2) Units of Variable Factor (Labour)	(3) Units of Total Output	(4) Average Product of Labour (3/2)	(5) Marginal Product of Labour $\Delta 3/\Delta 2$
9	1	12.0	12.0	
9	2	17.0	8.5	5.0
9	3	20.8	6.9	3.8
9	4	24.0	6.0	3.2
9	5	26.8	5.4	2.8
9	6	29.4	4.9	2.6
9	7	31.9	4.6	2.5
9	8	34.0	4.2	2.1
9	9	36.0	4.0	2.0
9	10	37.9	3.8	1.9

With one input held constant, the marginal and average products of the variable input eventually decline. Column 3 shows total output as more and more of the variable factor is used in combination with a fixed quantity of a fixed factor. **[43]** The average product, which is total product divided by the number of units of the variable factor (labour), declines continuously. The marginal product, which is the increase in total product as successive units of the variable factor are added, also declines continuously.

(Those who have studied microeconomics will recall that a micro production function, such as is discussed in Chapters 8 and 9, relates the output of *one firm* to the factors of production employed by *that firm.*)

The production function above—indicated by F_T—tells us how much GDP will be produced for given amounts of labour and physical capital employed, given levels of human capital, and a given state of technology. Using the notation F_T is a simple way of indicating that the function relating L, K and H to GDP depends on the state of technology. For a given state of technology, changes in either L, K or H will lead to changes in GDP. Similarly, for given values of L, K and H, changes in T will lead to changes in GDP. **[42]**

When discussing economic growth, we focus on the changes in potential output and ignore short-term fluctuations of output around potential. Hence GDP in the aggregate production function can be interpreted as potential income.

Early neoclassical growth theory dealt with economic growth when technological knowledge remained unchanged. There were no innovations: no new ways of making things and no new products. As a result, the relation between inputs and output, as shown by the aggregate production func-

tion, did not change. Since T was assumed to be constant, the aggregate production function could simply be written as

$$GDP = F(L, K, H)$$

indicating that growth in GDP was due only to changes in labour, physical capital, or human capital. The key aspects of what is called the neoclassical model are that the aggregate production function displays *diminishing returns* when either factor is increased on its own and *constant returns* when all factors are increased together (and in the same proportion).

To understand these important concepts, suppose that the population of the country grows while the stock of capital remains constant.[3] More and more people go to work using a fixed quantity of capital. The amount that each new unit of input adds to total output is called its *marginal product*. The operation of the **law of diminishing returns** tells us that the employment of equal additional amounts of labour will eventually add less to total output than the previous unit. In other words, each additional unit of labour will sooner or later produce a dimin-

---

[3]For this discussion, we combine physical capital and human capital together so that we can think of a single factor called "capital."

ishing marginal product. This famous relation is referred to as *diminishing returns to a single factor,* and it is illustrated in Table 33-3 and Figure 33-3.

The law of diminishing returns applies to any factor that is varied while the other factors are held constant. Hence successive amounts of capital added to a *fixed supply of labour* will also eventually add less and less to GDP.

According to the law of diminishing returns, the increment to total production will eventually fall steadily whenever equal increases of a variable factor of production are combined with another factor of production whose quantity is fixed.

The other main property of the neoclassical aggregate production function is called **constant returns to scale.** This says that if the amounts of labour and capital are both changed in equal proportion, total output will also change in that proportion. For example, 10 percent increases in the amounts of both

labour and capital used will lead to a 10 percent increase in GDP.

Sources of Growth in the Neoclassical Model

Now consider each of the sources of growth on the list at the beginning of this section. To begin, we let each source operate with the others held constant.

Labour-Force Growth. Over the long term, we can associate labour-force growth with population growth (although in the short term, the labour force can grow if participation rates rise even though the population remains constant). As more labour is used, there will be more output produced. The law of diminishing returns tells us that sooner or later, each further unit of labour to be employed will cause smaller and smaller additions to GDP. Eventually, not only will the marginal product of labour be falling, but the average product will fall as well. Beyond that point, although economic growth continues in the sense that total output is growing, living standards are falling in the sense that average GDP *per head of population* is falling. If we are interested in growth in living standards, we are concerned with increasing real GDP *per person.*

In the neoclassical growth model, whenever diminishing average returns applies, increases in population on their own are accompanied by increasing GDP but falling living standards.

Growth in Human Capital. Capital often means physical capital, the plants and equipment that embody current technological knowledge. Another kind of capital is also of great importance to the growth process. This is **human capital,** the knowledge and skills embodied in people.

Human capital has several aspects. One involves improvements in the health and longevity of the population. Of course, these are desired as ends in themselves, but they also have consequences for both the size and the productivity of the labour force. There is no doubt that improvements in the health of workers have increased productivity per worker-hour by cutting down on illness, accidents, and absenteeism.

A second aspect of the quality of human capital concerns technical training—from learning to operate a machine to learning how to be a scientist. This training depends on the current state of knowledge, and advances in knowledge allow us not only to build more productive physical capital but also to create

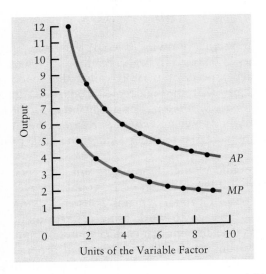

FIGURE 33-3
**The Average and Marginal Products
of a Variable Factor**

The average and marginal products of any variable factor decline as successive units of that factor are added to a fixed amount of another factor. This figure shows marginal and average products of a variable factor declining as more and more units of the factor are used. It plots the data from columns 4 and 5 from Table 33-3.

more effective human capital. Training is clearly required if a person is to operate, repair, manage, or invent complex machines. More subtly, there may be general social advantages to an educated population. Productivity improves with literacy. The longer a person has been educated, the more adaptable, and hence the more productive in the long run, that person is in the face of new and changing challenges.

A third aspect of human capital is its contribution to growth and innovation. Not only can current human capital embody in people the best current technological knowledge, but by training potential innovators, it leads to advances in our knowledge and thus contributes to growth.

Growth in Physical Capital. Increases in the amount of capital on their own affect GDP in a manner similar to population growth alone. Eventually, each successive unit of capital will add less to total output than each previous unit of capital.

There is, however, a major contrast with the case of labour-force growth because it is output *per person* that determines living standards, not output per unit of capital. So as capital increases, living standards increase because output is rising while the population is constant. Indeed, per capita output can be increased by adding more capital to a constant labour force as long as its marginal product *exceeds zero*. However, because the increases in capital are subject to diminishing returns, successive additions to the economy's capital stock bring smaller and smaller increases in per capita output.

In the neoclassical model, the operation of diminishing returns means that capital accumulation on its own brings smaller and smaller increases in real per capita GDP.

Balanced Growth with Constant Technology. Now consider what happens if labour and capital (and human capital) grow at the same rate. In this case, the neoclassical assumption of constant returns to scale means that GDP grows in proportion to the increases in inputs. As a result, per capita output (GDP/L) remains constant. Thus growth in labour and capital leads to growth in total GDP but unchanged per capita GDP.

This "balanced growth path" is not, however, the kind of growth that concerns people interested in explaining rising living standards. Since increases in living standards are determined largely by increases in

per capita output, it is clear that this balanced growth path is unable to explain rising living standards.

In this constant-technology neoclassical model, the only way for growth to add to living standards—that is, the only way to have increases in per capita GDP—is for the *per capita* capital stock to increase. That is, the capital stock must be growing faster than the labour force. More capital *per person* will increase the marginal product of labour and allow increases in per capita output. However, the law of diminishing returns dictates that the rise in per capita output brought about by successive equal increases in the per capita capital stock will inexorably diminish. This means that raising living standards becomes more and more difficult as capital accumulation continues.

Balanced Growth with Changing Technology. We have been discussing growth with technology held constant, and we concluded in such a model that balanced growth was not consistent with increases in living standards. But if we now allow technology to change in a specific way, we can change that result. Balanced growth in per capita output is possible in the neoclassical model if technological change is *labour augmenting*. This is technological change that increases the marginal product of labour by more than it increases the marginal product of other factors.

As an example, suppose that technological change is increasing labour productivity by 3 percent per year (and not increasing the productivity of other factors at all). Instead of having more labour due to population growth, we now have the same number of workers but each worker is more productive. If we were to measure the labour force in terms of *efficiency units* (how much each worker can produce), the *effective* labour force would be growing at 3 percent per year. If the capital stock is also growing at 3 percent per year, then balanced growth is possible. The property of constant returns to scale means that total output will be increasing at 3 percent per year. But since the actual number of workers is constant, then per capita output—and thus the standard of living—is increasing.

Measured Technological Change

New knowledge and inventions can contribute markedly to the growth of potential national income, even without net capital accumulation. To illustrate this point, suppose that the proportion of a society's resources devoted to the production of capital goods is just sufficient to replace capital as it wears out. If the old capital is merely replaced in the same form, the capital stock will be constant, and there will be no increase in the capacity to produce. However, if there is a growth of knowledge so that as old equipment wears out, it is replaced by different and more productive equipment, national income will be growing.

Increases in productive capacity that are created by installing new and better capital goods are called technical changes that are *embodied* in capital goods. The historical importance of this type of **embodied technical change** is clear: The assembly line and automation transformed most manufacturing industries, the airplane revolutionized transportation, and electronic devices now dominate the information-technology industries. These innovations, plus less well known but no less profound ones—for example, improvements in the strength of metals, the productivity of seeds, and the techniques for recovering basic raw materials from the ground—create new investment opportunities.

Less obvious but nonetheless important are technical changes that are embodied in *human* capital. These are changes that result from a better-educated, more experienced labour force; better management practices and techniques; improved design, marketing, and organization of business activities; and feedback from user experience leading to product improvement.

Changes in national income that cannot be accounted for by changes in the quantities of physical and human capital and in the size of the labour force are attributed to changes in what is called *total factor productivity (TFP)*. It stands for increases in output that cannot be accounted for by any of the sources cited. Although it is sometimes associated with technological change, it does not measure all of such change because much of it shows up as embodied in new physical and human capital.

Many—perhaps most—innovations are embodied in either physical or human capital. These innovations cause continual changes in the techniques of production and in the nature of what is produced. Looking back over the past century, firms produce very few products today in the same way that they did in the past, and much of what is produced and consumed is in the form of new or vastly improved products. Major innovations of the twentieth century include the development of such key products as the telephone, radio, television, the automobile, the airplane, plastics, CD players, refrigerators, washing machines, coaxial cable, xerography, the electron microscope, the telecommunications satellite, the computer, the transistor, and the silicon chip. It is hard for us to imagine life without them.

The modern understanding that technological innovation is at the heart of the growth process has led to two important developments in many economists' views on growth. The first is that technological change is largely endogenous to the economic system. The second is that investment that increases the capital stock may encounter increasing rather than diminishing returns. These insights have led to new growth theories that go far beyond the neoclassical growth model.

Different Types of Growth

The foregoing discussion suggests that a country can experience growth in two quite different ways. First, if the country experiences rapid labour-force growth and high rates of accumulation of either human or physical capital, then that country can experience a high growth rate of real per capita GDP *even in the absence of technological improvements.* Second, a country could have only modest rates of growth of labour and capital, but still have high growth rates of real per capita GDP *so long as it experiences high rates of technological improvement.* The first hypothetical country experiences growth largely by increasing the amount of factor inputs; the second experiences growth largely through technological change.

Are these two different types of growth equivalent, or is there an important difference between them? The answer is that in terms of *living standards,* the second form of growth is better because the technological improvements mean that more output is possible without increasing the amount of inputs. In contrast, the first type of growth is only occurring because of an increase in factor inputs, and it is important to keep in mind that there are opportunity costs associated with increasing the amount of labour and capital used in production. For example, individuals that are employed in producing output are not able to enjoy their leisure. Also, as we said earlier, the stock of physical capital can only be increased by foregoing current consumption.

FURTHER SOURCES OF GROWTH

So far we have looked at increases in labour and capital and at innovation as stimulators of growth. Contemporary studies suggest that other sources of growth are also important. The effects of these others appear as shifts in the aggregate production function, so that any given number of hours of labour operating with a given amount of capital produce more and more output as time passes.

Institutions

Almost all aspects of a country's institutions can foster or deter the efficient use of a society's natural and human resources. Social and religious habits, legal institutions, and traditional patterns of national and international trade are all important. So, too, is the political climate.

Some historians of economic growth attribute much of the growth of western economies in the postmedieval world to the development of *new institutions*, such as the joint-stock company and the limited-liability corporation. Many students of modern growth suggest that institutions are as important today as they were in the past. They suggest that the societies that are most successful in developing the new institutions that are needed in today's knowledge-intensive world of globalized competition will be the ones at the forefront of economic growth.

The Role of Government

Governments can play an important role in the growth process.

First, the government needs to provide the framework for the market economy. This framework includes such things as well-defined property rights providing protection from arbitrary confiscation, the security and enforcement of contracts, law and order, a sound currency, and the basic rights of individuals to locate, sell, and invest where and as they please.

Second, governments need to provide *infrastructure*. For example, transportation and communications networks are critical to growth in the modern globalized economy. Some of the facilities, such as roads, bridges, and harbours, are usually provided directly by governments. Others, such as telecommunications, rail, and air services, can be provided by private firms, but government regulations and competition policy may be needed to prevent the emergence of growth-inhibiting monopolies in these areas.

Education and health are important forms of public expenditure. Creating human capital is essential to creating a high standard of living. This requires general education, trade schools, and other appropriate institutions for formal education as well as policies to encourage firms to provide the appropriate amount of on-the-job training.

Finally, emphasis can be placed on poverty reduction because poverty can exert powerful antigrowth effects. People in poverty will not develop the skills needed to join a productive labour force, and they may not even respond to incentives that are provided. Malnutrition in early childhood can affect a person's capacities for life. Thus policies that reduce poverty may lead to higher rates of economic growth.

RECENT THEORIES OF ECONOMIC GROWTH

In the neoclassical model, innovation alters the relationship between the amount of output producible from a given level of factor inputs. But this innovation is itself unexplained (it is assumed to be measured by the amount of growth that cannot be accounted for by anything else). This view holds that technological change is *exogenous*. It has profound effects on economic variables, such as GDP, but it is not itself influenced by economic causes. It just happens.

ENDOGENOUS TECHNOLOGICAL CHANGE

Yet research by many scholars in recent decades has established that technological change is responsive to such economic signals as prices and profits; in other words, it is *endogenous* to the economic system. Though much of the earliest work on this issue was done in Europe, the most influential overall single study was by an American, Nathan Rosenberg, whose trailblazing book *Inside the Black Box* argued this case in great detail.[4]

Technological change stems from research and development and from innovating activities that

---

[4]Nathan Rosenberg, *Inside the Black Box: Technology and Economics* (Cambridge: Cambridge University Press, 1982).

put the results of R&D into practice. These are costly and highly risky activities, undertaken largely by firms and usually in pursuit of profit. It is not surprising, therefore, that these activities respond to economic incentives. If the price of some particular input such as petroleum or skilled labour goes up, R&D and innovating activities will be directed to altering the production function to economize on these inputs. This process is not a substitution of less expensive inputs for more expensive ones within the confines of known technologies; rather, it is the development of new technologies in response to changes in relative prices. Rosenberg shows, first, that R&D designed to apply known basic principles is responsive to economic signals and, second, that *basic research* is itself responsive. One reason for the latter is that the basic research agenda is strongly influenced by practical issues of the day. For example, basic research in solid-state physics became popular, and was heavily funded, only after the development of the transistor.

There are many important implications of this new understanding that, to a great extent, growth is achieved through costly, risky, innovative activity that occurs to a significant extent in response to economic signals. We now discuss some of these implications.

The Complexity of the Innovation Process

The pioneering theorist of innovation, Joseph Schumpeter (1883–1950), developed a model in which innovation flowed in one direction, from a pure discovery "upstream" to more applied R&D, then to working machines, and finally to output "downstream."

In contrast, modern research shows that innovation involves a large amount of "learning by doing" at all of its stages.[5] What is learned downstream then modifies what must be done upstream. The best innovation-managing systems encourage feedback from the more applied steps to the purer researchers and from users to designers.

This interaction is illustrated, for example, by the differences between the Japanese automobile manufacturers and their North American competitors in the handling of new models. North American design has traditionally been centralized: Design production teams develop the overall design and then instruct their production sections what to do, as well as asking for bids from parts manufacturers to produce according to specified blueprints. As a result, defects in the original design are often not discovered until production is under way, causing many costly delays and rejection of parts already supplied. Japanese firms involve their design and production departments and their parts manufacturers in all stages of the design process. Parts manufacturers are not given specific blueprints for production; instead, they are given general specifications and asked to develop their own detailed designs. As they do so, they learn. They then feed information about the problems they are encountering back to the main designers while the general outlines of the new model are not yet finalized. As a result, compared to North American car firms, the Japanese usually design a new product faster, at less cost, and with far fewer problems when production is finally begun.[6]

The Location of Innovation

Innovation typically takes place in different parts of the producer-user chain in different industries—as shown, for example, by the research of Eric von Hippel of MIT. In some industries, manufacturers make most of the product innovations. In other industries, users make most of them. In yet others, the innovating is done by those who supply components or materials to the manufacturer.

Unless these differences are appreciated, public policy designed to encourage innovation can go seriously astray. Von Hippel provides an example:

> Consider the current concern of U.S. policymakers that the products of U.S. semiconductor process equipment firms are falling behind the leading edge. The conventional assessment of

---

[5]This phenomenon, whereby costs per unit of output fall steadily over time as firms learn how to manage new technologies, is discussed in more detail in Chapter 35.

[6]A detailed account of this issue can be found in J. Womack, D. Jones, and D. Roos, *The Machine That Changed the World* (New York: Ransom Associates, 1990). North American firms have recently begun to adopt some of these Japanese practices.

this problem is that these firms should somehow be strengthened and helped to innovate so that U.S. semiconductor equipment users (makers of semiconductors) will not also fall behind. But investigation shows that most process equipment innovations in this field are, in fact, developed by equipment *users*. Therefore, the causality is probably reversed: U.S. equipment builders are falling behind because the U.S. user community they deal with is falling behind. If this is so, the policy prescription should change: Perhaps U.S. equipment builders can best be helped by helping U.S. equipment users to innovate at the leading edge once more.[7]

The message for economists and policymakers is important: An understanding of the details of the innovating process in each industry is needed if successful innovation-encouraging policies are to be developed.

Costly Diffusion

The *diffusion* of technological knowledge from those who have it to those who want it is not costless (as it was assumed to be in Schumpeter's model). Firms need research capacity just to adopt the technologies developed by others. Some of the knowledge needed to use a new technology can be learned only through experience by plant managers, technicians, and operators. We often tend to think that once a production process is developed, it can easily be copied by others. Indeed, some advanced economic theories use the hypothesis of replication, which holds that any known process can be replicated in any new location by using the same factor inputs and management as are used in the old location. In practice, however, the diffusion of new technological knowledge is not so simple.

For example, some economists argue that most industrial technologies require technology-specific organizational skills that cannot be "embodied" in the machines themselves, instruction books, or blueprints. The needed knowledge is *tacit* in the sense that it cannot be taught through books and can only be acquired by experience—much like driving a car or flying an airplane. Acquiring tacit knowledge requires a deliberate process of building up new skills, work practices, knowledge, and experience.

The fact that diffusion is a costly, risky, and time-consuming business explains why new technologies take considerable time to diffuse, first through the economy of the originating country and then through the rest of the world. If diffusion were simple and virtually costless, the puzzle would be why technological knowledge and best industrial practices did not diffuse very quickly. As it is, decades can pass before a new technological process is diffused everywhere that it could be employed.

Market Structure and Innovation

Because it is highly risky, innovation is encouraged by a strongly competitive environment and discouraged by monopoly practices. Competition among three or four large firms often produces much innovation, but a single firm, especially if it serves a secure home market protected by trade barriers, seems much less inclined to innovate.[8] The reduction in trade barriers over the past several decades and the increasing globalization of markets as a result of falling transportation and communication costs have increased international competition. Whereas one firm in a national market might have had substantial monopoly power three or four decades ago, today it is more likely to be in intense competition with firms based in other countries.

Government interventions that are designed to encourage innovation often allow the firms in an industry to work together as one. Unless great care is exercised and unless sufficient foreign competition exists, the result may be a national monopoly that

---

[7]Eric von Hippel, *The Sources of Innovation* (New York: Oxford University Press, 1988), pp. 9–10.

[8]Although the ideas of Joseph Schumpeter lie behind much of modern growth theory, this emphasis on competition seems on the surface to conflict with his ideas. The apparent conflict arises because the theories available to Schumpeter in his time offered only two market structures, perfect competition and monopoly. He chose monopoly as the structure more conducive to growth on the grounds that monopoly profits would be the incentive to innovate, and innovation itself would provide the mechanism whereby new entrants could compete with established monopolies. (He called this latter process "creative destruction.") Modern economists, facing a richer variety of theoretical market structures, find that competition among oligopolists is usually more conducive to growth-enhancing technological change than is monopoly.

will discourage risk taking rather than encourage it, as is the intention of the policy.

The United Kingdom provides many examples of this mistaken view of policy. For example, British policy in the 1960s

> . . . operated under the faulty theory that encouraging British companies to merge would create world-class competitors. Consolidation of steel, automobiles, machine tools, and computers all led to notable failures. A program of research support for industry . . . proved disastrous. The British government tried to choose promising technologies and gave direct grants to firms to develop them. Most of the choices were failures. . . . [In contrast,] unusually low levels of regulation in some service industries have avoided disadvantages faced by other nations and allowed innovation and change . . . in auctioneering, . . . trading and insurance. British firms in these industries have been among the most innovative in the world.[9]

Shocks and Innovation

One interesting consequence of endogenous technical change is that shocks that would be unambiguously adverse to an economy operating with fixed technology can sometimes provide a spur to innovation that proves a blessing in disguise. A sharp rise in the price of one input can raise costs and lower the value of output per person for some time. But it may lead to a wave of innovations that reduce the need for this expensive input and, as a side effect, greatly raise the productivity of labour.

Sometimes individual firms will respond differently to the same economic signal. Sometimes those that respond by altering technology will do better than those that concentrate their efforts on substituting within the confines of known technology. For example, in *The Competitive Advantage of Nations,* Michael Porter tells the story of the consumer electronics industry, in which U.S. firms moved their operations abroad to avoid high, rigid labour costs. They continued to use their existing technology and went where labour costs were low enough to make that technology pay. Their Japanese competitors, however, stayed at home. They innovated away most of their labour costs and then

built factories in the United States to replace the factories of U.S. firms that had gone abroad!

Innovation as a Competitive Strategy

Managing innovation better than one's competitors is one of the most important objectives of modern firms that wish to survive. Firms often fail because they do not keep up with their competitors in the race to develop new and improved products and techniques of production and distribution. Success in competition often depends more on success in managing innovation than on success in adopting the right pricing policies or in making the right capacity decisions from already known technological possibilities.

THEORIES BASED ON INCREASING RETURNS

We saw earlier that neoclassical theories assume that investment is always subject to diminishing returns. New growth theories emphasize the possibility of *historical increasing returns to investment:* As investment in some new area, product, power source, or production technology proceeds through time, each new increment of investment is more productive than previous increments. A number of sources of increasing returns have been noted. These fall under the two general categories of *fixed costs* and *knowledge.*

Fixed Costs

There are three reasons why there may be an important fixed-cost component to the amount of investment undertaken in an industry or region.

1. Investment in the early stages of development of a country, province, or town may create new skills and attitudes in the workforce that are then available to all subsequent firms, whose costs are therefore lower than those encountered by the initial firms. (For those who have studied microeconomics, the early firms are conferring a positive externality on those who follow them, as described in Chapter 18.)

2. Each new firm may find the environment more and more favourable to its investment because of

---

[9]Michael Porter, *The Competitive Advantage of Nations* (New York: Free Press, 1990), p. 507.

the infrastructure that has been created by those who came before.

3. The first investment in a new product will encounter countless problems both of production and of product acceptance among customers that, once overcome, cause fewer problems to subsequent investors.

All of these cases, and many more that could be mentioned, are examples of a single phenomenon:

Many investments require fixed costs, the advantages of which are then available to subsequent firms; hence the investment costs for "followers" can be substantially less than the investment costs for "pioneers."

More generally, many of the sources of increasing returns are variations on the following general theme: Doing something really new is difficult, both technically and in terms of customer acceptance, whereas making further variations on an accepted and developed new idea becomes progressively easier.

We have already seen one reason for this rule: The costly knowledge developed by early pioneers often becomes available to followers at a much lower cost. A second reason concerns customers. When a new product is developed, customers will often resist adopting it, both because they may be conservative and because they know that new products usually have teething troubles. Customers also need time to learn how best to use the new product—they need to do what is called "learning by using." The first firms in the field with a truly new idea, such as personal computers, usually meet strong customer resistance, but this resistance erodes over time.

Slow acceptance of new products by customers is not necessarily irrational. When a sophisticated new product comes on the market, no one is sure if it will be a success, and the first customers to buy it take the risk that the product may subsequently turn out to be a failure. They also incur the costs of learning how to use it effectively. Many potential users take the not unreasonable attitude of letting others try a new product, following only after the product's success has been demonstrated. This makes the early stages of innovation especially costly and risky.

These points lead to the following overall result:

For many reasons, successive increments of investment associated with a new set of innovations often yield a range of increasing returns as costs that are incurred in earlier investment expenditure provide publicly available knowledge and experience and as customer attitudes and abilities become more receptive to new products.

The implications of these ideas have been the subject of intense study ever since they were first embedded in modern growth models by Paul Romer of the University of California and Maurice Scott of Oxford University.[10] Probably the most important contrast between these new theories and the neoclassical theory concerns investment and income. In the neoclassical model, diminishing returns to capital implies a limit to the possible increase of per capita GDP. In the new models, investment alone can hold a constant population on a "sustained growth path" in which per capita GDP increases without limit, provided that the investment embodies the results of continual advances in technological knowledge.

Knowledge

An even more fundamental change in the new growth theories is the shift from the economics of goods to the economics of *ideas*. Physical goods, such as factories and machines, exist in one place at one time. The nature of this existence has two consequences. First, when physical goods are used by someone, they cannot be used by someone else. Second, if a given labour force is provided with more and more physical objects to use in production, sooner or later diminishing returns will be encountered.

Ideas have different characteristics. First, once someone develops ideas, they are available for use by everyone simultaneously. Ideas can be used by one person without reducing their use by others. For example, if one firm uses a truck, another firm cannot use it at the same time; but one firm's use of a revolutionary design for a new suspension on a truck does not prevent other firms from using that design as well. Ideas are not subject to the same use restrictions as goods.[11]

---

[10]As with so many innovations, these new views have many historical antecedents, including a classic article in the 1960s by Nobel Prize winner Kenneth Arrow of Stanford University.

[11]For those that have studied microeconomics, knowledge has many aspects that make it a *public good*, as we discussed in Chapter 18.

Second, ideas are not necessarily subject to decreasing returns. As our knowledge increases, each increment of new knowledge does not inevitably add less to our productive ability than each previous increment. A year spent improving the operation of semiconductors may be more productive than a year spent improving the operation of vacuum tubes (the technology used before semiconductors).

The evidence from modern research is that new technologies are usually *absolutely factor-saving*—in other words, they use less of all inputs per unit of output. Furthermore, there is no evidence that from decade to decade the factor saving associated with increments of new knowledge is diminishing.

Modern growth theories stress the importance of ideas in producing what can be called knowledge-driven growth. New knowledge provides the input that allows investment to produce increasing rather than diminishing returns. Because there are no practical limits to human knowledge, there need be no immediate boundaries to finding new ways to produce more output using less of all inputs.

Neoclassical growth theories gave economics the name "the dismal science" by emphasizing diminishing returns under conditions of given technology. The modern growth theories are more optimistic because they emphasize the unlimited potential of knowledge-driven technological change to economize on all resource inputs and because they display constant or increasing returns to investment with constant population.

Insofar as these new ideas are correct, however, they refer to long-term trends. The dynamics of market systems cause growth rates to vary from decade to decade for reasons that are not fully understood. Over the long run, however, there seems no reason to believe that equal increments of human effort must inevitably be rewarded by ever-diminishing increments to material output.

ARE THERE LIMITS TO GROWTH?

Many opponents of growth argue that sustained world growth is undesirable; some argue that it is impossible. A bumper sticker reads, "Economic growth is a cancer on society." Of course, all terrestrial things have an ultimate limit. Astronomers predict that the solar system itself will die when the sun burns out in another 5 billion or so years. To be of practical concern, a limit must be within our planning horizon.

RESOURCE EXHAUSTION

The years since World War II have seen a rapid acceleration in the consumption of the world's resources, particularly fossil fuels and basic minerals. World population has increased from under 2.5 billion to nearly 6 billion in that period; this increase alone has intensified the demand for the world's resources. Furthermore, the single fact of population growth greatly understates the pressure on resources. As economic development spreads to more and more countries, living standards are rising, in some cases at a rapid rate. As people attain higher incomes, they consume more resources. So not only are there more people in the world, but many of those people are consuming increasing quantities of resources.

The technology and resources available in the mid 1990s could not possibly support the world's population at a standard of living equal to that of the average European family. For example, the annual consumption of oil would increase more than 10-fold. It is evident that resources and our present capacity to cope with pollution and environmental degradation are insufficient to accomplish this rise in living standards with present technology.

Most economists, however, agree that absolute limits to growth, based on the assumptions of constant technology and fixed resources, are not relevant. As modern growth theory stresses, technology changes continually, as do stocks of resources. For example, 40 years ago, few would have thought that the world could produce enough food to feed its present population of nearly 6 billion people, let alone the 10 billion at which the population is projected to stabilize sometime in the twenty-first century. Yet this task now seems feasible.

There will never be full protection from the vagaries of nature or from willful or ignorant mismanagement. However, in the mid 1990s, the developed world struggles not with a food shortage but with a food glut. A mere 3 percent of European, U.S., and Canadian labour applied to limited farmland with modern technology is producing more food than the world markets can consume. The problem in the mid 1990s is how to reduce subsidized production, not how to produce more. Although globally there is enough food for everyone, severe problems arise when primarily agricultural economies suffer drought and other natural disasters or wars and other humanly contrived disasters. The problem, then, is not to produce more food worldwide but to be sure that it is available where it is needed.

It is possible that 50 years from now, the global energy problem will be as much a thing of the past as the global food shortage problem is today. Technology could by then have produced a cheap, nonpolluting energy source (possibly based on solar energy or nuclear fusion). This is not likely to happen, however, until existing supplies of petroleum become scarce enough to force its price up well above present levels—high enough to provide strong incentives to spend major amounts on R&D related to alternative energy sources.

Furthermore, research into technological change shows that the typical innovation in production processes uses less of all inputs per unit of output. Thus technological change is part of the solution, not part of the problem. The problem is too many people aspiring to levels of consumption that cannot be sustained with *existing technologies.*

The future is always uncertain, and it is instructive to recall how many things that we accept as commonplace today would have seemed miraculous a mere 25 years ago.

Yet there is surely cause for concern. Although many barriers can be overcome by technological advances, such achievements are not instantaneous and are certainly not automatic. There is a critical problem of timing: How soon can we discover and put into practice the knowledge required to solve the problems that are made ever more imminent by the growth in the population, the affluence of the rich nations, and the aspirations of the billions who now live in poverty?

There is no guarantee that a whole generation will not be caught in transition between technologies, with enormous social and political consequences. One positive outgrowth of concern over environmental issues is the recent attention given to the concept of sustainable development, discussed further in Application 33-3.

RENEWABLE RESOURCES

One possible limitation to growth relates to renewable resources. The demands placed on them threaten to destroy their natural recuperative cycle. Throughout history, for example, fishermen were a small part of the predatory process. Now the demands of nearly 6 billion people have made fish a scarce resource, threatening to destroy the fish-generating capacity of many oceans.[12]

POLLUTION

A further problem is how to cope with pollution. Air, water, and soil are polluted by a variety of natural activities, and for billions of years the environment has coped with these. The earth's natural processes had little trouble coping with the pollution generated by its 1 billion inhabitants in 1800. But the nearly 6 billion people who now exist put demands on pollution abatement systems that threaten to become unsustainable. Smoke, sewage, chemical waste, hydrocarbon emissions, spent nuclear fuel, and a host of other pollutants threaten to overwhelm the earth's natural regenerative processes.

Conscious management of pollution and renewable resources was unnecessary when the world's population was 1 billion people, but such management has become a pressing matter of survival now that nearly 6 billion people are seeking to live in the same space and off the same resources.

CONCLUSION

The world faces many problems. Starvation and poverty are the common lot of citizens in many countries and are not unknown even in countries such as Canada and the United States, where average living standards are very high. Growth has raised the average citizens of advanced countries from poverty to plenty in the course of two centuries—a short time in terms of human history. Further growth is needed if people in less-developed countries are to escape material poverty, and further growth would help ad-

---

[12]For those who studied microeconomics, we discuss the problem of overfishing as an instance of overuse of common property resources in Chapter 18.

APPLICATION 33-3

THE BRUNDTLAND COMMISSION AND "SUSTAINABLE DEVELOPMENT"

In 1983, the United Nations created the World Commission on Environment and Development (called the Brundtland Commission after its chairman, Gro Harlem Brundtland) to examine global environmental and development problems and design solutions. In its 1987 report, *Our Common Future,* the commission outlined a broad agenda for integrating economic development and environmental policy. It stressed the view that economic growth and environmental protection are interdependent: Growth cannot long continue at the present rate of environmental degradation.

The report introduced the concept of *sustainable development,* defined as "development that meets the needs of the present without compromising the ability of future generations to meet their own needs." Robert Solow, who received the Nobel Price in 1987 for his work on economic growth, has recently proposed a somewhat more precise definition of sustainability: ". . . a sustainable path for the national economy is one that allows every generation the option of being as well off as its predecessors."* Clearly, natural resources and environmental quality are important to achieving sustainability.

*Robert Solow, "An Almost Practical Step Toward Sustainability," *Resources for the Future,* Washington, D.C., October 8, 1992.

The idea that economic growth is limited by "nature" is not new. In the early 1970s, a group called "the Club of Rome" focused on the limits to growth arising from the supply of natural resources: It extrapolated from the shortages in oil, caused by the formation of OPEC and the attendant price increases, that industrialized countries faced an imminent absolute limit to growth. This prediction was refuted by experience as higher prices for fuel led to increases in both total supply and the efficiency with which it has been used.

The bounds to growth envisioned by the Brundtland Commission are not absolute but rather a function of the present state of technology and the capacity of the biosphere to absorb the effects of human activity. The environment imposes limits to the growth that can occur with any specific technology because it is the fundamental capital on which economic development is based. As technology and economic organization improve, the stream of wealth that flows from this stock of "environmental capital" can continue to increase. The concept of sustainable development stresses the role of the environment as capital that, if exhausted, cannot be replaced.

Regardless of whether an institution is a government agency, a small firm, or a transnational corporation,

vanced countries to deal with many of their pressing economic problems.

Rising population and rising per capita consumption, however, put pressure on the world's natural ecosystems, especially through the many forms of pollution. Further growth must be sustainable growth, which must in turn be based on knowledge-driven technological change. Past experience suggests that new technologies will use less of all resources per unit of output. But if they are dramatically to reduce the demands placed on the

earth's ecosystems, price and policy incentives will be needed to direct technological change in more "environmentally friendly" ways. Just as present technologies are much less polluting than the technologies of 100 years ago, the technologies of the twenty-first century must be made much less polluting than today's.

There is no guarantee that the world will solve the problems of sustainable growth, but there is nothing in modern growth theory and existing evidence to suggest that such an achievement is impossible.

the Brundtland Commission's message applies: All institutions that affect the environmental base of the economy must respect the needs of future generations.

According to the commission, governments need to expand their role in the collection and dissemination of information and, where possible, should produce an annual account of the nation's environment and resource base "to complement the traditional annual fiscal budget and economic development plans." The idea is that the environment is part of our capital, and when we degrade it, we reduce our ability to generate real income in the future, as occurs when a machine used for producing consumer goods depreciates.

Some of the Brundtland Commission's recommendations require increased government involvement in economies in order to produce and enforce environmental regulations. Although it recognizes the value of economic incentives in generating the cost reductions that flow from more efficient use of resources, the commission also feels that there are limits to the ability of competitive industry to reduce waste voluntarily: "Regulations imposing uniform performance standards are essential to ensure that industry makes the investments necessary to reduce pollution and waste and to enable [firms] to compete on an even footing."

In other cases, what is required is *less* government intervention, and the report calls on governments to examine whether existing policies and subsidies contribute to resource-efficient practices. For example, agricultural policies that protect farmers in the European Union and other industrialized countries are criticized for being "studded with contradictions that encourage the degradation of the agricultural resource base and, in the long run, do more harm than good to the agricultural industry." The solution lies in "reducing incentives that force overproduction and noncompetitive production in the developed market economies and enhancing those that encourage food production in developing countries."

Recommendations are made for reforming international organizations, in which an "extensive institutional capacity exists that could be redirected toward sustainable development." The efficacy of existing institutions is reduced by their "fragmented" nature and a "weakness of coordination." Key to these reforms is the requirement that sustainable development be made central to the mandate of all international bodies such as UN agencies, the International Monetary Fund, and the World Bank.

Our Common Future is a hopeful document, but its hope is tempered with the realization that unless major conservation initiatives are acted on quickly, the current serious rate of environmental degradation will soon start to harm the health and welfare of all of us.

SUMMARY

A. THE NATURE OF ECONOMIC GROWTH

- Real national income can be increased on a once-and-for-all basis from the demand side by removing recessionary gaps and from the supply side by reducing structural impediments and economic inefficiencies. Sustained increases, however, are due mainly to economic growth, which continuously pushes the *LRAS* curve outward, thereby increasing potential income.

- Growth is frequently measured by using rates of change of potential real national income per person or per hour of labour employed. The cumulative effects of even small differences in growth rates become very large over periods of a decade or more.

B. BENEFITS AND COSTS OF ECONOMIC GROWTH

- The most important benefit of growth lies in its contribution to the long-run struggle to raise living standards and to escape poverty. Growth also facilitates the redistribution of income among people.
- Growth, though often beneficial, is never costless. The opportunity cost of growth is the diversion of resources from current consumption to capital formation. For individuals who are left behind in a rapidly changing world, the costs are higher and more personal.

C. ESTABLISHED THEORIES OF ECONOMIC GROWTH

- Investment has short-term effects on national income through aggregate demand and long-term effects through growth in potential national income. Saving reduces consumption and aggregate demand and therefore reduces national income in the short run, but in the long run, saving finances the investment that leads to growth in potential income.
- Countries with high rates of national saving are also countries with high rates of investment and thus high rates of real per capita GDP growth.
- The neoclassical theory of growth displays diminishing returns when one factor is increased on its own and constant returns when all factors are increased together. In a balanced growth path, the quantity of labour, the quantity of capital, and per capita national income all increase at a constant rate.
- Changes in per capita output that cannot be accounted for by changes in the levels of physical and human capital and in the size of the labour force are attributed to changes in what is called total factor productivity (TFP). Although it is sometimes associated with technological change, TFP does not measure all of such change because much of it shows up as embodied in new physical and human capital.

- In the neoclassical growth model, technological change is assumed to be exogenous—unaffected by the size of the labour force or the size of the capital stock.

D. RECENT THEORIES OF ECONOMIC GROWTH

- Recent growth theory treats technological change as an endogenous variable that responds to market signals. The diffusion of technology is also endogenous. It is costly and often proceeds at a relatively slow pace.
- Some modern growth theories display constant or increasing returns as investment increases on its own. This investment confers externalities such that successive increments of investment may add constant or even successively increasing amounts to total output.

E. ARE THERE LIMITS TO GROWTH?

- The critical importance of increasing knowledge and new technology to the goal of sustaining growth is highlighted by the great drain on existing natural resources that has resulted from the explosive growth of population and output in recent decades. Without continuing technological change, the present needs and aspirations of the world's population cannot come anywhere close to being met.
- Rising population and rising real incomes place pressure on resources. Although not all resources will be exhausted, particular resources, such as petroleum, will be. Furthermore, resources that renewed themselves without help from humans when the world's population was 1 billion people can easily be exhausted unless they are consciously conserved as the world's population approaches 6 billion.
- This enormous increase in population has similar effects on pollution: The earth's environment could cope naturally with much of human pollution 200 years ago, but the present population is so large that pollution has outstripped nature's coping mechanisms.

KEY CONCEPTS

The cumulative nature of growth
Benefits and costs of growth
Short-run and long-run effects of investment and saving
The aggregate production function

Diminishing returns and constant returns
Balanced growth
Total factor productivity
Endogenous technical change

Increasing returns to investment
The economics of goods and of ideas
Resource depletion and pollution

DISCUSSION QUESTIONS

1. Economic growth is often studied in macroeconomic terms, but in a market economy, who makes the decisions that lead to growth? What kinds of decisions and what kinds of actions cause growth to occur? How might a detailed study of individual markets be relevant to understanding economic growth?

2. Discuss the following quote from a newspaper article that appeared in the summer of 1989: "Economics and the environment are not strange bedfellows. Environment-oriented tourism is one creative way to resolve the conflict between our desire for a higher standard of living and the realization that nature cannot absorb everything we throw at it. The growing demand for eco-tourism has placed a premium on the remaining rain forests, undisturbed flora and fauna, and endangered species of the world."

3. Use a UN publication to discover the per capita GDP in the world today. If growth were stopped in every country, could output be redistributed to raise living standards in the poorer countries to levels near those currently enjoyed in the developed countries? Would a massive redistribution of income among nations be politically and economically feasible?

4. The Overseas Development Council recently introduced "a new measure of economic development based on the physical quality of life." Its index, called PQLI, gives one-third weight to each of the following indicators: literacy, life expectancy, and infant mortality. Although certain countries, such as the United States and Canada, rank high on both the PQLI and on an index of per capita real national income, some relatively poor countries, such as Sri Lanka, rank much higher on the PQLI index than much richer countries such as Algeria and Kuwait. Discuss the merits or deficiencies of this measure.

5. "The case for economic growth is that it gives man greater control over his environment, and consequently increases his freedom." Explain why you agree or disagree with this statement by Nobel laureate W. Arthur Lewis.

6. Consider a developed economy that decides to achieve a zero rate of growth for the future. What implications would such a "stationary state" have for the processes of production and consumption and for human inventive activity?

7. Suppose that solar energy becomes the dominant form of energy in the twenty-first century. What effects will this have on the growth rates of Africa and Northern Europe?

8. Discuss the following newspaper headlines in terms of the sources, costs, and benefits of growth.

   a. "Stress addiction: 'Life in the fast lane' may have its benefits"
   b. "Education: An expert urges multiple reforms"
   c. "Industrial radiation risk higher than previously thought"
   d. "Developments in the field of management design are looking ahead"
   e. "Ford urged by federal safety officials to recall several hundred thousand of its front-wheel-drive vehicles because of alleged fire hazards"

9. Dr. David Suzuki, an opponent of further economic growth, has argued that despite the fact that "in the twentieth century the list of scientific and technological achievements has been absolutely dazzling, the costs of such progress are so large that negative economic growth may be right for the future." Policies to achieve this include "rigorous reduction of waste, a questioning and distrustful attitude toward technological progress, and braking demands on the globe's resources." Identify some of the benefits and costs of economic growth, and evaluate Suzuki's position. What government policies would be needed to achieve his ends?

10. Nonrenewable resources such as oil, coal, and other minerals are in finite supply. If we continue to use these for the production of current goods and services, are we jeopardizing the standard of living for some future generation? Why or why not?

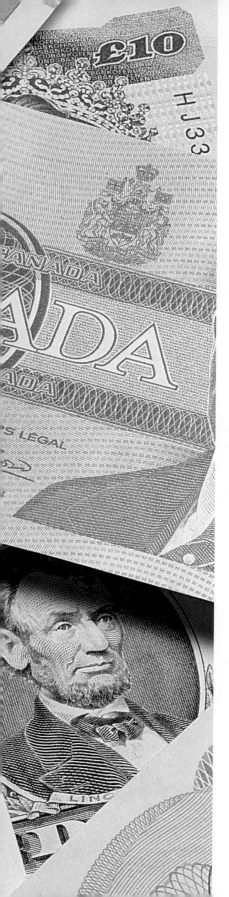

CHAPTER 34

GROWTH IN THE DEVELOPING COUNTRIES

In the comfortable urban life of today's developed countries, most people have lost sight of the fact that a short time ago—very short in terms of the life span of the earth—people were nomadic food gatherers, garnering an existence as best they could from what nature threw their way. It has been only about 10,000 years since the Neolithic agricultural revolution, when people changed from food gatherers to food producers. Throughout most of subsequent human history, civilizations have been based on a comfortable life for a privileged minority and unremitting toil for the vast majority. Only within the past two centuries have ordinary people become able to expect leisure and high consumption standards—and then only in the world's economically developed countries.

THE UNEVEN PATTERN OF DEVELOPMENT

Close to 6 billion people are alive today, but the wealthy parts of the world—where people work no more than 40 or 50 hours per week, enjoy substantial leisure, and have a level of consumption at or above *half* that attained by Canadians—contain no more than 20 percent of the world's population. Many of the rest struggle for subsistence. Many exist on a level at or below that endured by peasants in ancient Egypt or Babylon.

The richest countries with the highest per capita incomes are referred to by the United Nations as **developed countries.** These include the United States, Canada, most of the countries of Western Europe, South Africa, Australia, New Zealand, Japan, and a few others. The poorer states are referred to by the UN as the **developing countries** and include a diverse set of nations. (The developing countries are also sometimes referred to as the *underdeveloped* or *less developed* countries.) Some, such as Vietnam, Argentina, and China, are growing very rapidly, while others, such as Ethiopia and Papua New Guinea are actually experiencing negative growth rates of real per capita income. Between these two is another group of nations, called the **newly industrialized countries (NICs).** They include South Korea, Singapore, Taiwan, and Hong Kong. These countries have grown rapidly and typically have per capita incomes close to 50 percent of those found in the developed nations. Several other countries in Southeast Asia are close behind the NICs. These include Indonesia, Malaysia, and Thailand.

Seeing the problem of raising per capita income in a poorer country as one of economic development recognizes that the whole structure of its economy often needs to be altered to create economic growth. This is a complex task; many countries remain undeveloped today despite decades of effort by their governments to get them on a path of sustained growth.

Data on per capita incomes throughout the world (as shown in Table 34-1) cannot be accurate down to the last $100 because there are many problems in comparing national incomes across countries. For example, homegrown food is vitally important to living standards in developing countries, but it is excluded from or at best imperfectly included in the national income statistics of most countries. In Norway, significant amounts of GDP go to heating houses during cold winters. Such heating is not necessary in countries that have warm climates. Nevertheless, the data reflect enormous real differences in living standards that no statistical inaccuracies can hide. The *development gap*—the discrepancy between the standards of living in countries at either end of the distribution—is real and large.

Figure 34-1 provides another way of looking at inequality. It shows the geographical distribution of per capita income. The map reveals why modern political discussions of income distribution often use

TABLE 34-1
Income and Population Differences Among Groups of Countries, 1993

GNP Per Capita (US$)	(1) Number of Countries	(2) GNP (US$ millions)	(3) Population (millions)	(4) GNP Per Capita (US$)	(5) Percentage of World Population	(6) Percentage of World GNP
Less than $695	59	1,165,000	3,094	380	56.0	4.8
$696 to $2,785	69	1,635,000	1,099	1,490	19.9	6.7
$2,786 to $8,625	42	2,153,000	498	4,320	9.0	8.9
$8,625 or more	39	19,304,000	834	23,150	15.1	79.6
World	209	24,257,000	5,525	4,390	100.0	100.0

The unequal distribution of world income is shown in columns 5 and 6. The poorest half of the world's population earns less than 5 percent of world income. The richest 15 percent earns nearly 80 percent of world income.
(Source: World Bank Atlas 1995.)

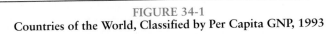

FIGURE 34-1
Countries of the World, Classified by Per Capita GNP, 1993

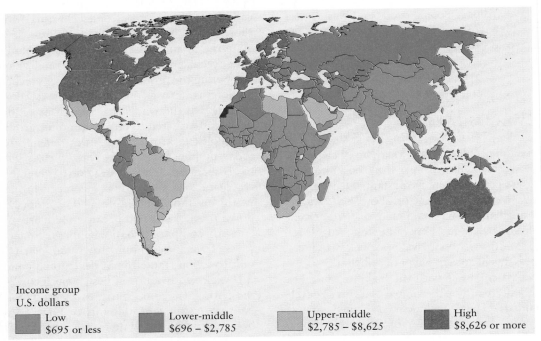

Income group
U.S. dollars

Low	Lower-middle	Upper-middle	High
$695 or less	$696 – $2,785	$2,785 – $8,625	$8,626 or more

There is a sharp geographical division between "North" and "South" in the level of income per capita. The nations of the world are classified here according to four levels of measured per capita GNP. The poorest group, shown in blue, represents 56 percent of the world's population. The wealthiest group, shown in red, includes North America, Europe, and Japan and represents only 5 percent of the world's population.

the labels *North* and *South* to refer to the rich and the poor nations, respectively.

The consequences of low income levels can be severe. In rich countries like Canada and the United States, variations in rainfall are reflected in farm output and farm income. In poor countries, variations in rainfall are often reflected in the death rate. In these countries, many people live so close to a subsistence level that slight fluctuations in the food supply bring death by starvation to large numbers. Other, less dramatic characteristics of poverty include inadequate diet, poor health, short life expectancy, and illiteracy.

For these reasons, reformers in developing countries feel a sense of urgency not felt by their counterparts in rich countries. Yet, as Table 34-2 shows, some of the poorest countries in the world are among those with very low or negative growth rates of per capita GDP, with the following consequence:

The development gap has been widening for the very poorest countries.

As we shall see, this is a problem of both output and population. It is also an international political problem. What are the causes of underdevelopment, and how may they be overcome?

IMPEDIMENTS TO ECONOMIC DEVELOPMENT

Per capita income grows when aggregate income grows faster than population. Many forces can impede such growth. Here we study a number of possible impediments.

INADEQUATE OR INEFFICIENTLY USED RESOURCES

A country's supply of natural resources is important. A country with infertile land and inadequate supplies

TABLE 34-2
The Relationship Between the Level and the Rate of Growth of Per Capita Income, 1985–1993

Growth of GNP Per Capita, 1980–1989 (% per year)	Number of Countries[a]	GNP (US$ million) 1993	Population (millions) 1993	GNP Per Capita (US$) 1993
Less than 0	63	1,862,000	995	870
0 to 0.9	24	1,757,000	328	5,362
1.0 to 1.9	30	12,803,000	1,048	12,220
2.0 to 2.9	16	890,000	112	7,950
3.0 or more	31	6,711,000	2,853	2,350

The very poorest countries spend much of their increase in income on a rising population. Hence their increase in income per capita is less than half that of the countries that are already richer. The gap in income between rich and many of the very poor countries is not closing.

[a]Countries with more than 1 million population.

(Source: World Bank Atlas 1995.)

of natural resources will find growth in income more difficult to achieve than one that is richly endowed with such resources.

How these resources are managed also matters. When farmland is divided into many small parcels, it may be much more difficult to achieve the advantages of modern agricultural techniques than when the land is available in huge tracts for large-scale farming. Fragmented land holdings may result from a dowry or inheritance system or may be politically imposed. One of the populist policies following the Mexican Revolution early in the twentieth century was the redistribution of land from large landowners to ordinary peasants. Today, however, fragmented land ownership prevents Mexican agriculture from producing at costs low enough to compete in international markets. The Mexican government now faces an agonizing choice between allowing its populist land reforms to be reversed or continuing to protect a large agricultural sector whose inefficiency is increasing relative to competing suppliers.

Although abundant supplies of natural resources can assist growth, they are neither sufficient to ensure growth nor necessary for it. Some countries with large supplies of natural resources have poor growth performance because the economic structure encourages waste. Prime examples are the former Soviet Union, Argentina before the 1990s, and Uganda. In contrast, other countries have enjoyed rapid rates of economic growth based on human capital and entrepreneurial ability despite a dearth of natural resources. Prime examples are Switzerland in earlier centuries, Japan over the past 100 years, and Singapore, Hong Kong, and Taiwan since the end of World War II.

When one discusses inefficiency in resource use, it helps to distinguish between two kinds of economic inefficiency, which are studied in microeconomics. *Allocative inefficiency* occurs when factors of production are used to make an inefficient combination of goods. There is too many of some goods and too few of others. This means that the society is at the wrong point on its production possibility boundary. If resources are reallocated to produce less of some and more of other types of goods, some people can be made better off while no one is made worse off.

Productive inefficiency occurs when factors of production are used in inefficient combinations. Given the prices of capital and labour, some production processes use too much capital relative to labour, while others use too little. This means that the society is inside its production possibility boundary. If factor combinations are altered, more of all goods can be produced.

Monopolistic market structures, as well as taxes, tariffs, and subsidies, are some important sources of the distortions that lead to both allocative and productive inefficiencies.

INEFFICIENT AGRICULTURE

A developing country whose labour force is mainly devoted to agriculture has little choice but to accept this basic allocation of resources. It can build up its industrial sector, and if its efforts are successful, the proportion of the population devoted to urban pursuits will rise. But the change will come slowly, leaving a large portion of the country's resources in rural pursuits for a long time to come.

It follows that policies to help the agriculture sector raise productivity are an important part of the development strategy in any agriculture-based poor country. These can fill the dual purposes of raising incomes of rural workers and reducing the cost of food for urban workers.

A developing country's government may choose to devote a major portion of its resources to stimulating agricultural production, say, by mechanizing farms, irrigating land, using new seeds and fertilizers, and promoting agricultural research and development. Modern developments of new crops and new growing techniques put a premium on agricultural research and development (R&D) so that a country can adopt, and usually adapt, other country's agricultural innovations. Also, nonfood agricultural and forest products are becoming increasingly important, and R&D expenditures are often needed if these are to become established products. If successful, the country will stave off starvation for its current population, and it may even develop an excess over current needs and so have a crop available for export. A food surplus can earn foreign exchange to buy needed imports.

In the past several decades, India, Pakistan, Taiwan, and other Asian countries have achieved dramatic increases in food production through the application of new technologies and the use of new seed in agricultural production. This has been referred to as the *green revolution.*

The gains from this strategy, while large at first, are subject to diminishing returns. Further gains in agricultural production have an ever-higher opportunity cost, measured in terms of the resources needed to irrigate land and to mechanize production. Critics of reliance on agricultural output argue that newly developing economies must start at once to develop other bases for economic growth.

Many developing countries (as well as many developed ones) suffer from misguided government intervention in the agriculture sector. In India, for example, the government—motivated by a desire to *diversify* agricultural production by increasing the number of crops under cultivation—has encouraged crops such as oilseeds and sugarcane, in which India has a comparative *dis*advantage, and discouraged crops such as rice, wheat, and cotton, in which India has a strong comparative advantage. It has subsidized food prices, thus giving large benefits to the urban population. About 8 percent of all Indian government spending is on subsidies that go to fertilizers, farmers' debt payments, and urban food consumption.

RAPID POPULATION GROWTH

Population growth is one of the central problems of economic development. For example, in the decade from 1982 to 1992, Ecuador and Papua New Guinea had population growth rates of 2.1 and 1.9 percent per year alongside GDP growth rates of 0.4 and 1.5 percent, respectively. Hence they experienced *negative* growth rates of *per capita* GDP (of −1.7 and −0.4 percent per year). Many developing countries have rates of population growth that are nearly as large as their rates of GDP growth. As a result, their standards of living are barely higher than they were 100 years ago. They have made appreciable gains in aggregate income, but most of the gains have been literally eaten up by the increasing population.

The critical importance of population growth to living standards was perceived early in the nineteenth century by Thomas Malthus (1766–1834). He asserted two relations concerning rates of increase. First, food production tends to increase in an *arithmetic* progression (e.g., 100, 103, 106, 109, 112, where the increments in this example are 3 *units* per period). Second, population tends to increase in a *geometric* progression (e.g., 100, 103, 106.09, 109.27, 112.55, where the increase in this example is 3 *percent* per period). Consequently, Malthus argued that under conditions of natural growth, population will always tend to outrun the growth in food supply. The difference in our example may not seem like much after only five periods. But after 20 periods, the arithmetic progression in food supply has increased it to 160, whereas the geometric progression in the population has increased it to 181.

Malthus's prediction helped to earn economics the sobriquet "the dismal science." And in some poor areas of the world, the predictions ring all too true, even today. Where agricultural methods are fairly traditional so that food production increases only slowly, population tends to increase at more rapid rates. The result is subsistence living, with population held in check by low life expectancies and periodic famines.

Fortunately, over most of the world, Malthus's predictions have been proved false. Two reasons are paramount. First, Malthus underestimated the importance of technological change, which has increased agricultural productivity at a *geometric* rate in many countries, a rate far higher than the rate at which the demand for food has been growing in most advanced countries. Second, he underestimated the extent of voluntary restrictions of population growth due both to the widespread use of birth control techniques and other changes in behaviour such as delayed marriages. As a result, population has grown more slowly than the production of food (and most other things) in developed countries. In these places, living standards have been rising rather than falling.

For the more advanced industrialized countries, Malthusian pressures are not a problem today. For many poor countries, where people subsist on what they grow for themselves, the tendency for the growth in population to outstrip the growth in the food supply makes Malthusian pressures a current threat.

Figure 34-2 illustrates actual and projected world population. By now, the population problem is almost completely limited to developing countries. About 97 percent of the expected growth in the world's population between now and 2050 will be in the developing countries of Africa, Asia, and Latin America.

INADEQUATE HUMAN RESOURCES

Numbers of people matter, and so do their training and experience. A well-developed entrepreneurial class, motivated and trained to organize resources for efficient production, is often missing in poor countries. The cause may be that managerial positions are awarded on the basis of family status or political patronage rather than merit, it may be the prevalence of economic or cultural attitudes that do not favour acquisition of wealth by organizing productive activities, or it may simply be an absence of the quantity or quality of education or training that is required.

In today's world, much production is knowledge-intensive. This puts a premium on a well-educated workforce. The ability to read, do basic calculations, operate electronic equipment, and follow relatively complex instructions are important requirements for much modern labour. Failure to develop such essential labour skills can be an important cause of lack of growth.

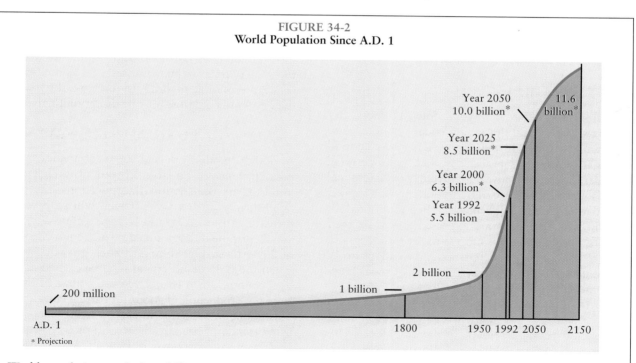

FIGURE 34-2
World Population Since A.D. 1

World population reached 5.5 billion in 1992 and is projected to rise to 10 billion by the middle of the next century. The population of industrialized countries has nearly stabilized. But in developing countries, population is skyrocketing. Up to 97 percent of population growth between now and 2050 will occur in developing countries. By that time, total world population will have reached 10 billion. Birth and death rates among present populations allow estimates to be made up to about the middle of the next century with reasonable accuracy. The projection to 11.6 billion by 2150 is much more conjectural and highly uncertain.

(Source: United Nations Population Fund.)

Poor health is another source of inadequate human resources. When the labour force is healthy, less working time is lost, and more effective effort is expended.

INADEQUATE PROPERTY RIGHTS

Secure property rights are necessary if individuals and firms are to be willing to make long-term investments. Uncertainties about ownership and individuals' rights and obligations make long-term investment especially risky. For example, a firm may buy a piece of land and build a factory on it and then, three years down the line, find that the person who sold the land did not have secure title to it or that the company is now liable for pollution caused decades before by parties unknown. Such situations, in which property rights are not secure, increase uncertainties and so reduce the expected payoff from investment. The former communist countries of Eastern Europe are currently finding that the absence of secure property rights and of limited liability protections against the past actions of others are severe disincentives to growth-inducing investment. (Recall our discussion of some of these issues in Application 3-1 in Chapter 3.)

CULTURAL BARRIERS

Traditions and habitual ways of doing business vary among societies, and not all are equally conducive to productivity. Often in developing countries, cultural forces are a source of inefficiency. Sometimes personal considerations of family, past favours, or traditional friendship or enmity are more important than market incentives in motivating behaviour. In a traditional society in which children are expected to stay in their parents' occupations, it is more difficult for the labour force to change its characteristics and to adapt to the requirements of growth than in a society in which upward mobility is itself a goal.

Structuring incentives is a widely used form of policy action in market-oriented economies. However, if people habitually bribe the tax collector rather than pay taxes, they will not be likely to respond to policies that are supposed to work by raising or lowering taxes. All that will change is the size of the bribe.

The fact that existing social, religious, or legal patterns may make growth more difficult does not in itself imply that they are undesirable. Instead, it suggests that the benefits of these patterns must be weighed against the costs, of which the limitation on growth is one. When people derive satisfaction from a religion whose beliefs inhibit growth or when they value a society in which every household owns its own land and is more nearly self-sufficient than in another society, they may be quite willing to pay a price in terms of foregone growth opportunities.

Many critics argue that development plans, particularly when imposed by economists coming from advanced countries, pay too little attention to local cultural and religious values. Even when they are successful by the test of increasing GDP, this may be at too great a cost in terms of social upheaval for the current generation.

A country that wants development must accept some alteration in traditional ways of doing things. However, a trade off between speed of development and amount of social upheaval can be made. The critics argue that such a trade off should be made by local governments and should not be imposed by outsiders who understand little of local customs and beliefs. An even more unfavourable possibility is that the social upheaval will occur without achieving even the expected benefits of GDP growth. If the development policy does not take local values into account, the local population may not respond as predicted by Western economic theories. In this case, the results of the development effort may be disappointingly small.

INADEQUATE DOMESTIC SAVINGS

Although modern development strategies call in many instances for a large infusion of foreign capital imported by transnational corporations, the rise of domestically owned firms, which will reap some of the externalities created by foreign technology, is one key to sustained development. This requires a supply of domestic savings to finance their growth.

If more domestic capital is to be created at home by a country's own efforts, resources must be diverted from the production of goods for current consumption. This implies a reduction in current living standards. If living standards are already at or near the subsistence level, such a diversion will be difficult. At best, it will be possible to reallocate only a small proportion of resources to the production of capital goods.

Such a situation is often described as the *vicious circle of poverty*: Because a country has little capital per head, it is poor; because it is poor, it can devote few resources to creating new capital rather than to producing goods for consumption; because little new capital can be produced, capital per head remains low, and the country remains poor.

The vicious circle can be made to seem an absolute constraint on growth rates. Of course, it is not; if it were, we would all still be at the level of the early agricultural civilizations. The grain of truth in the vicious-circle argument is that some surplus must be available somewhere in the society to allow saving and investment. In a poor society with an even distribution of income, in which nearly everyone is at the subsistence level, saving may be very difficult, but this is not the common experience. Usually there is at least a small middle class that can save and invest if opportunities for the profitable use of funds arise. Also, in most poor societies today, the average household is above the physical subsistence level. Even the poorest households will find that they can sacrifice some present living standards for a future gain. For example, presented with a profitable opportunity, villagers in Ghana planted cocoa plants at the turn of the century, even though there was a seven-year growing period before any return could be expected.

In developing countries, one resource that is often in abundance is labour. Profitable home or village investment that requires mainly labour inputs may be made with relatively little sacrifice in current living standards. Unfortunately, this kind of investment often does not appeal to local governments, which are too often mesmerized by large and symbolic investments, such as dams, power-generating stations, and steel mills.

INADEQUATE INFRASTRUCTURE

Key services, called **infrastructure,** such as transportation and a communications network, are necessary for efficient commerce. Roads, bridges, railways, and harbors are needed to transport people, materials, and finished goods. Phone and postal services, water supply, and sanitation are essential to economic development.

The absence of a dependable infrastructure can impose severe barriers to economic development.

Many governments feel that money spent on a new steel mill shows more impressive results than money spent on such infrastructure investments as automating the telephone system. Yet private, growth-creating entrepreneurial activity will be discouraged more by the absence of good telephone communications than by the lack of domestically produced steel.

INTERNATIONAL DEBT

The 1970s and early 1980s witnessed explosive growth in the external debt of many developing nations. Since the mid 1980s, most of these countries have experienced difficulties in making the payments required to service their debt. "Debt rescheduling"—putting off until the future payments that cannot be made today—has been common, and many observers feel that major defaults are inevitable unless ways of forgiving the debt can be found.

The trend toward increased debt started when OPEC quadrupled the world price of oil in 1973. Because many developing nations relied on imported oil, their trade balances moved sharply into deficit. At the same time, the OPEC countries developed massive trade surpluses. Commercial banks helped to recycle the deposits of their OPEC customers into loans to the developing nations. These loans financed some necessary adjustments and some worthwhile new investment projects. However, a large part of the funds were used unwisely; wasteful government spending and lavish consumption splurges occurred in many of the borrowing countries.

A doubling of energy prices in 1979 led to a further increase in the debt of developing nations. The severe world recession that began in 1981 reduced demand for the exports of many of these countries. As a result, they were unable to achieve many benefits from the adjustments and investment expenditures that they had made. Furthermore, sharp increases in real interest rates (caused in part by the widespread fight against inflation) led to increased debt-service payments; as a result, many countries could not make their payments.

The lending banks had little choice but to reschedule the debt—essentially lending the developing nations the money to make interest payments while adding to the principal of the existing loans. The International Monetary Fund (IMF) played a central role in arranging these reschedulings by making further loans and concessions conditional on appropriate policies of adjustment and restraint. These conditions were intended to limit wasteful government expenditure and consumption and thus to increase the likelihood that the loans would eventually be repaid. Critics of the IMF's role argued that much of the restraint resulted in reduced investment and hence that the IMF's conditions were counterproductive.

During the mid 1980s, the world economy recovered, inflation fell, and real interest rates fell. As a result, the developing countries' export earnings grew, their debt service obligations stabilized, and the crisis subsided. A sharp fall in the price of oil, which started in late 1985, further eased the problems of the oil-importing nations, but it also created a new debt problem.

Throughout the period of rising energy prices in the 1970s, a number of oil-exporting developing nations—including Mexico, Venezuela, and Indonesia—saw in those high prices new opportunities for investment and growth. Based on their high oil revenues, their ability to borrow improved. Their external debt grew, and they were able to avoid many of the adjustments that the oil-importing developing nations had been forced to undertake. When oil prices fell, however, these oil exporters found themselves in difficult positions. Today, although the debt is no longer rising, it remains an enormous burden on developing nations. Often the borrowed money produced little or no benefit, going either to develop industries that did not turn out to be viable or to provide graft to the ruling classes. Today, those who benefited little or not at all from the funds are saddled with the need to pay taxes to service the debt. This produces an enormous drag on further development.

DEVELOPMENT POLICIES

The past decade has seen a remarkable change in the views of appropriate policies for industrial development. The views that dominated development policies during the period from 1945 to the early 1980s have given way to a new set of views that reflect the experience of the earlier period.[1]

THE OLDER VIEW

The dominant approaches toward development strategies from 1945 to the early 1980s were inward-looking and interventionist.

The policies were inward-looking in the sense that replacing imports was the primary goal of fostering local industries. These local industries were usually protected with very high tariffs and supported by large subsidies and favourable tax treatment. The exchange rate was almost always pegged, usually at a level which overvalued the currency (that is, the exchange rate was pegged *below* its free-market value). As we will explain

in detail in Chapter 37, fixing the exchange rate below its free-market level raises the domestic currency prices of exports and lowers the prices of imports, which leads to an excess demand for foreign exchange. The argument for keeping export prices high was that foreign demand for traditional exports was inelastic so that (as we saw in Chapter 5) raising their prices would raise the amount received by their sellers. The excess demand for foreign exchange caused by the overvaluation of the currency led to a host of import restrictions and exchange controls such as import licenses and quotas issued by government officials.

Many governments were hostile to foreign investment and made it difficult for multinational firms to locate in their countries. For example, many had local ownership rules requiring that any foreign firm wanting to invest there must set up a subsidiary in which local residents would own at least half of the shares. Much new investment was undertaken by government-owned industries, while subsidization of privately owned local industries was often heavy and indiscriminate. Industrial activity was often controlled, with a license being required to set up a firm or to purchase supplies of scarce commodities. Much investment was financed by local savings, which were sometimes made voluntarily and sometimes forced by the state. One way of doing the latter was for a state marketing board to be empowered to buy all the outputs of traditional export industries (such as cocoa in Ghana) at very low prices, sell them abroad at high prices, and use the profits so generated to finance government-owned industries.

This whole set of measures is often referred to as being *inward-looking* and based on *import substitution*. Strictly, import substitution refers to the attempt to build local industries behind protectionist walls to replace imports. Often, however, the term is used more generally to refer to the entire battery of related measures just described.

These interventionist measures gave great power to government officials, and not surprisingly, corruption was rife. Bribes were needed to obtain many things, including state subsidies, licenses, and quotas. As a result, many resources were allocated to those who had the most political power and were willing to pay the highest bribes, rather than to those who could use the resources most efficiently.

Heavy subsidization of private firms and state investment in public firms required much money, and the tax structures of many poor countries could not provide sufficient funds. As a result, inflationary fi-

[1]This section draws heavily from "Globalization and Developing Countries," Main Discussion Paper for the United Nations Symposium in The Hague, March 30, 1992, report by the Rapporteur.

nancing was often used.[2] Persistent inflation was a major problem in many of these countries. Inflation was almost always in the double-digit range and quite often soared to *several hundred* percent per year.

Most of the economies where these policies were employed fell short of full central planning and full state ownership of resources. As a result, there was still some private initiative and some profit seeking through normal market means. But the overall policy thrust was interventionist and inward-looking.

THE RISE OF THE NEW VIEW

During the 1980s, four important events contributed to a reappraisal of this development model. First, developing countries that had followed these policies most faithfully had some of the poorest growth records. Second, the GDP growth rates of the more industrialized countries of Eastern Europe and the Soviet Union that had followed interventionist approaches to their own growth were visibly falling behind those of the market-based economies. Third, Taiwan, Singapore, South Korea, and Hong Kong, which had departed from the accepted model by adopting more market-based policies, were prospering and growing rapidly. Fourth, the globalization of the world's economy led to an understanding that countries could no longer play a full part in world economic growth without a substantial presence of multinational corporations within their boundaries. Given the size of developing countries, this meant the presence of foreign-owned multinationals. We now discuss each of these four events in more detail.

Experience of the Developing Countries

Highly interventionist economies fared poorly in the 1950s, 1960s, and 1970s. Economies as varied as Argentina, Myanmar (Burma), Tanzania, Ethiopia, and Ghana were all interventionist and all grew slowly, if at all. In Ethiopia, the emperor was overthrown, and the new government adopted rigid Soviet-style policies. Attempts to collectivize agriculture led, as they had 50 years previously in the Soviet Union, to widespread famine. Some countries, such as Ghana, Nigeria, and Myanmar, started from relatively strong economic positions when they first gained their independence but

later saw their GDPs and living standards shrink. Other countries, such as India and Kenya, sought a middle way between capitalism and socialism. They fared better than their more highly interventionist neighbours, but their development was still disappointingly slow.

Experience of the Socialist Countries

Earlier in this century, many observers were impressed by the apparent success of planned programs of "crash" development, of which the Soviet experience was the most remarkable and the Chinese the most recent. Not surprisingly, therefore, many of the early development policies of the poorer countries sought to copy the planning techniques that appeared to underlie these earlier socialist successes.

In recent decades, however, the more developed socialist countries began to discover the limitations of their planning techniques. Highly planned government intervention seems most successful in providing infrastructure and developing basic industries, such as electric power and steel, and in copying technologies developed in more market-oriented economies. However, it is now seen to be much less successful in providing the entrepreneurial activity, risk taking, and adaptivity to change that are key ingredients to *sustained* economic growth and technological change.

The discrediting of the Soviet approach to development was given added emphasis when the countries of Eastern Europe and the former Soviet Union abandoned their system *en masse* and took the difficult path of rapidly introducing market economies. Although China, the last major holdout, has been posting impressive growth figures, two very "nonsocialist" reasons are important in explaining its performance. First, over 90 percent of the population is engaged in basically free-market agriculture—because that sector has long been free of the central-planning apparatus that so hampered agriculture in the former Soviet Union. Second, while the state-controlled industries suffer increasing inefficiencies and absorb ever-larger proportions of the state budget in subsidies, a major investment boom is going on in China's Southeast coastal provinces. Here foreign investment, largely from Japan and the Asian NICs, is introducing a rapidly growing and highly efficient industrialized market sector.

Experience of the NICs

South Korea, Taiwan, Hong Kong, and Singapore— the so-called Asian Tigers—have turned themselves

---

[2] Under inflationary finance, the government sells newly created bonds to the central bank, which pays for them with newly created money. The increase in money supply creates inflation, as we saw in Chapter 30.

from relative poverty to relatively high income in the course of less than 40 years.

During the early stages of their development, they used import restrictions to build up local industries and to develop labour forces with the requisite skills and experiences. In the 1950s and early 1960s, however, each of the four abandoned many of the interventionist aspects of the older development model. They created market-oriented economies with less direct government intervention than other developing economies, who stuck with the accepted development model.

Korea and Singapore did not adopt a laissez faire stance. Instead, both followed quite strong policies that targeted specific areas for development and encouraged those areas with various economic incentives. In contrast, Hong Kong and Taiwan have had somewhat more laissez faire attitudes toward the direction of industrial development.

After local industries had been established, all four adopted outward-looking, market-based, export-oriented policies. This tested the success of various policies to encourage specific industries by their ability to compete in the international marketplace. With industries designed to serve a sheltered home market, it is all too easy to shelter inefficiency more or less indefinitely. With export-oriented policies *not based on subsidies*, the success of targeted firms and industries is tested in international markets, and unprofitable firms fail.

Each country has experienced great successes and some failures of policy. Taiwan was typical in demonstrating the value of the new market-oriented approach when in the period from 1956 to 1960, following the advice of the Western-trained Chinese economist S. C. Tsiang, its government abandoned most of the apparatus of the older development model and moved to market-oriented policies. Before long, the growth rate increased, and the country started on a path that has taken it from a per capita GDP of about 10 percent of that of Canada in 1955 to one of close to 50 percent in the early 1990s. Today, Taiwan has become a major foreign investor as its less skill-intensive industries migrate to mainland China and other locations in Southeast Asia. In Taiwan, wages are rising, making low-skill-intensive manufacturing uneconomical and pushing local industries to higher-value-added lines of production that can support higher wages and hence higher living standards for the workers.

Not far behind the NICs is a second generation of Asian and Latin American countries that have also adopted more market-oriented policies and have seen substantial growth follow. Indonesia, Thailand, the Philippines, Mexico, Chile, and Argentina are examples. Even Vietnam and Laos are liberalizing their economies as communist governments come to accept that a market economy is a necessary condition for sustained economic growth.

Globalization of Trade

We discussed globalization briefly in Chapter 1; you may find it useful to reread that discussion now. At the heart of globalization lies the rapid reduction in transportation costs and the revolution in information and communication technology that has characterized the past two decades. One consequence has been that the internal organization of firms, multinational or not, is changing to become less hierarchical and rigid and more decentralized and fluid. Another consequence is that the strategies of transnational corporations (TNCs), which span national borders in their organizational structures, are driving globalization and much of economic development. Because most trade, and much investment, is undertaken by TNCs, no country can develop into an integrated part of today's world economy without a substantial presence of TNCs within its borders. This is now recognized, and most aspiring developing countries generally put out a welcome mat for TNCs. Some countries, such as India, still put major obstacles in the way of foreign investment. But even in these cases, the attitudes are softening so that foreign investment is increasingly tolerated and even encouraged.

Historically, only a few countries, notably Japan and Taiwan, have industrialized without major infusions of foreign direct investment (FDI). Moreover, these cases took place before the globalization of the world's economy. It is doubtful that many (or any) of today's poor countries could achieve sustained and rapid growth paths without a substantial amount of FDI brought in by foreign-owned transnationals. Without such FDI, both the transfer of technology and foreign networking would be difficult to achieve.

Developing countries have gradually come to accept the advantages of dropping their traditional hostility to FDI. First, FDI often provides somewhat higher-paying jobs than might otherwise be available to local residents. Second, it provides investment that does not have to be financed by local savings. Third, it links the local economy into the world economy in ways that would be hard to accomplish with new firms of a purely local origin. Fourth, it provides training in worker and management skills that come from working with large firms linked into the global market. Fifth, it can provide advanced technology that is not easily transferred outside of the firms that are already familiar with its use.

Today, virtually all developing economies encourage foreign TNCs to locate within their borders. Where governments used to worry that their countries had too much FDI, they now worry that there may be too little.

ELEMENTS OF THE NEW VIEW

As a result of these various experiences, a new consensus on development policy has emerged. The revised model calls for a more outward-looking, international-trade-oriented, and market-incentive-based route to development. It calls for accepting market prices as an instrument for the allocation of resources. This means abandoning both the heavy subsidization and the pervasive regulations that characterized the older approach.

One of the most important parts of this new consensus is an acceptance of the beneficial role played by competition (in its broadest sense) as a defender of the public interest and as a stimulus to growth-creating innovation. The other side of the coin is recognition of the harmful effects of market power, whether of private firms, closed-shop union agreements, communications media, government institutions, or government-owned industries.

Another important part of the consensus is that it is more efficient to locate economic activities in the private rather than the public sector (unless there are compelling reasons for doing otherwise, as there may be with a range of "social services" such as medical and hospital care and public goods, such as infrastructure). Some of the reasons that lie behind this presumption are the incentives for efficiency when managers are responsible to owners who are risking their own wealth; the constraint provided by the need to be profitable, which acts as a rapid cutoff device when failure is evident; and the corrective for inefficiency provided by the possibility of a hostile takeover.

Another part of the new consensus concerns activities that are required of the government. Two basic classes of activity are important. First, the government needs to provide the framework for the market economy that is given by such things as well-defined property rights secure from arbitrary confiscation; security and enforcement of contracts; law and order; a sound currency; ensuring the basic rights of individuals to locate, sell, and invest where and how they wish; and the provision of infrastructure.

Second, state activity is needed to resolve conflicts of interest, to handle market failures, and to redistribute income in line with currently accepted ideas of social justice. Redistributive policies cannot be judged in isolation (nor can growth policies). Instead, they must be constantly scrutinized for their impacts on growth, and where these are significant, trade offs need to be consciously made.

The new view has many aspects, and we can detail only a few of the most important. The first concerns the changed attitude to foreign direct investment undertaken by TNCs. FDI is now understood to be capable of changing a country's comparative advantages and improving its firms' competitiveness in many ways.

The Importance of FDI

FDI provides a major source of capital. This capital tends to be allocated to areas where experienced international operators feel that the chances of success are best. The capital brings with it up-to-date technology that would be hard to develop domestically or even transfer to home-owned firms. It would be difficult to generate this capital through domestic saving, and if it were so generated, it would be difficult to import the necessary technology from abroad. The modern growth research discussed in Chapter 33 has shown that the transfer of technology to firms with no previous experience of using it is a far more difficult, risky, and expensive task than was formerly thought. Also, when capital is obtained through loans or grants from foreign governments, there is a risk that its allocation will be in the hands of administrators inexperienced in commercial activities and motivated by political concerns.

Over a long period of time, FDI creates many externalities in the form of benefits available to the whole economy that the TNCs cannot appropriate as part of their own income.

These externalities include transfers of general knowledge and of specific technologies in production and distribution, industrial upgrading, work experience on the part of the labour force, the introduction of modern management and accounting methods, the establishment of finance-related and trading networks, and the upgrading of telecommunications services. FDI in services affects the host country's absolute advantage by raising the productivity of capital and enabling host countries to attract new capital on favourable terms and by creating services that can be used as strategic inputs in the traditional export sector to expand the volume of trade and to upgrade production through product and process innovation.

In today's world, the range of products in which a country is internationally competitive appears to be affected more and more by the nature of its investment. It is difficult to compete in globalized trade without being a part of the vast, informal but powerful network of information and communications among TNCs.

By improving competitiveness through technology transfer and the effects of myriad externalities, foreign as well as domestic investment can alter the country's volume and pattern of trade in many income-enhancing directions.

The Washington Consensus

The so-called "Washington consensus" describes the conditions that, according to the newer views, are necessary for a poorer country to get itself on a path of sustained development. These views are accepted by a number of international agencies, including the World Bank, the IMF, and several UN organizations. The main elements of this consensus are as follows:

1. Government should adopt sound fiscal policies that avoid large budget deficits financed by bonds sold to the central bank, which cause rapid inflation.

2. The tax base should be broad, and marginal rates should be moderate.

3. Markets should be allowed to determine prices (including the exchange rate) and the allocation of resources. Trade liberalization is desirable, and import licensing, with its potential for corruption, should be avoided.

4. Targeted protection for specific industries and a moderate general tariff, say, 10 to 20 percent, may provide a bias toward widening the industrial base of a developing country. Such protection should be for a specified period that is not easily extended.

5. Industrial development should rely to an important extent on local firms and on attracting FDI and subjecting it to a minimum of local restrictions that discriminate between local and foreign firms. (Of course, restrictions will be required for such things as environmental policies, but these should apply to all firms, whether foreign-owned or locally owned.)

6. An export orientation (as long as exports do not rely on permanent subsidies) provides competitive incentives for the building of skills and technologies geared to world markets, permits realization of scale economies, and provides access to valuable information flows from buyers and competitors in advanced countries.

7. Education, health (especially for the disadvantaged), and infrastructure investment are desirable forms of public expenditure. Creating the appropriate factors of production is critical to creating comparative advantages in products that can be exported. This means general education, trade schools, and other appropriate institutions for formal education as well as assistance to increase on-the-job training within firms. Because future demands are hard to predict and subject to rapid change, a balance must be struck between training for specific skills and training for generalized and adaptive abilities.

8. Finally, emphasis needs to be placed on poverty reduction for at least two reasons. First, poverty can exert powerful antigrowth effects. People in poverty will not develop the skills to provide an attractive labour force, and they may not even respond to incentives when these are provided. Malnutrition in early childhood can affect a person's capacities for life. Second, although economic growth tends to reduce the incidence of poverty, it does not eliminate it.

DEBATE BEYOND THE WASHINGTON CONSENSUS

The basic Washington consensus on outward-looking, market-oriented, fiscally sound economic policies provides what many people believe are necessary conditions for a country to achieve a sustained growth path in today's world—which in most cases require that it is able to attract quite a large volume of FDI.

The policies suggested by the Washington consensus relate primarily to the behaviour of governments themselves.

Sufficient or Just Necessary?

There is substantial debate around one crucial issue: Are the conditions of the Washington consensus *suf-*

ficient to encourage the kinds and volumes of both domestic and foreign investment needed to develop comparative advantages in higher-value-added industries, or are they merely *necessary?*

Some observers believe that these conditions are sufficient. In their view, all a country needs to do is to meet these conditions. Domestic saving will finance domestic investments, FDI will flow in, and a sustained growth path will be established. Other economists worry that many countries may have only limited ability to attract FDI, to benefit from it, and to create sufficient domestic investment, even after fulfilling the necessary conditions of the Washington consensus. The latter set of economists point to the experience of some African countries where TNCs operated extractive industries that despoiled the countryside and left little permanent benefit behind them; they merely extracted the available resources and then left. Others point out that there is a major difference between pure extractive enterprises and manufacturing enterprises, the latter having more potential spillovers to the local economy than the former.

What does happen after the conditions of the consensus are fulfilled will depend in part on the existing endowments of the country in question. If large supplies of natural resources or cheap, well educated labour are available, fulfilling these conditions may be sufficient. Commentators who call for policies beyond those of the Washington consensus argue that for some countries, a past history of nongrowth, plus the absence of externalities that go with a reasonably developed industrial sector, may require that the government adopt a more active set of *integrated* trade, technology-transfer, and innovation policies. This set of policies would be aimed at encouraging the development of human and technological capabilities and building international competitiveness.

Policies that go beyond the Washington consensus are directed at the interactions between governments and the private sector, particularly as represented by TNCs.

Implications of Modern Growth Theory

What is at issue in the debate just described is related to the newer views on economic growth that were discussed in Chapter 33. The key new view is that *endogenous* technological innovation is the mainspring of economic growth. Things emphasized by economists for centuries, such as aggregate saving and investment, are still essential, but technological change is now considered to lie at the core of the growth process.

As we saw in Chapter 33, technological change is a costly process that is undertaken mainly by firms in pursuit of profit and responds to economic incentives. Research and development are by their nature risky and uncertain activities. The technological path followed by firms and industries is evolutionary in the sense that it develops as experiments and errors are made.

For developing countries, one of the most important of the many new insights stemming from research into the growth process is that adopting someone else's technology is often not a simple, cost-less task. Substantial R&D capacity is needed to adapt other people's technology to one's own purposes and to learn how to use it—except where the technology uses only very simple machines that can be operated by unskilled labour. For one reason, much of the knowledge required to use a technology is tacit; it can be obtained only from learning by doing and by using. This creates difficulties in imitating the knowledge, as well as uncertainty regarding which modifications will work in any new situation. This is true even when technology moves from one firm to another in the same industry and the same country. The problems are greater when technology moves across industrial or national borders. The difficulties of adopting new technologies also become more difficult the more complex and information-intensive the technology becomes.

It follows that all knowledge is not freely tradable. Neither a firm nor a government can go out and buy it ready-to-use. Acquiring *working* technological knowledge requires both investment (sometimes in large, indivisible lumps) and the experience that allows workers and management slowly to acquire the needed tacit knowledge.

Usable new knowledge comes to a developing country through a slow and costly diffusion process.

What May Be Needed

The foregoing view of technological change suggests to some economists a major reason why active government policies that go beyond the Washington consensus may be needed.

Protection of the Domestic Market. Such policies can work at the early stages by establishing a protected domestic market through tariffs and other import restrictions. Virtually every country that has moved to a sustained growth path in the past, including the United States, Canada, Japan, and all of the NICs, has used im-

APPLICATION 34-1

SOUTH KOREA'S DEVELOPMENT POLICY: A CASE STUDY*

In the late 1950s, South Korea seemed unable to generate adequate levels of exports and savings. Policymakers solicited foreign aid and sought to manage the flow of imports. The currency was overvalued at a fixed rate on the foreign exchange market, tariff rates were high, and quantitative import restrictions abounded. These policies, which discouraged exports and encouraged import substitution, were close to the old model of appropriate development policy discussed in the text.

The economy was dominated by agriculture and mining, and the manufacturing sector supplied only simple consumer products. Exports amounted to about 3 percent of GNP and consisted almost entirely of primary products and various minerals. Then came policy reforms that stretched over several years, starting in 1960. They centred on fostering exports from both existing and new industries.

Today, South Korea is dominated by the manufacturing sector. Major industries established since 1960 range from chemicals and electronics to automobiles and heavy electrical equipment. Exports exceed 40 percent of GNP, with manufactured products constituting over 90 percent of the total.

EXISTING INDUSTRIES

For well-established industries, the reforms ensured that production for export would be no less profitable than production for the domestic market. This was accomplished by insulating export activity from the adverse consequences of policies motivated by domestic concerns.

Capital and intermediate inputs used in export production could be imported without tariffs and were not bound by the quotas that applied to imports for other purposes. Tradable inputs were ex-

*This box is based on Larry E. Westphal, "Industrial Policy in an Export-Propelled Economy: Lessons from South Korea's Experience," *Journal of Economic Perspectives*, 4, 3, (1990): 41–60.

empt from indirect taxes. The currency was no longer overvalued.

The government enabled exporters to borrow working capital from state-owned banks in proportion to their export activity. Additional incentives were granted in the form of direct tax reductions, preferential interest rates, and privileged access to import licenses. The export incentives were administered fairly uniformly across all industries. They were granted equally to "indirect exports"—inputs produced and sold domestically that are destined to be used in export production. (This policy was a major innovation rarely found in developing nations.)

The government also used publicly announced quarterly export targets for individual commodities, markets, and firms. At a minimum, the targets have been useful in keeping the government well informed about export performance so that timely changes could be made in incentives.

These measures seem on balance to have been neutral among specific established export industries. They encouraged exports in general without the government having to pick specific winners in advance. No doubt, however, the policies encouraged producers to move to the export sector from the competing import sector, where the distortionary policies still applied.

NEW INDUSTRIES

The South Korean government has selectively intervened to promote targeted new (infant) industries, typically by supporting the creation of large-scale establishments that were accorded temporary monopolies and received access to credit on preferential terms, as well as exemptions from most taxes (including tariffs).

Protection for nonexport sales has been the dominant incentive to infant industries. Targeted industries have been protected by import controls, which enable them to practice discriminatory pricing. Export targeting requires that infant industries sell a growing proportion of their output at world prices, as either direct or indirect exports. This forces them to increase productivity rapidly.

The first producers of fertilizer, petrochemicals, and refined petroleum products were state-owned enterprises. So was the first integrated steel mill, which is generally considered to be one of the most efficient mills in the world. *New public enterprises have been expected to achieve international competitiveness quickly.* They have been managed as autonomous profit-seeking entities and have contributed to government revenues.

THE CONTRIBUTION OF INDUSTRIAL POLICY

The South Korean experience shows that industrial policy can work. Selective intervention seems to have contributed to the nation's remarkable success by accelerating the rate of growth with little if any compensating loss in efficiency. The enormous uncertainty in selecting infant industries for promotion was resolved by using information gained during implementation to evaluate intentions and by judging new industries on their ability to export (in a regime in which export promotion policies were neutral with respect to specific exports).

Viewing this apparently successful experience, an economist will naturally ask, "What South Korean market failures has selective intervention successfully overcome?"

Some economists argue that market imperfections associated with technological transfer are unimportant because developing countries face an abundant supply of available technology. But elements of technology are far from being perfectly tradable. Moreover, the tacitness of much technology creates problems in communication over long distances and across social boundaries, problems that can be overcome only at substantial cost.

1. The tacitness of much knowledge makes some elements inherently nontradable. Peculiarities in local resources, institutions, and local technological practices cannot be understood without being experienced.

2. Because of the imperfect tradability of technology, externalities related to technological development can be quite extensive. There are economies of scope in the application of many of the capabilities acquired in the course of industrialization.

3. An initial entrant's investments to master new technology may greatly reduce costs for subsequent nearby entrants. The returns to particular technological efforts may be largely inappropriable because a significant share of them derive from the application of the newly acquired element in a cascade of subsequent technological changes.

In short, if it is used appropriately, selective intervention seems able to increase a country's ability to capture dynamic economies associated with the introduction and exploitation of modern technology.

LESSONS

South Korea's industrial performance owes much to the government's reliance on free-market institutions to provide for flexibility in resource allocation. It has resulted in many highly profitable ventures that were either not foreseen or not actively promoted by the government.

But South Korea's industrial performance also owes a great deal to the government's promotional policies toward exports and to its initiatives in targeting industries for development. Selective intervention has driven the fast-paced evolution of South Korea's industrial structure by fostering vertical integration at the national level and by promoting greater diversification of end-product mix.

The belief that selective intervention has outlived its usefulness led the South Korean government to alter its policies. Selective intervention has lost the support of the South Korean public, who prefer democratic government to economically enlightened dictatorship. The trend appears to be away from selective interventions, and it remains to be seen whether South Korea's economic performance will continue to be exceptional.

port substitution in its early stages of industrialization. A protected home market provides a possible solution to the problem of coping with the enormous externalities involved in building up an infrastructure of physical and human capital as well as the required tacit knowledge and abilities. Even if all the specific infant industries that are protected by the import substitution policy do not grow into self-sufficient mature industries, the externalities may still be created and become available for a second generation of more profitable firms.

Protection of the home market from international competition can, however, pose serious problems unless it is selective and temporary. Investment may occur mainly in areas where comparative advantage never grows. High costs of protected industries may create a lack of competitiveness in other domestic industries whose inputs are the outputs of the protected industries. Some potential comparative advantages may not be exploited because of the distorting effects of existing tariffs, and—as always—consumers bear much of the cost in terms of high prices of protected outputs.

Innovation Policies. Trade restrictions do not provide the only route to building industrial and R&D capacity by encouraging technological diffusion and creating structural competitiveness. Other methods include the much-needed public investment in infrastructure and in human capital and many other things such as the provision of adequate financial schemes to favour investment in physical and intangible assets, procurement and tax incentives, provision of technical and marketing information, consulting services for assisting firms in industrial restructuring and in the adoption of new technologies and organizational techniques, support services in design, quality assurance and standards, schemes for training and retraining personnel, and facilities for start-up companies.

Advocates of such a policy package stress the importance of having these incentives as part of a more general innovation and competition policy in order to encourage technological transfer to the local economy (such transfers are riddled with market failures arising from their externalities). Linkages among firms, and between firms and universities and research institutions, both within the country and with the rest of the world, are also important.

Policies that encourage the development of small- and medium-size enterprises are important to any development strategy. These tend to be locally owned and tend to be the vehicle by which know-how and best practices are transferred from TNCs to the local economy. They are also the sector most vul-

nerable to excessive red tape, rules and regulations, profit taxes, and other interferences that raise the cost of doing business.

A Cautionary Note. There is no doubt that the governments of many poor countries have been highly interventionist—and some still are. Hence a good first strategy is often to diminish the government's place in the economy. There is no point adopting a new, relatively rational technology promotion strategy if existing government interventions are irrational and heavy. The unproductive interventions must be cleared away first. This does not mean, however, that if a government were starting from scratch, the best objective would be to minimize its place in the economy.

Whatever methods are chosen, selective intervention is a delicate instrument, highly dangerous in inept hands, and even when in practiced hands, much damage can be done.

The intervention needs to be carefully tailored to get specific results and to reduce the opportunities for small groups to gain at the expense of others. To meet these objectives, most assistance should, as a rule, be terminated after specified periods of time. It is also important to leave room for the market to generate, and support, unforeseen opportunities.

Application 34-1 provides a case study of South Korea's experience with some of the policies that go beyond the Washington consensus.

CONCLUSION

According to the World Bank's *World Development Report,* about 1.1 billion residents of the developing countries were in poverty in the year 1985. In reviewing this report, *The Economist* argued: "With luck and a lot of policy changes in rich and poor countries alike, that figure might be cut to about 800 million by the year 2000."[3] That may not seem like a large change at first sight, but it is when put into the perspective of the rapidly growing world population. The 1.1 billion that the World Bank reckoned to be in poverty in 1985 made up about one-third of the developing countries' total population. The 800 million would be only 18 percent of the estimated population of these same countries in the year 2000. The predicted change would substantially reduce the

---

[3]All calculations from *The Economist* in this section are from the July 21, 1991 issue.

probability that a person born into the developing world in 2000 would be born into poverty and condemned to a life of acute deprivation.

According to *The Economist*, the World Bank's prescriptions fall into two categories:

1. Create new economic opportunities for the poor. Because the poor's main source of income is what they are paid for their labour, this means promoting labour-intensive economic growth.

2. Equip the poor to grasp these opportunities. This calls for adequate provision of basic social services such as primary education, health, and family planning.

The World Bank also points out that one of the most damaging economic distortions in many developing countries is excessive taxation of farming. This hits the very part of the economy on which most of the poor depend for their livelihood.

The World Bank's report suggests that a major reduction in poverty is possible worldwide. What is needed is the acceptance of the new consensus on the importance of market determination and of reducing state control and state ownership of business activity. This, plus a large dose of enlightened policies to bring education, health, and jobs to ordinary people and improved technology to the nations' firms, could pay enormous dividends in reducing poverty and suffering. The next decade will show how much of that hopeful potential will be realized.

SUMMARY

A. THE UNEVEN PATTERN OF DEVELOPMENT

- About one-quarter of the world's population still exists at a level of bare subsistence, and nearly three-quarters are poor by Canadian standards. Although some poorer societies have grown rapidly, the gap between the very richest and very poorest remains large and is not decreasing.

B. IMPEDIMENTS TO ECONOMIC DEVELOPMENT

- Impediments to economic development include excessive population growth; resource limitations; inefficient use of resources; inadequate infrastructure; excessive government intervention; and institutional and cultural patterns that make economic growth difficult.

C. DEVELOPMENT POLICIES

- The older model for development policies included heavy tariff barriers and a hostility to foreign direct investment (FDI) to protect the home market for local firms; many government controls over, and subsidization of, local activities; and exchange rates pegged at excessively low values (overvalued currencies) with imports regulated by licenses.
- The newer view holds that heavy indiscriminate protection of home markets should be avoided, protection that does exist should be targeted to sectors that have a real chance of creating comparative advantage and that the protection be only for a moderate period of time so that market tests of success and failure can be allowed to op-

erate. Moreover, competition is viewed as an important spur to efficiency and innovation, quantitative controls should be avoided, and production of most goods and services should be in the private sector (except where there are strong reasons for preferring the public sector).

- Part of this new view is given in the Washington consensus, which calls for sound fiscal and monetary policies; broad-based taxes levied at moderate rates; market determination of prices and quantities; discriminating use of infant industry protection for moderate time periods; an acceptance of FDI and the presence of TNCs; active government provision of education, health care, and infrastructure; and antipoverty programs to help in human resource development and to aid citizens who are left behind by the growth process.
- An active debate turns on whether the conditions of the Washington consensus are sufficient, or just necessary, to establish a country on a sustained growth path. Analysts who regard it as sufficient feel that once unleashed, natural market forces will create sustained growth.
- Analysts who regard the conditions of the Washington consensus as necessary but not sufficient point to substantial externalities and pervasive market failures in the diffusion of technological knowledge from advanced to less advanced nations. They argue that foreign firms will not invest enough because they cannot capture in their profits many of the benefits they confer on the local economy (externalities) and that much of the technological know-how will not diffuse to local firms because such knowledge is not easy to transfer. These economists call for active government innovation policies to augment investment and to assist the transfer of technological know-how and practice to the local economy.

KEY CONCEPTS

Impediments to economic development
The vicious circle of poverty
The NICs

TNCs and FDI
The Washington consensus

Externalities and market failures in the
diffusion of technology

DISCUSSION QUESTIONS

1. In 1990, India had masses of people living at or near the poverty level. Yet surveying recent major reforms in that country, *The Economist* had this to say:

   > The experience of the 1980s showed that poverty begins falling swiftly in India when the rate of growth reaches 5%. A sustained GDP growth rate of 9% a year would free most Indians from truly grinding poverty by 2000, and make 1 billion of them middle-class by 2020. That is not impossible. India has plenty of entrepreneurs—and plenty of savings. Yet the government may lack the will to seize the chance. The government has so far shrunk from four huge challenges: reform of the labour market, of the financial system, of agriculture and of its own finances.

   a. Why can developing nations such as India hope (if they get the conditions right) for sustained growth rates as high as 8 to 9 percent while developed countries such as Canada, the United States, or Germany cannot?

   b. Which of the possible obstacles to growth discussed in this chapter does *The Economist* not seem to think important?

   c. What does *The Economist* see as the major obstacle to rapid growth in India?

   d. Given the last sentence in the quotation, can you guess what some of India's policies with respect to the labour market, the financial system, agriculture, and public debt might have been at the time of writing (May 1992)?

2. In his *Essay on the Principle of Population as it Affects the Future Improvement of Society,* first published in 1789, Thomas Malthus wrote:

   > This natural inequality of the two powers of population and of production in the earth . . . [forms] the great difficulty that to me appears insurmountable in the way to perfectibility of society. All other arguments are of slight and subordinate consideration in comparison of this. I see no way by which man can escape from the weight of this law which pervades all animated nature. No fancied equality, no agrarian revolutions in their utmost extent, could remove the pressure of it even for a single century.

   Discuss Malthus's "insurmountable difficulty" in view of the events of the past 100 years.

3. To what extent does the vicious circle of poverty apply to poor families that are living in the richest developed countries like Canada or the United States? Consider carefully, for example, the similarities and differences facing a poor family living in Vancouver and one living in Ghana, where per capita income is less than $400 per year. Did it apply to Canadian immigrants who arrived at the turn of the century with $10 in their pockets?

4. Would removing all restrictions on immigration into the advanced countries help to improve living standards in the developing nations? How might this policy change affect living standards in the advanced countries?

5. "Just about the most important thing the advanced countries could do to help the developing nations is to remove all restrictions on imports from those countries." Is this good advice from the point of view of the developing countries? Which groups in advanced countries do you think might support such advice, and which might oppose it?

6. "High coffee prices bring hope to impoverished Latin American peasants," reads the headline. Mexico, Kenya, and Burundi, among other developing countries, have the right combination of soil and climate to increase their coffee production greatly. Discuss the benefits and risks to them if they pursue coffee production as a major avenue of their development.

7. History has shown that rapid development of less developed countries is often accompanied by some measure of devastation of the country's natural resources. Can you provide some examples? Must this always be the case? How can the developed countries help to stem the devastation? Why don't they help more than they do at present?

PART ELEVEN

INTERNATIONAL ECONOMICS

Does a country always benefit from free trade? If so, why do so many people appear to believe the opposite? Can government policy influence a country's pattern of comparative advantage? What is "dumping," and who, if anyone, is hurt by it? What is "trade creation" and "trade diversion," and how does this relate to NAFTA? How is Canada's exchange rate determined? Is Canada's current account deficit a problem, or does it merely reflect strong growth domestically? How is the conduct of macroeconomic policy altered in an open economy? Does international capital mobility make monetary and fiscal policy more or less effective? Is there any connection between the government's budget deficit and the country's current account deficit? These are the sorts of questions you will be able to answer after reading the final four chapters of this book.*

Chapter 35 explores the *gains from trade,* and how these gains are based on the important concept of *comparative advantage.* You will learn the reasons why a country might have a *comparative advantage* in a particular product, and how some government policies can have the effect of changing a country's pattern of comparative advantage. You will also be introduced to a country's *terms of trade,* the relative prices at which a country trades with the rest of the world.

In Chapter 36, the focus is on *trade policy.* You will learn about the case for *free trade* as well as the case for *protectionism* (you will also encounter some common but fallacious arguments for protectionism). We then examine some *methods of protection,* such as *tariffs, quotas,* and *nontariff barriers.* The Chapter then examines current trade policy in Canada, with an obvious emphasis on the North American Free Trade Agreement.

Chapter 37 introduces you to the *exchange rate* and the *balance of payments.* You will learn about the *foreign exchange market* and about why the balance of payments *always balances.* The important distinction between *fixed exchange rates* and *flexible exchange rates* will be discussed in detail, and you will understand the kinds of events that lead to an *appreciation* or a *depreciation* of the Canadian dollar.

In Chapter 38, the emphasis is on the conduct of macroeconomic policy in an open economy. You will learn why *international capital mobility* is so important to the conduct of policy. You will also see that there is indeed a close connection between the government's budget deficit and the country's current account deficit—the so-called *twin deficits.* Finally, the chapter ends with a discussion of how exchange rates and capital mobility have entered into the past two decades of monetary policy.

---

*Chapters 37 and 38 do not appear in *Microeconomics.*

CHAPTER 35

THE GAINS FROM INTERNATIONAL TRADE

Canadian consumers buy cars from Germany, Germans take holidays in Italy, Italians buy spices from Africa, Africans import oil from Kuwait, Kuwaitis buy Japanese cameras, and the Japanese buy Canadian lumber. *International trade* refers to exchanges of goods and services that take place across international boundaries.

The founders of modern economics were concerned with foreign trade problems. The great eighteenth-century British philosopher and economist David Hume (1711–1776), one of the first to work out the theory of the price system as a control mechanism, developed his concepts mainly in terms of prices in foreign trade. Adam Smith (1723–1790) in his *Wealth of Nations* attacked government restriction of trade. David Ricardo (1772–1823) developed the basic theory of the gains from trade that is studied in this chapter. The repeal of the Corn Laws—tariffs on the importation of grains into the United Kingdom—and the transformation of that country during the nineteenth century from a country of high tariffs to one of complete free trade were to some extent the result of agitation by economists whose theories of the gains from international trade led them to condemn all tariffs.

In this chapter, we inquire into the gains to living standards that result from trade. We find that the source of the gains from trade lies in differing cost conditions among geographical regions. World income is maximized when countries specialize in the products in which they have the lowest opportunity costs of production. These costs are partly determined by natural endowments, geographical and climatic conditions, partly by public policy, and partly by historical accident. We then go on to discuss the terms on which trade takes place—which refers to the amount that must be exported to obtain a given amount of imports.

SOURCES OF THE GAINS FROM TRADE

First, we need to define a few terms. An economy that engages in international trade is called an **open economy**; one that does not is called a **closed economy.** A situation in which a country does no foreign trade is called one of **autarky.** The advantages realized as a result of trade are called the **gains from trade.**

The source of such gains is most easily visualized by considering the differences between a world with trade and a world without it. Although politicians often regard foreign trade differently from domestic trade, economists from Adam Smith on have argued that the causes and consequences of international trade are simply an extension of the principles governing domestic trade. What is the advantage of trade among individuals, among groups, among regions, or among countries?

INTERPERSONAL, INTERREGIONAL, AND INTERNATIONAL TRADE

To begin, consider trade among individuals. Without trade, each person would have to be self-sufficient; each would have to produce all the food, clothing, shelter, medical services, entertainment, and luxuries that he or she consumed. A world of individual self-sufficiency would be a world with extremely low living standards.

Trade among individuals allows people to specialize in activities they can do well and to buy from others the goods and services they cannot easily produce. A good doctor who is a bad carpenter can provide medical services not only for his or her own family but also for an excellent carpenter without the training or the ability to practice medicine. Thus trade and specialization are intimately connected. Without trade, everyone must be self-sufficient; with trade, each person can specialize in what he or she does well and satisfy other needs by trading.

The same principles apply to regions. Without interregional trade, each region would be forced to be self-sufficient. With trade, each region can specialize in producing products for which it has some natural or acquired advantage. Plains regions can specialize in growing grain, mountain regions in mining and forest products, and regions with abundant power in manufacturing. Cool regions can produce wheat and other crops that thrive in temperate climates, and hot regions can grow such tropical crops as bananas, sugarcane, and coffee. The living standards of the inhabitants of all regions will be higher when each region specializes in products in which it has some natural or acquired advantage and obtains other products by trade than when all regions seek to be self-sufficient.

This same basic principle also applies to nations. A national boundary seldom delimits an area that is naturally self-sufficient. Nations, like regions or persons, can gain from specialization. More of the goods in which production is specialized are produced than residents wish to consume, while less domestic production of other goods that residents desire is available.

International trade is necessary to achieve the gains that international specialization makes possible.

This discussion suggests one important possible gain from trade.

With trade, each individual, region, or nation is able to concentrate on producing goods and services that it produces efficiently while trading to obtain goods and services that it does not produce efficiently.

Specialization and trade go hand in hand because there is no motivation to achieve the gains from specialization without being able to trade the goods produced for goods desired. Economists use the term *gains from trade* to embrace the results of both.

We will examine two sources of the gains from trade. The first is differences among regions of the world in climate and resource endowment that lead to advantages in producing certain goods and disadvantages in producing others. These gains occur even though each country's costs of production are unchanged by the existence of trade. The second source is the reduction in each country's costs of production that results from the greater production that specialization brings.

GAINS FROM SPECIALIZATION WITH GIVEN COSTS

To focus on differences in countries' conditions of production, suppose that there are no advantages arising from either economies of large-scale production or cost reductions that are the consequence of learning new skills. In these circumstances, what leads to gains from trade? To examine this question, we shall use an example involving only two countries and two products, but the general principles also apply when there are many countries and many products. This discussion provides an elaboration of the points made in Extension 3-1 in Chapter 3 on comparative and absolute advantage.

A Special Case: Absolute Advantage

The gains from trade are clear when there is a simple situation involving absolute advantage. **Absolute advantage** involves comparing the quantities of a specific product that can be produced using the same quantity of resources in two different regions. One region is said to have an absolute advantage over another in the production of product X when an equal quantity of resources can produce more X in the first region than in the second.

Suppose that region A has an absolute advantage over region B in one product, while region B has an absolute advantage over region A in another. This is a case of *reciprocal absolute advantage*: Each country has an absolute advantage in one product. In such a situation, the total production of both regions can be increased (relative to a situation of self-sufficiency) if each specializes in the product in which it has the absolute advantage.

Table 35-1 provides a simple example, using hypothetical data for wheat and cloth production in Canada and in England. In the example, total world production of both wheat and cloth increases when each country produces more of the good in which it has an absolute advantage. As a result, more wheat and more cloth are obtained for the same use of resources.

These gains from *specialization* make the gains from *trade* possible. England will now be producing more cloth and Canada more wheat than when they were self-sufficient. Thus Canada will be producing more wheat and less cloth than Canadian consumers wish to buy, and England will be producing more cloth and less wheat than English consumers wish to buy. If consumers in both countries are to get cloth and wheat in the desired proportions, England must export cloth to Canada and import wheat from Canada.

A First General Statement: Comparative Advantage

When each country has an absolute advantage over the other in a product, the gains from trade are obvi-

---

TABLE 35-1
Gains from Specialization with Absolute Advantage

Part A: Amounts of wheat and cloth that can be produced with 1 unit of resources in Canada and England

	Wheat (bushels)	Cloth (metres)
Canada	10	6
England	5	10

Part B: Changes resulting from the transfer of 1 unit of Canadian resources into wheat and 1 unit of English resources into cloth

	Wheat (bushels)	Cloth (metres)
Canada	+10	−6
England	−5	+10
World	+5	+4

When there is a reciprocal absolute advantage, specialization makes it possible to produce more of both commodities. Part A shows the production of wheat and cloth that can be achieved in each country by using 1 unit of resources. Canada can produce 10 bushels of wheat or 6 metres of cloth; England can produce 5 bushels of wheat or 10 metres of cloth. Canada has an absolute advantage in producing wheat, England in producing cloth. Part B shows the changes in production caused by moving 1 unit of resources out of cloth and into wheat production in Canada and moving 1 unit of resources in the opposite direction in England. There is an increase in world production of 5 bushels of wheat and 4 metres of cloth; worldwide, there are gains from specialization. In this example, the more resources are transferred into wheat production in Canada and into cloth production in England, the larger the gains will be.

---

ous. But what if Canada can produce both wheat and cloth more efficiently than England? In essence, this was David Ricardo's question, posed nearly two centuries ago. His answer underlies the theory of comparative advantage and is still accepted by economists as a valid statement of the potential gains from trade.

To start with, suppose that Canadian efficiency increases 10-fold above the levels recorded in the previous example, so that a unit of Canadian resources can produce either 100 bushels of wheat or 60 metres of cloth. English efficiency remains unchanged (see Table 35-2). It might appear that Canada, which is now better than England at producing both wheat and cloth, has nothing to gain by trading with such an inefficient foreign country. But this is wrong. That it *does* have something to gain is shown in Table 35-2. Even though Canada is 10 times as efficient as in the situation of Table 35-1, it is still possible to increase world production of both wheat and cloth by having Canada produce more wheat and less cloth and England produce more cloth and less wheat.

TABLE 35-2
Gains from Specialization with Comparative Advantage

Part A: Amounts of wheat and cloth that can be produced with 1 unit of resources in Canada and England

	Wheat (bushels)	Cloth (metres)
Canada	100	60
England	5	10

Part B: Changes resulting from the transfer of one-tenth of 1 unit of Canadian resources into wheat and 1 unit of English resources into cloth

	Wheat (bushels)	Cloth (metres)
Canada	+10	−6
England	−5	+10
World	+5	+4

When there is comparative advantage, specialization makes it possible to produce more of both commodities. The productivity of English resources is left unchanged from Table 35-1; that of Canadian resources is increased 10-fold. England no longer has an absolute advantage in producing either commodity. Total production of both commodities can nonetheless be increased by specialization. Moving one-tenth of 1 unit of Canadian resources out of cloth and into wheat and moving 1 unit of resources in the opposite direction in England causes world production of wheat to rise by 5 bushels and cloth by 4 metres.

What is the source of this gain? Although Canada has an absolute advantage over England in the production of both wheat and cloth, the *margin* of advantage differs in the two products. Canada can produce 20 times as much wheat as England by using the same quantity of resources but only 6 times as much cloth. Canada is said to have a *comparative advantage* in the production of wheat (and a comparative disadvantage in the production of the cloth). This statement implies another: England has a comparative advantage in the production of cloth and a comparative disadvantage in the production of wheat.

One of the theory's key propositions is this:

The gains from specialization and trade depend on the pattern of comparative, not absolute, advantage.

A comparison of Tables 35-1 and 35-2 refutes the notion that the absolute *levels* of efficiency of two regions determine the gains from specialization. The key is that the margin of advantage one region has over the other must differ between products. Total world production can then be increased if each region specializes in producing the product in which it has a comparative advantage.

Comparative advantage is necessary as well as sufficient for gains from trade. This means that *if* there is comparative advantage then there *are* gains from trade; it also means that if there is *no* comparative advantage then there are *no* gains from trade. This is illustrated in Table 35-3, showing Canada with an absolute advantage in both products and neither country with a comparative advantage over the other in the production of either product. Canada is 10 times as efficient as England in the production of wheat and in the production of cloth. Now there is no way to increase the production of *both* wheat and cloth by reallocating resources within Canada and within England. Part B of the table provides one example of a resource shift that illustrates this. *Absolute advantage without comparative advantage does not lead to gains from trade.*

A Second General Statement: Opportunity Costs

Much of the foregoing argument has used the concept of a unit of resources. It assumes that units of resources can be equated across countries so that statements such as "Canada can produce 10 times as much wheat with the same quantity of resources as England" are meaningful. Measurement of the real resource cost of producing products poses many difficulties. If, for example, England uses land, labour, and capital in proportions different from those used in Canada, it may not be clear which country gets more output per unit of resource input. Fortunately, the proposition about the gains from trade can be restated without reference to so fuzzy a concept as units of resources.

To do this, go back to the examples of Tables 35-1 and 35-2. Calculate the *opportunity cost* of wheat and cloth in the two countries. When resources are fully employed (so that production takes place on the country's production possibilities frontier), the only way to produce more of one product is to produce less of the other product. Table 35-1 shows that a unit of resources in Canada can produce 10 bushels of wheat *or* 6 metres of cloth. From this it follows that the opportunity cost of producing a unit of wheat is 0.60 units of cloth, while the opportunity cost of producing a unit of cloth is 1.67 units of wheat. These data are summarized in Table 35-4. The table also shows that in England, the opportunity cost of a unit of wheat is 2 units of cloth, while the opportunity cost of a unit of cloth is 0.50 units of wheat. Table 35-2 (which shows the same pattern of *comparative* advantage as Table 35-1) also gives rise to the opportunity costs in Table 35-4.

TABLE 35-3
**Absence of Gains from Specialization
When There Is No Comparative Advantage**

Part A: Amounts of wheat and cloth that can be produced with 1 unit of resources in Canada and England

	Wheat (bushels)	Cloth (metres)
Canada	100	60
England	10	6

Part B: Changes resulting from the transfer of 1 unit of Canadian resources into wheat and 10 units of English resources into cloth

	Wheat (bushels)	Cloth (metres)
Canada	+100	−60
England	−100	+60
World	0	0

Where there is no comparative advantage, no reallocation of resources within each country can increase the production of both commodities. In this example, Canada has the same absolute advantage over England in each commodity (10-fold). There is no comparative advantage, and world production cannot be increased by reallocating resources in both countries. Therefore, specialization does not increase total output.

The sacrifice of cloth involved in producing wheat is much lower in Canada than it is in England. World wheat production can be increased if Canada rather than England produces it. Looking at cloth production, we can see that the loss of wheat involved in producing one unit of cloth is lower in England than in Canada. England is the lower-cost (that is, lower opportunity cost) producer of cloth. World cloth production can therefore be increased if England rather than Canada produces it. This situation is shown in Table 35-5.

The gains from trade arise from differing opportunity costs in the two countries.

Although Table 35-4 was calculated from Table 35-1 (or Table 35-2), we do not need to be able to compare real resource costs to calculate comparative advantages. The existence of a production possibility boundary implies opportunity costs, and the existence of different opportunity costs implies comparative advantages and disadvantages.

The conclusions about the gains from trade arising from international differences in opportunity costs may be summarized as follows:

1. Country A has a comparative advantage over country B in producing a product when the opportunity cost of production in country A is

TABLE 35-4
**Opportunity Cost of Wheat and Cloth
in Canada and England**

	Wheat (bushels)	Cloth (metres)
Canada	0.60 metres cloth	1.67 bushels wheat
England	2.00 metres cloth	0.50 bushels wheat

Comparative advantages can be expressed in terms of opportunity costs that differ between countries. These opportunity costs can be obtained from Table 35-1 or Table 35-2. The English opportunity cost of 1 unit of wheat is obtained by dividing the cloth output of 1 unit of English resources by the wheat output. The result shows that 2 metres of cloth must be sacrificed for every extra unit of wheat produced by transferring English resources out of cloth production and into wheat. The other three cost figures are obtained in a similar manner.

lower. This implies, however, that it has a comparative *dis*advantage in the other product.

2. Opportunity costs depend on the relative costs of producing two products, not on absolute costs. (Notice that the examples in Tables 35-1 and 35-2 each give rise to the opportunity costs in Table 35-4.)

3. When opportunity costs are the same in all countries, there is no comparative advantage and there is no possibility of gains from specialization and trade. (You can illustrate this for yourself by calculating the opportunity costs implied by the data in Table 35-3.)

4. When opportunity costs differ in any two countries and both countries are producing both products, it is always possible to increase production of both products by a suitable reallocation of resources within each country. (This proposition is illustrated in Table 35-5.)

GAINS FROM TRADE WITH VARIABLE COSTS

So far, we have assumed that unit costs are the same whatever the scale of output, and we have seen that there are gains from specialization and trade as long as there are interregional differences in opportunity costs. If costs vary with the level of output, or as experience is acquired via specialization, *additional* sources of gain are possible.

Scale and Imperfect Competition

Real production costs, measured in terms of resources used, generally fall as the scale of output increases.

TABLE 35-5
Gains from Specialization
with Differing Opportunity Costs

Changes resulting from each country's producing 1 more unit of a commodity in which it has the lower opportunity cost

	Wheat (bushels)	Cloth (metres)
Canada	+1.0	−0.6
England	−0.5	+1.0
World	+0.5	+0.4

Whenever opportunity costs differ between countries, specialization can increase the production of both commodities. These calculations show that there are gains from specialization, given the opportunity costs of Table 35-4. To produce 1 more bushel of wheat, Canada must sacrifice 0.6 metres of cloth. To produce 1 more metre of cloth, England must sacrifice 0.5 bushels of wheat. Making both changes raises world production of both wheat and cloth.

The larger the scale of operations, the more efficiently large-scale machinery can be used and the more a detailed division of tasks among workers is possible. Small countries such as Switzerland, Belgium, and Israel whose domestic markets are not large enough to exploit economies of scale would find it prohibitively expensive to become self-sufficient by producing a little bit of everything at very high cost.

Trade allows small countries to specialize and produce a few products at high enough levels of output to reap the available economies of scale.

Very large countries, such as the United States, have markets large enough to allow the production of most items at home at a scale of output great enough to obtain the available economies of scale. For them, the gains from trade arise mainly from specializing in products in which they have a comparative advantage. Yet even for such countries, a broadening of their markets permits achieving scale economies in subproduct lines, such as specialty steels or blue jeans.

One of the important lessons learned from patterns of world trade since World War II has concerned imperfect competition and product differentiation. Virtually all of today's manufactured consumer goods are produced in a vast array of differentiated product lines. In some industries, many firms produce this array; in others, only a few firms

produce the entire array. In either case, they do not exhaust all available economies of scale. (Students who have studied microeconomics may recall this from Chapter 12.) This means that an increase in the size of the market, even in an economy as large as the United States, may allow the exploitation of some previously unexploited scale economies in individual product lines.

These possibilities were first dramatically illustrated when the European Common Market (now known as the European Union or EU) was set up in the late 1950s. Economists had expected that specialization would occur according to the theory of comparative advantage, with one country specializing in cars, another in refrigerators, another in fashion clothes, another in shoes, and so on. This is not the way it worked out. Instead, much of the vast growth of trade was in *intra-industry* trade. Today, one can buy French, English, Italian, and German fashion goods, cars, shoes, appliances, and a host of other products in London, Paris, Bonn, and Rome. Ships loaded with Swedish furniture bound for London pass ships loaded with English furniture bound for Stockholm, and so on.

What free European trade did was to allow a proliferation of differentiated products, with different countries each specializing in different subproduct lines. Consumers have shown by their expenditures that they value this enormous increase in the range of choice among differentiated products. As Asian countries have expanded into North American and European markets with textiles, cars, and electronic goods, North American and European manufacturers have increasingly specialized their production and now export textiles, cars, and electronic equipment to Japan even while importing similar but differentiated products from Japan.

Learning by Doing

The discussion so far has assumed that costs vary only with the *level* of output. But they may also vary with the *accumulated experience* in producing a product over time.

Early economists placed great importance on a concept that we now call *learning by doing*. They believed that as countries gained experience in particular tasks, workers and managers would become more efficient in performing them. As people acquire expertise, costs tend to fall. There is substantial evidence that such learning by doing does occur. It is

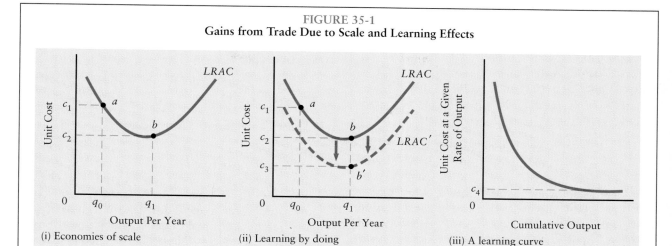

FIGURE 35-1
Gains from Trade Due to Scale and Learning Effects

Specialization may lead to gains from trade by permitting economies of larger-scale output, by leading to downward shifts of cost curves, or both. Consider a country that wishes to consume the quantity q_0. Suppose that it can produce that quantity at an average cost per unit of c_1. Suppose further that the country has a comparative advantage in producing this product and can export the quantity q_0q_1 if it produces q_1. This may lead to cost savings in two ways.

As shown in part (i), the increased level of production of q_1 compared to q_0 permits it to *move along* its cost curve from a to b, thereby reducing costs per unit to c_2. This is an economy of scale.

As shown in part (ii), as workers and management become more experienced, they may discover means of increasing productivity that lead to a downward shift of the cost curve. This is learning by doing. The downward *shift,* shown by the arrows, lowers the cost of producing every unit of output. At output q_1, costs per unit fall to c_3. The movement from a to b' incorporates both economies of scale and learning by doing.

Part (iii) shows a **learning curve,** which is another way of showing the effects of learning by doing. This curve shows the relation between the costs of producing a given output *per period* and the total accumulated output over the whole time during which production has taken place. Growing experience with making the product causes costs to fall as more and more is produced. When all learning possibilities have been exploited, costs reach a minimum level, shown by c_4 in the figure.

particularly important in many of today's knowledge-intensive high-tech industries.

The distinction between this phenomenon and the gains from economies of scale is illustrated in Figure 35-1. It is one more example of the difference between a movement along a curve and a shift of the curve.

Recognition of the opportunities for learning by doing leads to an important implication: Policymakers need not accept *current* comparative advantages as given. Through such means as education and tax incentives, they can seek to develop new comparative advantages.[1] Moreover, countries

cannot complacently assume that their existing comparative advantages will persist. Misguided education policies, the wrong tax incentives, or policies that discourage risk taking can lead to the rapid erosion of a country's comparative advantage in particular products. So, too, can developments in other countries.

SOURCES OF COMPARATIVE ADVANTAGE

We have seen that comparative advantage is the source of the gains from trade. But why do comparative advantages exist? Since a country's comparative advantage depends on its opportunity costs, we could also ask: Why do different countries have different opportunity costs?

---

[1]Of course, they can also foolishly use such policies to develop industries in which they do not have and will never achieve comparative advantages.

Different Factor Endowments

What has become the traditional answer to this question was provided early in the twentieth century by two great Swedish economists, Eli Heckscher and Bertil Ohlin, the latter subsequently being awarded the Nobel Prize in economics for his work in the theory of international trade. Their explanation for international cost differences is now incorporated in the so-called Heckscher-Ohlin model. According to their theory, the international cost differences that form the basis for comparative advantage arise because factor endowments differ across countries.

To see how this works, consider the prices for various types of goods in countries *in the absence of trade*. A country that is well endowed with fertile land but has a small population (like large parts of Canada) will find that land is cheap but labour is expensive. It will therefore produce land-intensive agricultural goods cheaply and labour-intensive goods, such as machine tools, only at high cost. The reverse will be true for a second country that is small in size but possesses abundant and efficient labour (like Japan). As a result, the first country will have a comparative advantage in agricultural production and the second in goods that use much labour and little land. Another country that is unusually well endowed with energy will have low energy prices. It will thus have a comparative advantage in such energy-intensive goods as chemicals and aluminium.

According to the Heckscher-Ohlin theory, countries have comparative advantages in the production of products that are intensive in the use of the factors of production with which they are abundantly endowed.

This is often called the *factor endowment theory of comparative advantage.*

Different Climates

Modern research suggests that this theory has considerable power to explain comparative advantage but that it does not provide the whole explanation. One obvious additional influence comes from all those natural factors that can be called *climate* in the broadest sense. If you combine land, labour, and capital in the same way in Nicaragua and in Iceland, you will not get the same output of most agricultural goods. Sunshine, rainfall, and average temperature also matter. If you seek to work with wool or cotton in dry and damp cli-

mates, you will get different results. (You can, of course, artificially create any climate you wish in a factory, but it costs money to create what is freely provided elsewhere.)

Climate, interpreted in the broadest sense, affects comparative advantage.[2]

Acquired Comparative Advantage

There is today a competing view. In extreme form, it says that comparative advantages exist but are typically *acquired*, not nature-given, and can change. This view of comparative advantage is *dynamic* rather than static. New industries are seen to depend more on human capital than on fixed physical capital or natural resources. The skills of a computer designer, a videogame programmer, a sound mix technician, or a rock star are acquired by education and on-the-job training. Natural endowments of energy and raw materials cannot account for the leadership in computer technology of Silicon Valley in California, for Britain's prominence in modern pop music or Canada's prominence in communications technology. When countries find their former dominance (based on comparative advantage) in such smokestack industries as cars and steel declining, their firms need not sit idly by. Instead, they can begin to adapt by developing new areas of comparative advantage.

Contrasts

This modern view is in sharp contrast with the traditional assumption that cost structures based largely on a country's natural endowments lead to a given pattern of international comparative advantage. The traditional view suggests that a government interested in maximizing its citizens' material standard of living should encourage specialization of production in goods where it currently has a comparative advantage. If all countries follow this advice, the theory predicts, each will be specialized in a relatively narrow range of distinct products. The British will produce engineering products, Canadians will be producers of resource-based primary products,

---

[2]Of course, if we consider "warm weather" a factor of production, then we could simply say that countries like Nicaragua are better endowed with that factor than countries like Iceland. In this sense, explanations of comparative advantage based on different climates are really just a special case of explanations based on factor endowments.

Americans will be farmers and factory workers, Central Americans will be banana growers, and so on.

There are surely elements of truth in both extreme views. It would be unwise to neglect resource endowments, climate, culture, social patterns, and institutional arrangements. But it would also be unwise to assume that all of them were innate and immutable.

To some extent, these views are reconciled by the theory of human capital which is a topic we discussed in Microeconomics. Comparative advantages that depend on human capital are consistent with traditional Heckscher-Ohlin theory. The difference is that this type of capital is acquired through conscious decisions relating to such matters as education and technical training.

IS COMPARATIVE ADVANTAGE OBSOLETE?

In the debate preceding the signing of both the Canada-U.S. Free Trade Agreement and the North American Free Trade Agreement (NAFTA), some opponents argued that the agreements relied on an outdated view of the gains from trade based on comparative advantage. The theory of comparative advantage was said to have been made obsolete by the new theories that we have just discussed.

In spite of such assertions, comparative advantage remains an important economic concept. At any one time, the operation of the price system will result in trade that follows the current pattern of comparative advantage. This is because comparative advantage is reflected in international relative prices, and these relative prices determine what goods a country will import and what it will export. For example, if Canadian costs of producing steel are particularly low relative to other Canadian costs, Canada's price of steel will be low by international standards, and steel will be a Canadian export (which it is). If Canada's costs of producing textiles are particularly high relative to other Canadian costs, Canada's price of textiles will be high by international standards, and Canada will import textiles (which it does). So there is no reason to change the view that Ricardo long ago expounded: *Current comparative advantage is a major determinant of trade under free-market conditions.*

What has changed, however, is economists' views about the *determinants* of comparative advantage. It now seems that current comparative advantage may be more open to change by private entrepreneurial activities and by government policy than used to be thought. Thus what is obsolete is the belief that a country's current pattern of comparative advantage, and hence its current pattern of imports and exports, must be accepted as given and unchangeable.

The theory that comparative advantage determines trade flows is not obsolete, but the theory that comparative advantage is completely determined by forces beyond the reach of public policy has been discredited.

It is one thing to observe that it is *possible* for governments to influence a country's pattern of comparative advantage. It is quite another to conclude that it is *advisable* for them to try. The case in support of a specific government intervention requires that (1) there is scope for governments to improve on the results achieved by the free market, (2) the costs of the intervention be less than the value of the improvement to be achieved, and (3) governments will actually be able to carry out the required interventionist policies (without, for example, being sidetracked by considerations of electoral advantage).

THE TERMS OF TRADE

So far, we have seen that world production can be increased when countries specialize in the production of the products in which they have a comparative advantage and then trade with one another. We now ask, how will these gains from specialization and trade be shared among countries? The division of the gain depends on what is called the **terms of trade,** which relates to the quantity of imported goods that can be obtained per unit of goods exported. They are measured by the ratio of the price of exports to the price of imports.

A rise in the price of imported goods, with the price of exports unchanged, indicates a *fall in the terms of trade;* it will now take more exports to buy the same quantity of imports. Similarly, a rise in the price of exported goods, with the price of imports unchanged, indicates a *rise in the terms of trade;* it will now take fewer exports to buy the same quantity of imports. Thus the ratio of these prices measures the amount of imports that can be obtained per unit of goods exported.

In the example of Table 35-4, the Canadian domestic opportunity cost of 1 unit of cloth is 1.67 bushels of wheat. If Canadian resources are transferred from wheat to cloth, 1.67 bushels of wheat are given up for every metre of cloth. But if Canada could obtain its

EXTENSION 35-1

THE GAINS FROM TRADE ILLUSTRATED GRAPHICALLY

International trade leads to an expansion of the set of goods that can be consumed in the economy in two ways:

1. by allowing the bundle of goods consumed to differ from the bundle produced; and,

2. by permitting a profitable change in the pattern of production.

Without international trade, the bundle of goods produced is the bundle consumed. With international trade, the consumption and production bundles can be altered independently to reflect the relative values placed on goods by international markets.

The graphical demonstration of the gains from trade proceeds in two stages.

STAGE 1: FIXED PRODUCTION

In each part of the figure, the black curve is the economy's production possibility boundary. If there is no international trade, the economy must consume the same bundle of goods that it produces. Thus the production possibility boundary is also the consumption possibility boundary. Suppose that the economy produces, and consumes, at point a, with x_1 of good X and y_1 of good Y, as in part (i) of the figure.

Next suppose that with production point a, good Y can be exchanged for good X internationally. The consumption possibilities are now shown by the line tt drawn through point a. The slope of tt indicates the quantity of Y that exchanges for a unit of X on the international market—the terms of trade.

Although production is fixed at point a, consumption can now be anywhere on the line tt. For example, the consumption point could be at b. This could be achieved by exporting y_2y_1 units of Y and importing x_1x_2 units of X. Because point b (and all others on line tt to the right of a) lies outside the production possibility boundary, there are potential gains from trade. Consumers are no longer limited by their own country's production possibilities. Let us suppose that they prefer point b to point a. They have achieved a gain from trade by being allowed to exchange some of their production of good Y for some quantity of good X and thus to consume more of good X than is produced at home.

STAGE 2: VARIABLE PRODUCTION

There is a further opportunity for the expansion of the country's consumption possibilities: With trade, the production bundle may be profitably altered in response to international prices. The country may pro-

cloth on more favourable terms by trading, then there would be gains to producing and exporting wheat in order to pay for the imports of cloth. Suppose, for example, that international prices were such that 1 bushel of wheat exchanged for (was equal in value to) 1 metre of cloth. At those terms of trade, Canada could obtain 1 metre of cloth for every bushel of wheat exported. It would get more cloth per unit of wheat exported than it could obtain by moving resources out of wheat into cloth production at home. These terms of trade would thus favour specializing in the production of wheat and trading it for cloth on international markets.

Similarly, in the example of Table 35-4, English consumers would gain if they could obtain wheat abroad at any terms of trade more favourable than 2 metres of cloth sacrificed. If the terms of trade permitted

the exchange of 1 bushel of wheat for 1 metre of cloth, the terms of trade would favour England's obtaining its wheat by exporting cloth rather than producing it at home: a unit of wheat would then cost 2 units of cloth sacrificed when produced at home compared to only 1 unit of cloth when obtained through trade.

In this example, both Canada and England gain from trade. Each can obtain units of the product in which it has a comparative disadvantage at a lower opportunity cost through international trade than through domestic production. The way in which the terms of trade interact with the gains from trade is illustrated graphically in Extension 35-1.

Because actual international trade involves many countries and many products, a country's terms of trade are computed as an index number:

duce the bundle of goods that is most valuable in world markets. That is represented by the bundle d in part (ii). The consumption possibility set is shifted to the line $t't'$ by changing production from a to d and thereby increasing the country's degree of specialization in good Y. For every point on the original consumption possibility set tt, there are points on the new set $t't'$ that allow more consumption of both goods—for example, compare points b and f. Notice also that except at the zero-trade point d, the new consumption

possibility set lies *everywhere above the production possibility curve.*

The benefits of moving from a no-trade position, such as a, to a trading position such as b or f are the *gains from trade* to the country. When the production of good Y is increased and the production of good X decreased, the country is able to move to a point such as f by producing more of good Y, in which the country has a comparative advantage, and trading the additional production for good X.

(i) Stage 1: Fixed production

(ii) Stage 2: Variable production

$$\text{Terms of Trade} = \frac{\text{Index of Export Prices}}{\text{Index of Import Prices}} \times 100$$

A rise in the index is referred to as a *favourable* change in a country's terms of trade (sometimes called a terms of trade *improvement*). A favourable change means that more can be imported per unit of goods exported than previously. For example, if the export price index rises from 100 to 120 while the import price index rises from 100 to 110, the terms-of-trade index rises from 100 to 109. At the new terms of trade, a unit of exports will buy 9 percent more imports than at the old terms.

A decrease in the index of the terms of trade, called an *unfavourable* change (or a terms of trade *deterioration*), means that the country can import

less in return for any given amount of exports, or, equivalently, it must export more to pay for any given amount of imports. For example, the sharp rise in oil prices in the 1970s led to large unfavourable shifts in the terms of trade of oil-importing countries. When oil prices fell sharply in the mid 1980s, the terms of trade of oil-importing countries changed favourably. The converse was true for oil-exporting countries.

Canada's terms of trade since 1970 are shown in Figure 35-2. As is clear, the terms of trade are quite variable, reflecting cyclical changes in the relative prices of different products. Also clear from the figure is that Canada's terms of trade have displayed a long-term improvement over the past 25 years.

FIGURE 35-2
Canada's Terms of Trade, 1970–1995

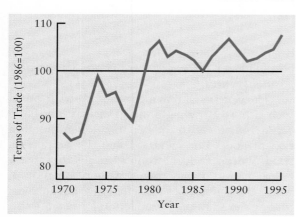

Canada's terms of trade have been quite variable over the past 25 years, but they have also displayed a long-term improvement. The data shown is Canada's terms of trade—the ratio of an index of Canadian export prices to an index of Canadian import prices. As the relative prices of lumber, oil, wheat, electronic equipment, textiles, fruit, and other products change, the terms of trade naturally change. For Canada, however, there has also been a trend improvement in the terms of trade over the past 25 years.

(Source: Economic Reference Tables, Department of Finance, August 1995.)

SUMMARY

A. SOURCES OF THE GAINS FROM TRADE

- One country (or region or individual) has an absolute advantage over another country (or region or individual) in the production of a specific product when, with the same input of resources in each country, it can produce more of the product than can the other.
- Comparative advantage is the relative advantage one country enjoys over another in the production of various products. It occurs whenever countries have different opportunity costs of producing particular goods. World production of all products can be increased if each country transfers resources into the production of the products in which it has a comparative advantage.
- In a situation of reciprocal *absolute* advantage, the total production of both products will be raised if each country specializes in the production of the product in which it has the absolute advantage. However, the gains from trade do not require absolute advantage on the part of each country, only comparative advantage.
- The most important proposition in the theory of the gains from trade is that trade allows all countries to obtain the goods in which they do not have a comparative advantage at a lower opportunity cost than they would face if they were to produce all products for themselves; this allows all countries to have more of

all products than they could have if they tried to be self-sufficient.
- As well as gaining the advantages of specialization arising from comparative advantage, a nation that engages in trade and specialization may realize the benefits of economies of large-scale production and of learning by doing.
- Classical theory regarded comparative advantage as largely determined by natural resource endowments that are difficult to change. Economists now believe that some comparative advantages can be acquired and consequently can be changed. A country may, in this view, influence its role in world production and trade. Successful intervention leads to a country's acquiring a comparative advantage; unsuccessful intervention fails to develop such an advantage.

B. THE TERMS OF TRADE

- The terms of trade refer to the ratio of the prices of goods exported to the prices of those imported. This determines the quantity of imports that can be obtained per unit of exports. The terms of trade determine how the gains from trade are shared.
- A favourable change in the terms of trade—a rise in export prices relative to import prices—means that a country can acquire more imports per unit of exports, and vice versa.

KEY CONCEPTS

Interpersonal, interregional, and international specialization

Absolute advantage and comparative advantage

Opportunity cost and comparative advantage

The gains from trade: specialization, scale economies, and learning by doing

The sources of comparative advantage

Factor endowments

Acquired comparative advantage

The terms of trade

DISCUSSION QUESTIONS

1. Adam Smith saw a close connection between the wealth of a nation and its willingness "freely to engage" in foreign trade. What is the connection?

2. One critic of the North American Free Trade Agreement argued that "it can't be in our interest to sign this deal; Mexico gains too much from it." What does the theory of the gains from trade have to say about that criticism?

3. Canada, the United States, and Mexico are clearly separate countries. Does this fact imply a lower standard of living in each of the three countries compared to the situation where they are united into a single new country? If Quebec were to separate from the rest of Canada, would this fact alone mean that Quebec and (the new) Canada would have a lower standard of living (ignoring the costs of upheaval that would be associated with the actual separation)?

4. One product innovation that appears imminent is the electric car. However, development costs are high, and economies of scale and learning by doing are both likely to be operative. As a result, there will be a substantial competitive advantage for those who develop a marketable product early. What implications might this have for government policies toward North American automobile manufacturers' activities in this area? Should the Canadian or U.S. governments encourage joint efforts by Chrysler, Ford, and GM, even if this appears to lessen competition between them?

5. Studies of Canadian trade patterns have shown that industries with high wages are among the largest and fastest-growing export sectors. Does this contradict the principle of comparative advantage?

6. Predict what each of the following events would do to the terms of trade of the importing country and the exporting country, other things being equal.

   a. A blight destroys a large part of the coffee beans produced in the world.

   b. The Koreans cut the price of the steel they sell to Canada.

   c. General inflation of 10 percent occurs around the world.

   d. Violation of OPEC output quotas leads to a sharp fall in the price of oil.

7. Heavy Canadian borrowing abroad has several times led to a high value of the dollar and thus a rise in the ratio of export prices to import prices. Although this is called a favourable change in the terms of trade, are there any reasons why it may not have been a good thing for the Canadian economy?

8. Suppose that the situation described in the accompanying table exists. Assume that there are no tariffs and no government intervention and that labour is the only factor of production. Let X take different values—say, $10, $20, $40, and $60. In each case, in what direction will trade have to flow in order for the gains from trade to be exploited?

Country	Labour cost of producing 1 unit of	
	Artichokes	Bathtubs
Inland	$20	$40
Outland	$15	$X

9. Suppose the following table shows the production of wheat and corn in Brazil and Mexico assuming no trade between the countries.

	Brazil	Mexico
Wheat	90 bushels per acre	50 bushels per acre
Corn	30 bushels per acre	20 bushels per acre

   a. Which country, Brazil or Mexico, maintains an absolute advantage in the production of wheat? Of corn?

   b. Which country, Brazil or Mexico, maintains a comparative advantage in the production of wheat? Of corn?

   c. Assuming constant returns to scale, draw the appropriate production possibilities curve for each country. In the absence of trade, assume each country has exactly 1 million acres of farmland and devotes exactly half towards the production of each commodity. How much of each commodity does each country produce without trade?

   d. Give an example (using specific figures) of how specialization and trade could benefit both countries.

10. Are there always benefits to specialization and trade? When are the benefits greatest? Under what situations are there *no* benefits from specialization and trade?

CHAPTER 36

TRADE POLICY

Conducting business in a foreign country is not always easy. Differences in language, in local laws and customs, and in currency often complicate transactions. Our concern in this chapter, however, is not with these complications but with government policy toward international trade and related matters, which is called **trade policy** or **commercial policy.** At one extreme is a policy of free trade, which means an absence of any form of government interference with the free flow of international trade. Any departure from free trade designed to protect domestic industries from foreign competition is called **protectionism.**

802

This chapter begins by restating the case for free trade and then goes on to study various valid and invalid arguments that are commonly advanced for some degree of protectionism. After that, we study the many modern institutions designed to foster freer trade on either a global or a regional basis. We conclude by studying one such institution that is of central importance to Canada—the North American Free Trade Agreement (NAFTA).

THE THEORY OF TRADE POLICY

Today, most governments accept that a relatively free flow of international trade is desirable for the health of their individual economies. But heated debates still occur over trade policy. Should a country permit the completely free flow of international trade, or should it seek to protect some of its local producers from some of the foreign competition that they face? If some protection is desired, should it be achieved by tariffs or by nontariff barriers? **Tariffs** are taxes designed to raise the price of foreign goods. **Nontariff barriers (NTBs)** are devices other than tariffs that are designed to reduce the flow of imports; examples are quotas and customs procedures that are deliberately more cumbersome than necessary.

THE CASE FOR FREE TRADE

The case for free trade was presented in Chapter 35. Comparative advantages arise whenever countries have different opportunity costs. Free trade allows all countries to specialize in producing products in which they have a comparative advantage. This in turn maximizes world production and hence maximizes average world living standards (as reflected by the world's per capita GDP).

Free trade does not necessarily make everyone better off than they would be in its absence. For example, reducing an existing tariff often results in individual groups receiving a smaller share of a larger world output so that they lose even though the average person gains. If we ask whether it is *possible* for free trade to improve everyone's living standards, the answer is "yes." But if we ask whether free trade always does so, the answer is "not necessarily."

There is abundant evidence that significant differences in opportunity costs do exist and that large gains are realized from international trade because of these differences.

What needs explanation is the fact that trade is not wholly free. Why do tariffs and other barriers to trade continue to exist two centuries after Adam Smith and David Ricardo stated the case for free trade? Is there a valid case for some protectionism?

THE CASE FOR PROTECTIONISM

Two kinds of arguments for protection are commonly offered. The first concerns national objectives *other than* maximizing total income; the second concerns the desire to increase one country's national income, possibly at the expense of the national incomes of other countries.

Objectives Other than Maximizing National Income

It is possible to believe that a country's national income is maximized with free trade and yet rationally oppose free trade because of a concern with other policy objectives.

Noneconomic Advantages of Diversification. Comparative advantage might dictate that a small country should specialize in producing a narrow range of products. The government might decide, however, that there are distinct social advantages in encouraging a more diverse economy. Citizens would be given a wider range of occupations, and the social and psychological advantages of diversification may more than compensate for a reduction in per capita output below what they would be with complete specialization of production according to comparative advantage.

Risks of Specialization. For a very small country, specializing in the production of only a few products—though dictated by comparative advantage—might involve risks that the country does not wish to take. One such risk is that technological advances may render its basic product obsolete. Everyone understands this risk, but there is debate about what governments can do about it. The pro-tariff argument is that the government can encourage a more diversified economy by protecting industries that otherwise could not compete. Opponents argue that governments, being naturally influenced by political motives are poor judges of which industries can be protected in order to produce diversification at a reasonable cost.

National Defence. Another reason for protectionism concerns national defence. It is argued, for example, that the United States needs an experienced commercial shipping industry in case of war and that this industry should be fostered by protectionist policies even though it is less efficient than the foreign competition. Current U.S. policy does this by forbidding foreign ships from transporting cargo between any two U.S. ports. Opponents of this measure argue that it has little to do with national security and much to do with increasing the incomes of ship owners and their crews at the expense of all those who use those ships.

Protection of Specific Groups.   Although free trade—and specialization according to comparative advantage—will maximize per capita GDP over the whole economy, some specific groups may have higher incomes under protection than under free trade. An obvious example is a firm or an industry that is given monopoly power when tariffs are used to restrict foreign competition. If a small group of firms and their employees find their incomes increased by a substantial amount when they get tariff protection, they may not be concerned that income for everyone else in the economy falls by a small amount. They get a much larger share of a slightly smaller total income and end up better off. If they gain from the trade restrictions, they will lose from free trade.

A similar argument can apply to larger groups. Consider the ratio of skilled workers to unskilled workers. There are plenty of both types throughout the world. Compared to much of the rest of the world, however, Canada has more skilled and fewer unskilled people. When trade is expanded because of a reduction in tariffs, Canada will tend to export goods made by its abundant skilled workers and import goods made by unskilled workers. (This is the basic prediction of the *factor endowment theory* of comparative advantage that we discussed in Chapter 35.) Because Canada is now exporting more goods made by skilled labour, the demand for such labour rises. Because Canada is now importing more goods made by unskilled labour, the demand for such labour falls. This specialization according to comparative advantage raises average Canadian living standards, but it will also tend to raise the wages of skilled Canadian workers relative to the wages of unskilled Canadian workers.

If increasing trade has these effects, then reducing trade by raising trade barriers can have the opposite effects. Raising trade barriers may raise the relative wages of unskilled Canadian workers, giving them a larger share of a smaller total GDP. The conclusion is that trade restrictions can improve the *relative* earnings of one group whenever the restrictions increase the de-

mand for that group's services. This is done, however, at the expense of a reduction in *overall* national income and hence the country's average living standards.

This analysis is important because it reveals both the grain of truth and the dangers that lie behind the resistance to reductions in trade restrictions on the part of some labour groups and some organizations whose main concern is with the poor.

What is the conclusion from the foregoing discussion? Other things being equal, most people prefer more income to less. However, economists cannot say that it is irrational for a society to sacrifice some income to achieve other goals. But economists can do three things when presented with such arguments for adopting protectionist measures. First, they can ask if the proposed measures really do achieve the ends suggested. Second, they can calculate the cost of the measures in terms of lowered living standards. Third, they can see if there are alternative means of achieving the stated goals at lower cost in terms of lost national income.

Maximizing One Country's National Income

Next we consider several arguments for the use of tariffs when the objective is to make a country's national income as large as possible.

To Alter the Terms of Trade.   Tariffs can be used to change the terms of trade in favour of a country that makes up a large fraction of the world demand for some product that it imports. By restricting its demand for that product through a tariff, it can force down the price that foreign exporters receive for that product. The price paid by domestic consumers will probably rise but as long as the increase is less than the tariff, foreign suppliers will receive less per unit. For example, a 20 percent U.S. tariff on the import of Canadian softwood lumber or natural gas might raise the price paid by U.S. consumers by 12 percent and lower the price received by Canadian suppliers by 8 percent (the difference between the two prices being received by the U.S. treasury).

Imposing tariffs to alter the terms of trade reduces world output. It can, however, make it possible for a single country to gain because its gets a sufficiently larger share of the smaller world output. However, if foreign countries retaliate by raising their trade restrictions, the ensuing trade war can easily leave every country with a reduced national income.

In many modern cases, the U.S. has left the exporting country to apply its own export-restricting measures. The effect of such export restrictions, as we shall see later in this chapter, is to turn the terms of trade in favour of the exporting country at the expense of the importing one.

To Protect Against "Unfair" Actions by Foreign Firms and Governments. Tariffs are used to prevent foreign industries from harming domestic industries by employing predatory practices. Two common practices are subsidies paid by foreign governments to their exporters and price discrimination by foreign firms, which is called *dumping* when it is done across international borders. These practices are typically countered by levying tariffs called *countervailing duties* and *antidumping duties*. The circumstances under which dumping and foreign subsidization provide a valid argument for such tariffs are considered in detail later in this chapter.

To Protect Infant Industries. The oldest valid argument for protectionism as a means of raising living standards concerns economies of scale. It is usually called the **infant industry argument.** An infant industry is nothing more than a new, small industry. If such an industry has large economies of scale, costs will be high when the industry is small but will fall as the industry grows. In such industries, the country first in the field has a tremendous advantage. A newly developing country may find that in the early stages of development, its industries are unable to compete with established foreign rivals. A trade restriction may protect these industries from foreign competition while they grow up. When they are large enough, they will be able to produce as cheaply as foreign rivals and thus be able to compete without protection.

Most of the now industrialized countries developed their industries initially under quite heavy tariff protection. This group included Canada, the United States, Germany, and South Korea. Once the industrial sector was well developed, all of these countries moved to reduce their levels of protection moving a long way toward freer trade.

To Encourage Learning by Doing. Learning by doing, which we discussed in Chapter 35, suggests that the pattern of comparative advantage can be changed. If a country learns enough by producing products for which it currently has a comparative *dis*advantage, it may gain in the long run by specializing in those products, developing a comparative advantage as the learning process lowers their costs.

Learning by doing is an example of what in Chapter 35 we called dynamic comparative advantage. The success of such *newly industrializing coun-*

tries (NICs) as Hong Kong, South Korea, Singapore, Taiwan, Indonesia, and Thailand seemed to many observers to be based on acquired skills and government policies that created favourable business conditions. This gave rise to the theory that comparative advantages can change and that they can be developed by suitable government policies, which can, however, take many forms other than restricting trade.

Some countries have succeeded in developing strong comparative advantages in targeted industries, but others have failed. One reason such policies sometimes fail is that protecting local industries from foreign competition may make the industries unadaptive and complacent. Another reason is the difficulty of identifying the industries that will be able to succeed in the long run. All too often, the protected infant grows up to be a weakling requiring permanent protection for its continued existence. Or else the rate of learning is slower than for similar industries in countries that do not provide protection from the chill winds of international competition. In these instances, the anticipated comparative advantage never materializes. One way of accomplishing these goals without the risk of protecting failures is to give other forms of assistance to the industries but insist that they compete in international markets from the outset. This assists industries without insulating them from the need to be internationally competitive.

To Create or Exploit a Strategic Trade Advantage. A major new argument for tariffs or other trade restrictions is to create a strategic advantage in producing or marketing some new product that is expected to generate pure profits. To the extent that all lines of production earn normal profits, there is no reason to produce goods other than ones for which a country has a comparative advantage. Some goods, however, are produced in industries containing a few large firms where economies of scale provide a natural barrier to entry. Firms in these industries can earn high profits even over long periods of time. If protection of the domestic market can increase the chance that one of the protected domestic firms will become established and thus earn high profits, the protection may pay off. This is the general idea behind the modern concept of *strategic trade policy,* and it is treated in more detail in the next section.

Strategic Trade Policy

In the past dozen or so years, another group of arguments *against* free trade have evolved; these arguments are based on the existence of imperfect competition and increasing returns to scale that arise from the presence of high fixed costs.

Implications of High Fixed Costs.

Many of today's high-tech industries have large fixed costs of product development. For a new generation of civilian aircraft, silicon chips, computers, artificial intelligence machines, and genetically engineered food products, a very high proportion of each producer's total costs goes to product development. These are fixed costs of entering the market, and they must be incurred before a single unit of output can be sold.

In such industries, the actual costs of producing each unit of an already developed product may be quite small. Even if average variable costs are constant, the large fixed development costs mean that the average total cost curve has a significant negative slope over a large range of output. It follows that the price at which a firm can expect to recover its total cost is negatively related to its expected volume of sales—the larger its sales, the lower the price that it can charge and still cover its full costs.

In such industries, a large number of firms, each of which has a relatively small output, could not cover their fixed costs. However, a small number of firms, each of which has a high output, could do so. Furthermore, it is possible for these firms to make large profits, whereas the entry of one more firm would cause everyone to suffer losses. In this case, the first firms that become established in the market will control it and will earn the profits.[1]

The production of full-sized commercial jets provides an example of an industry that possesses many of these characteristics. The development costs of a new generation of jet aircraft have increased with each new generation. If the aircraft manufacturers are to recover these costs, each of them must have large sales. Thus the number of firms that the market can support has diminished steadily until today there is room in the world aircraft industry for only two or three firms producing a full range of commercial jets.

---

[1]The reason for this is found in the indivisibility of product development costs. For example, if $500 million is required to develop a marketable product, a firm that spends only $300 million gets nothing. To see why this creates the potential for profits, suppose that the market is large enough for the product to be sold at a price that would cover variable costs of production and also pay the opportunity costs of $1.25 billion worth of capital. Further suppose that the capital required for actual production is negligible. In this case, two firms with a total of $1 billion of capital invested in development costs will enter the market and earn large profits. However, if a third firm entered, making the industry's total invested capital $1.5 billion, all three firms would incur losses.

Argument for Protection.

The characteristics just listed are sometimes used to provide arguments for protecting such industries. Suppose, for example, that there is room in the aircraft industry for only three major producers of the next round of passenger jets. If a government subsidizes a domestic firm, this firm may become one of the three that succeed. In this case, the profits that are subsequently earned may more than repay the cost of the subsidy. Furthermore, another country's firm, which was not subsidized, may have been just as good as the three that succeeded. Without the subsidy, however, this firm may lose out in the battle to establish itself as one of the three surviving firms in the market. Having lost this one battle, it loses its entire fight for existence.

This example is not unlike the story of Airbus, a European producer of commercial jet aircraft. Airbus received many direct subsidies (and they charge that their main competitor, Boeing, received many indirect ones). Whatever the merits of the argument, several things are clear: The civilian jet aircraft industry remains profitable, there is room for only two or three major producers, and one of these would not have been Airbus if it had not been for substantial government assistance. (It is not clear, however, if profits earned by Airbus will ever cover the enormous subsidies paid by governments during earlier stages of design and production.)

Debate over Strategic Trade Policy.

Airbus provides an example where strategic trade policy was successful in permitting a group of countries to succeed in an industry with high worldwide profits. (Whether Airbus can compete without subsidies, in the long run, remains to be seen.) The Japanese automobile industry is another example. It was protected from foreign competition all through its early stages of development in the 1950s and 1960s. In the 1980s it had reached such levels of technological efficiency that it went on to become a serious competitive threat to European and North American automobile producers.

High-definition television (HDTV) is an example of the failure of such a policy. During the 1980s, the Japanese government provided extensive subsidies to the development of HDTV (which, when it is introduced, will have much higher video quality than current television). The U.S. government did not provide such subsidies, despite widespread concern from the U.S. electronics industry that it would lose out to Japan in an important market. As it happened, however, a number of U.S. firms, acting on their own, developed a technique for HDTV that is superior to the subsidized Japanese version, and the U.S. standard for HDTV is generally expected to dominate the global market.

Just as the Airbus story seems to support proponents of strategic trade policy, the HDTV story seems to support the opponents. Opponents argue that strategic trade policy is nothing more than a modern version of age-old and faulty justifications for tariff protection. Once all countries try to be strategic, they will all waste vast sums trying to break into industries in which there is no room for most of them. Domestic consumers would benefit most, they say, if their governments let other countries engage in this game. Consumers could then buy the cheap, subsidized foreign products and export traditional non-subsidized products in return. The opponents of strategic trade policy also argue that democratic governments that enter the game of picking and backing winners are likely to make more bad choices than good ones. One bad choice, with all of its massive development costs written off, would require that many good choices also be made in order to make the equivalent in profits that would allow taxpayers to break even overall.

The Importance of International Competition. In today's world, a country's products must stand up to international competition if they are to survive. Over time, this requires that they hold their own in competition for successful innovations. Over even so short a period as a decade, firms that do not develop new products and new production methods fall seriously behind their competitors in many industries. Using case studies covering many countries, economists such as Michael Porter of Harvard University have shown that almost all firms that succeed in holding their own in competition based on innovation operate in highly competitive environments. Protection, by reducing competition from foreign firms, reduces the incentive for industries to fight to succeed internationally. If any one country adopts high tariffs unilaterally, its domestic industries will become less competitive. Secure in its home market because of the tariff wall, its protected industries are likely to become less and less competitive in the international market. As the gap between domestic and foreign industries widens, any tariff wall will provide less and less protection. Eventually, the domestic industries will succumb to the foreign competition. Meanwhile, domestic living standards will fall relative to foreign ones as an increasing productivity gap opens between domestic protected industries and foreign, internationally oriented ones.

Although restrictive policies have sometimes been pursued following a rational assessment of the ap-

proximate cost, it is hard to avoid the conclusion that more often than not, such policies are often pursued for political objectives or on fallacious economic grounds, with little appreciation of the actual costs involved. The very high tariffs in Canada and the United States during the 1920s and 1930s are a conspicuous example. The current pressure on the governments of Canada, the United States, and the EU to "do something" about the competition from Japan, Korea, and other Pacific Rim countries may well be another.

FALLACIOUS ARGUMENTS FOR PROTECTIONISM

We have seen that there are generally gains from trade, although trade does not necessarily make everyone in a country better off. We have also seen that there are some situations in which there are valid arguments for restricting trade. For every valid argument, however, there are many fallacious arguments—many of these are based, directly or indirectly, on the misconception that in every transaction there is a winner and a loser. Here we review a few such arguments that are frequently advanced in political debates concerning international trade.

Keep the Money at Home

This argument says that if I buy a foreign good, I have the good and the foreigner has the money, whereas if I buy the same good locally, I have the good and our country has the money, too. This argument is based on a common misconception. It assumes that domestic money actually goes abroad physically when imports are purchased and that trade flows only in one direction. But when Canadian importers purchase Japanese goods, they do not send dollars abroad. They (or their financial agents) buy Japanese yen and use them to pay the Japanese manufacturers. They purchase the yen on the foreign exchange market by giving up dollars to someone who wishes to use them for expenditure in Canada. Even if the money did go abroad physically—that is, if a Japanese firm accepted a shipload of Canadian $100 bills—it would be because that firm (or someone to whom it could sell the dollars) wanted them to spend in the only country where they are legal tender—Canada.

Canadian currency, or any other national currency, ultimately does no one any good except as purchasing power. It would be miraculous if Canadian money could be exported in return for real goods. After all, the Bank of Canada has the power to create as much new Canadian money as it wishes (at almost zero direct cost). It is only because Canadian money can buy Canadian products and Canadian assets that others want it.

Protect Against Low-Wage Foreign Labour

This argument says that the products of low-wage countries will drive Canadian products from the market, and the high Canadian standard of living will be dragged down to that of its poorer trading partners. Arguments of this sort have swayed many voters over the years.

As a prelude to considering them, stop and think what the argument would imply if taken out of the international context and put into a local one, where the same principles govern the gains from trade. Is it really impossible for a rich person to gain by trading with a poor person? Would the local millionaire be better off if she did all her own typing, gardening, and cooking? No one believes that a rich person gains nothing by trading with those who are less rich.

Why, then, must a rich group of people lose when they trade with a poor group? "Well," some may say, "the poor group will price its goods too cheaply." Does anyone believe that consumers lose from buying in discount houses or supermarkets just because the prices are lower there than at the old-fashioned corner store? Consumers gain when they can buy the same goods at a lower price. If the Mexicans pay low wages and sell their goods cheaply, Mexican labour may suffer, but Canadians will gain by obtaining imports at a low cost in terms of the goods that must be exported in return. The cheaper our imports are, the better off we are in terms of the goods and services available for domestic consumption.

The gains from trade depend on comparative, not absolute, advantages. World production is higher when any two countries specialize in the production of the goods for which they each have comparative advantages than when they both try to be self-sufficient.

Might it not be possible, however, that Mexico will undersell Canada in all lines of production and thus appropriate all the gains for itself, leaving Canada no better off, or even worse off, than if it had no trade with Mexico? The answer is no. The reason for this depends on the behaviour of exchange rates, which are discussed in Chapter 37. As we shall see in that chapter, equality of demand and supply in foreign exchange markets ensures that trade flows in both directions. In the meantime, the reason a country cannot import for long without exporting may be stated intuitively as follows: Imports can be obtained only by spending the currency of the country that makes the imports. Claims to this currency can be obtained only by exporting goods and services or by borrowing. Consequently, lending and borrowing aside, imports must equal exports. All trade must be in two directions; we can buy only if we can also sell.

In the long run, trade cannot hurt a country by causing it to import without exporting.

Trade, then, always provides scope for international specialization, with each country producing and exporting the goods for which it has a comparative advantage and importing the goods for which it does not.

Exports are Good; Imports are Bad

Exports create domestic income; imports create income for foreigners. Thus, other things being equal, exports tend to increase our total national income, and imports tend to reduce it. Surely, then, it is desirable to encourage exports by subsidizing them and to discourage imports by taxing them. This is an appealing argument, but it is incorrect.

Exports raise national income by adding to the value of domestic output, but they do not add to the value of domestic consumption. In fact, exports are goods produced at home and consumed abroad, while imports are goods produced abroad and consumed at home.

The standard of living in a country depends on the goods and services available for consumption, not on what is produced.

If exports really were "good" and imports really were "bad," then a fully employed economy that managed to increase exports without a corresponding increase in imports ought to be better off. Such a change, however, would result in a reduction in current standards of living because when more goods are sent abroad but no more are brought in from abroad, the total goods available for domestic consumption must fall.

The living standards of a country depend on the goods and services consumed in that country. The importance of exports is that they provide the resources required to purchase imports, either now or in the future.

Create Domestic Jobs

It is sometimes said that an economy with substantial unemployment, such as Canada during much of the

1990s, provides an exception to the case for freer trade. Suppose that tariffs or import quotas cut the imports of Japanese cars, Korean textiles, German kitchen equipment, and Polish vodka. Surely, the argument maintains, this will create more employment in Canadian industries producing similar products. This may be true—but it will *reduce* employment in other industries.

The Japanese, Koreans, Germans, and Poles can buy from Canada only if they earn Canadian dollars by selling things to Canada (or by borrowing dollars from Canada).[2] The decline in their sales of cars, textiles, kitchen equipment, and vodka will decrease their purchases of Canadian lumber, cars, software, banking services, and holidays in Canada. Jobs will be lost in Canadian export industries and gained in industries that formerly faced competition from imports. The major long-term effect is that the same total of employment will merely be redistributed among industries. In the process, living standards will be reduced because employment expands in inefficient import-competing industries and contracts in efficient exporting industries.

Protection is an ineffective way to increase employment or reduce unemployment. It does, however, lead to a redistribution of a given amount of employment.

METHODS OF PROTECTION

We have now studied some of the many reasons why governments may wish to provide some protection to their domestic industries. Our next task is to see how they do it. What are the tools that provide protection?

Two main types of protectionist policy are illustrated in Figure 36-1. Both cause the price of the imported good to rise and its quantity demanded to fall. They differ, however, in how they achieve these results. The caption to the figure analyzes these two types of policy.

POLICIES THAT DIRECTLY RAISE PRICES

The first type of protectionist policy directly raises the price of the imported product. A tariff, also often called an import duty, is the most common policy of

_____
[2]They can also get dollars by selling to other countries and then using their currencies to buy Canadian dollars. But this only complicates the transaction; it does not change its fundamental nature. Other countries must have earned the dollars by selling goods to Canada or borrowing from Canada.

this type. Other such policies are any rules or regulations that fulfill three conditions: They are costly to comply with; they do not apply to competing, domestically produced products; and they are more than is required to meet any legitimate purpose other than restricting trade.

As shown in part (i) of Figure 36-1, tariffs affect both foreign and domestic producers, as well as domestic consumers. The initial effect is to raise the domestic price of the imported product above its world price by the amount of the tariff. Imports fall. As a result, foreign producers sell less and so must transfer resources to other lines of production. The price received on domestically produced units rises, as does the quantity produced domestically. On both counts, domestic producers earn more. However, the cost of producing the extra production at home exceeds the price at which it could be purchased on the world market. Thus the benefit to domestic producers comes at the expense of domestic consumers. Indeed, domestic consumers lose on two counts: First, they consume less of the product because its price rises, and second, they pay a higher price for the amount that they do consume. This extra spending ends up in two places: The extra that is paid on all units produced at home goes to domestic producers, and the extra that is paid on units still imported goes to the government as tariff revenue.

POLICIES THAT DIRECTLY LOWER QUANTITIES

The second type of protectionist policy directly restricts the quantity of an imported product. A common example is the **import quota,** by which the importing country sets a maximum of the quantity of some product that may be imported each year.

A relatively new measure that is becoming increasingly popular is the **voluntary export restriction (VER),** an agreement by an exporting country to limit the amount of a product that it sells to the importing country.

Canada, the United States, and the European Union have used VERs extensively, and the EU makes frequent use of import quotas. Japan has been pressured into negotiating several VERs with Canada, the United States, and the EU in order to limit sales of some of the Japanese goods that have had the most success in international competition. For example, in 1983, the United States and Canada negotiated VERs whereby the Japanese government agreed to restrict total sales of

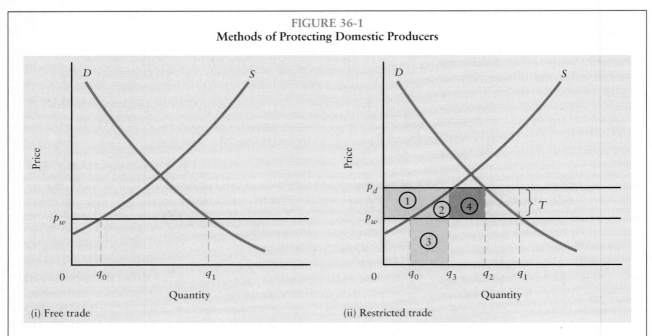

FIGURE 36-1
Methods of Protecting Domestic Producers

(i) Free trade

(ii) Restricted trade

The same reduction in imports and increase in domestic production can be achieved by using either a tariff or a quantity restriction. In both parts of the figure, D and S are the domestic demand and supply curves, respectively, and p_w is the world price of some product that is both produced at home and imported.

Part (i) of the figure shows the situation under free trade. Domestic consumption is q_1, domestic production is q_0, and imports are q_0q_1.

Part (ii) shows what happens when protectionist policies restrict imports to the amount q_3q_2. When this is done by levying a tariff of T per unit, the price in the domestic market rises by the full amount of the tariff to p_d. Consumers reduce consumption from q_1 to q_2 and pay an extra amount, shown by the shaded areas 1, 2, and 4, for the q_2 that they now purchase. Domestic production rises from q_0 to q_3. Because domestic producers receive the domestic price, their receipts rise by the three light-shaded areas, labelled 1, 2, and 3. Area 3 is revenue that was previously earned by foreign producers under free trade, while areas 1 and 2 are now paid by domestic consumers because of the higher prices they now face. Foreign suppliers of the imported good continue to receive the world price, so the government receives as tariff revenue the extra amount paid by consumers for the $q_3 q_2$ units that are still imported (shown by the dark shaded area, 4).

When the same result is accomplished by a quantity restriction, the government—through either a quota or a voluntary export restriction (VER)—reduces imports to q_3q_2. This drives the domestic market price up to p_d and has the same effect on domestic producers and consumers as the tariff. Since the government has merely restricted the quantity of imports, both foreign and domestic suppliers get the higher price in the domestic market. Thus foreign suppliers now receive the extra amount paid by domestic consumers (represented by the shaded area labelled 4) for the units that are still imported.

Japanese cars to these two countries for three years. When the agreements ran out in 1986, the Japanese continued to restrict their automobile sales by unilateral voluntary action, which they still do over ten years later. This episode is further considered in Application 36-1.

At one time or another, most of the rapidly growing countries of Asia have seen the United States place quantitative restrictions on the sales of some of their products that were most successful in penetrating the U.S. market.

NOMINAL AND EFFECTIVE TARIFF RATES

The tariff rate charged on each product, called the **nominal tariff rate,** does not necessarily show the degree of protection given to that product. Nominal rates frequently understate the degree of protection offered to domestic manufacturing industries, and a better measure is provided by what is called the **effective tariff rate.**

Nominal and effective tariff rates differ whenever imported raw materials or semifinished goods carry a different tariff rate than imports of the final goods that embody these intermediate products.

To illustrate this important point, consider an example drawn from Canadian-U.S. trade before these countries' free trade agreement began eliminating tariffs. Office furniture was manufactured in both the United States and Canada using Canadian wood. There was no tariff applied to the wood entering the United States, but the manufactured furniture was subject to a 10 percent tariff. When the product was manufactured in Canada, the raw material accounted for half the cost of the final product, and the other half was value added by Canadian manufacturers. Because of the 10 percent tariff, a unit of output that cost $100 to produce in Canada sold in the United States for $110 (in Canadian dollars).

Now consider the position of a U.S. manufacturer who was less efficient than its Canadian competitor. Say that the U.S. firm's production costs were 20 percent higher than those of the Canadian firm. Thus to produce one unit of output, the raw material cost the U.S. firm $50, but its other costs—including the opportunity costs of its capital—were $60 (i.e., 20 percent higher than the Canadian manufacturer's costs of $50). This gave the U.S. firm a final price of $110, which was just low enough to compete against the tariff-burdened Canadian import.

In this example, a U.S. tariff of 10 percent on the value of the final product is sufficient to protect a U.S. firm that is 20 percent less efficient than its Canadian competitor. To measure this effect, the effective tariff rate expresses the tariff as a percentage of the *value added* by the exporting industry in question. Thus the effective U.S. tariff rate on the Canadian furniture in our example is 20 percent, whereas the nominal tariff rate on furniture is only 10 percent.

TRADE-REMEDY LAWS AND NONTARIFF BARRIERS

As tariffs were lowered over the years since 1947, countries that wished to protect domestic industries began using, and often abusing, a series of trade restrictions that came to be known as nontariff barriers (NTBs). The original purpose of some of these was to remedy certain legitimate problems that arise in international trade, and for this reason, they are often called *trade-remedy laws*. All too often, how-

ever, they are misused to become potent means of simple protectionism.

The Escape Clause

One procedure that can be used as an NTB is the so-called escape clause action. A rapid surge of some imports may threaten the existence of domestic producers. These producers may then be given temporary relief to allow them time to adjust. This is done by raising tariff rates on the product in question above those set by international agreements. The trouble is that, once imposed, these "temporary" measures are hard to eliminate.

Dumping

Selling a product in a foreign country at a lower price than in the domestic market is known as **dumping**. Dumping is a form of price discrimination studied in the theory of monopoly. Most governments have antidumping duties designed to protect their own industries against what is viewed as unfair foreign pricing practices.

Dumping, if it lasts indefinitely, can be a gift to the receiving country. Its consumers get goods from abroad at less than their full cost of production. Dumping is more often a temporary measure, designed to get rid of unwanted surpluses, or a predatory attempt to drive competitors out of business. In either case, domestic producers complain about unfair foreign competition. In both cases, it is accepted international practice to levy antidumping duties on foreign imports. These duties are designed to eliminate the discriminatory elements in their prices.

Unfortunately, antidumping laws have been evolving over the past three decades in ways that allow antidumping duties to become barriers to trade and competition rather than to provide redress for unfair trading practices. Several features of the antidumping system that is now in effect in many countries make it highly protectionist.

First, any price discrimination is classified as dumping and is subject to penalties. Thus prices in the producer's domestic market become, in effect, minimum prices below which no sales can be made in foreign markets, whatever the circumstances in the domestic and foreign markets.

Second, following a change in the U.S. law in the early 1970s, many countries' laws now calculate the "margin of dumping" as the difference between the price that is charged in that country's market and the

IMPORT RESTRICTIONS ON JAPANESE CARS: TARIFFS OR QUOTAS?

Voluntary export restrictions (VERs) have been commonly used by the European Union, Canada, and the United States to limit Japanese imports in key industries where the Japanese have a strong competitive advantage, such as cars and electronics. The Japanese have agreed to such arrangements because for any given volume of trade restrictions, they are far more profitable to the Japanese than most alternative arrangements.

People who are strong supporters of free trade criticize such arrangements, which certainly shield several North American and European industries from intense Japanese competition and greatly raise the price of the affected products to North American and European consumers and producers who use such goods.

The issue raised in this box concerns alternative methods of restricting the import of Japanese cars into Canada. Given that trade is to be restricted, what does economic theory predict to be the relative merits of VERs and tariffs? In both cases, imports are restricted, and the resulting scarcity supports a higher market price. With a tariff, the extra market value is appropriated by the Canadian government. With a VER, the extra market value accrues to the goods' suppliers—in this case, the Japanese car makers and their Canadian retailers.

Both cases are illustrated in the accompanying figure. We assume that the Canadian market provides a small enough part of total Japanese car sales to leave the Japanese willing to supply all the cars that are demanded in Canada at their fixed list price. This is the price p_0 in both parts of the figure. Given the Canadian demand curve for Japanese cars, D, there are q_0 cars sold before restrictions are imposed.

In part (i), Canada places a tariff of T per unit on Japanese cars, raising their price in Canada to p_1 and lowering sales to q_1. Suppliers' revenue is shown by the light shaded area. Government tariff revenue is shown by the dark shaded area. In part (ii), a VER of q_1 is negotiated, making the supply curve of Japanese cars vertical at q_1. The market-clearing price is p_1. The suppliers' revenue is the whole shaded area ($p_1 \times q_1$). In both cases, the shortage of Japanese cars drives up their price, creating a substantial margin over costs. Under a tariff, the Canadian government captures the margin. Under a VER policy, however, the margin accrues to the Japanese manufacturers.

Although this is a simplified picture, it captures the essence of what actually happened between 1983 and 1986 when the Japanese agreed to restrict their sales of cars in Canada and the United States. First, while sellers of North American cars were keeping prices as low as possible, and sometimes offering rebates on slow-selling models, Japanese cars were listed at healthy profit margins. Second, while it was always possible for the buyer of a North American car to negotiate a good discount off the list price, Japanese cars usually sold for their full list price.

foreign producers' "full allocated cost" (average total cost). This means that when there is global excess capacity in some industry so that the profit-maximizing price for all producers is below average total cost (but above average variable cost), foreign producers can be convicted of dumping. This gives domestic producers enormous protection whenever the market price falls temporarily below average total cost.

Third, law in the United States (but not in all other countries) places the onus of proof on the accused. Facing a charge of dumping, a foreign producer must prove within the short time that is allowed for such a defence that the charge is unfounded.

Fourth, U.S. antidumping duties are imposed with no time limit, so they often persist long after foreign firms have altered the prices that gave rise to them. The United States, and to a lesser extent Canada and the EU, have been world leaders in turning antidumping policies increasingly into trade barriers. Unfortunately, more and more of the world's trading countries are copying U.S. law, and U.S. and Canadian exporters are finding themselves increasingly subjected to the kinds

Third, because Japanese manufacturers were not allowed to supply all of the cars that they could sell in Canada, they had to choose which types of cars to supply. Not surprisingly, they tended to satisfy fully the demand for their more expensive cars, which have higher profit margins. This change in the "product mix" of Japanese cars exported to North America raised the average profit per car exported.

The VERs were thus costly to North American consumers and profitable to Japanese auto manufacturers. It has been estimated that North American consumers paid about $150,000 (U.S.) per year for each job that was saved in the North American automobile industry and that most of this went to Japanese producers! (This cost to consumers per job saved is typical of what is found in many industries where VERs or their equivalents have been used.) Of course, this amount is spread over a great many consumers, so each does not notice the amount of his or her contribution. Nonetheless, $150,000 per year could do a lot of things, including fully retraining the workers and subsidizing their transfer to industries and areas where they could produce things that could be sold on free markets without government protection.

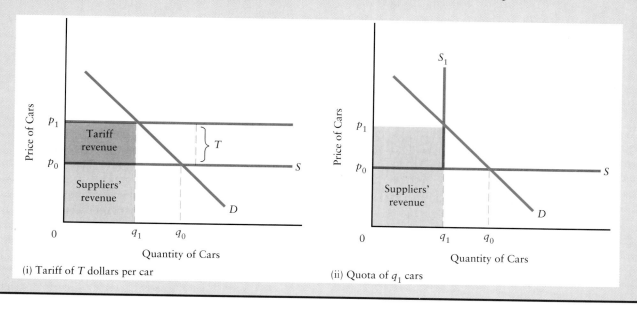

(i) Tariff of T dollars per car

(ii) Quota of q_1 cars

of antidumping duties formerly used mainly by the United States, Canada, and the EU.

Countervailing Duties

Countervailing duties, which are commonly used by the U.S. government but much less so elsewhere, provide another case in which a trade relief measure can sometimes become a covert NTB. The countervailing duty is designed to act, not as a tariff barrier, but rather as a means of creating a "level playing field" on which fair international competition can take place. Privately owned domestic firms rightly complain that they cannot compete against the seemingly bottomless purses of foreign governments. Subsidized foreign exports can be sold indefinitely at prices that would produce losses in the absence of the subsidy. The original object of countervailing duties was to counteract the effect on price of the presence of such foreign subsidies.

If a domestic firm suspects the existence of such a subsidy and registers a complaint, its government is required to make an investigation. For a countervailing duty to be levied, the investigation must determine, first, that the foreign subsidy to the specific industry in question does exist and, second, that it is large enough to cause significant injury to competing domestic firms. (A similar determination by domestic authorities is required before antidumping duties are imposed.)

There is no doubt that countervailing duties have sometimes been used to remove the effects of "unfair" competition that are caused by foreign subsidies. Many governments complain, however, that U.S. countervailing duties are often used as thinly disguised barriers to trade. At the early stages of the development of countervailing duties, only subsidies whose prime effect was to distort trade were possible objects of countervailing duties. Even then, however, the existence of equivalent domestic subsidies was not taken into account when decisions were made to put countervailing duties on subsidized imports. Thus the United States levies some countervailing duties against foreign goods even though the foreign subsidy is less than the domestic subsidy. This does not create a level playing field.

Over time, the type of subsidy that is subject to countervailing duties has evolved until almost any government program that affects industry now risks becoming the object of a countervailing duty. Because all governments, including most U.S. state governments, have programs that provide direct or indirect assistance to industry, the potential for the use of countervailing duties as thinly disguised trade barriers is enormous.

CURRENT TRADE POLICY

In the remainder of the chapter, we discuss trade policy in practice. We start with the many international agreements that govern current trade policies and then look in a little more detail at the NAFTA.

Before 1947, any country was free to impose tariffs on its imports. However, when one country increased its tariffs, the action often triggered retaliatory actions by its trading partners. The 1930s saw a high-water mark of world protectionism as each country sought to raise its employment and national income by raising its tariffs. The end result was lowered efficiency, less trade, but no more employment or income. Since the end of World War II, much effort has been devoted to reducing tariff barriers, both on a multilateral and on a regional basis.

THE GENERAL AGREEMENT ON TARIFFS AND TRADE (GATT)

One of the most notable achievements of the post–World War II era was the creation of the General Agreement on Tariffs and Trade (GATT). The principle of the GATT is that each member country agrees not to make unilateral tariff increases. This prevents the outbreak of tariff wars in which countries raise tariffs to protect particular domestic industries and to retaliate against other countries' tariff increases. The last such round of mutually destructive tariff wars occurred in the 1920s and 1930s. The GATT countries, which numbered 117 in 1996, also meet periodically to negotiate on matters affecting foreign trade and related matters and to agree on across-the-board tariff cuts.

The three most recently completed rounds of GATT agreements, the Kennedy Round (completed in 1967), the Tokyo Round (completed in 1979), and the Uruguay Round (completed in 1994), have each agreed to reduce world tariffs substantially, the first two by about one-third each and the last by about 40 percent.

The Uruguay Round agreement was the culmination of years of negotiation. The agreement created a new body, the World Trade Organization (WTO), to replace the GATT. It also created a new legal structure for multilateral trading under which all members have equal mutual rights and obligations. Until the WTO was formed, developing countries that were in the GATT enjoyed all the GATT rights but were exempt from most of its obligations to liberalize trade—obligations that applied only to the developed countries. Now, however, all such special treatments are to be phased out over the seven years ending in 2002. There is also a new dispute settlement mechanism with much more power to reach and enforce effective rulings over nontariff barriers than existed in the past.

The Multifiber Agreement, which greatly restricts the ability of developing countries to export textiles in which they have a major comparative advantage, is to be phased out over 10 years. There are much stronger rules for trade in services, the protection of foreign investment, and intellectual property. There is also a much improved mechanism for settling disputes about alleged infractions of WTO agreements.

From the point of view of most of the world's countries, the big failure of these talks was in not getting a major liberalization of trade in agricultural goods. Such an agreement was resisted by the EU and Canada. The EU has a scheme called the Common Agricultural Policy (CAP) which provides general support for most of its agricultural products. The CAP has made Europe self-sufficient in many agricultural products that it used to import from developing nations and it also creates large surpluses which the EU sells abroad at heavily subsidized prices. This causes major harm to agricultural producers in less developed countries whose governments are too poor to compete with the EU in a subsidy war.

Canada, which has free trade in many agricultural commodities, was concerned to maintain its supply management over a number of industries including poultry, eggs, and diary products. These schemes, which we described in Chapter 6, are administered by the provinces who restrict domestic production and thus push domestic prices well above world levels. The federal government made them possible by imposing quotas on imports of these products at the national level.

Canada, the EU, and a number of other countries that lavishly protect some or all of their domestic agricultural producers, were finally forced to agree to a plan to end all import quotas on agricultural products. In a process called "tariffication" these quotas have been replaced by "tariff equivalents," which are tariffs that restrict trade by the same amount as the quotas did. Canadian tariff equivalents are as high as several hundred percent in some products, showing just how restrictive the Canadian policy is. The hope among countries which are pushing for freer trade in agricultural commodities is that pressure will build to reduce these very high tariffs over the next few decades. As we shall see later in this chapter, the tariffication caused more immediate problems for Canada.

All in all, however, the successful completion of the Uruguay Round represented a major victory for the supporters of a strong, rule-based, multilateral trading system.

TYPES OF REGIONAL AGREEMENTS

Regional agreements seek to liberalize trade over a much smaller group of countries than the WTO membership. Three standard forms of regional trade-liberalizing agreements are *free trade areas, customs unions,* and *common markets.*

A **free trade area** (FTA) is the least comprehensive of the three. It allows for tariff-free trade among the member countries, but it leaves each member free to levy its own trade policy with respect to other countries. As a result, members must maintain customs points at their common borders to make sure that imports into the free trade area do not all enter through the member that is levying the lowest tariff on each item. They must also agree on rules of origin to establish when a good is made in a member country and hence is able to pass tariff-free across their borders and when it is imported from outside the FTA and hence is subject to tariffs when it crosses borders within the FTA.

A **customs union** is a free trade area plus an agreement to establish a common trade policy with the rest of the world. Because they have a common trade policy, the members need neither customs controls on goods moving among themselves nor rules of origin. Once a good has entered any member country it has met the common rules and regulations and paid the common tariff and so it may henceforth be treated the same as a good that is produced within the union.

A **common market** is a customs union that also has free movement of labour and capital among its members. The European Union is by far the most successful example of a common market.

TRADE CREATION AND TRADE DIVERSION

A major effect of regional trade liberalization is to reallocate resources. Economists divide these effects into two categories, *trade creation* and *trade diversion*.

Trade creation occurs when producers in one member country find that they can export to another member country as a result of the elimination of the tariffs. For example, as the Canada-U.S. free trade agreement eliminated most cross-border tariffs, some U.S. firms found that they could undersell their Canadian competitors in some product lines, and some Canadian firms found that they could undersell their U.S. competitors in other product lines. As a result, specialization occurred, and new international trade developed. This trade, which is based on (natural or acquired) comparative advantage, is illustrated in Table 36-1.

Trade creation represents efficient specialization according to comparative advantage.

Trade diversion occurs when exporters in one member country replace foreign exporters as suppliers to another member country. For example, trade diversion occurs when U.S. firms find that they can undersell competitors from the rest of the world in the Canadian market, not because they are the cheapest source of supply, but because their tariff-free prices are lower than the tariff-burdened prices of imports from other countries. This effect is a gain to Canadian firms but a loss to Canada overall, which now has to export more goods for any given amount of imports than before the trade diversion occurred. Similarly, trade diversion occurs when Canadian producers win out over

TABLE 36-1
Trade Creation and Trade Diversion

Producing Country	Canadian Delivered Price Without Tariffs (dollars)	Canadian Delivered Price with a 10 percent Tariff (dollars)
Trade creation		
Canada	40.00	40.00
United States	37.00	40.70
Trade diversion		
Taiwan	20.00	22.00
United States	21.50	23.65

Regional tariff reductions can cause trade creation and trade diversion. The table gives two cases. In the first case, a U.S. good, which could be sold for $37.00 in Canada, has its price increased to $40.70 by a 10 percent Canadian tariff. The Canadian industry, which can sell the good for $40.00 with or without a tariff on imports, is protected against the more efficient U.S. producer. When the tariff is removed by the Canada-U.S. free trade agreement, the U.S. good wins the market by selling at $37.00. Trade is created between Canada and the United States by eliminating the inefficient Canadian production solely for a protected home market.

In the second case, Taiwan can undersell the U.S. in the Canadian market for another product when neither is subject to a tariff (column 1) and when both are subject to a 10 percent tariff (column 2). But after the Canada-U.S. free trade agreement, the U.S. good enters Canada tariff-free and sells for $21.50, whereas the Taiwanese good, which is still subject to the Canadian tariff, continues to sell for $22.00. The U.S. good wins the market, and Canadian trade is diverted from Taiwan to the U.S. even though Taiwan is the lower-cost supplier (excluding the tariff).

competitors from the rest of the world in the U.S. market because they are not subject to a tariff in that market while their nonmember competitors are. This effect benefits Canadian firms at the expense of U.S. consumers. Table 36-1 also illustrates trade diversion.

From the global perspective, trade diversion represents an inefficient use of resources.

THE HISTORY OF FREE TRADE AREAS

The first important free trade area in the modern era was the European Free Trade Association (EFTA). It was formed in 1960 by a group of European countries that were unwilling to join the European Common Market (the forerunner of the European Union) because of its all-embracing character. Not wanting to be left out of the gains from trade, they formed an association whose sole purpose was tariff removal. First, they removed all tariffs on trade

among themselves. Then each country signed a free-trade-area agreement with the EU. This made the EU-EFTA market the largest tariff-free market in the world (over 300 million people). In recent years almost all of the EFTA countries have entered the EU.

In 1988, a sweeping agreement was signed between Canada and the United States, instituting free trade on almost all goods and most nongovernment services and covering what is the world's largest flow of international trade between any two countries. In 1993, this agreement was extended into the North American Free Trade Agreement (NAFTA) by renegotiating the Canada-U.S. agreement to include Mexico. Provision is made within the NAFTA for the accession of other countries with the hope that it may eventually evolve into a Western Hemispheric Free Trade Area (WHFTA) by taking in most, or even all, of the countries of South and Central America. The first accession was to have been Chile. But at the beginning of 1996, the negotiations for its entry into NAFTA were being held up by domestic political considerations in the United States.

Australia and New Zealand have also entered into an association that removes restrictions on trade in goods and services between their two countries. The countries of Latin America have been experimenting with free trade areas for many decades. Most earlier attempts failed, but in the past few years, more durable FTAs seem to have been formed, the most successful of which is Mercosur, which includes Argentina, Brazil, Uruguay, and Paraguay. Whether these will remain stand-alone agreements or evolve into a WHFTA remains to be seen.

THE NORTH AMERICAN FREE TRADE AGREEMENT (NAFTA)

The NAFTA is merely an extension of the Canada-U.S. free trade agreement with some important improvements based on the experience of the earlier agreement. It is a free trade area and not a customs union; each country retains its own external trade policy, and rules of origin are needed to determine when a good is made within the NAFTA and so allowed to move freely among the members. We now look in detail at various aspects of the NAFTA.

National Treatment

The fundamental principle that guides the NAFTA is the principle of *national treatment*. This means that countries are free to establish any laws they wish and that these can differ as much as desired among member countries, with the sole proviso that these laws must not discriminate on the basis of nationality. So the United States can have tough environmental laws or standards for particular goods, but it must enforce these equally on Canadian, Mexican, and U.S. firms and on domestically produced and imported goods. The idea of national treatment is to allow a maximum of policy independence while preventing national policies from being used as barriers to trade and investment. This principle of maximizing policy independence subject to removing trade barriers is opposite to the EU's philosophy, which seeks to harmonize as many policies as possible in order to create an all-encompassing economic union.[3]

Other Major Provisions

First, all tariffs on trade between the United States and Canada are to be eliminated by 1999. Canada-Mexico and Mexico-U.S. tariffs are to be phased out over a 15-year period that started in 1994. Also, a number of nontariff barriers are eliminated or circumscribed.

Second, the agreement guarantees national treatment to foreign investment once it enters a country while permitting each country to screen a substantial amount of inbound foreign investment before it enters.

Third, all existing measures that restrict trade and investment that are not explicitly removed are "grandfathered," a term referring to the continuation of a practice that predates the agreement and would have been prohibited by the terms of the agreement were it not specifically exempted. This is probably the single most important departure from free trade under the NAFTA. Under it, a large collection of restrictive measures in each of the three countries are given indefinite life. An alternative would have been to "sunset" all of these provisions by negotiating dates at which each would be eliminated. From the point of view of long-term trade liberalization, even a 50-year extension would have been preferable to an indefinite exemption.

Fourth, a few goods remain subject to serious nontariff trade restrictions. In Canada, the main examples are supply-managed agricultural products, beer, textiles, and the cultural industries. Restrictions for the Canadian supply-managed agricultural products may be short-lived because of their tariffication under the Uruguay round of GATT. Textile restriction comes under the Multifiber Agreement which is

being phased out over a 15-year period under the Uruguay round. So beer and culture are the only Canadian restrictions that seem secure at the moment. In the U.S., textiles, shipping between U.S. ports, and banking were shielded from free trade in good and services.

Fifth, trade in most nongovernmental services is liberalized by giving service firms the right of establishment in all member countries and the privilege of national treatment. There is also a limited opening of the markets in financial services to entry from firms based in the NAFTA countries.

Finally, a significant minority of government procurement is opened to cross-border bids.

Dispute Settlement

From Canada's point of view, by far the biggest setback in the negotiations for the Canada-U.S. FTA was the failure to obtain agreement on a common regime for countervailing and antidumping duties. In view of that failure, no significant attempt was made to deal with this issue in the NAFTA negotiations. The U.S. Congress has been unwilling to abandon the unilateral use of these powerful weapons.

In the absence of such a multilateral regime, a dispute settlement mechanism was put in place. Under it, the domestic determinations that are required for the levying of antidumping and countervailing duties are subject to review by a panel of Canadians, Americans, and Mexicans. This international review replaces appeal through the domestic courts. Panels are empowered to uphold the domestic determinations or refer the decision to the domestic authority—which in effect is a binding order for a new investigation. The referral can be repeated until the panel is satisfied that the domestic laws have been correctly and fairly applied.

This is pathbreaking: For the first time in its history, the United States has agreed to submit the administration of its domestic laws to binding scrutiny by an international panel that often contains a majority of foreigners.

Results

The Canada-U.S. FTA aroused a great debate in Canada. Supporters looked for major increases in the security of existing trade from U.S. protectionist attacks and for a growth of new trade. Detractors predicted a flight of firms to the U.S., the loss of Canadian competitiveness, and even the loss of Canada's political independence.

---

[3]This principle was qualified to some extent by the negotiation, after the main treaty was signed, of a side agreement between the United States and Mexico establishing minimum standards of environmental protection in Mexico.

CANADA-U.S. TRADE DISPUTES

Although more than 95 percent of Canada-U.S. trade in goods and services passes between the two countries without dispute or hindrance, some items have been beset by persistent disputes. Here is a brief discussion of three of the most important.

SOFTWOOD LUMBER

Canada exports large amounts of softwood lumber to the United States. And U.S. producers have persistently claimed that Canadian Provincial government policies provide a concealed subsidy which should be evened out with a countervailing duty. The main bone of contention is *stumpage,* which is the royalty that governments charge the logging companies for cutting timber on government-owned land. In the U.S., stumpage fees are set by open auction. In Canada, the fees are set in private negotiations between logging companies and the government. U.S. critics argue that the much lower Canadian stumpage fees that emerge from this process are a subsidy from the government to its powerful friends in the lumber industry. Canadians argue that the higher U.S. stumpage fees reflect the higher services that U.S. government provides for their lumber companies by way of infrastructure that Canadian lumber companies must provide for themselves.

Just before the Canada-U.S. FTA was finalized, the Canadian government imposed an export tax on lumber going to the U.S. to forestall the imposition of a U.S. countervailing duty. When this tax expired, Canada did not renew it and the U.S. imposed a countervailing duty. Two dispute settlement panels found in Canada's favour, but largely on the grounds of narrow technicalities. The U.S. then changed its laws to remove what they saw as the loopholes that the Canadians had used. In 1996, under the threat of another countervailing duty, the Canadian government left negotiations to the provinces who reached separate accommodations with the U.S. authorities to use taxes to limit exports to current levels.

Who wins and who loses? The restriction raised prices in the U.S. market making U.S. users of lumber clear losers, and U.S. lumber producers clear winners. The effect on the Canadian lumber industry depends on the elasticity of demand for Canadian lumber in the U.S. market. Providing that U.S. demand is sufficiently inelastic, Canadian lumber producers are winners—just as the Japanese car producers were winners from their voluntary export restrictions to the North American market.

SUPPLY-MANAGED AGRICULTURAL INDUSTRIES

We have seen that supply management by the Canadian provinces in the poultry and dairy indus-

During this great debate, the official opposition, the Liberal party, opposed the agreement. Later, when the NAFTA was negotiated, they advocated major renegotiation of that agreement before it was approved. In 1993, after the NAFTA had been negotiated, but before the enabling legislation had been passed, the Liberals won a massive electoral victory over the Conservatives who had negotiated both the Canada-U.S. FTA and the NAFTA. After only a short time, however, the new Liberal government announced that it would approve the NAFTA exactly as the Conservatives had negotiated it and would

make no attempt to withdraw from the Canada-U.S. FTA. Political debate then ended. When the major party to oppose the agreements accepted them as soon as it came into power, both agreements ceased to be major political issues.

By and large, both the Canada-U.S. FTA and NAFTA agreements have worked out just about as expected by their supporters—although it is still too early to determine their very long-term effects. Industry has clearly restructured in the direction of export orientation in all three countries. All three countries are importing more from and exporting tries substantially raises the prices paid by Canadian consumers. For years, the federal government had supported these policies by imposing import quotas on the managed products, without which their prices would be driven down to world levels. The federal government successfully negotiated exemptions for these quotas under the Canada-U.S. FTA. In the Uruguay round of GATT negotiations despite spirited resistance, the federal government was forced to agree to "tariffication" of these quotas. The U.S. then took the position that although the quotas had been exempt under the FTA, their tariff equivalents were not. After all, the U.S. argued, all tariffs without exception are to be removed by 1999 under the FTA. At the time of writing, the debate continues without an obvious resolution.

Who wins and who loses? Although it would be a political victory for the U.S. if Canada were forced to remove the massive tariffs currently levied on supply-managed agricultural products, it would also be a clear victory for Canadian consumers who pay much more than world prices for these protected products.

CULTURAL INDUSTRIES

Canada has always sought to support its magazines, book sellers, film distributors, and other cultural industries from U.S. competition. Although there was never any pressure to prevent governments on both sides of the border from subsidizing the performing arts, such as music and drama, protection of the cultural industries more widely defined was a serious bone of contention during the FTA negotiations. In the end, Canada got exemption for all of its broadly defined cultural industries.

Who wins and who loses? The Canadian exemption for its cultural industries was a mixed blessing because, unlike business, professional and trades persons, Canadian performing artists did not obtain the right extended under the FTA's "temporary access" provision to enter the U.S. on temporary visas to do specific jobs for up to two years. These would have been available to performing artists had it not been for the blanket exemption of the Canadian cultural industries. The clear winners were the owners of Canadian magazines and other Canadian-made cultural products that would otherwise have had to compete with U.S. products in the Canadian market.

The U.S. continues to be highly critical of Canadian cultural protectionism. The Canadian government replies that, without this protection, Canada-only publications could not compete with U.S. products which had already covered their fixed cost in the U.S. market and were then marginally adapted to the Canadian market.

This is a debate which will very probably go on for years if not decades.

more to each other. This is particularly true between Canada and the United States, where the great majority of tariffs have already been removed (some at the outset in 1989, some over a 5-year period ending in 1994, and the rest over a 10-year period which will end in 1999). As the theory of trade predicts, specialization has occurred in many areas, resulting in more U.S. imports of some product lines from Canada and more U.S. exports of other goods to Canada. Total trade—in both directions—increased sharply between the United States and Mexico during the first two years of NAFTA; it also increased, although much less sharply, between Canada and Mexico.

It is hard to say how much trade diversion there will be. The greatest potential is with Mexico, which competes in the U.S. and Canadian markets with a large number of products produced in other low-wage countries. South-East Asian exporters to the United States and Canada have been worried that Mexico would capture some of their markets by virtue of having tariff-free access denied to their goods. Most estimates predict, however, that trade creation will dominate over trade diversion.

Foreign investment has increased, particularly in Canada and Mexico, although it will be years before the magnitude of the induced increase in foreign investment can be reasonably estimated. A recent government report estimated that the bulk of the new jobs created in Canada over the next several years would be created by foreign rather than domestic investment. This made the fears of a NAFTA-induced flight of foreign capital from Canada look ill founded.

Most transitional difficulties were initially felt in each country's import-competing industries, which is what theory predicts. An agreement such as the NAFTA brings its advantages by encouraging a movement of resources out of protected but inefficient import-competing industries, which decline, and into efficient export industries, which expand because they have better access to the markets of other members countries. Southern Ontario and parts of Quebec had major problems as some traditional exports fell and resources had to be moved to sectors where trade was expanding. Eight years after the agreement however, Southern Ontario was booming again and its most profitable sectors were those that exported to the United States. Taking the 40 industries that account for virtually all of Ontario's foreign trade, exports to the U.S. were up in all but two (while exports to the rest of the world expanded significantly in only about 10). Similarly with imports: they increased in all but seven categories, all of which were relatively insignificant in total trade.

Finally, the dispute settlement mechanism seems to have worked well. A large number of disputes have arisen and have been referred to panels. Panel members have usually reacted as professionals rather than as nationals. Most cases have been decided on their merits with Canada winning significantly more than half the cases, the rest of the decisions being in favour of the United States. Allegations that decisions were reached on national rather than professional grounds have only been seriously raised in one case. There, the single U.S. panellist asserted forcibly that the two Canadian panellists acted in a prejudicial manner.

Nonetheless, as Application 36-2 shows, several long-term disputes still disturb the generally tranquil state of trading relations between Canada and the U.S.

THE FUTURE OF CANADIAN TRADE POLICY

Although the United States has been one of the staunchest defenders of the free-market system, many American voices have recently advocated moves that would reduce the influence of market forces on international trade and increase the degree of government control over that trade. It is ironic to see enthusiasm for state-managed trade growing in the United States just as the former Socialist countries of Eastern Europe have at last agreed that free markets are better regulators of economic activity than any government. The strength of the movement toward managed trade will become clearer during the next 5 or 10 years.

The Canadian government opposes these nonmarket pushes coming from the United States. As a small trading nation with about a third of its total GDP accounted for by international trade in goods and services, trade policy will always be at the centre of any Canadian government's policy. Whatever they have said while in opposition, no Canadian government in modern times has departed from the policy of liberalizing trade and, more recently, of liberalizing investment flows as well.

The breakup of the world into a set of trading blocks that did more and more trade within the block and less and less with outside countries would be to the disadvantage of most countries, particularly the smaller ones. Bilateral bargaining between groups of nations tend to involve large countries while leaving the smaller ones on the sidelines. For these reasons, among many others, Canada as a small trading nation has an enormous stake in the preservation of the liberalized multilateral trading regime.

Such high stakes ensure that Canadian policy makers will regard the WTO as Canada's best friend in pushing for more liberalized international trade and as its best defence against protectionist pressures (as they earlier regarded its predecessor the GATT). Regional agreements are seen as supplements rather than as alternatives to the multilateralism of the WTO. The Canada-U.S. FTA and the NAFTA give Canada increased access to what is by far its largest market and shields that access to a great extent from protectionist sentiments in the United States.

Canada prospers or suffers as its trading sector prospers or suffers. For this reason, maintaining a healthy trading sector will remain, as it has been for decades, a prime concern of Canadian policy markers, who wish to maintain and enhance the country's material prosperity.

SUMMARY

A. THE THEORY OF TRADE POLICY

- The case for free trade is that world output of all products can be higher under free trade than when protectionism restricts regional specialization.
- Protection can be urged as a means to ends other than maximizing world living standards. Examples of such ends are to produce a diversified economy, to reduce fluctuations in national income, to retain distinctive national traditions, and to improve national defence.
- Protection can also be urged on the grounds that it may lead to higher living standards for the protectionist country than a policy of free trade would. Such a result might come about by using a monopoly position to influence the terms of trade or by developing a dynamic comparative advantage by allowing inexperienced or uneconomically small industries to become efficient enough to compete with foreign industries.
- A recent argument for protection is to operate a strategic trade policy whereby a country attracts firms in oligopolistic industries that, due to scale economies, can earn large profits even in the long run.
- Some fallacious protectionist arguments are that (a) mutually advantageous trade is impossible because one trader's gain must always be the other's loss; (b) buying abroad sends our money abroad, while buying at home keeps our money at home; (c) our high-paid workers must be protected against the competition from low-paid foreign workers; and (d) imports are to be discouraged because they lower national income and cause unemployment.

B. METHODS OF PROTECTION

- Trade can be restricted either by policies that directly raise prices such as tariffs or that operate in the first instance on quantities such as import quotas and voluntary export restrictions.
- As tariff barriers have been reduced over the years, they have been replaced in part by nontariff barriers. The two most important are antidumping and countervailing duties which, although they can provide legitimate restraints on unfair trading practices, are also used as serious nontariff barriers to trade.

C. CURRENT TRADE POLICY

- The General Agreement on Tariffs and Trade under which countries agree to reduce trade barriers through multilateral negotiations and not to raise them unilaterally, has greatly reduced world tariffs since its inception in 1947. At the end of the Uruguay round, the GATT was succeeded by the World Trade Organization (WTO).
- Regional trade-liberalizing agreements such as free trade areas and common markets bring efficiency gains through trade creation and efficiency losses through trade diversion.
- The NAFTA is the world's largest and most successful free trade area, and the European Union is the world's largest and most successful common market.

KEY CONCEPTS

Free trade and protectionism
Tariffs and nontariff barriers
Voluntary export restrictions (VERs)
Countervailing and antidumping duties
The General Agreement on Tariffs and Trade (GATT)

The World Trade Organization (WTO)
Common markets, customs unions, and free trade areas
Trade creation and trade diversion

The North American Free Trade Agreement (NAFTA)

DISCUSSION QUESTIONS

1. Some Canadians opposed Canada's entry into NAFTA on the grounds that Canadian firms could not compete with the goods produced by cheap Mexican labour, which at the current exchange rate is earning less than $2 per hour in Mexico's highest wage sectors. Comment on the following points in relation to the above worries:

   a. Many Mexican goods entered Canada tariff-free before the NAFTA, and where they did not, the average Canadian tariff was about 10 percent.

   b. "Mexicans are the most expensive cheap labour I have ever encountered"—statement by the owner of a Canadian firm who is moving back from Mexico to Canada.

c. The theory of the gains from trade says that a high-productivity, high-wage country can gain from trading with a low-wage, low-productivity country.

d. International equilibrium could not be one in which Mexico undersold all Canadian-made goods in the Canadian market.

e. Technological change is rapidly reducing labour costs as a proportion of total costs in many products; in many industries that use high-tech production methods this proportion is already well below 20 percent.

2. Many Canadian opponents of the Canada-U.S. FTA and the NAFTA worried that it would cause an exodus of Canadian-based firms to the U.S. or Mexico. Suppose you are advising a foreign firm that is considering locating in one of the NAFTA countries to serve the North American market. Rank the following arrangements as to the attraction they offer for Canada as a location for this foreign investment (other things being equal). Which were within the control of Canadian policy makers and which beyond their control?

a. There are no regional trade-liberalizing agreements between any of the three countries (the status quo as of 1985).

b. The only agreement is the Canada-U.S. FTA (the status quo in 1990).

c. The U.S. has separate agreements with Canada and Mexico (which would have happened if Canada had stayed out of NAFTA).

d. The only agreement is a bilateral one between the U.S. and Mexico (which would have happened if Canada had cancelled the Canada-U.S. FTA and kept out of the NAFTA).

e. There is a single NAFTA agreement between the three countries (the status quo as of 1996).

3. Should Canada and the U.S. trade with countries with poor human rights records? If trade with China is severely restricted because of its lack of respect for human rights, who will be the gainers and who the losers? Argue the cases that this policy will help, and that it will hinder, human rights progress in China.

4. It has been calculated that the voluntary export agreement to reduce the import of Japanese cars into the North American market cost North American consumers $150,000 per job saved in North American automobile firms. Do consumers pay the cost? Who benefits? What alternatives are there to protecting jobs in the auto industry?

5. "What unfair trade has done to an American community" was the headline of a recent full-page ad in the *New York Times*. The ad claimed that subsidized and "dumped" steel imports from unstated foreign countries were unfairly driving U.S. steel plants out of business. Although not specifically mentioned in the article, Canadian steel companies were at the time facing antidumping duties on their sales to the United States. What foreign practices might justify this claim? What apparent dumping might represent perfectly fair competition? What U.S. legislation or other practices could provide relief, whether justified or not, to the U.S. firms?

6. What are some of the things that would happen if all countries tried to increase their domestic employment by imposing major restrictions on all imports?

7. "U.S. consumer is seen as big loser in new restraints on imported steel," said a recent *Wall Street Journal* headline. The big gainers from the quota limitations on imported steel were predicted to be U.S. producers, who would sell more, and foreign producers, who would sell less but at a higher price; the big losers would be U.S. consumers. Explain carefully why each of these groups might gain or lose.

8. Suppose Canada and the United States had imposed prohibitive tariffs on all imported cars over the past three decades. How do you think this would have affected the North American automobile industry? The Canadian and U.S. public? The kinds of cars produced by North American manufacturers?

9. Import quotas and voluntary export agreements are often used instead of tariffs. What real difference, if any, is there between quotas, voluntary export restrictions (VERs), and tariffs? Explain why lobbyists for some import-competing industries (cheese, milk, shoes) support import quotas while lobbyists for others (pizza manufacturers, soft drink manufacturers, retail stores) oppose them. Would you expect labour unions to support or oppose quotas?

10. Over the past several years, many foreign automobile producers have built production and assembly facilities in Canada and in the United States. What are some advantages and disadvantages associated with shifting production from, for example, Japan to Canada? Will these cars still be considered "imports"? What is beginning to happen to the definitions of "foreign made" and "domestic made"?

CHAPTER 37

EXCHANGE RATES AND THE BALANCE OF PAYMENTS

As we saw in Chapter 21, the external value of the Canadian dollar has fluctuated considerably over the past 25 years. It fell sharply between 1983 and 1988, and then increased until 1992 when it was back at the level of the early 1980s. Between 1992 and 1996, the value of the Canadian dollar fell again.

In this chapter, we ask what it means to speak of the "external value of the dollar," what causes this value to change, and what implications such changes have for the economy. We examine the important difference between *flexible* and *fixed* exchange rates, and what the role of the Bank of Canada is under each system. The discussion will bring together material on three topics studied elsewhere in this book: the theory of supply and demand (Chapter 4), the nature of money (Chapter 27), and international trade (Chapter 35).

We also examine a country's balance of payments—the record of transactions in goods and assets with the rest of the world. We examine what is meant by a balance of payments deficit or surplus, and what role the central bank plays in determining it.

THE EXTERNAL VALUE OF THE DOLLAR

Fluctuations in the value of the Canadian dollar are a matter of concern to such varied groups as Japanese firms that want to build factories in Canada, Canadians who want to buy French government bonds, German exporters who send automobiles to Canada, and Canadians who hope to sell computer software in Saudi Arabia or engineering services in Brazil. They also matter to Canadian tourists who cash their traveler's cheques in London, Athens, or Bangkok. Some of the causes of these fluctuations are well understood, and some are still a source of debate and even controversy.

FOREIGN EXCHANGE TRANSACTIONS

We have seen that money is vital in any sophisticated economy that relies on specialization and exchange. Yet money as we know it is a *national* matter, one that is closely controlled by national governments. If you live in Sweden, you earn kronor and spend kronor; if you run a business in Austria, you borrow schillings and meet your payroll with schillings. The currency of a country is acceptable within the borders of that country, but usually it will not be accepted by households and firms in another country. The Stockholm bus company will accept kronor for a fare but not Austrian schillings. The Austrian worker will not take Swedish kronor for wages but will accept schillings.

The situation is similar in Canada, except that our proximity to the United States leads many Canadian sellers—especially in the tourist industries—to accept payments in U.S. dollars. But in this case, the sellers are just providing an extra service to their customers. Because U.S. dollars are so well known and so common, Canadian merchants are willing to accept them and then do what the customer would otherwise have had to do: take the U.S. money to the bank and exchange it for Canadian money. Ultimately, it is Canadian dollars that are used in Canada.

When Canadian producers sell their products, they require payment in Canadian dollars. They must meet their wage bills, pay for their raw materials, and reinvest or distribute their profits. There is no problem when they sell to Canadian purchasers. However, when they sell their goods to Japanese importers, either the Japanese must exchange their yen to acquire dollars to pay for the goods, or the Canadian producers must accept yen. They will accept yen only if they know that they can exchange the yen for the Canadian dollars that they require. The same holds true for producers in all countries: They must eventually receive payment for the goods that they sell in terms of the currency of their own country.

In general, trade between nations can occur only if it is possible to exchange the currency of one nation for that of another.

THE EXCHANGE RATE

International payments involve the exchange of currencies between people who have one currency and require another. Suppose that a Canadian firm wishes to acquire 3,000 Japanese yen for some purpose. The firm can go to its bank or to some other seller of foreign currency and buy a cheque that will be accepted in Japan as ¥3,000. How many Canadian dollars the firm must pay to purchase this cheque will depend on the value of the Canadian dollar in terms of yen.

The exchange of one currency for another is called a *foreign exchange transaction*. The term *foreign exchange* refers to the actual foreign currency or various claims on it, such as bank deposits or promises to pay, that are traded for each other. The **exchange rate** is the price of the foreign currency in terms of Canadian dollars—it is the number of Canadian dollars required to purchase 1 unit of the foreign currency. For example, in January 1996 the price of 1 Japanese yen was 1.31 Canadian cents or 0.0131 Canadian dollars. This means that the exchange rate between yen and Canadian dollars was 0.0131. A more familiar example is the Canadian-U.S. exchange rate. In January 1996, the Canadian-dollar price of 1 U.S. dollar was $1.32—this means that the exchange rate between U.S. and Canadian dollars was 1.32.

Note that we could just as easily define the exchange rate in the opposite way. We could define the exchange rate as the number of units of foreign currency that could be purchased with 1 Canadian dollar. In our example from January 1996, the exchange rate between the yen and the Canadian dollar would then be 76.2—the number of yen that could be purchased with 1 Canadian dollar. The exchange rate between the U.S. and Canadian dollars would then be 0.757—the number of U.S. dollars that could be purchased with 1 Canadian dollar.

In this book, however, we will *always* define the exchange rate in the way economists normally do to be the Canadian-dollar price of 1 unit of foreign currency. This makes it clear that foreign currency, like any good or service, has a price. In this case, the price of the "good" has a special name—the exchange rate.

A rise in the external value of the Canadian dollar—an **appreciation** of the Canadian dollar—means that it takes *fewer* Canadian dollars to purchase 1 unit of foreign currency. For example, if the Canadian dollar appreciates (against the yen) from 0.0131 to 0.0125, it costs *fewer* Canadian dollars to purchase 1 Japanese yen. Thus an appreciation of the Canadian dollar implies a *fall* in the exchange rate (a fall in the price of foreign currency). Conversely, a fall in the external value of the Canadian dollar—a **depreciation** of the Canadian dollar—means that it takes *more* Canadian dollars to purchase 1 unit of foreign currency. Using the U.S.-Canadian exchange rate as an example, if the Canadian dollar depreciates (against the U.S. dollar) from 1.32 to 1.35, it costs *more* Canadian dollars to purchase 1 U.S. dollar. Thus a depreciation of the Canadian dollar implies a *rise* in the exchange rate (a rise in the price of foreign currency).

An appreciation of the Canadian dollar implies a fall in the exchange rate; a depreciation of the Canadian dollar implies a rise in the exchange rate.

Going back to our yen example, suppose that today it was possible to purchase 100 yen for 1 Canadian dollar. In this case, the Canadian dollar would have appreciated since January 1996 (the exchange rate would have fallen from 0.0131 to 0.01). However, if today it was only possible to purchase 70 yen for 1 Canadian dollar, then the Canadian dollar would have depreciated since January 1996 (the exchange rate would have increased from 0.0131 to 0.0143).

Because the exchange rate expresses the value of one currency in terms of another, when one currency appreciates, the other must depreciate.

When the Canadian dollar appreciates in terms of the Japanese yen, the yen depreciates in terms of the Canadian dollar. Similarly, when the dollar depreciates in terms of the yen, the yen appreciates in terms of the dollar.

THE BALANCE OF PAYMENTS

Later in this chapter, we will discuss the determination of the exchange rate by analyzing the demand and supply for foreign exchange that arise as a result of international transactions in goods, services, and assets. We begin, however, with a discussion of the balance-of-payments accounts, which is the record of a country's transactions with the rest of the world. This will set the stage for our later discussion of exchange-rate determination.

BALANCE-OF-PAYMENTS ACCOUNTS

To know what is happening to the course of international trade, government statistical agencies (like Statistics Canada) keep track of the transactions between countries. The record of such transactions is made in the **balance-of-payments accounts.** For computing Canada's balance of payments, each transaction, such as the exports or imports of goods, or the purchase or sales of assets, is classified according to whether the transaction generates a *payment* or a *receipt* for Canada.

Table 37-1 shows the major items in the Canadian balance-of-payments accounts for 1994. Transactions that represent a receipt for Canada, such as the export of a product or the sale of an asset abroad, are recorded in the balance-of-payments accounts as a *credit* item. Transactions that represent a payment for Canada, such as the import of a product or the purchase of an asset from foreigners, are recorded as a *debit* item.

There are three main categories to the balance of payments: the *current account,* the *capital account,* and the *official financing account.* We examine each account in turn.

The Current Account

The **current account** records transactions arising from trade in goods and services. It also includes net investment income that residents of one country earn from assets issued to them by foreigners. The current account is divided into two main sections.

The first section, called either the **trade balance** or the **balance of trade,** records payments and receipts arising from the import and export of goods, such as computers and cars, and services, such as legal or architectural services. (Tourism constitutes a large part of the trade in services.) Canadian imports of goods and services require a payment to foreigners and thus are entered as debit items on the trade account; Canadian exports of goods and services generate a receipt from foreigners and thus are recorded as credit items.

The second section, called **capital-service account,** records the payments and receipts that represent income on assets. When Canadians pay income to the foreign owners of assets located in Canada, this requires a payment to foreigners and thus is entered as a debit item. When Canadians receive income earned from their assets located abroad, this is a receipt from foreigners and thus enters as a credit item.

As shown in Table 37-1, Canadian exports of goods and services were just under $250 billion in 1994, and Canadian imports of goods and services were about $244 billion. The trade account therefore had a surplus of about $6 billion—in other words, in

TABLE 37-1
Canadian Balance of Payments, 1994
(billions of dollars)

CURRENT ACCOUNT

a) Trade Account	
Merchandise exports	+217.9
Service exports	+31.5
Merchandise imports	−202.8
Service imports	−40.9
Trade balance	+5.7
b) Capital-Service Account	
Net investment income (including unilateral transfers)	−28.0
Current Account balance	**−22.3**

CAPITAL ACCOUNT

Net change in Canadian investments abroad [capital outflow (−)]	−12.5
Net change in foreign investments in Canada [capital inflow (+)]	+30.2
Capital Account balance	**+17.7**

OFFICIAL FINANCING ACCOUNT

Changes in reserves [increases (−)]	+0.7
Statistical Discrepancy	+3.9
Official Financing balance	**+4.6**
Balance of Payments	**0.0**

The overall balance of payments always balances, but the individual components do not have to. In 1994, Canada had an overall trade surplus (including trade in goods and services) of $5.7 billion. There was a deficit of $28 billion on the capital-service account. There was thus a $22.3 billion deficit on current account. There was also a surplus on the capital account because capital imports exceeded capital exports. The capital plus current account surplus is what is commonly referred to as the balance of payments, and in 1994, there was an overall deficit of $4.6 billion. This is exactly matched by the official financing balance plus the statistical discrepancy. The statistical discrepancy entry compensates for the inability to measure some items accurately.

(Source: Economic Reference Tables, Department of Finance, August 1995.)

1994 Canada sold $6 billion more worth of goods and services to the world than it bought from the world. But in terms of the capital-service account, things were the other way around. The table shows that Canadians paid $28 billion more to foreigners in investment income than they received from foreigners. The current account balance, the sum of the trade and capital-service accounts, had a deficit of $22 billion.

The Capital Account

The second main division in the balance of payments is the **capital account,** which records transactions related to international movements of financial capital. The purchase of foreign assets by Canadians is treated just like the purchase of foreign goods. Since purchasing a foreign asset requires a payment from Canadians to foreigners, it is entered as a debit item in the Canadian balance-of-payments accounts. Note that when Canadians purchase foreign assets, financial capital is leaving Canada and going abroad, and so this is called a *capital outflow* or *capital export.*

The sale of Canadian assets to foreigners is treated just like the sale of Canadian goods to foreigners. Since selling a Canadian asset abroad generates a receipt for Canada, it is entered as a credit item in the Canadian balance-of-payments accounts. Note that when Canadians sell assets to foreigners, financial capital is entering Canada from abroad, and so this is called a *capital inflow* or *capital import.*

As shown in Table 37-1, in 1994, Canadians increased their holdings of assets abroad by $12 billion, resulting in a capital outflow of that amount. At the same time, foreigners increased their holdings of assets in Canada by $30 billion, resulting in a capital inflow of that amount. The net capital inflow resulted in a surplus in the capital account of $18 billion.

Short-Term and Long-Term Capital Flows. The capital account is often divided into two categories that distinguish between movements of short-term and long-term capital. *Short-term capital* is money that is held in the form of highly liquid assets, such as bank accounts and short-term treasury bills. If a nonresident merchant buys Canadian dollars and places them in a deposit account in Montreal, this represents an inflow of short-term capital into Canada, and it will be recorded as a credit item on short-term capital account. *Long-term capital* represents funds coming into Canada (a credit item) or leaving Canada (a debit item), to be invested in less liquid assets, such as long-term bonds, or in physical capital, such as a new automobile assembly plant.

Portfolio Investment and Direct Investment. The two major subdivisions of the long-term part of the capital accounts are *direct investment* and *portfolio investment.* **Direct investment** (also called *for-eign direct investment*) relates to changes in nonresident ownership of domestic firms and resident ownership of foreign firms. Thus one form of direct investment in Canada is capital investment in a branch plant or a subsidiary corporation in Canada in which the investor has voting control. Another form is a takeover, in which a controlling interest in a firm, previously controlled by residents, is acquired by foreigners. **Portfolio investment** is investment in bonds or a minority holding of shares that does not involve legal control.

Changes in Official Reserves

The final section in the balance of payments represents transactions in the *official reserves* that are held by the Bank of Canada and is called the *official financing account* or the *official settlements account.* These transactions reflect the financing of the balance on the remainder of the accounts. The central banks of most countries, including Canada, hold financial reserves that they can use in the foreign exchange market. (Recall from Chapter 27 that these reserves are assets for central banks.) Some of these reserves are held in gold, some in foreign currencies or claims on them, and some in an international currency, called *special drawing rights (SDRs).*

The Bank of Canada, operating on behalf of the government, can intervene in the market for foreign exchange to influence the Canadian dollar's exchange rate (we will see later how it does this). For example, to prevent the external value of the dollar from falling, the Bank of Canada must purchase Canadian dollars and sell foreign exchange. It can do so only if it holds reserves of foreign exchange. When the Bank of Canada wishes to stop the value of the dollar from rising, it enters the market and sells dollars. In this case, the Bank purchases foreign exchange, which it then adds to its reserves.

Since foreign exchange is an asset for the Bank of Canada, it follows that when the Bank of Canada enters the foreign exchange market to buy or sell foreign exchange, it is simply buying or selling an asset. And we deal with that transaction in the same way we deal with the other asset transactions in the capital account. Specifically, when the Bank purchases foreign exchange (and sells Canadian dollars) in the foreign exchange market, this transaction represents the purchase of an asset from abroad, and thus it enters as a debit item in the balance of payments. Conversely, when the Bank sells foreign exchange (and purchases Canadian dollars), this transaction represents the sale of an asset to foreigners, and thus it enters as a credit item in the balance of payments.

Table 37-1 shows that in 1994 the Bank of Canada *reduced* its reserves of foreign exchange by $0.7 billion; it therefore sold more foreign exchange during the year than it purchased.

THE MEANING OF PAYMENTS BALANCES AND IMBALANCES

We have seen that the balance-of-payments accounts show the total amount of receipts (credit items) and payments (debit items) in each category of transaction. It is also common to calculate the *balance* on separate items or groups of items. The concept of the balance of payments is used in a number of different ways, so we must approach this issue in a series of steps.

In what follows, it will be useful to keep in mind the relationship between the foreign exchange market and the transactions that appear in the balance-of-payments accounts. When Canadians sell goods or assets to foreigners, the foreign currency used by the foreign purchasers must somehow be converted to Canadian dollars which can then be used by the Canadian sellers. This means that foreign currency will be *supplied* to the foreign exchange market (and Canadian dollars will be demanded). Conversely, when Canadians purchase goods or assets from foreigners, the Canadian dollars must somehow be converted to the appropriate foreign currency. This means that foreign currency will be *demanded* in the foreign exchange market (and Canadian dollars will be supplied).

With this in mind, we now examine the concept of "balance" in the balance of payments.

The Balance of Payments Must Balance Overall

Notice that the balance-of-payments accounts record *actual* transactions, not *desired* transactions. For example, it is quite possible that at the existing exchange rate between dollars and yen, holders of yen would *want* to purchase more Canadian goods or assets than Canadians would *want* to sell. This means that those same holders of yen *want* to sell more yen than holders of dollars *want* to buy. In this situation, the quantity of yen supplied exceeds the quantity demanded. However, holders of yen cannot *actually* sell more yen than holders of dollars *actually* buy;

every yen that is sold must have been bought by someone.[1]

It follows that if we add up the value of all *actual* receipts from foreigners from:

1. exports of goods and services;

2. sales of assets (capital imports); and

3. sales of foreign exchange by the Bank of Canada,

these must be exactly equal to the value of all *actual* payments made to foreigners for

1. imports of goods and services;

2. purchases of assets (capital exports); and

3. purchases of foreign exchange by the Bank of Canada.

This means that *the balance of payments must always balance.*

For some of the discussion that follows, it will help to have this important relationship in the form of a simple equation. We let C, K, and F stand for current account, capital account, and official financing account (items 1, 2, and 3 respectively), and use the subscripts R and P to denote whether the transaction represents a "receipt" or a "payment" for Canada. Now we can use these symbols to write an expression showing that the value of all receipts must equal the value of all payments:

$$C_R + K_R + F_R = C_P + K_P + F_P \qquad [1]$$

We can convert this into an expression relating the various balance-of-payments accounts simply by rearranging terms. Subtracting the three terms that represent payments from Canada to abroad (C_P, K_P, and F_P) from both sides of Equation 1 yields

$$(C_R - C_P) + (K_R - K_P) + (F_R - F_P) = 0 \qquad [2]$$

The three terms in parentheses are the current account surplus, the capital account surplus, and the balance on the official financing account. Equation 2 shows that the three balances must sum to zero. Extension 37-1 illustrates this with a hypothetical example.

---

[1]From this comment it should be clear that the "balancing" of the balance of payments in no way requires clearing (equilibrium) in the foreign exchange market. We discuss equilibrium in the foreign exchange market later in the chapter.

The overall balance of payments must balance: the current account plus the capital account plus the official financing account must sum to zero.

Payments on Specific Parts of the Accounts Need Not Balance

Although the overall balance of payments must balance, the same zero balance does not have to hold on subsections of the accounts. We now look at the balances on *parts* of the accounts—balances that may be positive or negative. We do this first in relation to particular countries and then in relation to particular subsections of the account.

Bilateral (Country) Balances. When all foreign countries are taken together, a country's balance of payments must balance, but a country can have bilateral surpluses or deficits with individual foreign countries or with groups of countries. In general, the **multilateral balance of payments** refers to the balance between one country's payments to and receipts from the rest of the world. When all items are considered, every country must have a zero multilateral payments balance with the rest of the world, although it can have bilateral surpluses or deficits with individual countries.

Subsection Balances. The balance on current account is the sum of the balances on the trade and capital-service accounts. As a carryover from a long-discredited eighteenth-century economic doctrine called *mercantilism,* a current account surplus (where receipts exceed payments) is sometimes called a *favourable balance of payments,* and a current account deficit (where payments exceed receipts) is sometimes called an *unfavourable balance of payments.* Mercantilists, both ancient and modern, believe that a country's gains from trade arise only from having a "favourable" balance of trade—that is, by exporting more goods and services than it imports. But this misses the central point of comparative advantage which we explored in Chapter 35—that countries gain from trade because trade allows each country to specialize according to its comparative advantage. The gains from trade have *nothing* to do with whether the volume of exports exceed the volume of imports (or vice versa). The modern resurgence of mercantilism is discussed in Extension 37-2.

The balance on capital account gives the difference between receipts generated by the sale of assets to foreigners and the payments made to purchase assets from foreigners. A surplus, or "favourable" balance, on capital account means that a country is a *net importer* of capital, whereas a deficit, or "unfavourable" balance, means that a country is a *net exporter* of capital. Notice that a deficit on capital account merely indicates that a country is accumulating assets abroad. For a rich country to accumulate foreign assets that will earn income in the future may be a desirable situation. So once again we observe that there is nothing necessarily unfavourable about having an "unfavourable" balance on any of the payments accounts.

The balance on the official financing account indicates the change in the Bank of Canada's holding of foreign exchange assets (including gold). If the Bank of Canada buys more foreign exchange than it sells, then this adds to its reserves of foreign exchange. This accumulation of assets, just like the purchase of foreign bonds by the private sector, is a capital outflow and is thus a debit item in the balance of payments. Thus a deficit on the official financing account means that the Bank of Canada has purchased more gold and foreign exchange than it has sold; a surplus means that the Bank has sold more foreign exchange than it has bought.

The Relationships Among Various Balances

Two important implications follow directly from our observation that the overall payments must balance:

1. The terms *balance-of-payments deficit* and *balance-of-payments surplus* must refer to the balance on some part of the payments accounts. The terms make no sense if they are applied to the overall balance of payments.

2. A deficit on any one part of the accounts implies an offsetting surplus on the rest of the accounts.

We now consider two important applications of these statements. The first application concerns the balance on the official financing account and the combined balance on the current plus capital accounts; the second concerns the separate balances on current and capital accounts. Keep in mind that we use the word *overall* when referring to the balance of payments *including the official financing account.*

Official Financing and the Rest of the Accounts. We said above that the term "balance-of-payments deficit" does not strictly make sense since the balance of payments must balance overall. But such a term is nonetheless often used. What does this mean?

EXTENSION 37-1

WHY THE BALANCE OF PAYMENTS ALWAYS BALANCES: AN ILLUSTRATION

TRADE BETWEEN TWO COUNTRIES

Suppose that the sole international transaction made this year by a small country called Myopia was an export to Canada of Myopian coconuts worth $1,000. Further suppose that the Myopian central bank issues a local currency, the stigma, but does not operate in the foreign exchange market, so there is no official financing. Finally, suppose that Myopia's self-sufficient inhabitants want no imports. Surely, then, you might think that Myopia has an overall "favourable" balance on its current account of $1,000, which is a current account receipt (C_R) with no balancing item on the payments side.

To see why this conclusion is wrong, we must ask what the Myopian exporter of coconuts did with the Canadian dollars that he received for his coconuts. Let us suppose that he deposited them in a bank in Montreal. This transaction represents a capital export from Myopia. Myopians have accumulated claims on foreign exchange, which they hold in the form of a deposit with a foreign bank. Thus there are two entries in the Myopian accounts: One is a credit item for the export of coconuts ($C_R =$

$1,000), and the other is a debit item for the export of capital ($K_P = \$1,000$). The fact that the same firm made both transactions is irrelevant. Although the current account shows a credit balance, the capital account exactly balances this with a debit item. Hence, looking at the balance of payments *as a whole*, the two sides of the account are equal. The balance of payments has balanced—as it must always do.

Consider now a slightly more realistic case. If the Myopian coconut exporter wants to turn his $1,000 into Myopian stigmas so that he can pay his coconut pickers in local currency, he must find someone who wishes to buy his Canadian dollars in return for Myopian currency. However, we have assumed that no one in Myopia wants to import, so no one wants to sell Myopian currency for current account reasons. But there may be a wealthy Myopian landowner who wants to invest $1,000 in Montreal by buying shares in Bombardier, a Canadian firm. To do so, she needs $1,000. The Myopian coconut exporter can sell his $1,000 to the landowner in return for stigmas. Now he can pay his local bills. The landowner sells her stigmas to the exporter in return

---

When people speak of a country as having a balance-of-payments deficit or surplus, they are usually referring to the balance of all accounts *excluding* official financing—that is, to the combined balance on current and capital accounts.

We can express the relationship between the balance of payments and the balance on the official financing account by subtracting the official financing balance ($F_R - F_P$) from both sides of Equation 2. This yields

$$(C_R - C_P) + (K_R - K_P) = -(F_R - F_P) \quad [3]$$

The two terms on the left-hand side are the current account balance and the capital account balance; their sum is what we have just called the balance of payments. When the left-hand side is positive, the balance of payments is in surplus, which means that transactions on the current and capital accounts (combined) generate more receipts to Canada than payments from Canada. This means that, for all transactions on the current and capital account taken together, more foreign exchange is being supplied to the foreign exchange market than is being demanded from it. Equation 3 shows that in this case of a "balance of payments surplus," the right-hand side of Equation 3 must also be positive. But this is only possible if the Bank of Canada is a net purchaser of foreign exchange (so that F_P is greater than F_R).

A balance-of-payments surplus means that the Bank of Canada is adding to its holdings of foreign ex-for Canadian dollars. Now she can buy the Canadian shares.

Once again, the Myopian balance of payments will show two entries, equal in size, but one is a credit and the other is a debit. There is a credit item for the export of coconuts (the sale of coconuts earned foreign exchange) and a debit item for the export of capital (the purchase of the Canadian shares required foreign exchange).

TRADE INVOLVING MANY COUNTRIES

In the preceding example, Myopia had a balance in what is called its *bilateral payments account* with Canada. The *bilateral balance of payments* between any two countries is the balance between the payments and the receipts flowing between them. If there were only two countries in the world, their overall payments would have to be in bilateral balance; that is, one country's payments to the other would be equal to its receipts from the other. However, this is not true when there are more than two countries involved.

Suppose that in the year following the one just discussed, Myopia again sells $1,000 worth of co-

conuts to Canada. But this time the wealthy landowner is not interested in investing in Canadian shares; instead, there is a Myopian who wishes to import ¥100,000 worth of umbrellas from Japan. (Suppose also that in the foreign exchange market, $1 trades for ¥100.) Finally, assume that a Japanese importer wishes to buy $1,000 worth of lumber from a Canadian company.

Now what happens, in effect, is that the Myopian coconut exporter sells his $1,000 to the Japanese lumber importer for ¥100,000, which the coconut exporter then sells to the Myopian umbrella importer in return for Myopian stigmas. (In the real world, the exchanges are all done through banks, but this is the effect.) Now the Myopian payments statistics will show a $1,000 bilateral payments surplus with Canada—receipts of $1,000 from Canada on account of coconut exports and no payments to Canada—and a bilateral deficit with Japan of ¥100,000 (equal in value to $1,000)—$1,000 of payments to Japan on account of umbrella imports and no receipts from Japan. However, when both countries are considered, Myopia's multilateral payments are in balance.

change reserves; a balance-of-payments deficit means that the Bank of Canada is reducing its reserves.

What we have just said implies that the balance of payments can be in deficit or surplus *only if* the central bank changes its foreign exchange reserves. But such changes clearly require that the central bank be intervening in the foreign exchange market. If the central bank does not intervene in the foreign exchange market, the official financing balance must be zero, and there can then be no deficit or surplus in the balance of payments; as we shall see in the next section, this imposes a strict relationship between the capital and current accounts.

The Current and Capital Account Balances. Suppose that the Bank of Canada does not engage in

any foreign exchange transactions. This means that the official financing account is zero because both F_R and F_P in Equation 3 are zero.

Now any deficit or surplus on current account must be matched by an equal and opposite surplus or deficit on capital account. For example, if a country has a current account surplus, the net foreign exchange supplied for those current account transactions must be matched by a net foreign exchange demanded for transactions in the capital account. The foreign exchange may be used to buy foreign assets or merely stashed away in foreign bank accounts. In either case, there is an outflow of capital from Canada.

We can see this clearly if we return to Equation 3 and set F_R and F_P equal to zero to indicate no transactions by the Bank of Canada. This yields

EXTENSION 37-2

IS IT TRADE VOLUME OR TRADE BALANCE THAT MATTERS?

Media commentators, political figures, and much of the general public often judge the national balance of payments as they would the accounts of a single firm. Just as a firm is supposed to show a profit, the nation is supposed to secure a balance-of-payments surplus, with the benefits derived from international trade measured by the size of that surplus.

This view is related to the *exploitation doctrine* of international trade: One country's surplus is another country's deficit. Hence one country's gain, judged by its surplus, must be another country's loss, judged by its deficit.

People who hold such views today are echoing an ancient economic doctrine called *mercantilism*. The mercantilists were a group of economists who preceded Adam Smith. They judged the success of trade by the size of the trade balance. In many cases, this doctrine made sense in terms of their objective, which was to use international trade as a means of building up the political and military power of the state, rather than as a means of raising the living standards of its citizens. A balance-of-payments surplus allowed the nation (then and now) to acquire foreign exchange reserves. (In those days, the reserves took the form of gold. Today, they are a mixture of gold and claims on the currencies of other countries.) These reserves could then be used to pay armies, to purchase weapons from abroad, and to finance colonial expansions.

People who advocate this view in modern times are called *neomercantilists*. Insofar as their object is to increase the power of the state, they are choosing means that could achieve their ends. Insofar as they

are drawing an analogy between what is a sensible objective for a business, interested in its own material welfare, and what is a sensible objective for a country, interested in the material welfare of its citizens, their views are erroneous because their analogy is false.

If the object of economic activity is to promote the welfare and living standards of ordinary citizens, rather than the power of governments, the mercantilist focus on the balance of trade makes no sense. The law of comparative advantage shows that average living standards are maximized by having individuals, regions, and countries specialize in the things that they can produce comparatively best and then trading to obtain the things that they can produce comparatively worst. The more specialization there is, the more trade occurs.

In this view, the gains from trade are to be judged by the *volume* of trade rather than by the *balance* of trade. A situation in which there is a large volume of trade even though each country has a zero balance of trade can thus be regarded as quite satisfactory. Furthermore, a change in commercial policy that results in an equal increase in both exports and imports will generate gains because it allows for specialization according to comparative advantage, even though it causes no change in either country's trade balance.

To the business interested in private profit and to the government interested in the power of the state, it is the balance of trade that matters. To the person interested in improving average living standards, it is the volume of trade that matters.

$$(C_R - C_P) + (K_R - K_P) = 0 \qquad [4]$$

Of course, another way to write Equation 4 is to subtract the capital account surplus $(K_R - K_P)$ from both sides to get

$$(C_R - C_P) = -(K_R - K_P) \qquad [5]$$

This expresses in equation form what we have just stated in words: Any balance on current account must be matched by a balance on capital account of equal magnitude but opposite sign. For example, if a deficit on current account occurs (that is, if the left-hand side of Equation 5 is negative), it must be matched by a surplus on capital account (a capital inflow). Similarly, if a surplus on current account occurs, it must be matched by a deficit on capital account (a capital outflow).

Consider how Equation 5 has applied to Canada. For most if not all of Canada's history, Canada has been importing capital and hence experiencing a surplus on capital account. Equation 5 tells us that it must therefore have a deficit on current account. Furthermore, since the mid 1970s, when the Canadian government started running large budget deficits, the borrowing requirements of the government led to a substantial increase in the capital inflow into Canada making increases in the current account deficit inevitable. The link between the government's budget deficit and the country's current account deficit is examined in more detail in Chapter 38.

National Asset Formation.   In Chapter 24, we defined national asset formation to include net exports. Equation 5 allows us to restate the logic of this definition quite directly. According to Equation 5, a current account surplus implies a capital account deficit of the same magnitude. This capital account deficit arises because Canadian residents are acquiring assets abroad, and these assets are part of Canadian national asset formation. The current account balance itself consists of both net exports and payments for capital services, such as interest, dividends, and profits on investment abroad.[2] Generally, any change in the current account, whether due to a change in net exports or due to a change in net payments for capital services, will cause a one-for-one change in the capital account and in national asset formation.

Actual and Desired Transactions.   The discussion in this section has focused on *actual* transactions as measured in the balance-of-payments accounts. How do these relate to *desired* transactions in international markets? As we shall see, the exchange rate plays a key role in reconciling actual and

desired transactions. As a first step in understanding this, we now turn to a discussion of how the exchange rate is determined.

THE FOREIGN EXCHANGE MARKET

For the sake of simplicity, we continue using an example involving trade between Canada and Japan and the determination of the exchange rate between their two currencies, dollars and yen. The two-country example simplifies things, but the principles apply to all foreign transactions. Consequently, in our discussion, *yen stands for foreign exchange in general, and the price of yen in terms of dollars stands for the exchange rate in general.*

When ¥75 is equal in value to $1, a Japanese importer who offers to buy $4 with yen must be offering to sell ¥300. Similarly, a Canadian importer who offers to sell $4 for yen must be offering to buy ¥300.

Because one currency is traded for another in the foreign exchange market, it follows that a demand for foreign exchange implies a supply of dollars and that a supply of foreign exchange implies a demand for dollars.

For this reason, a theory of the exchange rate between dollars and yen can deal either with the demand and supply of dollars or with the demand and supply of yen; both need not be considered. We will concentrate on the demand, supply, and price of yen. Thus the market we will be considering (in general terms) is the foreign exchange market—the "product" is foreign exchange (yen in our case) and the "price" is the exchange rate (the Canadian-dollar price of yen).

We develop our example in terms of the demand and supply analysis first encountered in Chapter 4. To do so, we need only to recall that in the market for foreign exchange, transactions that generate a receipt for Canada in its balance of payments represent a *supply* of foreign exchange (foreign exchange is being supplied by the foreigners who purchase Canadian goods or assets). Conversely, transactions that are a payment from Canada in the balance of payments represent a *demand* for foreign exchange (foreign exchange is being demanded by the Canadians who are purchasing foreign goods or assets).

---

[2]These payments for capital services are exactly the difference between GDP and GNP. GNP includes payments for capital services that accrue to, or are incurred by, domestic residents, whereas GDP does not.

We begin by focusing only on the demand and supply of foreign exchange arising from the current and capital accounts. Later we turn to the important role of official financing by the Bank of Canada. But for now, suppose that the Bank of Canada makes no transactions in the foreign exchange market.

THE SUPPLY OF FOREIGN EXCHANGE

The supply of foreign exchange in the foreign exchange market arises from all international transactions that represent a receipt in Canada's balance of payments.

Canadian Exports

One important source of supply of foreign exchange is foreigners who do not currently hold Canadian dollars but who wish to buy Canadian-made goods and services. A Japanese importer of lumber is such a purchaser; an Austrian couple planning a vacation in Canada is another; the Russian government seeking to buy Canadian steel is a third. All are sources of supply of foreign exchange, arising out of international trade. Each potential buyer wants to sell its own currency in exchange for Canadian dollars which it can then use to purchase Canadian goods and services.

Capital Inflows

A second source of supply of foreign exchange comes from foreigners who wish to purchase Canadian assets, such as government or corporate bonds, or plant and equipment currently located in Canada. To buy Canadian assets, holders of foreign currencies must first sell their foreign currency and buy Canadian dollars in foreign exchange markets.[3] In recent years, foreign households and firms have invested tens of billions of dollars in Canadian securities and real estate. This has required the conversion of foreign currencies into Canadian dollars. The resulting transactions are called *long-term capital flows*.

In Chapter 29 we discussed how the Bank of Canada's efforts to reduce inflation in the early

1990s pushed Canadian interest rates well above those in the United States. With the increase in Canadian rates relative to U.S. rates, floods of "foreign money" came into Canada to buy short-term treasury bills and notes, certificates of deposit, and other securities. The buyers were seeking a high return on their liquid assets, but first these buyers had to convert their U.S. dollars, yen, guilder, marks, and francs into Canadian dollars in the foreign exchange market. When people sell financial assets in one country for foreign exchange that they then use to buy short-term financial assets in another country, the transactions are called *short-term capital flows*.

Reserve Currency

Firms, banks, and governments often accumulate and hold foreign exchange reserves, just as individuals maintain savings accounts. And these reserves may be in several different currencies. For example, the government of Nigeria may decide to increase its reserve holdings of Canadian dollars and reduce its reserve holdings of yen; if it does so, it will be a supplier of yen (and a demander of Canadian dollars) in foreign exchange markets.

The Total Supply of Foreign Exchange

The supply of foreign exchange (or the demand for Canadian dollars) by holders of foreign currencies is the sum of the supplies for all of the purposes just discussed—for purchases of Canadian exports, for capital inflow to Canada and for the purchase of Canadian dollars to add to currency reserves.

Furthermore, because people, firms, and governments in all countries purchase goods and assets from many other countries, the demand for any one currency will be the aggregate demand of individuals, firms, and governments in a number of different countries. Thus the total supply of foreign exchange (or the demand for Canadian dollars) may include Germans who are offering marks, Japanese who are offering yen, Greeks who are offering drachmas, and so on. For simplicity, however, we continue with our two-country example and use only Canada and Japan.

THE SUPPLY CURVE FOR FOREIGN EXCHANGE

The supply of foreign exchange on the foreign exchange market is represented by a positively sloped

---

[3]Capital inflows also arise when Canadians sell foreign assets. In this case, Canadians enter the foreign exchange market and sell the foreign currency received for the assets and buy Canadian dollars.

FIGURE 37-1
The Market for Foreign Exchange

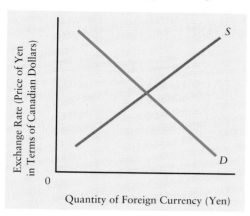

The demand for foreign exchange is negatively sloped, and the supply of foreign exchange is positively sloped, when plotted against the exchange rate, measured as the Canadian dollar price of one unit of foreign currency. The demand for foreign exchange is given by the negatively sloped green line D. It represents the sum of transactions on both current and capital accounts that require payments to foreigners, C_P and K_P (the purchase of goods, services and assets from foreigners).

The supply of foreign exchange is given by the positively sloped red line S. It represents the sum of transactions on both current and capital accounts that represent receipts from foreigners, C_R and K_R (sales of goods, services, and assets to foreigners).

A depreciation of the Canadian dollar is a rise in the exchange rate (moving up the vertical axis); an appreciation of the dollar is a fall in the exchange rate (moving down the vertical axis).

curve, such as the one shown in Figure 37-1. This figure plots the Canadian-dollar price of yen (the exchange rate) on the vertical axis and the quantity of yen on the horizontal axis. Moving up the vertical scale, more dollars are needed to purchase 1 yen—the dollar is depreciating. Moving down the vertical scale, fewer dollars are needed to purchase 1 yen—the dollar is appreciating.

Why is the supply curve for foreign exchange positively sloped? Consider the supply of foreign exchange derived from foreign purchases of Canadian exports. If the dollar depreciates, it takes fewer yen to purchase 1 Canadian dollar. Thus for a given

Canadian-dollar price of the product, the yen price has fallen. Japanese consumers will therefore buy more of the cheaper Canadian goods and will thus supply more foreign exchange for this purpose. In the opposite case, when the dollar appreciates, the yen price of Canadian exports rises. Japanese consumers will buy fewer Canadian goods and thus supply less foreign exchange.[4]

Similar considerations affect other sources of supply of foreign exchange. When the Canadian dollar depreciates (a high exchange rate), Canadian assets and securities become attractive purchases, and the quantity purchased will rise. As this happens, the amount of foreign exchange supplied to pay for the purchases will increase.

The supply curve for foreign exchange is positively sloped when it is plotted against the exchange rate; a depreciation of the Canadian dollar (a rise in the exchange rate) increases the quantity of foreign exchange supplied.

THE DEMAND FOR FOREIGN EXCHANGE

The demand for foreign exchange arises from all international transactions that represent a payment in Canada's balance of payments. What sort of international transactions generate a demand for foreign exchange (and a supply of Canadian dollars)? Canadians seeking to purchase foreign products will be supplying Canadian dollars and purchasing foreign exchange for this purpose. Holders of Canadian securities may decide to sell their Canadian holdings and shift them into foreign assets. If they do, they will sell Canadian dollars and demand foreign exchange. Similarly, a country with dollar reserves of

---

[4]We have assumed here that the foreign price elasticity of demand for Canadian exports is greater than one (so that a price change leads to a proportionately larger change in quantity demanded). This is a common assumption in the analysis of international trade. In the case of Canada (and other small countries) it is common to go further and make the "small open economy" assumption—that the country faces *given world prices* for both its exports and imports. In this case, the foreign price elasticity of demand for exports is infinite, which means that the exporting country can export all that it wishes at the given world price.

foreign exchange may decide to sell dollars in order to demand some other currency.

THE DEMAND CURVE FOR FOREIGN EXCHANGE

When the Canadian dollar depreciates, the Canadian-dollar price of Japanese goods rises. It takes more dollars to buy the same Japanese good, so Canadians will buy fewer of the now more expensive Japanese goods. The amount of foreign exchange being demanded by Canadians in order to pay for imported Japanese goods will fall.[5] In the opposite case, when the Canadian dollar appreciates, Japanese goods become cheaper, more are sold, and more dollars are spent on them. Thus more foreign exchange will be demanded to pay for the extra imports. This same argument applies in exactly the same way to the purchases of foreign assets. Figure 37-1 shows the demand curve for foreign exchange.

The demand curve for foreign exchange is negatively sloped when it is plotted against the exchange rate; an appreciation of the Canadian dollar (a fall in the exchange rate) increases the quantity of foreign exchange demanded.

THE DETERMINATION OF EXCHANGE RATES

Recall that the demand and supply curves in Figure 37-1 do not include official financing transactions (the demands or supplies for foreign exchange by the Bank of Canada). The demand curve represents the transactions in the current and capital accounts that generate a demand for foreign exchange (C_P and K_P); the supply curve represents the transactions in

the current and capital accounts that generate a supply of foreign exchange (C_R and K_R).

To complete our analysis, we need to incorporate the role of official financing transactions. Three important cases need to be considered:

1. When there are no official financing transactions by the central bank, the exchange rate is determined by the equality between the supply and demand for foreign exchange arising from the capital and current accounts. This is called a **flexible exchange rate.**

2. When official financing transactions are used to "fix" the exchange rate at a particular value, there is said to be a **fixed exchange rate.**

3. Between these two "pure" systems are a variety of possible intermediate cases, including the *adjustable peg* and the *managed float*. In the **adjustable peg system,** governments set and attempt to fix specific values for their exchange rates, but they explicitly recognize that circumstances may arise in which they will change that value. In a **managed float,** the central bank seeks to have some stabilizing influence on the exchange rate but does not try to fix it at some publicly announced value.

Canada has used a flexible exchange rate (with some managed floating) throughout most of the period since the end of the Second World War. There were, however, two periods in the 1940s and the 1960s when it operated under fixed rates. We now examine the operation of flexible and fixed exchange rates.

FLEXIBLE EXCHANGE RATES

Consider an exchange rate that is set in a freely competitive market, with no intervention by the central bank. Like any competitive price, this rate fluctuates according to the conditions of demand and supply.

Suppose that the current exchange rate is so high (say, e_1 in Figure 37-2) that the quantity of foreign exchange supplied exceeds the quantity demanded (equivalently, we could say that the quantity of Canadian dollars demanded exceeds the amount supplied). There is thus an abundance of foreign exchange and a shortage of Canadian dollars. This ex-

---

[5] As long as the price elasticity of demand for imports is greater than one, the fall in the volume of imports will exceed the rise in price, and hence fewer dollars will be spent on them. This condition (and the one in the previous footnote) is related to a famous long-standing issue in international economics, called the *Marshall-Lerner condition.* In what follows, we take the standard approach of assuming that both the price elasticity of demand for imports and the price elasticity of the demand for Canadian exports exceeds one. This guarantees that the slopes of the curves are as shown in Figure 37-1.

FIGURE 37-2
Fixed and Flexible Exchange Rates

The exchange rate adjusts so that the current account and capital account together are equal to the level of official financing; in the absence of any official financing, there is a flexible exchange rate and the current account and capital account sum to zero. The demand for and supply of foreign exchange are as in Figure 37-1. If official financing is zero, there is a flexible exchange rate. It will adjust to equate the demand and supply of foreign exchange; this occurs at E_0 with an exchange rate of e_0.

If the exchange rate is higher than that, say at e_1, the supply of foreign exchange will exceed the demand. The exchange rate will fall (the dollar will appreciate) until it reaches e_0, where balance is achieved at E_0. If the exchange rate is below e_0, say at e_2, the demand for foreign exchange will exceed the supply. The exchange rate will rise (the dollar will depreciate) until it reaches e_0, where balance is achieved at E_0.

The government can fix the exchange rate by using its official financing transactions to meet the excess demands or supplies that arise at the fixed value of the exchange rate. For example, if it chooses to fix the exchange rate at e_1, there will be a balance-of-payments surplus because receipts (on current and capital accounts) will exceed payments. The central bank will thus purchase foreign exchange (and sell dollars) to meet the excess supply. Alternatively, if the central bank chooses to fix the exchange rate at e_2, there will be a balance-of-payments deficit because receipts (on current and capital accounts) will be less than payments. The central bank will thus sell foreign exchange (and buy dollars) to meet the excess demand.

change (the exchange rate) to fall. As the exchange rate falls—an appreciation of the Canadian dollar—the yen price of Canadian goods rises, and this leads to a reduction in the quantity of foreign exchange supplied. Also, as the exchange rate falls, the Canadian-dollar price of Japanese goods falls, and this leads to an increase in the quantity of foreign exchange demanded. Thus the excess supply of foreign exchange leads to a fall in the exchange rate which in turn reduces the amount of excess supply. Where the two curves intersect, quantity demanded equals quantity supplied, and the exchange rate is at its equilibrium value.

What happens when the exchange rate is below its equilibrium value? The quantity of foreign exchange demanded will exceed the quantity supplied (or the quantity of Canadian dollars supplied will exceed the quantity demanded). With foreign exchange in excess demand, its price will naturally rise, and as it does the amount of excess demand will be reduced until equilibrium is reestablished.

A foreign exchange market is like other competitive markets in that the forces of demand and supply lead to an equilibrium price at which quantity demanded equals quantity supplied.

Recall that we have been assuming that there is no official financing by the central bank, so that demand and supply in the foreign exchange market represent transactions only on the current or capital account. We now consider a system of fixed exchange rates in which official financing plays a central role in the analysis.

FIXED EXCHANGE RATES

When official financing transactions are used to fix the exchange rate at a particular value, the current account and the capital account do not necessarily sum to zero. The balance on official financing has to be whatever is necessary to offset the balance of payments deficit or surplus that arises.[6] This is also shown in Figure 37-2.

The gold standard that operated for much of the nineteenth century and the early part of the

cess supply of foreign exchange, just as in our analysis in Chapter 4, will cause the price of foreign ex-

---

[6]This can be seen directly from Equation 3. Note that the central bank must give up control of its foreign exchange reserves when it chooses to fix the exchange rate.

twentieth was a fixed exchange rate system. The Bretton Woods system, established by international agreement in 1944 and operated until the mid 1970s, was a fixed exchange rate system that provided for circumstances under which the value of the currency had to be lowered (a *devaluation*) or raised (a *revaluation*). It was thus an adjustable peg system; the International Monetary Fund (IMF) has its origins in the Bretton Woods system, and one of its principal tasks was approving and monitoring exchange rate changes. The European Exchange Rate Mechanism (ERM) of the early 1990s was also a fixed exchange rate system for the countries in the European Union; their exchange rates were fixed to each other but floated as a block against the U.S. dollar and other currencies. Revival of this system is currently under debate in Europe.

In the remainder of this chapter, we focus on flexible exchange rates which exist today in most countries including Canada. Application 37-1 examines fixed exchange rates in more detail.

CHANGES IN EXCHANGE RATES

What causes exchange rates to vary? The simplest answer to this question is changes in demand or supply in the foreign exchange market. Anything that shifts the demand curve for foreign exchange to the right or the supply curve for foreign exchange to the left leads to a rise in the exchange rate—a depreciation of the Canadian dollar. Conversely, anything that shifts the demand curve for foreign exchange to the left or the supply curve for foreign exchange to the right leads to a fall in the exchange rate—an appreciation of the Canadian dollar. This is nothing more than a restatement of the laws of supply and demand, applied now to the market for foreign exchange; it is illustrated in Figure 37-3.

What causes the shifts in demand and supply that lead to changes in exchange rates? There are many causes, some transitory and some persistent. We will mention several of the most important ones.

A Rise in the Domestic Price of Exports

Suppose that the Canadian-dollar price of Canadian paper rises. What this will do to the supply of foreign exchange (or the demand for Canadian dollars) depends on the price elasticity of foreign demand for the Canadian product. If the demand for Canadian paper is elastic, perhaps because other countries supply the same product in world markets, the total amount spent on Canadian paper will decrease and hence less foreign exchange will be supplied to purchase Canadian paper. This implies that the supply curve for foreign exchange will shift to the left and the dollar will depreciate. This is illustrated in part (ii) of Figure 37-3. If the demand is inelastic (say, because Canada is the only country that produces this particular kind of paper), then more will be spent, the supply of foreign exchange to pay the bigger bill will shift the supply curve to the right, and the dollar will appreciate. This is also illustrated in part (ii) of Figure 37-3.

A Rise in the Foreign Price of Imports

Suppose that the yen price of Japanese-produced automobiles increases sharply. Suppose also that Canadian consumers have an elastic demand for Japanese cars because they can easily switch to Canadian-made substitutes. Consequently, they spend fewer yen for Japanese automobiles than they did before and hence demand less foreign exchange. The demand curve for foreign exchange shifts to the left, and the dollar will appreciate. If the demand for Japanese cars were inelastic, total spending on them would rise, and the demand for foreign exchange would shift to the right, leading to a depreciation of the Canadian dollar. This is illustrated in part (i) of Figure 37-3.

Changes in the Overall Price Levels

Suppose that instead of a change in the price of a specific export, such as cars or paper, there is a change in *all* prices because of a general inflation. We consider separate cases, each corresponding to a different pattern of Canadian relative to foreign inflation.

Equal Inflation in Both Countries.   Suppose that inflation is running at 10 percent in both Canada and Japan. In this case, the yen prices of Japanese goods and the dollar prices of Canadian goods both rise by 10 percent. At the *existing* exchange rate, the dollar prices of Japanese goods and the yen prices of Canadian goods will each rise by 10 percent, and hence the relative prices of imports and domestically produced goods will be unchanged in both countries. There is now no reason to expect a change in either country's demand for imports at the original exchange rate, so the inflation in the two countries leaves the equilibrium exchange rate unchanged.

APPLICATION 37-1

MANAGING FIXED EXCHANGE RATES

This box provides some details on how a central bank operates a regime of fixed exchange rates.

Suppose for purposes of illustration that the Bank of Canada fixed the exchange rate between the narrow limits of, say, C\$1.28 to C\$1.32 to the U.S. dollar. The Bank then stabilizes the exchange rate in the face of seasonal, cyclical, and other fluctuations in demand and supply, entering the market to prevent the rate from going outside the permitted band. At the price of 1.28 (Canadian dollars), the Bank offers to buy any amount of U.S. dollars; at the price of 1.32 (Canadian dollars), the Bank offers to sell any amount of U.S. dollars. When the Bank buys foreign exchange, its exchange reserves rise; when it sells foreign exchange, its reserves fall.

We make the following observations:

1. If the demand curve cuts the supply curve in the range 1.28 to 1.32, then the Bank need not intervene in the market.

2. If the demand curve shifts to D_1, then the Bank must sell U.S. dollars from its reserves to the extent of q_4q_1 in order to prevent the price of U.S. dollars from rising above 1.32.

3. If the demand curve shifts to D_2, the Bank must buy U.S. dollars to the extent of q_2q_3 in order to prevent the price of U.S. dollars from falling below 1.28.

If, on average, the demand and supply curves intersect in the range 1.28 to 1.32, then the Bank's foreign exchange reserves will be relatively stable, with the Bank buying U.S. dollars when the demand is abnormally low and selling them when the demand is abnormally high. Over a long period, the average level of reserves will then be fairly stable.

If conditions change (for example, there is more rapid inflation in one country than in the other), the Bank's foreign exchange reserves will rise or fall more or less continuously. Suppose that the average level of demand becomes D_1, with fluctuations on either side of this level. The average drain on reserves will then be q_4q_1 *per period*. But this situation cannot continue indefinitely because the Bank only has a limited amount of foreign exchange reserves. In this situation, the Bank has two alternatives: It can change the fixed exchange rate so that the band of permissible prices straddles the new equilibrium price, or it can try to shift the curves so that the intersection is in the band 1.28 to 1.32. To accomplish this, it must restrict demand for foreign exchange: It can impose import quotas and foreign-travel restrictions, or it can seek to increase the supply of U.S. dollars by encouraging exports.

The Bank can induce movements of short-term capital to assist in its policy of fixing the exchange rate in spite of fluctuations in the demand for and supply of foreign exchange. Assume, for example that in the figure, the demand for U.S. dollars is D_1 and the supply S, so that there is a potential loss of reserves of q_4q_1 per period. The Bank can raise the short-term rate of interest and attract short-term capital. This shifts the supply of U.S. dollars to the right. If the curve is shifted to cut D_1 vertically above q_1, the inflow of short-term capital just covers the potential shortfall, and the exchange reserves are not run down. Provided the Bank guessed correctly that the demand was abnormally high, the policy will work. If the demand now falls to produce a free-market rate within the permitted range, the Bank can lower interest rates, as it no longer needs to attract short-term capital to cover the excess demand for foreign exchange at the maximum permitted exchange rate.

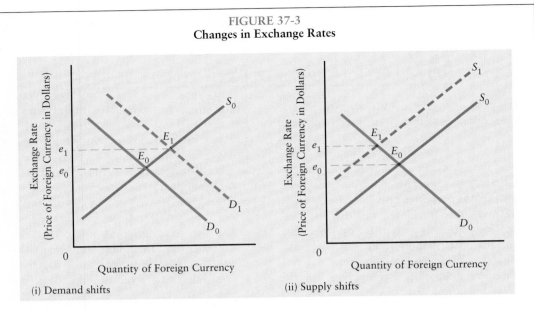

FIGURE 37-3
Changes in Exchange Rates

(i) Demand shifts

(ii) Supply shifts

An increase in the demand for foreign exchange or a decrease in the supply will cause the dollar to depreciate (the exchange rate to rise); a decrease in the demand or an increase in supply will cause the dollar to appreciate (the exchange rate to fall). The initial demand and supply curves D_0 and S_0 are as in Figures 37-1 and 37-2. Equilibrium is at E_0 with an exchange rate of e_0. An increase in the demand for foreign exchange as shown by a rightward shift in the demand curve from D_0 to D_1 in part (i), or a decrease in the supply of foreign exchange as shown by a leftward shift in the supply curve from S_0 to S_1 in part (ii), will cause the dollar to depreciate. In both parts, the new equilibrium is at E_1, and the depreciation is shown by the rise in the exchange rate from e_0 to e_1. Conversely, a decrease in the demand for foreign exchange or an increase in the supply of foreign exchange will cause the dollar to appreciate.

(This argument forms the basis of what is called the *purchasing power parity* theory of exchange rates, which will be discussed in more detail later.)

Inflation in Only One Country.   What will happen if there is inflation in Canada while the price level remains stable in Japan? The dollar price of Canadian goods will rise, and they will become more expensive in Japan. This will cause the quantity of Canadian exports, and therefore the amount of foreign exchange supplied by Japanese importers, to diminish. This means that the supply curve for foreign exchange shifts to the left.[7]

At the same time, Japanese goods in Canada will have an unchanged Canadian-dollar price, while the price of Canadian goods sold in Canada will increase because of the inflation. Thus Japanese goods will be more attractive compared with Canadian goods (because they have become relatively cheaper), and thus

more Japanese goods will be bought in Canada. At any exchange rate, the amount of foreign exchange demanded to purchase imports will rise. This means that the demand curve for foreign exchange shifts to the right.

Canadian inflation that is unmatched in Japan will therefore cause the supply curve for foreign exchange to shift to the left and the demand curve for foreign exchange to shift to the right. As a result, the equilibrium exchange rate *must* rise—there is a depreciation of the Canadian dollar relative to the yen.

Inflation at Unequal Rates.   The two foregoing examples are, of course, just limiting cases of a more general situation in which the price levels change in both countries. The arguments can readily be extended when we realize that it is the *relative* size of the changes in prices in two countries that determines whether home goods or foreign goods look more or less attractive. If country A's inflation rate is higher than country B's, country A's exports are becoming relatively expensive in B's markets while im-

---

[7]We maintain the assumption, outlined in footnotes 4 and 5, that the foreign and domestic demands for imported goods are elastic.

ports from B are becoming relatively cheap in A's markets. This causes the price of A's currency to fall—A's currency depreciates relative to B's.

If the price level in one country is rising relative to that in another country, the equilibrium value of its currency will be falling relative to that of the other country.

Capital Movements

Major capital flows can exert strong influences on exchange rates. For example, an increased desire by Canadians to purchase Japanese assets (a capital export for Canada) will shift the demand curve for foreign exchange to the right, and the dollar will depreciate. This is illustrated in part (i) of Figure 37-3.

A movement of investment funds has the effect of appreciating the currency of the capital-importing country and depreciating the currency of the capital-exporting country.

This statement is true for all capital movements, short-term or long-term. Because the motives that lead to large capital movements are likely to be different in the short and long terms, however, it is worth considering each separately.

Short-Term Capital Movements.   An important motive for short-term capital flows is a change in interest rates. International traders hold transactions balances just as do domestic traders. These balances are often lent out on a short-term basis rather than being left idle. Naturally, the holders of these balances will tend to lend them, other things being equal, in markets where interest rates are highest. Thus if one country's short-term interest rate rises above the rates in other countries (say, because that country undertakes a contractionary monetary policy), there will tend to be a large inflow of short-term capital into that country in an effort to take advantage of the high rate, and this will tend to appreciate the currency. If the short-term interest rate should fall in one country (say, due to a monetary expansion in that country), there will tend to be a shift in capital away from that country and its currency will tend to depreciate.

A second motive for short-term capital movements is speculation about the *future value* of a country's exchange rate. If foreigners expect the Canadian dollar to appreciate in the near future, they will rush to buy assets that pay off in Canadian dollars; if they

expect the Canadian dollar to depreciate, they will be reluctant to buy or to hold Canadian securities.

Long-Term Capital Movements.   Long-term capital movements are largely influenced by long-term expectations about another country's profit opportunities and the long-run value of its currency. A Japanese firm would be more willing to purchase a Canadian factory if it expected that the dollar profits would buy more yen in future years than the profits from investment in a Japanese factory. This could happen if the Canadian firm earned greater profits than the Japanese firm, with exchange rates remaining unchanged. It could also happen if the profits were the same but the Japanese firm expected the Canadian dollar to appreciate relative to the yen.

Structural Changes

An economy can undergo structural changes that alter the equilibrium exchange rate. *Structural change* is an all-purpose term for a change in cost structures, the invention of new products, changes in preferences between products, or anything else that affects the pattern of comparative advantage. Consider two examples.

Suppose that the reluctance of firms in one country to adopt technological innovations results in that country's products not improving as rapidly as those produced in other countries. Consumers' demand (at fixed prices) will shift slowly away from the first country's products and toward those of its foreign competitors. This will cause a gradual depreciation in the first country's currency because fewer people want to buy that country's goods and thus fewer people want to buy that country's currency.

Another example relates to the discovery of valuable mineral resources. Prominent examples are the development of natural gas in The Netherlands in the early 1960s, the development of North Sea oil in the United Kingdom in the 1970s, and the recent discovery of a massive nickel deposit in Voisey's Bay, Newfoundland, in 1995. If firms in one country make such a discovery and begin selling these resources to the rest of the world, then the foreign purchasers must supply their foreign currency in order to purchase the currency of the exporting country. This leads to an appreciation of the currency of the exporting country.

Anything that leads to changes in the pattern of trade, such as changes in costs or changes in demand, will generally lead to changes in exchange rates.

THE BEHAVIOUR OF EXCHANGE RATES

One surprise to supporters of the move to floating exchange rates following the demise of the Bretton Woods system (of fixed exchange rates) in the early 1970s has been the degree of exchange rate volatility. Why have exchange rates been so volatile? This question remains at the centre of debate and controversy among researchers and policy commentators. In this section, we provide only a cursory view of this and related questions about the behaviour of exchange rates.

PURCHASING POWER PARITY

The theory of **purchasing power parity** (**PPP**) holds that over the long term, the value of the exchange rate between two currencies depends on the two currencies' relative purchasing power. The theory holds that a currency will tend to have the same purchasing power when it is spent in its home country as it would have if it were converted to foreign exchange and spent in the foreign country. Another way to say the same thing is that the price of *identical baskets of goods* should be the same in the two countries when the price is expressed in the same currency. If we let p_C and p_J be the price levels in Canada and Japan, respectively, and let e be the price of yen in terms of Canadian dollars (the exchange rate), then the theory of purchasing power parity can be expressed as

$$p_C = e \times p_J \qquad [6]$$

This simply says that if a basket of goods in Japan costs ¥100,000 and the exchange rate is 0.013 (0.013 Canadian dollars per yen), then that same basket of goods in Canada should cost $1,300 (0.013 × 100,000 = 1,300).

The idea behind PPP is a simple one. Suppose that Equation 6 did *not* hold—specifically, suppose that p_C was greater than $e \times p_J$, so that Canadian-dollar prices in Canada exceed the Canadian-dollar prices of the same goods in Japan. In this case, people would increase their purchases of Japanese goods and reduce their purchases of Canadian goods. This would have the effect of depreciating the Canadian dollar (a rise in e); and this would continue until the equality was reestablished.

The *PPP exchange rate* is the value of the exchange rate which makes Equation 6 hold. That is, the PPP exchange rate (between the Canadian dollar and the yen) is given by

$$e^{PPP} \equiv p_C/p_J \qquad [7]$$

PPP in the Long Run

If, at existing values of relative price levels and the exchange rate, the Canadian dollar has a higher purchasing power in Canada than in Japan (p_C is less than $e \times p_J$), the Canadian dollar is said to be *undervalued* relative to purchasing power parity (this means that the actual exchange rate is *above* the PPP exchange rate). According to the theory, the Canadian dollar would appreciate (e would fall) in the future. In this case, there is an incentive to sell foreign exchange and buy the Canadian dollar in order to take advantage of its higher purchasing power in Canada. This will itself lead to an appreciation of the Canadian dollar.

Similarly, if the Canadian dollar has a lower purchasing power in Canada than in Japan (p_C is greater than $e \times p_J$), the Canadian dollar is said to be *overvalued* relative to purchasing power parity (this means that the actual exchange rate is *below* the PPP exchange rate). According to the theory, the Canadian dollar would depreciate (e would rise) in the future. In this case, there is an incentive to buy foreign exchange and sell the Canadian dollar in order to take advantage of its higher purchasing power in Japan. This will itself lead to a depreciation of the Canadian dollar.

According to the theory of purchasing power parity, the exchange rate is determined by the relative price levels in the two countries.

Note that the PPP exchange rate is itself not constant. If inflation is higher in Canada than in Japan, for example, then p_C will be rising faster than p_J and so the PPP exchange rate will be rising. Conversely, if inflation is higher in Canada than in Japan, then p_C will be rising more slowly than p_J and so the PPP exchange rate will be falling.

If the actual exchange rate (e) changes along with the PPP exchange rate (e^{PPP}), the competitive positions of producers in the two countries will be unchanged. Firms that are located in countries with high inflation rates will still be able to sell their outputs on international markets because the exchange rate adjusts to offset the effect of the rising domestic prices.

A Caveat About PPP

The logic surrounding the theory of purchasing power parity is sound, but care must be taken in applying this logic. Recall when we explained Equation 6 that we defined p_C and p_J as the prices of *identical baskets of goods* in Canada and Japan, respectively. Given that the goods are the same, the argument that the prices should (eventually) be equated across the two countries is sensible—if the prices are not equated across the two countries, then there would be an incentive to purchase in the cheaper country rather than in the more expensive country, and this would lead to changes in the exchange rate until Equation 6 *did* hold.

The problem is that when we apply the theory of purchasing power parity to *national price indices*, such as the Consumer Price Index or the Implicit GDP Deflator, the two baskets of goods are typically *not* the same. There are two reasons for this.

Different Countries Produce Different Goods. Suppose we try to apply the theory of PPP to the Canada-Japan exchange rate and we use the GDP deflators from the two countries as the measures of prices. Recall from Chapter 21 that the GDP deflator is an index of prices *of the goods produced within the country.* But Canada and Japan clearly produce very different goods. The price of forest products will have a large weight in the Canadian GDP deflator, but almost no weight in the Japanese GDP deflator; in contrast, the price of electronic equipment will have a much larger weight in the Japanese GDP deflator than in the Canadian one.

The implication of these differences for the theory of PPP is important. As long as changes in the *relative* prices of goods occur, such as a change in the price of forest products relative to electronic equipment, then p_C (the Canadian GDP deflator) will change relative to p_J (the Japanese GDP deflator) *even though the prices of individual goods might be equated across the two countries.* Thus differences in the structure of the price indices between two countries means that using a PPP exchange rate computed on the basis of Equation 7 will be misleading.

The Importance of Nontraded Goods. The previous discussion emphasized that the *baskets* of goods across two countries might differ even though the products in the baskets were the same. But even if Canada and Japan produced exactly the same range of goods, so that the various weights in the GDP deflators were the same, there is still a reason why the basket of goods in Canada differs from the basket of goods in Japan. Some of the goods produced in Canada are *nontraded goods,* such as haircuts and restaurant meals. Nontraded goods are also produced in Japan. But since nontraded goods cannot be traded (by definition), there is nothing that will force their prices to be equal across the two countries. If haircuts are more expensive in Tokyo than in Toronto (as they are), we do not expect people to shift their consumption of haircuts away from Tokyo toward Toronto, and thus we should not expect the exchange rate to move to make Equation 6 hold.

The conclusion of this discussion is not that the logic of Equation 6 is faulty, but that we must be very careful in selecting the price indices we use when we apply the theory of purchasing power parity. We know that countries have different patterns of production and thus have different structures to their national price indices. In the presence of changes in relative prices of various products, this means that the national price indices can change in ways that will not lead to changes in the exchange rate. Similarly, the presence of nontraded goods implies that some differences in prices across countries will not lead to changes in the location of demand and thus changes in the exchange rate.

PPP in the Short Run

Even if all countries produced the same goods, and even if there were no nontraded goods, the theory of PPP must be viewed as a theory of exchange rates *in the long run.* In the short run, the role of speculation becomes very important for understanding deviations of the actual exchange rate from the PPP exchange rate.

Some economists argue that speculators stabilize the actual value of exchange rates within a narrow band around the PPP value. The argument is that because everyone knows that the "normal" value is the PPP rate, speculators who are seeking a profit when the rate deviates from its PPP level will quickly force the rate back to that level. To illustrate, suppose that the PPP exchange rate of the dollar in terms of yen is $1 = ¥80 and that the dollar appreciates so that the actual rate is $1 = ¥125. Speculators will rush to buy yen and sell dollars at $1 = ¥125, expecting to sell yen for dollars later when the rate returns to its PPP level of $1 = ¥80. This very action will raise the demand for the yen and help push its value back toward its PPP level.

Such speculative behaviour would stabilize the exchange rate near its PPP value if speculators could be sure that the deviations would be small and short-lived. However, the experience with flexible exchange rates has been that the swings around the PPP rate have been wide and have lasted for long periods. Whatever the causes of these wide and persistent swings, they serve to reduce the inherent stabilizing nature of speculation. For example, if the dollar fell below its PPP value of $1 = ¥80, speculators would know that it could go lower and stay there for quite a while before returning to PPP. In that case, it might be worth speculating on a price of, say, $1 = ¥75 next week rather than a price of $1 = ¥80 in some indefinite future.

The wide swings in exchange rates that have occurred mean that speculative buying and selling cannot be relied on to hold exchange rates close to their PPP values.[8]

INTEREST RATES AND EXCHANGE RATE "OVERSHOOTING"

Differences in interest rates between countries, due to differences in monetary and fiscal policies as well as other factors, can trigger large capital flows as investors seek to place their funds where returns are highest. These capital flows will in turn result in swings in exchange rates. Some economists argue that this is the fundamental reason for the wide fluctuations in exchange rates that have been observed.

To illustrate, suppose that the Bank of Canada introduces a tight monetary policy, perhaps to reduce Canadian inflation. As we saw in Chapter 29, this will lead to an increase in Canadian interest rates. Suppose that this tight monetary policy causes Canadian interest rates to rise 4 percentage points above those in Japan.

The interest rate differential will lead to a capital inflow into Canada. Canadian and foreign investors alike will sell assets denominated in Japanese yen and buy Canadian dollar assets that earn higher interest. These capital inflows will lead to an increased demand for dollars on the foreign exchange market as investors exchange yen for dollars to buy Canadian assets. The increased demand will in turn lead to an appreciation of the Canadian dollar.

A tight monetary policy will lead to higher interest rates, a capital inflow, and an appreciation of the currency.

When will the process stop? It will stop only when the *expected* return on Canadian and foreign assets are again roughly equalized; as long as the return on Canadian assets is above that on foreign assets, the capital inflows will continue, and the upward pressure on the dollar will continue. The key is that the *expected* return includes not only the interest earnings but also the gains or losses that might arise because of changes in the exchange rate during the period of the investment. A foreign investor holding a Canadian asset will receive Canadian dollars when the asset is sold and will at that time want to exchange Canadian dollars for foreign currency. If the value of the dollar has fallen, that will be a source of loss that has to be balanced against the interest income in assessing the net return on holding the asset.

In response to a monetary contraction, the appreciation of the Canadian dollar will continue until it has appreciated enough so that investors expect a future depreciation that just offsets the interest premium from investing funds in Canadian dollars.

Suppose that investors believe that the PPP rate is $1 = ¥100, but as they rush to buy dollars to take advantage of higher Canadian interest rates, they drive the rate to, say, $1 = ¥125. (Because $1 now buys more yen, the dollar has appreciated, and because it takes more yen to buy $1, the yen has depreciated.) They do not believe that this rate will be sustained and instead expect the Canadian dollar to lose value. If foreign investors expect the dollar to depreciate at 4 percent per year, they will be indifferent between lending money in Vancouver and doing so in Tokyo. The extra 4 percent per year of interest that they earn in Vancouver is exactly offset by the 4 percent that they expect to lose when they turn their money back into their own currency.

A monetary or fiscal policy that raises domestic interest rates above world levels will cause the external

---

[8]For an excellent and very readable discussion of some issues relating to the use of purchasing power parity, see Rudiger Dornbusch, "Purchasing Power Parity" in *The New Palgrave: A Dictionary of Economics* (The Stockton Press: New York, 1987).

APPLICATION 37-2

Beggar-My-Neighbour Policies, Past and Present

During the Great Depression of the 1930s, concern over massive unemployment came to dominate economic policies in almost every country. All measures, including exchange rate manipulations, seemed fair game for dealing with unemployment. Many of the policies adopted were acts of desperation. Governments, hoping to gain short-term advantages before their policies provoked the inevitable reaction from others, tended not to consider the long-term effects that the policies they adopted would have on their trading partners.

The use of devaluations to ease domestic unemployment rested on a simple and superficially plausible line of analysis: If a country has unemployed workers at home, why not substitute home production for imports and thus give jobs to one's citizens instead of to foreigners? One way to do this is to urge Canadians to "buy Canadian." Another probably more effective way is to lower the prices of domestic goods relative to those of imports. Putting a tariff on imports does this, as does devaluation of one's currency—both make foreign goods more expensive. Of course, if this policy works, other countries will find *their* exports falling and unemployment rising as a consequence. Because such policies attempt to solve one country's problems by inflicting them on others, they are called **beggar-my-neighbour policies**, often described as attempts to "export unemployment." In a situation of inadequate world demand, a beggar-my-neighbour policy on the part of one country can work only in the unlikely event that other countries do not react by changing their policies to protect themselves.

During the 1930s, industrialized countries engaged in a series of "competitive devaluations." One country would devalue its currency in an attempt to reduce its imports and stimulate exports, but because other countries were suffering from the same kinds of problems of unemployment, retaliation was swift, and devaluation followed devaluation. The simultaneous attempt of all countries to cut imports without suffering a comparable cut in exports is bound to be self-defeating.

These policies, along with other restrictive trade policies such as import duties, export subsidies, quotas, and prohibitions, led to a declining volume of world trade and brought no relief from the worldwide depression because they did nothing to raise world aggregate demand.

To avoid a recurrence of the beggar-my-neighbour policies of the 1930s, trading nations designed some important institutions. The International Monetary Fund (IMF) was supposed to reduce the chances of competitive devaluations, and the General Agreement on Tariffs and Trade (GATT) was supposed to reduce the chances of competitive increases in tariffs and other trade restrictions. These institutions worked well for over 30 years.

Throughout the 1980s it was clear that great pressure was being put on the whole postwar fabric, designed to encourage trade and discourage beggar-my-neighbour policies. Many countries negotiated unofficial quotas that restricted the importation of Japanese cars. European agricultural protectionism threatened to wreck the GATT negotiations and remains the focus of considerable debate. As we saw in Chapter 36, however, these pressures were overcome, at least for the time being, with the ratification of the Uruguay Round of the GATT in 1994.

value of the domestic currency to appreciate enough to create an expected future depreciation that will be sufficient to offset the interest differential.

If interest differentials are to persist, the exchange rate must change relative to its PPP value; this is often referred to as *overshooting* of the exchange rate.

One implication of this theory is that a central bank that is seeking to use its monetary policy to attain its domestic policy targets may have to put up with large fluctuations in the exchange rate. In our example, the high Canadian interest rates were the result of a restrictive monetary policy, resulting in appreciation of the dollar. The overshooting of the dollar beyond its PPP rate would put export and import-competing industries under temporary but severe pressure from foreign competition because Canadian goods would be expensive relative to imported goods. The resulting fall in demand for Canadian goods would open up a recessionary gap, providing a further mechanism by which the restrictive monetary policy is transmitted to the rest of the economy. This was discussed in Extension 28-3 in Chapter 28.

The other side of this coin is that when one country tightens its monetary policy—leading to an appreciation of its currency—this may create inflationary pressure abroad. Though Canada is too small a country for this effect to be important, countries like the United States are certainly large enough

for this to matter. Imagine a situation where the Fed (the U.S. central bank) decides to implement a contractionary monetary policy. U.S. interest rates rise, foreign capital flows into the United States, and the U.S. dollar appreciates. But the appreciation of the U.S. dollar obviously implies a depreciation of other currencies, like the Canadian dollar. This stimulates Canadian exports to the U.S. and puts upward pressure on Canadian prices and wages. Canadian authorities are now faced with the uncomfortable choice of either accepting this increased inflation in Canada or raising their own interest rates (by tightening monetary policy) and thus dampening the depreciation of the Canadian dollar.

In the early 1980s, when a tight monetary policy was initiated in the United States, many central banks from other countries (including Canada) chose the latter option, and the tight U.S. monetary policy was then quickly imitated in other countries. This combined monetary contraction contributed to the severity of the world recession. Some related issues are discussed further in Application 37-2.

SUMMARY

A. THE EXTERNAL VALUE OF THE DOLLAR

- International trade normally requires the exchange of the currency of one country for that of another. The exchange rate between the Canadian dollar and some foreign currency is defined to be the number of Canadian dollars required to purchase 1 unit of the foreign currency—it is the price of that foreign currency.
- A rise in the exchange rate is the same thing as a depreciation of the Canadian dollar in terms of foreign currency; a fall in the exchange rate is an appreciation of the Canadian dollar in terms of foreign currency.

B. THE BALANCE OF PAYMENTS

- Actual transactions among the firms, households, and governments of various countries are kept track of and reported in the balance-of-payments accounts. In these accounts, any transaction that represents a receipt for Canada (Canadians sell goods or assets to foreigners) is recorded as a credit item. Any transaction that represents a payment for Canada (Canadians

purchase goods or assets from foreigners) is recorded as a debit item.
- If all transactions are recorded in the balance of payments, the sum of all credit items necessarily equals the sum of all debit items because the foreign exchange that is bought (for the payment items) must also have been sold (for the receipt items).
- Major categories in the balance-of-payments accounts are the trade account, the capital-service account, the current account (which is equal to the trade account plus the capital-service account), the capital account, and the official financing account.
- When a country is said to have a balance of payments deficit (or surplus), what is meant is that the sum of current and capital accounts is a deficit (or surplus). That is, it excludes the transactions on the official financing account. If official financing is zero, a balance on current account must be matched by a balance on capital account of equal magnitude but opposite sign.
- There is nothing inherently good or bad about deficits or surpluses. Persistent deficits or surpluses cannot be sustained because the former will eventually exhaust a country's foreign exchange reserves and the latter will do the same to a trading partner's reserves.

C. THE FOREIGN EXCHANGE MARKET

- The supply of foreign exchange (or the demand for Canadian dollars) arises from Canadian exports of goods and services, long-term and short-term capital flows into Canada, and the desire of foreign banks, firms, and governments to use Canadian dollars as an international medium of exchange or as part of their reserves.
- The demand for foreign exchange (or the supply of Canadian dollars to purchase foreign currencies) arises from Canadian imports of goods and services, capital flows from Canada, and the desire of holders of Canadian dollars to decrease the size of their holdings.
- A depreciation of the Canadian dollar lowers the foreign price of Canadian exports and increases the amount of foreign exchange supplied (to purchase Canadian exports). Thus the supply curve for foreign exchange is positively sloped when plotted against the exchange rate.
- A depreciation of the Canadian dollar also raises the dollar price of imports from abroad and hence lowers the amount of foreign exchange demanded to purchase foreign goods. Thus the demand curve for foreign exchange is negatively sloped when plotted against the exchange rate.

D. THE DETERMINATION OF EXCHANGE RATES

- When the central bank does not intervene in the foreign exchange market (zero official financing), there is a flexible exchange rate. Under fixed exchange rates, the central bank intervenes in the foreign exchange market to maintain the exchange rate at or near an announced value. To do this, the central bank must hold sufficient stocks of foreign exchange reserves.
- Under a flexible, or floating, exchange rate, the exchange rate is determined by supply and demand for the currency. This is simply an application of the laws of supply and demand that we studied in Chapter 4; the item being bought and sold is foreign currency.
- The Canadian dollar will appreciate in foreign exchange markets if there is an increase in the supply of foreign exchange (an increase in demand for Canadian dollars) or if there is a reduction in demand for foreign exchange (a reduction in supply of Canadian dollars). The opposite changes will lead to a depreciation of the Canadian dollar.
- These changes are caused by changes in such things as the prices of imports and exports, the rates of inflation in different countries, capital movements, structural conditions, and expectations about the future exchange rate.

E. THE BEHAVIOUR OF EXCHANGE RATES

- The theory of purchasing power parity (PPP) predicts that exchange rates should adjust so that the purchasing power of a given currency is the same in different countries. Another way to say this is that the price of an identical basket of goods should be equated in different countries (when expressed in the same currency).
- Care must be taken in applying the theory of PPP. Specifically, if price indices (such as the GDP deflator) from different countries are used as the basis for computing the PPP exchange rate, then it must be recognized that differences in the structure of price indices across countries, together with the presence of nontraded goods, can be responsible for persistent deviations of the actual exchange rate from this measure of the PPP exchange rate.
- In addition to deviations from PPP due to differences in the structure of price indices, there are short-term explanations for why PPP may not hold. One important reason is the overshooting of exchange rates in response to policy-induced changes in interest rates. A monetary contraction in Canada will raise Canadian interest rates and create an inflow of foreign capital. This capital inflow will cause an appreciation of the Canadian dollar large enough so that the expected future depreciation exactly offsets the higher Canadian interest rate.

KEY CONCEPTS

Foreign exchange and exchange rates
Appreciation and depreciation
Balance-of-payments accounts
Current and capital accounts
Changes in official reserves

Mercantilist views on the balance of trade and volume of trade
Sources of the demand for and supply of foreign exchange
Fixed and flexible exchange rates

Purchasing power parity
PPP exchange rate
PPP and nontraded goods
Exchange rate overshooting

1. What is the probable effect of each of the following on the exchange rate of a country, other things being equal?

   a. The quantity of oil imports is greatly decreased, but the value of imported oil is higher due to price increases.
   b. The country's inflation rate falls well below that of its trading partners.
   c. Rising labour costs of the country's manufacturers lead to a worsening ability to compete in world markets.
   d. The government greatly expands its gifts of food and machinery to underdeveloped countries.
   e. A major boom occurs with rising employment.
   f. The central bank raises interest rates sharply.
   g. More domestic oil is discovered and developed.

2. In the mid 1980s, money wages increased substantially faster in Canada than in the United States. Many Canadians expressed the fear that their rapidly rising costs would price them out of U.S. markets. Would this have made sense if the value of the Canadian dollar was fixed relative to the U.S. dollar? Did it make sense given that the exchange rate was actually free to vary on the market?

3. In mid 1992, German interest rates soared above those in many other European countries and in the United States. For the United States, this led to a steady and substantial devaluation of the U.S. dollar relative to the deutsche mark; for many of the European currencies, a crisis occurred in the foreign exchange markets. For example, the United Kingdom was forced to raise interest rates temporarily and ultimately had to withdraw the pound sterling from the European Exchange Rate Mechanism, which had involved a commitment to maintain the pound-deutsche mark exchange rate within a narrow range. Why were the U.K. and U.S. experiences so different?

4. Indicate whether each of the following transactions increases the demand for foreign exchange, the supply of foreign exchange, or neither in foreign exchange markets. How would you expect the transaction to affect the value of the Canadian dollar?

   a. IBM moves $10 million from bank accounts in Toronto to banks in Paris to expand operations in France.
   b. The Canadian government extends a grant of $3 million to the government of Peru, which Peru uses to buy farm machinery from a Canadian firm.
   c. Canadian investors, responding to higher profits of U.S. rather than Canadian corporations, buy stocks through the New York Stock Exchange.
   d. Several highly indebted countries stop interest payments on their large debts to Canadian banks.
   e. Lower interest rates available in Toronto than in London encourage British firms to borrow in the Toronto money market, converting the proceeds into pounds sterling for use at home.

5. "If a country solves its balance-of-payments problems, it will have solved its foreign trade problems." Discuss this statement.

6. Canada's trade surplus with the United States (or the U.S. trade deficit with Canada) is the cause of considerable concern to some U.S. politicians. Many economists, however, argue that U.S. policymakers should not be concerned with reducing the U.S. trade deficit with Canada primarily because there is no reason to expect a balance between any two countries. Comment on the need for policies to address the U.S. trade deficit with Canada.

7. Outline the reasoning behind the following 1989 newspaper headline: "Sterling strengthens as British interest rates rise."

8. "Under a flexible exchange rate system, no country need suffer unemployment, for if its prices are low enough, there will be more than enough demand to keep its factories and farms fully occupied." The evidence suggests that flexible exchange rates have not generally eliminated unemployment. Can you explain why? Can changing exchange rates ever cure unemployment?

9. For well over a decade, Canada has had to sell bonds abroad to finance its excess of government plus investment spending over tax revenue plus private-sector saving.

   a. What are the implications for the capital and the current accounts?
   b. Why, when this dissaving first appeared, was the main current account effect on the balance of trade?
   c. Why, over time, would the main current account effect switch to the investment-income side of the current account (interest payments)?

10. What must be the balance on current account when Canada is a major importer of foreign capital? Does it matter if this capital is used to build productive facili-

ties, as it largely was in the late 1970s, or to finance government borrowing (to finance current spending), as it largely was in the late 1980s and early 1990s?

11. On November 27, 1995, a letter to the *Globe and Mail* said that "the economy of this once wonderful country is in the sewer and the politicians keep on tinkering, not knowing how to fix it." The letter proposed a 20 percent devaluation of the Canadian dollar, and argued that the immediate effects would be (among other things):

- a dramatic rise in exports
- a dramatic fall in imports
- a large inflow of new foreign investment

What do you think of the proposal? What would the Bank of Canada have to do to achieve a 20 percent devaluation of the Canadian dollar? If such a devaluation were to take place, is it possible to have the effects claimed by the author of the letter? Explain.

CHAPTER 38

MACROECONOMIC POLICY IN AN OPEN ECONOMY

In earlier chapters, we considered the effects of monetary and fiscal policy on income and prices, in both the short run and the long run. In Chapters 35 through 37 we developed the basics of international trade, trade policy, the exchange rate, and the balance of payments. Here we put the pieces together, elaborating our model of macroeconomics and macroeconomic policy in the context of an economy that engages in trade and in international financial transactions.

In this chapter, we explore some of the issues that arise in such an open economy. When we focus on *open-economy* issues in macroeconomics, new complications arise. These include the behaviour of the exchange rate and its influence on the balance of trade and national income, the nature and extent of foreign borrowing, and the impact on the economy of changes in the terms of trade or in foreign national income, interest rates, and inflation. As we shall also see, the response of the economy to economic policies may be altered in an open economy, as opposed to the closed-economy response emphasized so far in this book.

There are three issues which are of special interest. The first concerns the effectiveness of monetary policy in an open economy. The second concerns the effectiveness of fiscal policy in an open economy. The third, related to the second, is the relationship between government budget deficits (or surpluses) and trade deficits (or surpluses). Our interest in that relationship arises from the experience of the past 15 years. In the early 1980s, the Canadian economy slid into a deep recession, and the decline in economic activity contributed to an increase in government budget deficits. Later in the decade, and indeed, into the mid 1990s, large government budget deficits were accompanied by large current account deficits. These events lead to discussion of the so-called *twin deficits*. Just how tightly the two deficits are related is one of the key issues in economic policy.

In the first section of this chapter, we focus on the relationships among the balance of trade, aggregate demand, and national income and on the role of the exchange rate. To make the exposition clearer, we start by considering these phenomena under the assumption that there is *no international capital mobility*. In this case, exchange rates are determined entirely by the supply and demand for foreign exchange *from current account transactions* (goods and services) and by official transactions by the central bank. Later in the chapter, we allow for capital mobility (capital account transactions), permitting us to consider a model that matches the real world quite closely.

THE BALANCE OF TRADE AND NATIONAL INCOME

Suppose that there are no international capital flows in the world economy, so that the only international activities involve the exchange of goods and services

across national boundaries. What are the implications of this international trade for the determination of national income and for the role of economic policies?

We start by comparing the basic macroeconomic equilibrium condition for a closed economy with that for an open economy. Recall that in a closed economy, the equilibrium condition is that national income equals desired aggregate expenditure. In an open economy, we use the same equilibrium condition to analyze the multiplier relating changes in equilibrium national income to changes in autonomous expenditure. In the case of the multiplier in an open economy, we distinguish between an open economy that maintains a fixed exchange rate and one that has a flexible exchange rate.

In studying national income under various circumstances, we find that changes in the price level arising from shifts of the aggregate demand curve (with an upward-sloping *SRAS* curve) complicate but do not change the basic results. Hence, for simplicity, we focus our discussion on shifts in the *AD* curve *with a given price level*; in terms of the terminology in Chapters 23 and 24, we will focus on the size of the *simple multiplier*.

A CLOSED ECONOMY

For a closed economy (an economy that does not engage in international trade), there are only three sources of expenditure: consumption (C), investment (I), and government purchases (G). Hence the equilibrium condition is that in which real national income equals desired aggregate expenditure:

$$Y = C + I + G \qquad [1]$$

We saw in Chapter 25 that this equation underlies the aggregate demand (AD) curve (see Figure 25-2). Recall in particular that the *simple multiplier* gives the size of the horizontal shift in the *AD* curve following a change in autonomous spending. The simple multiplier is equal to $1/(1 - z)$, where z is the marginal propensity to spend out of national income. As we saw in Chapter 24, for our closed economy, z is equal to $b(1 - t)$, where b is the marginal propensity to consume and t is the income-tax rate.

We want to study what happens when there is an increase in aggregate demand. This could be due to an expansionary fiscal policy (an increase in government purchases or a reduction in taxes), an expansionary monetary policy (which lowers the interest rate and thus increases desired investment), or it could be due to an increase in autonomous expenditure on the part of the private sector (an increase in autonomous consumption or investment). Such an increase in aggregate demand implies a rightward shift in the AD curve and hence an increase in national income as illustrated in part (i) of Figure 38-1 by the shift from AD_0 to AD_{closed}.

AN OPEN ECONOMY WITH A FIXED EXCHANGE RATE

Now consider an open economy (one that engages in international trade). For the moment, to simplify the exposition, we suppose that the central bank adjusts its official financing transactions so as to maintain a fixed exchange rate. As we saw in Chapter 37, this means that the balance of payments (the sum of the current and capital accounts) can take on a value different from zero; because we have also simplified our analysis at this stage by supposing that there are no international capital movements, the balance of payments is equal to the balance of trade.[1]

In Chapter 24, we saw that incorporating exports (X) and imports (IM) into the analysis results in the equilibrium condition:

$$Y = C + I + G + (X - IM) \qquad [2]$$

The inclusion of the balance of trade or net export term $(X - IM)$ in the determination of desired aggregate expenditure has two important implications.

Automatic Stabilizer

Because imports rise with national income, the simple multiplier is reduced; that is, there is a smaller horizontal shift in the AD curve following an increase in autonomous spending than would occur in a closed economy. Recall that the simple multiplier is given by $1/(1 - z)$, where z is the marginal propen-

---

[1]With no capital flows, the capital account is clearly zero. This leaves only the current account. But if there are no capital flows, then there is also no investment income or payments in the current account and so the current account balance is just equal to the balance of trade.

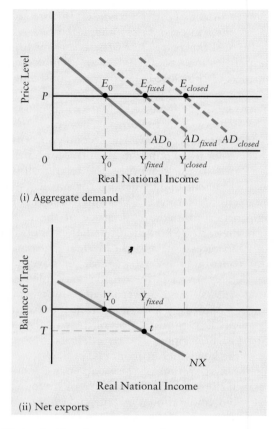

FIGURE 38-1

The Simple Multiplier in an Open Economy with a Fixed Exchange Rate

(i) Aggregate demand

(ii) Net exports

Under fixed exchange rates and zero capital mobility, the simple multiplier is smaller than it would be in a closed economy; the responsiveness of net exports to national income provides an automatic stabilizer. In part (i), aggregate demand is initially given by AD_0, and the price level is P. An increase in autonomous spending then shifts the AD curve to the right; the size of the horizontal shift is given by the simple multiplier. In a closed economy, the AD curve shifts to AD_{closed}, the new equilibrium is at E_{closed}, and the new equilibrium level of national income is Y_{closed}.

In an open economy with fixed exchange rates and no capital mobility, the simple multiplier is smaller. The AD curve shifts by less, to AD_{fixed}; the new equilibrium is at E_{fixed}, and the new equilibrium level of national income is Y_{fixed}, less than Y_{closed}.

In part (ii), the balance of trade is shown by the negatively sloped line NX. At Y_0, there is a zero balance of trade; the rise in income to Y_{fixed} in the open-economy fixed-exchange-rate case causes a movement along NX, and there is a trade deficit of T.

sity to spend; in an open economy, the marginal propensity to spend is reduced because of the *marginal propensity to import*. This reduction in z increases the denominator $(1 - z)$ and thus reduces the size of the simple multiplier. The simple open-economy multiplier is shown in part (i) of Figure 38-1 as the shift from AD to AD_{fixed}, which is smaller than the closed-economy multiplier shown by the shift from AD_0 to AD_{closed}.[2]

As we saw in Chapter 26, anything that reduces the size of the multiplier, and thus reduces the sensitivity of national income to autonomous changes in spending, is called an *automatic stabilizer*.

Under fixed exchange rates, international trade, by reducing the multiplier, acts as an automatic stabilizer.

The source of the difference between the closed- and open-economy multipliers is shown in part (ii) of Figure 38-1. In an open economy, the increase in national income caused by an increase in aggregate demand implies a movement along the net export function. Thus, following the change in AD, there is a fall in net exports (as imports increase) which then works to reduce equilibrium national income.

Export Multiplier

Equation 2 shows (as we discussed in Chapter 24) that in an open economy, a change in the level of exports will cause national income to change. A change in the level of exports can occur for many reasons, including a change in the terms of trade (i.e., a change in the price of a county's exports relative to its import goods) or a change in the level of economic activity in a country's trading partners. These will lead to a shift in the AD curve and hence to a change in the equilibrium level of national income.

Under fixed exchange rates, changes in exports cause changes in aggregate demand and equilibrium national income.

The link between a change in exports and a change in equilibrium national income is referred to as the *export multiplier*. It is just a straightforward

application of the concept of the multiplier from Chapter 24—the only difference is that in this case the autonomous expenditure that is initially changing is expenditure on Canadian exports by foreigners rather than expenditure by domestic residents for consumption, government purchases, or investment. One reason why the export multiplier is important is that it helps us think about how the levels of economic activity are related across trading partners. For example, a boom in the United States can be transmitted to Canada (its largest trading partner) via increased demand for Canada's exports.

The operation of the export multiplier is shown in Figure 38-2. An autonomous increase in exports shifts up the net export function, as shown in part (ii). (The net export function shifts upward by the amount of the autonomous increase in exports.) This generates a shift in the aggregate demand curve which increases equilibrium national income, as shown in part (i). What is the overall effect on the trade balance? On the one hand, the autonomous increase in exports suggests a movement toward a trade surplus. On the other hand, the resulting increase in national income leads to an increase in imports and this suggests a movement toward a trade deficit. As it turns out, however, it *must* be the case that the initial increase in exports is larger than the induced increase in imports.[3] The trade balance at the new equilibrium level of national income (Y_1 in Figure 38-2) must be a trade surplus. Thus, in contrast to the effects of an autonomous increase in domestic spending (which leads to a trade deficit), an autonomous increase in exports leads to a trade surplus.

In Figures 38-1 and 38-2, the analysis assumed a given price level. A more complete analysis would take account of the effects of a positively sloped *SRAS* curve so that any shifts in the AD curve lead to changes in the price level. As noted before, this

---

[2]The simple open-economy multiplier is $1/[1 - b(1 - t) + m]$, where m is the marginal propensity to import. Because m is positive, the denominator is increased and hence the simple open-economy multiplier is smaller than the simple closed-economy multiplier, $1/[1 - b(1 - t)]$.

[3]To see why the initial increase in exports must be larger than the induced increase in imports, note that the change in net exports is given by $\Delta NX = \Delta X - \Delta IM$. But we know that the change in imports is equal to the change in equilibrium income (ΔY) times the marginal propensity to import (m). Furthermore, we know that ΔY is equal to ΔX times the simple multiplier. Putting this together yields

$$\Delta NX = \Delta X - (\Delta Y)(m) = \Delta X - \frac{m}{1 - b(1 - t) + m} \times \Delta X$$

The fraction in this expression is less than one (as long as $b(1 - t)$ is less than one, which it is). This immediately implies that the induced increase in imports is less than the increase in exports.

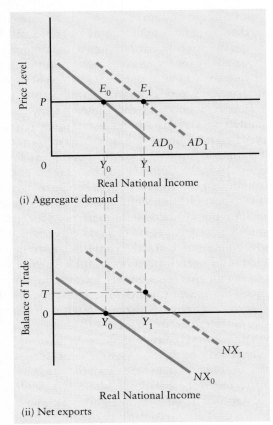

FIGURE 38-2
The Export Multiplier with a Fixed Exchange Rate

(i) Aggregate demand

(ii) Net exports

An autonomous increase in exports leads, under fixed exchange rates, to an increase in equilibrium national income and to a trade surplus. Initially, aggregate demand is given by AD_0 in part (i) and the net export function is given by NX_0 in part (ii). The price level is P, equilibrium is at E_0, equilibrium national income is Y_0, and there is a zero balance of trade.

Following an autonomous increase in exports, the net export function shifts to the right to NX_1 in part (ii). This causes the aggregate demand curve to shift to the right to AD_1 in part (i). The new equilibrium is at E_1, with equilibrium national income rising to Y_1. At the new equilibrium level of income there is a trade surplus of T.

complicates but does not change the basic results. For readers who wish to work through this more complicated case, the analysis is presented in Extension 38-1.

FLEXIBLE EXCHANGE RATES

The automatic stabilizer role provided by the balance of trade and the potential for the export multiplier to transmit disturbances from one economy to another are key aspects of a fixed exchange rate system. As such, they are especially relevant to the historical analysis of periods earlier in this century when the world was essentially on fixed exchange rates and to a study of the economies of countries that agree to operate with fixed exchange rates, as some members of the EU currently do. However, to study the economies of countries such as Canada and most other industrialized countries, it is important to examine flexible exchange rates.

As we saw in Chapter 37, with a flexible exchange rate, the balance of payments will be zero even when there are no official transactions by the central bank in the foreign exchange market. Let us suppose that the central bank allows the currency to float so that there are no official transactions. In the simplified model of this section, where there are no international capital flows, a zero balance of payments means that the balance of trade must also be zero. As we will see, this has dramatic implications for open-economy multiplier analysis.

Automatic Stabilizer

Look again at Figure 38-1, which shows the situation following an increase in autonomous spending. (In this section, we restrict our attention to the implications for changes in autonomous *domestic* spending, G or I; we return shortly to the implications of changes in export spending, X.) Following an increase in autonomous domestic spending, aggregate demand and national income have increased, *and* the increase in income has caused a trade deficit.

Under flexible exchange rates, however, the trade deficit following an increase in domestic spending cannot be sustained.[4] The increased demand for imports resulting from the stimulus to aggregate demand means that there is an excess demand for foreign exchange as Canadians try to sell Canadian dollars in order to obtain foreign exchange with which to buy imports. As a result, the Canadian dollar depreciates.

---

[4]In fact, it would never occur. There would be a tendency for a deficit to emerge, and this would set in motion the reactions discussed in the rest of this section.

AGGREGATE SUPPLY AND THE OPEN-ECONOMY MULTIPLIER

Here we consider the implications of incorporating a positively sloped *SRAS* curve into the analysis of the open-economy multiplier of Figure 38-1.

The basic analysis is presented in the accompanying figure. Because the *SRAS* curve does not shift in response to the change in autonomous spending, the change in national income is directly related to

(i) AD shifts due to increase in autonomous spending

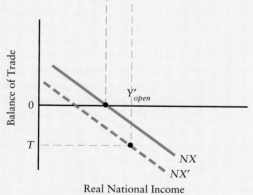

(ii) NX shifts due to rise in the price level

the shift in the *AD* curve. Hence the results from the fixed-price-level analysis of Figure 38-1 appear to carry through to this case.

When national income *and the price level* change in response to a change in autonomous spending, the following is true:

The change in national income following a change in autonomous expenditure is smaller because of the positively sloped *SRAS* curve.

But this is true in both the closed economy and the open economy. Further, the presence of the positively sloped *SRAS* curve does not alter the *relative* change in national income in the two cases—the multiplier is still smaller in the open economy than in the closed economy. (This is true for the same reason as in the fixed-price case: the rise in Y increases imports and thus net exports act as an automatic stabilizer.)

In the open economy, the rise in national income following an increase in autonomous spending also leads to a trade deficit. But there are two separate effects. First, for the given *NX* curve in part (ii), the rise in national income increases imports and thus leads to a trade deficit (this is a movement along the *NX* curve). The second effect comes from the change in the price level. From the discussion in Chapter 37, recall that a change in the price level changes the level of net exports. Specifically, for a given exchange rate, a rise in the Canadian price level makes foreign goods cheaper relative to Canadian goods, and thus leads consumers to buy more imports (and leads foreigners to buy fewer Canadian goods). This shifts the *NX* curve *down* to *NX'* in part (ii). Thus the overall effect of the change in autonomous spending is to increase the trade deficit to *T*.

The depreciation of the Canadian dollar will lead to an increase in exports as Canadian-produced goods become more competitive on world markets and to a decrease in imports as imported goods become more expensive. This in turn leads to a shift of the net export function upward and to the right; the depreciation of the Canadian dollar means that at any level of national income, net exports are higher. This is shown in Figure 38-3.

How much does the dollar depreciate, and how much does the net export function shift? As we saw in Chapter 37, the dollar *must* depreciate by enough

FIGURE 38-3
The Simple Multiplier in an Open Economy with a Flexible Exchange Rate

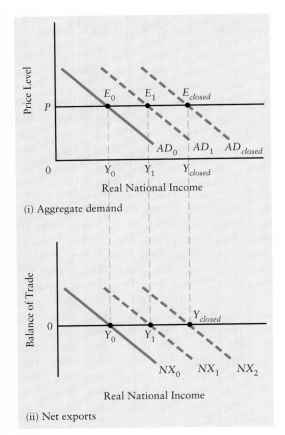

(i) Aggregate demand

(ii) Net exports

Under flexible exchange rates and zero capital mobility, the balance of trade is always zero, and hence the open-economy multiplier is identical to the closed-economy multiplier. No automatic stabilizer role is provided by net exports. Aggregate demand is initially given by AD_0, and the price level is P. Equilibrium is at E_0, and the equilibrium level of national income is Y_0.

An increase in autonomous spending then shifts the AD curve to the right; at the initial exchange rate, this is a shift to AD_1. National income would rise to Y_1 and there would be a trade deficit. The resulting depreciation of the dollar causes the NX curve to shift to the right, say, to NX_1, causing the AD curve to shift further to the right.

At the new equilibrium, national income and the exchange rate must be such that the balance of trade is zero. This occurs when the AD curve shifts by the amount it would shift in a closed economy, so that the new equilibrium is at E_{closed} and the NX curve shifts to NX_2.

to ensure that the market for foreign exchange clears, which means that net exports are zero. If national income were to remain constant at its new level (Y_1 in Figure 38-3), the answer would be that the net export function would shift by enough to make the balance of trade zero at that new level of national income. The dollar would depreciate by the amount necessary to cause just that shift in the net export function.

However, the process does not end there. The increase in exports following the depreciation leads to a further increase in aggregate demand. This of course leads to a further increase in national income, which in turn causes a movement along the new net export function. This increase in imports then gives rise to a further depreciation of the Canadian dollar.

This process comes to a halt when the new level of national income and the new exchange rate are compatible with equilibrium in the market for domestic output (as required by Equation 2) and the balance of trade is zero (as required by the flexible exchange rate in the absence of international capital flows). It might appear that finding the new equilibrium and assessing the final multiplier impact of the increase in autonomous spending will be difficult. But further examination of Equation 2 reveals a surprising and simple answer.

Because the exchange rate adjusts until net exports are zero, the economy behaves as if it were a closed economy.

This means that the AD curve continues shifting until it is coincident with the closed-economy curve AD_{closed} in Figure 38-3 and the equilibrium level of income is equal to Y_{closed}, the level that would have occurred in the closed economy. The NX curve shifts so that the balance of trade is zero when income is at its new equilibrium level, Y_{closed}.

With zero capital mobility and flexible exchange rates, the simple multiplier in an open economy is the same as that for a closed economy.

This means that the expansion of imports associated with the increased income resulting from an increase in domestic autonomous spending does not provide an additional automatic stabilizer for the economy (as it did under fixed exchange rates). This is true because the currency depreciation that accompanies the expansion of income serves to maintain a zero balance of trade. That is, the depreciation leads to increases in exports and decreases in imports that exactly offset the increase in imports resulting from the expansion of income.

Export Multiplier

Now consider the effects of an increase in Canadian exports resulting, say, from a boom in one of Canada's trading partners. The effects under fixed exchange rates, shown in Figure 38-2, are an increase in national income and a trade surplus.

Again, the nonzero balance of trade is not sustainable under flexible exchange rates. The trade surplus implies an excess supply of foreign exchange (or an excess demand for Canadian dollars) and thus leads to an appreciation of the Canadian dollar and a fall in net exports. This fall in net exports in turn reduces aggregate demand, causing the *AD* curve to shift to the left. As long as there is a trade surplus, the Canadian dollar continues to appreciate and the *AD* curve continues to shift to the left.

Once again, the solution to this apparently complicated interaction can be seen quite simply by reference to Equation 2, and again the answer is a surprising one.

Because the exchange rate adjusts until net exports are zero, any autonomous change in exports is reversed by subsequent exchange rate movements. The economy behaves as if the autonomous change in exports had never occurred.

In terms of Figure 38-2, the appreciation causes the *NX* and *AD* curves to shift to the left until they have been restored to their original position.

With zero capital mobility and flexible exchange rates, the export multiplier is zero.

The initial autonomous increase in *X* is offset by a combination of a decline in *X* and an increase in *IM* due to the appreciation of the dollar. As a result, the trade account remains in balance, and there is no net change in desired aggregate expenditure or, consequently, in national income.

THE INSULATION PROPERTIES OF FLEXIBLE EXCHANGE RATES

These results lead many economists to argue that a flexible exchange rate *insulates* an economy from foreign disturbances that cause the demand for the home economy's exports to change. That is why a flexible exchange rate is often said to cushion the domestic economy against cyclical variations in economic activity in other countries.

To see this insulation property at work, consider a simple example. Suppose that the United States (Canada's largest trading partner) goes into a recession. The decline in U.S. income will lead to a reduction in Americans' demand for Canadian goods, such as softwood lumber, nickel, engineering services, or telecommunications equipment. The fall in Canadian exports will reduce income in Canada through the multiplier effect. However, if the value of the Canadian dollar is allowed to respond to market forces, it will depreciate because Canada's trade deficit reflects an excess demand for foreign exchange (or an excess supply of Canadian dollars). This depreciation of the Canadian dollar will stimulate demand for Canadian exports and encourage Canadians to substitute Canadian goods for now more expensive imported goods. Thus the depreciation will provide a stimulus to demand in Canada that will offset the depressing effect of the U.S. recession.

This insulation property, combined with the result that flexible exchange rates increase the multiplier for changes in domestic expenditure (which enhances the effectiveness of domestic stabilization), provides the basis for many economists' advocacy of flexible exchange rates. However, as we shall see in the next section of this chapter, these results depend crucially on the simplifying assumption that there is no capital mobility.

INTERNATIONAL CAPITAL MOBILITY

In the previous discussion we assumed *no capital mobility,* meaning that there was no international trade in assets (either bonds or physical capital). This implied that capital account transactions did not occur. Under fixed exchange rates, this meant that the current account was balanced by the central bank's official transactions in the foreign exchange market. Under flexible exchange rates (with no official transactions by the central bank), this meant that the exchange rate adjusted until the current account was balanced. We now allow for international trade in assets such as bonds or physical capital—that is, we allow for *capital mobility*. Not surprisingly, the presence of capital account transactions makes the analysis more complicated.

As we saw in Chapter 37, capital flows are influenced by domestic interest rates. An increase in Canadian interest rates will attract an inflow of foreign capital; a fall in Canadian interest rates will have the opposite effect as capital moves elsewhere to take advantage of the now relatively higher foreign rates. When foreign investors buy securities that are issued by Canadian corporations or governments or when they invest in Canadian industry, the capital inflow causes an increase in the demand for Canadian dollars in the foreign exchange market (an increase in the supply of foreign exchange). Conversely, the acquisition of foreign assets by Canadians represents a capital outflow and causes an increase in the supply of Canadian dollars to the foreign exchange market (an increase in demand for foreign exchange).

As we shall now see, this responsiveness of international capital flows to changes in interest rates affects the mechanism by which monetary and fiscal policies influence the economy and thus alters the effectiveness of those policies. The operation of these policies can not only differs sharply from the closed-economy results emphasized earlier in this book but also differs from the simplified open-economy results with no international capital mobility that we have studied so far in this chapter.

Due to the dominance of flexible exchange rates in the world today, we continue to focus on the case of flexible exchange rates.

THE ROLE OF CAPITAL MOBILITY

Capital mobility complicates the analysis in the first part of this chapter in two related ways. First, the balance of payments (the sum of the current account and capital account) is no longer just equal to the balance of trade. The presence of capital mobility means that we must include the capital account when we think of the balance of payments. Second, the effect of a domestic demand disturbance on the balance of payments, and hence on the exchange rate, depends not only on its impact on national income but also its impact on interest rates.

Here we focus on the different effects that monetary and fiscal policy have when the exchange rate is flexible and international capital flows exist. The key to this difference is something that we have already encountered earlier in this book—the different effects that the two policies have on interest rates.

In a closed economy, monetary and fiscal policies that have the same influence on income have opposite effects on interest rates.

We saw in Chapter 29 that expansionary monetary policy exerts its influence on income primarily by *reducing* interest rates and thereby stimulating interest-sensitive expenditure. We saw in Chapter 32 that expansionary fiscal policy increases national income and, by driving up the demand for money, leads to *increases* in interest rates. Because monetary and fiscal policies have opposite effects on interest rates, it is important to distinguish between them when considering an open economy with interest-sensitive international capital flows.

Monetary Policy and the Capital Account

The effects of monetary policy on the capital account of an open economy are related to the interest rate effects that it would have in a closed economy. For example, expansionary monetary policy reduces interest rates; in an open economy, this leads to a capital outflow as foreign and domestic investors seek to sell Canadian assets and buy higher-yielding foreign assets.

An expansionary monetary policy will put downward pressure on interest rates and lead to an outflow of capital, thereby moving the capital account toward a deficit. A contractionary monetary policy will have the opposite effects.

Fiscal Policy and the Capital Account

Similarly, the effects of fiscal policy on the capital account of an open economy are related to the interest rate effects that it would have in a closed economy. For example, expansionary fiscal policy pushes interest rates up; in an open economy, this leads to a capital inflow as foreign and domestic investors seek to sell foreign assets and buy higher-yielding Canadian assets.

An expansionary fiscal policy will put upward pressure on interest rates and lead to an inflow of foreign capital, thereby moving the capital account toward a surplus. A contractionary fiscal policy will have the opposite effects.

THE EFFECTIVENESS OF MONETARY POLICY

Suppose that current output is less than potential output and the Bank of Canada seeks to remove this recessionary gap by expansionary monetary policy. The Bank conducts an open-market purchase of bonds, thereby increasing commercial-bank reserves. Through an expansion of commercial-bank lending, this increases the money supply and thus reduces interest rates. This stimulates interest-sensitive expenditure and leads to an increase in national income.

With zero capital mobility, as shown earlier in this chapter, the increase in national income leads to a rise in imports and thus to a trade deficit. This in turn leads to a depreciation of the dollar, and a further increase of aggregate demand and national income.

With capital mobility, however, lower Canadian interest rates will cause an outflow of capital and hence a deficit on the capital account. This will reinforce both the deficit on the trade account and the pressures for the dollar to depreciate, stimulating exports and reinforcing the expansion in national income. Income will be stimulated not only by the fall in interest rates but also by the increased demand for domestically produced goods (exports) brought about by a depreciation of the Canadian dollar. The initial monetary stimulus will be *reinforced* by the effects of currency depreciation.

Under flexible exchange rates, monetary policy is a powerful tool for influencing national income and employment. Because capital flows are interest-sensitive, a depreciation of the currency is an additional channel through which an increase in the money supply stimulates aggregate demand.

THE EFFECTIVENESS OF FISCAL POLICY

Consider again the case where current output is less than potential output. But now the government seeks to remove this recessionary gap by expansionary fiscal policy. An increase in government expenditures or a reduction in taxes (or both) will increase national income through the multiplier effect and reduce the size of the recessionary gap. As we saw earlier in this chapter, this will also cause a movement along the net export function, leading to a reduction in net exports (the rise in national income increases imports and thus reduces net exports).

In the absence of capital mobility, the reduction in net exports leads to a depreciation of the dollar; this depreciation, in turn, reverses the decline in net exports and thus reinforces the fiscal stimulus, increasing the size of the fiscal multiplier. With the introduction of capital mobility, however, we need to consider the impact of the fiscal stimulus on the capital account of the balance of payments.

Recall the analysis from Chapter 32 of a fiscal expansion in a closed economy. In a closed economy, a fiscal stimulus causes domestic interest rates to rise. This causes interest-sensitive private expenditures to fall, partially offsetting the initial expansionary effect of the fiscal stimulus. As we saw in Chapter 32, this *crowding-out effect* plays an important role in the analysis of fiscal policy in a closed economy.

In an open economy, the crowding-out effect involves an additional channel because of induced effects of international capital flows on net exports. Higher domestic interest rates will induce a capital inflow; if, as is likely, this capital inflow is larger than the balance-of-trade deficit induced by the expansion of national income, it will cause the domestic currency to appreciate.[5] This will depress demand by discouraging exports and by encouraging the substitution of imports for domestically produced goods. The initial expansionary effect of the fiscal stimulus will be offset to a considerable extent by the effects of currency appreciation; crowding out due to fiscal policy will be achieved in part by decreased net exports.

Under flexible exchange rates and capital mobility, the crowding out of net exports will reduce the effectiveness of fiscal policy.

THE TWIN DEFICITS

We have just argued that in an open economy with flexible exchange rates and international capital mobility, a fiscal expansion in Canada causes an increase in Canadian interest rates, an increase in demand for Canadian dollars as foreigners are induced to purchase high-yield Canadian assets, and thus an

---

[5]It is theoretically possible that the increase in the current account deficit will exceed the increase in the capital inflow so that the overall balance of payments moves into deficit. However, the rapid integration of world capital markets in recent years has made capital flows very sensitive to interest rates, so the case treated in the text is the more likely one.

appreciation of the Canadian dollar. As the fiscal expansion leads to an increase in Canadian national income, there is an increase in imports; as the Canadian dollar appreciates, imports rise further and exports decline. Thus the fiscal expansion leads to a capital inflow and to a reduction in net exports. The capital inflow shows up in the balance of payments as a capital account surplus; the decline in net exports shows up as the accompanying current account deficit.

We have thus established a link between the government's budget deficit and the current account deficit—what is often referred to as the *twin deficits*. This link can be seen by recalling some simple national-income accounting. You may recall that in Chapter 23 we made an important distinction between *actual* and *desired* expenditure; it is *actual* values on which national-income accounting is based. From the expenditure approach to measuring national income, recall that GDP is equal to the sum of *actual* consumption, investment, government purchases, and net exports. We have

$$GDP = C_a + I_a + G_a + (X_a - IM_a) \quad [3]$$

where the subscript "a" denotes that these are actual as opposed to desired values.

Now recall that *Gross National Product (GNP)* is equal to GDP plus net income generated from investments abroad. We define net investment income in the following way. Let R_F denote the receipts by Canadians from foreigners for investment income generated abroad; similarly, let P_F denote payments to foreigners for investment income generated in Canada. Then Canada's *net* investment income from abroad is $R_F - P_F$. This gives the relationship between GNP and GDP as

$$GNP = GDP + (R_F - P_F) \quad [4]$$

This tells us that when *net* receipts from abroad are zero ($R_F = P_F$) then GDP equals GNP. However, when net receipts are negative (as they have been in Canada for many years), GNP is less than GDP. The interpretation is that of all the goods and services that are *produced within* Canada in a given year (GDP), some of them are used to pay foreigners (interest on bonds or profits generated from the physical capital they own). As a result, the value of output available for consumption by domestic residents (GNP) is less than the value of output produced by domestic residents (GDP). Note that $(R_F - P_F)$ appears in the current account under the heading "net investment income" (see Table 37-1 in Chapter 37).[6]

Now, substituting Equation 3 into Equation 4 yields the following expression for GNP.

$$GNP = C_a + I_a + G_a + (X_a - IM_a) + (R_F - P_F) \quad [5]$$

Equation 5 shows the *composition* of GNP. We now think about the *disposition* of GNP—that is, how people dispose of (or spend) GNP. For this, note that GNP must be equal to consumption plus saving plus taxes. After all, since GNP is a measure of income accruing to domestic residents, there are only three things that can be done with income—it is either spent, saved, or paid to the government in taxes. In equation form, this disposition of GNP is represented as

$$GNP = C_a + S_a + T_a \quad [6]$$

It is now a simple matter to combine Equations 5 and 6. Also, since we know that we are talking here about *actual* rather than desired values, we simplify by omitting the "a" subscripts. This yields

$$C + S + T = \\ C + I + G + (X - IM) + (R_F - P_F) \quad [7]$$

which can be simplified to be

$$(S - I) + (T - G) = (X - IM) + (R_F - P_F) \quad [8]$$

The right-hand side of Equation 8 is the trade surplus $(X - IM)$ plus net investment income from abroad $(R_F - P_F)$. Thus the right-hand side is simply the current account balance. If the right-hand side is positive, then there is a current account surplus; if negative, then there is a current account deficit.

---

[6]From Table 37-1 in Chapter 37, the value of $(R_F - P_F)$ in Canada for 1994 was $-\$28.9$ billion, meaning that Canadians paid $28.9 billion more in investment income to foreigners than they received from foreigners. Some of this reflects the debt-service payments on the approximately $150 billion worth of Canadian government debt held by foreigners; much also reflects the profits that are remitted to foreigners that own firms located in Canada.

The left-hand side of Equation 8 has two terms. The first is the excess of private saving over private investment $(S - I)$. The second is the excess of government taxes (net of transfers) over purchases $(T - G)$—the government budget surplus. Since the budget surplus is the amount being saved by the government (public saving), then the left-hand side of Equation 8 is simply the excess of *national* saving over investment.

Equation 8 tells us that if the country saves more than it invests, then there must be a current account surplus. Why is this true? In a closed economy, domestic investment must be financed by domestic saving—it would be *impossible* for saving to exceed investment in a closed economy (in a closed economy, the right-hand side of Equation 8 is clearly zero). But in an open economy, if the country saves more than it invests, the extra saving must "go somewhere"—it must be saved abroad. But saving abroad means that domestic residents are purchasing foreign assets, either bonds or physical capital. This is a capital outflow—a capital account deficit (which is matched by a current account surplus).

A country that has national saving in excess of domestic investment must have a capital account deficit and a current account surplus.

Conversely, if the country saves less than it invests, then there must be a current account deficit. If the country saves less than it invests, then the extra investment must be financed somehow—it must be financed with foreign capital. This means that domestic residents are selling assets to foreigners. This is a capital inflow—a capital account surplus (which is matched by a current account deficit).

A country that has national saving less than domestic investment must have a capital account surplus and a current account deficit.

We started this section by mentioning the twin deficits—the connection between the government's budget deficit and the current account deficit. Equation 8 shows us this connection. What is clear from Equation 8 is that *for a given value of $(S - I)$, a one dollar increase in the government's budget deficit must be matched by a one dollar increase in the current account deficit.* In the previous section you learned the *mechanism* for how an increase in the government deficit leads to the current account deficit. That mechanism involved changes in interest rates and changes in the exchange rate. In describing that mechanism, we did so within the context of the model of national income determination that we have developed throughout this book.

What you have seen here, however, is not based on any model of the determination of national income. Equations 3 through 8 come only from national-income accounting *definitions*. What these equations say is that this precise relationship between government deficits and current account deficits *must exist*, even if the changes in interest rates and exchange rates we discussed above are small or slow in occurring.

An increase in the government budget deficit, for a given value of $(S - I)$, must be matched by an equal increase in the current account deficit. A decrease in the government budget deficit, for a given value of $(S - I)$, must be matched by an equal decrease in the current account deficit.

INSULATION PROPERTIES REVISITED

We have seen that international capital mobility enhances the effectiveness of monetary policy under flexible exchange rates but mitigates the effectiveness of fiscal policy. Consider the implications for the effects of an export boom; recall that in the absence of capital mobility, flexible exchange rates insulate the economy from the effects of such a boom because the export multiplier is zero.

The initial effect of an increase in exports on national income and the balance of trade is as shown in Figure 38-2: National income rises, and there is a trade surplus. The rise in national income causes an increase in the demand for money, an increase in the domestic interest rate, and hence a capital inflow. This reinforces the pressures caused by the trade surplus for the currency to appreciate and therefore to offset the expansionary impact of the export boom.

Capital mobility does not upset the ability of flexible exchange rates to insulate an open economy from the effects of shifts in the demand for its exports.

Suppose, however, that the boom in the foreign country also gave rise to an increase in foreign interest rates. This would lead to a capital outflow from Canada as funds moved in response to the higher foreign interest rates and hence to a *depreciation* of the Canadian dollar. The depreciation would in turn lead to an increase in net exports and an increase in national income.

International capital mobility, by linking domestic and foreign interest rates, provides a channel by which business cycles tend to be correlated across countries.

This accords with the experience of the international economy over the past two decades when the widespread adoption of flexible exchange rates has witnessed a continued correlation of booms and recessions in the major industrial economies.

RECENT CANADIAN POLICY

Canadian macroeconomic policy has several times encountered some of the issues we have discussed in this chapter. We take up the story at the beginning of the 1980s.

IMPORTED MONETARY RESTRAINT: 1980–1983

In the early 1980s, Canadian monetary policy and exchange-rate management were made difficult by the high average level, and volatile behaviour, of U.S. interest rates. A rise in the U.S. interest rate tends to cause outflows of short-term capital from Canada and a resulting depreciation of the Canadian dollar. This can be avoided only if Canadian interest rates are allowed to rise to match the increases in U.S. interest rates. Intermediate positions allow for *some* rise in Canadian interest rates and *some* depreciation of the Canadian dollar.

In 1980, U.S. interest rates rose dramatically. Canadian rates also rose, but by less than those in the United States. The resulting interest differential caused funds to move from Canada to the United States and, as a result, the Canadian dollar began to depreciate. When another round of U.S. interest rate increases occurred in 1981, Canadian interest rates were allowed to rise along with U.S. rates, and the exchange rate remained relatively stable.

Although nominal interest rates in the United States fell in 1983, real interest rates remained high. The Bank of Canada walked a middle ground between maintaining high Canadian real interest rates and allowing a depreciation of the Canadian dollar.

Though the Canadian dollar depreciated (a rise in the exchange rate) slowly but steadily from 1982 on, it was widely agreed that monetary policy in Canada was tighter than it would have been in the absence of the very tight U.S. monetary policy. By not allowing the full adjustment to be taken on the exchange rate, the Bank of Canada imported some of the tight U.S. monetary policy in terms of high Canadian interest rates. This caused a substantial fall in inflation in the 1982–1984 period, but also made the 1982 recession more severe than it would otherwise have been.

RECOVERY AND STABLE INFLATION: 1984–1987

During the period 1984–1987, the Bank of Canada was able to reap the benefits of the monetary tightness that it had pursued in the first years of the decade. The economy experienced a sustained recovery, inflation remained stable in the 4 percent range, and interest rates fell dramatically. As a result, the central focus of monetary policy was the reentry problem discussed in Chapter 29—the Bank managed to accommodate the recovery-induced growth in the demand for money while not rekindling inflation. The exchange rate did not play a central role in the overall design or execution of monetary policy in this period, although exchange rate fluctuations were large.

DISINFLATION AND APPRECIATION: 1987–1991

In 1988, the Governor of the Bank of Canada, John Crow, announced the policy of gradually reducing the rate of inflation from its plateau of around 4 percent to zero. Unfortunately, at the same time, the economy was developing an inflationary gap as a result of the longest sustained expansion since World War II. By mid 1989, the inflation rate had crept up to over 6 percent.

Containing the rising inflation and reducing the rate toward zero required a tight monetary policy. Interest rates were driven to unprecedented margins over U.S. rates. At several times during the period, Canadian rates were 4 percentage points above corresponding U.S. rates, and once the margin exceeded 5 percentage points! Attracted by the high Canadian interest rates, short-term investment funds flooded into Canada, leading to a substantial appreciation of the Canadian dollar. Exporters complained of their difficulties in selling profitably in the United States and of the high cost of funds at home. The Bank argued that, although unfortunate, these pressures were the inevitable consequences of the need to fight inflation. Critics argued that the cure was worse than the disease and called for the Bank to accept the higher inflation rate as the cost of letting the dollar and interest rates fall significantly.

Subsequent research showed that Canadian exports to the United States continued to increase despite the substantial appreciation of the Canadian dollar. One possible explanation is that the stimulus of falling American tariffs brought about by the Canada-U.S. Free Trade Agreement (beginning in 1989) was stronger than the depressing effects of the appreciating Canadian dollar. In contrast, there were few increases in exports to other countries where there were no tariff cuts. The high external value of the Canadian dollar also seemed to have had some effect in forcing Canadian firms to adopt productivity-increasing measures to stay competitive in foreign markets.

PRICE STABILITY: 1992–?

As we discussed in Chapter 29, the Bank of Canada and the federal department of finance jointly issued formal inflation targets beginning in late 1991. The initial target was for inflation to be in the 2–4 percent range by the end of 1992, with the 2-percentage-point range declining thereafter. By late 1992, it was clear that the battle against inflation had been won; indeed, for all of 1992, the actual inflation rate was *below* the lower bound of the target range. As inflation fell, interest rates were allowed to tumble. The Canadian dollar depreciated as some funds that had been attracted by the high Canadian interest rates now departed. The stimulus to exports of the depreciated Canadian dollar was welcomed, as were lower interest rates for domestic Canadian borrowers.

For the next four years, interest rates fell slowly and the Canadian dollar remained roughly stable. As the formal target for inflation fell to the 1–3 percent range by the end of 1995, actual inflation was hovering around 2 percent. At the time of writing in mid 1996, the inflation rate was slightly above 1 percent, interest rates are low by historical standards, and the exchange rate was relatively constant in the range of $1.30–$1.32 per U.S. dollar.

By the middle of 1996, the widespread view of the Bank's policies was that they were indeed successful in eliminating inflation, and that no permanent damage seemed to have been done to Canada's export industries. Debate no longer centred over whether the Bank could achieve its objectives but over whether the price was worth it in terms of a recession made longer and deeper by the policy of price stability.

SUMMARY

A. THE BALANCE OF TRADE AND NATIONAL INCOME

- Under fixed exchange rates and zero capital mobility, the responsiveness of imports to national income reduces the size of the autonomous spending multiplier and thus acts as an automatic stabilizer. In this case, national income and net exports move in opposite directions; increases in national income are accompanied by a rise in imports (and thus a fall in net exports).
- Under fixed exchange rates and zero capital mobility, changes in exports lead to a change in equilibrium national income; this is called the export multiplier. In this case, national income and net exports move in the same direction; increases in national income are accompanied by an increase in net exports.

- Under flexible exchange rates and zero capital mobility, the exchange rate adjusts until the balance of trade is zero. This means that net exports do not influence desired aggregate expenditure. As a result, the economy behaves as if there were no international trade. No automatic stabilizer role is played by imports, and the export multiplier is zero.
- The fact that the export multiplier is zero is the basis for the view that flexible exchange rates insulate the domestic economy from foreign disturbances.

B. INTERNATIONAL CAPITAL MOBILITY

- International capital mobility means that capital flows, and hence the capital account balance, must be included in the analysis of open-economy macroeconomics. Capital flows depend on interest rates, especially on interest rate differentials from one country to another. This means that the capital account is influenced by both fiscal and monetary policy because both influence domestic interest rates. Capital mobility also means that the current account balance can be different from zero; the current account deficit will equal net capital inflows.

- Under a flexible exchange rate, monetary policy is effective in influencing national income. When capital flows are highly interest-elastic, a monetary expansion will lower domestic interest rates and thus lead to a capital outflow. This will lead to a depreciation of the domestic currency, thus stimulating net exports and enhancing the expansionary effect of the initial monetary policy.

- Under a flexible exchange rate, fiscal policy is generally less effective in increasing national income than it would be in a closed economy. A fiscal expansion will push up interest rates (as the rise in national income leads to an increase in money demand). This will lead to a capital inflow and thus an appreciation of the domestic currency. This appreciation will reduce net exports, thus reducing the expansionary effect of the initial fiscal policy.

- Simple national income accounting shows the relationship between the government's budget deficit and the current account deficit.

$$(S - I) + (T - G) = (X - IM) + (R_F - P_F)$$

The left-hand side is the excess of national (private plus public) saving over domestic investment. The right-hand side is the current account balance. This equation says that for a given amount of $(S - I)$, a 1-dollar increase in the government budget deficit must be matched by a 1-dollar increase in the current account deficit.

C. RECENT CANADIAN POLICY

- Tight monetary policy during 1980–1981 had the predicted effects of high Canadian interest rates, a strong Canadian dollar, a severe recession, and a reduction in inflation. The same pattern occurred in the early 1990s, when the Bank of Canada drove inflation down to around 1 percent at the cost of higher interest rates, a stronger Canadian dollar, and a deeper recession than would have occurred if the 4 percent inflation had been tolerated. The anti-inflation policy succeeded, and debate centred on whether the benefits of *having* low inflation exceeded the costs of *achieving* low inflation.

KEY CONCEPTS

Net exports as an automatic stabilizer under fixed exchange rates
The export multiplier under fixed exchange rates

The insulation of the domestic economy under flexible exchange rates
The role of capital mobility

Fiscal and monetary policy and capital flows and flexible exchange rates
The twin deficits

DISCUSSION QUESTIONS

1. Explain how a country can influence the external value of its currency by

   a. direct intervention in the foreign exchange market,
   b. fiscal policy, and
   c. monetary policy.

2. Despite a formal commitment to flexible exchange rates, the Bank of Canada often acts to stabilize the exchange rate and thus to "mimic" policies of other major countries, especially the United States. Why might the Bank of Canada oppose both a depreciation and an appreciation of the Canadian dollar? Can you cite any episodes in which the Bank of Canada has faced this dilemma in the past two or three years?

3. Suppose that the Canadian government budget deficit remains high so that national saving remains low but that the rising Canadian national debt causes a sharp fall in the desire on the part of foreigners to purchase Canadian government bonds. Outline the key macroeconomic effects of this shift. What policies might you recommend to deal with these consequences?

4. Beginning in the early 1990s, Canadian governments (both federal and provincial) started "attacking" their fiscal deficits. Explain what a reduction in Canadian government budget deficits is likely to do to Canada's current account balance and the external value of the dollar.

5. In a column in the *Wall Street Journal,* U.S. economist Herbert Stein argued that much of the concern about the U.S. current account deficit was misplaced because the accompanying capital inflow had resulted in a stock of productive capital in the United States that was $700 billion higher than it would otherwise have been. What is the basis for such a statement?

6. Consider the following two potential sources of appreciation of the Canadian dollar:

   a. contractionary monetary policy followed by the Bank of Canada and
   b. foreign inflation.

   Explain how each could lead to dollar appreciation. What are the differences for the economy? How would you distinguish between the two?

7. If the European countries were to adopt a common currency as dictated by the Maastricht Treaty, each country would essentially have a fixed exchange rate with its European partners. If France were to double its exports (other things equal) over a short period of time, what effect would this have on its partners? What if its exports were to fall by 50 percent? What implication does this suggest about European economic integration?

8. In the weeks immediately preceding the Quebec Referendum in October 1995, foreigners sold off large holdings of Canadian-dollar bonds and then sold off their holdings of Canadian dollars. This led to sudden depreciation of the Canadian dollar in foreign exchange markets. Explain what was happening in the current account and capital account, assuming that the Bank of Canada was not making any official foreign exchange transactions.

MATHEMATICAL NOTES

1. The rule of 72 is an approximation, derived from the mathematics of compound interest. Any variable X with an initial value of X_0 will have the value $X_t = X_0 e^{rt}$ after t years at a continuous growth rate of r percent per year. Doubling the value of X requires $X_t/X_0 = 2$, and this requires $r \cdot t = 0.69$. A "rule of 69" would thus be correct for continuous growth. The rule of 72 was developed in the context of compound interest, and if interest is compounded only once a year, the product of r times t for X to double is approximately 0.72.

2. Because one cannot divide by zero, the ratio $\Delta Y/\Delta X$ cannot be evaluated when $\Delta X = 0$. However, as ΔX *approaches* zero, the ratio $\Delta Y/\Delta X$ increases without limit:

$$\lim_{\Delta X \to 0} \frac{\Delta Y}{\Delta X} = \infty$$

3. Many variables affect the quantity demanded. Using functional notation, the argument of the next several pages of the text can be anticipated. Let Q^D represent the quantity of a commodity demanded and

$$T, \overline{Y}, N, \hat{Y}, p, p_j$$

represent, respectively, tastes, average household income, population, income distribution, the commodity's own price, and the price of the jth other commodity.

The demand function is

$$Q^D = D(T, \overline{Y}, N, \hat{Y}, p, p_j), \qquad j = 1, 2, \ldots, n$$

The demand schedule or curve is given by

$$Q^D = d(p) \,\Big|\, T, \overline{Y}, N, \hat{Y}, p_j$$

where the notation means that the variables to the right of the vertical line are held constant.

This function is correctly described as the demand function with respect to price, all other variables being held constant. This function, often written concisely as $q = d(p)$, shifts in response to changes in other variables. Consider average income: if, as is usually hypothesized, $\partial Q^D/\partial \overline{Y} > 0$, then increases in average income shift $q = d(p)$ rightward and decreases in average income shift $q = d(p)$ leftward. Changes in other variables likewise shift this function in the direction implied by the relationship of that variable to the quantity demanded.

4. Quantity demanded is a simple and straightforward but frequently misunderstood concept in everyday use, but it has a clear mathematical meaning. It refers to the dependent variable in the demand function from note 3:

$$Q^D = D(T, \overline{Y}, N, \hat{Y}, p, p_j)$$

It takes on a specific value whenever a specific value is assigned to each of the independent variables. The value of Q^D changes whenever the value of any independent variable is changed. Q^D could change, for example, as a result of a *ceteris paribus* change in any one price, in average income, in the distribution of income, in tastes, or in population. It could also change as a result of the net effect of changes in all of the independent variables occurring at once. Thus a change in the price of a commodity is a sufficient reason for a change in Q^D but not a necessary reason.

Some textbooks reserve the term *change in quantity demanded* for a movement along a demand curve, that is, a change in Q^D as a result only of a change in p. They then use other words for a change in Q^D caused by a change in the other variables in the demand function. This usage is potentially confusing because it gives the single variable Q^D more than one name.

Our usage, which corresponds to that in more advanced treatments, avoids this confusion. We call Q^D *quantity demanded* and refer to any change in Q^D as a *change in quantity demanded*. In this usage it is correct to say that a movement along a demand curve is a change in quantity demanded, but it is incorrect to say that a change in quantity demanded can occur *only because of* a movement along a demand curve (because Q^D can change for other reasons, for example, a *ceteris paribus* change in average household income).

5. Similar to the way we treated quantity demanded in note 3, let Q^S represent the quantity of a commodity supplied and

$$C, X, p, w_i$$

represent, respectively, producers' goals, technology, the product's price, and the price of the *i*th input.

The supply function is

$$Q^S = S(C, X, p, w_i), \qquad i = 1, 2, \ldots, m$$

The supply schedule or curve is given by

$$Q^S = s(p) \, \Big|_{C, X, w_i}$$

This is the supply function with respect to price, all other variables being held constant. This function, often written concisely as $q = s(p)$, shifts in response to changes in other variables.

6. Equilibrium occurs where $Q^D = Q^S$. For *specified values of all other variables,* this requires that

$$d(p) = s(p) \qquad [6.1]$$

Equation 6.1 defines an equilibrium value of p; hence, although p is an *independent* or *exogenous* variable in each of the supply and demand functions, it is an *endogenous* variable in the economic model that imposes the equilibrium condition expressed in Equation 6.1. Price is endoge-

nous because it is assumed to adjust to bring about equality between quantity demanded and quantity supplied. Equilibrium quantity, also an endogenous variable, is determined by substituting the equilibrium price into either $d(p)$ or $s(p)$.

Graphically, Equation 6.1 is satisfied only at the point where the demand and supply curves intersect. Thus supply and demand curves are said to determine the equilibrium values of the endogenous variables, price and quantity. A shift in any of the independent variables held constant in the d and s functions will shift the demand or supply curves and lead to different equilibrium values for price and quantity.

7. The definition in the text uses finite changes and is called *arc elasticity.* The parallel definition using derivatives is

$$\eta = \frac{dq}{dp} \cdot \frac{p}{q}$$

and is called *point elasticity.* Further discussion appears in the Appendix to Chapter 5.

8. The propositions in the text are proved as follows. Letting TR stand for total revenue, we can write

$$TR = p \cdot q$$

It follows that the change in total revenue is

$$dTR = q \cdot dp + p \cdot dq \qquad [8.1]$$

(Recall that total revenue of the firm and total expenditure by consumers are identical, so the following applies equally to total expenditure.) Multiplying and dividing both terms on the right-hand side of Equation 8.1 by $p \cdot q$ yields

$$dTR = \left[\frac{dp}{p} + \frac{dq}{q} \right] \cdot (p \cdot q)$$

Because dp and dq are opposite in sign as we move along the demand curve, dTR will have the same sign as the term in brackets on the right-hand side that dominates—that is, on which percentage change is largest.

A second way of arranging Equation 8.1 is to divide both sides by dp to get

$$\frac{dTR}{dp} = q + p \cdot \frac{dq}{dp} \qquad [8.2]$$

From the definition of point elasticity in note 7, however,

$$q \cdot \eta = p \cdot \frac{dq}{dp} \qquad [8.3]$$

which we can substitute into Equation 8.1 to obtain

$$\frac{dTR}{dp} = q + q \cdot \eta = q \cdot (1 + \eta) \qquad [8.4]$$

Because η is a negative number, the sign of the right-hand side of Equation 8.4 is negative if the absolute value of η exceeds unity (elastic demand) and positive if it is less than unity (inelastic demand).

Total revenue is maximized when dTR/dp is equal to zero. As can be seen from Equation 8.4, this occurs when elasticity is equal to -1.

9. The axis reversal arose in the following way. Alfred Marshall (1842–1924) theorized in terms of "demand price" and "supply price," these being the prices that would lead to a given quantity being demanded or supplied. Thus

$$p^d = d(q) \qquad [9.1]$$
$$p^s = s(q) \qquad [9.2]$$

and the condition of equilibrium is

$$d(q) = s(q)$$

When graphing the behavioural relationships expressed in Equations 9.1 and 9.2, Marshall naturally put the independent variable, q, on the horizontal axis.

Leon Walras (1834–1910), whose formulation of the working of a competitive market has become the accepted one, focused on quantity demanded and quantity supplied *at a given price*. Thus

$$q^d = d(p)$$
$$q^s = s(p)$$

and the condition of equilibrium is

$$d(p) = s(p)$$

Walras did not use graphical representation. Had he done so, he would surely have placed p (his independent variable) on the horizontal axis.

Marshall, among his other influences on later generations of economists, was the great popularizer of graphical analysis in economics. Today, we use his graphs, even for Walras's analysis. The axis reversal is thus one of those historical accidents that seem odd to people who did not live through the "perfectly natural" sequence of steps that produced it.

10. The distinction made between an incremental change and a marginal change is the distinction for the function $Y = Y(X)$ between $\Delta Y/\Delta X$ and the derivative dY/dX. The latter is the limit of the former as ΔX approaches zero. Precisely this sort of difference underlies the distinction between arc and point elasticity, and we shall meet it repeatedly—in this chapter in reference to marginal and incremental *utility* and in later chapters with respect to such concepts as marginal and incremental *product, cost,* and *revenue.* Where Y is a function of more than one variable—for example, $Y = f(X,Z)$—the marginal relationship between Y and X is the partial derivative $\partial Y/\partial X$ rather than the total derivative, dY/dX.

11. The hypothesis of diminishing marginal utility requires that we can measure utility of consumption by a function

$$U = U(X_1, X_2, \ldots, X_n)$$

where $X_1, \ldots, X_n$ are quantities of the n goods consumed by a household. It really embodies two utility hypotheses: first,

$$\partial U/\partial X_i > 0$$

which says that the consumer can get more utility by increasing consumption of the commodity; second,

$$\partial^2 U/\partial X_i^2 < 0$$

which says that the marginal utility of additional consumption of some good declines as the amount of that good consumed increases.

12. Because the slope of the indifference curve is negative, it is the absolute value of the slope that declines as one moves downward to the right along the curve. The algebraic value, of course, increases. The phrase *diminishing marginal rate of substitution* thus refers to the absolute, not the algebraic, value of the slope.

13. The relationship between the slope of the budget line and relative prices can be seen as follows. In the two-commodity example, a change in expenditure (ΔE) is given by the equation

$$\Delta E = p_C \cdot \Delta C + p_F \cdot \Delta F \qquad [13.1]$$

Expenditure is constant for all combinations of F and C that lie on the same budget line. Thus along such a line we have $\Delta E = 0$. This implies

$$p_C \cdot \Delta C + p_F \cdot \Delta F = 0 \qquad [13.2]$$

and thus

$$-\Delta C/\Delta F = p_F/p_C \qquad [13.3]$$

The ratio $-\Delta C/\Delta F$ is the slope of the budget line. It is negative because, with a fixed budget, one must consume less C in order to consume more F. In other words, Equation 13.3 says that the negative of the slope of the budget line is the ratio of the absolute prices (i.e., the relative price). Although prices do not show directly in Figure 7A-3, they are implicit in the budget line: Its slope depends solely on the relative price, while its position, given a fixed money income, depends on the absolute prices of the two goods.

14. *Marginal product,* as defined in the text, is really *incremental* product. More advanced treatments distinguish between this notion and marginal product as the limit of the ratio as ΔL approaches zero. Marginal product thus measures the rate at which total product is changing as one factor is varied and is the partial derivative of the total product with respect to the variable factor. In symbols,

$$MP = \frac{\partial TP}{\partial L}$$

15. We have referred specifically both to diminishing *marginal* product and to diminishing *average* product. In most cases, eventually diminishing marginal product implies eventually diminishing average product. This is, however, not necessary, as the accompanying figure shows.

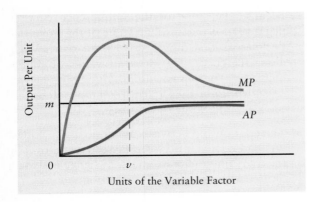

In this case, marginal product diminishes after v units of the variable factor are employed. Because marginal product falls toward, but never quite reaches, a value of m, average product rises continually toward, but never quite reaches, the same value.

16. Let q be the quantity of output and L the quantity of the variable factor. In the short run,

$$TP = q = f(L) \qquad [16.1]$$

We now define

$$AP = \frac{q}{L} = \frac{f(L)}{L} \qquad [16.2]$$

$$MP = \frac{dq}{dL} \qquad [16.3]$$

We are concerned with the relationship between these two. Where average product is rising, at a maximum, or falling is determined by its derivative with respect to L:

$$\frac{d(q/L)}{dL} = \frac{L \cdot (dq/dL) - q}{L^2} \qquad [16.4]$$

This may be rewritten

$$\frac{1}{L} \cdot \left[\frac{dq}{dL} - \frac{q}{L} \right] = \frac{1}{L} \cdot (MP - AP) \qquad [16.5]$$

Clearly, when MP is greater than AP, the expression in Equation 16.5 is positive and thus AP is rising. When MP is less than AP, AP is falling. When they are equal, AP is neither rising nor falling.

17. The text defines *incremental cost.* Strictly, marginal cost is the rate of change of total cost with respect to output, q. Thus

$$MC = \frac{dTC}{dq}$$

From the definitions, $TC = TFC + TVC$. Fixed costs are not a function of output. Thus we may write $TC = Z + f(q)$, where $f(q)$ is total variable costs and Z is a constant. From this we see that $MC = df(q)/dq$. MC is thus independent of the size of the fixed costs.

18. This point is easily seen if a little algebra is used:

$$AVC = \frac{TVC}{q}$$

but note that $TVC = L \cdot w$ and $q = AP \cdot L$, where L is the quantity of the variable factor used and w is its cost per unit. Therefore,

$$AVC = \frac{L \cdot w}{AP \cdot L} = \frac{w}{AP}$$

Because w is a constant, it follows that AVC and AP vary inversely with each other, and when AP is at its maximum value, AVC must be at its minimum value.

19. A little elementary calculus will prove the point:

$$MC = \frac{dTC}{dq} = \frac{dTVC}{dq} = \frac{d(L \cdot w)}{dq}$$

If w does not vary with output,

$$MC = \frac{dL}{dq} \cdot w$$

However, referring to note 16 (Equation 16.3), we see that

$$\frac{dL}{dq} = \frac{1}{MP}$$

Thus

$$MC = \frac{w}{MP}$$

Because w is fixed, MC varies negatively with MP. When MP is at a maximum, MC is at a minimum.

20. As we saw in note 17, $MC = dTVC/dq$. If we take the integral of MC from zero to q_0, we get

$$\int_0^{q_0} MC \, dq = TVC(q_0) + Z$$

The first term is the area under the marginal cost curve; the constant of integration, Z, is fixed cost.

21. Strictly speaking, the marginal rate of substitution refers to the slope of the tangent to the isoquant at a particular point, whereas the calculations in Table 9A-1 refer to the average rate of substitution between two distinct points on the isoquant. Assume a production function

$$Q = Q(K,L) \qquad [21.1]$$

Isoquants are given by the function

$$K = I(L,\overline{Q}) \qquad [21.2]$$

derived from Equation 21.1 by expressing K as an explicit function of L and Q. A single

isoquant relates to a particular level of output, Q. Define Q_K and Q_L as an alternative, more compact notation for $\partial Q/\partial K$ and $\partial Q/\partial L$, the marginal products of capital and labour. Also, let Q_{KK} and Q_{LL} stand for $\partial^2 Q/\partial K^2$ and $\partial^2 Q/\partial L^2$, respectively. To obtain the slope of the isoquant, totally differentiate Equation 21.1 to obtain

$$dQ = Q_K \cdot dK + Q_L \cdot dL$$

Then, because we are moving along a single isoquant, set $dQ = 0$ to obtain

$$\frac{dK}{dL} = -\frac{Q_L}{Q_K} = MRS$$

Diminishing marginal productivity implies $Q_{LL} < 0$ and $Q_{KK} < 0$, and hence, as we move down the isoquant of Figure 9A-1, Q_K is rising and Q_L is falling, so the absolute value of MRS is diminishing. This is called the *hypothesis of a diminishing marginal rate of substitution*.

22. Formally, the problem is to maximize

$$Q = Q(K,L)$$

subject to the constraint

$$p_K \cdot K + p_L \cdot L = C$$

To do this, form the Lagrangean,

$$\mathscr{L} = Q(K, L) - \lambda(p_K \cdot K + p_L \cdot L - C)$$

The first-order conditions for finding the saddle point on this function are

$$Q_K = \lambda \cdot p_K \qquad [22.1]$$
$$Q_L = \lambda \cdot p_L \qquad [22.2]$$
$$p_K \cdot K + p_L \cdot L = C \qquad [22.3]$$

Dividing Equation 22.1 by Equation 22.2 yields

$$\frac{Q_K}{Q_L} = \frac{p_K}{p_L}$$

That is, the ratio of the marginal products, which is -1 times the MRS, is equal to the ratio of the prices, which is -1 times the slope of the isocost line.

23. Marginal revenue is mathematically the derivative of total revenue with respect to output, dTR/dq. Incremental revenue is $\Delta TR/\Delta q$.

However, the term *marginal revenue* is used loosely to refer to both concepts.

24. For notes 24 through 26, it is helpful first to define some terms. Let

$$\pi_n = TR_n - TC_n$$

where π_n is the profit when n units are sold.

If the firm is maximizing its profits by producing n units, it is necessary that the profits at output q_n be at least as large as the profits at output zero. If the firm is maximizing its profits at output n, then

$$\pi_n \geq \pi_0 \qquad [24.1]$$

The condition says that profits from producing must be greater than profits from not producing. Condition 24.1 can be rewritten as

$$TR_n - TVC_n - TFC_n$$
$$\geq TR_0 - TVC_0 - TFC_0 \qquad [24.2]$$

However, note that by definition

$$TR_0 = 0 \qquad [24.3]$$

$$TVC_0 = 0 \qquad [24.4]$$

$$TFC_n = TFC_0 = Z \qquad [24.5]$$

where Z is a constant. By substituting Equations 24.3, 24.4, and 24.5 into Condition 24.2, we get

$$TR_n - TVC_n \geq 0$$

from which we obtain

$$TR_n \geq TVC_n$$

This proves Rule 1.

On a per-unit basis, it becomes

$$\frac{TR_n}{q_n} \geq \frac{TVC_n}{q_n} \qquad [24.6]$$

where q_n is the number of units produced.

Because $TR_n = q_n \cdot p_n$, where p_n is the price when n units are sold, Equation 24.6 may be rewritten as

$$p_n \geq AVC_n$$

25. Using elementary calculus, we may prove Rule 2.

$$\pi_n = TR_n - TC_n$$

each of which is a function of output q. To maximize π, it is necessary that

$$\frac{d\pi}{dq} = 0 \qquad [25.1]$$

and that

$$\frac{d^2\pi}{dq^2} < 0 \qquad [25.2]$$

From the definitions,

$$\frac{d\pi}{dq} = \frac{dTR}{dq} - \frac{dTC}{dq} = MR - MC \quad [25.3]$$

From Equations 25.1 and 25.3, a necessary condition for attaining maximum π is $MR - MC = 0$, or $MR = MC$, as is required by Rule 2.

26. To prove that for a negatively sloped demand curve, marginal revenue is less than price, let $p = p(q)$. Then

$$TR = p \cdot q = p(q) \cdot q$$

$$MR = \frac{dTR}{dq} = q \cdot \frac{dp}{dq} + p$$

For a negatively sloped demand curve, dp/dq is negative, and thus MR is less than price for positive values of q.

27. The equation for a downward-sloping straight-line demand curve with price on the vertical axis is

$$p = a - b \cdot q$$

where $-b$ is the slope of the demand curve. Total revenue is price times quantity:

$$TR = p \cdot q = a \cdot q - b \cdot q^2$$

Marginal revenue is

$$MR = \frac{dTR}{dq} = a - 2 \cdot b \cdot q$$

Thus the MR curve and the demand curve are both straight lines, and the (absolute value of the) slope of the MR curve ($2b$) is twice that of the demand curve (b).

28. A monopolist, selling in two or more markets, will set its marginal cost equal to marginal revenue in each market. Thus the condition

$$MC = MR_1 = MR_2$$

is a profit-maximizing condition for a monopolist that is selling in two markets. In general, equal marginal revenues will mean unequal prices because the ratio of price to marginal revenue is a function of elasticity of demand: The higher the elasticity, the lower the ratio. Thus equal marginal revenues imply a higher price in the market with the less elastic demand.

29. The marginal revenue produced by the factor involves two elements: first, the additional output that an extra unit of the factor makes possible and, second, the change in price of the product that the extra output causes. Let Q be output, R revenue, and L the number of units of labour hired. The contribution to revenue of additional labour is $\partial R/\partial L$. This, in turn, depends on the contribution of the extra labour to output $\partial Q/\partial L$ (the marginal product of the factor) and $\partial R/\partial Q$ (the firm's marginal revenue from the extra output). Thus

$$\frac{\partial R}{\partial L} = \frac{\partial Q}{\partial L} \cdot \frac{\partial R}{\partial Q}$$

We define the left-hand side as marginal revenue product, *MRP*. Thus

$$MRP = MP \cdot MR$$

30. The proposition that the marginal labour cost is above the average labour cost when the average is rising is essentially the same proposition proved in note 16. Nevertheless, let us do it again, using elementary calculus.

    The quantity of labour depends on the wage rate: $L = f(w)$. Total labour cost is $w \cdot L$. Marginal cost of labour is

$$\frac{d(w \cdot L)}{dL} = w + L \cdot \frac{dw}{dL}$$

Rewrite this as

$$MC = AC + L \cdot \frac{dw}{dL}$$

As long as the supply curve slopes upward, $dw/dL > 0$; therefore, $MC > AC$.

31. In general, for any growth rate per unit of time, g, and starting value, P_0, the price level at time t, P_t, will be $P_0(1 + g)^t$. This is the formula for *compound* growth at rate g per unit of time. For small values of g, $(1 + g)^t$ will be very close to $(1 + tg)$. But as g gets larger, so does the difference. For example, if prices are growing at 2 percent per month, the annual growth will be $(1.02)^{12} = 1.268$, yielding a growth rate of 26.8 percent per year. This is considerably more than 24 percent, which is just the monthly rate times 12. Generally, annual rates of growth are calculated by compounding rates of growth that are measured over shorter or longer periods than one year.

32. In the text, we define *MPC* as an incremental ratio. For mathematical treatment, it is sometimes convenient to define all marginal concepts as derivatives: $MPC = dC/dY_D$, $MPS = dS/dY_D$, and so on.

33. The basic relationship is

$$Y_D = C + S$$

Dividing through by Y_D yields

$$\frac{Y_D}{Y_D} = \frac{C}{Y_D} + \frac{S}{Y_D}$$

and thus

$$1 = APC + APS$$

Next, take the first difference of the basic relationship to get

$$\Delta Y_D = \Delta C + \Delta S$$

Dividing through by ΔY_D gives

$$\frac{\Delta Y_D}{\Delta Y_D} = \frac{\Delta C}{\Delta Y_D} + \frac{\Delta S}{\Delta Y_D}$$

and thus

$$1 = MPC + MPS$$

34. The total expenditure over all rounds is the sum of an infinite series. If we let A stand for autonomous expenditure and z for the marginal propensity to spend, the change in autonomous expenditure is ΔA in the first round, $z \cdot \Delta A$ in the second, $z^2 \cdot \Delta A$) in the third, and so on. This can be written as

$$\Delta A \cdot (1 + z + z^2 + \ldots + z^n)$$

If z is less than 1, the series in parentheses converges to $1/(1 - z)$ as n approaches infinity. The total change in expenditure is thus $\Delta A/(1 - z)$. In the example in the box, $z = 0.80$; therefore, the change in total expenditure is five times ΔA.

35. This involves using functions of functions. We have $C = C(Y_D)$ and $Y_D = f(Y)$. So, by substitution, $C = C[f(Y)]$. In the linear expressions that are used in the text, $C = a + bY_D$, where b is the marginal propensity to consume. $Y_D = hY$, so $C = a + bhY$, where bh is thus the marginal response of C to a change in Y.

36. This is easily proved. The banking system wants sufficient deposits (D) to establish the target ratio (v) of deposits to reserves (R). This gives $R/D = v$. Any change in D of size ΔD has to be accompanied by a change in R of ΔR of sufficient size to restore v. Thus $\Delta R/\Delta D = v$, so $\Delta D = \Delta R/v$, and $\Delta D/\Delta R = 1/v$. This can be shown also in terms of the deposits created by the sequence in Table 27-7. Let v be the reserve ratio and $e = 1 - v$ be the excess reserves per dollar of new deposits. If X dollars are initially deposited in the system, the successive rounds of new deposits will be $X, eX, e^2X, e^3X, \ldots$. The series

$$X + eX + e^2X + e^3X + \ldots$$
$$= X \cdot [1 + e + e^2 + e^3 + \ldots]$$

has a limit

$$X \cdot \frac{1}{1 - e} = X \cdot \frac{1}{1 - (1 - v)} = \frac{X}{v}$$

This is the total new deposits created by an injection of X of new reserves into the banking system. For example, when $v = 0.20$, an injection of $100 into the system will lead to an overall increase in deposits of $500.

37. Suppose that the public wishes to hold a fraction, c, of deposits in cash, C. Now suppose that X dollars are injected into the system. Ultimately, this money will be held either as reserves by the banking system or as cash by the public. Thus we have

$$\Delta C + \Delta R = X$$

From the banking system's reserve behaviour, we have $\Delta R = v \cdot \Delta D$, and from the public's cash behaviour, we have $\Delta C = c \cdot \Delta D$. Substituting into the above equation, we get the result that

$$\Delta D = \frac{X}{v + c}$$

From this we can also relate the change in reserves and the change in cash holdings to the initial injection:

$$\Delta R = \frac{v}{v + c} \cdot X$$

$$\Delta C = \frac{c}{v + c} \cdot X$$

For example, when $v = 0.20$ and $c = 0.05$, an injection of $100 will lead to an increase in reserves of $80, an increase in cash in the hands of the public of $20, and an increase in deposits of $400.

38. The argument is simply as follows, where prime marks stand for first derivatives:

$$M^D = F_1(T), \qquad F_1' > 0$$
$$T = F_2(Y), \qquad F_2' > 0$$

Therefore,

$$M^D = F_1(F_2(Y)), \text{ or}$$
$$M^D = H(Y), \qquad H' > 0$$

where H is the function of the function combining F_1 and F_2.

39. Let $L(Y, r)$ give the real demand for money measured in purchasing power units. Let M be the supply of money measured in nominal units and P an index of the price level, so that M/P is the real supply of money. Now the equilibrium condition requiring equality between the demand for money and the supply of money can be expressed in real terms as

$$L(Y, r) = \frac{M}{P} \qquad [39.1]$$

or in nominal terms by multiplying through by P,

$$P \cdot L(Y, r) = M \qquad [39.2]$$

In Equation 39.1, a rise in P disturbs equilibrium by lowering M/P, and in Equation 39.2, it disturbs equilibrium by raising $P \cdot L(Y, r)$.

40. The relations involved here are discussed in note 1.

41. The time taken to break even is a function of the *difference* in growth rates, not their *levels*. Thus had 4 percent and 5 percent or 5 percent and 6 percent been used in the example, it still would have taken the same number of years. To see this quickly, recognize that we are interested in the ratio of two growth paths:

$$\frac{e^{r_1 t}}{e^{r_2 t}} = e^{(r_1 - r_2)t}$$

42. A simple example of a production function is $GDP = z(LK)^{1/2}$. This equation says that to find the amount of GDP produced, multiply the amount of labour by the amount of capital, take the square root, and multiply the result by the constant z. This production function has positive but diminishing returns to either factor. This can be seen by evaluating the first and second partial derivatives and showing the first derivatives to be positive and the second derivatives to be negative.

For example,

$$\frac{\partial GDP}{\partial K} = \frac{z \cdot L^{1/2}}{2 \cdot K^{1/2}} > 0$$

and

$$\frac{\partial^2 GDP}{\partial K^2} = -\frac{z \cdot L^{1/2}}{2 \cdot K^{3/2}} < 0$$

The production function also displays constant returns to scale, as can be seen by multiplying both L and K by the same constant, θ, and seeing that this multiplies the whole value of GDP by θ:

$$z(\theta L \cdot \theta K)^{1/2} = z(\theta^2 \cdot LK)^{1/2} = \theta z(LK)^{1/2} = \theta \cdot GDP$$

43. The values are derived from the production function,

$$\text{output} = 4(KL)^{1/2}$$

in which both factors have the same average and marginal products.

GLOSSARY

absolute advantage   The situation that exists when a given amount of resources can produce more of some commodity in one country than in another.

absolute price   The amount of money that must be spent to acquire one unit of a commodity. Also called *money price*.

acceleration hypothesis   The hypothesis that when national income is held above potential, the persistent inflationary gap will cause inflation to accelerate, and when national income is held below potential, the persistent recessionary gap will cause inflation to decelerate.

adjustable peg system   A system in which exchange rates are fixed in the short term but are occasionally changed in response to persistent payments imbalances.

administered price   A price set by the conscious decision of the seller rather than by impersonal market forces.

adverse selection   Self-selection, within a single risk category, of persons of above-average risk.

AE See *aggregate expenditure*.

agents   Decision makers, including households, firms, and government bodies.

aggregate demand   Total desired purchases by all the buyers of an economy's output.

aggregate demand *(AD)* curve   A curve showing the combinations of real national income and the price level that makes aggregate desired expenditure equal to national income; the curve thus relates the price level to the total amount of output that will be demanded.

aggregate demand shock   Any event that causes a shift in the aggregate demand curve.

aggregate expenditure *(AE)* Total desired expenditure on final output of the economy;

$$AE = C + I + G + (X - IM),$$

representing the four major components of aggregate desired expenditure.

aggregate expenditure *(AE)* function   The function that relates aggregate desired expenditure to actual national income.

aggregate production function   The relation between the total amount of each factor of production employed in the nation and the nation's total output, its GDP.

aggregate supply   Total desired sales by all the producers of an economy's output.

aggregate supply *(AS)* curve   See *short-run aggregate supply curve* and *long-run aggregate supply curve*.

aggregate supply shock   Any event that causes a shift in the aggregate supply curve.

allocative efficiency   A situation in which no reorganization of production or consumption could make everyone better off (or, as it is sometimes stated, make at least one person better off while making no one worse off).

appreciation   A rise in the external value of the domestic currency in terms of foreign currencies; a fall in the exchange rate.

a priori   Literally, "at a prior time" or "in advance"; that which is prior to actual experience.

arc elasticity   A measure of the responsiveness of quantity to a change in price over an interval of the demand curve. It is usually defined by the formula

$$\eta = \frac{\Delta q / q}{\Delta p / q}$$

An alternative formula often used where computations are involved is

$$\eta = \frac{(q_2 - q_1)/(q_2 + q_1)}{(p_2 - p_1)/(p_2 + p_1)}$$

where p_1 and q_1 are the original price and quantity and p_2 and q_2 are the new price and quantity. With negatively sloped demand curves, elasticity is a negative number. The above expressions are therefore usually multiplied by -1 to make measured elasticity positive.

autarky   A situation in which a country engages in no foreign trade.

automatic fiscal stabilizers   Actions that automatically lessen the magnitude of the fluctuations in national income caused by changes in autonomous expenditures.

autonomous expenditure Elements of expenditure that do not vary systematically with national income or the interest rate, but are determined by forces outside of the theory.

average cost (AC) See *average total cost.*

average fixed cost (AFC) Total fixed costs divided by the number of units of output.

average product (AP) Total product divided by the number of units of the variable factor used in its production.

average propensity to consume (APC) The proportion of income devoted to consumption; total consumption expenditure divided by total disposable income ($APC = C/Y_D$).

average propensity to save (APS) The proportion of disposable income devoted to saving; total saving divided by total disposable income ($APS = S/Y_D$).

average revenue (AR) Total revenue divided by quantity sold; this is the market price when all units are sold at one price.

average tax rate The ratio of total taxes paid to total income earned.

average total cost (ATC) Total cost of producing a given output divided by the number of units of output; it can also be calculated as the sum of average fixed costs and average variable costs. Also called *cost per unit, unit cost, average cost.*

average variable cost (AVC) Total variable costs divided by the number of units of output.

balanced budget A situation in which current revenue is exactly equal to current expenditures.

balanced budget multiplier The change in equilibrium national income divided by the tax-financed change in government expenditure that brought it about.

balance-of-payments accounts A summary record of a country's transactions with the rest of the world, including the buying and selling of goods, services, and assets.

balance of trade The difference between the value of exports and the value of imports of goods and services.

bank notes Paper money issued by commercial banks.

bank rate The rate of interest at which the Bank of Canada makes loans to the chartered banks.

barter A system in which goods and services are traded directly for other goods and services.

beggar-my-neighbour policies Policies designed to increase a country's prosperity at the expense of reducing prosperity in other countries.

benefit-cost analysis A technique for evaluating government policies. The sum of the opportunity cost to all parties is compared with the value of the benefits to all parties.

black market A situation in which goods are sold illegally at prices that violate a legal price control.

bond A debt instrument carrying a specified amount and schedule of interest payments and (usually) a date for redemption of its face value.

break-even price The price at which a firm is just able to cover all of its costs, including the opportunity cost of capital.

budget balance The difference between total government revenue and total government expenditure.

budget deficit Any shortfall of current revenue below current expenditure.

budget deficit function A relationship which plots the government's budget deficit as a function of the level of national income.

budget line Graphical representation of all combinations of commodities (or factors) that a household (or firm) may obtain if it spends a specified amount of money at fixed prices of the commodities (or factors). In the theory of the firm, this is usually called an *isocost line.*

budget surplus Any excess of current revenue over current expenditure.

business cycle Fluctuations of national income around its trend value, after seasonal fluctuations have been removed, that follow a wavelike pattern.

C See *consumption expenditure.*

capacity The level of output that corresponds to the firm's minimum short-run average total cost.

capital A factor of production consisting of all manufactured aids to further production, including plant, equipment, and inventories.

capital account A part of the balance-of-payments accounts that records payments and receipts arising from the import and export of long-term and short-term financial capital.

capital consumption allowance See *depreciation.*

capital-labour ratio A measure of the amount of capital per worker.

capital-service account In the balance of payments, this account records the payments and receipts that represent income on assets (such as interest and dividends).

capital stock The aggregate quantity of capital goods.

cartel An organization of producers who agree to act as a single seller in order to maximize joint profits.

central bank A bank that acts as banker to the commercial banking system and often to the government as well. In the modern world, usually a government-owned and operated institution that controls the banking system and is the sole money-issuing authority.

centrally planned economy See *command economy.*

ceteris paribus Literally, "other things being equal"; usually used in economics to indicate that all variables except the ones specified are assumed not to change.

change in demand A change in the quantity demanded at each possible price of the commodity, represented by a shift in the whole demand curve.

change in quantity demanded A change in the specific quantity bought, represented by a change from one point on a demand curve to another point, either on the original demand curve or on a new one.

change in quantity supplied A change in the specific quantity supplied, represented by a change from one point on a supply curve to another point, either on the original supply curve or on a new one.

change in supply A change in the quantity supplied at each possible price of the commodity, represented by a shift in the whole supply curve.

Classical dichotomy The view that national income is determined only by the real sector of the economy and that changes in the money supply lead only to changes in the price level.

clearing house An institution where interbank indebtedness, arising from the transfer of cheques between banks, is computed and offset and net amounts owing are calculated.

closed economy An economy that has no foreign trade.

Coase theorem The idea (originally put forward by Ronald Coase) that as long as property rights are clearly assigned, externalities need not result in allocative inefficiency.

collective bargaining The process by which unions and employers arrive at and enforce agreements.

collusion An agreement among sellers to act jointly in their common interest, for example, by agreeing to raise prices. Collusion may be overt or covert, explicit, or tacit.

combine laws Laws that prevent firms either from combining into one unit or from cooperating so as to behave monopolistically.

command economy An economy in which the decisions of the government (as distinct from households and firms) exert the major influence over the allocation of resources.

commercial bank A privately owned, profit-seeking institution that provides a variety of financial services, such as accepting deposits from customers and making loans and other investments.

commercial policy See *trade policy*.

common market A customs union with the added provision that factors of production can move freely among the members.

comparative advantage The ability of one nation (region or individual) to produce a commodity at a lesser opportunity cost than another nation (region or individual).

comparative statics The derivation of predictions by analyzing the effect of a change in some exogenous variable on the equilibrium position.

competition policy Policy designed to prohibit the acquisition and exercise of monopoly power by business firms.

complements Commodities that tend to be used jointly. The degree of complementarity of any two goods is measured by the size of the negative cross elasticity between the two goods.

concentration ratio The fraction of total market sales (or some other measure of market occupancy) controlled by a specified number of the industry's largest firms, four-firm and eight-firm concentration ratios being most frequently used.

constant-cost industry An industry in which costs of the most efficient size firm remain constant as the entire industry expands or contracts in the long run.

constant returns (to scale) A situation in which output increases in proportion to inputs as the scale of production is increased. A firm in this situation, and facing fixed factor prices, is a *constant-cost firm*.

Consumer Price Index (CPI) A measure of the average prices of goods commonly bought by households.

consumer surplus The difference between the total value that consumers place on all units consumed of a commodity and the payment that they must make to purchase that amount of the commodity.

consumption The act of using commodities, either goods or services, to satisfy wants.

consumption expenditure In macroeconomics, household expenditure on all goods and services. Represented by the symbol C as one of the four components of aggregate expenditure.

consumption function The relationship between total desired consumption expenditure and all the variables that determine it; in the simplest cases, the relationship between consumption expenditure and disposable income and consumption expenditure and national income.

contestable market A market in which there are no sunk costs of entry or exit so that potential entry may hold profits of existing firms to low levels—zero in the case of perfect contestability.

cooperative outcome A situation in which existing firms cooperate to maximize their joint profits.

corporation A form of business organization in which the firm has a legal existence separate from that of the owners, and ownership and financial responsibility are divided, limited, and shared among any number of individual and institutional shareholders.

cost To a producing firm, the value of inputs used to produce output.

cost-effectiveness analysis Analysis of program costs with the purpose of finding the least-cost way to achieve a given result. See also *benefit-cost analysis*.

cost minimization An implication of profit maximization that firms choose the method that produces specific output at the lowest attainable cost.

CPI See *Consumer Price Index*.

cross elasticity of demand (η_{XY}) A measure of the responsiveness of the quantity of one commodity demanded to changes in the price of another commodity:

$$\eta_{XY} = \frac{\text{percentage change in quantity demanded of good } X}{\text{percentage change in price of good } Y}$$

cross-sectional data A set of measurements or observations made at the same time across several different units (such as households, firms, or countries).

crowding out The offsetting reduction in private expenditure caused by the rise in interest rates that follows an expansionary fiscal policy.

crown corporations Business concerns owned by the government.

current account A part of the balance-of-payments accounts that records payments and receipts arising from trade in goods and services and from interest and dividends that are earned by capital owned in one country and invested in another.

current-dollar GDP Gross domestic product valued in prices prevailing at the time of measurement; year-to-year changes in current-dollar GDP reflect changes both in quantities produced and in market prices. Also called *nominal GDP*.

current-dollar national income See *nominal national income*.

customs union A group of countries who agree to have free trade among themselves and a common set of barriers against imports from the rest of the world.

cyclical unemployment Unemployment in excess of frictional and structural unemployment; it is due to a shortfall of actual national income below potential national income. Sometimes called *deficient-demand unemployment*.

cyclically adjusted deficit *(CAD)* An estimate of the government budget deficit (expenditure minus tax revenue), not as it actually is but as it would be if national income were at its potential level.

debt Money owed to one's creditors; from a firm's point of view, the portion of its money capital that is borrowed rather than subscribed by shareholders.

debt-service payments Payments which represent the interest owed on a current stock of debt.

decision lag The period of time between perceiving some problem and reaching a decision on what to do about it.

declining-cost industry An industry in which costs of the most efficient size firm decline as the entire industry expands (or rise as the entire industry contracts) in the long run.

decreasing returns (to scale) A situation in which output increases less than in proportion to inputs as the scale of a firm's production increases. A firm in this situation, with fixed factor prices, is an *increasing-cost firm*.

deflation A situation in which there is a reduction in the general price level—the rate of inflation is negative.

demand The entire relationship between the quantity of a commodity that buyers wish to purchase (per period of time) and the price of that commodity, other things being equal.

demand curve The graphical representation of the relationship between the quantity of a commodity that buyers wish to purchase (per period of time) and the price of that commodity, other things being equal.

demand for money The total amount of money balances that the public wishes to hold for all purposes.

demand for money function See *liquidity preference function*.

demand inflation Inflation arising from excess aggregate demand, that is, when national income exceeds potential income.

demand schedule A table showing the relationship between the quantity of a commodity that buyers wish to purchase (per period of time) and the price of that commodity, other things being equal.

demogrants Social benefits paid to anyone meeting only minimal requirements such as age or residence; in particular, *not* income-tested.

deposit money Money held by the public in the form of demand deposits with commercial banks.

depreciation (1) A fall in the external value of domestic currency in terms of foreign currency; that is, a rise in the exchange rate. (2) An estimate of the amount by which the capital stock is depleted through its contribution to current production. Also called *capital consumption allowance*.

depression A persistent period of very low economic activity with very high unemployment and high excess capacity.

derived demand The demand for a factor of production that results from the demand for the products that it is used to make.

developed countries The higher-income countries of the world, including the United States, Canada, Western Europe, Japan, Australia, and South Africa.

developing countries The lower-income countries of the world, most of which are in Africa, Asia, and Latin America. Also called *underdeveloped countries* or *less-developed countries*.

differentiated product A group of commodities that are similar enough to be called the same product but dissimilar enough so that all of them do not have to be sold at the same price.

diminishing marginal rate of substitution The hypothesis that the marginal rate of substitution changes systematically as the amounts of two commodities being consumed vary.

direct burden Amount of money for a tax that is collected from taxpayers.

direct investment See *foreign direct investment*.

discouraged workers People who would like to work but have ceased looking for a job and hence have withdrawn from the labour force because they believe that no jobs are available for them.

discretionary fiscal policy Fiscal policy that is a conscious response (not according to any predetermined rule) to each particular state of the economy as it arises.

disequilibrium The situation of a market in which there is excess demand or excess supply.

disequilibrium price A price at which quantity demanded does not equal quantity supplied.

disposable personal income (Y_D) GNP minus any part of it not actually paid to households minus personal income taxes paid by households plus transfer payments to households; personal income minus personal income taxes.

dividends Profits paid out to shareholders of a corporation. Sometimes called *distributed profits*.

division of labour The breaking up of a production process into a series of specialized tasks, each done by a different worker.

double counting In national income accounting, adding up the total outputs of all the sectors in the economy so that the value of intermediate goods is counted in the sector that produces them and every time they are purchased as an input by another sector.

dumping In international trade, the practice of selling a commodity at a lower price in the export market than in the domestic market for reasons unrelated to differences in costs of servicing the two markets.

duopoly An industry that contains only two firms.

durable good A good that yields its services over an extended period of time.

economic efficiency See *allocative efficiency* and *productive efficiency*.

economic growth Increases in real potential GDP.

economic profits or losses The difference between the revenues received from the sale of output and the opportunity cost of the inputs used to make the output. Negative economic profits are economic losses. Also called *pure profits* or *pure losses*, or simply *profits* or *losses*.

economic rent The surplus of total earnings over what must be paid to prevent a factor from moving to another use.

economies of scale Reduction of average total costs resulting from an expansion in the scale of a firm's operations so that more of all inputs are being used.

economies of scope Economies achieved by a firm that is large enough to engage efficiently in multiproduct production and associated large-scale distribution, advertising, and purchasing.

economy A set of interrelated production and consumption activities.

effective tariff rate The tax charged on any imported commodity expressed as a percentage of the value added by the exporting industry.

efficiency wage A wage paid to a worker that exceeds the minimum required in order to induce him to work for the firm. This is profitable for the firm if the higher wage increases the worker's productivity.

elastic demand The situation in which, for a given percentage change in price, there is a greater percentage change in quantity demanded; elasticity greater than unity.

elasticity of demand (η) A measure of the responsiveness of quantity of a commodity demanded to a change in its market price:

$$\eta = \frac{\text{percentage change in quantity demanded}}{\text{percentage change in price}}$$

With negatively sloped demand curves, elasticity is a negative number. The above expression is therefore usually multiplied by -1 to make measured elasticity positive. Also called *demand elasticity* and *price elasticity*.

elasticity of supply (η_S) A measure of the responsiveness of the quantity of a commodity supplied to a change in its market price:

$$\eta_S = \frac{\text{percentage change in quantity supplied}}{\text{percentage change in price}}$$

embodied technical change Technical change that is intrinsic to the particular capital goods in use and hence can be used only when new capital, embodying the new techniques, is built.

employment The number of adult workers (15 years of age and older) who hold jobs.

endogenous variable A variable that is explained within a theory. Sometimes called an *induced variable* or a *dependent variable*.

ends The goals that one seeks to attain.

entry barrier Any natural barrier to the entry of new firms into an industry, such as a large minimum efficient scale for firms, or any firm-created barrier, such as a patent.

envelope Any curve that encloses, by being tangent to, a series of other curves. In particular, the envelope cost curve is the *LRAC* curve, which encloses the *SRATC* curves by being tangent to each without cutting any of them.

equalization payments Transfers of tax revenues from the federal government to the low-income provinces to compensate them for their lower per capita tax yields.

equilibrium condition A condition that must be fulfilled if some market or sector of the economy, or the whole economy, is to be in equilibrium.

equilibrium differential A difference in factor prices that persists in equilibrium, with no tendency for it to change.

equilibrium price The price at which quantity demanded equals quantity supplied.

equity capital Funds provided by the owners of a firm, the return on which depends on the firm's profits.

excess burden The value to taxpayers of the changes in behaviour that are induced by taxes; the amount that taxpayers would be willing to pay, over and above the direct burden of taxes, to abolish the taxes.

excess capacity The amount by which actual output falls short of capacity output (which is the output that corresponds to the minimum short-run average total cost).

excess-capacity theorem The property of long-run equilibrium in monopolistic competition that firms produce on the falling portion of their average total cost curves so that they have excess capacity measured by the gap between present output and the output that coincides with minimum average total cost.

excess demand A situation in which, at the given price, quantity demanded exceeds quantity supplied.

excess reserves Reserves held by a commercial bank in excess of its target reserves.

excess supply A situation in which, at the given price, quantity supplied exceeds quantity demanded.

exchange rate The number of units of domestic currency required to purchase one unit of foreign currency.

excise tax A tax on the sale of a particular commodity; may be a specific tax (fixed tax per unit of commodity) or an ad valorem tax (fixed percentage of the value of the commodity).

execution lag The time that it takes to put policies in place after a decision has been made.

exogenous variable A variable that influences endogenous variables but is itself determined by factors outside the theory. Sometimes called an *autonomous variable* or an *independent variable*.

expectational inflation Inflation that occurs because decision makers raise prices (so as to keep their relative prices constant) in the expectation that the price level is going to rise.

expectations-augmented Phillips curve The relationship between unemployment and the rate of increase of money wages or between national income and the rate of inflation that arises when the demand and expectations components of inflation are combined.

exports The value of all goods and services sold to firms, households, and governments in other countries.

external economies of scale Scale economies that cause the firm's costs to fall as industry output rises but are external to the firm and so cannot be obtained by the firm's increasing its own output.

external value of the dollar The value of the dollar expressed in terms of foreign currencies; a rise in the dollar's external value is reflected by a fall in the exchange rate. See *exchange rate*.

externality An effect, either good or bad, on parties not directly involved in the production or use of a commodity. Also called *third-party effects*.

factor markets Markets in which the services of factors of production are sold.

factor mobility The ease with which factors can be transferred between uses.

factors of production Resources used to produce goods and services; frequently divided into the basic categories of land, labour, and capital.

fiat money Paper money or coinage that is neither backed by nor convertible into anything else but is decreed by the government to be accepted as legal tender and is generally accepted in exchange for goods and services and for the discharge of debts.

final demand Demand for the economy's final output.

final goods Goods that are not used as inputs by other firms but are produced to be sold for consumption, investment, government, or exports during the period under consideration.

financial capital Money that a firm raises to carry on its business, including both equity capital and debt. Also called *money capital*.

fine tuning The attempt to maintain national income at its full-employment level by means of frequent changes in fiscal or monetary policy.

firm A unit that employs factors of production to produce goods and services.

fiscal policy The use of the government's tax and spending policies in an effort to influence the behaviour of GDP.

fixed exchange rate An exchange rate that is maintained within a small range around its publicly stated par value by the intervention of a country's central bank in foreign market operations.

fixed factor An input that cannot be increased beyond a given amount in the short run.

fixed investment Investment in plant and equipment. Also called *business fixed investment*.

flexible exchange rate An exchange rate that is left free to be determined by the forces of demand and supply on the free market, with no intervention by the monetary authorities.

foreign direct investment (FDI) Nonresident investment in the form of a takeover or capital investment in a domestic branch plant or subsidiary corporation in which the investor has voting control. Also called *direct investment*.

foreign exchange Actual foreign currencies or various claims on them, such as bank balances or promises to pay, that are traded on the foreign exchange market.

foreign exchange market The market where different national currencies, or claims to these currencies, are traded.

45° line In macroeconomics, the line that graphs the equilibrium condition that desired aggregate expenditure equals actual national income, $AE = Y$.

fractional-reserve system A banking system in which commercial banks keep only a fraction of their deposits in cash or on deposit with the central bank.

free good A commodity for which the quantity supplied exceeds the quantity demanded at a price of zero; therefore, a good that does not command a positive price in a market economy.

free-market economy An economy in which the decisions of individual households and firms (as distinct from the government) exert the major influence over the allocation of resources.

free trade The absence of any form of government intervention in international trade, which implies that imports and exports are not subject to special taxes or restrictions levied merely because of their status as "imports" or "exports."

free trade area (FTA) An agreement among two or more countries to abolish tariffs on all or most of the trade among themselves while each remains free to set its own tariffs against other countries.

frictional unemployment Unemployment caused by the time that is taken for labour to move from one job to another.

full employment Employment that is sufficient to produce the economy's potential output; at full employment, all remaining unemployment is frictional and structural.

function Loosely, an expression of a relationship between two or more variables. Precisely, Y is a function of the variables $X_1, \ldots, X_n$ if, for every set of values of the variables $X_1, \ldots, X_n$, there is associated a unique value of the variable Y.

functional distribution of income The distribution of national income among the major factors of production.

G See *government purchases*.

gains from trade The increased output due to the specialization according to comparative advantage that is made possible by trade.

game theory The theory that studies rational decision making in situations in which one must anticipate the reactions of one's competitors to the moves that one makes.

Giffen good An inferior good for which the negative income effect outweighs the substitution effect so that the demand curve is positively sloped.

goods Tangible commodities, such as cars or shoes.

goods markets Markets in which outputs of goods and services are sold. Also called *product markets*.

government All public officials, agencies, and other organizations belonging to or under the control of local, provincial, or federal governments.

government purchases All government expenditure on currently produced goods and services, exclusive of government transfer payments. Represented by the symbol G as one of the four components of aggregate expenditure.

Gresham's law The theory that "bad," or debased, money drives "good," or undebased, money out of circulation because people keep the good money for other purposes and use the bad money for transactions.

gross domestic product (GDP) National income as measured by the output approach; equal to the sum of all values added in the economy or, what is the same thing, the values of all final goods produced in the economy. It can be valued at current prices to get *nominal GDP* or it can be valued at base-year prices to get *real GDP*, which is also called *GDP at constant prices*.

gross investment The total value of all investment goods produced in the economy during a stated period of time.

gross national product (GNP) The value of total incomes earned by domestically based producers and factors of production.

gross tuning The use of macroeconomic policy to stabilize the economy such that large deviations from full employment do not occur for extended periods of time.

homogeneous product In the eyes of purchasers, a product every unit of which is identical to every other unit.

Hotelling's rule Determines the optimal rate of extraction of a nonrenewable resource as one such that the price rises at a rate equal to the interest rate.

household All of the people who live under one roof and who make joint financial decisions or are subject to others making decisions for them.

human capital The capitalized value of productive investments in persons; usually refers to value derived from expenditures on education, training, and health improvements.

I See *investment expenditure*.

IM See *imports*.

implicit GDP deflator An index number derived by dividing GDP, measured in current dollars, by GDP, measured in constant dollars, and multiplying by 100. In effect, a price index, with current-year quantity weights, measuring the average change in price of all the items in the GDP.

import quota A limit set by the government on the quantity of a foreign commodity that may be shipped into that country in a given time period.

imports The value of all goods and services purchased from firms, households, or governments in other countries.

imputed costs The costs of using factors of production already owned by the firm, measured by the earnings they could have received in their best alternative use.

income-consumption line (1) A curve showing the relationship for a commodity between quantity demanded and income, *ceteris paribus*. (2) A curve drawn on an indifference curve diagram and connecting the points of tangency between a set of indifference curves and a set of parallel budget lines, showing how the consumption bundle changes as income changes, with relative prices being held constant.

income effect The effect on quantity demanded of a change in real income, holding relative prices constant.

income elasticity of demand (η_Y) A measure of the responsiveness of quantity demanded to a change in income:

$$\eta_Y = \frac{\text{percentage change in quantity demanded}}{\text{percentage change in income}}$$

incomes policy   Any direct intervention by the government to influence wage and price formation.

income-tested benefits   Social benefits paid to recipients who qualify because their income is less than some critical level.

increasing-cost industry   An industry in which costs of the most efficient size firm rise as the entire industry expands (or fall as the entire industry contracts) in the long run.

increasing returns (to scale)   A situation in which output increases more than in proportion to inputs as the scale of a firm's production increases. A firm in this situation, with fixed factor prices, is a *decreasing-cost firm*.

incremental cost   See *marginal cost*.

incremental product   See *marginal product*.

incremental revenue   See *marginal revenue*.

indexation   Automatic change in any money payment in proportion to the change in the price level.

index number   An average that measures change over time of such variables as the price level and industrial production; conventionally expressed as a percentage relative to a base period, which is assigned the value 100.

indifference curve   A curve showing all combinations of two commodities that give the household equal utility and between which the household is thus indifferent.

indifference map   A set of indifference curves based on a given set of household preferences.

induced expenditure   Elements of expenditure that are explained by variables within the theory. In the aggregate desired expenditure function, it is any component of expenditure that is related to national income. Also called *endogenous expenditure*.

industry   A group of firms that produce a single product or group of related products.

inelastic demand   The situation in which, for a given percentage change in price, there is a smaller percentage change in quantity demanded; elasticity less than one.

infant industry argument   The argument that new domestic industries with potential for economies of scale or learning by doing need to be protected from competition from established, low-cost foreign producers so that they can grow large enough to achieve costs as low as those of foreign producers.

inferior good   A good for which quantity demanded falls as income rises—its income elasticity is negative.

inflation   A rise in the average level of all prices.

inflationary gap   A situation in which actual national income exceeds potential income.

infrastructure   The basic installations and facilities (especially transportation and communications systems) on which the commerce of a community depends.

injections   Income earned by domestic firms that does not arise out of the spending of domestic households and income earned by domestic households that does not arise out of the spending of domestic firms.

innovation   The introduction of an invention into methods of production.

inputs   Intermediate products and factor services that are used in the process of production.

interest   The payment for the use of borrowed money.

interest rate   The price paid per dollar borrowed per period of time, expressed either as a proportion (e.g., 0.06) or as a percentage (e.g., 6 percent). Also called the *nominal interest rate* to distinguish it from the *real interest rate*.

intermediate products   All outputs that are used as inputs by other producers in a further stage of production.

intermediate targets   Variables that the government cannot control directly and does not seek to control ultimately, yet that have an important influence on policy variables.

internal economies of scale   Scale economies that result from the firm's own actions and hence are available to it by raising its own output.

internal value of the dollar   The purchasing power of the dollar measured in terms of domestic goods and services; changes in the internal value of the dollar are measured by changes in an index of Canadian prices (such as the consumer price index).

internalization   A process that results in a producer or consumer taking account of a previously external effect.

invention   The creation of something new, such as a production technique or a product.

inventories   Stocks of raw materials, goods in process, and finished goods held by firms to mitigate the effect of short-term fluctuations in production or sales.

investment expenditure   Expenditure on the production of goods not for present consumption.

investment goods   Goods that are produced not for present consumption, such as capital goods, inventories, and residential housing.

involuntary unemployment   Unemployment due to the inability of qualified persons who are seeking work to find jobs at the going wage rate.

isoquant   A curve showing all technologically efficient factor combinations for producing a specified amount of output.

isoquant map   A series of isoquants from the same production function, each isoquant relating to a specific level of output.

Keynesians   Economists who tend to believe (following the views of John Maynard Keynes) that during recessions, expansionary fiscal policy is more effective than expansionary monetary policy in raising national income.

Keynesian short-run aggregate supply curve   A horizontal aggregate supply curve indicating that when national income is below potential, changes in national income can occur with little or no accompanying change in prices.

labour A factor of production consisting of all physical and mental efforts provided by people.

labour force The total number of persons employed in both civilian and military jobs, plus the number of persons who are unemployed.

labour-force participation rate The percentage of the population of working age that is actually in the labour force (either working or seeking work).

labour union See *union.*

Laffer curve A relationship between the revenue yield of a tax and the tax rate imposed. Named after its originator, Arthur Laffer.

laissez faire Literally, "let do"; a policy advocating the minimization of government intervention in a market economy.

land A factor of production consisting of all gifts of nature, including raw materials and land, as understood in ordinary speech.

law of diminishing returns The hypothesis that if increasing quantities of a variable factor are applied to a given quantity of fixed factors, the marginal product and average product of the variable factor will eventually decrease.

learning curve A curve showing how a firm's costs of producing at a given rate of output fall as the total amount produced increases over time as a result of accumulated learning.

legal tender Anything that by law must be accepted for the purchase of goods and services or in discharge of a debt.

less-developed countries (LDCs) See *developing countries.*

limited liability The limitation of the financial responsibility of an owner (shareholder) of a corporation to the amount of money that the shareholder has actually invested in the firm by purchasing its shares.

limited partnership A form of business organization in which the firm has two classes of owners: general partners, who take part in managing the firm and are personally liable for all of the firm's actions and debts, and limited partners, who take no part in the management of the firm and risk only the money that they have invested.

liquidity preference (LP) function The function that relates the demand for money to the rate of interest. Also called the *demand for money function.*

logarithmic scale A scale in which equal proportional changes are shown as equal distances (for example, 1 cm may always represent doubling of a variable, whether from 3 to 6 or 50 to 100). Also called log scale, ratio scale.

long run A period of time in which all inputs may be varied but the basic technology of production cannot be changed.

long-run aggregate supply (LRAS) curve A curve showing the relationship between the price level and the total quantity of output supplied when all markets have fully adjusted to the existing price level; a vertical line at $Y = Y^*$.

long-run average cost (LRAC) curve The curve showing the lowest possible cost of producing each level of output when all inputs can be varied.

long-run industry supply (LRS) curve A curve showing the relationship between the market price and the quantity supplied by a competitive industry when all the firms in that industry are at the minimum of their *LRAC* curves.

Lorenz curve A graph showing the extent of departure from equality of income distribution.

M1 Currency plus demand deposits plus other chequable deposits.

M2 M1 plus saving deposits at the chartered banks.

M2+ M2 plus deposits held at institutions that are *not* chartered banks.

macroeconomics The study of the determination of economic aggregates, such as total output, total employment, the price level, and the rate of economic growth.

managed float A situation in which the central bank intervenes in the foreign exchange market to smooth out some of the large, short-term fluctuations in a country's exchange rate, while still leaving the market to determine the exchange rate in the longer term.

marginal cost (MC) The increase in total cost resulting from raising the rate of production by one unit. Mathematically, the rate of change of cost with respect to output. Also called *incremental cost.*

marginal-cost pricing Setting price equal to marginal cost so that buyers are just willing to pay for the last unit bought the amount that it cost to make that unit.

marginal efficiency of capital (MEC) The rate of return on one additional unit of physical capital.

marginal efficiency of investment (MEI) function The function that relates the quantity of desired investment to the rate of interest.

marginal physical product (MPP) See *marginal product.*

marginal product (MP) The change in quantity of total output that results from using one unit more of a variable factor. Mathematically, the rate of change of output with respect to the quantity of the variable factor. Also called *incremental product* and *marginal physical product (MPP).*

marginal propensity to consume (MPC) The change in consumption divided by the change in disposable income that brought it about; mathematically, the rate of change of consumption with respect to disposable income ($MPC = \Delta C/\Delta Y_D$).

marginal propensity not to spend The fraction of any increment to national income that is not spent on domestic production (1 minus the marginal propensity to spend; that is, $1 - \Delta AE/\Delta Y$).

marginal propensity to save *(MPS)* The change in total desired saving divided by the change in disposable income that brought it about ($\Delta S/\Delta Y_D$).

marginal propensity to spend The fraction of any increment to national income that is spent on domestic production; measured by the change in aggregate expenditure divided by the change in national income ($\Delta AE/\Delta Y$).

marginal rate of substitution *(MRS)* (1) In consumption, the slope of an indifference curve, showing how much more of one commodity must be provided to compensate for the giving up of one unit of another commodity if the level of satisfaction is to be held constant. (2) In production, the slope of an isoquant, showing how much more of one factor of production must be used to compensate for the use of one less unit of another factor of production if production is to be held constant.

marginal revenue *(MR)* The change in a firm's total revenue resulting from a change in its rate of sales by one unit. Mathematically, the rate of change of revenue with respect to output. Also called *incremental revenue*.

marginal revenue product *(MRP)* The addition of revenue attributable to the last unit of a variable factor ($MRP = MP \times MR$). Mathematically, the rate of change of revenue with respect to quantity of the variable factor.

marginal tax rate The fraction of an additional dollar of income that is paid in taxes.

marginal utility The additional satisfaction obtained by a consumer from consuming one unit more of a good or service; mathematically, the rate of change of utility with respect to consumption.

market Any situation in which buyers and sellers can negotiate the exchange of goods or services.

market-clearing price The price at which quantity demanded equals quantity supplied so that there are neither unsatisfied buyers nor unsatisfied sellers; the *equilibrium price*.

market economy See *free-market economy*.

market failure Failure of the unregulated market system to achieve allocative efficiency or social goals because of externalities, market impediments, or market imperfections.

market for corporate control An interpretation of conglomerate mergers, leveraged buyouts, and hostile takeovers as mechanisms that place the firm in the hands of the parties who value it most.

market sector The portion of an economy in which commodities are bought and sold and in which producers must cover their costs from sales revenue.

market structure All features of a market that affect the behaviour and performance of firms in that market, such as the number and size of sellers, the extent of knowl-

edge about one another's actions, the degree of freedom of entry, and the degree of product differentiation.

means The methods of achieving one's goals.

median The value within any set of data at which half of the observations are greater and half are less. Thus half of a population earns income above the median income, and half earns income below the median.

medium of exchange Anything that is generally acceptable in return for goods and services sold.

merger The purchase of either the physical assets or the controlling share of ownership of one firm by another. In a *horizontal merger*, both firms are in the same line of business; in a *vertical merger*, one firm is a supplier of the other; if the two are in unrelated industries, it is a *conglomerate merger*.

microeconomics The study of the allocation of resources and the distribution of income as they are affected by the workings of the price system and by government policies.

minimum efficient scale *(MES)* The smallest output at which long-run average cost reaches its minimum; all available economies of scale in production and/or distribution have been realized at this point.

minimum wages Legally specified minimum rate of pay for labour in covered occupations.

mixed economy An economy in which some decisions about the allocation of resources are made by firms and households and some by the government.

Monetarists Economists who stress monetary causes of cyclical fluctuations and inflation.

monetary base The sum of currency in circulation plus reserves of the commercial banks; equal to the monetary liabilities of the central bank.

monetary equilibrium A situation in which the demand for money equals the supply of money.

monetary policy The central bank's attempt to influence the economy by changing the level of reserves in the banking system.

money A medium of exchange that can also serve as a store of value and a unit of account.

money capital See *financial capital*.

money income Income measured in monetary units per period of time. Also called *nominal income*.

money market deposit account (MMDA) A chequable deposit account at a nonbank financial institution that earns a relatively high interest rate.

money market mutual fund (MMMF) A liquid financial instrument that earns a high yield and is chequable but is subject to transaction restrictions.

money rate of interest See *interest rate*.

money substitute Something that serves as a temporary medium of exchange but is not a store of value.

money supply The total quantity of money in an economy at a point in time. Also called the *supply of money*.

monopolist A firm that is the only seller in a market.

monopolistic competition Market structure of an industry in which there are many firms and freedom of entry and exit but in which each firm has a product somewhat differentiated from the others, giving it some control over its price.

monopoly A market containing a single firm.

monopsony A market situation in which there is a single buyer.

moral hazard A situation in which an individual or a firm takes advantage of special knowledge while engaging in socially uneconomic behaviour.

multilateral balance of payments The balance of payments between one country and the rest of the world taken as a whole.

multinational enterprises (MNEs) See *transnational corporation*.

multiplier The ratio of the change in equilibrium national income to the change in autonomous expenditure that brought it about.

NAIRU Short for *nonaccelerating inflation rate of unemployment*. The rate of unemployment associated with potential national income and at which a steady, nonaccelerating or nondecelerating inflation can be sustained indefinitely. Also called the *natural rate of unemployment*.

Nash equilibrium An equilibrium that results when each firm in an industry is currently doing the best that it can, given the current behaviour of the other firms in the industry.

national asset formation The sum of investment and net exports.

national income The value of total output (in a given period of time) and of the income that is generated by the production of that output.

national saving The sum of public saving and private saving; all national income that is not spent on government purchases or private consumption.

natural monopoly An industry characterized by economies of scale sufficiently large that one firm can most efficiently supply the entire market demand.

natural rate of unemployment See *NAIRU*.

natural scale A scale in which equal absolute amounts are represented by equal distances.

near money Liquid assets that are easily convertible into money without risk of significant loss of value and can be used as short-term stores of purchasing power but are not themselves media of exchange.

negative income tax (NIT) A tax system in which households with income below some critical level receive payments from the government that are based on the amount by which their income is less than the critical level.

net domestic product Gross domestic product less capital consumed in the production of GDP.

net exports The value of total exports minus the value of total imports. Represented by the expression $X-IM$ as a component of aggregate expenditure, where X is total exports and IM is total imports. Net exports is denoted by the symbol NX.

net investment Gross investment minus replacement investment.

net taxes Total tax revenue minus transfer payments, denoted T.

neutrality of money The doctrine that the money supply affects only the absolute level of prices and has no effect on relative prices and hence no effect on the allocation of resources or the distribution of income.

New Classical economics An approach to explaining macroeconomic fluctuations in which fluctuations in economic activity are explained by shocks to technology and tastes rather than to markets that fail to clear.

newly industrialized countries (NICs) Countries that have industrialized and grown rapidly over the past 40 years to achieve per capita incomes roughly half of those achieved in Canada or the United States.

nominal interest rate See *interest rate*.

nominal national income Total national income measured in dollars; the money value of national income. Also called *current-dollar national income*.

nominal tariff rate The tax charged on any imported commodity.

noncooperative outcome An industry outcome reached when firms calculate their own best policy without considering competitor's reactions.

nonmarket sector The portion of the economy in which goods are provided freely so that producers must cover their costs from sources other than sales revenue.

nonrenewable resource Any productive resource that is available as a fixed stock that cannot be replaced once it is used. Also called an *exhaustible resource*.

nonstrategic behaviour Behaviour that does not take account of the reactions of rivals to one's own behaviour.

nontariff barriers (NTBs) Restrictions other than tariffs designed to reduce the flow of imported goods.

normal good A good for which quantity demanded rises as income rises—its income elasticity is positive.

normal profits The opportunity cost of capital and risk taking just necessary to keep the owners in the industry. Normal profits are usually included in what economists (but not businesspersons) call *total costs*.

normative statement A statement about what ought to be as opposed to what actually is. See also *positive statement*.

NX See *net exports*.

oligopoly An industry that contains two or more firms, at least one of which produces a significant portion of the industry's total output.

open economy   An economy that engages in international trade.

open-market operations   The purchase and sale of securities (usually short-term government securities) on the open market by the central bank.

opportunity cost   The cost of using resources for a certain purpose, measured by the benefit given up by not using them in their best alternative use.

output gap   Actual national income minus potential national income. Also called the *GDP gap*.

outputs   The goods and services that result from the process of production.

overnight rate   The interest rate that commercial banks charge each other for very-short-term loans.

partnership   A form of business organization in which the firm has two or more joint owners, each of whom takes part in the management of the firm and is personally responsible for all of the firm's actions and debts.

paternalism   Intervention in the free choices of individuals by others (including governments) to protect them against their own ignorance or folly.

pay equity   A government policy designed to eliminate the wage differentials between workers in different jobs who nonetheless appear to have similar levels of skills and responsibilities.

per capita output   GDP divided by total population.

perfect competition   A market structure in which all firms in an industry are price takers and in which there is freedom of entry into and exit from the industry.

personal income   Income of individuals before allowance for personal income taxes on that income.

Phillips curve   Originally, a relationship between the percentage of the labour force unemployed and the rate of change of money wages. Now often drawn as a relationship between actual national income and the rate of price inflation.

physical capital   See *real capital*.

point elasticity   A measure of the responsiveness of quantity to a change in price at a particular point on the demand curve. The formula for point elasticity of demand is

$$\eta = \frac{dq}{dp} \cdot \frac{p}{q}$$

With negatively sloped demand curves, elasticity is a negative number. The above expression is usually multiplied by -1 to make elasticity positive.

point of diminishing average productivity   The level of factor use at which average product reaches a maximum.

point of diminishing marginal productivity   The level of factor use at which marginal product reaches a maximum.

policy instruments   The variables that the government can control directly to achieve its policy objectives.

policy variables   The variables that the government seeks to control, such as real national income and the price level.

poll tax   A tax that takes the same absolute amount from each person, independent of the level of their income. Also called a *lump-sum tax*.

portfolio investment   Foreign investment in bonds or a minority holding of shares that does not involve legal control.

positive statement   A statement about what actually is (was or will be), as opposed to what ought to be. See also *normative statement*.

potential income (Y^*)   The real gross domestic product that the economy could produce if its productive resources were fully employed at their normal levels of utilization. Also called *potential GDP*.

poverty line   The official government estimate of the annual family income that is required to maintain a minimum adequate standard of living.

poverty trap   Occurs whenever individuals have little incentive to increase their pre-tax income because the resulting loss of benefits makes them worse off.

precautionary balances   Money balances held for protection against the uncertainty of the timing of cash flows.

present value (*PV*)   The value now of one or more payments to be received in the future; often referred to as the *discounted present value* of future payments.

price ceiling   A government-imposed maximum permissible price at which a commodity may be sold.

price-consumption line   A line connecting the points of tangency between a set of indifference curves and a set of budget lines where one absolute price is fixed and the other varies, money income being held constant.

price controls   Government policies that attempt to hold the price in a particular market at a disequilibrium value.

price discrimination   The sale by one firm of different units of a commodity at two or more different prices for reasons not associated with differences in cost.

price elasticity of demand   See *elasticity of demand*.

price floor   A government-imposed minimum permissible price at which a commodity may be sold.

price index   A number that shows the average of some group of prices, expressed as a percentage of the average in some base period. Price indexes are used to measure the price level at a given time relative to a base period.

price level   The average level of all prices in the economy, usually expressed as an index number.

price maker   A firm that administers its prices. See *administered price*.

price taker   A firm that can alter its rate of production and sales without significantly affecting the market price of its product.

price theory   The theory of how prices are determined; competitive price theory concerns the determination of prices in competitive markets by the interaction of demand and supply.

primary budget deficit The difference between the government's overall budget deficit and its debt-service payments.

principal-agent problem The problem of resource allocation that arises because contracts that will induce agents to act in their principals' best interests are generally impossible to write or too costly to monitor.

principle of substitution The principle that methods of production will change if relative prices of inputs change, with relatively more of the cheaper input and relatively less of the more expensive input being used.

private cost The value of the best alternative use of resources used in production as valued by the producer.

private saving Saving on the part of households—the part of disposable income that is not spent on current consumption.

private sector The portion of an economy in which goods and services are produced by nongovernmental units, such as firms and households.

procyclical Moving in the same direction as the business cycle—up in booms and down in slumps.

producer surplus The difference between the total amount that producers receive for all units sold of a commodity and the total variable cost of producing the commodity.

product differentiation The existence of similar but not identical products sold by a single industry, such as the breakfast food or automobile industry. See *differentiated product*.

production The act of making commodities—either goods or services.

production function A functional relation showing the maximum output that can be produced by each and every combination of inputs.

production possibility boundary A curve that shows which alternative combinations of commodities can just be attained if all available resources are used; it is thus the boundary between attainable and unattainable output combinations. Also called *production possibility curve*.

production possibility curve See *production possibility boundary*.

productive efficiency Production of any output at the lowest attainable cost for that level of output.

productivity Output produced per unit of some input; frequently used to refer to labour productivity, measured by total output divided by the amount of labour used.

product markets Markets in which goods and services are sold. Also called *goods markets*.

profit (1) In ordinary usage, the difference between the value of outputs and the value of inputs. (2) In microeconomics, the difference between revenues received from the sale of goods and the value of inputs, which includes the opportunity cost of capital, so that profits are *economic profits*. (3) In macroeconomics, profits exclude interest on borrowed capital but do not exclude the return on owner's capital.

progressive tax A tax that takes a larger percentage of income the higher the level of income.

proportional tax A tax that takes a constant percentage of income at all levels of income and is thus neither progressive nor regressive.

protectionism Any government policy that interferes with free trade in order to give some protection to domestic industries against foreign competition.

proxy An order from a shareholder that transfers the right to vote to a nominee, usually an existing member of the board of the firm.

public goods Goods or services that, if they provide benefits to anyone, can, at little or no additional cost, provide benefits to a large group of people, possibly everyone in the country. Also called *collective consumption goods*.

public saving Saving on the part of governments. Public saving is exactly equal to government budget surpluses, or government revenues less government expenditures.

public sector The portion of an economy in which goods and services are produced by the government or by government-owned agencies and firms.

purchasing power of money The amount of goods and services that can be purchased with a unit of money. The purchasing power of money varies inversely with the price level.

purchasing power parity (PPP) The theory that over the long term, the exchange rate between two currencies adjusts to reflect relative price levels (relative purchasing power).

quantity demanded The amount of a commodity that households wish to purchase in some time period.

quantity supplied The amount of a commodity that producers wish to sell in some time period.

rate of inflation The percentage rate of increase in some price index from one period to another.

rate of return The ratio of net profits earned by a firm to total invested capital.

rational expectations The theory that people understand how the economy works and learn quickly from their mistakes so that even though random errors may be made, systematic and persistent errors are not.

ratio scale See *logarithmic scale*.

real capital The physical assets that a firm uses to conduct its business, composed of plant, equipment, and inventories. Also called *physical capital*.

real income Income expressed in terms of the purchasing power of money income, that is, the quantity of goods and services that can be purchased with the money income. It can be calculated as money income deflated by a price index.

real interest rate   The money rate of interest corrected for the change in the purchasing power of money by subtracting the inflation rate.

real national income   National income measured in constant dollars so that it changes only when quantities change.

recession   A downturn in the level of economic activity. Often defined precisely as two consecutive quarters in which real GDP falls.

recessionary gap   A negative output gap; that is, a situation in which actual national income is less than potential income. Also called a *deflationary gap*.

regressive tax   A tax that takes a lower percentage of income the higher the level of income.

relative price   The ratio of the money price of one commodity to the money price of another commodity; that is, a ratio of two absolute prices.

renewable resources   Productive resources that can be replaced as they are used up, as with physical capital; distinguished from nonrenewable resources, which are available in a fixed stock that can be depleted but not replaced.

rent seeking   Behaviour whereby private firms and individuals try to use the powers of the government to enhance their own economic well-being.

replacement investment   The amount of investment that is needed to maintain the existing capital stock intact.

required reserves   The reserves that a bank must, by law, keep either in currency or in deposits with the central bank.

reserve ratio   The fraction of its deposits that a commercial bank holds as reserves in the form of cash or deposits with a central bank.

resource allocation   The allocation of an economy's scarce resources of land, labour, and capital among alternative uses.

retained earnings   See *undistributed profits*.

Ricardian equivalence   The proposition that the method of financing government spending (taxes or borrowing) has no effect on national saving because private saving will just offset any government dissaving. Hence, if the government raises its current deficit, private agents will save enough to cover the future taxes required to repay the increased debt, leaving national saving and *AD* unchanged.

satisficing   A hypothesized objective of firms to achieve levels of performance deemed satisfactory rather than to maximize some objective.

saving   All disposable income that is not consumed. See *private saving, public saving,* and *national saving*.

scarce good   A commodity for which the quantity demanded exceeds the quantity supplied at a price of zero; therefore, a good that commands a positive price in a market economy.

scatter diagram   A graph of statistical observations of paired values of two variables, one measured on the horizontal and the other on the vertical axis. Each point on the coordinate grid represents the values of the variables for a particular unit of observation.

search unemployment   Unemployment caused by people continuing to search for a good job rather than accepting the first job that they come across after they become unemployed.

sectors   Parts of an economy (such as the agricultural or manufacturing sectors).

sellers' preferences   Allocation of commodities in excess demand by decisions of the sellers.

services   Intangible commodities, such as haircuts or medical care.

shareholders   See *stockholders*.

short run   A period of time in which the quantity of some inputs cannot be increased beyond the fixed amount that is available.

short-run aggregate supply (*SRAS*) curve   A curve showing the relation between the price level and the quantity of output supplied on the assumption that all factor prices are held constant.

short-run equilibrium   Generally, equilibrium subject to fixed factors or other things that cannot change over the time period being considered. For a competitive industry, the price and output at which industry demand equals short-run industry supply, and all firms are maximizing their profits. Either profits or losses for individual firms are possible.

short-run supply curve   A curve showing the relationship between quantity supplied and market price, with one or more fixed factors; it is the horizontal sum of marginal cost curves (above the level of average variable costs) of all firms in a perfectly competitive industry.

shut-down price   The price that is equal to a firm's average variable costs. At prices below this, a profit-maximizing firm will produce no output.

simple multiplier   The ratio of the change in equilibrium national income to the change in autonomous expenditure that brought it about, calculated for a constant price level.

single proprietorship   A form of business organization in which the firm has one owner who makes all the decisions and is personally responsible for all of the firm's actions and debts.

size distribution of income   The distribution of income among households, without regard to source of income or social class of households.

slope   The ratio of the vertical change to the horizontal change between two points on a curve.

social benefit   The contribution that an activity makes to society's welfare.

social cost The value of the best alternative use of resources available to society as valued by society. Also called *social opportunity cost*.

social regulation The regulation of economic behaviour to advance social goals when competition and economic regulation will fail to achieve those goals.

special drawing rights (SDRs) Financial liabilities of the International Monetary Fund, held in a special account generated by contributions of member countries. Members can use SDRs to maintain supplies of convertible currencies when these are needed to support foreign exchange trades.

specialization of labour The specialization of individual workers in the production of particular goods and services, rather than producing everything that they consume.

speculative balances Money balances held as a hedge against the uncertainty of the prices of other financial assets.

stabilization policy Any policy designed to reduce the economy's cyclical fluctuations and thereby to stabilize national income at a desired level.

stagflation The coexistence of high rates of unemployment with high, and sometimes rising, rates of inflation.

stockholders The owners of a corporation who have supplied money to the firm by purchasing its shares. Also called *shareholders*.

stock market An organized market where stocks and bonds are bought and sold. Also called *securities market*.

strategic behaviour Behaviour designed to take account of the reactions of one's rivals to one's own behaviour.

structural unemployment Unemployment due to a mismatch between characteristics required by available jobs and characteristics possessed by the unemployed labour.

substitute Any good that can be used in place of another good to satisfy similar needs or desires. The degree of substitutability is measured by the magnitude of the positive cross elasticity between the two goods.

substitution effect A change in the quantity of a good demanded resulting from a change in its relative price (while holding constant real income).

supply The entire relationship between the quantity of some commodity that producers wish to sell (per period of time) and the price of that commodity, other things being equal.

supply curve The graphical representation of the relationship between the quantity of some commodity that producers wish to sell (per period of time) and the price of that commodity, other things being equal.

supply inflation A rise in the price level originating from increases in costs that are not caused by excess demand in the domestic markets for factors of production.

supply of labour The total number of hours of work that the population is willing to supply. Also called the *supply of effort*.

supply of money See *money supply*.

supply schedule A table showing the relationship between the quantity of some commodity that producers wish to sell (per period of time) and the price of that commodity, other things being equal.

tacit collusion Collusion that takes place with no explicit agreements. See *collusion*.

takeover The purchase of one firm by another.

takeover bid See *tender offer*.

target reserve ratio The fraction of its deposits that a commercial bank wants to hold as reserves.

tariff A tax applied on imports.

tax bracket A range of income for which there is a constant marginal tax rate.

tax expenditures Tax provisions, such as exemptions and deductions from taxable income and tax credits, that are designed to induce market responses considered to be desirable. They are called expenditures because they have the same effect as directly spending money to induce the desired behaviour.

tax incidence The location of the burden of a tax; that is, the identity of the ultimate bearer of the tax.

tax-related incomes policy (TIP) Tax incentives for labour and management to encourage them to conform to wage and price guidelines.

tax-rental arrangements An agreement by which the federal government makes a per capita payment to the provinces for the right to collect income taxes.

technological change Any change in the available techniques of production.

tender offer A time-limited offer to buy some or all of the outstanding common stock of a corporation from its stockholders at a specified price per share in an attempt to gain control of the corporation. Also called *takeover bid*.

term See *term to maturity*.

term deposit An interest-earning bank deposit, legally subject to notice before withdrawal (in practice, the notice requirement is not normally enforced) and until recently not transferable by cheque. Also called *savings deposit* and *time deposit*.

terms of trade The ratio of the average price of a country's exports to the average price of its imports, both averages usually being measured by index numbers; it is the quantity of imported goods that can be obtained per unit of goods exported.

term to maturity The period of time from the present to the redemption date of a bond. Also called simply the *term*.

time-series data A set of measurements or observations made repeatedly at successive periods (or moments) of time.

total cost (TC) The total cost to the firm of producing any given level of output; it can be divided into *total fixed costs* and *total variable costs*.

total fixed cost *(TFC)* All costs of production that do not vary with level of output.

total product *(TP)* Total amount produced by a firm during some time period.

total revenue *(TR)* Total receipts from the sale of a product; price times quantity.

total utility The total satisfaction resulting from the consumption of a given commodity or group of commodities by a consumer in a period of time.

total variable cost *(TVC)* Total costs of production that vary directly with level of output.

tradable emission permits Government-granted rights to emit specific amounts of specified pollutants that private firms may buy and sell among themselves.

trade balance See *balance of trade.*

trade creation A consequence of reduced trade barriers among a set of countries (typically signatories to a free trade agreement) whereby trade within the group is increased and trade with the rest of the world remains roughly constant. Thus the increase in trade among group members is an increase in total world trade.

trade diversion A consequence of reduced trade barriers among a set of countries whereby trade within the group replaces trade that used to take place with countries outside the group.

trade policy A government's policy involving restrictions placed on international trade. Also called *commercial policy.*

trade union See *union.* Also called *labour union.*

transactions balances Money balances held to finance payments because payments and receipts are not perfectly synchronized.

transactions costs Costs incurred in effecting market transactions (such as negotiation costs, billing costs, and bad debts).

transfer payment A payment to a private person or institution that does not arise out of current productive activity; typically made by governments, as in welfare payments, but also made by businesses and private individuals in the form of charitable contributions.

transmission mechanism The channels by which a change in the demand or supply of money leads to a shift of the aggregate demand curve.

transnational corporations *(TNCs)* Firms that have operations in more than one country. Also called *multinational enterprises (MNEs).*

treasury bill The conventional form of short-term government debt. A promise to pay a certain sum of money at a specified time in the future (usually 90 days to 1 year from date of issue).

two-part tariff A method of charging for a good or a service, usually a utility such as electricity, in which the consumer pays a flat access fee and a specified amount per unit purchased.

U See *unemployment.*

undistributed profits Earnings of a firm that are not distributed to shareholders as dividends but are retained by the firm. Also called *retained earnings.*

unemployment The number of persons 15 years of age and older who are not employed and are actively searching for a job, denoted *U.*

unemployment rate Unemployment expressed as a percentage of the labour force.

union An association of workers authorized to represent them in bargaining with employers. Also called *trade union* and *labour union.*

unit cost Cost per unit of output, equal to total cost divided by total output. Also called *average total cost.*

utility The satisfaction that a consumer receives from consuming some good or service.

value added The value of a firm's output minus the value of the inputs that it purchases from other firms.

variable Any well-defined item, such as the price of a commodity or its quantity, that can take on various specific values.

variable factor An input that can be varied by any desired amount in the short run.

very-long run A period of time that is long enough for the technological possibilities available to a firm to change.

voluntary export restriction *(VER)* An agreement by an exporting country to limit the amount of a good exported to another country.

wage and price controls Direct government intervention into wage and price formation with legal power to enforce the government's decisions on wages and prices.

wealth The sum of all assets minus liabilities.

withdrawals Income earned by households and not passed on to firms in return for goods and services purchased, and income earned by firms and not passed on to households in return for factor services purchased.

X See *exports.*

TIME LINE OF GREAT ECONOMISTS

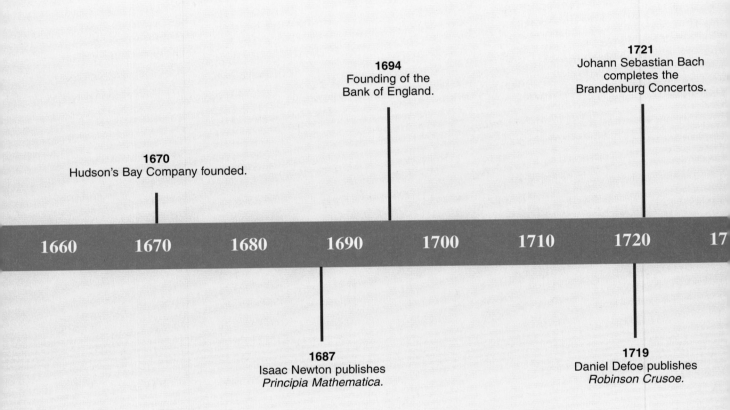

1721
Johann Sebastian Bach
completes the
Brandenburg Concertos.

1694
Founding of the
Bank of England.

1670
Hudson's Bay Company founded.

1660   1670   1680   1690   1700   1710   1720   17

1687
Isaac Newton publishes
Principia Mathematica.

1719
Daniel Defoe publishes
Robinson Crusoe.

Adam Smith (1723–1790)

Adam Smith was born in Kircaldy, Scotland and was raised by his mother alone, as his father had died before his birth. His intellectual promise was discovered early and Smith was sent to study at Oxford, after which he returned to Scotland, obtaining an appointment as professor of moral philosophy. Smith became one of the leading philosophers of his day and lectured on natural theology, ethics, jurisprudence, and political economy to students who travelled from as far as Russia to hear his lectures.

In 1759, Smith published *The Theory of Moral Sentiments,* his attempt to identify the origins of moral judgment. It is here that Smith writes of the motivation of self-interest and of the morality which holds it in abeyance. After its publication, Smith left his post at the university to embark on a grand European tour as a tutor to a young aristocrat. He returned to Scotland in 1766 and lived the remainder of his life in scholarly retirement. During this time Smith wrote *An Inquiry into the Nature and Causes of The Wealth of Nations* (1776), which was to become the foundation for much of modern economics and which continues to be reprinted today.

The three main features of Smith's analysis are the division of labour, the analysis of price and allocation, and the nature of economic growth. Smith was able to incorporate these concepts into a framework for analyzing the economic questions of income growth, value, and distribution. This intellectual contribution to economic thought was made at a time when national outputs of Great Britain and Europe were increasing and the industrial revolution was in its early stages. Smith's idea of a self-regulating economy operating within a market system was a new one in the mid-eighteenth century and propelled economic inquiry onto an entirely new path.

Smith's work also marked the beginning of what is called the Classical period in economic thought, which continued for the next 75 years. This school of thought was centred on the principles of natural liberty (laissez-faire) and the importance of economic growth as a means of bettering the conditions of human existence.

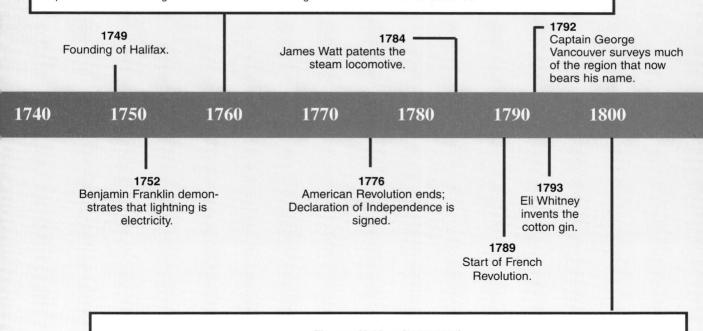

1749
Founding of Halifax.

1784
James Watt patents the steam locomotive.

1792
Captain George Vancouver surveys much of the region that now bears his name.

1740   1750   1760   1770   1780   1790   1800

1752
Benjamin Franklin demonstrates that lightning is electricity.

1776
American Revolution ends; Declaration of Independence is signed.

1793
Eli Whitney invents the cotton gin.

1789
Start of French Revolution.

Thomas Malthus (1766–1834)

Thomas Malthus was born into a reasonably well-to-do English family. He was educated at Cambridge and from 1805 until his death he held the first British professorship of political economy in the East India Company's college at Haileybury. In 1798 he published *An Essay on the Principle of Population as it Affects the Future Improvement of Society,* which was revised many times in subsequent years until finally he published *A Summary View of the Principle of Population* in 1830.

It is these essays on population for which Malthus is best known. His first proposition was that population, when unchecked, would increase in a geometric progression such that the population would double every twenty-five years. His second proposition was that the means of subsistence (i.e., the food supply) cannot possibly increase faster than in arithmetic progression (increasing by a given number of units every year). The result would be population growth eventually outstripping food production, and thus abject poverty and suffering for the majority of people in every society.

Malthus's population theory had tremendous intellectual influence at the time and became an integral part of the Classical theory of income distribution. However, it is no longer taken as a good description of current or past trends.

David Ricardo (1772–1823)

David Ricardo was born in London to parents who had immigrated from the Netherlands. Ricardo's father was very successful in money markets and Ricardo himself had earned enough money on the stock exchange that he was very wealthy before he was thirty. He had little formal education, but after reading Adam Smith's *The Wealth of Nations* in 1799, he chose to divide his time between studying and writing about political economy and increasing his own personal wealth.

Ricardo's place in the history of economics was assured by his achievement in constructing an abstract model of how capitalism worked. He built an analytic "system" using deductive reasoning that characterizes economic theorizing to the present day. The three critical principles in Ricardo's system were (1) the theory of rent, (2) Thomas Malthus's population principle, and (3) the wages-fund doctrine. Ricardo published *The Principles of Political Economy and Taxation* in 1817, which dominated Classical economics for the following half-century.

Ricardo also contributed the concept of comparative advantage to the study of international trade. Ricardo's theories regarding the gains from trade had some influence on the repeal of the British Corn Laws in 1846—tariffs on the importation of grains into Great Britain—and the subsequent transformation of that country during the nineteenth century from a country of high tariffs to one of completely free trade.

1837
Rebellions in
Upper and
Lower Canada.

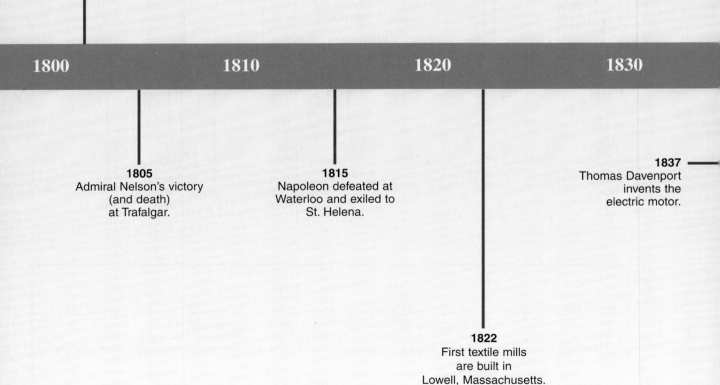

1800 **1810** **1820** **1830**

1805
Admiral Nelson's victory
(and death)
at Trafalgar.

1815
Napoleon defeated at
Waterloo and exiled to
St. Helena.

1837
Thomas Davenport
invents the
electric motor.

1822
First textile mills
are built in
Lowell, Massachusetts.

Karl Marx (1818–1883)

Karl Marx was born in Trier, Germany (then part of Prussia) and studied law, history, and philosophy at the universities of Bonn, Berlin, and Jena. Marx travelled between Prussia, Paris, and Brussels where he worked at various jobs until finally settling in London in 1849 where he lived the remainder of his life. Most of his time was spent in the mainly unpaid pursuits of writing and studying economics in the library of the British Museum. Marx's contributions to economics are intricately bound to his views of history and society. *The Communist Manifesto* was published with Friedrich Engels in 1848, his *Critique of Political Economy* in 1859 and in 1867 the first volume of *Das Kapital.* (The remaining volumes, edited by Engels, were published after Marx's death.)

For Marx, capitalism was a stage in an evolutionary process from a primitive agricultural economy toward an inevitable elimination of private property and the class structure. Marx's "labour theory of value" held the central place in his economic thought, whereby the quantity of labour used in the manufacture of a product determined its value. He believed that the worker provided "surplus value" to the capitalist. The capitalist would then use the profit arising from this surplus value to reinvest in plant and machinery. Through time, more would be spent on plant and machinery than for wages, which would lead to lower profits (since profits only arose from the surplus value from labour) and a resulting squeeze in the real income of workers. Marx believed that in the capitalists' effort to maintain profits in this unstable system, there would emerge a "reserve army of the unemployed." The resulting class conflict would become increasingly acute until revolution by the workers would overthrow capitalism.

1844 Electric telegraph opens between Washington and Baltimore.

1846 Britain repeals the Corn Laws.

1859 Charles Darwin publishes *On the Origin of Species.*

1861–1865 The U.S. Civil War.

1867 British North America Act establishes the Dominion of Canada. Alfred Nobel invents dynamite.

1869 Opening of the Suez Canal.

1840   **1850**   **1860**   **1870**

1840 Act of Union unites Upper and Lower Canada.

John Stuart Mill (1806–1873)

John Stuart Mill was born in London and was the son of James Mill, a prominent British historian, economist and philosopher. By the age of twelve he was acquainted with the major economics works of the day and at thirteen he was correcting the proofs of his father's book, *Elements of Political Economy.* J. S. Mill spent most of his life working at the East India Company—his extraordinarily prolific writing career was conducted entirely as an aside. In 1848 he published his *Principles of Political Economy,* which updated the principles found in Adam Smith's *The Wealth of Nations* and which remained the basic textbook for students of economics until the end of the 19th century. In *Principles,* Mill made an important contribution to the economics discipline by distinguishing between the economics of production and of distribution. He was able to point out that economic laws had nothing to do with the distribution of wealth, which was a societal matter, but had everything to do with production.

Previous to Mill's *Principles* was his *A System of Logic* (1843), which was the century's most influential text on logic and the theory of knowledge. His essays on ethics, contemporary culture, and freedom of speech, such as *Utilitarianism* and *On Liberty,* are still widely studied today.

Leon Walras (1834–1910)

Leon Walras was born in France, and was the son of an economist. After being trained inauspiciously in engineering and performing poorly in mathematics, Walras spent some time pursuing other endeavours, such as novel writing and working for the railway. Eventually he promised his father he would study economics and by 1870 he was given a professorship in economics in the Faculty of Law at the University of Lausanne in Switzerland. Once there, Walras began the feverish activity that eventually led to his important contributions to economic theory.

In the 1870s, Walras was one of three economists to put forward the marginal utility theory of value (simultaneously with William Stanley Jevons of England and Carl Menger of Austria). Further, he constructed a mathematical model of general equilibrium using a system of simultaneous equations which he used to argue that equilibrium prices and quantities are uniquely determined. Central to general equilibrium analysis is the notion that the prices and quantities of all commodities are determined simultaneously because the whole system is interdependent. Walras's most important work was *Elements of Pure Economics* published in 1874. In addition to all of Walras's other accomplishments in economics (and despite his early poor performance in mathematics!), we today regard him as the founder of mathematical economics.

Leon Walras and Alfred Marshall are regarded by many economists to be the two most important economic theorists who ever lived. Much of the framework of economic theory studied today is either Walrasian or Marshallian in character.

Carl Menger (1840–1921)

Carl Menger was born in Galicia (then part of Austria) and he came from a family of Austrian civil servants and army officers. After studying law in Prague and Vienna, he turned to economics and in 1871 published *Grundsatze der Volkswirtschaftslehre* (translated as *Principles of Economics*) for which he became famous. He held a professorship at the University of Vienna until 1903. Menger was the founder of a school of thought known as the "Austrian School," which effectively displaced the German historical method on the continent and which survives today as an alternative to mainstream Neoclassical economics.

Menger was one of three economists in the 1870s who independently put forward a theory of value based on marginal utility. Prior to what economists now call the "marginal revolution," value was thought to be derived solely from the inputs of labour and capital. Menger developed the marginal utility theory of value in which the value of any good is determined by individuals' subjective evaluations of that good. According to Menger, a good has some value if it has the ability to satisfy some human want or desire, and *utility* is the capacity of the good to do so. Menger went on to develop the idea that the individual will maximize total utility at the point where the last unit of each good consumed provides equal utility—that is, where marginal utilities are equal.

Menger's emphasis on the marginal utility theory of value led him to focus on consumption rather than production as the determinant of price. That is, Menger focused only on the demand for goods and largely ignored the supply. It would remain for Alfred Marshall and Leon Walras to combine demand and supply for a more complete picture of price determination.

1885
The last spike is driven on the Canadian Pacific Railway.

1880
Thomas Edison invents the electric light bulb.

1876
Alexander Graham Bell invents the telephone.

| 1870 | 1875 | 1880 | 1885 |

Alfred Marshall (1842–1924)

Alfred Marshall was born in Clapham, England, the son of a bank cashier, and was descended from a long line of clerics. Marshall's father, despite intense effort, was unable to steer the young Marshall into the church. Instead, Marshall followed his passion for mathematics at Cambridge and chose economics as a field of study after reading J. S. Mill's *Principles of Political Economy*. His career was then spent mainly at Cambridge where he taught economics to John Maynard Keynes, Arthur Pigou, Joan Robinson and countless other British theorists in the "Cambridge tradition." His *Principles of Economics,* published in 1890, replaced Mill's *Principles* as the dominant economics textbook of English-speaking universities.

Marshall institutionalized modern marginal analysis, the basic concepts of supply and demand, and perhaps most importantly the notion of economic equilibrium resulting from the interaction of supply and demand. He also pioneered partial equilibrium analysis—examining the forces of supply and demand in a particular market provided that all other influences can be excluded, *ceteris paribus*.

Although many of the ideas had been put forward by previous writers, Marshall was able to synthesize the previous analyses of utility and cost and present a thorough and complete statement of the laws of demand and supply. Marshall refined and developed microeconomic theory to such a degree that much of what he wrote would be familiar to students of this textbook today.

It is also interesting to note that although Alfred Marshall and Leon Walras were simultaneously expanding the frontiers of economic theory, there was almost no communication between the two men. Though Marshall chose partial equilibrium analysis as the appropriate method for dealing with selected markets in a complex world, he did acknowledge the correctness of Walras's general equilibrium system. Walras, on the other hand, was adamant (and sometimes rude) in his opposition to the methods that Marshall was putting forward. History has shown that both the partial and the general equilibrium approaches to economic analysis are required for understanding the functioning of the economy.

Thorstein Veblen (1857–1929)

Thorstein Veblen was born on a farm in Wisconsin to Norwegian parents. He received his Ph.D. in philosophy from Yale University, after which he returned to his father's farm because he was unable to secure an academic position. For seven years he remained there, reading voraciously on economics and other social sciences. Eventually, he took academic positions at the University of Chicago, Stanford University, the University of Missouri, and the New School for Social Research (in New York). Veblen was the founder of "institutional economics," the only uniquely North American school of economic thought.

In 1899, Veblen published *The Theory of the Leisure Class,* in which he sought to apply Charles Darwin's evolutionism to the study of modern economic life. He examined problems in the social institutions of the day, and savagely criticized Classical and Neoclassical economic analysis. Although Veblen failed to shift the path of mainstream economic analysis, he did contribute the idea of the importance of long-run institutional studies as a useful complement to short-run price theory analysis. He also reminded the profession that economics is a *social* science, and not merely a branch of mathematics.

Veblen remains most famous today for his idea of "conspicuous consumption." He observed that some commodities were consumed not for their intrinsic qualities but because they carried snob appeal. He suggested that the more expensive such a commodity became, the greater might be its ability to confer status on its purchaser.

1889–1902
South African
(Boer) War.

1896
Klondike
gold rush.

1890   1895   1900   1905

1903
The Wright Brothers'
first successful
flight.

Vilfredo Pareto (1848–1923)

Vilfredo Pareto was an Italian, born in Paris, and was trained to be an engineer. Though he actually practiced as an engineer, he would later succeed Leon Walras to the Chair of Economics in the Faculty of Law at the University of Lausanne.

Pareto built upon the system of general equilibrium that Walras had developed. In his *Cours d'économie politique* (1897) and his *Manuel d'économie politique* (1906) Pareto set forth the foundations of modern welfare economics. He showed that theories of consumer behaviour and exchange could be constructed on assumptions of ordinal utility, rather than cardinal, eliminating the need to compare one person's utility with another's. Using the indifference curve analysis developed by F. Y. Edgeworth, Pareto was able to demonstrate that total welfare could be increased by an exchange if one person could be made better off without anyone else becoming worse off. Pareto applied this analysis to consumption and exchange, as well as to production. Pareto's contributions in this area are remembered in economists' references to *Pareto optimality* and *Pareto efficiency.*

Joseph Schumpeter (1883–1950)

Joseph Schumpeter was born in Triesch, Moravia (now in the Czech Republic). He was a university professor, later a Minister of Finance in Austria, and in 1932 he emigrated to the United States to avoid the rise to power of Adolf Hitler. He spent his remaining years at Harvard University.

Schumpeter was a pioneering theorist of innovation and emphasized the role of the entrepreneur in economic development. The existence of the entrepreneur meant continuous innovation and waves of adaptation to changing technology. He is best known for his theory of "creative destruction," where the prospect of monopoly profits provides owners the incentive to finance inventions and innovations. One monopoly can replace another with superior technology or a superior product, thereby circumventing the entry barriers of a monopolized industry. He criticized mainstream economists for emphasizing the static (allocative) efficiency of perfect competition—a market structure which would, if it could ever be achieved, retard technological change and economic growth.

Schumpeter's best known works are *The Theory of Economic Development* (1911), *Business Cycles* (1939), and *Capitalism, Socialism and Democracy* (1943).

1908
Ford introduces the Model-T.

1910
National Hockey Association is formed (predecessor to NHL).

1914
Opening of the Panama Canal.
First World War begins.

1917
Bolshevik Revolution in Russua brings Lenin to power.

1918
Treaty of Versailles ends the First World War.

1905   1910   1915   1920

John Maynard Keynes (1883–1946)

John Maynard Keynes was born in Cambridge, England. His parents were both intellectuals and his father, John Neville Keynes, was a famous logician and writer on economic methodology. The young Keynes was educated at Eton and then at Kings College, Cambridge, where he was a student of Alfred Marshall and Arthur Pigou. His career included appointments to the Treasury in Britain during both the First and Second World Wars, a leading role in the establishment of the International Monetary Fund (through discussions at Bretton Woods, New Hampshire, in 1944), editorship of the *Economic Journal* from 1911 to 1945, all in addition to his academic position at Kings College.

Keynes published extensively during his life but his most influential work, *The General Theory of Employment, Interest, and Money,* appeared in 1936. This book was published in the midst of the Great Depression when the output of goods and services had fallen drastically, unemployment was intolerably high and it had become clear to many that the market would not self-adjust to achieve potential output within an acceptable period of time. Fluctuations in economic activity were familiar at this point, but the failure of the economy to recover rapidly from this depression was unprecedented. Neoclassical economists held that during a downturn both wages and the interest rate would fall low enough to induce investment and employment and cause an expansion. They believed that the persistent unemployment during the 1930s was caused by inflexible wages and they recommended that workers be convinced to accept wage cuts.

Keynes believed that this policy, though perhaps correct for a single industry, was not correct for the entire economy. Widespread wage cuts would reduce the consumption portion of aggregate demand which would offset any increase in employment. Keynes argued that unemployment could only be cured by manipulating aggregate demand, whereby increased demand (through government expenditure) would increase the price level, reduce real wages, and thereby stimulate employment.

Keynes's views found acceptance after the publication of his *General Theory* and had a profound effect on government policy around the world, particularly in the 1940s, 1950s, and 1960s. As we know from this textbook, Keynes's name is attached to much of macroeconomics, from much of the basic theory to the Keynesian short-run aggregate supply curve and the Keynesian consumption function. His contributions to economics go well beyond what can be mentioned in a few paragraphs—for, in effect, he laid the foundations for modern macroeconomics.

Edward Chamberlin (1899–1967)

Edward Chamberlin was born in La Conner, Washington and received his Ph.D. from Harvard University in 1927. He became a full professor at Harvard in 1937 and stayed there until his retirement in 1966. He published *The Theory of Monopolistic Competition* in 1933.

Before Chamberlin's book (which appeared more-or-less simultaneously with Joan Robinson's *The Economics of Imperfect Competition*), the models of perfect competition and monopoly had been fairly well worked out. Though economists were aware of a middle ground between these two market structures and some analysis of duopoly (two sellers) had been presented, it was Chamberlin and Robinson that closely examined this problem of imperfect markets.

Chamberlin's main contribution was explaining the importance of product differentiation for firms in market structures between perfect competition and monopoly. Chamberlin saw that though there may be a large number of firms in the market (the competitive element), each firm created for itself a unique product or advantage that gave it some control over price (the monopoly element). Specifically, he identified items such as copyrights, trademarks, brand names, and location as monopoly elements behind a product. Though Alfred Marshall regarded price as the only variable in question, Chamberlin saw both price and the product itself as variables under control of the firm in monopolistically competitive markets.

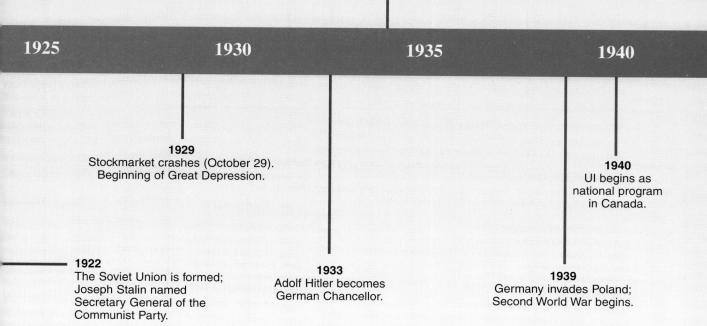

1925 **1930** **1935** **1940**

1929
Stockmarket crashes (October 29).
Beginning of Great Depression.

1940
UI begins as
national program
in Canada.

1922
The Soviet Union is formed;
Joseph Stalin named
Secretary General of the
Communist Party.

1933
Adolf Hitler becomes
German Chancellor.

1939
Germany invades Poland;
Second World War begins.

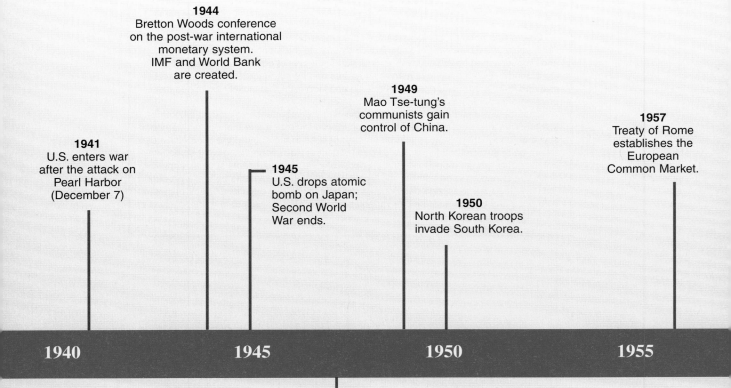

1941
U.S. enters war
after the attack on
Pearl Harbor
(December 7)

1944
Bretton Woods conference
on the post-war international
monetary system.
IMF and World Bank
are created.

1945
U.S. drops atomic
bomb on Japan;
Second World
War ends.

1949
Mao Tse-tung's
communists gain
control of China.

1950
North Korean troops
invade South Korea.

1957
Treaty of Rome
establishes the
European
Common Market.

1940   **1945**   **1950**   **1955**

1959
Fidel Castro
overthrows
Fulgencio Batista
in Cuba.

Freidrich August von Hayek (1899–1992)

Friedrich von Hayek was born in Vienna and studied at the University of Vienna where he was trained in the Austrian tradition of economics (a school of thought originating with Carl Menger). He held academic positions at the London School of Economics and the University of Chicago. He returned to Europe in 1962 to the University of Freiburg in what was then West Germany and the University of Salzburg in Austria. He was awarded the Nobel Prize in Economics in 1974.

Hayek contributed new ideas and theories in many different areas of economics but he is perhaps best known for his general conception of economics as a "coordination problem." His observation of market economies suggested that the relative prices determined in free markets provided the signals that allowed the actions of all decision makers to mesh—even though there was no formal planning taking place to coordinate these actions. He emphasized this "spontaneous order" at work in the economy as the subject matter for economics. The role of knowledge and information in the market process became central to Hayek, an idea which has grown in importance to the economics profession over the years.

Hayek's theory of business cycles provided an example of the breakdown of this coordination. A monetary disturbance (e.g., an increase in the money supply) would distort the signals (relative prices) by artificially raising the return to certain types of economic activity. When the disturbance disappeared, the boom caused by these distorted signals would be followed by a slump. Although Hayek's business-cycle theory was eclipsed by the Keynesian revolution, his emphasis on economics as a coordination problem has had a major influence on contemporary economic thought.

Hayek was also prominent in advocating the virtues of free markets as contributing to human freedom in the broad sense as well as to economic efficiency in the narrow sense. His *The Road to Serfdom* (1944) sounded an alarm about the political and economic implications of the then-growing belief in the virtues of central planning. His *Constitution of Liberty* (1960) is a much deeper philosophical analysis of the forces, economic and otherwise, that contribute to the liberty of the individual.

INDEX

Federal Government Expenditures, Revenues, and Deficit, 1970–1994

(i) Revenues and expenditures

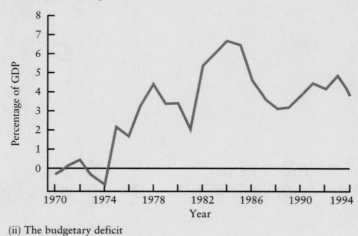

(ii) The budgetary deficit